A CAVALCADE OF INTERNATIONAL CRICKETERS

William Gilbert Grace, the
'father' of modern
batsmanship.

A CAVALCADE OF INTERNATIONAL CRICKETERS

MORE THAN 1500 TEST PLAYERS

BRIAN CROWLEY

SIDGWICK & JACKSON
LONDON

Dedicated to Roger Page

Other cricket books by Brian Crowley

The Springbok and the Kangaroo
Currie Cup Story
Calypso Cavaliers
Cricket's Exiles — The Saga of South African Cricket
Calypso Whirlwind
A History of Australian Batting
A History of Australian Bowling and Wicket-keeping

First published in Great Britain in 1988 by
Sidgwick & Jackson Limited

ISBN 0-283-99689-7

Typeset by Setrite Typesetters, Hong Kong
Printed in Hong Kong

for Sidgwick & Jackson Limited
1 Tavistock Chambers
Bloomsbury Way
London WC1A 2SG

Contents

Acknowledgements

The people mentioned here assisted in the production of this book. My heartfelt thanks are expressed to all of them: Roger Page for the use of his personal library; Rex Harcourt, honorary librarian to the Melbourne Cricket Club, for kind permission to use the MCC library and facilities (especially the Mervyn Shaw, Frank Laver and Ernest Bean Collections); Charlie Wat for his statistics and many suggestions; Pat Mullins and Ern Toovey for suggestions and information; Don Richards of The Herald & Weekly Times Ltd, Melbourne and Noel Mengel, editor of *Australian Cricket* for help with pictures; and to my wife, Esther, for assisting in the editing of the original manuscript. All additional photographic reproductions and retouching by Tristan Hast.

Preface

There's music in the names I used to know,
And magic when I heard them, long ago
— Thomas Moult

'The instinct to throw and to hit is the basis of man's primitive armoury', writes H S Altham in his *A History of Cricket*, and he goes on to state that this basic instinct was the genesis of cricket. The current offering was probably inspired just over 30 years ago when I became enthralled by Beldham and Fry's marvellous record of some of the giants of the 'Golden Age' of cricket. *Great Batsmen — Their Methods at a Glance*, and its companion volume, *Great Bowlers and Fielders*, were published by Macmillan, London, in 1905 and 1906 respectively, and they are quoted and their photographs are still used in all serious cricket history publications. George William Beldham, apart from being the pioneer cricket action photographer, batted with distinction for Middlesex during the early 1900s; Charles Burgess Fry was, in his own right, one of the 'Golden Greats' of batting. Their partnership provided for posterity an unsurpassed introduction to the style and methods of some of the greatest players of the 19th and early 20th century.

The number of cricketers who have appeared in Test cricket since the turn of the century is immense when compared with those who had played when Beldham and Fry produced their two great volumes. In *A Cavalcade of International Cricketers* I am only able to present an 'overview' of international batsmen, bowlers, wicket-keepers and fielders down the years which will, I trust, lead readers into a closer study of individual players through use of the wonderful body of cricket literature which has been built up over the years.

At the time when *Great Batsmen* and *Great Bowlers and Fielders* were published, countries like New Zealand, India and West Indies had not gained Test status and the players discussed were all from England, Australia and South Africa. This work covers the competitors of all Test-playing nations, including the relative newcomers, Pakistan and Sri Lanka. It also does not overlook the turn-of-the century importance of the great American Philadelphia XI. And lest I be accused of male chauvinism, there are chapters devoted to some of the remarkably talented international women cricketers who have appeared since the first women's Test was played in 1934.

Regrettably, for reasons of space, one or another personality may have been excluded. I apologise in advance to any reader who may miss a particular favourite.

Brian Crowley

THE BATSMEN

The Batsmen

Introduction

'Stand well up to the wicket; keep your left shoulder well forward; practise constantly and put your whole heart into it'

— W G Grace

The 'father' of modern batsmanship, Dr William Gilbert Grace, was once of the opinion that good batsmen are born, not made. He later altered his view and stated in his book *Cricket* that ':ny long experience tells me it is not so'. Acknowledging that the first prerequisite for a good batsman is the 'gifts of eye and wrist', 'WG' goes on to affirm that to acquire all-round proficiency, coaching and constant practice are essential.

Confirmation of these basic gifts and the quality of concentration and application is contained in the stories of every single one of the world's most outstanding batting champions. Grace himself practised with enthusiastic regularity. The most prolific batsman of all time, Sir Donald Bradman, practised long hours as a boy and always placed great emphasis on regular work in the nets.

Genius has been described as '10 per cent inspiration and 90 per cent perspiration' and examples abound of leading batsmen who constantly worked at their game, demonstrating in their dedication that there is never an easy and simple road to the top.

Sir Learie Constantine, that superlative all-rounder who created the mould for the archetypal West Indies cricketer, once stated, 'Cricket is an Art, apart from the fact that it is a Game'. He wrote these words as part of an attempt to counter the cautious 'scientific' approach that has taken hold in some cricketing quarters.

In what is probably one of the best two or three cricket books ever written, C L R James in his *Beyond a Boundary* states simply and emphatically, 'Cricket is first and foremost a dramatic spectacle. It belongs with the theatre, ballet, opera and the dance'.

Many eminent cricket writers of the past, like Sir Neville Cardus and R C Robertson-Glasgow to name but two, have echoed the viewpoint that cricket is indeed not a 'subject' for study but an experience of the spirit to be played with delight and joy.

All the great batsmen have, in their own unique fashion, and with few exceptions, given the impression that they have *enjoyed* playing cricket. It is an unfortunate modern trend in certain quarters that cricket is no longer considered just a game or a form of art but a business, and certain players give the impression that their interest lies more in remuneration than runs.

W G Grace not only revolutionised batting but maintained his own immense personal enthusiasm for the game until well past middle age. Australia's *non-pareil*, Victor Trumper, would most likely have done the same if his health had been sound and if he had not been claimed so young. MacLaren, Ranjitsinhji, Jessop and Fry all demonstrated wonderful skill and enjoyment when batting. Macartney and Hobbs made style and entertainment their priorities. In his quest for total domination Sir Donald Bradman could never be accused of abandoning the true spirit of the game. And so, down the years, a devotion to the *art* of batting has been carried forward by Hammond, Headley, Merchant, Hutton, Miller, Harvey, Compton, Nourse, Weekes, Worrell, Walcott, Sutcliffe, Sobers, Gravenay, the Chappells, Gavaskar, Turner, Boycott, Zaheer Abbas, Pollock, Border, Richards (Barry) and Richards (Viv), to name but a few of the marvellous entertainers who have graced international cricket.

Changes to the laws of cricket down the years have affected batting style — but the truly gifted players have adapted swiftly to new requirements, legal and otherwise. During the past century only three major codes of the laws of cricket have emerged: in 1947, the code which had stood since 1884 was firmly torn apart to satisfy more modern requirements, and in 1980 another re-structured code of laws was published. There were a number of major changes made between 1884 and 1947 and, after introduction of the post-war 1947 code, there arrived a multiplicity of experimental laws covering limitation on leg-side fielders, length of boundaries and the taking of the new ball. The dragging and throwing controversy of the 1950s created the need for a revision of the law pertaining to fairness of delivery. This is a subject which has again begun to rear its head in relation to the modern practice of short-pitched fast bowling in line with the batsman.

Improvement in the care of cricket pitches, allied with the spread of professionalism through countries outside England, has resulted since the 1970s in what may some day be termed as a 'New Golden Age' of batsmanship. This resurgence in run-making had to be countered in some way by captains and bowlers but exciting as it may be to some onlookers to witness batsmen weaving and ducking to avoid injury from balls directed at their bodies, the current pre-dilection for sustained short-pitched bowling directed at the batsman can only, in the long run, ruin cricket; it inhibits the glorious stroke-play which is the hallmark of good and great batsmen.

In the end, commonsense must prevail and cricket (and batsman-ship in particular) will continue to delight both player and spectator for many more years to come. In *A History of Cricket*, E W Swanton states: 'Bowlers and wicket-keepers, however brilliant, cannot by the nature of their work captivate the spectator in quite the same way as the greatest batsman.' Indeed it is the scoring of runs by batsmen of class and character that the game of cricket is all about.

1

Before the Tests

'I have always felt that if the Civil War had not broken out in 1861 and if communications were as easy in the nineteenth century as they later became, it is almost certain that cricket would have been played nationwide in the United States'

— John I Marder

The first-ever international cricket match between representative teams from two separate countries did not occur at the Melbourne Cricket Ground, scene of the famous inaugural England-Australia clash in March 1877. Nor was the first Test ball bowled on the hallowed turf of Lord's or any other great English cricket centre. The venue for the first recorded international cricket encounter was in fact the field used by the St George's Club 'near Bloomingdale Road' in the City of New York, identified by John I Marder, in his *The International Series — The Story of the United States versus Canada at Cricket*, as the present site of the New York University Medical Center, on East 31st Street.

The teams were the United States and Canada; the date, 24 September 1844, nearly 20 years prior to the American Civil War and not too long after Queen Victoria had ascended England's throne. And when Canada's opening batsman D Winckworth faced up to the opening left-handed under-arm delivery sent down by America's champion bowler H Groom, it was almost a full 15 years before any English team was to venture overseas.

There is a much earlier reference to what may be construed as some kind of international cricket encounter on the North American continent. The New York *Weekly Post Boy* reported a match between XI of London and XI of New York as early as 1751 but it is probable that both teams were drawn from residents of the city.

It remains a pity that the North Americans, after an early enthusiastic beginning, did not take to the noble game. One can only speculate as to what the development of cricket may have encompassed if the American flair for publicity and promotion had been introduced during the 1920s and 1930s. The *American Cricketer*, which had an unbroken run from 1877 to 1929, was in effect the first cricket magazine and, as a monument to what might have been, one of the most important cricket book and memorabilia collections of the world is housed in the C C Morris Memorial Library in Haverford, Pennsylvania.

Canada beat the United States by 23 runs in that first great double-innings game played over two days on American soil. According to Marder, betting on the game was 'spirited and heavy' and more than $100,000 depended on the result – a fortune for those days. With a few breaks here and there, the USA-Canada fixture became an annual event between 1844 and 1912. Then, after a gap of 50 years, the contest was resumed in 1963, with the introduction in 1985 of a triangular tournament to include the island of Bermuda. By the end of 1983 the United States had won 32 out of 62 matches, with Canada claiming 22 and eight games remaining unfinished.

Most notable of the encounters recorded as being drawn, and the first to embrace an international incident, was the 1846 clash in New York. In Canada's second innings a batsman named Helliwell hit the ball high in the air in the direction of the bowler, one Samuel Dudson of Philadelphia. Dudson was making ready to catch the ball when he was horrified to see the batsman charging full tilt in his direction. The poor bowler was knocked to the ground and missed the catch. After a few moments Dudson painfully picked himself up and hurled the ball at his attacker. While the other players restrained the two antagonists from further conflict, Helliwell claimed innocence, believing that he was acting within the laws of the game. It had indeed been legal until 1787 for the batsman to 'charge' the bowler if there was a possibility of a catch being made but the Canadian batsman's notion of the law was years out of date. The Canadians refused to go on with the game and settled their bets under protest.

In September 1859 Fred Lillywhite, son of a famous cricketing family, organised under sponsorship from a Mr W P Pickering of Montreal and a Mr R Waller of New York the first English touring team, which set sail from Liverpool on 7 September 1859 and finally docked at Quebec in Canada after a stormy two-week passage.

Lillywhite's team was captained by the famed George Parr of Nottingham and included such legendary cricketing names as John Wisden (originator of the cricketers' 'bible'); William Caffyn (whose coaching later revolutionised Australian cricket); H H Stephenson (the first man to captain an England team in Australia); Tom Lockyer (the 'father' of wicket-keeping); old Tom Hayward (uncle of the Test batsman with the same name); the 'crack' Surrey batsman Julius Caesar; devil-may-care express bowler John Jackson (who blew his nose so loudly that he was nicknamed 'Foghorn'); Robert Carpenter (batsman and outstanding point fielder); Alfred 'Ducky' Diver (a brilliant long-stop) and Jemmy Grundy (a famous songster and a superbly accurate bowler).

So, like the first international match, the opening international tour took place on the North American continent. However, according to an old Christmas card in the collection of a well-known American cricket personality, France was almost the venue for such a visit by an English cricket team a full 70 years before Lillywhite's men sailed from Liverpool harbour.

Karl A Auty, who died in Chicago in 1959 aged 81, possessed what has been described as an outstanding cricket book collection and was the editor of an early Chicago cricket annual. He also collected Christmas cards and one included the following message to a now unknown recipient: 'It is interesting to note that a Surrey (England) team on its way to play exhibition games in Paris in 1789 was at Dover ready for the crossing, but turned back when met there by their host, the Duke of Dorset, H B M Ambassador, who had fled from Paris before the coming outbreak of the French Revolution. Otherwise this would have been the first team ever to leave Britain's shores to play cricket abroad, thus depriving the 1859 team of that distinction.'

William Caffyn, one of Lillywhite's 'pioneers' and a member of the first England cricket team to sail south to the Antipodes in 1862 (sponsored by Melbourne restaurateurs Spiers & Pond and captained by H H Stephenson), was one of the early major influences in the development of Australian cricket in general, and Australian batting in particular. Another key member of Stephenson's side, Charles Lawrence, stayed on to coach in Sydney and was described as an 'altruistic cricket missionary'.

Lawrence staked a personal claim to fame when he arranged the introductory Australian overseas venture — a tour of England by a team of Aborigines in 1868, a full 10 years before the first official Australian side visited the 'Mother Country' in 1878. Despite certain technical limitations in their play, the Aborigines were not completely overawed by the strange conditions encountered in England and won as many matches as they lost. Their best batsman was Johnny Mullagh who hit 1670 runs at 23.65. Lawrence made 1156 runs at 20.16, next was J Cuzens with 1358 at 19.9, and the highest average among the rest was 9.33 by opening batsman, Bullocky.

A third early Australian cricketing 'father' (with Caffyn and Lawrence) should also be mentioned in relation to the development of the early Aboriginal cricketers. The imposingly tall and bearded T W Wills was an all-round sportsman who, aided by his cousin, Henry Colden Harrison, devised the game of Australian Rules Football to assist cricketers in keeping fit during winter. Thomas Wentworth Wills was born near Canberra in 1835 but learnt his cricket at Rugby Public School in England (he captained the First XI) and went on to hone his skills at Cambridge University and play matches for Gentlemen of Kent and the MCC.

After a tragic incident in which his father and 18 others were massacred by Aborigines in Queensland, Wills settled in Victoria where he demonstrated his depth of soul and broadness of vision by coaching and captaining various Aboriginal cricket teams. His Aboriginal team played a match against the prestigious Melbourne Cricket Club and toured New South Wales before he handed his charges over to Charles Lawrence for the famous England venture. Wills died of self-inflicted bayonet wounds at the age of 44 after a bout of prolonged drinking, a habit he had taken to after his father had been so brutally killed some 20 years previously.

Before the start of what was to become known as 'Test' cricket, there were a number of international tours to and from the 'home' of cricket, England. The incomparable W G Grace was seen in action in both Australia and North America, where home bowlers frequently despaired of taking the great batsman's wicket.

When Lillywhite and Parr took their pioneering team to North America in 1859 the fine batting of openers Tom Hayward and Robert Carpenter ensured success for the visitors. Although an erratic judge of a run, 'Old Tom' Hayward was a strong on-side player, while Carpenter was acknowledged as the best back-foot batsman of his century. In the two matches that might be termed 'internationals', one against XXII of the USA at Hoboken, New York, and the other against XXII of Canada and USA at Rochester, the runs scored by these two grand players were generally sufficient to match the combined totals of their opponents and the England XI won each game with an innings to spare.

The star batsman for H H Stephenson's combination in Australia in 1861–62 was William Caffyn, who excelled with the cut stroke, and when George Parr took his team to Australia during the 1863–64 English winter, his old comrades-at-arms, Carpenter and Hayward, were once more the leading England run-getters. In 1872 W G Grace first ventured overseas on a tour of North America and the story of his feats and those of his contemporaries will unfold in the following chapter.

Other than the Aborigines in 1868, another unusual pre-Test visit to England was made jointly by two teams of American baseballers in 1874 – the Athletic Club and the Boston Club. A combined America XVIII taken from these two teams faced the MCC at Lord's in a cricket match and fared well. MCC, batting 12, scored 105, and the American XVIII reached 107 all out, with a top-score of 23 by A G Spalding, which *Wisden* described as containing 'a splendid on-drive...and two or three other hard cracks'. A G Spalding was, incidentally, founder of the sporting goods business which carries his name to this day.

Despite these colourful anecdotes from early times and other lands, the history of international batting is inextricably woven into the fabric created by the first great international cricket series – England versus Australia, and the ties which were later established by these two original opponents with other first-class cricket countries. The term 'Test match' was initially used to describe the matches played between H H Stephenson's 1861−62 English team and each of the colonies. These games were invariably played against teams of eighteen or more and it was not until the fourth visit to Australia in 1876−77 that an England team played overseas on equal terms.

The first such important eleven-a-side match, played at Melbourne Cricket Ground on 15, 16, 17 and 19 March 1877, was described in *The Australasian* of 17 March 1877 as a 'Grand Combination Match − England versus Victoria and New South Wales'. The England XI was, in effect, James Lillywhite's professional touring team and the match was only later designated 'Test match' status. It was the Melbourne *Argus* that first coined the word 'Test', on 16 September 1884, to describe international cricket between England and Australia. The Australians won this historic encounter by 45 runs − and, in a *déjà vu* replay 100 years later, again beat England by exactly the same margin when the Centenary Test was played at Melbourne on 12, 13, 14, 16 and 17 March 1977.

What is virtually a Test cricket industry has grown out of that initial Melbourne encounter just over 100 years ago with seven nations − England, Australia, West Indies, New Zealand, India, Pakistan and the newly-arrived Sri Lanka − at present competing on the international stage. South Africa awaits impatiently in the wings for another opportunity to participate in the great cricket drama, while Zimbabwe, a team which struggled against the South African provincial teams during its Currie Cup days, is favoured as a leading candidate for early inclusion in the international cricketing cast.

2

Days of Grace

'Through W G Grace, cricket, the most complete expression of popular life in pre-industrial England, was incorporated into the life of the nation'

— C L R James

W G Grace was both the finest cricketer of his day and a social phenomenon whose influence on the Victorian period was possibly as profound as that of the Queen after whom the age was named. This great, bearded giant of a man was the first of a handful of cricketers to become a legend in their own lifetime. C L R James, a leading West Indian social innovator and the finest cricket writer to come from the Caribbean, once stated that he could not accept any social history of Victorian England which fails to find a place for the best-known Englishman of his time. According to James, 'WG' transformed a game which was the creation of a pre-Victorian England into a national institution. In effect, no cricketer other than Sir Donald Bradman has so dwarfed his contemporaries as did the larger-than-life Dr William Gilbert Grace.

WG arrived too early to participate in Test cricket in his prime, but without him the game as we now know it might never have existed. His innovative genius introduced the still existing batting technique of both forward and back play and, during the twilight of the champion's career, the fabulous 'Golden Age' of batsmanship was born.

The creator of modern batting was born on 18 July 1848. He made his Test debut against Australia at Kennington Oval, London, in September 1880, at the age of 32, and promptly put together the first Test century by an England batsman. By lunchtime on the opening day he had scored 82 and, reaching his 100 soon after the interval, went on to raise 152 out of the 281 for four wickets total at his dismissal, ensuring a victory for the home country in the first Test played on English soil.

Grace enjoyed the company of two of his four brothers (he also had four sisters) in this historic Test match. Dr Edward Mills Grace wore side-burns and a moustache and was known as 'The Coroner'. Seven years older than WG and a grand attacking right-hand batsman, he helped his younger brother raise 96 for the first wicket in their only Test together. George Frederick Grace, two years younger than WG, tall, handsome and muscular, suffered the ignominy of scoring a

Opposite: The champion batsman Dr W G Grace shows his style.

pair of 'ducks' in his only international outing. The only other instance of three brothers appearing together in a Test came 89 years later when the brothers Mohammed, Hanif, Mushtaq and Sadiq, played for Pakistan against New Zealand at Karachi in October 1969.

Another of WG's team companions at the Oval, A G Steel, described the great man's innings of 152 as an absolute delight in timing; 'the crispness of his strokes perfection'. C B Fry wrote in *Great Batsmen* that although the champion's sheer technical skill may not have been quite up to the standard of several subsequent players like K S Ranjitsinhji and Victor Trumper, 'neither of these nor any other batsman have begun to equal W G in the matter of the number of huge scores he made, nor in the length of time he maintained his undisputed supremacy'. Bradman is still the only other player to deserve similar comment.

For nearly 40 years the 'Grand Old Man' bestrode the cricketing world like a Colossus. A list of his major batting feats reads like something out of a boy's own paper: *Highest Score*: 344 for MCC v Kent at Canterbury in 1876; *most runs in a season*: 2739 in 1871 at an average of 78.25 (the next best aggregate that season was Henry Jupp's 1068 at 24.27; the next highest average was Richard Daft's 37.66 for Notts); *first batsman to hit 10 centuries in a season*: 1871; *first player to perform the 'double'*: 1664 runs and 140 wickets in 1874; *first batsman to score 1000 runs in a month*: 1024 in August 1871; *first batsman to reach 1000 runs in May*: 1016 in 1895; *first batsman to reach 20,000, 30,000, 40,000 and 50,000 runs in a career*; *first player to hit 100 centuries in a career*. Between 1865 and 1908, for Gloucestershire, MCC, London County and England, W G Grace four times exceeded 2000 runs in a season and reached 1000 on 23 occasions. His final first-class career batting figures read: *Matches*; 869, *Innings*; 1478, *Not Out*; 104, *Runs*; 54,210, *Highest*; 344, *Average*; 39.30, *Hundreds*; 124.

During his prime, from 1865 (when he turned 17) to 1887 (when he was 39), Grace scored 30,986 runs at 45.17 an innings — figures comparable with almost anyone. In 1895 and 1896 he enjoyed two remarkable, successive 'Indian' summers when he twice topped 2000 runs, at ages 47 and 48. In 1902, *the year he turned 54*, WG hit 1187 runs at 39.28 and he kept playing in first-class cricket until 1908. He compiled a score of 166 the day after his 56th birthday and, two years later, when he was 58, the 'Old Man' played his final major innings — 74 for Gentlemen versus Players.

His feats are the more remarkable as for much of his early career he batted on sub-standard pitches which would not now be considered for use in the lowest grades of cricket. A marvellous athlete, he used his extraordinary reflexes and strength of arm to so dominate the hitherto unplayable fast bowlers of his day that few were inclined to pitch the ball within his reach. Alfred Shaw, himself an all-time 'great', once commented: 'When I hear comparisons made between Dr W G Grace and some of the great batsmen of the present day (1902), I feel it necessary to remind the new generation that the Doctor had not only better bowlers to face, but worse wickets to bat upon.' Shaw goes on to relate how Grace dealt with a shooter or a ball that flew up around the ribs and praises the master batsman for his wonderful eye and his ability to handle every variety of ball.

In his *Jubilee of Cricket* K S Ranjitsinhji notes that, 'Before W G batsmen were of two kinds, a batsman played a forward game or he played a back game'. Each player also usually had one speciality stroke and was weak when playing others. Grace simply combined all the good points of all his batting contemporaries and proceeded to astound them all by having a stroke for every ball bowled to him. 'Ranji' goes on to state, 'I hold him (WG) to be, not only the finest player born or unborn, but the maker of modern batting. He turned the old one-stringed instrument into a many-chorded lyre'.

The 'Champion' was a few weeks past his 38th birthday when he scored 170 in the 1886 Oval Test against Australia. George Giffen, who bowled 62 overs for Australia during the England innings, was particularly impressed with WG's ability to deal with a ball slightly over-pitched on the middle or leg-stump. In his biographical *With Bat and Ball* Giffen describes this stroke as 'a beautiful swinging hit' and refers to it as one of Grace's great strokes.

Perhaps the most curious of all descriptions of WG's style, and one which delighted his own sense of humour, is contained in *'WG' – Cricketing Reminiscences & Personal Recollections* (written by the 'Old Man' in collaboration with Arthur Porritt and published in 1899). After a fine innings at Montreal during a trip to Canada in 1872 the local newspaper described Grace as a 'large-framed, loose-jointed man' who was 'quick-sighted, sure-handed and light-footed' in spite of an awkward and shambling gait. The report goes on to say that WG always opened the batting and 'to see him tap the ball gently to the off for one, draw it to the on for two, pound it to the limits for four, drive it beyond the most distant long leg for six, looks as easy as rolling off a log'.

Apocryphal stories about WG abound and have been oft repeated. He has been accused of gamesmanship and unsporting tactics, claims which may have some foundation in his known intense 'play to win' attitude on the field. This attitude was created in his family environment. His mother, Martha Grace, was a formidable lady who inspired her offspring to always go for the best (and was WG's first coach and critic during their backyard family matches).

H V Hordern, Australia's first great googly bowler, once batted together with W G Grace, for London County in 1908. Hordern was unaware that, although WG was always keen to run for his own first scoring stroke, the 'Grand Old Man' refused to do so for anyone else. The Australian recalled that he was twice forced to scramble home with a baseball slide on his stomach – once for WG to get *his* opening run and then when his eminent partner sent him scurrying back when Hordern thought he had his own safe first single!

WG was a popular man among men and possessed a fine sense of fun. George Giffen tells of a splendid ball from Australian medium-pacer Bob McLeod which just shaved WG's leg stump in a Test at Melbourne. The English giant wagged his beard as if to indicate that he was out and, with the 20,000 crowd shouting and clapping their delight, took three strides towards the pavilion – 'but the old man turns round and asks for block for the next stroke. Then the crowd is silent and crestfallen, for a rise has been got out of them, and they don't like that'. WG was accustomed to having his own way and his fiery temper often got the better of him. As Porritt puts it, 'He detested Radicals in politics, and disliked umpires who ever gave him out lbw'.

An example of WG's opinionated streak was an incident involving famous baseball pitcher 'Long John' Healey in London in 1887. The famed Chicago White Sox baseball side visited England that year as part of a world tour and, when the two champions were introduced, WG immediately gave his opinion of baseball players in general, and baseball pitching in particular. The cricketer claimed that he could hit any ball pitched by a baseball player and a contest was duly arranged. Curving the ball every-which-way, the White Sox player proceeded to strike out WG with three successive pitches. The fourth pitch made history for, in contrast to the oft told tale of Ernie Jones, the Australian fast bowler, the ball passed right through a startled WG's luxurious beard. Long John Healey pitched 21 balls before England's champion got the hang of it and despatched the ball almost out of the ground.

The names Grace and Gloucestershire were synonymous and, until the arrival of South African Mike Procter in the late 1960s, no player so dominated that county's affairs as did Grace, as batsman, bowler and a surprisingly excellent fielder. It is indeed something of a shame that Test cricket arrived too late for WG truly to demonstrate his finest, but he nevertheless did score 1098 runs in 22 matches (36 innings, two not outs) for an average of 32.29 (impressive for his day) with a highest innings of 170. Placed alongside the performances of contemporary batsmen, from 1877 (the year of the first-ever Test) until 1899, when Grace finally retired from Test play, the Grand Old Man's final figures are remarkable for someone whose best years were already passed when international cricket started. Charles Fry wrote in his *Book of Cricket* that he doubted if there would ever again be such a cricketer, 'In the mythology of cricket he is Jupiter the King'.

Of the batsmen to appear for England before W G Grace first played in Test cricket, the popular, clean-hitting George Ulyett lasted longest and was considered by WG himself to be worthy of inclusion in any eleven of the day. 'Happy Jack' Ulyett once jokingly claimed that Yorkshire played him for his whistling and good behaviour, and that England picked him as WG's opening partner because the good doctor needed confidence.

Ulyett's vigorous play made him first choice on three tours to Australia. A crowd favourite, he once hit the ball over the old Lord's pavilion and, at Melbourne in 1881−82, reached his peak Test performance with scores of 149 and 64 off the bowling of Spofforth, Garrett, Boyle, Palmer and Giffen − as star-studded an attack as has ever represented Australia. Ulyett was a grand fast bowler in his own right, a true all-rounder who might have revelled in limited overs cricket.

Ulyett played for James Lillywhite's all-professional England XI in that historic inaugural Test at Melbourne in March 1877. In a low-scoring game, England's highest in the first innings was Surrey's Henry Jupp with 63. Jupp was known as 'Young Stonewall' and was a tough character who was best in stylish defence but could also drive well. John Selby, the Nottinghamshire opener, deputised behind the stumps for the absent Pooley in the famous Melbourne game, and top-scored with 38 in the second innings. On a second tour to Australia with Shaw and Shrewsbury's 1881−82 team, Selby went home early, allegedly accused of having misbehaved with the wife of fellow Notts team-mate W H Scotton.

Scotton was an obdurate left-handed opening batsman who partnered W G Grace in a 170-run stand when the champion made 170 against Australia at the Oval in 1886. The dour Nottinghamshire player's contribution to the partnership was just 34 runs in four hours and at one stage in his innings he failed to score for more than an hour. In 1884, also at Kennington Oval, Scotton saved England when he stood fast against Spofforth and company after Australia had started the match with a massive 551 all out. A chanceless five and three quarter hours at the crease ended with his score on 90, but not before he and the eminently more enterprising Walter Read had made the game safe with a last-ditch 151-run stand for the ninth wicket. As was the case with a number of leading turn of the century cricketers, Scotton took his own life in a fit of depression after losing his place in the Nottinghamshire eleven at the age of 37.

W G Grace named Walter William Read as 'one of the great batsmen of the age' and it remains a mystery as to why 'WW' went in at number 10 at the Oval in 1884. If it was not because of some malady, perhaps England's captain, Lord Harris, was inspired in some strange way to hold Read back in a bid to save the day. Or perhaps Read had been injured when taking over the wicket-keeping gloves on the first day when Lord Harris had in desperation called on regular stumper Alfred Lyttelton to bowl.

An alert batsman who was not averse to the despatching of a loose ball for four from the start of an innings, Read played for England in 18 Tests. He was noted for his ability to place the ball on the leg side and was a punishing front-foot player. Read was England's 'compromise' captain when two separate teams joined forces for a Test at Sydney in 1887–88. He also led a side to South Africa in 1891–92; England won both Tests.

The prolific Walter Read, who once hit 338 for Surrey versus Oxford University, was accused of being a 'shamateur' in that he played for his county as an amateur but was paid a handsome salary (when placed against the normal professional's remuneration) as 'assistant secretary'; it being considered at the time unsuitable for an 'educated man' to become a professional cricketer. Like Read, the Middlesex and England captain Andrew Ernest Stoddart, lacking personal funds, experienced difficulty in maintaining amateur status. Even the mighty Dr W G Grace had been paid match fees, or been given assistance in the employment of a locum, to supplement his meagre income as a medical doctor who frequently neglected his practice in order to play cricket.

Ten days in August 1886 established 23-year-old Andrew Stoddart as a batsman of the highest class. In a single day he hit 485 (then a new world record for any class of cricket) in a club match for Hampstead versus Stoics. An innings of 207 followed in Stoddart's next club fixture, and then came successive innings of 98 versus Gloucestershire and his maiden first-class century, 116, for Middlesex versus Kent. A new star had been born and the multi-talented athlete had established his reputation as a cricketer to match his prowess in rugby.

A free and aggressive stroke-player, 'Stoddie' delighted in taking an attack by the scruff of its neck. He reserved some of his finest Test batting for Australian audiences, with 134 at Adelaide in 1891–92 and 173 at Melbourne in 1894–95 among his best efforts. Sir Pelham Warner considered Stoddart to be one of the best captains under whom he played, a leader with 'an infinite capacity for taking pains, and an eye for the smallest detail'. Tragically 'My dear victorious Stod', as he was called in a contemporary ballad, experienced hard financial times after giving up first-class cricket and declining health contributed towards his decision to end his own life at the age of 52.

The influential Honorable George Robert Canning, 4th Baron Harris, has been described as the most able cricket administrator and 'missionary' of his time. Canning inherited the honour of captaining England in the first Test played against Australia on home soil. As a dashing right-handed batsman and an outstanding fielder, Lord Harris did not do justice to his talents in international contests but scored nearly 10,000 first-class runs and took a number of wickets as a useful change bowler.

Autocratic and imperious, he was not always appreciated but was singular in his devotion to the fostering of cricket and did much for the game in India while Governor of Bombay between 1890 and 1895.

The correct but rather defensive Alfred Perry Lucas assisted WG in a 120-run second wicket stand at the Oval in 1880, after travelling to Australia with Lord Harris in 1878–79. Something of an all-rounder, Lucas and the tall Nottinghamshire professional William Barnes were two of the England XI's mainstays during the 1880s. Barnes often scored at a rapid pace and was particularly strong in cutting. In Australia in 1884–85 he came close to heading both England's batting and bowling tables and was the cornerstone around which a 3–2 series victory was constructed. An intractable character, Barnes was frequently warned by Notts county officials to refrain from arriving at the cricket ground in an intoxicated condition.

Other professionals to make their mark during the 1880s included Lancashire left-hander 'Merry' Johnny Briggs and Yorkshire's cavalier William Bates. George Giffen judged Briggs as 'one of the most formidable of Australia's opponents'. Bates was a hard driver all round the wicket and both he and Briggs could have played for England as either batsman or bowler. Bates's career came to a premature end when he received an eye injury during net practice at the Melbourne Cricket Ground in 1887. Briggs, an epileptic, once suffered a seizure during a Test and eventually died in an asylum.

Allan Gibson Steel was the most successful of the early amateur batsmen at Test level. Seemingly nerveless and always enterprising, Steel was a schoolboy cricketing prodigy and a member of the famed 1878 Cambridge University XI which beat the Australians at Lord's by an innings and 72 runs. Steel's contribution to the win was a brilliant 59 run out plus five wickets as opening bowler. He was indeed a grand all-rounder at all levels. His quick-footed driving brought the Lancashire amateur two Test hundreds, 135 not out at Sydney in 1882–83 and 148, also against Australia, at Lord's in 1884. Unfortunately his career as a barrister prevented A G Steel from being able to devote sufficient time to cricket to fulfil adequately his wonderful early potential.

The names Hornby and Barlow have been immortalised in verse by Francis Thompson. Tiny but truculent, Albert Neilson ('Monkey') Hornby was an adventurous batsman but a poor runner between the wickets who failed at international level. His Lancashire opening partner, Richard Gorton Barlow, in total contrast, was the epitome of the 'stonewaller' who once batted for more than two and a half hours at Nottingham scoring only five runs. Barlow, unlike Hornby, became a consistent player in 17 Test matches. He was indeed a superb all-rounder, batting right-handed but bowling left-arm at medium pace. On retirement from active play he became a leading Test umpire.

During the 1880s the brothers Studd became famous as a dashing cricketing family. In all there were five Studd brothers, A H, C T, G B, H W and J E K plus an elder half-brother, E J C Studd. All appeared in first-class cricket but only two, Charles Thomas Studd and George Brown Studd, appeared for England. Neither brother quite made the grade in Test cricket and C T Studd, the most talented batsman in the family, cut short a blossoming cricketing career, after achieving the double at the age of 23, to devote himself to work as a missionary in China, India and, finally, the Congo. G B Studd also became a missionary in China, and later in India and the USA, while younger brother J E K (Kynaston) Studd was Lord Mayor of London in 1928 and 1929.

A nephew of H H Stephenson (the man who took the first England team to Australia) has been described as representative of a 'new school of professionals' who came to the fore during the latter part of the 19th century and who were marked for their articulate sobriety and well-groomed endeavour. John Maurice Read was an enterprising middle-order right-handed batsman who toured Australia on four occasions and was a member of Major Wharton's pioneering team to South Africa in 1888–89. In *Cricket*, W G Grace notes that J M Read was a difficult man to dismiss when set but that his tendency to favour the pull shot often led to his downfall. Suffice to note that his overall Test record was not impressive, although Read was always noted as a fighter in a tight situation.

Another outstanding professional of the time, William Gunn, has become a part of cricket legend as much for his beautiful batting style as for his skill as 'the finest bat-maker in Christendom', as Sir Pelham Warner puts it in his *Book of Cricket*. Sir Neville Cardus describes William Gunn as 'the last of the "classical" batsmen', pointing out that the so-called classical period of batsmanship was marked by forward play 'and a gracefulness that can without misuse of language be called lyrical'. Standing 6 ft 3 in (190 cm), the Nottinghamshire champion was a hard and clean striker who used his great height to get well to the pitch of the ball. He set a pattern of strict technical perfection, with high backlift and a perfectly straight swing and follow-through. A double-international, Gunn played soccer for England and through his renowned Gunn and Moore bat-making enterprise rose from humble beginnings to become a man of wealth and prestige. Ironically, he enjoyed some of his most fruitful batting partnerships for Nottinghamshire and England with Arthur Shrewsbury, who with Alfred Shaw, the England bowler of old, was his rival in the sports goods business.

Unlike his (in Shrewsbury's own opinion) more slap-dash and

careless sports goods partner, Alfred Shaw, the precise and hard-working Shrewsbury was as much a perfectionist in business as at the wicket. Together with Shaw and James Lillywhite he organised four major tours to Australia and also managed to establish himself as the greatest professional batsman of his time, in both Test and county cricket, ranking second only to W G Grace. Grace would indeed virtually refuse to lead an England XI which did not include 'my Arthur' as first-choice opening batsman.

Shrewsbury's approach to batting was in the scientific mould, witnessed in recent years in batsmen like Geoff Boycott. On a bad wicket he would either go right back and play his stroke at the last possible moment or come forward as far as possible to the pitch of the ball. Shrewsbury was an excellent late cutter, but also knew the value of leaving certain balls alone, and became pre-eminent in the effectiveness and range of his leg-side shots. Some of his best Test innings were played on shocking pitches and his patience when batting was phenomenal. In 23 Test matches Arthur Shrewsbury amassed 1277 runs at 35.47 and can count among his finest innings his match-winning 164 against Australia on a bowlers' wicket at Lord's in 1886 and his 106, also versus Australia, in 1893 on a difficult, drying pitch.

Bald as a coot and painfully aware of it, Shrewsbury wore a cap on the field, a bowler hat in the street and a nightcap in bed, which caused his team-mates to joke that nobody had ever seen the top of his head. A serious man, too intense in fact, Arthur Shrewsbury shot himself when faced with terminal illness.

The tiny 5 ft 4 in (162 cm) Bobby Abel was unfortunate to be a late starter in international cricket and may have scored many more than the 744 runs he made in 13 Tests for England if given an earlier opportunity. WG rated him as being a top flight batsman and 'The Guv'nor', as Abel was known, started a tradition of great Surrey professional batsmen, continued after him by Tom Hayward and Jack Hobbs.

Abel made a useful start to his international career against Australia in 1888 when England revenged a first Test defeat at Lord's by taking the next two matches, at the Oval and Old Trafford, by an innings. The little Surrey player excelled in the second Test to top score with a neatly made 70 run out. During the winter which followed, at the age of 32, he went to South Africa under the captaincy of C Aubrey Smith (later Sir C Aubrey Smith of Hollywood fame) and stood head and shoulders above his colleagues as the batting star of the tour. In South Africa Abel scored 120 in the Cape Town Test, a match in which Lancashire's Johnny Briggs took 15 wickets in a day to create a world record which still stands.

Abel was described as a batsman who drove hard and with frequency. He was also a fine cutter, but his speciality was his stroke-play on the leg-side. *Wisden* records that 'Very few batsmen have excelled him in scoring in front of short leg with brilliant and safe forcing strokes off his legs', a description which may well have fitted the leg-side play of Peter May in the 1950s.

At Sydney in 1891—92, Lord Sheffield, sponsor of the England team, was so delighted with Abel having carried his bat for 132 not out (in a total of 307) against Australia in the second Test that he promptly presented him with a cheque for 50 pounds. Abel, like Shrewsbury and Gunn, was in fact something of an entrepreneur and, apart from capitalising on gold-mine shares when in South Africa, went into the manufacture of bats and other cricket equipment in a plant adjoining a shop he ran at the Oval.

Two other outstanding professional batsmen appeared for England during the period in which W G Grace was still active in international cricket. The six foot (183 cm) tall Yorkshire-born Albert Ward was snatched up by rival Lancashire after only a few matches for his home country, to the annoyance of the White Rose's peppery skipper, Lord Hawke. Stylish but a rather slow scorer, Ward became Lancashire's most dependable batsman for 10 seasons and, when honoured with selection for England at the Oval in 1893, responded with a competent innings of 55. Under A E Stoddart in 1894—95, England won an enthralling series 3—2 and Ward, J T Brown, A C MacLaren and Stoddart provided the run-scoring base for bowlers Tom Richardson and Bobby Peel. Ward himself scored 75 and 117 at Sydney in a thriller opening match in which England followed-on and then won by a meagre 10 runs.

In contrast to Ward, the short and stocky John Thomas Brown was an entertaining batsman and a key figure in Yorkshire's Championship-winning side of the turn of the century. Jack Brown twice scored more than 300 runs in a first-class innings but was, during an age of batsmanship, limited to eight Tests for England. Particularly adept at handling short-pitched rising deliveries, his greatest moment in international cricket was at Melbourne in 1894—95 when he scored 140 and added 210 with Ward during England's successful bid to score 297 runs for victory in the fourth innings.

On England's various tours to Australia prior to 1900 there was an initial dominance by professional batsmen due to the fact that most of the earlier combinations were organised by paid players. Some amateur batsmen got their chance in the odd home Test match and Grace, Lucas, Lord Harris, Steel and W W Read all proved their worth at one time or another. But the closest England came to a representative eleven was when two rival teams toured Australia, sponsored respectively by G F Vernon and the Lillywhite/Shaw/Shrewsbury enterprise, and joined forces for a Test match at Sydney.

In 1891—92 Lord Sheffield arranged a tour by what would have been almost a full strength England team were it not for the absence of Shrewsbury and William Gunn, who both refused the terms offered. W G Grace at 43 years of age captained Sheffield's team and had under his command batsmen like Abel, Stoddart and J M Read, but the averages for the 1891 county season reveal the names Shrewsbury and Gunn at the top of the table.

A E Stoddart's 1894–95 combination won the Ashes in a nail-biting series but did not include Grace, Abel, Gunn or the up-and-coming Stanley Jackson. It was not until 1897–98 that a side reasonably worthy of being called All-England made the voyage to Australia. This was also the one and only occasion on which K S Ranjitsinhji ventured out on a major overseas tour and the amazing Indian batting charmer became an instant drawcard. By 1903–04, when the MCC sent its first official party to Australia, it became more or less customary for England to pick the best possible players available.

3

The Philadelphians

'For almost one hundred years the game of cricket was a distinctive element in the social life of Philadelphia'

– J A Lester

The initial enthusiasm for cricket on the North American continent was great and it is appropriate to end the story of the 'Grace Era' with some mention of the various Philadelphian teams of the 19th and early 20th centuries which frequently challenged and, on some occasions, overcame teams from England and Australia.

In his *Century of Philadelphia Cricket*, J A Lester submits that Benjamin Franklin himself brought back with him to the United States of America from England a copy of the Laws of Cricket which he presented to the Young America Club in Boston in 1867. Cricket in New York had existed long before that date and an even earlier reference to cricket in Pennsylvania is contained in a booklet published by W R Wister, who became known as the 'grandfather of American cricket'. William Rotch Wister recalls that the first cricket he saw played was in 1842 at Philadelphia.

By 1878 Philadelphia was strong enough to take on (in an equal 11-a-side match) D W Gregory's Australians who had defeated MCC at Lord's – and held their august visitors to a draw. Batting star for the Philadelphians was Robert S Newhall, who, together with six of his brothers, had dominated Philadelphian cricket and the annual USA versus Canada matches for a number of seasons. R S Newhall is described in the 1885 *Wisden* as 'A fine bat, hitting with freedom in all directions'. Older brother Charles A Newhall was the fastest bowler in America and took five wickets in the Australians' first innings and eight wickets in the match. Robert Newhall reportedly jumped out of his crease and thumped the first ball bowled to him by 'The Demon' Fred Spofforth to the off boundary and scored 84, the best innings of the match, before he was eventually dismissed by Frank Allan.

In 1884 the first 'Gentlemen of Philadelphia' team was on its way to tour England. The 1885 *Wisden* records: 'From the time Mr R A Fitzgerald's unbeaten team of amateurs visited America and Canada in 1872, the principal supporters of cricket in Philadelphia have never wavered in their desire to one day see the pick of the exponents of the noble game in the City of the Quakers pay a visit of instruction to old England.' One of the grand successes for the Gentlemen of

Philadelphia in 1884 was a 168-run win over the Gentlemen of Gloucestershire, W G Grace et al. The Gloucestershire and England champion hit 41 in the first innings and took 14 wickets in the match, but to no avail, the batting of Philadelphia's R S Newhall, J Allison Scott and John B Thayer junior eliciting much praise from their opponents.

The next Gentlemen of Philadelphia tour to England, in 1889, marks the start of what came to be called the 'Patterson Period' in American cricket. George S Patterson was the contemporary W G Grace of Philadelphian batting, whose technique was based on a sound defence and good clean hitting all round the wicket. In a thrilling two-run win over Hampshire, the Philadelphian carried his bat through each of his side's two completed innings; 35 not out (out of 91) in the first, and 106 not out (out of 229) in the second.

George Patterson was again in grand form when Lord Hawke's eleven of amateurs was soundly thrashed by the Americans at Manheim, Philadelphia, in 1891. In 1897, on the first visit to England by the Gentlemen of Philadelphia rated as 'first-class', he hit 162 against Nottinghamshire, but took second place in the batting averages to John Lester. J A Lester was to in 1952 write *A Century of Philadelphia Cricket* and was as fine a cricketer as any produced in

The Gentlemen of Philadelphia in England in 1897: (left to right) back row: J B King, H L Clark, F H Bohlen, M C Work (manager), H C Thayer, C Coates; middle row: P H Clark, E M Cregar, G S Patterson (captain), F W Ralston, A M Wood; front: L Biddle, J A Lester, B Baily, F H Bates.

the USA during the 'Golden Age of Philadelphian Cricket'. He is described in *Wisden* as 'a watchful batsman who could hit well and had plenty of strokes and strong defence'. An Harvard Ph. D., Lester was a leading Pennsylvania educationist.

Another batsman in the 1897 Philadelphian team was Francis H Bohlen, more than six foot tall (183 cm), and a strong driver who was to tour England again in 1903 and 1908. One of Frank Bohlen's most notable innings, however, was played against Jack Blackham's Australian team which visited America in 1893 — and was thrashed soundly by the Philadelphians by an innings and 68 runs. Even though the tourists virtually went straight to the ground after disembarkation and a railway trip from New York, Philadelphia's score of 525 off an attack including George Giffen, Hugh Trumble and George Trott must give some indication of the ability of the home batsmen of the time. The explosive, hard-hitting Bohlen was fortunate to be dropped three times but scored 118 in four hours and again played well when the Australians squared matters with a six-wicket win in a return bout.

Five of Blackham's team returned to the USA with George Trott's eleven of 1896 and a powerful Australian side, including Giffen, S E Gregory, Hugh Trumble, Frank Iredale, Joe Darling, Ernest Jones and Clem Hill, came off best in the first two matches of a three-game series against Philadelphia. Some grand bowling by all-rounder John Barton King brought the locals some consolation when they took the final match.

At his best in the early 1900s Philadelphia's John King, in the opinion of many well-known judges of the game, was, with Sydney Barnes, a first choice bowler in any World XI. He was also a capable run-maker who often opened both batting and bowling and made the only score over 50 in an innings and 26-run win over Gloucestershire in 1903, the largest margin win by the Philadelphians over an English county side. During the same season King hit 98 and 113 not out against Surrey (and took six wickets) in another famous victory. His finest season in England came in 1908 when he astonished the cricket world with 120 wickets at 10.61 runs apiece in first-class games to head the England bowling table. John Lester was the Philadelphians' leading batsman on the 1903 and 1908 tours, receiving most support from King, Bohlen, the aggressive N Z Graves, A M Wood, a patient gatherer of runs, and the enthusiastic C C Morris, who still holds the record first-class score for an American cricketer — 164 versus Nottinghamshire at Trent Bridge in 1903. 'Christy' Morris maintained his love for cricket through a long life. He died in 1971 aged 88 and his devotion to the game was immortalised when the Cricket Library and Collection at Haverford College was named after him.

The power of Philadelphian cricket was nearing its end when, in

George Stuart Patterson, the 'WG' of Philadelphian cricket.

1912, a useful Australian XI (captained by E R Mayne and containing other Test players in C E Kelleway, S H Emery, T J Matthews, S E Gregory, J W MacLaren, W J Whitty and W Carkeek) was beaten by two runs at Manheim and when, in 1913, the Germantown Cricket Club XII won an exciting two-wicket victory over another Australian team that included Mayne, Herbie Collins, Charles Macartney, Warren Bardsley, Emery and Arthur Mailey. Veteran Philadelphian Percy H Clark, who used to open the bowling with J B King in former years, scored a vibrant 82 in the Germantown encounter, of which 64 runs came in sixes and fours. This was to be the last famous innings played for a Philadelphian club against an international eleven.

Australia's first great 'bosey' bowler, H V Hordern, spent a number of happy seasons playing cricket in Philadelphia and was next best bowler to King on the 1908 tour of England. In his biographical *Googlies*, Hordern notes that the Philadelphian batsmen were influenced from two directions, in that, from the one side they received the benefit of coaching from men like George Woolley (a relation of the famous Frank Woolley of Kent and England) and Australian Tom Warne, and from the other possessed the natural eye and hitting ability of the baseball player. Many of the Philadelphians played both sports and the baseball influence was often evident in their stance at the wicket. As Hordern puts it 'the American batsman had a stance all of his own, not over attractive but quite effective', a stance borrowed from baseball and not unlike that used by present-day players like Graeme Gooch and Clive Rice. '. . . up would go the bat and stay there, until he decided in the fraction of time available, what stroke would be made'.

Between 1894 and 1914 America was one of the world's leading cricket countries. One of the reasons the game lost its impetus and eventually collapsed to become regarded as something of a novelty sport may have been the fact that, for the most part, the great Philadelphian team consisted of virtually the same players between 1890 and 1910, with few opportunities provided for rising young hopefuls, and a resultant drop in standards when the older men retired virtually *en masse*.

4

Murdoch's men

'No matter how tight the hole we were in, Billy, with a smile of assurance and a cheering word, would go in himself and often master the bowling with his splendid defence'

– George Giffen

An early Australian protégé of English coach William Caffyn holds the singular cricket record of having scored the first run and the first-ever Test Match century, after facing the first ball bowled in international cricket. At the Melbourne Cricket Ground on 15 March 1877, Charles Bannerman, England-born but Australian raised, scored a single from the second ball he faced from England's legendary Alfred Shaw. He went on to make a famous 165 and, later in his career, became the first Australian to register three figures in England, New Zealand and North America.

Charles Bannerman was a strong leg-side hitter and a powerful driver who seldom lifted the ball. His historic debut Test innings ended at 165 after 85 minutes when a ball sent down by Jack Ulyett split the seecond finger of his right hand. The percentage of runs scored by Bannerman off the bat (69.6 per cent) remains to this day the highest individual proportion of any Test innings.

It has been claimed that Australia's first opening batsman was prone to 'burning the candle at both ends' and, after one trip to England with the Australian team, bad health forced him to retire prematurely.

Bannerman's position as leading Australian batsman was soon challenged by William Lloyd Murdoch, who made his own Test debut in the second Melbourne match of 1876–77. As a run-getter, Murdoch was to become spoken of in the same breath as W G Grace himself and, in his *Cricket*, published in 1891, Grace describes 'Billy' Murdoch as 'the best batsman that ever represented Australia'. George Giffen wrote that Murdoch had all the attributes of a great batsman and that 'it was an education to watch how he drove or cut the ball along the sward, seldom mistiming his stroke one iota'.

Murdoch captained Australia in the first Test match played in England at Kennington Oval in 1880, and topped WG with a brilliant 153 not out when Australia followed-on after the England champion had scored a first innings 152. Short but thickly built, Murdoch was described as a technically correct batsman with free footwork, essential on the unpredictable pitches of the time. Particularly adept at cutting and when executing the off-drive, he was also noted for playing a peculiar under the leg, or 'dog-leg', stroke that baffled both the bowler and the leg-side fielders. His placing and timing were described as 'wonderfully skilful' and, all in all, Murdoch must go down in history as the first Australian seriously to challenge Grace's hitherto pre-eminent position. He was also a highly skilful and popular captain of Australia.

Originally a wicket-keeper, Murdoch made his first trip to England as understudy to Jack Blackham but eventually gave the gloves away to concentrate on his batting. A man of immense personal charm, robust and popular, he was a crowd favourite and the Sydney spectators rioted when he was given run out in a dubious decision against Lord Harris's 1878−79 English team.

After 18 Tests for his country of birth, and the distinction of hitting the first double-century in a Test match, 211 at the Oval in 1884, Murdoch was considered, at 36, too old for the Australian side. He answered his critics by emigrating to England to captain Sussex and gain an England cap and by scoring his final first-class 100 when 49.

In *Giants of the Game* his Sussex companion, C B Fry, describes Murdoch as being 'as active as most men half his age and every bit as keen'. The buoyant Australian's end came as a surprise at age 56 when he suffered a stroke while watching a Test match against South Africa at Melbourne in 1911. His sad passing was poignantly described by his former Australian team-mate, Tom Horan. Writing in *Cricket* under his pseudonym, 'Felix', Horan affirmed: 'In the history of Australian cricket no sadder shock has ever been experienced than we all felt when the sad news came back from the hospital that the great old warrior had gone to his account.'

Alexander Chalmers Bannerman, like brother Charles before him, reached a number of cricketing milestones which can never be matched, but there the family comparison ends. Charles Bannerman was by all accounts a fine, free-scoring stroke-player while A C 'Alick' Bannerman became the most famous (or infamous) of all Australian stonewallers (barring perhaps Charles Kelleway who rejoiced in the nickname 'Rock of Gibraltar'). W G Grace claimed that 'Alick' Bannerman was 'a treasure to his side but tedious to watch'.

His career highlights included: participation in the match in which the Australians defeated MCC at Lord's in 1878; the first Test match on English soil in 1880; and the Oval Test match against England in 1882 which eventually gave birth to the Ashes legend. He defended for seven and a half hours during the 1892 Sydney Test against England, and during one period of play took only five runs off 204 balls bowled to him by William Attewell, his patient effort ensuring an Ashes win for Australia.

'Billy' Murdoch
demonstrates his famous
'dog-leg' stroke.

In sharp contrast to 'barn-door' Bannerman's solid approach, the
London born P S McDonnell batted with debonair and energetic
flair. The opposing methods of these two fine Australian batsmen
were put on display in 1881−82. Bannerman (a dour 70) and
McDonnell (a dashing 147) added 199 for the fourth wicket and their
stand bettered by 92 runs the first Australian century partnership in

Test cricket which had been hoisted by Tom Horan (124) and George Giffen (30) at Melbourne in 1881–82.

Percy Stanislaus McDonnell could perhaps be called the 'Trumper' of his day. He was regarded by the severest of English critics as a player of style and culture during a period in cricket history when many Australians were written off as mere sloggers.

George Giffen, the man who had given McDonnell the name 'Greatheart', expressed great sorrow when his admirable compatriot died at only 36, ironically, from heart disease. The 6 ft 1 in (185 cm) McDonnell had a remarkable Test batting record in an age of relatively low scoring and enjoyed series averages against England of 50.33 in 1881–82 and 57.50 in 1884–85.

Superbly proportioned 6 ft 6 in (198 cm) George John Bonnor was known in his time as 'The Colonial Giant' or 'The Colonial Hercules' and certainly lived up to his name. There was little formality about Bonnor's forthright play, although he did at times revert to orthodoxy, usually to the chagrin of his fellows. According to the *Wisden* 'they claimed that his business was to hit, and that when he failed to fulfill his proper mission he was no use'.

Bonnor 'killed' good length balls with his great reach and when he hit he did so 'flat-footed'. His prodigious driving rivalled that of the famous English hitter C I Thornton. One of Bonnor's most famous hits resulted in his dismissal against England at the Oval in 1880, *after the batsmen had already turned for their third run.* Poor Fred Grace who waited all the time to make his catch died two weeks after the match and it was said that his heart may well have stopped beating while he was waiting for the ball to drop from such a tremendous height!

At the Sydney Cricket Ground during the 1884–85 Ashes series Bonnor, coming in at number eight with Australia six down for 119, struck a furious 128, reaching his century mark in just 100 minutes. This remained the fastest hundred in Tests until England's J T Brown reached the target in 95 minutes in 1894–95. And the big-hitting Australian played during an era when hits *over* the boundary counted only four (and later, five) – to achieve a six, the ball had to be thumped right out of the ground!

Tom Horan relates a delightful story in *The Australasian* (24 November 1883) of a plot against the Melbourne pavilion clock involving Bonnor: 'It appears that 30 to one has been laid that the giant will neither hit nor break the clock this season ... and a well-known player who has taken the odds is determined that Bonnor shall have plenty of practice to enable him to perform the feat'. Horan goes on to warn the Melbourne Cricket Club committee of 'the dreadful conspiracy complotted and contrived against their beloved clock', and it seems an end was put to Bonnor and his supporters' ambitions towards the MCG timepiece.

The tall and imposing Hugh Hamon Massie was another forcing right-hander of character. He started the 1882 Australian tour of England (having been the last player to be chosen for the trip) with two hours and 49 minutes of mayhem during which he decimated the Oxford University bowlers to register a mammoth 206 out of 265. The final hundred came while fast bowler 'Jonah' Jones contributed five runs.

Massie generally opened the innings (often in the company of Alick Bannerman), it being the custom at the time to send a stone-waller and a hitter in together, a contrast in styles which frequently proved successful. His one famous Test innings in a rather disap-pointing international career was a brilliantly struck 55 that set up Australia's shock first victory on English soil at Kennington Oval in 1882.

In his day 'JJ' Lyons was considered the best Australian all-round hitter and George Giffen contended that 'Bonnor could drive as powerfully, Massie could make the cover hit as effectively, and McDonnell could hit as hard on the off, but none of them possessed the power to blaze away all round the wicket in so marked a degree as South Australia's John James Lyons'. Lyons's favourite ground was Lord's — he slammed 55 runs in 45 minutes there in the 1890 Test against England; in the same year, against MCC, he rattled up 99 out of 117 in 75 minutes; and, in 1893, again against the MCC, he scored 149 out of 181 in only 90 minutes.

George Giffen was himself one of Australia's finest all-rounders. He was South Australia's first notable cricketer and an inspiration to men like Lyons and the later heroes, Clem Hill and Joe Darling. The dominating Giffen was worth his place in any side as a batsman alone and compiled four double-centuries with a highest of 271 against Victoria at Adelaide in 1891–92.

Although Billy Murdoch had earlier rated comparison with the immortal WG as a batsman, it was Giffen who became widely acknowledged with his awesome all-round ability, as the 'W G Grace of Australia'. The good doctor himself rated his Antipodean counter-part very highly and stated in his *Cricket*: 'he has certainly proved himself to be the best that has yet visited England'.

The cool, confident and high-scoring Giffen appeared untroubled by nerves. His patience in defence was marked while his attacking stroke-play was splendid, all round the wicket. He used a high grip on the bat handle and, from a peculiar stooping stance, was able to launch into the fiercest drives, the product of an immensely strong, wide-shouldered physique. Australia's 'WG' was equally adept off front and back foot and was noted as much for the leg-glance as for his powerful cover-driving.

Ray Robinson wrote in *On Top Down Under* that nothing on two legs could outdo George Giffen for stamina, 'not even an Olympic

Great all-round ability made George Giffen into Australia's 'WG'.

runner from Kenya'. And it was total dedication to the task on hand that resulted in this immaculate and brilliant turn-of-the-century player becoming the first Australian to reach 1000 runs and 100 wickets in Test matches.

Victoria's Thomas Patrick Horan, the first Irishman to play for Australia (he was born in County Cork, within easy distance of the

Blarney Stone), was another consistent performer during the early years of Australian cricket. Against England at Melbourne in 1881–82 he and Giffen added 124 in a fifth-wicket stand which represented the first instance of a Test century partnership in Australia.

The short and thick-set Irishman had a round, good-humoured countenance, framed by a luxuriant set of mutton-chop whiskers and a breadth of brow that illustrated his above average intelligence. He also wore brown pads 100 years before the advent of World Series Cricket and the multi-coloured 'pyjama game'.

In 1884–85 Horan took over the Australian captaincy of a substitute eleven when Murdoch's team refused to play against England because their demand for 50 per cent of the gate had not been agreed to. As 'Felix', Tom Horan later produced a lasting contribution to Australian cricket literature in the columns of *The Australasian* and various other journals.

The genial but superbly effective George Henry Stevens Trott, was another Victorian who first appeared during the 1880s, although some of his best work was to come when he captained Australia from 1896 to 1898. Giffen and Trott were two fine players with the same first name, who both captained Australia and shared another common practice — walking in order to keep fit. For Giffen, however, it was by choice; Trott was merely following the demands of his chosen vocation as a postman.

Harry Trott adjusted his style of play to the conditions of the day. His greatest innings was probably the 143 he hit off England (and the mighty fast bowler Tom Richardson) at Lord's in 1896. He seldom became flustered and his elegance of style was evident even when he was forced to 'stonewall' in an attempt to save his side. If there could be one criticism of his attitude to the game it was that he tended to throw things away when the occasion was unimportant or the going a little too easy.

One of Trott's predecessors as Australian captain, H J H 'Tup' Scott, cut short his own Test career at the age of 28 when he remained in England to study medicine after an unhappy tour in 1886. Scott's tenure as skipper had been marked by team squabbles. As a batsman he was no stylist but made 102 against England at the Oval in 1884, adding 207 for the third wicket with W L Murdoch.

S P 'Sammy' Jones was, in contrast to Scott, an early Australian stylist who proved a popular figure with his home crowds at Sydney as a youngster and went on to take part in the famous 1882 Ashes Test. Known for his watchful defence and an elegant array of strokes, he played in a dozen Tests for Australia.

Two left-handers who first made their mark as bowlers and then developed into fairly regular Test batsmen were the Victorians William Bruce and Dr J E Barrett. Another fine left-hander, Henry Moses, did not fulfil his potential by remaining consistently unavailable to tour England. 'Harry' Moses was still rated as Australia's first truly outstanding left-hand batsman and will go down in history as one of the great 'might-have-beens'.

Ultra-defensive Harry Donnan was also one of the last of the round-arm bowlers and made one trip to England, but was a poor fielder and could not hold down a Test position. The short and strong Jack Worrall was an aggressive right-hander who played in eleven Tests and represented Victoria 65 times but is perhaps best remembered for his prowess as an Australian Rules footballer and for his alleged coining of the expression 'bodyline' when he was a Melbourne sportswriter during the 1932–33 Jardine tour. He also took over as 'Felix' in *The Australian* when Tom Horan passed away.

A more dashing batsman of the period was Harry Graham, whose unorthodox brilliance brought him 107 in his first Test at Lord's in 1893 and visions of a bright future at top level. Unfortunately he could not maintain his form in later seasons and, although he remained a crowd pleaser, Graham failed to secure his initially anticipated place among the immortals of Australian cricket. A hard driver who frequently changed his stroke at the last moment, he was also known as a daring runner between the wickets.

Sydney-born Francis Adams Iredale was an eminently more resourceful batsman, equally at home in defence or attack, although labelled a shaky starter. When set, his stroke-play was as commanding as any of his contemporaries and *Wisden* records that Iredale could cut stylishly and drive gracefully. A late developer, he made his debut for New South Wales when 21, had his initial outing in Test cricket in 1894–95, but waited until he was 29 before making his first trip to England in 1896. Iredale's 'great variety of strokes' impressed, among others, the illustrious K S Ranjitsinhji and on the 1896 tour, the New South Wales batsman rivalled S E Gregory, Joe Darling and Clem Hill as Australia's most consistent performer. He hit 108 in the second Test at Manchester, his second three-figure innings for Australia (he scored 140 in the 1894–95 Adelaide Test). After a short but brilliant career Iredale retired in 1902 and was later secretary of the NSW Cricket Association and author of *Thirty-Three Years' Cricket*. A testimonial 'Australia versus The Rest of Australia' match was played in his honour in 1922.

Although A E Trott (or 'Albertrott' as he was dubbed by cartoonist 'Rip') played most of his first-class cricket in England (he represented both Australia and England in Test matches), he was born in Victoria and first made his mark as an Australian. Known mainly as a bowler, Trott was also responsible for some of the more spectacular big-hitting feats in cricket history. For MCC versus Sussex at Lord's in 1899, one of his massive blows struck the MCC coat-of-arms atop the towers of the pavilion. Against his touring fellow-Australians, he bettered this by placing a ball from Monty Noble right over the top of the Lord's pavilion, a feat that has never been equalled. Alas, this larger than life character with the grandfather of all handlebar moustaches took his own life at the age of 41 after a series of illnesses.

Chosen for Australia against England in 1894–95 as a bowler, Trott played successive innings of 38, 72 and 85, all not out, in his first two Test outings. His average of 102.50 for Australia places him ahead of 'The Don' himself!

During the 19th century it was fairly common practice for Australia to play three or four flat-footed hitters. With some exceptions like Murdoch and McDonnell, most batsmen fell into either one of two categories: a slogger or a stonewaller. During the remainder of the 'Golden Age' of batsmanship, the art of stroke-play was to take on a new sophistication to complement the improvement in playing conditions and in bowling skills.

5

Golden years

'...the age which began a little before the turn of the century and ended with the outbreak of the First World War was a true golden age, not only for cricket, but for many other good things'

— A A Thomson

The batsmen of the so-called 'Golden Age of Cricket' have frequently been cited as the finest in terms of sheer genius and refinement in the art of run-making ever to grace the playing fields of England. W G Grace had been for decades the most famous man in England, more well known even than Gladstone and the Prince of Wales, and his influence on the life of his country might even be claimed to have been as potent as was that of Winston Churchill during the dark years of the Second World War. But when it came to batsmanship, some of the disciples who followed the Grand Old Man were to exceed the master in skill, and to lead the way into a new golden dawn of run-making of an order never before witnessed in international cricket.

Sir Neville Cardus once called A C MacLaren 'the noblest Roman of them all', and claimed that there never was a batsman who performed with more grandeur. A contemporary 'golden great', C B Fry, wrote in 1905: 'It is commonly remarked of really great batsmen that the better the bowling the better they play' and went on to note that MacLaren was one of those very best players who was 'armed at all points and ready to meet any bowling upon any wicket'. In his own autobiography W G Grace heaps praise on MacLaren, both as a batsman and as an outstanding and popular leader of men and Sir Pelham Warner, in his *Book of Cricket*, affirms that most Australians were of the opinion that 'MacLaren is the finest batsman we have ever sent them' and that there were many who would lay even money that the English captain would score a century every time he went in to bat at Sydney. Warner states that MacLaren's attitude to bowlers was one of, 'I am here to hit you, and I mean to lose no time about it'.

Archibald Campbell MacLaren was the son of the treasurer of the Lancashire Cricket Club, born to play cricket so to speak, and first demonstrated his mettle when he scored 55 and 67 at the age of 15 for Harrow versus Eton, at Lord's in 1887. At 23 he took over the Lancashire captaincy and in 1894–95 played his first game for England as a member of A E Stoddart's team in Australia. Until the final deciding game of a thriller of a series, the imperious young English stroke-player was something of a failure. At Melbourne he set England up for ultimate victory with a brilliant first innings 120. When MacLaren returned to Australia in 1897–98 (and captained England in three of the five Tests when Stoddart was unavailable), he made up for earlier failure in no uncertain manner.

R C Robertson-Glasgow describes MacLaren in *More Cricket Prints* as a 'magnifico' of a batsman whose hallmark was freedom of style. A wonderful front-foot driver and a brilliant back-foot player, he excelled with the hook and the cut. MacLaren's high back-lift made him instantly recognisable from the boundary and his uncanny ability to force runs on the leg-side was the despair of the poor bowler trying to contain him. The Australians of 1897–98, players and spectators, were time after time given a full demonstration of all his marvellous strokes. Prince Ranjitsinhji, who also travelled with Stoddart's side that year, regarded his team companion as the best of all batsmen on hard wickets. MacLaren's tour record confirmed this

Archie MacLaren coming down the wicket to drive, the epitome of the 'Golden Age' batsman.

high opinion. On his favourite Australian ground at Sydney, scores of 142 and 100 versus New South Wales were followed by 109 and 50 not out in the first Test, and 65 in the fifth Test, plus 61 and 140 in a return State encounter. MacLaren also hit 124 against Australia at Adelaide and 181 versus Queensland at Brisbane to give him six centuries and 1037 runs (average 54.57) for the tour.

In 1901–02, as organiser and sole selector for another England tour of Australia, MacLaren astonished everyone by calling on the unknown Lancashire League bowler Sydney Barnes to join his side, an act of foresight which introduced the cricketing world to a man who was to become acknowledged as probably the best bowler of all time.

At the age of 50, a now portly A C MacLaren and his personally selected eleven took on the might of Warwick Armstrong's 1921 team at Eastbourne and beat the hitherto unconquered Australians. Armstrong had seen his pair of express bowlers, Gregory and McDonald, scythe through their opponents like experienced harvesters taking in ripe corn, and no fewer than 30 players were pressed into service by England's panicky selectors. MacLaren's scratch XI fought back after being bowled out for just 43 runs in its first innings to win by 28 runs, thanks to a brilliant 153 by former South African champion all-rounder Aubrey Faulkner, who had not played first-class cricket for nearly 10 years, and decisive fast bowling from Norfolk's Michael Falcon and Cambridge University's C H Gibson, whom many thought should have played for England that year.

MacLaren did not play when WG captained England in his own final Test at Trent Bridge in 1899, but took over the reigns for the first time in the second Test at Lord's in a home game against Australia. At his call was one of the most glittering batting elevens ever to represent England. MacLaren's opening partner was C B Fry: first wicket down came K S Ranjitsinhji, then followed C L Townsend (in place of William Gunn), F S Jackson, T W Hayward, J T Tyldesley and G L Jessop, an awsome array of talent who would have all been challengers for a place in any World XI of the time.

When Colonel The Honourable Sir Francis Stanley Jackson, PC, GCIE died in 1948, in his 77th year, tributes to the former soldier, politician, Governor of Bengal and captain of England flowed in. A *Wisden* eulogy named him 'one of the finest cricketers ever seen in England'; Sir Pelham Warner, in a letter to *The Times*, recalled Jackson as the model cricketer, 'immaculate in his flannels and his beautifully cleaned pads and boots, with his neat trim figure every inch a cricketer'; Wilfred Rhodes called his former skipper 'a model all-round cricketer' whose movements, whether batting, bowling or fielding, were always stylish and graceful; officiating at his funeral service Canon F H Gillingham, a former Essex player, stated that Sir Stanley was 'the most honest man I ever knew'.

A 1932 appraisal of 'Jacker' by Lord Hawke, former Yorkshire captain, relates the story of Stanley Jackson's first season in the England XI. Such was the embarrassment of batting riches at the time that WG was forced to ask the young Yorkshire amateur to bat number seven in the second Test against Australia at the Oval after Jackson had scored 91 at number four on his debut in the previous Lord's match. The newcomer to the English side responded with an elegant innings of 103, top score in the match. Jackson was a complete all-rounder whose personal performance during the 1905 season has seldom been approached. Like Aubrey Faulkner (South Africa), Garfield Sobers (West Indies) and Ian Botham (England), he was able to influence the result of an entire series through his own outstanding deeds in all departments of the game.

In what has been described as 'Jackson's Year', the highly adaptable Stanley Jackson, who appeared to have a stroke for every ball, headed England's batting with an average of 70.28 and topped the bowling list while captaining his country to an Ashes victory over Australia. His second innings 140, coupled with a first innings bowling analysis of 5/52, turned the opening Test at Trent Bridge after England had trailed on the first innings; at Lord's he claimed another 4/50 analysis in a rain-ruined game; he hit 144 not out at Leeds to prevent any Australian hopes of a recovery; then, at Old Trafford, England went up 2−0 thanks to their skipper's 113; and, finally, at the Oval, Jackson scored 76 in a 151-run first day partnership with C B Fry to dash Australian hopes of salvaging lost pride.

Fry was another uniquely gifted batsman who typified the Golden Age. He was also a brilliant academic and an athlete of incredible versatility. Sir Neville Cardus once wrote of him: 'The cricket field has seen no sight more Grecian than the one presented by C B Fry'. H S Altham asserted that, even when he was a pupil at Repton School, 'Fry's remarkable endowment of body, mind and personality dominated his generation'.

Charles Burgess Fry was a classical scholar and a triple blue at Oxford University, winning his colours for cricket, soccer and athletics, and, but for injury, would also have claimed a rugby blue. He played soccer for England, and for Southampton in the 1902 FA Cup Final, and for 21 years held the world long jump record. He was, for a time, a schoolmaster at Charterhouse, but preferred journalism and edited his own magazine. In later life Fry stood unsuccessfully for parliament, but represented India at the League of Nations. He was even once offered the throne of Albania, but declined, preferring to devote 42 years of his life to the work of the Royal Navy training ship *Mercury* at Southampton. Above all, he played cricket and other games because he loved them, and never for personal gain. As captain of England in 1912, at the age of 40, he did not lose a match. If he had made himself available to tour Australia he would surely have led his country on many more occasions. Charles Fry died in 1956 at the age of 84 and to the end he was, as Cardus puts it so succinctly, 'an inexhaustible virtuoso at the best of all indoor games, conversation'.

'Dave' Nourse, the 'Grand Old Man' of South African cricket, claimed that C B Fry was 'the most correct in style of any batsman I have seen'. This opinion of a classical scholar whose rational mind became reflected in his strictly orthodox batsmanship was shared by all who observed him in action. He was certainly one of the most scientific players in the history of the game: his hands held close together at the top of the bat handle; his stance at the wicket a model of perfection; his back-lift straight and high; his command of every stroke, be it in attack or defence, a copy-book example for any young apprentice batsman; his tactics strictly allied with the state of the game.

In 1901 C B Fry became the first batsman to score six successive first-class centuries. This feat has never been bettered, and has only been equalled by Sir Donald Bradman (1938−39) and the South African Mike Procter, in 1970−71. The full details of the remarkable achievements of these three fine batsman at intervals of almost four decades runs as follows:

C B Fry (1901)

106	Sussex v Hampshire	(Portsmouth)
209	Sussex v Yorkshire	(Hove)
149	Sussex v Middlesex	(Hove)
105	Sussex v Surrey	(Kennington Oval)
140	Sussex v Kent	(Hove)
105	Rest v Yorkshire	(Lord's)

Sir D G Bradman (1938−39)

118	Bradman's XI v Rigg's XI	(Melbourne)
143	Sth Australia v NSW	(Adelaide)
225	Sth Australia v Queensland	(Adelaide)
107	Sth Australia v Victoria	(Melbourne)
186	Sth Australia v Queensland	(Brisbane)
135 (n.o.)	Sth Australia v NSW	(Sydney)

M J Procter (1970−71)

119	Rhodesia v Natal B	(Bulawayo)
129	Rhodesia v Transvaal B	(Salisbury)
107	Rhodesia v OFS	(Bloemfontein)
174	Rhodesia v NE Transvaal	(Pretoria)
106	Rhodesia v Griqua West	(Kimberley)
254	Rhodesia v W Province	(Salisbury)

A partnership between Charles Fry and his Sussex and England

Charles Fry, the most talented of all English athletes and a supreme Golden Age batsman, demonstrates the straightest of back-lifts.

team companion and life-long friend K S Ranjitsinhji revealed a fascinating contrast in styles. Fry played according to strict principles dictated by his well-ordered mind; 'Ranji' expressed a personal and instinctive genius which reflected the esoteric character of his race. George Giffen once declared: 'Ranji, call him a batsman? Why he's a bloomin' conjurer!'

Kumar Shri Ranjitsinhji, who later was to become ruler of his Indian State as His Highness Shri Sir Ranjitsinhji Vibhaji, Jam Sahib of Nawanagar, was a batsman whose quickness of stroke often defeated the eye of the beholder. A razor keen cricketer who loved every moment he spent on the field, the dignified and modest Indian Prince introduced a new, intuitive dimension to batsmanship, and not a few strokes of his own invention. His placement of the ball, particularly on the leg-side, was considered magical. No opposing captain could safely place a field for him, for in a flash he would alter his position and with perfect timing send the ball on its way through an unoccupied gap.

Ranji's most famous scoring innovation was the leg-glance, and it is said that to perfect the stroke and simultaneously to overcome his fear of fast bowling, he would peg his back foot to the ground and pay a set of speedsters to hurl the ball at him. He thus developed the art of wrist-work in his batting to such an extent that he could send scudding past fine-leg a ball that had pitched on the middle stump. The Indian batting wizard in fact scored most of his runs square and behind the wicket, but was not afraid to jump out and drive when necessary. In an article published in *The Cricketer International* (December 1983), contemporary wicket-keeper A G Pawson described 'keeping to K S Ranjitsinhji. (Pawson, born 30 May 1888, was then the oldest surviving English first-class cricketer, second only to Rupert de Schmidt of Western Province, who was born 24 November 1883). According to Pawson, the distinctive difference between batsmen in the Ranji class and other players of his time was the fact that he 'slighted the ball so much quicker, judged its length perfectly and moved into position with time to spare'.

The Rajput Prince was, amid some controversy, first invited to play for England against Australia at Old Trafford in 1896. He silenced his critics with innings of 62 and 154 not out. On his only trip to Australia, in 1897–98, he followed 100s against South Australia and New South Wales with a scintillating 175 in the first Test at Sydney. In 15 Tests for England Ranji hit 989 runs at 44.95, but it was not the runs he made which electrified those privileged to watch him perform, it was the manner in which he made them. His greatest friend, C B Fry, once wrote: 'The brightest figure in the cricket world is Kumar Shri Ranjitsinhji, whom we all love for his supple wrist, silk shirt and genial ways.'

As a footnote, it has been suggested that the revered Mohandas K Gandhi, the 'Father of India', may have enjoyed a cricketing connection which had a vague link with K S Ranjitsinhji. Ranji went to school in Rajkot at the Rajkumar College; Gandhi was very close by at the Albert School, also in Rajkot (it has since been renamed the Mohandas K Gandhi College). According to local legend, Gandhi played cricket as a schoolboy on the Rajkumar College field. (The only reference that I have been able to trace which points to the likelihood that the famous Gandhi did in fact play cricket at school is in his own *The Story of My Experiences with Truth* (Phoenix Press, London, 1949) in which Gandhi writes: '. . . I never took part in any

It was said that K S Ranjitsinhji never made a 'Christian stroke' in his life. Here 'Ranji' plays his famous leg-glide, a stroke he invented.

exercise, cricket or football, before *they were made compulsory.*' (my italics).

Unlike his 'gentlemen' contemporaries, imperturbable Surrey professional Tom Hayward did not raise his bat high before taking appropriate action but regulated his back-lift to accommodate the stroke he intended playing. A contemporary once called him 'a solid rock against which many a bowler has dashed in vain' and Thomas Walter Hayward, nephew of 'Old Tom' Hayward of 1859 fame, certainly provided evidence to support this assessment of his batting proficiency. From 1895 onwards, for 20 successive seasons he totalled in excess of 1000 runs in an English season, on 10 occasions going on to 2000 runs, and twice topping the 3000 mark. His 3518 runs in 1906 remained unbeaten until 1947 when Denis Compton and Bill Edrich both passed the milestone. On 40 occasions Hayward assisted Jack Hobbs to post 100 for the first wicket for Surrey. For England he fell just one run short of 2000 in 35 Tests, at an average of 34.46.

When it came to handling fast bowling, one of his England captains, Sir Pelham Warner, regarded Tom Hayward as being in the same class as W G Grace and Ranjitsinhji. Undemonstrative, and florid of face beneath his military moustache, he was the perfect professional batsman of his time, and the first 'Player' to post 100 centuries, only WG having achieved the feat before him. Typical of Hayward's professional dedication was his calm and confident match-saving 130, coming in at number six against Australia at Old Trafford in 1899 after the amateur luminaries Fry, Ranji, MacLaren and Jackson had all failed against fiery 'Jonah' Jones and crafty Monty Noble. In the final Test of the same series, at the Oval, Hayward compiled a patient 137, adding 185 with F S Jackson for the first wicket, and 131 with Ranjitsinhji for the second.

The 'big, ruddy-cheeked and bashful' Tom Hayward (as he was described in a *Daily Mail* report on his wedding day) married, at the age of 42, a famous woman detective, the tall and beautiful blonde Matilda Mitchell, an expert at disguises in her job as an agent for the South-Western Railway Company. This happy alliance occurred just before his 22nd and final season in first-class cricket.

On observing for the first time a new young Lancashire batsman, W G Grace was said to have remarked: 'He's a good lad, and when he learns to play with a straight bat he'll do.' John Thomas Tyldesley, by all accounts, never did learn to play with a straight bat but nevertheless became one of England's most accomplished batsmen in 31 Tests, in which he scored 1661 runs. Johnny Tyldesley (whose even more prolific brother Ernest was to follow him into the England XI) was a rarity among professional batsmen of the day in that he preferred to 'go for the bowling', as *Wisden* puts it. In this attitude he was similar to Yorkshire's David Denton, another attacking player of the day who, apart from a century against South Africa in 1909—10, was not as consistent as Tyldesley at Test match level.

Batting with a style and artistry that was usually reserved for amateur batsmen, Johnny Tyldesley enjoyed a brilliant career in 507 matches for Lancashire over 29 seasons. During what many people have called the finest Test series of all time, the England-Australia clash of 1902, Tyldesley went gaily to a cut-and-thrust 138 in just over four hours after MacLaren, Fry and Ranjitsinhji had been removed for just 35 runs in the first match at Birmingham. On a Melbourne 'sticky-dog' wicket in 1903—04, he played a masterful 62 in an England second innings of 103 after having scored 97 in the first innings, an innings which he personally regarded as his most satisfying in Test cricket.

The 1902 English season produced a number of legendary cricketing feats. In the first Test at Edgbaston rain spoilt the chance of a result after Tyldesley had scored his 138 out of an England total of 376 and Yorkshire's left-arm 'twins' Wilfred Rhodes (7/17) and

George Hirst (3/15) had bundled Australia out for an all-time low score of 36. The second game, at Lord's, was also washed out with two Englishmen out for no score in the first innings and MacLaren and Ranji going strong in a 102-run third-wicket partnership. At Bramall Lane, in the only Test ever played in the City of Sheffield, the brilliant batting of Trumper and Hill, followed by some devastating bowling from J V Saunders, Noble and Hugh Trumble, saw England crumble and Australia take the series lead with a 143-run victory. But not before Gilbert Laird Jessop, whom C B Fry described as 'The batsman who does nearly everything a batsman ought not to do — with consummate success', had, in his own unique and almost insolently unorthodox fashion, smacked 50 in 45 minutes.

Jessop was left out of the next Test at Old Trafford, where poor Fred Tate dropped a crucial catch and Australia won by the slimmest of margins — three runs. Trumper was again at his regal best in this match with an innings of 104, but England's Stanley Jackson was just as impressive while taking 128 off the Australian trundlers. By the final game of the series, at Kennington Oval, all the Englishmen could hope for was to salvage a little lost pride. So began the finest of Tests until the nail-biting tied matches between Frank Worrell's West Indians and Richie Benaud's Australian XI at Brisbane in December 1960 and the Madras tied Test between Kapil Dev's Indians and Allan Border's Australians in September 1986.

At the Oval Australia's bowlers put on a grand rescue act to take the first innings score to 324, after George Hirst had been among the wickets early on. England then collapsed again to Hugh Trumble (8/65) and the visiting side started their second knock holding a 141-run first innings lead. With fast bowler Bill Lockwood moving into top gear, the home team fought back to dismiss Australia for 121. Needing 263 to win England once again collapsed in ignoble fashion (this time to the teasing left-arm deliveries of Jack Saunders) and all appeared lost when the short but powerful Jessop strode in to take guard and then crouch low into his peculiar waiting stance. The scoreboard showed that five wickets were gone for only 48 runs.

During a tour of the USA in 1897, the style and attitude of 'Croucher' Jessop had been immortalised by one Ralph D Paine in a verse published in a Philadelphia newspaper:

At one end stocky Jessop frowned,
The human catapult,
Who wrecks the roofs of distant towns
When set in his assault.

On 13 August 1902, Gilbert Jessop, the most noteworthy of all famous hitters, proceeded to play the innings of his life. Not unaccustomed to rattling along at a personal rate of 70 or 80 runs an hour, the Gloucestershire ace pulled, cut and drove as if he were indulging in a village green knockabout, demolishing an hitherto invincible Australian bowling attack. His 50 arrived after just 43 minutes, and then Jessop accelerated in his onslaught on Armstrong's wilting bowlers. With Jackson moving along at a quieter pace in support, 109 runs were added before the sixth wicket fell, and England was suddenly in with a chance. Full of dependable Yorkshire grit, George Hirst came in to join the rampant Jessop. Not to be outdone, he immediately pulled Warwick Armstrong for a couple of fours before yielding the strike to his impatient partner. Jessop responded with two hits off Trumble straight into the pavilion, spaced by a couple of twos for good measure. His score stood at 96 and, when Hirst gave him the strike again against Armstrong, Jessop played a delightful cut shot to the boundary to reach his 100 in a new record time of 75 minutes. Pandemonium reigned as hats were thrown in the air and everyone looked for an umbrella or walking stick to wave in acclamation.

Perhaps Jessop's concentration was upset by the prolonged applause. Just two balls later, after sweeping Armstrong once more to the leg boundary, he gave Noble an easy catch at short-leg. He had scored 104 out of 139 runs added while he was at the wicket in only 77 minutes — a record for England-Australia Tests (in terms of time) which stands to this very day and has only been bettered in international cricket by Jack Gregory, who smote a century in 70 minutes for Australia against South Africa at Johannesburg in 1921–22.

England still required 76 runs to win when Jessop departed, but Yorkshire determination won through in the end. Hirst made 58 not out and watched from the other end as Wilfred Rhodes, last man to bat, drove the winning run between Trumble and Duff at mid-on, and continued on his way to the pavilion.

Gilbert Jessop's final Test record was hampered by a predeliction for sea-sickness which saw him refuse several invitations to tour overseas.

For many years Jessop held the world record for the fastest double-century in first-class cricket — 120 minutes, for Gloucestershire versus Sussex at Hove in 1903. He reached 100 in 70 minutes and his final innings of 286 took 175 minutes. This feat was equalled in 1976 by Clive Lloyd for West Indians versus Glamorgan at Swansea. The West Indian captain topped 100 in 80 minutes and hit his second century in 40 minutes.

In January 1985, India's 22-year-old R J Shastri bettered Jessop's long-held record when he reached his 200 in 113 minutes off 123 balls. During the course of his 200 not out for Bombay versus Baroda at the Wankhede Stadium in Bombay, Ravi Shastri also equalled the record set up in 1968 by Sir Garfield Sobers for Nottinghamshire versus Glamorgan of six consecutive sixes in a six-ball over.

One of the acknowledged great all-rounders of all time, George Herbert Hirst, aggressive right-hand batsman and left-arm fast-medium bowler supreme, was a superb puller and hooker of the ball (and the only man ever to have scored 2000 and taken 200 wickets in the same season) but a player who only came good with the bat in Tests in rare occasions.

Somerset professional Leonard Charles Braund was an almost automatic choice in England's teams between 1901 and 1908 and was also a member of the famous 'Golden XI' of 1902 that included MacLaren, Fry, Ranjitsinhji, Jackson, J T Tyldesley and Jessop, perhaps the finest England batting line-up of all time. After marking his Sydney debut against Australia with an innings of 58 and seven wickets, Braund came close to scoring 1000 runs and taking 50 wickets in his 23 Tests.

At the turn of the century, and carrying on well into the between-wars period, it was customary for England to field virtually two separate teams — one for the serious business of matching the 'old enemy' Australia, and another to face the burgeoning newcomers like South Africa, New Zealand, West Indies and India. During the English winter of 1929—30, two English teams, neither of which could be called representative, actually played two separate Test series simultaneously, one in New Zealand and the other in the West Indies. When it came to touring Australia, first-choice players such as Grace, Fry, Jackson and Jessop were seldom, and in some cases never, available to embark upon the venture.

When Lord Hawke took an English contingent to South Africa in 1898—99 he included in his side the 25-year-old Oxford and Middlesex batsman P F Warner who was later knighted and became an outstanding cricket personality until his death in 1963. In an obituary in *Playfair Cricket Monthly* of March 1963, Sir Neville Cardus recalled that 'Nearly 60 years ago "Plum" Warner was every schoolboy's hero'. With his colourful harlequin cap and 'cherubic' boyish appearance, Pelham Warner reflected an image of the typical public school cricketer. Although somewhat frail of physique, Warner was a sound right-hand batsman who believed in the observance of first principles. Against South Africa at the Old Wanderers Ground in Johannesburg in 1898—99, he became one of a select few batsmen to score a century on first Test appearance when he carried his bat in the second innings for 132 not out in a total of 237. He captained England in the thrilling 1905—06 match against South Africa when the home team won their first Test and series and, in all, led his country in 10 Tests.

Off the field, Sir Pelham Warner's achievements in the fostering of the game he so loved were monumental. Besides founding and editing *The Cricketer* magazine (which has enjoyed a continuous run from 1921 to the present time), he wrote many cricket books, co-managed the MCC on the notorious bodyline tour of 1932–33, served as an England selector, was cricket correspondent for the *Morning Post* for 12 years and for 16 years served as President of the MCC. He was a man known for his charm and sincerity towards all who met him.

Frederick Luther Fane, an attractive and stylish right-hander, was eminently successful when he toured South Africa with Warner in 1905–06 and hit 143 off the South African googly bowlers at Johannesburg. Fane also took over as captain of the MCC when A O Jones fell ill on the 1907–08 tour of Australia and led England in three Tests.

John Neville Crawford, one of the most talented of the 'might-have-beens', was another player first to represent England under P F Warner in South Africa in 1905–06. A school prodigy and an all-rounder of immense potential, he first appeared for Surrey when only 17, went to South Africa when he was 19, and headed England's bowling averages in Australia in 1907–08 but batted low in the order with little result. He later moved to Australia and played in the Sheffield Shield after a dispute when he was captain of Surrey.

Another new English player in Warner's 1907–08 team played an unforgettable debut Test innings at Sydney which may never be equalled. In seven hours and 10 minutes, the graceful Reginald Erskine Foster produced a record-making 287; then the highest score ever in Test cricket and still the best for a player batting in his first Test innings. All-rounder Len Braund aided Foster in a 192-run stand for the fifth wicket and Wilfred Rhodes added 130 in a last-wicket which remains a world Test record.

Incidentally, Rhodes is one of the three all-time 'adaptable' batsmen (the others are Vinoo Mankad (India) and S E Gregory (Australia)) who have batted in every position from number one to number 11 in a Test match.

Warner describes R E Foster as a wonderful driver and cutter, with the strongest of wrists, who 'seemed to be able to make the bowling dance to his own pleasure and whim'. 'Tip' Foster was one of seven Worcestershire brothers whose combined cricketing skills caused their county to become known as 'Fostershire'. He was also a brilliant soccer forward, who gained an England cap at that sport, and an excellent golfer and racquets player. R E Foster never again quite scaled the batting heights he had reached at Sydney in December 1903 and died of diabetes at the age of 36.

Leicestershire professional Albert Ernest Knight, one of very few men from his county to be chosen for England, top-scored in Australia with 70 not out on a rain-ruined pitch at Sydney during the crucial fourth Test of 1903–04. England won the match and series but Bert Knight never again played for England. He was a devout lay Methodist preacher who apparently prayed before going in to bat and the story goes that Lancashire bowler Walter Brearley complained that Knight was taking an unfair advantage. A E Knight's book *The Complete Cricketer*, published in 1906, is considered something of a classic and was described in *Wisden* as 'grandiose in style, containing much startling metaphor'.

Other notable county batsmen of the period who did not quite make their mark when selected for England included Middlesex amateur C P McGahey, Nottinghamshire captain A O Jones (he captained MCC in Australia in 1907−08 but missed three Tests through illness), and old William Gunn's nephew, John Gunn, a left-handed all-rounder from the same county. John Gunn's younger brother, George Gunn, was destined to become a legend in his own time.

George Gunn was a man and a cricketer akin in character to Australia's Charles Macartney. No other person, and certainly no opposing bowler, could dictate terms to him. If it were not for indifferent health and his original and whimsical character, the younger nephew of William Gunn may indeed have been noted in the annals of the game as one of the half-dozen greatest batsmen of all time. Peculiarly enough, it was an attempt to recuperate from illness which took him to Australia in 1907−08 and into Test cricket as a substitute batsman when England's skipper A O Jones fell ill.

The Nottinghamshire pro who, as R C Robertson-Glasgow put it 'mocked equally the rules of batting and the Rules of Cricket', proceeded to score 119 and 74 at Sydney in the first Test, 65 at Adelaide and 122 not out at Sydney in the final game of the rubber, hitting 462 runs in all at 51.33 − a fair performance for an 'invalid'. At the age of 50 he went with the MCC to the West Indies and added 322 with Andrew Sandham, then 10 years his junior, for the first wicket against Jamaica, and 173 with the same partner in the Test at Kingston. If he had lived in another age, the eccentric and unconventional George Gunn (he was considered 'sacrilegious' by some of cricket's hierarchy) would surely have played many more games for England.

Fast bowlers hated the sight of George Gunn. His method against them was unique and highly impudent: as the bowler ran in, so too would Gunn move forward with a crab-like motion, and then, instead of putting the ball back over the bowler's head as might be expected from his position at almost mid-pitch, he would flick the ball away to long-leg or third-man with a casual turn of the wrist. Cardus rated him the 'wittiest' batsman who ever lived and one who played the game 'for fancy's sake', stonewalling for a period just because the bowler knew he was capable of hitting the cover off the ball, and then smacking the best ball of the match to the boundary fence with a stroke 'as impudent as a coxcomb'.

He delighted in teasing the bowler and tempting the fieldsmen to run him out but, above all, he was capable if the mood took him of reducing the most famous bowling attack to shreds with a range of strokes which, as Cardus wrote in *Good Days*, 'apparently included them all, ancient and modern, with, of course, variations of his own thrown in to lend savour'.

A number of other notable English batsmen were introduced to Test cricket between the 1907−08 Australian summer and the start of the First World War. Kent amateur Kenneth Lotherington Hutchings was another fine example of Golden Age batsmanship and his 126 at Melbourne in 1907−08 even overshadowed the excellent 83 compiled by the coming 'master', J B Hobbs. Lieutenant K L Hutchings was killed in northern France in 1916, one of the thousands of young cricketers, a generation, cut off in their prime.

Joseph Hardstaff senior, the Nottinghamshire professional, survived two wars and saw his son, Joe Hardstaff junior, also gain an England cap. Nicknamed 'Hotstuff' in Australia during 1907−08, Hardstaff senior was a sturdy, free-scoring right-hander who headed the tour averages with 1384 runs at 51.25 but was not again called upon to play for his country.

The MCC side to Australia in 1911−12 included a number of all-rounders whose batting could be considered above average. Frank Rowbotham Foster once scored 305 in a day for Warwickshire versus Worcestershire in 1914. On the 1911−12 tour he formed, with Sydney Barnes, a fearsome match-winning bowling combination and in 11 Tests averaged 23.57 with the bat. John William Hearne lasted longer than Foster to play for England in 24 Tests in which he scored 806 runs at 26.00 and took 30 wickets with his leg-breaks and googlies. J W H T Douglas was to become England's first post-war captain and a stubborn batsman whose initials clearly suggested his style of play and were immediately converted into 'Johnny Won't Hit Today' by a quick-humoured Australian barracker. The six foot (183 cm) tall Douglas was a fighter of great quality who twice led England in Australia. He died in a brave attempt to save his father from drowning when a ship in which they were travelling collided with another in dense fog.

Four other members of Douglas's team ('JWHT' took over from elected captain 'Plum' Warner when the latter became ill) − Wilfred Rhodes, C P Mead, Frank Woolley and John Berry Hobbs − belonged as much to the new era which was to arise after the conclusion of the First World War as they did to the Golden Age of batting, which was now drawing swiftly to a close as the clouds of conflict drifted across the Channel to hover over the playing fields of England.

Some writers have claimed that if one person were to be selected as a typical example of Edwardian Golden Age batsmanship, he would be Lancashire amateur Reginald Herbert Spooner. Sir Neville Cardus recorded that he was 'uncapable of awkwardness' and that 'his strokes would have honoured the lawns of a royal palace'. Wounded during the Boer War, Spooner returned to play rugby for his country and to make his cricket Test debut against Australia in 1905. He played elegant and powerful innings of 52 and 79 in his two games of the series. Rarely available for first-class or Test cricket thereafter, he returned to the England XI at Manchester in 1909 to score 58 in 90 minutes in an innings described by *Wisden* as 'superb'. Three years later (at Lord's in 1912) he scored a delightful 119 against South Africa, even though he had not played for England in the interim.

Reggie Spooner, it has been said, did not just play with style, he *was* style and spectators delighted in just watching him play, regardless of the number of runs he scored. The 1904 *Wisden* (he was one of the 'Five Cricketers of the Year') states that there were few batsmen who could compare with him and that not even L C H Palairet 'is better worth looking at'. Palairet was of course the wonderfully stylish Somerset batsman who, in county matches, provided a model of the Golden Age batsman but was given few opportunities to perform at international level.

6

Trumper's reign

'You can never speak to an Australian about Victor Trumper without seeing his eyes glisten with pride and affection; Trumper will always remain for your true Australian the greatest batsman that ever lived'
— Sir Neville Cardus

There has been some disagreement about the precise dating of the 'Golden Age of Cricket' but it is now generally accepted that it began in 1895 (W G Grace's 'Indian summer' at the age of 47) and ended in 1914, with the outbreak of war and the subsequent passing of the amateur influence, particularly in batsmanship. Patrick Morrah writes in *The Golden Age of Cricket*, recalling the end of the great age: 'Cricket has always reflected the mood of the nation. Edwardian opulence had vanished and with it opulent batting.' If a batsman was to be selected as the undisputed Australian representative of that vanished 'opulent' era, the choice could only be Victor Thomas Trumper.

Of Victor Trumper's countless admirers, two are particularly notable for their wonderful prose about the great batsman. One is the Englishman Sir Neville Cardus, dubbed by Jack Fingleton 'the Victor Trumper of the writing world', the other is the Australian Arthur Mailey, googly bowler, journalist, author and cartoonist. Each has been quoted on scores of occasions, but any tribute to Victor Trumper would remain incomplete without reference to their most famous statements about him. Recalling Trumper's burial, when the Sydney streets were jammed with thousands of mourners and the list of pall-bearers read like a 'Who's Who' of Australian cricket, Cardus wrote: 'It was like a Royal funeral, and rightly so. For Victor was the Prince of batsmen.'

Mailey's most touching reference to Trumper illustrated the googly bowler's own debut as a young colt in first grade cricket in Sydney when he was first called upon to bowl to his hero. The master batsman effortlessly despatched the young spinner's first two deliveries to the boundary; Mailey's third ball, a 'bosey', beat Trumper's swinging bat with the great man out of his crease. The stumper made no error and Trumper acknowledged that the ball had been too good for him. Mailey's reaction, however, was not one of elation: 'There was no triumph in me as I watched the receding figure. I felt like a boy who had killed a dove.'

C B Fry, himself one of the finest stylists of all time, commented that Trumper 'has no style, yet he is all style'. Trumper possessed a seemingly limitless range of strokes to combat all conditions. His influence on his fellows was immense. He defied all orthodox rules, yet he played every shot with a minimum of effort and with maximum effect, with a unique combination of eye, wrist and foot. Trumper's perfect natural balance is most evident in the superb action shots taken by G W Beldham which record a glimpse of the remarkable beauty of his movement. The position of Trumper's feet when hooking reveals a smooth and quick movement before execution of the stroke from well inside the path of flight, with the placing of his back foot governed by the line of the ball. When preparing to drive, Trumper held his arms close to the body and always followed through fully and effectively. Not averse to despatching to leg a ball pitched outside the off-stump, he used his wrists to cut deliveries pitched in line with the wicket. In one photograph he can be seen shifting the grip of his right hand down to the shoulder of the bat when preparing for a back stroke. Peculiarly enough, Warwick Armstrong asserts in his analysis of the great batsman that 'sliding the right hand down the handle of the bat in playing back has never been practised by such forceful back players as Trumper, Clem Hill, Hobbs, Spooner, Macartney and others'.

Australian captain Monty Noble wrote that Trumper's intention was to 'spoil a bowler's length'. The outstanding feature of his batting was his 'ability to get into the proper position which made those strokes possible'. According to Noble, one of the most effective of these was made to a fast ball well up on the middle stump. The bat would meet the ball at half-volley and, with a flick of the wrist at the moment of contact, the ball would be forced along the ground at great pace forward of short leg. Few batsmen before or after Trumper have approached his skill in improvisation of a shot. He played all the known strokes and added those of his own design.

Trumper scorned any thoughts of playing himself in. If the first ball deserved to be hit for four, he did so. To quote Alan Gibson in *Jackson's Year*: 'But then no rules, no generalisations can ever be applied to Trumper. He will always be the most enchanting, and the most maddening, cricketer of them all.' A E Knight's tribute to Trumper reads: 'In Victor Trumper we have seen the very poetry and heard the deep and wonderful music of batsmanship.'

The measure of Trumper's genius is not to be found in figures alone, for it has been said he frequently gave his wicket away when he thought he had scored enough. Claims that he did not go for a big score once he had reached 100 may be somewhat belied by the fact of his first three-figure innings of 292 not out (for New South Wales versus Tasmania at Sydney in 1898–99) and his undefeated 300 against Sussex at Hove in 1899. In Tests Trumper's high scores included 185 against England in 1903–04 and 214 against South

A wonderful action study by George Beldham of Australia's nonpareil, Victor Trumper.

Africa in 1910—11, both not out. When Australia visited England during an unusually rainy summer in 1902, he aggregated a staggering 2570 runs — including 11 centuries, the finest of which was his 104 on a dreadful wicket at Old Trafford when England lost by a mere three runs.

As a man, Trumper was universally admired, although according

to some accounts he was known as a 'scruffy genius' who batted in crumpled shirts and creams. Tom Horan reflects a different impression: '...what particularly attracted my attention...was the remarkably neat way in which his shirt sleeves were folded. Not loose, dangling down...It is a small thing, perhaps, to some, but to me it counts and suggests a good deal.'

Victor Trumper was a teetotaller and non-smoker and a family man. Australian colleague Frank Iredale wrote that he was a man, 'in whose presence you felt it good to live'. His modesty was indeed sometimes misunderstood.

Trumper died at the age of 37 after suffering severely from acute kidney failure. Memory of his feats will remain fresh as long as the game of cricket continues to be played.

Of Trumper's batting contemporaries, the diminutive Sydney Edward Gregory actually preceded the great batsman into the Australian XI by almost 10 years but his career remains very much a part of the Golden Age of Australian batting. 'Little Tich' Gregory first played against England at Lord's in 1890 at the age of 20 and remained a fixture in the Australian eleven for more than two decades. During the twilight of his career he captained, at age 42, a virtual Australia Second XI when six other senior players withdrew for the 1912 Triangular Series against England and Australia. Gregory's 58 Tests for his country remained a record until Ray Lindwall exceeded that figure 44 years later.

At 5 ft 4 in (162 cm), and wearing a big moustache (some say to convince people that he was indeed an adult) the dapper little Australian was a technically correct batsman. The son of Ned Gregory (who had appeared in the first-ever Test match), he was born on the site of the present Sydney Cricket Ground, and used a bat manufactured in his home town to run up the first double-century in Test match cricket — 201 against England on the SCG in 1894—95, in the first Test to run into six days.

The Gregory family is certainly the most celebrated cricketing clan produced by Australia. Ned Gregory's brother David William led Australia in the first Test at Melbourne in 1877; Syd's younger brother Charles (also a very short man, who died aged 32) was the first Australian to score 300 runs in one day's play (318 of his eventual 383 for New South Wales versus Queensland at Brisbane in 1906). Charles did not play in a Test but old Dave's nephew Jack Gregory was to become acknowledged during the 1920s and 1930s as Australia's greatest all-rounder. In all, the Gregory family supplied four Test players (two of whom captained Australia) and seven New South Wales players.

Victor Trumper's regular opening partner for Australia was Reginald Alexander Duff, one of the most exciting stroke-players. This superb attacking right-hander showed his original style during a

Test debut against England at Melbourne in 1901–02 which saw him called to bat at number 10 in Australia's second innings, after skipper Joe Darling had juggled his order on a difficult pitch. Duff posted 104, adding 105 with Clem Hill for the ninth wicket and taking part in a blistering last wicket hand of 120 with Warwick Armstrong. By the end of the series, Duff was opening the batting with Trumper.

Their partnership prospered until Duff fell on hard times and dropped out of the Australian team after the 1905 tour of England. He ended his cricketing career, aged only 27, in the manner he had begun – his farewell 146 at the Oval in 1905 is still regarded as one of the finest Test innings ever played by an Australian batsman.

Australia's turn of the century batting line-up was immensely powerful: Trumper, Duff, Hill, Syd Gregory, Darling, Noble, Armstrong, with such grand players as A J Y Hopkins, wicket-keeper J J Kelly, Hugh Trumble and all-rounder Charlie McLeod to follow.

During the early part of his career C E McLeod played for Australia as a batsman who could bowl (he hit 112 as opener at Melbourne in 1897–98), but batted at number 11 at Adelaide in 1901–02. Wicket-keeper and ace bowler Hugh Trumble was an above average batsmen and all-rounder 'Bert' Hopkins was considered classy enough to be included in the Beldham and Fry book.

Clem Hill, though born in the same year as his right-handed counterpart, won his first Test cap three years before Trumper and has been described as the best left-hander to play for either Australia or England. His father scored the first century on the Adelaide Oval in the same year that Clem was born and, all in all, seven Hill brothers were selected at one time or another for South Australia. Clem was the sole left-hander in the Hill brood and also the only one to play Test cricket. His 188 against England at Melbourne in 1897–98 still remains the highest innings by a batsman under 21 in Australia-England contests.

Self-possessed and cool, he watched the ball so closely that C B Fry commented: 'Even his free and enterprising strokes might be called careful.' Charles Macartney considered it a wonderful experience to field to Hill's exemplary batting and said that his leg-glancing and on-side play, as well as his 'hefty' drives through the covers, 'will always live in my memory'. Giffen prophesied early on with great accuracy that Hill was 'a boy who would not spoil himself'. The South Australian left-hander went on to become Australia's most prolific scorer prior to the arrival of Ponsford and Bradman after the First World War.

During much of his Test career Clem Hill played under the leadership of a kindred left-hander, the robust and powerful Joe Darling, one of Australia's toughest captains and a batsman to rank

Clem Hill was Australia's first outstanding world-class left-hander.

alongside the very best. He adjusted his play to suit the circumstances and could stonewall with great patience or revert to all-out attack.

Darling made particular mince-meat of the attack A C MacLaren brought with him to Australia in 1897−98. Using the likes of Tom Richardson, Hirst, Hearne and Briggs as his butcher's chopping block during his own golden summer, the left-hander became chief slaughterer of bowlers in a 4−1 Australian series victory after England had won the first Test. He also became the first left-hander to reach three figures in a Test; the first player to score 500 runs in a series; the first to score 20 fours in a Test; and the first to reach his century with a six (which in those days still entailed hitting the ball right out of the ground). And, to top it all, Darling's fifth Test 100 arrived in just 91 minutes, which remains the fastest for Australia versus England (England's record holder is G L Jessop − 75 minutes). So much for the batsman described as the ace stonewaller of his time.

Another of Victor Trumper's distinguished Australia XI colleagues, Montague Alfred Noble, proved, by all accounts, true to his aristocratic sounding name. Sir Neville Cardus once commented that 'M A

Noble was in the classic school through and through', but went on to confirm that he was also a player of his day 'for it is possible to be classic without being pedantic'. His style was a blending of orthodox principle and natural development. In 1898 K S Ranjitsinhji described Noble as an essentially off-side player, 'playing forward and back with much force', but just a few years later George Giffen asserted that the young batsman had a distinctly good defence and that 'when set he scores all round the wicket very rapidly'.

Noble was noted for his wonderful sportsmanship and pursuit of cricketing ethics and, with almost 2000 Test runs plus 121 Test wickets, remains one of Australia's greatest Test all-rounders.

W W Armstrong (who revelled in the second half of his career in the name 'The Big Ship') was another grand all-rounder whose crowning achievement was to lead Australia to eight consecutive victories, a feat only passed in 1984–85 by Clive Lloyd and his pace-packed West Indians.

If the slim and lanky Warwick Windridge Armstrong of the turn of the century had been able to see into his own cricketing future, he would scarcely have recognised the giant 22-stone (140 kg) frame that was to make him into such a dominating captain and personality. C B Fry notes that Armstrong 'Mark I' was 'built for driving'. The earlier version of this magnificent player was tall and already powerful, although still reasonably slim. Armstrong batted without fuss or exaggerated effort, with a good sense of timing and, according to C B Fry, with a 'fullness of swing'. He was a strong square-cutter who relished fast bowling and was, for a man who became so large, always quick and neat on his feet.

The attractive left-handed Victorian Vernon Ransford, who hit more than 1200 runs in 20 Tests and delighted spectators with his cover drive and strong leg-side hitting, had an instantly recognisable crouching stance. His sound defence allied with his stroke-making also made him one of Australia's most accomplished left-handers. On a series of damp wickets in England during 1909, Ransford rivalled Warren Bardsley in scoring runs and a dashing 143 not out on a difficult wicket at Lord's brought high praise from all quarters.

Roger Joseph Hartigan was one of the few Queenslanders to play for Australia before the war and took part in what has come to be called 'The Great Adelaide Rescue'. Coming in at number eight in the second innings against England at Adelaide in 1907–08, he was joined by a patently ill Clem Hill with Australia only 102 in the lead and with three wickets to fall. On the next morning, after just four hours play, the dashing Hartigan was finally out for 116. His match-winning stand with an ailing Clem Hill had created the still existent Australian record of 243 for the eighth wicket which was, at the time, the highest partnership so far for *any* wicket in Test cricket. Australia gained a famous victory after one of the most astounding of all Test recoveries but Roger Hartigan played just one more game for his country and, after an unsuccessful trip to England, faded from the scene.

Sir Neville Cardus once commented that Charles George Macartney was 'a sort of Bradman *de luxe*, Bradman plus wit and genius for improvisation'. Like Sir Donald, Macartney had the 'killer' instinct and tempered it with flair and creativity. It was manifestly apparent that the most lasting influence on his cut and thrust stroke-play had come from the great master who had preceded him. Of those who followed Trumper, Macartney probably came closest to emulating the style and genius of the acknowledged 'Prince' of batsmen.

Macartney like Trumper possessed several strokes for every type of ball and was only satisfied when in total control. His domination of bowlers was ruthless and his self-confidence was overwhelmingly apparent in every move. Short and stocky, with blacksmith fore-arms, his habit of raising the bat high after taking guard, stretching himself so to speak, indicated to the bowler that Macartney was a shade better than just ready and able to handle anything on offer.

One of Macartney's most damaging feats with the willow was a world record 345 runs in one day against Nottinghamshire in 1921. Fourteen other batsmen have performed this feat but Macartney's 345 remains the most in a day by any batsman in a first-class game. Sir Donald Bradman's 309 for Australia versus England at Leeds in 1930 is the only instance ever in a Test match (he was out next day for 334). The full list of players who have scored 300 runs in a single day's play is:

345	C G Macartney	Aust v Notts at Nottingham	1921
334	W H Ponsford	Vic v NSW at Melbourne	1926−27
333	K S Duleepsinhji	Sussex v Northants at Hove	1930
331*	J D B Robertson	Middlesex v Worcester at Worcester	1949
325*	B A Richards	S Aust v W Aust at Perth	1970−71
322+	E Paynter	Lancs v Sussex at Hove	1937
318	C W Gregory	NSW v Qld at Brisbane	1906−07
316+	R H Moore	Hants v Warwicks at Bournemouth	1937
315*	R C Blunt	Otago v Canterbury at Christ'ch	1931−32
312*	J M Brearley	MCC U-25 v N Zone at Peshawar	1966−67
311*	G M Turner	Worcester v Warwicks at Worcester	1982
309*	D G Bradman	Australia v England at Leeds	1930
307*	W H Ashdown	Kent v Essex at Brentwood	1934
306*	A Ducat	Surrey v Oxford U at the Oval	1919
305*	F R Foster	Warwicks v Worcester at Dudley	1914

* = not out at end of day's play
+ = Paynter's 322 and Moore's 316 were both scored on the same day: 28 July 1937.

Macartney was known universally as the 'Governor-General' and the first time he was asked to open the innings for Australia, against South Africa in 1910–11, he responded with scores of 137 and 56. Like his famous left-handed peer Warren Bardsley, he also reserved some of the best for his autumn years. A fortnight after Bardsley had become the oldest Australian batsman to hit a Test 100 (193 not out at Lord's at the age of 42 years 201 days), Macartney, just two weeks prior to his own 40th birthday, scored a century in 103 minutes *before lunch* on the opening day at Headingly, Leeds. This was but the second of the three successive 100s he tallied against England during his farewell Test series.

As cocksure as Macartney could be, so was his fellow stroke-player Warren Bardsley the most solemn of men. Arguably Australia's foremost left-hander, Bardsley was the most serious minded of people, so glum at times in fact that even 'poker-face' Herbie 'Horseshoe' Collins was once heard to say, 'Cheer up Bards – it can't be that bad'. But after one of Bardsley's all too frequent long tenures at the crease, it was usually the fielding side who ended up looking sad.

Warren Bardsley batted in copy-book style: an upright stance, perfect footwork and an eminently straight bat. Few batsmen stood as erect with such a high grip on the bat handle, and fewer still possessed as great a variety of elegantly played shots. When compared with his immediate predecessor in left-handed skill, Clem Hill, it could be said that where Hill was more proficient at cutting past point, Bardsley compensated by being more fluent in hitting through the covers and to leg.

Bardsley hit the headlines when he became the first batsman to score two centuries in a Test – 136 and 130 against England at Kennington Oval in 1909. He toured England four times in all, twice hitting more than 2000 runs, and during his famous 193 not out at Lord's in 1926, he carried his bat in a total of 383. As recorded before, that was in his 43rd year when he also captained Australia for the first time, a fitting end to an honourable career.

Four basic styles were prominent in Australian batsmanship prior to the First World War. There were the flat-footed hitters; the individualistic stylists like Trumper and Macartney; the correct stroke-players, typified by Bardsley; and to complete the picture, that uncompromising and oft agonising but eminently useful breed the 'stonewaller'.

Charles Kelleway was perhaps the last of the true stonewallers. R C Robertson-Glasgow observed that he was 'deaf of opinion, contemptuous of style except as servant of effect'. Spectators, whether appreciative or volubly abusive of his efforts, did not concern Kelleway. His sole interest was the demands of the game which for him invariably meant a protracted demonstration of unyielding defence by the acknowledged last-ditch expert. Of more modern players only

Charles Macartney was cast in the Trumper mould as a brilliant attacking batsman.

England's 'Barnacle' Bailey was cast in a similar mould. Although his batting must have been a painful sight for onlookers, Kelleway was an invaluable member of the Australian XI.

As it turned out, Kelleway, Macartney and Bardsley, in their different styles were, together with 'Big Ship' Warwick Armstrong, to provide the backbone of the first post-war Australian XIs of 1920–21 when they carried through to a new generation the legacy that had been granted them by the great batsmen of the 'Age of Trumper'.

7

Early South Africans

'The white population of the Union of South Africa is still no greater than a large town in a prosperous and progressive industrial centre, and yet its record in the cricket field has been as bewildering to our own people as to our rivals in other parts of the Empire'
— Abe Bailey — September 1915

The origin of cricket in South Africa is clearly linked with the British military presence from 1795 onwards. One of the first notable batsmen to appear for a South African team in a match against an international touring side was a major in the British Army stationed at Maritzburg when Lord Hawke's team arrived during the 1895–96 season. Robert Montagu Poore raised the first century against a touring team when he scored 112 for Maritzburg XV and his second-wicket stand of 184 with Charles Hime remained the highest against an overseas team for 15 years.

Poore was later a brigadier-general, and the only man to have ever been invited to play for both sides in a Test match season. When Lord Hawke's second team arrived in 1888–89, the English officer greeted them with another century, an undefeated 107 for a Natal XV. Hawke was so impressed that he immediately invited Poore to play for England in the forthcoming 'Test' series. Fortunately for the home team, Poore's commanding officer refused him leave of absence unless he turned out for South Africa.

A huge man, Poore developed his cricket while stationed in India and in 1899 at the age of 33, he created a sensation during his one full season in English county cricket when he scored 1551 runs at the phenomenal average of 91.23, including 304 for Hampshire versus Somerset. The well-built soldier preferred frontal attack and was particularly fearless when faced by fast bowlers. When asked how he would have dealt with bodyline bowling his swift reply was: 'Fixed bayonets and charge the blighters!'

South Africa's first home-born batsman of quality was Augustus Bernard Tancred, who opened for his country in its first Test against England at Port Elizabeth in 1888–89 and whose two younger brothers, L J Tancred and V M Tancred, were also to gain international caps in later years. A player who possessed both a sound defence and an impressive array of attacking strokes, South Africa's early champion averaged 35.40 for his 708 runs in first-class cricket, a quite remarkable figure for the period and the local conditions.

Matches in South Africa were then played on matting pitches, usually stretched over gravel, and it was not until the 1930s that turf wickets came into general use.

A B Tancred's most remarkable international batting feat was his 26 not out, after having come in first, in a total of 47 all out at Newlands, Cape Town when England won the second Test of 1888–89 by an innings and 202 runs. The local batsmen could do little with the crafty bowling of Johnny Briggs who claimed 15 wickets for 28 runs in the match. Their only other batsman of outstanding ability was Charles Vintcent whose brilliant innings of 87 had been instrumental in a Kimberley XVIII's shock win over the visitors at Kimberley. Unfortunately Vintcent failed in the Tests.

When W W Read took a party of cricketers to South Africa in 1891–92, all was carried before them and the home eleven (without A B Tancred) was conclusively thrashed in the single Test played at Cape Town. For a 15-year-old schoolboy who trudged in to face the England bowlers at the very end of a long list of batsmen playing for a Transvaal XVIII, it was the first great opportunity to impress his elders.

James Hugh Sinclair was still a pupil at Marist Brothers School when he cracked the first ball bowled to him by Kent left-hander Fred Martin defiantly to the boundary for four. Although he was caught in the deep going for another big hit off the following delivery, Sinclair had posted notice of his intention to become a mighty smiter of the cricket ball. During the next decade bowlers from both England and Australia were to cringe before the tremendous punishing power of his onslaughts.

The sight of South Africa's 6 ft 4 in (193 cm) giant walking in to take strike was always greeted with great delight by spectators in England and Australia as well as in his own country. Sinclair believed in one prime batting axiom – attack the bowling from the start. Apart from a rather unusual stance, the alert Sinclair based his batting on orthodox principles, employing a high backlift and ever ready to jump out and drive the ball straight. The bat, it was recalled by Sir Pelham Warner, looked like a cane in his brawny hands, 'but his hits flew like golf drives from the tee'.

Sinclair's first great international innings was a blistering 106 out of a South African total of 177 at Cape Town in the second of two Tests against England in 1898–99. He had already scored 86 in the opening match at Johannesburg and no other South African batsman went past 40 during a series in which former Australian bowler Albert Trott and Yorkshire's Schofield Haigh proved virtually unplayable. The performance of notching the first-ever Test 50 by a South African, and then raising the first South African Test century, was made all the more remarkable by the fact that at Cape Town Sinclair also became the first South African bowler to claim six

Jimmy Sinclair hit South
Africa's first Test century
and was his country's
answer to Gilbert Jessop.

wickets in an innings. However, his most famous feat was still to
come.

Against Joe Darling's 1902–03 Australians Sinclair made a lone
attempt to save the final Test at Cape Town. Australia was already
one-up in the three-Test series and, when the home side followed on
at Newlands 167 runs in arrears, all appeared lost. Although Australia
did finally claim the match and series, it was the batting of big
Jimmy Sinclair which made this game memorable. Of classic build

and proportion, the South African hero proceeded to use his great strength and skill to scatter the Australian attack to all corners of the Newlands boundary.

Striking eight fours and six sixes, he swept to his 100 in only 80 minutes, just five minutes short of Gilbert Jessop's world record. According to a one-time South African cricket team manager, 'Billy' Simkins, one of Sinclair's hits landed in an adjoining field which was occupied by a ferocious young bull and some five minutes were lost getting the ball back into play.

At one point Sinclair struck 34 runs from eight balls received — 4, 4, 6 off Howell and 2, 4, 4, 6, 4 off Hopkins — which may be about the most devastating example of hitting in Test cricket.

Genial Jimmy Sinclair was much-loved, the 'South African Trumper' so to speak, and when he died at 37, his funeral was attended by thousands of mourners. Apart from being a hitter accomplished enough to compare with Jessop, James Hugh Sinclair was, above all, known as gentle and loving. Allegations made by an English cricket historian, Major Rowland Bowen, that Sinclair once cruelly taunted the South African all-rounder Charles Llewellyn over his skin colour proved to be fabricated nonsense.

In any event, Llewellyn's own daughter scotched all previous claims that her father was not a white man in a letter to *Cricketer International* in 1976: 'My father, who often recalled his cricketing days, certainly never referred to any ostracism, except for one incident which concerned the Australian player Warwick Armstrong.' The occasion referred to had nothing to do with skin-colour; Armstrong was upset that a man who had played for South Africa (versus England in 1898–99) had now (in 1902) been included in England's 14-man squad for the Birmingham Test. According to Llewellyn's daughter, Armstrong's actual sarcastic comment was, 'I thought we were playing England, not South Africa', and 'was the only offensive remark referred to by my father'.

The truth is that Natal-born Charles Bennett Llewellyn was a cricketer classy enough to have played for South Africa *and* been considered for England in an era when her line-up included such illustrious Golden Age names as MacLaren, Fry, Ranjitsinhji, Jackson, Tyldesley, Lilley, Hirst, Jessop, Braund, Lockwood and Rhodes — the batting order of the team which ultimately played against Australia at Birmingham and which in the eyes of many represents the greatest team England ever put into the field.

Llewellyn was an aggressive middle-order left-handed batsman who could count an innings of 90 for South Africa versus Darling's Australians at Johannesburg in 1902–03 as his best Test effort. As an all-rounder (Llewellyn bowled left-arm spinners) he was one of the best three or four of his day and he three times achieved a 'double' in an English county season. Ironically 'Buck' Llewellyn's highest score was an innings of 216 for Hampshire versus the touring South Africans in 1901.

As a Test-playing nation, South Africa only really started during the 1902–03 season when Joe Darling brought his team to the Cape after their wonderful 1902 season in England. On the Old Wanderers mat in Johannesburg, South Africa scored 454 off an attack which included Jones, Armstrong, Trumble, Hopkins and Noble and Australia was forced to follow-on. Following the family tradition of positive batsmanship, Louis Joseph Tancred (A B Tancred's younger brother) made a sparkling 97 to come the closest a South African has been to scoring a 100 on debut in an official Test (S J 'Jimmy' Cook, in his first game for his country in 1981–82, hit 114 for South Africa versus Graham Gooch's 'Rebel' England XI, at the New Wanderers in Johannesburg, a performance which will sadly remain officially unrecognised).

L J Tancred's effort was reinforced by Llewellyn's 90, a dashing 44 from Jimmy Sinclair and consistent down-the-line performance from several batsmen who were destined to become members of South Africa's own early 'Golden XI' of 1905–06. The consistent and dogged W A Shalders and the more adventurous Maitland Hathorn played their part, as did wicket-keeper E A Halliwell, while a rugged left-hander called Nourse weighed in with a well struck 72 after coming in at number eight.

Arthur William Nourse, known as 'Dave' throughout his long cricketing life, seldom again batted as low down in the order as in his first Test in October 1902. This remarkably indestructible character was to be a number one selection in South Africa's Test elevens for the next 23 years, to play in 45 consecutive international games and to produce a son who was destined to become an even more accomplished Test batsman than his father. As late as the summer of 1935–36, he appeared for Western Province (aged 56) against the touring Australian team during a season when Grimmett and O'Reilly had created all sorts of problems for South Africa's batsmen. Jack Fingleton, a member of V Y Richardson's Australian side, recalled in his *Cricket Crisis* that Dave Nourse played a 'capital half-century innings' against them and 'gave an object lesson to the young Springboks on how to play against class bowlers...He played each ball quietly and with a spirit of determination.'

Dave Nourse counted his finest batting as his 93 not out against England at Johannesburg in 1905–06. He and captain Percy Sherwell added 48 runs in an undefeated partnership for the 10th wicket to ensure South Africa's first victory in a Test match, with the winning run coming off the very last ball of the match. Nourse later wrote that he was conscious only of a sea of faces around him as he waited for Bert Relf to bowl that fateful final delivery to his skipper: '...and when Relf bowled a full toss on the leg side to Sherwell, from which the winning hit was made, I heard Warner say, "Good God, Bert!"'

Percy Sherwell, who batted at number 11 in a team of batsmen in 1905−06, scored a match-saving 115 at Lord's in 1907 as an opener. Such was the batting ability of South Africa's team at the time that the order could have been reversed without any reduction in overall run-scoring potential.

Other new batsmen in that versatile 1905−06 team included Gordon Charles White, a stylist described by his opponents as the best batsman in South Africa, and Sibley John Snooke, another long-lived player who scored a century against Australia at Adelaide in 1910−11 and who made a surprise comeback to the South African XI against England in 1922−23 after having last played in the 1912 Triangular Tournament. White batted impressively for 81, 147 and 73 in the Tests against Warner's 1905−06 team and was also one of the famous South African googly bowling quartet who so startled England in 1907. Of the other three 'bosey' men, Reggie Schwarz and Ernie Vogler were both more than average batsmen while George Aubrey Faulkner was a pre-eminent batsman and one of the acknowledged greatest all-round cricketers of all time.

The London *Times* obituary described Faulkner as 'one of the dominating figures in South African cricket' and his incredible performances in his few Test series certainly confirmed this high rating. Faulkner eased his way into international cricket against Pelham Warner's 1905−06 England team. He batted only reasonably fluently low down in the impressive South African batting order but bowled with penetration in a variety of styles. Touring with the South Africans in England in 1907, he topped 1000 runs and remained an integral part of the four-pronged googly offensive. By 1909−10, when the next MCC team came to South Africa, Faulkner had developed into a world-class performer.

Although his batting style conveyed an impression of awkwardness, Aubrey Faulkner was an intense student of the game. Very few players of his time scored runs with more assurance and he was an extremely difficult player to dislodge. A measure of his proficiency was demonstrated when he played his remarkable innings of 153 for A C MacLaren's XI against the Australians at Eastbourne in 1921 after a 10-year break from first-class cricket. Faulkner was overheard 'coaching' himself throughout his long innings against Armstrong's bowlers and his batting improved with every ball faced.

Against England in 1909−10, Faulkner put up an all-round performance which has only been approached in recent years by Garfield Sobers and Ian Botham, scoring 545 runs at 60.55 and taking 29 wickets at 21.89 in the five Tests. In a summing up of the tour, his team-mate Gordon White wrote that although Faulkner may have appeared a bit cramped in style at the start of an innings, 'he was

Aubrey Faulkner was a
world-class all-rounder who
scored South Africa's first
Test double-century.

only taking the measure of the bowling, and once he had played himself in would score all round the wicket with fine strong shots'. One of Faulkner's best strokes was a pull shot along the ground and some of his methods were 'peculiarly his own'.

The author was fortunate to spend some time with Tom Reddick, a former Nottinghamshire batsman and a wonderful cricket coach who assisted Basil D'Oliveira to play professional league cricket in England. In his youth Reddick worked at Aubrey Faulkner's famed indoor cricket school in London, 'for 30 shillings a week and my lunch', and spoke of the South African's profound influence on English players like K S Duleepsinhji, Bob Wyatt, Freddie Brown, R W V Robins and I A R Peebles, all of whom attended his coaching classes.

Reddick claimed that Australia's brilliant left-hander Clem Hill described Aubrey Faulkner as 'the most effective batsman to visit the Antipodes'. The South African's tour record in Australia in 1910–11 has still to be bettered. In all first-class matches on that visit Faulkner scored 1534 runs at 59.00 (Eddie Barlow came close to beating this in 1963–64 with 1523 at 66.21) but it was in the Test matches that Faulkner was seen at his very best with 732 runs at 73.20 per innings.

Many of the great players of his time attended Faulkner's school and Tom Reddick recalled 'rubbing shoulders' with the likes of Douglas Jardine, Walter Hammond, Warren Bardsley and 'Plum' Warner. Aubrey Faulkner's young assistant was also the first person to discover Faulkner's body after having found a note on his desk explaining that Faulkner intended to take his own life.

An opening batsman who accompanied Faulkner in Percy Sherwell's side of 1910–11 will be remembered by his Australian opponents for his Test 100s at Adelaide and Sydney as well as for the fact that in a subsequent encounter in South Africa, fast bowler Ted McDonald once dismissed him hit wicket when the ball broke his bat. John William Zulch was a sound right-hander with a good range of strokes who was one of the few consistent players to support Faulkner in 1910–11. His innings of 105 at Adelaide contributed towards South Africa's first Test victory over Australia and his 150 when South Africa followed on in the final match at Sydney was a dogged effort against a formidable bowling attack. 'Billy' Zulch was already 36 when the 1921–22 Australians visited South Africa to play three Tests and the hit-wicket incident occurred in the second clash at Johannesburg. Umpire Arthur Laver told the South African opener that his bat was split at the top, but Zulch decided to bat on through the two overs left before close of play. It was a decision he regretted when a ball from McDonald sent a splinter from his bat flying into the stumps to dislodge the bails.

South Africa's remaining outstanding batsman of the Golden Years period was unfortunate to have his career interrupted by the First World War, but not before he had become one of the few men to come close to mastering England's bowling supremo, Sydney Barnes. Herbert Wilfred Taylor must be counted alongside Faulkner, Dudley Nourse, Graeme Pollock and Barry Richards as the best half-dozen or so batsmen produced by his country. England leg-spinner Ian Peebles, who as a young man played in two Test series against Taylor, wrote in *World of Cricket* that the South African was 'the ideal model for all aspiring batsmen'. Up until his death in 1973, 'Herby' Taylor remained a profound influence on all South African players, as an example during his own heyday, and as a guide and mentor in his later years.

A man of immense personal charm and modesty, Taylor batted with an orthodox and controlled method that stood him in good stead, even when he was approaching his 50s and still playing regular cricket. With his style based mainly on back play, his bat was always dead straight, his footwork neat, nimble and copybook correct, his stroke-making incisive in its run-scoring efficiency. Louis Duffus, doyen of South African cricket writers, delighted in talking about Taylor and his duel with Sydney Barnes. According to Duffus, the England master bowler became so frustrated at having to bowl for endless hours at an unyielding Taylor that he once threw the ball down in a fit of pique and stalked off the field for a shower and rub-down, muttering audibly, 'It's Taylor, Taylor, all the time!'

Referring to the Taylor-Barnes duel, Sir Neville Cardus remarks in his *Days in the Sun* (1924 edition): 'If the best batsman in the world is the cricketer who proves himself more accomplished than anyone else against the best bowling in the world, H W Taylor, the South African captain, has strong claims to be out in front even of our own Hobbs.'

In *Giants of South Africa Cricket*, one of the two best books on the game in South Africa (the other is Louis Duffus's *Cricketers of the Veld*), former *Cape Times* sports editor Chris Greyvenstein describes his own last interview with Herby Taylor shortly before the great batsman's passing. Taylor spoke of the first time he faced Barnes, in England in 1912 during the Triangular Tournament. In a very wet season, and on uncovered wickets, Taylor, Faulkner and Dave Nourse, technically the best equipped South African batsmen, struggled throughout against Barnes and left-hander Frank Foster. On his home matting wickets, when England toured South Africa in 1913–14, Taylor found it an easier matter to deal with his famous foe. The famous Barnes 'walk-off' incident was, according to Herby Taylor, prompted when he and Dave Nourse were batting together for Natal against the Englishman and he decided to go after the visitors' ace bowler: 'I decided then and there to try and hit him out of the attack and, from his next three overs, I took 32 runs.' Taylor

South Africa's Herby
Taylor once tamed the
mighty England bowler
Sydney Barnes.

went on to say that England's captain Johnny Douglas helped a little by keeping Barnes on too long. Taylor's tactics proved successful for South Africa's champion batsman scored 91 and 100 and Natal won the match by four wickets. In the Tests that season Taylor added scores of 109, 70, 93, 42 and 87 against Barnes and the other England bowlers.

Herby Taylor scored close to 3000 runs in his 42 Tests for South Africa and, for an older generation, remains 'technically' the best batsman to have played for his country. His emphasis on correctness of technique was most certainly carried forward in Natal and South African cricket to produce the latter day genius of the likes of Barry Richards, Graeme Pollock and Mike Procter.

8

Hobbs — The Master

*'How many men whose names you never knew
Are proud to tell their sons they saw you play'*
— John Arlott

Sir Pelham Warner described Jack Hobbs as 'a professional who bats exactly like an amateur', a perfect statement of truth if viewed within a certain time-frame; particularly if consideration is given to the distinction once made between 'Gentlemen' and 'Players', and the fact that the former were generally allowed to bat much as they pleased while the latter were expected to score runs with prudent consistency in order to earn their daily keep.

John Berry Hobbs was the first professional cricketer to become a knight, an honour which came his way as much for his qualities of character as for his pre-eminent position as England's leading batsman for a quarter of a century. His influence on batsmanship was not confined to his own country. W G Grace introduced forward *and* back play as the essential for an accomplished batsman; Hobbs, with his uncomplicated, upright and flexible style, provided the bridge between the classical stroke-player of the Golden Age and the scientific 'accumulators' of runs who were to follow him. Although he was the complete 'natural' and unburdened with any excessive accent on theory, Jack Hobbs batted with few flourishes and relied primarily on fleetness of foot and an absolutely straight bat.

When the South African googly 'menace' arrived in England for the first time in 1907, classical performers like A C MacLaren were seen to 'lunge forward majestically at these weird barbarians' (as Cardus put it) and miss the ball nearly every time it turned in unexpected ways. MacLaren even wrote to the press to complain that the googly would 'bring dignity and beauty of style in batsmanship to an end'. Hobbs, on the other hand, proceeded to reorganise his method to cope with the new type of attack. Like Grace before him, and Bradman after him, Hobbs never allowed any bowler to gain dominance.

The Surrey 'master' did not allow the state of the pitch to affect his ability to score runs either. He was equally at home on the difficult wickets of a wet English summer as on the rock-hard Australian turf or the coir matting still prevalent in South Africa. Hobbs's undiminished run-making ability on all types of wickets and under all conditions has led some notable critics to place him ahead of Bradman when it comes to selecting the best batsman of all time.

Like all the truly great batsmen, Hobbs positioned himself perfectly and played his stroke at the last possible moment, though perhaps using his wrists more frequently (and effectively) than others might have. He always performed with such calm dignity and poise and made batting look so easy that his fans expected him to make runs every time. Hobbs seldom let them down, for Surrey or for England. His courage was immense. Only once did he leave the field after being struck by the ball while batting (versus Australia at Adelaide in 1908 when he received a painful blow 'in the region of the abdomen' from a ball bowled by J V Saunders). Considering the number of innings he played for England as an opening batsman (102 innings – 5410 runs – average 56.94), it is a tribute to Hobbs's brilliant footwork that he was only eight times incapacitated in any way by a blow from the ball. His dour Yorkshire-born partner Herbert Sutcliffe suffered more frequently as a target for the likes of Australia's Jack Gregory and Tim Wall. In his 84 Test innings Sutcliffe was struck 18 times, with no fewer than six of these blows being sustained from balls bowled by Wall in England in 1930 and during the 1932–33 bodyline series.

Learie Constantine recalls that he first played against Hobbs when the great batsman was well into middle age but that his soundness of method even then maintained his position among the foremost batsmen of the age. The West Indian was particularly impressed with Hobbs's ability to take a single off almost any ball bowled to him, which resulted in the score mounting unnoticably but with regularity. Other notable shots played by the English master batsman included a perfectly timed cut stroke to anything pitched short outside the off-stump, a unique square drive past or behind point off a half-volley and a wristy deflection between square and fine-leg off a ball pitched up on the leg-stump. Although his game was based on a mastery of back play, he hooked and drove with the best of them. Jack Hobbs scored 197 first-class centuries – 27 more than his nearest rival, 'Patsy' Hendren. The most remarkable thing about this achievement is that no fewer than 98 of these 100s were scored *after he had reached the age of 40*. When most players do not seem to last much beyond their mid-30s (with apologies to Mr Boycott), it seems unlikely that anyone will beat this record, or Hobbs's career aggregate of 61,237 runs (average 50.65). The now-retired Boycott would have had to score 1000 runs per season for another 10 or 12 years (and remain a first-class player to the age of 57 or so) to better this.

In Test cricket Hobbs was supreme, from his debut against Australia at Melbourne on New Year's Day 1908 until his final game at the Oval (also against Australia) in 1930. During this time only injury or illness kept him out of the England team. In his *Jack Hobbs – Profile of 'The Master'*, John Arlott refers to him as 'the poor

John Berry Hobbs shows
his elegant style as he jumps
out to drive.

man's son who became the finest batsman in the world, earned a
knighthood and bore it with innate modesty and dignity'. In just 23
words, one of cricket's finest writers creates a complete cameo portrait of a player and a man who can, without any hesitancy, be listed
among the first half-dozen of the most accomplished cricketers of all

time. The following words from a poem by W H Thompson provide a fitting final tribute to Sir John Berry Hobbs, knight and master batsman:

His earthly innings shall continue
Though he hath left our shore
A great and gracious memory
Will push along his score.

Hobbs's initial opening partners in Test cricket included such illustrious players as F L Fane and George Gunn (in Australia during the 1907–08 English winter), and A C MacLaren, Tom Hayward and C B Fry (in England in 1909). Then, in 1909–10, on the South African matting wickets, he found the first of his two regular first-wicket companions, a man of many parts who had started his own Test life as a number 11 batsman and a left-arm spinner who could vie for an all-time best crown.

Wilfred Rhodes was all Yorkshire grit, born into cricket in a county that for 50 years considered itself to *be* English cricket. This remarkably versatile performer took seven wickets on his debut against Australia at Trent Bridge in 1899, W G Grace's final Test. When he was called to bowl for the England team at the Oval in 1926, Rhodes was two months short of his 50th birthday and three of his team-mates in the England XI – A P F Chapman (the captain), G T S Stevens and Harold Larwood – had not been born in 1899! Sir Neville Cardus once remarked in reference to Wilfred Rhodes: 'That man's life and deeds take the breath away.'

As his batting improved so did Rhodes rise in the order and, in South Africa in 1909–10, he accompanied Hobbs to the crease for the first time to face up to the South African googly attack at the Old Wanderers ground in Johannesburg. England's score stood at a healthy 159 when the Yorkshireman was finally beaten and bowled by Ernest Vogler for 66 (with Hobbs still undefeated), and a new partnership had been born. In the final Test of that series, at Cape Town, England's new-found opening duo added 221 for the first wicket. Against Australia at Adelaide in the third Test of 1911–12, they scored a 147-run stand and then topped previous accomplishments with a massive new Test record of 323 at Melbourne in the following game. It was not until 1948–49 that Len Hutton and Cyril Washbrook broke this English first-wicket Test record with 359 against South Africa at Johannesburg. The Yorkshire all-rounder made his highest Test score (179) in partnership with Hobbs, who scored 178 and was first out after only 268 minutes at the wicket. Rhodes went on to partner number three batsman George Gunn in a century stand that saw the score to 425 before the second wicket fell.

Perhaps Wilfred Rhodes's own attitude to batsmanship is best summed up in the words he uttered to TV talk show host Michael

Parkinson when in his 90s. Parkinson records in his *Cricket Mad* that the then blind Rhodes (who still went to 'watch' cricket and could follow the game well by listening to ball hit turf and bat hit ball) made the following remark: 'Tha' knows one thing I learned about cricket: tha' can't put in what God left out. Tha' sees two kind of cricketers, them that uses a bat as if they were shovelling muck and them that plays proper....'

If there were a more proficient pair of openers at running between the wickets than Hobbs and Rhodes it would be Hobbs and his second great Test opening companion, Herbert Sutcliffe, another product of that northern English county whose name was for so many years synonymous with cricket. Sir Pelham Warner wrote that Hobbs and Rhodes enjoyed an understanding concerning running that 'was so perfect that seldom did they call for a run'. Walter Hammond, who was himself fleet of foot between the wickets and in the field, considered himself fortunate to have had the opportunity to observe two of the 'best ever' at running between the wickets in the first Tests in which he himself took part. Hammond was of course referring to number two partnership — Hobbs and Sutcliffe.

Jack Hobbs was already 41 and Sutcliffe rising 30 when the new 'South-North' duo first opened together for England. South Africa's bowlers of 1924 were given a glittering preview of the star performances that were to follow during the following seven Test series in which England was involved. At Edgbaston Hobbs guided his new young companion in a 'baptism' stand of 136. England scored 438 and South Africa were immediately put out for 30 by England's new-ball bowlers, Arthur Gilligan and Maurice Tate. An improved follow-on innings of 390 could not save the match for the Springboks. Then, at Lord's in the second Test of the series, Hobbs strode majestically to 211. His new aide-de-camp Sutcliffe made 122 in a 268-run first-wicket partnership and, with Frank Woolley hitting up 134 not out and 'Patsy' Hendren weighing in with an undefeated 50, England totalled 531 for just two wickets. The firm of Hobbs and Sutcliffe was well and truly in business.

A first impression of Herbert Sutcliffe's batting revealed a detached and unemotional approach. The Yorkshireman viewed each ball as a separate challenge and promptly put the previous delivery out of his mind when facing up to the next, even when he may have been dropped at slip, survived a leg-before-wicket appeal or almost clean-bowled. His calm, unruffled temperament frustrated opposing bowlers as much as his stroke-making capability. Ray Robinson once recalled how in one over against Jack Gregory's quick bowling Sutcliffe snicked two successive balls to the boundary and was dropped at slip off the next. At the end of that torrid over, unperturbed and with no sign of emotion on his countenance, the English opener 'leaned serenely on his bat, with legs crossed, happy in the knowledge that eight runs had been added to the score and he was still there'. R C Robertson-Glasgow referred to him as 'the sort of man who would rather miss a train than run for it, and so be seen in disorder and heard breathing heavily'.

Although Sutcliffe was mentally all Yorkshire, his batting style was out of character when compared with the accepted White Rose model of all dour grit. He was a debonair player in his youth with flowing off-side strokes and an imperious hook which left no doubt as to the destination of the ball. As he grew older and wiser he learnt every aspect of the defensive art — the straightest of straight bats and an uncanny ability to detect which delivery could be left to go by — which eventually brought him 4555 Test runs at an average of 60.73, the highest so far by an English batsman. But Sutcliffe never forgot how to switch from defence to all-out attack when the occasion demanded it. He actually preferred facing fast bowling to slow and was a master of the hook stroke with the ability to place the ball anywhere between fine-leg and square-leg, depending on the position of the fieldsmen. Sutcliffe's off-driving was described as splendid and his placement of the ball was superb.

He shared 11 first-wicket century stands with Jack Hobbs, with three in a row in Australia in 1924—25 during a series in which Sutcliffe scored 734 runs (average 81.55, and including scores of 59 and 115 at Sydney, and 176 and 127 at Melbourne in his first four innings).

Their most famous match-winning stand came at Melbourne in 1928—29 on what has been described as one of the most 'spiteful' rain-affected pitches ever seen at the MCG. England required 332 in the final innings to clinch the match and rubber, and the general opinion was that under the prevailing conditions the visitors would be fortunate to reach 100. In 1974, aged 80, Sutcliffe recalled in an interview with former Yorkshire and England fast bowler Bill Bowes that both he and Hobbs, on an unpredictable and treacherous pitch, were frequently struck by the ball: 'It was almost a case of waiting until the ball pitched and then improvising some sort of shot. Runs didn't matter. We had to try and stay there until the wicket eased. . . .' And they did, in no uncertain fashion. Hobbs was eventually out leg-before to Don Blackie for 49 when the total had reached 105. Sutcliffe went on to score a magnificent 135 and England won by three wickets.

With his Yorkshire opening partner Percy Holmes, he broke the then world first-wicket record of 554 (set up by J T Brown and J Tunnicliffe for Yorkshire versus Derbyshire in 1898) when the two added 555 for Yorkshire versus Essex at Leyton in 1932 — an achievement only bettered in 1976—77 in Pakistan when Waheed Mirza and Mansoor Akhtar added 561 for Karachi Whites versus Quetta. Unfortunate to play at the same time as Hobbs, the unlucky

Opposite: Hobbs of Surrey (right) and Yorkshire's Herbert Sutcliffe, possibly the greatest opening partnership of all time.

Holmes was only seven times chosen to represent England. He and Sutcliffe enjoyed an uncanny understanding of when a run was on and they kept the score moving with quickly-taken singles.

Herbert Sutcliffe was a model of the perfect professional cricketer. A player who commanded the highest rate of the day, he gave full entertainment value for the money paid him. There was no hint of the histrionics or 'prima donna' behaviour that has in recent years become the vogue among so many players whose performances often fail to match monetary expectations.

The man who became known as 'Hobbs's other partner', the long-lived Andrew Sandham (who died in 1982, aged 91) was, like Percy Holmes, unfortunate to have a cricketing career which ran parallel with those of Hobbs and Sutcliffe. He (and Holmes) would have been first-choice openers if they had been available for some of the England XIs of later years. In fact, the humorous and dignified 'Little Master', as Sandham came to be called, averaged 38.21 for the 879 runs he scored in 14 Test matches, although one great innings accounted for almost 40 per cent of his final aggregate. He played a mammoth innings of 325 against West Indies at Kingston in 1929–30 in an England total of 849 and it was the genius of a new young Caribbean star, George Headley, that saved the game for the West Indies. Sandham assisted Jack Hobbs in no fewer than 63 century stands for the first-wicket for Surrey.

When Hobbs first went to South Africa in 1909–10, a team companion was a lanky young Kent all-rounder who made his England debut in the fifth Test against Australia at the Oval the previous summer and who became world-renowned for his grace in batting style. Sir Neville Cardus described the batsmanship of Frank Edward Woolley as 'somehow luminous'. The crowd always greeted his appearance with joyous appreciation. Few batsman, left- or right-handed, have so consistently combined elegance and power in their stroke-play as left-hander Woolley and his closest model (according to observers who saw both men play) was wonderful South African left-hander, Graeme Pollock who, at 41, remains the scourge of all the 'rebel' bowlers who have dared to venture to his troubled land during the past few seasons. In his later years, Woolley was a frequent visitor to the Cape and an admirer of Pollock's talent.

Like Hobbs and others before him, Woolley was also a long-lived player. His first game for Kent was played in 1906, his final first-class effort came in 1939. During the intervening years nobody could match him for sheer uninhibited style. It is said that Woolley never appeared to strike the ball, it just flowed off his blade, a product of perfect timing and a full straight swing of the bat. Scorning averages and aggregates, he played each ball strictly on merit, regardless of the position of the game. Woolley batted for batting's sake. Sir Donald Bradman described him as a player unafraid of failure. In a salute to the England left-hander on his 80th birthday in 1967, the Australian supremo referred to an innings of 219 in four hours by Woolley (then 42) against New South Wales in 1929 as 'one of the most majestic and classical innings I have seen, with every stroke in the book played with supreme ease'. Former England googly bowler Ian Peebles regarded each innings by Woolley as 'an event', stating that 'There was always something almost dramatic about the appearance of this majestic figure'.

Woolley's positive attitude to the game is contained in a recollection by the Kent and England batsman/wicket-keeper Leslie Ames of an occasion when they together faced an awkward bowler on a rain-affected pitch. 'We'd better get at him before he can get started' was Woolley's immediate advice to his younger colleague.

Perhaps Frank Woolley's finest hour in Test cricket was during the second Test of the 1921 Ashes series in England. Gregory and McDonald had twice bowled the home XI out for under 200 in the first game at Trent Bridge and were rampant again at Lord's when the tall Englishman came out to face them with two wickets gone for 24. The scoreboard soon read three for 25 when McDonald clean bowled the stubby and stubborn Alfred Ernest Dipper. Finding a willing and brave partner in Johnny Douglas, the Kent hero proceeded to bat as if he were playing on a village green. It was a case of Woolley versus Australia as he cut, drove, pulled and placed his way to 95 before Arthur Mailey had him stumped going to raise his century. When England were again struggling in the second innings, Woolley carried on where he had left off to score a wonderful 93 before holing out to his old foe, Mailey. The obdurate Alf Dipper of Gloucestershire, playing in his second and final Test, stayed with him while 94 was added for the second wicket and, of the other England batsmen, only the never-say-die Honourable Lionel Hallam Tennyson went down fighting with a well-struck 74 not out. The immensely powerful Tennyson (later Lord Tennyson) was one of the few English batsmen of courage that season and, in the next match at Headingly, he was honoured with the England captaincy and played a heroic one-handed epic against Gregory and McDonald after being injured in the field.

In cold figures Frank Woolley scored 3283 Test runs at an average of 36.07 (and took 83 wickets with his left-arm slows) and is second only to Hobbs in terms of first-class runs with 58,969 at 40.75. But, as Sir Neville Cardus once put it, 'The score-board does not get anywhere near the secret of Woolley'. Cardus goes on to say that some of Woolley's innings 'stay with us until they become like poetry which can be told over and over again'.

A contemporary England left-hander, whose style of play was the antithesis of Woolley's, enjoyed a career which virtually paralleled that of the Kent hero. When Hampshire's faithful Charles Philip

Mead, then aged 41, went to Australia with Percy Chapman's 1928–29 MCC team he was greeted by one local official who claimed to have watched Mead's 'father' play for England in 1911–12. The amused Philip Mead had to inform the Australian that it was in fact he himself who had, 17 years earlier, made his first trip to Australia.

R C Robertson-Glasgow, who was frequently forced to bowl at Mead in county matches, described his immovable opponent as 'an awful sight' who 'pervaded a cricket pitch...occupied it and encamped on it!' His bat always appeared wider than others' and Mead the batsman was himself, in physical terms, the broadest of batsmen. A creature of habit he was said to have worn out dozens of cap peaks through his ritual of touching his cap four times, tapping his bat four times, and shuffling his feet (yes, four times) before facing up to the poor bowler who could see 'neither daylight nor stumps between bat and pad'. But, clumsy as he may have looked, Phil Mead was a master at footwork and always beautifully balanced, whether cutting with delicacy or driving with immense strength and power.

Mead's appearance of solidity belied the fact that he was a quick scorer who averaged around 40 an hour in his longer innings. Because of his unique appearance and style he simply *looked* as if he were perpetually stonewalling. He was unafraid of fast bowling and played innings of 47 and 182 not out in the last two Tests against Gregory and McDonald in 1921 after having been previously overlooked by the England selectors while they tried 30 players in a five-match rubber. In 17 Tests for England he scored 1185 runs at 49.37 and suffered throughout his long career (1905 to 1936) from inconsistent treatment by the selectors. Mead also stands in fourth place in the list of overall first-class run aggregate with a total of 55,061 at 47.67, just ahead of Grace, Hammond and Sutcliffe of those players who have reached 50,000 runs.

Hobbs, as stated earlier, heads the overall first-class run-makers' table, with Woolley in second place. In third position is another contemporary batsman of the 1920s and 1930s, Elias Henry Hendren, or 'Patsy' as he was known to all his fans, at home and overseas. The right-handed Hendren's first-class aggregate stands at 57,611 (average 50.80) and in Test cricket he was far more successful than either of the left-handers Woolley and Mead, with 3525 runs at 47.63. Apart from his run-scoring ability, Hendren was possibly the first international to wear a helmet of sorts when called upon to face fast bowling.

In his *Cricket in the Sun*, Sir Learie Constantine claims that Hendren first resorted to wearing a 'helmet' when the West Indians were playing the MCC at Lord's in 1933, shortly after the bodyline rumpus in Australia. Constantine and Mannie Martindale had been skittling the home team, and bouncing the odd ball or two on the leg-stump. According to Constantine, the 'crash helmet' worn by Hendren consisted of a normal cricket cap padded with thick rubber, and with the peaks of two other caps coming down to guard temples and ears, but 'the effectiveness of the shield remained doubtful, as he never headed even one!'.

Hendren did not play in the three-Test series against West Indies that season but was, for the most part, a regular England fixture in 51 Tests between 1920 and 1935. He was a thrilling and aggressive batsman similar in style and temperament to Denis Compton. In the West Indies in 1929–30 he hit four double-centuries and compiled 1765 runs at 135.76 an innings on the tour, with 693 at 115.50 in the four Tests. No wonder Constantine and his mates came after him at Lord's in 1933! In Australia Hendren also had a wonderful record. On each of his three visits to the Antipodes he scored more than 1000 runs at an average of more than 60 runs an innings. A courageous and talented hooker, he was particularly adept handling the fast ball rising sharply at throat or chest. Hendren's answer was to hit the ball off his back foot with devastating ferocity. He could also drive effectively off either foot. Above all else, he was a happy-natured man who revelled in any opportunity at clowning on the field to enliven a dull situation. Roberston-Glasgow wrote in *Cricket Prints*: 'I think he most enjoyed doing something outrageous when the scene was all majesty and strain.'

Patsy Hendren scored 170 first-class centuries, which places him second to Hobbs. Third on the list is Walter Hammond with 167. And when it comes to overall run aggregate, Hammond, with 50,551 runs at 56.10, joins the illustrious 'group of seven' who have topped 50,000. The list reads as follows:

Batsman	Career	Runs	High score	Average	100s
J B Hobbs	1905–1934	61,237	316*	50.65	197
F E Woolley	1906–1938	58,969	305*	40.75	145
E H Hendren	1907–1938	57,511	301*	50.80	170
C P Mead	1905–1936	55,061	280*	47.67	153
W G Grace	1865–1908	54,210	344	39.30	124
W R Hammond	1920–1951	50,551	336*	56.10	167
H Sutcliffe	1919–1945	50,138	313	51.95	149

* = not out

In the modern era, only Geoff Boycott appeared to have any chance of reaching the magic 50,000. Boycott turned 45 during the 1985 English season but was still batting with prolific consistency and came second to Viv Richards (1836 runs – average 76.50) in the first-class averages with 1657 runs at 75.32. An injury in 1986 put him out for the remainder of the season after he had scored 992 runs at 52.21 and then he retired. Boycott's full first-class record is:

Career	Inngs	N.O.	Runs	H.S.	Avrge	100s
1962–1986	1014	162	48,426	261*	56.83	151

9

Runs galore
and a tragic loss

*'Many of the records with which Ponsford astonished the cricket world
have been surpassed by Bradman, but if a newcomer were to burst into
first-class cricket with performances like Ponsford's he would be hailed
as likely to outdo the mighty Don'*

— Ray Robinson

International cricket resumed after the First World War for Australia
in an exceedingly positive fashion. England's team over the seasons
1920 to 1925, on paper, contained batting promise aplenty, but
proved incapable of consistent scoring against the Australian fast
bowlers Gregory and McDonald and that happy-natured googly
wizard Arthur Mailey.

The war had also taken its toll of England's bowlers and a make-
shift attacking force fell apart when faced by the rapid-fire battery of
a formidable 'something old something new' Australian batting line-
up.

Led for the first time by the ubiquitous Warwick Armstrong,
Australia batted down to wicket-keeper Bert Oldfield at number 10
and promising young run-getters like Taylor, Pellew and the more
mature Ryder appeared in the bottom half of the order, following big
guns Macartney, Bardsley, Kelleway, Armstrong, Herbie Collins and
Jack Gregory.

Herbert Leslie Collins was not an inexperienced colt when he first
donned Australian colours. When Charles Kelleway left England
under something of a cloud in 1919, the dapper little Lance-Corporal
Collins deftly took over the reins to skipper the Australian Imperial
Forces XI with merit and unselfish determination. He was the popular players' choice and his election as captain was supported by a
major, three captains and a lieutenant, all of whom subsequently
played under him. His work with the AIF side proved to be of
inestimable value to Australian cricket. When the team eventually
returned home after playing in England and South Africa, the national selectors and captain Warwick Armstrong were presented with a
pool of experienced players from whom to choose their Test XI.

Bookmaker Collins celebrated his first Test in 1920—21 with a
winner — he became the fifth Australian to score a century on debut
and the oldest at the age of 31. One of his numerous nicknames,

'Squirrel', described well his aptitude for collecting runs quietly and unobtrusively. After only 12 Tests Collins diligently raised his run-pile to 1000, the first Australian to do so in so few outings. With a limited range of shots and little or no style, he was, however, a courageous batsman who frequently demonstrated his limitless patience and quiet confidence. Collins was given the nickname 'Horse-shoe' by England captain Arthur Gilligan after the Australian five times in a row won the toss during 1924–25.

Another of Warwick Armstrong's key players was that grand fast-bowling and hard-hitting left-hander Jack Gregory, whose breakdown with torn knee ligaments at Brisbane in 1928 brought the first severance of the Gregory family tie with Australian Test cricket since old Dave Gregory captained his country in 1878.

In *Collins's Men*, an account of the 1926 Australian tour of England, A E R Gilligan described John Morrison Gregory as a player whose

Jack Gregory carried on the family tradition as a Test cricketer for Australia and held the fastest Test century record for more than 60 years.

'energy is the keynote of his cricket existence' and when the Australian all-rounder walked in to bat, no matter the match or occasion, he was 'openly out for runs, all the time and every time'. Gregory was an optimistic and cheerful player who lived by one rule alone – go for a win, 'no matter what the wicket and bowling or the position of the game'. It seems fitting therefore that such a player should have, for more than 65 years, held the world record for the fastest Test century.

This breathtaking feat was accomplished in the company of the normally snail-paced prodder Herbie Collins – against South Africa at Johannesburg in 1921–22. And the pair added 209 in only 97 minutes, a world record time for a double-century partnership. Collins hit 203 in unfamiliar style and Gregory scored his hundred in just 70 minutes. Using the modern method of calculating fast scoring – runs scored off balls received – Gregory reached his target in an amazing 67 balls. After 65 years Viv Richards bettered Gregory's outstanding effort in a thrilling, bludgeoned innings against David Gower's hapless England team at the current West Indian captain's home ground in St John's, Antigua during the fifth West Indies versus England Test in April 1986. It may take as many years again (if ever) for anyone to approach the Caribbean master's miraculous hitting spree that took him to his century in just 56 balls. The time taken by both Richards and Gregory was 70 minutes.

Next in line in the Test hitting stakes are: Roy Fredericks (West Indies) – 71 balls, versus Australia at Perth, 1975–76, G L Jessop (England) – 76 balls, versus Australia at the Oval, 1902, C H Lloyd (West Indies) – 85 balls, versus India at Bangalore, 1974–75.

England's Ian Botham is way behind Viv Richards, Gregory and Fredericks. In 1981, the England all-rounder reached his centuries versus Australia at Manchester and Leeds in 86 and 87 balls respectively.

Gregory was a tremendous driver who used his forearms more than wrists and, peculiarly enough, unlike most great batsmen, did not use the 'long handle' but gripped his bat handle fairly low down.

Two other Australians of the 1920s, 'Nip' Pellew and Johnnie Taylor, first came to notice with the AIF team as remarkably quick fieldsmen, each with safe hands and a superb throw. John Morris Taylor, a small right-hander, was a polished stroke-player who total-led 541 in 10 innings against England in the 1924–25 home series. Clarence Everard 'Nip' Pellew was a comparative failure on two tours of England and, again like Taylor, reserved his best effort for a single home rubber, when he scored two centuries against England in 1920–21.

Jack Ryder had just begun to make his mark when war broke out in 1914 but, although his success was limited to home rubbers, a late entry into the Test arena did not prevent him from becoming one of

Australia's finest batsmen. After what must have been a disappointing start the slim and lanky 6 ft 1 in (185 cm) Ryder went on to average 51 in 20 Tests.

According to Ray Robinson 'a long-handled grip helped give him a drive like a slamming gate' and, during the course of a lambasting 201 not out against England at Adelaide in 1925, one of his hammerblows so badly bruised the hands of 'Tich' Freeman that the fieldsman 'swooned'. In the second innings of that game Ryder hit 88 to become the first player to score a double-century and a 50 in one Test.

The 1922 *Wisden* describes Thomas James Edwin Andrews as being the best batsman on the Australian side after Macartney and Bardsley. Unfortunately Tommy Andrews (who was described as a batsman with a 'crowd pleasing style' who seemed to make a habit of getting out in the 90s in Tests) did not flourish to the extent which was at first anticipated, with recurring ill-health impeding his progress.

The period 1920 to 1940 produced some of the highest totals ever reached in first-class cricket. Victoria's uncompromising Bill Ponsford started the trend and shattered most existing batting records in a manner that was an uncanny portent of that which was to follow during the Bradman era. William Harold Ponsford is the only cricketer to have twice topped 400 runs in a first-class innings and his initial assault on the Everest of batsmanship in 1922–23 saw him better A C Maclaren's mighty 424 for Lancashire versus Somerset at Taunton in 1895. Ponsford went on, five years later, to better his own 429 for Victoria against Tasmania at the Melbourne Cricket Ground with an innings of 437 versus Queensland (again at the MCG) in 1927–28.

Ponsford played two further innings exceeding 300. Only Bradman himself, with six scores over 300, has done better and the only other batsman to touch 300 four times is England's Wally Hammond, also before 1940.

Bradman, of course, went ahead of Ponsford in the individual stakes when he hit 452 not out for New South Wales versus Queensland at Sydney during the 1929–30 season and, some 30 years later, Pakistan's little master Hanif Mohammed topped them all with 499 not out for Karachi against Bahawalpur. It is, however, perhaps not quite fair to compare Hanif's effort with the others as the quality of the Bahawalpur bowlers could scarcely be compared with those available to most of Australia's leading States between 1920 and 1940.

Ponsford's first attempt at posting a triple-hundred provided the inspiration for Victoria to race through to the highest team total in first-class cricket – 1107 versus New South Wales at Melbourne in 1926–27.

Ponsford was the only batsman of his time, or any time for that matter, who could be compared with Bradman when it came to sheer efficiency in run-making but, like the Don, he did falter when faced with Larwood's bodyline attack.

The Australian opener was not lonely in his failure during the notorious 1932–33 season but returned to bow out of Test cricket triumphantly in 1934 with 181 at Headingly followed by 266 at the Oval in his final game. In both of these innings he shared in massive stands with one D G Bradman.

With footwork that was likened to a boxer's, Ponsford moved into his shots from an initially relaxed but crouching two-eyed stance with what has been described as a 'crab-like mobility'. Spin bowlers feared him most of all, and against this type of attack he may have been a finer batsman than Bradman. His record shows that only top-drawer fast bowling caused Ponsford any trouble and his first-class tally of a shade less then 14,000 runs at 65 runs an innings clearly indicates that the Victoria and Australia opener deserves mention among the very best batsmen.

With the unselfish and quietly efficient William Maldon Woodfull, a remarkable defensive right-hander with, as Arthur Gilligan put it, 'no flash and not much sparkle', Ponsford formed a partnership that became accepted as Australia's most effective opening combination between the wars. Woodfull's scornful dismissal of any hint of his-trionic display in his batting earned for him, perhaps unjustly, a

The talented Bill Ponsford set the pattern for high-scoring between the wars.

reputation as a slow scorer. His record proves otherwise. Although he was not a dasher, he was considered 'unbowlable' early in his career and certainly succeeded in the prime function of batsmanship – the making of runs and plenty of them. In his footwork Woodfull moved with a shuffle and swung his bat stiff-shouldered but, despite this awkward style, always seemed to get into the right position at the right time. Bill Woodfull and Bill Ponsford shared no fewer than 20 century partnerships – 16 for the first wicket.

For a man of Woodfull's sensitivity the whole bodyline affair was a painfully emotional experience. True at all times to his own fine character, as Australia's captain he totally refused to retaliate in any way to Jardine's tactics, which he contended were totally unfair and without consideration for the true spirit of the game.

South Australia's two unrelated Richardsons, Arthur and Victor, made a joint Test match debut against England at Sydney in 1924–25 for the first match of the series. Arthur Richardson scored 98 in the second innings at the SCG before offering a return catch to England leg-spinner 'Tich' Freeman; Victor made up for his 'cricketing brother's' disappointment by notching 138 in the second Test at Melbourne. The Richardson careers then ran concurrently for a while until Arthur dropped out of international cricket in 1926 after finally reaching a belated maiden Test century at the age of 37, the oldest player to achieve the feat.

A right-hander who played in spectacles, Arthur John Richardson was six years older than his namesake, and a dour and defensive batsman who tuned his game to the circumstances of the day. A popular character, he travelled the world in search of cricket and during one stay in the Caribbean coached future Test stars John Stollmeyer and Gerry Gomez. Victor York Richardson was a cheerful character who is described in E W Swanton's *World of Cricket* as a player who 'in many ways did not conform to the ordinary type of Australian cricketer and at times seemed to have more in common with an English amateur of the old school'. Grandfather of the famous Chappell brothers, he did not quite reach the heights he might have in international cricket. As with the rest of Australia's batsmen his courage was sorely tested by Jardine and the England pace barrage in 1932–33.

Vic Richardson was always of the opinion that bodyline bowling should be attacked from the start and possibly set himself up as a prime target when he had the temerity to hook Harold Larwood for six during an innings of 231 for South Australia versus MCC during the previous tour in 1928–29. When he finally gave away his playing career he turned to cricket broadcasting, becoming a favourite commentator whose good humoured asides in the company of Alan McGilvray (who was himself a fine performer at Sheffield Shield level) lightened even the dullest games.

Every so often an unusually brilliant stroke-player appears to give spectators some inkling of what it must have been like to witness Victor Trumper in all his glory. Charles Macartney was such a player; the graceful Alan Kippax was another, of whom A G Moyes once wrote: 'Kippax is remembered, perhaps, more for his delightful style than for the runs he made.'

The operative word is 'style' and here Kippax did differ somewhat from his acknowledged boyhood hero in that, unlike Trumper, he was an orthodox player, although it was said that he did stretch orthodoxy to its limit.

In *Between Wickets* Ray Robinson paints a wonderful comparative word picture of the two great batsmen. Both were around 5 ft 11 in (180 cm) and Kippax, who had watched the earlier champion as a teenager, modelled his stance at the wicket on Trumper. This similarity even extended to the folding of shirtsleeves halfway up the forearm. Feet comfortably spaced and weight evenly balanced, a high grip on the bat handle and left shoulder pointing a little outwards, if the heads on photographs of each were covered there may be difficulty in telling one from the other.

Alan Falconer Kippax was a prolific run-getter for New South Wales but for a batsman of his high talent an average of 36 for just over 1000 runs in 22 Tests was not a fair measure of the impact he made on his contemporaries.

In every cricketing age there have been one or two exceptional players whom the fates have taken from us at an early age. One was a batsman whose name had already become a household word wherever cricket is played when he was summarily cut off while on the threshold of what promised to be a uniquely brilliant cricketing career. To repeat the words of Johnny Moyes, 'When the Great Umpire gave Archie Jackson out at the age of 23, cricket lost one of the most graceful players it has ever known'.

It can perhaps be claimed that had Archibald Jackson not died so young he may well have gone on to excell even Bradman as a Test match batsman. To this very day those who were privileged enough to watch the slim, quiet and dignified Archie Jackson at the crease speak of him with an almost reverent admiration and awe. David Frith questions whether Jackson's premature death may have caused his legend to become 'gilded' but goes on to assert that 'A wealth of evidence substantiates the expectation and eventual manifestation of Jackson's splendour'.

Jackson was the youngest batsman, at 19 years and 152 days, to score a century in Tests between Australia and England. His grand 164 debut against England at Adelaide in the fourth Test of 1928–29 ensured a ticket to tour England in 1930. But his debilitating illness was taking hold and though he reached 1000 runs on the tour, Jackson was rarely at his brilliant best. His only remaining international tour was against the West Indies XI on their inaugural Australian trip in 1930—31.

One can only wonder at what the result might have been for Australian cricket if Jackson had survived to play alongside Bradman into the 1930s and 1940s. Perhaps Mr Jardine would have been prompted to search for another Larwood or two?

10

England falters

'O Batsman, rise and go and stop the rot'
— Siegfried Sassoon

In the face of a terrifying Australian new-ball combination, the man with the kangaroo spring, Jack Gregory, and panther-like Ted McDonald, England's post-First World War batsmen flinched and fell like ninepins. Many were called to arms — few survived the first battles. An early and unlucky casualty was Lancashire's Yorkshire-born Joseph William Henry Makepeace, who was known throughout his career and after simply as 'Harry' Makepeace. On his one tour to Australia, the dour and almost strokeless Makepeace (Cardus wrote that he 'accumulated his runs by stealth') played in four Tests, scoring 117 and 54 at Melbourne in the fourth match. Makepeace's only major problem was his age — he was almost 40 when he tallied up his first Test century, a record age for a debut Test 100. In fact, he did better than some of his more illustrious peers but was never again asked to play for England.

Makepeace was a double-international who played soccer for England in 1912. It has been said that when he first took his Lancashire partner, the equally patient left-hander Charles Hallows (14 years his junior and who later played in two Tests) out to bat in a Lancashire-Yorkshire 'Roses' match, he was heard to mutter, 'Now remember la'ad, no fours before loonch'.

There was some confusion regarding the names and initials of Essex opener 'Jack' Russell, who followed his father (a wicket-keeper) into the county eleven. There is no doubt about his quality as a batsman. Known throughout his career as A C (Albert Charles) Russell, it has since been established that his full name was Charles Albert George. C A G Russell became the first England batsman to hit two centuries in a Test against South Africa, at Durban in the fifth Test of the 1922–23 series, matching the feat of Australia's Warren Bardsley at the Oval in 1909. According to *Wisden*, Jack Russell played defensively for more than five hours to reach his first innings 140 (he must have been quite a hare by some post-war standards) and, in his second effort 111, he batted nearly four and a half hours without fault. Perhaps he simply gave the illusion of batting slowly while nevertheless keeping the scoreboard ticking over swiftly?

When he was chosen as one of *Wisden*'s 'Five Cricketers of the Year' in 1923, his biographer recorded that he was an exceptional player and a master of on-side play but that he was rather 'utilitarian' and his batting lacked the 'quality that fascinates...One cannot imagine people jumping into taxi-cabs and rushing off to Lord's or the Oval because they had seen on the tape that he was not out at lunch-time'. Russell compiled three other Test hundreds and had a rather remarkable final Test record of 910 runs at 56.87.

The Essex batsman's opening partner in the two last Tests of 1921 was the ubiquitous all-rounder George Brown of Hampshire who was, at one and the same time, a left-handed opening or middle-order batsman, a right-arm medium-pace bowler, a wicket-keeper for England and a fearless and spectacular silly mid-off fieldsman. Brown's face was described as like that of an American Indian chieftain, chipped out of granite. According to John Arlott, this tall and immensely powerful man walked 60-odd miles with a tin trunk holding his cricket gear on his shoulders to take part in a trial for his county. Arlott also tells of the time that George Brown became a target for Kent fast bowler Arthur Fielder after the Hampshire giant had himself bounced a few at the Kent batsman. Apparently Brown stood erect when Fielder let his first bumper go and, taking the ball on his chest with an almighty thud, said 'He isn't fast' and went on to score a quick 50. Brown fared admirably against the Australian fast bowlers in 1921 but was another of the players of the time who suffered somewhat from selectorial blunders and never quite reached his potential at Test level. Facing Gregory and McDonald at their finest and fiercest, he played consecutive innings of 57, 46, 31, 32 and 84 (the last three as opening batsman) and kept wicket in his three Tests of 1921.

Of the players who went with the England party to Australia in 1920–21 when cricket was resumed after the First World War, Percy George Henry Fender was a leg-break bowler, scintillating slip fieldsman and a character of quality who had more than a few pretensions as a batsman. Although 'Percy George' did not quite demonstrate his hitting capabilities to any great extent in Test cricket he created, in 1920, a fast scoring record that was to remain unchallenged for more than 50 years. He employed his strong driving, sure square cutting and audacious pull-stroke to such effect for Surrey versus Northamptonshire at Northampton in 1920 that he scored his century in just 35 minutes, five minutes better than G L Jessop's 100 in 40 minutes for Gloucestershire versus Yorkshire at Harrogate in 1897. It is thought that Fender's first 91 runs actually came in 29 minutes before tea and that he completed his 100 shortly after the interval.

It has been reliably estimated that Fender's 100 came off a maximum of 46 balls (and possibly only 42) so that his record still stands as the quickest in terms of balls faced. In 1977, Yorkshire's fast bowler Chris Old struck 100 off 72 balls (37 minutes) during the death-throes of a drawn match with Warwickshire. Then, in 1983, young Lancashire all-rounder Steve O'Shaughnessy raced to his century in 35 minutes against Leicestershire at Old Trafford, to equal Fender's time. However, O'Shaughnessy needed 54 balls to reached the coveted ton which leaves Fender as the number one hitter of all time.

Percy Fender was probably the best county captain never to lead his country in a Test match. He was also the cartoonists' delight. Thin and tall, with horn-rimmed spectacles and a big black moustache, he was almost a dead ringer for Groucho Marx. Add a slightly stooping carriage and a long sweater which perpetually hung about his knees and there can be no surprise that the ace cartoonist of the day, Tom Webster, regarded Fender as his favourite cricket character. In conversation, Fender apparently voiced strong opinions on everything under the sun, usually in what has been described as a 'circulatory' fashion.

When the 22-year-old O'Shaughnessy visited his 91-year-old fellow centurion in 1983, Fender claimed emphatically that he had always thought that his own feat had been accomplished in 34 minutes! Brian Bearshaw, who was present at the meeting, records in *Wisden Cricket Monthly*: 'It would have been impolite, as well as pointless, to have mentioned that many of us at Old Trafford, including the batsman himself, had thought O'Shaughnessy's century had also been inside the recorded 35 minutes.'

Much was expected of another 1921 season Test debutante, the stylish Surrey right-hander Donald John Knight. Unfortunately this public schoolboy prodigy who batted in the classic manner suffered a severe blow to the head while fielding in 1920 and dropped out of first-class cricket in 1922. He was one of the five openers used by England with scant result during the first three Tests of 1921. The others included Percy Holmes, England soccer international Alf Dipper, Harold Hardinge and even Frank Woolley, in what was an unfamiliar role.

Another England football international who put in a brief appearance as a batsman during that depressing (for England) 1921 rubber was Surrey's Andrew Ducat, whose contribution to his only Test was three and two. Ducat died of heart failure in 1942, aged 56, while batting in a club match.

Lancashire's faithful Ernest Tyldesley was one of the few new batsmen introduced in 1921 who did not immediately fade into oblivion. On the contrary, this entertaining and talented performer went on to average 55.00 in his 14 games for England and was unfortunate to be already 32 when he first gained an England cap. As R C Robertson-Glasgow puts it in *More Cricket Prints*: 'I doubt if the greatness of Ernest Tyldesley's batting was ever wholly recognised or adequately rewarded.' A younger brother of former England player

J T Tyldesley (who was 16 years his senior), G E Tyldesley was so organised in style and stroke that he (as Cardus puts it) made 'all the other Lancashire batsmen seem pedestrian'. Ernest Tyldesley played for his beloved Red Rose county on 573 occasions, more than anyone else in history. That he played in only 14 Tests was England's loss.

In South Africa in 1927–28 (he was already 38), Ernest Tyldesley scored 520 in the Tests (average 65.00), the best on either side, but was touching 40 when taken to Australia for the first time in 1928–29 and played in only one Test there. Courteous in manner, his gentle nature belied his ability at hooking fast bowlers to the boundary. He stood up fearlessly to men like Gregory, McDonald and Larwood. Brought up in the Lancashire 'school' of Johnny Tyldesley, MacLaren and Spooner, he considered it natural and necessary to play great strokes, no matter the quality of the bowling. A A Thomson once wrote that Ernest Tyldesley showed in his batsmanship 'not only how charmingly strokes could be made but how easy they could be made to look'.

When he took the MCC team to South Africa in 1922–23, F T Mann provided the first half of the only father-son combination both to captain England. Frank Thomas Mann's Test career began and ended in South Africa (he scored 281 runs in the series at 35.12); his son F G Mann also skippered England in South Africa (1948–49) and in two further Tests against New Zealand in 1949. According to Sir Pelham Warner there could have been fewer better hitters than Mann senior. He was reputed to have once hit the ball out of Lord's and into St John's Wood Road and, against Yorkshire, once drove Wilfred Rhodes for three sixes in one over that landed on top of the Lord's pavilion.

Arthur William Carr, captain of Nottinghamshire for 16 seasons, was acknowledged as a hard hitter, with both bat and words. A wonderful straight-driver he did not get going against South Africa and, when picked to captain England against Herbie Collins's Australians in 1926, batted only once (score 13) in four Test matches. He is remembered most that year for having dropped Charlie Macartney at slip off the fourth ball the batsman faced at Headingley. Macartney went on to reach his century before lunch. Always prone to the use of provocative speech, Carr was dropped as England captain for the final Oval Test. In 1934, when he persisted in supporting Harold Larwood after the bodyline ruckus, he was axed by Nottinghamshire.

Carr's successor as England captain was the debonair and cavalier 'Percy' Chapman, who in Sir Neville Cardus's estimation was 'every schoolboy's summer night's dream of the ideal cricketer'. Arthur Percy Frank Chapman introduced an air of adventure into the England captaincy, always prepared to back up his attacking policy with personal batting of blazing courage that smacked of schoolboy impudence. A left-hander of huge proportions he was, when still young and before his weight increased, able to use consistently his great reach to drive the ball back past the bowler with stunning effect. Like his Kent team-mate Frank Woolley, he also possessed a late squarish off-drive which startled the bowler who thought the ball was already through to the wicket-keeper.

Chapman was a 'natural' as a batsman, as a captain and as one of the most spectacular close fielders of all time, particularly when standing in the gully. He led England to an unexpected Ashes triumph at the Oval in his first Test as captain (thanks, in part, to the six wickets taken by recalled veteran Wilfred Rhodes) and commanded the all triumphant England combination of 1928–29 which so handsomely took the first four matches of the rubber against Australia before they were finally stopped by a Bradman century in the fifth Test at Melbourne. Chapman, however, missed this final game in which England was captained by left-arm spinner J C White, the star bowler of the series.

When Percy Chapman next led England his team faced Bradman at his most prolific. Although the charismatic England skipper pounded a thrilling 121 in the second Test at Lord's in 1930, he was dropped for the deciding match at the Oval, handing over the reigns of office to R E S Wyatt.

'Bob' Wyatt had, incidentally, in the company of Walter Hammond made his Test debut against South Africa three years previously as a member of Colonel R T Stanyforth's 1927–28 MCC team. The enthusiastic Robert Elliott Storey Wyatt played and enjoyed his cricket in Australia, New Zealand, South Africa, India, West Indies and even the Argentine in an age when most of the more proficient and well-known England Test performers opted out of most overseas tours, other than to Australia.

He may never have enjoyed the privilege of being called a great batsman but Bob Wyatt was indeed a great cricketer — a sound right-hand batsman, a right-arm medium paced bowler and a brilliant close fielder, whom Arthur Gibson, in a profile to celebrate his subject's 80th birthday, named 'the Complete Cricketer'. Robertson-Glasgow called him 'part artist, part workman', whose batsmanship alternated between 'a solid, almost stodgy, orthodoxy' and six-hitting freedom. In his 40 Test matches for England, Wyatt compiled 1839 runs at an average of 31.70, figures which do not place him in the pre-eminent class. He was, nevertheless, a dogged fighter whose loyalty to team and captain was never in question.

An amateur batsman of the 1930s who played in only one Test series against Australia (and one each against West Indies and India) nevertheless batted in so fine a fashion as to be rated among the best batsmen of the day. Sir Neville Cardus describes (in *Good Days*) an innings of 82 by Cyril Frederick Walters, made against Australia at Lord's in 1934, which must rank as one of the most exquisite ever played in an Anglo-Australian Test match: 'Walters was charming; he used his feet to Grimmett, and his strokes were timed to perfection ...lifted himself up, thrust forward his front foot, and drove O'Reilly to the off like a king...'.

In that 1934 series, C F Walters captained England in the first Test when Wyatt was injured and scored 401 runs at 50.12 against a formidable bowling attack which included Wall, McCabe and Chipperfield in support of the 'master' spin duo Grimmett and O'Reilly. He played Test cricket over a period of only two years – 1933 to 1934 – but ended with 784 runs at an average of 52.26 in 11 Tests.

Cyril Walters (right) walking out to open the England innings with Herbert Sutcliffe in 1934.

His debut Test innings of 51 was played against West Indies at Lord's in June 1933; in February 1934 he scored 59 and 102 in a Test against India at Madras; he partnered Herbert Sutcliffe in two century first-wicket stands against Australia in 1934 (only twice in nine starts did the pair fail to raise at least 40 runs), then Walters played his final game for Worcester midway through the 1935 season and was not seen again. At the age of only 30 one of England's finest opening batsmen had retired 'for domestic reasons'.

However before Walters arrived and left, another great amateur batsman appeared who, through phenomenally high scoring, changed the face of international batting — and provided a portent of what was to follow when a new young batting genius emerged in Australia.

11

And a new champion appears

'From the moment he walked from the pavilion to begin his innings, he looked the master...and the moment he faced up to bowling that had held difficulties for the other batsmen, that bowling appeared to lose its venom'

— Sir Leonard Hutton

Sir Neville Cardus apparently delighted in writing about Wally Hammond whom he once described as 'A Sculpture of Elegance and Strength'. It was perhaps the combination of these two attributes which placed England's champion of the 1920s and 1930s in the very highest category of international batsmanship. In another tribute to Hammond, the doyen of cricket writers summed up the great player as follows: 'Some judge batsmen by the number of their runs, others by the manner of their making. By either criterion W R Hammond, England's captain, must rank among the great.'

Walter Reginald Hammond is one of the few select cricketers whose deeds in Test and first-class cricket place him in the same bracket as the likes of W G Grace, Victor Trumper, Sir Donald Bradman and, more recently, Sir Garfield Sobers. There can be little doubt that the unprecedented huge scoring by Hammond in Australia in the Tests of 1928–29 might have added some fire to the future ambitions held by Bradman himself. His full Test record that year was: 44, 28, 251, 200, 32, 119 not out, 177, 38 and 16 — total runs: 905; average 113.12. Only Bradman has bettered these figures. The list of players who have totalled 800 runs or more in a Test series makes interesting reading:

Batsman	Tests	I	Not out	Runs	H.S.	Average		
D G Bradman	5	7	0	974	334	139.14	A v E	1930
W R Hammond	5	9	1	905	251	113.12	E v A	1928–29
R N Harvey	5	9	0	834	205	92.66	A v SA	1952–53
I V A Richards	4	7	0	829	291	118.42	WI v E	1976
C L Walcott	5	10	0	827	155	82.70	WI v A	1954–55
G St A Sobers	5	8	2	824	365★	137.33	WI v P	1957–58
D G Bradman	5	9	0	810	270	90.00	A v E	1936–37
D G Bradman	5	5	1	806	299★	201.50	A v SA	1931–32

★ = not out

Bradman is the only batsman who has achieved the feat more than once, and in two different countries. The Australian also came closest to scoring 1000 runs in a series, although it would be interesting to speculate what Viv Richards may have accomplished if the 1976 England-West Indies rubber had consisted of five instead of four matches.

When it came to playing shots, Hammond did not merely execute a cover stroke of beauty and absolute perfection — he *was* the cover drive, in every fibre of his bat and being. His back-play was described as 'not less than perfect' and he could hit straight with a combination of power and grace seldom seen before or since his time. 'He moved to the ball like a panther on the kill' was Australian writer A G Moyes's evocative summing-up of Hammond's temperament, grace and power.

Though virtually self-taught, Hammond was, throughout his distinguished career, a strict observer of all the first principles of batsmanship. In his more daring youth he reminded spectators of the glory of a past golden age; in his prime he mellowed but continued to exhibit an easy and powerful array of strokes. It has been claimed that Hammond did not know how to hook. Fact was that when he was chosen in the Test XI, he accepted the responsibility of being England's major scoring hope and eliminated all risky shots. Hammond was certainly as capable a hooker as any of his contemporaries, as he so wonderfully demonstrated for Gloucestershire versus Lancashire at Old Trafford in 1927.

Australian fast bowler Ted McDonald had routed Gloucestershire in its first innings with a 7 for 82 haul; Hammond had made 99 before touching a McDonald express to be caught by the wicket-keeper. Lancashire gained a 101-run lead but thoughts of ultimate victory were soon shattered. In a glorious display, Hammond proceeded to thrash McDonald's bowling as it had never been pounded before. When McDonald pitched the ball up, Hammond drove him straight to the boundary (at one point five consecutive balls were thus treated); when the fast bowler pitched short, the batsman went back and hooked again and again, with power and perfect timing. *Wisden* records that Hammond hit four sixes and 22 fours in his chanceless 187 made in just five minutes over three hours — a personal run rate of 60 runs an hour against one of the finest fast bowlers who ever drew breath. Poor Ted McDonald must have left the field a weary man, if his final bowling figures are anything to judge by: 36 overs, one maiden, 165 runs, 2 wickets!

In *Between Wickets*, Ray Robinson also reminds us that 'Hammond playing Grimmett was one of the grandest contests in the game'. Although recording that Grimmett was unfortunate in having a number of catching and stumping chances missed off Hammond during the England batsman's prosperous days in Australia in

1928–29, Robinson notes that 'More often than not the Englishman's smooth footwork enabled him to thwart the veteran's stratagems...', which confirms perhaps that Hammond must have won that particular round against the wily Grimmett.

Walter Hammond's first-class aggregate of 50,551 (average 56.10) has already been discussed; his Test record was 7249 runs at 58.45. Both figures bear testimony to his undoubted class. At Auckland, against New Zealand in 1932–33, he set a world record Test score of 336 not out in the second game of a two-match series, after scoring 227 at Christchurch in the first Test. In all he topped 200 on seven Test occasions. Hammond scored more than 300 runs in four of his first-class innings (only Bradman with six has beaten this) and shares with Pakistan's Zaheer Abbas the record of seven times having scored a century in each innings of a match. As a lively right-arm medium-paced bowler, he also claimed 732 first-class wickets. His slip catching has not been equalled – for Gloucestershire versus Surrey at Cheltenham in 1928 he took 10 catches, *and scored a century*

England and Gloucestershire's between-wars champion batsman Walter Hammond demonstrating his immaculate cover drive. New Zealand statisticians Pat Culpin and Mark Kerly have made a recent claim that a re-check of the scorebook shows Hammond's Auckland score as 337 not out, not 336. If this is so, Hammond will move into equal third place, with Hanif Mohammed, behind Sir Garfield Sobers (365 not out) and Sir Len Hutton (364) in the list of highest Test innings.

in each innings of the match! A giant indeed, and one of the game's undisputed 'immortals'.

Walter Hammond was judged one of the *Wisden* 'Five Cricketers of the Year' in 1928; so was Douglas Robert Jardine, who had made his first trip to Australia in the great batsman's company under the captaincy of Chapman in 1928–29. Unlike Hammond, who came from a middle-class background and was compelled to become his own early tutor in the game, Jardine was 'to the manor born', so to speak. *Wisden* recorded that he provided 'a striking instance of heredity at cricket', referring to his father, M R Jardine, who in his day was a fine batsman for Oxford University and Middlesex.

The six-foot (183 cm) Jardine was blessed with a strong physique and particularly powerful forearms to add to his inherited gifts of footwork and style. He stood up to fast bowling with the best of them. Sir Learie Constantine confirms in *Cricket in the Sun* that, when he and Mannie Martindale employed bodyline tactics in 1933, 'The leg-trap stuff did not work at Old Trafford, mainly because Douglas Jardine played it in the proper manner and stood up to it and eventually collected quite a creditable century off it'. Constantine does, however, go on to reflect his own puzzlement at the time at the tactics dictated to him by West Indies skipper G C Grant as it was clear that Jardine was primarily a leg-side player and it may have been more profitable to concentrate on his off-stump. Jardine was in effect as determined and unrelenting as a batsman as he was a captain and scored 1296 runs in 22 Tests at 48.00 an innings, although his only Test century was the one against West Indies at Manchester in 1933.

Jardine was right-handed, aristocratic and from the south of England. The batsman who replaced him for the third Test against West Indies at the Oval in 1928 was a left-handed Yorkshire professional, definitely working class, but a man destined to be labelled at one time the 'spinal column' of the England batting order. Morris Leyland (his first name has been incorrectly spelt Maurice) suggests two forms of motive power – the quiet civilian type and the hard-working hauler.

Morris Leyland exhibited the qualities of both vehicles and in batting was certainly a player of two parts. A A Thomson put it in a nutshell in the obituary he wrote when Leyland died in 1967: 'Because so many of his grandest efforts have been made with his broad back to the wall, he has often been seen as his side's rescuer-in-chief, but his batting was by nature an attacking weapon.' Ray Robinson was even more colourful in his tribute to the Yorkshireman who so frequently proved to be a thorn in Australia's side when he spoke of '...Leyland of the broad bat, broad back and broad smile', who scored seven 100s against Australia (one less than Herbert Sutcliffe, and in 12 fewer innings) and 'was as determined a dogfighter as

Herbert himself and could be more forceful, with forearms like an Olympic runner's calves'.

Stubborn as his batting may have been in times of dire distress, Leyland was also hugely equipped to push the score along when it needed hurrying. There was an apparent gaiety in his jaunty gait and optimistic mien. Quick on his feet, he was a wonderful driver of the ball, as well as being in possession of all the usual left-hander's square strokes on off and leg-side. He was a major force in the English batting line-up for eight seasons (with three tours to Australia), having made up for a debut 'duck' at the Oval in 1928 with a grand 137 and 53 not out at Melbourne in his first Test in Australia. In all, Leyland scored 2764 Test runs at 46.06 an innings.

Running into the 1930s, England possessed an incredibly powerful batting potential – Hobbs (soon to retire), Sutcliffe, Hammond, Woolley, Hendren, Chapman, K S Duleepsinhji, Leyland and Wyatt, with plenty of strong reserve strength still awaiting the call to arms.

Although his career was short, Kumar Shri Duleepsinhji reintroduced some Indian magic into the English batting line-up, to follow the tradition laid down by his esteemed uncle, the incomparable K S Ranjitsinhji. Like his revered predecessor, 'Duleep' was noted for his mastery of footwork and was called a 'prince of style'. In just eight seasons (he did not play the full programme in two) he hit 50 centuries, and was barely 27 when persistent ill-health cut short his career.

Jawansinhji Jadeja Duleepsinhji (as Duleep was known in his native India) was blessed with natural gifts of eye, timing and fleetness of foot from an early age. At Cheltenham School, Cambridge University and when he played for Sussex he was known affectionately as 'Mr Smith' by all who gave up trying to pronounce his name, and by all the others who loved Duleepsinhji equally for the wonderful entertainment he introduced into every cricket match in which he participated. Herbert Sutcliffe contended that there was no better team man and that Duleep 'was never out for personal glorification, his great concern being for the success of the team'.

Ray Robinson recalls in *Between Wickets* that 'Of his many strokes the most entrancing was the cut, played with fascinating frequency'. K S Duleepsinhji batted with ease and maturity from an early age; he murdered slow bowling and only Australia's Clarrie Grimmett sometimes got the better of him. He did not fear the fast stuff either, as was witnessed at Lord's in 1930 when Duleep took 173 off an Australian attack spearheaded by the pacy Tim Wall in the Indian batsman's first Test against the old enemy. In his 12 Tests for England, Duleepsinhji scored 995 runs at 58.52, and as most of his innings were played against Australia, this was an exceptional result.

Another famous Indian prince followed Duleepsinhji into the England XI to play in the bodyline series of 1932–33 and, if Duleep had been fit, there would have been two Indian batsmen in the MCC team that season. Iftikhar Ali Khan, the Nawab of Pataudi (or 'Pat' as he was known to all) celebrated his first Test cap with a century against Australia at the Sydney Cricket Ground but lost his place after two matches. He played one more game for England, versus Australia at Trent Bridge in 1934, and then waited patiently for another dozen years before re-entering Test cricket as captain of India in 1946. During his five and a half hour 100 at Sydney the 'Hillites' dubbed Pataudi 'potatoes' instead of his usual 'Pat'. Not quite in the same class as Duleep, he was a prolific and graceful runmaker for Oxford University and Worcestershire and an all-round sportsman who represented Oxford at cricket, hockey and billiards. His son, Nawab of Pataudi junior (or Mansur Ali Khan as he later became known) was to become one of India's finest post-Second World War captains and a batsman who exceeded his father in skill and performance.

When Pataudi was dropped by Jardine in 1932–33 due to his 'lack of enterprise', his place was taken by a doughty Lancashire left-hander who gained his place in the tour party only when Duleepsinhji dropped out, but who was to have 'hero' written all over his countenance before the series was out. Edward Paynter was Lancashire through-and-through. Ray Robinson called him 'a bashful record-breaker'; Robertson-Glasgow referred to him as a batsman who 'feels as if he can do it, and nearly always does'. Quiet but firm; undemonstrative but highly effective. Paynter's former Lancashire colleague Cyril Washbrook, who himself was a distinguished England opening bat, described his batting method as hardly correct or stylish, 'being a complete law unto himself in his method of playing all types of bowling'.

Although short of stature (5 ft 5½ in − 166 cm) 'Eddie' Paynter was never seen to flinch at fast bowling, even though he was sometimes compelled to deal with a bouncer with both his feet off the ground. Washbrook contends that the left-hander did not bother to try and 'read' leg-breaks and googlies from the bowler's hand, but played from the pitch and, above all else, hit the ball hard and frequently. As Cardus put it: 'His bat could move as straight as Oswaldthistle Sunday School', or 'drive unethically across the virtuous line of the ball...'

Paynter enjoyed batting against Australia − he averaged 84.42 against them in seven Tests. It is a tragedy that he was not more frequently asked to play. He entered Test cricket at 30 and the Second World War put an effective end to his first-class career. The Paynter Test innings which has gone down in history was his do-or-die effort at Woolloongabba, in a Brisbane heatwave in 1932–33, when he arose from a bed of sickness like Lazarus from the dead and, pale as a corpse, wended his way to the middle. The England first innings was also ailing, but Paynter shrugged off the combination of tonsilitis and sunstroke which had put him in a hospital bed the night before (after a day in the field in searing heat) and, under the shade of a big floppy white hat, kept his end going for the 90 minutes left to the close of the third day. He was rushed from the ground back to hospital. Next morning, with his team still 69 in arrears, Paynter arose once more from his sick bed to bat for a further two and a half hours. He contributed 83 runs to the cause and England gained a 16-run first innings lead. The plucky Lancastrian then fielded for a couple of hours in the afternoon, but after that it was back to bed (and a diet, it is said, of chicken and champagne) until the sixth day of the match. His captain called again, and Mr Paynter arose from his hospital bed for the third time to complete an England victory with a six-hit into the stand!

In all Test cricket, Eddie Paynter scored 1540 runs for an average of 59.23 and played innings of 216 not out (versus Australia at Nottingham in 1938) and 243 (versus South Africa at Durban in 1938–39). When Len Hutton made 364 at the Oval against Australia in 1938, and England totalled a world record 903 for seven wickets declared, Eddie Paynter contributed the only 'duck' of the innings. Perhaps conditions were too easy for a batsman who relished a fight. At the age of 50 he played his final first-class innings when called in as a replacement in an injury-hit Commonwealth XI in India in 1950–51. Although he had not played any regular first-class cricket since 1939, the little left-hander responded with an innings of 75 not out.

Paynter's cricketing drama was played out during what has been described as an infamous period in Anglo-Australian Test cricket. Douglas Jardine, aided and abetted by Harold Larwood and Bill Voce, had introduced the bodyline theory to counter the amazing high scoring of one Donald George Bradman. Before moving on to the story of the 'greatest of them all' in the following chapter, here is a quick look at some of the remaining English Test batsmen of the 1930s.

Nottinghamshire professional Joe Hardstaff junior assisted Len Hutton in a 215-run sixth-wicket stand against Australia at the Oval in 1938, during which Hutton reached his own world record score of 364. Hardstaff was the famous son of a famous father who had played for England against Australia in 1907–08 but, in contrast to his father who was well-knit and short in stature, 'Young Joe' was a tall and elegant stylist. Powerful and fluent, he possessed a fine sense of balance, used his wrists admirably when playing his shots and had natural grace of stroke and movement. He claimed two major Test innings: 205 not out versus India at Lord's in 1946 and 169 not out at the Oval in 1938. Hardstaff junior toured Australia under Walter Hammond in the first Anglo-Australian encounter after the Second

The controversial England bodyline captain Douglas Jardine was also a batsman of quality.

World War and was also a member of G O B Allen's 1936−37 'peace-making' mission to Australia − the first MCC tour after the bodyline squabble.

A young professional batsman who travelled with Allen's team in 1936−37 but who never quite succeeded at Test level was Arthur Edward Fagg. He suffered from rheumatic fever which affected his form and cut short his tour to Australia in 1936−37 but his name is firmly imprinted in cricket's record for an astounding performance for Kent versus Essex at Colchester in 1938 when he hit a *double-*

century in each innings of the match. Fagg's mighty feat of scoring 244 and 202 not out in the same game may never be equalled.

'Gubby' Allen was himself a highly competent all-rounder who complemented his fine fast bowling with some usefully robust attacking batsmanship and rescued England on more than one occasion. His highest Test innings was a blistering 122 against New Zealand at Lord's in 1931 after he had come in at number nine. With wicket-keeper Leslie Ames, he added 246 runs for the eighth wicket — a world record which exists to this day. Apart from captaining England on the 1936—37 peace-making mission to Australia, G O B Allen became an acknowledged pillar of the English cricket establishment and an administrator of energy and excellence.

Leslie Ethelbert George Ames was one of Allen's 1936—37 peace-makers, and a veteran of the bodyline tour in 1932—33. He was also probably the best wicket-keeper/batsman of all time and was, without a shadow of doubt, worth his place in any England XI of his day for batting alone. He hit 1000 runs for Kent in an English season 17 times and rated the following comment from Douglas Jardine after a brilliant innings of 120 against Australia at Lord's in 1934: 'Ames seems to hit a cricket ball as naturally and, incidentally, as hard as almost anyone playing, with the possible exception of Hammond at his best.' In 47 Tests, Ames added 2434 runs at 40.56 to his 97 victims behind the stumps.

Middlesex captain Robert Walter Vivian Robins was a leading English googly bowler of the 1930s but also an all-rounder of great ability who toured with Allen's 1936—37 team. Against South Africa at Old Trafford in 1935 he put up a grand rescue act by making 108 in a little over two hours.

Another all-rounder in the 1936—37 MCC team was Derbyshire's Thomas Stanley Worthington who had shared a record 266-run fourth wicket stand with Walter Hammond against India at the Oval in 1936 (Worthington scored 128). He failed when tried as an opening batsman in three Tests in Australia.

Charles John Barnett, the dashing and imaginative Gloucestershire opener was, in contrast, one of the few real successes of Allen's 1936—37 combination. He batted with consistency throughout and could count an innings of 129 at Adelaide in the fourth Test as his best of the series. Robertson-Glasgow described his batting as 'strong, free, yet controlled'. Unafraid to use his strokes at the start of an innings, Barnett was a fine driver and cutter of the ball. At Trent Bridge in 1938 he raced to 98 not out at lunch against Australia, and reached his 100 off the first ball of the afternoon. He was the first to reach his century in the only innings in which four batsmen have reached three figures in an England-Australia match. The four centurions in England's 658 for 8 wickets declared were: C J Barnett (126), L Hutton (100), E Paynter (216 not out) and D C S Compton (102).

Between the wars, England's selectors appeared to use Test matches against countries like South Africa, New Zealand, West Indies and India as 'trial' matches for the more serious contests against Australia. Touring teams sent to countries other than Australia were in some instances almost Second XI status. But there was no doubt of the quality of batsmen like E H 'Ted' Bowley (Sussex), Nottinghamshire opener Walter Keeton, Denis Smith (Derbyshire), Wilfred Barber (Yorkshire), Norman Oldfield of Lancashire (Northamptonshire after the war), Somerset's mighty hitter Harold Gimblett and the unfortunate A H ('Fred') Bakewell of Northamptonshire, a superb natural stroke-player who took 107 off the West Indian fast bowlers at the Oval in 1933 but whose career was brought to an abrupt end when he injured his right arm in a motor accident in 1936. J H ('Jim') Parks had one Test against New Zealand in 1937 when his son, also James, was just six years old. Parks junior went on to play for England in 46 Tests after the Second World War.

High-class amateur batsmen who either went on minor tours or played in the occasional Test match at home included: E W Dawson (Cambridge and Leicestershire), the hard-hitting G B Legge (Oxford and Kent), Glamorgan's stylish Maurice Turnbull, D C H Townsend (son of C L Townsend who played for England in 1899), N S Mitchell-Innes (Oxford and Somersetshire), Surrey captain E R T Holmes and the Reverend E T Killick (Cambridge and Middlesex) who died in 1953 while playing in a cricket match between two teams of clergymen.

Dashing Kent amateur Bryan Herbert Valentine averaged 64.85 in his seven Tests (he did not play against Australia) and scored 136 against India at Bombay in 1933–34 and 112 against South Africa at Cape Town five years later. Known as Kent's 'Laughing Cavalier', he was considered unfortunate not to have graduated to England-Australia Test matches, and perhaps the England captaincy.

Finally, the bespectacled Yorkshire wicket-keeper/batsman Paul Anthony Gibb played as an amateur before the war before taking up employment with cricket-philanthropist Sir Julien Cahn. Prematurely bald and a teetotaller with an acknowledged passion for ice-cream, Gibb was a shy and reserved personality but a splendid defensive opening batsman who scored two centuries against South Africa in 1938–39, including an innings of 120 in the famous 'Timeless Test'.

After the war, Gibb toured once with the MCC, to Australia in 1946–47, before retiring and was lured back into county cricket in 1951 as a professional for Essex and visited India with a Commonwealth team. Gibb saw out his last days virtually incognito as a bus driver and collapsed and died at the Guildford bus station in 1978, aged 64.

12

Australia's answer: 'The Don'

'Arguments about who is the best batsman in history are a pointless charade: Bradman is not only the best, he leaves the rest of the field out of sight . . .'

– H A Pawson

Donald George Bradman, 'The Don', was at all stages of his career the undisputed champion of his time. He destroyed all bowlers who challenged him at State and Test level for more than 20 years, right into his early 40s. Then, when he finally gave away his bat and gloves and was knighted for his services to the game, Sir Donald Bradman moved competently into a new role as administrator and selector.

No player has ever approached this remarkable individual's relentless dedication and almost unnatural talent when it came to run scoring. So much has been written about the unchallenged greatest batsman of them all that any new attempt can only cover old ground. It may, indeed, be sufficient merely to record the fact that he ended with the incredible Test average of 99.94; throughout his career he scored at a run-rate per hour which was phenomenal by any standards; for 20 years he reigned supreme as the best player in the world and 'murdered' all bowlers who faced him.

Irving Rosenwater, in his *Sir Donald Bradman*, speaks of the four ingredients of Bradman's genius: the first ingredient was *unwavering concentration*, a quality cultivated at an early age when he practised at home with a golf ball and a cricket stump for a bat; the second was a *magnificent sportsman's eye*, the trigger for his uncanny reflexes; then *quickness of foot* – an immediate and appropriate positional response; and, finally, his imperturbable *temperament*; probably the most important of all.

Some of Bradman's contemporaries may have clashed with him on a personal basis for some reason or other but no attempt was ever made to denigrate his unparalleled cricketing skill. Jack Fingleton claimed that he could not recall a single player who ever denied the great man's batting genius. When Bradman first toured England in 1930, there were a few critics, like Percy Fender and Maurice Tate, who questioned his unorthodoxy but, as Fingleton puts it, 'Don noted these criticisms and dealt with them in the best possible manner – with the bat'.

It was a single failure by Bradman, against Verity at Lord's in

Donald George Bradman is caught at the wicket by George Duckworth to end his record-breaking innings of 334 at Leeds in 1930.

1934, which prompted the myth that he was unsure on difficult wickets. Sir Jack Hobbs was of the opinion that on good pitches Don Bradman was undoubtedly the most accomplished batsman in world cricket and 'probably on all wickets if given the opportunity to get used to the wet ones'. The only occasion on which he (and the rest of the Australian batsmen) really faltered was against Jardine's relentless and unique bodyline battery in 1932–33, and even then Bradman averaged well over 50 runs an innings in four Test matches.

A shade under 5 ft 7 in (170 cm) according to Ray Robinson, Bradman was the supreme individual player, who gripped his bat as no other and used it as an offensive weapon to smash opposition attacks into submission. Seldom was he content with a defensive answer to any cricketing challenge; Bradman seemed to have an instinctive knowledge of where each fieldsman was placed and A G Moyes wraps it up very adequately when he states that this is where Bradman excelled, 'he could beat the field, get runs off nearly every ball and in so doing perplex the bowler, weary the fieldsmen, and drive the opposing captain frantic in his effort to stop the stream of runs'.

There was indeed something quite alarming about the power and range of his stroke play. Equally at home on either side of the wicket, he could cover-drive with the same effect off either front or back foot. He was also a marvellous exponent of the cut stroke, both square and late, but it was as a hooker that he rose clearly above all his contemporaries, all those who had come before him and possibly all who have followed. According to H S Altham, Bradman could 'direct this stroke at will anywhere...hardly ever lifting the ball'.

As long as cricket is played, controversy will continue to surround the infamous bodyline tour of 1932–33, when an England captain devised a tactic with the express intention of bringing to a halt the flow of runs from the bat of one Donald George Bradman. In England in 1930 Bradman so humbled the English bowlers with his amazing aggregate of 974 runs (the closest anyone has ever come to 1000 in a series) in five Test matches that a method had to be found to curb his prolific scoring. Then came Douglas Jardine and his swift-as-the-wind fast-bowling aide Harold Larwood, and Bradman's aggregate in 1932–33 dropped to 396 at an average of 56.57 per innings, an effective fall of almost 60 per cent.

In *Beyond the Boundary* (written in 1963), C L R James states: 'Bodyline was not an incident, it was not an accident, it was not a temporary aberration. It was the violence and ferocity of our age expressing itself in cricket.' One can only guess what Mr James's thoughts may have been had he watched his fellow West Indians operating under Clive Lloyd and Viv Richards around the grounds of Australia, England and the Caribbean in recent years. There is no doubt that bodyline type bowling is a 'violent' practice – there can surely be little difference between the fast short-pitched stuff sent down by Larwood (and Constantine) in the 1930s and the sustained bumper attacks launched by Lindwall and Miller, Lillee and

Thomson and a long line of West Indians from Wes Hall to Malcolm Marshall since the Second World War.

Modern practice is at variance with that employed by the England fast bowlers under Douglas Jardine in only the matter of the number of fielders placed in catching positions on the leg-side. The England captain's field setting almost completely inhibited the batsman from countering the bombardment on his body by hooking the ball safely away to the leg boundary. There is also, of course, a limit now on the number of short-pitched balls permitted in each over (when the ruling is strictly applied by umpires). The main difference today is in the number of fast bowlers employed. Under Jardine, England had two men, Larwood and Voce, hurling the ball down short of a length and in line with the body — with another fine fast bowler, Gubby Allen, consistently refusing to participate in the bodyline tactic. Today, few international teams go into a Test match with less than three express bowlers. The West Indies, of course, usually play four such men who are all capable of bowling short and fast for sustained spells.

After some of the bodyline furore had been dispelled, revenge came for Bradman (and Bill Ponsford) in England during 1934. At Leeds (where in 1930 he scored 309 runs in one day off Larwood, Tate, Geary and Tyldesley) Bradman posted a monumental 304, his second triple-century in Tests, with two sixes and 43 fours. At the Oval, Bradman and Ponsford raised a new world record for the second wicket, their 451 coming in only 316 minutes, and Australia went on to win the match (and the Ashes) by 562 runs. In Australia's total of 701 Ponsford made 266 and Bradman 244. No one else reached 50.

Against England in Australia in 1936−37, Bradman led a remarkable Australian recovery after the visiting side had decisively won the first two Tests, playing innings of 270, 212 and 169 in the remaining three matches which Australia won with ease. In 1931−32 five Bradman innings brought an incredible 806 runs at an average of 201.50 against South Africa, including 299 not out at Adelaide Oval and 226 at Brisbane in the first Test played at the 'Gabba'. West Indies and, after the war, India also felt the full might of the great man's batting.

By the end of his long career Sir Donald had scored 117 centuries (the only Australian to reach 100) of which no fewer than six exceeded 300. In addition there were 31 other scores over 200 and his first-class average of 95.14 an innings was not much short of his unbelievable Test average of 99.94. This final Test figure would have been an incredible 100 were it not for an especially fine delivery by England spinner Eric Hollies in his farewell innings at Kennington Oval. He was, as all the cricket world knows, bowled second ball for a duck.

Bradman's perfect balance
in playing forward.

During the 1932—33 bodyline series there was another Australian batsman who demonstrated unsurpassed guts, determination and skill in facing up to the thunderbolts of Larwood and company. Stanley Joseph McCabe may never have made his runs in the enormous quantities that Bradman did but to call him a 'less gifted' player than Bradman is unjust. When it came to *quality* of batsmanship, McCabe had few peers.

A description of three epic Test innings (described by Ray Robinson as the three greatest Test innings seen in the decade before the war) − at Sydney in 1932−33, at Johannesburg in 1935−36 and at Trent Bridge in 1938 − will aptly illustrate the courage, style and character of this most talented player.

Bodyline, it can be said, brought out the bravest and the best in Stan McCabe and, for a few brief hours at the Sydney Cricket Ground in December 1932, it seemed as if an Australian had found the answer to the persistent and pernicious short-pitched fast bowling of Harold Larwood and Bill Voce. McCabe played a truly heroic hand but, alas, was unable to maintain his do-or-die form amid the increasing tensions of the remainder of the bodyline series. Jack Fingleton records that 'the crowd surged into ecstasies that day at the temporary slaying of the giant Larwood'. Meeting fire with fire, McCabe hooked, cut, drove and hooked again to reach 187 not out in an Australian total of 360 after coming in with the scoreboard showing 4 for 87.

Ray Robinson portrayed the event in stirring prose: 'Without a flinch he stood up to the fearsome bowling; he hooked the short balls as if there were no danger to his ribs and skull, and as if he were unaware of the battalion of catch-awaiting fieldsmen, covered by outer scouts ready for the lofted ball.'

About an inch (2.5 cm) taller than Bradman, McCabe was described as a batsman with a balanced stance whose bat 'came down from exactly over the middle stump'. The cheerful Australian used his batting weapon like a swashbuckler's cutlass to rout the best bowlers of his time. He relished facing up to pace and was always ready to drive the over-pitched ball, without ever losing the ability to position himself for the hook − a shot of which he was an acknowledged master, possibly even the equal of Bradman.

The second of McCabe's glorious contributions to cricket lore, believe it or not, caused *the opposing fielding captain to appeal against the light* for fear of losing what had appeared at first to be a safely drawn match! Surely no batsman has been paid a higher compliment than this. Australia had gone in at the old Wanderers ground in 1935−36 needing a formidable 399 at a run-a-minute. McCabe tore into the Springbok attack to reach his hundred before lunch. By mid-afternoon all looked lost for South Africa. Then came South African skipper Herby Wade's startling but successful appeal against the light, from the field, with McCabe on 189 not out and Australia just 100-odd runs off their winning target.

McCabe's third 'miracle' innings, at Trent Bridge in 1938, gave, according to *Wisden*, 'an epic turn to the game'. It had been all roses for England on the first two days as the home batsmen moved inexorably towards their huge final total of eight for 658 declared. Australia, at the close of the second day, was placed precariously at 138 for three with main hopes Bradman, Jack Fingleton and Bill

Australia's Stan McCabe played a couple of the most memorable Test innings of all time.

Brown all back in the pavilion. Assisted by the tail-enders, McCabe introduced a new dimension to a dying game, *by scoring 232 in under four hours while eight partners made 38 between them*. McCabe displayed absolute genius in keeping his fellows away from the bowling and, during the final stages of his run-riot, hit 44 off three overs from leg-spinner Doug Wright. Australia's rescuer faced the strike in eight of the final 10 overs and smacked 72 out of the 77 added for the last wicket with Fleetwood-Smith, who did little but carry his bat and run.

A number of Australian batsmen between the two wars had a rather short life at the top. Victorian captain K E Rigg, left-handed South Australian H C 'Slinger' Nitschke and a bevy of Victoria left-handers, L P J 'Leo' O'Brien, the dashing L S Darling and E H 'Slogger' Bromley were all tried at various times without coming anywhere close to the standard of success enjoyed by players like McCabe. O'Brien, with Darling and Bromley, was brought in during the bodyline series and delights in telling the tale of how he dropped his 'holy medal' while batting against the Englishman and how he and Bill Voce went down on hands and knees to search for it.

Although he failed dismally against the English bodyline attack, there was one young batsman tried by Australia in 1932−33 who fought his way back into prominence. In the face of criticism of his journalistic activities and misgivings about his batting style, John Henry Webb Fingleton eventually silenced most of his detractors with plenty of runs on the board. Although never classed as an elegant batsman, he was eminently effective. As David Frith put it in Fingleton's obituary eulogy, titled 'Roundhead batsman, Cavalier writer': 'Almost as if by way of making amends for his unspectacular batting style throughout the 1930s, Jack Fingleton emerged after the war as one of cricket's most colourful writers.'

Fingleton played one innings of note in 1932−33 − his gutsy 83 at Melbourne in the second Test − but followed with an ignominious 'pair' at Adelaide that put him out of contention for the remainder of the series. During one innings in the bodyline series, Fingleton became most upset when his rosary, which he carried in his pocket at all times, was crushed by a Larwood missile.

The fact that he fought back so admirably and went on to register more than 1000 runs in Tests at an average of 42.46 certainly confirms Fingleton's faith and fortitude. Four of his five Test 100s came in successive innings.

Later in life Jack Fingleton became revered as both a cricket and a political commentator and touched the hearts of millions when he aided his old 'enemy' Harold Larwood to settle in Australia 17 years after the bodyline series.

Fingleton's main Test opening partner, Bill Brown, ran with professional sprinters to keep reactions sharp and learn quickness off the mark, the hallmark of the truly professional batsman. William Alfred Brown would have slotted very comfortably into the English county groove had he chosen to do so. He was a classy, unruffled and assured type of batsman whose consistent day-by-day contributions to his country's cause were a prominent feature of the 1934 and 1938 Australian tours in England.

A brilliant 206 not out at Lord's in 1938 was a highpoint of an exceptional Test career. A strong back player, Brown was also a classic driver of the ball. During the previous 1934 tour, Brown's best effort had also been reserved for Lord's — a remarkable 105 when no-one else made 40 and Hedley Verity was spinning the ball like a top on a particularly nasty 'turner'.

Arthur Gordon Chipperfield was a surprise choice for the 1934 side to England after only three first-class games for New South Wales. He was chosen primarily for his brilliant work in the slips and his inclusion in Bill Woodfull's team was at the expense of Jack Fingleton. A useful aptitude for off-spin bowling rendered Chipperfield a most valuable 'bits-and-pieces' utility man in the Australian battle scheme. A watchful right-hander who could hit hard when required, he enjoyed an outstanding but unlucky debut Test match. Not out at lunch on the second day after batting just over three hours to save Australia from collapse, he was caught behind the wicket three balls after the interval without addition to his score, and became the first player to score 99 in his first Test innings. 'Chipper' Chipperfield made amends in his first Test against South Africa a year or so later by hitting a grand 109 at Kingsmead, Durban.

C L 'Jack' Badcock scored more than 1600 runs in first-class games in England in 1938 but experienced a nightmare run of failures in the Test matches, his eight Test innings producing a run of 9, 5, 0, 0, 4, 5 not out, 0 and 9.

The last Test against England just before the start of the Second World War must have weighed heavily on Bradman's mind over the next seven years. England totalled 903 for 7 wickets declared (Hutton 364, Leyland 187, Joe Hardstaff 169 not out) and with Bradman (injured while bowling) and Fingleton unable to bat, Australia was thrashed by an innings and 579 runs.

The war took away many of Australia's young cricketers and few were mourned as much as the talented Ross Gregory, who had missed the 1938 tour but played in two Tests in 1936–37 proving that he was a fine stroke-playing right-hander. He was killed at the age of 26 while on active service with the RAAF.

Two particularly fine batsmen survived to play in Australia's post-war team. Arthur Lindsay Hassett has always lived in danger of being under-rated both as a batsman and as a captain of Australia because he was to some extent overshadowed by Bradman. Yet the dapper little 5 ft 6 in (167 cm) Victorian stroke-player can be counted as one of the prime re-activators of post Second World War cricket in general and Australian cricket in particular. As skipper of the Australian Services team and the 'Victory Tests' Australian XI in 1945, he led his men with quiet but dedicated skill and, in the process, made friends for Australia wherever he and his merry band went to play cricket. He was a man of immense goodwill who revelled in the art of entertaining and whose self-appointed post-war task appeared to be to prevent the game he loved from becoming a substitute for war.

A member of Hassett's 1945 Services XI, 'Dick' Whitington, in a biography of Hassett, sums up the character of his beloved skipper: 'This is the story of a man who, because he loves cricket, came to be a cricketer; and of a cricketer who, because he loves life, came to be a man whose company all men seek.'

The impish Lindsay Hassett could count among his friends captains and kings but always found time to prick the bubble of pomposity, no matter the individual concerned. The pranks he played upon unsuspecting fellow cricketing tourists are legend, but were always performed with a sense of playful good humour and offended no-one. On the field, beneath the cheerful exterior, was a cool cricketing brain of great quality.

Because of his lack of inches Hassett quickly learnt to concentrate on back-foot play and to leave the flowing front-foot drive to his taller colleagues. He was always unwilling to accept the limitations imposed by his stature. The cut, the pull, the deflection and the hook were the main weapons in his armoury and, in defence, he could be as impregnable as a castle wall. His 3073 Test runs at an average of 46.56 is testimony to his effectiveness.

Although by preference a number three batsman, Hassett took over the opening role in his farewell series, against England in 1953, as Arthur Morris's partner, and topped the batting average list. Sir Neville Cardus labelled Hassett 'a born cricketer' for whom even stonewalling was a matter of humour, for himself if not for the crowd.

Sydney George Barnes was possibly as disliked as Hassett was popular, but he was a belligerent batsman and fearless close fielder of the highest class. His many clashes with the Australian Board of Control and its selection committee may have soured his existence but there was never any doubting Barnes's immense ability as a cricketer. A naturally aggressive batsman, he was in his early seasons a wonderful player of off-side strokes. Then came a ship-board accident on the way to England in 1938 in which Barnes fractured a wrist that forced him to alter his methods, and which resulted in an improvement in his back-foot and leg-side play. Barnes was renowned for his powerful hook and his impeccable sweep shot and, with his ability to drive, cut and leg-glance, he was as complete a batsman as any skipper could hope for.

Later in his career this former Sydney street urchin, who had been transformed into an object of sartorial splendour on his first overseas tour, adjusted his approach to batting so drastically that he was barracked for spending long scoreless hours sitting on the splice. Many of Barnes's slower innings were played on orders from above, or according to the demands of the game, and much of the criticism directed at him may have been unfounded.

In England in 1948, Barnes suffered a severe blow while fielding but came second to Arthur Morris, and ahead of Bradman, in the Test batting averages. He was then dropped from the Australian team against John Goddard's West Indies side after the Control Board had vetoed the selectors' choice. A long legal wrangle followed when the cricketer sued a detractor for defamation of character and called in the Australian Cricket Board to give evidence.

Barnes won his case, but his playing career had come to an end. He turned to commentating and journalism, and lost his few remaining friends in Australian cricket through his disparaging remarks. Finally, an overdose of sleeping pills was the recorded cause of Sydney Barnes's death in 1973. His Test batting figures reveal the unusually high career average of 63.05 with a top score of 234.

Another prominent pre-war performer, batsman/wicket-keeper Donald Tallon, scored heavily for Queensland in Sheffield Shield cricket and was unfortunate to miss out on a pre-war England tour. After the war he was to become Australia's number-one stumper, and it is sometimes forgotten that he was an above average batsman who might have played for Australia for his batting alone.

In any event, Hassett and Barnes were, with Bill Brown and Sir Donald Bradman, two of four Australian batsmen whose Test careers extended beyond the Second World War — as was the case in 1920 when four batsmen (Armstrong, Macartney, Bardsley and Kelleway) survived the hostilities to carry the fight into another era.

13

A 'black Bradman' and a West Indian Lord

'Pride of place in my list goes to Bradman, but George is not far behind. In fact, it is my belief that if he had lived his cricketing life in England or Australia he would not be behind anyone'
— C L R James

West Indian cricket fans of the 1930s may have laughed at the title 'black Bradman', as Jamaica's George Alphonso Headley was known to the cricketing world — they considered the Australian master as being a 'white Headley'! And they probably had good reason, for their own hero never failed in international cricket in any of the Test series he graced between 1929 and 1939.

Figures may not always reflect the truth, but in the case of Headley they certainly provide a strong reflection of the facts about his batting: in just 22 Tests he totalled 2190 runs at 60.83, with 10 centuries and a top score of 270 not out against England at Kingston in 1934 — and for virtually the whole of his Test career he played in West Indian XIs that struggled to match the strength of their opponents. Headley twice hit two separate 100s in a Test. On his first visit to England in 1933 he scored 169 not out in the Manchester Test and totalled 2320 first-class runs on the tour. In Australia in 1930–31 he hit two centuries in the Tests, including a lone undefeated hand of 102 out of 193 at Brisbane after the first wicket had fallen at 13. Back home in the West Indies his tall scoring became legend.

Strangely enough, were it not for a certain passport officer's lack of urgency, the cricketing world may have been denied the opportunity of witnessing the flawless technique of the little West Indian maestro who is still regarded by many as the finest batsman ever to come out of the Caribbean. It had been planned for the Panamanian-born 18-year-old to travel to the United States to study dentistry, but a delay in receiving his travel document from Panama meant that he was able to join the Jamaican XI for matches against the Honourable L H Tennyson's team in 1927–28. Headley proceeded to post scores of 71 in the first match at Sabina Park, a dazzling 211 in the third game at Melbourne Park and an elegant 71 in the fifth and final match at Sabina Park.

Headley's double-century feat was enshrined in Jamaican and West Indian cricket lore in a verse composed by George B Wallace, who was known as the 'People's Poet'. A segment of the verses ran as follows:

> Headley, G played that day as he'd never played before,
>   He made a DOUBLE CENTURY, and then ELEVEN more,
> The Englishmen surrounded him, with every trick they tried,
>   But Headley, G defiantly, as steadily defied.
>
> Barbados has its Challenor G, Trinidad their famed St Hill,
>   Demarara its mighty Browne, and various others still,
> But Jamaica is now their masters — we have the greatest three
>   The West Indian Captain Nunes...Martin...and Headley G.

Two seasons later, the strongest MCC team to visit the Caribbean thus far arrived in the West Indies, and George Headley was plummeted forward into his Test career. Sailing south to Barbados, instead of north to the USA, the young Jamaican proceeded to save the first Test with a second innings 176 to become the youngest West Indian to score a century in a Test; doubled up with scores of 112 and 123 at Georgetown in the third game, as West Indies swept to victory after England had gone one-up in the second Test at Port of Spain; and in a final *pièce de résistance*, Headley became West Indies' youngest double-centurion with a second innings 223 at Kingston in the fourth Test. This last effort was made all the more remarkable by the fact that England had totalled a mammoth 849 in its first innings (Sandham 325) and declared in its second innings to leave West Indies 835 in arrears. Headley saved the day, and West Indies were 408 for 5 wickets when rain stopped play in a game which stretched out over nine days (excluding a Sunday break), two of which were washed out.

C B Fry once said that George Headley's middle name should be 'Atlas', because, as their only batsman of world class, he so often 'carried' the West Indian team. Against England at Lord's in 1939 he repeated his century in each innings feat with scores of 106 and 107 — only one other West Indian batsman passed 30. He either opened the innings or frequently came in with one wicket down and the shine still on the ball.

Below average height, Headley was essentially a back-foot player in defence, but in attack he could come down the wicket and drive as well as any batsman. He was a master at placement of the ball, could cut with precision and possessed a devastating on-drive off the back foot. In his *Cricket and I*, Sir Learie Constantine notes that Headley, 'although one of the smallest of first-class cricketers...made some of the loveliest of straight drives one could hope to see', and added that Headley would drive anything flighted to him 'over the bowler's head up against the sight screen, sometimes first bounce and sometimes full for six'.

But it was as a hooker that Headley most caught the eye. C L R James records a conversation he had with the little West Indian master in later years after the West Indian batsmen had failed to cope with bouncers bowled at them by Lindwall and Miller in Australia in 1951—52. Apparently Headley was a quietly spoken man who never raised his voice, but on this occasion he made an exception: '"West Indians couldn't hook," he says, his eyes blazing, "*West Indians!*"'

The chain-smoking Headley always sat quietly in the pavilion awaiting his turn to bat. He was all concentration on the business in hand and ignored the mundane utterings of his fellow players. At the wicket he was all sparkling footwork and flashing bat, and as sure of eye and timing as Bradman. Although it may be conceded that The Don was a better player all round, on a wet wicket Headley was his superior. In *Beyond a Boundary*, James gives a table for Headley of his scores made in England on uncertain pitches — in 13 such innings Headley passed 50 seven times and on only three occasions did he fail to reach double figures. Ray Robinson made a similar log for Bradman in his *Between Wickets* and this shows that only once did the Australian master pass 50 in 15 innings on rain-affected wickets and failed to reach double figures seven times.

Headley was never known to play defensively unless with a vital reason for doing so. His normal method of defence was to go on to the attack. Before Headley, the first outstanding West Indian batsman, George Challenor, had been a white man. Headley was the first great black West Indian batsman and he set a standard of free and aggressive batsmanship for all who followed him.

His cricketing life was not without problems. He was the first black man chosen to captain West Indies, against England at Bridgetown in 1947—48, an appointment which sparked controversy at a time when race was still a major issue in the islands. Like Constantine, he encountered racial prejudice when he was approached to play Lancashire League cricket. Constantine records in *Cricket in the Sun* that Lord Tennyson wrote a letter to the press which contained the following statement: 'This trafficking in foreign players is unwholesome, if not positively offensive. I make no mistake when I declare that every native boy with an aptitude for cricket dreams of the coming of the day when he will be "bought" by some English Boss.' Perhaps Tennyson was still sour at the treatment his own bowlers got from Headley back in 1927—28, and again in 1931—32 when the little Jamaican took 344 not out off his Lordship's attack and added 487 in an unbroken stand with Clarence Passailaigue, who scored 261 not out!

According to Headley's Jamaican contemporary, author John J Figueros, questions of colour, class and intense inter-territorial rivalry bedevilled cricketing relationships in the West Indies in Headley's

George Headley, the 'black Bradman', demonstrates his relaxed and comfortable stance.

time and some of the things that happened then are now difficult to believe. Colour and class certainly entered into consideration when it came to choice of captain, who would frequently travel first-class while the team travelled second. Unbelievably, on one trip to Barbados and British Guiana, Headley and Constantine were even forced to share a bed.

Headley also had his occasional ups and downs with officials at home in Jamaica but was an honoured citizen of Jamaica and a Member of the British Empire (MBE) when he passed away in 1983. He experienced what has been described as a rather distant relationship with his son, who was left behind in England at the age of 14 when George Headley returned, by public demand, from his league engagements in England to play for West Indies in 1947−48. Ronald George Alphonso Headley only saw his father again on four brief occasions but went on to play for Worcestershire from 1958 to 1974 as a classy left-hand batsman and ultimately represented West Indies in two Test matches against England in 1973.

The black George Headley succeeded the white George Challenor as the pre-eminent West Indian batsman and, if he had had Headley's opportunities, Challenor may have been recorded in the international cricket record books with as much emphasis as Headley. By all accounts Challenor must have been a grand player; Constantine certainly thought very highly of him and his opening partner P H 'Tim' Tarilton: 'I have bowled at Hobbs and Sutcliffe at the Oval and against Woodfull and Ponsford at Sydney, but Tarilton and Challenor batting for Barbados at the Kensington Oval were worthy to stand in that great company'. Unfortunately Challenor (already 40) played in only one Test series − West Indies' first, in England in 1928. Tarilton was by then already 43 and did not tour that season.

Before Challenor and Tarilton, the West Indies boasted a string of fine batsmen who scored prolifically in inter-colonial matches or made their mark on early England tours. Men like Percy Goodman, Harry Ince and H B G Austin from Barbados, Charles Ollivierre from the little isle of St Vincent (who remained in England after the 1900 West Indies tour to play for Derbyshire for seven seasons), J K Holt senior from Jamaica and Andre Cipriani from Trinidad were the forerunners of the long line of West Indian batsmen.

Another Trinidad player who also arrived on the scene a bit too early to make his mark in Test cricket was the six foot (183 cm) tall, strong and stylish Wilton St Hill, who played in only three internationals but is mentioned by C L R James in the same breath as Sobers, Headley and the three Ws, Worrell, Weekes and Walcott.

The steady Jamaican left-hander Frank Reginald Martin had more opportunities than some of the other early West Indian batsmen and could count an innings of 123 not out against Australia in the fifth Test at Sydney in 1930−31 as his crowning achievement. His 100, plus a century from Headley, gave West Indies its first Test win against Australia. 'Freddie' Martin was described as a difficult player to dislodge and he went on three tours with West Indian teams, to Australia in 1930–31 and twice to England, in 1928 and 1933.

Trinidad's Clifford Archibald Roach was an adventurous right-hand opener, second only to George Headley as a batsman in the early West Indies series. He totalled more than 1000 runs on his two tours to England (1928 and 1933) and, at Georgetown in 1929–30, playing a dazzling innings of 209 in under five hours against an England attack that included Voce and Rhodes. In the opening match of that rubber, at Bridgetown, Roach had led off with the first-ever century by a West Indian in a Test match. He never again quite approached his debut form in subsequent series.

Barbados's James Edward Derek Sealy became the youngest cricketer ever to represent West Indies (17 years, 122 days) when the schoolboy was chosen for the Bridgetown Test against England in 1929–30. He was an outstanding utility player who was used at various times as a stylish and attacking batsman, a bowler of outswingers and a wicket-keeper. He later revealed that during his debut innings of 58 he received frequent advice and encouragement from one of the umpires, old England batsman Joe Hardstaff senior. Derek Sealy was at one time considered as fine a prospect as Headley but failed to fulfill the promise of youth.

One of West Indies' leading pre-war wicket-keepers, Ivan Barrow, claims the distinction of scoring the first century for his country during a Test in England. He opened the batting with Headley in the second Test at Old Trafford in 1933 and the two batsmen raced neck-and-neck for their coveted three-figure target. At one point Headley had 99, Barrow 94 and it looked as if the former would be first. His fellow Jamaican then took six runs from an over by Hammond and pipped him at the post. The slimly-built Barrow later in life became a prominent horse-racing personality and commentator.

The Grant brothers from Trinidad both captained West Indies in between-wars Tests. The elder, George Copeland Grant, was like his younger brother a Cambridge Blue and led West Indies in all 12 Tests in which he participated. A plucky right-hander of optimistic mien, 'Jacky' Grant was at his best in a fight and scored 53 and 71, both innings not out, in a vain attempt to save the day against Australia in the first Test of 1930–31. A much-travelled player, he appeared for Rhodesia in the South African Currie Cup competition in 1931–32.

The tall and handsome Rolph Stewart Grant captained West Indies in England in the 1939 tour cut short when war with Germany appeared certain. He was a remarkable all-round sportsman who kept goal for England at soccer and was at one time Trinidad's heavyweight boxing champion. His only feat of note with the bat in

Test cricket came at Old Trafford in 1939 when he opened the innings and proceeded to hit 47 out of 56 in 38 minutes, including three sixes from off-spinner Tom Goddard on a rain-affected pitch, before being caught in front of the sightscreen.

Of all the pre-war batsmen, one of the strangest stories, when it comes to a matter of intervals between appearances, was that of George McDonald Carew from Barbados. A sound right-handed opener, he scored a duck in his first appearance in January 1935 — against England on a 'sticky' pitch at Kensington Oval, Bridgetown. Carew waited patiently for more than 13 years, until February 1948, when he was again picked to play for West Indies, this time at Queen's Park Oval, Port of Spain. Wearing a chocolate-coloured felt hat and chewing gum incessantly like an American GI, he vented his frustration on the England attack and smashed 107 in an opening stand with Andy Ganteaume. Carew appeared in only two more Tests, the following match of the England series at Georgetown, and against India at Calcutta in 1948−49. His opening partner at Port of Spain in 1948, Andrew George Ganteaume from Trinidad, was less fortunate and is still awaiting a second chance!

Poor Andy Ganteaume also scored a century in the game against England that marked his debut Test, was dropped for the next game, and was never again called to play for West Indies. He claimed in later years that he was unfairly treated to accommodate establishment players.

The 1939 West Indies tour of England was abandoned at the close of a three-match Test series, and with seven more tour matches still to be played, when the clouds of war began to drift across the Channel. J B Stollmeyer and G E Gomez were fortunate to be picked again for West Indies eight years later, when Test cricket was resumed after the war; other newcomers V H Stollmeyer and K H Weekes, both of whom made auspicious entries into international cricket, had to remain content with their brief encounter with Test cricket.

The quick-scoring opener Victor Humphrey Stollmeyer from Trinidad was just 23 years old when he shrugged off early tour tonsillitis to hit 96 in his only Test innings in the third and final match of the 1939 rubber at the Oval. Almost immediately after his arrival at the wicket, a bad call by Vic Stollmeyer saw the great George Headley run out. To make amends the new player stayed put and shared a brilliant 163-run fifth-wicket stand with the barrel-chested Jamaican Kenneth Hunnell Weekes, an unorthodox left-hander who scored freely all round the wicket. *Wisden* remarks on the partnerships between 'Bam Bam' Weekes and his partner in the following terms: 'The left-hander and V Stollmeyer quickly took complete control and the bowling received drastic punishment.' The first 200 runs of the innings had come in 230 minutes; Weekes and

Stollmeyer then raised 110 in the next hour, with 43 runs coming off four overs from seam bowlers Nicholls and Perks, and the entire 163 partnership was accomplished in just 100 minutes. Kenneth Weekes went on to hit 137 in his second and final Test.

West Indies had lost the first Test of that series at Lord's (despite a Headley twin effort of 106 and 107) and rain had helped them force a draw in the second Test at Manchester. Although the match ended in another draw, their effort at the Oval provided a fitting climax to pre-war West Indies Test cricket.

England had been dismissed for 352 on the first day of the three-day Test and the entertaining West Indian reply made sure of a draw at least. Victor Stollmeyer's younger brother, 18-year-old J B Stollmeyer, scored 59 and shared a 113-run second wicket stand with Headley; then came Headley's run out and, after 19-year-old Gerry Gomez had left early, the Vic Stollmeyer-Weekes partnership ensued. A blistering onslaught by the famous Learie Constantine followed and West Indies ended with 498. England took no chances on the final day and batted through to the end, with centuries from Hutton and Hammond.

Jeffrey Baxter Stollmeyer can be recorded as one of West Indies' premier Test batsmen. In *West Indian Cricket*, Christopher Nicole states that most of Jeff Stollmeyer's innings can be described 'in terms rare in cricket, lovely, elegant, soft and charming...not the type to break a bowler's heart'. The tall, cultured and well-proportioned Stollmeyer was a pleasure to observe at the crease. He has been described as a 'batsman's batsman', a player who executed all of the strokes, off back and front foot, with due observance of the tenets of orthodoxy. While some of the other young West Indian batsmen fell away during the war years, Stollmeyer continued to concentrate on his game and to log some huge scores in domestic cricket, including an inning of 324 for Trinidad versus British Guiana at Port of Spain, when he and Gerry Gomez (190) added 434 for the third wicket — a feat which remains a West Indian first-class record.

Thus, when Test cricket resumed in 1947—48, Jeffrey Stollmeyer was an automatic selection for the West Indies XI. He formed with Jamaica's left-handed Allan Rae one of the finest opening partnerships in cricket history. Their achievements for the first wicket played no little part in preparing the way for the prolifically scoring Worrell, Weekes and Walcott, who followed in the batting order. Jeffrey Stollmeyer eventually became a senator in the Trinidad legislature and, as did his old batting partner Rae, a respected president of the West Indies Cricket Board of Control.

Stollmeyer's fellow teenage team-mate in the 1939 team, Gerald Ethridge Gomez, has also been notable as a West Indies cricket administrator since he retired from active cricket, and has been a well-respected radio commentator on the game. Gerry Gomez started off as a batsman pure and simple, dependable rather than stylish, but no less effective for it. After the war, in India in 1947–48 he began to emerge as a true all-rounder and for a period was, at medium pace, the stock bowler of the West Indies team. As a batsman who followed the likes of Stollmeyer, Rae, Worrell, Weekes and Walcott in the order, he was usually forced to tailor his game to the needs of the day. If there had been an early collapse (which was not a very frequent occurrence other than in Australia in 1951–52) he would be compelled to knuckle down and save the day; when he came in with plenty of runs already on the board, he was expected to maintain the momentum.

Gomez's best Test season was in Australia in 1951–52 when Worrell, Weekes and company failed consistently to master the short-pitched bowling of Miller and Lindwall. Although his highest score in 10 innings was only 55, he rarely failed and took 10 wickets in the fifth Test at Sydney. Gerry Gomez hit his only Test century against India at New Delhi in 1947–48.

One essentially important West Indian player has been kept for the end of this chapter because, through sheer force of character and stunning ability as a dynamic cricketer, he typified what has now become the popular image of a West Indian cricketer – a player who was, in fact, a perfect model for all future West Indian cricketers.

This description fits only one man: Learie Nicholas Constantine. His incredible 'rags-to-riches' story sounds like fiction – a tale of a barefoot plantation boy, grandson of a slave, who rose to play Test cricket, became a barrister and a social activist, represented his country as High Commissioner in London, received a knighthood and, finally, took his seat in the House of Lords so that, when he passed on to the Elysian fields, it was as Baron Constantine MBE, Peer of the Realm. He remained throughout an inspiration to all cricketers, young and old, to all politicians and administrators and, perhaps most important, to all those who are born without social and financial advantage.

The vision of Learie Constantine the cricketer is of a tearaway fast bowler, an 'electric heels' fielder and catcher and an habitual six-hitter with every stroke in the book plus more than a few unique to his own brand of genius. As this book is about batting, Constantine's skill as bowler and fielder will be left aside for the moment.

His father was Lebrun Samuel Constantine, an estate overseer whose own father had been a plantation slave and who had toured England twice as a batsman during the early 1900s. In Trinidad 'Old Cons' was one of the most loved cricketers of his time; kindly but firm, in character and conviction. He was also one of the best island batsmen of the time who scored the first century by a West Indian in England; a useful bowler, fine fielder and a wicket-keeper (he kept for the first-ever representative West Indies XI against A Priestley's

West Indian Learie Constantine was probably the most audacious cricketer of all time.

English team at Port of Spain in February 1897).

Although figures will show that Learie Constantine was not the most prolific batsman of *his* time, he can certainly lay claim to having been the most electrifying and the most famous of improvisors.

Learie Constantine's stroke-playing was never premeditated – he endeavoured to score off each ball he faced and, if a conventional shot would not accomplish his purpose, he would invent one on the spur of the moment. C L R James recalls seeing him bat against Hammond in Trinidad one day and, having played forward to a ball pitched outside off stump and moving in to his body, he found himself crowded for a stroke and, bending over backwards to give himself room, cut the ball to the left of point for four. 'What made us sit up and take notice was that he had never in his life made such a stroke before...'. When he once cracked Queensland Aboriginal fast-bowling terror Eddie Gilbert for a six to square leg, the bemused

Gilbert shook his head in wonder at the stroke employed and came straight across to congratulate Constantine — and told him that it was the first time he had ever been hit for six!

In that final Oval Test before the war, Constantine played the last notable innings in pre-war Test cricket in, as *Wisden* records it, 'the mood suggesting his work in Saturday afternoon League cricket'. The description of his innings of 79 that day (made out of the 109 added for the last four wickets) continues: 'He revolutionized all the recognised features of cricket and, surpassing Bradman in his amazing stroke play, he was absolutely impudent in his treatment of bowling shared by Nichols and Perks.' Both the bowlers mentioned were new-ball bowlers of fair pace. Constantine hit one six straight back over Perks's head which will forever remain in the memories of those who were fortunate enough to witness the blow. He was eventually dismissed going for a six over the wicket-keeper's head!

Sadly, Learie Constantine's Test batting performances of note were few and far between but his amazing big-hitting capability will remain enshrined in the two innings he played for West Indians versus Middlesex at Lord's in 1928. After slamming 86 in an hour in the West Indians' first innings, he casually claimed seven Middlesex second innings wickets for 57 to set his side up for victory. Then, to round the game off (and make it 'Constantine's match') the Trinidad hitter unleashed an unprecedented array of dazzling strokes to reach a spectacular 103 — in an hour! One of his hits was a *cover-drive* for six off England fast bowler Gubby Allen, another shot, off his back foot, broke a finger on the bowler Hearne's hand before scudding through to the boundary fence.

Constantine became a barrister and his book *Colour Bar* was published in 1954. In 1966 he joined the Race Relations Board and was elected to the peerage. When Lord Constantine died in 1969, his body was flown back to his home island, Trinidad, where its arrival was greeted by a guard of honour and a 19-gun salute. He was buried with the ceremony of a State funeral. His memory remains as the West Indian cricketer who was West Indian cricket, just as Grace was English cricket.

14

New Zealand newcomers

'In the nigh on 140 years it (cricket) has been faithfully followed and played in New Zealand, 90 were spent in achieving Test-match status'
— T P McLean (in *World of Cricket*)

Cricket in New Zealand has been recorded as far back as 1840 and a number of the early England teams visiting Australia also sailed further east to fulfill a few fixtures. In 1878, Murdoch's Australian team went to New Zealand and met with resistance when they insisted that Canterbury field 22 men as was the custom. Canterbury wanted to play 11 men but compromised at 15 and to the surprise and disgust of Murdoch and company Canterbury won the match! It was to be some years before New Zealand were to meet other cricketing nations on equal terms and even longer before Test-status would be granted and a maiden international victory gained.

A number of batsmen in the early years distinguished themselves against various touring combinations. Canterbury left-hander Daniel Reese was an early batting hero. Aged 23, he hit 20 boundaries in a sparkling four-hour 148 against Lord Hawke's XI at Basin Reserve, Wellington in 1902–03, off an attack that included two Test bowlers. Against South Australia at Adelaide in 1913–14, when Reese was 34, he scored 96 and 130 not out. Wicket-keeper Edmund Vernon Sale collected a more patient 109 not out off Sim's awesomely powerful Australian team in the same season. Against a strong MCC team at Christchurch in 1922–23, the veteran opener David Collins cover drove the first ball for four and went on to a chanceless 102 in 133 minutes. Famed New Zealand big-hitter 'Ces' Dacre also shone in the same match.

When the New Zealand side visited England for the first time in 1927, Charles Christian Ralph Dacre was one of the stars of the team. No Tests were played but Dacre hit two of the 19 centuries scored by New Zealanders that season, including a grand 107 against the MCC at Lord's. *The Times* described him as 'a natural forcing batsman who never descends to vulgar hitting'. Dick Brittenden writes in *New Zealand Cricketers* that Dacre 'nearly always scored at astonishing speed, but there was nothing slap-dash about it'. Dacre never player in an official Test but did play for Gloucestershire from 1928 to 1936.

Six other New Zealand batsmen who had accompanied Dacre to England in 1927 found places in the first-ever official New Zealand

Test series against England in 1929–30: C S Dempster, M L Page, R C Blunt, T C Lowry, J E Mills and C F W Allcott.

Cyril Francis Walter Allcott was an all-rounder who never quite made it as a Test batsman. The painstaking Milford Laurenson 'Curly' Page went on to play 14 Tests for New Zealand (he was captain in seven of them) and scored 104 at Lord's in his country's first Test in England. John Ernest Mills was a left-hander whose style was described as straight and beautiful. In 1929–30, on his Test debut in the second match of the series, he made 117 against England at Wellington (to become the first New Zealander to score a Test century) and helped Dempster add 276 for the first wicket – a record which still stands. He seldom again reached the same form in international matches but scored heavily on two tours of England.

Thomas Coleman Lowry was New Zealand's captain for its first two series, home and away against England. Although he did not score heavily in his seven Tests, he was strong in attack, as a batsman and a popular captain and team manager. A magnificent utility player, 'Tom' Lowry also kept wicket and bowled right-arm slow. He was a Cambridge Blue and played a fair number of matches for Somerset in English county cricket. His Somerset colleague R C Robertson-Glasgow referred to Lowry as 'a leader in a thousand'.

Roger Charles Blunt was in batting style the antithesis of his surname. He was, indeed, one of the most graceful of performers and, according to Brittenden, 'his fluent, wristy stroke-making... suggested the lean elasticity of an Indian batsman'. Originally chosen as a leg-break bowler pure and simple, he developed into one of the classiest batsmen in the New Zealand side and could rate an innings of 96 in the first New Zealand Test played on English soil at Lord's in 1931 as his best international effort. His all-round performances on the previous non-Test 1927 trip to England brought selection as one of *Wisden*'s 'Five Cricketers of the Year' – an honour few New Zealand players have achieved. The 1928 *Wisden* states: 'Those who bowled against him...expressed the opinion that he was one of the hardest men on the side to get out....'

According to Sir Pelham Warner in 1945, Charles Stewart Dempster 'stands out as the best batsman New Zealand has given to the game'. Indeed, C S Dempster was the first truly world-class batsman produced by New Zealand. In his 10 Tests for New Zealand, Dempster scored 723 runs in 15 innings (four not outs) for a remarkable average of 65.72. After two tours of England with the New Zealand team he joined Leicestershire in the County Championship and, in all, he hit 1000 runs five times in a season. For the spectator it was not the number of runs scored that was important, it was the manner in which they were made.

Dempster was the batsman for the occasion. Small in stature, and with a hint of the bow-legged in his walk, at the crease he was quick

C S Dempster, New
Zealand's first outstanding
Test batsman.

of eye and swift of foot. A neat, compact batsman, his timing was usually perfect and he possessed all the strokes. He drove with extraordinary power, seldom lifting the ball, and was the acknowledged mainstay of New Zealand's batting during the first few series of initiation into international cricket. During his famous first-wicket stand with John Mills in New Zealand's innings at Wellington in January 1930, Mills was first to his 100 but Dempster soon followed and went on to raise 136. He added an 80 not out in the second innings for good measure and New Zealand had the best of a drawn game. In England in 1931 he led off with scores of 53 and 120 at Lord's. In his final Test appearance, against England at Eden Park, Auckland in 1932–33, he scored a defiant 83 not out (in a total of 158) after coming in with two wickets down for no runs.

Of Scottish descent, Dempster was proud to be chosen in 1934 to represent Scotland at cricket. He later toured a couple of times with Sir Julien Cahn's XI but did not play representative cricket after 1933.

Other New Zealanders who batted with some success in the first Test series included three leading all-rounders, A W Roberts, G L 'Dad' Weir and F T Badcock, while John Lambert Kerr was a solid right-handed opener who disappointed in his first Test in England in 1931 but was, outside of the Tests, one of the batting mainstays of the New Zealand team during the next visit to England in 1937.

The versatile left-hander Henry Gifford Vivian can be counted as one of the successes of the 1931 England tour, during the course of which he made his Test debut aged 18 years and 267 days, the second youngest player to appear for New Zealand (the youngest was Australian born googly bowler D L Freeman who played against England at Christchurch in 1932–33 aged 18 years 197 days). The highly articulate 'Gif' Vivian's batting was all dash and sparkle. His added value as a left-arm 'Chinaman' bowler made him one of New Zealand's best all-rounders. At Wellington in 1931–32 the ruddy-faced New Zealander enjoyed a miracle Test hitting 100 and 73 and taking four South African first-innings wickets for 58.

Although his two Test appearances against England in 1932–33 brought meagre reward, Auckland's aggressive right-hand opener Paul Erskine Whitelaw claimed a place in New Zealand's record books when he hit 195 for Auckland versus Otago at Dunedin in 1936–37 and added 445 in 268 minutes for the third wicket with W N Carson (who made 290), a performance which remained a world record until beaten by Khalid Itirza (also 290) and Aslam Ali (236) who put together a 456-run third-wicket stand for United Bank versus Multan at Karachi, Pakistan, in 1975–76. W N Carson, incidentally, did not appear for his country in a representative game.

Four young batsmen were introduced to the Test arena when New Zealand played its last rubber before the Second World War in

England in 1937. One of the four, Denis Andrew Robert Moloney, would count his three Tests in England that year as the sum total of his Test career. The remaining three, W A Hadlee, W M Wallace and M P Donnelly, would carry their careers forward into the post-war era. The bespectacled Moloney was in fact the leading New Zealand all-rounder in England in 1937 and hit a defiant 64 in the first Test at Lord's when his side was battling to avert the follow-on. Hadlee, Wallace and Donnelly were batsmen pure and simple and their feats at Test level merit separate and closer examination.

Like Moloney, Walter Arnold Hadlee wore spectacles when he played cricket. The tall and enthusiastic 'Wally' Hadlee was a cricket fanatic before he became a Test cricketer. As a schoolboy he filled many an exercise book with cricket notes and records; as a batsman, Dick Brittenden recalls, he was 'a sight for the cricketing gods'. Graceful and handsome driving was the hallmark of Hadlee's play. An immaculate cricketer, he was instantly recognisable at the wicket through his habit of plucking at the point of his shirt collar while waiting for the bowler to get back to his mark.

His best pre-war Test batting performance was a plucky 93 against England at Old Trafford in 1937 when the other New Zealanders had failed, bar Vivian. In 1945–46 Walter Hadlee succeeded M L Page as captain in the first Test after the war. This was a match against Australia which was not regarded as a full international at the time but was elevated to Test match status at a meeting of the then Imperial Cricket Conference in March 1948. This curious procedure affected the debut details of a string of New Zealand and Australian players, a number of whom did not appear in a Test again.

W A Hadlee scored his one and only Test 100 against England at Christchurch in 1946–47. In 1949, he took a star-studded batting side to England, possibly the most powerful run-scoring combination ever to sail forth from New Zealand. Hadlee was an inspirational captain, at times accused of being too severe and autocratic but always prepared to match his own devotion and skill against the demands he made on others. His feat of holding a superior England side to a draw in four Tests in 1949 represented a combination of his own fine tactical skill and a tribute to the batting strength of the New Zealand team. It also resulted in the increase of Test match play in England from the customary three days to four days and eventually to the present five days.

Of Wally Hadlee's five cricketing sons, three have represented New Zealand: D R (Dayle) Hadlee and R J (Richard) Hadlee in Test cricket proper, and B R (Barry) Hadlee in the Prudential World Cup. Hadlee senior has himself become prominent with the New Zealand Cricket Council.

Walter Mervyn Wallace scored heavily against the counties on his two tours of England but disappointed in the Tests. Known as

Mervyn or 'Flip', he was an inveterate and immaculate stroke-player who perhaps did not have the patience needed to succeed at the highest level. Mervyn Wallace would frequently bat beautifully until he reached 30 or 40 and then get himself out, but never, it was said, with a crude stroke. A short and happy-natured man with a craggy face, he favoured the cover-drive and could also hook and pull with exuberant effect. He started the 1949 England tour in Bradman-like fashion, hitting 727 runs with four centuries in his first eight innings.

Of the batsmen who appeared for New Zealand before the Second World War, two stand out as personalities whose skill placed them in a class with the best from any of the other cricket-playing countries. One was the right-handed 'Stewie' Dempster, the other was a left-hander who could rank with the best of his type of all time. Martin Paterson Donnelly was, with Mervyn Wallace, regarded as one of the 'discoveries' of the 1937 England tour. The young left-hander was barely 19 when the tour started but finished second in the batting averages, behind the 20-year-old right-handed Wallace. C B Fry rated him in the class of Clem Hill and Frank Woolley. At Lord's in 1945, he played a masterful innings of 133 for a Dominions XI versus England that was matched that season only by a dazzling 185 from Australia's Keith Miller in the same game.

In 1946 Donnelly went up to Oxford University, hit 142 in the University match at Lord's and continued to bat with such brilliance the following season that he was picked as one of the *Wisden* elect in 1948, to become the third New Zealander to be so honoured (the others being R C Blunt and C S Dempster). He was described as 'the world's best present-day left-handed batsman'.

Martin Donnelly at first sight did not look the picture of an accomplished batsman. Below average height, he faced the bowling with a stance which was all bent knees and waist and (as Ray Robinson puts it) 'stern jutting insultingly toward short-leg'. The moment the bowler let go of his delivery there was a total transformation: 'Feet and body glided and turned into position naturally, whether he was cutting, cover-hitting, driving, hooking, flicking the ball off his toes or using his own speciality, a confident nudge wide of mid-on to the boundary.' He used all the strokes and like the Englishman Denis Compton, was not afraid to move right down the wicket to create the pitch of the delivery he wanted to hit.

In 1949 when still only 32, Donnelly took part in his second and final Test series (he never played Test cricket in his own country) and went well past 50 in four out of the six innings he played in four Tests against England. He started with 64 at Leeds in his only innings in the first Test; swept to 206 at Lord's in the second Test, batting three and a half hours for his first 100 and then racing to his double-century in another 145 minutes, hitting 26 fours in all; scored 75 and 80 in the third Test at Manchester, where he batted with

Opposite: Martin Donnelly was another gifted world-class stroke-player whose career for New Zealand was interrupted by war.

138

great responsibility in the second knock to ensure three draws in a row; then, at the Oval in the fourth and final drawn match of the series, he failed for the first time with scores of 27 and 10 (a 50 in each innings from Wallace and fine batting by openers Bert Sutcliffe and Verdun Scott and the 21-year-old John Reid ensured that England would have no chance of taking the rubber).

So effectively did Donnelly (462 runs in the Tests at 77.00 and 2287 on the tour at 61.81) and Bert Sutcliffe (423 at 60.42 and 2627 at 59.70, respectively) bat that a tour report related that 'bowlers seldom could have viewed their prospects with optimism' when faced by the tall-scoring New Zealand left-handed duo. Sutcliffe was considered in 1949 to have been an even greater batsman than Donnelly himself and his exploits and those of Scott, Reid and the other postwar New Zealand batsmen will be dealt with in a later chapter.

As for Martin Donnelly, at the age of 32 he gave away cricket to take up a business appointment in Australia. He returned to play his final first-class match during the 1960−61 season, when he flew to Auckland from Sydney to join a Governor-General's XI against the MCC and batted much in his old vintage style. As Gerald Brodribb wrote of him in *World of Cricket*: 'His cricket career was short: memories of it will endure.'

15

Indian magic

'Cricket enjoys, and has enjoyed for some time, a unique status in Indian society'

— Richard Cashman

It would not be far from the truth to claim that of all the cricket-playing nations India is a country whose people are, to a very large extent, enthralled by the game of cricket. So much is this the case that the major players of the day are accorded a status in keeping with that enjoyed by the most popular film stars. It is therefore paradoxical to record that when the game was first introduced into the Indian sub-continent by its British rulers, it was a sport organised exclusively around the clubs set up for European members of the British Raj.

Indian cricket clubs were initially forced to play using cast-off cricket equipment from the European clubs and Indians versus British matches were few and far between, with no thought of a combined Indian-European XI. In 1877 a team of Parsees beat a European XI at Bombay and were so taken with their success that they eventually arranged a trip to England in 1886, after an earlier tour to Australia did not proceed. The Parsees' enthusiasm for the game did not match their prowess and they won only one match of the 28 played in England.

Although a number of English amateur teams toured India during the late 1800s, most matches were played against British military and civilian resident teams and a representative 'All India XI' versus Lord Hawke's 1892 team consisted predominantly of European cricketers. Inspiration was then drawn from the feats of the mighty K S Ranjitsinhji in England and when the Indian Princes took over from the British as patrons of the game during the 1890s, Indian cricket began to flourish, although it was some years before Indian players of truly first-class and Test standard began to appear.

The then existing 'Presidency' matches played between teams from the European and the Parsee communities were soon extended into a triangular tournament when the Hindus formed their own eleven in 1907. The Muslims joined in 1912 to form the quadrangular tournament and a combined Christian-Jewish XI made it into a pentangular competition in 1937.

Staged in Bombay, the various tournaments provided some opportunity to select candidates for various All India teams that played in unofficial 'Tests' prior to elevation to full status in 1932, when India toured England and played its debut official Test at Lord's. A single performance by a Hindu batsman playing against Arthur Gilligan's MCC touring side at the Bombay Gymkhana ground in December 1926 may have prompted the Imperial Cricket Conference seriously to consider the admission of India as a Test-playing nation, alongside England, Australia, South Africa, West Indies and New Zealand. It is certainly safe to say that the fanatically fit and athletic Cottari Kanakaiya Nayudu was the first great Indian batsman to play in a Test for the country of his birth.

C K Nayudu was 31 when he faced up to Gilligan's bowlers at Bombay during the 1926−27 season and acknowledged as the finest batsman playing in India. The MCC big-hitter Guy Earle had made a hurricane 130 runs in 90 minutes on the first day, including eight huge sixes, and 'C K', coming in at number five, did not disappoint his fans crowding the stands and embankments, adjacent rooftops and trees around the ground. *Wisden* records that 45,000 watched the two days' play in the match.

The lithe Indian batsman smacked the third ball he faced from left-arm spinner Boyes back over the bowler's head for six. During the next over from the same bowler he placed the ball right into the pavilion. When he was asked to contend with medium-pacer Astill at the other end, Nayudu responded by carting the ball over the sight-screen and onto the 'maidan', the large expanse of lawn adjoining the field. Other MCC bowlers tried included Tate, Wyatt and Mercer but to no avail; the Indian continued on his merry way, with spectators delighting in returning the ball after it had been smacked to or over the boundary. Finally, when he had thrashed 153 runs out of 187 added while he was at the crease in only 115 minutes (and created a new world record for that time with 11 sixes in his innings; he also hit 13 fours), Nayudu was caught in the outfield by Boyes when going for another big hit. A newspaper cartoon next day portrayed a group of spectators huddled on the ledge of the Bombay clock tower. The caption read 'Don't hit us C K − We're not playing.'

C K Nayudu's record of 11 sixes has since been surpassed by a number of batsmen − the current first-class record holder is New Zealand's J R Reid who hit 15 sixes in an innings of 296 for Wellington versus Northern Districts at home in 1962−63. Ravi Shastri during the course of his record double-hundred at Bombay in January 1985 hit 13 sixes − the current Indian record. In all cricket, the record is believed to be 36 in an innings of 253 not out played by D Hope for Standard Bank versus Lever Brothers in Durban, South Africa, in 1939−40. Another South African, the England player Basil D'Oliveira, once hit 28 sixes in an innings of 225 (made in 90 minutes) for his Cape Town club Croxley, versus Mariedahl in

C K Nayudu, the 'father' of Indian cricket and a wonderful attacking batsman.

1953−54 — this feat represents the most sixes hit by a Test cricketer playing in any class of cricket. West Indian Gordon Greenidge (twice) and Pakistan's Majid J Khan (once) have hit 13 sixes in a first-class innings.

Former pupils from the Hislop Collegiate High School in Nagpur may not have recognised their erstwhile schoolmate destroying the formidable MCC bowlers at Bombay in 1926−27. As a schoolboy batsman, C K was known as 'a plodder, a bore to watch'. India and the cricketing world can thank the famous Ranji for C K's transformation into a six-hitter supreme. The story goes that Nayudu's father, who attended Cambridge University with K S Ranjitsinhji, compelled his son to change his mental attitude towards batting when his old friend criticised the lacklustre style of a boy who possessed all the natural, physical qualities of a potentially great batsman.

Nayudu senior included concentrated physical exercise to supplement net practice and his son was soon set on a lifelong path of supreme physical fitness and regular training. C K Nayudu's cricketing road was to take him to a height of achievement which led to him becoming known as the 'Father of Indian Cricket'. He was to India what W G Grace was to England, what Trumper was to Australia, what Headley was to the West Indies.

Rusi Modi, one of India's finest post-war players, described the tall and well-proportioned C K Nayudu as a stylist, like Trumper and Spooner. 'He thrilled the crowd as well as the connoisseurs.' He played every stroke with an easy grace with the cut and the pull to mid-wicket as his personal favourites. He was unafraid of fast bowlers (his answer to the short-pitched ball was to hook unmercifully) and simply murdered spin bowlers who were not of the highest standard.

Because of his fanaticism about fitness he broke bowlers' hearts for 48 years — from his debut first-class match for the Hindus in 1916−17 at the age of 21 (C K hit the first ball bowled he faced, from expatriate Australian Frank Tarrant, for six) until his final first-class game for the Maharashtra Governor's XI in 1963−64. In 1957, when he was 62, he hit 81 in the Ranji Trophy competition including two magnificent sixes off Vinoo Mankad. This represents the longest first-class career in history — the mighty W G Grace takes second place with 47 seasons.

In international cricket C K received few opportunities at a time when India was offered only the occasional Test or tour. He led India's first Test at Lord's in 1932, although he was not the official tour captain (or even vice-captain), the honour having been bestowed for political reasons on the Maharajah of Porbandar, with another member of the Indian aristocracy, K S Ganshyamsinhji of Limbdi, chosen as official tour deputy. It was common knowledge that neither of these worthies were skilled enough to play in the Lord's Test and

Nayudu led his team with verve. He used his pace attack (Nissar, Amar Singh and Jahangir Khan) with hostile effect until England was saved by Douglas Jardine, and then, despite an injury, C K top-scored in India's first innings. Against Jardine's 1933–34 England team to India, Nayudu used Nissar and Amar Singh (both slippery customers) in a 'bumper war' − Jardine's reply was to instruct Northants left-hander 'Nobby' Clark to retaliate.

In 1936 C K was again overlooked as captain for the tour of England − another prince with sketchy cricketing qualifications, the Maharajkumar of Vizianagram, was chosen for the job. On his 1932 trip to England he added 65 wickets (taken with slow-medium cutters) to 1618 first-class runs scored on the tour; in 1936 C K scored 1102 runs and took 51 wickets.

Considered a martinet by some, C K Nayudu was revered by others − a fearless player, a man of tremendous ego and an autocratic leader who expected from his players absolute fitness and dedication to the task in hand. He upheld these twin principles in his own life and carried forward his immense enthusiasm for cricket into his later work as an Indian Test selector and as vice-president of the Indian Cricket Board of Control. His disregard for physical discomfort was illustrated during a Ranji Trophy match at Bombay in 1951 when he was 56 years old. A rising delivery from Test pace bowler Phadkar hit him in the mouth. Spitting out several broken teeth, the veteran campaigner swept the pieces away with his bat and told the bowler to get on with the game.

C K was already touching 37 when he made his Test debut and took part in all seven games played by India between 1932 and 1936. His highest Test score of 81 came in his final innings, at the Oval against England, after a severe blow to the solar plexus by a ball from fast bowler Gubby Allen. According to *Wisden*, wristy off-side strokes were a feature of his 150-minute stay at the crease.

Colonel C K Nayudu was employed for many years by the cricket-mad Maharaja of Indore who, as Rusi Modi records, once remarked: 'I may be the ruler of Indore, but C K is undoubtedly the king of outdoor games.' There could be no greater tribute paid to the father of Indian cricket.

His brother C S Nayudu was a Test leg-spinner; another brother, C L, and C K's son and grandson all played first-class cricket, while his daughter is a cricket radio commentator.

Of the Indian Test batsmen who played supporting roles to C K Nayudu in the first Tests played by India, the tiny Naoomal Jeoomal was a plucky right-hand opener who squared up doggedly to the fast bowling of Voce and Bowes in his country's first Test at Lord's in 1932 to score 33 and 25. His own oft stated axiom was: 'Playing fast bowling is not so much an art of choosing the balls to hit as choosing the balls to leave alone.'

Another of C K's contemporaries, Syed Wazir Ali, was described by D R Jardine as the best-dressed cricketer he had ever come across. A sportsman to his fingertips, Wazir was an attractive and powerful stroke-player who sometimes opened the innings. Wazir Ali was the elder brother of Test all-rounder S Nazir Ali and father of Pakistani Test cricketer Khalid Wazir.

Batsmen who came and went without raising much dust on the international scene included S H M Colah; the turbanned Lall Singh, the only Malaya-born player to represent India; and P E Palia. India's leading bowler of the day, L N Amar Singh, was also a bold hitter who earned the name of 'India's Jessop'. In India's first-ever Test at Lord's in 1932 he gave a grand display of free hitting when scoring 51 (the first half-century for India in a Test) and added 74 in 40 minutes with Lall Singh. At the Oval in 1936 Amar Singh smacked 44 out of 51 in half an hour in the third Test against England. One of the great disappointments for India in Test cricket was the Bombay stylist L P Jai whom C G Macartney considered the best Indian batsman when an Australian team visited the sub-continent in 1935–36.

The adventurous Jai made his international debut (it was his only Test) in a match against England at Bombay in 1933–34 which also marked the appearance of two of India's finest players of all time. 'Lala' Amarnath was India's first truly great all-rounder and he scored a century on debut which also represented the first-ever (and the fastest) three-figure score for India in a Test; Vijay Merchant was to be acknowledged during the 1930s as the Indian version of Don Bradman.

Nanik Bhardwaj Amarnath was known simply as 'Lala' throughout his long and stormy career which started when he first appeared for the Hindus in 1929–30 and ended with his final match in the Ranji Trophy in 1960–61. His Test career extended from 1933–34 to 1952–53 but, because of the few series played before the Second World War, the intervention of the war itself and sundry clashes with officialdom, Amarnath only played in 24 Test matches for his country.

In his *Great Indian Cricketers* Partab Ramchand sums up the character and style of Lala Amarnath in one sentence: 'He made brilliant centuries, bowled like no one else in his time, fielded in an agile manner that belied his build, and led his side as shrewdly and wisely as only he could.' Above all else, Amarnath was outspoken and something of an activist who clashed frequently with petty officialdom while fighting for better conditions for his fellow players.

His disdain of authority saw him sent home 'for disciplinary reasons' during the 1936 India tour of England, on the eve of the first Test and at a time when he was already established as the most successful all-rounder in a struggling team with 613 runs in 20

Lala Amarnath was the first Indian to score a century on Test debut and later the father of two Test players.

innings and 32 wickets at 21 runs apiece. The fact that Lala Amarnath was completely exonerated at a post-tour judicial hearing points to one of the monumental tour blunders of all time. Later research has indicated that his dismissal from the 1936 tour was the outcome of a language problem. Apparently the team captain, the Maharajkumar of Vizianagram, completely misunderstood a remark made by Amarnath in Punjabi, a language His Highness did not understand.

The 'stormy petrel' of Indian cricket began his Test career, aged 22, with a dashing display at Bombay in 1933—34 when he thrashed an impressive looking England attack (including Nicholls, Clark and Verity) for 118 (21 fours), reaching his 50 in 56 minutes and his 100 in 117 minutes — an Indian record which still stands. His batting that day was likened to the cavalier type of play of a Macartney or a Trumper. For once the mightly C K Nayudu was overshadowed as his younger partner dominated a 186-run third-wicket stand, to which the veteran batsman contributed only 67 runs.

In England in 1946 Lala Amarnath surprisingly emerged as India's most dangerous strike bowler — he used only a three-pace run-up and bowled off the wrong foot — and headed the bowling averages. As a batsman, he could not get going in the Tests although he scored consistently in the other tour matches. This pattern was to be repeated in Australia in 1947—48 when he opened the tour with scores of 0, 144, 94 not out, 228 not out, 16, 10, 7, 172 not out and 20 (691 runs at 115.12) in the preliminary State matches but scored only 140 runs in his 10 Test knocks. Four of India's best players of the day, Merchant, R S Modi, Mushtaq Ali and Fazal Mahmood, declined the tour and as the side's leading batsman, first-choice new ball bowler and captain, the strain began to tell.

At Bombay in 1948—49, during the final Test of the India-West Indies series, the now veteran Lala Amarnath gave a remarkable exhibition of cricketing versatility by batting, bowling, fielding and keeping wicket in the same Test. Regular keeper Probir Sen was injured early on in West Indies' first innings and Amarnath donned the gloves after having already bowled as first change. Not content as a mere makeshift 'keeper, the Indian captain went on to take five catches in the match.

Towards the end of his career (after having captained India against Pakistan at the age of 41), Lala Amarnath became a Test selector and retired from active play as one of the most popular players (from both his colleagues' and fans' point of view) ever to represent India. Two of his sons, Mohinder and Surinder, have followed him into the Test XI, a third, Rajinder, has appeared regularly in Indian domestic first-class cricket.

Of the pre-war Indian batsmen, Amarnath and Mushtaq Ali were the dashers; Vijaysingh Madhavji Merchant was the supreme accumulator of runs. Merchant scored with such prolific consistency as to be compared with Don Bradman himself. A brief glance at Merchant's Ranji Trophy record reveals that between 1934–35 and 1950–51 he scored 3639 runs at an average of 98.35. When it comes to his final batting average in all first-class cricket, his name ranks second only to Bradman. On two tours of England (1936 and 1946) he virtually carried India's batting. His Test chances were severely limited and although his Test aggregate of 859 runs at 47.72 is not in the Bradman class, his record would have been greater had Merchant been born Australian or English, as was also the case with West Indian George Headley.

A short man, Merchant did not allow his limitations of physique to hinder him in play. He made up for lack of inches with sparkling and text-book perfect footwork. A quick eye allowed for playing the ball late and his cutting, both square and late was superb. Unafraid to hook or drive the faster bowlers, he was a master at playing the ball pitched on his legs and at executing the finest of leg-glances. As Rusi Modi puts it: 'In an innings by Vijay, every point of fine batsmanship was there...'.

Plagued by illness Merchant missed the 1947–48 Australian tour and played his final Test innings against England in the first Test of 1951–52. Although illness prevented further participation in the series, the Indian champion batsman bowed out of big cricket with the then highest innings in Test cricket by an Indian batsman – he scored 154 in seven and a half hours. In his biography of the Indian batting master, Dr Vasant Naik sadly notes: 'After seeing that knock which was replete with delicate late cuts, occasional drives and dainty placements, hardly anybody imagined that this was to be the last Test effort by the prince among Indian batsmen...'.

Vijay Merchant was aided in many a first-wicket battle by the quicksilver bat of Syed Yacubali Mushtaq Ali, the 'Idol of Indore', whose batting is described by Ray Robinson as that of 'a tiger on hot bricks'. Australian Servicemen touring India in 1945 called him 'Muchjack Alley' because of his liking for the strike. It is unlikely that a spectator would ever be found who would complain if Mushtaq were to face up to every single ball bowled while he was at the wicket.

Mushtaq Ali batted like a jack-in-the-box who, with a total disregard for the basic rules of batting, delighted in prompting 'heart-failure' among fans and colleagues. Tall, slender and charismatic at the crease, he could play with orthodox efficiency if desired but preferred to dance merrily down the track (with no regard for the bowler's reputation) and charm his admirers with a display of flamboyant and effective strokes – and was frequently dismissed when going for an impossible shot. Rusi Modi describes his character beautifully: 'The ladies' man who attracted hundreds of yards of ninon silk and georgette and tons of grease paint.' A dazzlingly

unorthodox 112 at Old Trafford in 1936 was his most memorable Test knock.

Mushtaq, at 6 ft 1 in (185 cm), was one of the few tall Indian cricketers. The tallest to play for India were fast bowler Ladha Ramji (6 ft 4 in − 193 cm) and the 'record-holder', the Maharaja of Patiala (6 ft 5 in − 195 cm), who as the then 20 year-old Yuvaraj of Patiala scored 24 and 60 against Jardine's England side in the third Test of the 1933−34 series at Madras.

Dr Dilawar Hussein, who opened the innings and scored 59 and 57 in his debut Test at Calcutta in 1933−34, was, at 6 ft 2 in (188 cm), a little shorter than Ramji and Patiala, and the Doctor of Philosophy had unwearying patience as the hallmark of his rather ungainly batsmanship. While at Cambridge University in 1936, he was pressed into service as a wicket-keeper for the third Test at the Oval and scored 35 and 54. He later became a founder-member of the Board of Control of Cricket in Pakistan and served as a Pakistan Test selector.

Of the remaining Indians who played Test cricket before the war only Cotar Ramaswami, an extraordinary all-round sportsman, batted with sufficient consistency to press for inclusion in this roundup of early Indian Test batsmen. The sturdily built left-handed Ramaswami was already more than 40 when he first played for India against England in 1936. After a poor start to the tour, he batted with great determination in the last two Tests at Manchester and the Oval and, with successive scores of 40, 60, 29 and 41 not out, headed the Test batting averages.

Fourteen years previously, a much slimmer Cotar Ramaswami distinguished himself by taking part in two Davis Cup ties for India − the only man to play both Test cricket and Davis Cup tennis. In 1922 he partnered Dr A H Fyzee to win doubles rubbers against Romania and Spain. In 1923 Ramaswami won the England Grass Court Championship and in 1934 represented India in an international tennis competition against a British team. He has also served as a Test selector and as Indian team manager.

Although struggling for the most part against superior opposition, pre-war Indian cricket survived the storms and controversies related to the diverse customs of India's many religious and language groupings to produce a line of truly accomplished batsmen of international class − from C K Nayudu through to Amarnath, Merchant and Mushtaq Ali.

Tha last three mentioned were to carry their Test careers past the dark days of world war to provide the inspiration and example required to produce a post-war generation of Indian batsmen − who were destined to surpass most of the achievements of their eminent predecessors.

Opposite: M Merchant had a Bradman-like average in Indian domestic cricket and seldom failed in a Test.

151

16

Hutton's Oval epic

'Cricket has always been so much part of my existence that it has occupied my thoughts to the exclusion of other things'
— Sir Leonard Hutton

Leonard Hutton's famous Oval epic, during which the Yorkshire and England batsman stayed at the wicket for almost three full days to compile a new Test record score of 364, began on Saturday 20 August 1938 and ended on Tuesday 23 August after 13 hours and 17 minutes of batting time. At this point England had compiled an unassailable score (unprecedented in Tests) of 903 for seven wickets declared. The Australians were patently exhausted and, with both Bradman and Fingleton unable to bat in either of the subsequent Australian innings because of injury, England swept through to what remains the highest winning margin in a Test — an innings and 579 runs. Morris Leyland helped Hutton in a 382-run second-wicket partnership (the highest for any wicket in an England-Australia Test) and Hammond assisted in raising a further 135 runs before the third wicket fell at 546. A minor 'collapse' was then checked by the Hutton-Hardstaff stand of 215 for the sixth wicket and Hardstaff went ahead to put on 106 for the seventh wicket with wicket-keeper Arthur Wood.

The Pudsey-born Hutton was encircled by Yorkshire grit during his 1938 record-making innings at the Oval — there were five Yorkshiremen in the England XI: Hutton, Leyland, Wood, Verity and Bowes — and an unexpected change in the batting order by England captain Walter Hammond may have been the inspired move which gave his young opening batsman the confidence to soldier on after the first wicket had fallen at 29. Hutton and Barnett had raised 219 in the first Test at Trent Bridge but thereafter various combinations of opening pairs had consistently failed. Leyland had batted at around number five for all his years for England; now he came in at first wicket down to partner a rather shaky Hutton whose previous Test at Lord's had seen him dismissed for scores of 4 and 5. Leyland had in fact not played in any of the previous Tests that season but England needed stability at the top after several poor starts. The full score-card reads:

Yorkshire and England's Leonard Hutton combats the spin of Bill O'Reilly during his epic innings of 364 versus Australia at the Oval in 1938.

ENGLAND v AUSTRALIA
at Kennington Oval, London, 20, 22, 23, 24 August 1938

England

L Hutton c Hassett b O'Reilly	364
W J Edrich lbw b O'Reilly	12
M Leyland run out	187
W R Hammond lbw b Fleetwood-Smith	59
E Paynter lbw b O'Reilly	0
D C S Compton b Waite	1
J Hardstaff jr not out	169
A Wood c and b Barnes	53
H Verity not out	8
Extras (byes 22, leg-byes 19, wides 1, no-balls 8)	50
Total (77 wickets declared)	903

K Farnes and W E Bowes did not bat
Fall of wicket: 29, 411, 546, 547, 555, 770, 876

Australia

	O	M	R	W
M G Waite	72	16	150	1
S J McCabe	38	8	85	0
W J O'Reilly	85	26	178	3
L O B Fleetwood-Smith	87	11	298	1

S G Barnes	38	3	84	1
A L Hassett	13	2	52	0
D G Bradman	2.2	1	6	0

Australia 201 (W A Brown 69, W E Bowes 5/49)
and **123** (K Farnes 4/63)

England won by an innings and 579 runs

Sir Leonard Hutton was the second professional cricketer to be knighted. Sir Jack Hobbs was the first and the pre-war Hutton was a batsman who was in many ways similar to his famous predecessor. Both were stylists of great natural ability who played without fuss but with instinctive consistency. The post-war Hutton was as consistent a run-getter as before the hostilities but a shortened left arm (the result of a war-time accident) forced an adjustment in method. However, he remained the supreme batting technician, a perfect model for all young batsmen.

Alan Ross once wrote: 'Self-sufficiency, I suppose, is one of the true marks of the artist and Hutton has been self-sufficient as a cricketer to a point of often seeming disinterested.' Hutton's son, Richard (who followed his father into the England team without substantial success), claims that there has always been a certain eccentricity about his father and recalled in an article in *The Cricketer* his father's reaction to the news telephoned from abroad that he (Richard) was about to be married: '...in his woe-ridden manner, he informed me that only that very day the government had been forced to take-over British Leyland and the rates were doubling.' When Richard Hutton repeated that he was getting married, the conversation concluded with the remark by his father that 'he would be having trouble with my mother that night!' Richard goes on in his article to assure his readers that his mother had never, in her whole life, been trouble to anyone and was delighted with the news of the forthcoming wedding. Perhaps Sir Leonard Hutton worked according to the axiom 'hope for the best but expect the worst', and was thus always ready and able to face up to any crisis, on or off the cricket field.

Trevor Bailey contends that the two finest batsmen who played for England both before and after the war were Hutton and Denis Compton — for the former, batting was a profitable business, for the latter it always remained a game. In a tribute to Hutton in *Playfair Cricket Monthly*, Bailey claims that press and public placed an intolerable load on their batting hero by considering 'anything less than a century a failure'. Hutton was perhaps unfortunate to play for most of his England career during a period when, apart from a very select few, most of England's batting representatives were auspicious for their failures alone.

Bailey contends that one of the most fascinating features of Hutton's batting was its technical perfection, 'which was so good that he remained interesting to watch even when he was scoring slowly'. He goes on to record that when bowling against Hutton, he was frequently astonished to note how swiftly the scoreboard total was mounting: 'He would take a single here, run one down to third man, and tuck the ball neatly off his legs for two, while always at the back of my mind was the knowledge that a bad delivery would simply be despatched to the boundary.'

With the needs of England foremost in his mind, the post-war Hutton eliminated many of his pre-war strokes. For instance, because of his shortened left arm he considered it unsafe to hook with freedom. In one of his essays Cardus commented: 'This defensive resourcefulness, based on a perfect and calculated technique, was certainly part of his genius: he made no moves that were not absolutely certain of success.'

Occasionally the great man would be seen performing in a different mode. A classic and well quoted example was his onslaught on Lindwall and Miller in full cry at Sydney in 1946—47 when he scored 37 out of 49 in 24 minutes with an array of strokes that left both Australian fast bowlers flat-footed. In 1950—51, on an atrocious and totally unplayable Brisbane 'sticky dog', he came in at number eight when England was chasing 193 in the second innings and hit a magnificent 62 not out, an innings which will remain one of the most remarkable ever played in Australia.

Hutton's major scoring feats adorn the pages of every *Wisden* and every other record book published during the two decades between 1934 and 1955. In 79 Tests for England he totalled 6971 runs at an average of 56.67, and many of his innings were back-to-the-wall affairs when he virtually carried the batting single-handedly for a losing team. When he became captain of England, as the first professional player to hold the post, he immediately won back the Ashes from Australia in England in 1953; he then led his country to a draw in the West Indies; and in 1954—55, took a young team to Australia and thrashed his old opponents three matches to one. He retired after that great success in Australia and was knighted for his services to cricket in 1956.

Sir Leonard Hutton had a tough apprenticeship in his native Yorkshire and learned his lessons well to become the natural successor to an eminent Yorkshire line that began with the great amateur Sir Stanley Jackson and continued through John Tunnicliffe, Herbert Sutcliffe and Geoffrey Boycott. All of the players mentioned were noted for their watchfulness, for their dedication to first principles, and for their refusal to allow any situation or bowler to dominate

Australian captain Don Bradman congratulates Hutton on passing Bradman's own record Test score of 334. Joe Hardstaff is the other batsman.

them. One could easily envisage a Hutton or a Sutcliffe (or a Boycott) serenely carrying on with their innings until after the last trumpet has been sounded.

Hutton's major post-war opening partner was a Lancashire professional who also made his international debut for England before the war, in one Test versus New Zealand at the Oval in 1937. When Cyril Washbrook played for Lancashire at Headingly, Leeds, the partisan Yorkshire crowd hated the sight of him and wished him out every ball during the course of his many long innings played against their revered county on the beloved home turf. But they respected him as a batsman of the highest order and when he appeared in his England cap as first-wicket partner to Len Hutton, the Yorkshire crowd applauded him as enthusiastically as they did their own hero. And never was their applause as long and deafening as on that occasion in 1956 when, as a Test selector who had not played for England for six years, he was recalled to a side trailing 0−1 in an Ashes series against Australia. Aged 42, he scored a determined 98 to assist Peter May in turning the series around.

Washbrook was something of a Jekyll and Hyde batsman. One day he could be seen quite content in playing a supportive and primarily defensive role as opening partner to Len Hutton; on the next he might be blazing away with great panache for Lancashire, dictating the course of his county's destiny by putting the opposition bowlers to the sword. His driving off either foot evoked comparison with A C MacLaren in its certainty and placement. His hook was a perfect example of effortless timing that resulted in unexpected power. He was a master of the push to mid-wicket and the nudge down to third man.

Above all else, Washbrook was a student of the game who always looked like a cricketer, from his jauntily angled cap down to the placement of his feet as he took strike. In 1946−47 against Australia, Washbrook aided Hutton in three consecutive first-wicket century partnerships. Against South Africa in 1948−49, at Johannesburg, the pair added 359. In 37 Tests Washbrook aggregated 2569 runs and averaged 42.81. For Lancashire he was superb − his record 14,000 pounds benefit in 1948 reflected the value placed on his contribution to the county.

17

A timeless Test — and the end for a time

'The little gods that preside over England's lovely cricket fields looked down with favour on the bronzed visitors from the veld'

— Louis Duffus

When South Africa played its first post-First World War Test against Australia in 1921–22, only three experienced batsmen were present: Herby Taylor, 'Dave' Nourse and J W Zulch. Of the newcomers, only tiny Charles Newton Frank did anything of note. The prematurely wizened Frank batted for almost two days at Johannesburg in the second Test to score 152 to save the match. The story goes that, when he was due to go in to bat, his employer allowed the remainder of the staff to watch him, on the understanding that they would return to work when Frank was dismissed. There must have been much hilarity all round when Charlie Frank's workmates' few hours off turned into a two-day vacation.

Most of the new batsmen again failed but one debutante against England in 1922–23, Robert Hector Catterall, was to go on to a fairly lengthy and distinguished Test career. Although 'Bob' Catterall was by no means a 'great' South African batsman in the class of Faulkner, Taylor, Mitchell, Dudley Nourse and, later, McGlew, Barlow, Pollock and Richards, he was an enterprising and correct right-hander who treated cricket as a game and not a business.

His forthright attitude sometimes drew criticism but Catterall enjoyed a particularly fine first tour of England in 1924 as a free-scoring middle order batsman, twice hitting 120 in the Tests, at Edgbaston and at Lord's, and topping the Test batting averages with 471 runs at 67.28. On his second trip in 1929 he took over the role of a more defensive opening batsman.

In a year that proved distressing for South African batsmen, one of the few successes of the 1924 England tour was the former Cambridge University batsman, Manfred Julius Susskind. A tall and ungainly player who was often condemned for his persistent habit of padding away off-side deliveries, 'Fred' Susskind scored more than 1000 runs in a wet summer and averaged 33.50 in his one and only Test series. The 1924 Edgbaston Test remains one that South Africans prefer to forget. Facing an England total of 438, the visiting team was unceremoniously despatched for a grand total of 30 by Arthur Gilligan and

Maurice Tate. Only a century from Catterall and the dogged batting of Susskind restored some sense of dignity in the follow on.

South Africa's new captain that year was Hubert Gouvaine Deane, a useful batsman and a leader who did much to shape the successful Springbok XI of 1935 for his successor as captain, Herby Wade. 'Nummy' Deane can count his 93 at the Oval in 1929 as his best Test innings, during the course of which he and Taylor added a South African Test record 214-run partnership for the fourth wicket.

Deane's 1929 Springbok side boasted a string of new names, most of whom justified their choice with reasonable performances at international level — players like the tall and handsome D P B Morkel, who emerged as the best all-rounder of the combination; the hard-hitting E L Dalton; J A J Christy, a tall and powerful right-hander who combated Larwood and Tate with great verve at Lord's in the second Test; and opening batsman I J Siedle, who was the oldest living Springbok Test player at the time of his death in 1982 at the age of 79. A reserved man, 'Jack' Siedle possessed an enviable defence and a good range of scoring strokes but his Test career was hampered by injury and illness.

Two new outstandingly aggressive batsmen who made a lasting impression on the 1929 England tour were 'Tuppy' Owen-Smith and 'Jock' Cameron, who went on to become one of the most notable wicket-keeper/batsmen of all time, to captain his country, and then to succumb tragically to illness and an early demise at the age of 30.

At Headingly in the third Test of 1929, the South African first innings was in total disarray at the close of the penultimate day. When Dr Harold Owen-Smith was informed by his room companion Bruce Mitchell that the morning papers said only rain or a century could save South Africa, he decided on the latter and posted a thrilling 100 before lunch, sharing a helter-skelter last-wicket South African record stand of 103 in three minutes over the hour with number 11 'Sandy' Bell.

Louis Duffus in *Cricketers of the Veld* describes the ebullient and cheerful Owen-Smith as 'More like a lad setting off for a day's picnic at a swimming pool than a Test match hero'. His nickname 'Tuppy' was derived from tuppence (or twopence) and related to his size, for he looked for all the world like a mischievous schoolboy out on a prank.

Horace Brackenridge Cameron has been described as arguably South Africa's finest wicket-keeper/batsman — he was most certainly the best of his kind before the Second World War. Since then, Johnny Waite and Denis Lindsay must challenge for the crown, although Cameron will remain the most spectacular hitter of all South Africa's glovemen.

Duffus describes Cameron perfectly: 'Some players have etched their autograph over cricket's pitch with a fine delicate hand. Some

have scrawled it, and some composed the letters with painstaking care. Cameron wrote his with bold, lavish strokes. Mitchell sometimes scores his boundaries as though he were ashamed of them. Cameron has no such shyness in his rugged methods. Mitchell's batting appeals to the aesthetic, to the connoisseur, Cameron's to primitive instincts.'

The most famous Cameron story has been told many times, but no reference to the great South African cricketer would be complete without it. Against Yorkshire at Sheffield in 1935, Cameron had to contend with the famous left-arm spinner Hedley Verity on a pitch helpful to spin. The Springbok 'keeper scored 45 and 103 not out and his batting was the decisive factor in a big win by the Springboks. But even if the South Africans had failed, the match will always remain 'Cameron's match'. In the course of making his second innings century, Cameron struck Verity for 30 runs in one over — three successive fours, followed by three successive sixes. With typical Yorkshire wit, the home wicket-keeper Arthur Wood remarked dryly to the stunned Verity as the players crossed at the end of the over: 'Had 'im in two minds then, didn't thee Hedley? 'E didn't know whether to hit thee for four or for six.'

Jock Cameron was a rugged character with infinite courage. He could defend when necessary and presented a lifeless bat for an hour and a half at Leeds during the 1935 third Test, when South Africa were holding on to their 1−0 series lead. During this game one of the other South African batsmen, Eric Rowan, was struck on the head by a ball from fast bowler Bowes. Cameron's remark before facing up to the same bowler was: 'If you hit me, Bowes, I'll come down the pitch and hit you over the head with this bat.'

As a wicket-keeper Cameron was regarded equal to Australia's Bert Oldfield; as a captain he was one of South Africa's most popular leaders when he took the Springboks to Australia in 1931−32. He became ill on the boat home from the 1935 England tour and died, aged 30, just a few days after landing in South Africa. His untimely death shocked South Africa and may well have contributed towards the listless, lacklustre performances put up by his former comrades during the 1935−36 season when Vic Richardson brought an Australian team to tour South Africa.

South African cricket reached its pre-war peak at Lord's, the home of cricket, in 1935 when the Springboks for the first time defeated England in a Test series played on English soil. The leg-break and googly bowling of a player of Greek origin, Xenophon Constantine Balaskas, proved a decisive factor in that famous win (Balaskas was also no mean batsman and once scored 122 not out in a Test in New Zealand), but it was the batting of 26-year-old Bruce Mitchell that set the seal on the South African Lord's success.

It was the second tour of England for the young Springbok opening

Opposite: Bruce Mitchell (right) coming out to open the innings for South Africa with Jack Siedle.

batsman. On the previous occasion in 1929 he was faced for the first time with the prospect of batting on only turf wickets. At that time in South Africa, matting stretched over turf or gravel was still the norm. The 20-year-old Mitchell soon showed his temperament and skill and ended the tour with most runs for his team.

A graceful player with a remarkable defence and perfect footwork, Mitchell was often accused of slow scoring by critics who failed to realise that he was frequently South Africa's only hope of survival on unfamiliar English wickets. He played a number of epic innings in his Test career which illustrated to perfection his skill, stamina, style and outstanding determination. In difficult situations and on treacherous wickets Mitchell was superb — few of his South African colleagues ever came close to matching him.

At Edgbaston in 1929, playing in his first Test, Mitchell grafted painstakingly for seven hours for 88 runs. His classic 164 not out in five and a half hours at Lord's in 1935 was a faultless display of concentration and determination. At the Oval in 1947, England left South Africa with 451 to win in the fourth innings of the game and Mitchell, not content with just batting it out, was 189 out at stumps and South Africa was only 28 runs short of its target with three wickets still to fall.

In 42 Test matches Bruce Mitchell totalled 3471 runs at 48.88 — the highest aggregate for a South African. He shares South Africa's record first-wicket Test partnership of 260, versus England at Newlands, Cape Town, in 1930—31, with Jack Siedle.

Three other young batsmen who toured with Herby Wade's 1935 Springbok team in England were to stay on the scene for a number of years and provide the foundation for South Africa's first post-war teams. (Herbert Frederick Wade was, incidentally, a useful forcing right-handed batsman who never quite came up to Test class but who has been recorded as one of South Africa's best captains). Of the trio, Eric Rowan and Dudley Nourse did not shine in the Tests but were destined for greater moments in later years; the third player, Ken Viljoen, scored a match-saving century in the fourth Test at Manchester in what was to be his best Test series.

Kenneth George Viljoen was a polished right-hander who had entered first-class cricket as a prodigy of 16 and who notched his first Test 100 against Australia in 1931—32 when he was barely 21. His 111 at Melbourne in the third Test was the only three-figure innings played by a South African in a Test that season. In 1935, Viljoen scored 124 at Manchester and averaged 40 for the series and, although he did not score heavily in international cricket thereafter, was a fairly regular member of South African teams until the start of the war and, again, during the 1947—49 period. As South African manager on subsequent tours to Australia and England, he helped Jack Cheetham rebuild South African cricket during the 1950s when many seasoned players retired after the 1951 tour of England.

The fearless and cocky Eric Alfred Burchell Rowan will always remain as one of the real characters of South African cricket. Unfortunately, he was frequently at odds with South African cricket administrators because of his forthright manner and missed out on two overseas tours, to England in 1947 and to Australia in 1952–53, 'for reasons other than cricket'.

Superbly confident in all he approached, Rowan was a teetotaller and a fitness fanatic who was still worth his place in the Test team at the age of 42. According to former Springbok captain Jackie McGlew, who toured as a novice with Nourse (captain) and Eric Rowan (vice-captain) in 1951, Rowan 'programmed himself to score runs in ceaseless profusion'.

From an easy and watchful stance, Eric Rowan developed a virtuosity of footwork that has seldom been excelled. He drove fluently and pulled powerfully but did not ignore the value of runs to be scored through a neat leg-glance or a chopped cut through the slips, or through his own peculiarity — a spooned shot over the heads of close fielders on the leg-side. McGlew recalls that 'Against the fastest bowlers he was at his best because he was fearless and pugnacious'. Dudley Nourse rated his comrade-in-arms as 'brave almost to a degree of foolhardiness'.

Rowan demonstrated this pugnacity when faced with the full fury of Lindwall, Miller and big Bill Johnston in 1949–50. The Australians were sweeping through South Africa like an uncontrolled bushfire. South African cricket was at the crossroads, with the three best bats in the land, Mitchell, Nourse and Rowan himself, all touching 40 years. Mitchell's reflexes were no longer sharp enough to handle the Australian quickies and he was not chosen for the Tests; Nourse and Rowan batted like phoenixes reborn from the flames.

With virtually no support, Rowan battled through to a gritty 143 at Durban in the third Test and made three other 50s in the series. Nourse hit 65 and 114 in the second Test at Cape Town and made two more 50s. Only three other South African batsmen reached 50 in a Test.

In England in 1951, each of South Africa's two veteran players raised a double-century in the Tests. Nourse fought through to 208 in the first Test at Nottingham, batting with a strapped broken thumb; Rowan played a marathon innings of 236 at Leeds in the fourth game to create a new South African individual score record. He was already 42 years old.

Unfortunately, Eric Rowan's last overseas tour was marred by controversy. He was involved in a 'sit down' incident when batting against Lancashire at Old Trafford. Objecting to unwarranted slow hand-clapping from the crowd, he and Johnny Waite sat on their bats until it had quietened down. Later, he was involved in an incident with an abusive spectator — and gave back verbally as much as he got. There was talk of the manager Sid Pegler sending the veteran opening batsman home but good sense prevailed.

The double-century made by Dudley Nourse at Nottingham in 1951 was a gruelling nine-hour ordeal during which the South African captain was seen to grit his teeth against the pain caused by a metal pin in his broken right thumb. His other Test double-hundred, 231 versus Australia in 1935—36 at Johannesburg, was accomplished in under four hours and was notable for an exhibition of free and unfettered stroke-play that saw the mighty Grimmett and O'Reilly truly put to the sword.

Arthur Dudley Nourse was a famous son of a famous father, A W 'Dave' Nourse, the 'Grand Old Man' of South African cricket, who played 45 consecutive Tests for his country. Nourse junior played 34 Tests between 1935 and 1951 and scored 2960 runs at 53.81, with two double-centuries and seven 100s. But for the war, his record may have been even more remarkable. At the Old Wanderers ground in Johannesburg, over Christmas 1935, he reached his pinnacle as a forcing stroke-maker the like of which has only been matched in South Africa in recent years by Graeme Pollock and Barry Richards.

When Nourse came in to bat, South Africa had already lost three second-innings wickets for 90 and was still three runs behind the Australians' first innings total. In under five hours the 25-year-old turned the match around. According to *Wisden*, 'He often ran in to drive the slow bowlers and seldom has Grimmett suffered such severe treatment'. O'Reilly also received the 'treatment' when Nourse dissipated the Australian bowler's customary double leg-trap with what Duffus describes as 'bold virile strokes to the on'.

Nourse was 96 not out at close of play on the penultimate day and recalled that he spent the night wide awake, listening for the clock to strike each hour. By lunch time the next day he had made 179, but when Nourse was finally caught off the bowling of McCabe for 231 (36 fours), a remarkable match was not yet over. Set 399 to win, Australia went merrily along thanks to a blistering onslaught by Stan McCabe. Only impending rain and South Africa skipper Herby Wade's unprecedented appeal against the light from the field saved the day for the home team with Australia 274 for two wickets and McCabe on 189 not out.

Like all great batsmen, Dudley Nourse made full use of the crease when batting. A stocky man with the forearms of a blacksmith, he thumped the ball off his back foot with tremendous power. His cover drive was superb and his square cut went like a rifle shot. Nourse seldom went forward, other than when he moved down the pitch to drive a slow bowler. Never afraid to hook, even when facing Lindwall and Miller at the age of 40, his bravery was unquestioned — as was witnessed by his double-century against England with a severely

Dudley Nourse, famous son of a famous father, on his way to a double century for South Africa versus Australia at Johannesburg in 1935—36.

injured hand and when he was hit in the neck by a Miller bumper at Newlands in 1949−50, the third Miller bouncer in three consecutive balls! The first went by; the second hit Nourse on the shoulder; the third knocked him to the ground. He staggered to his feet, shrugged it off and battled on to score 100.

Dudley Nourse was a self-made cricketer; his famous Springbok father did not coach him and the first time he saw young Dudley bat was when they opposed each other on the field − 'Old Dave' for Western Province and Dudley for Natal. Nourse junior scored a century that day and his father was the first to congratulate him.

Test matches were few and far between before the war for South Africa. After the Australians departed there was a three-year wait for the 1938−39 MCC team. When the decision was made to play the final Test at Kingsmead, Durban, to a finish, nobody realised that the scene was being set for one of the most bizarre international matches of all time.

The Durban Test began with England one-up in the series − it ended 11 days later with no change in the series status quo! As *Wisden* records: 'Unparalleled in the history of the game this was in many ways an extraordinary match, emphasizing that there are no limits to the possibilities of what may occur in cricket: but it ended farcically, for insufficient time remained to finish the "timeless" Test.'

South Africa batted until well into the third day for a first innings of 530. England replied with 316 and South Africa went in again, to increase the lead to a massive 695, by scoring 481 in its second innings which was completed on the sixth day. On the seventh day England arose, after having been outplayed for nearly a week! The 22-year-old Bill Edrich, who to that point had experienced a dreadful succession of Test failures, went on to score 219 but by the close of the 10th! day (one day was lost due to rain) England, with 654 for five wickets, was still 41 runs short of the seemingly impossible target − and the game had to be abandoned so that the MCC team could catch a train to Cape Town to board their ship, the *Athlone Castle*, for England.

So ended one of the most protracted Tests in history which produced the longest first-class match in history and the highest match aggregate to that date (since twice beaten in Indian domestic cricket but still the highest for a Test).

Of the new South African batsmen to appear in the 1938−39 home series against England, first-choice wicket-keeper W W Wade, an aggressive right-hander, lost his place before the Timeless Test. He re-appeared for South Africa in 1948−49 and scored 407 runs (average 50.87) in the series that season against England with a top score of 125 in the final match at Port Elizabeth. The towering but affable Pieter van der Bijl made his own personal mark on the timeless Test in his one and only series. Alan Melville also scored well in that famous match and was to go on playing for South Africa after the war.

Pieter Gerhart Vintcent van der Bijl came from an old Cape cricketing family. More than six foot (183 cm) and a heavyweight boxing champion and rugby lock forward, he was an opening batsman known for his infinite patience and he must have driven England's bowlers to distraction during his 438 minutes at the wicket for a first innings 125 at Durban – the longest innings in a Test by a South African. In the second innings, van der Bijl was unfortunate to be dismissed just three short of his second 100 of the match.

The tall Pieter van der Bijl produced an even more towering offspring, 6 ft 7½ in (202 cm) Vintcent van der Bijl (South Africa's answer to Joel Garner), a massively talented seam bowler who broke every Currie Cup bowling record, bowled Middlesex to a County Championship victory in 1980 and decimated the batting line-ups of sundry English, Australian, Sri Lankan and West Indies 'rebel' teams who challenged him on his home turf.

The remaining pre-war South African batsman of stature who remains to be profiled can be catalogued as the most delightfully elegant of his country's players. Alan Melville, captain of Oxford University, Sussex, Natal, Transvaal and South Africa, was a batsman of whom E W Swanton once wrote: 'Alan Melville...will recall to the older generation a batsman of high talent and classic style...'.

An upright batsman, Melville was particularly at ease when playing fast bowling. He drove and hooked with grandeur and the operative words in any description of his batting will always remain 'classical style'. Melville was also a prolific scorer of runs. In only 11 Tests he totalled 894 runs at an average of 52.28. His stand of 319 with Dudley Nourse versus England at Trent Bridge in 1947 remains a record for South Africa's third wicket (or any other) in Test cricket.

Alan Melville's four Test centuries were made in consecutive innings – 103 versus England at Durban in 1938–39, followed by 189 and 104 not out in the same match at Trent Bridge in 1947 and 117 at Lord's (both games versus England). During the 1947 series in England and he totalled 569 runs at 63.22 an innings.

As a man of immense personal charm, Melville proved a fine captain and when he gave away the game because of persistent back trouble, served as a Test selector for a number of years.

Melville was his country's captain when South Africa's pre-war Test cricket ended with one of the strangest of all cricket matches. Time had run out in the timeless Test and, in Europe, time was beginning to run out for all cricketers who were preparing for a more serious and deadly contest that was to prevent all first-class cricket from being played for five long and wearisome years.

18

Shall we join the ladies?

'What matter that we lost, mere nervy men
Since England's women now play England's game?
Wherefore, immortal Wisden, take your pen
And write MACLAGAN on the scroll of fame'
— G D Martineau

In any discussion of international cricket it is sometimes overlooked that women's Test matches have been played since 1934, when players from Australia and England first joined in battle at Brisbane. And there have been a number of highly capable batswomen down the years, or batspersons as they may now have to be called, although most women cricketers prefer the customary term batsman, which in fact keeps women's cricket within the parameters laid out in the Laws of Cricket, which make provision for only the masculine striker of the ball.

For in-depth reference, two good books have been produced which outline the history of women's cricket in general and women's international cricket in particular: Nancy Joy's *Maiden Over* (1950) and *Fair Play* by Rachel Heyhoe Flint and Netta Rheinberg (1976).

The first great woman international cricketer was England's high-scoring Myrtle Maclagan who dominated the pre-war Anglo-Australian Test series like a Walter Hammond. In the first ever Test at Brisbane in December 1934, she scored 72 (after taking seven wickets for 10 runs in the first Australian innings); in the next match at Sydney she drove with great power to reach 119, the first Test century in women's cricket. As a hard-hitting right-handed bat, Myrtle Maclagan was superb — as a medium-fast bowler she was outstanding. Her first series record reads: 253 runs at 50.60; 20 wickets for 179 (average 8.95). England won that inaugural rubber 2−0 with Maclagan's main batting support coming from batsman/wicket-keeper E A 'Betty' Snowball, who hit 71 in a first-wicket stand of 154 with Maclagan at Sydney, and a delightful 83 not out at Melbourne, where her delicate leg-glides were a feature of play. Only one Australian passed 50 in the series. On the way home, a single Test was played against New Zealand at Christchurch and England gained a massive win by an innings and 337 runs, Betty Snowball hitting a blistering 189.

The Australians showed marked improvement when they toured England for the first time in 1937 where they squared the rubber. For the visitors, the stylish Hazel Pritchard batted with what was

Myrtle Maclagan,
all-rounder supreme, was
the 'Wally Hammond' of
English women's cricket.

described as 'her own inimitable delicacy of touch' with her main support from the powerful Kath Smith. Pritchard averaged 51.00 for her 306 runs in the three Tests; Smith tallied 214 at 35.66. Hazel Pritchard, the first of Australia's outstanding batswomen had deceptively strong wrists for a person of such delicate appearance. Her timing was excellent, as was her footwork, and she held the bat high up on the handle. One quaint Harold Gittins cartoon of the time bore the caption: 'Hard-hitting Hazel at the Oval, Australia's female Bradman, who makes boundaries look as easy as dabbing on lipstick.'

Myrtle Maclagan for England was again the Australians' main stumbling block. Displaying remarkable consistency, she hit 315 runs at an average of 63.00, with a top score 115 at Blackpool, a grand attacking innings that contained 15 fours. She also bowled more overs in the series than any other England bowler. Of the other England batsmen, Betty Snowball was again to the fore and at the Oval added 134 runs for the third wicket with the quick-scoring Molly Hide (64), who went on to become England's leading batswoman after Myrtle Maclagan.

Play was resumed in women's international cricket after the Second World War when an England side sailed to Australia in the 1948−49 season under the captaincy of Hide, after their male counterparts had twice been thrashed by Bradman's Australians, at home and in Australia.

Before the Australian-England series started, Australia visited New Zealand and won the only Test at Wellington. Una Paisley, a solid player whose favourite stroke was the cut, hit 108 for Australia (she hit another century against New Zealand at Adelaide in the 1956−57 season).

The three-match rubber in Australia ended with honours even, the home team's ace all-rounder, Betty Wilson, and England's Molly Hide dominating the series. Wilson scored the first century by an Australian in an international match versus England in the opening Test at Adelaide and then took nine wickets and scored 74 in the next game at Melbourne; she was by far Australia's most reliable player. Netta Rheinberg describes Betty Wilson in *Fair Play* as 'the finest woman cricketer in the world', at a time when Myrtle Maclagan was still playing but entering the last phase of her own outstanding career. According to Rheinberg, the Australian produced 'a standard of batting believed by many to be impossible for a woman' and that 'her stroke-play ran the whole gamut of orthodoxy'. Betty Wilson was still Australia's leading run-scorer almost 10 years later when she hit two centuries in the 1957−58 series against England.

During the 1948−49 series in Austtralia, England's Molly Hide, who had made a Test debut century against New Zealand in 1934−35, reached her own peak in Tests and ended with consecutive scores of 51 (at Melbourne) and 63 and 124 not out (at Sydney).

In England in 1951, Betty Wilson remained Australia's most prominent run-scorer (and wicket-taker) while, apart from the evergreen Maclagan and Molly Hide, Cecilia Robinson (105 in the first Test at Scarborough) came to the fore for the host team. Robinson's effort at Scarborough took four hours and 47 minutes — the slowest women's Test century on record. The patient Cecilia Robinson again did well with scores of 102 and 96 during the 1957–58 England tour of Australia.

Another prominent England player of the 1950s was Mary Duggan who logged two Test centuries and took over from Maclagan as her country's outstanding all-rounder.

South Africa entered the women's international scene when England visited the Cape in 1960–61. Eileen Hurley, who at 13 had hit the first recorded 100 in a women's league match in Johannesburg, made 96 not out for South Africa in the first Test at Port Elizabeth. South Africa's captain Sheila Nefdt also impressed with the bat and to left-hander Yvonne von Mentz went the honour of scoring her country's first Test century — a patient 105 not out in the fourth Test at Cape Town.

Captaining England for the first time against New Zealand in 1966, the highly talented Rachel Heyhoe (later Heyhoe Flint) was England's top run-maker when she hit 113 at Scarborough and aggregated 356 runs at an average of 59.33 in the three-game series. Ten years later, Rachel Flint was still going strong when she played successive innings of 110, 49, 12 and 179 (350 at 87.50) in a three-match series versus Australia. Her 110 at Old Trafford in the first Test was her own maiden Test hundred against Australia. At the Oval in the final game she played a second innings of 179 in 521 minutes to save England after Australia had led by 245 runs on the first innings.

As Rachel Heyoe, she first played cricket at age 14 and, in 1963, hit the first six in a women's Test match against Australia at the Oval. Netta Rheinberg describes this stroke as 'a beautifully timed shot over long-on, the ball travelling with surprising power for a slightly built person of short stature'. Rachel Heyhoe must be recorded as one of the half-dozen finest batswomen of all time and was also a tireless administrator and writer on the game who for a long time had her own column in *Cricketer International*. One of the more amusing incidents in her career occurred in a Test versus Australia at Scarborough in 1963 when she left her shoe in the middle of the pitch while taking a sharp single. A A Thomson, writing in *The Times*, referred to the incident as 'stealing a run like Cinderella'.

Another outstanding English champion woman cricketer emerged when England toured Australia and New Zealand in 1968–69 — and became the first woman cricketer to be accorded the honour of an article in *Wisden* (1970).

In a tribute to Enid Bakewell, who totalled more than 1000 runs and 100 wickets on the tour to Australia and New Zealand, Netta Rheinberg reminds her readers that it was a woman, W G Grace's cricket-loving mother, who first instilled the finer points of the game into her famous son's play.

Enid Bakewell, a small but athletically built blonde wife and mother, batted and bowled left-handed. In six Tests on the tour she totalled 601 runs at 54.63 and took 26 wickets. Not even the legendary Myrtle Maclagan had performed so remarkably.

For Australia, Miriam Knee and Lyn Denholm each reached 90 in an innings but the rest were inconsistent. New Zealand's captain, Patricia McKelvey, however, broke her country's run drought with a mammoth 155 not out in five and a half hours in the first Test at Wellington. Judi Doull then emulated her captain's century feat with a patient 103 in 249 minutes in the second match at Christchurch. Prior to this series, New Zealand's highest was by wicket-keeper Bev Brentnall, who came in at number eight in the second Test against England at Edgbaston in 1966 to score 84 not out.

Patricia McKelvey and Judi Doull were again in form when New Zealand travelled to South Africa in 1971–72, McKelvey logging her second Test century at Cape Town. South Africa's Brenda Williams scored 100 in the third Test at Johannesburg in what proved to be her country's last official Test.

In 1973 the first women's World Cup one-day competition was staged in England, with teams from England, Australia, New Zealand, Trinidad and Tobago and Jamaica supplemented by an International XI and a Young England XI.

Enid Bakewell dominated the final at Edgbaston with an innings of 118 as England swept through to beat Australia by 92 runs (England scored a phenomenal 279 for three wickets in 60 overs). Wisden records that Bakewell batted fluently and 'looked as relaxed as if she had been on the beach'; truly a remarkable cricketer by any standards. Three England players, Bakewell (twice), Rachel Heyhoe and Lynne Thomas recorded the four centuries made during the tournament.

The inaugural England-West Indies series took place in 1979 and the ubiquitous Enid Bakewell was again the chief architect of an England victory with scores of 68 and 112 not out in the Edgbaston Test. West Indies skipper Pat Whittaker (twice), Shirley-Anne Bonaparte and wicket-keeper Beverly Brown made 50s. Australia triumphed in the 1982 World Cup in New Zealand, in which the five teams, Australia, England, New Zealand, India and an International XI, were given live television coverage for the first time. England's Jan Southgate was the outstanding batsman of the tournament.

Australia toured India in 1983–84 for the first time and spectacular batting from the touring team's Jill Kennare (131), Peta Verco (105) and Karen Price (104 not out) helped create a new women's record Test total of 525 in the third Test at Ahmadebad.

Jill Kennare, Australia's
leading batswoman of the
1980s.

India's Chandra Nayudu (daughter of the famous C K Nayudu) is, incidentally, the first-ever woman cricket commentator to go on air in a men's first-class match. The vivacious Chandra Nayudu first took over the microphone when Tony Greig's MCC team played Bombay at Indore in 1976–77. Oddly enough, Greig had forgotten about that unique occasion in 1984 when much was made of the first appearance of actress Kate Fitzpatrick as a commentator on Australia's Channel 9 and she was incorrectly introduced as the first woman cricket broadcaster.

In 1984, in an unprecedented burst of scoring, a new and spectacular England batting star, Janette Brittin, using a David Gower bat, hit 338 runs (average 112.66) in three Tests against New Zealand plus a one-day international tally of 258 (average 129.00) – an overall record of 596 runs at 119.20! Shades of Bradman and Sobers. She continued her fine run when England toured Australia in 1984–85 to tally 429 runs (average 42.90) in a five-match series.

Australia's Jill Kennare (she prefers to be called a 'batswoman') emulated Betty Wilson's 1958 feat by scoring two centuries in the same series, including 100 at Bendigo, scene of the first-ever women's cricket match in Australia. She also scored 100s in two of the one-day internationals against England to challenge Jan Brittin for the title of best batswoman in current international cricket.

Another Australian, Denise Emerson, sister of Australian Test bowler Terry Alderman, scored 121 in the second Test at Adelaide and, with 453 runs in the series (average 50.33), outscored Jill Kennare (347 at 38.55). For England, Jan Southgate, Carol Hodges and Jackie Court were the most successful run-scorers after Jan Brittin.

The 1984–85 series celebrated 50 years of women's Test cricket and the fifth Test between Australia and England was played at Bendigo, venue of the first recorded match in Australia between two teams of women. In 1874, the *Bendigo Advertiser* recorded: 'The match evoked great enthusiasm and was watched by a large crowd, feelings being rather mixed about this new and daring innovation in feminine activities.' One can only wonder what the reporter's comments would have been if he could have viewed the Australian and England women's teams a 100 years later, taking the field in immaculate whites. In 1874 the women apparently wore coloured gear – 'Garibaldi jackets of vivid red hue . . . plus sailors hats with red bands'. The only difference in dress between the two teams was their hat bands – one side wore red, the other bright blue.

For 51 years the record score in women's Test cricket remained a blistering 189 by England's Betty Snowball versus New Zealand at Christchurch in 1934–35. Then, during the course of two consecutive seasons, it was beaten and raised. Betty Snowball had scored her 189 at a run a minute — and then got herself out because she thought the crowd would like to see someone else bat.

In 1986, versus England at Blackpool, India's ultra-cautious but skilfull Sandhya Agarwall occupied the crease for a 561 minutes to score a monumental 190.

Not to be outdone, next season, Australia's 23-year-old and tiny five-feet-in-her-socks Denise Annetts wrote a new page in the record book with an infinitely more entertaining but no less dedicated 193 in only 381 minutes (365 balls), also versus England, at Collingham. During the course of her unforgettable innings, Annetts hit 30 fours and created a new world partnership record of 309 with team-mate Lindsay Reeler (110 not out).

More confirmation of Australia's current pre-eminence in batting was given earlier on when a third high-scoring member of an exceptionally talented 1987 Australian team, Belinda Haggett, registered the highest score by a woman on Test debut — 126 in the first Test at Worcester.

19

Victory celebration

'Keith Miller is the most unpredictable cricketer I have played against. I am never quite sure what he is going to do next and I don't think he knows himself until he is about to do it'

— Sir Leonard Hutton

A team of Australian Servicemen toured England in 1945 under the genial and talented Lindsay Hassett and helped ease cricket towards a post-war recovery. A series of five 'Victory' matches was played between teams representing England and Australia (three games at Lord's; one each at Sheffield and Manchester) and the honours were even at the end (two wins each and a draw) in a fitting re-start to international cricket. No player on either side performed with as much charismatic verve as did a tall young Victorian batsman who had played a number of Sheffield Shield matches prior to the hostilities.

Keith Ross Miller was the major international find of the season in 1945 and the one player in the Services combination, other than Hassett himself, who looked equipped to claim a permanent place in the full Australian Test XI. In the 1946 *Wisden*, Norman Preston wrote that Miller was 'destined to become one of the great men of Australian cricket'. His prophecy was clearly vindicated during the following decade.

John Arlott has written: 'Keith was, and is, *potentially* the best batsman, the best bowler and the best fieldsman in the world.' It was as a batsman that one of Australia's most spectacular players first caught the imagination. With footwork that was as improvised as that of his fellow 'Brylcreem Boy', Denis Compton, Miller moved swiftly to the pitch of the ball and hit with tremendous power. And, like Compton again, it was not unusual for Miller to smack the best ball of the day to the boundary. According to Ray Robinson 'superb technique...enabled Miller to look for runs where others look for trouble'.

Smoothing down his mane of dark hair, Miller would relax into an easy stance at the wicket, as a natural and comfortable prelude to the launching of his attack on the bowling. The 'grandest player of cricket's grandest stroke' his straight drive was 'unrivalled in splendour'. Miller also hit on the off-side with regal delight and was the master of the late cut. Yet it was Miller's hook-shot that fired the

The glorious
straight-driving of
Australia's Keith Miller was
a feature of post-war
cricket.

imagination most. John Arlott describes this frightening shot as
comparable with that played by Bradman – 'but unlike it, because
this is Miller's hook. The characteristic of Bradman's hook is safety
and control, of Miller's, fierce power and speed'.

Dick Whitington once went on record to claim that Bradman
ruined Miller as a Test batsman by calling on the debonair all-
rounder to bowl too frequently on the 1948 tour of England. One of
Bradman's team, a subsequent Australian captain, Ian Johnson,
argued that Bradman's decisions were based entirely on team neces-
sity. According to Johnson (and probably Bradman), Miller was

more valuable as a bowler in a side that boasted run-getters of the calibre of Bradman himself, Hassett, Barnes, Brown and the left-handers Arthur Morris and Neil Harvey (plus a host of all-rounders other than Miller).

Keith Miller's glorious range of strokes brought him runs in every company and in every land in which he played. At the end of his career figures revealed that he had scored just short of 3000 runs and taken 170 wickets in 55 Tests. In all first-class cricket Miller hit 33 centuries, most in dashing fashion. When chosen as one of the 'Five Cricketers of the Year' in 1954, Keith Miller was fittingly described as Australia's finest all-rounder since M A Noble and it was noted that 'Even that Golden Age of cricket would have been enriched by a character as colourful as Keith Ross Miller'. John Arlott sums up Miller with insight and accuracy: 'When Keith Miller, the finest all-rounder in the world, found himself a public figure, he shrugged his shoulders and continued to be Keith Miller.'

Miller was the undoubted Australian batting star of the 1945 Victory celebrations − but when the Australian team was assembled for the first post-war Tests, the list of batting potential had grown to include a number of other players whose names will always be close to the top of a list of the best Australian batsmen.

As Test batsman, the left-handed opener Arthur Robert Morris has had few peers. Starting his career aged 18 with a century in each innings of his debut Sheffield Shield match just before the outbreak of war, he quickly re-established himself in 1946−47. Three 100s in successive innings off Hammond's sorely tested England bowlers placed Morris as automatic number one choice in the national XI.

Morris has naturally been compared with the other outstanding Australian left-handers. The most frequent of such comparisons has been made with Warren Bardsley − although Morris's back-lift was not quite as straight as his predecessor. Each batsman hit two centuries in a Test against England. Bardsley was, however, generally a one-tempo batsman − Morris was a two-in-one player, who could switch from defence to attack at will.

According to Ray Robinson few other batsmen have ever equalled Morris's ability to adapt to unfamiliar conditions. The left-hander was particularly adept in a counter-attack against aggressive fast bowling and was a fierce hooker of the bouncer. He played superbly in front of the wicket on the off-side and, like all truly great batsmen, executed his shots from a point of perfect balance. His leg-side play was brilliant and he possessed a powerful square cut. A truly elegant batsman, Morris used his near-perfect footwork to become one of the best of players against spin and frequently went yards down the pitch to disturb a bowler's length.

His Achilles' heel was discovered by one English bowler. Morris's nemesis was the indefatigable Alec Bedser who frequently dismissed the Australian with his finger-spun quick leg-cutter that moved in from the off to the left-hander after Morris had followed too far the initial late out-swing of the ball.

However Bedser was way off the mark when Morris assisted his captain, Don Bradman, to take Australia through to a miraculous win at Leeds in 1948 in what was possibly the best innings, in terms of sheer determination, that the left-hander ever played for Australia. The impossible was achieved when Australia, thanks to a massive 301-run stand from Morris (182) and Bradman (173 not out), actually scored 404 runs for three wickets in under six hours on the final day.

Sir Neville Cardus considered Australia's second great post-war left-hander, Neil Harvey, a batting artist: 'You will no more arrive at a complete idea of his cricket by adding up the runs that he makes than you will realize the quality of Mozart's music if you add up all the crochets and quavers.'

On all wickets, Robert Neil Harvey was possibly the best Australian batsman of his time. His branded answer when faced with a dire situation was first illustrated against England at Headingly, Leeds, in 1948. The tender 19-year-old joined Keith Miller with Australia at three for 68 and facing an England total of 496. The two young cavalier batsmen proceeded to scatter the English attack and Harvey went on to his century with 17 fours.

In 1956, once again in the company of his old companion-at-arms Keith Miller, Harvey was one of the pitifully few Australian batsmen who had any perception of how to handle Laker on the turning tracks at Headingly, Old Trafford and the Oval.

Although at times prone to play risky shots, Harvey's fabulous eye and reflexes made sure thay his habits did not prove too costly. Against anything less than the best of bowling he would put his right foot down the pitch and slash across the flight of the ball — a devastating stroke. Glorying in the attacking game, he played all the strokes with compact force, revelling in the drive, square-cut and pull shots. Ray Robinson described Harvey's batting as being akin to that 'of a boy playing schoolmates' bowling on a vacant block, hitting as many balls as he can....'.

Neil Harvey's unshakeable temperament came out strongly against South Africa on a spinners' wicket at Kingsmead, Durban, in 1949–1950. The tantalising off-breaks of Hugh Tayfield had hustled Australia out for a first innings low of 75. In the end Australia needed 336 to win in the final innings — a daunting task indeed against Tayfield and dead-accurate Springbok left-hander 'Tufty' Mann.

For five and a half hours Harvey displayed uncharacteristic patience, accelerating his scoring as the time went by. His amazing 151 not out carried Australia through to victory completely against the run of play.

Neil Harvey, the most brilliant of Australian stroke players, pulls the ball to the boundary.

This writer's own best personal memory of Neil Harvey's glorious batsmanship was the almost disdainful 178 he took off Dudley Nourse's South African attack in the Newlands Test during the same 1949−50 tour. No matter where fast bowler Cuan McCarthy or spinners Tayfield and Mann put the ball, Harvey made his own length and cracked it away.

Neil Harvey came from a family of six boys, three of whom played together in the Victorian Sheffield Shield XI. Eldest brother Mervyn Roye Harvey was indeed an enterprising right-handed opening batsman who actually preceded his younger brother Neil into the Australian Test team for just one game when he replaced an injured Sid Barnes for the fourth Test against England at Adelaide in 1946−47.

Bradman's team to England in 1948 raised Australian all-round scoring to a new dimension. Sir Donald has himself claimed that his 1948 combination bore comparison with any of its predecessors. Even if there had been no Lindwall or Miller to pulverise England's batsmen into submission, the chances are that the powerful Australian batting would have proved sufficient to win the series. Morris (87.00), Barnes (82.25), Bradman (72.57), Harvey (66.50) and Hassett (44.28) all averaged more than 40 in the Tests and all-rounders Miller, Sam Loxton, Ian Johnson and Ray Lindwall all weighed in when required to do so. Ian Johnson and Ray Lindwall were both highly talented batsman who may well have reached Test level for their run-making ability alone if they had not both been such excellent wicket-takers.

The popular Samuel John Everett Loxton was an all-rounder who took second place to Lindwall as a bowler but whose batting entertained all who watched him play. Loxton batted like a jolly pirate swinging his cutlass; he frequently taunted opposing fast bowlers to bounce them at him so that he could hit the ball over the fence. His best effort in 1948 consisted of 93 in the Test at Headingly that included five enormous sixes and nine fours and ruined England's chance of a win.

Although he never went to England on tour, New South Wales opener John Rodger Moroney (a painstaking right-hander who was often criticised for his cautious attitude) is one of the select Australian batsmen to score two centuries in a Test, as opening partner to Arthur Morris at Ellis Park, Johannesburg, in 1949−50. Partly due to his lacklustre fielding but mainly because of his stonewalling tendencies, John Rodger Moroney could not hold his place in the Test team.

The tall and sapling-slender Graeme Blake Hole, of the awkward looking stance, was a young stroke-player of the day who flattered early on in his career, only ultimately to deceive but one of the biggest batting disappointments for Australia during the first decade after the war was the failure of boy prodigy Ian David Craig.

Craig was looked upon with similar awe to that inspired by the young Trumper, the young Jackson and the young Bradman but his international career went onto a slippery downward slide. He did, however, create a record by becoming Australia's youngest international captain.

Ken Archer's younger brother, Ronald Graham Archer, eventually took over from Keith Miller as all-rounder in the Australian XI but a persistent back problem hampered his progress. A solid hitter of the ball, Ron Archer went to England twice and impressed with his full-blooded driving and whole-hearted square cutting in 19 Tests, without fulfilling his initial promise.

A batsman who was to recall memories of the dour days of Alick Bannerman and Charles Kelleway did ultimately make the grade for Australia during the 1950s. James Wallace Burke's first love was golf but when it came to cricket his strokes were all too frequently set aside for a push and a prod that brought him more than 1000 Test runs but few friends in the crowd. Sydney's famous 'Hill' barrackers were oft heard to cry 'Go home, Burke!' even before the batsman had taken guard.

Capable of turning it on when the occasion warranted, Burke excelled with the on-drive but for most of the time was content to let the ball hit the bat. A low grip and nifty footwork helped him in his back-play tactics against Laker in 1956 when he headed the Australian averages and looked best equipped to stave off the disaster that eventually ended in such overwhelming rout.

One of Burke's famous dead-bat efforts earned him the dubious world record of the slowest ever piece of Test batting when he crawled his way to 28 not out in 250 minutes against England at Brisbane in 1958−59 − in response, no doubt, to an equally boring but 'less successful' dead-bat display from England's 'Barndoor' Bailey. Jimmy Burke ended his own life tragically in 1979 with a shotgun.

The first decade after the Second World War had seen Australian batsmanship slump from a positon of commanding superiority to a scene of faltering and fumbling against the off-spin of England's Jim Laker. But a revival was around the corner, inspired by a new leader whose own aggressive attitude provided an inspiration to his men and helped to set the stage for the most thrilling Test of all time.

20

The terrible twins

'They go together in English cricket, as Gilbert
and Sullivan go together in English opera'
— R C Robertson-Glasgow

During the 1947 season a war-weary England shrugged off the gloom of rationing and rebuilding and delighted at the dashing exploits of Denis Charles Scott Compton and William John Edrich. For both county and country, the 'Terrible Twins' ran riot in an unprecedented run-scoring spree which was as exciting for its entertainment value as for its contribution to the innings totals of Middlesex and England.

The reference by Robertson-Glasgow to Gilbert and Sullivan was amplified by the statement: '. . .it should not be doubted that, in the art of giving pleasure to an English audience, both pairs lack rival.' Compton and Edrich served their early batting apprenticeship prior to the war; they faced unflinchingly an Australian fast-bowling bombardment of frightening aspect immediately after the conflict; during the summer of 1947 they rejoiced at their survival: 'To bowlers, Compton and Edrich became the daily task, and maybe, the nightly vision.'

It would seem fitting first to record the figures and then discuss the art. In 1947 Denis Compton scored 3816 first-class runs at 90.85 with 18 centuries (both records still stand); Bill Edrich totalled 3539 at 80.43 with 12 centuries. Both passed the record of 3518 runs (13 centuries) set by Tom Hayward in 1906.

In five Tests against South Africa, Compton played innings of 65, 163, 208, 115, 6, 30, 53 and 113 — total 753 at 94.12; in four Tests, Edrich hit 57, 50, 189, 191, 22 not out and 43 — total 552 at 110.40. In other matches against the touring South Africans, Compton made scores of 18, 97, 154, 34, 101 and 30; Edrich, 67, 133 not out, 64 and 54 — their combined totals in all matches against the tourists was: Compton — 1187 runs at 91.30; Edrich — 870 at 108.75. Three South African batsmen (Nourse, Mitchell and Melville) scored seven Test 100s between them and each averaged more than 60 for the five Tests — yet England, because of the even more phenomenal scoring by Compton and Edrich, easily won the rubber 3–0.

Sir Neville Cardus once described Denis Compton as 'a great improvisor, instinctive and free'. Trevor Bailey rates Bill Edrich 'a complete batsman with a magnificent defence. . .and a wide range of attacking strokes'. Compton was the innovative genius who thumbed

Denis Compton
demonstrates his famous
sweep shot.

his nose at batting convention and batted with carefree disdain in all situations; Edrich was a batsman of talent who worked at his game to raise himself to the highest standard. His old opponent Dudley Nourse of South Africa summed up Denis Compton completely: 'He can keep the crowd on tenterhooks, his opponents in a fever of expectation of his dismissal at any moment, can almost send his batting partner into an apopleptic fit (Compton was a notoriously risky runner between the wickets), and score a century as though it was just some ordinary everyday matter which he takes in his stride.' John Arlott described Compton as a batsman who 'simply *plays* — like a boy striking at a rubber ball with a paling from a fence — for fun'.

Compton at the crease produced a dazzling (and for the bowler, frustrating) display of classical drives, cuts and pulls combined with a variety of shots he seemed to make up on the spur of the moment. Cardus describes once watching Compton dance down the pitch to drive an anticipated leg-break, with the spin, to the off. Only when the ball hit the pitch did the batsman realise it was in fact a googly. 'Compton had to readjust his entire physical shape and position at the last split second.' Falling flat on his chest, Compton found time to sweep the ball to the leg-boundary. 'It was a case of delayed science.' Various versions of the famous Compton sweep shot became the trade mark of every substantial innings he played.

It must be clearly recorded that, although Compton played many a stroke which finds no place in the textbook, he almost always did so from a basis of orthodox first principle − perfect balance, feet correctly placed and body and head over the ball as his bat swung into a full follow-through.

Compton's sparkling footwork as he moved down the wicket (sometimes as the bowler was still running in) made a mockery of any slow bowler's intended length. Against the quick stuff he was as brave and adept as any other batsman. At Trent Bridge in 1948 (when Lindwall and Miller were sowing the seeds of fearful apprehension in the England batting ranks and the home country faced a first innings arrears of 344) Compton (184) and Hutton (74) stood up to the blistering bombardment in a rearguard action.

Compton handled the fast short-pitched bowling with admirable dexterity until he decided at the last second to leave a bouncer from Miller alone (after losing sight of it against the dark pavilion background − it was described as the fastest ball bowled by Miller all summer) and, overbalancing, trod on his stumps.

At Old Trafford a month later, England's debonair hero returned to score 145 not out after being forced to retire with the England score on 33 for two wickets. Compton was helped from the field, blood streaming from a cut above his eye, after mistiming a hook from a Lindwall bouncer that saw the ball fly from bat's edge to his forehead. His great innings continued when the England total had reached 119 for five wickets and he saw his side through to a total of 363, in a match which might have provided England its only win of the season but for rain.

As the years advanced and he experienced severe knee problems necessitating several operations, Compton adjusted his style and continued to score readily (other than a disastrous Test season in Australia in 1950−51). In 78 Tests he gathered 5807 runs at 50.06, with a devastating 278 versus Pakistan at Nottingham in 1954 as his highest innings. For MCC versus North-Eastern Transvaal at Benoni, South Africa, in 1948−49 he plundered 300 in only 181 minutes − the fastest first-class triple-century on record.

The writer was privileged to watch Compton bat at his peak in South Africa during 1948−49, and saw him score his final 100 in any class of cricket. During 1964−65, Denis Compton accompanied Mike Smith's MCC team to South Africa as a newspaper correspondent. He was prevailed upon to play in a Sunday charity match at Newlands, Cape Town, for a Press XI versus a full-strength Western Province team. When the 47-year-old and no longer very trim Compton came to the wicket, Western Province captain Peter van der Merwe put his wicket-keeper, John Ferrandi, on to bowl. A succession of sweetly-timed late-cuts, glorious sweeps and vintage cover-drives to the boundary resulted. Ferrandi was quickly replaced by Springbok bowlers Jimmy Pothecary and Harry Bromfield — but the old master was now in full flow. Ninety minutes later Compton posted his 100 with his own very special sweep-shot to the leg boundary.

Bill Edrich was small, nimble, built like a boxer and a born fighter. According to Tevor Bailey, this characteristic was 'the most outstanding feature of his batting, and indeed his life'. Edrich was at his best when the chips were down, when there was serious business at hand at the wicket. Off the field, he was the life and soul of the party — if a party, heaven forbid, looked like ending before dawn, he would provide his own cabaret act to keep the festivities going.

He was a member of an illustrious cricketing family from Norfolk that frequently fielded an XI composed entirely of Edriches. Brothers, Eric and Geoffrey (both Lancashire) and Brian (Kent), all played county cricket. His cousin John Edrich followed him into the England XI. Edrich's father — known in Norfolk as 'Father William' — was an avid cricket fan whose four sons and one nephew scored 221 first-class centuries between them.

Aged 16, Bill Edrich experienced a baptism of fire in his first big match for Norfolk versus All India in 1932. The 6 ft 2 in (188 cm) and decidedly quick Mohammed Nissar severely tested the pint-sized Norfolk schoolboy with a succession of bouncers. Not afraid to go on the hook, Edrich made top score of 20 in a first innings total of 49 (Nissar 6/14) and added a defiant 16 in the second, when Nissar took another eight wickets for 43. When he was called upon to combat Lindwall and company after the war, Edrich had not forgotten how to hook.

Certainly no stylist, he plundered many of his runs with lusty pulls and hooks. His small stature brought limitations in forward play and he used the straight drive less frequently than most batsmen of class. One of his most punishing strokes was what can only be described as a 'pull-drive' which would send the ball soaring to the right of long-on. Off the back foot he was superb and his fierce and frequent hooking was the combined result of courage and timing. On a bad wicket, Edrich was at his best, his quick-footed efficiency a rare counter to the turning and popping ball.

Overcoming a dreadful start to his Test career (his first 11 innings produced only 88 runs; his 12th innings was a brilliant 219 versus South Africa in the 'Timeless Test'), Edrich became, with Hutton, Compton and Cyril Washbrook, one of England's few reliable scorers at Test level during the first years after the war. From time to time he was dropped from the England team, only to return when those who replaced him could not match his guts and determined skill. In

Bill Edrich (right) walking in to bat with Reg Simpson of Nottinghamshire and England.

1966, at the age of 50, he captained Minor Counties against the touring West Indians and hooked and pulled his way to a second innings 61 (four sixes and six fours) in just 40 minutes.

Hard as some of the choices tried, after the first four (Hutton, Washbrook, Edrich, Compton), England's batting larder was distinctly bare during the 1940s and into the 1950s. Lancashire's left-handed John Thomas 'Jack' Ikin, Warwickshire's first professional captain Horace Edgar Dollery, the phlegmatic left-hander John Frederick 'Jack' Crapp (Gloucestershire) and belligerent Gloucestershire opener George Malcolm Emmett were all tried with small result.

An opening batsman with hard luck was John David Benbow Robertson of Middlesex. For his county, this handsome and correct right-hander frequently matched the brilliance of Edrich and Compton. In 11 Tests during the Hutton-Washbrook period, he scored 881 runs at 46.36, was picked to replace an injured Washbrook against New Zealand at Lord's in 1949, scoring 121, but was dropped when Washbrook reported fit for the next game and did not play again in the series!

A number of able county batsmen experienced their only outing for England when the MCC toured the West Indies in 1947–48, including Washbrook's Lancashire opening partner, the rather introverted Winston Place; prolific Northamptonshire opener Dennis Brookes (who returned home early with a chipped finger bone); Gerald Arthur Smithson (a left-hander and a former coal miner from Yorkshire); and Lancashire amateur Kenneth Cranston.

Reserve wicket-keeper (and a future secretary and president of the MCC) Stewart Cathie Griffith was sent in as a makeshift opening batsman in the Port of Spain Test. To the amazement of colleagues and opponents alike, he scored a determined 140, but never again approached this kind of form in any class of cricket.

Three of England's post-war captains occasionally weighed in with useful scores in Test matches but did not play with the consistent skill required at international level. Norman Walter Dransfield Yardley had the unenviable task of trying to combat Bradman's famous 1940s XI. As a Test batsman, he put up some plucky displays – his best innings was 99 against South Africa at Trent Bridge in 1947. Francis George Mann emulated his father, F T Mann, by taking an MCC team to South Africa. A forcing player like his father, F G Mann played a decisive innings of 136 not out against South Africa at Port Elizabeth in 1948–49. England's succeeding captain, Frederick Richard Brown, went to Australia under Jardine for the 1932–33 bodyline tour. His next visit to Australia was as captain of England in 1950–51.

The most often told tale about England's 1950–51 skipper concerns the Australian vegetable seller who called out to his potential customers that his cabbages had 'hearts as big as Freddie Brown's'. In his batting and bowling on that tour (Australia proved far superior to England at all points), Brown displayed admirable guts and application.

Two Glamorgan professionals, the enterprising left-hander Allan John Watkins (known as 'Friar Tuck' because of his build and balding pate) and William Gilbert Anthony Parkhouse, played in a smattering of games for England during the 1940s and 1950s but neither made much progress.

England's ace wicket-keeper Thomas Godfrey Evans was a swashbuckling batsman who on more than one occasion hit England out of a crisis. At Lord's versus India in 1952 Evans hit 98 runs before lunch and went to 104 after the interval.

His 104 against West Indies at Old Trafford in 1950 included 16 fours — Evans and Trevor Bailey saved the England innings with a sixth-wicket partnership of 161 runs. Godfrey Evans's world record 95 minutes sojourn at the crease before scoring a run against Australia at Adelaide in 1946—47 proved a sharp contrast to some of his later efforts — and was more in the style of his Old Trafford partner, 'Barnacle' Bailey.

Trevor Edward Bailey was a batsman whose style of play placed him in a similar category to the stonewallers of past eras. His four and a half hour crawl to the initial 50 of his first Test century (versus New Zealand at Christchurch in 1950—51) occasioned E W Swanton to write that Bailey's innings was 'a joyless burlesque of the art of batting'. As England's leading all-rounder of the 1950s, Trevor Bailey thrived on crisis. At Lord's in 1953 he and Yorkshire left-hander Willie Watson batted for almost a day against Australia to save England; Bailey made 71 in four hours. At Brisbane in 1958—59, again versus Australia, he sorely frustrated the Australian team and put the 'Gabba crowd to sleep with the slowest 50 of all time — 357 minutes. Bailey eventually made 68 in 458 minutes! Against South Africa at Headingly in 1955 he stayed put for two hours for just eight runs. With his perpetual forward defensive prod as virtually his only 'stroke', Bailey became the uncontested 'Johnny One-Note' of international cricket.

Bailey for Essex was frequently seen in a different mood and could force the pace when the occasion demanded it. He was the last player to score 2000 runs and take 100 wickets in a season (1959).

Bailey's collaborator in the famous 1953 Lord's rescue act against Australia offered a pleasing contrast in style. Yorkshireman Willie Watson was a left-hander of class who made the art of batting look simple and who provided the additional bonus of unusual fleetness of foot when running between wickets — which was not too surprising for a soccer left half who gained four caps for England. Apart from his Lord's century, Watson scored 116 against West Indies at Kingston in 1953—54.

On his Test debut against South Africa at Durban in 1948—49, the tall and striking Reginald Thomas Simpson failed miserably (5 and 0) and was consigned to the reserves' bench for the remainder of the series. Given another opportunity in the third Test against New Zealand at Manchester the following summer, the Nottinghamshire amateur produced brilliant form which saw him race from 50 to 103 in just 27 minutes. He three times hit New Zealand's much-fancied left-arm spinner Tom Burtt over the ropes and was caught on the boundary by Donnelly going for another six.

Simpson was to play a number of important innings during the remainder of his Test career but none surpassed his memorable 156 not out in the fifth Test at Melbourne on England's rather ill-fated 1950—51 tour of Australia when he was one of the few batsman to handle the mystery spin of Jack Iverson with any aplomb.

At a time when a distinction was still made between the status of amateur and professional cricketers (or Gentlemen and Players), Simpson played as one of the former. It was not to be long before England's batting, which had for the first decade after the war relied almost exclusively on professionals like Hutton, Washbrook, Edrich and Compton, would be dominated by a bevy of 'amateur' performers who had learnt the art of batsmanship at the two English universities that boasted first-class status.

21

The 'W' formation

'Seldom, if ever, has one country possessed three middle order batsmen of the calibre of Weekes, Worrell and Walcott'

— Trevor Bailey

The popular image of the islands of the Caribbean which make up the cricketing entity known as West Indies is certainly colourful and enchanting. Sun-drenched, palm-fringed beaches, crystal clear water and sapphire bays, high mountains with flamboyant trees and birds of a thousand species, exotic fruits and unique song and dance that typify the inherent attitudes of the happy inhabitants.

From the 7000 square kilometre Jamaica (George Headley's island), with a population of just over two million, to the mainland shores of Guyana (Clive Lloyd, Kanhai, Kallicharran) on the continent of South America; from the tiny Antigua (birthplace of the mighty Viv Richards and Andy Roberts) to the festival island of Trinidad (birthplace of the incomparable Lord Learie Constantine) there can be heard everywhere, throughout a long and lazy summer, the sweet sound of bat striking ball and the enthusiastic and frequently raucous response of the West Indian cricket spectators.

One of the smallest of the islands is the most prolific spawning ground of cricketers of quality, in terms of players per square kilometre, on planet Earth. It is also the birthplace of the legendary three 'Ws' — Worrell, Weekes and Walcott.

Barbados is a pear-shaped tropical island, 34 kilometres long and about 22 kilometres across at its widest point. Its image on postcards captures scenes of palm-fringed sandy white beaches, with sugar plantations stretching into the interior of the island. In every one of the parishes into which the island of Barbados is divided, the central feature is the cricket ground — and the abiding passion, the religion of its people, is cricket. No other place in the world of comparable size has produced so many outstanding first-class and international cricketers.

H B G (later Sir Harold) Austin became the 'King of Barbados' during the early 1900s — as a batsman and as a captain who at the age of 48 led both Barbados and West Indies against the 1925–26 MCC touring team. Then came George Challenor (known by the enthusiastic Barbadian crowds as 'Lord Runs-Come') and Tarilton, Hoad, Ince, C A Browne and the first of the great Barbados fast bowlers, George Francis and Herman Griffith.

The powerful Clyde Walcott is the only batsman to score a century in each innings in two Tests (West Indies versus Australia in 1954–55).

During the Second World War, three young batsmen, born within a mile of each other (and within a period of 18 months), first caught the attention of the selectors and the Barbados fans — Frank Mortimer Maglinne Worrell, Clyde Leopold Walcott and Everton de Courcy Weekes were, during the 1950s, to raise Barbados cricket tradition to unprecedented heights and to set the stage for the appearance of the finest of all Barbadian players, Sir Garfield Sobers, perhaps the most talented and versatile cricketer of all time.

Clyde Walcott was the first of the 'W' formation to emerge. As a schoolboy batsman he was superb, possibly the greatest produced by Barbados. With his former schoolmate Frank Worrell, he took part in an unbroken 574-run fourth-wicket stand for Barbados versus Trinidad at Port of Spain in 1945–46 which remains the West Indian record stand for all wickets. Walcott scored 314 not out (he had just turned 20) and Worrell (then aged 21) made 255 not out.

During the period Walcott was asked to keep wicket for Barbados and West Indies between 1947 and 1951 (when 'Sammy' Guillen took over midway through the tour of Australia), he only occasionally displayed his great batting talent in Test cricket. When he gave away the gloves, he was for a time the undisputed top West Indian batsman.

Walcott failed as a batsman in his first series against England, at home in 1947–48. He had a good tour of India in 1948–49 but played only one Test innings of note in England in 1950. Then came a disastrous tour to Australia in 1951–52 (the West Indian batsmen failed to a man) but, against India in the West Indies in 1952–53, the big Barbadian hit two centuries (plus a 98) and was magnificent when England toured in 1953–54. On his home Barbados turf at Bridgetown in the second Test, he smashed his way to a match-winning 220 in six and a half hours and put such force into his driving and cutting that some of the English fieldsmen complained afterwards of bruised hands. Walcott added two more centuries at Port of Spain and Kingston and aggregated 698 (average 87.25) to top the batting list for the rubber.

Even better was to follow against Australia in 1954–55. Batting with great courage in what proved in the end to be a lost cause (Australia took the series 3–0), Clyde Walcott overshadowed all his compatriots (including Weekes and Worrell) and compiled 827 runs in 10 Test innings. Playing for British Guiana in an island game against the tourists, he made 51 in the first innings and, had he not been unable to bat in the second innings because of injury, might well have boosted his tally of runs against Australia that season to the 1000 mark.

On two occasions against Australia in 1954–55 Walcott scored a century in each innings – 126 and 110 in the second Test at Port of Spain (West Indies forced a draw) – and 155 and 110 in the final game at Kingston where Australia scored 758 for eight wickets declared and won the match by an innings.

Standing 6 ft 2 in (188 cm), the muscular and superbly fit Clyde Walcott looked almost as broad as he was tall and may have stood comparison with Muhammed Ali had he been a heavyweight boxer. Walcott's method in batting matched his boxer's build. Off either foot, he must have been just about the hardest striker of the ball the game has known. Starting from a low crouching stance, he would stand erect to play his strokes. Driving and cutting were the hall-marks of his batting but he could hook with great power anything pitched short of a length. One of Walcott's most attractive shots was a delayed drive off the front foot that sent the ball scudding to the boundary, backward of point. He was also one of the few batsmen in the world who has been successful at striking a six off the back foot and over the head of long-off.

When he moved from Barbados to coach and play in British Guiana (now Guyana) in the mid-1950s, Walcott helped change the balance of cricket power in the West Indies and inspired an upsurge of batting talent on the mainland that produced players like Rohan Kanhai, Basil Butcher, Roy Fredericks, Alvin Kallicharran and Clive Loyd. As manager of West Indian teams, he has proved diplomatic, popular and efficient.

Of the three famous Ws, the batting of Everton Weekes bore closest comparison to that of George Headley or Sir Donald Bradman.

Like Headley, Weekes was short and compact and relied primarily upon back foot play; like Bradman, he would attack bowlers relentlessly during long occupations of the crease. If Weekes did not perhaps quite possess the full range of strokes that Headley boasted, he was quick of foot and eye and was seldom tied down by bowlers and generally then only on a difficult wicket. His cuts and pulls travelled to the boundary like pellets from a shotgun; he would lean back to smack the good length ball to the off or on-side fence.

In England in 1950, Weekes's county match scoring was phenomenal. He hit 304 not out against Cambridge University in a little over five hours after the university had totalled 594 for four wickets declared (West Indies replied with 730 for three wickets on what must have been the grandfather of all 'feather bed' pitches!). Weekes added four double-centuries and two centuries (including 129 in the Nottingham Test) and averaged 79.65 for his 2310 runs on the tour. In his review of the West Indies' 1950 tour of England, John Arlott referred to Everton Weekes as a player to whom batting was 'a continual adventure'. Trevor Bailey considered bowling to him on a good pitch a 'nightmare'.

A comparative failure in the early Tests against the 1947–48 England team, Weekes scored 141 in the final game of that series at Kingston and then added four more Test 100s in a row during the 1948–49 tour of India that followed (after haivng almost been left out of the West Indies touring party!). Weekes remains the only batsman to score five Test centuries in succession. In New Zealand in 1955–56 he made three consecutive Test centuries.

In his final Test series, the quiet, good-natured and highly revered Everton Weekes fittingly scored 197 against Pakistan at Bridgetown in 1957–58. Only a record 16 hours and 13 minutes encampment at the crease by diminutive Hanif Mohammed could save the match for Pakistan. Weekes continued to play for Barbados for a while – the only one of the island's famous trio to stay at home. Walcott had moved to Guyana; Frank Worrell played most of his domestic cricket for Jamaica.

Frank Worrell was the third member of the 'W' triumvirate. When he died tragically at the age of 42, Worrell was mourned throughout the cricketing world; his name stands alongside those of Lord Constantine, George Headley and Sir Garfield Sobers at the top of the West Indies cricketing tree.

Sir Frank Worrell first gained his place in the Barbados team as a slow left-arm bowler when he was barely 18. Aged 19, he scored 308 not out for Barbados versus Trinidad at Bridgetown (after J B Stollmeyer had made 210 for the visiting team) and added a record unfinished 502 for the fourth wicket with his skipper, John Goddard (218 not out). The new West Indies record stood only for a couple of years – in 1945–46 Worrell's wonderful 574-run partnership with

Everton Weekes was an enthusiastic stroke-player for the West Indies who dominated bowlers for a decade from 1948.

Walcott against Trinidad established both players as batsmen of rare skill and promise.

Walcott and Weekes employed power of stroke to build their big scores; Worrell was the artist who gathered his runs with gentle and consumate grace. John Arlott described him in 1950 as '. . .a batsman with little time for any batting but the best'. Calm and elegant in his command of stroke-play, Worrell was a master batsman on a good wicket. Once he had overcome the impetuosity of youth, his strict orthodoxy gave him the technique to handle most conditions. Worrell himself was once recorded as saying that he was unable to hit across the line, even if he wanted to or thought he should. If he had any weakness, it may have been against very fast bowling at the start of an innings. Trevor Bailey, for one, contends that Worrell was a much better player of slow bowling than of pace.

As is the case with all great batsmen, Worrell's sense of balance and timing was clean and efficient. He was a master of the late cut and played every other stroke in the book with natural ease. His sound technique enabled him to continue to score with consistency as he entered middle age, a milestone he was destined never to pass. It was one of cricket's greatest tragedies that Sir Frank Worrell, the second of three great West Indian cricketers to be knighted, should depart for higher realms, a victim of leukaemia, a few months short of his 43rd birthday.

Worrell's highest Test score (261 in the third Test at Trent Bridge, Nottingham) provided the high point of the 1950 West Indies visit to England — the tour which first established West Indies as an international cricketing power. At the other end of his eminent career, as West Indies' first black captain on tour, he aided Australia's Richie Benaud in breathing new life into international cricket as a whole, following a period which was for the most part marked by slow scoring and unenterprising on-the-field tactics in Test cricket.

Frank Worrell was the complete cricketer. A batsman of beauty and skill, an accurate left-arm bowler, a useful fielder and one of West Indies' most renowned captains. Clayton Goodwin writes in his *Caribbean Cricketers*: 'As Shakespeare said — some men in their lives play many parts. Worrell was one of the few to do it all at the same time.'

The Test batting records of Worrell, Weekes and Walcott bear comparison with the majority of international batsmen of note, past and present:

Opposite: Frank Worrell was a great West Indies captain and an elegant, world-class batsman.

	Tests	Innings	Not out	Runs	H.S.	Average	100s
E deC Weekes	48	81	5	4455	207	58.61	15
C L Walcott	44	74	7	3798	220	56.68	15
F M M Worrell	51	87	9	3860	261	49.48	9

They all 'fired' together on a number of occasions in a particular

Test innings. Against India at Sabina Park, Kingston, in 1952–53, the trio each reached centuries in the same Test innings – Worrell 237, Weekes 109 and Walcott 118. They repeated the feat against England at Port of Spain in 1953–54, with Weekes this time providing the double-century (206) and Worrell (167) and Walcott (124) contributing their share to a record score against England – 681 for eight wickets declared.

By the time West Indies went to England for their second post-war visit in 1957, Weekes and Walcott were beginning to decline, but Worrell excelled with a marvellous 191 not out at Nottingham in the third Test when he opened the batting and carried his bat undefeated in an innings of 372.

The famous 'three Ws' had now moved into a supportive role to the new young West Indian batting heroes Sobers, Hunte, Kanhai and O G Smith. Weekes and Walcott soon retired. Worrell missed a couple of Test series but returned to score 197 in a 399-run partnership with Sobers against England at Bridgetown in 1959–60. He then took over the West Indies captaincy from Gerry Alexander for the 1960–61 tied Test tour and was still batting with skill and determination in his final series, versus England, in 1963.

Above all else, Sir Frank Worrell introduced a new element of 'nationhood' among the previously frequently bickering players from different islands and countries which came together as the West Indies cricket team. His marvellous leadership transformed West Indian cricket and set the model for Gary Sobers to follow when he took over during the 1960s.

When Worrell's 1960–61 team in Australia left the field at Melbourne after the final Test, the crowd thronged the entrance to the players enclosure in their thousands and chanted: 'We want Frank! We want Frank!' When the dapper West Indian captain appeared, smiling and attired, as always, in a neat grey suit, a spontaneous chorus of 'For he's a jolly good fellow' arose from the throats of the thousands present who had just witnessed the closing moments of one of the most absorbing series in international cricket history.

Of the West Indies batsmen contemporary with Worrell, Weekes and Walcott, most were overshadowed by the celebrated trio. Jeff Stollmeyer and Gerry Gomez were the only two to have appeared before the war and their careers have already been dealt with. The bespectacled Robert Julian Christiani (younger brother of pre-war Test wicket-keeper Cyril Christiani) was an exciting and quick-footed right-handed stroke-player who doubled as reserve wicket-keeper to Walcott. West Indies' 1950s skipper, John Douglas Claude Goddard, a resolute left-hander from Barbados, frequently bolstered the lower order.

Another left-hander, Jamaica's Allan Fitzroy Rae, became the perfect opening partnership foil to right-handed Jeffrey Stollmeyer for a couple of series. Tall, and originally a hard-driving stroke-maker, Rae refurbished his style to provide top-order stability and a safe launching pad for the fireworks of those who followed him in the batting order. In the Herbert Sutcliffe tradition, he was prepared to hit a bad ball hard but placed greatest emphasis on security and tenure at the crease. Rae came second only to Worrell in the 1950 Test batting averages although he failed in Australia in 1951−52.

Roy Edwin Marshall was from Barbados and, like Bob Christiani, played in spectacles. He made his debut during the ill-fated series in Australia in 1951−52 but was lost to West Indies cricket when he joined Hampshire. Marshall was an enterprising opener, as was yet another bespectacled player, Bruce Hamilton Pairaudeau (British Guiana) who scored a century in his first Test but later emigrated to New Zealand.

A more successful opener for West Indies was Jamaica's J K Holt junior who made his Test debut aged 30 against England at Kingston in 1953−54 and scored 94 in his first innings. His dismissal, leg-before-wicket to Brian Statham, provoked a home crowd reaction which saw the wife and son of the umpire assaulted by spectators who disagreed with the decision. In the next Test at Bridgetown, Holt added 222 with Frank Worrell and eventually made 166, his highest Test score.

One of the most notable rearguard batting actions in the history of Test cricket was performed by two West Indians who were not chosen primarily as batsmen. Against Australia at Bridgetown in 1954−55, all-rounder Denis St Eval Atkinson (219) and wicket-keeper Cyril Clairmonte Depeiza (122) defied the Australian attack for more than a day to raise the still existing world record seventh wicket stand of 347 runs and save the game for West Indies. Atkinson went on a number of overseas tours with West Indian teams and captained West Indies in seven Tests. Depeiza only played in a handful of games for his country.

The era of West Indian cricket dominated by the 'W' formation eventually came to a close. The effortless grace of Worrell, the compact power of Weekes and the majestic brute force of Walcott represented all that is best in batsmanship and each player, in his own unique style, contributed something of lasting value for those West Indian batsmen who followed.

One of the outstanding features of the play of all three was their ability to hit the *good* ball to the boundary, thus making it an impossible task for most opposition bowlers to contain them. They preferred attack to defence, were always run hungry and, above all else instilled a sense of fun and enjoyment into every innings they played − a quality which has always been the hallmark of cricket in the tiny island of Barbados.

22

Mankad's marathon and an Indian tiger

'Already cricket is a hundred years old in India and there is every sign that it will endure'

— Sujit Mukherjee

It was not until 1946 that India's cricketers put aside the differences which had plagued the earlier teams and played together with a previously non-existent sense of team spirit. The 1932 and 1936 teams had as chosen leaders Indian princes who would never have been picked to play for their country if selection had been based solely on cricketing ability. The 1946 combination was again captained by a prince — but this time it was the Nawab of Pataudi, a true cricketer, and a batsman of fine quality who had during the earlier part of his career been chosen on merit to play for England.

Although they failed to extend England in the three Tests, the 1946 Indians made friends all round. Early in the tour two bowlers, Chandra Sarwate (124 not out) and Shute Bannerjee (121), combined in an amazing 249-run stand for the 10th wicket against Surrey at the Oval. Sarwate was an all-rounder with some pretensions as a batsman; Bannerjee was a regular number 11.

India's leading batsman remained the dependable Vijay Merchant. Flashy and unpredictable Mushtaq Ali opened with Merchant in the Tests, but had a poor overall tour record. Pataudi, although coming close to 1000 runs for the season, failed in the Tests. Lala Amarnath's main worth in the three games against England was as a bowler and it was left to three newcomers to international cricket, Vijay Hazare, 'Vinoo' Mankad and Rusi Modi, to provide Merchant with run-making support.

Mulwantrai Himatlal Mankad had made some impression as a teenage all-rounder before the war. He was now India's leading bowler — a tireless left-arm spinner who bowled nearly twice the number of overs achieved by any other Indian in England in 1946. Mankad took 129 wickets and scored 1120 runs, a rare double for a touring cricketer (he is the only Indian ever to have totalled 1000 runs and 100 wickets in a season).

In Australia in 1947–48, Mankad also scored readily (including two Test centuries — he was the first Indian to score a century against Australia — and took 61 first-class wickets.

The stockily built Mankad was known as Vinoo (a corruption of his family nickname 'Minu') and for many years his actual first names and initials were ignored in the record books. Each of his two cricketing sons, A V M Mankad (the Test cricketer) and R V Mankad, has Vinoo as his official second name.

Vinoo Mankad played in 44 Tests for India and scored more than 2000 runs (to add to his 162 Test wickets). Against New Zealand in 1955–56, he posted a double-century twice – 223 at Bombay and

Vinoo Mankad (left) and Pankaj Roy are holders of the world record Test opening partnership, 413 for India versus New Zealand at Madras in 1955–56.

231 at Madras, where he and the equally stocky Pankaj Roy (173) created a world record opening stand of 413.

The finest of Mankad's eight Test scores of 100 or more will remain his historic 184 at Lord's in 1952 after he had been drafted into the Indian side for three Tests while engaged in Lancashire League cricket. Even though England eventually ran out victors by eight wickets, the Lord's Test that season will always be remembered as 'Mankad's match'.

An adaptable player who tailored his technique to suit the state of the game, Mankad batted belligerently for 72 in India's first innings, hitting a six high over the sightscreen early on in his innings and rarely missing an opportunity to score. He was always watchful in defence but could hit to leg, cover-drive or late-cut with excellent placement and timing. In reply to India's first innings 235, England proceeded to amass a total of 537 and India looked to be heading for an innings defeat.

Mankad had bowled no fewer than 73 overs in England's long innings (he took five wickets for 196) but now batted like a man inspired. Scorning defensive tactics, he took the fight to the England bowlers. Two of his partners departed before he found a willing assistant in Vijay Hazare. The pair added 211, of which Hazare contributed a meagre but watchful 49. Mankad was superb; the first ball he received from googly bowler Roley Jenkins was pulled for six. He also hit 19 fours and was only dismissed because of sheer exhaustion when he was bowled by Jim Laker with his score on 184 (made out of 270 in four and a half hours). England was eventually left to make 77 to win, which they accomplished for the loss of two wickets — but not before the indefatigable Vinoo Mankad had completed a further 24 overs (his figures, with the English batsmen looking for runs, were 24−12−35−0!).

The cricket corespondent of *The Times* waxed eloquent about Mankad's feat at Lord's: 'Mankad's performance in this match has been something to remember for a long time. For endurance and skill it has possessed all the breadth of the plains of his homeland and all the heights of the Himalayas.'

Mankad's only successful supporter at Lord's was Vijay Samuel Hazare who must be marked down as one of India's best batsmen of all time. Hazare scored 2192 runs at 47.65 in 30 Tests and in all first-class cricket tallied in excess of 18,000. He hit two triple-centuries and eight double-centuries and his stand of 577 with Gul Mohammed for Baroda versus Holkar at Baroda in 1946−47 stands as the world record partnership for any wicket.

In his autobiography, Hazare rates the 49 he scored in Mankad's company at Lord's among his own best Test innings. India's batsmen found themselves in dire trouble that year against the unaccustomed pace of new young England tearaway fast bowler Freddie Trueman.

Only Hazare, Mankad and the 20-year-old Vijay Manjrekar made any progress during a four-match series.

Of his seven Test centuries, Hazare's highest was his monumentally patient 164 not out in 515 minutes versus England at New Delhi in 1951−52. This was Vijay Merchant's final game for India and the pair added a new Indian record third wicket partnership against England of 211 (Merchant scored 154 − the stand lasted 330 minutes).

Hazare's finest match was against Australia at Adelaide in 1947−48. His scores of 116 and 145 represented a personal triumph and the first occasion on which an Indian batsman has scored two separate 100s in a Test (S M Gavaskar has since performed the feat three times).

Perhaps through force of circumstances Hazare was primarily a defensive batsman. During his Test career India was generally struggling and he was frequently the only player to offer any resistance. He possessed an equable temperament, judged each ball strictly on its merits and was a collector of runs who used most of the orthodox strokes but committed himself to risky strokes like the hook shot only when he was absolutely certain of the end result. Although Hazare played all the strokes, as Rudi Modi has so nicely put it: 'few of them set the Thames on fire as those of Amarnath and Mushtaq Ali did.'

Rusi Sheriyar Modi was himself a patient right-hander; tall, slim as a reed and light on his feet and noted for his wristy stroke-play, he enjoyed a brief but highly successful spell at the top in international cricket.

He hit 203 in an unofficial Test against Lindsay Hassett's Australian Services XI in 1945−46 and, against West Indies in 1948−49, played consecutive Test innings of 112, 80, 87 and 56, and averaged 56.00 for his 10 innings in the series. Modi was unfortunate to play in only two more Tests for India.

When India went to Australia in 1947−48, a surprise batting success in the Tests was the team's new-ball bowler, Dattatraya Gajaran Phadkar. A genuine all-rounder, 'Dattu' Phadkar scored 123 in the first innings of the Adelaide Test that was graced by Hazare's twin 100s (the pair added 188 for the sixth wicket). Phadkar also scored three 50s in his four Tests in Australia and was elated when he dismissed the great Bradman leg-before-wicket at Melbourne.

A number of Indian batsmen came and went in quick succession during what was for India a shaky period in the 1940s and 1950s. Others stayed for longer but did not establish themselves as Test cricketers − players like H R Adhikari (a lieutenant-colonel in the Indian army who was considered second only to Neil Harvey as a cover fieldsman), A G Kripal Singh (100 not out in his first Test but little thereafter), and his younger brother, A G Milka Singh. Then there was R H 'Deepak' Shodhan, a dashing left-hander who made a fighting 110 against Pakistan at Calcutta in 1952−53 in his first Test but was soon discarded, and the determined right-hander Madhav L Apte, who batted with remarkable courage as an opening batsman to score 460 runs at 51.11 in five Tests in the West Indies in 1952−53 but was axed by the fickle Indian selectors on his return home.

A player who scored with admirable consistency in Tests and who could also bat in a style reminiscent of C K Nayudu was the tall and strong Pahlan Ratanji Umrigar, who rejoiced in the nickname 'Polly' throughout his career. Although Polly Umrigar, like Hazare, was forced by circumstance to temper his aggressive flair when playing Test cricket, he frequently provided glimpses of batting grandeur, especially when he went down the wicket to play the lofted drive. Batting against a Commonwealth XI in 1950−51 he went to his century at Madras with two successive straight sixes off Frank Worrell.

Rusi Modi rates Umrigar's 102 in the third Test at Bombay of the 1952−53 India-Pakistan rubber as the finest Test innings he has witnessed. With Pakistan's ace medium-pacers Fazal Mahmood and Mahmood Hussain seaming the ball as if the pitch was made of oil-covered glass, Umrigar threw caution aside and raced to his century in 165 minutes, adding 183 with the more patient Vijay Hazare who ended with 146 not out. Umrigar's on the field dedication was monumental; during play, no bowler was his friend − off the field he was smiles all round.

Vinoo Mankad's partner in the 413-run first wicket stand against New Zealand at Madras in 1955−56 was a batsman who scaled the heights and plunged to the deepest depths during his Test career. Pankaj Khirodroy Roy (father of Pronab Pankaj Roy who toured England in 1982) scored two centuries against England in his debut series in India in 1951−52. In England in 1952, the unfortunate Pankaj Roy ended his Test series summer with four 'ducks' on the trot and in the four matches played against England, failed to score in five out of seven innings.

The Indian selectors uncharacteristically persevered with him and Roy ended up with more than 2000 Test runs. A patient player who eschewed the flamboyant and flashy, he played two memorably brave innings against West Indies at Kingston in 1952−53 when he saved the fifth Test with scores of 85 and 150.

The best Indian player of fast bowling during the 1950s was undoubtedly the tough and versatile Vijay Laxman Manjrekar. In his first Test overseas, versus England at Leeds in 1952, he went on the attack against Trueman and Bedser and slammed 19 fours in his 133 made out of 249 in 270 minutes.

Although Majrekar was to add another six Test centuries to his final tally (and scored more than 3000 Test runs), his 133 at Leeds in 1952 must remain his finest and one of the greatest innings ever played by an Indian batsman. He was one of the few Indian batsmen (or batsmen from any country for that matter) who actually relished fast bowling and who competently handled England's Trueman and West Indies' Wesley Hall at their most menacing.

The foundation of Manjrekar's play was a solid defence and from this technically proficient base, he would launch out and employ whatever stroke was required to combat the given delivery. Like all great batsmen he always seemed to have plenty of time to play all the shots in the book. His ability to concentrate on the task in hand was legend and the severest critic would be hard pressed to find flaw in his technique.

Had he not suffered a fractured skull when ducking into a lifting ball bowled by Charlie Griffith at Bridgetown in 1961–62, the dogged left-hander Nariman Jamshedji Contractor may have gone on to play in as many again as the 31 Tests in which he appeared.

Contractor made a century in each innings of his debut first-class match (152 and 102 not out for Gujarat versus Bombay in 1952–53) to join Australia's Arthur Morris – another left-hander and the only other player to have done the same.

The Indian left-hander first appeared for his country against New Zealand in 1955–56 but started making his mark only in the early 1960s. In 1961–62 he captained India to a 2–0 home series victory over England after having come to the fore during the previous season's rubber against Australia, in the course of which he scored his one and only Test century at Bombay. Then came the Bridgetown incident and the sad abrupt end to his Test career.

A chequered Test career was also the lot of the extrovert right-hander Motganhalli Laxmanarsu Jaisimha. Slim and stylish, he was judged too reckless to open in Tests. Strangely enough, one of his most remembered Test knocks was a deadly dull eight hours and 20 minute occupation of the crease against Pakistan at Kanpur in 1960–61 for 99 run out. Flown to Australia as a reinforcement in 1967–68, Jaisimha virtually went straight from the plane to Woollangabba and played courageous innings of 74 and 101 which kept India's hopes alive.

The volatile Abbas Ali Baig will be remembered for his batting against England in 1959 when he was called from Oxford University to join the Indian team after Manjrekar was injured. He responded with a sparkling Test debut 112 at Old Trafford in the fourth Test and although he played in a few more Tests, Baig never again touched his Manchester debut form.

Enterprising Indian all-rounder Chandrakant Gulabrao Borde was more of a batsman than a bowler (he scored more than 3000 Test runs, including five centuries). 'Chandu' Borde's peak Test effort was a patient nine-hour 177 not out against Pakistan at Madras in 1960–61. His most outstanding Test was against West Indies at

Delhi in 1958—59 when he squared up bravely to the speed of Gilchrist and Hall and scored 109 and 96, missing his second century when he hit his own wicket when going for the boundary in the last over of the day.

Gulabrai Sipahimalani Ramchand was a strongly built player who could claim to be a genuine all-rounder. A forceful back-foot batsman, 'Ram' Ramchand hit two Test centuries — a dashing 106 not out against New Zealand at Calcutta in 1955—56 and a captain's knock of 109 at Bombay when he skippered India against Australia in 1956—57.

Raghunath Gangaram Nadkarni was best known as a supremely accurate left-arm spin bowler who frequently slowed down a Test by pinning the opposition batsmen down with his immaculate length. As a determined left-handed batsman he produced equally tedious but highly effective results. Tall for an Indian, he was a meticulous dresser who batted and bowled with his shirt-sleeves buttoned at the wrist. Against England at Kanpur in 1963—64 (during a series in which each of five Tests ended in a draw), 'Bapu' Nadkarni was encamped at the crease for a total of 11 hours for his innings of 52 not out and 122 not out, the second effort being his only Test century.

The handsome Salim Aziz Durani once starred in a film and on the cricket field he played with the debonair flair exhibited by Australia's Keith Miller. A left-handed batsman of many moods and a slow left-arm spin bowler, Salim Durani has been described as an erratic genius with a charismatic appeal that made him a crowd favourite. His sole Test century came against West Indies at Port of Spain in 1961—62.

Rusi Framroz Surti was another left-handed all-rounder, a sort of 'poor man's Sobers', who batted with great vigour and bowled at medium pace or slow and was outstanding in the covers. Rusi Surti never made a Test century but suffered the indignity of being missed twice at 99 against New Zealand at Auckland in 1967—68 — and was then out caught without adding the single needed to reach three figures! The exuberant Surti enjoyed a particularly fine tour of Australia and New Zealand and then moved to Australia to play for Queensland in 35 matches.

Two of India's wicket-keepers were also Test batsmen of note during the 1960s. Budhisagar Krishnappa Kunderan was an exciting stroke-player who could bat anywhere in the order. 'Budhi' Kunderan hit two Test centuries but his most memorable Test effort was a blazing 79 in 92 minutes off the West Indian fast bowlers at Bombay in 1966—67.

The second stumper and batsman, Farokh Manekha Engineer, would have challenged for a place in any Test side as a batsman alone. Known in England as 'Rooky', Engineer was one of cricket's characters and was a strong leg-side player whose prime Test performance came towards the end of his 14-year international career when he opened the batting and hit 121 and 66 against England at Bombay in the fifth Test of the 1972−73 home series.

One of the most forceful of India's batsmen in the 1960s and 1970s was the dedicated Dilip Narayan Sardesai, whose brilliant 200 not out against New Zealand at Bombay in 1964−65 prompted one of the most remarkable recoveries in Test history. With India following on 209 runs in arrears, Sardesai took over and an undefeated double-century enabled India captain Pataudi to declare at a mammoth 463 for five wickets. New Zealand was struggling to avoid defeat at 80 for eight wickets in their second innings when stumps were drawn.

In the West Indies in 1970−71, Dilip Sardesai hit 212 in the first Test at Kingston, 112 in the second at Port of Spain and 150 in the fourth match at Bridgetown to give him a series aggregate of 642 runs at 80.25. A cool-headed individual, Sardesai's batting was noted for its flowing cover-drives and delicate glances.

Until the arrival of batsmen like Sardesai and Engineer, India's Test innings were notable for dour defensive play. Another aggressive stroke-player of high quality followed in his eminent father's footsteps to breathe a new sense of purpose into Indian batting. Were it not for the tragic loss of his right eye in a car accident while at Oxford University, this exciting player might have gone on to even greater achievements. What remains as a remarkable illustration of sporting bravery is the fact that the Nawab of Pataudi junior (or Mansur Ali Khan as he later became known) became a Test batsman and captain of his country *after* he had lost the sight of one eye.

'Tiger' Pataudi was indeed a courageous man and an adventurous batsman whose nickname illustrated his character most aptly. In Australia he collected the added *nom de guerre* 'Long John Silver' when, at Melbourne in the first Test of 1967−68, with his one glass eye and only one good leg (he had a hamstring injury) he defied the fastest balls bowled at him by the Australians to score 75 and 85. Pataudi performed with such splendour that day that the question was asked in the Melbourne press: 'How much would he have scored with two good eyes and on two sound legs?'.

Forced to reajust his batting stance and method, he never lost sight of his original ambition to emulate his revered father and play Test cricket. In the process, Pataudi became one of the strongest leg-side players in Indian cricket. Ever-willing to loft the ball in an effort to score, he made it difficult for an opposing captain to set a field to him.

Like all good batsmen, 'Tiger' Pataudi based his batting style on orthodox principles, but, as do all players of exceptional genius, he added more than a few strokes of his own device. Apart from a penchant for leg-hits into the stand, either through a lofted shot over

The Nawab of Pataudi Junior lost an eye in a car accident but still went on to become a star Test batsman.

long-on or a pull-drive over mid-wicket that was his own speciality (and very un-Indian in conception and execution), his timing and stroke-play to the off was excellent. And working according to the principle that if he could lose an eye and still play Test cricket, he could face up to anything, Pataudi junior became one of the best post-war players of fast bowling.

'Tiger' Pataudi hit six Test centuries in his 46 games for India, but not one of these knocks surpassed in courage and excellence his batting in Australia in 1967—68. He also became the youngest captain in international cricket when he took over leadership of India at age 21. He is also the only Test captain who flew on tours and to home Test matches in his own private jet! When he scored an unusually brilliant 148 against England in a back-to-the-wall situation at Leeds in 1967, the *Daily Mail* was prompted to applaud his batting with the banner headline: 'His Magnificent Highness The Nawab Of Headingley And Pataudi'.

Pataudi junior and Pataudi senior are the only father and son combination to each be honoured as one of *Wisden*'s 'Five Cricketers of the Year'. Only two sets of fathers and sons have captained their country at cricket – the Pataudis for India and F T Mann and F G Mann for England.

After the old aristocratic titles were dropped in India, the younger Pataudi continued to play under the name Mansur Ali Khan. His Test career for India extended from 1961 to 1975 and his inspiration produced a legacy for India's young batsmen.

Another Indian prince who played Test cricket in the 1960s was the Maharajkumar Banswara, who played under the name Hanumant Singh. In the fourth Test versus England at New Delhi in 1963—64, Hanumant became the first Indian to score a century in the first innings of his debut match. The 105 not out this well-organised right-hander made at Delhi proved to be his only three-figure knock in Tests, although he made scores of 94 against Australia and 75 not out and 82 against New Zealand in the 1964—65 Indian season.

Hanumant Singh and Nawab of Pataudi junior were destined to be the last Indian cricketing princes to play Test cricket before the former State rulers were stripped of their powers in a move by the Indian Government to stabilise democracy in their ancient land.

23

New Zealand heroes

'At his best, Sutcliffe is the very epitome of elegance and cricketing culture. Explosive is about the best word to describe the cricket of John Reid'

— R T Brittenden

For a couple of decades after the Second World War, New Zealand batting was dominated by two players who would have found a place in any Test side from any country, and at any time in cricket history.

It is remarkable to note that the left-handed stylist Bert Sutcliffe and the explosive right-handed John Richard Reid were, for the majority of their time in Test cricket, members of a losing team. How much better they might have performed (and what a delight to cricket statisticians they would have been) if they had been born in England or Australia.

Bert Sutcliffe was the star of the New Zealand tour of England in 1949. English bowlers had already experienced the whiplash of his bat in 1946–47. Against the touring MCC team, the 24-year-old left-hander played two stunning knocks for Otago — 197 and 128 — from an attack which included Voce, Bedser and Wright. He followed up with 58 on his Test debut at Lancaster Park, Christchurch, and in 1949 put the English county bowlers to the sword. Against Essex, Sutcliffe hit 243 and 100 not out in the same match; in all games he scored seven centuries; on the tour he totalled 2627 at 59.70; in the four Tests he averaged 60.42 for 423 runs. *Wisden* described him as a more brilliant batsman than Martin Donnelly.

Good-looking and golden-haired, Bert Sutcliffe caught both eye and imagination with his confident and classy style. In contrast to most left-handed stroke-players, it was his dazzling off-side shots which most impressed. He could also hook and pull with the best.

Adulation failed to turn the head of this modest though confident player. R T Brittenden notes in *New Zealand Cricketers*: 'No New Zealand cricketer has captured the public imagination as he has... To say that Sutcliffe is a fine batsman is rather like suggesting Sir Winston Churchill has made some good speeches.'

In Test cricket, Bert Sutcliffe made runs wherever he played. His best Test score was an uncharacteristically subdued nine-hour 230 not out against India at Delhi in 1955–56 — then a New Zealand Test record.

In domestic cricket he was virtually unbowlable. With Don Taylor he set a world record for Auckland versus Canterbury in 1948–49 of

New Zealand's Bert Sutcliffe was felled by a bouncer from South African fast bowler Neil Adcock at Johannesburg in 1953–54 but returned from hospital to hit off-spinner Tayfield out of the ground.

first-wicket stands of 220 and 286 in the same match (Sutcliffe scored 141 and 135, Taylor 99 and 143). Don Taylor only played in three Tests — he made 43 and 77 against West Indies at Wellington in 1955—56 after having been overlooked by the selectors since his debut in 1946—47. For Otago versus Auckland in 1950—51 Sutcliffe (275) and Les Watt (96) added 373 for the first wicket. Sutcliffe twice topped 300 in New Zealand cricket — 355 for Otago versus Auckland in 1949—50 and 385 for Otago versus Canterbury in 1952—53.

When the New Zealand batsmen found themselves struggling in South Africa in 1953—54 against the extreme pace of Neil Adcock and the guileful off-spin of Hugh Tayfield, Sutcliffe played one of his greatest innings in distressing circumstances. On the second morning, Sutcliffe was hit on the head by a bouncer from Adcock before he had scored and was rushed to hospital. Returning later with his head bandaged, and finding the New Zealand innings well and truly on the skids, Sutcliffe proceeded to lambast the bowling to such good effect that seven of his hits off Tayfield soared over the boundary fence, three of the sixes coming in one over from the hitherto virtually unplayable off-spinner.

Sutcliffe eventually made 80 not out in this do-or-die effort but to no avail. South Africa won easily against a side which was not only depressed because of the injury to Sutcliffe (and to Lawrie Miller, who was also sent to hospital for an X-ray after being hit by Adcock), but because fast bowler Bob Blair had received news just prior to play of the death of his fiancée in the 1953 Christmas Eve train disaster in New Zealand.

All-rounder John Reid was far and away the best New Zealand player on that 1953—54 tour to South Africa — conditions seemed to suit his style of play. In 1953—54 he hit 1012 runs and took 51 wickets; on a return trip in 1961—62 he totalled 1915 at 68.39 (a record for South Africa), with 546 runs in the Tests at an average of 60.64. His best Test innings that tour, a blazing 142 in the fourth Test at Johannesburg, set the veld on fire and was only ended by a miraculous diving catch at cover by 'Golden Eagle' Colin Bland, who picked the ball up inches off the ground from a full-blooded cover-drive.

The feature of Reid's batting was indeed his hammer-blow driving in an arc from cover-point to long-off. He was possessed of a devastating square cut and was a safe and sure hooker. Reid often hit his team out of trouble, seldom bothering to play himself in for too long a period before unleashing his range of strokes. If he had any weakness it might have been his impatience against good spin bowling; fast bowlers he didn't mind, medium-pacers he murdered, but accurate spinners were a test for Reid's pugnacious and impetuous temperament.

John Reid frequently carried New Zealand's frail batting on his broad and muscular back.

South African fast bowler Peter Pollock, who made his own Test debut against the 1960−61 New Zealanders, once recalled Reid taking his life into his own hands when faced by Tayfield in a pre-Test provincial game, in an effort to prove that the ace Springbok spin bowler was over the hill. Reid's ploy worked for Tayfield was left out of the Tests.

A remarkable fact about the life of the athletic and robust John Reid is that in his late teens he spent four months in hospital with rheumatic fever which, for a time, left his heart weakened. He was nursed in hospital by the young woman who later became his wife and recovered so completely that he became known as something of an 'ironman' of international cricket.

During the period 1945 to 1964 very few New Zealand batsmen made much of an impression in Test cricket, other than those who toured England in 1949. Of the 1949 players, Verdun John Scott was a tall, determined opening batsman with a short backlift who partnered Bert Sutcliffe in some useful stands for the first wicket. Another 1949 team member was Frank Brunton Smith, another right-hander but one who lived dangerously and frequently hit across the line. Smith played in two of the 1949 Tests and scored 96 (in two hours) and 54 not out (50 minutes) in the first Test at Headingley.

New Zealand wicket-keeper F L H Mooney was also a useful batsman in the 1949 side and all-rounder Geoff Rabone contributed occasional runs. Geoffrey Osbourne 'Boney' Rabone captained New Zealand in South Africa in 1952−53 and contributed a patient and chanceless 107 in six hours in the first Test at Durban.

Lawrence Somerville Martin Miller was a lanky left-hander who batted in the Ken Mackay defensive style in South Africa in 1953−54 and in England in 1958 but his run tally did not match that of his Australian counterpart; Murray Ernest Chapple was slightly more aggressive but frequently flattered only to deceive and could not average 20 in his 14 Tests; Matt Beresford Poore looked the part of a stroke-player of class but never reached 50 in a Test; John Edward Francis Beck was run out for a rather fortunate 99 (he was dropped four times) against South Africa at Cape Town in 1953−54 when he was 19 but did not progress.

Spencer Noel McGregor batted for five hours and 40 minutes against Pakistan at Lahore in 1955−56 to reach 111, his only three-figure total in international cricket but, like a few others before and after him, failed to average 20 in all Tests.

Other New Zealand batsmen who put together an occasional Test 50 or 100 but could not match the scoring capacity of opponents from other countries included: Parke Gerald Zinzan Harris ('Zin' Harris hit 101 against South Africa at Cape Town in 1961−62); Noel Sherwin Harford (93 and 64 on debut against Pakistan at Lahore in 1955−56 but little else afterwards); left-hander John William

Guy (102 in more than seven hours against India at Hyderabad in 1955–56); the painfully slow John William D'arcy who toured England in 1958; William Rodger Playle (also a 1958 tourist who failed in Tests and eventually settled in Australia and appeared for Western Australia); John Trevor Sparling, an all-rounder who only once made 50 (in three hours at Old Trafford in 1958); Paul Thomas Barton (a stylish 109 against South Africa at Port Elizabeth in 1961–62); and Michael John Froud Shrimpton (highest Test score 46).

Two batsmen who first appeared for New Zealand towards the end of the Reid-Sutcliffe era were destined to provide more substantial results in Test cricket. Barry Whitley Sinclair was a dogged right-hander who supplied some much-needed stiffening to the New Zealand middle order for five or six years (1962 to 1968) and captained his country in three Tests. Sinclair made centuries against South Africa, Pakistan and England and frequently averted total collapse when others were falling around him. In 21 Tests he totalled 1148 runs.

Graham Thorne Dowling was a keen student of the game who also became one of New Zealand's best captains. A methodical and well-organised right-hander, Dowling scored three Test centuries (all against India) and topped 2000 runs in his 39 games for New Zealand.

Dowling first came into the New Zealand team for the 1961–62 South Africa tour and contributed scores of 74 and 58 in his debut Test at Johannesburg. In 1964–65 he scored 129 versus India at Bombay; at home against India in 1967–68 Dowling reached his personal peak with innings of 143 in the first Test at Dunedin and 239 in 556 minutes (five sixes, 28 fours) in the second match at Christchurch, to set a new New Zealand record for Tests. Graham Dowling was the first representative of a new line of New Zealand batsmen who were to begin to approach the skill of Sutcliffe and Reid and achieve true international status as regular run-scorers during the Tests played by New Zealand in the 1970s and 1980s.

24

Enter Pakistan and the family Mohammed

'Pakistan's cricket history is contemporary. From humble beginnings sound progress has been made'

— Abdul Hafeez Kardar

Northern India was the home of a string of fine cricketers long before the nation of Pakistan was converted from a dream into a reality — players like Wazir Ali, Nazir Ali, Mohammed Nissar, Jahangir Khan (father of the exciting batsman Majid J Khan), Dilawar Hussain, Naoomal Jeoomal, Baqa Jilani and Amir Elahi (who played Tests for both India and Pakistan). All made their mark in Indian cricket, some in the international arena.

Pakistani cricket began with the partition of India in 1947 when four provincial cricket associations which previously fell under the aegis of the India Board were left high and dry, without funds or administration, to fend for themselves. That Pakistan should have graduated towards acceptance as a Test-playing country in just five years was little short of a miracle.

A H Kardar, one of the leading early sponsors of cricket in his country, became Pakistan's first captain in an official Test. As a young man he was a free-hitting left-hander who toured England rather unsuccessfully with the Indian team under the Nawab of Pataudi in 1946 after having made big scores against Lindsay Hassett's powerful 1945 Australian Services team.

Kardar stayed awhile in England, gained an Oxford University Blue and played for Warwickshire before returning to Pakistan to lead his country to an historic win in an unofficial Test over the touring MCC team in 1951–52.

Prior to this match, Pakistan was led in two notable unofficial Tests by a former prominent player in Indian domestic cricket, Mohammed Saeed. Against the all-powerful West Indies team in 1948–49, Saeed and future Pakistan Test opening batsman Imtiaz Ahmed both hit centuries. Nazar Mohammed, father of the current Pakistan opening batsman Mudassar Nazar, also scored well and was destined, with Imtiaz, to represent his country in its first official Test.

Next season, veteran England wicket-keeper George Duckworth brought his Commonwealth XI to Pakistan and Nazar Mohammed and Mohammed Saeed again played with skill and determination. After a season's gap, two unofficial Tests were played against the MCC in 1951−52 − and Pakistani cricket suddenly came of age when the second match at Karachi ended in a victory for the home team after a draw at Lahore in the first.

At Lahore, the dependable Nazar Mohammed got things moving with a fine knock of 66 and 16-year-old schoolboy wicket-keeper/batsman Hanif Mohammed defied the English attack for two and three-quarter hours for 26 in a first-wicket stand of 96. Pakistan's 'Little Master' improved thereafter in every innings he played. Other major contributions in the drawn first Test came from three future Pakistan international players − M E Z Ghazali (86), the dashing Maqsood Ahmed (137) and the new captain, Kardar (48).

The second game at Karachi brought an MCC collapse agaainst swing and pace bowling of Fazal Mahmood (Pakistan's 'Bedser') and Khan Mohammed. Imtiaz Ahmed extricated his team from a shaky first innings collapse with a top score of 43 and, left with 285 to win in the fourth innings of the match, Pakistan's batsmen knuckled down to bat consistently down the order the second time around to gain a meritorious four-wicket win which assured Pakistan success in its application for admittance to the Imperial Cricket Conference and participation in Test cricket proper. Most of the players chosen for Pakistan's first couple of official Test series (India 1952−53; England 1954) appeared in the early pioneer encounters against the West Indies, the Commonwealth XI and the MCC.

Obdurate opening batsman Nazar Mohammed was forced to retire aged 32 in 1953, just prior to Pakistan's first tour to England in 1954, when he suffered a serious arm injury. He carried his bat through the innings for 124 not out for Pakistan versus India in 1952−53 in his country's second official Test. Nazar's score came out of a total of 331 and was a painstaking affair lasting 515 minutes. His son, Mudassar Nazar, is the holder of the 'slow century' world record in Tests − 557 minutes. Nazar was appointed Pakistan's national cricket coach when he was forced to give up active play and had an official hand in the coaching of his now famous son.

The dynamic Imtiaz Ahmed was a player who was as likely to hit a six in the first over of a match as the last. During his playing days the trim and supple Pakistani wicket-keeper/batsman was a flight-lieutenant in the Pakistan Air Force. As a batsman he was frequently flying high; against the 1950−51 Commonwealth XI in India he hit 300 not out for a Prime Minister's XI at Bombay to save the game after his team had been forced to follow on.

His highest Test score was an innings-saving 209 against New Zealand at Lahore in 1955−56, after having come in late at number eight with the scoreboard reading 111 for six wickets. It was the first double-century in a Test by a Pakistan batsman and contained 28 fours. Imtiaz scored a bold 122 in the match at Kingston, Jamaica, in which Sir Garfield Sobers logged his Test record 365 not out to beat Sir Leonard Hutton's 1938 score.

Shy but determined, Imtiaz Ahmed played in 41 Tests for Pakistan (he holds the unique distinction of having appeared in each of Pakistan's first 39 Tests) and was virtually a permanent fixture from the first game against India in 1952–53 until he bowed out of international cricket a decade later. He twice hit 1000 runs on an England tour and scored more than 2000 Test runs and claimed 93 Test wicket-keeping victims.

Maqsood Ahmed was another dashing batsman — a natural hitter who sent the inaugural 1954 England tour off to a flying start with a blistering 111 in a little over two hours against Worcestershire. Unfortunately his impetuosity often proved his downfall and Maqsood's Test record belied his ability, although he came whisker-close to an official Test century against Pakistan at Lahore in 1954–55 when he was stumped off Indian leg-spinner Subash Gupte for 99.

The stroke-playing Alim-ud-Din was an exciting opener who failed in the Tests on his trips to England (1954 and 1962) and West Indies (1957–58) but who made plenty of runs in home-based rubbers. Like Maqsood, he started the 1954 England tour in dashing style with a century in each of his first two games but could not maintain the momentum into the Tests. Alim-ud-Din eventually scored two Test centuries, both at Karachi.

Much was also initially expected of Waqar Hassan after the accomplished right-hander had played a succession of sturdy knocks against India in 1952–53 at the age of 21. Although he went on to represent Pakistan in 21 Tests, Waqar infrequently batted with the skill and authority of which he was capable.

Mrs Amir Bee must be just about the most famous cricket mother since Martha Grace, mother of the famous W G Grace and his two cricketing brothers. Of her five children who survived to adulthood, four played Test cricket for Pakistan and the fifth was 12th man versus New Zealand at Dacca in 1955–56, after having been assured the evening before the match that he would be playing on the following morning Maqsood Ahmed played in his place).

The odd man out, Raees Mohammed, was a prolific right-handed run-getter in Pakistan's domestic competitions. According to Keith Miller, who once batted with him in a flood-relief match in Pakistan, Raees was as good as most Test batsmen. The other Mohammed brothers were Hanif, Wazir, Mushtaq and Sadiq who, between them, scored 10,938 runs and made 29 centuries in 173 Tests for Pakistan. In 1961, the five brothers appeared together in the same first-class match in the Ayub Zonal Trophy — Raees, Hanif and Mushtaq in one team and Wazir and Sadiq for the opposition.

Hanif Mohammad, at the age of 17, Pakistan's first batting champion.

Whenever one of her sons scored a century, Mrs Amir Bee would distribute sweets to all neighbourhood children as an expression of her happiness. Her husband Shaikh Ismail was also a cricket enthusiast, although not much of a player.

The Mohammed impact on Pakistan cricket has been phenomenal and unique. Although pairs of brothers have played for other countries (plus the three Graces for England), there is no other instance of four brothers representing their country. And with the elevation to Test status in recent seasons of Hanif's son, Shoaib Mohammed, the family record becomes even more remarkable. Hanif has two more sons, Shahid and Asif, who have already played first-class cricket for Pakistan International Airways in Pakistan domestic competition.

In England in 1954, little Hanif Mohammed was called 'Bambino' by his team-mates. This appellation was soon altered to 'The Master' when the neat and adroit Hanif began reeling off scores the likes of which had not been witnessed from a Pakistani batsman before.

When Hanif Mohammed was defying the West Indies attack at Bridgetown to save the first Test of the 1958−59 tour, his mother said a prayer for every minute of his innings. Mrs Amir Bee must have broken all praying records during the nearly three days that her son was at the wicket. Hanif batted for 973 minutes to score 337 − the longest innings in Test history, beating Len Hutton's Oval epic of 797 minutes by nearly three hours!

Hanif's remarkable innings came when Pakistan followed on 473 runs behind West Indies. Thanks to Hanif's tenacity and skill, Pakistan amassed 657 for eight wickets in its second innings and the game ended in a draw.

Hanif Mohammed's innings could not top Sir Leonard Hutton's 364 (Sobers was to beat this record during the third Test of the same West Indies-Pakistan series) but the Pakistani batting wizard does hold the world record score for all first-class cricket. His 499 (he was run out going for his 500th run) for Karachi versus Bahawalpur in January 1959 beat Don Bradman's 452 not out for New South Wales versus Queensland in 1929−30.

Only one other Pakistani batsman, Aftab Baloch (who played two Tests with a top score of 60 not out), has topped 400 in a first-class match − 428 for Sind versus Baluchistan at Karachi in 1973−74. On his Test debut against New Zealand in 1969−70, Aftab was, at 16 years and 191 days, the second youngest international cricketer of all time. The youngest was Hanif's brother, Mushtaq Mohammed, who was chosen for Pakistan versus West Indies at Lahore in 1958−59 when only 15 years and 124 days.

Hanif Mohammed was a natural cricketer who, when the mood took him and circumstances permitted, would step out of his normally defensive shell and use his quick reflexes and fleetness of foot to unleash a variety of excellent shots. Early on in England in 1954, the short and slightly-built Pakistan mainstay was tested by English fast bowlers with short pitched bouncers. Few tried the trick twice, for Hanif quickly demonstrated that he could hook as well as anyone – and better than most. John Arlott described Hanif's hook shot as 'quick as light' but with his team's interests taking first priority, Hanif, after his first couple of seasons, transformed himself from a stroke-making boy prodigy into one of the best and most mature and capable defensive players the world has ever seen.

Older brother Wazir Mohammed, although not in the same class as Hanif, put up a couple of outstanding Test batting performances and thrived in the West Indies in 1958–59 when he hit 106 in the third Test at Kingston, 97 not out in the fourth match at Georgetown and a six and three-quarter hour innings of 189 in the last Test at Port of Spain, which Pakistan won by an innings and one run.

Brother number three, Mushtaq Mohammed, was almost as famous as Hanif. Barely out of short pants when he made his first-class debut at 13 years and 41 days, at 15 years and 124 days he played his first Test, versus West Indies at Lahore in 1958–59, and at 17 years and 82 days became the youngest player in history to score a Test century – 101 versus India in the fifth Test at Delhi in 1960–61.

The stocky Mushtaq was a fluent stroke-player and a calm and composed performer whose only idiosyncrasy at the crease was a twirl of the bat between strokes. Although only 5 ft 7 in (170 cm), he was strongly built and nimble on his feet, always quick to get to the pitch of the ball. He possessed an entertaining variety of off-side strokes – late and square drives and cuts and a pistol shot cover drive. To hook fast bowling, he would move beautifully inside the line of the ball. When there was need to defend, he could alter his play accordingly.

Mushtaq was always the player for a crisis and a much-travelled cricketer who played in Pakistan, England, West Indies, Australia, New Zealand, Sri Lanka and Zimbabwe, taking part in 500 first-class matches between 1956 and 1982.

The youngest of Mrs Amir Bee's cricketing progeny was Sadiq Mohammed who followed brother Mushtaq into county cricket (Sadiq played for Gloucestershire) after making his Test debut against New Zealand in 1969–70. A much freer player that any of his brothers, Sadiq is also the only left-hander in the brood. Small and stocky like his brothers, the quietly spoken Sadiq also made his first-class debut as a schoolboy, aged 14 years and nine months.

Sadiq Mohammed enjoyed a fruitful season in Australia and New Zealand in 1972–73 when he scored 137 at Melbourne in the second Test against Australia and 166 versus New Zealand in the first Test of the following series at Wellington. In 1976–77 he continued to show his liking for conditions in the southern hemisphere when he scored another 100 against Australia in the second Test at Melbourne, after missing the first game at Sydney.

He tended to live dangerously and Sadiq's defence did not match that of Hanif or Mushtaq. The left-handed Mohammed brother was often prone to offer catches to opposing slip or gully fieldsmen through flashing his bat outside the off stump. This flaw in Sadiq's batting may well have occurred because he was not born left-handed and only started batting thus as a boy when older brother Hanif pointed out that there was more scope for left-handers in Pakistan cricket.

Of the other fine batsmen who appeared for Pakistan in the 1950s and 1960s Saeed Ahmed was an upstanding right-hand stroke-player and one of his team's most consistent performers before his career ended under a cloud when he was sent home early from a tour to Australia in 1972—73 for alleged misbehaviour. Against West Indies in the Caribbean in 1957—58, Saeed was second only to Hanif Mohammed as a scorer of runs (508 at 56.44 in the Tests). Among his more memorable performances was a brilliant 150 in the fourth Test at Georgetown and at Lahore in 1959—60 he executed one of the most classic rescue attempts (albeit unsuccessful) of all time when he batted for six hours for 166 against Australia.

Others who appeared for Pakistan at this time included wicket-keeper Abdul Kadir who scored 95 and shared a first-wicket stand of 249 with the well-seasoned Warwickshire county professional Khalid Ibadullah versus Australia at Karachi in 1964—65. 'Billy' Ibadullah scored 166 in his first Test outing but only played in three Tests thereafter before becoming an outstanding cricket coach. The Ibadullah-Kadir 249-run stand remains Pakistan's best in Tests.

Javed Burki disappointed on two tours of England but played one innings of note when he captained Pakistan in England in 1962—101 at Lord's in the second Test when he was joined in a face-saving stand by left-arm spinner Nasim-ul-Ghani who rose above himself also to notch 101. Against England in Pakistan in 1961—62, Burki played painstaking innings of 138 at Lahore and 140 at Dacca during a three-match series that was notable for unenterprising batsmanship by both teams.

Of the two rather more exciting batsmen who remain to be discussed, Asif Iqbal Razvi, whose uncle Ghulam Ahmed was a leading Indian off-break bowler, literally burst onto the international cricket scene in England in 1967 when he played an innings in the third and final game of a three-Test series at the Oval which has seldom been matched by any batsman from any country for its sheer audacity.

Plans were already being made for the staging of a limited overs exhibition match to entertain the crowd who were expecting (as was the England team) an early end to the proceedings. With the scoreboard showing 53 runs for seven wickets, in strode the smiling cavalier figure of Asif Iqbal. Soon the score stood at 65 for eight; but three hours and 10 minutes later it was an unbelievable 255 for nine, when Asif Iqbal was stumped for 146 brilliant runs (the highest score ever by a number nine batsman) when going for another big hit to add to his two sixes and 21 fours. Driving with impudent grandeur, and hooking and cutting skilfully, the 24-year-old Pakistani, who was in the team as a bowler who could bat a little, reached his century in 139 minutes with his 14th four.

Popular Pakistani leg-spinner and sometime captain Intikhab Alam Khan was a more than useful hitter ('Inti' could count a score of 138, including four sixes, against England among his many achievements) but, for once in his career, Pakistan's resident big-hitter was content to pat and prod the odd single and give his young partner the strike.

Although England won in the end, the match will always remain Asif's. Referring to a similar effort by Asif when he scored 76 at number nine in the first Test at Lord's (and was the dominant partner in a 130-run stand with Hanif Mohammed), *Wisden* recorded that the young Pakistani was 'rapidly becoming the agent of the impossible'. When his innings ended, hundreds of Pakistani spectators rushed the pitch and hoisted their hero shoulder high. The game was held up for five minutes before a squad of police rescued Asif, who had been bruised and battered by his excited admirers.

Asif Iqbal's noble effort at Lord's was the first of 11 centuries for Pakistan − in Australia in 1976−77 he was in superb form with 152 not out at Adelaide and 120 at Sydney − but his subsequent efforts could not match the sheer audacity of his innings at the 'Home of Cricket'.

When Asif Iqbal made his Test debut against Australia at Karachi in 1964−65, it was as an opening bowler who shared the new ball with another young debutante, also destined to become one of Pakistan's finest batsmen and a player of world class.

Majid Jahangir Khan was the son of pre-war Indian fast bowler Dr M Jahangir Khan and a cousin to former Pakistan captain Javed Burki and the current skipper Imran Khan. It was not to be too long before this unlikely opening bowler was no longer given the new ball. Instead, he was given room to mature as a batsman who was quickly developing a very high standard of technical proficiency and power.

Majid was a magnificent attacking batsman who used the drive, cut, pull and hook with devastating effect. On his first tour to England with Pakistan in 1967, he cracked a spectacular 147 not out against Glamorgan at Cardiff in 89 minutes − a tour knock that was only equalled by Asif's Oval effort. Majid hit 13 sixes in that innings, a feat that has been equalled by very few other batsmen, and only bettered by New Zealand's John Reid when he struck 15 sixes in his 296 for Wellington versus Northern Districts at Wellington in 1962−63.

Majid Khan made close to 4000 runs and hit eight centuries in Tests but was, in his later career, something of a wayward genius

The stylish and powerful off-drive of Majid Jahangir Khan.

whose final figures did not reflect his enormous talent. He did almost invariably exhibit a batting majesty that was a model for all future Pakistani batsmen.

One record held by Majid Jahangir Khan worth emulating is the fastest Test hundred for Pakistan, versus New Zealand at Karachi in 1976–77. Majid's time was 113 minutes (he reached 50 in 65 minutes) and he reached his century before lunch on the first day.

25

University connections

'The amateur, he who plays the game when he can for the love of it alone...'

— A E Knight

There were many fine players at both the major English cricketing universities of Cambridge and Oxford during the first decade or so following the Second World War. New Zealand's Martin Donnelly, who played for Oxford, has been rated as the best university batsman ever. There were also plenty of young English batsmen of class who had their initial crack at first-class bowling while resident at either Oxford or Cambridge.

England all-rounder Trevor Bailey was a Cambridge product of the 1940s together with the dogged England batsman D J Insole. Douglas John Insole was powerful and no charmer when it came to batting but he had a resolute approach and scored 110 not out against South Africa at Durban in 1956–57 when he was fellow Cambridge player Peter May's vice-captain in the MCC team.

P B H May was a member of the incredibly strong Cambridge batting combination which scored 594 for four wickets declared on a perfect batting wicket at Fenner's against the 1950 West Indians. J G Dewes (183) and D S Sheppard (227) led off with a first-wicket partnership of 343 and G H G Doggart (71), May (44 not out) and M H Stevenson (53 not out) piled on the agony before the Cambridge captain declared. On a farcical wicket, the West Indians replied with 730 for three – Christiani 111, Stollmeyer 83, Worrell 160, Weekes 304 not out and K B Trestrail 56 not out!

In an interview in *Wisden Cricket Monthly* (January 1983), the Right Reverend David Stuart Sheppard, Bishop of Liverpool, recalled that when he and Dewes went out to face the West Indian bowlers at Cambridge in 1950, the tourists' wicket-keeper initially stood back for fast bowler Hines Johnson 'further away than I've ever seen a wicket-keeper stand before'. The opening ball sent down by Johnson hardly lifted from the dead pitch and bounced three times before reaching the wicket-keeper. The West Indian fast bowler immediately lost all interest in proceedings which began to unfold on the dead Fenner's wicket as first Cambridge and than West Indies piled on the runs.

George Hubert Graham Doggart played a remarkable debut first-class innings of 215 not out for Cambridge versus Lancashire in 1948. An attractive stroke-player, he played in two Tests against West Indies in 1950 but was not picked again for England. In 1981, Doggart succeeded his old Cambridge comrade Peter May as president of the MCC.

Doggart (219) and the left-handed John Gordon Dewes (204) once added 429 for the second wicket for Cambridge versus Essex at Fenner's in 1949 – an English first-class record until J A Jameson (240 not out) and R B Kanhai (213 not out) bettered it in an unfinished stand of 465 for Warwickshire versus Gloucestershire at Birmingham in 1974.

Dewes actually made his first-class debut in one of the unofficial Victory Tests against Australia at Lord's in 1945 but could not come to grips with Test-class bowling when given his chance against Australia (in 1948 and 1950–51) and West Indies (1950).

David Sheppard found runs easy to get on that batsman's paradise wicket at Cambridge but when he first went to Australia with Freddie Brown's team in 1950–51, he found the tracks and the bowlers a different proposition and was a failure. This tall and classical batsman, who delighted onlookers with his graceful off-side play, had to wait a few years before he was able to right matters.

Sheppard appeared intermittently for England in a few home Tests and after his ordination into the Anglican priesthood, was recalled in 1956 at Old Trafford (veteran Cyril Washbrook had been brought back in the previous Test at Leeds) to help bolster an ailing England batting order. Sheppard responded with a splendid 113, but his appearances in first-class cricket thereafter were severely limited by clerical duties.

In 1962 he scored a century in the last Gentlemen versus Players match at Lord's and was prevailed upon to tour Australia with another Cambridge Blue, E R Dexter, and his MCC team in 1962–63. The cricketing cleric rose to the occasion; asked to open the batting, he scored a determined second innings 113 in the second Test at Melbourne to give England the victory which ultimately enabled the visitors to square the rubber. The Reverend Sheppard then returned to his other calling and later became Bishop of Liverpool.

When Peter Barker Howard May gave up playing first-class cricket at the age of 32, his retirement coincided with the abolition of amateur status in English county cricket. His final season of 1962 also saw the end of the traditional Gentlemen versus Players match at Lord's, which first took place in 1806 and ran for a total of 137 matches at the MCC headquarters. Peter May's timing was perhaps of some symbolical significance – he was considered by many worthy judges to be England's finest post-war amateur batsman, if not the best English batsman to emerge since first-class play restarted in 1945. It is also interesting to note that of the great university batsmen of the 1950s, May was probably the most professional in his attitude to the scoring of runs.

Although May did not come from a cricketing family and did not conform to the specifications of the natural athlete, he was, from the moment he was first seen batting in the school nets at Charterhouse, marked down as an England prospect of rare talent; he was an instinctive cricketer.

May's rise from school to Cambridge Blue to Test team (via Surrey in the County Championship) was meteoric. He entered university in 1950, in 1951 he was playing for England against South Africa at Headingley and in his first Test innings scored 138. A dream debut with more to follow.

He toured the West Indies and Australia under the leadership of Len Hutton (May was vice-captain in Australia in 1954–55) and, at the age of 26, was offered the England captaincy when Hutton, suffering from lumbago, stood down against South Africa in 1955. May led England to a win in his first series as skipper and with Denis

The perfect forward defensive stroke of Peter May of England.

Compton carried the English batting. Later in his term as England leader he was to suffer some bitter setbacks but, other than a lacklustre performance in South Africa in 1956–57 (and a disturbing trip to the West Indies in 1959–60 when he returned home early because of illness), he was generally England's most reliable batsman.

The power of Peter May's cover drive was first felt in international cricket by the Australians in 1954–55 when he and Colin Cowdrey, the two amateur novices in the English team, delighted their captain Hutton, charmed the Australian spectators with their sweet stroke-play and gave the England bowlers a run-base to work from.

Ted Dexter, who graduated into the England XI under May, writes in his *From Bradman to Boycott* that May hit the ball with a tremendous thump, 'there was no doubt about his murderous inten-tions when he went out to bat'. Trevor Bailey, writing in *Playfair Cricket Monthly*, contended that Peter May 'made others look ordi-nary, dwarfing them by execution and presence'. Gordon Ross des-cribed him as 'cricketer *par excellence*, a classical batsman with a ruthless approach to his run-making'.

If one shot of May's were to be selected as typical of the player, it would probably be his booming on-drive, a stroke he played with apparent ease but which invariably sent the ball to the fence with tremendous speed and power. He scored with great freedom in an arc from cover point to mid-wicket, with wonderful timing his key-note, off either front or back foot. The former cricket correspondent of *The Times*, John Woodcock (in *Wisden* 1971), recalls that the most memorable stroke he saw May play was at Lord's, 'when from the middle of the ground he hit a medium-pacer high into the Mound Stand, over extra cover and off the *back* foot'.

The author will always carry an indelible impression of an innings of 162 played by May against Western Province at Cape Town in 1956–57 (I was keeping score for the overseas press and had my attention on every ball bowled to him). Against a competent attack, the great England batsman unfolded almost every shot in the book, from a delicate late cut to a leg-glance of perfection, with every stroke in between – with the exception perhaps of the hook and the sweep, shots May did not need to play because of his wonderful ability at driving off either foot and his uncanny sense of timing and placement when 'working' the ball through mid-wicket.

At Edgbaston in 1957, Peter May destroyed forever the mystery and myth which up to that time had surrounded the spin bowling of the West Indian Sonny Ramadhin. In the process (and in the com-pany of Colin Cowdrey) he also played one of the greatest captain's innings of all time – only matched, perhaps, by Gary Sobers's 254 for Rest of the World versus Australia at Melbourne in 1971–72.

Deciding from the start to refrain from trying to 'read' Ramadhin's hand in the act of delivering the ball, May and Cowdrey played the little Trinidadian as they would any off-break bowler. With England starting its second innings 288 runs in the arrears (Ramadhin took seven for 49 in England's first), caution was the initial watchword but as May and his willing back-up Cowdrey progressed, so too did they begin to open up, driving and cutting with great freedom. Their stand of 411 for the fourth wicket remains the world record. Peter May remained undefeated on 285 when the English innings was declared; Cowdrey was out for 154. At the end of the match, West Indies, at 72 for seven wickets, was struggling to avoid defeat.

In 66 Tests, May scored 4537 runs at 46.77 and hit 13 centuries. He retired too early but gave service to the game later as president of the MCC.

Michael Colin Cowdrey was given his initials by a cricketing father with a personal vision of his son as a Test player. At school, Cowdrey played like a storybook hero. Aged 13 and playing with boys three or four years his senior, he won a match for Tonbridge School versus Clifton at Lord's by making top score (75) and taking eight wickets for 91 in Clifton's two innings. At Oxford University he continued, as a batsman, to dwarf his contemporaries. At the age of 21 he found himself, together with Peter May, on his way to play for England in Australia.

Cowdrey senior was there to bid farewell but when the team arrived in Perth, news came through that he had died from a heart attack. At Melbourne in the third Test versus Australia, the bereaved young Oxford University and Kent batsman was to play the innings of his life – and record the first of his 22 Test centuries.

With Lindwall and Miller firing well on a pitch which produced uneven bounce, the young Cowdrey came in with two wickets gone for only 21 runs (including May for a duck). Within a short period the scoreboard displayed 41 for four wickets but 'Barnacle' Bailey stuck for a couple of hours as Cowdrey began skilfully to work the ball off his legs and to unleash the occasional majestic drive off the fast bowlers, straight and through the covers. When Richie Benaud dropped one of his leg-breaks a little short, a Cowdrey late-cut brought up his 50 in 103 minutes, out of 69 runs scored while he was at the wicket.

Bailey departed but chunky wicket-keeper Evans took over as support to the youthful batsman. When Cowdrey reached the 80s, a Lindwall bouncer caught him unawares and the batsman winced as the ball thumped into his torso, despite the protection of his already ample figure. Medium-pacer Ron Archer trapped Evans leg-before when Cowdrey had just entered the 'nervous 90s'. Cowdrey was not deterred: a crashing drive straight back past Archer brought him his 15th four and took his score to 97. A forcing shot to leg off the back foot from the following delivery brought three runs and Cowdrey's first Test century. The applause was deafening. The young man's

Colin Cowdrey of Kent and England played the most beautiful cover drive since Wally Hammond.

century had come out of 158 and five wickets had fallen while he was batting.

Colin Cowdrey went on to play many fine Test innings but his first will always remain the jewel in the crown for in his later years he often became bogged down in a defensive mode. In his record 114 Tests for England (India's 'Sunny' Gavaskar with 118 took over the world crown in 1986), Cowdrey made 7624 runs at 44.06 with 22 centuries. In all first-class cricket he exceeded 40,000 runs and joins the select 100 club with 107 centuries (May, incidentally, hit 85 100s). He played Test cricket in every official Test-playing country.

His first of four tours to Australia was in 1954–55, aged 21; his final trip was a nostalgic affair in 1974–75 when, touching 42, Cowdrey was called to try and bolster an England batting line-up that was flinching and faltering in the face of thunderbolts from Lillee and Thomson. Even then, the portly middle-aged Cowdrey looked best equipped of all England's batsmen to handle the Australian fast bowlers. If ever there was a batting thoroughbred, his name was Michael Colin Cowdrey. Sir Neville Cardus paid his own tribute to Cowdrey with the words: 'I have seen batsmanship by Cowdrey that had a pedigree quality, fit for a place in a cricketers' Debrett's.'

The third post-war university player who can be noted as a batsman of unusual quality was the tall and erect Edward Ralph Dexter, known to all as 'Lord Ted'. In his first year at Cambridge University, the imperious Dexter already had people talking of a new batting star whose style and technique matched that of any of the famous pre-war batsmen.

In 1962 John Arlott described Dexter as the hardest orthodox hitter in the game – the Cambridge and Sussex batsman had truly taken over from Peter May. Dexter's height and reach contributed much to his punishing powers. He was able to drive not only the half volley but any ball close to a good length as well. Dexter employed cut and hook sparingly. As with Peter May, his preference was always the majestic flowing drive, anywhere between cover point and mid-wicket.

Dexter was a handsome adventurer whose lifestyle echoed his batting method. A pilot (he flew his own private plane), brilliant amateur golfer, writer and broadcaster, horse and greyhound owner, fashion model and businessman, he was also known to enjoy riding motorbikes. As a batsman, Dexter preferred to go onto the attack when faced with a challenge, although he always based his play on sound orthodox principles and could defend when necessary.

The contrasts in his attitude to batting were contained in two of his greatest Test innings. At Edgbaston in 1961 in the first Test against Australia, he batted with flawless majesty in England's second innings when his side trailed by 321 runs. Dexter's 180 in 345 minutes was a glorious exhibition of driving and contained 31 fours. This innings saved the match for England. At Old Trafford in 1964 in the fourth Test against Australia, he put his head down for eight hours for 174 (and added 246 with Ken Barrington, who made 256) when England was faced with a mammoth Australian total of 656 for eight wickets declared (Bobby Simpson 311).

But Dexter's two most memorable Test innings were a breath-takingly valiant 76 versus Australia at Old Trafford in 1961 (84 minutes, one six, 14 fours) and a daring 70 off Hall and Griffith at their fiercest versus West Indies at Lord's in 1963. In the latter knock he reached 50 in 48 minutes and made his 70 off 73 balls in 81 minutes. Any true description of Dexter's batting at its best must include the word 'explosive'.

In all, Ted Dexter scored 4502 runs at 47.89 in his 62 Tests (nine centuries) and also took more than a few useful wickets with his fast-medium bowling, sent down with an action reminiscent of Keith Miller's.

When Ted Dexter saved England in the 1961 Edgbaston Test he was assisted by another famous university batsman, the left-handed Raman Subba Row of Cambridge and Surrey (and later, Northamptonshire). The resolute Subba Row contributed a patient 112 in 460 minutes at Edgbaston and, during a short but fruitful Test career, scored 984 runs at 46.85 in 13 matches for England. Subba Row's aggregate of 468 runs at 46.80 versus Australia in 1961 remained his best Test series performance.

Of the remaining university batsmen of the 1950s and 1960s, Donald Bryce Carr (Oxford) played two Tests in India in 1951–52 and later became prominent in English first-class cricket administration; Roger Malcolm Prideaux from Cambridge might have played in more than three Tests if the England's tour to South Africa in 1968–69 had not been cancelled; and Welshman Anthony Robert Lewis, also Cambridge, captained England in eight Tests in India, Pakistan and Sri Lanka in 1972–73 and hit 125 versus India at Kanpur.

Yet another Cambridge batsman, the exciting left-hander Robert William Barber, like Subba Row, enjoyed a short but prolific spell in Test cricket. A no-nonsense hitter who almost always went onto the attack from the first ball, opener 'Bob' Barber provided a pleasing contrast to the normal dour English version of a number one batsman. After a controversial time as Lancashire's captain, Barber joined Warwickshire and immediately became an England prospect. Taken to South Africa in 1964–65, he hit 290 runs in four Test innings (top score 97) and in Australia in 1965–66, played one of the most outstanding Ashes series innings ever when he raced to 185 out of 303 in the third Test at Sydney in 296 minutes, to set England up for an innings victory.

Oxford University's tall and bespectacled Michael John Knight Smith was a man of enormous concentration who played some grand innings in his 50 matches for England. Mike Smith captained England in precisely half of his games for his country and could count three centuries among the 2278 runs he scored in international cricket. In 1972 he was recalled to the England team for three Tests versus Australia at the age of 39 after having officially retired from Test cricket in 1967.

A number of amateurs without connections with either Cambridge or Oxford were picked by England before amateur status was abandoned in 1962. Of these players, Peter Edward Richardson, a short and pugnacious left-hander from Worcestershire (he later played for Kent) was an amateur who batted like the popular version of the typical professional. A patient and skilful opener Richardson gave England excellent service in 34 Tests, although he failed when taken to Australia in 1958–59.

In his first Test versus Australia at Trent Bridge in 1956, the fair-haired left-hander made 81 and 73, adding 151 with Colin Cowdrey for the first wicket in the second innings. Richardson's younger brother, Derek Walter Richardson, played one Test for England in 1957.

With the abolition of amateur status in 1962, the dominance of the two great universities waned. By the mid-1960s Cambridge and Oxford, as cricketing forces, bore little resemblance to the heyday of university cricket (and free and stylish university batsmanship in particular) which existed prior to the war and immediately afterwards, particularly during the halcyon days of May, Cowdrey and Dexter in the 1950s. For the next decade or so, batting emphasis would become rooted in a professional watchfulness that was more reflective of the methods of the 'Players' of the day than of the erstwhile 'Gentlemen'.

26

Professional pride

'The first-class professional cricketer is usually a well-made, strong-looking man, ranging from twenty to thirty-five, with agreeable quiet manners'

— A G Steel (1904)

Two professional England batsmen of the late 1950s and early 1960s stood head and shoulders above their contemporary paid county players. One of these outstanding run-scorers, Tom Graveney, was an elegant front foot player who delighted fans with his style of batting and the vast number of runs scored for Gloucestershire, Worcestershire and England. The other, Ken Barrington, son of an army man, soldiered on in the service of his country and his county (Surrey) through thick and thin, with a strictly controlled and determined approach that would have done Napoleon proud.

Thomas William Graveney was a batting artist who was as close to a complete batsman as anyone could be. Yet for long periods in his distinguished career, he found difficulty in holding a regular place in the England XI. In county cricket Graveney was king. For Gloucestershire and for England his batting evoked memories of Walter Hammond. Sir Neville Cardus once wrote of him: 'No batsman not truly accomplished is able to play a characteristic Graveney innings.'

In form, Graveney was batsmanship personified, immaculate in appearance and with an effortless balance and a timing in stroke execution that was pure magic. He favoured front-foot play in the old style and this perhaps counted against him when England teams to tour Australia were being chosen. His record in Australia certainly did not reflect his ability.

He scored only one Test century against the 'old enemy', but that was a glorious innings of 111 in two hours 40 minutes in the fifth Test of the 1954–55 series at Sydney when Australia's captain, Ian Johnson, asked England to bat first on a rain-affected pitch. Most of the 14 fours struck by Graveney in that knock came from magnificent straight drives.

Graveney's highest Test innings was also an affair of thundering magnificence. In an unprecedented heat wave at Trent Bridge, Nottingham, he thrashed the West Indies bowlers to the tune of 258 runs in just under eight hours. Driving with tremendous power and making full use of his great height, Graveney struck 30 boundaries in this innings.

Opposite: The elegance and control of Tom Graveney of Gloucestershire and England.

After a disappointing trip to Australia in 1962−63, Graveney was dropped (many thought permanently) from the England team. In 1966, with England wickets being skittled all round like nine-pins by the West Indian quick bowlers, he was recalled in an act of desperation, a week prior to his 39th birthday.

In a clear demonstration of the axiom that class will always win out, a rejuvenated Tom Graveney led the way in an England fightback with scores of 96 and 30 not out in a drawn second Test at Lord's and 109 and 32 in the third Test at Trent Bridge, which West Indies won but only after England (thanks to Graveney, Cowdrey and Test newcomer Basil D'Oliveira) had put up some sort of fight.

Graveney, and England, failed in the fourth Test at Leeds but with the tough as old teak Brian Close taking over the captaincy at the Oval, England stormed back with a heartening innings and 34 runs victory in the final match of the series. The England win was built around the batting of the veteran Graveney whose 165 run out would not have been possible without the aid of one of the three tailenders in the England XI.

For the first time in Test history the last three wickets produced 361 runs. At 166 for seven wickets, all appeared lost but Graveney and the England wicket-keeper J T Murray (112) added 217 in four and a half hours. John Murray actually doubled his aggregate of runs for England while moving to his first and only Test century. Graveney soon followed Murray into the dressing room, but all was not lost for England. Two unlikely batting heroes, Ken Higgs and John Snow, England's new-ball bowlers, proceeded to frustrate Sobers and company by adding 128 runs for the final wicket.

In 79 Tests for England (spaced over nearly 20 years), Tom Graveney hit 4882 runs at 44.38 with 11 centuries. In all first-class cricket he topped 100 centuries.

In 1962 John Arlott wrote an appreciation of Kenneth Frank Barrington which contained the following summary: 'The soundest of judges of cricketers are their opponents; and there is little doubt that, in the dressing room of county cricket, the bowlers would rank Ken Barrington the best English professional batsman now playing.'

Judged by his incredibly consistent performances in 362 matches over 16 seasons for Surrey, and in 82 Tests played for England between 1955 and 1968 (plus 89 assorted tours and other games), Ken Barrington was a cricketers' cricketer. The uncomplaining workhorse batted as if England's whole future depended upon him. As Christopher Martin-Jenkins put it so aptly in Barrington's obituary notice in *Cricketer International* (May 1981): 'He was a Master and a servant of cricket.' Ironically, it was perhaps Ken Barrington's unfailingly loyal and conscientious dedication to English cricket which brought both his phenomenal aptitude for run-gathering and his

Barrington reaches his hundred with a rare six in the fifth Test versus Australia at Melbourne in 1956–66. His Surrey and England team-mate John Edrich watches from the other end.

early death from a heart attack. Barrington experienced a minor heart attack while playing in a double-wicket tournament in Australia in 1968 and he decided to retire. The strain invoked by the decision of the Guyana Government to refuse to admit England's Robin Jackman entry in 1980–81 due to that player's South African coaching connections must have preyed on the sensitive mind of assistant manager Barrington. The ever-popular Ken Barrington died in Barbados within days of the Guyana furore.

Ken Barrington was always present when England played a Test match. His numerous rescue acts are legend. His father was a soldier and he himself became known as 'The Colonel'. At the crease, Barrington of the Roman nose was generally in command. He seldom failed in a Test, and never in a whole series, once he had established himself as a permanent fixture in the England team.

Barrington's batting method was based on a principle of safety first. He gradually eliminated from his armoury all strokes considered a risk. Yet he could score swiftly when the occasion warranted it. In the final Melbourne Test of the 1965–66 series in Australia, the burly batsman moved from 63 to 102 off 21 balls, reaching his century with a massive six. In 1965 he was dropped from the England team after scoring 137 in the first Test against New Zealand (in over seven hours) as a disciplinary measure – because he had batted with too much caution. Barrington returned for the third match of the series and thumbed his large nose at the selectors with an infinitely more aggressive innings of 163 in 339 minutes (he added a record 369 for the second wicket with John Edrich, who made 310 not out).

In all, Ken Barrington scored 6806 Test runs at the high average of 58.67. His top score was his 256 in 11 hours and 25 minutes against Australia at Old Trafford in 1964. In Australia he batted with superb consistency. On two tours to that country he headed both Test and first-class batting tables. In 1962–63 he averaged 72.75 for the Tests and 80.13 in all games in Australia; in 1965–66 his figures were: Tests, 66.28; all matches, 67.57.

Australian wicket-keeper Wally Grout once said that when Ken Barrington walked out to bat for England you could see a Union Jack trailing behind him. He was England's man, and a model of the perfect professional cricketer and batsman.

When it comes to talk of bravery on the cricket field, the name of Brian Close inevitably springs to mind, particularly when it comes to discussion of 'suicide' close-to-the-wicket fielding.

Judged by his overall results, Dennis Brian Close was not a very successful Test batsman but during his rather chequered Test career for England, the tough and stubborn Yorkshireman did play one or two courageous knocks worth recording.

In 1963, Close played what was described at the time as a 'heroic' innings of 70 against Hall and Griffith at Lord's, driving poor Wes

Hall to distraction by moving down the pitch to the giant West Indian fast bowler. In 1976 he was brought back into the England team at the age of 45 to square up to a new squad of West Indies speedsters. Again at Lord's on a lively wicket, the fearless left-hander (late of Yorkshire but now skipper of Somerset) put together scores of 60 and 46 against terrifying bowling from Andy Roberts and Michael Holding.

Between 1949, when he first appeared against New Zealand, and his swan-song effort in 1976, Brian Close played only 22 games for England − less than one Test per year − a poor return for a gutsy player who for the most part gave more than full value when he was chosen.

Geoffrey Pullar of Lancashire was, like his Yorkshire counterpart, a left-hander. Pullar had an upright and easy style that allowed him to make full use of his height. He was also a man of phlegmatic temperament who did yeoman service for England as an opener in 28 Tests between 1959 and 1963. 'Noddy' Pullar hit four Test centuries, his best effort being 175 versus South Africa at the Oval in 1960. For his county he was originally a middle-order batsman but was promoted to partner opener Colin Cowdrey with great success on the 1959−60 tour of the West Indies. Sadly, Pullar returned home early from the 1962−63 tour of Australia with an injured knee and, prone to injury thereafter, lost any further chance of playing for England.

When John Murray was injured in 1963, James Michael Parks established himself as England's wicket-keeper but was also a sparkling right-handed batsman who scored nearly 2000 Test runs and hit two centuries for England. Jim Parks was a thrilling stroke-player who frequently made runs when his team was in a tight corner and may have been even more successful as a batsman were he not burdened with England's wicket-keeping duties.

Fast bowler Barry Rolfe Knight might also have scored more Test runs had he been a specialist batsman. Slim, trimly built and a vigorous stroke-player, Knight hit Test centuries against New Zealand and India.

The Middlesex left-hander Peter Howard Parfitt was a batsman of class who played with an exceptionally straight bat. His quiet pugnaciousness was part of his Norfolk heritage and there was much of the Edrich approach in his play. A well-travelled cricketer, Parfitt toured with England teams to all the major cricket countries other than the West Indies but failed against Australia and relied upon his three centuries against a struggling Pakistan in 1962 to boost his overall Test average to 40.91.

During the years when England's middle order (apart from Graveney and Barrington) was generally occupied by amateur batsmen, it was mainly professional opening batsmen who were given some opportunities in international games. Unfortunately, few made any lasting impression on Test cricket. Clement Arthur Milton (Gloucestershire) and Michael James Stewart (Surrey) were inconsistent in both run-making and appearances for England. The tiny and neat Arthur Milton was a watchful right-hander who scored 104 not out in his first Test against New Zealand at Leeds in 1958 but broke a finger in Australia in 1958−59 and did little thereafter. Cheerful 'Micky' Stewart played in eight Tests and scored 385 runs at 35.00 without logging a century, but was worth his place in any team as a fielder alone.

John Brian Bolus was a defensive opener who played for three counties, Yorkshire, Nottinghamshire and Derbyshire. Prematurely grey and always seen in rather bulky pads, his overall Test record was fairly impressive − 496 runs at 41.33. Most of Bolus's runs for England were made against a thin Indian attack in 1963−64. Bolus made his Test debut against West Indies the summer before and displayed guts and character when he on-drove Wesley Hall for four off the first ball he faced.

Philip John Sharpe was a Yorkshireman who will be remembered in Test cricket as much for his slip fielding as for his cheerfully courageous batting. Brought into the England team when others failed against West Indies pace in 1963, Sharpe batted in the third Test at Edgbaston to score 85 not out and followed up with scores of 63 and 83 in the final match of the series at the Oval. After a few seasons in the wilderness, he was chosen against the next West Indies team in 1969 and scored 86 at Lord's. Against New Zealand (also in 1969), Sharpe aggregated 270 runs at 67.50 but was not picked again.

One of the most dependable of all England's openers started his career when distinction was still made between amateur and professional status. John Hugh Edrich, of the famous Norfolk bloodline and first cousin to Bill Edrich, could be described as a left-handed Barrington in style and attitude, but there the comparison ended. Edrich was also short and squarely-built but had handsome good looks and flashing white teeth to provide a sharp contrast to the perpetual creases of worry that adorned Barrington's brow.

As batsmen, the two Surrey players *were* similar in approach. Like the right-handed Ken Barrington, left-handed Edrich progressively eliminated all risky strokes from his repertoire until he became a virtually unsinkable ship in the England battle order. In his 77 Tests, Edrich scored 5138 runs at 43.54 with 12 centuries with a very large proportion of these runs, and seven of his Test hundreds, made against Australia.

Early in his Test career John Edrich was still regarded as a fairly adventurous opening batsman (in 1965 he struck 310 not out against New Zealand at Leeds with five sixes and 52 fours) but a blow on the head from South African fast bowler Peter Pollock in 1965 altered his attitude somewhat.

Self-discipline and concentration became his watchwords and, as John Woodcock wrote in the 1978 *Wisden*, 'At different times in the last fifteen years, Australian bowlers have found him as stubborn and inflexible as anyone, qualities they admire more than finesse'. On the 1965–66 tour of Australia, Edrich scored two Test centuries and totalled 375 runs in the series at 46.87; in 1970–71 he bettered this effort with 648 runs at 72.00 (and again two centuries); in 1974–75 he was a Lillee injury victim and batted courageously with a couple of broken ribs in the fourth Test at Sydney but was unable to score as heavily as in previous seasons.

Two fine attacking professional right-handers both of whom cut their Test teeth against the West Indies fast bowlers of 1966 were also each, in their own way, the subject of an unusual story of trial and personal triumph.

As an exceptionally large 17-year-old schoolboy, the robust Colin Milburn slammed 101 quick and skilfully made runs for Durham versus the touring Indian team at Sunderland in 1959. Colin Milburn did not allow his 'Billy Bunter' image to affect his batsmanship. At every opportunity, he would tuck into the task of scoring runs with the same skill and haste as his fictional counterpart could be pictured tucking into a sumptuous birthday feast.

When he was chosen as one of the 'Five Cricketers of the Year' in 1967, Milburn was described in *Wisden* as 'both a scientific hitter and a character'. 'Ollie' Milburn based his batting on technical soundness but was ever-ready to unleash a savage square-cut or a thunderous drive. He was also one of the most fearless and devastating hookers of fast bowling to have ever walked onto a cricket field.

With England sliding to certain defeat against West Indies in the first Test of 1966 at Manchester, Milburn, playing in his debut international, rode his luck (he was dropped three times) and contributed a belligerent and defiant hand of 94, including hooking feared Wesley Hall for six. In the following Test at Lord's, the burly England opener again played a brilliant second innings knock. This time he hit 126 not out in three hours with three sixes and 17 fours. In his first Test versus Australia at Lord's in 1968, Milburn struck 83 in two and a half hours, pulling Garth McKenzie for six early on and scoring his last 68 runs in only 85 minutes.

Sadly, Colin Milburn, like the young Nawab of Pataudi, lost an eye in a car crash, just as the heavyweight Englishman, at 28, was reaching his prime as one of the outstanding hitters of all time. Pataudi lost his right eye but was able to go on and build a grand Test career as a batsman; Milburn lost his left eye and there was no way he could have continued effectively at top level without achieving the impossible task of teaching himself to bat left-handed.

That Colin Milburn did return after four painful years to play a few matches again for Northamptonshire provided a lasting tribute to the courage of a man who was always a fighter.

The story of Lord Learie Constantine's rise from barefoot plantation boy to Test cricketer and a peer of the realm is the only cricketing rags-to-riches tale to parallel that of Basil Lewis D'Oliveira. D'Oliveira's transition from what he later described as the 'Burma Road' wickets he was forced to play on as a young man in Cape Town, South Africa, to the hallowed turf of the famous Lord's itself, where he made his Test debut for England versus West Indies in 1966, represented the pinnacle event in a heart-warming story of triumph over adverse personal circumstances.

Born within the framework of social and racial strictures created by the original British rulers of the Cape, and enshrined in the statute books in 1948 by the Afrikaner Nationalist architects of the 'apartheid' policy, the gentle-natured but determined Basil D'Oliveira concentrated most of his youthful energy on sport.

Even before he arrived in England in 1960 to play for the central Lancashire League club Middleton, D'Oliveira was already something of a legend in local 'non-white' cricket in South Africa. His 225 in 90 minutes with 28 sixes in a club match in Cape Town in 1953–54 was just one of his many amazing batting efforts. When he was 24 he led a South African 'non-white' XI and easily headed the batting table against a touring Kenya-Asian XI. On a return tour to East Africa, D'Oliveira stood head and shoulders above his batting colleagues and opponents alike.

D'Oliveira was already 29 when he arrived in England in 1960, his fare paid by a public subscription organised by cricket-mad Cape Town Indian barman the late D N 'Bennie' Bansda (Bansda and the late Syd Reddy formed a publishing team which produced the only cricket annuals to contain records of black cricket in South Africa).

By the time he had graduated from League to County Championship cricket for Worcestershire and then into the England side, the South African expatriate, now a British citizen, was already touching 35, an age when most players start looking to retirement. The fact that he had 'made a mistake' with his date of birth details when joining Middleton (everyone thought he was 33 when chosen for England) probably contributed towards his selection for the Lord's Test of 1966. He was to play for England as resident middle-order batsman and sometime all-rounder for the following six years.

In his debut series against West Indies in 1966, D'Oliveira produced a quality and style of batsmanship that he was to carry forward for the remainder of his international career. Run out for 27 in his only innings at Lord's, he hit a quick-fire 76 (14 fours) and 54 (10 fours) at Trent Bridge in the third Test. At Leeds in the next game, with Hall and Griffith at their fastest, he played a brilliant knock of 88, including four sixes and eight fours. One of his magnificent straight drives left Wes Hall flat-footed when it sailed over the fast bowler's head and over the sightscreen for six.

Basil D'Oliveira, the South African who played for England, was a grand attacking batsman who maintained his personal dignity throughout a protracted political controversy.

D'Oliveira relied on the strength of his forearms when playing his shots. His backlift was negligible, a result perhaps of having been forced as a young man to play on pot-holed and bumpy pitches where it was never certain how the ball would bounce. Usually slow at the start while he was getting his eye in, D'Oliveira would gradually accelerate his range and power of stroke-play.

He had an unhappy time when taken to the West Indies by England in 1967–68 but did well in Ceylon and Pakistan in 1968–69 (on a replacement tour when the scheduled South African visit was cancelled) and enjoyed a fine season in Australian in 1970–71, where he hit a particularly grand century in the fifth Test at Melbourne.

The sad story of the cancellation of England's proposed 1968–69 visit to South Africa has been covered in great depth in many publications. D'Oliveira was initially left out of the England touring party. He was then called up to replace an injured Tom Cartwright. D'Oliveira had 'demanded' recognition in the best way he knew – while the England selectors were agonising over the political implications of choosing a black South African for a tour to South Africa, he played a defiant match-winning knock of 158 in the fifth Test of 1968 versus Australia at the Oval.

Then came the political posturing of South African Prime Minister Vorster, pandering to the prejudices of a National Party congress in Bloemfontein. Throughout the controversy, D'Oliveira carried himself in a manner which was a credit to the man and an example for all people to follow, regardless of their personal and political prejudices.

27

Australian victory but cricket wins

'...that greatest of all Tests...breathed new and lusty life into the ailing spectre of a once great game'

— J H Fingleton

Cricket in general and batsmanship in particular drifted into a lack-lustre defensive groove during the mid- to late-1950s and the dead-bat displays put up by the Burkes and the Baileys, the Mackays and the McGlews bored the crowds to distraction, sending them off to seek other entertainment.

Successive seasons saw the breaking of the slowest Test century record (P E Richardson, 488 minutes, England versus South Africa at Johannesburg, 1956—57; D J McGlew, 545 minutes, South Africa versus Australia at Durban, 1957—58). At Leeds in 1955, Trevor Bailey batted for two hours for England against South Africa for just eight runs and 458 minutes for 68 versus Australia at Brisbane in 1958—59. For Australia, Burke took 250 minutes over 28 not out versus England at Brisbane in 1958—59 and Mackay scored 31 in 264 minutes at Lord's in 1956.

Even such an inherently fine stroke-player as Colin Cowdrey now presented a forward defensive batting style that was a pale reflection of the classical wonder he displayed when scoring his first Test century at Melbourne in 1954—55.

A drastic remedy was required — a transfusion of bold new blood to save an ailing game. As if in answer to the prayers of all true lovers of cricket, two great captains (opposing each other in Australia in 1960—61) provided the inspirational leadership that raised the game once more to the heights experienced during previous 'golden ages'. The efforts of Benaud's Australians and Worrell's West Indians in that one glorious Australian summer of 1960—61 brought a revival of attacking cricket that was, with one or two notable but highly effective exceptions, to become a positive and regenerative influence on the next couple of generations of Test batsmen. Although the home team eventually took the honours in the 1960—61 Australia-West Indies series, in the end result the winner was cricket.

Sir Frank Worrell's famous West Indies XI of 1960—61 did not feel the full effect of Richie Benaud's own grand flowing drive on too many occasions, but the Australian captain's contribution to the Brisbane spectacular which set the whole new positive process in motion was both decisive and dramatic.

In partnership with crashing left-hander Alan Davidson, Benaud pulled the Australians out of the fire to set the match up for its ultimate nail-biting finish. When little Joe Solomon threw down a single stump to dismiss Ian Meckiff with the scores dead level, thus was created the first Test tie in history.

What that famous match illustrated above all else was that the attitude of the captains can elevate any game of cricket from a dull war of attrition into a worthy contest.

As Alan Davidson, one of the major participants, later put it, the first contest of the 1960—61 Australian-West Indies series was 'a great Test played between two great teams, led by two great gentlemen of cricket, Frank Worrell and Richie Benaud'.

The career of Sir Frank Worrell has been discussed in an earlier chapter. Richard Benaud came from a cricketing family. His father Lou Benaud was, like his eldest son, a leg-break bowler and a veteran Sydney first-grader who once took 20 wickets in a match. Younger brother John Benaud followed Richie into the Australian side as a tall, free-hitting batsman who thumbed his nose at contrary selectors by hitting 142 (including 93 before lunch) off Pakistan at Melbourne in 1972—73 after having been told that he was to be dropped for the next Test (he found himself at odds with the New South Wales Cricket Association and the Australian Cricket Board over the use of the subsequently common ripple-soled boots).

Richie Benaud the batsman was a fine sight to see. One of his especially grand innings turned the tide in the first Test against South Africa at Johannesburg in 1957—58. The mean South African giant Peter Heine terrorised Australia's openers with his fast short-pitched bowling and Australia slumped to 62 for four wickets. Benaud's quick-fire 122 saved the day, the match and probably the series and, on the final day, 'Slasher' Mackay's four-hour crawl to 65 not out put paid to any aspirations the Springboks might have had of starting the series with a win.

That season in South Africa under Ian Craig saw the making of Richie Benaud as a Test match all-rounder and, given the captaincy, he led Australia to a shock 4—0 victory over Peter May's 1958—59 Englishmen. He never looked back: Benaud lost only four of his 27 Tests as Australian captain.

As a young batsman in the West Indies in 1955, Benaud blasted his way to 121 in 78 minutes (just eight minutes short of Jack Gregory's world record) in the fifth Test at Kingston, in an innings which saw five Australian centuries in a total of 758 for eight wickets (which has only been surpassed by England's seven for 903 declared at the Oval in 1938).

During the famous tied Test, one of Australia's finest all-rounders helped Benaud turn the match. Good enough to play for Australia as either a pulverising left-handed batsman or as a match-winning fast bowler, Alan Keith Davidson has since become chairman of the New South Wales Cricket Association and has served as a national selector. As a Test batsman, his vigorous stroke-play, in which he utilised to the full his immense strength of arm and body, made this tireless 'ironman' of cricket an invaluable member of the Australian XI.

One of Davidson's most memorable efforts came during a 98-run last-wicket partnership with fellow fast-bowler Garth McKenzie against England at Old Trafford in 1961. The burly left-hander carted several balls out of the park as part of his contribution to a new Australian Test record.

Richie Benaud was a member of Ian Johnson's 1956 side that was so demoralised by the off-spin of Jim Laker (and by left-hander Tony Lock) during a season when Australian post-war cricket reached its nadir. With him were a few other up-and-coming players who would soon help boost their country's cricket fortunes. Three batsmen who toured with the young Benaud in 1956 were Burke's opening partner Colin McDonald as well as 'Slasher' Mackay and Peter Burge.

When Benaud first took over the Australian captaincy, Colin Campbell McDonald had already established himself as Australia's number one. He faced up to fearsome fast bowlers like Wes Hall with great courage and skill. Essentially a back-foot player, McDonald hardly lifted his bat when preparing for a stroke, a tactic allowing that extra split second necessary to combat great pace. In attack his square cut was superb and he seldom lifted the ball, preferring to hit crisply along the ground.

McDonald formed a highly rated opening partnership in 18 Tests with dour Jimmy Burke. One of their best efforts was a decisive 190 start to the second Test against South Africa at Newlands in 1957–58 that finally put paid to any Springbok hopes of taking the series. In 1958–59, the pair added 171 on the opening day at Adelaide Oval in the fourth Test against England, with Burke contributing a watchful 66 (McDonald made 170).

When Worrell's men arrived for their famous 1960–61 series, Burke had departed the scene and young Bobby Simpson was promoted to open with McDonald. The new pair proved a success on debut with an 84-run stand at Brisbane. In the crucial final Test at Melbourne, McDonald was given a fine farewell to Test cricket in what proved to be a match-winning 146-run first-wicket stand with his new partner.

Before Simpson's arrival, McDonald teamed up with a couple of opening batsmen who never quite fulfilled their potential at Test level. After playing in four Tests on the tour of Pakistan and India in

1959–60, Gavin Byron Stevens contracted a severe case of hepatitis and was sent home, never again to appear in first-class cricket. Leslie Ernest Favell played in 19 Tests for an average of 27 runs per innings – a disappointing result for a crowd pleaser who did not allow himself to be shackled by orthodoxy in his quest for quick runs. Favell's hook shot and back-foot cutting were quite spectacular and Ray Robinson was once heard to lament that this exciting player was the best opener of his time never to have been taken to England.

Three of the main batting king-pins in Benaud's Australian combination of the 1960s were players of divergent temperament and style: gum-chewing Kenneth Donald 'Slasher' Mackay, left-handed and awkward and with a slightly withered arm, was the modern-day heir to the dead-bat 'skills' of the stonewallers of the past; dashing Norman Clifford O'Neil was the tall and handsome 'superstar', unfortunate to have played before the age of television when he might have set hearts aflutter in many lounge rooms, as well as at every ground on which he appeared; and the imposing Peter John Purnell Burge, whom Ray Robinson called the 'jumbo jet' of cricket and whose bat resounded with a 'clunk' each time he struck the ball.

A description of the 'stroke' repertoire of Ken Mackay may well require a re-writing of the conventional batting text book. In Test cricket 'Slasher' seldom actually 'hit' the ball – it was a case of a little nudge here and a deflection there with the occasional weird and wonderful looking improvisation of a drive when least expected by frustrated bowler and somnambulant spectator.

Yet the number of runs he scored belies the claim that Mackay was the complete stonewaller. Quite early in his career he took 203 off a New South Wales attack which included Miller, Davidson and Benaud, in 435 minutes with 24 fours! Mackay's prime asset was his superb temperament and it should be noted that his highly individual method was greatly valued by his various captains. He was the one man who could save them when all else failed.

Ken Mackay scored 1507 runs for his country at 33.48 an innings and, with his equally original medium-paced 'wobbles', claimed 50 wickets at 34.42 – figures that confirm his undoubted effectiveness. As it was once put in the *Manchester Guardian*: 'Mackay is like the common cold – there is no cure for either'.

It is perhaps unfortunate that newspaper economics frequently call for the superlative when a lesser epithet might suffice. Every now and then a young batsman is hailed as the 'second Bradman'. Such a headline certainly assists in selling more newspapers but the benefit of a sensational early build-up to a young batsman is questionable.

Norman O'Neill was once hailed by the press as a new Don Bradman. He was unable to live up to such expectations but certainly produced some of the most exciting Australian batsmanship of the 1960s. O'Neill retired at 30 when he might reasonably have expected to play for Australia for at least a half-dozen more seasons. The tension at the top had apparently become too great.

Shrewd judges like Walter Hammond and E W Swanton observed early on the seeds of greatness in the young New South Wales batsman's play, but both warned of his nervous temperament. O'Neill was described as a complete batsman – quick into position; a superb back-foot player; always anxious to display his wide range of shots.

In his first Test against England at Brisbane in 1958–59, O'Neill played a decisive match-winning knock of 71 not out that was described at the time as 'an object lesson in hitting the ball'. His debut series brought a batting average of 56.40. O'Neill's first Test century was a highly responsible (if somewhat out of character) innings of 181 in the tied Test at Brisbane in 1960–61, without which Australia would not have come close to matching West Indies.

Former England skipper Ted Dexter has described Peter Burge as 'the man I would most like to have in any team batting number five or six when a cause is apparently lost, because he might just be the man to turn the match entirely on his own'. Burge was a no-nonsense hitter who based his batting on correct principles, a thundering hook and booming straight drive, and more than once rescued Australia from the brink when the rest were falling about him like boulders in an avalanche.

Unlike many Australians of his time, Burge enjoyed coming onto the front foot and with his strong and correct defence was the perfect choice to play in England. One of his most notable Test knocks started in low gear and then moved smoothly into top in the company of Norm O'Neill when Australia were caught in a stop-start situation on three for 88 in the fifth Test versus England at the Oval in 1961.

O'Neill batted gloriously in that innings and at one stage hit 67 off 74 balls. Burge kept his end going with 13 off 90 balls. The pair added 123 in under two hours off a strong and well-balanced England attack. When O'Neill was out for a well-deserved 100, Burge took the initiative and, excelling with the hook against Brian Statham and the sweep to counter the spin of David Allen and Tony Lock, moved with great majesty to a magnificent 181. His innings made certain that England would have no further chance of taking the Ashes.

On his next England tour in 1964, Burge scored a thundering 160 in the third Test at Headingley, during the course of which he made a devastating assault on the second new ball.

In each cricketing generation a number of highly competent players find themselves elevated to Test level but then fail to perform with sufficient consistency to hold their place in top company. One was the thick-set classy right-hander Graeme Thomas. Another was Perth teacher John Walter Rutherford, a defensive right-handed opener who was the first Western Australian player to appear in a

Test and the first to be picked for an England tour.

Robert Maskew Cowper was an all-rounder of great talent whose batting at Melbourne in 1965–66 will forever enshrine his name in Test cricket records. 'Wallaby' Cowper made a dream comeback to the Australian XI for the final Test in 1965–66 after he was inexplicably dropped for the fourth match of the series.

A right-hander in everything else but batting, Cowper took part at Melbourne in what E W Swanton described as 'an interminable left-handed stand...(with Bill Lawry)...that effectively doused English prospects'. Displaying supreme self-discipline in the face of an England total of 485 (and with Simpson and Thomas back in the pavilion for 36) Cowper and Lawry frustrated all attempts to dislodge them until 212 runs had been added for the third wicket. Lawry then left the scene having scored 592 runs in the series (and an incredible 979 in all matches against M J K Smith's England side).

It was left to Bob Cowper to continue the fight, which he did, for 12 hours and seven minutes – the third longest innings in Anglo-Australian Test history, beaten only by Sir Len Hutton's 364 in 13 hours and 17 minutes at the Oval in 1938 and Bobby Simpson's 12 hours 42 minutes for 311 at Old Trafford in 1964. Cowper's 307 also became the highest Test innings ever played in Australia – and a personal pinnacle that he never again approached.

William Morris Lawry has been labelled a 'stonewaller'. There is no gainsaying that the obdurate left-hander was at times a frustratingly slow scorer, and dull to watch in the extreme, but he was at his best a batsman who was technically capable of scoring effectively all round the wicket.

His method for Australia was usually governed by the requirements of the match, although it might be said that when he became Australia's captain he contributed much to the tempo of play. The word 'inexorable' describes a Lawry innings most aptly – relentless in the extreme when the going was rough; similar to the comic-book hero who gave him his nickname – 'The Phantom'.

Sir Leonard Hutton was particularly impressed with Lawry's patience after a plodding but match-winning first Test century at Lord's in 1961. Lawry's autobiography is titled *Run-Digger*, and that is precisely what his game was all about, although it must be acknowledged that he very frequently succeeded when others failed, especially when conditions were not to the liking of the batsmen.

Results have shown that the Lawry-Bob Simpson combination provided the most effective Australian first-wicket partnership in history. The most remarkable partnership ever put together by the two great Australian openers was their 382 against West Indies at Bridgetown in 1964–65, when the home side was already leading 2–0 in the series. Lawry and Simpson batted throughout the first day for 263 and on the second they became the first opening pair to each score a double century. Their stand of 382 remains Australia's best for the first wicket and is only 31 runs short of the world record set up by Vinoo Mankad and Pankaj Roy for India versus New Zealand at Madras in 1955–56.

In his *Ted Dexter Declares* the former England captain reveals the tactic he used to frustrate Bill Lawry during the 1962–63 series in Australia. Observing that the Australian opener was seldom inclined to cut the ball, Dexter ordered his bowlers to direct their deliveries just short of a length and outside the off-stump. The ploy worked and Lawry's run-rate was cut to an even slower pace than usual, although the England bowlers still experienced much difficulty in removing him altogether.

Bill Lawry may have been boring to watch at times but he certainly did his job as an opener and stayed put while his team-mates got on with the business of scoring runs.

When Bill Lawry and Bobby Simpson posted their famous 382 partnership at Bridgetown in 1965, there were two comparative batting failures of the day, one right-handed and the other left, who contributed only nine runs to Australia's massive six for 650. Tall and elegant Brian Booth was the right-hander and he was going through a bad patch after striking a handsome 117 off the West Indies pace attack at Queen's Park Oval, Port of Spain, a few weeks previously; the broad framed Barry Shepherd, whose inelegant but powerhouse play made him a spectators' favourite, was the left-hander, playing his first hand of the series. Booth was in the middle of his eminently distinguished career as a regular Test choice – Shepherd remained a 'utility' player who received few chances.

Left-hander Barry Kenneth Shepherd totalled 502 runs at 41.83 an innings in nine Tests for Australia and it was unfortunate that his opportunities were so limited. By the time the Western Australian first donned his Australian cap he had already hit two double centuries in Shield cricket including a spectacular affair in the company of Rohan Kanhai at Perth in 1961–62.

Brian Charles Booth was a sparkling batsman whose stroke-play (as Ray Robinson put it), 'upheld a charming tradition of the batsmanship of Sydney'. Here was a batsman who could claim his heritage from the long line established by Trumper. Extracts from Robinson's description of Booth's batting could have been written for Trumper: 'His effortless style owed much to unhesitating footwork...His grip made good use of his reach...a full range of graceful on shots...cover drives and square drives placed to advantage...and he cut well.' Here was an enterprising and talented batsman whose deeds gave pleasure in abundance to players and specatators alike.

One of Brian Booth's most courageous innings was the 117 he made at Port of Spain off the frightening thunderbolts of Hall and

Griffith when batting with a more dour Bob Cowper. The pair added 225 after Norm O'Neill had been 'struck out' when defending his head from a vicious Griffith lifter, and made the game safe for Australia.

Booth was accepted in his day as one of the most fearless and competent players of pace bowling. Progress to his chanceless top Test score of 169 against Goddard's South Africans at Brisbane in 1963–64 was punctuated by a series of fearsome bouncers from 'Big Dog' Peter Pollock during the opening overs. Booth remained cool, collected and rigid in his determination; as Ray Robinson later put it in his essay on one of God's finest batsmen: 'loose shots had no more place in his career than loose living'.

As a humble man of high principles 'Sam' Booth was respected by friend and foe alike. After saving his side in his inimitable unhistrionic fashion one day he was referred to by a newspaper writer as 'Sam Booth, Australia's one-man Salvation Army'. That there was a touch of evangelism about his play came as no real surprise. In 1984 Brian Booth toured Australia in the company of his former opponent Trevor Goddard of South Africa as part of a Christian Crusade. In 29 Tests, Booth scored 1773 runs at 42.21, with five centuries.

When World Series Cricket, or the 'Packer circus' as it came to be called, was first played in 1977–78 it was not commonly known that as early as 1975 Kerry Packer had approached former Australian skipper Bobby Simpson to captain a 'special' Australian XI. Simpson declined the offer and pointed Packer in Ian Chappell's direction. Ironically, the next time Simpson and Packer met the former was again captain of the official Australian team.

To come out of retirement at the age of 42, having played his last Test match 10 years previously and with only participation in grade cricket to back up any claims of form and fitness was indeed a remarkable achievement. But Robert Baddeley Simpson was a remarkable player – determined right-handed opening batsman, immaculate slip fielder, accurate leg-spin bowler and unyielding captain.

When he was chosen as 12th man for New South Wales at 16, a snap decision by skipper Keith Miller put rookie substitute Simpson into the slips. Two dazzling catches followed in short order, and settled the new player's fielding position for life. And Bobby Simpson's unusual slip fielding gift may well have been the key to his first chance at Test level.

Batting anywhere between number five and number eight for Ian Craig's team in South Africa in 1957–58, the new cap only once reached 50 in his first Test series. A move to Perth set him up as an opening batsman and he proceeded to remind old-timers of their years spent watching Bradman and Ponsford logging up double-100s galore. The new Western Australian's 1959–60 Sheffield Shield re-

cord was a minor batting marvel with consecutive scores of 98, 236 not out, 230 not out, 79, 98, and 161 not out — a total of 902 at an average of 300.66! In between Shield engagements, Simpson also hit four and 246 not out for a Combined XI versus South Africans, which gave him an early season run tally of 1152 at 288.00.

When he returned to New South Wales a couple of years later, Simpson came close to a repeat performance by starting the 1963–64 season with innings of 359 versus Queensland at Brisbane, 247 not

Bobby Simpson came out of retirement to captain Australia against India in 1977–78 and was still his country's best available Test batsman at the time.

out against his old mates, Western Australia, at Sydney and 135 (run out) off Victoria at Melbourne (his final Shield tally was 784 at 112.00).

As he grew older and wiser Simpson was seen to become more side-on in style and to develop his back-foot play at the expense of more entertaining but ever more risky front foot strokes. In order to consolidate his position in the Australian XI he schooled himself as an opener who would sell his wicket dearly, realising that his best chances lay in the unwanted post. His forward defence was a model for posterity, bat almost scraping the white off his pad. Generally, Bobby Simpson used an orthodox technique, other than when he was confronted by bowlers of the pace of Wesley Hall on an unfriendly pitch. He would sway right back in rather ungainly fashion to dodge bouncers and wait for the safer ball to play.

Doug Walters batted magnificently in Tests in Australia but usually struggled overseas. Here he fends off a Procter bouncer in unusual fashion at Cape Town in 1969–70.

Waiting for his first Test century must have been a frustrating business for this outspoken but supremely dedicated player. There were 50s aplenty before he finally hit pay dirt, against England at Manchester in 1964. Simpson stood guard at the crease for more than two days to reach 311 in the longest innings ever played by an Australian. His three-figure drought had been broken, on the ground which has seen more 'rain' than most others.

Simpson went on to add another nine Test centuries, including a memorable and highly nostalgic 176 against India at Perth in 1977−78 during his amazing comeback season at the age of 42.

The Australian veteran handled the legendary and magical Indian spin quartet of Prasanna, Bedi, Chandrasekhar and Venkataraghavan with consumate ease, but struggled a few months later under bombardment from the West Indian fast bowlers in their own native islands when Australia toured the West Indies in 1977−78.

Simpson may have failed as a batsman during his final farewell but the brave champion of the past, who had been resurrected to lead his country once again, succeeded hands down in his primary task of keeping the flag waving through a period of grave crisis.

It was a trying time indeed for the 'establishment', whose very foundations were being shaken by the heavy artillery at Kerry Packer's command. Cricket was being propelled forward at an alarmingly rapid rate into the age of commercial television − into an age where the old values of playing the game for the game's sake were lost in dim memory, and the prime motivation had become a scramble for TV ratings.

28

Sir Gary and his men

'Garfield Sobers, as all the cricketing world knows, is a very special case. His marks in class, judged by all and sundry, are amazingly high, on the verge of perfection'

— Ted Dexter

The famous Brisbane tied Test in December 1960 was off to a thrilling start with a century from Garfield Sobers that not only had the crowd roaring their approval of its thunderous excellence, but which was a knock that bears comparison with any of the greatest attacking innings.

As Sobers went on his merry and merciless way, visions were conjured up of McCabe's innings at Johannesburg in 1935, and at Nottingham in 1938; of the innings Dudley Nourse played at Johannesburg in 1935 when the South African put Grimmett and O'Reilly to the sword; of Colin Cowdrey's jewel at Melbourne in 1959.

We have since witnessed Graeme Pollock's resounding 125 at Headingley in 1965, and more than a few knocks by Ian Botham and Viv Richards that may compare, but Sobers's century in 125 minutes at Brisbane proved to be a turning point in international batsmanship, a quantum leap from a period in Test cricket when safety-first was the by-word into a new more enterprising age.

Sobers's first 50 in his great masterpiece came in only 57 minutes, with eight fours; in completing his 100 he struck 15 fours and was eventually out for 132, having presented Lindsay Kline with an easy catch off controversial fast bowler Ian Meckiff from what was described as the worst ball of the day: a wide full toss outside the leg-stump. Jack Fingleton records that the West Indian master batsman 'stood at the crease as if unable to believe that he had fallen to such a ball and such a stroke'.

Sir Neville Cardus once called Sir Garfield St Auburn Sobers 'the most renowned name of any cricketer since Bradman's high noon', and considered the West Indian as an even more famous player than Bradman because of his unique genius in every department of the game — prolific left-handed batsman; fast-medium left-arm new ball bowler, who could 'seam' the ball with the best of them; slow orthodox left-arm spinner (or back-of-the-hand purveyor of the 'Chinaman'); slip fielder in the Simpson class; and an astute captain. Garfield Sobers, as a cricketer, was indeed all things to all men. Apart from Australia's Keith Miller, there was certainly no all-rounder of his time or before his time who could approach his abounding flair and skill. As Gordon Ross once summed it up: 'It is difficult to imagine any ball game at which Gary Sobers could not be head and shoulders above his contemporaries.'

In Kenneth Gregory's *In Celebration of Cricket*, the master batsman, Sir Donald Bradman, is quoted as follows: 'With his long grip of the bat, his high-back lift and free swing, I think, by and large, Gary Sobers consistently hits the ball harder than anyone I can remember.' There could be no better, or more authoritative assessment of Sobers the batsman.

When Gary Sobers first came into big cricket he was warned that fast bowlers like Miller and Lindwall would 'find him out' by pitching the ball short in an effort to hit his body. Sobers's answer was to bat in the nets without pads and gloves to give himself confidence. When he was batting, the great West Indian left-hander put spectator entertainment high on his list of priorities. Like all true batting geniuses, he was able to score as easily off a good ball as off a bad one. He hooked with fluid and contemptuous power; his full-blooded square cut was lethal; he was a master at placing the ball with a wristy stroke wide of mid-on; and coming down the pitch to drive, he was for all the world like a left-handed Victor Trumper.

Garfield Sobers enjoyed a meteoric rise from near-poverty in Barbados to fame and fortune on the cricket field. Born one of seven children of a merchant seaman who died in the war when Gary was only five, he was raised with his brothers and sisters by a determined mother. He was through some strange freak of nature born with an extra finger on each hand, which were surgically removed during boyhood. Throughout his distinguished Test and first-class career he was noted for his enjoyment of cricket and for his dignified behaviour and became Sir Garfield Sobers, the third West Indian cricketing knight, in 1975 (the others are Lord Constantine and Sir Frank Worrell).

Where most batsmen might have been content with one supremely memorable effort in their international careers, Sobers played more than a handful of 'innings of a lifetime'. Assisted by his first-cousin David Holford, the West Indian maestro saved West Indies versus England at Lord's in 1966 with an innings of 163 not out that will long be remembered. The Sobers-Holford stand lasted five hours and 20 minutes, thwarted any England hope of gaining ascendency and created a West Indies record stand for matches versus England of 274 runs. From the moment he took guard, Sobers was complete master of the situation. Holford followed his example and posted 105 not out, his sole Test century. David Anthony Jerome Holford was, incidentally, a leg-break bowling all-rounder who was known for his fighting qualities in 24 Tests for West Indies.

At Melbourne, over the New Year in 1971–72, Sobers as captain

of a World XI played what was perhaps the greatest captain's innings of all time. *Wisden* records his 254 in 376 minutes (two sixes, 35 fours) as 'an unforgettable display, combining such elegance of stroke play, power and aggression that the crowds responded ecstatically'.

South Africa's Peter Pollock, who contributed 50 to a helter-skelter 186-run eighth-wicket stand with the West Indian, regarded Sobers's innings as being on a par with his brother Graeme Pollock's devastating 125 versus England at Headingly in 1965, and with Pollock's equally majestic 274 versus Australia at Durban in 1969–70.

One mighty Sobers innings remains to be discussed – his towering 365 not out for West Indies versus Pakistan at Kingston, Jamaica, in 1957–58 that beat Sir Leonard Hutton's Test record score of 364, made in 1938 for England versus Australia. Although the Pakistan attack (with the exception of world-class medium-pacer Fazal Mahmood) may not have been a particularly lethal combination in Test terms, this feat by a 21-year-old comparative newcomer to international cricket was the highly meritorious result of skill, determination and application.

A month or so earlier, Pakistan's Hanif Mohammed had batted for 973 minutes at Bridgetown to score 337 and pass Hutton's longest Test innings record (in terms of time at the crease). Sobers's monumental knock lasted only 608 minutes (as opposed to Hutton's 797 minutes) with his first 100 coming in 197 minutes, 200 in 327 minutes, 300 in 530 minutes and 350 in 596 minutes. Sobers hit one five, 38 fours, six threes, 30 twos and 130 singles. The full score-card reads as follows:

WEST INDIES v PAKISTAN
at Kingston, Jamaica, February 26–28, March 1, 3, 4 1958

Pakistan 328 (Imtiaz Ahmed 122, Saeed Ahmed 52, Wallis Mathias 77, E St E Atkinson 5/42) and **288** (Saeed Ahmed 44, A H Kardar 57, Wazir Mohammed 106)

West Indies

C C Hunte	run out	260
R B Kanhai	c Imtiaz b Fazal	25
G St A Sobers	not out	365
E deC Weekes	c Hanif b Fazal	39
C L Walcott	not out	88
Extras (byes 1, leg-byes 8, wides 4)		13
Total (three wickets declared)		790

The wonderful elegance, eye and timing of Garfield Sobers, holder of the world record Test score of 365 not out for West Indies versus Pakistan in 1957–58.

O G Smith, E St E Atkinson, F C M Alexander, L R Gibbs, T Dewdney and R Gilchrist did not bat.
Fall: 87, 533, 602

Pakistan bowling:	O	M	R	W
Mahmood Hussain	0.5	0	2	0
Fazal Mahmood	85.2	20	247	2
Khan Mohammed	54	5	259	0
Nasim-ul-Ghani	14	3	39	0
A H Kardar	37	2	141	0
Wallis Mathias	4	0	20	0
Alim-ud-din	4	0	34	0
Hanif Mohammed	2	0	11	0
Saeed Ahmed	6	0	24	0

West Indies won by an innings and 174 runs

Sir Garfield Sobers's record Test score may one day be beaten; another of his batting records has been equalled but cannot be bettered. At Swansea in 1968, for Nottinghamshire versus Glamorgan, Sobers struck six consecutive sixes off a six-ball over sent down by M A Nash. This feat was equalled by Ravi Shastri for Bombay versus Baroda in a Ranji Trophy match at Bombay in 1984–85. Poor Malcolm Nash may never be remembered as a steady left-arm seam bowler who took 993 wickets for Glamorgan between 1966 and 1983. In 1977, F C Hayes of Lancashire and England smacked him for 34 in a six-ball over at Swansea.

At the end of his record 93 Tests for West Indies, Sir Garfield Sobers had scored 8032 runs at 57.78 (he was the first player in Test history to reach 8000 runs – a feat since equalled by Geoff Boycott (England) and Sunil Gavaskar (India). He also took 235 Test wickets and 407 catches.

For the major portion of his record-breaking innings at Kingston, Sobers was partnered by fellow Barbadian Conrad Cleophas Hunte, a delightful naturally aggressive right-hander who displayed enormous self-discipline when asked to tone down his stroke-playing exuberance to open the batting for West Indies in Test matches. Strong off his legs, Hunte was a grand hooker and could also drive with power and panache.

At Kingston, Hunte contributed a splendid 260 and he and Sobers added a West Indies record 446 for the second wicket (Hunte was eventually run out with the total at 533 for two wickets). During the 1957–58 West Indies-Pakistan series, Hunte totalled 622 runs at 77.75 an innings. Sobers totalled 824 at 137.33 – the highest by a West Indian in a Test rubber.

Other famous Hunte innings in Tests included a dashing 110

against Australia in the second Test at Melbourne in 1960–61 and a brilliant 182 versus England in the first Test at Old Trafford in 1963. In Australia in 1964–65, he was such a consistent scorer in the Tests that he totalled 550 runs (average 61.11) with a top score of only 89.

The 1956–57 West Indies-Pakistan encounter was the last occasion on which Sobers played with his close friend O'Neill Gordon Smith in a home Test series. Their final Test outing together came in Pakistan in 1958–59. In September 1959 'Collie' Smith died in a car accident in England also involving his friend Gary Sobers, who escaped relatively unscathed. Smith's body was flown back to his home, Jamaica, where 60,000 attended the funeral. It has been said that Collie Smith may have become as great a player as Gary Sobers.

Smith made an auspicious Test debut against Australia at Kingston in 1954–55 when he batted audaciously to take 44 and 104 off a powerful attack spearheaded by Lindwall and Miller. A marvellous player of shots in the Headley-Weekes style, he also held the nick-name 'Jim' for a while – as a front-line off-break bowler, whose hero was Jim Laker, he was a true Test-class all-rounder.

As a Test batsman, O G Smith reached the personal pinnacle of his tragically short career when he made a highly responsible 161 for a struggling West Indies versus England in the first Test of 1957, scoring at great speed after reaching his century. In the third Test at Trent Bridge, he played a lone second innings hand of 168, out of 296 runs added while he was at the wicket.

Rohan Babulal Kanhai was a highly inventive player who added a few strokes of his own to a full repertoire of conventional shots. Kanhai was one of the most exciting batsmen on view when Worrell took his team to Australia in 1960–61 – a bustling bundle of energy who delighted in going on the attack when the chips were down. At Adelaide in the fourth Test he hit 117 and 115 in scintillating style, carting Benaud's hapless bowlers to all corners of the oval. Kanhai's first 100 (two sixes, 11 fours) came in a little over two hours and he and Frank Worrell added 107 in an hour.

Twice he hit a Test double-century – 256 (his personal highest) versus India at Calcutta in 1958–59 and 217 versus Pakistan at Lahore in the same season. Kanhai also hit three double-centuries for Warwickshire and, in 1974 at Edgbaston, created a new world record second-wicket stand with John Jameson. The pair added an unbeaten 465 and both players scored more than 200 – Kanhai 213 not out, Jameson 240 not out.

Later in his career, Kanhai played and coached in South Africa, as an employee of the non-racial South African Cricket Board. His presence in the land of the Springbok went largely ignored by white cricket fans. The writer recalls watching him score a brilliant 100 for Transvaal versus Western Province on one of Basil D'Oliveira's 'Burma Road' wickets in Cape Town. Apart from Gerald Mallinick, then chairman of the 'rebel' white Green Point Cricket Club which had defied government policy by admitting black players, there was no other white man present.

Two other outstanding West Indian batsmen who were contemporary with Kanhai and/or Sobers also enjoyed cricketing connections with South Africa. Alvin Isaac Kallicharran went to South Africa initially as a paid professional for Transvaal, and then played alongside Lawrence George Rowe in the 'rebel' West Indies XI the latter captained on a blockade-busting tour.

Jamaica's Lawrence Rowe made a stunning debut for West Indies versus New Zealand at Kingston in 1971–72 when he became the first and only batsman in history to score a 100 *in each innings* of his first Test. Not content with twin centuries, the stocky Jamaican stroke-player converted the first of his two famous innings into a double-century. Only four batsmen have scored a double-century and a century in the same Test. Rowe is the only player to do so in his first game. The full list reads:

K D Walters (Aust)   242 and 103   v W. Indies at Sydney,
                                                          1968–69
S M Gavaskar (India)   142 and 220   v W. Indies at Port of Spain,
                                                          1970–71
L G Rowe (W. Indies) 214 and 100★ v N. Zealand at Kingston,
                                                          1971–72
G S Chappell (Aust)   247★ and 133 v N. Zealand at Wellington,
                                                          1973–74

★ = not out

Lawrence Rowe is the only batsman to score a double century and a century in his debut Test, West Indies versus New Zealand at Kingston in 1971–72.

Rowe also played a remarkable innings of 302 when he opened the batting against England at Bridgetown in the third Test of the 1973–74 series, but later experienced problems with his eyesight, frequent injuries and a curious allergy to grass which frequently put him out of action.

In South Africa in 1982–83 and 1983–84, he delighted Test-starved fans with his rapid scoring in the one-day internationals against South Africa but, apart from a magnificent 157 at Durban in the first 'Test' of the second rebel tour, failed in first-class matches played against the Springboks.

Alvin Kallicharran (a left-handed version of Kanhai and also from Guyana) was another comparative failure with the breakaway West Indian teams in South Africa after previously setting the veld alight when batting for Transvaal in the Currie Cup competition. He did well enough in local South African cricket to rival his Transvaal team-mate, Graeme Pollock, in thrilling stroke production.

Like fellow Guyanan Rohan Kanhai, the dapper Kallicharran was a batsman of great flair and temperament who based his play on an orthodox technique but could play any of the unorthodox strokes one has come to associate with the best West Indian batsmen. He began his Test career against New Zealand in 1971–72 with a hurried 100 not out, after his innings had been interrupted midway by a bottle-throwing incident.

Kallicharran also hit a thrilling 100 against England at Port of Spain in the first Test of the 1973–74 season – and was the principal player in a peculiar run out controversy involving England's South African born all-rounder Tony Greig. Kallicharran was not out on 142 just before the close of the second day when his batting partner, Bernard Julien, successfully fended the last ball away to Greig, fielding at silly point. Thinking that proceedings were over for the day, but with the ball technically not yet 'dead', Kallicharran strolled out of his crease on his way to the pavilion. Greig immediately threw the ball at the stumps, appealed and Kallicharran was given run out by Umpire Sang Hue. After angry crowd reaction, Sang Hue was persuaded, off the field, to reverse his decision and Kallicharran duly took his position at the wicket next morning. He was dismissed early on for 158.

'Kalli' took over as captain of West Indies for nine Tests during the wholesale defection of players to World Series Cricket in Australia.

Three middle-order right-handers of varying styles – Basil Butcher, Joe Solomon and Seymour Nurse – provided the West Indian XI of the 1960s with a solid backbone of run-making potential. The quietly confident Basil Fitzherbert Butcher (Guyana) was a methodical and wristy player who drove and cut with great discretion and was a regular West Indies choice in 44 Tests. His highlight Test innings was a thundering 133 in a West Indies total of 229 at Lord's in 1963.

Joseph Stanislaus Solomon was less successful and far more reserved than Butcher but will be recalled for his wicket-shattering throw that caused the famous tie at Brisbane.

Seymour McDonald Nurse was a big and powerful driver from Barbados whose batting bore comparison with great entertainers of the past like Weekes and Walcott. The enthusiastic Seymour Nurse based his technique on orthodox principles but was slow in establishing a regular spot in the West Indies team until he hit a double-century at Bridgetown in 1964−65 during the Test in which Simpson and Lawry performed the same feat for Australia. Against New Zealand in 1968−69 he hit 95 and 168 (in 215 minutes) in the first Test at Auckland and followed with his career best 258 (eight hours) in the third Test at Christchurch. Trinidad left-hand opener Michael Conrad Carew shared a 231-run stand with Nurse against New Zealand at Christchurch. This was 'Joey' Carew's only Test century although he had enjoyed a consistent run against Australia earlier in the season. Not afraid to go down the pitch and drive 'mystery' slow bowler Johnny Gleeson, he hit 90 at Adelaide to inspire a previously fumbling West Indian batting line-up to compile a stunning second innings score of 616.

Another Trinidad-born opener, Charles Alan Davis, was even more impressive that Carew. In just 15 Tests, Charlie Davis logged 1301 runs at an average of 54.20, hitting four centuries. He was a fluent stroke-player in inter-territorial matches but reverted to a sheet-anchor role in international games. His most memorable match-saver came at Bridgetown in 1971−72 in the third Test versus New Zealand when he and skipper Garfield Sobers put together an amazing rescue act, adding 254 in a sixth-wicket stand. Sobers made 142 and Davis was eventually run out for 183 after 602 minutes at the crease, during the course of which he recorded the slowest West Indies Test century − 386 minutes.

Against India in 1970−71, despite his two-eyed stance, Davis was one of the few West Indian batsmen to combat the off-spin of Prasanna and Venkataraghavan with any confidence and his omission from subseqent West Indies teams after two Tests in Australia in 1972−73 remains a mystery.

Charlie Davis's older brother, Bryan Alan Davis, was another sound right-hander who opened for West Indies in four Tests against Australia in 1964−65.

When Conrad Hunte left the scene, the bespectacled George Stephen Camacho was given an opportunity to open for West Indies in five Tests versus England in 1965−66. Hunte had three different partners (Nurse, Carew and the West Indies wicket-keeper Deryck Murray) and scored 328 runs at 32.80. He again performed adequately in England in 1969 as opening partner to Roy Fredericks.

Deryck Lance Murray (Trinidad) was a watchful right-hander

who ended up with close to 2000 runs in his 62 Tests to supplement his immense wicket-keeping contribution. Two other West Indian wicket-keepers of the 1960s, one a West Indies captain, were batsmen of more than average ability: Franz Copeland Murray Alexander (Jamaica) was the last white man to captain West Indies. When 'Gerry' Alexander handed over the leadership to Frank Worrell in 1960–61, he continued in the team as wicket-keeper and played a succession of grand knocks against Australia in 1960–61 including at least one innings of 50 or more in each of the five Tests; Desmond Michael Lewis was Alexander's successor as wicket-keeper for Jamaica but his career coincided with that of Derryck Murray. In his only Test series versus India in the Caribbean in 1970–71, Lewis batted with panache to log innings of 81 not out, 88 and 72 in successive Tests.

Roy Clinton Fredericks was an opening batsman of unusual brilliance whose career spanned the period from the late 1960s and into the early 1970s. This explosive left-handed dynamo from Guyana was small but wiry and tough. At Perth in 1975–76 he played one of the great innings in Test history when he flayed an Australian attack headed by Lillee and Thomson on a very fast wicket.

Reaching his century off only 71 balls in under two hours, Fredericks raced on to a glorious 169 in only 212 minutes (145 balls) with a six and 27 fours, his contribution coming out of the 258 runs scored by West Indies.

Fredericks played all the shots — from a whispy late cut to thunderous drives and hooks and a cheeky leg-glance. The man who later became Guyana's Minister for Sport never had an unsuccessful tour or Test series. He enjoyed two distinct styles as a Test batsman: his 150 against England at Edgbaston in the second Test of 1973, for instance, was in sharp contrast to his Perth fireworks, an eight and a half hour long yawn. All the other West Indies batsmen played and missed against the English seam attack that day and without Fredericks there would have been a debacle.

An acknowledged West Indies batting 'great', Clive Hubert Lloyd began his Test career during the 1960s in the company of Sobers, Hunte and Kanhai. The evergreen Lloyd belonged just as easily to the era that was to follow, when the all-wonderful eye and timing that is the trademark of West Indian batsmen was carried forward into the 1980s. The latter part of Lloyd's career also paralleled that of a player whose batting performances were to be compared with the best produced by such heroes as Headley and Sobers and the outstanding stories of 'King Viv' Richards and 'Supercat' Lloyd will follow.

29

South Africa's 'golden age' — and a lost generation

'...it was Pollock who went on to rewrite the record books...Richards who captured the imagination of the cricket world'

— Trevor Bisseker

There have been four major periods of particularly high achievement in South African cricket and each has been of relatively short duration. At the turn of the century, for a brief season or two, the famed googly quartet initiated South Africa's first Test rubber victory; at Lord's in 1935 South Africa gained its first Test and series win over England; in 1952–53, under the inspired leadership of Jack Cheetham, the Springboks became the finest fielding side in the world and shared series with Australia and England; the final days of glory in official international cricket came during the heady days of the mid-1960s and early 1970s when the Springboks for the first time possessed a team equal to any in the world.

During the 1940s and into the 1950s South African batting was still dominated by the old guard: Nourse, Melville, Eric Rowan and Viljoen. Few new batsmen of ability emerged before 1951 and it was not until John Erskine Cheetham took his team of untried rookies to Australia in 1952–53 that a new breed of South African batsmen began to demonstrate their class.

Jack Cheetham was not a true Test batsman, but nevertheless he was a fighter of limitless courage and initiative and worth his place in the Springbok team as skipper and brilliant close fielder. Fielding was the keynote of Cheetham's team — his 1952–53 combination has been acknowledged as probably the best fielding side ever to be seen in Australia.

Three young batsmen were 'blooded' in England under Dudley Nourse in 1951. 'Jacky' McGlew, John Waite, Roy McLean and Russell Endean were destined, together with others like Ken Funston and Headley Keith, to form a competent Test match batting line-up over the next few years.

The graceful and talented John Henry Bickford Waite was originally picked for the 1951 Springbok team as second wicket-keeper to Russell Endean. His pre-Test form as an opening batsman and as a 'keeper of the highest promise found him going in with old campaigner Eric Rowan at the start of the South African innings in the first Test at Nottingham. Not until the closing days of his long international career (1951 to 1965), was he ever considered anything but first choice on the South African selectors' list, as wicket-keeper and as a batsman who was at the time probably South Africa's most gifted player on a turning wicket.

'Johnny' Waite played in 50 Tests – a remarkable record for a South African when consideration is given to the fact that the Springboks' matches were limited to games against England, Australia and New Zealand and Test series were few and far between.

Waite was one of the three Springboks to score centuries in the Manchester Test of 1955. Another who did so was the 6 ft 3 in (190 cm) Paul Lyndhurst Winslow, whose big hitting in his 108 in a little over three hours recalled memories of Jessop and Cameron. Winslow went to his 100 with a six off Tony Lock over the sightscreen that, according to Jack Cheetham, landed in a car park a full 50 yards out of the field. Earlier in the tour, Winslow had emulated 'Jock' Cameron's 1935 feat when he struck Jack Ikin of Lancashire for 30 in an over and altogether hit 40 off eight successive balls. Despite scores of 81 and 139 for Rhodesia versus Ian Craig's 1957–58 Australian team, Winslow did not play for South Africa after that 1955 series in England.

Derrick John McGlew was the third Springbok to post a century in the 1955 Manchester Test, having retired injured early in his innings and then returned to take his score to 104 not out at the close. Jacky McGlew was well named – when everyone else was failing he could generally be counted upon to stick around. He can perhaps be considered as one of South Africa's batting greats. To quote *Wisden*: 'The terse comment "McGlew's still there" was sufficient to encourage hope or temper enthusiasm, according to whichever camp allegiance lay.'

When Cheetham took his side to Australia in 1952–53, McGlew provided consistent stability at the start of the innings in the Tests against Australia and, in New Zealand on the way home, broke Dudley Nourse's South African individual record with an almost chanceless 255 not out in the Test at Wellington. McGlew was seldom to look back during the rest of his international career.

The diminutive Jacky McGlew made up for his lack of height with seemingly unlimited powers of concentration and endurance. He was rock-steady in defence and could unfold a wide range of strokes all round the wicket when the occasion demanded.

Of his seven Test centuries the most infamous was a 545-minute crawl against Australia in the third Test at Durban in 1957–58. His first 50 took 313 minutes. McGlew's all-time slow record was 'beaten' by Pakistan's Mudassar Nazar who batted for 557 minutes to reach his 100 against England at Lahore in 1977–78.

The positive batting of the other 'Mac' in Cheetham's team, Roy Alastair McLean, provided a complete contrast to the unhurried style generally adopted by McGlew. Although never as prolific a scorer as his Natal team-mate, McLean was certainly the more entertaining.

Roy McLean's most telling contribution to the Springbok cause came at Melbourne in 1952−53 when he scored 81 in 90 minutes and 76 not out in 80 minutes in wonderfully bold fashion to bring South Africa victory (and a drawn series) against Australia − after the visiting team had faced an Australia first innings total of 520! McLean was a great crowd favourite wherever he played; his batting style carried the glamour of a Nourse or a Hammond − balance, timing, a superb cover drive plus a dynamite square cut. He was also unafraid of quick bowling and a marvellous hooker of the short-pitched ball.

William Russell Endean was a more dour performer who accumulated his runs in unspectacular fashion. The Australian bowlers found it difficult to either break his concentration or penetrate his defence in 1952−53 and Endean became the sheet-anchor of Cheetham's team. His monumental seven and a half hour 162 not out in South Africa's second innings of the second Test at Melbourne brought South Africa back into the game and the series after defeat in the first Test at Brisbane. He headed both tour and Test averages with 438 runs at 48.66 and 1496 runs at 55.40, respectively.

Known as 'Endless' Endean, he was, like McGlew, McLean, Cheetham (and just about every other member of the Springbok team) a world-class fielder in any position. He is also one of the few players in history who have been given out 'handled ball' in a Test − he diverted a ball bowled by Laker with his hand, against England at Newlands, Cape Town, in 1956−57. Peculiarly enough, it was on Endean's appeal that Len Hutton was given out 'obstructing the field' when he prevented the South African wicket-keeper from taking a catch at the Oval in 1951.

Other useful batsmen in Cheetham's team included the balding Kenneth John Funston, an attacking middle-order batsmen who sometimes matched McLean stroke for stroke; all-rounder John Cecil Watkins; and steady left-hander Headley James Keith.

The Test career of Trevor Leslie Goddard spanned two eras in South African cricket. He first came into the team at the end of Cheetham's successful reign as captain (in England in 1955) and was still a member of the side captained by Ali Bacher in 1969−70, which so thoroughly thrashed Bill Lawry's Australians.

During the interim Goddard gave fine service as a dogged left-hand opening batsman; a left-arm seam bowler who frequently took the new ball, and then reverted to the role of stock bowler when the shine was gone; a brilliant fielder anywhere; and South Africa's captain in Australia in 1963−64 and in a total of 13 Tests.

Although tall, Goddard had a preference for back foot play and was acknowledged for more than a decade as one of the most difficult batsmen to dismiss on the international circuit. Surprisingly, it took him 62 Test innings to record his first century. Goddard averaged 34.46 in Tests and his great value was as a resolute opening batsman at first partnering Jacky McGlew and then the up-and-coming Eddie Barlow.

The Goddard-Barlow partnership started in Australia in 1963—64 and only ended in 1969 (with one lapse in 1965 when Goddard was unavailable for an England tour). Then young Barry Richards appeared on the scene, Barlow dropped down the order and Goddard went in first with Richards, until the left-handed veteran retired at the end of the third Test, and Barlow and Richards teamed up for the final Test of the series against Australia in 1969—70.

When McGlew suffered injury during the series against England in South Africa in 1956—57 a determined young Rhodesian opener, Anthony John Pithey, came into the team. Pithey later batted with great patience in Australia in 1963—64 and further demonstrated his endurance with a six-hour 154 for South Africa versus England at Cape Town in 1964—65.

The 1960 Springbok tour of England was a disaster, marred by political demonstrations and the throwing incident at Lord's which saw young fast bowler Geoff Griffin put out of big cricket for good. To top it all, South Africa toured without many of the old guard batsmen and replacements like Colin Wesley, Jon Fellows-Smith, a youthful Peter Carlstein and Syd O'Linn were clearly out of their depth in Test cricket.

The others did little, and with men like McGlew and Goddard also struggling, South Africa's batting drifted into the doldrums. Only Roy McLean, on his last overseas tour, continued to hold high the South African batting torch. After a brief resurgence during the 1950s, the flame of South African batsmanship appeared to be flickering — but within a few years it would be burning more brightly than ever.

Although such players as Graeme Pollock and Barry Richards have become acknowledged as all-time greats, if one player were to be chosen as representative of the resurgence in South African cricket during the swinging 1960s, it would have to be Edgar John Barlow.

Eddie Barlow was known throughout his long first-class career as 'Bunter' because of his spectacles and round-faced ruddiness. Comparison with the indolent Greyfriars fat boy ended from the shoulders down. During the major part of his playing days, the energetic Eddie Barlow possessed the muscularly trim figure of an athlete who always placed fitness and training at the top of his schedule. It was only later when he was approaching his 40s, but still playing as well as ever, that Eddie let his waistline enjoy some leeway.

With his positive approach, Eddie Barlow helped transform South African cricket in the 1960s.

The secret of Eddie Barlow's cricketing success was his positive mental attitude. His immediate reply when asked what he thought of the Lillee-Thomson fast bowling threat (this was in early 1975 when the Australian pair had just completed their destruction of the 1974−75 England team) was: 'Do you think Barry (Richards) and I would be intimidated by them? No way, we would go out and hit the buggers!'

Eddie Barlow was certainly not a classical batsman in the Barry Richards mould. He was a roundhead and cavalier all rolled into one. He observed sound basic principles and added a few of his own specialities: like his cheeky slice high over the slips' heads which would reach the boundary first bounce and leave opposing fast bowlers flat-footed and fuming. Barlow simply exuded pugnacious belligerence as he peered tauntingly through his owlish spectacles at the approaching bowler. Basically a back-foot player, he excelled with cuts, pulls and back-foot drives.

Barlow's stock phrase to newspaper reporters was 'Nice guys finish last'. His team-mates revered him and called him their inspiration. Peter Pollock says that without Eddie Barlow's 'nothing is impossible if you believe you can do it' approach, South African cricket may not have reached the dizzy heights it did in the 1960s. He never captained South Africa in an official Test yet Eddie Barlow would have made a superb Springbok leader. When Ali Bacher retired from first-class cricket soon after leading his men to a 4−0 victory over Bill Lawry's 1969−70 Australians, Barlow was denied his chance by the politicians.

Barlow played the innings of his life in the fourth Test at Adelaide in 1963−64. Together with 19-year-old Graeme Pollock, he decimated an Australian attack led by McKenzie and Benaud in a South African record 341-run third-wicket partnership. The ebullient right-handed Barlow hit 201; Graeme Pollock, with left-handed grace and power, struck 175 and as *Wisden* records it, 'threw his bat at the ball even more joyously than his partner'.

In the second match of the South Africans' 1963−64 Australian tour, the confident Barlow declared his aggressive intentions with 209 at Perth against a Combined XI. In the same innings Robert Graeme Pollock, not yet 20, scored 127 not out in 108 minutes, an innings of such magnificent quality that it caused Sir Donald Bradman himself to state, 'If you ever score a century like that again I hope I'm there to see it'.

Veteran Australian cricket writer Phil Wilkins 23 years later journeyed to Johannesburg to see how a 42-year-old Graeme Pollock would cope with the bevy of eager fast bowlers in Kim Hughes's 'rebel' Australian team. After observing the South African master batsman at work against Hughes's men, Wilkins returned to Australia and happened to view the Jackson Pollock painting purchased for the Australian National Gallery for $1.3 million, and now worth an estimated $24 million − the famous (or infamous) 'Blue Poles' that was apparently 'concocted, stamped on, slapped on, scraped on by Jackson Pollock'. Wilkins's closing remark in his appreciation of Graeme Pollock in Ken Piesse's *Cricketer* reads: 'At Wanderers I saw another Pollock, a Pollock beyond price. Michaelangelo could not have painted it.'

As the various 'rebel' teams who have visited South Africa over the past few years have discovered, 'Ou Baas' Pollock has lost very little of the skill which made him the most talked about batsman in international cricket in the 1960s. (The appellation 'Ou Baas' is Afrikaans for 'the Old Master' and a title of great respect.) As England fast bowler John Lever put it when asked about Pollock's batting form after he had toured South Africa with SAB England XI in 1981−82: 'It's the same old Pollock − down the track and smack!'

This writer can still recall the look of absolute dumbfoundedness on the face of another English XI bowler, former Test new-ball exponent Les Taylor, when Pollock casually flicked a good length ball of his, on middle stump, into the leg-side stand during the first of the one-day internationals of 1981−82. On the same ground a year later, the 'aging' Pollock carted much-fancied West Indies fast bowler Sylvester Clarke for four successive fours, to leave the big West Indian as nonplussed as his English counterpart.

At Wanderers, Johannesburg, in 1983−84, Pollock played two innings on a fiery and unpredictable pitch in the third unofficial Test against Lawrence Rowe's West Indies XI (captained on the day by Alvin Kallicharran) which defied all known cricket science. With the Springbok batsmen struggling to avert physical injury against a customary West Indies short-pitching four-pronged fast attack on a slippery wicket, Pollock, in cool and collected manner, hit 41 off 31 balls in the first innings and 46 off 33 balls in the second. So fierce

Still going strong at 43, Graeme Pollock is South Africa's greatest Test batsman of all time and arguably the best-ever left-hander in the world.

was his attack on the aggressive Hartley Alleyne that the bowler was seen to refuse when asked by his captain to continue bowling.

In his *Sort of a Cricket Person*, quoting his own press report of the time, E W Swanton refers to the 125 runs Pollock made against England at Trent Bridge in 1965 (in two hours and 20 minutes out of 160 runs made while he was batting) as follows: 'An innings was played here today by Graeme Pollock which in point of style and power, of ease and beauty of execution, is fit to rank with anything in the annals of the game.'

At Newlands, Cape Town, in 1966–67 a lame Graeme Pollock, restricted in his normally free footwork, played an innings of 209 against Australia in the second Test of that season, with 30 fours (he could not run) in six hours and out of 331 made while he was at the crease. At Kingsmead, Durban, in 1969–70, again against Australia, Pollock and a young Barry Richards (in his first Test) added 103 runs in an hour for the third wicket. Pollock went on to reach his South African record Test score of 274, hitting a five and 43 fours and batting, in all, for only 417 minutes.

But of all the great innings this writer has witnessed the South African master play down the years – from his first Currie Cup match at Newlands in 1961 when, at the age of 16, he scored 60 and 53 right up to his amazing forays against various mercenary XIs of the 1980s – Pollock's most memorable knock will remain his scintillating 90 against Australia in the first Test at Johannesburg in 1966–67.

Graeme Pollock's assault on Bobby Simpson's bowlers at the Wanderers ground lifted an ailing Springbok side and set the stage for the phenomenal run of scoring that was to follow from the flashing bat of Denis Lindsay. Pollock's first scoring stroke was a six off Tom Vievers and, with his team in a perilous position, he and skipper Ali Bacher went on the attack to add 91 in an hour before Bacher was given run out following a dubious umpiring decision. South Africa went on to a world Test record second innings score of 620, won the match and, eventually, its first ever series against Australia.

Pollock is essentially a very correct player, with a classic side-on stance that keeps him in a perfect position to hit the rising ball 'on the up'. Tall at just over 6 ft 2 in (188 cm), he stands waiting with his feet about 20 inches (50 cm) apart and, when his right foot moves down the track, he makes his own length and can produce what must surely be as devastating a drive through an arc from extra cover to long off as has even been witnessed. The Springbok left-hander is equally effective on the off-side when he rocks into his back foot shots. He can hook or pull anything short on the leg, and flick to leg with great power anything pitched up to him from middle to leg stump.

One of Pollock's most spectacular shots off a slightly short of a length ball from a slow bowler is to hit it with a straight bat, high wide and handsome to the left of mid-on, more often than not for a six into the crowd. With his wide range of bludgeoning attacking shots he remains an ideal limited overs cricketer as well as a formidable proposition in the game of longer duration.

In January 1983 at Cape Town, the writer watched South Africa's two greatest world-class batsmen, Graeme Pollock and Barry Richards, bat against Lawrence Rowe's team in the first match with some claims to international status played between teams from South Africa and West Indies and recorded the event as follows: 'The first morning was pure magic — Barry Richards, in almost indolent fashion, unleashed a series of sweetly timed hooks, drives and cuts which left the West Indian fieldsmen standing and their much vaunted pace attack astounded. Until he was comprehensively bowled by Ezra Moseley, after majestically cover-driving that bowler to the Oaks' fence to raise his hundred, Graeme Pollock batted with all the glory of old.'

Pollock scored exactly 100 runs (14 fours — 159 balls) that day; Barry Anderson Richards made a sweet 49, before he appeared to wake up from a personal reverie that had perhaps placed him in a real Test encounter, locked in combat with official Test match bowlers, to realise suddenly that it was not the genuine article and virtually to give his wicket away with a lazy shot.

In the *Hampshire Handbook* for 1977, Henry Blofield wrote: 'Barry Richards is undoubtedly the supreme batsman of his generation and arguably he is the best the game of cricket has ever known.' Richards only batted in one Test series for South Africa, versus Australia in 1969—70 and logged 508 runs at an average of 72.57. One can only wonder if Mr Blofield's high praise would have been confirmed in figures if Richards had been allowed to continue playing at Test level for the next 10 or 12 years.

In matches for Natal, Hampshire and in one season for South Australia, he reigned supreme. He is the only South African batsman to have scored 1000 runs or more in a home season on five occasions (a daunting target in a season of just 10 or 12 first-class matches). Graeme Pollock has done it four times; four other players, Jimmy Cook, Peter Kirsten, Colin Bland and Denis Lindsay, have done it once only.

In recognition of his marvellous batting in his debut season for Hampshire in the English County Championship in 1968 (2395 runs), Richards was picked as one of the 1969 *Wisden* 'Five Cricketers of the Year'. The young South African's off and cover driving was compared with that of Walter Hammond; his square cut was a savage blow that left no doubt as to the destination of the ball; his leg-side shots were exhilarating and almost cruelly effective. Blofield asks: 'I wonder if any batsman has given bowlers an inferiority complex quicker than Richards?' Supremely confident, almost disdainful in very smooth movement, Barry Richards very rarely looked as if he was anything other than in complete control of the situation, regardless of what reputation an opposing bowler might enjoy.

When it comes to an affirmative exhibition of high batting art, Barry Richard's *pièce de résistance* must remain the innings played for South Australia versus Western Australia at Perth in 1970−71 when, through the sheer arithmetic of his performance, he placed himself in the same bracket as the high scorers of the between-the-wars years.

Against a bowling attack which reads like a Test line-up: McKenzie, Lillee, Tony Lock, Mann, Inverarity and Brayshaw, the then 25-year-old Richards raced to 325 runs on the first day. Next day, he took his score to 356 (one six, 48 fours) in 372 minutes. Dennis Lillee's final bowling analysis (in his own Test debut season against England) was 18−1−117−0!

During that golden 1970−71 Australian summer, Barry Richards hit 1538 runs at 109.86 per innings, including scores of 224, 146 and 23 in his two matches against Ray Illingworth's touring MCC team.

When he was in the right frame of mind Richards, like Bradman, was considered almost impossible to get out but, after that wonderful year in Australia, the South African visibly became more and more dispirited when he saw his country's chances of ever returning to the Test fold dwindling. Hylton Ackerman, a former Western Province captain and a talented hard-hitting left-hand batsman who scored a century for a World XI against Australia at Brisbane in 1971−72, recalled that he once observed Richards playing as a professional in Holland. Apparently none of the spectators even recognised the South African Test opener.

If Eddie Barlow could be regarded as the motivating grand vizier and Graeme Pollock as the uncrowned king, Barry Richards was the undisputed crown prince of South African batsmanship. Although the writer did not see Bradman or Sobers bat, other than on film, he did see Pollock and Richards at their peak, and again in their 'waning' years, and will therefore leave this life one day fully content in the knowledge that he has observed the art of batsmanship in its highest possible form.

Unfortunately for South Africa's opponents of the time, Richards, Pollock and Barlow were not the only world-class South African batsmen around in the 1960s.

Kenneth Colin Bland may be best remembered as the 'Golden Eagle', a name he earned as possibly the best outfielder of all time, but he was also a commanding right-handed stroke-maker who looked every bit as handsome a player as Pollock or Richards when he got his batting into gear.

When the MCC visited South Africa in 1964−65, Bland hit 572

runs at 71.50 in the Tests. Always ready to loft the ball, he was particularly severe on the English off-break bowlers Titmus and Allen. In 1965 he was chosen alongside the Pollock brothers as one of *Wisden*'s 'Five Cricketers of the Year' but made a sad departure from the Test scene when he badly damaged his knee running into the boundary fence at Wanderers during the first Test of the 1966–67 series against Australia.

Denis Thomson Lindsay, whose father played for South Africa as wicket-keeper in 1947, was, like Bland, a tall upstanding stroke-player whose favourite stroke was the hook shot off short-pitched fast bowling. Australia's lanky Dave Renneberg will have special cause to remember South Africa's wicket-keeper/batsman. In the fourth Test of the 1966–67 series against Australia Lindsay twice cracked Renneberg, bowling with a new ball, into the stand just backward of square leg.

Lindsay's 1966–67 form was phenomenal. In the first Test at Johannesburg he rode his luck after being dropped at 10 and his supremely impudent 182, including five sixes, a five and 25 fours set a pattern for the remainder of the series. On the way to his 606 runs at 86.57 for the series he passed Indian B K Kunderan's 525-run record for a wicket-keeper/batsman in a Test series.

South African captain Peter Laurence van der Merwe, inelegant but effective, and the tall all-rounder Herbert Roy 'Tiger' Lance played a few fine supporting hands during the 1960s while Dr Aron Bacher, van der Merwe's successor as Springbok captain, set the ball rolling for South Africa in 1966–67. Bacher struck a thundering 235 off Simpson's Australian team for his home province Transvaal (which became the first South African team ever to beat an Australian XI on South African soil).

'Ali' Bacher was a free-scoring right-hander who played three or four decisive innings in his 12 Tests for South Africa. He was forced to give away active play in his late 20s when he underwent heart surgery but has in recent years become a prime mover in the organisation of 'rebel' tours to South Africa.

Two younger players whose careers were sorely affected by South Africa's isolation from Test cricket from 1970 onwards did sufficiently well from the chances they were given to be noted down as batsmen of unusual ability. As a schoolboy in Natal, Michael John Procter was considered as good a batsman as his close friend and contemporary Barry Richards. Procter at the crease certainly evoked visions of Dudley Nourse or Roy McLean. His cover drive had a touch of Hammond about it and, when he started playing for Gloucestershire as their most prolific all-rounder since W G Grace, Jessop and Hammond, the county supporters took him to heart. Later, when he was made county captain, it was not unusual to hear the county referred to as 'Proctershire'.

Mike Procter, all-rounder supreme, holds a joint world record of six successive first-class centuries with Sir Donald Bradman and C B Fry.

In Tests proper, Procter did not get much of an opportunity to show his paces as a brilliant attacking batsman (aggregate 226, average 25.11). As a bowler he was magnificent — 41 wickets in seven Tests at an average of 15.02 each. Outside Tests he batted with grand assurance to equal the Bradman-Fry record of six first-class centuries in a row. His all-round feats for Gloucestershire saw him named the 'White Sobers' and his big hitting has only been equalled in recent seasons by Ian Botham. A relaxed and popular player, Mike Procter was a fine leader of men who always put the needs of his side ahead of his personal ambitions.

Brian Lee Irvine was a classy left-hander who also sought solace in English county cricket after a brief flirtation with Test cricket, and the chagrin of being picked for tours to England and Australia that were subsequently cancelled. If it were not for politics in sport, the name of Lee Irvine may have gone in the history books as South Africa's finest left-hander after Graeme Pollock.

In his only Test series, versus Lawry's 1969—70 Australians, Irvine scored 353 runs in seven innings at an average of 50.42 with his maiden Test century coming in the final game at Port Elizabeth in under three hours. In that innings, Richards made 126 and Lindsay reached 50 in 48 minutes.

For Essex and Transvaal, Irvine remained a high scoring batsman until he retired aged 32 in 1977, and was also a wicket-keeper of more than average ability.

One of South Africa's finest cricketers of the past 15 years or so, the giant and lovable fast bowler Vintcent van der Bijl has recently published an autobiography entitled *Cricket in the Shadows*. He tells the sad tale of a player and a generation who were denied the opportunity to display their prowess in the highest of cricket's forums — the Test match arena.

South African cricket entered its new dark age in the early 1970s. The door was firmly closed to South African teams who wished to venture overseas. Matches against touring sides of any worth were few and far between and eventually came to a complete halt. A sporting dyke, with special emphasis on cricket, had been built around the beleagured Republic of South Africa. It was not until the early 1980s that a crack was made in the retaining wall and the waters of hope for South Africa's Test-thirsty cricket players and public were seen to trickle through.

Then, during the 1981—82 season, the dam burst and an English XI of near-Test strength arrived to do battle with the Springboks. 'Rebel' teams appeared from the West Indies and Australia, and even a brave but woefully weak combination from Sri Lanka. At last some recognition was given to South African players, including batsmen like Peter Kirsten, Kenny McEwan and Clive Rice, who had become household names in English county cricket. But what of the others, that lost generation who were denied all opportunity for recognition?

Batsmen like Hylton Ackerman and Chris Wilkins joined Irvine, Richards, Procter and company to make a mark in English cricket, and are therefore not totally forgotten by the outside world. Hylton Michael Ackerman was a dashing left-hander who, as a teenager, hit a century in less than two hours for Border versus MCC in 1964−65. He also had a successful tour to Australia with a replacement World XI when the 1971−72 South African tour was cancelled.

Christopher Peter Wilkins was a belligerent right-hander who, in a Currie Cup match, once smacked the first ball sent down by big fast bowler Garth le Roux for six − by flicking a short pitched delivery over the astounded wicket-keeper's head in a vast parabola and into the crowd behind him at long-stop.

David Dyer, Lorrie Wilmott, Andre Bruyns and left-hander Darryl Bestall were all Test material batsmen in their respective styles who may have made it into international cricket during the 1970s. Those who survived into the 1980s took their chances well against the various rebel teams. Some, like Allan Lamb, Chris Smith (both England) and Kepler Wessels (Australia), sought foreign pastures and were eventually picked in Tests for other countries.

Peter Kirsten scored a string of double centuries for Derbyshire, has made runs against all the 'rebel' teams and is South Africa's leading contemporary batsman after Graeme Pollock.

Peter Noel Kirsten came into the Western Province team around the same time as Lamb, and in the minds of many remains a finer batsman than the England player. Kirsten scored prolifically in England and compiled five double-centuries for Derbyshire. He captained South Africa against the rebel Sri Lankan and West Indies teams and was his team's most reliable batsman after Graeme Pollock; Essex professional Kenneth Scott McEwan would have walked into an England XI of the late 1970s as an exciting stroke-player; Clive Edward Butler Rice did some grand all-round work for the 'Packer circus' during World Series Cricket years and is currently South Africa's captain — and a one-day batsman of particular power whose superlative feats brought South Africa back from 0—2 against Hughes's first Australians to a 6—4 victory in the one-day games.

As a captain and all-rounder for Nottinghamshire, Rice was superb for 13 seasons before his retirement from county cricket, ironically, just when he had qualified to play for England. In 1984 he beat such eminent challengers as Ian Botham (England), Kapil Dev (India), Richard Hadlee (New Zealand) and Malcolm Marshall (West Indies) in a world all-rounders tournament to astound the bookmakers.

Henry Richard Fotheringham, an amply proportioned red-haired right-hander, forms with Stephen James Cook one of South Africa's best post-war opening partnerships. 'Jimmy' Cook has been South Africa's first choice number one since Barlow hung up his boots and Cook scored 114 in his first 'international' against the SAB English XI at Johannesburg in 1981—82 (the first and only South African to score 100 on debut in a representative non-limited overs match).

Mandy Yachad partnered Cook on his own international debut in a one-day game versus the West Indies XI in 1983—84. The pair added 155 in less than even time and Yachad went on to register 123 not out and become the second South African batsman to score a century on his first appearance in any international match.

Another atacking right-hander, Kevin Alexander McKenzie, rid himself of years of frustrated ambition when, at the age of 35, he scored 220 runs in rapid fashion in four 'Test' innings against the 1985—86 Australian team, including a magnificent match-winning century in the final game at Port Elizabeth.

The list goes on and on. Will the world ever hear of Adrian Kuiper, Roy Pienaar and Darryl Cullinan, three of the best of the younger South African batsmen of today? As Shakespeare said through the mouth of Macbeth:

'Come what come may,
Time and the hour runs through the roughest day.'

Hopefully, if and when South Africa sees itself through its present political crisis, then may the great Springbok batting tradition be carried forward again into true Test match cricket.

30

Silver Fern rising fast

'We have had some great players, and very many more who have played their cricket well, and with spirit'

– R T Brittenden

The 1965 Test series in England marked the final departure from international play of Bert Sutcliffe and John Reid, New Zealand's two major batting mainstays of the post-war period and two of the finest players ever to wear the Silver Fern on their cricket caps. It was to be some while before a line of reasonably consistent performers again arose.

Of the up-and-coming men who made their entry into Test cricket when Sutcliffe and Reid were still active, the lean and slightly stooping Bevan Ernest Congdon was destined to become not only one of his country's finest captains, but a batsman to rank with some of the very best New Zealanders of the past.

Congdon was a slow developer at Test level, but once he discarded the early flamboyancy inherent in his play, he established himself as a batsman of great character and concentration, and a shrewd and tough captain. He made his debut against Pakistan in a home series in 1964–65 but only really came into his own in a series in the West Indies in 1971–72 when he took over as captain from an injured Graham Dowling for the third Test at Bridgetown and went on to aggregate 531 for the series (average 88.50), second only to Glenn Turner who had experienced his own first season of exceptional high scoring.

Retaining the captaincy in 1973, Congdon twice came within a whisker of leading New Zealand to its first Test victory on English soil. He was the key player in a bold bid for victory at Trent Bridge when New Zealand was left to score an impossible 479 in 560 minutes for victory; the final England winning margin was only 38 runs. Congdon was magnificent, stroking his way to 176 in just under seven hours, his straight driving an outstanding feature of this long innings.

The stubborn Victor Pollard, a right-hander like Congdon, stayed with his captain while 177 runs were added for the fifth wicket and went on to score the first of two centuries he made in his own finest series.

At Lord's in the second Test, New Zealand started its second innings 298 in arrears but another wonderful Congdon effort saved the day. The New Zealand skipper made a slow but certain 175 in 535 minutes. Support came from the enterprising Mark Burgess, who hit 105 in attractive style, and Pollard, who was left undefeated on 105 and amazed the opposition by charging fast bowlers Snow and Arnold when they took a second new ball. This was in effect the talented Pollard's only great season as a Test batsman. The even-natured and entertaining Mark Gordon Burgess went on to take his century tally for New Zealand to five.

New Zealand's visit to the West Indies in 1971–72, because of ultra-defensive batting, became one of the most boring international tours and Test series ever. Every match played was left drawn (bar one against Bermuda which was, strictly speaking, not part of the West Indies) including the five Tests. Ironically, the tour also represented a statistical highpoint for New Zealand's batsmen.

In 13 first-class matches, six New Zealand batsmen scored 12 centuries between them, including nine three-figure scores in the five Tests versus West Indies. Congdon hit four 100s (two in the internationals) and aggregated 988 runs at an average of 89.81 for the tour to head the batting table. Next on the average list was the obdurate Glenn Turner with the figures 1214 runs, average 86.71. The remarkable factor about this latter performance was that in his 13 tour innings Turner hit four double-centuries, two of them coming in the Tests.

The 1971–72 Caribbean venture proved the making of Glenn Maitland Turner as an international batsman of stature who possessed formidable powers of concentration and run-making skills. Although he had been scoring with admirable consistency for Worcestershire in the English County Championship for a few years, had already scored a Test century versus Pakistan (110–Dacca 1969–70), and had carried his bat for 43 not out through a completed Test innings versus England at Lord's in 1969, the name Glenn Turner was still far from familiar.

Turner played what was described at the time as 'an astonishing innings' of 223 not out (he carried his bat through a completed innings of 386) in the first Test at Kingston. This was the match in which West Indian Lawrence Rowe marked his Test debut with scores of 214 and 100 not out and it was only Turner's amazing display, plus a fifth day 100 from Mark Burgess that saw New Zealand through to a draw.

The fourth game of the series at Georgetown found Turner at his defensive best (after he had already logged 259 versus Guyana in the pre-Test territorial fixture). When time was lost on the first two days through rain and a bottle-throwing incident, Sobers declared West Indies' first innings at 365 for seven wickets after having batted well into the third morning. Turner's response was to kill the match when he proceeded to bat for virtually the rest of the available

Opposite: Glenn Turner is one of only three non-England players to reach 100 first-class centuries (and the only New Zealander to do so) along with Sir Donald Bradman and Pakistan's Zaheer Abbas.

playing time for 259 in 702 minutes, adding a record 387 with T W Jarvis for the first wicket. Turner's aggregate for the series was 672 runs at an average of 96.00. Without him, New Zealand would have surely been thrashed conclusively in at least three of the Tests played.

Because of his Bradman-like run-making, Glenn Turner suddenly became a cricketing celebrity. He was to go on in an almost inexorable style to reach a number of milestones previously unattained by a New Zealand batsman. He was not an entirely defensive batsman; when he first arrived in England to play for Worcestershire, Turner lacked a range of offensive strokes but this deficiency was soon rectified when he was compelled to alter his method and attitude to accommodate the requirements of one-day limited over cricket. Although he kept his hands a little far round the back of the bat handle to please the purist, the New Zealander was able to hit through the covers effectively and could score freely on both sides of the wicket. His driving through mid-wicket was particularly effective and, above all else, Turner always played with the straightest of straight bats.

Of his major batting feats, Turner's two centuries in a Test in the second game of the 1973–74 rubber against Australia was particularly meritorious – his 101 and 110 not out gave New Zealand a David and Goliath type first Test victory over the much-fancied Australian team led by Ian Chappell. His feat did much to foster a new confidence among New Zealand's cricketers in the years to follow.

In 1982 at the age of 35, the New Zealand run-machine became the first New Zealander and the 19th first-class batsman to reach 100 first-class centuries. He did this while compiling his own personal career best score – a mammoth 311 not out for Worcestershire versus Warwickshire at Worcester. This innings in itself created a couple of new records: it was the highest 100th century, beating W G Grace's 288 in 1895 and it was the highest score for Worcestershire.

Turner also became only the second non-English batsman to achieve the feat (Sir Donald Bradman was the first; Zaheer Abbas of Pakistan has since joined the exclusive 100 club) and he scored his 311 in one day, to join another elite group of batsmen. Turner made 128 before lunch and 126 between lunch and tea. It was his final season with Worcestershire and on hand to bring him a celebratory gin and tonic was his old coach from Dunedin days, the former Pakistani batsman Billy Ibadulla.

Glenn Turner was a shrewd and dedicated player whose password was consistency. He provided a model of professionalism and dedication for a new breed of New Zealand batsmen to follow. Although his Test appearances were curtailed late in his career when he clashed with New Zealand authorities, he remains the outstanding New Zealand post-war batsman after Bert Sutcliffe and John Reid and, in some areas, was even superior to that brilliant pair as a relentless gatherer of runs.

In a continual search for new scoring talent during the 1960s and 1970s, batsmen came and went. Men like R W Morgan; left-handed Graham Ellery Vivian (son of H G Vivian of the 1931 New Zealand team); Bruce Alexander Grenfell Murray, hockey international; Keith Thomson; Brian Frederick Hastings (who scored 1510 runs in 31 Tests); and the ginger-haired Terrence Wayne Jarvis, a cultured stroke player who made 182 of his 625 Test runs in one monumental innings in partnership with Glenn Turner at Georgetown in 1971−72 (Jarvis occupied the crease for nearly two days in the 387-run New Zealand first-wicket record).

Two Parker brothers gained Test caps. The elder, Norman Murray Parker, made his debut for New Zealand as a batsman when his younger brother, John Morton Parker, was captaining his country for the first time in the third Test against Pakistan at Karachi in 1976−77. Norm Parker failed but brother John was a regular in 36 matches between 1972 and 1981, modelling his play on Glenn Turner's.

Eye problems brought an abrupt end to the promising career of the Sutcliffe-like left-hand opener Rodney Ernest Redmond. In an incredible debut performance against Pakistan in the third and final 1972−73 Test at Auckland he cut, pulled and drove his way to a stunning 107 in a first innings opening stand of 159 with Glenn Turner in 132 minutes; in the second innings, Redmond smacked another quick 56. Chosen to make the trip to England in 1973, the exciting new left-handed prospect experienced difficulty with his contact lenses, did not appear in a Test, and was forced to give up the game two years later.

John Francis Maclean Morrison replaced an injured Glenn Turner at Sydney in 1973−74 and scored 117 in only his second game for New Zealand. Thereafter he was in and out of the national side, making his final Test appearance in the 1981−82 home series versus Australia.

Much was expected of the short and stocky Graham Neil Edwards, as a wicket-keeper and as a right-handed batsman who could hit with exceptional firmness. 'Jock' Edwards did not fulfill his potential but was a delightful comical character who always helped raise team spirits when the going got tough.

New Zealand's wicket-keepers of the period were more than competent batsmen. Kenneth John Wadsworth, who died tragically of cancer when 29, was a positive-minded competitor who did not reach his peak as batsman and 'keeper. Warren Kenneth Lees played an heroic innings of 152 when New Zealand faced a Pakistan total of 565 for nine wickets declared in the third Test at Karachi in 1976−77. Current New Zealand wicket-keeper Ian David Stockley Smith has followed his predecessors' example and stroked his way to a fine 113 not out in the third Test against England at Auckland in 1983−84.

All-rounder and fast bowler Bruce Richard Taylor became the first man in history to score a century and take five wickets in an innings in his debut Test. The 6 ft 2 in (188 cm) Taylor smacked 105 runs in 158 minutes against India in the second Test at Calcutta in 1964−65, adding 163 with Bert Sutcliffe. He then went on to bag five wickets for 86 in the Indian first innings. In scoring New Zealand's fastest Test century (versus West Indies in the first Test at Auckland in 1968−69), the belligerent Taylor reached his 100 in 86 minutes with his fifth six, a towering hit off fast bowler Edwards.

Towards the end of the 1970s and running into the 1980s, a number of New Zealand batsmen, following the example offered by Glenn Turner and Bev Congdon, tightened up their techniques to form a core group of competent scorers who became a credit to New Zealand and international cricket.

Geoffrey Philip Howarth, a charismatic captain, lost his Test batting touch at 35 and his place in the New Zealand team after a lacklustre trip to the West Indies in 1984−85. However, he was one of New Zealand's finest captains and a technically efficient batsman who could gear his play to the needs of the hour. Howarth's major Test batting pinnacle came in the third Test versus Australia at Auckland in 1977−78 when his twin-centuries, 122 and 102, saw him emulate Glenn Turner's 1973−74 feat.

Howarth led New Zealand to an unprecedented 1−0 victory over West Indies in a stormy series in 1979−80, during which the phlegmatic New Zealand skipper kept a cool head throughout. As a popular skipper he always appeared to be in control − as Peter Webbs puts it in *The New Zealand Cricket Player*, 'like a grand master directing his chessmen'.

The tall gangling Jeremy Venon Coney first gained a reputation as New Zealand's 'bits and pieces' player but his all-round play in England in 1983, both in the Prudential World Cup and in the subsequent Test series against England, earned him a place amongst *Wisden*'s 'Five Cricketers of the Year', an honour few of his countrymen have achieved.

Coney's early doggedness as a batsman remained but he added the classic, old-fashioned drive wide of mid-on − realising that a half-volley is a gift. This new approach was superbly demonstrated at Wellington in January 1984 when Coney stroked his way to his own personal best Test score of 174 not out against England in the first Test.

As an unconventional 18-year-old, Coney made his first-class debut for the New Zealand Under-23 XI against Auckland and arrived at the match in 'flower-power' clothing and shoulder-length hair. Sent to Australia as a replacement for the injured Glenn Turner in

December 1973, he apparently arrived without his own bat, and spent the money the team manager gave him to buy one on a guitar! A more mature Jeremy Coney has now displayed great verve as New Zealand's captain and remains one of the most reliable of contemporary Test batsmen.

Nine seasons for Derbyshire and nearly 50 Tests makes left-handed opener John Wright one of New Zealand's most experienced players. He was beset with the problem of falling into a defensive groove early on, and then being unable to 'go for his shots' when his eye was in. Happily Wright 'came right' against Australia at Christchurch during the 1981–82 series when he drove superbly on his way to 141 out of an innings total of 272 at Christchurch in the third Test.

Wright's success in various limited over tournaments, from the Prudential World Cup in England through to the Australian Benson & Hedges World Series, has also kept his name to the fore. If he had

John Wright has proved an extraordinarily reliable left-handed performer for New Zealand, in Tests and in one-day internationals.

not been brilliantly run out by England's Derek Randall for 69 when going at full blast in the 1979 World Cup semi-final, he would surely have taken New Zealand to Lord's to contest final honours with the mighty West Indians.

Bruce Adrian Edgar is an accountant and it showed in his cool handling of the new ball as a skilful left-handed Test opener. He first toured in England in 1978 and passed 1000 runs in his 17th Test but when New Zealand made its first-ever tour of Sri Lanka in March 1984 he suddenly lost his place. This proved to be a reasonably brief lapse for a fine player. In Australia in 1985–86, the talented Edgar came second to Martin Crowe in the Test batting averages and again worked effectively at the top of the order with his old opening partner, John Wright.

Another fine New Zealand left hander, John Fulton Reid, is a popular and successful player and unrelated to former New Zealand captain John Reid. In his early career J F Reid has suffered from inconsistent selection decisions but struck a golden patch during the third Test versus Sri Lanka at Colombo in 1983–84, to end with 180 and ensure a winning total for New Zealand.

A schoolmaster who dislikes leaving New Zealand, Reid declined to tour the West Indies in 1984–85, after playing outstanding innings of 148 and 158 not out in the three-match home series that New Zealand won against Pakistan, but he returned to the team for the Tests against Australia in 1985–86.

The intelligent and articulate Martin David Crowe must be a future candidate for the New Zealand captaincy. A very correct but extremely exciting stroke-player, he has begun to realise his vast potential as a Test batsman of above average quality. First chosen for New Zealand against Australia in 1981–82 at 19, Martin Crowe went quietly about his way of serving his apprenticeship in the team before launching out to become the current batting supremo of New Zealand cricket.

In Australia in 1985–86, Martin Crowe's thrilling 188 in the first Test at Brisbane helped set New Zealand up for an historic first win on Australian soil, a victory which was also achieved through the magnificent bowling of Richard Hadlee who took 15 wickets in the match. At Georgetown, Guyana, in 1984–85, the young stroke-player played a responsible innings of 188 off a rampant Marshall, Garner and Holding that must rank as one of the best hands against the fearsome West Indies pace men in recent years. It would appear that the young New Zealand hero has the cricketing world at his feet.

Jeffrey John Crowe (four years older than the talented Martin and current Test captain) followed his brother into the New Zealand team. A fair-haired right-hander, John Crowe has still to score consistently enough in Tests to ensure automatic selection for New Zealand. The Crowe brothers, whose father D W Crowe played for

Martin Crowe is his country's young batting champion and may become New Zealand's best ever.

Wellington and Canterbury, first played together in a Test match against England at the Oval in 1983.

The dynamic and aggressive Richard John Hadlee is also a member of a famous cricketing family. His father, Walter, and two of his three older brothers, Dayle and Barry, have represented New Zealand in Tests or limited overs internationals. After his amazing crickket in Australia in 1985−86 (and the fact that he scored a double of 1000 runs and 100 wickets in England in 1985), he must be a leading candidate for the title of world best Test all-rounder alongside Ian Botham, Kapil Dev and Imran Khan.

Hadlee is only the ninth player to complete the Test double of 150 wickets and 1500 runs. He holds the New Zealand 'best bowling' record with nine for 52 against Australia at Brisbane in 1985–86 and hit his maiden Test century (103) versus West Indies at Christchurch in 1980. To complete the impressive family picture, Richard's wife Karen, also an all-rounder, has played for New Zealand's women's team.

Another of New Zealand's faithful and long-serving all-rounders of the past decade, Bernard Lance Cairns, a husky giant of a man, delighted spectators with his huge six-hitting antics before retiring at the end of the 1985–86 series in Australia. Cairns had the biggest hands in the business and became one of the characters of New Zealand cricket.

The tall New Zealand off-spin expert John Garry Bracewell is also no mean performer with the bat. In 1983–84 he recorded his maiden first-class century with 104 not out for Auckland against the touring England team. Against Australia at Sydney in 1985–86, he came in at number 10 and scored a defiant 83 not out, adding a New Zealand record 124 for the last wicket with left-arm spin bowler, Stephen Boock. Then, in England in 1986, Bracewell followed a quick-fire 100 against Northamptonshire with an inspired 110 in the Second Test at Trent Bridge (batting at number eight) to lift himself well and truly into the Test all-rounder class.

For the future, it seems as if the youthful Kenneth Robert Rutherford, a sound right-hander, may be fighting his way back into international cricket after a dreadful start to his career. Taken as a 19-year-old to the West Indies in 1984–85, Rutherford suffered the shattering experience of making a pair of ducks in his first Test at Port of Spain and followed this with a depressing sequence of 4, 0, 2, 1 and 5 in the remaining three Tests. Towards the close of the 1986 England tour he hit a blistering 317 off 245 balls in 230 minutes (8 sixes, 45 fours) versus D B Close's XI at Scarborough, the fifth fastest triple-century ever.

Rutherford was not the lone failure against the fearsome West Indies fast bowlers, although it should be recorded that Martin Crowe, Jeremy Coney and John Wright did, on occasion, play innings of high character and determination. Two other interesting new-comers in the New Zealand team are the Kenya-born and former Worcestershire stroke-player Dipak Narshibhai Patel and another exciting right-hander, Andrew Howard Jones, who hit his maiden Test hundred versus Australia in 1987–88.

One can also say with confidence that players like Congdon, Turner, Wright, Edgar, Howarth, Coney and Martin Crowe lose little compared with New Zealand giants of the past like Dempster, Donnelly, Sutcliffe and Reid. With a new professionalism now apparent in the play of its batsmen, the land of the Silver Fern will continue to challenge strongly the other cricketing nations.

31

Mr Forever

'Would that half a dozen others had Boycott's dedication...'
— Robin Marlar

Like Old Father Time perched atop the pavilion at Lord's, Geoffrey Boycott, OBE, went on, and on...and on, seemingly forever and amen. He remained at the top of the tower as a batsman of high professional standards for close to a quarter of a century, and, until injury took its toll during the 1986 season and he retired, looked likely to continue his frustration of bowlers for another few years.

It might be stated that Boycott and controversy have shared the longest opening partnership in the game. Notwithstanding any claims England's South African former captain and all-rounder Tony Greig might have, Yorkshire's Geoffrey Boycott has, through weight of runs and length of argument, taken the crown as the most controversial cricketer since the Second World War.

Geoffrey Boycott is also one of the finest and most successful batsmen of all time, a player who will not lie down, no matter the odds, but who has frequently spoilt his chances by steering his own course when an element of compromise might have been better for the game of cricket.

Acrimony and personal criticism have often surrounded Boycott. Life must be difficult indeed for a singularly minded man whose abiding preoccupation is the scoring of runs, to find himself embroiled in media debate; thrust into the limelight because of supreme dedication to his profession. Actors, politicians and sports people have become regarded as public property — an intrusion which is perhaps a sign of a still immature society that may not have developed past its puberty, notwithstanding any social and scientific claims to the contrary.

The words 'supreme technician' spring immediately to mind when one thinks of the batting of Geoffrey Boycott. Other contemporary or near-contemporary batsmen may be more artistic, like Greg Chappell or Gower, others more explosive, like Viv Richards, but batsmen like Boycott (and 'Sunny' Gavaskar) are, because of their unyielding dedication to safety of method, generally the most dependable of the lot.

'Conservative' is another epithet which might be applied to Boycott's orthodox approach although, when the occasion calls for it, he can cut loose and shake an opposition attack like a terrier does a

captive hare. His batting has progressed through different stages —
as an artist moves through different colour or media periods. Technically superlative, Boycott exhibits the twin gifts of a talented but
conservative representational artist — deft precision and intense concentration — as he builds an innings stroke by stroke until he has
covered his canvas (and the scoreboard) with sufficient runs.

A statistical resume of the batting feats of Boycott reveals such a
wealth of achievement that it is practical here to reveal only some of
the highlights of his long and profitable career:

- In 108 Tests (before he was effectively banned for playing in
  South Africa in 1981–82), he has scored 8114 runs at 47.72 with
  22 centuries — only India's Sunil Gavaskar (9572 runs at 50.64 in
  118 Tests, with 33 centuries) has exceeded his aggregate).
- He is one of only nine players who have scored 20 or more Test
  centuries.
- By the end of the 1986 English season, he had scored 151 first-
  class centuries — only the pre-war Hobbs, Hendren, Hammond
  and Mead, all of whom played far more innings than Boycott,
  have passed this figure.
- He is the only batsman to average more than 100 in an English
  season twice.
- He has hit 10 double-centuries in first-class cricket.
- With an aggregate of 48,426 runs he came closest of the modern
  batsmen to joining the six batsmen (all pre-war) who have totalled
  more than 50,000 first-class runs. Next in line, Warwickshire's
  43-year-old Dennis Amiss, took his first-class total to 43,423 in
  1987.
- He was dropped from the England side for slow scoring immediately after registering his highest Test score, 246 not out versus
  India at Headingley, Leeds in 1967.

Boycott was one of the last major English batsmen to start wearing
a helmet when the protective headpiece became the vogue. This was
long after he had been accused of withdrawing from Test cricket for
a while for fear of fast bowling. Trevor Bailey is, incidentally, one
former player who has publicly decried the use of a batting helmet
(*Wisden* 1981): 'Obviously a helmet makes batting, which I personally
never considered even a vaguely dangerous occupation, less dangerous;
just as wearing one in a car...would reduce the risk of injury
following a road accident.' A current batting supremo who disagrees
with the former England all-rounder is Graeme Pollock, who started
his career before helmets became the vogue and once told the author
that he thought it logical and sensible that a batsman who values his
own skin should wear whatever protection is available.

Although he has a large group of devoted supporters, Geoffrey
Boycott has never been a popular player among his team companions.
He has been accused time and again of being a supremely selfish

Geoffrey Boycott of
Yorkshire and England
displays the best defensive
technique in the business.

player who is more concerned with his own performance than the
needs of his team. Notwithstanding this accusation, the times he has
been virtually the sole agent of an England victory bid, or has almost
single-handedly saved the day for his country, are legend. When the
scales are finally balanced, it may be fair to contend that without
Geoff Boycott, English cricket would have been the poorer over the
past 24 years.

Boycott stayed away from Test cricket for a couple of years by choice; Dennis Leslie Amiss was ever willing to battle for his country but was 'excommunicated' by the English cricket establishment after joining Kerry Packer's World Series circus in 1977, and became an even more condemned cricketer when he joined Boycott and company on a 'rebel' trip to South Africa in 1981—82. England, in fact, willingly dispensed with the services of almost a complete generation of capable batsmen when a three-year ban was imposed on the players who flew south to do battle with the Springboks.

In his first 12 games for England, Amiss faltered and failed to average 20 runs per innings; in his next 20 games he scored more than 2000 runs (eight centuries) and averaged more than 70. During the calendar year 1974, he compiled 1379 Test runs including scores of 174 versus West Indies in the first Test of 1973—74 at Port of Spain and a nine and a half hour epic which produced 262 not out (he carried his bat through the England innings) in the next match at Kingston. Each of these two amazing efforts was achieved in the second innings of a match in which England was struggling to avoid defeat.

Then came a depressing period against Australia, and Dennis Lillee, when the Warwickshire batsman could not get things together for a while, and the legend was born that Amiss was vulnerable to extreme pace (as if nine out of 10 of the other batsmen on the international circuit at the time were immune to the high speed and skill of bowlers like Lillee, Thomson and Michael Holding!).

Amiss fought his way back in a magnificent comeback against the West Indies (and a rampant Holding and Roberts) in the fifth Test of the 1977 series at the Oval. Playing a lone hand, he batted with noble aggression, cover-drive flowing and his steel-wristed flicks through mid-wicket racing to the boundary, in a display which came close to matching the innings of 291 played by West Indies' Viv Richards in the same match. Dennis Amiss's 203 out of 342 took only 320 minutes and contained 28 fours and he remains as one of those unfortunate players who might have achieved even greater things if it were not for selectorial prejudices and politics which were out of his control. In 1986 Amiss finally joined the elect 'century of centuries club' when he posted his 100th for Warwickshire versus Lancashire at Egbaston, the 21st player to reach this milestone.

When Anthony William Greig came into first-class cricket in South Africa in 1965—66 Eddie Barlow was fast becoming the new 'guru' of South African cricket, preaching a gospel of get-up-and-go self-reliance and self-confidence which ran contra to the previously held image of a rather reserved and submissive South African cricketer. Perhaps Tony Greig was influenced in his attitudes by Barlow. When he was asked to take over the leadership of an ailing England side in 1975, he immediately inspired a new sense of urgency in his team that was akin to the super-optimistic approach of a Barlow or a Peter Pollock.

Leaving his South African connections aside to join Sussex, the 6 ft 7 in (200 cm) Greig became, in his own right, a dynamic captain of England and a batsman of verve and courage who stood up straight to the fastest bowlers of the day and was always prepared to hand out as much punishment as he received.

Primarily a front-foot player who used his height and reach to expert advantage, Greig's thunderous lofted straight drive was the outstanding feature of his play. He became an instant crowd favourite when he first appeared in India, the West Indies and Australia. Greig notched his first Test century at Bombay in 1972−73 and hit two centuries (and won the final match and rubber with his slow-medium off-turners) against West Indies in the Caribbean in 1973−74. In Australia in 1974−75, when England's batsmen started to fall like bottles hanging on the wall, he played a defiant innings of 110 at Brisbane which had the crowd on their feet, after they had started off by hooting him for his aggressive antics on the field.

Tony Greig became one of the prime movers behind Kerry Packer's World Series cricket. To the establishment set, he was a despicable mercenary rebel; to many of his fellow players he was something of a saint come to lead them to new and more lucrative pastures. The blessings for cricket of the World Series episode have been mixed and, on the whole, not as dreadful as was first anticipated. Tony Greig continues his involvement in the game which he still holds close to his heart. Of those who chose the Packer road he had more to lose than most and was the only major figure in the venture who failed to return to Test cricket when the burnt bridges were repaired.

An interesting feature about his final batting figures is the fact that his Test batting average exceeds his overall first-class average − an indication, perhaps, that Tony Greig was a player who preferred a challenge.

Greig took over as England captain from the much-maligned Michael Henry Denness of Scotland, Kent and later Essex who was unfortunate to be made captain just at the time when Lillee and Thomson were reaching their peak and England's batting strength was not quite up to the task of combating the Australian speed duo. To compound his problems, Denness, normally a player of quality with a good range of shots, frequently faltered in Tests. Though he did enjoy one particular high moment when he returned to the England team for the sixth match of the 1974−75 series in Australia (after having dropped himself from the previous Test because of his poor batting form) and scored a brilliant 188 which set England up for an innings victory.

England's resident wicket-keeper of the 1970s is regarded by respected judges as possibly the best gloveman of all time. Alan Philip Eric Knott was also a gritty Test-class batsman who could

have played for England for his run-scoring ability alone. Knott scored many of his runs when England was in a tight corner or when fast scoring was needed. Because of his sparkling footwork, he was a particular asset against the Indian spin bowlers and an even greater player of fast bowling, particularly when Lillee and Thomson were cutting their fearsome swathe through the English batting line-up in 1974–75.

Keith William Robert Fletcher was known to his friends as 'the gnome', for both his looks and perhaps because of his dogged and restrained batting. Although he ended his Test career with more than 3000 runs and seven centuries, Fletcher seldom gave full reign to the stroke-playing powers he exhibited when playing for Essex. Fletcher captained England on the troubled tour to India and Sri Lanka in 1981–82 when some of his team were secretly privy to a plan that was being hatched to send an unofficial England XI to South Africa.

Three of the England players who chose to go with Boycott, Amiss and others to South Africa were batsmen of great character, two of whom have recently found their way back into the England team after a three-year exile.

The graceful Robert Andrew Woolmer of Kent was a Cowdrey look-alike in girth and style who was not picked for England again after his South African excursion. On his painfully slow passage to a score of 149 versus Australia in the fourth Test at the Oval in 1975, Woolmer logged the slowest century for England in an Anglo-Australian Test – 426 minutes.

A second South African tour 'rebel', Peter Willey (Northamptonshire and Leicestershire), of peculiar two-eyed stance, has reserved his best Test batting performances for encounters with West Indies and was picked in the 1985–86 team sent to the Caribbean under David Gower. On his previous trip he scored a brave and resolute 102 not out in the fourth Test at St John's with only the tailenders to support him.

The remaining batsman involved in the South African affair, Graham Gooch, resumed his position as England's number one opener batsman and will be dealt with in a later chapter.

Other batsmen who appeared for England during the 1970s, before or during the reign of Tony Greig, included Yorkshiremen John Harry Hampshire (a debut 107 versus West Indies at Lord's in 1969) and Raymond Illingworth (who was to become a famous England captain and who also scored a century in the Test at Lord's in 1969). Brian William Luckhurst of Kent was a workmanlike right-handed opener who was first picked for England aged 31 in a series against a Rest of the World side raised in 1970 to replace the banned South African team. His success in this replacement rubber saw him given a berth to Australia in 1970–71 where he became one of England's

Opposite: Tony Greig stood up to the fire of Australia's Lillee and Thomson at their best, excelled in the West Indies and India and led England at home and abroad with verve and skill.

most reliable performers and scored 455 runs at 56.87 in five Tests, including centuries at Perth and Melbourne. The prematurely grey and bespectacled David Stanley Steele was a Northamptonshire opener who, at the age of 33, was brought into the England side struggling against the fast bowling of Lillee and Thomson in 1975. He played six innings against Australia for 365 runs (average 60.83) but drifted away after appearing against West Indies the following season.

Fun-loving Derek William Randall of Nottinghamshire livened many a dull day with his antics on the field. He played a couple of Test innings of great note but failed frequently and recently found himself on the reserve bench in the England 'B' team. In the Centenary Test at Melbourne in 1977, Randall single-handedly kept England in the game with an audacious 174. The Australian spectators took him to heart when he 'tennis-batted' one Lillee bouncer to mid-wicket for four, and then fell over backwards and did a reverse roll when trying to avoid another.

Randall's innings that day at Melbourne was one of the cricket classics of all time. His dour, but ultimately match-winning, 150 in 589 wearying minutes versus Australia in the fourth Test at Sydney in 1978–79 was a marvellous demonstration of discipline and stamina.

England's batting during the 1970s and into the early 1980s was generally defensive and remained particularly vulnerable against top quality fast bowling. During the 1980s a number of unusually gifted attacking players were to appear whose style of batting was more akin to that of the amateur university players of the 1950s than that of the professional line represented by Geoff Boycott.

32

The Chappell influence

'A cricketer of effect rather than the graces'
— John Arlott

Ian Chappell took over the Australian captaincy from Bill Lawry for the final match of a depressing series in 1970—71 when the Australian batsmen faltered and flinched for the most part against the extreme pace of John Snow. The axing of Lawry coincided with the arrival of Lillee on the Test match circuit and Ian Chappell began the leadership cycle of his career by boldly asking England to bat first at the Sydney Cricket Ground. His ploy did not work but England was made to battle strongly to gain a 62-run win as a new spirit of enthusiasm and confidence became evident among the members of the Australian team.

The success Ian Chappell enjoyed as a captain sometimes obscures reference to the fact that he was also one of the finest Australian batsmen. A bit slow off the mark at first in Test cricket, he batted low in the order in his first couple of Tests against England and failed miserably in South Africa in 1966—67. Chappell blames his lack of success on that first tour to South Africa on advice taken from Australian skipper Bobby Simpson to give away his hook shot.

A player who naturally employed 'cross-bat' shots — the hook, the pull and the cut — more than most, Chappell was sometimes accused of being less than correct in his methods but he came right in the end when he re-introduced his favourite attacking stroke.

Following a couple of outstanding batting triumphs against West Indies in Australia and in India, Chappell again experienced trouble with his hook when he went to South Africa a second time, in 1969—70. There the pace of Peter Pollock and Mike Procter found his technique lacking in innings after innings and his meagre contribution to an overall Australian disaster was only 92 runs in eight excursions to the crease.

Giant South African seam bowler Vintcent van der Bijl (undoubtedly the finest South African bowler never to have played in an official Test), writes about the Australian's problem in his *Cricket in the Shadows*. Apparently, when Ian Chappell returned to South Africa on a third occasion, as a member of the International Wanderers in 1976, van der Bijl, recalling the Australian's disastrous 1969—70 performance, tested him with a vicious bouncer — which was immediately smacked through mid-wicket for four.

When van der Bijl later questioned Chappell about the change, Ian Chappell replied that a lack of genuine fast bowlers in Australian domestic cricket around 1970 had given him little opportunity at the time to practice his hook shot against real pace. Shrugging off the trauma of his South African failure Chappell went on from strength to strength as a batsman and as captain of Australia to total 5345 runs in 75 Tests (and to win 15 out of his 30 games as captain with only five losses to his debit).

A comparison of the styles of the two most successful Chappell brothers, Ian and Greg, suggests that Gregory Stephen Chappell, a strong and firm personality in his own right, may have found it necessary to assert himself by playing in a style different from that of his already well-known brother. Ian was a square-on player who preferred back-foot shots; Greg can be listed alongside the great technical front-footed stylists of the past. Famous England all-rounder Trevor Bailey has described Greg Chappell as technically the most correct of all Australian batsmen produced since the Second World War, and possibly the most accomplished.

Unlike his older brother, Greg Chappell served no long batting apprenticeship in the Australian team but went out and made a century in his very first innings, versus England in the second Test at Perth in 1970—71. He is one of the few players who have ended a Test match career with an average exceeding 50 per innings and, in all first-class games, hit 74 centuries (Ian Chappell logged 59), a remarkable effort for a batsman who had only two seasons as an English county cricketer (with Somersetshire in 1968 and 1969).

Greg Chappell was a marvellous timer of the ball, particularly to anything pitched on the leg-side, be it a long-hop or a half-volley or anything in between. If there was one element in his batting style that could be subject for criticism, it was his known liking for front-foot play, an asset under English conditions but often a dangerous practice on Australian wickets, especially when facing up to West Indian whirlwind express bowlers.

Because of his own unique batting genius, Greg Chappell would usually succeed with his forward play but, according to some observers, the emulation of his style by lesser mortals has created something of a deleterious influence among certain contemporary players.

During the 1983—84 season Greg Chappell lifted his Test batting aggregate beyond that achieved by Sir Donald Bradman and became in the process the first Australian to top 7000 runs in international cricket. Bradman, however, remains as undisputed champion of all time — his 6996 Test runs were scored at an average of 99.94 an innings; Greg Chappell's 7110 Test runs were made at an average of 53.86.

As Australia's captain, Ian Chappell gathered a devoted group of players who formed a tightly-knit and talented squad from which the Test team was chosen. One player, Ian Ritchie Redpath, was a batsman of class who had preceded his skipper into the Australian team. The young Victorian featured in a 219-run opening stand with State team-mate Bill Lawry and was unfortunate to be dismissed for 97 in his first Test outing against South Africa at the Melbourne Cricket Ground in 1963–64.

Keith Stackpole described Ian Redpath as 'an ornament to cricket' because of his immense love for the game, while Ian Brayshaw labels him 'a team man for all occasions'. 'Redder' Redpath was an unruffled player with unlimited patience, cast in the mould of Alick Bannerman, Woodfull and Barnes. Frequently overlooked by the Australian selectors for no logical reason, he would quietly go about the business of collecting runs whenever he was given an opportunity to represent his country.

Australia's Ian Chappell shelved his hook shot for a while, but later became one of the world's leading batsmen.

Rugged Keith Raymond Stackpole played his first Test as a leg-spinner who could bat and, coming in at number eight against England at Adelaide in 1965–66, hit 43 to celebrate being chosen for his country. The effervescent 'Stackie' was still languishing low down in the order (at number seven) when he swept to his first Test century, a rapid-fire 134 against South Africa at Cape Town in 1966–67.

Two years later he joined Bill Lawry at the top of the batting order for the first time. Three 50s in his first four knocks as a Test opener settled Stackpole's batting position for the remainder of his international career.

Fundamentally a back-footed right-hander who revelled in the hook and the cut, Stackpole was as unlike his more sedate front-footed left-handed partner, Bill Lawry, as Falstaff and the Lord Chief Justice. His best Test score was a blazing 207 in the first Test versus England at Brisbane in 1970–71.

An opener of the time who did not quite make it at Test level was Robert John Inverarity, dubbed by England writer E W Swanton as Mr 'Inforeverty', who made his first appearance as an 18-year-old rookie for Western Australia in 1962 and, at 41, played his final first-class game for his adopted South Australia in 1984–85. With a square-cut for four versus New South Wales at Newcastle in 1984–85, Inverarity overtook Sir Donald Bradman's record for runs scored in Sheffield Shield cricket, but he needed 256 innings (average 39.33) to overhaul Bradman's 8926 runs in 96 innings at 110.20.

If he had been able to carry forward his Australian form onto the playing fields of England, Kevin Douglas Walters may well have become rated as one of the great batsmen of Australian cricket history. Doug Walters kept on totting up huge scores in home-based Tests but rarely impressed on four tours of England between 1968 and 1977.

But the worth of a player to his side is not always counted by runs alone. If there were some method to measure the morale-boosting entertainment value that Walters provided, on the field and in the dressing room, he could still find himself listed as one of the very best cricketers produced by his country.

When it came to a matter of technique 'Freddie' Walters was frequently unorthodox in his approach. His method depended upon eye, timing and reflexes, and he preferred all-out assault as his counter to a threatening situation. A natural match-winner, Walters was able to turn the course of events within a short period of time.

Among his more outrageously effective shots was what Trevor Bailey has called his 'come-to-attention shot'. This consisted of a hit through mid-wicket that was preceded by a peculiar heels-together step that brought both feet facing the bowler. Two years in the army at a crucial period in his career was said to have affected his technique.

On firm wickets Walters could drive, cut and hook with safety but when the ball moved about (as in England), his less than straight backlift caused him to play too much across the line.

Walters was the fifth Australian to score a century in the first innings of his first Test when he smacked England's bowlers for 155 at Wooloongabba in 1965—66. At Sydney, versus West Indies in 1968—69, he scored 242 and 103 to become the first batsman to score a double-century and a century in the same Test.

A former wicket-keeper who gave the gloves away to become one of the finest cover-points ever seen in Australian cricket was also a batsman of note during the Chappell era. Ross Edwards may not have been a natural batsman but he certainly possessed the qualities most admired by fellow cricketers — temperament plus the ability to rise to the occasion.

A grim determination to succeed at Test level was the main ingredient in Edwards's self-made batting mix. In 1972, as stop-gap opener when Bruce Francis fell ill before start of play in the third Test at Nottingham, he ended the day with a chanceless 170 not out in 330 minutes. Edwards scored more than 1000 Test runs at an average exceeding 40, and probably saved half as many again in the field.

A more naturally gifted batsman than Edwards was the handsome Andrew Paul Sheahan but unfortunately this brilliant stroke-player never came fully to terms with the task of scoring runs consistently at Test level. Something of a glamour boy among Australian cricketers during the late 1960s, Sheahan reserved most of his best batting for Victoria.

The tall, self-composed and methodical Richard Bede McCosker was transformed by Ian Chappell from a relatively obscure but prolific number three for New South Wales into an opening batsman for Australia after the departure of Keith Stackpole had left a large gap in the Australian batting line-up.

McCosker proved a success in England in 1975 and batted heroically in the second innings of the Centenary Test against England at Melbourne in March 1977 when he scored valuable runs at number 10 after having his jaw broken by a Bob Willis bouncer in the first innings.

Graeme Donald Watson, a competitive all-rounder, was the third batsman to partner Stackpole during the 1972 Tests in England (the others were Bruce Francis and Ross Edwards)' after a remarkable recovery from a near fatal accident on the cricket field only a few months before. Playing for Australia against a World XI at Melbourne in January 1972, Watson was felled by a beamer from Tony Greig. Taken straight to hospital, the Australian batsman remained on the critical list for days and holds the dubious distinction of twice being carried off the Melbourne Cricket Ground on a stretcher — the other occasion being when he was injured during an Australian Rules football match.

McCosker's opening partner for the 1977 Centenary Test was fellow New South Wales batsman Ian Charles Davis, whose first appearance on the scene suggested that a new champion in the tradition of the Trumpers and Jacksons may have been found. The slightly built, blond and good-looking Davis impressed with his ability to drive fast bowling straight and along the ground off the back foot, but he made no real impact in Test cricket and experienced a miserable time as a batsman on his one tour to England in 1977. Another opener, left-hander Alan Turner, was a solid and compact player, noted for his strong leg-side play and a slashing and effective square cut. Turner's one gold-letter day came against West Indies at Adelaide in 1975–76 when he comprehensively collared Windies pacemen Andy Roberts and a young Michael Holding in an innings of 136.

A number of all-rounders like the pugnacious left-handed hitter Gary Gilmour and spin bowlers Kerry O'Keefe and Terry Jenner added depth to Ian Chappell's Australian team of the early 1970s but one of the main contributors to Australia's run-base in the late order was wicket-keeper 'Bacchus' Marsh.

Many of Australia's long line of glovemen have been reasonably talented batsmen – from Jack Blackham and Bert Oldfield through to Tallon, Langley and Jarman – but it is probably fair to contend that other than Don Tallon, none was good enough to take his place purely as a batsman in the Australian team.

Ian Brayshaw claims that 'any close analysis of the reasons behind the success of Australian teams under Ian Chappell would soon isolate Rodney William Marsh as a major factor'. The impact this grand player has made behind the stumps is discussed in a later chapter. A brief analysis of his batting prowess certainly cannot be overlooked.

A Bill Lawry declaration deprived Rodney Marsh of the first-ever century in a Test by an Australian wicket-keeper when Marsh was left high and dry on 92 not out versus England at Melbourne in the third Test of 1970–71. In England in 1972 the roly-poly 'Mr Everywhere' again came close to his goal with a defiant and bludgeoning 91 (four sixes, nine fours) in two hours at Old Trafford. Six months later Marsh set the record straight with a brilliant 118 off Pakistan at Adelaide.

The 1975–76 season saw the 'Chappell era' move into new gear when Ian Chappell handed over the Australian captaincy against West Indies to his younger brother. Greg Chappell's initial stint as skipper of his country was to be short-lived. Older brother Ian took over again when the 'Packer circus' started in earnest two years later.

Of the batsmen who came under Greg Chappell's influence, the

Opposite: Greg Chappell has scored most Test runs for Australia and must be placed on the list of the top 10 batsmen to play for his country.

red-haired and amply proportioned right-hander Gary John Cosier flavoured his first appearance in the Test match cauldron with a spicy 109 off the West Indian bowlers at the Melbourne Cricket Ground. The bulky, wise-cracking Cosier lacked consistency and an occasional burst of success was interspersed with periods of failure.

Polished left-hander Graham Yallop made his debut against West Indies two years before the Packer revolution but also elected to support the Australian Cricket Board when the mass 'defection' took place. How ironical that eight years later he should partake in a 'rebel' tour to South Africa.

Yallop battled gamely in the West Indies with Simpson's second-string team in 1977–78. When Australia's veteran caretaker captain refused the Australian Board's terms for 1978–79, Yallop took over the leadership against Mike Brearley's well-drilled England XI. Although he scored most runs for Australia that season, Yallop's inexperience as captain showed up sharply. Unfriendly media response did not assist his cause and he has since played irregularly for Australia – but has scored heavily when given the chance. Yallop's Test innings of a lifetime was a magnificent 268 off Pakistan in 1983–84 in front of his home crowd at the Melbourne Cricket Ground.

Among the remaining pre-Packer Test players, Craig Stanton Serjeant was a well-built right-hander who hit his maiden Test 100 against West Indies at Georgetown in 1977–78 but could not hold his place in the Australian team while David William Hookes remains an irrepressible but enigmatic stroke-playing left-hander. Hookes first drew banner headlines when he smacked a surprised England captain Tony Greig for five consecutive fours during the 1977 Centenary Test. What the tall and strongly-built Hookes lacks in technical perfection he makes up for in enthusiasm and determination but his progress at Test level has been somewhat disjointed.

But he remains an exciting and entertaining batsman whose record of the fastest century in Australian cricket may stand for many years. Hookes reached that famous 100 off 34 balls in only 43 minutes in the second innings of a South Australia-Victoria match at Adelaide in 1982–83. His feat was made even more remarkable by the fact that he actually scored two centuries (137 and 107) in the game.

The advent of World Series cricket created unexpected opportunities for budding young Australian batsmen. Bobby Simpson played chaperone to no fewer than 14 Test debutantes during the 1977–78 India series, plus the tour to the West Indies that followed in the same season, including left-handed opener Paul Anthony Hibbert, the bearded Alan David Ogilvie, and leg-spinning all-rounder Anthony Longford Mann (who surprised both his fellows and the Indian bowlers during the second Test at Perth in 1977–78 when he clobbered his way to 105 to become the first night-watchman in history to score a Test century).

Against India, the dashing Peter Michael Toohey placed the ball with great power and looked to be the find of the series. Recovering from a broken thumb on the subsequent trip to the West Indies, he made 122 and 97 in the final riot-ruined Test at Kingston but never again matched that heady achievement.

Dogged opener John Dyson lasted a while longer in the Australian team. A batsman cast in the Woodfull mould, Dyson could also supply an attractive array of strokes on demand and scored a defiant 127 not out against the West Indies at Sydney in 1981–82. When he failed to gain a spot in the 1985 Ashes squad, Dyson sought greener fields in South Africa with Kim Hughes's rebels.

It has been claimed that only the introduction of the batting helmet in cricket has kept alive South Australia's impulsive hooker Rick Darling. The highly-strung Warwick Maxwell Darling infrequently produced the form that saw him picked for Australia in 1977–78. His opening partner on his debut Test at Adelaide in 1977–78, Graeme Malcolm Wood, was one of the few Packer interlude newcomers who managed to hold a place in the Australian team when the air was finally cleared and the World Series players returned to the mainstream for the 1979–80 season.

Wood weathered many a storm to become one of his country's most seasoned players. A gritty left-hander with a strong will to win, he frequently confirmed his ability to handle quick bowling, although he has been criticised constantly for 'suicidal' running between the wickets. Wood's high point in Test cricket was reached at Lord's in 1980 when he fought his way to a grand 112 in the Centenary Test against England.

Bruce Malcolm Laird was a plucky opener who combined for a while with Wood in a fruitful first-wicket partnership. A consistent right-handed grafter, Laird was unfortunate to suffer an achilles tendon injury after a grand start against West Indies in 1979–80. As an expert at dealing with pace bowling, he would have been an automatic choice both during and after the WSC split if he had remained with the establishment.

One major batsman who made his first Test appearance shortly before World Series Cricket deserves more than a fleeting mention. The sensitive and talented Kimberley John Hughes has seldom found himself far removed from controversy during his exceptionally distinguished career for Australia.

It is perhaps only his own apparent hesitancy at the start of an innings that has prevented this oft explosive right-hander from being accepted in the same class as Greg Chappell. And it has, ironically, been an unfortunate and bewildering captaincy policy that has led to the frustration that came so dramatically to a boil when Hughes tearfully resigned from the Australian leadership in 1984–85.

Kim Hughes did not enjoy an exceptionally exciting first Test series against India in 1977–78 and was injured before he could get going on Simpson's West Indies tour that followed. An uncharacteristically slow maiden Test century came against England the following season but, given the captaincy of Australia for the first time on a trip to India in 1979–80 (just before the return of the World Series players), Hughes celebrated in expansive fashion with 594 runs in the Test series. Handing the captaincy back to a now re-legitimised Greg Chappell, Hughes continued his fine batting run against the West Indies in Australia the same season.

The 12 months between September 1979 and September 1980 were to be the happiest and most uncontroversial of Hughes's career. His brilliant stroke-play was the most memorable feature of the Lord's Centenary Test in 1980 and saw Hughes chosen as one of the *Five Cricketers of the Year*. Kim Hughes was the man of the moment with what *Wisden* described as 'a smorgasbord of strokes'. His first innings 100 included three sixes and 14 fours and, as if not content with the shots he had demonstrated in his original cordon bleu class, Hughes 'tickled the palate with a lot of new ones' in the second innings. England fast bowler Chris Old, for instance, was said to have been left gasping in disbelief when Hughes landed the ball on the pavilion top deck after hitting on the run three strides down the pitch. Now it seems certain that Kim Hughes and several other highly competent Australian batsmen will be permanently lost to Australian cricket because of their decision to play in South Africa.

One other major Australian batsman who first played during the 'Chappell' period remains to be reviewed. Allan Border, in his capacity as current Australian captain and resident batting supremo, belongs to the current generation and will be discussed in a later chapter.

33

World Series interlude

'...a remarkable series of events which shattered the staid and well-ordered corridors of cricket like a nuclear explosion'
— Peter McFarline

The revelation that Australian media tycoon Kerry Packer had signed most of the world's leading cricketers to take part in a series of privately organised international matches in Australia in 1977–78 shattered the resident cricket establishments in all the major cricketing countries. Bar one that is, for South Africa was still languishing in the wilderness of isolation and its cricketers and administrators looked on Mr Packer's gambit as a grand opportunity to show the world that there were still some very good Springbok players around.

The story of the covert preparations that led to the formation of the so-called 'Packer circus' and the denouncement of that epsiode in cricket's history has been amply chronicled over the years. Suffice to say that, for the best part of two years, the world's most outstanding players were lost to official Test cricket. The matches played under the auspices of World Series Cricket (WSC) were not accorded first-class status. The cricketers who took part in these games were most certainly first-class players and many of the official Tests played during 1977–78 and 1978–79 must themselves become dubious entries in a fair-minded directory of international cricket.

The pros and cons regarding the status of the WSC matches have been frequently discussed and it is accepted that, due to the technical definition of a first-class match as being 'a match of three days' duration (or more) between two sides of eleven players officially adjudged first-class', the WSC games cannot be accepted as first-class. The operative words in the definition of a first-class match are 'oofficially adjudged first-class'. This judgement can only be made by an official 'governing body', such as the foundation members, full members and associate members of the International Cricket Conference, which means that there is no way that the WSC matches can be made first-class without a retrospective amendment to the articles of the ICC.

Incidentally, South Africa, in terms of the ICC guidelines, is still regarded as a foundation member of that organisation and the proposed move by the Australian Cricket Board to regard matches played in South Africa by an Australian 'rebel' team as not first-class is 'illegal' in terms of the rules and regulations of the international cricket administrative body, of which South Africa was also a founder member.

Whether or not the games played by WSC in Australia and the West Indies in 1977−78 and 1978−79 are ever accorded the honour of first-class recognition remains unimportant, other than as a statistical event. The matches themselves were toughly fought contests between extremely powerful sides and produced some excellent cricket and more than a fair amount of high quality batsmanship. Unable to use regular cricket venues, the matches were played at the Showground in Sydney, VFL (Victoria Football League) Park in Melbourne, Football Park in Adelaide and Gloucester Park in Perth.

In the first WSC season, Australia played two 'series' of three matches each against West Indies and a combined World XI (which included West Indian players). In the first round, three centuries were logged, all in the third match at Football Park in Adelaide − Ian Chappell (141) and Bruce Laird (106) for Australia; Viv Richards (123) for West Indies.

The second round brought some phenomenal scoring with South African Barry Richards in great form (including a stunning 207 at Perth). Greg Chappell then made the WSC top score of the year when he smashed 246 not out at Melbourne in a match that provided Australia with its only win in three games. Rick McCosker (129) helped Greg Chappell add 199 for the second wicket in Australia's first innings. The younger Chappell had made 174 in the previous match at Sydney and Viv Richards played innings of 119 (at Sydney), 177 (at Perth) and 170 (at Melbourne).

At Perth the World XI raced to 625 against Australia (B A Richards 207, Gordon Greenidge 140, I V A Richards 177) in only 113.3 overs − a rate of 5.5 runs an over!

In 1978−79 a full three-team tournament was held involving Australia, West Indies and a WSC World XI in which each side played three games, the World XI running out easy winners in each of their fixtures.

The WSC World XI was reinforced by the inclusion of the South Africans Clive Rice and Garth Le Roux (Graeme Pollock and top South African spin bowler Denys Hobson travelled to Australia but were left out after a ruling that only regular professional South Africans were eligible).

Barry Richards smacked a match-winning 101 not out versus Australia at Sydney while another South African, left-hander Kepler Wessels, played admirably for Australia, scoring 126 versus West Indies at Melbourne. Another left-hander, David Hookes, hit 116 and 56 off the West Indies attack at Melbourne and was Australia's only consistent batsman.

In a feast of run-making, other successful World XI batsmen included the Pakistanis Asif Iqbal (who captained the team and

Politics denied Barry
Richards his opportunity in
international Test cricket
but the South African
demonstrated his class in
Packer's World Series
Cricket.

scored 107 versus West Indies at Sydney), Majid Khan and Zaheer
Abbas. For West Indies, Viv Richards disappointed but Lawrence
Rowe batted magnificently against the World XI at Sydney (he
scored 85) and hit the highest score of the season (175) versus
Australia at Melbourne.

The Australian and West Indies teams then travelled to the Caribbean for a rubber of five full 'supertests'. A rather stormy series
marred by rain and riots ended with each side claiming one victory;
three games were drawn. 'Supercat' Clive Lloyd demolished the
Australian bowlers in the first 'Supertest' at Kingston, hitting 56 and
197 (West Indies won by 369 runs). With Australia in the driving
seat (Ian Chappell 61 and 86, Greg Chappell 45 and 90), the second

game at Bridgetown was interrupted by a spate of bottle-throwing and had to be left drawn. At Port of Spain in the third match, Bruce Laird (122) and Greg Chappell (150) gave Australia sufficient runs to force victory. Then bad weather and the worst rioting experienced in the series ruined the fourth game at Georgetown, after Greg Chappell (113 for Australia) and Collis King (110 for West Indies) had posted centuries. More rain spoilt the final 'supertest' at St John's, but not before Greg Chappell (104 and 85), Rodney Marsh (a whirlwind second innings 102 not out) and Lawrence Rowe (135) had left their mark.

The following Australian season, things were back to 'normal', the Packer interegnum not quite forgotten (or in some quarters forgiven). Kerry Packer's company PBL Marketing took over the promotion of cricket for the Australian Cricket Board, and his television network gained sole rights to screen the game in Australia.

One on-the-field legacy of the 'Packer circus' remained in what is now known as the Benson & Hedges World Series of international limited over one-day matches. Limited over cricket had been one of the outstanding features of the original WSC and is now an integral and highly necessary part of international cricket's financial base. The truncated version of the game certainly calls for some modification in batting attitude and style with, at times, a scorning of the basic principles of batsmanship.

One-day cricket has come to stay and certainly has its highly lucrative and entertaining place in the structure of modern cricket, but any move towards it becoming the *only* form of international cricket would ultimately bring with it, according to most sound judges, such a fall in skill and standards that the death-knell would be heard of cricket as a spectator sport.

One important innovation that was fostered by Mr Packer to protect his investment, after he had observed Australia's David Hookes being struck on his bare head by a bouncer, was the batting helmet − a piece of equipment that has since become as much part and parcel of the game as the bat and pads themselves.

Off the field, the Packer demarche has certainly resulted in an elevation of the status and earning potential of the players themselves, which history may eventually record as a justification for the entire operation.

34

'Sunny'

'...a run machine, one of the greatest batsmen India has produced'
— Dilip Vengsarkar

Leading Indian batsman Dilip Vengsarkar first batted together with Sunil Manohar Gavaskar in a first-class match for Bombay when only 18 years old and scarcely out of short pants. In an article in *Cricket Lifestyle*, Vengsarkar describes his esteemed Test team companion as a player 'who shows a scant regard for records and who goes about shattering them in a dedicated manner as though he was born into the world solely for the purpose'.

'Sunny' Gavaskar has now retired from Test cricket as the only player to have topped 10,000 Test runs — a unique and remarkable record which places him beyond even the great Sir Donald Bradman, whom he has also beaten in the matter of Test hundreds (34 to Gavaskar; 29 to Bradman).

Of current players, only Allan Border appears as a possible challenger for the 10,000-run mark. At the age of 32, Border has now passed 7000 and, if he lasts as long as Gavaskar did (the Indian retired aged 39), the Australian may still find himself at the top of the tree one day.

With Gavaskar easily leading the field, the top five Test run-getters of all time are (as at end of 1986–87 season):

Batsman	Tests	Innings	NO	Runs	H.S.	Avrge	100s
S M Gavaskar (India)	125	214	26	10,122	236*	50.16	34
G Boycott (England)	108	193	23	8,114	246*	47.63	22
G S Sobers (W Indies)	93	160	21	8,032	365*	57.78	26
M M Cowdrey (England)	114	188	15	7,624	182	44.07	22
C H Lloyd (W Indies)	110	175	14	7,515	242*	46.68	19

A comparison of Gavaskar with Sir Donald Bradman reveals that apart from the huge disparity in average runs per innings (Gavaskar 50.16; Bradman 99.94), Bradman scored 29 centuries in his first 51 Tests — it took Gavaskar 94 Tests to reach the same target. Gavaskar's record-breaking 30th Test century was also his highest — 236 not out versus West Indies in the sixth Test at Madras in 1983–84.

Sir Donald stands alone when it comes to a discussion of Test batsmen but (to repeat again the oft-quoted words of English poet

John Donne) '...comparisons are odious', and there can be no just disparaging of the achievements put up by the little Indian batting master from Bombay (or Mumbai as it has recently become known). One fact of life in modern Test cricket that Sir Donald did not have to contend with (other than in the notorious 1932−33 bodyline series) is the seemingly inevitable battery of three or four fast bowlers in almost every international cricket team, a phenomenon which Gavaskar has usually handled with great courage and aplomb.

When it comes to a matter of style, the first thing one notices about the tiny 5 ft 4½ in (164 cm) Sunil Gavaskar's batting method is the straightness of his bat. If there is a stroke he appears to enjoy playing above all others it is possibly the front-foot straight drive. But in an age of predominantly short-pitched fast bowling, he has been forced to become a master of back-foot play. More of a utilitarian craftsman than an artist, his one shot which can be described as 'graceful' is the square cut. His one occasionally risky stroke is his hook into the air.

Gavaskar must surely be one of the finest players of fast bowling in the world and it seems peculiar that he has often had to be cajoled into opening the innings for India. At 37, he is perhaps wary of the possibility that his sharp reflexes may be on the wane.

Against the West Indies fast bowlers on their home Caribbean turf in 1970−71 in his own first Test series, the 21-year-old sun-hatted Gavaskar totalled 774 runs (the most by an Indian in a series) at an average of 154.80 in only four Tests (injury kept him out of the first game). He has seldom looked back and only illness or injury has kept him out of the Indian team for any length of time. In Australia in 1977−78 he scored three centuries in five Tests and confirmed his liking for the conditions with two big scores (166 not out − first Test, Adelaide; 172 − third Test, Sydney) in the three-match 1985−86 series.

A breakdown of the broad-batted Gavaskar's Test century scores reveals that he has reached three figures against each of the countries India has played. The list reads: West Indies − 13; Australia − eight; Pakistan − five; England − four; New Zealand − two; Sri Lanka − two; total − 34. The high proportion of centuries against West Indies confirms his ability in handling fast bowling. He is also the only batsman to have scored three Test double-centuries against West Indies. Gavaskar is also the only batsman to have three times scored a century in each innings of a Test.

Sunny Gavaskar's brother-in-law, Gundappa Rangnath Viswanath, was, with Gavaskar, one of the twin-pillars of India's run-scoring in the 1970s. Even smaller than the man whose sister he married, Viswanath marked his debut versus Australia in the second Test at Kanpur in 1969−70 with a second innings 137.

He was a dynamic and stylish little batsman who even made a

Opposite: The diminutive Indian master Sunil 'Sunny' Gavaskar has now scored more Test runs and centuries than any other player.

defensive stroke into a thing of beauty. The tiny 5 ft 2 in (157 cm) 'Vishy' played drives that reminded onlookers of Hazare at his best; his cuts evoked memories of Manjrekar. The gutsy little Indian was also a daring hooker against quick bowling and played a delightfully delicate leg-glance. Rusi Modi called him 'a classical batsman with a ruthless approach to the game....'.

Against England in the fifth Test at Bombay in 1972−73, Viswanath became the first Indian batsman who scored a century on debut to add a second century to his bag. The previous century on debut men, Lala Amarnath (1933−34), Deepak Shodhan (1952−53), Kripal Singh (1955−56) Abbas Ali Baig (1959) and Hanumant Singh (1963−64) never again scored a hundred in a Test.

The 6 ft plus (183 cm) and well built Ajit Laxman Wadekar was an attacking left-hander who made his debut against West Indies in 1966−67, a few years before Gavaskar and Viswanath, and distinguished himself by hooking the great fast bowler Wes Hall for six into the stand at Madras.

The name 'Ajit' translates into 'unbeatable' and, in 1971, Wadekar led India in its first Test series win in England. Wadekar played some decisive cricket and in a low-scoring and crucial final Test, his batting proved almost as valuable to India as the magical spin bowling of Bhagwat Chandrasekhar. Wadekar and his team returned home to a heroes' welcome.

In 1972−73 he repeated his 1971 leadership feat when he captained India to a home series victory after England had won the first Test at Delhi. Wadekar also played two exceptional innings that year − 90 at Kanpur in the fourth Test and 87 at Bombay in the fifth.

The amply-proportioned son of past Indian cricketing great Vinoo Mankad made his debut as an opening batsman in Wadekar's 1971 team. Ashok Vinoo Mulwantrai Mankad enjoyed one outstanding series against Australia in India in 1969−70 when he scored 347 runs in eight innings with a top score of 97 at Delhi in the third Test.

Another Indian opener who can count a score of 97 as his best in Tests is the phlegmatic and diminutive Chetandra Pratap Singh Chauhan who appeared in 40 Tests following his debut versus Australia in India 1969−70. Chetan Chauhan played his best Test cricket on two trips to Australia, in 1977−78 and 1980−81. On the second tour, in a three-match Test series, he logged his top score of 97 at Adelaide.

The lanky and bespectacled Anshuman Dattajirao Gaekwad is the son of former Indian captain D K Gaekwad and an opening batsman who has been in and out of the Indian team since his debut against West Indies in 1974−75. A D Gaekwad has scored two widely spaced Test centuries − 102 versus West Indies at Kanpur in the sixth Test of 1978−79 and 201 versus Pakistan at Jullundar in 1983−84.

When Chetan Chauhan decided to settle in Australia for a while, his opening spot was initially taken by the ebullient Krishnamachari Srikkanth, an irrepressible dasher of a batsman who is a student of numerology. The impetuous Indian opener, who sings film songs or *slokas* to himself while batting, comes from a family who have a strong belief in numerology — he added an 'h' to his original name Srikkant to attract more favourable 'vibes'!

'Krish' Srikkanth has made a name for himself in limited overs cricket, but was an inconsistent performer in Tests until he made an effort to tighten up his defence in Australia in 1985—86. Batting with a refreshing blend of responsibility and panache, Srikkanth came right when in Australia and logged his first Test century at Melbourne in just over three hours.

India has not been short of classy middle-order batsmen over the past decade or so: men like Brijesh Parsuram Patel, a scintillating but rather wayward stroke player; the consistent Yashpal Sharma, a short man but a strong on-side player; and the tall and debonair Sandeep Madhusudan Patil.

Patil is an Indian film star and something of a national idol. He is also a wonderful attacking right-hander who batted with great flair when he was still in the Indian team and played a couple of unforgettably powerful Test innings. India's current number one wicketkeeper, Syed Mutjaba Hussan Kirmani, has often batted well in a crisis and has hit three Test centuries.

The 6 ft 3 in (190 cm) and highly talented all-rounder Ravishankar Jayadritha Shastri has compiled six Test 100s to date. As a left-arm spin bowler and a versatile right-hand batsman who can bat anywhere in the order, the cool and unruffled Shastri was accused of slow batting in the Tests against England in 1984—85 but went to the other extreme for Bombay versus Baroda when he raced to 200 in 113 minutes off 123 balls to beat by seven minutes the world record for a double-hundred. The Indian hitter also equalled Sir Garfield Sobers's record of six sixes in one over, off spinner Tilak Raj, and became the fifth batsman in history to score 13 sixes in an innings (the record is 15 sixes by New Zealander John Reid).

Sobers's record six hits off Glamorgan's Malcolm Nash were recorded by television cameras; Shastri's effort will remain only in the memories of those who witnessed it — there were about 1000 spectators present in the vast Wankhede Stadium but not a television camera in sight.

Mohinder Bhardwaj Amarnath, one of two Test-playing sons of India's first Test centurion Lala Amarnath, was for a while something of an enigma in international cricket. The impressively orthodox 'Jimmy' Amarnath made his debut for India as early as 1969—70 as an opening bowler versus Australia and soon established a regular place in the Indian team. He then sustained a fractured skull in

1979, trying to hook New Zealander Richard Hadlee when the Indians played Nottinghamshire on their England tour. For years he had refused to wear a helmet, preferring to don a solar topee in imitation of his famous father.

When recalled by his country's selectors in 1983, Amarnath had altered his orthodox side-on batting stance to an open-chested one, and surprised the cricketing world with more than 1000 Test runs in a calendar year, including 598 in the Caribbean against the blistering West Indies pace attack and with bold and frequent hooking a feature of his batting.

Then, inexplicably, Amarnath became every bowler's sitting duck with a run of five noughts in six Test innings against the West Indies in India in 1983–84. He has since recovered from this traumatic experience and reached his 10th Test century against Australia in 1985–86.

Mohinder's older brother by two years, Surinder Bhardwaj Amarnath, was a wristy left-handed batsman who had a brief spell in the Indian team between 1975 and 1980 and who emulated his famous father when he became the seventh Indian batsman to score a century on his Test debut (124 versus New Zealand in the first Test at Auckland in 1975–76).

Of the current powerful and talented India batting line-up, Dilip Balwant Vengsarkar, at 30, can already be classed as a veteran international cricketer. Since his 1975–76 debut, Vengsarkar has been an automatic choice for the Indian Test team.

One of India's more reliable performers, he is a tall, upright player who handles pace bowling with particular efficiency. Vengsarkar holds the honour of being the only Indian batsman to have hit more than one Test century at Lord's (he has now hit three). During the calendar year 1979, he compiled 1174 Test runs. Against the West Indians in the third Test at Calcutta in 1978–79, Vengsarkar (157 not out) and Sunil Gavaskar (182 not out) notched an Indian record-breaking partnership for all Tests of 344 runs for the second wicket.

Dilip Vengsarkar's 157 in the first Test against England at Lord's in 1982 was a brilliant affair when India was in a tight corner. The Indian stroke-player took the fight to the English bowlers when he hit 86 between lunch and tea with some gloriously powerful shots. Vengsarkar's great effort set the scene for what *Wisden* described as a 'spectacularly violent piece of batting' from ace all-rounder Kapil Dev.

As a pace bowler, Ramlal Nikhanj Kapil Dev is, for an Indian, quite unique and can be placed alongside Malcolm Marshall, Imran Kahn, Dennis Lillee and Richard Hadlee as one of the most potent new-ball exponents of the past decade. In batting, Kapil Dev generally dispenses with all preliminaries and launches straight into all-out attack. The consistency and clarity of his hitting is perhaps only

Opposite: Mohinder Amarnath has weathered many ups and downs in his Test career for India but his final figures are impressive.

Ravi Shastri is still going strong for India in Tests and in the Ranji Trophy equalled Gary Sobers's famous six-hitting record.

Mohammad Azharuddin is India's shining batting star of the future.

rivalled by Viv Richards and Ian Botham at their best. His method is uncomplicated, his timing superb.

During his rapid-fire innings of 89 out of 117 runs added in 15 overs at Lord's in 1982, Kapil Dev was well on course for the fastest ever Test century. He was out after facing only 55 balls and hit 13 fours and three sixes. Kapil then took England's first three wickets in four overs and, as *Wisden* put it, 'enjoyed as glorious a session of play as any immortal of the game'.

India's current young batting supremo is the 5 ft 11 in (180 cm) and slender Mohammed Azharuddin who, at 21, made an unprecedented start to a Test career with a century in each of his first three matches (versus England in 1984–85). Known to his team-mates as 'Ajju', he is the only Muslim in the current Hindu dominated Indian team and called by Indian writer R Mohan 'the bashful prophet'.

Azharuddin burst onto the cricket scene like a warrior riding in from the desert with flashing scimitar. The majestic young stylist has since kept on waving his magic bat to torment his opponents and delight his many followers. Although he has enjoyed little formal coaching, Azharuddin's technique is nigh faultless. He has, it must be said, that indefinable quality of genius that seems to be the prerogative of the natural-born cricketer. He confesses to never having read a book on cricket and affirms that he did not receive any coaching at school. When he attended official coaching camps run by the South Zone cricket authorities (under Lala Amarnath) at the age of 17, he confesses: 'There was nothing new that I learnt.'

He has not yet quite lived up to the vision he created of a new international batting maestro against England in 1984–85, but Mohammed Azharuddin is the bearer of the Indian batting torch into the future — together with players like Arun Lal and Raman Lamba, and the rising stars, Vijay Raman, Ajay Sharma and Sanjay Manjrekar (son of Vijay).

35

The Red Lion

'Anyone watching the Sri Lankans on their England tour must have been struck by their seemingly old-fashioned approach to the game'
— Wisden 1982

The writer's first impression of Sri Lankan batsmen came at Newlands, Cape Town, in October 1982 when a pair of tiny openers proceeded to hook, cut and drive from the very first ball sent down to them in a reckless devil-may-care style that was, at one and the same time, highly entertaining and nail-bitingly risky.

The rebel 'Arosa Sri Lanka' team which played in South Africa was a weak combination somewhat short of 'first-class' standard and the flashy stroke-play of its batsmen soon led to their downfall.

The next encounter with Sri Lankan batsmen was at Sydney Cricket Ground in January 1985 in a limited over match. The sight of pint-sized Aravinda de Silva 'charging' Australia's number one paceman Geoff Lawson and driving the bowler back over his head for a glorious six will always remain clearly etched in my personal file of outstanding cricketing memories.

As Sidath Wettimuny so effectively demonstrated in his record-breaking 10 and a half hour plus innings at Lord's in 1984, not all Sri Lanka's batsmen are of the impatient breed but, by and large, the typical cricketer from the island State that was previously called Ceylon is noted for his carefree and exhilarating 'get-on-with-the-game' batting method.

Cricket in Sri Lanka has a long history. The *Colombo Journal* of 5 September 1832 contained a notice calling on all those who wished to form a cricket club to meet and the Colombo Cricket Club was formed on 8 September 1832.

Down the years there have been a succession of exciting batsmen who have performed with skill and success against the occasional touring team passing by sea through Colombo, on the Indian mainland and in club, university and county cricket in England.

Men like F C 'Derrick' de Saram, who played for Oxford University and was by all reports the finest pre-war batsman from Ceylon. De Saram hit a dazzling 128 for Oxford off the 1934 touring Australians and, according to *Wisden*, treated Clarrie Grimmett 'with a disrespect of which few Test batsmen have shown themselves capable'. Described as a 'complete batsman' who combined wristy stroke-play with a strong defence, de Saram played for and captained Ceylon between 1949 and 1954. In 1962, at the age of 50, he was sentenced to a long term of imprisonment for conspiring to overthrow the Singalese government of the day. He died in 1983, aged 70.

Other pre-war Ceylon batsmen of note were Dr Churchill Gunasekara (who also played for Middlesex); L D S 'Chippy' Gunasekara, a left-handed opening batsman who skippered Ceylon against Jack Ryder's Australians in 1935; S S 'Sargo' Jayawickreme, who rivalled de Saram as a batsman between the wars; P D McCarthy; and Mahadevan Sathasivam.

De Sarem, Jayawickreme and Sathasivam all played for Ceylon against the touring West Indies team in 1948−49. De Sarem hit 94 in the second of two first-class matches. M Roderigo, an opener, carried his bat for 135 not out in a total of 318 in the first match against West Indies.

C I Gunasekara was another batsman who did well against the West Indies and against Commonwealth teams. When the MCC made made its first post-war tour of the Indian sub-continent in 1951−52, he scored 135 and helped Australia's Keith Miller add 207 runs in 150 minutes for the fourth wicket for a Commonwealth XI at Colombo.

Between 1952−53 and 1982−83, Ceylon (Sri Lanka after 1970−71) played an annual match versus the Indian State of Tamil Nadu, as well as fairly regular unofficial 'Tests' against India and Pakistan. Many good batsmen emerged from these encounters and, prior to Sri Lanka's first Test against England at Colombo in 1981−82, names like Michael Tissera, P Derek Heyn, Stanley Jayasinghe and Anura Tennekoon were very prominent. The copybook Tissera was, with Jayasinghe, a leading run-getter during the early 1960s. Stanley Jayasinghe joined Leicestershire in 1961 and four times scored more than 1000 runs in English county cricket seasons.

A number of Sri Lankan-born batsmen appeared in county cricket, including Clive Clay Inman (Leicestershire), who holds the world record for the fastest 50 in a first-class match, and Ladislaw 'Laddie' Outschoorn, who scored more than 15,000 runs for Worcestershire between 1946 and 1959 but did not appear in his home country.

Anura Punchi Banda Tennekoon was a dashing batsman who led Sri Lanka in the first two Prudential Cup world limited over tournaments in England in 1975 and 1979. When Sri Lanka replied to Australia's mammoth 328 for five wickets in a preliminary round match at the Oval in 1975 with 276 for four wickets, Anura Tennekoon hit 48 in fine style. In 1968−69 he hit 101 against an MCC team at Colombo.

Future official Test batsmen who played in the first two Prudential Cup tourneys included Sri Lanka's first Test captain, Bandula Warnapura, current skipper Duleep Mendis, Arnura Ranasinghe (with Warnapura a 'defector' to South Africa in 1982−83), Roy Dias and Ranjan Madugalle.

S R de S (Sunil) Wettimuny, older brother of Sri Lanka's current opening batsman, Sidath Wettimuny, was also an accomplished opener and unlucky to have played his best cricket before his country was accepted into the Test fold. In the famous Prudential preliminary against Australia at the Oval in 1975 he hit a sparkling 53 before retiring after twice being hit by balls from Jeff Thomson.

In England in 1981, during a non-Test tour, Sidath Wettimuny, Duleep Mendis, Roy Dias and others gave spectators a foretaste of the sparkling, if at times reckless, stroke-play that has become the hallmark of Sri Lankan batting.

Bandula Warnapura, Sri Lanka's captain in its first historic Test versus England at the Saravanamuttu Oval in Colombo in February 1982, had the singular honour of facing the first ball bowled to a Sri Lankan in a full official international match, but when he chose to lead the breakaway Sri Lankan team in South Africa, effectively severed all further connection with official Test cricket. His opening partner in that first Sri Lankan Test was to achieve great success in international cricket and make some history of his own at the home of cricket, Lord's.

Sidath Wettimuny, a technically correct player, was a first-choice opener after being capped against England 1981−82 and until his premature retirement following the 1986−87 tour of India. The son of an author of Buddhist books, he has an ideal temperament for the big occasion.

Wettimuny notched his country's first Test 100 − a brilliant 157 off the Pakistan attack at Faisalabad in 1981−82. A year later, against New Zealand at Christchurch, he carried his bat through a Test innings for 63, the first Sri Lankan to do so. In addition, he opened that innings with his younger brother Mithra, a family affair which last occurred when the brothers W G and E M Grace opened for England at the Oval in 1880.

In the inaugural England-Sri Lanka Test on English soil at Lord's in 1984, the consistent opener played a monumental innings of 190 (the highest score by a batsman playing his first Test in England), giving a classical demonstration of text book batting while occupying the crease for 637 minutes.

Sidath Wettimuny claims that one of the greatest influences on his batsmanship has been the English 'Golden Age' batsman, C B Fry. His father, Ramsey Wettimuny, was chief engineer to the Ceylon Transport Board and, when he visited England he brought back with him C B Fry's 1912 publication, *Batsmanship*. Wettimuny senior then built what is believed to be Sri Lanka's first indoor cricket school and proceeded to instil into his sons Fry's principles of batsmanship.

Cheery and chubby Louis Rohan Duleep Mendis was named by his cricket-loving parents after the great Indian batsman K S Duleepsinhji. The 5 ft 4 in (162 cm) batsman has certainly justified the choice of name. With a distinctive cavalier approach to batting,

The patient Sidath Wettimuny scored a century in Sri Lanka's first Test at the home of cricket, Lord's.

Mendis reached his personal peak when he joined the immortal Sir Donald Bradman and West Indian Everton Weekes as one of only three players to hit two 100s in a Test match against India (105 and 105 at Madras in 1982–83).

In September 1985, Mendis created a sensation when he and Roy Dias each hit second innings match-saving 100s in the third Test at Kandy. A draw in the final game of a three-match series versus India created history: Sri Lanka's first series victory (with a first-ever Test win in the second game at Colombo).

Mendis has played in all three World Cup tournaments in England and claimed the Man of the Match award in a surprise win for Sri Lanka over India in 1979. Sri Lanka's leading Test batsman is an aggressive stroke-player who is particularly quick when going on the hook, but he was forced to adjust his technique after the insertion of a permanent steel pin in his right index finger, broken by a ball from Dayle Hadlee at Christchurch in 1983.

In Sri Lanka's first Test in England at Lord's in 1984, he struck a quick-fire 100 off only 113 balls (including three hooked sixes off Ian Botham) and followed up with another rapid innings of 94 off 97 balls when Sri Lanka batted a second time.

Main support for Mendis and Sidath Wettimuny in Sri Lanka's early Test years has come from the 5 ft 6 in (167 cm) package of batting dynamite, Roy Luke Dias. A right-hander like Mendis and Wettimuny, Dias is a dedicated cricketer who hails from a family of sportsmen. He hit his maiden Test 100 against Pakistan in Sri Lanka's fourth international outing (versus Pakistan in the third Test at Lahore in 1981–82) and included four 50s in his first six Tests.

Dias is a stylish, correct player who loves to get on with the game and who usually walks in with the knowledge that he already has runs in the bank following his impeccable fielding in the covers.

Two Sri Lankan batsmen, right-hander Ranjan Madugalle and left-hander Arjuna Ranatunga, captain and vice-captain respectively of the 1987–88 team to Australia, both played in the inaugural Test versus England in 1981–82 and each scored his first Test century versus India in the first Test at Colombo in 1985–86.

The dashing Arjuna Ranatunga was, at 18 years and 78 days, the youngest Sri Lankan to play in a Test when he scored 54 in his debut innings against England (leg-spin bowler Sanjeeva Weerasinghe, at 17 years 189 days, is now the youngest Sri Lankan Test player). Ranjan Senarath Madugalle is a less flamboyant player but an automatiic Sri Lankan choice since that country's entry into Test cricket.

Reserve wicket-keeper Sampathage Amal Rohita Silva opened the innings in Sri Lanka's first Test on English soil at Lord's in 1984. Dismissed for eight in the first innings, the left-handed Amal Silva batted with rare aplomb to score 102 not out second time around. Against India in 1985–86, the quicksilver gloveman again distinguished himself with a century and at least three world records: nine catches in a Test in two successive Tests; 22 dismissals (21 caught, one stumped) in a three-match series; a century plus nine dismissals in a single Test. Silva has also made something of a name for himself as a limited overs expert.

Another Sri Lankan wicket-keeper/batsman, Don Sardha Brendon Priyantha Kuruppu, played in 22 limited overs internationals before gaining his first Test cap versus New Zealand at Colombo in April 1987. He immediately celebrated the occasion, and consolidated his position in the Sri Lankan team with a record-shattering 201 not out. A fine timer of the ball, Kuruppu has, in one-day games, often batted in an electrifying fashion. In his sole Test innings he played completely out of character for 777 weary (for the New Zealand bowlers) minutes — the third longest knock in Test history, behind Hanif Mohammed (337 in 970 minutes) and Len Hutton (364 in 797 minutes). It was the longest innings ever by a player on debut and Sri Lanka's first Test double-hundred. His 201 not out (out of 397 for 9 wickets) was also the slowest double-century in Tests, 'beating' Anshuman Gaekwad of India, 652 minutes versus Pakistan at Jullunder in 1983–84.

Kuruppu set a host of other records: first Sri Lankan to score a century on debut; highest Test score by a Sri Lankan; first wicket-keeper to score a Test double-century on debut. And, by opening the batting and keeping wicket, he became the first Test player to be on the field all five days in his first Test — with pads on throughout!

The irrepressible, hard-hitting Pinnaduwage Aravinda de Silva is regarded as something of a Sri Lankan batting prodigy and was chosen for his country's team to contest the Asia Cup in Sharjah at the age of 18. His exuberant batting and keen fielding made de Silva an instant crowd favourite during the Benson & Hedges Series and World Championship of Cricket in Australia in 1984–85.

On a short tour of Pakistan in 1985–86, Aravinda de Silva hit 122 in the first Test at Faisalabad (including two sixes off fast bowler Imran Khan) and a defiant 105 in the second game at Karachi. He is, with three other exciting new stroke-players — left-hander Asanka Gurusinghe (who has already claimed his first Test hundred), Roshan Mahanama (a dashing opening bat and a superb fielder), and the all-rounder Baba Roshan Jurangpathy — a leading Sri Lankan batting hope of the future. Jurangpathy is the first member of Sri Lanka's Malay community to play at Test level, a sign of hopefully changing times when perhaps the previous preference given to Sri Lankan (or Singalese) players will disappear and Sri Lanka's other races like the Malays and Tamils will receive equal consideration when it comes to cricket.

And hopefully the tiny island country which rests like a jewel at the tip of India, and boasts a flag with an emblazoned red lion, will continue to provide Test cricket with a host of sparkling and adventurous batsmen.

36

'Zed'

'It seems a long time ago that Zaheer made his first impact...when scoring a double century against England at Edgbaston in 1971'
— David Gravenay

Syed Zaheer Abbas of Pakistan is one of those remarkable batsmen, like Bradman, Boycott, Gavaskar, who always seemed to be at the wicket and was ever prepared to make or break a new record every other week. The even-tempered 'Zed' has been described as the supreme artist at the crease. If his career were to be judged by figures alone, he would certainly warrant ranking among the 20 or so greatest batsmen of all time.

His world records include 100 in each innings of a game on eight occasions and he is the only batsman to four times tally a century *and* a double century in the same first-class match. This record is even more impressive considering his four centuries/double-centuries were achieved without being dismissed — 216 not out and 156 not out versus Surrey and 230 not out and 104 not out versus Kent (both in 1976), 205 not out and 108 not out versus Sussex in 1977 and 215 not out and 150 not out versus Somerset in 1981 (all innings were played for Gloucestershire in the English County Championship).

As far back as 1971 Zaheer achieved ranking as one of *Wisden*'s 'Five Cricketers of the Year', an honour bestowed mainly because of a phenomenal 274 in the first Test versus England at Birmingham — the Pakistan record score against England. He was the first Pakistani to score more than 5000 runs in Tests (Javed Miandad has since achieved this feat) and is the first Asian player to reach 100 centuries in first-class cricket.

It was a case of 'Zaheer who?' when the slim, unknown, bespectacled Pakistani, a few weeks short of his 24th birthday, peered owlishly at the England bowlers through large-lensed glasses and stroked his way to 274 in 550 minutes (38 fours) in a total of 608 for seven wickets declared.

Awaiting each delivery with a slightly raised bat, Zaheer in his early days was particularly strong on the leg-side. Later on he added to his stroke repertoire and his Gloucestershire captain, Mike Procter, was once heard to mention that Zaheer 'appears to have no weaknesses, and no particular strengths'. Equally capable off either back or front foot, his driving through the covers and straight was magnificent. Zaheer's sweep through midwicket and behind square was a

A youthful Zaheer Abbas, Pakistan's scorer of a century of centuries, hooks to leg with flowing vigour.

distinct feature of his play and even in defence his strokes usually carried enough power to gain a run or two if there was a misfield.

Zaheer Abbas fittingly reached his hundredth century during an innings of 215 for Pakistan versus India in the first Test at Lahore in 1982–83. His record at the Gaddafi Stadium in Lahore is pheno- menal. In 1984–85 versus India, his 168 not out in the first Test took him past 1000 Test runs on the ground and he thus became only the 12th batsman to pass four figures in Tests at one venue. Zaheer reached his 1000 runs (1019 runs to be exact – average 113.22) at Lahore in his 13th Test innings there – Australia's Sir Donald Bradman and Greg Chappell jointly hold the record for one venue of 1058 runs (at Melbourne – average 117.55) and 1006 runs (at Brisbane – average 111.78) respectively, with the target for each batsman reached in only the 11th innings played on the ground in question. The *most* runs scored on one ground in Tests is Sir Donald Bradman's 1671 at Melbourne in 17 innings (average 128.54).

The match against England at Edgbaston in 1971 that contained Zaheer Abbas's great scoring feat also marked the entry into Test cricket of an 18-year-old all-rounder, Imran Khan Niazi, who has since developed into a player of such vast talent that he would be worthy of a place in any international team as either batsman or bowler.

Until a stress fracture to his left shin laid him low for a period, 'Immy' Khan was considered by most critics to be the best of the modern fast bowlers. As a batsman he is a forthright and handsome striker of the ball who generally takes the attack to the bowler, although handicapped to some extent because of trouble with his left arm which was broken when he fell from a tree as a boy.

Playing against India in the third Test at Faisalabad in 1982–83, the current Pakistan captain claimed 11 wickets in the match and hit 117 to become only the second player in history to score a century and take 10 wickets (or more) in a Test (Ian Botham did it for England versus India at Bombay in the Golden Jubilee Test of 1980).

A handsome athlete with a charismatic personality usually reserved for film stars, Imran's jet-set bachelor lifestyle has provoked much comment but the Pakistani captain and ace all-rounder is an unas- suming man who enjoys Western ways but, as a devout Muslim, remains a teetotaller.

Following a clash on the field in the second Test at Perth in 1981–82 with Australian fast bowler Dennis Lillee, the short but thick-set Javed Miandad Khan lost the Pakistani captaincy. Miandad remains Pakistan's current leading batsman.

The Miandad-Lillee confrontation at Perth was one of the most undignified events ever in Test cricket. Miandad had turned a Lillee delivery to leg and was running through for a comfortable single when his path was obstructed by Lillee. A fracas ensued, during which the big Australian fast bowler aimed a kick at his much shorter opponent. A furious Miandad responded by threatening Lillee with his bat. Lillee was suspended for two limited over internationals; Miandad refused to apologise, and eventually lost the Pakistan captaincy.

Javed Miandad is an audacious stroke-player (his square and off drives are among the most powerful in the game) and a quick runner between the wickets, who appears to delight in taunting his opponents to take a shy at the stumps in response to his cheeky antics at the crease. But to quote former Aussie wicket-keeper Rod Marsh, 'he's too bloody quick, too bloody cunning'.

At Hyderabad, Pakistan, in 1982−83, Javed Miandad and Mudassar Nazar equalled the Test record partnership for any wicket when they put on 451 against India in the fourth Test − matching the Bradman-Ponsford stand for Australia versus England in the fifth Test at the Oval in 1934. Miandad's contribution to the partnership was a Test career best 280 not out; Mudassar was dismissed for 231.

At 19 years and 119 days, Miandad became the youngest batsman to score a century in his debut innings when he swept to a brilliant 163 versus New Zealand in the first Test at Lahore in 1976−77.

Mudassar Nazar's father, Nazar Mohammed, opened the batting for Pakistan in its first-ever Test. Known to his team-mates as 'Mud', Mudassar holds the dubious distinction of having scored the slowest-ever Test century (557 minutes against England in the first Test at Lahore in 1977−78), but has since developed into an attractive stroke-player. He has improved beyond all recognition as a bowler − he was given the name 'the Man with the Golden Arm' when he took six wickets in an amazing spell against England at Lord's in 1982.

Like his father Nazar Mohammed (Pakistan's first Test century scorer), Mudassar carried his bat undefeated through a complete innings when he made 152 not out in a total of 323 against Pakistan's arch foe India in the fifth Test at Lahore in 1982−83. Mudassar Nazar's highest Test score remains his 231 made in the world record partnership with Javed Miandad at Hyderabad in 1982−83.

Muddassar's current Test opening partner is Mohsin Hasan Khan, an exciting but consistent stroke-player of some elegance who is a particularly capable performer against pace bowling. Mohsin Khan made his first-class debut in 1970−71, and then had to wait for nearly eight years for his first call to Test duty.

An attacking opener with a wide range of strokes, he attained his career peak at Lord's in 1982 when he became the first Pakistani to reach a double-100 in a Test on that famous ground. Mohsin straight drove the first ball bowled to him (by Ian Botham) for four and his 491-minute innings was resplendent with cover drives and forcing shots off his legs.

Middle-order left-hander Wasim Hasan Raja has seldom lived up to the form he showed during one outstanding season in the West Indies in 1976–77. In five Tests in the Caribbean against the pace attack of Roberts, Croft and Garner, the enterprising Wasim Raja hit 517 runs at an average of 57.44 (including 14 sixes). Wasim has, perhaps, been unfortunate to be a contemporary of the many fine stroke-players available to the Pakistani selectors over the past 10 years and has, at times, battled to hold his place in the team.

Tall and muscular Haroon Rashid Dar and the enigmatic but gifted stroke-player Mansoor Akhtar have also struggled to hold places in the powerful Pakistani batting order, despite some outstanding performances. Mansoor Akhtar and Waheed Mirza hold the world opening stand record of 561 made for Karachi Whites versus Quetta in 1976–77.

Wicket-keeper Taslim Arif in only his third match for Pakistan scored 210 not out versus Australia at Faisalabad in 1979–80. He had opened the batting after having been behind the stumps throughout a 617 total raised by Australia and was, in effect, on the field throughout the entire drawn match. He played only a few more Tests before fading from the scene.

The bright and bubbly 5 ft 6 in (167 cm) Qasim Omar was born in Kenya and is the first African-born player to represent Pakistan. He soon became a favourite of the Australian spectators in 1983–84 with his enthusiasm and distinctive Afro hairstyle (hidden by his white helmet when batting) making him instantly recognisable. In the Tests against Australia, Qasim Omar batted with great courage, character and skill and handled the Australian pace bombardment of Lillee, Lawson and Hogg with far more aplomb than most of his more illustrious colleagues.

After consolidating his position in the Pakistan team, raising his highest score (210) against India in the second Test at Faisalabad in 1984–85 and logging another double-century against Sri Lanka in 1985–86, Qasim was summarily dropped following an off-field controversy involving the alleged use of drugs by some (unidentified) Test cricketers.

The exciting Salim Malik, who handles fast bowling with particular bravado, has already at the age of 22 played in 27 Tests. In Australia in 1983–84 he scored two Test 50s and followed up with a grand run against England the same season, including 116 and 76 in the second Test at Faisalabad and a total of 322 runs in six innings.

Salim certainly seems destined to take over the number three or four batting spot in the powerful Pakistani line-up. When scoring his 116 against England at Faisalabad in March 1984 he became only the third player in history to compile three Test centuries before his 21st birthday: George Headley (West Indies) scored four and Graeme Pollock (South Africa) three.

The explosive Javed Miandad, a prolific scorer for Pakistan in Tests, goes onto the drive.

Other youthful batsmen like Hanif Mohammed's son Shoaib Mohammed, Wasim Raja's younger brother, the dashing Rameez Raja, opener Rizwan-uz-Zaman — plus the teenagers Asif Mutjaba and Ijaz Ahmed — have had some taste of Test cricket and, together with Salim Malik, appear destined to form the core of Pakistan's batting strength in coming years.

37

Borderline
and a new pop hero

'Down under we're not talkers, for our skill
Lies all in action. Take us as we stand...'
— Anon., 1899

World Series Cricket had run its course by 1979 and Australia's top players returned to the official fold. A number of cricketers who had maintained their loyalty to the board and had gained Test recognition during the breakaway period were suddenly cast aside. Some even found difficulty in retaining their places in State teams when the 'rebels' were again available.

The pressure was on, and the competition for batting spots in the Australian team keen. Some of the more senior batsmen started falling by the wayside (culminating in Greg Chappell's own retirement after the 1983—84 season) and a stream of young players were thrust into the limelight. Few have come up to scratch and it has been left to one man to try and hold Australia's batting together.

In every cricketing age there are usually one or two batsmen who stand out as torch-bearers for their peers. Australia's current batting supremo is its chunky captain, Allan Robert Border who despite the struggle of leading a weak team, seems to grow each day in stature as batsman and leader. As a batsman Border has always been more than worth his place in the Australian team, right from the day of his debut against England in 1978—79.

During the 1986—87 series versus New Zealand Border quietly moved past the Australian Test run records of all-time greats, Sir Donald Bradman and Greg Chappell. This has not been his only achievement in a marvellous career. His four centuries on the trot to give an early impetus to the 1985 tour of England (followed by 597 runs at 66.3 in the six-match series) will not easily be forgotten. Nor will Border be forgotten by Pakistan's bowlers of 1979—80, who must have thought they were suffering from double-vision when he played innings of 150 not out and 153 in the third Test at Lahore. An aggregate of 533 runs during the 1981 series in England gained him a place among the *Wisden* elect. His many other feats in Test and first-class cricket could fill a volume on their own.

Sure-footed against spin and a brave behind-the-line player against pace, Allan Border is the Australian man for all seasons.

His courageous batting took him to the top of the calypso hit parade in the West Indies in 1983–84. In the five Tests (West Indies won three and two were left drawn) Border battled his way to 521 runs, more than twice the aggregate of any other Australian batsman. 'Big Bird' Joel Garner seemed to have added yards to his pace that season and took 31 wickets in the series – aided by Marshall and Holding at their intimidatory best. Yet Border stood fast while everyone else faded and played his comfortable array of strokes with customary free movement.

Although at times a little flashy against rising deliveries outside the off-stump, Border is as complete a batsman as could be expected of Australia's current number one player. His driving on both sides of the wicket is a joy to behold and he has never been afraid to go on the hook, despite one or two mishaps that have resulted in stitches on temple and forehead.

Border's air of confidence when batting could become one of the most important influences on Australian batsmen of the future. Emulation has always been the name of the game.

But what support is there for Allan Border? The strong Gregory Michael Ritchie, a bold adventurer of a batsman, headed both Test and tour averages on an otherwise disastrous Australian trip to Pakistan in 1982–83 (he hit three sixes and nine fours in an unbeaten 106 in the second Test at Faisalabad). He was then overlooked for the 1983–84 home series versus Pakistan but was picked for the tour to the West Indies the same season. Like everyone else bar Allan Border, Ritchie produced meagre returns in the Caribbean and had to wait until the fifth Test of the 1984–85 season to get another chance.

An upright player who knows the value of putting bat to ball, he has thrown off his former 'fat-cat' image and was picked for the 1985 Ashes trip and immediately took his chances in England to establish himself as Australia's leading run-getter after Border. However, further successes against India and New Zealand in 1985–86 failed to consolidate a permanent position in the Australian team.

When Wayne Bentley Phillips gave away his wicket-keeping gloves he simultaneously lost his place in the Australian eleven. As an attacking left-handed batsman of great promise he thrashed the Pakistan attack for 158 on his debut in 1983–84, driving and square-cutting with particular vigour. He again batted with vigour in England in 1985 before falling away during the ensuing Australian summer.

Phillips and the explosive left-hander David Hookes (who has never quite transferred his Sheffield Shield form to Test level), took part in an amazing 462-run unbroken fourth-wicket stand for South Australia versus Tasmania at Adelaide in 1986–87 — a new Australian record for any wicket. Phillips scored 213; Hookes a massive 306.

Of the younger batsmen taken to England by Border in 1985,

Opposite: Australia's current batting supremo, Allan Border, has always been strong on the leg side.

rugged little right-hander David Clarence Boon has emerged as Australia's number one Test opening batsman, after patchy form lower in the order. First tried in his new unfamiliar position against India in the first Test at Adelaide in 1985–86, Boon blossomed as a controlled and cool-headed performer, scoring 123 in a little over five and a half hours.

When Wayne Phillips failed at the head of the order, 'Daniel' Boon was given a new partner, Geoff Marsh, for the third and final Test at Sydney. The pair immediately set about compiling a partnership of 217, the first Australian opening stand to exceed 100 since 1981–82, and Boon went on to his second Test hundred and was finally out for 131. Marsh scored 92.

Geoffrey Robert Marsh waited long for his opportunity to represent Australia and has taken his chances with both hands, registering his own first Test century in New Zealand towards the end of the 1985–86 season. He made his debut for Western Australia as a 19-year-old in 1977–78 and finally got the call to play for Australia following the mass defection to South Africa in 1985–86. Marsh is a well-organised player whose devotion to his task is one of his strongest points.

All-rounders like Simon Patrick O'Donnell and Stephen Rodger Waugh have also been given a chance in recent years. O'Donnell is now sadly sidelined through cancer. Waugh has played a few Test innings of note without accumulating the quantity of runs that should fit his undoubted stroke-playing talent.

The defection of players like Hughes, Yallop, Dyson and Smith to play in South Africa was compounded by the retirement from Test cricket and return to his home country by Kepler Wessels following a disagreement over terms with the Australian Cricket Board. Kepler Christoffel Wessels is a man of strong and definite character who waited patiently for his Australian Test squad selection. He was given his first chance against England at Brisbane in 1982–83 and the tough South African-born left-hander immediately established himself as Test-class opener with a dedicated debut innings of 162 that laid the foundation for an Australian victory.

As a dour gatherer of runs, and a left-hander who uncharacteristically favours off-side stroke-play, Wessels is not everyone's favourite batsman but his courage is unquestioned. What Wessels may lack in terms of stroke-making range, he more than compensates in terms of sheer guts and determination. For personal training he spars with professional boxers and, like any good ring man, is adept at lifting himself off the canvas to continue a fight.

There was no better illustration of this aspect of Wessels's character than his incredible recovery against Clive Lloyd's 1984–85 West Indian fast bowlers. After Joel Garner had dismissed the Australian opener four times in five encounters (including three ducks), certain sections of the press began in their inimitable fashion to bay for his blood. Wessels's reply came in the form of a defiant 61 followed by successive efforts of 98, 70, 90 and 0.

In the final Test at Sydney (when good old-fashioned leg-spin bowling from Bob Holland finally baffled the West Indians) the tough-as-nails left-hander set up Australia's fine win with a magnificent 173. After playing in the first Test against New Zealand at Brisbane in 1985–86, Wessels departed the international scene of his own accord when he became dissatisfied with the remuneration offered by the Australian Cricket Board.

A surprise resurrection of an all but totally forgotten opener during the 1984–85 season provided the initial inspiration the Australian team needed finally to break a long run of West Indian victories in Test cricket. Andrew Mark Jefferson Hilditch had last played in a Test in 1978–79. When he was recalled against Clive Lloyd's team for the fourth Test at Melbourne in 1984–85, he batted for nearly a whole day to score a dogged 113 in Australia's second innings (he made 70 in the first) and earn his country a draw after three straight losses.

Unfortunately Hilditch gained the reputation of being a 'hapless hooker' on the tour of England that followed in 1985 and has since lost both form and favour.

The major batting event of the 1985–86 season was the sudden rise in stature of the exuberant Gregory Richard John Matthews, a left-hander of character who had for a couple of seasons been experiencing a shaky existence on the fringe of the Australian team, with an occasional match thrown in to keep him primed.

Greg Matthews threw off a previous 'pop and punk' image against New Zealand in the first Test at Brisbane, to take on the aspect of Australia's current cricketing hero. By the end of the season, the banners flapping in the breeze on the stands at Sydney and Melbourne bore the legend: 'Matthews for PM'. The extrovert Matthews had suddenly become transformed from a sometimes irritating cricket eccentric into the most popular player in Australia.

With New Zealand's Richard Hadlee firing on all pistons, Australia crashed to an ignominious defeat at Brisbane, but not before the defiant Matthews had thrilled the crowd with a belligerent 115 in 229 minutes (205 balls, 10 fours, one six) and helped his skipper in a face-saving stand of 197 for the sixth wicket.

Chipping in here and there with a wicket or two taken with his increasingly confident and crafty off-turners (or 'donkey-drops' as Bill O'Reilly calls them), Matthews continued his grand form with a dogged 50 against New Zealand in the second Test at Sydney, and a never-say-die century in the second Test against India at Melbourne that will long live in the memories of all those privileged to see it.

All appeared lost for Australia at 109 for five wickets on the opening day (it soon became 127 for six) when the jaunty but determined figure of Matthews emerged from the pavilion. Left-arm spinner Ray Bright provided initial support in a 66-run stand; numbers 10 and 11, Bruce Reid and Dave Gilbert, defended like a pair of opening batsmen. Matthews, his every movement cheered by an adoring following, batted cautiously and sensibly at first and then raced to exactly 100 not out, off 152 balls in 195 minutes, out of 135 runs added while he was at the wicket. Reid stayed with him for half an hour; Gilbert for 50 minutes.

At 96, the crowd groaned and then cheered as their new hero mis-hit a ball just out of reach of mid-wicket and took two runs. He edged the next just wide of wicket-keeper Kirmani, through the vacant first slip position, and sprinted off like a hare to get the two runs needed for his century. Running back for the second run, Matthews punched the air and waved his bat in ecstasy to the Southern Stand crowd. He had made 46 out of 52 runs added on the second morning. Pandemonium reigned for more than a few minutes.

The previous 12 months had seen a rather bleak period in Australian cricket. Crushing defeats by Clive Lloyd's West Indians at home had been followed by an equally depressing showing in England. Then, Richard Hadlee and New Zealand had for the first time in history humbled a rebel-depleted Australia on the Aussies' home turf.

Matthews was the unlikely hero who stepped forth in his bouncy and up-beat fashion to prove that with unbridled enthusiasm as his major asset, a seemingly average all-rounder could raise his play, and his batting in particular, to provide an example and a model for all future Australian cricketers to follow. As his team-mate Greg Ritchie put it: 'It's a confidence thing and his confidence is sky-high.'

When it comes to confidence, there are few to beat Australia's current number two run-maker (after skipper Allan Border), the upright, belligerent and frequently sparkling Dean Mervyn Jones. Unlucky to make his Test debut at 22 during a trying tour of the West Indies in 1983–84, Jones was left out in the wilderness for a few seasons but came back with a vengeance in 1986–87.

Logging what is destined to become a legendary double-hundred in the famous tied Test versus India at Madras, and going on to score 511 at 56.77 in five Tests and 623 at 47.92 in the limited over internationals that followed versus England, he made the number three spot in the current Australian batting order his very own — at least for the forseeable future.

Jones has seemingly overcome a serious knee operation and could one day succeed Allan Border as Australian captain. He certainly has no current rival for the position of Australia's batting supremo when Border finally decides to retire. Of the rising young Australians, the superbly-equipped Michael Robert John Veletta has scored prolifically for Western Australia and made a promising international debut during the 1987–88 season.

38

Botham tilts the scales

'Ian did so much in so short a time that his few inevitable set-backs were doubly disappointing'

— Alec Bedser

One hundred years hence, if all else is forgotten about England's Ian Terrance Botham, his mighty deeds in the Ashes series of 1981 will surely survive the sands of time. The mighty England all-rounder has since stumbled on more than a few occasions (particularly when faced by the West Indies fast bowlers) but, if Ian Botham had never played in another Test series in his entire cricketing career, his performances in that one golden year would place his name alongside those of the greatest players of the past.

1981 was Botham's year, as much as 1947 was Compton's and Edrich's. He is known to his friends as 'Guy the Gorilla', not because of the much publicised punch-ups but related to a party costume he once used in Australia. The Australians of 1981 probably saw him more as a kind of cricketing Tarzan who was constantly on hand to save England when the pot was boiling and the victory meal about to be prepared.

Botham was still a much-maligned captain of England when the 1981 series started. He contributed little as England slid to ignoble defeat in the first two Tests. Botham made an inglorious 'pair' at Lord's and resigned forthwith as England captain — a decision that was to herald a dramatic transformation in his own play and in England's cricketing fortunes.

Mike Brearley, Botham's predecessor (and a major influence in Botham's development as a Test cricketer) was prevailed upon to resume Test cricket and once again take command of the ailing England team.

John Michael Brearley was acknowledged by friend and foe alike as possibly one of the greatest Test captains of all time although as a Test batsman he was patently out of his class. Bob Willis, his former deputy and a subsequent England captain, writes in his *Lasting the Pace*: 'Because Brearley was never quite of true Test calibre as an opening bat, his England sides usually carried the extra batsman.' Willis goes on to contend that England was usually left with only four front-line bowlers and that Ian Botham was overbowled to a degree that was ultimately damaging to his form and effectiveness.

There is no gainsaying the fact that, for the most part, Brearley enjoyed a full measure of loyalty from his England teams and that he was a major inspiration, though he was perhaps fortunate never to be called upon to captain England against West Indies. One of Mike Brearley's lasting memorials to the game of cricket will be the batting helmet, a piece of equipment of which he was an early pioneer.

But back to Botham and his golden year. With England one down and four to go (it was a six-match rubber), Brearley took over the reigns for the third Test at Leeds. The drama was about to start; the three principle actors were to be Botham, Brearley and Bob Willis and the English phoenix was soon to rise from its ashes.

At Leeds Botham took six wickets for 95 before England followed on, 227 runs behind, after folding like a pack of cards to fast bowlers Lillee, Alderman and Lawson. Botham gave some glimpse of what was to come in a gallant and swift innings of 50. The game appeared over when he strode in again with England's second innings scoreboard at 105 for five wickets. This soon became 135 for seven, but then the miracle began. With young fast bowler Graham Dilley propping up one end (and later producing a series of stunning left-handed drives), Botham moved into a last-ditch assault. He proceeded in the most astonishing fashion to alter the course of the match and his glorious straight hitting and square cutting decimated the field set by opposing captain Kim Hughes.

Botham's thunderous hooks and pulls had the crowd constantly on its feet as he raced to 145 not out at the close of the fourth day. Dilley made a surprisingly convincing 56 in a 117-run stand in 80 minutes. Another bowler, and left-handed batsman, Chris Old, stayed while 67 was added; Willis stuck around for a last-wicket partnership of 37.

On the final morning, Botham took his score to 149 not out (two sixes, 27 fours), before Willis was dismissed and England's show of defiance apparently over. Australia needed just 130 runs to win; it would all be over long before the tea interval.

Botham disposed of Australian opener Wood at 13. The score moved to 56 without further loss and Australia seemed to be coasting along. Brearley made Willis change ends, to bowl with the wind. The lanky fast bowler galloped in like a thoroughbred and added his own hour of glory to that already logged by Botham. In one of the most astounding turnarounds in cricket history, Australia collapsed to 111 all out (Willis eight for 43), and England won by 18 runs to keep the series alive.

The fourth game at Edgbaston saw Botham snatch five wickets for 11 runs in Australia's second innings and England won another tight encounter by 29 runs. At Manchester in the fifth Test, the amazing England all-rounder played another glorious rescue innings of 118 in 123 minutes. The England hero hit six sixes — a record for Anglo-

Australian Tests − and 13 fours off 102 balls (he reached his 100 in 86 balls). When Lillee and Alderman took the second new ball, Botham ran amok. He hooked Lillee for three sixes and a lusty pull off Alderman landed far back in the pavilion crowd. He plundered 66 runs off eight overs bowled by the two Australian fast bowlers.

Although Australia fought back in a second innings of 402 (Yallop 114, Border 123), England were home again by 103 runs to seal the series. Botham took five wickets in the match.

Botham's final figures for six Tests read: 399 runs (average 36.27) and 34 wickets (at 20.58 each); omitting his lacklustre first two games as captain, his figures would have been: 365 runs (average 52.14) and 28 wickets (at 19.32).

It is perhaps unfortunate that Botham should have set such a high personal standard − he is expected to be able to turn any match at any time. It cannot be an easy task to walk across water every time.

In his personal life, Ian Botham has had his problems, mostly with the media. As a batsman, he has still to pass successfully through the ultimate testing fire − the West Indies fast bowlers. This new phenomenon of four fast bowlers up and at the batsman constantly is unparalleled in international cricket and when it comes in future years to a comparison of batsmen of different ages, it will not be an

Ian Botham, a split second before bat strikes ball.

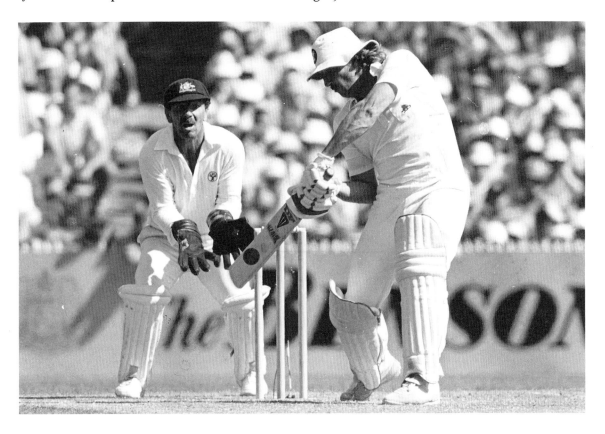

easy task to decide. The batsman of the 1980s has perhaps the most difficult of all forms of bowling to cope with in more than 100 years of international cricket.

During the 1985 English season, for Somerset and England Ian Botham launched into the biggest six-hitting blitz in cricket history. His 80 sixes for the season far exceeded the record of 66 set up by Somerset's Arthur Wellard in 1935 (Wellard also exceeded 50 sixes in three other seasons). Botham's overall scoring rate (including that in six Tests against Australia) was remarkable − 1530 runs off 1226 balls in 1521 minutes, a rate of 124.8 runs per 100 balls and 60.4 runs per hour, with boundaries accounting for 74.2 per cent of his aggregate runs.

Still only in his early 30s, it is hoped that this superlative cricketer will continue to entertain us with his outrageous hitting for at least another decade.

One of England's most capable players against fast bowling is the South African-born Allan Joseph Lamb who now plays for Northamptonshire. Against a West Indies battery in 1984 that included such big guns as Marshall, Garner and Holding (with some reserve

South African-born England representative Allan Lamb is a magnificent player against fast bowling.

support from Davis, Baptiste and Small), the short but thickly-built Lamb scored three centuries in a five-Test series. It was not just the runs he made, it was also the manner he employed.

Allan Lamb's 1984 performances against West Indies pace represent the apogee of his Test career to date and his centuries at Lord's, Leeds and Manchester were all defiant and doughty knocks, made when England was virtually pinned to the boards.

The writer recalls watching Allan Lamb bat in his debut first-class match for Western Province as a schoolboy in 1972−73. The young batsman scored 58 runs and from the moment he took guard looked and batted like a reincarnation of a Dudley Nourse or a Roy McLean. He is and always has been an attacking batsman and an instinctive stroke-player. Lamb was raised in the cricketing school created at Newlands by Eddie Barlow and, in the Barlow tradition, he looks for runs off every ball.

In isolation, South African cricket in the 1970s was tough. Transvaal and Western Province (and sometimes Natal) fielded teams that would not disgrace themselves if pitted against any of the Test countries playing today. Lamb learnt his cricket in a hard school and discovered early on that he would have to take his knocks and get on with the game. Dropped by England after the 1987 World Cup, Lamb went home to South Africa for a season with Orange Free State — and promptly shattered the existing Currie Cup highest innings record.

Another current England batsman with South African connections who is also a fine attacking player, normally unafraid of fast bowling, is Graham Alan Gooch of Essex. After his 1981−82 excursion to South Africa as skipper of a rebel team, Gooch was effectively banned from Test cricket for three years and has some catching up to do. Before his censure, he had already performed some mighty deeds for England, fighting back after a distressing start to his international career when he collected a dreaded 'pair' in his first Test versus Australia at Edgbaston in 1975.

Gooch went back to county cricket before getting his next chance against Pakistan in 1978 and then a tour to Australia in 1978−79. Things did not go too well for him on that tour, but Gooch was fast gaining a reputation as an explosive limited overs batsman. His testing time and his days of triumph came against West Indies in England in 1980 and in the West Indies in 1980−81.

Today's sternest test of a batsman is fast bowling and Gooch, with his peculiar bat up and waiting stance and ability to drive off either foot and cut and hook with clarity, has shown that he has what it takes. The stroke production contained in his 123 out of an England total of 269 in the second Test versus West Indies at Lord's in 1980 rivalled that of the West Indians themselves. At Bridgetown, Barbados in 1980−81 he again defied the West Indian fast bowlers who lopped

Graham Gooch is a
right-handed England
opener who has never been
afraid to lay bat on ball.

their way through the other England batsmen while he made 116. At Kingston, Gooch reached 103 out of 155 in the 40th over of the first day and went on to score a blazing 153 out of the 249 runs added while he was batting.

Gooch then decided to join forces with the SAB English XI that had been recruited by Geoff Boycott and others to tour South Africa. His thunderous batting was frequently the only factor standing between South Africa and victory and he was accepted as the best attacking English batsman to be seen in South Africa since Denis Compton and Ted Dexter.

After three years in the wilderness, Gooch regained his rightful place but like the other England batsmen must be rather shell-shocked after his experience in the Caribbean in 1986. Hopefully he will recover from the onslaught and continue to delight his many admirers.

During 1985, England and Leicestershire's current captain David Ivon Gower stroked his way majestically to 732 runs in the series against Australia — the record number of runs by an England captain against any country. Although he has occasionally found himself in the doldrums, there has never been any doubt about Gower's flawless pedigree as a Test match batsman.

The graceful left-handed Gower batted in 1985 with what has been described as a merciless authority. His three 100s in the series all exceeded 150 — only Walter Hammond of all English Test batsmen has matched this (versus Australia in 1928−29). Gower's crowning innings was an almost disdainful 215 in the fifth Test at Edgbaston. At the Oval in the final Test, he scored 157 and added 351 with Graham Gooch.

David Gower is an imperious stroke-player who would not have been out of place in cricket's Golden Age and, with his elegant air and curly blond locks, he is every schoolboy's batting hero. He passed a stern batting examination in the Caribbean in 1980−81 with a commendable 154 not out at Kingston but has since failed twice against the West Indies fast bowlers, in England in 1984 and in the West Indies in 1986. Still under 30, he remains England's most equipped and accomplished batsman.

Michael William Gatting is another player who has fought back after an uninspiring start to his career to earn the image of an English bulldog, a fighter of rare guts and quality. Like Botham, he is a vigorous striker of the ball with a sizzling square cut, a powerful and dismissive hook and a penchant for lofting the ball over the heads of the fielders. Gatting's first trip to Pakistan and New Zealand in 1977−78 brought his first England cap but an unmemorable start to his international career when he scored 5, 6 and 0 in his first three Tests.

For the next seven years he was in and out of the England team and was considered fortunate to be included in the party sent to

England's David Gower
displays left-handed
elegance in the old style.

India in 1984–85. Gatting came of age as a Test batsman, scoring 136 at Bombay in the first Test and 207 at Madras in the fourth and heading the Test batting table with an aggregate of 575 and an average of 95.83. He then continued his fine run against Australia in England in 1985 with two centuries and an average of 87.83 for the series, again topping the overall batting list.

Misfortune followed in the West Indies when first his nose and then his thumb were broken in gladiatorial exchanges with pace men Marshall, Garner, Holding and the frightening newcomer Patrick Patterson. Since those trying times Gatting's famous bulldog qualities have seen him emerge as a fighting captain of England and as his country's most consistent run-getter but a cloud now hangs over his future following a stormy, controversial passage through Pakistan in 1987–88.

Of the batsmen apparently no longer under consideration for the England team, the dour Kent right-hander Christopher James Tavare bats much in the fashion of the stonewallers of the past and must vie with Trevor Bailey for the title of most boring England batsman since the Second World War.

Against India at Madras in 1981–82, Tavare camped at the wicket for 332 minutes while scoring only 35 runs. In two innings versus Australia at Manchester in 1981 Tavare batted for 287 minutes for 69 in the first innings and 423 minutes for 78 in the second – 11 hours and 50 minutes for 147 runs!

Lancashire's more adventurous left-hander Graeme Fowler was unfortunate to be the player dropped to accommodate the returning Graham Gooch in 1985. By the end of 1985, the hapless 'Foxy' Fowler had not only lost his England place, but his position in the Lancashire team as well. Fowler's slide came just a few months after he had played a decisive innings of 201 off the Indian bowlers in the fourth Test of 1984–85 at Madras (and added 241 for the second wicket with Mike Gatting, who scored 207).

England introduced a string of new batsmen during the 1984 series against West Indies but Marshall, Garner and friends literally knocked most of them over like ninepins in a bowling alley. Terry Lloyd, the Warwickshire left-handed opener, was struck on the head by a Marshall flyer in the first Test at Birmingham and spent five days in hospital with blurred vision; Paul Terry (Hampshire) suffered a broken arm in the fourth Test at Manchester trying to avoid a bouncer from Winston Davis.

One exception was the phlegmatic Nottinghamshire left-handed opener Brian Christopher Broad who stuck to it through four Tests, with the ball constantly whistling about his ears, and averaged 24.37 in eight innings. To his chagrin, Broad was dropped for the 1984–85 India tour that followed, replaced by his Notts first-wicket partner Tim Robinson, whom it was thought would be a better bet on turning wickets. Broad's subsequent successes in Australia during the 1986–87 summer (including centuries in three consecutive Tests) came as a just reward for his resilience and determination.

The England selectors' assumption about the footwork skill of Robert Timothy Robinson proved to be correct. The tall and confident Robinson displayed a sound technique and started making runs from the moment he arrived in India. In the second Test at Delhi he batted eight and a half hours for 160 and ended the series second in the batting table to Gatting, with an aggregate of 444 and an average of 63.42.

Robinson continued to build on this solid foundation when Australia arrived in England in 1985. In the first Test at Leeds he set England up for victory with a dedicated 175; in the fifth match at the Oval he was, with a score of 148, one of three England batsmen to pass three figures in an innings of 595 for five wickets declared (Gower 215, Gatting 100 not out). Like his more experienced peers, Robinson returned battered and bruised from the West Indies in 1986, having added very few runs to his Test aggregate but will no doubt remain in consideration for some years to come. Broad was given sound opening support in Australia in 1986–87 by the resurrected Charles William Jeffrey Athey, a sound right-hander who won his first Test cap versus West Indies in 1980, moved from Yorkshire to Gloucestershire after suffering a loss of form, and eventually regained his England place in 1986.

After the 1986 West Indies debacle England's batting appeared to be in some state of disarray, but hopefully there will soon arise those players of character and courage equipped to carry English batsmanship forward into a new period of prosperity.

Young players recently blooded who may carry England's fortunes into the future include: Lancashire left-hander Neil Harvey Fairbrother (yes, named after the Australian left-hander); energetic Northamptonshire all-rounder David John Capel; and dour Yorkshire opener Martyn Douglas Moxon.

England's most exciting batting prospect of the future — and possibly the best batsmen under 25 in the world — is unhappily not yet qualified to play for his adopted country. Zimbabwe-born Graeme Hick has played some thundering innings for his original home country and for his county Worcestershire. His hitting powers are perhaps only second to those of Ian Botham among current English players.

In 1986, at 20, he became the youngest batsman ever to score 2000 runs in an English season. Under present rules, Hick will not be able to play for England until 1993.

39

'Supercat' and 'King Viv'

'Lloyd is a father figure to his team'
— Richie Benaud

'...Vivian Richards went into battle wielding his bat like a broadsword'
— Trevor McDonald

When a hulking young man from Guyana with exceptionally long arms first played for his adopted county, Lancashire, at Old Trafford in 1969, he was immediately dubbed 'Jungle Jim' by some dry-witted Lancashire supporter; after observation of the newcomer's lightning-quick run-in, pick-up and throw and, later, his easy free-hitting, the awkward-looking West Indian's soubriquet was swiftly altered to 'Supercat'. He is known to his many friends simply as Hubert.

Early impressions of Clive Hubert Lloyd will be linked with the vision of him fielding like two men in the covers. Towards the end of his career, due to advancing age and recurrent knee problems, the West Indies captain and elder statesman directed operations from the slips. But Clive Lloyd is most remembered for the way he has destroyed, with his power-house left-handed efficiency, so many bowling attacks at all levels of the game since his first-class debut in the Caribbean more than 20 years ago.

Lloyd is one half of the most prolific of all cricketing family connections. His first cousin Lance Gibbs, of the 'praying mantis' off-break bowling style, was almost 10 years his senior when the two first played together in a Test match for West Indies. By the close of the 1984–85 series in Australia their combined total of 189 Tests far exceeded the aggregate 172 international games played by Pakistan's *four* Mohammed brothers!

In 1983–84 at Kingston, Jamaica, versus Australia in the fifth Test, Clive Lloyd played his 100th Test (Sir Garfield Sobers is next best with 93) and voted himself into the elect 'century club', whose other three notable members are fellow-batsmen Colin Cowdrey (founder member with 114 Tests); little Sunny Gavaskar, the Indian wizard of the wicket who surpassed Sir Donald Bradman's 29 Test centuries record by scoring 236 not out against West Indies in his 99th Test in 1983–84 and has since raised his appearances to 118; and the prolific Geoffrey Boycott (108).

Clive Lloyd may be most remembered for his explosive hitting in

the limited over version of the game. He wielded his massive bat with a built-up grip as if it were a battle-axe, bludgeoning the very best of bowlers into submission.

Dennis Lillee for one will most certainly never forget that day at Lord's in the 1975 World Cup Final when Lloyd came in at 50 for three wickets and opened his account with a stunning hooked six off the fast bowler. With the dependable Rohan Kanhai as anchorman at the other end, Lloyd proceeded to demolish the hitherto cock-a-hoop Australian attack and turn the game around as the West Indian pair, captain and former captain, raised 149 in just 36 overs. Man of the Match Lloyd sailed through to reach 102 and West Indies claimed an historic 17-run victory in the first-ever World Cup.

It is quite amazing that a man who has at times experienced eyesight problems should have come so far in world-class cricket. As a lad of 12 he incurred an eye injury when breaking up a fight and has since had to wear spectacles. At times the West Indies executioner (of bowlers) appeared to be at a loss at the start of an innings but, once underway, his natural ease of movement took charge.

Lloyd's basic batting technique was based on orthodox principles and an unusually high backlift (similar to Sobers). His style was swashbuckling; he would hook a bouncer with supreme disdain; his cut past point would send the ball to the fence like a bullet from a shotgun; his driving on the rise could look deceivingly languorous, but the power and timing of his shot, and the manner in which he dissected the field, left little chance of intercepting the ball.

Clive Lloyd made his Test debut in December 1966 against India in the first Test at Bombay (he scored 82 and 78 not out) and hit 33 and 72 in his final game for West Indies versus Australia at Sydney over the New Year of 1984–85. In 110 Tests he logged 7515 runs at 46.67. The first of his 19 Test centuries (118) came against England in the first Test at Port of Spain in 1967–68; his highest Test innings (242 not out) was taken off the India attack in the fifth Test at Bombay in 1974–75; his final Test 100 (114) was a grand rescue attempt against Australia in the second Test versus Australia at Brisbane in 1984–85.

At Bangalore in the first Test versus India in 1974–75, Lloyd reached a century in 102 minutes off 85 balls to beat the West Indies fast-scoring century record of 110 minutes set by Kenneth 'Bam Bam' Weekes versus England in the third Test at the Oval in 1939. Lloyd went on to 163 off only 149 balls (two sixes, 22 fours) and his effort remains the fastest Test century on the Indian sub-continent.

As the most successful of all West Indies leaders, Lloyd captained what has been claimed to be the best West Indies team of all time. He has perhaps been fortunate to have had the support during the past decade of the most fearsome set of fast bowlers ever to stride onto a cricket field.

Opposite: West Indian record-making captain Clive Lloyd used a massive bat to hit as hard as any batsman in history.

His record as a Test skipper is awe-inspiring — he was the first captain in history to lead his team to victory in nine consecutive Tests — three against Australia in the West Indies in 1983—84, five out of five in England in 1984 and the first Test in Australia in 1984—85. He then went on to take the next two Tests against Australia to make it 11 in a row. Add to this an impressive list of one-day limited over wins (including two World Cups) and the credentials of one of the world's all-time best captains are convincingly confirmed.

Lloyd's 11 consecutive Test wins gave him the last laugh at critics who claimed that his phenomenal reign must surely be at an end when he hobbled off the field in 1980 with a severe hamstring injury.

Entering the twilight of his famous career seemed to have spurred Clive Lloyd on to even greater achievements. In 1983 he expressed great personal satisfaction at taking his native Guyana to Shell Shield honours. In 1984—85 his final triumph came during the Test series against Australia. His name stands firmly alongside those of Headley, Constantine, Worrell and Sobers on the West Indies roll of honour.

Dashing opening batsman Cuthbert Gordon Greenidge made his debut in the Bangalore Test that was marked by Lloyd's record century. He is another West Indian powerhouse player who hit two incredible double-centuries against England during a 5—0 'blackwash' of the home team in England in 1984.

His first effort in the company of a more subdued 'Larry' Gomes recalled the feats of Bradman and Arthur Morris at Leeds in 1948 when Australia reached a fourth innings three for 404 to beat England against the run of play. At Lord's in the second Test of 1984, West Indies reached a match-winning 344 for one wicket, with Gordon Greenidge pummelling his way to 214 not out in only five hours.

Then, during the fourth Test at Old Trafford, he played what has been described as one of the most technically perfect Test innings on record when he reached a 223 in under six hours, without providing a visible chance and with some glorious driving in an arc between cover and mid-wicket.

Although he was born in Barbados, Gordon Greenidge received his secondary schooling in England and originally played most of his first-class cricket for Hampshire. He was in effect eligible to play for England and one wonders what records may have been shattered by a Boycott-Greenidge combination if the English selectors had opted for his services!

Greenidge admits to gaining great benefit from opening the Hampshire innings for so many seasons with another masterful batsman, Barry Richards. He is only the second West Indian (George Headley was the first) to hit two centuries in a Test in England and, as the fastest scoring opening batsman in contemporary international

Gordon Greenidge of the West Indies remains one of the most technically correct of all Test batsmen.

cricket, is a superb limited over player who can chart the course of a match from the first ball bowled.

The left-handed Hilary Angelo Gomes from Trinidad has had what one critic has described as 'an unreasonable struggle' to establish his position in the West Indies team. Born into a cricketing family where his father encouraged his five boys to use their talents to the full, 'Larry' Gomes for years lived in the shadow of the little left-handed master Alvin Kallicharran. When finally given a chance in two Tests in England in 1976, Gomes failed but received a second opportunity when many players defected to the 'Packer circus' in 1977–78.

He responded with two centuries in successive matches against Bobby Simpson's touring 1977–78 Australians but again found himself on the bench when peace was made and the Packer players returned.

Then came a triumphant tour of Australia in 1981–82 when the left-hander was the only West Indian to post a Test century in the three international matches played (he averaged more than 78 for the series). This shy almost introverted player has seldom failed for West Indies since.

Gordon Greenidge has formed with fellow-Barbadian Desmond Leo Haynes one of the most effective Test opening partnerships of all time. A lively character, Desmond Haynes made a spectacular entry into the international scene with a brilliant 148 in a limited over game against Bobby Simpson's Australian team in the West Indies in 1977–78. His batting style has since undergone some modification and he is now the less ebullient half of the partnership.

The two openers are similar in build and look very much alike when wearing helmets, but their styles are markedly different, with Haynes at times the more flowing with a liking for the straight drive.

Greenidge's tall and solidly built younger partner holds the distinction of having scored a century in his first Test at Lord's, the second match of the 1980 series in England. After adding 37 with Greenidge for the first wicket, Haynes was joined by Viv Richards (145) in a stand of 223. Richards's own explosive century came in 125 minutes and when he was dismissed, Haynes continued calmly on his way to record what remains his highest Test innings, 184 in 515 minutes with 27 fours. Against India in the fourth Test at Bombay in 1983–84 Haynes became the fourth player to be given out 'handled the ball' in all Test cricket.

Two batsmen who eventually defected to play in South Africa alongside Lawrence Rowe and Alvin Kallicharran were fairly regular West Indies team members. The exuberant and outrageously unorthodox Collis Llewellyn King (Barbados) became the 'King of Wanderers' when he hit a spectacular century against South Africa in the Johannesburg 'Test' of 1982–83 (he hit 101 out of 146 in 133 minutes after coming in with the score at 39 for three wickets). His most bewildering shot was a *back-foot drive* off a well-pitched up ball, through a very wide arc from cover point to mid-wicket.

The more orthodox Guyanan Sheik Faoud Ahumul Fasiel Bacchus played one major innings of note for West Indies – a marathon 250 in eight and a half hours versus India in the sixth Test at Kanpur in 1978–79 – during his short Test career that preceded his trip to South Africa.

When incumbent West Indies wicket-keeper David Murray sold his gloves to South Africa in 1983, Peter Jeffrey Dujon from Jamaica quickly consolidated his place in the West Indies team as an agile wicket-keeper and a hard-hitting batsman who could have played for his run-scoring ability alone.

A gifted stroke-player, Jeff Dujon is a 'natural' as a batsman and behind the stumps. Coming in around number six or seven after the 'big guns', his consistent free-scoring ability has made him an invaluable member of the current West Indies match-winning combination.

Richard Benjamin Richardson is the latest player from the tiny island of Antigua to make it to the top (following fast bowler Andy Roberts and current captain and batting supremo Viv Richards). Richie Richardson has swiftly consolidated his place in the West Indies team with a string of solid performances against Australia and England after making his first appearance against India at Bombay in 1983–84.

Feared by fast bowlers for his sure hooking and cutting ability, he is a player who boasts a maturity far beyond his years. Against Australia in the West Indies in 1983–84, he averaged 81.75 – with a top score of 154 on his home ground at St John's, Antigua, where he and Viv Richards delighted the crowd with a massive 308-run record partnership. During 1985–86 Richardson established himself as possibly West Indies' leading batsman after Viv Richards with a series of stunning performances in the Tests against England in the Caribbean.

Augustine Lawrence 'Gus' Logie has been hailed in some quarters as a future West Indies 'great' but only gained his West Indies cap when a number of players went to South Africa in 1983. A wonderful outfielder, he has had few opportunities to show his class in Tests as a punishing batsman.

It can not be an easy task to follow players like Haynes, Greenidge, Richards, Gomes and Lloyd in the order. But now that Lloyd has gone, the little Trinidad stroke-player has his chance finally to establish himself, although he lost ground in 1986 when Barbados captain Charlie Best was picked for the vacant spot against England. Other young batsmen jostling Logie for a permanent place in the West Indies batting line-up include the pugnacious Trinidad opener Phillip Verant Simmons and the exciting Guyana all-rounder Carl Llewellyn Hooper, who struck his first Test century versus India in 1987–88.

Many superlatives have been used to describe the remarkable batting of Isaac Vivian Alexander Richards, the undisputed maestro of modern West Indies cricket, the best batsman of the day in world cricket and a player worthy of inclusion alongside the all-time greats. In 1976, on his first tour to England, the 24-year-old Antiguan prodigy hit brilliantly all round the wicket at Trent Bridge in the opening Test to reach 232 in 445 minutes with four sixes and 31 fours. At Manchester in the third Test, he compiled a second innings 135. Then, in the final Test at the Oval he scored a blistering 292 and, in the process, passed Sir Frank Worrell's West Indies record

No one can match the power of Viv Richards, the current 'king' of West Indies cricket and its captain.

for Tests in England — 261 at Trent Bridge in 1950.

Richards's seven Test innings in 1976 produced 829 runs at 118.42. England's captain Tony Greig had, in a moment of grave indiscretion, reportedly claimed before the West Indies team arrived in 1976 that 'we will make them grovel'. Viv Richards's verbal response was: 'Nobody talks to Viv Richards like that.' His more visible reply was plenty of runs on the board and total humiliation for the England cricket team.

Only three Tests were played on his next trip to England in 1980, but Richards scored with the same devastating consistency and power and logged 379 runs at an average of 63.16. In 1984, Viv Richards reserved his most amazing batting of the season for the Texaco

Trophy one-day encounter at Manchester. His 189 not out (five sixes, 21 fours) against England in that match is the record for limited over internationals and came off just 170 balls.

He has made runs by the bucketful wherever he has played and in every major cricketing country, in Test matches, in one-day internationals (his personal speciality) and in first-class games. Although no elegant artist like Sobers, Kanhai or Worrell, Richards has a masterful and complete technique. Exceptionally quick of eye and foot, he possesses the power of a Walcott off the back foot and, off the front, the savage driving capability of a Weekes.

England captain Mike Brearley once wrote in *The Cricketer International* that when Richards was in full flow, he felt helpless. This view of the batting maestro was confirmed in no uncertain manner when he slammed a century off 56 balls against England at St John's, Antigua, in 1985–86 to create a new Test record for big hitting that may well stand for all time. Richards ended the day with a dazzling 110 not out off 58 balls and one hit off Ian Botham carried an estimated 120 metres and landed in the top tier of the stand to the left of long off. The innings included six sixes and seven fours.

Ted Dexter claims that the main basis of Richards's powerful batting is his 'uncanny ability to time the ball fluently on the leg side off anything remotely pitched up on a line somewhere near the stumps'. This playing across the line would be fatal for less gifted batsmen but Richards is so sure-eyed and well-balanced that the impossible becomes the normal.

Viv Richards's father Malcolm was Antigua's leading fast bowler for many years, but had little hope of reaching higher honours when that tiny island was not yet part of a first-class cricket grouping. Young Vivian was chosen for Antigua in both cricket and soccer while still a teenager and at a tender age was already the idol of the crowds.

In his mature years, Viv Richards has become as much a representative of the struggle of the black races of the world for recognition as was Lord Learie Constantine and Sir Frank Worrell. He is also the undisputed West Indies batting supremo of the day, whose feats have become legend on almost every major cricket ground, from Bridgetown to Bombay, from Lord's to Lancaster Park, and from Sydney to St John's. Long may 'King Viv' continue to reign.

40

The Greatest?

'The great batsman lifts us out of our utilitarian selves: we admire his work for its beauty, not merely for its value in runs'
— Sir Neville Cardus

Each generation and each country has had its own heroes. The immortal W G Grace was the first great batting champion. Viv Richards is the current 'king'. In between we have had men like Trumper, Faulkner, Hobbs, Macartney, Taylor, Ponsford, Herbert Sutcliffe, Hammond, Bradman, Headley, McCabe, Merchant, Donnelly, Hutton and, after the Second World War, Miller, Compton, Morris, Harvey, Bert Sutcliffe, Weekes, Worrell, Walcott, Mankad, Manjrekar, May, Cowdrey, Hanif Mohammed, Simpson, Dexter, Pataudi, Sobers, Boycott, Pollock, Barry Richards, Zaheer, Turner, Greg Chappell, Gavaskar, Gower, Border (and more than one favourite has been omitted).

The poet Owen Meredith, Earl of Lytton, wrote, 'Genius does what it must, and Talent does what it can'. The fine line that exists between the man of genius and the man of talent has been described as being represented by the capacity of the former, through painstaking work and practice, to transmute his inherent talent into genius.

Perhaps the use of a set of criteria would assist in choosing the greatest batsman of all time. Owen Meredith provides us with two: 'Genius' and 'Talent' but in cricketing terms perhaps a more realistic formula would be to categorise players under three groupings: series dominators, match winners and match savers. The final choice would be a batsman who qualifies in all three categories, subject to a further breakdown into categories of 'Genius' and 'Talent' (and a third requirement that the batsman concerned would have been something of a 'legend' in his own time).

Even with the use of this complicated formula, it still remains obvious as to who will eventually claim pride of place. The heading of an earlier chapter quotes the words of H A Pawson concerning Sir Donald Bradman. The argument for Bradman as number one is further strengthened by the facts – his phenomenal Test batting average (99.94 in 80 innings); his run-scoring speed (around 50 runs an hour); and his almost complete dominance of Test cricket over some 20 years.

Bradman came through the infamous bodyline series with an

average of 56.57, which exceeds the career average of most other batsmen, so it might be safe to suggest that he would have coped fairly adequately with the modern four-pronged short-pitching pace attack. However, it remains unlikely that even a Bradman would have been able to maintain a Test average in the 90s if forced to contend with the West Indies fast bowling pack in every other series.

But there can be no real argument against the choice of Sir Donald George Bradman as the greatest international batsman of all time. So it may be best at this point to invite him to take his place on the dais as gold medallist and take a look at the candidates for silver and bronze.

To be democratic, we should choose one or two outstanding batsmen from each Test country. Any choice among English batsmen would narrow down to Sir J B Hobbs and W R Hammond (with Herbert Sutcliffe, Boycott and perhaps May and Compton pressing hard). Both Jack Hobbs and Walter Hammond were indisputable legends in their own time. The only other England batsman who would qualify in this regard is, of course, the great doctor himself, W G Grace, who stands alone as the 'Father of Modern Cricket' but whose actual Test career started too late for him to fully exhibit his genius in international play.

Australia's choice? Can there be any other first claimant but Victor Trumper? We already have Bradman, so Macartney, Ponsford, McCabe, Harvey, Greg Chappell and Border must be left out. All were or are batsmen of character and high talent, but none could surely lay claim to by the equal of the genius of Trumper.

Three names come up for West Indies: Headley, Sobers and Viv Richards (with the three 'Ws' in reserve). The first, George Headley, although a cricketing 'immortal' in any terms, was unfortunate to play when his team was generally unable to match the strength of the other Test-playing countries and he was frequently forced into the role of match-saver instead of match-winner. In another age, or playing for a stronger team, he would have challenged Bradman himself for the ultimate batting crown.

The charismatic Viv Richards has won enough matches for West Indies to qualify and who can leave Sir Garfield Sobers out of a short list of the greatest batsmen (or bowlers, or fielders) of all time? So the West Indies candidates for silver and bronze must be Sobers and Viv Richards.

South Africa? Five names spring immediately to mind: Faulkner, Taylor, Dudley Nourse, Graeme Pollock, Barry Richards. Aubrey Faulkner certainly dominated a couple of series (and won one in South Africa virtually on his own, as batsman and as bowler). Taylor was one of the few batsmen ever to master the immortal England bowler Sydney Barnes. Dudley Nourse found the answer to Clarrie Grimmett's spin. But none of these batsmen seemed quite to possess the genius of the more latter day Pollock and Richards. Graeme Pollock and Barry Richards certainly qualify in the 'legend' category. Richards has indeed been named by more than one famous critic as possibly the best batsman to appear since Bradman.

When it comes to New Zealand, the overall field is small but highly talented: C S Dempster, Martin Donnelly, Bert Sutcliffe, John Reid and Glenn Turner. Turner has scored more runs that any other New Zealander but has had more opportunities than the more dominating Sutcliffe. Although Glenn Turner outscored all others, Bert Sutcliffe must be the candidate, for his dominance and close to legendary status.

From India there is C K Nayudu (like W G, too early for a full Test career), V M Merchant, V L Manjrekar, the Nawab of Pataudi junior and S M Gavaskar. Merchant falls into the Headley class — a potential match-winner forced to become a match-saver. Manjrekar and Pataudi are of the same category. So the single choice must be Sunny Gavaskar, the man who beat Bradman's Test century record.

Pakistan is a relative newcomer to Test cricket but has already produced two 'legendary' batsmen, Hanif Mohammed and Zaheer Abbas. Zaheer was fortunate to play when Pakistan possessed a strong all-round team, so must qualify for our short list.

And to keep the choice fair and democratic, Sri Lanka's Duleep Mendis must be added.

The shortlist for the silver and bronze medals thus reads: Sir J B Hobbs, W R Hammond (England), V T Trumper (Australia), R G Pollock, B A Richards (South Africa), Sir G St A Sobers, I V A Richards (West Indies), B Sutcliffe (New Zealand), S M Gavaskar (India), Zaheer Abbas (Pakistan), L R D Mendis (Sri Lanka).

There can be little argument that, skilled and talented as they were or are, Gavaskar, Zaheer, Mendis and Bert Sutcliffe do not quite fulfil our predetermined criteria. Which leaves Trumper, Hobbs, Hammond, Sobers, Viv Richards, Pollock and Barry Richards. Take your pick. The writer's is Hobbs (silver) and Sobers (bronze) with Pollock next in line, followed by a dead-heat involving Trumper, Hammond, Barry Richards and Viv Richards.

The final choice then: gold medal — Sir Donald George Bradman; silver — Sir John Berry Hobbs; bronze — Sir Garfield Sobers. It is perhaps no coincidence that all three have been knighted for their services to cricket.

A batting line-up of all time greats might read: Hobbs, Trumper, Viv Richards, Bradman, Hammond, Graeme Pollock and Sobers. Add three bowlers (they select themselves): Bill O'Reilly, Sydney Barnes and Dennis Lillee. And, as it would take quite an attack to get past the first seven batsmen, we can go for the best gloveman, irrespective of his batting prowess — so Bert Oldfield gets the vote, to make a full all-time World XI: J B Hobbs, V T Trumper, I V A

Richards, Sir D G Bradman (captain), W R Hammond, R G Pollock, Sir G St A Sobers, W A Oldfield (wicket-keeper), W J O'Reilly, S F Barnes, D K Lillee. With 12th man duties going to Colin Bland (the greatest outfielder of all time?).

Statistician Charlie Wat has chosen the following team to beat our World XI, based on their potential to dismiss its great batting line-up and handle its bowlers: W H Ponsford, W M Woodfull, I M Chappell (captain), E deC Weekes, Sir F M Worrell, C L Walcott (wicket-keeper), K R Miller, W Rhodes, R R Lindwall, H Larwood, F R Spofforth, with 12th man Gus Logie of the West Indies.

There will be many alternative suggestions — but, in the end, it matters little, for what *is* important is that in every age we will have new champions to carry forward the traditions of excellence in batsmanship created by our heroes of the past.

THE BOWLERS

Contents

Introduction

'Bowling is just as artistic as many of the so-called higher arts and a great deal more manly and healthy...'

— F R Spofforth

The story of the evolution of bowling has been covered by a number of notable writers, from John Nyren and the Reverend James Pycroft in the 1800s and George Beldham and C B Fry, who recorded profiles in words and pictures of many of the 'Golden Age' greats in their *Great Bowlers and Fielders*, through to the contemporary David Frith, with his two separate studies, *The Fast Men* and *The Slow Men*, both published in the 1980s.

This work concentrates as much on the character and performance of the great international bowlers as on their actual method. A brief look at the evolution of bowling is followed by the story of international bowling, from the inaugural Melbourne Test of the 1876–77 Australian season (and the first ball in Test cricket bowled by England's Alfred Shaw) through to the days of Lohmann, Tom Richardson, Rhodes and Sydney Barnes of England; 'The Demon' Spofforth, Turner, Giffen, Noble and company of Australia (without forgetting Philadelphia's 'King of Swing', John Barton King).

The discovery by B J T Bosanquet of the googly and its adoption by South Africans like Faulkner, Vogler and Schwarz, and later development to a high art by Australians like Hordern, Mailey, Grimmett and O'Reilly and Englishmen, Freeman, Peebles and Wright is fully covered.

So too is the emergence after the First World War of fast bowling as an ultimate weapon when, initially, Gregory and McDonald (Australia) and then, Larwood and Voce (England), gave international cricket a foretaste of what has become the standard of modern Test cricket.

The fast bowling trend at top level was taken up immediately after the Second World War by Australia's Lindwall and Miller, and continued by Davidson, McKenzie and the fearsome Lillee and Thomson. England produced 'Fiery Fred' Trueman, Statham, 'Typhoon' Tyson, Snow and Willis. From South Africa came Adcock, Heine, Peter Pollock and Procter. The West Indies' tradition started by Constantine, Francis and Martindale in the 1930s was revived by

Hall, Griffith and Sobers and then taken to new levels of terrifying efficiency by the stream of quick men who came out of the Caribbean led by Andy Roberts in the 1970s. India's pre-war Mohammed Nissar and Amar Singh and current spearhead Kapil Dev gain mention, as do New Zealand's seam bowlers Blair, Motz, Taylor, Collinge and the latest 'king', Richard Hadlee. Pakistan's Imran Khan and Sarfraz Narwaz cannot be overlooked and the great medium-pacers are not neglected: Tate, Bedser, Bailey, Botham (England), Fazal Mahmood (Pakistan) and Cowie (New Zealand).

The master slow bowlers gain their rightful place: Verity, Laker, Lock, Wardle, Titmus, Underwood (England), Tayfield (South Africa), Ramadhin, Valentine and Gibbs (West Indies), Australia's mystery men Iverson and Gleeson, and the famed Indian quartet of Chandrasekhar, Prasanna, Bedi and Venkataraghavan, and their predecessor Gupte.

Before the Second World War (with some notable exceptions as witnessed in the heyday of Gregory and McDonald and during the bodyline fracas), the main emphasis in attack was on slow and medium-paced bowling; on art and patient device. Bowlers like Barnes, Rhodes, O'Reilly, Mailey and Grimmett were like poker players, ever seeking an opportunity to bluff their opponents. Since the 1939–45 War, a new pattern of play has emerged which perhaps exemplifies the quickened pace of life that has come in our technological age. That great traditionalist E H D Sewell once commented: 'There is real art in bowling opponents out or in getting them caught or stumped out by the clever-pitching of a well-spun ball. There is none whatever in trying to frighten them out.' One can only wonder what Mr Sewell's comments might have been had he witnessed the methods of some of the current fast bowlers in international cricket.

Whatever an individual bowler's choice of style in his effort to dislodge opposing batsmen, the fact remains that to become a bowler of international standing requires much effort and practice. And, as the Reverend Pycroft noted more than a hundred years ago, brawn without brains seldom succeeds — as has been amply demonstrated by the great international bowlers who have achieved success at a supreme level.

1

The evolution of bowling

'Bowling consists of two parts: there is the mechanical, and the intellectual part'

— James Pycroft (1851)

The early bowlers *bowled* the ball along the ground, making use of unpredictable rough surfaces to fool the batsman who was armed with a curved bat to combat the 'shooting' ball. In the beginning, there were only two stumps, with a single, long bail but the aptitude in the late 1700s of men like the amply-proportioned Edward 'Lumpy' Stevens to frequently beat the bat and put the ball between the sticks saw the introduction of a third stump.

During the famous Hambledon Era, bowlers began to give the ball some 'air' and to introduce the term 'flight' into cricket's vocabulary. Leg-break bowling, a natural development for a right-hander bowling under-arm, was introduced towards the close of the 18th century by men like Tom Boxall and Lamborn, who was known as 'The Little Farmer' and whose first name has been lost. The latter also developed an off-break and might, indeed, have been the true father of all googly bowlers.

Faster under-arm bowlers, like the celebrated David Harris, soon discovered the efficacy of the sharply rising ball as a weapon to disconcert the batsman. Harris was the finest bowler of the late 18th century and a bachelor who practised assiduously all year round and who bowled his last few seasons from his wheelchair when suffering from gout!

The opening half of the 19th century saw the first true 'giants' of the game emerge when William Lambert and William Clarke helped to raise the art of bowling (and of batting,) to new heights. 'Old Clarke' was the first of cricket's great captains and his All-England XI carried the cricket doctrine from one corner of England to the other. Clarke introduced scientific field-placing and his successor to the captaincy of the All-England XI, George Parr, was destined to lead the first England team abroad in 1859. Nicholas Wanostrocht, who wrote under the name 'Felix', even produced a booklet entitled *How to Play Clarke*, a compliment to that bowler's prowess not repeated for anyone else in cricket's long history.

Tom Walker, who joined Hambledon from Surrey, is recorded as the first player to try round-arm bowling. He was swiftly censured by the Hambledon committee. The frustrated Walker reverted to bowling very slow underhand lobs; he was also noted for his tedious batting.

Where Tom Walker failed in his attempt at introducing a new element to the art of bowling, the obdurate John Willes of Kent persisted with round-arm bowling, and courted unpopularity for 15 years until he was no-balled at Lord's in 1822 and effectively hounded out of the game. In his last big match for Kent versus MCC, Willes responded to his no-balling by throwing the ball to the ground and departing on horseback in high disgust at his treatment by the umpire. Willes, it was said, received the inspiration to bowl round-arm after observing the bowling action of his sister whose ballooning hooped skirts prevented her from employing a true under-arm action.

Willes's method was taken up by a number of top bowlers, with William Lillywhite and Jem Broadbridge of Sussex opposing tradi-tional die-hards like John Nyren, William Denison and Thomas Lord in their support of the new type of bowling.

In 1828 the Marylebone Cricket Club (MCC) altered the bowling rule to permit the raising of the bowler's hand as high as the elbow with the back of the hand uppermost, but Lillywhite and Broadbridge continued to flaunt the ruling by bowling at shoulder height.

In 1835, the MCC succumbed to popular demand and the law was altered to read: 'The Ball must be bowled, and if it be thrown or jerked, or if the hand be above the shoulder in the delivery, the umpire must call "No Ball".'

The advent of John Willes's protege, the 18-stone-plus (114 kg) Alfred Mynn ('The Lion of Kent'), a truly ferocious fast bowler who terrorised all but the finest of batsmen, induced the law-makers in 1845 to reinforce their ruling regarding height of the bowling arm at the moment of delivery.

Bowling was carried into its final stage of development by a rather unlikely 'rebel' – Edgar Willsher, the 14th child of a Kent farmer and who reputedly had one lung. Tall, slender and fastish left-arm, Willsher played for Kent for a quarter of a century. In 1862, bowling at the Oval for All-England XI versus Surrey, he was repeatedly no-balled by John Lillywhite (son of the man who had helped pioneer round-armers) for delivering the ball from above shoulder height. Willsher walked off the field followed by the eight other professionals in the All-England side. Play was suspended for the day and, on the next, Lillywhite was replaced as umpire and Willsher was allowed to continue bowling.

Just two years later, in 1864, the law pertaining to fairness of delivery was finally altered to permit the bowler to deliver the ball with his arm at any height, and the modern game of cricket as we know it was born.

Thus, when Australia faced up to England for the first time at Melbourne in March 1877 for the start of Test cricket proper, over-arm bowling had already been legal for a dozen years, though it should be recorded that the first-ever international cricket match had taken place a good 33 years prior to the famous Melbourne encounter.

In September 1844, teams representing the United States of America and Canada did battle in New York, and the man to bowl the opening ball in international cricket was H Groom, of the US, a left-hander who delivered the ball with an under-arm action. In 1859, the long-lived Groom played for XXII of USA versus the first England team to venture overseas, a side which included such famous English bowlers as tearaway 'Foghorn' John Jackson, H H Stevenson, Jemmy Grundy, William Caffyn and John Wisden, 'The Little Wonder' who has gained cricketing immortality through the publication to this day of *John Wisden's Cricketers' Almanack*, which he first released in 1864 and is now known simply as *Wisden Cricketer's Almanack*, the acknowledged 'cricketers' bible'.

2

First Ball

'It was the deadly length and straightness which did the mischief'
— 'F G' (in Bailey's Magazine, June 1895)

Alfred Shaw, the great England bowler of the 19th century, remarks in his *Cricket Reminiscences*: 'I set before myself the object of endeavouring to pitch the ball as nearly as possible in one place, with the idea of wearing off the turf, and making "a spot" off which I might have a chance of making the ball turn just sufficiently to beat the bat.'

Shaw goes on to state with due modesty that he 'very often succeeded' in his self-imposed task and that he never bowled a wide in his life, and could only remember having been no-balled once or twice ('one occasion being when the ground was wet and the foothold treacherous'). A remarkable feat indeed for a player who made his debut for Nottinghamshire in 1864 and played his final first-class match 33 years later, in 1897 when he was already 55 years of age.

Although it should be recorded that up until 1888 four balls per over was the rule in England (it became five in 1889 and then six in 1900), one of the most stunning facts about the long and distinguished first-class career of the portly Notts and England right-hander was that he bowled more overs than he conceded runs. He was also the man who sent down the first delivery in Test cricket — to set in motion the Anglo-Australian 'Ashes' series.

Looking rather disarmingly like a benign Victorian uncle, the neatly-bearded Alfred Shaw took more than 2000 first-class wickets. Although he himself scotched the legend that he could place the ball at will on a threepenny bit placed on the pitch, his control over length and direction was remarkable. Playing for Nottinghamshire versus MCC and Ground at Lord's in 1875, he clean-bowled the mighty W G Grace twice in the match while recording the amazing figures of 54−35−39−2 (first innings) and 41.2−36−7−7 (second innings), bowling in all 95.2 four-ball overs for just 46 runs and nine wickets.

In his biography Shaw acknowledges that 'WG', because of that great batsman's ability to play a shot for every type of ball bowled at him, was in the ace bowler's estimation the most difficult batsman of his time to dismiss. Grace was, in turn, a great admirer of Shaw's bowling and complimented its 'unvaried precision', commenting in

Alfred Shaw of England bowled the first ball in Test cricket to Australia's English-born Charles Bannerman at Melbourne on 15 March 1878.

his *Cricket* that, although he 'got more work on the ball from the off', Shaw 'could break both ways'.

Something of a businessman, Alfred Shaw was a joint promoter of four of the early England tours to Australia, although already 34 when Test cricket started. He played in only seven 'Tests', achieving the best figures for either side in the inaugural game at Melbourne with 55.3−34−51−3 in the first innings and 34−16−38−5 in the second. This outstanding feat was, however, not sufficient to prevent Australia gaining an historic 45-run victory.

Although he bowled the first ball in Test cricket, Shaw failed to gain the honour of capturing the first wicket − this distinction went to Yorkshire right-hander Allen Hill, whose main attributes as a bowler were a smooth action, good length and direction and a 'break-back' from the off at a brisk medium pace. Hill played in the two Tests engaged in by James Lillywhite's 1876−77 all-professional England team, taking seven wickets for 130 runs.

James Lillywhite junior was a member of a renowned cricketing family of whom five members played for Sussex. A slow left-arm bowler with a high action, he captained England in the 1876−77 Tests against Australia and helped Shaw and batsman Arthur Shrewsbury organise three subsequent visits to Australia. Lillywhite took eight wickets in his two Tests for England.

Of the other bowlers at James Lillywhite's command, Yorkshire's George Ulyett was a fast-bowling right-handed all-rounder who was not averse to employing the bouncer. 'Happy Jack' Ulyett took 50 wickets in his 25 Tests for England and was also a grand batsman who scored 949 Test runs, touring Australia five times.

James Southerton, a slow round-arm off-break bowler, remains the oldest Test debutante, appearing at Melbourne in 1876−77 aged 49 years 119 days. A key performer in Lillywhite's combination despite his age, he took seven wickets at 15.28 runs each in the two games against Australia.

The quick-tongued but popular Yorkshireman Tom Emmett also played in the first two Tests of 1876−77, but without much success as a left-handed round-arm fast bowler. Emmett started playing before over-arm bowling became legal and kept to his former style when he experienced difficulty with the new-fangled method that became the vogue midway through his career. He was one of the few bowlers of his time to trouble W G Grace, who was sometimes disturbed by a ball Emmett called his 'sostenuter', a fastish natural left-hander's leg-break pitched on the leg stump.

Two of Emmett's contemporary fast bowlers in the 1800s, George Freeman and George Tarrant, were also known to occasionally ruffle 'WG' with express deliveries. Neither played in a Test, although Tarrant, on tour with the second English team to Australia under George Parr in 1863−64, provided the inspiration that set F R Spofforth on a fast bowling path.

Grace was himself a wily round-arm bowler of no mean ability, but he did little of that in Tests. The 'Grand Old Man' took nearly 3000 first-class wickets with a combination of crafty skill and out-and-out gamesmanship. In modern parlance, he 'psyched' opposing batsmen out as much as he dismissed them with conventional bowling. With his stock ball a slow leg-break, 'WG' varied his length and flight and was a wonderful catcher off his own bowling.

Nottinghamshire left-hander Frederick Morley made his first Test appearance alongside 'WG' against Australia at the Oval in 1880, and complemented the champion's brilliantly decisive first innings for England of 152 with equally match-winning bowling of eight wickets for 146 runs.

Morley bowled at a fastish pace with a smoothly efficient action and might have performed well in Australia had he not cracked a rib when he was badly knocked about in a collision at sea en route to Australia with Ivo Bligh's team in 1882–83. The game and loyal Morley appeared in three games in Australia, although suffering from great pain, before pulling out, and died from 'congestion and dropsy' soon after returning home to England.

The six-foot-plus (183 cm) William Barnes was another Nottinghamshire player who bowled with good effect at around medium pace. Although picked for England primarily as a free-scoring batsman, 'Billy' Barnes took 51 wickets in 21 Tests (to add to his 725 runs). A 'difficult' character, he once refused to bowl in a Test when given the ball by England's captain and was sometimes involved in brawls because of his drinking habits, which also led to him being reprimanded by the Nottinghamshire committee.

Edmund 'Ted' Peate was the first in the long line of Yorkshire left-arm spin bowlers to become first choice for England in home Test matches. It was jokingly said Peate's batting was so poor that he went in at number 11 only because there wasn't a number 12. As a bowler, he was a supreme master of flight and length.

When still a teenager, Peate was a member of a touring group called 'Treloar's Clown Cricketers' which travelled the country to perform alongside clowns and acrobats. There was no clowning about when he was picked for England versus Australia in 1881–82 and took eight wickets for 57 runs in his third Test at Sydney. At the Oval in 1882, in his first home Test, Peate's eight wickets for 71 runs in the match failed to stop Australia from gaining a famous seven-run win (Spofforth took 14 wickets in the match).

Fellow-Yorkshireman Willie Bates was a grand all-rounder, a hard hitter who scored more than 600 runs in the 15 Tests in which he took 50 wickets at 16.24 runs apiece with his slow right-arm off-breaks bowled to an excellent length. Poor catching kept Billy Bates out of Tests in England but he went to Australia on five occasions. Bates's last visit there ended in tragedy when his sight was permanently impaired after a blow in the eye at net practice in Melbourne during the 1886–87 tour. In the second international of the 1881–83 tour, he became the first England bowler to claim a Test hat-trick when he dismissed McDonnell, Giffen and Bonnor in the first innings.

In that match Bates boasted figures of 7/28 and 7/74 and his 14 wickets ensured an innings win for England.

When Australia's batsmen moved relentlessly towards a mammoth score of 551 at the Oval in 1884, Lord Harris, England's captain, called upon all 11 of his players to bowl in an effort to dislodge the opposing skipper, W L Murdoch, who was on his way to the first double-century in Test cricket.

This included use of the home wicket-keeper, the Honourable Alfred Lyttelton, without success, on the first day of play (with England batsman W W Read keeping wicket). When called upon to bowl again on the second day, Lyttelton responded by sending down under-hand lobs and capturing four wickets, with W G Grace taking over duty behind the stumps. Lyttelton returned an analyis of 12−5−19−4, which remained his only performance as a bowler in Test cricket.

W W Read, normally an early-order batsman, came in to bat at number 10 in the England innings (and scored a match-saving 117, which indicates that he might well have injured himself slightly when keeping wicket to Lyttelton on the first day).

The short and stocky Robert Peel took over from Ted Peate as Yorkshire and England's left-arm spin bowler. As was the case with a number of professional cricketers of his time, Bobby Peel enjoyed a predilection for strong drink but his frequent carousing did not prevent him from bagging a century of wickets in only 20 Tests.

Peel began and ended his Test career with eight wickets in a match. In all, he exceeded that figure for England on five occasions with a best of 11 wickets for 68 in the Old Trafford Test versus Australia in 1888.

A better than ordinary left-handed striker of the ball, Bobby Peel was close to all-rounder status and worth his place in any side. It seems a shame that he is perhaps remembered as much for his many misdemeanours on and off the field as for his very fine bowling and useful batting. It has been alleged that the last straw as far as peppery Yorkshire skipper Lord Hawke was concerned came on the day when Peel, well 'in his cups', passed water on the pitch. There is no concrete evidence of this final event having ever taken place, but the recalcitrant left-arm spinner who had humbled Australia's best on so many famous occasions was certainly banned from Old Trafford and first-class cricket following an incident involving Lord Hawke in 1897.

In the match which marked Bobby Peel's Test debut at Adelaide in 1884−85, Lancashire's beloved little left-hander, the fun-loving Johnny Briggs, did not even get a bowl. This much-admired but ultimately tragic player, like Peel, claimed more than 100 Test victims with his guileful, round-arm slow medium spinners. According to W

G Grace, Briggs fielded to his own bowling ('and everybody else's') 'with the quickness of a cat' and the Lancashire left-hander gave added value with his aggressive batting, hitting the ball exceptionally hard for a man of his size.

The 5 ft 5 in (165 cm) 'Boy' Briggs claimed a hat-trick against Australia at Sydney in 1891–92 on the fourth of his six tours there with England teams. At Lord's in 1886 he took 11 Australian wickets for 74 runs and, in the first-ever Test series between tourists England and South Africa, in 1888–89, Briggs demoralised the local players with figures of 19.1–11–17–7 and 14.2–5–11–8–15 wickets in the match for only 28 runs, with South Africa being dismissed for totals of 47 and 43. Briggs had little need for fielders in that match: 14 of his victims were clean bowled and the remaining one dismissed leg-before-wicket!

Alas, poor Johnny Briggs suffered from a type of epilepsy and an attack of sunstroke while in Africa did not help matters. At captain A C MacLaren's behest the Lancashire all-rounder, then aged 37, was recalled to the England eleven for the third Test of 1899, having been overlooked for the first two matches. Briggs had taken 94 wickets in Anglo-Australian Tests and it has been claimed that the fast approaching coveted 100 victims triggered off an epileptic attack after he had taken three Australian wickets in the first innings of the match. Briggs was carried from the field following his seizure and was unable to bat, or bowl again, in what proved to be his final Test. Another epileptic attack, while watching a variety show in Leeds, saw the hapless England player committed to Cheadle Asylum.

Although he recovered sufficiently to play a wonderful season for Lancashire in 1900, Briggs had a relapse and died early in 1902 at the age of 39.

Of Johnny Briggs's contemporaries, players like William Attewell (an accurate and tireless right-arm medium pacer from Nottingham-shire) and Wilfred Flowers (also from Notts and a steady right-hand off-break exponent) gained the odd success in Test cricket without sealing a regular place in the England team.

The one-eyed John William Sharpe (he lost the use of one eye when a youth) arrived a little later, after he had moved from Notting-ham to play for Surrey. Although slightly built, Sharpe bowled with great vigour and success for Lord Sheffield's team in Australia in 1891–92, but wore himself out through trying to bowl too fast and soon faded from the scene.

The early England teams to South Africa included one or two bowlers of merit who did not gain recognition in the more prestigious England-Australia clashes. Among them was the Honourable Charles Aubrey Smith (later Sir C Aubrey Smith) who was to become a famous film actor and patron of cricket in Hollywood. R C Robertson-Glasgow says of him: 'If Sir Aubrey Smith could have joined the company of King Arthur, he would have introduced cricket and become captain of Camelot...'

More than six foot tall (183 cm), Smith was a right-arm fast-medium bowler whose curving run up to the stumps earned him the soubriquet 'Round the Corner' Smith. He toured Australia in 1887–88 and 1888–89 without playing in a Test, then captained the first English team to tour South Africa (sponsored by Major Warton) and took seven wickets in the first Test played between the two countries at Port Elizabeth.

Somerset's Arnold James Fothergill, left-arm medium-paced, took eight wickets in the two Tests versus South Africa in 1888–89. Another left-hander of medium pace, Kent's Frederick 'Nutty' Martin was chosen for England against Australia at the Oval in 1890 when both Peel and Briggs were unavailable. He took six wickets in each innings in a thriller that England eventually won by two wickets but was never again picked in a Test against Australia. His one other international came against South Africa at Cape Town in 1891–92 when he bowled unchanged with former Australian Test bowler J J Ferris, then playing for England, in the home team's second innings. In his two Tests, Martin took 14 wickets at 10.07 each.

Ferris was one of five Australians who have played for both Australia and England, the others being batsman and former Australian captain, W L Murdoch and all-rounders W E Midwinter, S M J Woods and Albert E Trott. Ferris, Murdoch, Woods and Trott all represented England in Tests versus South Africa after having played for Australia against England.

Billy Midwinter, an all-round player of rare talent, was Gloucestershire born, appeared for Australia in the first-ever Test at Melbourne in 1876–77 (he took five wickets for 78 runs in England's first innings with his medium pace spin bowling) and, touring Australia as a member of Alfred Shaw's England XI in 1881–82, opened the bowling with Peate in two Tests. He then switched back to play for Australia against England in 1882–83 and 1886–87 and again on tour in England in 1884. In a sad sequence of events, Midwinter suffered the triple loss of his wife and two daughters and their demise drove him insane. He was confined to an asylum and died at the age of 39.

One major England bowler of the late 1800s remains to be discussed: George Alfred Lohmann who, by all accounts, was probably the finest of all his country's pre-'Golden Age' trundlers. He was, however, also destined to leave this world prematurely, a victim of tuberculosis at the age of 36. No less a judge than C B Fry regarded it an honour to face up to Lohmann's impeccable bowling and W G Grace himself regarded the Surrey cricketer as the best all-rounder of his time.

Before his illness and untimely death, Lohmann built up a reputation as probably the best bowler in the world. In just 18 Tests he took 112 wickets at the low average of 10.75. Lohmann graduated from club to international cricket in two years and startled H J H Scott's 1886 Australians when he claimed 12 wickets in the third and final Test of the season at the Oval to give England a 3−0 clean sweep for the series.

One of the most striking figures ever to appear on a cricket field, the strong shouldered, handsome and blue-eyed Lohmann bowled right-arm with a high, over-the-top action that was at once rhythmical and effective. His pace was normally around medium, but he would occasionally unleash a faster delivery without any perceptible change to his smooth action.

One of Lohmann's most deceptive deliveries was a high curving ball which he let go just before his arm reached the top of its swing and which dipped rather sooner than the batsman expected. A master at pace variation, he was a difficult proposition on any type of wicket. Although he did not score many runs at Test level, George Lohmann's quick-footed batting and miraculous catching in the slips made him something of a 19th century Ian Botham in county games for Surrey.

Lohmann produced a long list of incredible bowling feats in Tests against Australia and South Africa. Following his debut 7/36 and 5/68 at the Oval in 1886, he bagged 16 wickets for 137 runs in the two Tests England played in Australia in 1886−87 (both played at Sydney) including 8/35 in Australia's first innings in the second match. In the only Test played by the 1887−88 England team in Australia (again at Sydney), Lohmann and Bobby Peel bowled virtually unchanged through the two home innings as England swept to a 126-run victory in a low scoring match. Peel's figures read: 5/18 and 5/40; Lohmann took 5/18 and 4/35.

Sydney again provided a happy hunting ground for England's ace bowler in 1891−92 when the dashing Lohmann, blonde locks and moustache glinting in the sun, virtually dismissed Australia single-handedly when taking eight wickets for 58 (43.2 overs, 18 maidens) in the second Test.

By 1892 health problems started to become apparent and Lohmann sailed to South Africa in the company of his good friend and fellow England cricketer, Maurice Read. There Lohmann took up residence at a sanatorium in the picturesque town of Ceres, near Cape Town, and then in the home of South African cricket enthusiast and sponsor J D Logan at Matjesfontein, in the Karoo, where the air was dry and clear.

Returning home in 1895, Lohmann rejoined Surrey and was then taken by Lord Hawke on a tour of South Africa during the English winter. In the three Tests he played in against South Africa in 1895−96, he claimed a phenomenal 35 wickets for 203 runs (average

George Lohmann was known as the 'WG' of the early England bowlers.

5.80), including 7/38 and 8/7 in the first Test at Port Elizabeth, 9/28 and 3/43 at Johannesburg, in the second, and 7/42 and 1/45 in the final match at Cape Town. The closest any international bowler has since come to this amazing performance in a three-match series was when New Zealand's Richard Hadlee netted 33 wickets for 401 runs (average 12.15) versus Australia during the 1985–86 season.

Lohmann appeared in only one more game for his country, against Australia at Lord's in the first Test of 1896, and would have played in the third and final game of the rubber at his county home ground, the Oval, were it not for a pay dispute.

George Lohmann's confrontation with the Surrey committee resulted in his moving to South Africa permanently (where he played for Western Province in the Currie Cup). When he returned to England in 1901 as manager of the South African touring team, his health had deteriorated to such an extent that it was clearly apparent that his days were numbered.

The 'WG' of English 19th century bowling died in South Africa a few months after returning to his new home following the 1901 tour. He was treated for his debilitating complaint during his final days at the British Military Hospital at Matjesfontein (the Anglo-Boer War had broken out two years before) where one of the medical orderlies who ministered to him was the future thriller writer of great fame, Edgar Wallace. George Lohmann was buried in the Matjesfontein Cemetery where a headstone, erected in his memory by the Surrey County Cricket Club and his many South African friends, still stands.

The passing of George Lohmann represented the end of an era in English cricket in general and bowling in particular. His brilliant cricketing career overlapped into what has become known as the 'Golden Age of Cricket' – and a new set of great England bowlers was making ready to adorn an era which some regard as the peak period in all of cricket's long history.

3

'The Demon' and 'The Terror'

'I verily believe he has frightened more batsmen out than many bowlers have fairly and squarely beaten'

— George Giffen

George Giffen, Australian Test all-rounder and captain, once wrote that Frederick Robert Spofforth 'looked the Demon every inch of him' and that when Spofforth meant business, 'the batsman had to look out for squalls'.

During his cricketing career Spofforth achieved many remarkable performances, but his most notable feat was to so humble England's batsman as to provide clear evidence of Australia's right to meet the 'enemy' on equal terms. And, as much as the indomitable W G Grace raised the standards of first-class batting to a higher level of proficiency than had been the case before his advent onto the cricket stage, so too did Spofforth bring a fresh dimension to the art of bowling, to inspire those who played with and against him to raise their own standards of performance.

'The Demon' bowler of the 19th century was born the son of a Yorkshireman in the Sydney suburb of Balmain in 1853, but spent much of his early childhood in New Zealand. The Spofforth legend started the day he claimed his 14th wicket in the match that saw Australia defeat England on English soil for the first time, at the Oval in 1882.

The story of the Ashes also began with this famous match when a mock obituary appeared in a racing journal *The Sporting Times*, proclaiming the death of English cricket and that the body would be cremated and the ashes sent to Australia. The Ashes themselves did not physically come into existence until some years later when some Melbourne women burnt a bail (some say a ball or stump) and placed the remains in an urn for England captain the Honourable Ivo Bligh (Lord Darnley) to take back to England in 1883.

In a low scoring Test at the Oval in 1882, Spofforth took seven wickets in England's first innings (he yorked 'WG' for 4) but Australia's own batting, apart from the display by opener Hugh Massie, was feeble in the extreme and England was ultimately called upon to score just 85 runs for victory. With the tally on 15, Spofforth knocked England captain 'Monkey' Hornby's off-stump out of the ground and castled Lancashire stone-waller Dick Barlow next ball.

With medium-pacer Harry Boyle sewing up the opposite end, Spofforth added seven more wickets to his first innings effort to end the match with 14/90, and not even a determined 32 from 'WG' himself could prevent the shock Australian seven-run win.

Four years previously, at Lord's in 1878, Spofforth and Boyle had stunned the English cricketing fraternity by bowling out a powerful MCC team for scores of 33 and 19 (the Australians won by 10 wickets). Spofforth bowled with superb control of length, used a deceptive 'breakback' and was, according to some observers, terrifically fast, although it is unlikely that he consistently bowled at a great pace. 'The Demon' was, however, considered unplayable on all but the best of pitches. According to Australian Test bowler William Cooper, who lived to see bodyline bowling, 'The Demon' was as fast as Larwood but only bowled his express delivery occasionally, and always gave Australian wicket-keeper Jack Blackham a signal beforehand.

Frank Iredale, one of Australia's most succesful batsmen of the 1890s, claimed that although he considered C T B Turner ('The Terror') to be the best all-round bowler produced by Australia in his time, Spofforth was always a more formidable proposition because of his ability to create the greatest amount of 'funk' among opposing batsmen.

Whereas everything about Spofforth — his athletic run-up, menacing action and his whole physique and bearing — suggested fire and strength, Turner relied upon a more conservative action, designed to conserve his energy, and depended upon his mastery of length, break and change of pace to get his wickets. 'The Demon' was once asked what advice he would give to a schoolboy bowler and his immediate reply was: 'Bowl with brains'.

Spofforth must have been a remarkable bowler indeed: 94 Test wickets at 18.41 runs each; 586 wickets during his five England tours at 13.08 each; and, altogether 853 first-class wickets at 18.41 each. Miracle figures, even in an age of lower scores than today. One thing certain is that during his own lifetime, Fred Spofforth was acknowledged by his fellow players and by spectators as the greatest bowler of his day.

Henry Frederick Boyle was once heard to say that if Spofforth was 'The Demon' then he (Boyle) was 'the very Devil himself'. Like Spofforth, Boyle certainly looked the part, with piercing eyes and a huge black spade-shaped beard. And even if Boyle had not been a fine bowler, he would have been as much remembered for his fearless and intimidating fielding close in on the leg-side to the bowling of his mate Spofforth. As a bowler 'Boyley' was the perfect foil to Spofforth; while Spofforth was at work digging a grave for the English batsmen at Lord's in 1878 and the Oval in 1882, Harry Boyle kept the coffin lid firmly shut at the other end with his unerring length and deceptive

Opposite: 'The Demon' in action: Frederick Robert Spofforth was the first great Australian bowler.

flight. With his right-hand round-arm deliveries, Boyle bowled so tightly that batsmen were prone to swing at Spofforth in frustration and get themselves out against a bowler who was also far too good to be carted in the ordinary fashion.

Boyle tallied 277 wickets on four trips to England, including 125 at 12.18 runs per wicket in 1882. He was also a more than useful batsman who tended to play with better results in England than in Australia.

Thomas William Garrett was one of the bowlers who provided support for Spofforth and Boyle in the early Tests against England and was a long-serving New South Wales and Australia player who had played in the first of all Test matches. Fast right-hand round-arm, with a beautifully easy action and a good yorker, Garrett was adept at gaining pace off the pitch and could move the ball both ways. 'WG' considered him the best Australian bowler on a good wicket, as he was able to keep going for long periods without losing his accuracy or length. At 18 years 232 days, he was the youngest Australian ever to play against England.

England-born slow left-hander Thomas Kendall was another bowler who represented Australia in the inaugural Test. He claimed seven wickets for 55 as the team from his land of birth tumbled to a 45-run defeat. Kendall experienced a chequered career thereafter and was, as far as is known, the first Australian player to be disciplined 'for reasons other than cricket' when he was sent home to Melbourne from Perth after having accompanied the Australians on the first leg of the 1878 tour to England. He moved to Hobart and was instrumental in the development of a number of young players who later made their mark in first-class cricket. The 'William Cooper Letters' published in *Wisden Cricket Monthly* reveal that Kendall was 'the best left-handed medium pace bowler Victoria has seen, when not in his cups'.

Another controversial inaugural Test participant was the powerful all-round sportsman, William Evans Midwinter − hard-hitting right-hand batsman, round-arm spin bowler, brilliant outfielder and a quarter-mile runner, crack rifle shot and adept billiards player. Midwinter, as recorded earlier, played at various times for both Australia and England and was at one time caught up in the middle of a tug-of-war between W G Grace, who wanted him to play for Gloucestershire, and Australia captain Dave Gregory and manager John Conway who insisted that he had arranged to make up the numbers in their 1878 Australian team. The argument ended in a farcical 'Keystone Cops'-type chase through London when 'WG' pushed Midwinter into his carriage and raced off, while Gregory, Conway and Harry Boyle allegedly pursued them in another carriage. In the end, after lengthy altercations, Grace got his way but was forced to apologise to the Australians for his behaviour. Grace's team (with Midwinter absent injured) was, incidentally, thrashed by the Australians when they met later in the same season.

John Henry Hodges was a Victorian fast-medium left-hander who joined in the attack with Garrett, Kendall and Midwinter at Melbourne in 1876–77 when the more capable and well-known Frank Allan was unavailable. Hodges, who had never played for Victoria, did well enough in his two Tests but was not considered when the Australian team was picked to tour England the following year. Allan won a place in the party to England and became feared as a left-arm swing bowler who was named by one critic as 'the bowler of the century'.

In an article entitled 'The Bowler and his Art', (*C B Fry's Magazine*, July 1905), the famous Australian cricketer Hugh Trumble confirms W G Grace's belief that bowlers are born and not made and cites the independent minded Frank Allan as an example. Francis Erskine Allan must have regretted his decision to attend an agricultural show instead of playing against England and never really made up for his lost opportunity, although he did remain the mainstay of Victoria's bowling attack for many years. He could not acclimatise to the cold weather conditions prevailing in England and was a comparative failure on the 1878 tour and played in only one Test for Australia, against England at Melbourne in 1878–79. At his best, it was claimed that Allan rated alongside Spofforth, Turner and J J Ferris, particularly on a fast wicket.

When the Australian XI next made the journey to England in 1880, Spofforth and Boyle were joined by another Victorian, George Eugene Palmer, who with them formed a deadly trio who sorely tested their international opponents over the next five years. Peculiarly enough, 'Joey' Palmer received his first big chance when Frank Allan missed the train that was to take him to play for Victoria against Lord Harris's England XI in 1878–79. The 18-year-old Palmer's dream debut consisted of nine wickets in the match, all clean-bowled, including His Lordship.

Palmer bowled right-arm medium pace with a wonderfully easy delivery. His stock ball was the natural off-break and on a perfect wicket he was even considered superior to Spofforth and Turner, although on a 'sticky dog' the other two were definitely more formidable. A well-disguised yorker was an added asset in Palmer's armoury but when he tried to develop a leg-break later in his career, his length and direction went sadly awry.

Although he missed the famous Ashes encounter, George Palmer could, when he finally retired, look back on a highly productive career that brought him 78 Test wickets (in 17 games) including a personal-best 7/65 in the first Test against England at Melbourne in 1882–83.

William Henry Cooper was a bowler who made up for lost time, after first taking to cricket at the age of 27 when his doctor advised him to get more exercise. Cooper developed an intense love of the game and became a slow round-arm right-hand bowler with a rather peculiar delivery who played in two Tests against Ivo Bligh's 1881–82 English XI (he took 9 wickets at 25.11) and was taken to England in 1884. Sadly, he severely strained the spinning finger on his right hand during a collision with team-mate Alick Bannerman when the Australians were indulging in a game of ship-board hockey en route to England. Cooper did not recover sufficiently and missed much of the tour.

Edwin Evans of New South Wales first played for his colony in 1874–75 but had to wait until 1886 for his initial England tour when already 38 and well past his best. In 1878, Lord Harris, writing after the 1878–79 English tour, claimed that Evans was 'certainly the best bowler we met in Australia'. A grand all-rounder, the large-framed Evans bowled slow-medium with a very high action. His length was usually perfect and he varied his pace and the angle of his arm effectively as an adjunct to his stock off-break.

During the 'Golden Age of Cricket' a number of players were at one time or another compared with the champion of champions, W G Grace, but few really deserved to be spoken about in the same breath. As a batsman, Billy Murdoch certainly looked like matching some of the great man's feats – but, although a capable wicket-keeper, he was not a bowler as was his English counterpart. However, there was a contemporary Australian all-rounder who through his mighty feats on the field of play undoubtedly warranted the title 'Australia's own WG'.

Like an Atlas supporting the globe, the broad-shouldered and moustachioed George Giffen carried South Australia on his strong back for many a long season and was also Australia's most noted all-round cricketer of the 19th century. As a batsman, Giffen had few peers and, if it were permitted, would have bowled happily all day from both ends.

His almost super-human double for South Australia versus Victoria at Adelaide in 1891 could stand well into the 21st century. Not even a supremo like Ian Botham seems capable of scoring 271 (in seven hours) and then claiming 16 wickets in the same match. Only Sir Garfield Sobers (or perhaps Mike Procter) might have achieved such a feat if the circumstances of the day had called for it.

Off a strictly measured run of eight paces, the superbly fit Giffen would vary the pace of his run-in to bowl, without ever signalling to the batsman what type of delivery could be expected. Slow-to-medium, the South Australian titan built his attack around the off-break, but employed variation in flight and pace as an adjunct. An 'over-spun' ball would whip straight through with the batsman playing for the break; a higher, slower delivery would get an opponent's feet in a tangle before it dipped unexpectedly; without change of action a quicker, shorter and straighter ball would trap the batsman leg-before when playing back.

Giffen was the first Australian to reach 1000 runs and 100 wickets in Test cricket and was always a cool and unruffled character, a dignified ornament to the game wherever and whenever he played.

On the day Charles 'The Terror' Turner and his talented side-kick 'The Tricky' Ferris played their opening roles for Australia, that old cricketing trouper and adept performer of the role of bowling villain, F R Spofforth, was making his own final curtain call. With new-boys Turner and Ferris bowling the old enemy, England, out for their lowest total ever in Test match cricket, 'The Demon' chipped in with but a single wicket, that of Johnny Briggs, when the Lancastrian left-hander looked to be leading a batting recovery.

Spofforth took just this single wicket in this his final Test at the Sydney Cricket Ground over New Year 1886−87. but Turner and Ferris claimed between them 17 of the 20 English wickets to tumble. A first innings 45 all out in that match remains the nadir of English batsmanship. Only George Lohmann reached double figures, coming in at number nine with the visiting team's total stuck at a miserable seven for 21.

Australian captain Percy McDonnell won the toss and was the first skipper in history to send his opponents in to bat in a Test. Turner and Ferris bowled unchanged through their debut innings.

Right-arm Charles Thomas Biass Turner went on to take 101 wickets (at 16.53 each) in only 17 Test matches and proved a worthy successor to Spofforth. Left-hander John James Ferris played eight Tests for Australia and took 48 wickets at 14.25 and, in his one and only Test for England (versus South Africa at Cape Town in 1891−92), netted 13 wickets for 91 runs.

Turner 'The Terror' is the only Australian bowler to have taken 100 wickets in an Australian first-class season, a feat he achieved in just 12 matches in 1887−88. In England he was the scourge of all but the finest of county and Test batsmen on three tours, twice in the company of Ferris, although the two Australian bowlers' superlative efforts were ultimately to no avail for England won the series courtesy of a string of dismal performances from Australia's batsmen.

A shade over 5 ft 9 ins (175 cm), Turner used what height he had but bowled with a curious chest-on action that did not quite satisfy the purists. Apart from his regular off-break he was, like Spofforth, a marvel at disguising his changes of pace and utilised a stunning yorker or quicker straight ball for surprise effect. He was unplayable on a sticky wicket and seemed to gather haste and lift off the pitch with an abrupt 'break-back'. Turner did not rely entirely upon his ability to bowl a batsman − he bowled for catches, especially in the slips, employing a faster Alec Bedser-type 'leg-cutter'. Yorkshire all-rounder Willie Bates was once heard to exclaim: 'I never saw a

Known as 'The Terror', C T B Turner of Australia was unplayable on a sticky wicket with his medium-paced off-breaks, leg-cutters and yorkers.

bowler break as much as does Turner from so fast a pace'.

'The Terror' lived to the ripe old age of 82 (he died in 1944) and in 1915 was one of the distinguished pall-bearers at Victor Trumper's funeral. The Sydney-born Ferris died in South Africa in 1900 during the Boer War, aged 33, after having played with Gloucestershire for whom, strangely enough, he performed with more success as a batsman than bowler.

Ferris bowled left-arm at a lively medium pace, mostly breaking across the batsman from leg; a ball pitched outside leg-stump would frequently pass outside the off-stump. Ferris also bowled a confusing variation that unexpectedly came into the batsman. Small but sturdily built, the left-hander was a tireless wicket-taker who made full use of his height and was unflappable when batsmen attacked his bowling.

Until Turner and Ferris stopped playing for Australia, genial Victorian postman George Henry Stevens Trott (an all-rounder in the Giffen image who was good enough to play for Australia as a batsman alone) was not given much to do with the ball in Test cricket. And when he became captain of his country, the popular 'Harry' Trott, unlike George Giffen, did not over-bowl himself. His brother, Albert Edwin Trott, was entirely a different character to his genial brother and is reported to have once cut Harry dead in the street.

As a batsman, 'Alberto' Trott degenerated into a pure slogger, forever endeavouring to emulate his own feat of once smacking the ball over the pavilion at Lord's. As a bowler he responded to his shock omission from the 1896 team to tour England (after a grand Test debut 8/43 at Adelaide in 1894–95) by bitterly stating: 'Very, well, I will go on my own account.' Australia's loss became Middlesex's gain and A E Trott became one of the most feared of bowlers on the English county circuit for 13 seasons. He also became one of the small band of players to represent two countries in Test cricket when he played for England on a trip with Lord Hawke's team to South Africa in 1898–99.

A tall man of forthright personality with huge hands and an even more imposing drooping moustache, Trott could be the life and soul of a party but, with a ball in his hand, all thoughts of conviviality disappeared. His fast yorker was considered a 'holy terror' and, as it might be followed by a slow off-break or leg-break, the batsman could never relax his concentration against a bowler who was 'unique in his variety' and who never minded how much he was hit as long as he eventually claimed the wicket. Stories abound about this unusual player who later ended his own life.

Samuel Moses James Woods was another Australian bowler of pace who, like Ferris and A E Trott, played for both his own country and for England. Also a fine rugby forward for England, the 6 ft 1 in (185 cm) 'Sammy' Woods was born in Sydney but spent the whole of his adult sporting life in England. A strong right-arm fast bowler who varied his pace well and bowled a devastating yorker, he was described by W G Grace as 'a giant in size, in strength, and in pluck'. Woods played three Tests each for Australia and England (and took five wickets for each country). He was the only Australian to play Test cricket for his country without ever having taken part in first-class cricket in Australia.

At the approaching close of the era which ran its course from the days of 'The Demon', F R Spofforth, to the times of 'The Terror', C T B Turner, new names began to appear to form the attacking strength of the various Australian Test elevens that received their batting inspiration from the one and only Victor Trumper during the first 'Golden Age' of Australian cricket between 1899 and the First World War.

4

Golden Age bowlers

'The really great bowler knows more of the game than anyone else'
— A E Knight

It has frequently been suggested that the 11 players who turned out for England versus Australia in the first two Tests of the summer of 1902 represented the strongest England XI of all time. A glance at the names on the scoresheets confirms the possible validity of such claims: A C MacLaren (captain), C B Fry, K S Ranjitsinji, Hon. F S Jackson, J T Tyldesley, A F A Lilley (wicket-keeper), G H Hirst, G L Jessop, L C Braund, W H Lockwood and W Rhodes. Magic names all, and almost every man a legend in his own lifetime.

England's 'Golden Age' batsmen are discussed elsewhere in this volume while stumper A F A Lilley has a place in the wicket-keeping and fielding section. Two of the 'Golden XI' bowlers made their Test debut together at Lord's in 1893. Both were all-rounders of class: the Honourable Frank Stanley Jackson (later Sir F S Jackson), a Yorkshire amateur, was one of England's finest and could be cited as the epitome, in character, skill and style of the 'Golden Age' of cricket; William Henry Lockwood, a professional, a 'rough diamond' and the most formidable of natural fast bowlers, was one of the most destructive bowlers ever to have played in a Test match.

Tall and strongly built, 'Jacker' Jackson bowled right-arm medium-fast, varying his pace subtly and turning the ball from the off. His action was superb, a model for young bowlers. Jackson did little with the ball in his first home Test against Australia, but hit 91 with the bat. Unavailable for tours of Australia, he nevertheless was a fixture in the England team for home internationals and the 1905 season remains 'Jackson's Year' following his heroic batting and bowling in the series played that year against Australia.

In 1905, Jackson headed England's batting with an average of 70.28 and bowled his team to a decisive victory in the opening match at Nottingham with first innings figures of 5/52. Playing in a team that was blessed with so many fine bowlers, Stanley Jackson did not always get a chance to turn his arm over, but seldom failed when he was needed as an attacker.

K S Ranjitsinhji considered Lockwood to be the most difficult fast bowler he ever faced, and not only because of the Surrey professional's sharp pace. Without perceptibly altering his action, Bill Lockwood was the master at sending down a devious slower ball that frequently had the baffled batsman mistiming his stroke. He also bowled a fierce 'break-back', a ball which pitched at great speed outside the off stump and caused the wicket-keeper to lunge to his left to take it on the leg-side. C B Fry notes in *Great Bowlers* that Lockwood was 'gifted with a perfect rotary action, swinging freely from the shoulder' and that his arm came over very high after a long, springy run that ended at the extreme off-side edge of the crease.

In 12 Tests for England Lockwood claimed 43 wickets at 20.55, his finest effort coming at Old Trafford in the fourth Test of 1902 when he produced figures of 6/48 and 5/28. This Manchester Test was a thriller (won eventually by Australia by just three runs) which can only be compared for sheer last-minute excitement with the famous tied Test between Australia and West Indies at Brisbane in 1960−61 and with the final match of the 1902 series, which England won in another nail-biting finish by one wicket.

England might have won the Manchester match (and the series) were it not for an unfortunate dropped catch by Sussex off-break bowler Federick William Tate, father of the illustrious between-wars England bowling giant Maurice Tate. Poor Fred Tate was playing in what turned out to be his only Test and dropped a skied hit off Australian captain Joe Darling at a crucial moment − a miss that lost the match.

Whenever the name Lockwood is mentioned, Surrey and England's Tom Richardson springs naturally to mind. Sir Neville Cardus once wrote that Lockwood and Richardson were 'surely the two most beautiful fast bowlers ever seen in action at the same time', which was frequent, for they played together for Surrey and must have looked like Australia's panther-like speedster Ted McDonald bowling from both ends.

The dark-eyed, black-mustachioed Thomas Richardson looked like a gypsy king. He was a simple-hearted, splendidly built giant of a man for whom bowling fast all day (and almost every day) off a long run-up, with a leap in his second last stride and a high classical action, was as natural as getting up in the morning. No captain could have wished for a more reliable and loyal ally. Known as 'Honest Tom' or 'Long Tom', Richardson simply had no notion of what it meant to give up trying − even if it was the final over of the day on the dullest of tracks and he had gone wicketless since play began in the morning.

Cardus notes that Lockwood would 'blow hot and cold' and needed to be emotionally stirred in order to rise to greatness; Richardson simply 'felled your wicket as the next woodsman fells his tree, regretfully maybe, but as part of the bright day's work'.

Richardson's endurance was legendary. In his first Test, versus Australia at Old Trafford in 1893, he bowled more than 60 overs and captured five wickets in each innings. Taken to Australia by A E Stoddart in 1894–95, he contributed 309.1 six-ball overs in the five Tests (England won 3–2) for 32 wickets at 26.53, frequently bowling 40 or more overs in an innings, including 53.3 five-ball overs in the first innings of the series. The remarkable thing about all this muscular effort was that Richardson apparently bowled as fast at the end of the day as at the start and at a time when only the one ball was available to the fielding side throughout the longest innings.

In one of the most sustained Test or first-class bowling spells of all time by a fast bowler, at Old Trafford in 1896, Tom Richardson sent down 68 overs (five-ball) in Australia's first innings (he took 7 wickets for 168) and 42.3 overs in the second innings (6/76) to give him 13 wickets, and near victory for England. Set to score 125 to win in the fourth innings, Harry Trott's Australians were almost wafted away by Richardson's whirlwind attack which brought the big fast bowler six of the seven wickets that fell before the visiting team struggled through to victory. If Tom Richardson's Test career had not been over when the 'Golden XI' was assembled in 1902, he would have been an automatic selection among that august company.

Of the other bowlers who did appear in 1902, the 'happy warrior' George Herbert Hirst, Yorkshire-made in every ounce of his fibre, was known as a fierce combatant on the field and a wonderfully sincere and kindly friend after stumps had been drawn for the day. George Hirst was an aggressive all-rounder (right-hand bat, left-arm fast-medium bowler) who was the model of the perfect professional – tough and skilful, loyal and humorous, with an integrity of purpose that was a shining influence for younger players.

It is unlikely that the all-round performances put up by George Hirst in county cricket will ever be equalled. He is the only player to achieve 2000 runs and 200 wickets in a season (1906) and, in all, performed the 'double' of 1000 runs and 100 wickets 14 times, a feat that has been bettered by only one man, fellow-Yorkshireman Wilfred Rhodes, who achieved the 'double' in 16 separate seasons.

With his devastating late-dipping in-swing his main attacking weapon, Hirst also enjoyed occasional success in Test cricket, but for a player of such undoubtedly high talent, he was something of a disappointment at international level. As a batsman he enjoyed some bright moments – notably his 43 and 58 not out that brought England its famous one-wicket victory in the fifth Test versus Australia at the Oval in 1902, when Hirst and Wilfred Rhodes added 15 runs for the last wicket after the former had told his partner: 'We'll get 'em in singles.' With the help of a couple of twos and threes, interspersed with the odd single, the two Yorkshire heroes won the day for England.

One of George Hirst's greatest Test bowling efforts also came in 1902. In the first Test at Edgbaston, he and Rhodes shot Australia

George Hirst, the amazing Yorkshire and England all-rounder who is the only man to ever score 2000 runs and take 200 wickets in a season.

out for just 36 runs. Hirst removed Trumper (clean bowled), Hill and Gregory for 15 runs, while left-arm spinner Rhodes mopped up the rest to finish with seven wickets for 17 runs.

Wilfred Rhodes followed in the footsteps of Ted Peate and Bobby Peel as the third of Yorkshire's long line of left-arm spin bowlers. He must also go down in history as one of the most renowned cricketers of all time. His life-span extended for almost a complete century, from his birth in 1877 to his death, aged 95, in 1973 and Rhodes's incredible playing career for Yorkshire lasted from 1898 until 1930. He made his Test debut at Trent Bridge in 1899 in the match that marked the close of W G Grace's international career, and the arrival of Australia's Victor Trumper. In 1929–30, at the age of 52, Rhodes toured the West Indies with the MCC and played his final Test at Kingston. During the intervening years he had taken part in 58 Tests, had batted in every position for England, from number one to number 11, had frequently been his country's main bowling hope, and had amassed 2325 runs and taken 127 wickets during an international career in which he altered his role for England as frequently as a chameleon changes its colour.

Rhodes the bowler was, as Sir Neville Cardus puts it, 'the artist and arch schemer of spin'. The fact that he took more wickets in

Wilfred Rhodes, another great Yorkshire and England all-rounder, is the greatest wicket-taker in history and presented the perfect example of the slow left-arm bowler's art.

first-class cricket than anyone else (4187−411 more that his nearest rival, A P Freeman) does not completely convey the sheer genius of his art. Always a miser when it came to giving away runs, he bowled with an economy of effort that suited his strictly utilitarian personal concept of how things should be ordered. In his earlier years, Rhodes could turn the ball at will on any surface, but preferred to employ all possible variations of flight. In later times, when he could no longer spin the ball as effectively as in his youth, his wonderful accuracy, length and flight continued to bamboozle the very best of batsmen. Rhodes was a bowler's bowler.

In his first Test in 1899, Rhodes batted at number 11. For the next decade he remained England's number one spin bowler, his finest hour coming at Melbourne in the second Test of 1903−04 when he took 15 wickets in the match for 124 on a pitch that resembled polished glass. His batting prowess improved all the time and Rhodes became one of Sir Jack Hobb's most effective opening partners until world war effectively stopped first-class cricket in 1914.

After the war, Yorkshire's need was again for a spin bowler and Rhodes, already more than 40, responded with typical workmanlike enthusiasm. In 1926 he was touching 49 when the desperate England selectors brought him back for the fifth and vital Test against Australia at the Oval. The old master exhibited all his old skill in the air, took six wickets in the match and England won the game and the Ashes.

Wilfred Rhodes was not just a cricketer − he *was* cricket. In his 90s, although totally blind, he attended cricket with keen regularity, frequently in the guiding company of the equally renowned Sydney Barnes, and was able to 'read' the state of the game purely by the sounds that were so familiar to him.

The fifth main bowler in England's premier 1902 eleven was the Somerset all-rounder Leonard Charles Braund, a powerful right-handed batsman who hit three Test centuries and a dual-purpose bowler who switched from right-arm fast medium to slow-medium leg-breaks at will. Braund was also one of the most brilliant of slip fielders to appear in a Test. He took five wickets in the second innings of his debut Test match versus Australia at Sydney in 1901−02 and ended with 21 wickets in his first series. Len Braund's crowning achievement with the ball came at Melbourne in the fifth Test of the 1903−04 rubber when he returned an amazing first innings analysis of 8/81 in a match that England lost by 218 runs.

Colin Blythe was a much-loved man of Kent who made his Test debut in Australia in 1901−02 and for some years rivalled Wilfred Rhodes for the post of England's top left-arm spinner. Seldom has a country produced simultaneously two bowlers of such excellence. Ranjitsinhji favoured Blythe but many others considered Rhodes the outstanding left-hander of the Edwardian age.

'Charlie' Blythe was a sensitive performer who was also devoted to his violin. His rhythmical bowling action reflected the touch of a musician and H S Altham writes that to watch him in action was 'an aesthetic experience'. The feature of Blythe's style was the full, free looping swing of his arm, which started with his left hand holding the ball at his hip pocket. He was deadly on a helpful wicket but, unlike Rhodes at his best, could sometimes be mastered when the conditions favoured the batsman.

Blythe took 100 wickets in 19 Tests, an indication of his effectiveness at the highest level. In the first Test of 1909 at Birmingham, he bowled virtually unchanged with George Hirst to dismiss Australia for 74 and 151. Blythe claimed figures of 6/44 and 5/58 and Hirst 4/28 and 5/58.

Against the strong South African batting line-up of 1907, Blythe bowled with wonderful skill in the second Test at Leeds after Aubrey Faulkner's new-fangled 'googlies' had sent the home side packing for a miserable 76 in their own first knock. Blythe's 8/59 kept the game alive for England (and held South Africa's first innings lead down to 34 runs). C B Fry then led an England batting recovery on a difficult pitch, and a second innings 7/40 stint by the elegant Kent and England left-hander saw South Africa bundled out in its second innings for England to gain a 53-run victory.

Colin Blythe was one of the many young Englishmen killed in action during the First World War and is commemorated by a monument at Canterbury, his home ground in Kent.

Of the remaining bowlers who played for England during the 'golden era', one of the most prominent was John Thomas Hearne (Middlesex), a right-arm medium pacer who headed England's Test bowling table in Australia in 1897–98 with 20 wickets at 26.90 and made history at Headingly in 1899 when he claimed a hat-trick, also against Australia. 'Old Jack' Hearne's victims that day were Clem Hill, Syd Gregory and Monty Noble, as distinguished a trio as could be found in any cricket match.

John William ('Young Jack') Hearne is thought to have been a distant cousin of 'Old Jack' and was a googly-bowling all-rounder whose career for Middlesex and England overlapped that of his namesake, but whose bowling at Test level was something of a disappointment. Known also as 'Nutty' Hearne, he suffered from ill-health and never quite fulfilled his enormous potential at international level.

Harding Isaac Young (Essex) was a deceptive left-arm medium pacer who claimed 12 victims in two Tests against Australia in 1899 but was not seen again in the England eleven. Kent's Walter Morris Bradley also played in only two Tests and was described as one of the fiercest of fast bowlers (he was a right-armer). However, he was a one-Test wonder who took six wickets on his debut appearance at

Old Trafford in 1899, and no wickets for plenty in his next and final game for England at the Oval.

In 1905 the England selectors called upon Derbyshire right-arm fast bowler Arnold Warren for just one match against Australia, the third Test at Headingly. The hostile Warren, on his day one of the fastest bowlers in England, wrecked the first Australian innings with 5/57. He then suffered a back strain and bowled with little fire in the second innings.

A subsequent loss of form saw Warren replaced after his one game by the lion-hearted, 15-stone (95 kg) Walter Brearley, a Lancashire stalwart and a genuine quick bowler whose eight wickets in his first Test on his beloved Old Trafford ground was instrumental in sending Australia slithering to an innings defeat. Brearley played in a few more games for England, but never repeated his debut fire and form.

Of the others who appeared briefly for England during the era, Edward George Arnold took 18 wickets in the 1903–04 series in Australia, although he did little else at Test level with his fast-medium deliveries; Albert Edward Relf of Sussex made little progress as a right-arm medium-pacer when taken to Australia in 1903–04 but took five wickets in an innings when picked against Australia at the Oval in 1909 and performed with credit on two tours of South Africa; John Richard Gunn, nephew of the famous 'Golden Age' batsman William Gunn, played half-a-dozen Tests versus Australia (only one in England) and took 18 wickets with his left-arm slow-medium deliveries; Kent right-arm fast bowler Arthur Fielder toured Australia twice with English teams, taking 25 Test wickets at 25.08 in 1907–08 but never played in a Test in England. Not considered much of a batsman, Fielder nevertheless stuck around long enough to help Frank Woolley set up an English last-wicket record stand of 235 runs for Kent versus Worcestershire in 1909, scoring his one and only first-class century in the process.

That 'prince' of left-handed stroke players, Frank Edward Woolley, was himself no mean performer as an orthodox left-arm spin bowler at Test and county level. Woolley certainly ranks among the best dozen or so all-rounders in cricket history. In Tests he added 83 wickets to his more than 3000 runs and, in all first-class cricket, had the commendable average of 19.85 for his 2068 wickets.

Another classy all-rounder of the early 1900s who might have played for England as either batsman or bowler was the bespectacled cricketing prodigy John Neville Crawford, who graced the Surrey and England elevens with his presence before migrating to play in Australia following a dispute with the Surrey authorities. Crawford was a fine batsman who excelled in driving, and was also a right-arm fast-medium bowler who bowled with a smooth action and moved the ball considerably. Australians considered him the finest orthodox medium-pacer to tour with an England team 'Down Under' when he bowled with untiring efficiency for a losing England team in 1907–08 to take 30 wickets in the series at 24.79.

Harry Dean of Lancashire, left-arm fast-medium, enjoyed one season of success for England when he appeared in three Tests in the Triangular Tournament of 1912 (between England, Australia and South Africa) and took 11 wickets at 13.90, including a 4/19 spell at the Oval that saw Australia put out for 65 in what had been scheduled as the first 'timeless Test' in England. As it turned out, England won within four days by 244 runs with Australia's batsmen struggling throughout against Dean, Sydney Barnes and Frank Woolley. The latter played a scintillating knock of 62 in a low-scoring encounter which produced only two other 50s, and then claimed bowling figures of 5/29 and 5/20.

Yorkshire's Schofield Haigh was a right-arm medium bowler with a sharp off-cutter that was deadly on a drying wicket. He took 24 wickets in 11 Tests, mainly against South Africa. He and Australian expatriate Albert Trott bowled out South Africa for 35 at Cape Town in 1898–99. Surrey's Walter Scott Lees, right-arm medium, took 26 wickets in his one and only Test rubber versus South Africa in 1905–06. Another player to perform well against South Africa was Northamptonshire's George Joseph Thompson. A larger-than-life character of tremendous energy who sported a large drooping moustache, Thompson bowled right-arm at a brisk pace with a windmill action off a short run-up. He made little impact when asked to play in one home Test against Australia, but took 23 wickets in the series when he went to South Africa in 1909–10. The tall and stylish Claud Percival Buckenham of Essex also bowled with verve in South Africa in 1909–10 to take 21 wickets in four Tests, but was never considered a prospect for England teams against Australia.

The 1909–10 trip to the Cape also marked the appearance of the last of the true 'lobsters', George Hayward Thomas Simpson-Hayward. Although Simpson-Hayward's style was representative of a method of bowling which had become an anachronism, he was a surprise success with his under-arm deliveries and he dismissed 23 South African batsmen in five Tests for only 18.26 runs apiece.

England's Golden Age continued through to the start of the First World War, but the tale still remains to be told of one of the major bowlers of the period who made his Test debut in Australia in 1901–02, having been selected to tour as a total unknown after only a handful of first-class games. The story of Sydney Barnes, a man who has been named by many sound judges as the best bowler of all time, certainly warrants a separate review.

5

Mostly from the off

'The original seam swervers and the spin swervers also have their place in the great development of bowling'

— M A Noble

Montague Alfred Noble was regarded as the greatest Australian all-rounder of his day and, apart from his flair for leadership and his superb fielding, would have held his place in the Australian XI for either batting or bowling. He along with England's George Hirst and others was one of the early exponents of a new variation in bowling that relied as much on 'swerve' or 'swing' as it did on actual spin and break.

C B Fry described Noble as one of the most artistic of bowlers, who had no superior when it came to winkling out batsmen on a plumb wicket and who could also make full and deadly use of a bad track. With a high and free action, Noble's bowling varied from medium to fast-medium, much in the style of Trumble, Howell, and other Australian right-handed off-break bowlers of the day. As Fry puts it in *Great Bowlers and Fielders*: 'He has made a complete study of the art of deceptive variation of pace and of the art of deceptive flight.'

Holding the ball between thumb and forefinger, Noble relied as much on swerve (swing in modern parlance) as he did on his spun off-break, and was a master of late movement, in the air and off the pitch. Ranjitsinhji commented that the Australian had a curious knack of making the ball 'curl' from off to on and, occasionally, from on to off, much in the way of a baseball pitcher.

One of the select few to have gathered more than 1000 runs and 100 wickets in Test cricket, Noble was a pillar of strength for Australia and New South Wales. The crowd dubbed him 'Mary Anne', after his initials, while his colleagues referred to him simply as 'Boots', because of feet that Ray Robinson claims were of 'heroic proportions'.

A man whom Sir Pelham Warner once described as 'one of the greatest bowlers that that great bowler-producing country, Australia, has sent forth' preceded Monty Noble as a seam and off-break bowler in the Australian team. At 6 ft 4 in (193 cm), the lanky and angular Hugh Trumble was a player who, because of his great height, prominent nose and saucer-like ears, could never be missed

Hugh Trumble was possibly the greatest of Australia's early medium-paced off-break bowlers.

on the field – or off it where he was even more distinguishable because of his taste in hats (wide brimmed Stetsons specially imported from America) and long bent-stemmed pipes. A character indeed, and by all accounts one of the most kind-hearted and gentlemanly of all Australia's cricketers.

Hugh Trumble was not only an outstanding bowler but also a wonderful student of the game. C B Fry wrote that he was a 'cunning and long-headed adversary, who knew every move of the game'. Using every inch of his long frame, and with a deliberate and easy action, Trumble bowled to an accurate length at medium pace. In the terminology of the time he 'got a lot of work on the ball', swinging it when new or breaking in sharply from the off when the shine was gone. Like Turner, he was a daunting proposition on a drying wicket and, on a plumb track, he effectively varied pace and length to remain a constant threat to the unwary batsman.

Trumble played for Australia for 14 years and took seven wickets (7/28) in his final Test outing against England on his home ground at Melbourne, including a hat-trick, the second of his international career. In 32 Test matches he totalled 141 wickets at 21.78 and will go down in the history books as one of the greatest bowlers of all time.

Another off-spinner of the time, Thomas Robert McKibbin, was as a man and player as popular as Trumble but lived out his career in the shadow of doubt about the legitimacy of his bowling action. McKibbin was able to effect a prodigious turn on the ball and had a particularly effective and deceptive faster one. This delivery was probably the one that labelled McKibbin as one of the early throwers. Although he was never 'called' in a first-class match, he was no-balled for throwing in a minor match in both England and Australia. McKibbin could also bowl an almost unplayable ball and had to be carefully watched at all times but was known to intersperse good deliveries with bad and could not to be placed in the same class as Hugh Trumble.

Doubts were also expressed at one time about the action of Australia's fastest turn-of-the-century bowler, Ernest 'Jonah' Jones. One brave Australian umpire, James Phillips, even had the courage to 'call' his country's pride and joy in a Test match. Jones, the rough hewn miner who had became the quickest and most ferocious bowler in the world, was more than a little upset at Phillips's temerity in naming him as a 'chucker'.

The most famous story about Ernie Jones concerns a ball he was said to have once bowled right through W G Grace's massive beard. In an interview about Jones published in the 1944 *Wisden*, Sir Stanley Jackson asserted that the offending delivery was aimed at Grace during the first match of the Australians' tour when he (Jackson) opened the batting together with the 'Grand Old Man' of cricket for

Lord Sheffield's XI at Sheffield Park, but that it did not pass *through* the great man's beard.

Jackson says he and Grace 'had to dance about a bit' when Jones let rip with 'short and bumpy stuff' on a very dry wicket. One ball apparently cracked Grace under the arm and another went head-high past him and over wicket-keeper Kelly to the boundary. 'WG' threw his head back to avoid this delivery, causing his beard to stick out, and giving the appearance of the ball passing through his whiskers. Grace immediately strode down the pitch and Jones apologised with: 'Sorry, Doctor, she slipped.' Incidentally, Jackson ended the innings with 95 not out and a cracked ribbed, compliments of Ernie 'Jonah' Jones, Australian fast bowler.

Sir Stanley claimed that it was absurd to suggest that Jones was a thrower and says that he had a beautiful action and was a very fine bowler indeed. Jones was certainly endowed with great strength but there were some claims that his pace would drop after a blistering first few overs. He toured England three times and in 19 Tests claimed 64 wickets at 29.01. Years later, when asked of his opinion of English fast bowler Harold Larwood, Jones was heard to mutter that Larwood 'wouldn't knock a dent in a pound of butter on a hot day.'!

A much underrated Australian bowler of the 1890s was the right-arm fast-medium Charles Edward McLeod, who played together with Jones and Hugh Trumble in many an Ashes tussle and who, on various separate occasions, enjoyed the privilege of opening both batting and bowling for his country. Charlie McLeod's best performances with the ball came on the firmer Australian pitches and Ranji recorded that he kept an admirable length, was 'deceptive in flight' and changed his pace cleverly.

The claim that bowlers are born and not made was most singularly vindicated through the immediate and most effective results obtained by 'Farmer Bill' Howell when he came at age 25 to Sydney with a team of country cricketers. His uncle, Edwin Evans, had been the best Australian all-rounder of the 1870s, so it can be claimed that cricket ran strongly in his genes. William Peter Howell was to become renowned as one of Australia's most eminent Test bowlers, despite having to play for most of his career in the same side as bowling genius Hugh Trumble.

On Australian wickets, the strongly built farm lad with the biggest of handle-bar moustaches used a skilful variation of flight and pace to deceive opposition batsmen into an act of self-destruction. In England his ability to impart massive spin to the ball enabled him to beat the bat consistently with vicious turn. The snap of Howell's strong fingers caused the ball to literally buzz in its flight towards the awaiting batsman — an appropriate delivery for a New South Wales bee-keeper. Quicker than Trumble, his main weapon was a devastating off-break but Howell also used a quick-turning leg-break. Even on the hard turf of Australia he could turn the ball more than his colleagues.

Howell also appreciated the value of the ball that whips straight on without turning and was of great value to a succession of Australian teams in England, except on a sticky wicket when his break was sometimes too great. When Joe Darling took his team to South Africa for the first time in 1902–03, Howell ensured success for Australia in a three-match Test series by taking 14 wickets at 12.42 in the two games he played.

In his *With Bat and Ball*, George Giffen describes Victoria's Frank Laver as an inelegant but effective batsman who was a safe field and a 'fair change bowler'. Laver's form in England in 1905 belied the last description as he topped the tour averages with 115 wickets at 18.19, although his batting had fallen away.

Laver, like Noble, used a peculiar and unusual grip on the ball with the inside of his first finger running along the seam and with only the ball of his thumb making contact. Although his action was dissimilar from that of Noble, he also appeared to base his movement of the ball on baseball principles. At 6 ft (183 cm), Laver was able to bring the ball down from a good height and swung it a little both ways at a brisk medium pace.

When the Australian Board of Control overlooked Laver as manager for the 1912 Triangular Tournament team, six of Australia's main players – Hill, Trumper, Carter, Cotter, Ransford and Armstrong – declined to tour. For years the players had made all their own touring arrangements, including choosing the team manager.

Two of Australia's leading bowlers were among the six who refused to take part in the tournament. Of the two, Warwick Armstrong was destined to become one of his country's most successful leaders after the 1914–18 War, while 'Tibby' Cotter was to be killed by a sniper during the Great War.

The short, compact and strong Albert Cotter was a right-arm fast bowler whose slinging action was similar to that of Jeff Thomson. Australia's first great 'bosey' champion, H V Hordern, recalls in his *Googlies* that even as a schoolboy Cotter was a much-feared pace bowler. Muscular and athletic, he started as a tearaway with a long run-up but later cut down his approach and, in the process, developed a vicious off-cutter, to the consternation of opposing batsmen. Cotter's delivery was described by Sir Pelham Warner as curious but scrupulously legitimate. However, although very fast, he could be rather erratic but would often make amends for wayward deliveries by suddenly producing a devastating leg-stump yorker, after a succession of short balls had skimmed the batsman's nose.

For eight or nine years Cotter was the spearhead of the Australian attack, with a career-best performance at Melbourne in 1903–04 when he took 6/40 to send England tumbling to 61 all out (Hugh Trumble took 7/28 in the second in his last Test match). He was also particularly effective when bowling in tandem with left-hander W J Whitty against South Africa in 1910–11.

Warwick Windridge Armstrong was another of those magnificent Australian all-rounders who would have gained Test selection for his prowess in either of the major departments of the game. As a relentless and adaptable batsman he had few peers; as a leg-spin bowler he was noted for his accuracy, an unusual attribute for one of his kind and was a sort of latter-day W G Grace when it came to psyching out his opponents.

As a leg-break bowler pure and simple, Armstrong did not turn the ball much and was therefore not in the same category as England's Len Braund or the father of the googly, B J T Bosanquet. He was, however, as deadly accurate in length and line as the best of the

Larger than life in more than one way, Warwick Armstrong was a superbly accurate leg-break bowler.

natural spinners and could bowl for long periods at just under medium pace without faltering. When conditions favoured batting and Armstrong found it difficult to extract much turn, he adopted a leg-theory of his own design whereby he would pitch most of his deliveries outside the leg-stump to a packed on-side field. His great accuracy inhibited batsmen from going on the attack and, as his patience was seemingly inexhaustible, catches on the leg-side came with regularity. On a helpful pitch Armstrong was another proposition. He would then bowl in order to hit the stumps and again his pin-point accuracy made him difficult to counter.

Kind of heart although definitely his own man, Armstrong was forever at odds with authority and always a champion of the players' cause. His post-career newspaper work was noted for its acid comment and must have created more enemies than friends but Armstrong was a man who could truly be described in substance and in character as larger than life.

Apart from a couple of classy but fairly conventional medium-pacers (and a few of that new-fangled breed of leg-spinners who chose to introduce the 'bosey' aberration into their bowling arsenal) the three remaining regular Australian XI bowlers of note before the First World War were all left-handers, albeit of differing style and inclination.

First to appear was the lanky Victorian John Victor Saunders, who cut a dapper figure with his military moustache and persistent left-arm medium paced bowling round the wicket off a run that curved in from mid-on. Saunders spun the ball prodigiously from leg and had all batsmen of his time in a state of fright when operating on a wet wicket. When he pushed through a faster ball there was some hint of a throw, but he was never called in the 14 Tests he played.

Second of the left-handers was the man whom it was hoped would become Saunders's successor. It was not to be, however, for Charles George Macartney had other ideas and became instead a batsman worthy of mention in almost the same breath as Victor Trumper. Because of his scintillating batting record it is frequently overlooked that, at the start of his career, Macartney was played by Australia mainly as a left-arm spin bowler of exceptional talent.

Left-hander number three was William James Whitty, whose new-ball partnership with 'Tibby' Cotter against South Africa in 1910–11 represented the first instance of two bowlers of above medium pace opening the bowling for Australia throughout a Test series. More's the pity that Whitty was unable to sustain his progress the following season when an English left-arm/right-arm pace combination (F R Foster and S F Barnes) humiliated the Australian batsmen at almost every turn. Fast-medium and using his height with good effect, Whitty was described by A J Richardson as 'the loveliest-actioned bowler I have ever seen'.

Whitty first went to England as a rookie on the 1909 tour, when the more mature right-armed fast medium John Denis Alphonsus O'Connor was expected to spearhead the Australian attack. O'Connor made an impressive Test debut against England in 1907−08 but failed to follow through and was not the success originally anticipated when taken to England. He bowled with a flat trajectory, from a jerky action that could never be termed classical and he relied mostly on the away-swinger, which was contrary to the practice of most of Australia's fast and medium-paced bowlers of the time.

A right-arm medium pacer who rendered Australia useful service in the early 1900s was Albert John Young Hopkins, a bits-and-pieces all-rounder who always seemed to be around somewhere in every game he played, be it as a forceful batsman, brilliant fieldsman in any position, or as a nagging bowler who was constantly changing his pace. Hopkins also bowled a good yorker and could move the ball a little both ways, which made him an ideal back-up bowler to the main attackers.

When Gervys Rignold Hazlitt died aged 27, he had not yet fulfilled the rich promise he had shown in the nine Test matches he played between 1907 and 1912. Gerry Hazlitt was a right-arm medium pacer who belonged to the old school of the Trumbles and Nobles. Tall and angular, he spun and cut the ball remarkably well and achieved his best Test figures on a drying Oval pitch in 1912 when he took seven wickets for 25 in 21.4 overs. Hazlitt's grand hour was to no avail though, as Australia slid to 65 all out and defeat against Harry Dean and Frank Woolley.

A leading batsman who could be classed as a genuine all-rounder was the dour Charles Kelleway, who successfully made the transition from a relentless stonewalling batsman to a sometimes hostile fast-medium right-hand bowler. As a batsman, Kelleway scorned any embellishments but, as a bowler, he used swing and swerve to such excellent effect that he was rated as Australia's foremost medium-pacer in the years immediately following the First World War. He made his initial Test appearance against South Africa in 1910−11 and, in all, took 52 wickets and scored 1422 runs in 26 outings for Australia.

When Test cricket resumed after the First World War, Kelleway and Armstrong were the only two pre-war Australian bowlers present in the Australian XI, then captained by Armstrong. Yet, for the first post-war years, Australia was to repeatedly get the better of its opponents, mainly because of the bowling of three new men, one slow and devious, the other two all fearsome fire and pace.

6

King of Swing

'If I had been given the selection of a World's Team in the years
1906–10, he would have been almost my first choice'
                                          – H V Hordern

Australia's first great 'googly' bowler H V Hordern spent some years living in the United States where he played cricket for the famous Philadelphia XI. In his autobiographical *Googlies*, Hordern claims that the only word to describe Philadelphian cricket at the time was 'magnificent'. In 1908 he went with the American team on a tour of England during which the Philadelphians gave an excellent account of themselves. In first-class matches on the tour, Hordern provided main support for an American-born bowler who would have walked into any contemporary Test team of the day.

John Barton King took 120 wickets at 10.61 in 14 matches in England in 1908 (87 of them at 11.01 in 10 first-class games). He headed the overall first-class bowling averages for the season during what was his third trip to England at the age of 34. As a younger man, when the Philadelphians visited England on two previous occasions in 1897 and 1903, he had already impressed the critics as a fast bowler who varied his pace cleverly with little change of his smooth action and who could swerve the ball alarmingly in the manner of a baseball pitcher.

Hordern describes his American team-mate as a 'phenomenal player' who, at 6 ft 1 in (185 cm) and around 180 lbs (81 kg), was a magnificent physical specimen, full of vigour and youth and with 'a brainy knowledge of the game'. The prematurely balding King was a marvellous all-rounder – a top-class hard-hitting batsman 'without actually being a champion', a splendid, athletic fieldsman and an undisputed world-class bowler.

He would come bounding in at great speed off a long run and, just before actual delivery, grip the ball with both hands high above his head, 'a la baseball pitcher', and follow through with what was described as 'the most perfect arm and body swing possible to imagine'.

King's most damaging delivery was a stinging late in-swinger that came in sharply during the last yard. A perfect length ball would frequently hit the turf outside off-stump and miss the leg-stump by inches. Although this fearsome in-swinger remained his main wicket-taker, Bart King used as variation a fast, straight ball (more often

than not a yorker) and an occasional outswinger which did not curve
as sharply as his deadly inswinger.

Hordern relates the story of how he was badly beaten by two or
three balls the first time he faced King in a club match in the USA.
He turned to the wicket-keeper to comment: 'I must be bilious
today, those balls looked wobbly to me.' The 'keeper replied with a
smile: 'You need not worry about your liver, young fellow. You will
always be bilious when Bart King is bowling.'

The Philadelphian fast
bowler John Barton King
would have walked into any
World XI of the late 1890s
and early 1900s.

King called his famous inswinger his 'angler' and reveals his serious intellectual approach to the technicalities of bowling in an article published in John A Lester's *A Century of Philadelphia Cricket*. King had powerful shoulders, long arms and lean hips but it was the strength in his fingers that produced his amazing ability to 'curve' a cricket ball. According to John Lester, the American champion could send a new cricket ball to the second storey window of a building just with 'a snip of two fingers and a thumb'. King himself relates that he was a baseball pitcher before he became a bowler and that 'right-hand outcurve pitching was like throwing an off-break' and would break from the off if allowed to hit the ground.

This type of pitching was known as the 'roundhouse' because the curve started when the ball left the pitcher's hand. It was replaced when pitchers developed the 'hook', a ball that travelled with little curve until the final 10 feet. King experimented in an effort to develop the same kind of ball in cricket and thus was born his 'angler'. Not satisfied with merely being able to swing the ball late and unexpectedly, the American went on to identify the points in his bowling technique which would aid him to gain complete control over the delivery − grip, relaxation during his approach, height of arm at point of delivery and a whole-hearted follow-through.

Touring England in 1897, Bart King, with figures of 7/13 and 6/102, wrecked a strong Sussex batting line-up at Brighton that included former Australian captain Billy Murdoch and the immortal K S Ranjitsinhji.

Ranji was clean-bowled first ball by a Bart King special, and in his inimitably charming fashion, the Indian prince exclaimed: 'That was a wonderful ball Mr King, and I wish you to accept my bat as a memento.'

Against Surrey at the Oval in 1903, King scored 98 (run out) and 113 not out and took six wickets in the match. His 5/40 and 4/38 at Manheim, USA, in 1912 saw an Australian team that included Test players S E Gregory, C E Kelleway, E R Mayne, S H Emery, T J Matthews, D B M Smith, J W MacLaren, W J Whitty and W Carkeek, toppled in an enthralling two-run victory for the Philadelphians.

When the Gentlemen of Ireland toured America in 1909 and played the Philadelphians, King bagged all 10 wickets for 53 runs on his home ground at Haverford *and* clean-bowled the not out batsman, G A Morrow, with a 'no-ball' − a feat which appears to be unprecedented and must represent a world record.

Bart King was one of the greatest bowlers and cricketers the world has seen. He was also noted as an avid leg-puller and a wonderful after-dinner speaker. His own favourite cricket story concerned an English stationmaster and porter whom he saw playing cricket when an 'express' train he was travelling on from London stopped at a small wayside station for coal and water. When the train failed to resume its journey after a reasonable period, King went to investigate and found the train's porter busy bowling to a bat-wielding stationmaster.

'What time does the express leave?', asked the American. The porter looked embarrassed, side-stepped the question and asked if King could bowl. Admitting that he had done a bit of bowling in his time, the cricketer took the ball and promptly clean-bowled the stationmaster. With a sigh of relief, the porter announced: 'Thank God, sir, and the express leaves immediately!'

Bart King was not the only fine Philadelphian bowler of the Golden Age. Percy H Clark, with an outswinger as his stock-in-trade, proved the perfect foil to King. Clark bowled with an easy action and also swung the ball abruptly in the last yard or so and reverted to off-breaks when the seam flattened.

In *Cricket* in the Badminton series of publications, E R Wilson, an England Test-player, writes that 'King and Clark of the Philadelphia eleven were as awkward a pair of bowlers as any batsman could wish to meet'. One of Clark's most outstanding efforts was his 5/102 and 5/112 which helped the Philadelphians beat Surrey in 1903 and his second innings 6/38 at Germantown, USA, in 1915 set a Germantown XII up for a thrilling two-wicket win over an Australian team that boasted players like H L Collins, C G Macartney, E R Mayne, W Bardsley, S H Emery and A A Mailey. Clark also hit a very quick 82 in his match.

In support of King and Clark, the big-hearted giant E M Cregar, over six foot (183 cm) and weighing 220 lbs (100 kg), was known as 'King of Bumpers'. Cregar's fast short-pitched deliveries would sometimes clear both batsman and wicket-keeper. Although not possessing the swing or the guile of King and Clark, Eddie Cregar was also noted for a clever slower delivery.

Of the earlier American players, the Newhall brothers were prominent (there were 10 Newhalls in all and seven played for Philadelphia). The six foot (183 cm) Charles A Newhall was noted as the fastest American bowler of his time and twice captured W G Grace's wicket in a match in America in 1872. Charles Newhall's most famous delivery was a fast 'break-back' known as his 'rib-roaster'. During the period 1868 to 1886, he played against all 10 overseas teams that visited Philadelphia and claimed 80 of the 159 wickets taken by the American side. Most of his brothers were batsmen and the fast left-hand Spencer Meade provided excellent back-up for Newhall in the early matches against touring teams.

Mead stayed at home when Newhall went with the first Gentlemen of Philadelphia team to England in 1884 but excellent bowling was seen from the slow left-hander William C Lowry, who took 110 wickets in all matches on that tour.

Philadelphian cricket started to fade away after 1908, going into a gradual decline prompted by the retirement of almost an entire generation of fine cricketers who had formed the core of the representative teams of the late 1890s and early 1900s, plus the upsurge of interest in baseball, a game that was to fast become America's national sport. Although American cricket has survived to the present day, it cannot claim the strength and skill of the balmy days when Bart King and his friends challenged some of the best teams from England and Australia and on more than one occasion ran out victors.

7

Enter Sydney Barnes

'In the opinion of his contemporaries Sydney Barnes was the best bowler of their day, and of any other they ever saw'

— Ian Peebles

In 1910 Sydney Francis Barnes was honoured by Wisden Cricketers' Almanack as one of the 'Five Cricketers of the Year' for his bowling during the 1909 season. Apart from his appearance in three Tests for England that year (in which he claimed 17 wickets at 20.00) and a match for Players versus Gentlemen at Lord's (he took 8 wickets for 55 runs), he took no part in any other first-class cricket in 1909. The majority of Barnes's cricket was played for lowly Staffordshire in the Minor Counties League, where he gathered 76 wickets at 6.77 runs apiece. No other major England bowler has been chosen for his country when not actively engaged by one of the major counties. Such was the worth placed on this phenomenal bowler's ability that there was no hesitation in calling upon him to make the transition from minor cricket to international cricket for the third Test against Australia at Leeds after England had been comprehensively beaten in the previous match at Lord's.

Commenting on Barnes's performance in the 1909 Gentlemen versus Players match, Sir Pelham Warner, a participant in the encounter, stated: 'Barnes did not bowl one really bad ball during the two innings of the Gentlemen and a finer bowler I have never played...'

For Barnes the unusual was frequently the commonplace, right from the time when he was first picked by A C MacLaren to tour Australia in 1901—02 (after having appeared for Lancashire in only one game during the 1901 English season and having spent the rest of his time in league cricket) right through to 1940 when he played his last club match at the age of 67. Years later, when Sydney Barnes was well into his 80s, he stood as umpire in a charity match. Former England spin bowler Ian Peebles (in *The Cricketer Spring Annual, 1968*) recalls the great man giving a demonstration of bowling between fall of wickets: 'The umpire, in uniform coat and trilby hat, skipped up a few springy paces and, with the most beautiful high wheeling action, delivered every variety of "request item". It was plain to any discerning eye that here indeed was the best ever.'

One of the keys to his success as a world-beater was physical fitness. Tall at 6 ft 2 in (188 cm), lean and rather gaunt, Barnes at his peak was essentially a fast to fast-medium bowler with a free and easy action with what C B Fry described as 'a peculiarly loose, long circular swing'. On the boat out to Australia in 1901 Barnes made it clear to England captain Archie MacLaren that he did not consider himself as purely a fast bowler, pointing out that 'in the cricket I had played I had to get results on any kind of wicket. . .if the wicket took spin I didn't bowl my heart out with fast stuff, but if the wicket was good and firm I did bowl faster. . .'

On his first trip to Australia a knee injury put Barnes out of the England team during the third Test and he did not play again on the tour but, through his performances in the first two games, he had already done enough to give notice of his arrival on the international bowling scene. At Sydney, Barnes's first victim was Victor Trumper, caught and bowled for two, and he took six wickets in his first outing in a Test. Then, in the second Test at Melbourne, he bowled almost throughout the match for figures of 6/42 and 7/121. He and Charlie Blythe put Australia out for 112 in its first innings but England capitulated in reply and was all out for 61 (Monty Noble 7/17). At second go, Australia totalled 353 and Barnes bowled 64 overs. England then failed again (all out 175 − Noble 6/60) and Australia won by 229 runs. After bowling only seven overs in the next Test at Adelaide, Barnes pulled up with the knee injury. He had taken 19 wickets at 17.00 in his first series and fast became one of the most talked about players in world cricket.

Although Barnes's home appearances in Tests were intermittent, he made his mark on just about every game in which he played. In his only Test in 1902 he took six wickets for 49 in Australia's first innings. In 1909 he went straight from league cricket into the third Test, again versus Australia, and ended up with 17 wickets at 20.00 in three matches. During the 1912 Triangular Tournament in England involving the home team, Australia and South Africa, he bagged 39 wickets in six Tests at 10.35 runs each, a stunning performance.

Notwithstanding his excellent figures in the 10 Tests he played in England (63 wickets at 13.38), it was in Australia (and later in South Africa) that Barnes really made his name as the finest bowler of his time, and perhaps of all time. On his second trip to Australia, in 1907−08, Barnes headed a painfully thin England attack and took 24 wickets at 26.08 for a losing side. In 1911−12 he returned and, with the assistance of left-hander F R Foster, proceeded to rout Australia. Barnes's most famous effort on that tour was his 'Melbourne miracle', when he bowled for an hour and 10 minutes before lunch on the first day of the second Test to end with figures of: *overs* 9 *maidens* 6 *runs* 3 *wickets* 4. He bowled Warren Bardsley with the first ball of the day, which went from the batsmen's foot on to the stumps (Barnes's comment was: 'He would have been lbw if it had not') and Kelleway was caught leg-before for two by a ball that dipped in late. Ace left-hander Clem Hill then faced what he later described as one of the most torrid overs he had encountered in a lifetime. Barnes, in an article published in *The Times* in 1953 to commemorate his 80th birthday, described the over thus: 'I gave him one that was an off-break to him and then an inswinger. Then I sent him one going away and he let it go. The last ball of the over pitched on his leg stump and hit the off.'

Barnes gained his fourth victim before lunch when Warwick Armstrong snicked a quick leg-break to wicket-keeper 'Tiger' Smith with the score at 11. His four wickets to that point had cost just one run. Eleven for four wickets soon became 33 for five after lunch, when Foster bowled Trumper. Australia might have been dismissed for under 50 were it not for the fact that England skipper Johnny Douglas was compelled to take his master bowler off. Barnes had been ill for some days before the start of the match and now reported that he was so dizzy that he could scarcely see the other end. When he was brought back he immediately had Roy Minnett caught by Hobbs at cover and ended the innings with figures of 23−9−44−5.

Sydney Barnes was able to move the ball both ways, in the air and off the pitch, and acknowledged a debt to Australia's Monty Noble who passed on to him some of the secrets of 'swerve'. Barnes himself insisted that the secret of swerving the ball was contained in the ability to apply finger spin. It was the pace at which he spun and swerved the ball that made him such a formidable opponent. One of the many variations he employed was a ball that seemed to stop in flight and then go on. He was also highly adept at gaining pace from the pitch and he always tried to make his leg-break indistinguishable from his sharply turning off-break. In *Great Bowlers and Fielders*, Barnes's leg-break is described thus: 'He had a natural power of bowling a ball which swung across from leg to the off after pitching, and he increased this cross swing by finger work so that it became something more than merely "going with the arm" and yet was not a genuine break.' Other observers claim that Barnes perfected what was in effect a 'forehand leg-break', something no other bowler has been seen to achieve.

H V Hordern played against Barnes in 1911−12 and claimed that the England bowler's action and delivery could be used as 'a model of perfection of the bowler's art'. The Australian also referred to the ball that would 'hurry up' off the pitch and stated that Barnes had 'every artifice, not only at his command, but under his control... every ball was different, all of a perfect length....'.

Barnes claimed 34 victims at 22.88 in the 1911−12 series in Australia and the bowling combination he formed with Warwickshire amateur left-arm fast bowler F R Foster ranks as one of the most effective ever seen in international cricket. Frank Rowbotham Foster

Sydney Barnes was first
picked for England as an
obscure league bowler but
immediately made his mark
and became what many
knowledgable judges have
described as 'the best
bowler of all time'.

was a classy all-rounder, a natural hitter who dispensed with the niceties of technique, but who was highly effective, and a bowler who came in off a short run to surprise batsmen with the remarkable velocity the ball attained once it had pitched. Wicket-keeper Smith, in fact, stood back for Foster, as he did for England's acknowledged fast bowler in the 1911—12 team, Bill Hitch of Surrey.

Foster bowled at what looked like medium-fast pace but the ball came off the pitch like that of a fast bowler. In England he had been considered a conventional left-arm seamer but, in Australia, he changed over to a constricting leg-theory attack which he exploited to the full (D R Jardine consulted Foster before embarking on his 'bodyline' venture in 1932—33). Perfect control of length and direction, allied with a sharp inswinger and his tremendous pace off the pitch had Australia's batsmen in all kinds of trouble.

In the five Tests of 1911—12, Foster took 32 wickets at 21.62. In 1912, the Barnes-Foster combination continued during the Triangular Tournament, but Frank Foster's cricket career was shattered when he was injured in a motor-cycle accident during the First World War, while still in his 20s, and he never played again at international level.

Barnes also received support in 1911—12 from his captain, Johnny Douglas, who bowled at fast-medium. Nearly six foot (183 cm) and strongly built, John William Henry Tyler Douglas was a fighter of immense character who wore his hair parted strictly down the middle and could intimidate an opponent with his square boxer's jaw and piercing blue eyes alone. If needed, he could bowl all day and he seldom lost pace or enthusiasm. He took over as England's captain in 1911—12 when Pelham Warner fell ill after one tour match and he led England from the front to regain the Ashes. Douglas's 4/50 in the second innings of the first Test at Sydney and his 5/46 (again in Australia's second knock) in the fourth game at Melbourne were both decisive contributions to England's cause in 1911—12. J W H T Douglas again captained England on the next tour to Australia in 1920—21 and a word play on his initials, coupled with his stubborn batting, earned him the title 'Johnny Won't Hit Today' Douglas. The never-say-die Douglas later drowned in an attempt to save his father following a collision between ships in fog.

The other fast bowler in Douglas's team, John William Hitch, was genuinely quick off a curious run-up that included a series of hops at the start. He did not live up to expectations on two tours of Australia in 1911—12 and 1920—21.

Sydney Barnes reserved his most remarkable international bowling performance for his last series (and the last before the First World War) when, at the age of 40, he shattered South Africa's batting by taking 49 wickets in only four Tests played in South Africa in

1913—14 (he missed the final match after a dispute over expenses for his wife and child who had accompanied him on the tour).

Barnes was not an entire stranger to South African conditions having played for and coached the Claremont Cricket Club in Cape Town in 1898—99. In the first Test of 1913—14 at Durban, Barnes took 10 wickets; at Johannesburg, in the second, he ran out with the startling figures of 8/56 and 9/103; in the third Test at Johannesburg he took eight in the match; and in the fourth, back at Durban, he rounded off with a decisive 7/56 and 7/88. Only five Test bowlers down the years have reached 40 or more wickets in a series. Barnes did it in only four Tests — all others needed five or six. The list reads:

	Tests	Runs	Wkts	Avrge	Season	Versus
S F Barnes (Eng)	4	536	49	10.93	1913—14	S. Africa
J C Laker (Eng)	5	442	46	9.60	1956	Australia
C V Grimmett (Aust)	5	642	44	14.59	1935—36	S. Africa
T M Alderman (Aust)	6	893	42	21.26	1981	England
R M Hogg (Aust)	6	527	41	12.85	1978—79	England

Only one South African batsman mastered Barnes at any time during the 1913—14 season. Herby Taylor scored consistently throughout the rubber for his province Natal (the only team to beat the MCC team), and frequently upset England's premier bowler with his skilful footwork on the matting wickets which were then still in use in South Africa.

Years later, Taylor claimed in various interviews that Barnes once threw the ball down during the Natal match at Durban, refused to bowl, and walked off the field muttering 'It's Taylor, Taylor, all the time'.

Barnes himself scoffed at these claims. When the stern and brooding Barnes was asked by the author of his biography, Leslie Duckworth, about the incident his swift reply was: 'Rot...no such thing. It took Taylor all his time to protect himself...' Taylor's tale, as colourful and true to character as it may be, remains unsubstantiated, but illustrates the fiery temperament of a man and a bowler who demanded of himself and all around him only the highest possible standards, and found it difficult to tolerate second best at any level.

Sydney Barnes, in some ways, lived before his time. In an age when the master-servant relationship still existed with regards to professional cricketers and their employers, he resented discipline imposed from without and would stand his ground if he thought he was in the right — and 'down tools' if the occasion warranted.

At Old Trafford, home of Lancashire cricket, Tom Reddick once asked Barnes if he found it necessary to work up a hatred of batsmen in order to bring out his best.

'No,' answered Barnes, 'I never hated anyone on the cricket field, but I disliked a few off it.'

The old bowler pointed towards the committee room and added: 'Those were the sort of people I got angry with. The Lancashire committee of my day never paid me enough!'

When he first played under the rather imperious A C MacLaren, there was some clash over field-placing but the England captain soon accepted that when Barnes was bowling, Barnes was the 'captain' and more than able to set his own field and decide upon his tactics. Throughout his long life he was his own man. He refused to continue playing for Lancashire because the county would not offer him certain financial guarantees which he considered necessary for the future of himself and his family. This act probably deprived Barnes of the opportunity to play in more Tests than he did, but his overall international bowling record still remains impressive: 189 wickets at 16.43 in 27 Tests. For Staffordshire and for various league and club teams he continued to take wickets by the bucketful every season until well into his 60s. At 48, while still engaged in minor cricket, Barnes was actually invited to tour Australia (in 1920–21) but declined. He was already 56 when he appeared for a Minor Counties XI versus the touring South Africans in 1929 and bowled unchanged for three hours to take 8/41 in 32 overs in the visitors' first knock.

Somerset amateur R J O Meyer also played in that match and old Nottinghamshire professional Tom Reddick once related to the writer a story told him by Meyer about Barnes's effort against the 1929 South Africans. By lunch time Barnes had taken two wickets and a local enthusiast offered him 25 pounds if he took all the remaining wickets in the innings. Springbok batsman Jack Siedle had retired ill, which meant Barnes could not achieve all 10 wickets but, when the last man came in he had taken all eight to fall.

Barnes drew a cross with his boot on the turf a couple of yards from the batsman and ordered Jack Meyer to stand there. Meyer did so and crouched low in readiness as Barnes came in to bowl at the South African number 11, fast bowler Sandy Bell. Barnes hit the required spot and the ball went from Bell's bat straight in, and out, of the hands of a red-faced Meyer. The master glared at the erring fielder and muttered appropriate threats. Barnes's subsequent remarks when Meyer proceeded to clean bowl Springbok number 10, Neville Quinn, with the first ball of his own next over were not recorded and were probably unprintable.

At 94, in the year of his death, the seemingly indestructible Sydney Barnes was almost as stern and erect as he was at 30. Can anyone claim that there was ever a greater bowler?

8

Birth of the Bosie

'But, after all, what is the googly? It is merely a ball with an ordinary break produced by an extraordinary method.'

— B J T Bosanquet

During a period when spin bowling reigned supreme, batsmen who had become confidently adept at countering the ball breaking in the direction of slip were suddenly confronted with a new phenomenon, what some have termed 'the Devil's own ball' — the apparent leg-break that defied all known science by turning in abruptly from the off.

The father of the googly (or the 'bosie', as Australians have preferred to call it, after the name of its prime creator) was not a bowler who could be measured as great when placed alongside his more talented disciples, although he did, with the sang-froid born of his Eton and Oxford upbringing, for a short period bamboozle some of the best batsmen in Test and first-class cricket.

Bernard James Tindal Bosanquet, a leading English amateur all-rounder of the late 19th century, discovered the googly quite by accident in 1897 when fooling around with a tennis ball in a billiard table game called 'twisty-twosty'. Up to that point he had been a plain and simple right-arm medium-paced bowler and his change to leg-breaks and googlies was not accompanied by the years of practice necessary for the making of a truly great spin bowler. Bosanquet's initial success was more due to the novelty of his new invention and it was left to those who followed him to perfect the art. Fittingly, though, his first attempt at a googly in a Test in Australia clean bowled the incomparable Victor Trumper.

Bosanquet describes the incident in an article in the 1925 *Wisden*: 'Two leg-breaks were played beautifully to cover, but the next ball (delivered with a silent prayer), pitching in the same place, saw the same graceful stroke played — and struck the middle stump instead of the bat!'

According to Bosanquet, the secret of bowling a googly consisted merely 'in turning the wrist over at the moment of delivery far enough to alter the axis of spin, so that a ball, which normally delivered would break from leg, breaks from the off.'

Before Bosanquet appeared on the scene, the googly, or something similar had been bowled from time to time, but he was the first

England's B J T Bosanquet discovered the googly by accident, while playing a game with a tennis ball on a billiard table, and started a bowling revolution when he displayed the strange new delivery in a Test.

player to use it consistently in first-class and Test cricket. Writing in the *Australasian*, T P Horan (he wrote as 'Felix') claimed that Australian Test bowler Frank Allan coined the term 'gooler' or 'googly' when referring to a slow high-tossed ball: 'The ball maybe looks infantile, or such as a child would bowl. Hence "goo". Then that infantile or childlike toss is supposed to hide some trick or stratagem. Hence "guile". Thus we have "goo-guile", which, by an easy process of contraction, changes into "googlie" [sic].'

The 'googlie' in the days of Frank Allan was definitely not the googly bowled by Bosanquet, although Horan does record that he was once shocked by an apparent leg-break bowled by Lancashire and England player A G Steel which turned sharply from the off. The ball bowled by Steel *was* apparently a genuine googly but its full significance was not recognised at the time.

Horan goes on to say that bowlers like W H Cooper, left-hander Tom Kendall, George Palmer and Harry Trott frequently mixed an off-break with the stock leg-spinning deliveries but that their change in action when doing so was discernible. Bosanquet himself wrote in the 1925 *Wisden* that English bowlers like William Attewell and E R Wilson had dismissed batsmen with balls which turned other than the way expected, but could never do so at will.

Bernard Bosanquet enjoyed a brief but lucrative period as a bowler of leg-breaks and googlies, and won a couple of Tests for England in the process. At Sydney in 1903−04 he won the deciding match of the series with a 6/51 spell and, at Trent Bridge in 1905, again versus Australia, he captured 8/107 in another win for England.

Although conceived by an Englishman, the googly was raised to a pre-eminent form of attack outside England. Aubrey Faulkner was one of the celebrated South African quartet who used Bosanquet's new type of ball to stunning effect in England during the wet 1907 season. Faulkner, together with Ernest Vogler, Gordon White and Reggie Schwarz (who differed from the other three in that he bowled the googly as his stock delivery) had mastered the freak new form of attack on their own responsive matting wickets in South Africa. They bowled South Africa to its first home Test series victory, against England in 1905−06, and with their deceiving break and unusual pace off the pitch, were a collective menace in England in 1907.

Famous as the man who pioneered the concept of the indoor cricket school, Faulkner states in his *Cricket − Can it be Taught?* that, when looking back on the four or five years he personally spent on mastering the leg-break and googly, he was highly amused at bowlers who complained that they had been trying to do the same thing all season and 'can't spin or control the ball anything like enough yet'. Faulkner comments that he wonders why 'this type of fellow ever chose cricket...I should have thought marbles was more in his line!'

Faulkner and company (with the exception of Schwarz) failed woefully on a foray to Australia in 1910−11 when, on hard pitches, the stroke-play of the swift-footed Victor Trumper and his colleagues made a mockery of their attempts at spinning the ball.

George Aubrey Faulkner, teetotaller, non-smoker and cricket theorist supreme, was South Africa's first world-class batsman. His added ability as a bowler of leg-breaks, googlies and even fast-medium yorkers made him a doubly formidable opponent. Although he failed as a bowler in Australia, Faulkner scored a record 732 runs in the Tests. Perhaps the strain of being his team's one reliable scorer proved too much for him to apply his full energy and attention to bowling. In South Africa he virtually single-handedly won the 1909−10 rubber against England, scoring 545 runs (average 60.55) and taking 29 wickets at 21.89 in one of the most outstanding Test series all-round performances in cricket history. Faulkner's Test bowling performances in England included 6/17 at Leeds in 1907 and 7/84 versus England at the Oval during the 1912 Triangular Tournament. This classy performer's 1754 runs and 82 wickets in 25 Tests stands high in the list of all-round international performances.

Aubrey Faulkner's pioneering indoor cricket school in London attracted many notable cricketers and a young man he once engaged as secretary/assistant coach, Ian Peebles, went on to bowl googlies for England and to become one of cricket's most knowledgable and informative writers.

Albert Ernest Edward Vogler bowled his leg-breaks and googlies with such skill and success in 1907 that England's captain R E Foster was moved to state that the South African was 'the greatest bowler playing cricket in either hemisphere at the present time...'.

Vogler only really came into his own as a Test bowler during that 1907 tour (15 wickets for 295 runs in three matches) and when the MCC visited South Africa in 1909−10. In the latter series, Vogler bowled in tandem with Faulkner and the two googly bowlers claimed between them 65 of the 88 England wickets to fall in five Tests. Vogler's efforts resulted in 36 wickets at 21.75 (a South African series record that stood until Hugh Tayfield broke it in 1956−57) including 5/87 and 7/94 in the first Test at Johannesburg. Vogler is the only South African bowler to have taken 10 wickets in an innings in a first-class match. His 10 for 26 for Eastern Province versus Griqualand West in 1906−07 formed part of an overall match analysis of 16 for 38 − all obtained during a single day's play. Vogler's 'wrong 'un' was particularly difficult to detect and few batsmen could 'read' his hand at the moment of delivery. Like Faulkner, he varied his pace and flight expertly and also included a slow but deadly yorker in his repertoire.

Vogler failed dismally in Australia in 1910−11; some say he saw most of the tour through the bottom of a beer bottle. Another member of South Africa's famous googly foursome, the English-born Reginald Oscar Schwarz, who used the googly as his stock ball and did not bowl a leg-break, was a resounding success in Australia with 25 wickets in the Tests at 26.04 and 59 wickets in all first-class matches.

Schwarz was the first South African to experiment with the googly when South Africa made a non-Test tour of England in 1904. He was not considered much of a bowler but headed the tour averages and passed his find on to the other South Africans.

The fourth South African googly bowler, Gordon Charles White, a soccer international, was more of a batsman that a bowler and was seldom given the ball in Tests, although he took his share of wickets in county matches in England in 1904 and 1907. Both White and

South African all-rounder
C B Llewellyn was possibly
the first left-arm slow
bowler of note to bowl the
'chinaman', the
left-hander's googly.

Schwarz were killed in action during the Second World War; Vogler retired from first-class cricket in 1912 but Aubrey Faulkner made his final appearance for South Africa at Lord's in 1924 when he was already 42. Six years later he committed suicide under mysterious circumstances.

Charles Bennett Llewellyn was an orthodox left-arm spinner when he first appeared for South Africa versus England in 1895–96. Llewellyn later added the left-hander's googly to his armoury and was, in effect, one of the first bowlers to bowl what later became known as the 'Chinaman'.

The term 'Chinaman' carries separate connotations in Australia and England. In Australia it refers to the left-hander's googly — the expected off-break that turned instead from leg to the right-handed batsman. In England it is used to describe the ordinary left-hander's off-break. It has been said that the term was coined when Ellis Achong, a left-handed West Indian bowler of Chinese descent, was seen spinning the ball out of the back of his hand, but any confirmed fact about its origin remains obscure.

Charles 'Buck' Llewellyn was, incidentally, considered good enough to be included in the 'Golden Age' England Test squad at Edgbaston in 1902, although he was omitted in the final selection. He was a prolific all-rounder for Hampshire and played with distinction in 15 Tests for South Africa.

Before the emergence of its googly quartet, South Africa's main bowler was the prodigious hitter James Hugh Sinclair. A right-arm fast bowler with a flowing high action, Sinclair twice claimed more than 100 wickets on a tour of England. He was the first South African to reach both 50 and 100 in Tests and the first player to score a century and take five wickets in the first innings of a Test (6/26 and 106 versus England at Cape Town in 1898–99).

Sinclair's main support in the early years came from James 'Bonnor' Middleton (slow-medium left-arm), George Alexander Rowe (slow left-arm) and South Africa's first genuine express bowler, J J 'Kodgee' Kotze.

Leading South African batsman of the turn-of-the-century period, Sibley John Snooke, was a useful right-arm fast-medium bowler who bowled South Africa to victory over England in the third of three Tests played in Johannesburg in 1905–06 with figures of 4/57 and 8/70. Snooke played his last Test in 1922–23 when he was already more than 40.

Another long-lived South African cricketer who, apart from his value as a consistent left-handed batsman, was a left-arm medium-paced bowler of no mean ability was the Springboks' 'Grand Old Man' of cricket, Arthur William Nourse. Known as 'Dave' Nourse throughout his 40-year first-class career stretching from 1896 to 1936, he played 45 consecutive Tests for South Africa over 22 years and was the father of Dudley Nourse, one of South Africa's half-dozen finest batsmen.

Following the demise of South Africa's much vaunted googly attack in Australia in 1910–11, men like C P Carter, S J Pegler and J M Blanckenberg took over as the lynch-pins of the Springbok attack. Claude Paget Carter, a slow left-hander, was particularly adept on South Africa's matting pitches. Sidney James Pegler was a medium-paced right-handed leg-break and off-break bowler of impeccable length and control but who did not bowl the googly. He headed the bowling for the 1912 Triangular Tournament with 29 wickets at 20.48 and, in 1924, when already 36 was prevailed upon to join the South African team in England after originally missing selection. Pegler responded by taking more wickets that anyone else in the team. James Manuel Blanckenberg was a superbly accurate tireless right-arm medium-pacer who was a formidable foe on matting wickets but failed in Tests in England.

As talented as bowlers like Pegler, Carter and Blanckenberg may have been, they could not match the mystery and effect produced by South Africa's four original 'bosie men' in England in 1907. South Africa's record overseas was to remain a rather dismal one until 1935, when a googly bowler of Greek descent was to twice bowl England out in a Test at Lord's.

It was, then, the Englishman Bernard Bosanquet who introduced the revolutionary googly to international play and the South Africans Faulkner, Vogler, Schwarz and White who improved on Bosanquet's new bowling method and changed the face of cricket. A series of outstanding Australian and English bowlers of varying style and character were destined soon to perfect the new art. Their tales unfold in the following chapter.

9

Perfecting the art

'There is a final drop of venom which transforms a good bowler into a great one'

— Hon. T C F Prittie

One lone Australian was ready to take over the googly bowling flame from the faltering South Africans who had found their nemesis in Australia in 1910–11 — a cricketing dentist who had up until then been playing for the most part on the continent of America. The Sydney-born Dr Herbert Vivian Hordern mastered the mysteries of the off-breaking leg-break while studying dentistry at Pennsylvania University. He also took the opportunity while living in the USA to tour England with the famous Philadelphian cricket team in 1908.

'Ranji' Hordern, whose nickname came as a result of his facial resemblance to the great Indian batsman, formed with swing bowler Barton King of Philadelphia one of the most formidable attacking duos of all time. As a leg-spin and googly bowler, Hordern would have been first choice for a world team during the period from 1906 to 1910, as would King have been as a fast bowler.

The world first became aware of Hordern's ability with the 'bosie' when an MCC team including South African R O Schwarz toured the United States and Canada in 1907. Hordern twice claimed five wickets in an innings against the visitors and Schwarz was stunned when he saw the Australian dentist bowl a googly.

Arthur Mailey was a Hordern admirer and records in his *10 for 66 and All That* that the cricketing dentist would continually massage his fingers to keep them flexible 'even when he was walking down the street or fighting his way through the south-coast jungle'. It was concern for his fingers, when related to his chosen profession, that caused Hordern to give away Test cricket after only two series in which he claimed 46 wickets at 23.36 in only seven Tests.

Taller than his successors in the Australian team, Mailey and Grimmett, and taking a much longer run than most bowlers of his kind, Hordern bowled with a smooth action and was perhaps closest to Bill O'Reilly in pace and method. A placid and even-tempered performer, his variations of flight and spin were subtly disguised and he very rarely offered up a loose ball, other than in an effort to dislodge a stubborn batsman. Sir Pelham Warner and C B Fry both rated Hordern the best googly bowler.

On his first appearance for Australia (versus South Africa in 1910–11) Hordern was faced by an in-form Aubrey Faulkner. He asked his captain, Clem Hill, if he might give away a few boundaries by feeding Faulkner his favourite shot, the cover-drive. Hill was dubious but agreed. Hordern bowled three consecutive half-volleys outside the off-stump, which Faulkner promptly hit for four each time, much to Hill's consternation. The fourth ball Hordern flighted a little higher, and it dropped a shade shorter; Faulkner holed out to Algy Gehrs, at extra cover, the ball travelling about a foot from the ground. Clem Hill rushed over to congratulate Hordern, but said: 'Well, it came off; but for heaven's sake *don't try it again*.'

After the First World War, Hordern discarded his uniform and went 'walkabout' for a while on the south coast of New South Wales and once bowled in a country match to a youth named Donald Bradman, who was also a burgeoning googly bowler.

Before war put an end to first-class cricket between 1915 and 1919, only one 'bosie' bowler other than Hordern made some sort of mark in Australian cricket. A G Moyes considered Sidney Hand Emery to be, on his day, the 'most devastating bowler of the bosie ever seen'. Unfortunately Emery's day did not come too frequently; fairly quick through the air, the restless 'Mad Mick' Emery could manage only 5 Test wickets at 49.80 runs apiece.

Emery was a member of the 1912 Australian team in the Triangular Tournament. One of his colleagues was leg-spinner Thomas James Matthews, who produced a 'Boys' Own' storybook performance at Manchester when he claimed two hat-tricks in the match, both on the same day against South Africa. No-one has since matched this feat. Short and perpetually sun-tanned, Matthews pitched his leg-breaks up to the batsman, compelling a stroke, but never mastered the googly.

One of the most important and certainly the most entertaining of Australia's outstanding googly bowlers made his first-class debut during the golden days of Victor Trumper, but did not play in a Test until after the First World War. Arthur Alfred Mailey looked upon Trumper as an idol and the googly bowler's description of their first meeting on the field (when he clean-bowled his hero third ball) is one of the finest and most poignant pieces in cricket literature.

Mailey's autobiographical *10 for 66 and All That* (the title alludes to his best bowling performance and not to any historical association) is as amusing as it is informative about the game and the players of his time. When he retired from Test cricket, the irrepressible Mailey became a journalist, artist and cartoonist who would have deserved the description 'outstanding' in any one of his four chosen disciplines.

Mailey was as proficient with his spin-bowling as he was with his colourful prose, or with his deft pencil. He was the Cardus of cricket cartoonists, acknowledged court-jester to the Australian cricket teams of the 1920s, and he was one of the finest bowlers who ever set foot on hallowed turf.

According to Ray Robinson, Mailey bowled like a millionaire and, in his effort to generate turn on Australia's iron-clad pitches, 'he had to put so much snap into his finger action that accuracy was left to take its chance'. In the matter of the many full-tosses he sent up to the batsman, only the perpetually dead-pan Mailey knew whether they were intentional − offered up as a lure for the unsuspecting batsman to catch hold of and mishit to a waiting fielder.

Apart from the annoyance of his dipping full-toss (he twice bowled Jack Hobbs with it) an inventory of Mailey's armoury would reveal every conceivable type of ball possible to produce when bowling with bent wrist from the back of the hand. A shuffling start to his short run-up ended in a classical side-on action, arm over the top at full height. As he sighted the batsman from behind his left shoulder, Mailey would swing his right arm over from behind his back, having hidden his missile for as long as possible. It was never easy to pick up his 'wrong 'un'; difficult to judge his flight and where the ball would ultimately pitch.

In today's efficiency conscious cricket, where runs-per-over is sometimes considered a more important statistic than balls-per-wicket, Arthur Mailey may not have prospered as he did during the 1920s. With Warwick Armstrong's powerful batting eleven providing a cascade of runs to bowl to, Mailey took 36 wickets in the eight innings against England in 1920−21. A peculiar statistic connected with his performance was that in seven of the eight English innings, the googly bowler was hit for more than 100 runs. His final average of 26.27 runs per wicket is testimony to his skill, and it can be noted that Australia won all five Tests in the series by overwhelming margins. In terms of runs-per-over, Mailey bowled throughout at the rate of 3.8 per six-ball over, but he snared an English wicket for every 40 balls bowled, a remarkable strike-rate by any standards. During his own most prolific series in terms of wickets taken, Dennis Lillee, against England in 1981, took 39 wickets in 12 innings while conceding 2.8 runs an over but he needed 48 balls for each of his wickets, a good 20 per cent more than Mailey.

During the 1920−21 series, Mailey also set the existing record for wickets per innings in a Test with his 9/121 during the fourth game at Melbourne. He took 13/236 in the match.

While Arthur Mailey was considered a bowling spendthrift, Clarrie Grimmett was an acknowledged bowling miser. For Mailey a full-toss was just another ball that might take a wicket, for Grimmett it was a delivery to be avoided as conscientiously as the plague. The parsimonious Clarence Victor Grimmett would be less likely to con-template using such an abomination of a ball as a bank manager would consider providing overdraft facilities to the local tramp.

Where Arthur Mailey would happily distribute largesse when bowling, awaiting an opportunity to snare his eventually over-confident opponent, Grimmett would make no such concession. He wanted the batsman's wicket and he was not prepared to trade runs.

Grimmett was one of Sir Neville Cardus's favourite characters whom he portrayed as a bowler who 'hides' his skill and 'is a master of surreptitious arts'. At first glance, Grimmett's action must have aroused a certain amount of puzzled laughter. What on earth was an old-fashioned round-arm type of bowler doing with a baggy Australian green cap covering his head? Was this the baggage-manager posing as a Test cricketer? The results of Grimmett's rather curious and antiquated action soon dispelled any notions that this little man may be an imposter. Ray Robinson referred to Grimmett as that 'mighty little bloke', who bowled with his cap on to hide his bald pate, and with his quick six-pace approach to the stumps, usually completed an over within two minutes.

If fortitude could be calculated in dollars, Clarrie Grimmett would have been a multi-millionaire. According to Ian Peebles, Grimmett was forced to spend years 'trying to convince the world he was a serious bowler'. At school he bowled fast, until a master noted his ability to bowl leg-breaks and forbade him from bowling anything else. Born and raised in Wellington, New Zealand, he was 23 when he migrated to Australia, after completing an apprenticeship as a signwriter. He moved from Sydney to Melbourne and then to Adelaide, before finally making his Test debut at the age of 34.

Although he turned his googly further than his leg-break, Grimmett did not frequently use his wrong 'un, preferring to baffle the batsman with what he termed his 'mystery ball'. It took years of practice to develop this puzzling delivery which dipped in flight and gathered pace off the pitch while shooting straight through as a top-spinner might. Grimmett practised with a tennis ball and gradually increased his distance of pitch, from a few yards initially, until he was able to bowl the delivery to the full 22-yards. He chose this ball as his surprise weapon because, unlike when bowling the googly, he did not have to drop his shoulder further than for his conventional leg-break.

Clarrie Grimmett's motto was 'never communicate your intentions'. He wrote a number of books on the art of bowling but Peebles claimed that Grimmett 'only told us how he took wickets himself' and that one might as well have read 'the wind on the art of blowing'. In 37 Tests Grimmett bagged 216 wickets at 24.21, a record that stood until eventually overhauled by the great Ray Lindwall. With 44 wickets in five Tests against South Africa in 1935–35, he heads the list for most wickets in a series by an Australian bowler.

Grimmett the wily and circumspect was short and slight; his famous partner-in-destruction, Bill O'Reilly, was tall, robust and

Opposite: New Zealand-born Clarrie Grimmett played for Australia and bowled his leg-breaks and bosies like a miser, regarding a full-toss as some sort of sacrilege.

menacing. Where Grimmett snared his victims with cool and calculated subterfuge, O'Reilly bore down upon his prey remorselessly with tallons drawn, perpetually prepared to strike.

As a hostile combatant 'Tiger' O'Reilly might be more easily compared with the relentless Englishman, Sydney Barnes — a man who gave and asked no quarter and regarded the mere presence of an undismissed batsman as a personal affront.

Unlike his little mate Clarrie Grimmett who always bowled with cap firmly placed on his head, O'Reilly's own hairless dome shone in the burning light of day, almost as if it were part and parcel of an act of defiance. Like the Englishman Barnes, Australia's O'Reilly bowled his leg-breaks at a pace somewhat above that normally associated with spin bowling. But he was seldom as quick as Barnes who could, at times, be described as around fast-medium. O'Reilly's stock leg-turner was sent down at medium-pace, his wrist curled much in the way of the conventional leg-tweaker, but straighter than that of, say, Grimmett or Mailey, with a resultant rolling action more than a spinning motion on the ball. His top-spinner was more of the spinner's variety, as was his googly which, according to observers, buzzed through the air.

From an early age O'Reilly attacked the stumps constantly and, as Johnny Moyes put it in *Australian Bowlers*, 'when he appealed it was not a request, but a demand for the blood of the victim'. Ian Peebles described him as 'good honest-to-God Irish-Australian, without malice, but red-blooded and certainly without hypocrisy'.

At his best when aroused, O'Reilly gained figures of 5/66 and 5/56 in the second 1938 Test versus England, at Headingly, Leeds, after he had been unexpectedly no-balled when bowling to Joe Hardstaff. Temper flaring, O'Reilly's next ball took Hardstaff's off-bail and the following delivery saw Wally Hammond caught by Bill Brown to start an England slide to disaster.

As a combination (the only two Australian slow bowlers of any great note to have hunted as a pair), Grimmett and O'Reilly were feared by batsmen everywhere until Grimmett, still going strong at the age of 45, was dropped from the Australian team in 1936–37 amid controversy. (His replacement, Francis Anthony Ward, made little impression in his four Test outings). From then on, until the outbreak of the Second World War, O'Reilly remained Australia's number one attacker and, according to most authorities, the finest bowler in world cricket. As a cricket writer, Bill O'Reilly has maintained his exceptional standards and remained an astute and knowledgable voice in the press-box.

The unusually gifted Leslie O'Brien Fleetwood-Smith was an unorthodox left-hander and a prodigious spinner of the ball who received his first Test chance against South Africa in 1935–36 and in 1936–37 claimed 19 wickets in three Tests against England.

Australia's Bill 'Tiger' O'Reilly was a hostile competitor who has been ranked alongside England's Sydney Barnes as among the best bowlers in history.

'Chuck' Fleetwood-Smith ended life a tragic figure and he died a derelict after having early in his life overcome disability on his way to becoming a Test cricketer. As a boy he was an aspiring *right-arm* fast bowler until an accident forced him to bowl with his left. Fleetwood-Smith spun the ball to an alarming degree, but his control sometimes deserted him. His main ball was the left-hander's off-break, a back-of-the-hand delivery that was the mirror counterpart of the right-handed spinner's wrist-spun leg-break. His well-hidden wrong 'un, the 'Chinaman', broke the other way with sudden venom and few batsmen were able to anticipate such a ball.

The tall and powerfully built left-hander did not relish having to bowl to anyone but the best of opponents and Fleetwood-Smith was often at odds with various captains when he failed to remove an obstinate tail-ender. His ability to turn the ball alarmingly on the deadest of pitches also meant that many deliveries beat bat and wicket. According to Bill O'Reilly, Fleetwood-Smith was the best left-arm spinner of his day and, had he been blessed with a sounder temperament, may well have been counted among the best of all time.

Only a handful of leg-break and googly bowlers played for Australia in Tests between 1910 and 1938 but Hordern, Mailey, Grimmett, O'Reilly and left-hander Fleetwood-Smith demonstrated back-of-the-hand spin bowling of a quality that has never since been seen in international cricket.

England's premier leg-break and googly bowler, Alfred Percy Freeman, reserved his best for county cricket and seldom made much of an impression in international cricket. Although his Test rewards remained meagre, 'Tich' Freeman must go down in history as one of the most remarkable of his breed.

Sir Neville Cardus named him as 'the cleverest of all leg-spinners' and, in an age of quick-footed batsmen, the tiny, balding Kent spinner snared in his cunning web 3776 first-class victims at 18.42 runs apiece. Many English county batsmen considered Freeman something of a magician who could neither be played nor hit. Australian batsmen, well fed on leg-breaks and 'boseys' in club and Sheffield Shield cricket, were not afraid of him.

Freeman's Test record in Austalia was rather woeful − 8 wickets for 459 runs − yet he remains the only bowler to have taken 300 wickets in a single English season (304 at 18.05 in 1928). He passed 200 wickets in each of the following seven seasons to create a record which must remain unassailable. Three times he took 10 wickets in an innings, a unique performance. Against South Africa in 1929 he twice took seven wickets in an innings, but was belted for 169 runs and no wicket in the final Test at the Oval.

A technical perfectionist, Freeman's craft revolved around perfect length and accuracy. On a responsive wicket he spun the ball sharply from leg-stump to off and employed a well-disguised googly and his top-spinner brought many wickets. Freeman spun the ball sufficiently well to remain a menace in England for more than two decades. On unresponsive brick-hard Australian wickets he could not match the spin of Australian bowlers, who literally made the ball buzz in the air and could probably extract life and bounce from a coffin lid.

When the England selectors lost interest in 'Tich' Freeman they tried a succession of slow bowlers, none of whom made a lasting impression in Test cricket. The red-faced Richard Knowles Tyldseley of Lancashire relied mainly on his top-spinner for variation and turned his leg-break alarmingly on most pitches. Like Freeman, he failed when taken to Australia but had a few days of success in home Tests against Australia and South Africa.

Schoolmaster Douglas Ward Carr made an amazing jump from club cricket to Test cricket at the ripe age of 37 in his debut season for Kent. Carr started the season in club cricket, took 51 wickets with his googlies in seven matches for his county, claimed 6/71 for Gentlemen versus Players at Lord's and was picked for the fifth Test versus Australia at the Oval.

England captain A C Maclaren, in his own last Test, gave Carr first over of the match and kept him on for an hour and a half after the spinner bowled Syd Gregory at nine and trapped Noble and Armstrong leg-before-wicket at 27 and 55 respectively. Bardsley and Trumper then righted the Australian innings in a century stand and Carr finished with the figures 34−2−146−5. He added a 35−1−136−2 stint in the second Australian innings when Bardsley hit his second hundred of the match and the game slipped away from England. Carr was never picked for England again but played for Kent until he was 42.

The charismatic and adventurous Percy George Herbert Fender holds the world record for the fastest century in first-class cricket and he supplemented this robust hitting with medium-paced leg-breaks and a very occasional wrong 'un. But like Freeman before him, the Surrey captain seldom troubled batsmen in Tests. Arthur Mailey was of the opinion that had 'Percy George' been born in Australia and nurtured on hard wickets, he would have ranked among the greatest.

Another talented county captain, Robert Walter Vivian Robins of Middlesex, took five wickets in his Test debut against South Africa at Lord's in 1929 and seven wickets in his first game versus Australia at Nottingham the following season. When he struck a length, which was not as frequent as he would have wished, 'Robbie' Robins was quite deadly with his leg-breaks and googlies, but failed to build on his promising start in international cricket.

The tall Scottish-born Ian Alexander Ross Peebles also played for Middlesex and later gained a reputation as a cricket writer of humour and great insight whose *Straight From the Shoulder* is the definitive work on throwing. He was also an above average googly bowler and an employee and protege of the celebrated Aubrey Faulkner.

Peebles's easy and flowing bowling action has been described as a model for all leg-spin bowlers and he is one of the few Test bowlers to have troubled the mighty Sir Donald Bradman. On his England debut at Old Trafford in 1930, Peebles, who possessed a most deceptive googly, dismissed Bradman for 14 after the great man had plundered 334 off England's attack at Headingley in the previous Test. At the Oval, in the final Test of 1930, Peebles sent down 71 overs to take six wickets for 204 in a marathon effort. Unfortunately, like so many other England leg-spin bowlers of the period, his subsequent Test performances were mediocre.

Carr, Fender, Robins and Peebles were amateurs, as was another remarkable 'one Test wonder', Charles Stowell Marriott, a Kent schoolmaster like Carr who bowled his leg-breaks and what was described as a 'rare' googly from a short, prancing run. 'Father' Marriott played his only Test against West Indies at the Oval in 1933, scored a duck, but claimed 11 wickets in the match for 96 runs. His only other recognition came when he was taken on a tour of India with the MCC in 1933–34 but he did not appear in the Tests.

Apart from 'Tich' Freeman, professional leg-break and googly bowlers were few and far between during the 1920s and 1930s — which is probably understandable since bowlers of that type can prove expensive luxuries on occasion and a paid player would be more conscious of the need for consistent performance. Of those professionals who did dare to take up leg-break bowling, five appeared in Test cricket before the Second World War, two played after the war, but only one really established himself as a consistently dangerous international bowler.

Middlesex's dry and lugubrious James Morton Sims and two Lancashire leg-spinners, the bespectacled former coal-miner Thomas Bignell Mitchell and the keen and lively Leonard Litton Wilkinson, all played for England at one time or another without troubling the best Test batsmen. William Eric Hollies (Warwickshire) played for England in the West Indies in 1934–35 but failed in Australia in 1950–51. He is remembered as the man who delivered the googly that bowled Sir Donald Bradman for a duck in that great man's final Test innings, thus preventing him from achieving a Test batting average of 100.

The remaining England leg-spinner of note was another Faulkner pupil, Douglas Vivian Parson Wright of Kent who, on his day, was regarded as a world-class bowler. According to R C Robertson-Glasgow (in his *Cricket Prints*), even Bradman once said he would like to have Wright on his side.

Doug Wright's long and peculiar hop-skip-and-jump approach to the stumps sometimes provoked unfavourable comment and his length and direction were frequently wayward. But when he got it all together he was deadly on any wicket. Bowling at a much faster pace that most leg-spinners, he would sometimes produce a truly unplayable ball which frequently beat bat, stumps and wicket-keeper. He is the only bowler to have seven times secured a hat-trick, although never in a Test.

Freeman wilted under severe attack from opposing batsmen but an assault on Wright generally resulted in an even more sustained effort by the bowler to dismiss the offending batsman. Of his Test match gems, Doug Wright's 7/105 versus Australia at Sydney in 1946–47 was his most meritorious, and would have won the match for England if a catch had not gone astray off Bradman in Australia's second innings.

Although he was a comparatively expensive bowler in terms of runs per over, Wright's strike-rate in wickets per balls bowled was impressive. As David Frith puts it in *The Slow Men*: 'The game never moved faster in terms of runs and wickets than when this man was in action.'

Since the days of Bosanquet and Faulkner, Hordern, Mailey, Grimmett and O'Reilly, Freeman through to Wright, leg-break and googly bowling has, with a few notable exceptions, become unfashionable in international cricket. For those cricket-lovers who thrived on the mystery and the excitement that is provided by a top-class googly bowler, the present age of pace and fire must, at times, appear tedious, strange as such a statement may sound. Gone, alas, are the days of 20 overs and more per hour, scintillating footwork and strokeplay, a run-rate of 300 or 400 runs per day, and the fall of a wicket to a devious 'heathenish' ball at the most unexpected moment.

10

A sign of things to come

'Genuinely fast bowling...finds out batsmen short of the highest class because their reactions are not quick enough to deal with it'
— John Arlott

Up to fairly recent times, before the word 'pack' became descriptive of international fast bowlers working in unison, it was customary to contend that the finest of fast bowlers usually hunted in pairs. Such a pair were two Australians who terrorised England's batsmen when Tests resumed after the First World War — the rangy, bounding and aggressive Jack Gregory and that 'most beautiful of fast bowlers' (as Cardus always called him), the silken-smooth and panther-like 'Ted' McDonald.

Before the formation of the Gregory-McDonald partnership, the most noteworthy speed combination in international cricket had probably been the Englishmen S F Barnes and F R Foster who so decimated Australia's batting line-up during the 1911–12 summer. Barnes and Foster were not out and out speed merchants like Gregory and McDonald, who relied as much on the effect of physical fear on opposing batsmen through their constant short-pitched bowling as they did on their ability as bowlers in the true sense of the description.

Jack Morrison Gregory seldom placed more than three fielders on the leg-side when he tested batsmen with his steepling bouncers and challenged them to hook or be damned, but he was pacy enough to achieve more hits than he was in turn hit. Charging in at full gallop he presented a frightening aspect to the apprehensive defender. Always bare-headed, even when swinging his thunderous bat as one of Australia's mightiest hitters, the 6 ft 3½ in (192 cm) Gregory bounded forward to the bowling crease in 10 great leaps. After an initial shuffling start, his ninth stride was described as a huge 'kangaroo hop', and his final delivery leap covered some nine feet.

Ray Robinson paints a frightening picture of what Gregory must have appeared like to the hapless batsman shivering in his block-hole: 'His towering figure and fierce expression — blue eyes bulging, teeth bared — were terrifying enough to scare the wits out of batsmen before he let fly with the ball.'

At Trent Bridge, in the first Test of 1921, Gregory rocked England back on its heels and set the pattern for what was to follow in the remainder of a one-sided series. In his first two overs, both maidens, he had D J Knight caught behind by Hanson Carter for 8 and clean-bowled Ernest Tyldesley and Patsy Hendren for a duck apiece. England did not recover until the fourth match of the rubber, by which time the Ashes were already well packaged for a return trip to Australia.

A dynamic player from a famous cricketing family, Jack Gregory held the world record for the fastest-ever Test century (in 70 minutes and 67 balls, versus South Africa at Johannesburg, 1920−21) until it was bettered by the West Indies' Viv Richards versus England in 1986. The Australian all-rounder would have been an instant success in the age of television.

In dramatic contrast to his wildly leaping and exuberant partner, Tasmanian-born Edgar Arthur McDonald, of splendid physique and taciturn temperament, moved in for the kill like a jungle cat silently gathering momentum before leaping upon its prey. Len Braund, former England all-rounder, frequently umpired when Ted McDonald was bowling for Lancashire and once told Neville Cardus that 'not until he was almost at the crease did you sort of *feel* he was there'.

After he gave away Test cricket for the regular employment offered by League and County appointments, McDonald would bowl 30 overs or more in a day as a matter of course. Yet according to contemporary accounts, he would leave no rough footmarks in the turf or on the pitch. As Cardus once put it 'he might well have bowled on a cat's paws'.

Feared even by that greatest of all players against quick bowling, George Gunn, the Lancashire McDonald took 205 wickets in his first full season for the county in 1925, bowling, at 33 years of age, 1249 overs in first-class cricket. A few current Australian and English fast bowlers have not yet achieved that number of overs in their entire careers!

Described as a 'detached smouldering man, handsome and heavy-lidded' McDonald made certain, during the 11 Test matches against England and South Africa, that there would seldom be a moment of respite for the beleaguered batsman. Australia's record for these matches bears testimony to the effectiveness of the terrifying duo: six wins (all in a row) versus England, then two draws against that country followed by a win and two draws against South Africa for a final record of *played* 11 *won* 7 *drawn* 4.

In the famous Nottingham Test of 1921, McDonald matched his mate Gregory when it came to taking England wickets (they each bagged eight) and went on to claim 27 for the series. McDonald did not play for Australia again after 1922, but Gregory continued to cause mayhem for a few more seasons, until he limped from the field after taking 3/142 in an England total of 521 at Brisbane in 1928−29. A persistent cartilage problem had finally exacted its toll.

McDonald continued to play for his adopted Lancashire until 1931

Australian Jack Gregory
was a frightening sight with
his great kangaroo leap
before delivery.

and took his first-class tally to 1395 wickets in the process. He died
in tragic circumstances, aged 45, when he was struck and killed by a
passing motor car while giving police details of an accident from
which he had just had a miraculous escape.

Although a number of capable fast bowling performers followed
Gregory and McDonald onto the Test match oval, Australia could

not at any other time prior to the Second World War put together another combination as exhilarating and dangerous. Hard as such talented and energetic fast bowlers like Tim Wall and Ernest McCormick tried, they were unable to quite match their predecessors.

At the height of the 1932–33 bodyline series, one Australian bowler, the boisterous Harry Houston 'Bull' Alexander, made some attempt to match the fire and bounce of England's Harold Larwood. Although fairly sharp, he was nowhere near as skilful as his English opponent and was thoroughly mastered by the England batsmen. Strong as an ox, Alexander did enjoy the dubious satisfaction of three times striking England captain Douglas Jardine on the body in one over (he also broke the bat of England vice-captain Bob Wyatt) but ended his one and only Test with figures of 1/154.

Bean-pole 6 ft 6 in (198 cm) Lisle Ernest Nagel, a right-hander who swung the ball alarmingly from his great height, also managed one Test during 1932–33. He dismissed two England century markers, Walter Hammond and the Nawab of Pataudi, but was later hampered by a persistent neck injury.

When compared with Gregory and McDonald, it was obvious that amiable Tim Wall lacked what Ray Robinson called 'that streak of savagery' that most great fast bowlers seem to need. Tall, dark and decidedly handsome, Thomas Wellbourne Wall bowled with a graceful high delivery. A big-hearted bowler, his approach to the stumps included a curious scissor-like movement in the middle of a 27-pace run, which he covered in 13 long strides with a vigorous kicking action described as being like that of 'a frisky colt'.

Wall's long and slow walk back to his mark made him the butt for much good-natured barracking from the spectators, but he kept at it for 12 years in first-class cricket and claimed 56 wickets in 18 Test matches, without ever bettering his debut 3/123 and 5/66 against England at Melbourne in 1928–29. Tim Wall's most auspicious contribution to the record books came when he took all 10 wickets for 36 for South Australia versus New South Wales (including Bradman for a duck) during the 1932–33 season.

No fewer than 13 men bowled for Australia during Wall's Test debut season, eight in their first international series. One was the tall and slim Hunter Scott Thomas Laurie Hendry. 'Stork' Hendry was a right-arm medium pacer who represented his country in 11 Tests as an all-rounder without ever quite hitting the headlines, but he provided solid support to the more visible players in the side. He was, in 1986, at 91 years of age, the oldest living Test cricketer in Australia.

The 1928–29 season, when Australia struggled from match to match against one of England's most powerful teams, introduced to Test cricket a couple of bowlers who by accepted cricketing age standards would have been considered over the hill and out of the race. One of these 'born-again' veterans was the left-handed Herbert

'Dainty' Ironmonger who had played for Victoria before the war, which started when he was already 31.

Ironmonger's true age remained a mystery for years and when he stepped onto the Exhibition Ground at Brisbane to bowl against A P F Chapman's England XI in 1928–29, he claimed to be 41. Ironmonger ended his Test career with 74 wickets at 17.97 (14 matches) and it was only discovered many years later that he had in fact been born in April 1883 and was more than 45 when he first donned an Australian cap.

A spin bowler of exceptional accuracy, Ironmonger had half of two fingers missing from his bowling hand, the result of a sawmill accident. On better pitches, Ironmonger was content to tie batsmen down until their own impatience brought their downfall; on a worn or wet wicket he would make most players look foolish. His most amazing bowling figures were against South Africa in 1931–32: 7.2–5–6–5 and 15.3–7–18–6 in the fifth Test at Melbourne. South Africa was dismissed for totals of 36 and 45!

The bulky and rather unathletic 'Dainty' Ironmonger gained his nickname because he looked as if he were carefully stepping on eggs when running in to bowl.

Ironmonger made his Test debut during the first Test of the 1928–29 series when everyone *thought* he was 41. The lively off-break bowler Donald Dearness Blackie made his first appearance, in the second Test at Sydney the same year, when everyone already *knew* that he was 46 years and 253 days old – the oldest player for Australia on debut. Ironmonger was in fact just 16 days younger than Blackie when he played in the first Test at Brisbane and, when he played his last game for Australia, versus England in 1932–33, was only 38 days short of his 51st birthday – a record beaten only by England's Wilfred Rhodes, who represented his country against West Indies at Kingston in 1929–30 aged 52 years and 165 days.

Starting his run-up near mid-off, the bow-legged Don Blackie was generally capable of wiping away any smile that may have appeared on the batsman's face when first sighting the bowler's curious and old-fashioned approach. He bowled an off-break as his main delivery but could turn the ball the other way as well, and bowled much in the style of the leading pre-First World War bowlers like Trumble, Howell and Noble. It has been claimed that 'Rock' Blackie bowled more than 40,000 balls in all classes of cricket during his exceptionally long and active career.

A G Moyes wrote that for St Kilda and Victoria Blackie and Ironmonger were 'as closely linked in cricket as Laurel and Hardy' and that they 'proved once again that spin and length, allied to flight and control, are wicket-taking ingredients in any age – and also *at* any age'.

Queenslander Percival Mitchell Hornibrook, a left-hander in various styles from slow to medium-fast, was given the new ball opposite Wall in the final encounter of the 1928—29 series and then went to England in 1930. At 6 ft 3 in (190 cm), Hornibrook was able to use his height effectively at a whippy fast-medium for a few overs, but then usually reverted to orthodox left-arm spin, like Bill Johnston of a later vintage. Bowling mainly spinners, Hornibrook took 93 wickets in England in 1930 (and bowled more overs than anyone else) but was not able to establish a consistent place in the Australian team. His best moment in Test cricket came at the Oval when he netted 7/92 in England's second innings, an effort which helped Australia secure the Ashes.

All-rounder Alan George Fairfax also played his first game for Australia at Melbourne in 1928—29 and performed with some success in England in 1930. Steady right-arm medium pace, Fairfax was also a competent batsman and an especially fine gully fieldsman noted for his spectacular catching.

Another 1930 tourist, Alexander Hurwood, did not bowl well enough to play in a Test that year but was brought into the Australian XI during the 1930—31 home series versus West Indies. A lively right-arm medium-pacer who would change to off-breaks off a short run, he played in just two 1930 Tests and was unfortunate to be dropped after taking 11 wickets at 15.45.

A couple of new faces came and went when South Africa sent its second team to Australia in 1931—32 but, with Grimmett and Iron-monger among the wickets in almost every Test, there was little opportunity for others. Tasmanian-born Laurence John Nash was the fifth new bowler tried by Australia against the South Africans and by far the most successful. Genuinely fast, and a grand competitor who was also a brilliant Australian Rules footballer, Nash took 4/18 and 1/4 during what proved to be exactly one half of a truly frustrating Test career. Having made his debut at 21, he then waited another five years for a second go — in the final and deciding match versus England in 1936—37. Nash responded with match figures of 5/104 to bring his wicket aggregate to 10 wickets at 12.60 in his two Tests.

Australian cricket now entered a period when bowling strategy revolved almost solely around the spin of Grimmett and O'Reilly, with some support from fast bowler Tim Wall and the medium pace of batsman Stan McCabe. There was little opportunity for anyone else, other perhaps than little Arthur Chipperfield who, like Arthur Richardson some years previously, was picked mainly for his batting but bowled off-spinners with constant enthusiasm and occasional success.

Hans Irving Ebeling (who enjoyed a 57-year association with the Melbourne Cricket Club and was a prime organiser of the 1977 Centenary Test) was given the new-ball just once, at the Oval in

1934, and though he continued to render more than useful service to Victoria, was not considered again for Australia.

'Chuck' Fleetwood-Smith came in as a third back-of-the-hand spinner when Australia sailed off to South Africa in 1935–36 while a new fast-bowling 'find', Ernie McCormick, took Wall's place. It is perhaps unfortunate that Ernest Leslie McCormick is remembered more for his predilection for sending down no-balls than for his bowling excellence.

The humorous 'Goldie' McCormick first lost his bowling rhythm when playing for Australia against Worcestershire in the opening match of the 1938 tour. In his first three matches McCormick sent down 54 no-balls in 48 overs and reached his century of no-balls in his tenth outing.

It was a disastrous time for a dedicated bowler whose opening overs just before the Second World War were, according to Ray Robinson, 'the fastest on earth'. McCormick's carefully marked-out run-up was to no avail; as Robinson put it: 'He always looked where he was firing but didn't always fire where he was looking.' And he could never keep his back foot behind the line. McCormick was bowling at a time when the 'back-foot' law still applied when it came to a no-ball – whereby the bowler had to deliver the ball with one foot on the ground behind the bowling crease, and with no limitation relating to the position of either of his feet behind the popping crease. The law as it now stands calls for the bowler to have 'some part of his front foot whether grounded or raised' behind the popping crease. In both instances the bowler must of course operate within the return crease.

Despite his no-ball problems McCormick, in terms of balls per wicket, had one of Australia's best strike-rates for a pre-war fast bowler, although he was fairly expensive due to his no-balls and other loose deliveries. McCormick was unfortunately also prone to muscular strain and lumbago, which placed added limitations on his ultimate effectiveness.

At 6 ft 4 in (193 cm) Morris William Sievers was taller than McCormick but did not rate in the same class of hostility. Sievers did experience a few moments of personal glory during his only Test series, against Allen's Englishmen in 1936–37. At Melbourne in the third Test, with England already leading 2–0 in the rubber, he used his height to remarkable effect in capturing five England first-innings wickets for 21 and Australia went on to win the match and recovered to win the series.

A right-hander of much gentler pace, Mervyn George Waite opened the bowling for Australia in the last two Tests played before the Second World War and was perhaps unfortunate to face England's new young batting star, Len Hutton. The English opener made 364 at the Oval and poor Waite had to be content with figures of 1/150 off 72 overs in an England total of 7/903 declared.

Merv Waite was the last debutante bowler to appear for Australia before war broke out in 1939 and cricket balls were exchanged for far more lethal missiles. When hostilities were finally brought to a close, Australia was destined to again recommence cricket proceedings with a pair of fast bowlers whose performances would match in skill and effect those put up by Gregory and McDonald immediately after the First World War.

'Ted' McDonald, the Australian speedster dubbed the 'most beautiful of fast bowlers' by Cardus.

11

Notts Express

'A breed of Larwoods, armed with eight or so fieldsmen on the leg or onside, would no doubt have put an end to cricket altogether'
— Sir Neville Cardus

When Test cricket resumed for England after the First World War, there was no Barness-Foster combination to spearhead the defence of the Ashes won so convincingly in 1911−12. A weak England attack retired battered and beaten from a campaign in Australia in 1920−21 and with no bowler having enhanced his reputation. Of the pre-war men, Rhodes had virtually given up bowling in Tests, Bill Hitch didn't last the pace, Johnny Douglas, England's captain, made scant impression and Jack Hearne and Frank Woolley lacked penetration and were dreadfully expensive. It was not until 1926, when a new fast bowling hope of unusual skill emerged, that England was to raise itself from the dust of defeat and again meet its old antagonist, Australia, on equal terms.

Among the 1920−21 newcomers, Henry 'Harry' Howell (Warwickshire), right-arm fast off a long run, and Abraham 'Abe' Waddington (Yorkshire), lively left-arm fast-medium, were not helped by inconsistent slip fielding and provided few headaches for the Australian batsmen. Of the spin bowlers who first appeared in the same series, Lancashire's unpredictable but highly talented Cecil Harry Parkin varied the pace and spin of his off-breaks with great skill and took most wickets (16 at 41.87) in the five Tests. Something of an eccentric, 'Ciss' Parkin frequently found himself in hot water following his many clashes with authority. In 1921 he was again England's leading bowler in a home series against Australia, with 16 wickets in four Tests, but his criticism of England's captain Arthur Gilligan in the press during the 1924 series versus South Africa saw him dropped from the England side for all time. Parkin was a born comedian who delighted in entertaining the crowd with his tricks with the ball between deliveries. Leg-spinners Percy Fender (Surrey) and Evelyn Rockley Wilson (Yorkshire) also toured under Johnny Douglas in 1920−21 but also made little impression.

The 1921 season saw a further drop in England's fortunes. With Jack Hobbs unavailable, the batsmen had no answer to the speed of Gregory and McDonald. Other than Parkin, England's bowlers fared little better. No fewer than 30 players were called up by England, the most in any rubber in history.

Newcomers introduced during the series (and who all failed) included such redoubtable county performers as Nottinghamshire googly bowler Thomas Leonard Richmond; Northamptonshire all-rounder and off-break bowler, Vallance William Crisp Jupp (who bagged five first-class hat-tricks); the 6 ft 5 in (195 cm) fast bowler Frederick John ('Jack') Durston and all-rounder Nigel Esme Haig from Middlesex; and Gloucestershire's long-lived Charles Warrington Leonard Parker.

'Charlie' Parker (or 'Parlie Charker' as he was often called) was an immaculate left-arm slow bowler who had figures of $28-16-32-2$ in his only Test innings and who certainly deserved to play for England again. A delightfully erudite man, the 6 ft (183 cm) and lean Charlie Parker bowled with a classical action and a machine-like precision.

Somerset left-arm orthodox spinner John Cornish White was the only newly introduced England bowler of 1921 who was to make some mark in international cricket. 'Farmer' White's career fell between that of Wilfred Rhodes and England's next great left-hander, Hedley Verity. White, who relied more on accuracy and pace variation than spin, astounded critics who doubted the wisdom of sending an orthodox left-arm spinner to Australia. He topped England's bowling table in $1928-29$ with 25 wickets at 30.40 and was a key member of a highly talented four-pronged attack (five with Walter Hammond's medium-pace) that helped to restore some of England's post-war honour.

Before a resurgence of England's fortunes towards the close of the 1926 season when the Ashes were wrested from Australia at the Oval, a few new bowlers were blooded in series against South Africa and Australia, at home and abroad. Hampshire's Alexander Stuart Kennedy and Lancashire's George Gibson Macaulay were two medium-pacers who bowled to good effect on the South African matting wickets in $1922-23$ — Macaulay bagged a wicket with his first ball in a Test at Cape Town. Middlesex amateur googly bowler and all-rounder Greville Thomas Scott Stevens also made his debut in one Test against South Africa in $1922-23$ and was one of the many to play against Australia in 1926. Although he appeared in 10 Tests, this attractive and highly talented player, who had been a schoolboy prodigy, failed to live up to the high expectations originally accorded him.

Enthusiastic Sussex skipper Arthur Edward Robert Gilligan, a right-arm fast bowler, also played in only one Test in South Africa in $1922-23$ but was destined to be something of a force in the England team when the Springboks visited England in 1924. At Edgbaston, in the first Test of 1924, Gilligan and fellow Sussex bowler M W Tate bundled South Africa out for just 30 runs in its first innings. A E R Gilligan gained figures of $6.3-4-7-6$ that day and took 11 wickets in the match. Some weeks later he received a blow over the

Maurice Tate, one of the finest swing bowlers in history, often carried England's attack on his broad back.

heart while batting. On doctor's orders he stopped bowling flat out, although he continued to open the bowling with new 'find' Tate for the remainder of the South African series and in Australia in 1924–25.

Maurice William Tate took four South African wickets for 12 runs (and eight wickets in the match) in his first Test outing. He went on to become one of England's finest bowlers of all time and thus vindicated the prophecy allegedly made by his father, Fred Tate, who dropped the catch that lost the match when he played in his one and only Test against Australia in 1902.

Sir Neville Cardus called Maurice Tate 'the last of the truly rustic cricketers'. Tanned brown with Sussex air and sunshine, wide shouldered, above average height and with huge feet that gave him a peculiar, farmer's gait, Tate, according to Cardus, 'might have just walked out of a hayfield'. The resemblance between Tate and a rustic farmer ended when he took a cricket ball in his hand. During a time in cricket history when manipulation of the seam was, as a practice, still in its infancy, big Maurice Tate was the first Test bowler to truly master the art of late swing. And he could do it, at will, both ways.

Tate ran in swiftly over about eight yards and delivered the ball with a smooth action that would have delighted any purist. With left arm fully extended, he began his swing with all his weight on the right foot. A bend of the back and roll of the shoulders would bring his arm over with unexpected momentum. He was one of those rare bowlers who seemed to be able to make the ball gather pace after it hit the pitch. Its speed through the air was around fast-medium but, off the ground, the ball flew through so fast that his slip fielders sometimes stood back further than for any other fast bowler.

The genial Maurice Tate carried England's bowling on his broad and able back much in the manner that Alec Bedser, a bowler of similar style and effect, did during the 1940s and early 1950s. Australia won the 1924–25 series against England by four matches to one. In a performance that brought back memories of 'Golden Age' fast bowler Tom Richardson, Tate toiled manfully through more than 300 overs and claimed 38 wickets at 23.18. The next most successful England bowler was Yorkshire left-arm spinner Roy Kilner (17 at 23.47) in his one prominent rubber for England.

Maurice Tate went on to take 155 wickets in 39 Tests at 26.16. He was also a grand attacking batsman who three times achieved the double of 1000 runs and 200 wickets, adding the more conventional 1000 runs and 100 wickets on a further five occasions. In Tests, Maurice Tate hit more than 1000 runs with a top score 100 not out against South Africa at Lord's in 1929.

Two bowlers who made their Ashes debut in 1926 were to form, with Tate and 'Farmer' White (and with occasional help from Wally Hammond), a formidable England attack when A P F Chapman sailed to do battle with Australia in 1928–29. One was Leicestershire's strong and cheerful George Geary, an accurate right-arm fast-medium bowler with a high delivery. The other was rising Nottinghamshire fast bowler Harold Larwood, who was already being dubbed a future match-winner.

George Geary first bowled for England with great effect on the matting pitches encountered in South Africa in 1927–28. A dedicated professional of the old school, he shrugged off the effects of a broken nose early on in the 1928—29 tour of Australia and rounded off the series with a marathon 81 overs (5/105 and 36 maidens) in Australia's first innings of the fifth Test at Melbourne. In his four Tests that season, Geary took 19 wickets at 25.10 to head the bowling averages. Similar in style to Tate, he bowled a deadly leg-cutter and an occasional slower off-break that whipped back off the pitch. Like Tate, Geary was also a more than useful batsman at international level.

John Arlott recalls in an article in *Wisden Cricket Monthly* (January 1980) that, as a young man, he watched Harold Larwood and his Nottinghamshire new ball partner Bill Voce experiment with short pitched bowling to a packed leg-side field in a Nottinghamshire versus Essex encounter at Leyton in 1932. Arlott's reaction at the time was: 'Surely they can't be trying this out for the Australian tour – the Australians are such good hookers.' On an easy pitch the Essex batsmen handled Larwood without much difficulty and the 'Notts express' did not take a wicket. There was no mention of the new tactic in the press but Arlott was again present later in the season when 'Lol' Larwood tried his new form of attack against Glamorgan at Cardiff.

Again the wicket was placid and Glamorgan's Maurice Turnbull hit 205, including three hooked sixes. Douglas Jardine, England's captain and the man who devised the now infamous bodyline plan to curb the mammoth run-scoring of Australia's Don Bradman, confirmed many years later that this Notts-Glamorgan game (in which Larwood took 5/78) was indeed the final dress rehearsal for what was to follow in Australia in 1932—33. When reminded that Turnbull's assault on Larwood seemed to prove that the new tactic was unsuccessful, Jardine pointed out that the fast bowler was merely getting into his rhythm to bowl the length that was required to make bodyline effective in Australia, where the pitches were harder and faster that in England.

Nottinghamshire captain Arthur Carr was in on the plan and had been a willing collaborator, even though it may have cost his county a couple of matches. When Jardine was asked why no-one had written about Larwood's bowling tactics at Leyton and Cardiff, his reply was: 'Perhaps nobody noticed.' A few months later, the whole world was taking notice when the new method employed by Larwood and Voce left in its wake a trail of battered, bruised and angry Australian batsmen.

A flood of books was published immediately after the controversial bodyline tour in 1932—33 and continued in the years that followed, including Jardine's own *In Quest of the Ashes* and Larwood's *Body-Line?*. A host of other works have included reference to the events in Australia of 1932—33. Even an entertaining although inaccurate television mini-series has been made on the subject. It should suffice here to merely log certain of the more important and striking occurrences during that tour.

A perfunctory glance at the composition of the MCC party to tour Australia in 1932–33 would have provided any astute observer with some indication of a special plan afoot. Apart from Larwood and his county companion Bill Voce, four other bowlers of above medium pace were included in the team of 17 players: Bill Bowes, 'Gubby' Allen, Maurice Tate and Walter Hammond. The six fast men formed a formidable pace and seam battery that has possibly only been equalled by some of the post-Second World War attacks from various countries.

Something had to be done about the almost superhuman run-scoring of one Donald George Bradman. There was nothing in the Laws of Cricket as they then stood which would inhibit Jardine from packing his leg-side field and instructing Larwood and the others to bowl short and in line with the batsman's body. All was dependent upon the conscience of the captain and the bowler. The object was to get batsmen to give catches to men in the close-in catching positions while defending their bodies, or to feed the well-stocked boundary patrol with lofted hook shots.

As it turned out, Allen, one of the fastest of Jardine's bowlers and the only amateur in the group, flatly refused to bowl bodyline. The fact that the Middlesex all-rounder was second only to Larwood as a wicket-taker with 21 wickets at 28.23 in the series was indicative of his fine qualities as a conventional fast bowler.

George Oswald Browning Allen proved to be a traditionalist all his life, as a dashing, forthright stroke-player, as a fast bowler with a classic sideways action and as an establishment oriented administrator who became something of an *eminence grise* at Lord's. Although he refused to follow the instructions of his friend, Douglas Jardine, and bowl bodyline, there was no doubting that Allen's complete loyalty always remained with his team. He played in all five Tests and frequently fielded in the Larwood and Voce leg-trap, taking seven catches in the series.

Four years later, Allen was picked to lead England on a conciliatory 'peace-making' tour of Australia in 1936–37. With the aid of left-hander Bill Voce, now delivering the ball in conventional style, the England captain bowled his team to victory in the first two Tests. Allen was thwarted during the remainder of the rubber through an amazing run of scoring by England's old nemesis, Don Bradman, the man for whom bodyline bowling had originally been designed. Bradman hit double-centuries in the third and fourth Tests and a century in the fifth Test of 1936–37 to engineer an amazing turn-about and triumph for Australia.

In 1932–33, Jardine first signalled his intentions in a pre-Test game in Melbourne versus an Australian XI which included Bradman, the number one target, and a number of other probable Test batsmen. There was mixed press reaction and certainly no immediate concerted outcry over the English tactics, an indication perhaps that Larwood and company did not give the Australians the full 'treatment' at Melbourne. But by the time of the first Test at Sydney, things were definitely on the boil following further 'demonstrations' of bodyline bowiing in various State matches.

Australia was without Bradman for the first Test due to ill-health and Larwood took 10 wickets in the match, with a mixture of bodyline and normal fast bowling, to yield England an easy victory. Only the doughty Stan McCabe gave as much as he got and his 187 remains as one of the finest dozen or so Test knocks of all time.

Jardine had played Larwood, Voce and Allen in the first Test. With Bradman back in the Australian team for the second match at Melbourne, Jardine brought in Bowes for spin bowler Verity to give England a five-man pace attack (Larwood, Voce, Allen, Bowes and Hammond).

The English fast bowlers pitched short on the leg-stump with regularity. A slow wicket hampered their efforts to a certain extent, although the crowd was vociferous in its barracking of Jardine and his bowlers. The delivery that trapped Bradman for a first-ball duck was not even a bumper but a wild long-hop sent down by Bowes which the Australian hero dragged onto his stumps.

In the second innings, Bradman hit 103 not out in an innings of 191 and there was rejoicing in the home camp at the 'defeat' of bodyline. Australia won the match and, for the moment, all seemed forgiven. It was in fact the point of no return.

The theory has been presented that, if the Australian authorities had pressed their case against bodyline immediately after the Melbourne Test, there may have been some positive response from the England camp. What was needed perhaps was some public protest at that point, but Bradman had scored a century and Australia had won, so there was none forthcoming.

At Adelaide in the third Test, a series of mishaps to Australia's batsmen resulted in near riot. Larwood started off bowling conventionally, but when a ball that was not really short of a length reared up and struck opening batsman Bill Woodfull, the Australian captain, a blow above the heart that sent him staggering away from the wicket, Jardine almost immediately placed a leg-trap field and instructed his key fast bowler to pitch the ball short and in line with the batsman's body, bodyline bowling.

With the second ball of his next over, Larwood knocked the bat out of a visibly shaken Woodfull's hands and the hooting and booing in the outer increased to a roar. For a moment it even looked as if the pitch might be invaded but good sense prevailed. Fortunately, Bradman was not hit that day (if he had, the crowd might well have taken over) but was caught in the leg-trap by Allen when defending his body. Years later Larwood was quoted as saying that he only once hit Bradman during the series − on the behind.

Opposite: Harold Larwood of Notts and England: the classic fast bowler's action.

454

Veteran Australian batsman Bill Ponsford padded about like an Eskimo, took a few painful blows but survived long enough to score 85. When wicket-keeper Bert Oldfield was pole-axed by a ball pitched in line with the stumps and not the batsman's body, the crowd again demonstrated angrily and it looked possible that play might be halted. Oldfield was helped from the pitch with a fractured skull, but he later admitted that the injury had been his own fault. He had simply not followed the cardinal rule when hooking of getting one's head inside the line of flight.

The Woodfull and Oldfield incidents were the nadir of the bodyline series but cabled protests by the Australian Board of Control to Lord's fell on deaf ears and nothing was done to prevail upon Jardine to alter his tactics. England won the series 4−1 and for the moment Bradman's run of high-scoring had been contained. When bodyline was later outlawed, the Australian batting master was to wreak a terrible vengeance on England's bowlers.

It has been claimed that bodyline might not have succeeded as an attacking weapon had not Jardine had the services of such a controlled fast bowler as Harold Larwood. Leg-theory bowling was not a new concept; Worcestershire's Charles Frederick Root had bowled his inswingers at a fast-medium pace to a packed leg-side field against Australia in England in 1926, but he was not as fast as Larwood. Larwood was something of a phenomenon in that he could bowl fast *and* with pin-point accuracy. Without these two essential ingredients, Jardine's bodyline tactics would not have so severely tested Australia's batsmen.

The son of a coalminer, Larwood was below medium height but as wiry as steel, if not exactly muscular. His eighteen-yard run up was a model of athletic control, gaining pace with every measured step and all easy flow and accelerating rhythm. There was no great leap in his delivery stride, but his left leg would lift high before pounding into the turf as his arm came over smoothly and he moved into a beautiful body swing that ended in a perfect follow through. And by all accounts, Larwood *was* fast − perhaps the fastest of them all. According to his England contemporary Ian Peebles, those who stood to him in the slips at Melbourne in January 1933, 'are convinced...that they saw the fastest spell ever delivered by man'. The current generation can indeed count themselves fortunate that the great fast bowler's action has been captured on film for all to witness.

Larwood took 33 wickets at 19.51 in the bodyline series and some say his figures would not have altered appreciably if he had bowled to an orthodox field. He remains the model of the perfect fast bowler. Sadly, he was not again to play Test cricket after the 1932−33 experience. Larwood was then still short of his 29th birthday and had had just six years in international cricket. Many years after the bodyline series, Larwood settled in Australia, assisted by one of his old opponents, Jack Fingleton. Although his and Jardine's tactics of 1932–33 were severely censured and resulted in changes to the laws, Larwood remains for most knowledgeable observers as much the perfect fast bowler as Bradman was the master batsman.

Main support for Larwood during the bodyline series came from his Nottinghamshire new-ball partner William Voce, who normally bowled fast left-arm over the wicket but reverted to left-arm round the wicket for leg-theory or bodyline purposes. Taller than Larwood, Bill Voce was big and brawny. He played in four of the bodyline Tests and took 15 wickets at 27.13, reserving his best Test performances for the peace-making tour under G O B Allen in 1936–37. In the first two Tests of 1936–37 Voce's outswinger was lethal and he claimed 17 Australian wickets for 133 runs. A laconic and jovial character, Voce was a gentle giant until handed the ball. When taken to Australia for a third time with Walter Hammond in 1946–47, he was already 37 and overweight and bore little resemblance to the menacing bodyliner of the 1930s.

Yorkshire's tall and bespectacled William Eric Bowes could swing the ball prodigiously and played a supporting role in 1932–33 but only appeared in one Test. An intelligent bowler who later became a famous cricket journalist, Bill Bowes enjoyed fair success in later Tests against Australia, England, South Africa and West Indies.

England's number one batsman of the time, Walter Reginald Hammond, was the fifth seam bowler used by Jardine during the 1932–33 series. Hammond's supportive work at a brisk medium-fast yielded nine wickets at 32.33 and, had he not been England's acknowledged batting champion of the 1930s, he might well have played Test cricket for his bowling and exceptional slip fielding alone.

The sixth bowler in Jardine's party was the immaculate Maurice Tate, who did not play in a Test that summer as his style of seam bowling did not fit into the bodyline scheme. It was a disappointing final Australian tour for a great Ashes campaigner whose remaining international cricket consisted of a couple of Tests against New Zealand and South Africa.

Left-hander Hedley Verity, of Yorkshire, a worthy heir to Wilfred Rhodes, was the main spin bowler in Jardine's team. Leg-spinners Tommy Mitchell and Freddie Brown hardly got a bowl and Verity, on the first of his two trips to Australia, took only 11 wickets in four Tests. Verity was hardly given the ball until the final game at Sydney, when he claimed eight wickets in the match for 95 runs. He was to end his Test career with a total of 144 wickets in 40 games for England.

More medium-paced than slow in the Derek Underwood fashion, Hedley Verity was a classical left-hander with an easy, cat-like run in. He spun the ball prodigiously to a perfect length and was never

Hedley Verity was one of England's finest left-arm spinners and a worthy Yorkshire heir to Wilfred Rhodes.

flustered when batsmen went on the attack. Verity's quick inswinging yorker could be unplayable and, when conditions called for it, he would beat the batsman as much with his teasing flight as with his actual turn off the wicket. Verity was rather a shy and retiring person, but an on-field perfectionist.

After rain he could be irresistible, as was witnessed when he took 7/61 and 8/43 in the second Test against Australia at Lord's in 1934. But for some, Verity's greatest value lay in his ability to keep his opponents guessing on the best of batting surfaces. He was never overawed by any batsman, including Bradman.

Hedley Verity twice claimed all 10 wickets in an innings. His analysis of $19.4-16-10-10$ for Yorkshire versus Nottinghamshire at Leeds in 1932 remains the most remarkable in first-class cricket history. He died from wounds received in battle as a prisoner of war in Italy in 1943. It was recorded that when Captain Hedley Verity was struck down by enemy fire he continued to encourage his men to 'keep going'; as Sir Neville Cardus once put it: 'Such was his philosophy and motto always, whether he happened to be playing for Yorkshire and England, or fighting for his country and for civilisation.'

During the 1920s and 1930s a number of outstanding county bowlers appeared for England in a Test or two against Australia or played in the odd game against South Africa without offering that consistency of performance needed to consolidate a place in the England eleven. In this category could be counted Gloucestershire off-break expert Thomas William John Goddard (who was still playing county cricket in 1952 when well past his 50th birthday); Nottinghamshire right-arm medium pacer Samuel James Staples; Leicestershire's William Ewart Astill (an all-rounder and an off-break bowler); Maurice Stanley Nichols of Essex (left-handed hitter of some ability and a right-arm fast bowler) — and a string of other new ball exponents like the huge, fun-loving Maurice James Carrick Allom (Surrey); Middlesex big-hitting number 11, Cedric Ivan James ('Big Jim') Smith; Alfred Richard Gover of Surrey (the famous coach in later years); Arthur William Wellard of Somerset; William Henry Copson (Derbyshire); Reginald Thomas David Perks (Worcesterhire).

Edward Winchester Clark of Northamptonshire was a left-arm fast bowler whose pace came close to that of Larwood but whose highly strung nature counted against him. The red-headed 'Nobby' Clark displayed his enthusiasm with much gesticulation when appealing or at the fall of a wicket in an age when on-field behaviour was somewhat more staid that is now the case. His best Test effort came in what proved to be his last game for England, the fifth Test versus Australia at the Oval in 1934, when Ponsford (266) and Bradman (244) hit double-centuries for the visiting team and the Northamptonshire left-hander ran out with figures of 2/110 and 5/98.

The only England fast bowler after Larwood to establish some sort of a permanent spot in the England XI was Essex amateur Kenneth Farnes. Well built and standing 6 ft 5 in (195 cm), Farnes bowled right-arm at a tremendous speed off a short 11 pace run up. In the brief period available before war broke out, Farnes bagged 60 wickets in 15 Tests at a time when pitches seldom aided bowlers and England's opponents possessed particularly strong batting line-ups. Farnes produced figures of 5/102 and 5/77 in his first Test versus Australia at Trent Bridge in 1934. After one more match he fell out because of injury and was next brought into England's team for the last two

Tests against Australia in 1936—37. Farnes responded with 11 wickets in the two matches, including an impressive 6/96 at Melbourne when three Australians scored 100s and the home team totalled 604.

Ken Farnes's final Test effort came in the famous Durban 'Timeless Test' versus South Africa in 1938—39 (he took five wickets in the match). This was just a few months before war broke out and all first-class cricket was temporarily abandoned. The handsome and debonair Pilot Officer Farnes was killed in an air crash during the Second World War. He was then barely 30 years old.

12

India keeping pace

'...Mohammed Nissar and Lala Amar Singh, the hammer and tongs of Indian bowling'

— Sujit Mukherjee

It may surprise many to know that the chief rival between the wars to Australia's pace duo of Gregory and McDonald and England's much-feared Larwood and Voce was the tall Indian pair of Mohammed Nissar and Amar Singh, notwithstanding any claims made by Learie Constantine and his West Indian colleagues.

The country which in later years was to produce some of the finest spin bowlers ever seen in international cricket started playing Test cricket in 1932 with virtually an all-pace attack of extremely high quality.

Laheem Shaheem Mohammed Nissar Mohammed was a giant-hearted performer of tremendous stamina and physique who relied mainly on sheer speed off a long but fluidly athletic run-up. He bowled the first ball for India in international cricket against England at Lord's in 1932 and, with the first and last balls of his second over in Test cricket, clean-bowled each of England's opening batsmen, the great Yorkshireman Herbert Sutcliffe and his county partner Percy Holmes. With Amar Singh firing successfully from the other end, England was in grave trouble until its skipper, the redoubtable Douglas Jardine of bodyline fame, came in to right matters with a brave and decisive knock. Mohammed Nissar came out of his Test baptism with figures of 5/93. When he and Amar Singh looked to be making another devastating breakthrough in England's second innings, it was again the unflappable Jardine who thwarted them with his second outstanding hand of the match. He had scores of 79 and 85 not out and England won this inaugural Test by 158 runs.

Nissar's next encounter with Jardine took place in India in 1933—34 and *Wisden* records that the Indian express merchant, 'keeping up a good pace...sent Jardine's off stump flying with a specially fast ball'. Nissar's 5/90 performance in England's first innings was to no avail as the home batsmen succumbed easily to the touring team's own fast bowling pair, Nichols and Clark.

At Calcutta, on a pacy wicket in the second Test, India's captain, C K Nayudu, instigated a 'bumper war' when he instructed Mohammed Nissar and Amar Singh to pitch the ball short in England's first innings. Jardine was one of the batsmen struck by a

Lala Amar Singh was India's first world-class bowler and formed a feared new-ball partnership with the giant Mohammed Nissar.

rising ball and, when it came to India's turn to bat, he instructed fast left-hander 'Nobby' Clark to bowl bouncers at the local batsmen.

Normally, Mohammed Nissar was known for his rather placid and kindly nature and gained something of a reputation as a 'gentleman bowler' who preferred to get his victims with good old-fashioned speed and swing, with the occasional vicious break back for variation while the shine was still on the ball. Eleven of his 25 Test victims were clean-bowled. With his high, easy action Mohammed Nissar was able to make the ball lift alarmingly off a good length and rarely resorted to the bouncer. In his early days he scorned conventional cricket flannels and wore the traditional salwar until it became apparent that he was sacrificing pace for tradition.

Big-hearted Mohammed Nissar only appeared in six Tests (out of the meagre seven played by his country before the war – he missed one through illness) but took 25 wickets bowling with the wind for a team that relied almost solely on his performances and that of his new-ball partner, Amar Singh. Bowling mainly into the breeze, the latter claimed 28 wickets in seven Tests – which gives the Indian fast-bowling pair 53 of the 84 wickets taken by a total of 16 men who turned their arm over for India between the wars.

Ladhabhai Nakum Amar Singh was the acknowledged best Indian bowler of the 1930s. Following his resoundingly successful first tour of England in 1932 (he claimed 111 first-class wickets), *Wisden* recorded of him that, 'more than one famous old cricketer said afterwards that Amar Singh was the best bowler seen in England since the war'.

In contrast to his Punjabi partner, Mohammed Nissar, 'Lala' Amar Singh's approach to the stumps was anything but tidy. But India's master bowler of the 1930s baffled many a batsman with his wide variety of deliveries off a short, disjointed run that one observer described as an 'utterly disorganised run-up which was more of a hurried scramble to somehow traverse the eight or ten yards to the bowling crease'. Relying on immense strength of back and shoulders for his power, Amar Singh varied his pace with magical precision and could make the ball swerve either way and dip sharply in flight.

Bowling against Jack Ryder's Australian team at Madras in 1935–36, Amar Singh clean bowled both Ryder and Charles Macartney with balls that were described as 'unplayable'. This event took place during the fourth 'Test' of an unofficial series when Amar Singh and Mohammed Nissar ran through the Australian eleven to put the tourists out for 107 runs and give India an unexpected victory.

In Test cricket proper, Amar Singh was noted for his marathon bowling spells, as one of India's two main strike bowlers and its major stock bowler. When England totalled 403 at Calcutta in 1933–34, he ended with figures of 54.5–13–106–4. At Madras, in the third and final Test of the same series, he excelled in a display of sustained accuracy that produced an analysis of 44.4–13–86–7.

When India visited England in 1936, Amar Singh was an established Lancashire League professional whose awesome performances rivalled those of the league 'king', Learie Constantine (Amar Singh was also a prodigious hitter of sixes). Called in to strengthen India for the three Tests, he claimed figures of 25.1–11–35–6 in England's first innings of a remarkable first Test at Lord's. Thanks to Amar Singh, India was, until the final day, in with a chance of victory in a low scoring match (India scored 147 and 93; England 134 and 108 for one wicket). In his first nine overs Amar Singh took four wickets for 13.

Lala Amar Singh died tragically of pneumonia at the age of 30 in 1940. His brother, the 6 ft 4 in (193 cm) Ladhabhai Ramji, was India's second tallest cricketer and a massive right-arm fast bowler of the Mohammed Nissar school who took the new ball with Nissar against England at Bombay in 1933−34 but did not take a wicket in this, his only Test.

Few other bowlers used in India's first Tests made much of an impression. Dr Mohammed Jahangir Khan, father of celebrated Pakistan Test batsman Majid J Khan, bowled right-arm off-cutters at a medium-fast pace. As India's main support bowler in the inaugural England−India Test at Lord's in 1932, he posted second innings figures of 30−12−60−4 but he did not take a wicket in his subsequent three Tests. India's first notable batsman, Cottari Kanakaiya Nayudu (India's 'WG'), was also a right-arm medium-pacer who could cut the ball from off and leg to good effect but whose best bowling efforts were reserved for matches other than Tests.

His younger brother, Cottari Subbanna Nayudu, was a classic leg-break and googly bowler who terrorised slow-footed batsmen in domestic cricket but could manage only two wickets for 359 runs in his eventual 11 Tests for India, some of which were played in England and Australia after the war.

Three major Indian batsmen who emerged before the Second World War were also good enough bowlers to warrant the title all-rounder for at least part of their career. The entertainingly unorthodox opening batsman Syed Yacubali Mushtaq Ali (slow left-arm) did not progress as a bowler and, after the war, played for India solely as a free-scoring batsman. Post-war middle order batting mainstay Vijay Samuel Hazare (right-arm medium), emerged as an all-rounder in some of the unofficial Tests India played before 1939 and remained a useful change bowler after the war.

Nanik Bhardwaj Amarnath, the 'stormy petrel' of Indian cricket and father of two Test batsmen, might have been India's leading bowler after Amar Singh and Mohammed Nissar in the 1936 Tests versus England had he not been sent home for disciplinary reasons before the series started.

'Lala' Amarnath came to notice as a bowler during net practice prior to the Test against England at Bombay in 1933−34 when he became the first Indian player to hit a century on international debut. Amarnath bowled his right-arm medium-paced swingers off a run-up that consisted of a few shuffles and a hop that ended with him bowling off what seemed to be the wrong foot. There was, however, nothing wrong with his stock in-dipper, and the occasional outswinger as a surprise weapon.

Vinoo Mankad was India's
finest all-rounder before
Kapil Dev and a left-arm
spin bowler of world class
who performed particularly
well in England and
Australia.

In England in 1946, and as India's captain in Australia in 1947—48, Amarnath stood out as his country's main bowling hope after left-arm spinner 'Vinoo' Mankad.

Mulwantrai Himatlal Mankad was known simply as Vinoo Mankad throughout his long and distinguished first-class career that started at 17 years of age in 1935 and ended almost a quarter of a century later. During this period India's first great spin bowler took 162 wickets in 44 Tests and scored 2109 Test runs to make him one of the outstanding international all-rounders in cricket history.

Mankad was a dashing and brave right-hand opening batsman who played a couple of the epic Test innings in cricket history. As a left-arm spinner he bowled with a slightly round-arm action, but with a side-on delivered in the Wilfred Rhodes mould. Mankad generally delivered the ball from the outside edge of the crease, but would vary his bowling position when sending down his deadly 'arm-ball', which was virtually an inswinger. Patience and endurance were his watchwords, allied with length and direction and subtle variation in flight and spin.

As the only Indian to have performed the double of 1000 runs and 100 wickets on an England tour, Mankad was one of the stars of India's first post-war team in 1946. In Australia in 1947—48, where he was the main bowler and hit two Test centuries, Mankad stood out as a world-class player in an obviously undermanned team. Ray Robinson cited the sturdily built Mankad as a leading contender in 1948 for the title of 'world's best bowler of the day'.

At Lord's in 1952, Mankad made, due to league cricket commitments, one of only three appearances that season for India. Although England won in the end, the match became known as 'Mankad's Test' when he played innings of 72 and 184 and bowled 97 overs to yield 5/231.

With Pankaj Roy, Mankad holds the world partnership batting record for any wicket in Tests (413 for the first wicket versus New Zealand at Madras in 1955—56 — Mankad 231). At Delhi in 1952—53, he posted his best bowling performance in Tests: 8/52 and 5/79 versus Pakistan in the first official Test played by that country.

In his *Some Indian Cricketers*, former Test batsman Rusi Modi records that Mankad, as a Test bowler, 'had to toil against Hammond, Hutton, Compton, Bradman, Morris, Hassett, Weekes, Walcott and his runs were scored against Trueman, Bedser, Wright, Lindwall, Miller and Johnston'. Stiff competition indeed, and sufficient evidence to place the name Vinoo Mankad high in the list of India's 'giants' of cricket.

Of Mankad's contemporary support bowlers, the right-arm fast-medium Dattatraya Gajanan Phadkar was also an all-rounder who hit a Test hundred against Australia in 1947—48 and was India's regular new-ball bowler in 31 Tests. 'Dattu' Phadkar's right-arm fast-medium swing bowling brought him 62 Test wickets; tall and distinguished looking, right-arm off-spinner Ghulam Ahmed was, for a few years, India's best spin bowler after Mankad. A cerebral player, he bowled with a fluid action and used variation of flight and length to 'think' his opponents out. His brightest Test day came at Calcutta in 1956–57 when his 7/49 saw a strong Australian team spun out for 177. The equally lanky but thin-as-a-reed Sadashiv Ganpatrao Shinde bowled two variations of the googly that were difficult to 'pick', but suffered from wayward length and direction and, apart from a 6/91 stint against England at Delhi in 1951–52, contributed little to India's post-war bowling cause.

Other than Phadkar, none of India's new ball bowlers of the 1940s and 1950s possessed sufficient pace to trouble the best batsmen. For instance, hard as he tried, Gulabrai Sipahimalani Ramchand, an accurate medium-paced bowler of mainly inswingers, could manage only 41 wickets at 46.34 in 33 Tests. The powerfully built 'Ram' Ramchand was, however, an energetic and dedicated all-rounder who hit two Test centuries. Of the others who were tried, Commandur Rajagopalachari Rangachari (right-arm fast with a peculiar round-arm action), and Oxford Blue Ramesh Vithaldao Divecha (also right-arm and a sometime off-break exponent) had their moments but, like Ramchand, lacked the speed to succeed at top level.

One of India's unlucky 'might-have-beens' was a bowler of genuine pace who only played in one Test despite many fine performances in domestic cricket. The heavily-built Sarbindu Surendrakumar Bannerjee (known during his playing days as Shute Nath Bannerjee) also took part in a memorable Indian record last-wicket stand of 249 with another sometime Test bowler, tiny leg-spinner Chandrasekhar Trimbak Sarwate, against Surrey at the Oval in 1946 – the only instance in which numbers 10 and 11 have each scored a century in a first-class match. Sarwate was a 'bits-and-pieces' player who batted anywhere from number one to number 11 and would switch with alacrity from bowling leg-breaks to off-breaks. His versatility did not, unfortunately, bring him much joy at Test level.

When Vinoo Mankad and Ghulam Ahmed were still at their peak during the early 1950s, they were joined by a young leg-break and googly bowler who was to become his country's bowling star of the next decade or so, and a herald of what was to follow during the 'Golden Age' of Indian spin bowling when a quartet of spin bowlers performed with legendary skill. The stories of Subhash Gupte and his four spinning heirs, Chandrasekhar, Prasanna, Bedi and Venkataraghavan are told in Chapter 24 of the bowling section.

13

Constantine and friends

'In attack the West Indians are most famed for their fast bowlers'
— Christopher Nicole

It seems that there has always been fast bowlers in the Caribbean; right from the time in 1896–97 when C P Cumberbatch and J 'Float' Woods helped Trinidad thrash the English touring team by 137 runs. 'Float' Woods was something of a local legend who preferred to bowl in his bare feet and who was once said to have secretly torn the soles off his boots when his captain insisted he wear boots on the field. Sir Pelham Warner considered Woods one of the fastest he faced and the barefoot Trinidadian express bowler of the 1890s must go down as the first in the long line of West Indian 'rib thumpers'.

At Scarborough in 1923, two of this very special breed, George John and George Francis, almost turned a lost cause into a sensational victory when they swept through a strong England batting line-up led by H D G Leveson-Gower. The English side had been left to score a mere 31 runs to win. The fearsome John–Francis combination sent their opponents reeling to 19 for six wickets. A sensational turnabout appeared imminent, but it was not to be. Leveson-Gower's team managed to score the required runs without further loss but, as a result of this amazing fast bowling assault, West Indies moved a step further towards full recognition as a Test-playing country.

By the time West Indies played its inaugural Test against England at Lord's in 1928, Trinidad's pride, George John, was no longer playing. In his heyday John was a fearsome proposition for opposing batsmen. Described as a genuine fast bowler, with a high action and a natural inswing, he was an intimidating bowler who followed through to within a few yards of the batsman, glaring darkly at his opponent all the way. C L R James, the most fluent of all West Indian cricket writers, commented in his *Beyond a Boundary*: 'He (John) was not the captain of his side but I never saw the captain take him off. John always took himself off.'

John's 1923 partner, George Nathaniel Francis, came from that amazing cricket 'nursery' on the tiny island of Barbados that has produced an abundance of world-class cricketers over the years, including the famous three 'Ws', Worrell, Weekes and Walcott; the incomparable Sir Garfield Sobers; and a seemingly inexhaustible supply of quality fast bowlers. Francis was an uncomplicated speedster

Opposite: Learie Constantine ended his days as a peer of the realm and was the archetypal model of the West Indian cricketer: tearaway fast bowler, outrageous big-hitter and 'electric-heeled' fieldsman.

who simply bowled as fast and as straight as he possibly could, although judges at the time considered him to be less speedy than George John.

George Francis sent down the first ball bowled by a West Indian in an official Test. Opening the bowling from the other end against England at Lord's in 1928 was a man who was the central character in one of the most amazing rags-to-riches stories of this and any century, and a fast bowler, unorthodox big-hitter and quicksilver fieldsman who provided a model for all future West Indian cricketers.

Born Learie Nicholas Constantine, son of a Trinidad plantation overseer who had himself represented early West Indian teams, this phenomenal man and player was to rise so far in status that he was eventually buried, in his native island with the ceremony of a State funeral, as Lord L N Constantine, MBE. When he once joined a private cricket tour of the United States, posters outside the grounds read: 'Come and see L N Constantine, the fastest bowler in the world. Incomparable as a fieldsman. A harder hitter than G L Jessop.'

As a 21-year-old in England in 1923, Constantine was, like John and Francis, a tearaway fast bowler pure and simple. Never afraid to test a batsman's courage and ability to hook with an early bouncer, he was sometimes accused of overdoing short-pitched bowling. Serving a cricket apprenticeship in the Lancashire League, he was to become one of the smartest of bowlers, varying from medium pace to outright fast, and a dangerous proposition no matter the conditions or strength of opposition.

When bowling fast, the long-armed and broad-shouldered Constantine covered his 19-yard run-up in long, athletic strides. He varied the height of his arm, not so much to alter his delivery, as he could bowl the desired ball no matter what his arm position, but to fool the batsman who was looking for some clue as to what was in store for him.

At Manchester in 1933, Constantine and powerful Barbados fast bowler 'Manny' Martindale gave Douglas Jardine and his English team a taste of bodyline bowling. Bowling to a leg-side field of six players, the two West Indians bounced them at Sutcliffe, Hammond, Jardine and company. One ball from Martindale cut Hammond's chin and England's number one batsman was struck three times. Jardine faced up to the fast leg-theory onslaught without flinching and scored 127, his innings evoking the comment in *Wisden*: '...he played it probably better than any other man in the world was capable of doing...'. It should be noted though that the wicket at Old Trafford, Manchester, could not be compared with the bodyline pitches of 1932–33 at Sydney, Adelaide or Melbourne and that, notwithstanding their accepted pace and skill, Constantine and Martindale were not as fast as Harold Larwood.

Before Martindale arrived to take the new ball with Constantine,

Manny Martindale joined Constantine to bowl 'bodyline' at England's Douglas Jardine at Manchester in 1933.

the short but robustly proportioned Herman Clarence Griffith, yet another Barbadian speedster, teamed up with Constantine and Francis to form a three-pronged pace attack in England in 1928 and Australia in 1930–31. Griffith was a fitness fanatic and, although not as fast as his team-mates, was a thinker, forever looking to trick a batsman out. Griffith's greatest moment in Test cricket came at Sydney in 1930–31 when he produced a grand delivery to bowl the great Bradman for a duck.

Emmanuel Alfred Martindale played for the same Barbados Empire

Club as Griffith and was, by all reports, a more consistently fast bowler than any of his colleagues. A near-perfect action combined with above average strength made Martindale a fiery performer; he broke the jaw of England captain R E S Wyatt with a bouncer at Kingston in 1934—35.

During the 1934—35 home rubber against England, Constantine and Martindale were joined by the massively-built Jamaican Leslie George Hylton, another right-arm no-nonsense all-out pace man. They were to form one of the most terrifying fast bowling trios in Test history. Hylton gained the dubious distinction of becoming the first Test player to be executed when he was hanged in 1955 for killing his unfaithful wife.

Of the less fiery West Indies pre-war bowlers, Cyril Rutherford ('Snuffy') Browne (Barbados and British Guiana) was an all-rounder who bowled steady leg-breaks at medium pace in Tests in England and the West Indies. He later became a magistrate and became the first black West Indian to be made an honorary member of the Marylebone Cricket Club. Rolph Stewart Grant from Trinidad captained the West Indies in 1939 and also played in Tests in the Caribbean as an all-rounder who bowled useful off-breaks. Another Trinidadian, Ellis Edgar Achong, a slow left-hander of Chinese ancestry, was thought to be the inspiration for the term 'Chinaman' (a left-hander's googly).

In the Test at Adelaide in 1930—31, Jamaican right-arm leg-break bowler Oscar Charles Scott dismissed four Australian batsmen for no runs during the course of nine balls and proved a useful adjunct to the fast bowlers on tours abroad and in a couple of home Tests. He put up a marathon performance against England at Kingston in 1929—30 when he came out of the match with figures of 80.2—13—266—5 (England totalled 849) and 25—0—108—4. O C Scott's son, Alfred Scott, played as a leg-break bowler for West Indies versus India at Kingston in 1952—53 but failed to take a wicket in his only Test.

When the West Indies made its last overseas tour to England before the Second World War, a surprise selection was the young Barbados googly bowler Carlos Bertram Clarke. Dr 'Bertie' Clarke's Test career was cut short by the war but, as a bowler of ability who was noted for his pace off the pitch, he achieved success after the war for Northamptonshire and later for Essex in the English county championship.

Before war put a temporary hold on serious cricket, it was the Caribbean pace bowlers who provided a nucleus for the West Indies Test attack, forming a model for later years. But, before pace was to predominate, a short post-war interregnum was to occur during which the spin wizardry of two virtual unknowns raised the West Indies cricket team to unexpected heights of achievement.

14

A Greek at Lord's

'I was just given a cricket ball, which became a part of me, and it all happened from there'

— Xenophon Balaskas

Apart from a few isolated accomplishments, South Africa struggled to overcome its two major traditional opponents England and Australia until the mid-1960s.

Before its departure from the international cricket scene South Africa, for political reasons, only played against three countries — the two mentioned plus New Zealand. This was because of, initially, segregation as introduced to the Cape by the British, and then apartheid, as the practice of racial separation came to be called when an Afrikaner Government entrenched existing practices into the statutes of the land.

Until the past two or three decades, British attitudes were rather more conservative than they now are. One can only wonder what the outcome might have been if a stand had been taken by the Imperial Cricket Conference (which included non-white countries as members) before the Second World War to force South Africa to play against teams from India and the West Indies. Indeed, as early as 1894, a very fine Cape Malay bowler, 'Krom' Hendricks, was left out of the first team sent from South Africa to tour England 'as a result of the greatest pressure by those in high authority in the Cape Colony' (the Cape was under British rule at the time). What might have been the outcome if a precedent had been set in 1894?

'Krom' Hendricks was not the only capable black South African bowler of his day. A number of pre-war players from the Cape were invited (but declined for various reasons) to play in England — like left-arm fast bowler C J Nicholls, who so impressed England's captain 'Plum' Warner in 1905; and the almost legendary (among Cape Malays) googly bowler Taliep Salie, who refused to play for Kent as he could get no assurance that there would be a mosque near the cricket ground.

Another notable South African-born googly bowler was called 'the black Greek' by a Yorkshire crowd that was furious when he bowled the South Africans to victory over the 'Tykes' with a spell of 8/99 at Sheffield in 1935. Xenophon Constantine Balaskas, born in Kimberley, South Africa, of Greek parents was a white man and a member of an official South African touring team.

Self-taught leg-break and 'bosie' expert Balaskas was one of the heroes of South Africa's famous win over England at Lord's in 1935 in the only decided Test of the series. Bowling unchanged for two and a half hours in England's first knock, and using his well-disguised top-spinner to excellent effect, the wily Balaskas ran out with an analysis that read 32–8–49–5 and South Africa gained a narrow first innings lead. Then followed one of the finest Test innings by a South African player, when Bruce Mitchell scored 164 not out in a total of 278 for seven wickets declared. England was left to score 309 to win. With the fast-medium 'Chud' Langton (4/31) scything through the upper order and Balaskas picking up the rest (27–8–54–4), England folded up to total only 151 and South Africa gained a famous victory by 157 runs – its only pre-war Test win overseas, other than two matches won in New Zealand in 1931–32.

That second Test of the 1935 series at Lord's proved to be the lively 'Bally' Balaskas's only international match of the season. He fractured an arm when fielding against Nottinghamshire in the next game and hardly played for the rest of the tour. A versatile cricketer who was in his later years a great supporter of young cricketing talent, he once hit a century in a Test in New Zealand.

The 1935 South African team boasted what was probably South Africa's best bowling attack since the famous days of the 'Golden Age' googly quartet. The two new-ball bowlers, 'Sandy' Bell and 'Bob' Crisp, were both fairly slippery customers.

The rather temperamental Alexander John Bell was mainly an inswing bowler who could operate for long spells if required and was one of the few South Africans to do well in Australia in 1931–32, when he took 23 wickets in the five Tests at 27.13. On the 1929 tour of England Bell, never considered much of a batsman, took part in a famous South African record 103-run last-wicket stand with H G O Owen-Smith. The chirpy 'Tuppy' Owen-Smith was thus able to reach a century before lunch – the only South African to do so in a Test.

Robert James Crisp was an athletic bowler and appreciably faster than Bell. In the Currie Cup tournament he twice bagged four wickets in four balls and, bowling from a good height with an easy, flowing action, could swing the ball both ways and lift it disconcertingly from the pitch. An adventurous soul, Bob Crisp twice climbed Mount Kilamanjaro, was wounded as a tank commander in the Western Desert during the Second World War and, suffering from cancer, opted out of society to live as a semi-recluse on a Greek island. Miraculously, he overcame his illness but stayed on his island, although he was seen from time to time in Cape Town and contributed some hilarious articles on cricket in Corfu to the *South African Cricketer* in 1971.

A third seam bowler of quality in the 1935 South African attack was the 6 ft 3 in (190 cm) Arthur Beaumont Chudleigh Langton, who varied his pace cleverly and took 115 wickets at 21.16 on the tour (Crisp claimed 107 at 19.58, the only other South African bowler to reach 100 wickets). 'Chud' Langton had a major part in the Lord's Test victory, assisting Bruce Mitchell to add 101 in South Africa's second innings and chipping in with six wickets in the match, including the vital scalps of Sutcliffe and Hammond in England's second innings.

Orthodox left-arm spinner Cyril Leverton Vincent provided some variation. Playing in four Tests in 1935, the 33-year-old veteran of the team took 18 England wickets. He also bowled well in Australia in 1931−32 and, at home in 1930−31, spun England out at Durban where his 6/51 was a personal best in a 25-Test career.

Prior to 1935, there were few South African Test bowlers who could be called match-winners. An exception was the tall, strong and one-eyed Eiulf Peter Nupen, of Norwegian parentage, a right-arm medium-pace bowler of off-cutters who was an absolute menace on his home matting wickets but disppointed on turf in England in 1924. With his fair hair and one blue eye, 'Buster' Nupen proved virtually unplayable on the mat at Old Wanderers, Johannesburg, in the first Test of the 1930−31 series against England. Such noteworthy England players as Hammond, Leyland, Wyatt and Hendren scratched around like old hens as Nupen, backed by left-hander Vincent, cut through them to take 11 wickets in the match. His reputation as a matting wicket bowler worked against him and Nupen was infrequently called upon to bowl for South Africa on turf.

Another fine bowler on matting was Neville Anthony Quinn, a superbly accurate left-arm medium pacer who was not exactly a match-winner at top level, but who could keep swerving and spinning the ball for long spells. He did, however, have some memorable moments on turf, notably when he took 6/19 against England at Headingley in 1929 and in Australia in 1931−32, when it was said that Don Bradman held his bowling in high regard.

The Lancashire-born Alfred Ewart Hall was another left-hander, but at fast-medium pace, who also revelled when bowling on matting wickets. Alf Hall never toured overseas with a South African team, but took part in three home series against England and played some cricket for Lancashire. At Cape Town in 1922−23, Hall humbled his former countrymen when he took 11 wickets on the mat in the second Test, including 7/63 in the second innings. His grand effort was in vain as England scraped through to win by one wicket.

Strong and wiry George Finlay Bissett enjoyed a short but highly lucrative Test career as a right-arm fast bowler of genuine pace, taking 25 wickets at 18.76 apiece in four home Tests against England in 1927−28. In the second Test of the series at Cape Town, he took 5/37 and 3/99 on his debut and, bowling with a gale behind him in the final Test at Durban, Bissett wrecked England's second innings in a 7/29 spell. Taken to England earlier, in 1924, Bissett suffered a foot injury and did not play in a Test.

A weak South African bowling attack was supplemented in 1924 by the inclusion for two Tests of a Cape Town-born Bradford League professional who had only played in one first-class match. George McDonald Parker bowled right-arm fast with great determination for figures of 37−2−152−6 in his first Test outing at Edgbaston (England scored 438 in its only innings of the match). At Lord's in the following Test, Parker's bowling was 'murdered' by Hobbs and Sutcliffe, but he took the only two England wickets to fall (24−0−121−2) in an innings of 531 for two declared. He was not called upon again and never appeared in a first-class match in the country of his birth.

When South Africa played its first match against New Zealand at Christchurch in 1931−32, leg-break and googly bowler Quintin McMillan eased away bad memories of the just completed series against Bradman and Australia (7/329 in four Tests) by taking nine wickets in the match for 127 runs. In the second of two Tests played in New Zealand, he added a further seven wickets to give him 16 at 20.18 in the last two matches of his short international career.

One of South Africa's most talented and most unfortunate pre-war bowlers was the right-arm fast-medium 'seamer' Norman Gordon who, at the age of 28, chose for his international debut the famous 'Timeless Test' series, South Africa's last before the war. During a season of phenomenally high scoring on the easiest of pitches, 'Mobil' Gordon (so called because of his sleek, oily hairstyle) bowled tirelessly to claim 20 wickets in the five Tests. This included a marathon stint of 55.2 overs for 174 runs and one wicket when England scored 654 for five in its second innings of the Durban crawl that was called off after 10 days so that the Englishmen could catch their ship home.

After the war, the 1947 South African team landed in England with a core of seasoned batsmen who had, for the most part, made their Test debuts during the 1920s or 1930s − but not one of their bowlers had played in international cricket before. They were to be greeted by Denis Compton and Bill Edrich on a run rampage. Each of the two Middlesex and England batsmen scored more than 3000 runs in first-class matches that season and, between them, look 1305 runs off the South African bowlers in five Tests.

The cool and confident fast-medium right-armer Lindsay Tuckett, who gained surprising pace off the pitch from a short run of about a dozen yards, toiled manfully throughout, sending down 252 overs in five Tests and taking 5/68 at Nottingham in his first Test outing. Tuckett's only worthwhile support came from two spin bowlers who must rank among the best of their kind to have played for South Africa in Test cricket. One of these players, bespectacled Norman

Bertram Fleetwood Mann, was destined to move on to other fields at the early age of 32 after playing in 19 Tests; the other, Athol Matthew Burchell Rowan, brother of Test batsman Eric Rowan, was to leave the game because of injury at the age of 30.

A placid but steel-willed orthodox slow left-hander, Norman 'Tufty' Mann had been at Cambridge University in 1939 when war broke out (he gained a golfing Blue but did not make the cricket side) and was rated by Denis Compton as a slow bowler of significance who was slightly slower than England's Derek Underwood, but spun the ball more. 'Tufty' Mann was a 'gentleman cricketer' and one of the few bowlers in Test cricket who applauded when an opposing batsman played a particularly fine shot.

A shortish man at 5 ft 9 in (175 cm), Mann presented a disarmingly frail profile but sent down 329.5 overs in five Tests in England in 1947 for just 603 runs (against Edrich and Compton!), or around 1.8 runs per over. In the first England innings of the series, at Nottingham, Mann returned figures of 20−13−10−0, keeping Compton and Edrich well in check. When the England pair went berserk at Lord's in the next match (Edrich 189, Compton 208), Mann's figures were 53−16−99−1. At Leeds (fourth Test) his first innings analysis read: 50−20−68−4; at the Oval (fifth Test): 64−28−93−4. Mann headed the South African Test bowling table and repeated the feat on the next tour in 1951.

His value did not lie entirely in his ability as a containing bowler of immaculate length and line; he was, in the right conditions, a match-winner as well. At Trent Bridge, Nottingham in 1951, a visibly ailing Mann and his 'partner-in-crime', Athol Rowan, spun England out for 114 to win the match for South Africa − Mann's figures: 24−16−24−4.

The 1951 England tour was 'Tufty' Mann's last encounter with international cricket. A year later he was dead from cancer. His health had always been suspect and was weakened by 20 months hidden in a tiny, filthy hut at the back of a pigsty, cared for by an elderly Italian couple and their niece after having escaped from a German POW camp during the war.

Athol Rowan was rated by some of the most knowledgable critics of his time as a world-class right-arm off-break bowler. Determined and strong-willed, he sometimes bowled with one leg in irons, a legacy of war wounds suffered in the Western Desert. Swerving and spinning the ball much in the manner of the Nobles and Trumbles of old, Rowan gained sharp turn from the off and also bowled a deceptive leg-cutter at close to medium pace.

Athol Rowan's most lucrative Test series in a truncated career came at home against England in 1948−49 when he took 24 wickets in five matches. When Lindsay Hassett's Australians arrived in South Africa in 1949−50, the off-spinner was expected to lead South

Athol Rowan was an
off-spin bowler of class who
sometimes bowled in
leg-irons; his career for
South Africa was cut short
by injury.

Africa's bowling challenge. At first it looked as if he would give the Australians all sorts of trouble. On a turning pitch at Johannesburg, Rowan, playing for Transvaal before the Tests started, spun out 15 of the tourists for 68, including an unplayable spell of 15.4−7−19−9 in the first Australian innings. No mean batsman, he looked to be taking his team to victory off his own bat when, turning for a run, his bad knee gave way and he was forced to retire injured. Australia scraped home by 15 runs and Athol Rowan was out of the Test rubber. That he recovered sufficiently to tour England once more in 1951 was a tribute to his great personal courage.

Ironically, the injury sustained by Athol Rowan at Johannesburg in 1949−50 opened the way for his successor, Hugh Tayfield, to take his place as an off-break bowler in the Springbok eleven. Tayfield responded with great success and went on to capture more Test wickets than any other South African bowler. Tayfield and an outstanding four-man attack that dominated South African bowling for a couple of series are covered in Chapter 21.

One other notable and controversial Springbok bowler who made his debut during the 1940s was the tall and gangling, 19-year-old, fair-haired Cuan Neil McCarthy who literally burst onto the international scene against England in 1948−49. In his very first Test − on his home ground at Kingsmead, Durban − McCarthy, off a long run-up and with his peculiar double-jointed action, bowled with such fiery pace that England's batsmen struggled to reach a second-innings winning target of just 128 runs. McCarthy took six wickets for 43 but England won by two wickets with a leg-bye off the very last ball of the match in a finish that has only been equalled for nail-biting by the famous tied Test at Brisbane in 1960−61 and the tie between India and Australia at Madras in October 1986.

In his first Test series versus England Cuan McCarthy took 21 wickets, but his speed made scant impression on the Australians who followed in 1949−50. The pace was certainly there but inexperience, plus a spate of dropped catches in the slips, saw him end the five-match rubber with but five wickets at 107.20 runs apiece.

Hampered by injury in England in 1951 and doubts over his bowling action (he was eventually no-balled once for throwing when playing for Cambridge University in 1952), McCarthy was never again a force in Test cricket.

South Africa's leading seam bowler in England in 1951 turned out to be the oldest Springbok to make a Test debut. At 40 years, 56 days, the trim, bespectacled right-arm Geoffrey Walter Ashton Chubb played his first Test at Nottingham, and followed through to take more wickets (21) in the series than anyone else and most wickets on tour (76). *Wisden* records that Geoff Chubb 'bowled medium pace with the enthusiasm of a man half his age'. The veteran who had started his first-class career before the war as an opening batsman, bowled 150 overs more than any of his younger colleagues in an inspired display of skill, stamina and enthusiasm.

Geoff Chubb never played Test cricket again; by the end of 1952, 'Tufty' Mann was sadly no longer of this world; Athol Rowan's injury had forced him out of the game; and Cuan McCarthy had retired prematurely from Test cricket under a 'chucker' cloud. The stage was thus set for the emergence of a Springbok bowling combination that would bear comparison with any quartet of bowlers ever to appear together in cricket history — and whose short spell together at the top provides a story on its own.

15

Seaming through to
the 'Seventies

'It has often been dismal, sometimes it has been dreadful, this road winding uphill all the way which New Zealand cricket has had to traverse'

— T P McLean

Before the Second World War official Test cricket involving New Zealand was limited to just 14 contests, some played against second- or third-string England elevens, a couple against a full strength South African team and none against Australia, India or West Indies, the remaining nations to take part in international cricket up to 1939. Nevertheless, some very fine players emerged from New Zealand and, when play resumed in 1945, there came a steady, if rather staggered improvement in its fortunes.

An interesting feature throughout has been the dominance of medium and medium-fast swing and seam exponents, with the occasional appearance of a truly fast bowler and the equally rare inclusion of a spin bowler or two of unusual merit.

The first ball bowled in Test cricket by a New Zealander was by the well-groomed all-rounder Frederick Theodore Badcock, who bore some resemblance to Australia's Keith Miller in looks and in his dashing style of play. Ted Badcock, with his sleek black hair and dazzling white boots, always looked the part of a cricketer, bowled his medium-paced inswingers with skill, batted with enterprise and fielded like two men. The keenest of cricketers and a devoted coach of young players, he was approaching 50 when seen in action in Services matches in England during the 1940s. When the New Zealand team landed at Fremantle, Australia, in 1954 on their way home from South Africa, they were greeted by the immaculate Ted Badcock who was still coaching and bowling with his old, practised skill.

The right-arm George Ritchie Dickinson, described as being as fast a bowler as any to represent his country, opened the bowling with Badcock in New Zealand's first Test venture against England at Christchurch in 1929–30. Dickinson did some of his best work before New Zealand was granted Test status, but bowled with sufficient skill to take eight wickets at 30.62 in his three Tests.

First change for New Zealand at Christchurch in 1929–30 was William Edward Merritt, a right-arm leg-break and googly bowler who had taken 107 wickets on a non-Test tour of England in 1927 and later played for Northamptonshire. Bill Merritt's length was often rather wayward but he could, on occasions, produce a ball to beat the best batsman. Roger Charles Blunt, another leg-break bowler and a graceful batsman who was a New Zealand mainstay in early Tests, also bowled well in his country's first international encounter to claim figures of 3/17 and 2/17, eventually heading the series bowling table with nine wickets at 19.00.

Left-arm orthodox spinner Cyril Francis Walter Alcott was also introduced to Test cricket in 1929–30 and formed, with Merritt, Blunt and newcomers I B Cromb and H G Vivian, the basis of New Zealand's bowling attack for its first Test tour of England in 1931. The sharp-witted and shrewd Ian Burns Cromb was a loose-limbed right-arm fast-medium bowler in the Maurice Tate tradition. Henry Gifford Vivian batted left-handed and bowled right-arm leg-breaks and was New Zealand's first truly outstanding all-rounder, who had made his Test debut at age 18.

Against South Africa at Wellington in 1931–32, H G Vivian hit 100 and 73 and took 4/58 in the visiting team's first innings. His son, Graham Ellery Vivian, also played for New Zealand as a left-hand bat and right-arm leg-spinner, making his debut versus India in 1964–65 six days past his 19th birthday, although he did not enjoy the same success as his father.

New Zealand's youngest-ever Test player was also a leg-break bowler. Australian-born Douglas Linford Freeman played the first of his two Tests against England at Christchurch in 1932–33 at the age of 18 years and 197 days but, like so many New Zealand hopefuls down the years, failed to trouble the top level batsmen.

The 1937 New Zealand tour of England saw the introduction of a couple of new seam bowlers. The persevering right-arm fast-medium John Angus Dunning and right-arm medium Albert William Roberts were little more than containing stock bowlers who seldom posed much of a problem for England's experienced batsmen. The strapping John Cowie was an entirely different proposition and was destined to become New Zealand's only pre-war world-class bowler.

Commenting on his 19 wickets at 20.78 in three Tests against England and 114 wickets at 19.95 on the tour, the usually conservative *Wisden* speaks of Jack Cowie in glowing terms: 'Had he been an Australian, he might have been termed a wonder of the age.' Nicknamed 'The Bull', the strongly-built Cowie bowled with a balanced mixture of determination, aggression, competitiveness and skill. Fast-medium right-arm, he had a good command of the out-swinger, extracted lift from the dullest of pitches, and threw in a vicious break-back from time to time, a reminder of fast-bowling

Jack Cowie was the first of New Zealand's long line of outstanding seam bowlers.

giants of the past like Tom Richardson and Bill Lockwood.

In only nine Tests Jack Cowie took 45 wickets and after the war he took six wickets in an innings in home Tests against both Australia and England. In England in 1949, he again headed New Zealand's

Test bowling with 14 wickets at 32.21. With his magnificent build, beautiful approach and delivery and highly competitive instinct Jack Cowie would have revelled — and succeeded enormously — in modern Test cricket.

The amply proportioned Thomas Browning Burtt was one of New Zealand's bowling exceptions — a left-arm spin bowler of high skill who proved to be Cowie's main support in England in 1949 (17 Test wickets at 33.41; a phenomenal 128 tour wickets at 22.88). Full of humour and wide of girth, Tom Burtt was happy to bowl all day. As Dick Brittenden, New Zealand's number one cricket writer, wrote in his *New Zealand Cricketers*: 'There is not much point in recalling Burtt's performances, for he simply made a habit of bowling innumerable overs and taking wickets all the time.'

Burtt had a rollicking sort of run and looked, according to Brittenden, 'rather like a sailor hurrying to catch a bus'. Far from being a graceful Verity or Blythe, Burtt was nonetheless a highly effective bowler at all levels and an enthusiastic if rustic batsman who played more than one innings of value.

Jack Cowie's new-ball partner in England in 1949 was the industrious Henry Butler Cave, an economical right-arm medium-pacer who bowled with a high-swinging windmill action. Harry Cave swung the new ball well and was prepared to bowl till he dropped from exhaustion, which was fairly frequent during his Test career when opposition batting was usually very strong. Cave played Test cricket for New Zealand for nearly a decade and his greatest value was as a containing bowler. Against India in 1955−56, he achieved a remarkable 118 maidens in 255 overs.

Two other useful seam bowlers in the 1949 New Zealand line-up were the right-arm medium-pace George Fenwick Creswell, who bowled mainly leg-theory with an awkward chest-on delivery, and the tall and fast John Arthur Hayes, a right-armer with a classic side-on action and a late outswinger. In his sole Test in 1949, Creswell took 6/168 in an England total of 482 at the Oval. Hayes's Test career highlight came when he took the wickets of West Indians Worrell, Weekes and Gomez in eight balls at Christchurch in 1951−52.

Two all-rounders of note, right-arm off-spinner Geoffrey Osborne Rabone and the versatile John Richard Reid, were also in the strong 1949 New Zealand combination and both were to captain their country. 'Bones' Rabone sometimes opened both batting and bowling (switching from medium-pace to off-breaks when the shine was off the ball). Against South Africa in 1953−54 he followed an innings of 107 in the first Test at Durban with a first innings 6/68 in 38.7 eight-ball overs in the next game against South Africa at Cape Town.

Reid remains one of New Zealand's half-dozen or so finest cricketers and certainly its most illustrious all-rounder. His powerful batting frequently carried his side. His medium-fast outswing and/or slower off-cutters won more than one match. John Reid's most decisive spell of bowling occurred in South Africa in 1961−62 when he led New Zealand from the front to win the final Test and tie the series with a marathon 45−27−44−4 stint. Reid also kept wicket on occasion and was a brilliant fielder, which made him something of a one-man team. At one point in his career he had scored more runs that any other New Zealander, taken most wickets, held most catches, scored most centuries, played for and captained his country most times.

The giant 6 ft 5 in (195 cm) Anthony Roy MacGibbon was New Zealand's first-choice new-ball bowler between 1950 and 1958. In South Africa in 1953−54 he was New Zealand's main strike bowler in a strong seam attack that included Guy Overton, Bob Blair and John Reid. Although handicapped by stomach problems during the tour, MacGibbon, who swung the ball both ways and used his height to gain sharp lift, took 22 Test wickets at 20.63. Known as 'Long Hop' or 'Split Pin', Tony MacGibbon took 70 wickets in 26 Tests for New Zealand, one of his finest efforts being 20 wickets at 19.45 in the series for a side that lost four out of five internationals in England in 1958.

Guy William Fitzroy Overton was another cheerful, diligent and loyal right-armer of considerable pace who sent down well-controlled inswingers and outswingers. The bow-legged Overton (he was a horse-riding sheep farmer) took nine wickets at 28.66 in his only three Tests, all played in South Africa in 1953−54.

For Robert William Blair, the South African tour of 1953−54 was a bittersweet experience. It confirmed his promise as a hostile right-arm fast bowler, but his success was dampened when he received news of his 19-year-old fiancée's death in a Christmas Eve train disaster back in New Zealand. This sad bulletin arrived in the middle of a Test at Johannesburg, but the brave Bob Blair joined a bandaged Bert Sutcliffe (returned from hospital after being hit on the head by an Adcock bouncer) in a rollicking 10-minute last-wicket stand of 33.

Blair relied on pace for his wickets, coming in from a long run and delivering the ball with a pronounced foot drag. A man of immense humour and one of New Zealand's cricket characters, his best Test performance came at the tail-end of his career when he took 7/142 in the match against the powerful 1963−64 South African team, dismissing the prolific opening bat Eddie Barlow cheaply in each innings.

Two lively right-arm medium-fast swing bowlers who put in some Test appearances during the time of MacGibbon and Blair were the strongly built Donald Derek Beard and the 6 ft 2 in (188 cm) and amply proportioned Kenneth William Hough. The flamboyant Beard's persistent swing brought him figures of 1/20 and 3/22 in the low-scoring match against West Indies at Auckland in 1955—56 that resulted in New Zealand's first-ever Test win. The even more uninhibited Ken Hough was built like a blacksmith and, despite his vast bulk, was an international soccer player. He had the satisfaction of twice clean bowling England's Colin Cowdrey for low scores in Tests in New Zealand in 1958—59

Although New Zealand's bowling emphasis lay mainly with seam and pace during the 1950s, some spin bowlers did appear and two were as good as any to have played for their country. Maths schoolteacher John Chaloner Alabaster approached his leg-break and googly bowling in a scientific way. Uncannily accurate for one of his type, he was used as a stock bowler and frequently bowled in tandem for Otago and New Zealand with another leg-spinner, the sharper-turning Alex Moir. Alabaster used a well-disguised top-spinner and a wrong 'un judiciously, reaching his peak in South Africa in 1961—62 when he claimed 22 wickets in the five Tests.

Shorter and more heavily built than Alabaster, the perky Alexander McKenzie Moir was a late developer. Playing in his first Test versus England at Christchurch in 1950—51 at age 31, Moir acquitted himself admirably to return figures of 56.3—16—155—6 (England scored 550) but, in an age when leg-spin bowling was becoming increasingly unfashionable, his chances thereafter were limited.

When Alabaster and Moir departed from Test cricket it became a definite case of New Zealand 'seaming into the '70s', with very few opportunities being given to spin bowlers at all. The 1961—62 tour of South Africa introduced three new pace bowlers of different method to spearhead the attack. Alabaster was still around as the sole spinner and the only other experienced Test bowler was the ubiquitous John Reid. But newcomers Dick Motz, Gary Bartlett and Frank Cameron acquitted themselves admirably and New Zealand was able to square the rubber (two wins each and one match drawn) for the first time in history.

Richard Charles Motz was a tenacious right-arm fast bowler who knew not the meaning of defeat and a magnificent scientific hitter who turned many a match, with the ball or off his own bat. The features of his energetic bowling were a good outswinger and pace off the pitch. In 32 Tests, Motz became the first 'Kiwi' to reach 100 wickets for New Zealand. He headed the tour averages in South Africa in 1961—62 and took 19 wickets at 26.57 in the Tests and thereafter became New Zealand's number one attacker.

On a short tour of England in 1965, Dick Motz bowled like a demon to take 54 first-class wickets in 14 games. In 1967—68, his best innings Test figures of 6/63 at Christchurch saw New Zealand beat India for the first time in a Test. As a hitter, 'Bon' Motz was a definite crowd favourite. Back trouble during the 1969 England tour caused him to retire from first-class cricket at the age of 29.

Dick Motz was a tireless seam bowler for New Zealand and a highly entertaining and effective scientific hitter.

Before the appearance in the 1970s of a young man named Richard Hadlee, the right-arm Gary Alexander Bartlett was named as probably the fastest of all New Zealand bowlers. There was, however, much criticism about the legitimacy of his action and his Test career was short, albeit reasonably effective. Although his ability to bounce the ball was used as a deterrent against similar attack from the South African fast bowler Peter Pollock in South Africa in 1961–62, Bartlett was not as effective there as Motz and Frank Cameron. Against India at Christchurch in 1967–68, Gary Bartlett complemented Dick Motz's first innings 6/63 with a match-winning 6/38 burst in the visitors' second innings, to bring New Zealand an historic first win over India.

The less pacy but infinitely more versatile Francis James Cameron served as New Zealand's stock bowler in South Africa in 1961−62, claiming 20 wickets at 24.65 in the Tests, and went on to garner 62 wickets in his 19 games for his country. At Cape Town in 1961−62, he helped his side towards its first win of the series with 5/48 in the home team's first innings. When Pakistan visited New Zealand in 1964−65, Cameron took 4/36 and 5/34 in the second Test at Auckland, his best Test effort.

When Dick Motz was unavailable because of injury for the third Test against South Africa at Auckland in 1963−64, Frank Cameron took the new ball with the broad-shouldered Robert Smith Cunis. The fast-medium right-arm Bob Cunis was a talkative player who often berated a batsman whom he had beaten but not dismissed. He was also an energetic worker for his country's cause and toiled faithfully to take 51 wickets in 20 Tests. In 1970−71 he took nine England wickets in a drawn Test at Auckland, including his career best of 6/76 in the first innings.

A left-arm fast-medium bowler of unusual stature, physically and in terms of wicket return, made his debut for New Zealand against Pakistan at Wellington in 1964−65. Richard Owen Collinge stood 6 ft 5 in (195 cm) in his socks and took five wickets in his first international game. Fourteen years later, in his final Test, versus England at Lord's in 1978, Collinge boosted his wicket haul to 116 (35 Tests) and was the most prolific wicket-taker in New Zealand Test cricket when he retired.

For more than a decade Collinge spearheaded the New Zealand attack. Coming in with huge strides off a long run that saw him flailing his arms in the air, the New Zealand left-hander must have presented a fearsome sight for any faint-hearted batsman. Accurate and able to swing the ball effectively, Collinge was a respected opponent on the international circuit for more than a dozen years, although he missed many Tests through his reluctance to tour over-seas because of family commitments.

Collinge enjoyed many days of success in Test cricket, but none could have given him greater satisfaction that when he clean bowled Geoff Boycott for one run with an unplayable fast inswinger at Basin Reserve, Wellington, in February 1978. This ball from the veteran fast bowler started an England slide to 64 all out and the first ever Kiwi Test win over the 'Mother Country'. Firing full bore from the other end was the new young fast bowling 'find', Richard Hadlee, who took 10 wickets in the match and whose own bowling trail of success at international level is the subject of a separate chapter.

Richard Hadlee's older brother, Dayle Robert Hadlee, was the first of former Test batsman Walter Hadlee's sons to play Test cricket for New Zealand. Dayle Hadlee started off at right-arm fast-medium but persistent back injuries forced him to reduce his pace and hampered his career, although he managed to gather 71 wickets in 26 Tests, bowling with accuracy and swing.

Five years before Dayle Hadlee first put in an appearance for New Zealand, another fast-medium bowler, the 6 ft 3 in (190 cm) Bruce Richard Taylor, stunned the cricketing world with a unique debut double against India at Calcutta of a century (in 158 minutes) and five wickets in an innings − the only player to do so in Test history.

An aggressive left-handed batsman, Taylor bowled right-arm with a high action, swinging both ways and was ever ready to use the bouncer to disturb a batsman. In 30 Tests he took 111 wickets at 26.60 and hit 898 runs, including a swashbuckling second century in 86 minutes, versus West Indies at Auckland in 1968−69. Taylor was known as a man who played the game hard and lived life to the full off the field. He bowled magnificently on rock-hard pitches in the West Indies in 1971−72, where his 27 wickets at 17.70 in four Tests contributed as much to a drawn series as the prolific run-making of New Zealand's ace opening batsman, Glenn Turner. At Bridgetown in the third Test Taylor's fiery 7/74 performance saw West Indies put out for only 133 in its first innings, and only magnificent second innings efforts from the incomparable Garfield Sobers and the obdurate Charlie Davis saved the day for the home eleven.

New Zealand's vice-captain on the West Indies tour, Bevan Ernest Congdon, was forced to take over leadership when skipper elect Graham Dowling became injured. Apart from being a leading runscorer, Congdon went on to become one of New Zealand's finest captains. The almost painfully thin and stooping Bev Congdon was also a right-arm medium-pacer who moved the ball a little each way. In 61 Tests, Congdon scored move than 3000 runs and took 59 wickets, many of them when a breakthrough was desperately needed.

Congdon depended heavily on left-arm spinner Hedley John Howarth and the more volatile Bruce Taylor in the West Indies in 1971−72. Older brother to recent New Zealand captain Geoff Howarth, Hedley Howarth was for 30 Tests his country's only real spin bowling hope. Although other spinners like fellow left-hander Bryan William Yuille (34 wickets in 17 Tests and a bowler of immaculate length) and off-spinner Victor Pollard (primarily a batsman after having been chosen as a bowler) occasionally produced worthwhile results, Howarth was the only New Zealand slow bowler of the 1970s to trouble batsmen of Test rating.

A smiling and philosophical character, Hedley Howarth just kept on bowling his orthodox slow left-arm breaks no matter the conditions or the quality of the opposition, much in the same manner as burly Tom Burtt had done some 20 or so years before. As the acknowledged work-horse of the 1971−72 team in the West Indies, Howarth sent down 338 overs in the five Tests, 138 more than his nearest rival, Congdon. After an exhausting spell against Sobers and Davis at

Bridgetown in the third Test, his figures read: $74-24-138-2$.

In his 30 Tests, Hedley Howarth captured 86 wickets at 36.95, a fairly ordinary return in itself and no indication of this dedicated player's worth as an instrument of containment when conditions were in favour of a strong opposition batting line-up.

Hedley Howarth was one of very few Kiwi slow bowlers of note during a Test history of more than 50 years in which New Zealand's cricket has been dominated by pace bowlers of varying degrees of speed, effectiveness and skill. The art of seam and swing has been seen to rule as far as New Zealand cricket is concerned and an account of the unprecedented feats of its greatest Kiwi exponent, Richard Hadlee, is in Chapter 31.

16

Bowling a maiden over

'...the first major influence of women on the game of cricket was the introduction of round-arm bowling'

– Netta Rheinberg

Recorded earlier in this volume is a version of cricket history which claims that John Willes got the idea of bowling round-arm while watching his sister, Christina Hodge, delivering the ball wearing a hooped skirt that prevented her from using the then customary under-arm mode. In *Fair Play – The Story of Women's Cricket*, Netta Rheinberg contends that Willes's sister denied any knowledge of such a story about the origin of round-arm bowling, but reconfirms a female first connection with the revolutionary form of bowling. Ms Rheinberg quotes from an article published in *Badminton Magazine* of December 1895 which tells the story of a Mrs Lambert being hampered when bowling by her attire and forced to bowl round-arm to her husband, William Lambert (a reference presumably to the famous early 19th century cricketer of the same name).

Other women of the 19th century also had a sort of midwifery and motherly hand during the birth and early development of cricket as we now know it. Notable among these ladies were Mrs Jane Walker, who begged her husband, Joseph Walker, a wool merchant, to form the Lascelles Hall Cricket Club for sons of poor weavers; it later became the nursery of Yorkshire cricket. The most famous of all cricketing ladies was of course Martha Grace, mother of W G Grace and his cricketing brothers. Mrs Grace could frequently be seen coaching her large brood (four boys, three girls and a couple of dogs to do the fielding) in the orchard where her husband, Dr Henry Grace, had cut down some trees to create space for a cricket pitch. Mrs Grace was also a regular spectator at cricket matches and could frequently be overheard making astute comments in a loud voice.

For supporters of women's cricket, 1934 was the auspicious year when the first international Test series between two teams of women took place. The venue was Brisbane and the first day's play saw Australia bowled out by England for a rather ignominious total of 47 runs. Chief architect of the Australian collapse in a bowling spell of 17−11−10−7 was the remarkable Myrtle Maclagan, considered the 'WG' or 'Wally Hammond' of women's cricket between the wars. When at school, she once wrote in her diary: 'Freeman [the Kent

Australia's Betty Wilson was known as the female Sobers and was probably the finest all-rounder in women's cricket history.

and England bowler] came and coached us and taught me to bowl so that the ball curled in the air.'

Myrtle Maclagan was also an outstanding batswoman who scored the first Test century in women's cricket and was a long-lived champion and still one of England's major players after the Second World War. She was a medium-fast bowler and a hard-hitter with the bat who could match most men stroke for stroke.

In the inaugural Test at Brisbane, Australian slow bowler Alice Palmer matched Maclagan's bowling feat by claiming seven wickets for 18 when England batted, but the visiting side ran out easy winners by nine wickets.

Another Australian slow bowler, Peggy Antonio, took 12 wickets in that first Anglo-Australian three-match series during the 1934–35 season, went on to become the outstanding woman bowler before the Second World War and is described in *Fair Play* as 'a woman who could spin the ball as well as any man'. A leg-spinner, the small, dark-haired Antonio was known as the 'girl Grimmett' and twice took six wickets in a Test innings.

When Australia visited England for the first time in 1937, Myrtle Maclagan was still England's spearhead bowler (and leading batswoman), but Peggy Antonio excelled for the tourists with 25 wickets in three Tests and was the bowler of the series.

An all-round feat of champion style saw England defeated by 186 runs at Adelaide in the first Test after the war. Australia's Betty Wilson scored 111 and then took 6/23 and 3/39 to make her mark in her first international outing. She soon became regarded as the finest Australian woman all-rounder in history and, in batting and bowling, showed high skill and a shrewd knowledge of the game.

For England, the talented Mary Duggan was fast becoming accepted as the all-round heir to Myrtle Maclagan's crown and is described by Rachel Heyhoe Flint (a later England captain and the first regular woman contributor to an international cricket magazine) as, 'Big in build, big in heart, kind, generous and gentle...' Mary Duggan was also a prolific scorer of runs and a left-hand fast bowler with a fine action who later changed to slow-medium deliveries.

Another outstanding England all-rounder was the petite but athletic, blonde, left-hander Enid Bakewell who made history in 1970 when she became the only woman cricketer to be profiled in *Wisden* following her phenomenal 1000 runs and 100 wickets on the England tour of Australia and New Zealand in 1968–69. As a left-handed bat, Enid Bakewell hit 601 runs in six Tests. As a left-arm spin bowler who bowled with skill and consistency and could drift the ball across the batsman and then straighten it sharply, the modest but alert Ms Bakewell claimed 26 Test wickets at 18.34.

Miriam Knee, one of Australia's best captains, was a cunning medium-pace bowler of note and a grand left-handed bat who performed well during the late 1950s and into the 1960s. During the 1968–69 season, another Australian, Anne Gordon, became the second woman bowler to reach 10 wickets in a Test. This was achieved with figures of 5/61 and 5/57 in the first match of the series at Melbourne.

South Africa entered the women's Test scene in 1960 and produced a couple of outstanding right-arm seam bowlers in Lorna Ward and

Jean McNaughton. New Zealand first met England and Australia during the early 1950s but made little impression until 1966 when a three-match series in England was drawn thanks in part to some fine work by new-ball bowler Jocelyn Burley. When India played its first international series against an Australia Under-25 XI in India in 1975, the 21-year-old Shanta Rangaswamy batted in great style and took 5/54 with her medium-pacers in the second 'Test' at Delhi, while the 19-year-old left-arm spinner Diana Eduljee took 6/40 in the first match at Pune. West Indies captain Pat Whittaker proved the cornerstone of her team, as batswoman and bowler, when it played its first series in England in 1979.

Running into the 1980s, prominent Australian wicket-takers included players like opening bowler Sharon Tredrea, left-arm spinner Lyn 'Lefty' Fullston, and Australia's skipper during the 1984−85 home series against England, veteran Raelee Thompson who, at 39, had played in more Tests (13) that any other Australian. Thompson, a right-arm fast-medium bowler, also became, in her final test before retiring, the second Australian to reach 50 Test wickets. The incomparable Betty Wilson heads the list with 66.

Current England bowling stars include the medium-fast Avril Starling, who took 5/36 to give England a surprise five-run victory against the run of play at Adelaide in 1984−85 and ended the series with 21 wickets − the most ever for England in a women's series − beating the 20 by Myrtle Maclagan (in 1934−35 v Australia) and Mary Duggan (1951 v Australia), both of whom achieved their totals in a three-Test series. Avril Starling's feat also equalled Australian Betty Wilson's world record of 21 wickets (achieved in a three-match rubber). Another England seamer, Jan Brittin, is also one of the most prolific woman run-scorers in history and left-arm spinner Gill McConway, on runs per wicket average, ended ahead of Avril Starling on the 1984−85 England bowling table with 17 wickets at 20.76.

There are many more fine women cricketers, and bowlers in particular, waiting to carry on the traditions started by John Willes's sister, Mrs Lambert and Martha Grace; carried forward by such 'giants' as Myrtle Maclagan and Betty Wilson; and continued by the current top performers in women's international cricket. In a rapidly changing world where women are taking their place alongside men in almost every human activity, it is perhaps not too far-fetched to contemplate a future when male and female Test cricketers may take the field together.

17

Bouncing back

'No batsman likes the bouncer, not even the occasional one...'
— Leslie Ames

Australia's Ray Lindwall and Keith Miller gave England a foretaste in 1946–47 of what might be expected when Don Bradman brought his team to England in 1948, although the overwhelming Australian victory in the first series between the two countries since 1938 was not entirely based on the use of fast bowling. In each Test of the 1946–47 series, the home country included at least three and sometimes as many four spin bowlers in their line-up, if left-hander Ernie Toshack is to be included in this category. But one can only speculate as to what misguided logic prompted the English authorities to persist, in 1948, with a ruling that allowed for a new ball to be taken after only 55 overs. This meant that England's batsmen would hardly be past the first trauma of a Lindwall and Miller onslaught when another became due. Bradman must have been supremely content to dispense with his wrist spinners and fill in the time between new-balls with his accurate 'containment' trio of Bill Johnston, Toshack and Ian Johnson. How Clive Lloyd would have beamed if the 55-over new-ball law had been operative in his day.

The 55-over experiment lasted just one season. It was changed to 65 overs in 1949 and, in 1955, the old '200 runs' new-ball limit returned, only to be amended once more the following season when the definition was enlarged to 200 runs *or* 75 overs. Finally, in 1961, as 'an experiment', the current 85-over new-ball ruling came into force.

In 1948, a shell-shocked England whose major cities had survived a blitz of terrifying proportions, was faced with a bombardment of a different nature on its cricket grounds. A certain apathy was also apparent in English cricket in 1948, the result in part of years of war and deprivation, but also induced according to some observers by a series of selection blunders. It seemed that all the Australian fast bowlers needed to do was to prise loose two or three of the main batting bricks in the England line-up and the whole wall would come tumbling down. The middle order were usually lacking in basic technique and, in some cases, the temperament and courage needed to handle top-drawer fast bowling.

As a young lad, Raymond Russell Lindwall observed the great English bowler Harold Larwood in full cry at the Sydney Cricket

Ground. The future Australian fast bowler never forgot the sight — and the lessons learnt through exposure to the full glory of a perfect fast bowler's action. With one minor variance Lindwall came, in general appearance and method, closest of all post-war fast bowlers to matching the style and delivery of the Nottinghamshire express. Larwood, in his final stride, would place his front foot parallel to the bowling crease, his right foot sliding forward; Lindwall's left toe would be pointed straight ahead as he swung his arm over with his back foot, like Larwood's, dragging over the line. Both bowled with perfect control over line and length.

By any standards Lindwall was one of the great fast bowlers. A masterful cricket tactician in his own right, he planned his bowling for the day from the moment he began limbering up in the dressing-room. Unlike his more spontaneous ally, Keith Miller, Lindwall may best be described as a technically ordered athlete. Through his mastery of pace, line, length and variation of movement, he kept batsmen under constant pressure.

At 5 ft 11 in (180 cm) and with not a touch of unwanted weight on his muscular boxer's frame, the fair-haired Lindwall was a sight for the gods as he came sprinting in on his 16-pace approach. His arm did not go over quite as high as some purists may have desired; he preferred his natural method and followed Bill O'Reilly's advice to leave well alone when it was suggested he should alter his action.

Lindwall's bouncer was an alarming missile that tested a batsman's reflexes and his courage as it bore into the throat like a hunting dog coming in for the kill. He never wasted it on unworthy individuals, but was never reluctant to bowl his short flyer at a batsman of class. The word 'waste' found no place in Lindwall's bowling vocabulary — for him every single ball was a potential wicket-taker. Other than his alarming bouncer, Lindwall was most feared for his late and vicious outswinger and for subtle, undetectable changes in pace which made him a formidable proposition no matter the conditions of pitch or day.

Ray Lindwall took 228 wickets (at 23.03) in 61 Tests and, as spearhead to the Australian attack, has only been matched in recent years by Dennis Lillee and Jeff Thomson. And if Ray Lindwall had never been a bowler at all, he would most likely have worn his baggy green cap as a stroke-playing batsman whose best feat for Australia was a thundering century in only 115 minutes against England at Melbourne in 1946/47.

In a foreword to R S Whitington's *Keith Miller — the Golden Nugget* England's famous batsman of contemporary age, Denis Compton, describes his first brush with Keith Ross Miller. The tall and debonaire glamour boy of Australian cricket had been brought on as a fifth bowling change during an Australian Services XI match at Lord's in 1943 and Compton, batting at the time, turned to

Services wicket-keeper Stan Sismey to ask: 'What does this chap do, Stan?' He was told by the 'keeper that the new man was 'not really a bowler' but that Compton might find him 'a bit quick'. Compton went on to record that he had personally not faced anything as fast since squaring up to Ernie McCormick during the Anglo-Australian Test series in 1938: 'A bit quick! The bowler took only a short run, but when he let the ball go, my hair nearly stood up on end.'

The 1953 *Wisden* described Keith Miller as 'a gifted athlete who is capable of being anything except dull'. Ray Robinson compared him to an Olympian god and called him 'the cricketer that all would like to be'. Like West Indian Garfield Sobers, the Australian all-rounder was, at one and the same time, possibly the best batsman, the best bowler and the best fielder in the world. According to Richie Benaud, Keith Miller was also the best captain never to have led his country and the finest skipper under whom he (Benaud) ever played.

When Australia's captain Don Bradman discovered what a fine match-winning partnership he had in Lindwall and Miller, he risked much criticism by using the latter for long bowling spells, some said

England was left shell-shocked during the 1940s when Australia's Ray Lindwall first appeared in Test cricket, to bring back memories of Larwood at his fastest.

to the detriment of the all-rounder's batsmanship. Bradman's logic was, and quite correctly, that team results were of primary consideration and that, with batsmen like Bradman himself, Hassett, Morris, Barnes, Brown, Harvey and Loxton already available, Miller could be spared to concentrate on his bowling. Allegations that there was bad blood between Bradman and Miller during the 1948 tour have since been refuted.

Loose-limbed and tall, and with a mane of thick black hair, the exuberant Miller was a 'natural' whose run-up was half as long as Lindwall's but he could send down a delivery as fast as Lindwall, and at times, some said even faster. In contrast to Lindwall's mostly lethal bouncers that threatened a batsman's very existence, many of Miller's short-pitched balls would fly way over the batsman's head, a result of his very high, classical action. But he bowled more of them than Lindwall, and delighted in doing so.

Miller *was* fast, and superbly accurate from his first ball, but would enjoy experimenting with anything from an off-break to a googly when conditions did not favour fast bowling. His record was phenomenal in an age when there was not an assured Test series (or two) every season; in 55 matches for Australia he claimed 170 wickets (at 22.97), and scored 2958 runs.

The third most important spoke in Bradman's 1948 bowling wheel of destruction was the tall and wiry 6 ft 2½ in (189 cm) left-arm fast-medium William Arras Johnston. On figures alone Johnston was the de facto principal bowler in the 1948 side. He equalled Lindwall's 27 wickets in the five Tests and, in 21 tour games, took 102 wickets at 16.42, as opposed to Lindwall's 86 wickets (at 15.68) in 22 matches. Johnston bowled 850.1 overs at a shade *under* two runs an over, Lindwall 573.1 overs at 2.35.

Throughout his career for Australia, Bill Johnston was the man to keep one end plugged solid, on good track or bad, no matter the conditions or the state of the game. He was three bowlers in one: with a new ball as dangerous, if not quite as speedy, as Lindwall or Miller; on a receptive wicket, a seam and swing menace; on a plumb pitch, left-arm medium to slow containment bowler.

When he first played for Australia against India in 1947–48 Johnston was given the new ball. In England in 1948 he was used strictly as the third strike bowler when either Miller or Lindwall tired or faltered, giving opposing batsmen no respite from pace. Taking a 10-pace approach to the wicket, Johnston would give a curious dipping motion before delivering the ball, fast-medium, over the wicket. His main delivery was the inswinger to a right-handed batsman, but he also sent down a sharp and late outswinger as his surprise weapon. Batsmen experienced difficulty in detecting which way the ball would swing and, when he dropped his pace, Johnston's leg-spinners would kick nastily.

As a batsman, Johnston was considered an entertainer, although his stay at the crease could seldom be described as being more than brief. In England in 1953, with the aid of his conniving team-mates who kept him away from the strike as much as possible, Australia's resident number 11 actually headed the tour batting table with 16 not outs in 17 innings and an average of 102.00!

The presence of another fine left-hander, Ernest Raymond Herbert Toshack, in the 1948 Australian bowling line-up allowed Bradman to exploit to the utmost the English ruling that allowed a new ball after just 55 overs. Another typical Australian over-the-wicket specialist (most English left-handers have preferred to bowl around the wicket), Toshack could be best described as a containing type of bowler on an easy wicket but one who was absolutely lethal on a 'sticky dog'.

Toshack's first headline performance was achieved on a typical Brisbane 'sticky' against England in 1946—47 when his 6/82 sent England slithering to a disastrous innings and 332 runs defeat in the Woollongabba mud. His bowling repertoire was based around a stock delivery which would cut across the batsman from off-stump to leg but also included a genuine leg-break and an occasional faster ball. Incidentally, Toshack shares a trivia-type record with Ray Lindwall in that neither ever bowled against Don Bradman in a match.

Of the remaining members of Bradman's 1948 bowling squad, Ian William Johnson was the only one to bowl a reasonable number of overs in the Tests. Used in a supportive role, the slow off-spinner only claimed seven wickets but, with his tight length and an added ability as ace slip fieldsman, was an integral part of the Bradman plan. In 1948, Johnson's most lucrative Test days lay ahead of him and he was to become captain of his country.

Unlike his off-turning predecessors of the past, Trumble and Noble, who both bowled at somewhere above medium pace, Ian Johnson was a genuine *slow* off-break bowler, a rare bird in the Australian cricketing aviary. Not really quick enough to take full advantage of a wet wicket, he was at his best on a harder or dustier pitch where he could use to the full his ability to bounce the ball and employ all the subtleties of flight.

Johnson's own bowling method counted against him in England in 1956 when Jim Laker so deceived leaden-footed Australian batsmen with his turn off the wicket that he took 49 wickets in five Tests. Johnson, on the other hand, was unable to get the ball to 'bite' on the soft pitches prevalent that year and had to be content with only six wickets in the entire rubber.

On the firmer wickets at home in Australia, and during tours of South Africa, West Indies and the Indian sub-continent, Ian Johnson was a far more formidable proposition. In 45 Tests he took 109 wickets at 29.19 runs apiece and certainly qualified as an all-rounder by gathering exactly 1000 runs.

Only one of two genuine wrist-spinners in the touring party was used by Bradman in the 1948 series. Douglas Thomas Ring would have prospered more fully in an age when spin was given priority over speed, but he twice claimed six wickets in a Test match innings and, with his ability as a grand striker of the ball, could certainly be classed as an all-rounder. The sturdy and studious Colin Leslie McCool, who bowled with a quaint, round-arm action, his arm often circling even lower than that of Clarrie Grimmett, was also a superb slip fieldsman and a free-scoring right-hand batsman who hammered 104 not out against England at Melbourne in 1946–47. McCool took 36 Test wickets at only 26.61 runs each and, like Ring, was denied opportunity because of the trend towards fast bowling vogue when both leg-spinners were in their prime.

Of the bowlers not aboard the boat to England in 1948 were a couple of spinners who had played for Australia two years before in 1946–47. Unorthodox left-hander George Edward Tribe played three Tests against Wally Hammond's 1946–47 tourists, but he lost control of his line and length and, as Ray Robinson described it, he became 'a lost Tribe'. Later in his career, Tribe became a successful all-rounder for Northamptonshire and was one of the stars of the Commonwealth teams that toured India in the mid-1950s. Bruce Dooland (who played with distinction for Nottinghamshire after a spell in the Lancashire League) also made a couple of Test appearances against England in 1946–47. But the competition among wrist-spinners for places in the Australian XI at the time (Ring, McCool, Tribe, Dooland) was such that Tribe and Dooland had no viable opportunity to further their international careers. On tour in India with the Commonwealth XI in 1950–51, Bruce Dooland hit two centuries in the unofficial Test series.

John Brian Iverson made his name famous as a 'mystery' spin bowler when England made its second post-war tour of Australia in 1950–51. Like B J T Bosanquet before him, the heavily-built 6 ft 2 in (188 cm) Iverson shook the cricket world by 'inventing' a new delivery. And he won his only series for Australia when he teased and tantalised Freddie Brown's batsmen to take 21 wickets at 15.23.

Iverson never played for Australia again but, allowing for the fact that he did not play major cricket until well into his 30s, could be well satisfied with his final results. As a bowler, his *piece de resistance* was an amazing delivery which he propelled on its way by flicking his middle finger, which had been neatly tucked *underneath* the ball. Iverson learned this cricket conjuring trick by experimenting with a celluloid table tennis ball and could bowl a leg-break or off-break by changing the position of his thumb.

Bill O'Reilly once wrote that Richie Benaud did not, as a leg-

Richie Benaud was one of Australia's best captains and kept googly bowling alive when seam bowling was more in fashion.

spinner, deserve to be counted among Australia's truly 'gifted' bowlers of that kind. Notwithstanding this apparently lone (though highly rated) opinion of him, it is not perhaps being too bold to suggest that Benaud did, for the best part of his playing career, almost singlehandedly keep alive in an age of seam, the leg-spin and googly heritage that was initiated by Hordern, Mailey, Grimmett *and* O'Reilly himself. Richie Benaud's finest Test bowling performance was achieved when the Australian captain employed a make-shift and unfamiliar technique to counter a nagging shoulder injury.

The scene was Old Trafford, Manchester, in 1961 with England needing 256 to win. At 150 for one wicket, and with the dour left-hander Subba Row in occupation at one end and England's dashing captain, 'Lord' Ted Dexter firing away at the other, Benaud decided to try bowling round the wicket. Although unable to spin the ball in his usual fashion, he pitched into the rough created by an England bowler's foothold. There followed an amazing England collapse that saw nine wickets tumble for 51 runs, Benaud gaining an analysis of 32−11−70−6, and Australia snatching victory from the jaws of defeat.

Under normal circumstances, Benaud's style of leg-spin bowling was of the classic nature: leg-break, googly and top-spinner, delivered with a high, free action. An advocate of persistent practice, he was a master of length and flight. Benaud could also bowl a puzzling delivery known as a 'flipper' (which was first developed by Bruce Dooland), a ball that cuts across from off to leg like a striking cobra having been spun out of the fingers − in effect, an off-spinning top-spinner. Benaud would also vary his attack constantly through use of pace and flight changes, often delivering the ball from different heights and angles in an effort to confuse the batsman. He was, above all else, a man who never gave up, no matter what the situation.

Colin Cowdrey has recorded that Benaud was more of a length bowler than a big spinner of the ball and that he was at his most dangerous 'bowling into a breeze blowing from the area of third man'. In all Test cricket, Richie Benaud claimed 248 wickets (at 27.03) and scored 2201 runs.

When the name Richie Benaud is mentioned, the name Alan Davidson springs immediately to mind. The career of Alan Keith Davidson ('Davo' to his mates) ran a close parallel to that of Benaud and the two all-rounders were often associated in match-winning performances, with bat, ball and in the field.

The partnership between these two grand players first prospered at the international level in South Africa in 1957−58. With a little help from their friends, 'Slasher' Ken Mackay and Jimmy Burke, Benaud and Davidson became pop heroes of the veld when they took Australia to a 3−0 win over a home team that had been counted firm favourites at the start of the series. On the tour, Benaud hit 817 runs at 51.06 and took 106 wickets at 19.40; Davidson made 813 runs at 54.20 and claimed 72 wickets at 15.13.

But, if any single match were to be chosen to illustrate the skills of these two great Australian all-rounders, it would have to be the famous tied Test against Frank Worrell's West Indies team at Brisbane in 1960−61. At Brisbane, left-handed 'Davo' carried the Australian bowling on his broad back on an unresponsive pitch to gain figures of 5/135 and 6/87, and hit 44 and 80, taking part in a second innings partnership with Benaud that set the match up for its thrilling climax. Australia eventually won that rubber against the West Indies, thanks mainly to the dynamic Davidson, who took 33 wickets at 18.54 in four Tests. Benaud was next best with 23 wickets at 33.86. Both players figured high in the batting averages.

The Benaud-Davidson bowling partnership was also very much in evidence when Peter May's England team was thrashed 4−0 in 1958−59. Although Australia's performance that season was marred by the 'chucking' controversy surrounding Ian Meckiff and Gordon Rorke, Benaud (31 wickets at 18.33) and Davidson (24 at 19.00) were the main reason for England's defeat.

Alan Davidson used his muscular six-foot (183 cm) frame to the full and bowled at a genuinely fast pace, although perhaps not quite up to the speed of Lindwall and Miller. Taking a short 15-pace run, he put back, arms, legs and all into a wheeling action that enabled him to extract lift from the deadest of tracks. What he may have lacked in style he made up for in almost super-human strength and resilience. As a batsman, Davidson's method was forthright and effective. Richie Benaud himself once wrote that, when Davidson had bat in hand, from a bowler or close fielder's point of view, it was a case of 'When you see that big right foot coming down the wicket, brother, you duck!'.

When Alan Davidson made his first cricketing trip for Australia to England in 1953, the young left-arm fast bowler's main challenger for a spot in the Test XI was the equally sturdily-built Queensland all-rounder Ronald Graham Archer. A right-hander who batted like a carbon-copy of Keith Miller, Archer could not, as a fast bowler, be regarded as 'quick' in the Lindwall sense of the term. Almost from the outset of his career Ron Archer fought a battle with a back problem, but claimed 48 wickets for Australia in 19 matches and often batted with skill and aplomb.

An unusual right-arm spin bowler who relied more on a lifting top-spinner than on any appreciable turn from off or leg was also a new boy in the 1953 Ashes team in England. John Charles Hill was already 30 when given his first chance in Test cricket and, in face of stiff competition from the likes of Ring and Benaud, was unable to establish a place in the Australian team.

A genuine fast bowler, the tall and well-built right-hander William Patrick Anthony Crawford was given a short run in the Australian team as Lindwall's aide when Australia went on to India after the 1956 England tour. Crawford had made his Test debut at Lord's, but pulled a muscle after only 29 balls. He grabbed seven wickets for 102 in two Tests against India before fading from the scene.

One of the most important bowlers in Richie Benaud's Test XIs of the late 1950s and early 1960s was one of the most unlikely of international bowlers, the perpetually gum-chewing Kenneth Donald Mackay. A uniquely phlegmatic and loyal player, 'Slasher' Mackay batted and bowled as if his very life depended upon the outcome of his unusual looking activity. Mackay's stamina was legend and he was used by Benaud to keep one end permanently plugged with his gentle but crafty right-arm medium-paced seamers, while the Australian captain and the other more recognised bowlers attacked from the other. Mackay ended with 50 good Test wickets to add to his doggedly accumulated 1507 runs.

A couple of Test bowlers of controversial action have been left for analysis in another chapter but there remain for mention a few spin bowlers who played for Australia during the 'Benaud' era. Of two unorthodox left-armers of the time, the agile Lindsay Francis Kline was the first to appear on the scene. Kline bowled the left-hander's off-break and googly with equal effect but, other than a useful performance alongside Benaud and Davidson in South Africa in 1957−58 and in India and Pakistan in 1959−60, did not quite reach the highest level as a Test bowler. Fellow left-hand 'Chinaman' bowler, the cheery little John Wesley Martin, was a far better bat than Kline and a player who might have become a leading Test all-rounder were it not for his frequently wayward bowling. A fairly prolific run-getter and wicket-taker for New South Wales, Johnny Martin sadly disappointed in most of his eight Tests for Australia.

Benaud's successor as Australian captain, Robert Baddeley Simpson, was another of those genuinely inspired players who might have played for his country as a batsman or as a highly capable leg-spin bowler (apart from his absolutely stunning ability in slips). In all first-class cricket Simpson took 349 wickets and frequently looked the part of a top drawer bowler in Shield and Test competition.

Six seam bowlers of varying pace complete the list of attackers who represented Australia during the Benaud reign. Three of these, Ian Meckiff, Gordon Rorke and Ken Slater, were, at one time or another, labelled 'chuckers' and Rorke was also criticised for his unusual drag when delivering the ball. Of the remainder, Ronald Arthur Gaunt and the massive 6 ft 3 in (190 cm) Desmond Edward Hoare, both right-arm fast-medium, failed in Tests. The right-arm fast Francis Michael Misson made his debut for Australia during the 1960−61 'tied Test' series against the West Indies and lasted some-what longer than Gaunt and Hoare. At a muscular 6 ft 3 in (190 cm) and revelling in the nickname 'Tarzan', Frank Misson played his best cricket at international level in support of Davidson and Garth McKenzie in England in 1961. When Benaud took his popular team to England that year, it included a strapping youngster of such magnificent physique that he was called 'Garth' by his team-mates, after the famous cartoon strip strongman. Graham Douglas McKenzie, right-arm fast bowler extraordinaire, was to become during the following 10 years the central pillar of the Australian bowling attack in more than 50 Tests.

As a 19-year-old, McKenzie literally burst onto the international scene when he surprised Sir Frank Worrell's 1960−61 West Indians with a 4/41 spell at Perth that took Western Australia to a 94-run win over the visitors at the start of their tour. Worrell was so impressed with the young fast bowler's pace and physique that he immediately predicted a great future for him.

McKenzie made his Test debut at Lord's in 1961, just two days before he turned 20, and celebrated his pending birthday by first assisting Ken Mackay in a 53-run ninth-wicket stand and then by proceeding to set Australia up for victory with a magnificent bowling spell of 29−13−37−5. A new Test bowling star had arrived.

By the time McKenzie had reached the age of 23, he had already

Australia's Graham McKenzie presents the perfect picture of a fast bowler's ideal follow through.

topped 100 wickets in Tests (in a shorter period of time that any other Australian bowler − 3 years, 165 days). Using his 6 ft 1 in (185 cm) to full advantage, he bowled off a fluid, long-striding nine-pace approach and used his unusual strength to generate great speed. The success of this fitness fanatic, teetotaller and non-smoker was based more on control, subtle change of pace and a magnificent outswinger than on pace.

Sadly, McKenzie's bowling declined in South Africa in 1969−70 after a gruelling tour of India where he had, as usual, virtually carried the Australian attack. Searing heat and the ever-present threat of crowd violence had taken its toll. The decision to arrange two major consecutive overseas tours contributed greatly to a fine bowler's departure from Test cricket when only 30. McKenzie ended his career with 246 Test wickets, two short of the then record-holder, Richie Benaud.

During his reign, the Australian fast bowling supremo of the 1960s received loyal support from a squad of fast-medium seam bowlers who, each in his own style, made a useful contribution to Australian cricket. The awkward chest-on delivery used by one of his main support bowlers was, for instance, the antithesis of McKenzie's own smooth and rhythmic style, but Neil James Napier Hawke provided a string of grand performances which resulted in 91 Test wickets in 27 games for his country.

A strong character in every sense of the term, Hawke may have topped his 100 wickets for Australia if he had not clashed with skipper Bill Lawry and decided, in 1968, to quit Test cricket and play in the Lancashire League. His best series performance came under the captaincy of Bobby Simpson, in the West Indies in 1964−65, when Hawke headed the averages with 24 wickets at 21.83, ahead even of the West Indies pair Griffith and Hall. Neil Hawke's brave fight against debilitating illness in recent years was an example to all.

Genial Alan Norman Connolly played a double role for Australia during McKenzie's days at the top. Another well-proportioned right-hander, he used the new ball when needed and then utilised his clever diversity of swing, cut and pace change to act as an ever-willing stock bowler. Connolly's most noble performance in international cricket was his 20 wickets at 26.10 in four Tests against Pollock and Richards in full cry in South Africa in 1969−70. With the lethargic and listless McKenzie completely out of luck and form, Connolly was forced to take over as senior seam bowler, his sole effective support coming from 'mystery' spinner, Johnny Gleeson. Connolly was the only bowler to twice take five wickets in an innings for his country.

Laurence Charles Mayne was another right-arm fast-medium bowler who experienced the frustration of trying to contain the rampant South Africans in 1969—70. Mayne had taken 4/43 and 4/56 in his first Test, versus West Indies at Kingston in 1964—65, but never matched his debut performance. Australian Rules football player Eric Walter Freeman, of South Australia, was another seam bowler who may prefer to forget the playing side of his South African visit in 1969—70. After the hiding he received at the hands of Pollock and company, Freeman dropped out of Test cricket. Lanky right-hand fast bowler David Alexander Renneberg came to similar grief on the previous Australian trip to South Africa, in 1966—67, when Springbok Denis Lindsay hooked him out of the park on more than a few occasions. An 'arm' bowler who did not use his strong physique efficiently, Renneberg never quite came to terms with the demands of Test cricket.

More impressive than Renneberg was the persevering Grahame Edward Corling. On the short side for a fast bowler, Corling bowled with a classic action reminiscent of Lindwall. But he lacked the pace of the fast bowling master and was not called up for Australia beyond the five Tests he played on his only tour to England in 1964.

Figures can sometimes be misleading when assessing a bowler's worth. A case in point would be the volatile Kenneth Douglas Walters who sent down a fair number of highly commendable overs for Australia without ever being talked about as a true Test all-rounder. Another top Australian run-maker, Robert William Cowper, was perhaps more of a genuine Test all-rounder than Walters and, with his flighty off-turners, took 36 Test wickets at 31.63 runs each.

Fast and fast-medium bowlers did not control events completely for Australia during the 1960s. Hefty Thomas Robert Veivers enjoyed one particularly busy season with his off-turners when Australia played in England in 1964. Although he only netted 11 wickets in the five-match series, Veivers broke all Australian records for number of balls bowled in an innings when he sent down 95.1 overs at Old Trafford. With Bobby Simpson contributing a dour 311, Australia had declared their first innings at 8 for 656 after batting into the third day. England's strong but tedious reply centred around the dead-bat technique of Ken Barrington, who eventually pushed, prodded and deflected his way to 256 in 685 minutes to take England to a total of 611.

Veivers bowled and bowled and, in one gargantuan spell, actually sent down 51 consecutive overs. His 571 balls in the England innings has only been exceeded by West Indies spinner Sonny Ramadhin, who bowled 98 overs (588 balls) against England, at Edgbaston in 1957. The popular Tom Veivers, whose left-handed hitting was always a delight to the spectators, was never again given a really extended bowling spell in Test cricket.

It was reputed that David John Sincock could produce the occasional 'unplayable' ball amid the erratic variety he sent up on his odd

Test appearance but, like so many of his kind, this wristy left-arm unorthodox bowler had as much success at maintaining consistent control of the ball as a small boy with his first yo-yo. A spectacular start to his first-class career was followed by a faltering follow-up and, in three Tests for Australia, Sincock totalled 8 wickets for 410 runs.

Right-arm googly bowler Peter Ian Philpott got his first chance at the big time after he had officially retired from first-class cricket, at the age of 29, and then returned to make an eventful comeback. Chosen unexpectedly for the 1964–65 West Indies tour, Philpott turned out to be the leading spinner in the party and played in all five Tests of a gruelling series. With 18 wickets at 34.94 in the Tests, he was second only to Neil Hawke in effectiveness, and overall on the tour was way ahead of Hawke (32 wickets) and the other Australian bowlers with 49 wickets in nine matches.

Philpott made an excellent start when given another chance, versus England in 1965–66 but, after taking 5/90 and 1/62 at Brisbane in a drawn match, faded somewhat in the next two games and lost his place in the Australian eleven. He may be most remembered in years to come as a cricket coach of great flair and inspiration.

Of Australia's leading batsmen who might also be considered trundlers of quality, Ian Chappell (leg-breaks) and Keith Stackpole (mostly top-spinners) filled in with useful effect from time to time, but it was only in 1968 that a new spinner appeared who could safely be compared to Benaud and the best slow bowlers of the past. To top it all, the new man was one of the variety known as a 'mystery' spinner, a perpetrator of unusual bowling tricks who used the bent-finger technique originally pioneered by Jack Iverson.

Like Iverson, John William Gleeson came rather late into Test cricket. He first played for New South Wales at 28, and a year later was chosen for Australia against India, in 1967–68, at Adelaide Oval. Johnny Gleeson did not cause much immediate consternation among batsmen who were, at home, accustomed to facing up to the magic of the likes of Bhagwat Chandrasekhar and a host of other spin bowlers of every hue and variety. It was not until the following season, when a Sobers-led West Indies team arrived, that the new mystery spinner came truly to the fore with 26 wickets in the five-match contest.

Although he was difficult to 'read' (Springbok Graeme Pollock for one admits that he was never able to fathom which way he would turn), Gleeson did not attain the figures he might have in Test cricket if he had been part of a spin-duo combination of the Grimmett-O'Reilly genus. His appearance on the Test scene occurred when the accent on pace and pace alone became the order of the day. One of Australia's finest off-spin bowlers, Ashley 'Rowdy' Mallett, was also around at the time and it was a case of Australia going in with one spinner at a time and seldom giving the two men a chance to operate in tandem.

Ashley Alexander Mallett was given his nickname to epitomise all that was foreign to his rather shy off-the-field nature. On the field he was as aggressive as any of his colleagues and gained a deserved reputation for his live-wire close fielding. Mallett did not prosper under the parsimonious captaincy of Bill Lawry, who, true to his own run-hungry nature, preferred to utilise bowlers who gave away nothing in their effort to trap a batsman into indiscretion. When his fellow spin-kinsman Ian Chappell took over the reins it was a different story and Mallett eventually became one of Australia's most successful off-break bowlers with 132 Test wickets.

Slim and 6 ft 3 in (190 cm), Mallett used his towering height with great skill and played first-class cricket from his first Shield game in 1967−68 right through to the 1980−81 season when he retired, aged 36.

During the 1970−71 season, when Ray Illingworth's England team defeated Australia 2−0 in a protracted and at times acrimonious series, a fast bowling 'find' who was destined to become a legend in his own time played his first Test for his country. Dennis Lillee eased himself into international cricket with 5 wickets for 124 at the Adelaide Oval, although a quick glance at the score-sheet of Lillee's first Test match could fool the uninformed.

The debut fast bowler's new-ball partner is listed as Thomson. It was, however, Thomson, A L ('Froggy' to his friends), and not Thomson, J R, who opened the bowling with Lillee at Adelaide. Alan Lloyd Thomson was a fiery character who bowled off the wrong foot after a staccato approach to the crease. Unfortunately his aggressive temperament was more potent than the pace he generated through the air and off the pitch and in four Tests Froggy Thomson's 12 wickets cost 54.50 runs apiece.

Pace humbled Australia in 1970−71, and the search was on for a bowler of speed to partner the new white hope, Dennis Lillee. Little did the departing English batsmen realise that in the not too distant future, they would be forced to face a pair of fire-breathing quickies comparable to the Gregory-McDonald and Lindwall-Miller rib-tickling acts of previous years.

18

Two little pals

'They gave the crowd plenty fun; Second Test and West Indies won . . .
The bowling was super-fine Ramadhin and Valentine.'
— Egbert Moore ('Lord Beginner')

When the West Indies won its first Test and series in England in 1950, the names Ramadhin and Valentine became forever enshrined in song in the 'Victory Calypso' written by Egbert Moore, who was known to his fans as 'Lord Beginner'. The two virtually unknown spin bowlers, one from Trinidad, the other from Jamaica, were serenaded on the streets of London and throughout the Caribbean islands and there were few who did not become familiar with the calypso chorus words: 'With those two little pals of mine, Ramadhin and Valentine.'

In his book on the 1950 West Indies tour, *Days at the Cricket*, John Arlott records: 'Ramadhin and Valentine, when the tour opened, were probably the greatest gamble that any touring side had ever taken for a Test series in England.' Up to the time when skipper John Goddard arrived in England with his Caribbean party towards the end of April 1950, the 21-year-old right-handed 'mystery' spinner, Sonny Ramadhin of Trinidad, and the 20-year-old slow left-arm orthodox Alfred Lewis Valentine from Jamaica, had between them taken part in barely half a dozen first-class matches.

By the end of the tour in September, the two unlikely West Indian heroes had humbled most of England's experienced batsmen and materially assisted the famous 'W' run-scoring formation of Worrell, Weekes and Walcott in gaining a shock 3−1 series victory. In a summing up of the season, the editor of *Wisden* wrote: 'Just as in the past there have been notable pairs of bowlers like Barnes and Foster, Hirst and Rhodes, Gregory and McDonald, Constantine and Martindale, Larwood and Voce, this West Indies couple became the talk of the cricket world.' (And, to add the names of another famous duo not included in the *Wisden* summation, not since the days of Grimmett and O'Reilly had a pair of spin bowlers so dominated a Test season.)

In all first-class matches Ramadhin took 135 wickets at 14.88 and Valentine 123 at 17.94; in the four Tests Valentine had 33 wickets at 20.42 and Ramadhin 26 at 23.23 − the remaining six regular bowlers used took 18 wickets between them at 39.66!

Sonny Ramadhin's hand was sometimes too quick for the batsman and, with his two-way spin, helped West Indies to a shock victory over England in 1950.

Until the first Test at Manchester Ramadhin and Valentine seldom bowled in tandem. At the Old Trafford ground they sent down between them almost 70 per cent of the overs bowled. Due to virtually the only batting lapse by the West Indians on the tour, England won the first Test by 202 runs — but with only one or two exceptions, England's batsmen were all at sea against the new Caribbean spin twins.

Valentine's remarkable debut figures of 50−14−104−8 in England's first innings remains a record for number of wickets taken in an innings on a Test debut. He might have bagged all 10 and he had

actually taken the first eight England wickets in a row before Ramadhin gained compensation for beating the bat all day without reward
by claiming the last two wickets. In England's second knock, the
tirelessly accurate Valentine again reached 50 overs with figures of
56−22−100−3, to give him 11 wickets for 204 in his first Test.
Ramadhin ended with match figures of four for 167, a result which
did not reflect the number of times he beat the bat but missed the
wicket.

The next Test at Lord's provided the inspiration calypso writer
Egbert Moore needed to eulogise his two 'little pals'. With the West
Indian batsmen (in particular burly Clyde Walcott) also putting their
game together, the tables were turned on England. This time
Ramadhin took most of the wickets while Valentine kept the batsmen
groping at the other end. Ramadhin's figures read: 43−27−66−5
and 72−43−86−6; Valentine returned 45−28−48−4 and 71−47−
79−3. Their combined figures reveal an incredible percentage of
maidens to overs and a run scoring rate of only 1.2 per over. And
England's batsmen included such worthies as Hutton, Washbrook
and Edrich!

The West Indies won by 326 runs at Lord's and went ahead in the
series when the next match at Nottingham was won by an equally
decisive 10 wickets (Worrell hit 261; Weekes 129). Ramadhin took
seven wickets in the match and Valentine five, with a rare first
innings breakthrough being made by new-ball bowlers Hines Johnson
and Frank Worrell in England's first innings.

In the final Test at the Oval West Indies won again, this time by
an innings and 56 runs, despite a brilliant 202 not out by England's
Len Hutton (he carried his bat through an innings of 344). And, it
was definitely a case of 'spin rules, OK?', with Valentine bagging
another 10−wicket haul, Ramadhin claiming four wickets and sometime off-spinning skipper John Goddard chipping in this time with a
match analysis of 5/36.

For a number of years the tiny, 5 ft 4 in (162 cm) Sonny Ramadhin
was regarded as something of a mystery spin bowler whose off-break
was almost impossible to detect from his leg-break. Both balls were
bowled from the back of his hand in the fashion of a normal leg-
breaker, but were finger spun rather than wrist spun. Ramadhin
bowled to an impeccable line and length and, like his pal Valentine,
was happy to keep going for as long as his captain needed him.

After his successful debut in England, the normally cheerful Sonny
Ramadhin came in for some stick from quick-footed batsmen in
Australia in 1951−52 (notably Harvey and Miller) and visibly lost
some of his former confidence and penetration. He continued to
produce the occasional match-winning spell for the West Indies until
1957, when England's Peter May and Colin Cowdrey, deciding to
treat him as a conventional off-break bowler, added 411 in England's

Opposite: The superbly
accurate Alf Valentine
formed with Ramadhin one
of the most effective spin
partnerships in Test
history.

512

second innings of the first Test at Edgbaston in one of the historic stands of Test history, and forever destroyed the myth of Ramadhin's mysterious two-way spin.

Ramadhin had mesmerised England's batsmen in the first innings with a return of 7/49 in 31 overs. During the long England second innings, Ramadhin sent down no fewer than 98 six-ball overs, a record in first-class or Test cricket, taking 2/179.

Although he kept his place in the West Indies team for another few seasons, Sonny Ramadhin was never again as successful as during the early 1950s. In 43 Tests he took 158 wickets at 28.98.

The tall, slim and bespectacled left-handed Alf Valentine delivered the ball with an easy action, almost square on to the batsmen, after just a couple of quick steps to the wicket. He was a length bowler par excellence who spun the ball so sharply that he had to treat his spinning finger each day with surgical spirits. Where Ramadhin failed against Australia's batsmen on their home turf in 1951–52, Valentine remained his team's most penetrative and least expensive bowler, taking 24 wickets at 28.79 in the Tests.

Valentine then went through a bad patch for a few years, exacerbated by illness during the 1957 tour of England, but came back strongly in Australia in 1960–61 when his experience made him an integral part of Frank Worrell's team. He was kept out of the West Indies team by the versatile Garfield Sobers on his final tour of England in 1963. In 36 Tests, Alf Valentine took 139 wickets at 30.32.

The inclusion of Ramadhin and Valentine in the 1950 West Indies team to tour England saw the omission of the bald-headed, short and stocky Wilfred Ferguson, a slow leg-break bowler from Trinidad who impressed against England in the Caribbean in 1947–48. On his home wicket at Port of Spain in 1947–48, Ferguson spun the ball so ably that he took 11 wickets in the match and was chief wicket-taker for West Indies in a four-match series with 23 at 24.65. Picked to tour India in 1948–49, and at home against England in 1953–54, he made little impression.

West Indies captain John Douglas Clyde Goddard was a Barbados all-rounder of note whose alternating medium-paced inswingers and slower off-breaks made him a useful fill-in bowler who gained the occasional success in Tests. But the most valuable bowler in the 1950 West Indies team, after Ramadhin and Valentine, proved to be a man who had toured England before the war as a batsman.

Gerald Ethridge Gomez, from Trinidad, was a reliable middle-order batsman who adapted his play well to suit the needs of his team. He suddenly emerged as a right-arm fast-medium bowler during the West Indies tour of India in 1948–49, taking 16 wickets in the Tests. The energetic Gomez's bowling opportunities in England in 1950 were limited, but when Ramadhin failed in Australia in 1951–52, Gomez took over as a stock seamer and produced his best international figures of 7/55 and 3/58, in the fifth Test in sweltering heat at Sydney. In his later years Gomez became a noted West Indies cricket administrator and has also stood as a Test umpire.

Denis St Eval Atkinson played for both Barbados and Trinidad and was another West Indies all-rounder of the period who put in some useful bowling work, with medium-paced right-arm off-cutters. He will, however, be remembered most for his participation with wicket-keeper Clairmonte Depeiaza in a match-saving 348-run seventh wicket stand against Australia at Bridgetown in 1954–55, during which Atkinson reached a double-century.

Of the West Indian fast bowlers who were around during the 1950s, the speediest was Hophnie Hobah Hines Johnson from Jamaica. The 6 ft 3 in (190 cm) right-arm Hines Johnson was already 37 when he played his first Test against England at Kingston in 1947–48, but maintained his pace throughout the match and, without resorting to bowling bumpers, took 5/41 and 5/55 on debut. Taken to England in 1950 at the age of 40, he played in two Tests but was given little work.

Prior Erskine Jones was a right-arm fast bowler from Trinidad who also played in only a couple of Tests in England in 1950 without being given much scope. Already 34 when he went to Australia in 1951–52, Jones was overworked when the West Indies spinners were mastered and did not appear again.

Another fast right-hander, Esmond Seymour Maurice Kentish, enjoyed a curious Test career in which he made his debut versus England at Kingston, Jamaica in 1947–48 (aged 31) and was then chosen again for one match against England at his home ground, Kingston, in 1953–54. In the second match, Kentish took 5/49 in England's second innings but was never picked again. Frank McDonald King, who played for both Barbados and Trindad, was another right-armer of the 1950s (and genuinely quick), who favoured the bouncer but, although given many opportunities, seldom did much in 14 Tests for West Indies.

In a round-up of the West Indian international bowlers of the 1950s, mention must be made of a man who, in his cricket and in his personal life, epitomised all that is best in West Indian cricket. Frank Mortimer Maglinne Worrell (later knighted for his services to cricket) was frequently given the new ball, bowling left-arm fast-medium with an easy action and swinging the ball with great control. Worrell also reverted to bowling left-arm spin at will and more than once put in a decisive spell in Tests with either method.

Although Worrell the batsman and all-rounder was a key member of the famous West Indies side of 1950, he belongs as well to another era when West Indies cricket began working up speed, metaphorically and factually, to the point where the team from the Caribbean was to become the undisputed best in world cricket.

19

Bedser, 'Fiery Fred', 'The Typhoon' and 'George'

'It has always been easier to obtain movement off the seam in England than in the other Test-playing countries...'

— Trevor Bailey

When England resumed Test cricket after the Second World War its bowling attack proved woefully under-equipped when asked to contain the likes of Bradman, Morris, Miller and company. There was, however, one man who stood head and shoulders above his fellow England bowlers, physically and in terms of performance. Day in, day out, Alec Victor Bedser was the one England attacker who could rank in skill and performance with the very best that Australia and any other country possessed.

Sir Neville Cardus called Alec Bedser the 'Gentle Giant', for others he was simply the 'Big Fella'. In the eyes of all of his contemporary players, he was the professional's professional. As Jim Laker, Bedser's Surrey and England colleague, once stated: 'In 1938 he decided to become a professional medium-fast bowler, and he subsequently became the best in the world.'

Bedser ran in over eight enormous strides, his approach to the wicket looking for all the world as if he were struggling to run uphill, and, as Laker puts it, 'every inch of his height and every ounce of his weight was contained in a perfect bowling action'. Such was the huge-framed Bedser's rhythm that he frequently exceeded 1000 overs in a season and rarely missed a match through injury.

He was not exclusively a new-ball bowler, as has been the case with some fast-medium bowlers, and could 'seam' an old ball with almost as much facility as when it was still shiny. Bowling to an awkward length that made a batsman waver as to whether to play forward or back, Bedser, as a result of his powerful body-swing, gained tremendous pace off the pitch. Any side-on photograph of Bedser at the moment of delivery conveys a perfect model for all bowlers: left arm pointed straight upwards; right arm diagonal — just prior to swinging round in a perfect circle.

The London *Times* cricket correspondent, John Woodcock, once commented: 'You always knew when Alec was in the mood. His head would start to bob about as he came in from his mark. Sometimes the earth would seem to shake. No one was safe on such days as these.'

Relying mainly on a controlled inswinger as his stock ball (to a leg-trap field), Bedser also became famous for his deadly leg-cutter, a delivery which inspired comparison with the great Sydney Barnes.

Bedser never gave up trying. After a sensational debut against India at Lord's and Old Trafford in 1946 (11 wickets in each of his first two Tests), he carried the England attack on his broad back in Australia in 1946−47. Receiving some support from leg-spinner Doug Wright, but little from anyone else (expect perhaps vice-captain Norman Yardley, who bowled his right-arm medium-paced deliveries to occasional surprising effect), Bedser was the only bowler to really trouble Bradman and his men. In England in 1948, the 'Big Fella' again spearheaded England's effort, and shouldered the main burden of its attack in a series that was again dominated by Australia.

After his many hours of toil for a losing team, Alec Bedser's reward eventually came when he bowled England to a turning-point

Alec Bedser, the 'Gentle Giant', was England's only bowling hope running into the 1950s.

victory with a brilliant 10-wicket haul in the fifth Test of 1950–51 against Australia at Melbourne (he took 30 wickets in the series at 17.10) and completed the job when England regained the Ashes during a 1953 home rubber.

The year 1953 represented the peak of Bedser's Test career. At Trent Bridge, in the first Test, only rain saved Australia after the big England bowler had taken seven wickets in each innings (7/55 and 7/44). As the series progressed, Bedser raised his total of wickets to 39 at 17.48, at the time a new record for an England bowler versus Australia. In the only decisive Test of the season at the Oval, which England won to take the rubber, Bedser had the satisfaction of dismissing both Australian openers, Hassett and Morris, early on the first day.

Gentle off the field but tough and competitive on it, Bedser always remained the perfect, conservative professional who knew and used all the tricks of his trade, but scorned the use of histrionics when appealing for a dismissal and encouraged his team-mates to do likewise. When he gave away playing he immediately began putting back into the game what he had received, as a Test selector and as president of Surrey County Cricket Club. His twin brother, Eric, has always been Alec Bedser's inseparable companion, at home and when touring abroad, and was himself a fine all-rounder who played many seasons for Surrey.

Of the seam bowlers who gave Alec Bedser support from time to time, Derbyshire's Clifford Gladwin was a lanky and lively bowler of mainly inswingers and an extrovert who coined the phrase, 'cometh the hour, cometh the man', when he won a famous Test against South Africa at Durban off the very last ball by allowing it to strike his amply padded behind and then running through for a sharp leg-bye. Gladwin was, unfortunately, no great success as a Test strike bowler. Nor was Lancashire's Richard ('Dick') Pollard, another right-arm fast medium bowler, who claimed 5/24 on his Test debut versus India in 1946 but was not quick enough to make any impression when taken to Australia in 1946–47.

Cliff Gladwin's new ball partner at Derbyshire, Herbert Leslie Jackson, was a true fast bowler who was unfortunate not to have played in Australia and who experienced a curious Test career of two matches spaced 12 years apart. Much feared as one of the meanest fast bowlers on the county circuit, Les Jackson had a Test against New Zealand in 1949, and then had to wait until 1961 to share the new ball with Fred Trueman at Leeds. Jackson's four wickets for 83 runs in that match, when he was already 40 years old, made something of a mockery of earlier selectorial decisions that had kept him out of Test cricket for a dozen years, when England was sorely pressed to find fast bowlers of class.

A similar case could be made for the less pacy, but no less effective

Derek Shackleton of Hampshire, a tireless and prolific wicket-taker at right-arm medium-pace who toured India in 1951−52 but only occasionally got the nod, for home Tests against West Indies and South Africa, and never appeared against Australia.

Harold James Butler, a fast-right arm bowler who succeeded Larwood in the Nottinghamshire county side, was another sometime Test cricketer who might have played more frequently for England were it not for the war and injury problems. Against South Africa at Leeds in 1947 Butler took seven wickets in the match, but broke down when taken to the West Indies in 1947−48 after he had played in just one more Test and added five wickets to his bag.

Another West Indies tourist in 1947−48 was Lancashire captain Kenneth Cranston, an all-rounder whose right-arm fast medium deliveries brought 18 wickets in eight Tests against South Africa (1947), West Indies and Australia (1948).

Bedser's first meaningful new-ball partner was Trevor 'Barnacle' Bailey, who supplemented his dour, defensive forward-prod batting and brilliant close fielding with more than lively right-arm fast-medium deliveries that brought him 132 wickets to add to his 2290 runs and 32 catches in 61 Tests.

Trevor Edward Bailey of Essex was a true all-rounder and a grand competitor who gave of his best when the chips were down. With his high, energetic action, Bailey was a finer sight as a bowler than as a batsman. On his Test debut versus New Zealand at Leeds in 1949, Bailey made the ball fly about quite alarmingly and took 6/118 against a powerful Kiwi batting line-up. He added figures of 6/84 in the third Test that season at Manchester and was soon being spoken of as England's new fast bowling hope. When he first went to Australia in 1950−51, Bailey took 13 wickets in the first two Tests before being sidelined by injury.

Although he never became a destructive fast bowler of the Larwood/Trueman type, Trevor Bailey certainly exerted his personality on every game in which he played and won more than one Test for England with his fine command of swing and cut. At Johannesburg in 1956−57, all reports predicted a South African victory after a poor England batting start, but Bailey proceeded to destroy the Springboks' middle order in the first innings and followed through with match-winning figures of 5/20 in the second. His most decisive Test bowling spell came against West Indies at Kingston in the final Test of 1953−54, when his stunning 16−7−34−7 performance on the opening day on a perfect batting strip ensured victory for England and evened the series.

When his side was struggling with injuries in Australia in 1950−51, brave-hearted England captain Frederick Richard Brown changed a life-long bowling style when he switched from his normal leg-breaks and 'googlies' to right-arm medium-fast cutters. The metamorphosis was so complete that a slow bowler who had failed to gain a Test place against Australia before the war (Brown was a member of Jardine's 1932−33 party) now became the most successful wicket-taker of the series after Alec Bedser. With 5/49 in the fifth Test at Melbourne his best effort (England won its only Test of the series), Freddie Brown, at the age of 40, took 18 wickets at 21.61, batted with immense courage and determination, and led his team from the front at a time when England's cricketing fortunes were dismally low.

Brown's performances in Australia in 1950−51 raised his team's morale and inspired a revival. He was, however, soon to hand over the England captaincy to the first professional player to lead his country on a regular basis, the experienced and Test-proven York-shireman Len Hutton.

Another Yorkshireman of rather more tender years had been intro-duced as Alec Bedser's opening partner with devastating results against India in 1952, and had sorely tested the Australian batsmen at the Oval in 1953 in a match that had at long last brought England the Ashes. Frederick Sewards Trueman had arrived and was destined to become the most consistently successful English bowler of true pace since Harold Larwood and, arguably, even perhaps the finest English all-round fast bowler in history.

'Fiery Fred' Trueman became to an entire generation of English cricket followers something of a symbol of the return of the genuine fast bowler to England's cricket fields, after a pace-starved post-war period. For the first six or seven overs, Trueman was the most destructive fast bowler of his time. The entire 1952 Indian team must bear witness to that fact − and all the other sides he destroyed during a 20-year career that took in 459 first-class matches and brought the fast bowler 2304 wickets.

The Indian batsmen of 1952 did not quite know what hit them. England won three of the four Tests played (and would have won the fourth but for rain) by huge margins. Trueman, in his debut series, took 29 wickets at 13.31 in seven innings, including a blistering 8/31 stint at Manchester.

At Leeds in the first Test, India's second innings scoreboard at one point read: Runs 0, Wickets 4. The *Daily Express* spoke of India's leading batsmen 'playing like blind men in a minefield' and described Trueman bowling to India's top player, Vijay Hazare, when the young bowler was on a hat-trick after having taken two wickets in two balls: 'He roared to the wicket, the ball sped like a bullet, Hazare waited for the crash of splintered wood or flesh and bone but heard only the rush of air and the smack of collision with Godfrey Evans's gloves. Says Trueman: "The first he saw of it was when Godfrey tossed it back to me".'

With big Alec Bedser offering encouragement from the other end,

The Indians of 1952 didn't know what hit them when Yorkshire's Freddie Trueman was given the new ball opposite Bedser. Trueman went on to take 307 Test wickets.

and no respite for the beleaguered visiting batsmen, Trueman was given his head, charging in and bowling at a speed not seen from an Englishman in 20 years. As Frank Tyson once commented, the 5 ft 10 in (178 cm) Trueman was 'no Greek statue', but his strong frame was supported by superbly muscular legs. Like Larwood before him, he had the broad back and arms of a coalminer (both men worked for a time in the pits) and his parabolic approach from the region of mid-off was smoothly punctuated with long athletic strides. Also like Larwood, Trueman's left arm went up high before his swinging delivery and follow through, his left foot slamming the turf, his metal-capped toe acting as a brake as he dragged his right foot behind him. His classic fast bowler's action, like that of Larwood and the Australian Lindwall, resulted in what Tyson describes in his *Great Bowlers* as a 'boomeranging out-curve'.

Down the years Freddie Trueman added many tricks to his bowling bag, compensating for any limitations imposed by age. At the end of his career Trueman was as dangerous a bowler as at the beginning. There was always the feeling that Freddie Trueman knew he was the greatest, that there was no doubt in his own mind that it was so, and that this totally positive attitude to his game ensured that he bowled at his best at all times.

It was perhaps not unexpected that a man of Fred Trueman's forthright and positive approach would have had some clashes with authority. He was, it has been claimed, left out of a number of England touring teams for reasons other than talent. It is a peculiar logic indeed that leads to the omission of the best bowler in the land simply because he is outspoken and refuses to bow to 'tin-pot' authority. Trueman first went to Australia in 1958−59 at the age of 27, more than six years after he had slaughtered the Indians. He should have toured with Tyson and Staham in 1954−55; if he had been an Australian, he would have not have been allowed to 'vegetate' for so long.

A record of Trueman's many fast bowling exploits of note would fill an entire volume. Among the best highlights were his 11 wickets for 88 in the Leeds Test of 1961 that sent Australia crashing to defeat and his 5/75 and 7/44 versus West Indies at Edgbaston in 1963 that gave England its only win in a series dominated by Hall, Griffith and Sobers. Trueman, with scant support, took 34 wickets at 17.47 in that 1963 series. In his 67 Tests, Freddie Trueman took 307 wickets at 21.57 and retired as the first player to have topped the 300 mark.

Off the field, Freddie Trueman remains his own man and a cricketing character whose humour, though sometimes a bit abrasive, is legend. The writer will certainly never forget an evening spent at the Breweries Pub, alongside Newlands cricket ground in Cape Town some years ago, when the Yorkshire and England bowler had the members of the Cape Town Sportswriters' Club in fits during three uninterrupted hours of stories and anecdotes.

The Trueman temperament is wonderfully illustrated in a story told by Yorkshire skipper Brian Close in his *I Don't Bruise Easily*. The final innings of a Scarborough Festival match in 1963 started with Trueman needing three wickets for his 100 for the season. He took a quick wicket at the start of the match to make it 98 but, to his disgust, was promptly taken off by Close who did not want to finish the match off too early. Close continues the story: 'Finally, when our opponents had reached 183 for 8, I called down to the boundary:

"Come on, Fred. Finish it off." He roared back: "Stick your so-and-so ball. I'm not bloody bowling." "Fair enough," I said.'

In *From Larwood to Lillee*, an appraisal of fast bowlers which he co-authored with Trevor Bailey, Fred Trueman states: 'Whenever there is talk about fast bowling, I always say without fear of contradiction that the quickest bowler I have ever seen, or played against, was Frank Tyson.' The 1956 *Wisden* confirms this lofty assessment: 'Not for a long time has a star burst upon the cricket firmament with such startling suddenness as has been the case with Frank Holmes Tyson, the Northamptonshire and England fast bowler.' But, like Halley's Comet, Tyson 'the terrible' was to be on view in Test cricket, in all his blazing glory, for just a few short seasons (and one in particular in Australia).

Former England captain Freddie Brown was the first to take note of the potential of the 22-year-old tearaway with the build of a boxer when Tyson made his first-class debut against the hapless Indian touring team in 1952. Running in from a mark that was placed about 70 yards from the wicket-keeper, the young fast bowler took only one wicket in that match, Indian opener Pankaj Roy for a duck. In the following season, Tyson rocked Australia's batsmen back on their heels when he took wickets with the second and fourth balls of a fiery first over bowled at them for his county, Northamptonshire. Wise Freddie Brown did not over-bowl his young protege and the Australians recovered from their initial shock. But the die had been cast; 14 months later the young Tyson was en route to Australia with Len Hutton's MCC team, and poor Fred Trueman was left at home.

Weathering the trauma of a 1/160 return in the first Test at Brisbane, Tyson, under the watchful and expert eye of Len Hutton, moved from strength to strength until not one Australian batsman could truthfully say that he was not overawed by the sheer power and speed of the new England 'find'.

At Sydney in the second Test, Tyson tilted a closely-fought game England's way with one of the most frightening bursts of pace bowling ever seen in Test cricket. Coming in off a shorter run that he had used in England, Tyson seemed to have gained in speed. After a rather stiff-jointed approach his left leg would kick high and then stamp down into the turf and he would rely for his velocity on sheer strength, his basic action lacking the body swing of more classical fast bowlers like Lindwall and Trueman.

Tyson took 4/45 and 6/85 at Sydney. In the following Test at Melbourne he was even more frightening, taking 7/27 in a second innings spell that sent the Australian batsmen reeling against the ropes like punch-drunk boxers. In the five Tests, Tyson grabbed 28 wickets at 20.82. If he could have 'dropped' his miserable first Test his figures would have read 27 wickets for 423 runs, average 15.66!

The Brisbane Test, incidentally, marked the beginning of the end for old war horse Alec Bedser, who took 1/131 and was then left out of the England team for the remainder of the rubber when Hutton decided he needed all-rounder Bailey as a back-up to Tyson and the quick and accurate Brian Statham. Bedser played in only one more Test, versus South Africa at Old Trafford in 1955.

So 1954—55 was Tyson's year, but the physical strain imposed on his body by an unorthodox action put horrendous strain on his legs and ankles. As Fred Trueman points out, 'once his terrific pace had gone, he had nothing to fall back on'. South African spectators wondered what all the excitement had been about when they saw a shadow of the former Tyson bowl in their country in 1956—57, although he did take eight wickets in the fifth Test at Port Elizabeth, but off a shortened run and at no more than fast-medium pace.

When he retired from cricket Frank Tyson migrated to Australia, scene of his brief but glorious cricket conquests. There he coached and wrote about the game he so loves before returning to England in 1987 after almost 30 years.

While Frank Tyson was firing away in all his fury downwind against the Australians in 1954—55, his 'partner-in-crime', the honest and reliable Lancashireman John Brian Statham, bowled into the breeze with a combination of what John Arlott terms 'supple speed and uncomplicated wisdom'.

Like Barnes, Wilfred Rhodes and Bedser before him, Brian Statham (or 'George' as he was universally known because of his facial resemblance to war-time entertainer George Formby) was a bowler's bowler who never gave less than his best. His surging 22-yard run, high action and curious double-jointed whip of the wrist during delivery were all part of a smooth and professional approach that carried him through thousands of overs for Lancashire and England during more than 20 years of cricket.

Although Frank Tyson enjoyed star billing in Australia in 1954—55, Brian Statham also had his moments. At Melbourne, in the third Test, he took 5/60 in Australia's first innings; at Adelaide in the fourth match, Statham made the essential breakthrough to victory when he removed McDonald, Miller and Maddocks in his first three overs on the final morning after having cut a hole in his left boot to allow an injured toe to move freely.

Brian Statham's 252 wickets in 70 Tests were taken against every one of the cricketing nations and against each he enjoyed more than one great moment of glory. The South Africans who faced him at Lord's in 1955 will never forget him, or how he dismissed their talented opener, little Jacky McGlew, for a 'king pair' — caught by 'keeper Godfrey Evans's first ball in the first innings; trapped leg-before-wicket first ball in the second. Against New Zealand at Auckland in 1954—55, his figures were 4/28 in the first knock and

Opposite: England's Frank Tyson was a short-lived but highly destructive 'Typhoon' and one of the fastest bowlers of all time.

524

9−3−9−3 in the second when the home team was bowled out for the all-time low Test score of 26 (Tyson 7−2−10−2; Appleyard 6−3−7−4; Wardle 5−5−0−1). Versus India in 1959, Statham bagged 17 wickets at just 13.11 apiece in three Tests; in three games against Pakistan in 1962, he took 16 at 17.37.

And when, at the age of 35, he was recalled to the England team in 1965 to try and counter the brilliant batsmanship of Graeme Pollock, Barlow and Bland after a couple of years in the outer, the ever-loyal, ever-willing Statham made sure that England would not lose the match with 24.2−11−40−5 in the Springboks' first innings.

After the tour, it was revealed that South African skipper Peter van der Merwe had instructed his men never to mention the names of Statham or Trueman, for fear that the England selectors may get it into their heads to choose one or both of the veteran fast bowlers, who, despite their years, were secretly more highly rated by the Springboks that any other seam bowlers in England at the time.

Trueman, Statham and, for a short period, Tyson were the more visible English fast bowlers of the 1950s and early 1960s. There were one or two others of reasonable pace, and a veritable army of seam exponents, ranging in pace from medium to fast-medium.

Surrey's Peter John Loader, right-arm, hostile and, on his day, as fast as anyone except perhaps Tyson, was unfortunate to play in the same era as so many fine English quick bowlers. At any other time when the cupboard was a little more bare he would have been an automatic choice. In South Africa in 1956−57, Loader looked infinitely more dangerous than, and outbowled, Frank Tyson.

The equally pacy Middlesex right-armer Alan Edward Moss was reputed to have once sent down a bouncer at Kingston, Jamaica, that hit the sight screen first bounce. 'Amos' was a great trier whose best spell in a Test came on his home ground, Lord's, in 1960 when he took 4/35 against South Africa as first change to Trueman and Statham.

Two Worcestershire bowlers who tried for England in the early 1960s were considered one of the most deadly strike forces in county cricket, but could not quite get a footing in international cricket. Both were right-armers; the faster of the two, big red-haired John Alfred Flavell was considered as quick as most on the county circuit, but was a disappointment in Tests against Australia in 1961 and 1964. Leonard John Coldwell was more of a medium-fast swing bowler in the Bedser mould who also failed when picked against Australia, but who had some days of success against Pakistan in 1962.

Alan Brown (Kent), David Robert Smith (Gloucestershire) and David William ('Butch') White were all right-armers of varying pace and method who toured India and Pakistan in 1961−62 without doing sufficiently well to merit further consideration.

Middlesex's right-arm fast John Sidney Ernest Price suffered frequently from injury but, when firing on all cylinders, would gain bounce from the deadest of tracks. He bowled with some result in India in 1963−64 as did, at times, the Essex all-rounder Barry Rolfe Knight. Knight, who later moved to Leicestershire, was a dashing batsman who hit two Test centuries and a right-arm fast-medium bowler who sometimes tested the best of batsmen. Knight toured Australia and New Zealand under Ted Dexter in 1962−63 and under Mike Smith in 1965−66, as well as playing the odd home Test as a third seamer. Sometime England captain and star attacking batsman 'Lord' Edward Ralph Dexter was himself a right-arm bowler of some ability and a useful partnership breaker at medium pace.

The unusually tall 6 ft 7½ in (202 cm) John David Frederick Larter was Tyson's successor as strike bowler for Northamptonshire and bowled right-arm at a good pace off 10 huge strides that covered 20 yards. Plagued by injury, Larter retired early, at the age of 27, having taken 37 wickets at 25.43 in 10 rather widely-spaced Tests for England.

Glamorgan's big and strapping left-arm quickie Ivor Jeffrey Jones, of smooth action and menacing pace, teamed up fairly successfully with Warwickshire's 6 ft 4 in (193 cm) robust, right-arm fast-medium David John Brown as England's spearhead in Australia in 1965−66. Jones retired a couple of years later when he tore the ligaments in his elbow, but Brown went on to take 79 wickets in 26 Tests, including a devastating 5/42 at Lord's in 1968 that saw Australia put out for 78. All-rounder Barry Knight grabbed 3/16 in the same innings.

Left-arm fast Frederick Edward Rumsey moved from Worcestershire to Somerset before being first picked for England against Australia in 1964. The rather bulky Fred Rumsey bowled well in a few more Tests against New Zealand in 1965, but then lost his place after the first Test against South Africa in the same season.

A younger and far more agile fast bowler of immense promise (he made his debut against New Zealand a couple of Tests previously) took the new ball in place of Rumsey in the second South African Test of 1965. The 1965 season also marked the close of Fred Trueman's long and distinguished sojourn as England's fast bowling supremo. But John Snow of Sussex was making ready to take on the old master's fast bowling mantle.

20

Laker's ten

'To have been a participant in "Laker's Match" is a milestone to remember. I am proud to have caught one of the celebrated nineteen and have mixed feelings having caught out the twentieth.'

— Colin Cowdrey

Surrey off-break expert James Charles Laker will always have his name enshrined in cricket's record books as the first bowler in history to take all 10 wickets in a Test innings. He achieved the impossible versus Australia at Old Trafford, Manchester, in the fourth Test of 1956, where he ended with figures of 9/37 and 10/53 in the match. Laker then went on to raise his total of wickets for the five match series to 46 at a phenomenal 9.60 each.

It is quite feasible that his 10 wickets in a Test innings record will one day be equalled, and that Laker's 19 wickets in the match may also one day be topped. For Laker, there was no breathtaking wait in anticipation that he might reach the magic 20. Early on in the Australian first innings, the amply proportioned but remarkably agile Colin Cowdrey had pocketed a catch at slip from Australia's dour Jimmy Burke off the bowling of the painfully unfortunate left-arm spinner Tony Lock. Throughout the two Australian innings, Lock matched his Surrey mate Laker ball for ball in skill and penetration to end the match with figures of one wicket for 106 (69 overs; 33 maidens). Amid opposition cries that the pitch had been specially tailored to suit the England off-break bowler, Laker's match return (on a wicket that Cowdrey later claimed was nowhere near as menacing as the results would have indicated) was the absolutely staggering 68−27−90−19!

The next best figures in Test cricket is the 17/159 performance put up by England's turn-of-the-century ace Sydney Barnes versus South Africa at Johannesburg in 1913−14. The list of bowlers who have taken 15 and more wickets in a single Test is:

19/90	J C Laker	Eng v Aust at Manchester	1976
17/159	S F Barnes	Eng v S. Africa at Johannesburg	1913−14
16/137	R A L Massie	Aust v Eng at Lord's	1972

15/28	J Briggs	Eng v S. Africa at Cape Town	1888−89
15/45	G A Lohmann	Eng v S. Africa at Pt Elizabeth	1895−96
15/99	C Blythe	Eng v S. Africa at Leeds	1907
15/104	H Verity	Eng v Aust at Lord's	1934
15/123	R J Hadlee	N. Zealand v Aust at Brisbane	1985−86
15/124	W Rhodes	Eng v Aust at Melbourne	1903−04

On his way to first innings figures of 9/37 against Australia at Manchester, the always serene and undemonstrative Jim Laker at one point claimed seven wickets for only eight runs while the last eight Australia wickets fell for 22. All out for 84, Australia followed on, facing an England total of 459. On his way to 89, Colin McDonald (before being almost inevitably caught off Laker) proceeded to play one of the finest rearguard innings of the Ashes series, holding firm for a little over five and a half hours.

Tony Lock admitted years later that, as the innings progressed, he became more and more tense because he had failed to take a wicket while his partner was picking them up like ripe cherries. Lock's co-ordination suffered, and so too did his chance of capturing the wickets he deserved.

In contrast, Laker bowled his off-breaks to perfection throughout the two Australian innings. As Colin Cowdrey recalled in an article in *The Cricketer International*: 'It was his perfect rhythm that I remember so well about Jim Laker's performance. He was never in a hurry; slow and precise in all his movements; no histrionics. A lovely approach to the wicket, high action and a solid follow through utterly without flourish.' Laker, it can safely be said, presented to the world the perfect off-break bowler's action.

Laker once commented in *Wisden Cricket Monthly* that he did not consider his 19/90 feat against Australia at Manchester his best international performance. He referred instead to his experience at Bombay in 1950−51 when, bowling for a Commonwealth team versus India, he sent down 50 overs in a single day and ended an Indian innings that lasted two days in high temperature and humidity, with figures of 64.5−34−88−5. Another startling Laker performance was his almost unbelievable 14−12−2−8 spell for England versus the Rest in a Test trial match at Bradford in 1950 (The Rest totalled 27). In Tests in England, his outstanding feats against all-comers are too numerous to recall. On the hard wickets of Australia, South Africa and the West Indies, Laker was not quite the force he had been on his softer home pitches. Nevertheless, his 193 wickets at 21.24 in 46

The perfect off-spinning action of England's Jim Laker, the only bowler to take 10 wickets in a Test innings.

Tests confirmed the credentials of a bowler whom many critics have named as the best of his type.

Some Test and county batsmen have claimed that Lancashire's Roy Tattersall was an even better off-break bowler than Laker. As tall as Laker, Tattersall's combination of pace, variation and accuracy made him a menace on the county circuit for a decade. Tattersall only appeared in 16 Tests, but took 58 wickets and on more than one occasion bowled England to victory, notably in matches against New Zealand and South Africa. But 'Tatt' was given little chance against Australia, although he made his Test debut there in 1950–51 when he and a youthful Brian Statham were flown out as replacements for an ailing team. Tattersall went on to take 6/44 in a Test against New Zealand at Wellington.

Sir Neville Cardus once wrote about Laker's Surrey and England 'spin twin', Graham Anthony Richard Lock, that he was 'always in the game'. As a left-arm foil to Laker against Australia in 1956, Tony Lock was superb. In two separate styles he was perhaps the premier left-arm orthodox spin bowler of his day, his only competition for the title coming from fellow-England player Johnny Wardle.

Tony Lock was another of those 'cricketers' cricketer' whose presence was always apparent in any match in which he played, whether bowling his pin-point accurate left-arm spinners, batting with belligerency or fielding like two men in his exclusive 'suicide' position on the leg side.

Sun gleaming on his prematurely balding brow, Lock bowled left-arm spinners from 1946 to 1950 with technical perfection. Then he altered his technique to suit the slow wicket at Surrey's home ground, the Oval, becoming almost medium-fast. And when Lock unleashed his faster one, it would stun batsmen with its new-ball pace through the air and off the pitch. Then came the dark days when 'Beau' Lock was called as a 'chucker' (he was no-balled for throwing in a Test at Kingston, Jamaica). Fighting back in typical fashion, he altered his action totally, reverting to the pluperfect left-arm spin bowler, with flight, length, line and spin predominating.

Tony Lock took 174 wickets at 25.58 in 49 Tests. At the age of 34, he responded to being omitted from the England team to tour Australia in 1962–63 by migrating to Australia. There he began a marvellous nine-year 'second' career for Western Australia, as a spin bowler and as a tough and inspiring captain who had a hand in the early development of a number of outstanding Australian Test players, including Dennis Lillee and Rodney Marsh. Lock's impact on Western Australian cricket was astonishing; he quickly led his State to Sheffield Shield honours and, in no time at all, Western Australia was supplying a third of the Australian side.

Tipping the scales at 17 stone (108 kg), towards the end of his career, Tony Lock became such a 'dinkum' Aussie that Jim Laker wrote the following about him during the 1976—77 Centenary Australia-England Test: '. . .I was never wholly sure whether he was on our side or not. His admiration for the professionalism of Geoff Boycott was patently obvious, yet there was no doubt that pride and joy was written all over his face when one of his own boys from Perth, Kim Hughes, was so rightly named as Man of the Match.'

Tony Lock's main rival for the left-hand spinner's berth in the England eleven was Yorkshire's John Henry Wardle, whom Jim Laker considered to be the best slow left-arm bowler he had seen on all types of wicket. Happy-go-lucky Johnny Wardle (or 'Happy go Johnny' as the title of his autobiography calls him) gained a reputation as one of cricket's great clowns; with a ball in his hand he was no joke. Although Tony Lock frequently got the nod ahead of him for Tests in England, Wardle was generally the superior performer in Australia, the West Indies and South Africa.

South Africans, for one, will want to forget the Wardle of 1956—57, who wrecked their strong-on-paper batting side with his unorthodox 'Chinaman' bowling. Wardle's strength lay in his ability to bowl in two distinct styles — mainly orthodox left-arm spin in England and back-of-the-hand left-hander's off-breaks (to the right-handed batsman), plus a marvellous 'bosie' when conditions overseas did not favour conventional spin.

For Yorkshire, Wardle carried on the long tradition of left-arm spin bowlers, following in the footsteps of Peate, Peel, Rhodes and Verity, although his forthright personality eventually saw him clash with county authority and saw his invitation to tour Australia in 1958—59 withdrawn. He nevertheless took 102 wickets at only 20.39 in 28 Tests. Had he been blessed with the temperament of a Rhodes or Verity, he would surely have taken many more.

One of the famous stories about Wardle and his on-field hi-jinks concerned a young West Indian batsman, in a match played on a matting wicket, who dropped his bat and gloves on the ground when the drinks appeared. Wardle promptly hid the bat under the mat and, when play was due to restart, pretended that he had hidden it under his jumper. A chase ensued, Wardle heading for the boundary with the young batsman after him!

During the height of the bottle-throwing incident which almost turned into a riot when England played West Indies at Georgetown in 1953—54, Wardle helped defuse the situation by collecting a half-dozen bottles, pretending to drink the contents, and then staggering around, acting 'drunk'.

Johnny Wardle made his Test debut against West Indies in 1947—48. Middlesex left-arm spinner John Albert Young preceded him into the England eleven versus South Africa in 1947, was not picked for the Caribbean tour, but for a couple of seasons was more or less first choice slow left-hander for England. Jack Young was a dapper little man and, like Wardle, something of a wit, but in a more subdued and subtle manner. Young's approach to bowling was totally professional, with an overriding emphasis on length and direction. Against Australia at Trent Bridge in 1948, he started his first spell against the tourists with 11 consecutive maidens (Bradman was batting at the time) but his overall Test record was disappointing and he soon gave way to Wardle and Lock.

Worcestershire's Richard Howorth, another raconteur of note but who reserved most of his wit for off-the-field occasions, played five Tests as a left-arm spinner against South Africa and West Indies in the 1940s. Dick Howorth was a fine left-hander of the traditional school (and an occasional seamer) whose career was interrupted by war. Howorth was already 38 when he made his bow for England with six wickets in the final Test of 1947 against South Africa. In the West Indies in 1947–48, Howorth teamed up with Jim Laker as one of England's only two successful bowlers on tour, taking 16 wickets in the four Tests. Noted for his calm demeanour, he was also a batsman of note who frequently opened for his county; he achieved the double of 1000 runs and 100 wickets three times.

Another county left-hand slow bowler who had a few games for England in the 1950s was Lancashire's Robert Berry, who took nine wickets in his first Test against West Indies at Old Trafford in 1950 but experienced a dreadful time on the hard Australian wickets in 1950–51. Bob Berry had to contend for a place in the Lancashire side with another left-hander, Malcoim Jameson Hilton who, with Roy Tattersall, bowled England to victory over India in the Test at Kanpur in 1951–52 but who received little chance in home Tests.

Of the very few post-war leg-break and googly bowlers to join pre-war men like Wright and Hollies as contenders for an England place, Howarth's Worcestershire team-mate Roland Oliver Jenkins was unlucky to miss out on a trip to Australia. When taken to South Africa in 1948–49, Jenkins, among the recognised bowlers, topped the bowling table for both Tests and tour and took 20 more wickets than anyone else. Employing a bowling action that has been described as 'reminiscent of a crab' or of a 'nautical roll', the broad-shouldered 'Roley' Jenkins was built like a middleweight boxer but behaved like a boy in his first prep school match whenever he claimed a wicket. His enthusiasm carried forward into Jenkins's batting and fielding to make him a valuable all-rounder.

Another googly bowler, Thomas Peter Bromley Smith from Essex, suffered a cruel hoax in 1933 when he received a telegram inviting him to play for England versus West Indies at the Oval. On arrival, a disappointed Smith discovered that the message was false and he had to wait another 13 years, when he was chosen against India in 1946. Peter Smith, who was later well known as a respected cricket writer, played a couple more Tests in Australia in 1946−47, but his three wickets in Tests cost 106.33 runs apiece.

Yorkshire's Edward Leadbeater was equally a failure as a leg-spinner cum 'bosie' bowler in India in 1951−52. The only other post-war leg-break bowler of any consequence to represent England in the 1950s and early 1960s was Lancashire's Thomas Greenough. Greenough came in to bowl off a long bouncing run to take 14 wickets in two Tests versus India in 1959, but was not picked for the Tests when taken on the following winter tour to the West Indies.

During the season that Frank Tyson's fast bowling terrorised Australia in 1954−55, Yorkshire's Robert Appleyard was one of two spin bowlers (the other was Wardle) to pick up some of the left-overs. But, in the crucial fourth Test at Adelaide, it was the medium-paced off-breaks of Bob Appleyard that actually set England up for victory. A tall man bowling with a high action, Appleyard's bounce contributed to Australia's second innings downfall at a stage when the game had been evenly balanced. During the course of six overs, in which he gave away just six runs, the quickish off-spinner removed Morris, Burke and Harvey − three of Australia's main batting hopes − thus paving the way for Tyson and Statham to quickly finish off the innings on the final morning and give England a chance to seal the series.

Another off-spinner who used his height very effectively was Gloucestershire's John Brian Mortimore, who acquitted himself well when flown to Australia as a late replacement in 1958−59, although his eventual overall Test record was unimpressive. Mortimore's Gloucestershire team-mate, David Arthur Allen, was very much more productive at Test level, with 122 wickets in 39 games for England against most of the other Test-playing countries. Allen was noted as a bowler who kept his length, and his cool, over long spells and was also a batsman of great courage who averaged more than 25 in Tests and was particularly capable against fast bowling. In South Africa in 1964−65, Allen bowled in tandem with another off-spinner, Freddie Titmus, to give England victory in the first Test at Durban. The two slow bowlers then carried out skipper Mike Smith's unenterprising but successful containment plan to ensure a draw in each of the remaining four matches.

In 1962−63, David Allen was one of three off-spin bowlers taken by England to Australia in what was something of an unprecedented move. Until South Africa's Hugh Tayfield bowled his flighted off-breaks with stunning effect in Australia in 1952−53, it had been the myth that off-break bowlers of the English flight and length variety would not thrive under Australian conditions. Master craftsman of the art Jim Laker was not wholly a success when taken to Australia in 1958−59, and was certainly no match-winner there. As it turned out, four years later in 1962−63, only one of the three off-break exponents in the England squad was anything of a success.

Freddie Titmus was an England off-break bowler of excellence who made a brave comeback after a severe foot injury.

Frederick John Titmus of Middlesex and England made his first-class debut at 16 and batted in a fashion that led one newspaper to conjure up visions of a new Compton. Although not living up to this intitial image, Fred Titmus remained throughout his Test and county career a prolific run-scorer to be rated as a true all-rounder. Titmus was a busy player who soon became a wily bowler of off-breaks, dropping the ball on the proverbial sixpence all day and employing all the available variations of length, float and drift, spin and cut in order to trap a batsman.

Against some very strong batting opposition in Australia in 1962–63, the small and ever-cheerful Titmus came second to Freddie Trueman in the Test bowling averages with 21 wickets at 29.33. At Sydney, in the third Test, he had figures of 7/79 in Australia's first innings, his best in international cricket. In the final Test, again at Sydney, a protracted spell from Titmus yielded 5/103 and prevented the home side from gaining a winning foothold.

Freddie Titmus was an automatic England choice until tragedy struck in the Caribbean in 1967–68 when he lost four toes in a boating accident. His balance totally upset, the England off-break bowler had to fight back determinedly to re-shape his bowling method and regain his Test place. That he did so, and that he was still in the England side in Australia during 1974–75 when he was already 42, was a tribute to the man's courage and determination. Freddie Titmus ended his 53-match Test career with 153 wickets and a batting average in the 20s and, when he came out of retirement to appear for Middlesex during the early 1980s, he became one of a small band to have played the first-class game over five decades.

The third off-break bowler in Ted Dexter's 1962–63 team took only one wicket in two Tests in Australia. He was, however, another exceptionally long-lived player whose deeds as off-break bowler, solid middle-order batsman and as tactician made him among his country's best all-rounders and captains.

Until his appointment as England's captain in 1969, when he was already 37, Yorkshire-born and bred Raymond Illingworth had been one of those might-have-been players who had promised much but seldom delivered at Test level. A move from Yorkshire to captain Leicestershire signalled a dramatic change in his fortunes when injury to Colin Cowdrey saw Illingworth chosen to lead England against West Indies. 'Caretaker captain' Illingworth led England so well that he won his first series and hardly ever looked back in 31 games as leader.

Stubborn and fearless, he was also highly popular with his men, who respected his profound knowledge of the game. As an off-break bowler, 'Illy' delivered the ball with a perfect action, reminiscent of Jim Laker's. He mixed his stock off-breaks with a puzzling 'away floater' and in 61 Tests took 122 wickets.

A whole new generation of England bowlers came under the tutelage and guidance of the man who had played Test cricket alongside the likes of Trueman, Statham and Tony Lock. The value of Ray Illingworth's contribution to England cricket remains inestimable. It can perhaps only be calculated in terms of the performances of those young players, and bowlers in particular, who received the benefit of his guiding hand and who continued to hold England's standard high after their formidable leader retired from Test cricket in 1973, at the age of 41.

In 1982, Ray Illingworth, at the age of 50 was recalled by his beloved Yorkshire to take over the leadership of a struggling side. He had achieved marvellous things as captain of Leicestershire and England. It seemed fitting that he should have his chance to lead the county which had originally nourished him.

21

Springbok quartet

'South Africa's real strength was their well-equipped attack'
— Wisden, 1956

Mention was made in the previous chapter of the marvellous bowling of South Africa's master off-spin bowler, Hugh Tayfield, in Australia in 1952–53. On that tour Hugh Joseph Tayfield, a man who never spared an opponent or himself, took more wickets in first-class and non first-class matches that any other touring bowler before or since. With 30 wickets at 28.10 in five internationals against Australia, he also materially assisted South Africa to win more than two Tests in a series played abroad. South Africa relied almost totally on Tayfield as their spearhead and main stock bowler. As an off-break bowler, his name must be mentioned in the same breath as Jim Laker's.

Tall and lissom, Hugh Tayfield used his considerable height to full advantage. The swing of his left arm led him into a superbly rhythmic delivery and his action was a model of poise and balance. Above all else, Tayfield's accuracy was legend and he possessed the stamina of two men, and he certainly needed the latter quality in Australia in 1952–53 when he sent down 5684 balls in first-class matches — 2000 more than his nearest Springbok team-mate.

Tayfield often operated to an unusually attacking field for a bowler of his type operating in Australia. Placing at least two and sometimes a squad of four men close in on each side of the batsman, 10 to 15 yards from the bat, he would challenge the Australian batsmen to drive his cleverly flighted deliveries. Tayfield would not have been able to do this without the unusual fielding talents of Jack Cheetham's Springbok team, rated by many knowledgeable critics as possibly the finest Test fielding side of all time. The offspinner was himself a remarkably fearless and agile close fielder who frequently took miraculous catches off his own bowling.

His most remarkable match performance in Australia was a marathon stint in the second Test at Melbourne when he bowled South Africa to victory with figures of 6/84 and 7/81. During one spell of 83 balls, Tayfield claimed the wickets of Harvey, Langley, Miller and Hole — without conceding a single run.

Tayfield's only support in 1952–53 came from a battery of game, medium-fast bowlers who sometimes bowled above their known ability as work-a-day seamers not quite of Test match class. The fair-haired right-arm fast-medium Edward Russell Henry Fuller took 3/74 and 5/66 in the fifth Test at Melbourne to help South Africa square the series; right-arm fast Michael George Melle was genuinely quick and took 6/71 in Australia's first innings of the first Test at Brisbane but did little thereafter; and all-rounders John Cecil Watkins and Anton Robert Andrew Murray, both very tall and right-arm medium-fast swing bowlers, each sent down support overs.

Earlier in his career, when chosen as a replacement for the injured Athol Rowan, a 21-year-old Tayfield humbled the Australian team at Durban with a 7/23 spell that saw his opponents put out for an ignominious 75 runs. In England in 1955, Tayfield took a staggering (for a visiting bowler) 143 first-class wickets on tour, including 26 at 21.84 in the five Tests versus England. It was Tayfield's bowling in at least one of the two Tests won that season that proved the decisive factor, although the inclusion of two or three new bowlers of high quality meant that the South Africans' tactical attack plan no longer revolved solely around their ace off-break bowler.

When England played a series in South Africa in 1956–57, Tayfield reached his peak with 37 wickets at 17.18 in five Tests, including a memorable South African record of 13 wickets for 192 (4/79 and 9/113) in the fourth game at Johannesburg. In a season dominated by the ball, Tayfield and the other main South African bowlers lost nothing when compared with England's wonderfully strong attack that year, which was drawn from a pool consisting of Statham, Tyson, Bailey, Loader, Wardle, Laker and Lock.

Hugh Tayfield remains South Africa's highest wicket-taker in Tests (170 at 25.91 in 37 Tests – a remarkable strike rate) and was an early example of the new, tough breed of South African cricketers. 'Toey' Tayfield was a distinctive character on the field, with his toe-tapping of the right foot before each delivery (and before facing each ball as a gritty and troublesome tailender) and in the way he would kiss the Springbok badge on his cap before handing it to the umpire at the start of an over.

When South Africa went to England in 1955, Tayfield was joined by a trio of bowlers – Neil Adcock, Peter Heine and Trevor Goddard – each of whom was, in his own right and in his own style, a world-class performer.

Neil Amwin Treharne Adcock, more than six foot (183 cm) tall, blond and strong, right-arm and exceptionally fast off a long but smooth run up, simply terrorised New Zealand's batsmen in South Africa when he made his Test series debut in 1953–54. On a fiery track at Johannesburg in the second Test, he sent New Zealanders Lawrie Miller and Bert Sutcliffe to hospital. Sutcliffe returned, head bandaged, to play an unforgettable innings of 80, with seven sixes, but could scarcely recall his time at the wicket. Tending to bowl short most of the time, Adcock was something of a disappointment in England in 1955, where the wickets did not favour such tactics. In South Africa in 1956–57 the story was a different one, when Adcock tidied up his length and line and took 21 wickets at a very low 14.90 in five Tests. He also bowled with great fire against the 1957–58 Australian team in South Africa, but excelled himself in England in 1960 when he virtually carried the South African attack.

With 108 wickets at 14.02 on the tour (including 26 at 22.57 in the Tests), Adcock raised himself above the controversy generated by his new-ball partner, Geoff Griffin, being called as a thrower, and became South Africa's sole penetrative bowler. With help from Tayfield and left-hander Goddard, Adcock frequently saw England put out for a reasonably low score, only to witness the advantage thus gained squandered through inept batting.

Of Neil Adcock's many fine bowling spells in Test cricket, his 6/43 burst against Australia at Durban in 1957–58 was his most destructive. In 26 Tests he took 104 wickets at 21.10. His antics as a batsman often caused merriment among his fellow players and there was always a toss up as to whether he would end his international career with more wickets than runs. Adcock had the last laugh, scoring 146 Test runs at an average of 5.40.

The first of Neil Adcock's Test new-ball partners of some note was the right-arm medium-fast David Ernest James Ironside, who swung the ball quite alarmingly in three Tests against New Zealand in 1953–54 to take 15 wickets at 18.33, but was not called upon by South Africa again. Adcock's second fast-bowling aide lasted a little longer and made a grand impression in his brief career.

One of the few Afrikaners to reach the top in cricket, the huge 6 ft 5 in (195 cm) tall Peter Samuel Heine was a right-arm fast bowler with a genuine 'killer' streak. Jim Laker, in his book *Over to Me*, relates an incident when Heine was heard to growl at obdurate England stonewaller Trevor Bailey: 'I want to hit you, Bailey...I want to hit you over the heart', and apparently meant every word of it!

Neil Adcock was the smooth tearaway, Peter Heine was the mean machine. As a pair, they were, for a brief period, possibly the biggest fast-bowling menace in international cricket. Bowling together for the first time against England on a well-grassed pitch at Lord's in 1955, Adcock quickly disposed of one opener and Heine's kicking deliveries from just short of a length had the Englishmen in all sorts of trouble. Heine ended with debut figures of 5/60. The Springbok fast bowling pair's effectiveness was again demonstrated in the next Test at Manchester when England's two openers made just seven runs between them in the match: Heine dismissed Don Kenyon for 5 in the first innings and 1 in the second; Adcock had Gravenay for scores of 0 and 1. In South Africa in 1956–57, Heine troubled England's batsmen sorely with his vicious bumper; Adcock with his

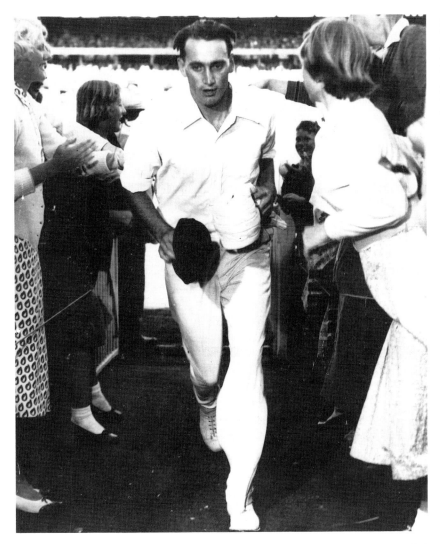

South African Hugh Tayfield, rated in the same category as England's Jim Laker as a world-class off-break bowler, leaves the field at Melbourne after taking 13 wickets in a Test versus Australia in 1952–53.

stamina, speed and accuracy. When the Australians arrived the following season, they were greeted by a fearsome barrage from South Africa's speed twins and it was again only bad batting by the Springboks that let them down and saw South Africa lose a series they had started as favourites.

Throughout, Hugh Tayfield rolled in his off-breaks with immaculate precision while the fourth spoke in South Africa's bowling wheel, left-arm medium-paced Trevor Leslie Goddard, South Africa's top all-rounder of the day, sewed up one end whenever called upon to do so.

Goddard was a left-handed version of England's right-handed 'Barnacle' Bailey and a defensive opening batsman with immense powers of concentration. He was worth his place in the Springbok team as a batsman or as a fielder alone. Tall and athletically spare,

Goddard bowled his medium-paced deliveries with a nagging accuracy that brought him 123 wickets at 26.22 in 41 games for South Africa (to add to his 2516 runs and 48 catches). Through 15 years of Test cricket he was always a great asset to his country.

Goddard bowled with an economy of effort that enabled him to continue for extraordinarily long spells and was seldom, if ever, 'collared' at any level. Coming into the South African eleven as a raw-boned rookie in 1955, he immediately surprised England's batsmen with his powers of containment, bowling with pin-point accuracy to a cleverly placed leg-side field and seldom wavering from his line that varied from on to just outside the leg-stump. In England's second innings in the fourth Test at Leeds, Goddard's figures of 62−37−69−5 reflect his effectiveness. On the final day he bowled unchanged from 11.30 am until the match was won by South Africa at 4.12 pm.

The combination of Adcock and Heine (both fast), Tayfield (off-breaks) and Goddard (left-arm medium to slow) gave South Africa for a couple of years one of the most balanced and feared attacks in international cricket − a quartet of fine bowlers who have indeed seldom been matched by any country. Until Heine departed the scene at the close of the 1957−58 season (he returned briefly for one Test against New Zealand in 1961−62), no other bowlers were required with only Springbok captain, Clive Berrange van Ryneveld occasionally being seen trundling down his leg-breaks and googlies.

When South Africa embarked upon what proved to be its fateful tour of England in 1960, it was without Peter Heine. In the big Afrikaner's place was the controversial Rhodesian pace bowler Geoffrey Merton Griffin, who in 1958−59 had already twice been no-balled for throwing in a South African domestic match. In the light of the drama that followed when he was called in a Test in England, it was, in retrospect, a mistake to even have considered him for the tour. Yet Tayfield, for one, was on the wane as a Test force and South Africa's reserve bowling was thin. Griffin was the only bowler of pace other than Adcock and, if he had not been picked, someone like the burly but barely medium-pace Jimmy Pothecary would have been forced to take the new ball with Adcock. As it turned out, after Griffen was 'chucked out' at Lord's, the right-armed seamer James Edward Pothecary (who had, as a schoolboy, once taken all 20 wickets in a match) did open the bowling in three Tests, but was never any great threat to the England batsmen.

The 'Griffin incident' was only one of the troubles encountered by the 1960 South African team in England. The Springboks were also at times asked to run the gauntlet of a growing band of anti-apartheid demonstrators. Sport was beginning to be used by politicians to press home their views and, after a brief new hour of glory during the mid- to late-1960s, South Africa was forced out of international cricket.

22

Thrown out

'There's no doubt in my mind that Griffin was crucified'
— Ian Meckiff

Whether or not right-arm bowler Geoffrey Merton Griffin was a 'chucker' is, in some ways, irrelevant. The South African authorities were at fault to send to England a suspect bowler, especially following England's experience against Meckiff and company in Australia in 1958—59 and the subsequent 'witch-hunt' of 'chuckers'.

Australia's Ian Meckiff, who was himself no-balled for throwing in a Test match, went on record in his *Thrown Out* as being of the opinion that the 'Griffin incident' was provoked with the 1961 Australian tour of England in mind. Meckiff claims that the English cricket writers were 'sharpening their claws' for the projected Australian tour and that Griffin was '. . . a straight out bunny as far as the English writers were concerned. . .'

The 1960 Geoff Griffin saga started well before the first Test ball was bowled. 'Called' in two separate first-class matches early on in the tour, Griffin sought advice from Alf Gover, one of England's top coaches, and took part in a three-day coaching course under his guidance; it was to no avail. Griffin passed muster in the first Test at Edgbaston, but was then no-balled 11 times for throwing by square-leg umpire Frank Lee in England's innings. Ironically, that was the innings the young Springbok claimed South Africa's one and only hat-trick in international cricket (if the 'double' hat-trick performance by Clive Rice and Garth le Roux against the 'rebel' Australian team in 1985—86 is ignored).

Then, in a farcical turn of events that might have contained all the ingredients of a set-up, the 21-year-old Griffin was no-balled for throwing by umpire Syd Buller during an exhibition match played to entertain the crowd after the Test proper had ended early. Buller no-balled Griffin four times in five balls. Umpire Lee then chimed in with another 'no-ball' shout when the bewildered bowler, in order to complete the over, switched to under-arm without notifying his intention.

Poor Geoff Griffin did not bowl again on the tour and the Test career of a dedicated young player was left in tatters scarcely before it had begun. Fair-haired Griffin, an outstanding athlete, had a permanently crooked right elbow as the result of an accident at school and, with the best will in the world, could not straighten it naturally.

In *Straight from the Shoulder*, the definitive work on the subject, Ian Peebles writes: 'Perhaps a reasonable comparison between the different techniques of bowling and throwing would be to liken the first to the swinging, sweeping motion of the flail as against the flicking of the whip, the human trunk providing the shaft in both cases, and the arm the lash.'

Peebles goes on to note that the vital point when a delivery can become a throw instead of a bowl is plainly apparent during the final moments before the ball leaves the bowler's hand. Right-arm bowlers with orthodox actions would present a picture of: sideways trunk, fully forward extended left arm, and almost a straight line through the shoulders to the fully extended right arm making ready for its circular motion before release of the ball — like a wheel with two spokes, if another comparison can be offered. And, as with a turning wheel, the bowling arm swings over straight and true to complete the circle after release of the ball.

To throw the ball over-arm, it becomes necessary to turn the trunk almost chest-on to the batsman (instead of presenting the left shoulder),

Geoff Griffin was 'called' for throwing at Lord's after he had taken South Africa's first hat-trick in Test cricket. He was then no-balled again for chucking in an exhibition game played after the Test and suffered the humiliation of completing his over under-arm.

which position makes it impossible for the swinging right arm to come over the top without bending and then straightening again with a whip-like action, unless the bowler is double-jointed. Many bowlers have been known to throw inadvertently when striving for speed or a bouncer and there are others who seem to have the physical capability of bowling fairly with an almost chest-on action.

There is no provision in the Laws of Cricket for a bowler with any kind of deformity that might prevent him from straightening his arm altogether. It must be clearly stated though that many judges of the day were of the opinion that Geoff Griffin was a thrower even without any reference to the fact that he was unable to fully straighten his arm naturally, and that his permanently bent elbow had nothing to do with the matter.

Geoff Griffin was not the first Test bowler to be no-balled for throwing but, until the Meckiff incident which followed a few years later, was certainly the most publicised.

Australia's turn-of-the-century fast bowler, fiery Ernie 'Jonah' Jones, was 'called' by tough and uncompromising umpire James Phillips at Adelaide and Melbourne way back in 1897–98. More than 50 years later, England's slow left-hander Tony Lock became the next domino to fall in the throwing game, called by umpire Perry Burke when bowling his 'faster' ball against West Indies at Kingston, Jamaica, in 1953–54. Pakistan Test off-spinner Haseeb Ahsan also fell foul of the throwing law in a Test when he was called in a match versus India at Bombay in 1960–61.

One of the most curious of throwing instances in Tests involved Indian all-rounder Syed Abidali, who was no-balled by umpire F R Goodall in the New Zealand versus India match at Christchurch in 1967–68 when he deliberately threw the ball in protest at the action of New Zealand's fast bowler Gary Bartlett, who had not been 'called'.

A fair smattering of other Test players have been 'called' for throwing in first-class cricket, including England's C B Fry, D J Insole and R T Simpson, Australia's I R Redpath and India's M R Rege, who were all primarily batsmen who did not bowl regularly.

South Africa's Cuan McCarthy was no-balled for throwing in a Cambridge University versus Worcestershire match in 1952, but after his Test career was over. England's Harold James Rhodes, right-arm fast, took nine wickets in two Tests before doubts about his action and a 'call' for throwing in the Derbyshire versus South Africans match during the witch-hunt season of 1960 kept him from further contention (he was 'called' again in a county match in 1961). Hampshire's D W 'Butch' White was also overlooked after a few Tests in India once he had been no-balled for throwing in a county game in 1960. Both Rhodes and White were again no-balled for throwing in 1965.

West Indies' fire-breathing quickie Charlie Griffith got the 'chucking' call for Barbados versus India at Bridgetown in 1961–62 and was perhaps fortunate not to have had his action censured on occasion during a Test.

Geoff Griffin celebrated his 21st birthday a couple of weeks before his hat-trick at Lord's and his subsequent dismissal as a chucker. He had played in just two Tests. Australia's Ian Meckiff was a little more fortunate. He had already played in 18 matches for Australia when he too was 'chucked' out of Test cricket, ironically enough during a game against South Africa, at Brisbane in December 1963.

Keith Miller, who considered himself as one of the 'last of the straight-arm bowlers' was, at first, a severe critic of his countryman, but was reported to have softened his attitude after the left-hander had made a concerted effort to correct his bowling technique. But the English cricket establishment could not be counted upon to reverse their own opinion of Australia's controversial fast bowler who had wrecked England's batting in Australia in 1958–59 and Meckiff, together with Gordon Rorke, was left out of the team for England in 1961. It should be recorded though that Meckiff and Rorke were perhaps dropped more because of injury than in some effort to please the English critics.

With Garth McKenzie established as new-ball partner to Allan Davidson after a successful time in England in 1961, Australia's 'hot-potato' was again left out of the pot when England returned the visit in 1962–63. Davidson, however, played his final series that summer and Meckiff was brought back for the first Test against Trevor Goddard's South Africans, at Brisbane in December 1963. He was to bowl just one agonising over.

Australian skipper Richie Benaud gave McKenzie first over before calling Meckiff in to bowl his first ball in Test cricket since his appearance in the famed tied Test against West Indies, also at 'The Gabba', in December 1960. The left-hander, who bowled with a permanently bent arm which, as was the case with Griffin, he *could not straighten*, was promptly called by square-leg umpire Col Egar for his second, third, fifth and ninth balls. Meckiff's first over of the match, and the final over of his Test career, lasted for 12 balls. Benaud came under much fire for taking an essential bowler off immediately and not trying him again in the match from umpire Lou Rowan's end. Perhaps he was influenced by administrators who considered that it was justifiable to sacrifice the career of one player for the overall good of the game.

Before he fell foul of a law that became operative midway through his career, Meckiff had turned in a number of match-winning performances for Australia. His best Test performance was a 6/38 blast that sent England crashing to defeat at Melbourne in 1958–59. The even-tempered Meckiff claimed emphatically that he was not a thrower, intentional or unintentional, and there were many who were appalled at the treatment this mild-mannered man received from elements in the media.

Sir Donald Bradman was one who went on record before the 1961 England tour as being shocked that a man could be condemned as a 'chucker' by overseas critics who had never seen him bowl and when he had not, as yet, even played in their country.

It seems that the law concerning throwing was altered to limit *all* bowlers with a suspicious action and that Griffin and Meckiff *were* used as scapegoats of a sort. Other bowlers who sent down the occasional dubious delivery, for instance Griffith of West Indies, were seemingly ignored at Test level and the whole furore centred around the doings of just two players.

The subject of throwing was no joke for the players whose Test careers were cut short because of renewed vigilance on the part of umpires and officials. Australia's Keith Nichol Slater was one of the unfortunates who got a taste of Test cricket before being hounded out of the representative game. Slater, a right-arm medium-paced cum off-break bowler, was twice no-balled for throwing in a first-class match and never considered again for Australia.

Two other Australian Test bowlers have been no-balled for throwing in recent years, but without any apparent detrimental effect to their careers. Leg-spinner Jim Higgs was 'called' when bowling for the Australia versus Leicestershire in 1975 and off-breaker Bruce Yardley received similar treatment for Australia versus Jamaica in 1977–78.

Had he been chosen again for Australia versus England after the stormy 1958–59 series, the amiable giant Gordon Frederick Rorke may well have joined Meckiff in the penalty box, and for more than one reason. Rorke was one of those unfortunate fast bowlers of the time who relied on the dragging of the back foot as part of his essential action and, because of his enormous height, his front foot was frequently placed well over the line of the popping crease when he let go of the ball.

Unlike the famous British stand in Zululand, the Australian version of Rorke's drift was soon cut short. It has even been alleged that the present front-foot law was devised to counter the action of just one bowler. Those who argue against the front-foot ruling claim that Rorke's unusual drag could never be duplicated by anyone who was unable to also physically match his incredibly strong 6 ft 5 in (195 cm) frame, and his resultant enormous stride.

Like Meckiff, Rorke was an enthusiatic cricket-lover who must have been severely disappointed at the length of his international career — just four Tests in which he claimed 10 wickets at 20.30 each.

There have been a number of notable players whose actions have been placed under suspicion but who were never actually penalised for throwing. In 1896, F R Spofforth, 'The Demon' bowler of old, wrote in *Wisden* that fellow Australian T R McKibbin (an off-break bowler) 'should never be allowed to play under the existing rule'.

Another off-break bowler to be labelled a chucker was the dour Australian opening batsman Jimmy Burke, whose action is described by Ian Peebles as looking like 'a constable laying his truncheon on a very short offender's head'. Largely because he was a change bowler in Test and State cricket, Burke was never called.

Throwing is no longer an issue in Test or first-class cricket but, for a short period of time, threatened to become a spark that would set alight another bonfire of controversy as big as bodyline. In his *Straight from the Shoulder*, Ian Peebles contends, quite rightly so, that a batsman beaten by a legitimate ball has no complaint. But he goes on to assert, again in total fairness, that, 'the cricketer who, albeit unintentionally, gains advantage by infringing the laws introduces an entirely different element'. Peebles also offers the opinion that a batsman facing up to a fair delivery should not, in effect, be in any danger of injury. With an eye on the methods used by some current international fast bowlers it can perhaps be claimed that we may now have another problem on our hands.

23

Working up speed

'Fast bowlers come in all shapes, styles and temperaments. Few have been as near to the ideal image as Wesley Hall'

— Clayton Goodwin

The Australia-West Indies Test match which ended in a tie in the last possible over at Brisbane in December 1960 has been acknowledged by most observers as the greatest game of international cricket ever staged.

In the 1961 edition of *Wisden*, noted English cricket writer E M Wellings even goes so far as to claim that it was the greatest game ever played with a ball. He was there to see it all; so was Jack Fingleton, who was so inspired by the dramatic proceedings that he wrote a whole book about that singular match. Fingleton devoted a chapter to the final few overs bowled by West Indies' giant fast bowler Wesley Winfield Hall. When Hall started his final over, Australia needed six runs to win and West Indies needed three wickets.

The image of the West Indian cricketer is one of batsmen with wonderful eye and timing, electric-heeled fielding and giant young athletes sprinting in to hurl the ball down at the highest possible velocity a human being is capable of. And it seems totally appropriate that the final over in what may remain cricket's finest match was bowled by a man who represents the archetypal model of the West Indian fast bowler.

At 6 ft 2 in (188 cm) and built like Muhammad Ali, Wes Hall came from Barbados, the island where cricket is considered a 'religion', and possessed all of the attributes of the great fast bowler — a natural athleticism, great strength and stamina, a classic side-on action, a full follow through and an equable temperament. Above all he was very, very fast and a fearsome prospect for the waiting batsman as he sprinted in from his distant mark, every muscle in his powerful frame flexing, big eyes bulging, teeth glinting and gold crucifix swinging in the sunlight and shirt hanging out. Wes Hall was simply all fast bowler. His pace was once measured at 91 mph (146 kph). He never knew what it was to give up and could be seen hurling the ball down as quickly in the last over of the day as he did in the first, bowling all the time as if he expected to take a wicket with each and every delivery. His steepling bouncer would test the best. And his happy-go-lucky nature meant that he was seldom rattled when some brave batsman dared to launch a counter strike.

Wes Hall's grand sense of humour was illustrated at Brisbane in 1960–61 when he walloped his way to a thundering 50 in the West Indies first knock and was then out stumped, playing an inglorious 'cow shot'. Jack Fingleton records that, on being upbraided by skipper Frank Worrell, Hall explained that he had thrown his wicket away in the interests of the team: 'Why man, I could've got a century easy. Wes Hall was right on top of the bowlers. Yes, sir. Then I suddenly think and say, "Wes, man, you not in this side as batsman only. You got to do some fast bowling." So I tell myself be satisfied with 50, man, and get out. So I got out.'

In India in 1958–59, Hall marked his Test debut by swiftly dismissing both opposing opening batsmen. He claimed 30 wickets in five Tests in India and then moved on to Pakistan to add another 16 in three matches to give him an overall 46 wickets at 17.76 in his first Test season (and Hall had only been picked for the tour when Frank Worrell withdrew at the last moment). Then followed 22 wickets in a tough home series against an England batting line-up of immense skill and depth in 1959–60 before the cricketers from the Caribbean set forth for the historic 1960–61 tour of Australia. On his first tour of Australia, Hall was simply magnificent. In the famous tied Test he returned figures of 4/140 and 5/63.

And so he went on, season after season, at home and abroad. For the next decade, Hall formed with Garfield Sobers, Charlie Griffith and off-spinner Lance Gibbs one of those dream Test attacks that every captain would wish to have under his command. In 48 Tests Wes Hall took 192 wickets at 26.38. There was no batsman in the world who did not respect him, as a bowler and as a man.

The season before Wes Hall made his Test debut in India, a slimly built but long-armed Jamaican speedster, Roy Gilchrist, so rattled Pakistan's batsmen in a series in the West Indies that the mighty little Hanif Mohammed, who scored 337 in the first Test at Bridgetown, was forced to drop down in the order from opening batsman to number four. In that first Test Hanif scored 354 runs in his two innings. During the remainder of the rubber, Gilchrist dismissed him five times and the Pakistani only added a further 274 runs in seven innings.

Gilchrist had played a previous series in England in 1957 and was fast gaining a reputation as something of a 'bad guy' who had no compunction about the use of fast head-high 'beamers' to intimidate batsmen. In India in 1958–59, the fiery-tempered Gilchrist (then aged 26) took 26 wickets against the 21-year-old Wes Hall's 30 and it looked as if West Indies had discovered a new-ball partnership of awesome dimensions. It was not to be; Gilchrist's temperament let him down and he was sent home as a disciplinary measure before the

The magnificently proportioned Wesley Hall was the first West Indian post-war fast bowlers of note.

Pakistan leg of the tour began and never again played in a Test.

Before Hall appeared on the scene Gilchrist had an assortment of new-ball partners, including Frank Worrell with his left-arm seamers in England in 1957 and the right-arm medium-fast Eric St Eval Atkinson (from Barbados and brother of Test all-rounder Denis Atkinson) and the strongly-built right-arm fast David Thomas Dewdney (Jamaica), against Pakistan in 1957–58. Eric Atkinson took 9 wickets at 13.22 in two games against Pakistan and went to India and Pakistan in 1958–59. Tom Dewdney played intermittently for West Indies between 1954 and 1959 with no great success. He was injured in a car accident in England in 1959 when Gary Sobers was also injured and the promising young West Indies all-rounder O G 'Collie' Smith was killed.

Trinidad's right-arm fast-medium Jaswick Ossie Taylor made his debut against Pakistan in the final Test of 1957−58 at Port of Spain and, with Gilchrist able to bowl only seven overs because of injury, returned figures of 36.5−6−109−5 in a Pakistan innings of 496. Taken to India and Pakistan in 1958−59, Taylor could not build on his fine start and was not picked again.

In England in 1959−60, and for some of the time in Australia in 1960−61, Hall was partnered by the strongly-built Jamaican Chester Watson, who was something of a disappointment despite his ability to generate surprising pace off a shortish run because of a whippy wrist action. Back in the West Indies in 1961−62, Hall opened the bowling against India with the loose-limbed right-arm fast Sven Conrad ('Charlie') Stayers from British Guiana, who also performed with only moderate success.

Jamaica's energetic right-arm fast-medium Lester Anthony King was brought in to partner Hall in the final Test against India at Kingston in 1961−62, took 5/46 and 2/18, and then had to wait another six years for his next and only other Test chance − against England at Georgetown 1967−68. Lester King also went on tours to England, India and Australia and New Zealand without playing in a Test.

Hall's first meaningful new-ball partner after Roy Gilchrist was the 6 ft 2 in(188 cm) and massively built Charles Christopher Griffith who, like Gilchrist, was to become surrounded by controversy, but who eventually played in 28 Tests and took 94 wickets.

Bowling off a deceptively lumbering run that gave no indication to the batsman that his pace would be equal to that of Hall, Charlie Griffith was a decidedly disturbing proposition whose bouncer lifted alarmingly and whose stinging yorker frequently left a batsman defenceless. There were, unfortunately, loud accusations that his two most lethal balls were bowled with an illegal action, especially after Indian captain Nari Contractor's career was cut short when he suffered a fractured skull after ducking into a Griffith lifter. Griffith was actually no-balled for throwing in the same Barbados versus India match.

Although Griffith was never 'called' for throwing in a Test, he had to live with an almost daily barrage of press speculation about his bowling technique. Griffith was a sensitive person who was deeply disturbed by the criticism of his bowling and who ultimately turned into a brooding, disillusioned man who deeply resented the accusations levelled at him.

There were, however, always signs of great companionship between 'Mr Nice Guy', Wes Hall, and 'Mr Ugly', Charlie Griffith. As a bowling combination they were devastating. They first bowled together against England on a feather-bed pitch at Port of Spain in 1959−60 but Griffith was then left out of the West Indies team until the tour of England in 1963. Their impact was immediate and quite frightening. *Wisden* recorded that Griffith's 'command of the yorker had not been equalled in this century' and, with many of England's batsmen favouring a 'two-eyed' stance, the giant Barbadian cut through them like a hot knife through butter to take 32 wickets at 16.21 in the five Tests, twice as many as Hall, whose 16 wickets cost 33.37 runs apiece. This was indeed Griffith's golden year: twice he took six England wickets in an innings and West Indies won the series 3−1.

West Indies captain Frank Worrell relied almost entirely on just four bowlers to dismiss England during the 1963 series − and not once did they let him down. To add to Griffith's 32 wickets and Hall's 16, off-spinner Lance Gibbs chipped in with 26 at 21.30 and all-rounder Garfield Sobers took 20 at 28.55. The four bowled nearly 900 overs between them. Worrell himself sent down 45 overs for three wickets. No-one else was needed or called upon.

Sir Garfield Sobers, like Griffith, was from the amazing island of Barbados which has produced more Test cricketers per square mile that any other place in the world. Sobers was also probably the greatest all-round cricketer of all time, perhaps even better than W G Grace.

As a batsman, Sobers holds the record for the highest Test innings, 365 not out versus Pakistan at Kingston in 1957−58. He totalled 8032 runs at 57.78 in 93 Tests and took 109 catches as a brilliantly athletic fielder in any position. As a bowler in three distinctive styles, Sobers claimed 235 Test wickets at 34.03, frequently using the new ball with his fast-medium to fast left-arm inswingers and later reverting to either orthodox left-arm slow (with a perfect left-hander's action) or unorthodox left-arm, back-of-the hand wrist spin. In all three styles he was a Test-class bowler. He first came into the West Indies side versus England at Kingston in 1953−54 as a 17-year-old left-arm spinner who could bat a bit.

Against England at Kingston in 1961−62, Sobers played innings of 104 and 50 and then won the match for West Indies with a bowling return of 5/63 in the final innings. In England in 1966, now captain of West Indies, the left-handed genius scored 722 runs at 103.14 in the five Tests and took 20 wickets at 27.25. At Leeds in the fourth Test, he scored a brilliant 174 (including 100 between lunch and tea) and, bowling in all three of his styles, took 5/41 and 3/39 to take West Indies to an innings victory. At Brisbane in 1968−69, Sobers took the new ball in Australia's second innings and gave West Indies its only win of the series with a 6/73 stint.

The fourth major West Indies bowler of the 1960s (and into the 1970s) was the lean Guyanese off-break expert, Lancelot Richard Gibbs, cousin of famous West Indian captain Clive Lloyd. (Between them the cousins played in 189 Tests − more than Pakistan's four famous Mohammed brothers combined.)

Lance Gibbs's bowling action was once described as approximating

Lance Gibbs has been the only West Indies spin bowler of any great note in the past 20 years or so and took more than 300 Test wickets with his off-breaks in an age of pace.

that of a human grasshopper. His action was rather unorthodox, chest-on and with left arm hanging by his side as the right arm came over high and clear. Exceptionally long fingers enabled Gibbs to obtain spin and bounce on the deadest of tracks and he was a resounding success in Australia. Gibbs had made his Test debut in India in 1958−59, but was originally chosen for the 1960−61 Australian tour as third spinner after Ramadhin and Valentine. Given his chance in the third Test at Sydney, he took three wickets in four balls and ended with a match analysis of 8/112. In the next Test at Adelaide, Gibbs bagged a hat-trick and ended the series with 19 wickets at 20.78 to top the West Indies bowling averages.

As an automatic selection thereafter, Lance Gibbs began spinning his way around the globe to gather 309 wickets at 29.09 in 79 Tests, taking five or more wickets in a Test innings on 18 occasions. His wicket total in Tests is by far the best for West Indies and, when he reached 308 in 1975−76, he broke the then existing record of 307 held by England's Freddie Trueman.

Another West Indian off-break bowler, O'Neil Gordon Smith, might have challenged Gibbs for a place at times. He was tragically killed in a car accident in England in 1959. Jamaica's 'Collie' Smith was, however, primarily a batsman of great ability who played innings of 44 and 104 on his Test debut against Australia at Kingston in 1954−55 and added three further centuries in his brief international career. Smith also took 48 wickets in his 26 Tests and could be described as a highly useful off-spinner who gained the second nickname 'Jim' because of the similarity between his bowling action and that of England's Jim Laker.

Touching 35, the Trinidad right-arm off-break bowler Jack Mollison Noreiga replaced an out of form Lance Gibbs for four Tests versus India in 1970−71. Noreiga bowled with dramatic effect in the second Test at Port of Spain to take 9/95 in India's first innings, but had started his career too late to capitalise on his initial, triumphant performance.

Of the other West Indian spin bowlers of the period, Gary Sobers's cousin, the Barbadian, David Anthony Jerome Holford, was a tall right-arm leg-break bowler and reliable batsman who occasionally put in a useful bowling performance in his 24 Tests. Three left-arm spinners of varying styles also appeared, but very infrequently made any sort of impact: Trinidad's Inshan Ali, an unorthodox back-of-the-hand exponent, took 5/59 against New Zealand at Port of Spain in 1971−72, but did little else; Raphick Rasif Jumadeen, orthodox left-arm and also from Trinidad, took 11 wickets in two Tests versus Australia in 1977−78 but proved rather expensive in his remaining games for West Indies; Elquemedo Tonito Willett, another orthodox left-hander hailing from the tiny island of Nevis, was the first Leeward

Islander to play for West Indies but only managed 11 wickets at 43.81 in five Tests.

When Trinidad's sometime left-arm spinner and useful left-arm seamer Bernard Denis Julien and Barbados all-rounder Keith Boyce were given the new ball in Tests during the the 1970s, the action signalled the end of an era. With Hall and Griffith no longer in the team, West Indies entered a period that was marked by a dearth of capable, genuine fast bowlers. Hard as Julien and Boyce, right-arm fast, tried, they could not match the speed and penetration of their predecessors. Julien was an energetic though inconsistent performer who later opted to play in South Africa. His 50 wickets in 24 Tests proved expensive at 37.36 runs each, but he hit two Test 100s and was a useful player. Boyce was rather more reliable and took 60 wickets in 21 Tests at 24.33, counting as his best innings a brilliantly struck 95 not out against Australia at Adelaide in 1975–76.

The lanky, raw-boned Vanburn Alonza Holder from Barbados also tried hard at right-arm fast medium and was more consistent as a bowler than either Julien or Boyce. Until the arrival of genuine quick bowlers like Joel Garner and Colin Croft, Holder played regularly and took 109 wickets at 33.28 in 40 Tests but, like Julien and Boyce, seldom worried opposing batsmen with his speed.

Other seam bowlers tried were the right-arm fast-medium Grayson Cleophas Shillingford from Dominica and long-serving Kent professional John Neil Shepherd, a right-arm medium-fast and a hard-hitting batsman originally from Barbados. But the ineffectiveness of West Indies fast bowlers during the latter half of the 1970s was reflected in a calypso of the time:

> *'West Indies tried Holder and Keith Boyce,*
> *Because they had no other choice.*
> *They even called on Uton Dowe,*
> *But I'm sure they sorry they bring him now.'*

The reference to Jamaica's right-arm fast-medium Uton George Dowe followed that bowler's dismal showing against Australia at Kingston in 1972–73. The harder he bowled his bouncers at Keith Stackpole, the harder he was hooked each time to the boundary. Dismayed at his performance, his home crowd began chanting: 'Dowe shalt not bowl!'

As far as fast bowling was concerned, West Indies reached a low point during the early 1970s, but the advent in 1973–74 of a little known bowler from Antigua heralded a change of fortunes. Little did the world realise at the time that the arrival of Anderson Roberts, the first Antiguan to play Test cricket, also signalled the start of a cricket era that would become completely dominated by a seemingly inexhaustible supply of fast bowling talent from the Caribbean islands.

24

Eastern magic

*'The art of bowling is an incommunicable natural gift which can be
perfected to almost any degree by practice'*

— K S Ranjitsinhji

In an earlier chapter it was pointed out that India's first great Test
bowlers were all of the fast and fast-medium variety. Today, India is
regarded as the home of spin and from the 1940s through to the
present day, a succession of practitioners of the magical art of flight
and turn have appeared out of the East in an abundance that has not
been matched by any other country.

The deeds of the likes of Vinoo Mankad and Ghulam Ahmed have
already been discussed. The next outstanding Indian spin bowler in
line was Subhashchandra Pandhrinath Gupte, a leg-break and googly
expert with wonderful control over flight, length and spin. The high
skill of Subhash Gupte has seldom been matched and he stood head
and shoulders above his colleagues during a time when the Indian
team was generally fighting a losing battle. He was the first truly
world-class Indian leg-spin bowler and one of the best ever seen in
international cricket.

Had Gupte been supported by a keen fielding side (one of India's
weak points during the 1950s) he might have even bettered his 149
wickets at 29.55 in 36 Tests. In fact, during his career he took more
than one third of all the wickets captured by Indian bowlers in Test
cricket — an incredible feat.

On the short side, Gupte was nevertheless an aggressive bowler
who was not merely content to contain batsmen with his command of
line and length. He spun his leg-break viciously and used a well-
disguised top-spinner to trap batsmen leg-before-wicket. His googly
was difficult to pick and Gupte experimented continually in his
efforts to deceive batsmen, never sheltering behind negative theories.

He first made his name and gained a new nickname in the West
Indies in 1952–53. Due to Gupte's 27 wickets at 29.22 (out of 62
wickets taken) and the determined batting of 'Polly' Umrigar and M
L Apte, India managed to hold the powerful West Indies team to
four draws in five games (West Indies took the series with a win at
Bridgetown in the second Test). A marathon spell of 66–15–162–7
on a batting wicket in the West Indies first innings at Port of Spain
saw the locals dub the little Indian spin wizard 'Fergie' Gupte, after
their own former Test leg-spinner, the bald-headed Wilf Ferguson.

Gupte always seemed to do well against West Indies. In India in 1958–59, he took 22 of the 53 wickets taken by the home bowlers in a five-match series, including his personal Test best of 9/102 in West Indies first innings of the second match on a matting wicket at Kanpur. India in turn collapsed to the pace bowling of big Wes Hall and poor Gupte's grand effort was to no avail.

Against New Zealand in 1955–56, the little spinner bagged exactly half the wickets taken by Indian bowlers during the series – 34 at 19.67. Next best Indian bowler was Vinoo Mankad with 12 wickets at 27.33. Gupte took five or more in an innings four times and India won the series with ease.

Towards the end of his career, Gupte was left out of a three-match home series against Australia in 1959–60 in favour of the right-arm off-break bowler Jasubhai Motibhai Patel, a hard spinner of the ball who had a jerky action caused by a wrist injury as a boy. At Kanpur, on a newly-laid turf wicket (replacing the matting used before at that venue), Jasu Patel startled the Australians by bowling India to a 119-run victory and claiming figures of 9/69 and 5/55 – his 14/124 was India's best-ever Test performance. Unfortunately, Jasu Patel's action came under suspicion and he only played in a few more Tests.

At Kanpur in 1959–60, Patel received most support from the medium-paced outswingers of all-rounder Pahlan Rantanji Umrigar. 'Polly' Umrigar was India's leading batsman for a half-dozen years and could also be a penetrative bowler on a helpful wicket. Indian seam bowlers of ability were few and far between at the time and Umrigar frequently took the new ball. Some others did have their moments, notably the medium-paced Surendranath and the rather quicker Ramakant Bhikaji Desai, both of whom were right-arm bowlers. The happy-natured Surendranath was called 'Surrender-not' by English crowds when he refused to give up when India was battling in England in 1959 (he topped the bowling averages with 16 wickets at 26.62). The slightly-built 'Tiney' Desai generated more pace that would be expected of a man of his size. In the absence of any other fast bowlers, he was frequently over-bowled by the Indian captains of the time, but enjoyed one particularly fine series when he took 21 wickets against Pakistan in 1960–61. A third occasional Indian Test new-ball bowler was the right-arm fast-medium Vasant Baburao Ranjane, who took 19 wickets in seven Tests without establishing a regular place.

But other than Ranjane, Desai and Surendranath, it was generally spin all the way for India during the 1950s and 1960s. Subhash Gupte's brother, Balkrishna Pandharinath Gupte, had a Test against each of Pakistan, England and New Zealand, but ended up with only three wickets for his efforts. In contrast to his older brother, 'Baloo' Gupte was a big, sturdy man but, like Subhash, was a leg-break and googly bowler whose flight and length was excellent. Leading batsman

Chandrakant Gulabrao Borde eventually took over from Gupte as resident leg-spinner for a time. Although he had his days of glory, he was not in the same consistent class as his predecessor and was infinitely more expensive. Another excellent leg-break bowler of the day, Vaman Vishwanath Kumar, was unfortunate in that his career coincided with that of Borde and the Guptes (and later, B S Chandrasekhar). Against Pakistan at New Delhi in 1960−61, Kumar took 5/64 and 2/68 in the first of his two Tests.

Left-arm spinner Vinoo Mankad's place in the Indian eleven was eventually taken over by the studious and determined Rameschandra Gangaram Nadkarni, another genuine all-rounder but a more defensive type of player than Mankad. 'Bapu' Nadkarni's tireless left-arm bowling spells of precise and immaculate length became something of a legend. Tall and dapper, and bowling with his sleeves buttoned, Nadkarni created a world Test record versus England at Madras in 1963−64 when he sent down 131 balls (21.5 overs) without conceding a run. His final analysis for the innings was the incredible 32−27−5−0! A patient left-hander, Nadkarni also headed the Indian batting averages for the series. In 1964−65 he had bowling figures of 5/31 and 6/91 versus Australia, again at Madras, and ended the three-match rubber with 17 wickets at 13.70. In 41 Tests Nadkarni scored 1414 runs and took 88 wickets at 29.07. He was also a fearless close fielder.

Another left-handed all-rounder, flamboyant Salim Aziz Durani, often bowled in tandem with Nadkarni. Salim Durani was a man of many parts. He once starred in a film and claimed that he felt more nervous at the time than when he stood guard in a Test match. A left-handed batsman of moods, who could one day be seen hitting the cover off the ball and the next quietly patting it back to the bowler, he was also a left-arm spin bowler whose lazy-looking action belied his ability to spin the ball and subtly vary his flight and pace changes. Durani played particularly well in the West Indies in 1961−62. He later lost his place to the up-and-coming Bishan Bedi, but not before he had scored more than 1000 runs and taken 75 wickets in 29 Tests.

Yet another versatile left-handed all-rounder of the 1960s was the energetic and talented Rusi Framroze Surti. An aggressive left-handed batsman who preferred to face fast bowling, Surti was an Indian version of Gary Sobers, bowling left-arm seamers with the new ball and then reverting to left-arm slow. Surti was an outstanding success in Australia and New Zealand in 1967−68 and later migrated to play for Queensland.

From the mid 1960s through to the later 1970s, India's out cricket was dominated by four spin bowlers, two off-spinners, one orthodox left-arm and one googly expert − who only once played altogether in the same Test but of whom there were seldom less than three present

Erapelli Prasanna was one of the two world-class off-break bowlers in India's famous spin quartet. He was noted for his subtle, looping flight variations.

in every India eleven from 1966 to 1979. Each of the four — the two off-breakers E A S Prassana and S Venkatagraghavan, left-hander B S Bedi and leg-breaker B S Chandrasekhar — was a truly world-class spin bowler who could rank alongside Mankad, Ghulam Ahmed and Gupte and bear comparison with any other bowler of their particular type in Test cricket history.

Right-arm off-spinner Erapalli Anatharao Srinivas Prasanna was the first of India's spin quartet to appear in a Test (versus England in India in 1961–62), but he failed for five years to gain a regular place. Bhagwat Subramanya Chadrasekhar, the leg-break and googly bowler who bowled with a withered right arm, made his debut against England in 1963–64 and made an immediate impact. Srinivasaraghavan Venkataraghavan, the second off-break merchant, played his first Test against New Zealand at home in 1964–65. Bishansingh Giansingh Bedi, left-arm spin bowler extraordinaire, teamed up with Chandrasekhar, Venkataraghavan and Prasanna during the India-West Indies series in India in 1966–67.

At Edgbaston, Birmingham, in 1967, the four spin bowlers all played together in the same Test (the third and final game of the series against England) for the first and only time. Thereafter it was ususally a case of three being chosen, with at least two out of the four men present in every Test played by India until the close of the 1979 series in England. Prasanna moved to Australia and was not chosen after the 1977–78 season; Bedi and Chandrasekhar retired after the 1978–79 series versus West Indies; Venkataraghavan went on to play in all five Tests on a tour of the Caribbean in 1982–83 during his own swansong series appearance. The influence of at least one of India's four amazing spin bowlers was thus apparent for two decades, from 1961–62 through to 1982–83.

In his *Great Indian Cricketers*, Partab Ramchand praises off-spinner Prasanna in colourful terms: 'In the late forties and early fifties it was Vinoo Mankad who fooled and beguiled batsmen to their doom. In the fifties, it was Subhash Gupte who made them look like clowns in a circus. And in the late sixties and early seventies it was Erapalli Prasanna, who with his sinuous deliveries, alluring as a vamp, led the gullible batsman to desperation and disaster.'

Prasanna bowled his off-breaks with a flowing action, spinning the ball in a high loop towards the batsman, with absolute control over line, length and flight. He forced batsmen to use their feet or perish. He beat them through the air or with unexpectedly sharp bounce and turn off the pitch. Prasanna was a 'head' bowler, forever scheming, always planning the downfall of his opponents. He played his 49 Tests in six countries and captured 189 wickets at 30.38. On tour in Australasia in 1967–68, he took 49 wickets in a total of eight Tests against Australia and New Zealand. In 1969–70, Prasanna put up something of a repeat performance for his home crowds in India with a combined 46 wickets in eight matches against the same two countries.

In contrast to Prasanna, the tall and lean Srinivas Venkataraghavan dug the ball in more, but also sent down his deliveries with a high, classical off-spinner's action after a very short approach to the wicket. The popular 'Venkat' was a quiet and unassuming but knowledgable personality who was captain of India in England in 1979 and has, since his retirement, become an able manager of Indian touring teams.

Venkat played in 55 Tests for India, taking 155 wickets at 35.67 and displaying a long-suffering attitude at the uncertainties of selection when India possessed four world-class spin bowlers, only two or three of whom could be played for the sake of the overall balance of the Test eleven. He was something of a success when taken to the West Indies in 1970−71 (22 Test wickets at 33.81). In 1971, an overweight Prasanna was left out of the team and a slimmer and fitter Venkataraghavan assisted Chandrasekhar and Bedi to take series honours in England. Venkat's contribution was 13 wickets at 26.92 in three Tests.

The Indian hero of that 1971 tour was the lean but not over tall Bhagwat Chandrasekhar, who was considered something of a freak when he was first seen bowling in Tests with a right arm that had been crippled by polio when he was only five years old. Chandrasekhar's story is one of an indomitable will that saw him overcome a physical disability that would have prevented most people from playing cricket at all, let alone Test cricket. He bowled with his withered right arm and, as an agile fieldsman, used his left arm for throwing. As former Indian Test batsman Rusi Modi once put it: 'Who could have imagined that...a victim of poliomyelitis would one day paralyse the best of batsmen in the game?'

'Chandra' bowled his leg-breaks and googlies faster than most of his kind and seldom operated without a slip and a couple of close-in fielders on the leg side. At one time he preferred to bowl mostly googlies and top-spinners, but later increased the frequency of his leg-breaks. Slim and bearded, Chandrasekhar took a fairly long run of about ten yards, after starting with the ball held in both hands in front of his face as if saying a silent prayer or supplication before setting out to bowl.

Chandrasekhar made his Test debut as a shy 18-year-old against England at Bombay in 1963−64 (his debut figures: 40−16−67−4) and, on his merry way around the world, collected no less than 242 Test wickets at 29.74 in his 58 matches for India. But his 6/38 spell against England on the fourth day of the match at the Oval in 1971 that brought India an unexpected match and series victory will always remain the high achievement of a brave and talented performer's illustrious career.

Bhagwat Chandrasekhar was a remarkable googly bowler who delivered the ball with a polio-withered right arm.

The fourth member of India's amazing spin-bowling squad of the 1960s and 1970s was the second outstanding Sikh left-arm spin bowler. Bishansingh Bedi had one of the most illustrious international careers ever enjoyed by an Indian cricketer. He took 266 wickets at 28.71 in 67 Tests and captained his country with great distinction in 22 games, winning six.

Bedi was only 15 when he made his first-class debut and, for a long time, had to contend for a place in the North Zone XI with another left-arm spinner of great skill, Rajinder Goel, the highest wicket-taker in the Ranji Trophy and still playing first-class cricket in 1985—86 when well into his 40s.

Bishen Bedi was a master through the air, finger-spun the ball hard from leg, and occasionally produced a ball that straightened unexpectedly to trap a batsman. His adept concealment of his 'arm' ball made him the most feared left-arm slow bowler in international cricket. Bedi's method was built on simple, basic principles — an easy, co-ordinated action, intelligent use of the width of the crease to vary his line and a deceiving arc in flight that was subtly altered from time to time through changes in the position of his arm.

The turbaned Bishansingh Bedi was known simply as 'Bish' or 'Pa'. He was a popular player but found it difficult to avoid controversy and frequently clashed with the Delhi and Indian national cricket authorities; he was even dropped from a Test versus West Indies at Bangalore in 1974—75 on the insistence of the Indian board's president, Purushottam Rungta, for having made 'indiscreet comments' when on tour under Ajit Wadekar in England in 1974. Bedi was known as a man who stood his ground when he felt he was in the right. As captain at Kingston in 1976, he declared India's first innings closed with six wickets down for 306 in protest at persistent short-pitched bowling at his tailenders by fast bowlers Holding and Daniel. Bedi, who batted right-hand in spectacles, then declined, with Chandrasekhar, to bat in the second innings when the game was a foregone conclusion in West Indies' favour and the two leading Indian bowlers were loathe to endanger their careers by having to face up to the questionable tactics of the West Indians. At Sahiwal, Pakistan, in 1978—79, Bedi led his team off the field and conceded a one-day international to the home team in protest at the umpires' reluctance to caution Imran Khan and Sarfraz Narwaz for intimidatory short-pitched bowling. Bedi was also the main protester against the use of Vaseline gauzes to shine the ball by two England bowlers in Madras in 1976—77.

As a bowler in Test cricket, Bishen Bedi was superb in series after series, at home and abroad. He reached a personal peak in the middle part of his career, against England in India in 1972—73 when he took 25 wickets at 25.28 to ensure a 2—1 series win for India. In 1976—77, Bedi again took 25 wickets (at 22.96) in a series versus

The turbanned Bishansingh Bedi, a colourful and dedicated player who often clashed with authority, was the finest left-arm spinner of his day.

England and added another 22 in three Tests against New Zealand in the same season. His best Test bowling performance was a 50−19−98−7 stint versus Australia at Calcutta in 1969−70.

Running into the 1980s, India's four famous spin bowlers all departed the international scene, and it was apparent that the reserve spin cupboard was relatively empty. India's spin attack would have been almost bare were it not for the presence in the wings of the near-veteran Dilip Rasiklal Doshi. The gentle and philosophical Doshi was a bespectacled orthodox left-arm spinner who had been toiling away in English county cricket for eight seasons while Bedi ruled the Test roost for India.

With Prasanna, Bedi and Chandrasekhar all gone, Doshi joined Venkataraghavan in the Indian team in 1979−80 and, at 32, was an instant success. Starting with 27 wickets at 23.33 in the series against the touring Australian team, Doshi added another 18 at 28.00 when India visited Pakistan the same year and a wicket in the Golden Jubilee Test versus England at Bombay at the end of the season gave him 46 wickets in his first 13 Tests. Doshi went on to play for India in England and Australasia and ended his rather belated 32-Test career with 113 wickets at 30.53.

India's current crop of spin bowlers has still to prove itself conclusively. A fair number of aspirants have come and gone in short order, but four players stand out among spinners to play in recent years. Ravishankar Jayadritha Shastri is an all-rounder of quality, a right-handed batsman who can suit his game to the circumstances and an accurate, orthodox slow left-arm bowler. Since his international debut in 1980, the 6 ft 3 ins (190 cm) Shastri has already established himself as a century-scoring batsman. As a bowler, his entry into the Test arena was certainly dramatic. Flown as a late replacement to New Zealand in 1980−81, he walked off the plane at Wellington and went straight into the Test side the following morning. Figures of 3/54 and 3/9 made an immediate impression and Shastri has been a more or less permanent fixture since.

'Ravi' Shastri possesses a cool temperament and goes about his game in a quiet, unruffled manner. He took the Man of the Series award in the 1984−85 World Championship of Cricket played in Australia and, at the close of the 1986 Test series versus Australia had topped 100 Test wickets.

Accused of slow batting in the Tests against England in 1984−85, Shastri went to the other extreme for Bombay versus Baroda the same year when he raced to 200 in 113 minutes off 123 balls to beat by seven minutes the world record for a double-hundred. The Indian also equalled Sir Garfield Sobers's record of six sixes in one over and became only the fifth batsman in history to score 13 sixes in an innings.

The jaunty 5 ft 6 in (167 cm) little Laxman Sivaramakrishnan's re-

As a teenager, the slimly built Laxman Sivarama-krishnan took 12 England wickets in a Test at Bombay but has still to live up to his early promise.

markably controlled leg-breaks and googlies brought him 12 wickets for 181 against England at Bombay in 1984–85. But he was since fallen from favour and was left out of the Indian team to tour England in 1986. Still under 21, Sivaramakrishnan (whose parents decided that for protection they would give him a name embodying all three main Hindu deities – Siva, Rama and Krishna) has time on his side and should soon make another bid for recognition. 'Sivu' Sivaramakrishnan's bowling style is markedly dissimilar to that of Chandrasekhar, his predecessor in the Indian team as a leg-break cum googly bowler, and more in keeping with the traditional image of a leg-spinner, somewhat in the Benaud mould.

Shivlal Nandlal Yadav made his debut as a right-arm off-break bowler versus Australia in the 1979—80 home series and impressed immediately with 24 wickets at 24.04 in five Tests. He then slipped somewhat until taken to Australia in 1985—86 when he was by far the most teasing and penetrative of India's spin bowlers, taking 15 wickets at 22.26 in three Tests. Other off-spinners like Gopal Sharma and Ashok Patel have been tried in recent seasons, but Yadav remains India's main hope in that department for the foreseeable future.

Maninder Singh, a left-arm protégé of Bishen Bedi, has now emerged as India's leading spin bowler after a dreadfully expensive start when first given his chance at the age of 20 in the West Indies in 1982. Picked to replace Sivaramakrishnan in 1986, the accurate and persistent Maninder can now probably be rated as the best slow left-hander in Test cricket today.

The departure of India's four world-class spin bowlers marked the end of a distinct era in India cricket when slow bowling took preference and bowlers of pace were scarcely visible at all in India's Test teams. Hard as all-rounders like Syed Sardarali Abidali (right-arm medium) and Eknath Dhondu Solkar (left-arm seam and occasional spin) tried they could not by any stretch of the imagination be classified as ideal new-ball bowlers. Both were, however, useful members of the Indian team who weighed in with runs and the odd wicket from time to time to add to their ability as fielders. Two other all-rounders, Madan Lal Udhouram Sharma (a live-wire right-arm medium fast bowler and hard-hitting batsman) and Karson Devjibhai Ghavri (left-handed bat and left-arm medium-pace seamer), also excelled at times. More recently, the persevering right-arm seamer and all-rounder Roger Michael Humphrey Binny has shown some excellent form in both Tests and one-day games.

India's current ace strike bowler, Ramlal Nikhanj Kapil Dev, is a vastly different proposition. Although not a bowler of high pace in the true sense of the word, Kapil Dev can be placed alongside Malcolm Marshall, Imran Kahn, Dennis Lillee and Richard Hadlee as one of the most penetrative new-ball exponents of the past 15 years. Tall and superbly proportioned, Kapil Dev has worried the best opening batsmen with his two-way swing and seam, generated from a model side-on action after an athletic approach to the wicket. He is quick enough to coerce batsmen to move onto the back foot, uses a lethal bouncer, and can obtain lift even off a good length.

The debonaire Kapil Dev has a film star quality about him and some of his performances have taken on the dimensions of a Hollywood (or Bombay) epic. Against Pakistan on 31 January 1980, he became, at 21 years 25 days, the youngest bowler in history to reach 100 Test wickets — beating the record held by Australia's Graham McKenzie by two years 138 days. Two days later, the irrepressible Kapil Dev became the youngest player, at 21 years 27 days, to reach

1000 runs in Test cricket — 99 days better than the previous best, Javed Miandad of Pakistan.

Kapil Dev's 100th wicket also set a record, having taken one year 107 days to reach since his debut against Pakistan at Faisalabad in October, 1978 — a full 267 days faster than England's Ian Botham took to reach the coveted 100. Wondrous deeds indeed from a captivating player whose maxim is attack from the start, as a free-hitting batsman and as a free-flowing fast-medium bowler.

As Indian captain, Kapil Dev's record has not until recently been as striking as his performances with bat and ball but, like many of

Kapil Dev is India's best all-rounder since Mankad and a right-arm fast-medium bowler of the highest class.

his team, time is well on his side as he was barely 26 years old when he led India in England in 1986.

As for new-ball support for Kapil Dev in future years, there are not too many prospects, although the keen but slimly-built Chetan Sharma (right-arm fast-medium with a whippy action) is a great trier, who grabbed 16 wickets in just two Tests in England in 1986 and troubled all of the batsmen. Indian cricket seems to be at some sort of crossroads. There are few spin bowlers around who may conceivably one day approach the class of Bedi, Venkataraghavan, Chandrasekhar and Prasanna. Kapil Dev remains the one and only bowler of pace who is feared at Test level. It has been claimed that a preference for limited over matches among the Indian schools (and a resultant emphasis on containment seam bowling) is preventing young spin bowlers from coming through to challenge at a higher level. Hopefully, steps will be taken to adjust the situation so that the world will not be denied the opportunity of soon witnessing in action the rightful heirs of the Mankads, the Guptes, the Bedis and the Chandrasekhars.

Mention must be made of India's latest spin bowling sensation, Narendra Hirwani, who made his first-class debut for Madhya Pradesh in the Ranji Trophy competition in 1984–85 as something of a youthful heavyweight. He has since lost 14 kilos. When he claimed a world-record 16 wickets for 136 (8/61 and 8/75) on Test debut versus West Indies at Madras in early 1988, the young leg-spin and googly wizard may have regretted his weight loss. His fans immediately offered to reward him with his weight in money!

Hirwani's amazing performance represents the best-ever bowling debut in a Test. His international potential was first noticed when he took 18 wickets for 324 runs in just two Youth Tests in Australia in 1986–87. His rise has been meteoric and hopefully his new brand of Eastern bowling magic will herald an elevation in India's Test cricket fortunes.

25

Pakistan Zindabad!

'Fazal cut through England as Alec Bedser might well have done to Pakistan'
— Alex Bannister

Pakistan's cricket history began amid the ecstasy and the agony of the birth of a new nation when India was partitioned in 1947. The Muslim state was now free and the cry was: 'Pakistan, Zindabad!'. Partition left little organised infrastructure at government level, let alone in the administration of cricket. That Pakistan should within five short years become a Test-playing country was commendable, and a lasting tribute to the persistent labours of men like Justice A R Cornelius and Pakistan's first cricket captain, the former Indian Test player, Abdul Hafeez Kardar. That Pakistan immediately produced a bowler of acknowledged world class was remarkable. That Fazal Mahmood, 'Pakistan's Alec Bedser', should bowl his country to victory in a Test on its first tour of England was little short of miraculous.

The scene was the fourth and final Test of the 1954 England-Pakistan series at the Oval. England was one-up in the series, with two matches left drawn because of rain. Abdul Kardar elected to bat when he won the toss and Pakistan collapsed, all out 133, against an up-and-coming trio of English fast bowlers, Statham, Tyson and Loader. Fazal Mahmood, who had played Ranji Trophy cricket in India at the age of 17, then took the ball to start what became an amazing unbroken bowling spell of 30−16−53−6 that saw England back in the dressing room for 130 runs. Apart from eight overs by Pakistan's spinners, the solidly-built Fazal was backed throughout by the taller and faster right-arm bowler Mahmood Hussain, a willing and able new-ball partner in most of Pakistan's early Tests. With the ball often rising from a length on a responsive pitch, Fazal Mahmood and Mahmood Hussain made the most of the conditions and all 10 Englishmen were out caught.

Pakistan's batsmen then struggled against Johnny Wardle's left-arm spin and England were eventually left with 168 to win, with two and a half hours still left on the fourth day plus the entire fifth. With a batting line-up of Hutton, Simpson, May, Compton, Graveney, there was little concern in the home camp that they would not be able to get the runs before close of play. It is no secret that most of England's players had already planned to catch a certain train home on the fourth evening.

It was not to be. Bowling as before, without any sign of show or outward threat, Fazal proceeded to once again bamboozle England's best with a dazzling show of varied pace and swing and darting leg-cutters and break-backs, all delivered with an economical action reminiscent of their own Alec Bedser. Although he was not as massive in build as Bedser, Fazal's method was similar. As Alex Bannister comments in *Cricket in North India*: 'To the casual observer he might even have appeared harmless, and just another bowler putting his arm over. But what guile and consummate skill went into every ball!'

In England's second innings, Fazal Mahmood returned figures of 30−11−46−6 to bring his match analysis to 12 wickets for 99 runs. The winning target was not reached on the fourth evening and, after 45 minutes on the fifth and final morning, a jubilant Pakistan emerged as victor by 24 runs. The Pakistanis had achieved what no other cricketing nation had done before them − a Test match victory and honours even in a series of three matches or more on their first visit to England.

The redoubtable Fazal Mahmood went on to take 139 wickets at 24.70 in 34 Tests. He had no equal on his home matting wickets at Karachi, were his bowling feats in Tests became legend. Against Australia in 1956−57, his 6/34 and 7/80 saw Pakistan defeat Australia in the first encounter between the two countries. On matting Fazal was often unplayable; on grass he could be equally devastating, as was witnessed at the Oval in 1954. He also captained Pakistan with distinction and was a useful lower-order right-handed batsman and a keen fielder. Fazal Mahmood can be named as one of the two early world-class Pakistani cricketers, the other being the diminutive opening batsman, Hanif Mohammed.

Fazal's new-ball aide at the Oval, Mahmood Hussain, was one of three excellent seam bowlers in the first Pakistan Test elevens. Confident and a willing work-horse, Mahmood Hussain was over-bowled at times, particularly in the West Indies in 1957−58, and his final Test figures of 68 wickets at 38.64 did not fully reflect his worth. The third seamer was the right-arm medium-fast Khan Mohammad, who was as big a threat on matting wickets as Fazal, but whose career suffered because of frequent muscular strains and injuries. Khan Mohammad nevertheless took 54 Test wickets at 23.92, including 21 at 15.86 in Pakistan's first home series against India in 1954−55.

Pakistani captain Abdul Hafeez Kardar was himself a useful slow left-arm bowler but, until the emergence of leg-spinner Intikhab Alam in the 1960s, Pakistan's spin bowlers, for the most part, struggled at Test level. There were, however, players like left-arm spinner Shuja-ud-din Butt, who was also a useful right-handed batsman, and the steady right-arm off-break bowler Zulfiqar Ahmed, who threw in the odd leg-break. Zulfiqar's Test career was short but prolific: 20 wickets at 18.20 in nine Tests − 19 of his wickets were obtained in three games against New Zealand in Pakistan in 1955−56.

Leg-break and googly bowler Khalid Hassan played his one and only Test in England in 1954 at the age of 16 years 352 days and was Pakistan's youngest Test player for three years. Off-break bowler Miran Bux, who played in two Tests versus India in 1954−55, is the oldest Pakistani player on debut − 47 years 284 days. The amusing and much-loved Amir Elahi was a leg-break and googly bowler who played in a Test for India in Australia in 1947−48 and became one of the 12 players to represent two countries when he took part in the first official India-Pakistan series in 1952−53.

Two teenage spin bowlers went through a Test baptism of fire when taken to the West Indies in 1957−58. Right-arm off-spinner Haseeb Ahsan and orthodox left-arm spinner Nasim-ul-Ghani bowled with great pluck, but little good fortune, against Gary Sobers and friends in a rampant mood. Haseeb Ahsan conceded 496 runs for his five wickets in the Caribbean and proved rather expensive in the 12 Test he eventually played for Pakistan. He also went through the agony of accusations about a suspect action and was no-balled for throwing in a Pakistan versus India Test at Bombay in 1960−61. The 17-year-old Nasim-ul-Ghani came through the West Indies ordeal with 19 Test wickets at 26.73, but his return in international matches thereafter was rather slim. He did, however, develop as a batsman and hit a century against England at Lord's in 1962.

Pakistan's first really outstanding international spin bowler was a modest man who led Pakistan in 17 Tests and was throughout his long career a universally popular character. The thick-set and prematurely balding Intikhab Alam Khan, under medium height but all muscle, wheeled his arm over to deliver tantalising leg-breaks, top-spinners and googlies in all conditions in Pakistan, in English county cricket and on tours overseas, suffering good fortune and bad with equanimity for 20 years. On the way, he picked up more than 1500 first-class wickets, including 125 at 35.95 in 47 Tests. 'Inti' was one of those individuals who just always seemed to be in the game and, as the resident big-hitter in the Pakistan team (he could also defend if necessary), he came close to 1500 Test runs at an average in the 20s.

As a Test bowler, Intikhab Alam began his career by bowling Australia's Colin McDonald with his first ball at Karachi in 1959−60. His first real match-winning showing was against New Zealand in 1964−65, also at Karachi, when he spun his way to figures of 3/53 and 4/39 and had the opposition batsmen in all kinds of trouble. In his first series as captain, Intikhab celebrated with a 10-wicket haul against New Zealand at Dacca (an identical 5/91 in each innings).

As skipper of Pakistan, the engaging Intikhab went unbeaten

through the England tour of 1974, his team holding its own in three drawn Tests. He also captained his country on his own second visit to Australia in 1972–73, but handed over to Mushtaq Mohammed before the two tours to Australia and West Indies in 1976–77. This latter tour proved a dreadfully unhappy trip for Intikhab, who found himself isolated when he refused to join other players in their demands for higher pay. He maintained his loyalty to Pakistani cricket and became manager of the team in 1982. His partnership with new skipper Imran Khan proved fruitful and helped raise Pakistani cricket to new levels of achievement.

Intikhab's successor as captain, Mushtaq Mohammed, was also a leg-break and googly bowler of class. The only one of the four renowned Mohammed brothers to bowl regularly, Mushtaq was, of course, one of Pakistan's leading batsmen who scored more than 3000 Test runs. Making his international debut aged 15 years 124 days (the youngest in history), Mushtaq Mohammed also claimed 79 Test wickets at 29.22 and, with his deceptive googly, was a match-winner under the right conditions.

Current leg-spin and googly practitioner in the Pakistan eleven is the enigmatic and temperamental Abdul Qadir Khan, an individualist who has at his command a variety of deliveries to supplement the conventional leg-break and googly. Qadir uses two versions of the

The enigmatic googly bowler Abdul Qadir of Pakistan is a world-beater on his day.

top-spinner and a Richie Benaud type 'flipper' and, when he took 6/133 against England at Edgbaston in 1982, one report commented that his 371 deliveries comprised 'every possible variation on a leg-spinner's theme'.

Although he has found it difficult at times to live up to his reputation as an embarrasser of batsmen in every Test series he has played, Abdul Qadir is one of the most entertaining bowlers of the day. One of his most outstanding series came in 1982–83 when his 22 wickets at 25.54 helped Pakistan win all three Tests versus Australia. Of his other major performances, Qadir's sensational 6/16 to dismiss West Indies for 53 runs at Faisalabad in 1986, his 7/96 versus England at the Oval in 1987 and his incredible 9/56 and 4/45 to humble England at Lahore in 1987–88 stand out.

Of Pakistan's more conventional spin bowlers, two orthodox left-arm spinners stand out. The economical and penetrating Pervez Sajjad Hassan (brother of Test batsman Waqar Hassan) took 59 wickets at 23.89 in 19 Tests between 1964 and 1973. At Auckland in 1964–65, Pervez Sajjad dismissed four New Zealand batsmen in 10 balls without conceding a run. The equally accurate and effective Mohammad Iqbal Qasim has taken 137 wickets at 29.16 in 41 Tests since his debut in 1976 but has not been picked regularly in recent seasons because of a preference for pace bowlers. Iqbal Qasim has done most of his finest work in home-based Test matches, although he has toured to all the other major countries except Sri Lanka. His best Test figures are 7/49 versus Australia at Karachi in 1979–80.

Off-break bowlers of Test class have been few in Pakistani cricket, but bowlers like Mohammed Nazir junior and Tauseef Ahmed have had their days of success. Mohammed Nazir was a good flighter of the ball who played in eight Tests in the 1970s and took 26 wickets at 24.42 Tauseef Ahmed, who turns the ball sharply, played his first Test against Australia at Karachi as a 19-year-old in 1979–80 and took 4/64 and 3/62. In Pakistan's two most recent series, versus Sri Lanka at home and in Sri Lanka in 1985–86, Tauseef Ahmed's off-breaks were decisive in two wins out of the three Tests in which he appeared. At Karachi, in the third Test of the home series in Pakistan, he took 5/54 in Sri Lanka's second innings and, at Kandy in the first Test of the away series, his 3/32 and 6/45 wrapped up the match for Pakistan.

Two leading batsman (other than Mushtaq Mohammed) have also been useful bowlers in Tests in support of the speed and seam oriented Pakistan attack. Saeed Ahmed, who scored nearly 3000 Test runs as a resplendent stroke-player, was not used much as a bowler when he first appeared, but later look 22 wickets at 36.45 with off-breaks. Dashing left-handed batsman Wasim Hasan Raja also came close to 3000 Test runs and bagged 51 wickets at 35.80 with his flighty leg-breaks and top-spinners.

As mentioned earlier, Pakistan's bowling attack has become reliant mainly on pace bowling but, after the decline of the great Fazal Mahmood in the early 1960s, there was, with one or two exceptions, something of a dearth of high-class seam bowlers. The list of those who took the new ball in a few Tests and then disappeared from the scene is quite a long one and includes: left-handed all-rounder Israr Ali; right-arm medium-fast Antao D'Souza; the energetic and quite fast right-armer Mohammed Farooq; Munir Malik, another hard-worker at right-arm fast-medium; and Arif Butt, also right-arm fast-medium, who took 6/89 in Australia's first innings at Melbourne in 1964−65. Two unlikely new-ball bowlers were the notable batting pair Majid Jahangir Khan and Asif Iqbal Razvi (both right-arm fast-medium at the time) who opened the bowling together on their joint Test debut versus Australia at Karachi in 1964−65. Asif Iqbal remained a useful change bowler throughout his career and took 51 Test wickets.

Saleem Altaf Bokhari was a more formidable and talented right-arm fast-medium bowler who came to stay for a while. With his ability to swing the ball both ways, Saleem Altaf bowled particularly well in Australia and New Zealand in 1972−73 and became a fine support seamer to the newly-emerged Sarfraz Narwaz and Imran Khan. He also provided aid in some Tests for the well-proportioned Asif Masood, who caused a flurry among England's batsmen in 1971 when he took 5/111 and 4/49 in the first Test at Edgbaston, after Zaheer Abbas's monumental innings of 274 had set Pakistan up with a first innings total of 608 for seven wickets declared. In the end England saved the game but Asif Masood, with his stuttering start to his run, his military demeanour and big black moustache flowing, was bowler of the match.

The arrival of Sarfraz Narwaz and Imran Khan brought new life into Pakistan's out cricket. The tall and strong Malik Sarfraz Narwaz was a bit of a maverick and a law unto himself who once had the temerity to bowl bouncers at Australia's fiery speedster Jeff Thomson. After a rather stiff approach with his back straight as a ram-rod, Sarfraz Narwaz used sheer strength to generate sufficient pace and lift to trouble most batsmen. He also swung the ball disconcertingly at times and moved it both ways off the seam. A thoroughly professional bowler, Sarfraz played for Northamptonshire for 12 seasons and in 55 Tests for Pakistan took 177 wickets at 32.75.

Sarfraz Narwaz's most stunning Test performance has seldom been approached in terms of match-winning effectiveness. Needing 382, Australia appeared to have victory well within its grasp at 305 for three wickets at Melbourne in 1978−79. The big Pakistani fast bowler then shortened his run and, bowling seam up, turned the match on its head in an amazing spell that brought him seven wickets for just one run in 33 balls and a final analysis of 9/86. Like

With his devastating
ieg-stump yorker, the
dashing Imran Khan is as
potent a fast bowler as any
in world cricket.

so many humpty-dumpties, the Australian batsmen tumbled from
305 for three to 310 all out and Pakistan won by 71 runs.

Imran Khan Niazi entered Test cricket as an 18-year-old rookie
right-arm fast-medium bowler in England in 1971. By 1976–77,
when New Zealand toured Pakistan, he had developed into a bowler
of genuine speed who formed with Sarfraz Narwaz as effective an
opening combination as was around in world cricket at the time.
Imran Khan has since become transformed into a glamorous figure in
world cricket, as a match-winning bowler and as a dashing right-
handed batsman whose performances have placed him on the short
list of the greatest all-rounders of all time.

He would be worth his place in any Test team as a batsman and fielder alone. But it is as a devastating fast bowler with the most vicious leg-stump yorker in the business that has made Imran Khan one of the most feared opponents on the international cricket circuit. Outside the West Indies, Imran Khan is one of a handful of genuine fast bowlers in modern Test cricket who are able to gain some sort of psychological advantage over their opponents, even before a ball has been bowled.

Imran Khan is able to beat batsmen by sheer speed through the air and off the pitch. Add to this his ability to bowl a virtually unplayable outswinger to complement his vicious in-dipping yorker and the attributes of a truly great fast bowler are apparent. Bending forward at the waist as he runs in to bowl, Imran provides an exhilarating athletic spectacle that has seldom been matched in any time period.

His outstanding bowling feats in Tests are many and include 14 wickets for 116 versus Sri Lanka at Lahore in 1981−82, which included his best innings analysis of 8/58. A shin injury prevented Imran from bowling for a couple of seasons. When he recovered, newspaper headlines read: 'Return of the Mighty Khan'. During the 1985−86 season he took 32 wickets at 16.93 in six home and away Tests with Sri Lanka, a team that is no pushover these days as far as batting is concerned. At 33 Imran Khan still has some time to improve on his already impressive Test bowling record of 264 wickets in 57 Tests at 22.19. He has also scored more than 2000 Test runs.

Up to 1983, Imran relied mostly on Sarfraz Narwaz as seam bowling support. Of the lesser lights, men like Ehtesham-ud-Din, the bespectacled Jalal-ud-din, Sikander Bahkt, Rashid Khan and Tahir Naqqash, all right-arm and ranging from medium to fast-medium, have been used as third and fourth seamers, with Sikander Bakht the only one of the group to play with any great regularity.

For the future there is the 22-year-old Azeem Hafeez and the 19-year-old Wasim Akram, both left-armers and both of whom have already made a distinct mark in Test cricket.

Azeem Hafeez is, like India's spin wizard B S Chandrasekhar, a handicapped player who has succeeded at the highest level. The 6 ft 2 in (188 cm) Pakistani left-arm fast bowler has a deformed right hand which has only one normal digit on it, the thumb, and his right arm is a good three inches shorter than the left. This has not prevented Azeem from becoming a fair fieldsman, although he does experience some difficulty when batting. After a grand debut against India in 1982−82, when he claimed 11 wickets in three Tests, Azeem captured the hearts of the Australian crowds in 1983−84 when Imran Khan was injured and unable to bowl and the brave young seamer was called upon to virtually carry Pakistan's pace attack. Against a strong Australian batting team, Azeem had figures of 27.3−5−100−5 at Perth, a marathon 38.2−8−167−5 at Adelaide, and topped Pakistan's bowling table despite a belated recall of veteran Sarfraz Narwaz.

Wasim Akram is a shy young man who arrived in New Zealand for his first overseas tour in 1984–85, minus a pair of proper bowling boots. He borrowed a pair and took 12 wickets in his two Tests, including 10/128 in the final match at Dunedin where he also cracked the skull of New Zealand all-rounder Lance Cairns with a bouncer. On the way home, the young left-arm pace bowler surprised Australia with a Man-of-the-Match 5/21 spell at Melbourne in a preliminary round of the World Championship of Cricket that ensured Pakistan's place in the semi-finals (and, eventually, in the final versus India).

Another integral member of Pakistan's present bowling line-up is a right-arm medium-paced seamer whose rather gentle looking deliveries contain more menace than is at first apparent and who has a unique connection with the beginnings of Pakistan as a Test-playing nation. At Lord's in 1982, Mudassar Nazar took 6/32 against England in an inspired spell that gave Pakistan its one Test win of the season; he is also one of his country's most prolific opening batsmen. His father, Nazar Mohammad, was the man who faced up to the first ball bowled in Pakistan's first-ever Test, against India at Delhi in October 1952, when Mudassar Nazar was just 16 years old.

26

Pollocked and Proctered

*'It was nine years of team spirit, of great individual feats, of some
brilliant cricket, some spine-tingling excitement and bitter frustration . . .'*
— Peter Pollock

The first cold winds of cricket isolation were felt by South Africa in
1968 when a politically expedient statement from Prime Minister
Vorster shut the door on the 1968–69 MCC team because of the
inclusion in the English team of South African-born black cricketer
Basil D'Oliveira, who was by then an English citizen. The wall of ice
around South Africa closed in even further when the proposed 1970
tour of England by the Springboks and then the 1971–72 visit to
Australia were also cancelled because of the threat of disruption of
cricket by political demonstrations.

It was to be 10 long years before a series of 'rebel' tours was
arranged to create a few cracks in the wall that was keeping South
Africa from participation in international competition.

It was rather ironic that, during the decade preceding South Africa's
banning from Test cricket, the Springboks played some of their
finest cricket and produced a team that was not only the best South
African team of all time but a challenger, at the time, for 'best in the
world'. The Springboks beat England in England in 1965, thrashed
Australia at home in 1966–67 and 1969–70 but it should be recorded
that the 'world title' claim would only have been truly validated if
South Africa had been able to meet a full-strength West Indies XI.
Perhaps the day is not too distant when such a contest will be
arranged. It remains a pity that such an event will come too late for
South Africa's own 'Golden Age' cricketers: Graeme and Peter Pollock,
Eddie Barlow, Barry Richards, Mike Procter and their many talented
team-mates of the past 20 years.

Before isolation, South Africa, between 1961 and 1970, produced a
number of world-class batsmen and bowlers who would rank with
the best from any country. One of these was a man who has been
acknowledged by most of his contemporary players as the main
inspiration behind the resurgence in South Africa's cricket fortunes
during the 1960s.

Although Edgar John Barlow was selected primarily as a gifted
and gutsy opening batsman (he was also a former wicket-keeper and
a brilliant slip fielder), he turned himself, through sheer willpower,

from an occasional change bowler into a right-arm medium-fast seamer who once stunned a full England eleven at Leeds when he claimed four wickets in five balls, including a hat-trick, and ended the match with 7/64 and 5/78. Barlow confessed at the time that his hat-trick was the first he had ever seen. His ace bowling performance came when he was playing for a powerful Rest of the World XI in 1970 that had been organised to replace the cancelled South African tour. As an all-rounder, the ebullient Springbok vied with the mighty Gary Sobers himself for top spot in the composite team.

Barlow was, like Lillee, Botham and a few others, one of those bowlers who genuinely expected to take a wicket with every ball he sent down. Spectacles glistening in the sun, every inch of his muscular, power-packed body straining, he always looked as though he could not get to the wicket and deliver the ball quickly enough. If he failed to take a wicket, Barlow would stand hands on hips glaring belligerently at the batsman, almost as if psyching his opponent into believing that the next delivery would get him for sure. Barlow bowled a booming outswinger that came to be known as his 'banana ball'. His first Test efforts were considered something of a joke — until a 5−2−6−3 spell at Adelaide in 1963−64 won a Test for South Africa. In 30 official Tests, Barlow took 40 wickets at 34.05 and frequently did not bowl at all. If the five matches played for Rest of the World versus England are included, his record reads: 60 wickets at 29.30. Barlow also scored more than 2500 Test runs.

Of South Africa's post-war fast bowlers, the most successful in terms of performance was Peter Maclean Pollock, right-handed older brother of the left-handed batting genius Graeme Pollock. Peter Pollock was genuinely fast and was a potential match-winner on tours to England and Australasia, as well as in his own country. In contrast, the other leading South African post-war quickies, Adcock, Heine, Mike Procter, Clive Rice and Garth le Roux, either did not play at all in Australia or (as was the case with the last three mentioned) appeared only in World Series Cricket there.

Fair-haired like his famous batting brother, Peter Pollock was a strapping 6 ft 2½ in (189 cm) and all fast bowler, in method, in purpose and in result. In Australasia in 1963−64, Peter Pollock's bowling was described as 'brute-force bowling flat out', with little variation but with loads of determination that brought him 25 wickets at 28.40 versus Australia in five Tests and 15 wickets at 17.20 versus New Zealand in three Tests. When he went to England in 1965, the older Pollock brother began to mature into the wily fast bowler he was to remain to the end of his truncated career, always scheming, but never reluctant to drop the ball short to test a batsman's nerve.

The Pollocks sometimes played like a two-man team in England in 1965 and won a vital Test at Nottingham with a minimum of help from the other nine Springboks. 'Little Dog' Graeme Pollock's first

Peter Pollock was a belligerent fast bowler who succeeded in Tests in four countries.

knock of 125 out of 160 in 140 minutes on a seamer's wicket remains one of the classic Test innings in history. 'Big Dog' Peter Pollock did the bowler's double — five wickets in each England innings — to give him match figures of 10/87 and to give England little hope of saving the game or the series.

In 28 Tests, Peter Pollock took 116 wickets at 24.18, more than any other South African fast bowler. He was also no mean player with the bat, as was witnessed at Melbourne in 1971−72 when he scored 54 and helped Gary Sobers add 186 runs for the eighth wicket for a World XI versus Australia.

When South Africa stormed to victory in its final two Test series before isolation (both played against Australia) in 1966−67 and 1969−70, Peter Pollock teamed up with a fast-bowler and all-rounder of such proportions that he was to become universally known as the 'White Sobers'. Sadly, the Test career of Michael John Procter was limited to just seven matches − all against Australia.

Built like the trunk of an oak, unruly thatch of fair hair bobbing in the breeze, Mike Procter came bounding in with long athletic strides, starting with a canter but ending in a full gallop. With his peculiar and apparently wrong-footed action, he defied all known principles of the bowling art to propel the ball towards the batsman as swiftly as anyone before or since. His arm came over high, brushing his right ear, but Procter used virtually no body-swing: it was sheer strength of arm and back that did the work. His stock delivery swung into the right-handed batsman; his bouncer was a frightening experience, the sort of ball a head-hunter from Borneo might bowl.

In three Tests against Australia in 1966−67, Procter took 15 wickets at 17.53. In 1969−70 he had 26 at only 13.57 in four games − a total of 41 at 15.02 in his seven Tests. No Australian batsman faced him with confidence. In South African domestic cricket and in English county cricket, he became something of a legend while for Rhodesia he hit six centuries in a row to equal the world record. His performances in English cricket were so immense that his county, Gloucestershire, became known as 'Proctershire'. There is no-one who would dare deny that 'Proccie', had he been given the opportunity, would have come closest to rivalling Sir Garfield Sobers as top Test all-rounder of the 1970s.

Peter Pollock, and later the Pollock-Procter combination, received grand support from a bevy of seam and pace bowlers who helped to form what was perhaps South Africa's most penetrative attack of all time. Against New Zealand in 1961−62, the 21-year-old tearaway Pollock vied for new-ball duties with men like Kenneth Alexander Walter and the 6 ft 5 in (195 cm) Rhodesian giant, Godfrey Bernard Lawrence, both right-arm fast. 'Goofy' Lawrence swung the ball prodigiously to take 8/53 in a New Zealand innings at Johannesburg in 1961−62, but lost his place to fellow-Rhodesian Joseph Titus Partridge for the 1963−64 Australasian tour. The bespectacled and tireless Partridge bowled his accurate right-arm inswingers to such

The strong and energetic Mike Procter produced astounding figures in seven Tests before South Africa's isolation from international cricket.

good effect at Sydney that he claimed 18 of his 25 wickets in the series against Australia. Another Springbok right-arm fast-medium seamer of great stamina was Sydney Frank Burke, whose two Tests were spaced three years apart, despite his having taken 11/196 in 80 overs in his debut game against New Zealand at Cape Town in 1961–62.

Batsman Herbert Roy 'Tiger' Lance was an above average right-arm fast-medium bowler who sometimes came on first change, while James Thomas Botten and Patrick Henry Joseph Trimborn were two pacy right-armers who might have thrived during the 1960s and 1970s if South Africa had not been isolated from international cricket. Jacky Botten bowled a useful outswinger and shared the new ball with Peter Pollock in England in 1965. Pat Trimborn also seamed the ball cleverly and played a major part in South Africa's win in the fifth Test against Australia at Port Elizabeth in 1966–67.

South Africa generally played only one spinner during the 1960s. The tall and accurate right-arm off-spinner Henry Dudley Bromfield had an analysis of 57.2–26–88–5 in England's first innings at Cape Town in 1964–65, but was seldom given much work in his nine Tests. Two other right-arm off-break bowlers, Michael Arthur Seymour and David Bartlett Pithey, were taken to Australia in 1963–64 but made little impression in Tests. 'Kelly' Seymour was a medico who retired from the game early and David Pithey was the brother of dour Springbok opening bat of the time, Tony Pithey. A fourth right-arm off-break bowler, Athanasios John Traicos, was born in Egypt of Greek parents and played in a couple of Tests in South Africa's last series, versus Australia in 1969–70. Traicos has since reappeared as one of the king pins of the Zimbabwe team that appears to be challenging for Test recognition.

Traicos was one of the original selections for the aborted 1970 South African tour of England, as was orthodox left-arm spinner Grahame Anton Chevalier, surely one of the unluckiest of Springboks. Grahame Chevalier took five wickets for 100 runs in the two innings of his only Test, at Cape Town, versus the 1969–70 Australians. He was then picked for the cancelled 1970 England tour and again for the cancelled 1971–72 Australian venture. Before Chevalier appeared, South Africa's leading left-arm spinner was the burly and jovial Atholl Henry McKinnon, a popular player who died of a heart attack in 1983 when manager of the touring West Indies XI.

Only three spin bowlers of note have appeared since South Africa departed the official Test arena. Denys Hobson and Alan Kourie have played in internationals against the 'rebel' English, Sri Lankan, West Indian and Australian sides. The third, Omar Henry, orthodox left-arm slow and a crowd-pleasing big hitter, is the only black player to appear for an official South African XI since South African cricket went completely non-racial in 1977. Denys Laurence Hobson has now retired from first-class cricket but was for a decade South Africa's leading spin bowler. A quickish leg-break and googly bowler of the Doug Wright type, he made a particular impression on former Australian captain Richie Benaud. Hobson actually travelled to Australia in 1978–79 at Kerry Packer's invitation to play in World Series Cricket but was, together with Graeme Pollock, prevented from doing so as he was not a full-time professional cricketer. South Africa's current leading spin bowler, orthodox left-hander Alan John Kourie, is a highly competitive all-rounder who has troubled all the visiting 'rebel' batsmen.

The list of South African bowlers denied international cricket is a long one and it seems that men like fast left-arm Donald Mackay-

The 6 ft 7½ in (202 cm) Vintcent van der Bijl was the greatest South African bowler never to have played in an official Test.

Coghill, spearhead of the Transvaal attack for half a dozen years when South African cricket was well and truly in the wilderness, may be forgotten by future generations. One of South Africa's finest bowlers of the past decade did so remarkably well in domestic cricket, for Middlesex in the English county championship and in the few unofficial international series in which he participated, that he was judged by the best critics as probably the greatest South African bowler never to have played in a regular Test.

The towering and avuncular 6 ft 7½ in (202 cm) Vintcent Adriaan Pieter van der Bijl, at the age of 32, bowled so magnificently for Middlesex in England in 1980 that his skipper, former England captain Mike Brearley, maintained that without the giant South African his county could never have won the championship that year. When the various mercenary teams from England, Sri Lanka and the West Indies arrived in South Africa, the veteran van der Bijl was not once mastered, and gave his opponents an object lesson in swing and seam, line and length and change of pace.

Lumbering in like an African bull elephant preparing for a charge, the balding 'Big Vince' van der Bijl brought his arm over high in his delivery, using his full height to rap batsmen's knuckles and chests, on the truest of pitches. For 15 seasons he dominated Currie Cup cricket; his 572 wickets in that competition exceeds the next best, Mike Procter, by 111 wickets. In his six unofficial international matches for South Africa during the 1980s, van der Bijl took 29 wickets at 19.86. He was truly one of the giants of South African cricket.

In the 'rebel' games, van der Bijl operated for most of the time opposite the massively built Garth Stirling le Roux, whose parents must have been blessed with uncommon foresight, for he looks uncommonly like the cartoon character who gave him his first name. The right-arm fast Garth le Roux tested the best when he played World Series Cricket in Australia in 1978−79 (he was named 'Player of the Series') and was still firing when Kim Hughes's Australian XI was overrun by the Springboks in 1985−86. At Johannesburg, in the third 'international', le Roux and his skipper, Clive Rice, each grabbed a hat-trick as the Australians were swept away for 61 all out in their second innings. In 15 'rebel' games for South Africa, le Roux has taken 59 wickets at 23.27.

Clive Edward Butler Rice, like Mike Procter, has done so enormously well in English county cricket that his name has become synonymous with that of Nottinghamshire, which he captained with great skill. As an all-rounder, Rice must be counted among the best three or four produced by his country. He thrived when he played World Series Cricket in Australia, as a hard-hitting right-hand batsman and as a nippy right-arm fast-medium bowler who could occasionally slip in a delivery of real pace. Although he suffered a neck injury that hampered his bowling for a couple of seasons, Rice, at the age of 36, confirmed against the 1985−86 and 1986−87 Australian team that he is still one of South Africa's top strike bowlers.

Of the younger South African pace bowlers who have gained recognition against the various 'rebel' sides, the left-arm fast-medium Stephen Thomas Jefferies has taken a bag of wickets and impressed with his speciality, a swinging, leg-stump yorker. Of the three new fast bowlers introduced against Hughes's Australians the quickest included the 6 ft 4 in (193 cm) Hugh Ashton Page, who was at one time the most talked-about young cricketer in South Africa but who has since failed to impress in English county cricket for Essex. Two other quickies from the veld have also played recently in England: the fiery Cornelius Johannes Petrus Gerhardus van Zyl (like former Springbok demon bowler Peter Heine, an Afrikaner from the Orange Free State) has appeared for Glamorgan and Alan Donald, also from Free State, has played for Warwickshire.

Whether players like Donald, Page and van Zyl will ever play in an official Test is an open question in a rapidly changing world where anything can happen, and sometimes overnight. The facts that do remain are that South Africa's isolation from Test cricket for more than a decade has been a tragedy for a whole generation of Springbok sportsmen, white and black − and a great loss, in terms of entertainment value, to the rest of the world.

27

Life with Lillee and Thomson

'...their names had become synonymous with pain and terror or triumph and revenge, depending upon one's nationality'

— David Frith

'Ashes to Ashes, Dust to Dust; if Lillee don't get ya, Thommo must!' were the words emblazoned on an Aussie supporter's t-shirt during the 1975 Prudential World Cup tournament in England. During the previous English winter, Australia's fearsome pair of fast bowlers, Dennis Lillee and Jeff Thomson, had so battered and bewildered England's batsmen that there was doubt about whether some would continue to play Test cricket.

Broken hands and split fingers abounded among the hapless Englishmen. A disturbing factor was the number of blows suffered by tail-end batsmen, who were frequently bombarded with a barrage of bouncers — a sight seldom before witnessed in Test cricket. According to Jim Laker, a bumper bowled by Lillee at tail-ender Geoff Arnold parted the England bowler's hair as he stood petrified and helpless. Lillee also once bowled a beamer at English fast bowler Bob Willis. By no stretch of the imagination could players like Arnold and Willis be described as a batting threat and the tactics employed by Lillee and Thomson in 1974–75 must always remain questionable.

Some English critics claimed that the umpires were grossly at fault for allowing the Australian pair to bowl in such an intimidatory fashion. There were few complaints from their Australian counterparts, who still held fresh memories of Tyson, Statham and Trueman and the more recent England express bowler, John Snow. Australians have in more recent times voiced some criticism of the tactics used by the current herd of magnificent West Indian fast bowlers. Memories are perhaps short. It seems that genuinely quick bowlers are always welcome when they are on your own side.

So much has already been penned about the ferociously competitive Dennis Keith Lillee that it is no easy task to produce any new and unfamiliar epithet with which to honour his achievements. There have been claims that 'Thommo' was the pacier of the Australian pair and for a while, possibly the fastest bowler of all time. It was, however, the wily Lillee who combined brains and brawn, stamina and skill, to became a legend in his own lifetime.

Breathing fire, the fast and furious young Lillee took 5/84 on

his debut against England at Adelaide in 1970–71. A spell in the Lancashire League followed and league batsmen of the time will verify that, when conditions suited him, Lillee could let slip with a burst of fast bowling as quick as had ever been seen north of the Mersey River. Then, when the proposed 1971–72 South African tour of Australia was cancelled, Lillee vented his frustration on a hastily invited Rest of the World XI. A great leap forward in his bowling came with a stunning 8/29 spell that put the World XI out for a lowly 59 at Perth and signalled the 'arrival' of a new force in international cricket.

In England in 1972, the still tearaway Lillee, an out-and-out express merchant with terrifying speed his main stock-in-trade, grabbed 31 wickets at 17.67 runs, a record at the time for an Australian fast bowler. Never afraid to use a menacing bouncer, Lillee was once quoted as saying that there was no use in bumping them if the intention was not to occasionally wing (and intimidate) the batsman.

Lillee was still flying high when he left Australia for the Caribbean in 1972–73. He came home in despair after just one Test (and 0/132) to be encased in plaster because of stress fractures in his spine. Then began one of the most remarkable of sporting comebacks. With the dedication of 10 men, Lillee stuck to an exhausting programme of exercises in an effort to cure his back injury. His return to big cricket in 1974–75 was little short of miraculous – and just in time to team up with Thomson to set up a new firm of Australian new-ball wreckers to compare with, in fire and effectiveness, Gregory and McDonald, Lindwall and Miller.

With the encouraging chant 'Lillee, Lillee, Lillee . . .' in his ears, the rejuvenated paceman and his new mate had the Englishmen ducking and diving for cover. At one end they were assailed by Jeff Thomson's rib-bruising thunderbolts. From the other, Lillee was bowling as fast as ever before, coming into his final stride with an athletic bounding leap which was almost as frightening as the delivery which came whizzing so swiftly past the batsman's ears.

Lillee was to slow down considerably after the World Series inter-regnum, but maintained his hostile, competitive approach right through to the end of his Test career. A master of the leg-cutter and of a superb out-swinger, Lillee still bounced the ball awkwardly after his pace finally slackened. But the truly marvellous quality in Lillee's bowling was his pin-point accuracy and the fact that he scarcely ever wasted a delivery. Every ball, so it seemed, was thought out in advance. By the time he retired in 1983, Dennis Lillee had achieved a new world record Test haul of 355 wickets at 23.92 in 70 games for Australia – a fitting memorial to the great courage and skill of a man who may well be the greatest Australian bowler of all time.

During a season when Richard Hadlee of New Zealand swept past

Opposite: Australia's Dennis Lillee is acknowledged as one of the finest fast bowlers in history and a candidate for the best of all time.

Lillee's 355 Test wickets, and looked like overhauling record-holder Ian Botham, Lillee made a sensational comeback to first-class cricket for Tasmania in early 1988.

It is certain that Lillee will not be mainly recalled for his various on-the-field indiscretions, such as the notorious clash with Pakistan's pint-sized Javed Miandad, who responded with upraised bat, ready to strike the big Australian, after Lillee had aimed a foot at his posterior. He will surely be remembered for his guts in mastering an injury which would have crippled most for life, to become the finest bowler of his time and a candidate for the short-list of the finest bowlers in cricket history.

The bowling action employed by Dennis Lillee's fearsome partner, Jeffrey Robert Thomson, has been likened to that of a slingshot. Although not copybook in the classic sense, Jeff Thomson's slinging and swinging action did bring him side-on before delivering the ball. When he first partnered Lillee, the young Thomson relied almost totally on extreme pace and body-threatening bounce to subdue opposition batsmen. The ball was hidden behind Thomson's body until his 'slingshot' delivery propelled his right-arm over, much in the manner of a javelin thrower. When he added an in-swinging bouncer, through the use of wrist movement, Thomson became virtually unplayable on a fast wicket. Much later he learned to use his wrist to also move the ball away towards the slips.

There have been almost as many articles, apocryphal or otherwise, about Jeff Thomson's joy at seeing a batsman writhe and bleed on the ground as that excellent fast bowler has taken wickets in Test cricket. At his quickest, Thomson was, as far as batsmen were concerned, for a few years one of the most avoidable of all Australian fast bowlers. West Indies captain Clive Lloyd was even once heard to quip: 'The best way to play Thomson is to get down the other end.'

Thomson's entry into Test cricket was as inauspicious as it was foolhardy when he hid the fact of a broken bone in his foot to make his debut against Pakistan at Melbourne in 1972–73. He took no wickets for plenty and had to wait until the 1974–75 series against England for his second chance. Thomson proceeded to take 33 wickets at 17.93 (Lillee had 25 at 23.82) and England retreated from the fray in a shambles, battered, bruised and thoroughly beaten.

A collarbone fracture (incurred when he collided with a fellow fielder) then kept Thomson out of action until the 1977 England tour. Lillee had already joined the breakaway World Series outfit and his erstwhile new-ball partner was left to carry his team's bowling attack on his broad back during the most disastrous tour of England ever undertaken by an Australian side. Thomson nevertheless took 23 wickets at 25.34 and was seldom mastered by the English batsmen.

For the next few seasons Thomson's appearances for Australia were intermittent and he had patently lost his previous zip and rib-

Opposite: Lillee's slingshot-actioned partner Jeff Thomson was a fearsome prospect in his heyday during the 1970s.

tickling effectiveness. But he made a renewed effort during 1981–82 and regained his Test place and, picked as a late selection to tour England in 1985, Thomson moved his wicket tally to 200 at 28.00 in 51 Tests.

One of Dennis Lillee's earlier new-ball partners chose Lord's as the venue for the match which will be remembered as his own. Unfortunately, the 6 ft (183 cm) Robert Arnold Lockyer Massie never again reached the heights he scaled in June 1972 when he stunned the cricketing world by taking 16 wickets (eight in each innings) in his very first Test match.

'Massie's Match' saw Australia draw even with England in what turned out to be a ding-dong battle for supremacy, after the home side had weathered a furious onslaught from Lillee to win the first Test at Manchester. (Massie did not play at Manchester, where Lillee opened with the powerful right-arm fast-medium David John Colley. This was Colley's one and only Test series in which he performed rather usefully as a late-order hitter and support seamer to Lillee and Massie).

Massie's debut Test at Lord's was the stuff of which schoolboys' dreams are made. Under a grey English sky, with the humidity high and a light wind blowing, he had the batsmen nonplussed and the spectators gasping in disbelief as ball after ball passed the groping bats. Bowling around the wicket, the Australian right-arm medium-pacer swung the ball both ways prodigiously, his outswinger frequently moving too much and too soon to touch bat or stumps. Massie bowled 'brick-wall' Geoff Boycott with a superb swinging yorker and scythed through the rest like a wheat-farmer at harvest time, after Lillee had removed numbers two and three in the England batting list. His incredible 8/84 and 8/53 performance brought a Fleet Street headline that boomed the message: 'MASSIECRE AT LORD'S'!

When he came home to a smiling Perth, the cheerful and unaffected Massie mysteriously lost his control and ability to swing the ball. He even lost his place in the Western Australia team and no amount of experimentation with his action could bring back the magic that had been demonstrated at Lord's. In his first Test Massie took 16 wickets for 137; in his remaining five games for Australia he totalled 15 for 510.

Ian Chappell must have been a concerned captain when Australia went to the West Indies in 1972—73. Lillee dropped out after the first Test with his back injury, while poor Bob Massie never even became a contender for a Test spot when he lost, simultaneously, his swing, his length, his line and his confidence. On wickets where fast bowling pays the best dividends, Chappell was left with two virtually untried seam bowlers, a trio of leg-spinners, plus his brother Greg as a medium-pace fill-in.

Thankfully for Australia, both of Chappell's young reserves bowled well above their normal ability to see their country annex the rubber. For Jeffrey Robert Hammond, brisk right-arm fast-medium, it was to be his one and only tour and Test series; for the tall and gangling

Max 'Tanglefoot' Walker, it was the send-off to a lengthy and lucrative Test match career.

Jeff Hammond was one of those unlucky players in Australian cricket who have been prevented by persistent injury from reaching their full potential as international cricketers. As Walker's main support, he claimed 15 West Indian wickets at 32.53 but, back in Australia, broke a bone in his foot and was then further hampered by a back ailment.

The tireless and ever cheerful Maxwell Henry Norman Walker grabbed his chance in the Caribbean in 1972−73 with both hands, with both of his unusually big feet and, in fact, with every fibre of his persevering body and soul. At 6 ft 4 in (193 cm), Walker bowled off the wrong foot at medium-fast, with a tangle of feet and arms and a flashing smile beneath a moustache that would have done a Mexican bandit proud, to capture 26 West Indies wickets at 20.73 in his first five-match Test outing.

Sidling in off a 13-stride run, Max Walker had the ability to bowl long spells of unerring accuracy. His unflagging approach kept batsmen on the defensive and an ability to make the ball lift awkwardly added to his additional wicket-taking menace. Like other men of such height, Walker was able to 'dig' the ball in and obtain bounce on the most placid of pitches, in the style of West Indian Joel Garner and South Africa Vintcent van der Bijl.

When Lillee returned to the Australian side, Walker cheerfully handed the new-ball back to the master and happily resumed as first-change bowler, when the shine had diminished and the batsmen had to be contained. Occasionally during his Test career Walker slipped in a spell of devastating match-winning bowling, more often than not against the run of play. A typical instance was a stunning 6/15 versus Pakistan at Sydney in 1972−73 when the visiting team were quite confident that they would get the 159 runs needed to win for the first time on Australian soil. With ironman Lillee contributing 23 overs unchanged at the other end, Australia won by 52 runs.

The popular Max Walker became something of a local hero at the Melbourne Cricket Ground. In 1974−75 he bowled his heart out there against England to net 8/143 in a total of 529 after Lillee had left the field with an injury. In his 34 Tests for Australia big Max Walker took 138 wickets at 27.47, but his value to the team never lay in statistics alone. He was, above all else, a great team-man who always gave of his absolute best.

When it comes to bowling, Greg Chappell, one of Australia's truly great batsmen, may well be most remembered for the day he sparked an uproar by asking his younger brother, Trevor Chappell, to roll down an under-arm 'grubber' to prevent the last New Zealand batsman from hitting the six required to win a one day limited over international. But as a nagging right-arm medium-pacer Greg

Chappell was, in his own right, often difficult to handle and quietly claimed 47 wickets to add to his record 7110 runs in Test cricket.

Two left-arm seamers of note also played useful supporting roles for Australia during the 1970s as back-up to Lillee, Thomson and Walker. The immensely strong left-handed all-rounder Gary John Gilmour was an aggressive seam bowler and big hitter who gave away big cricket before he turned 30. His slanted and viciously late left-arm inswingers were never more potently revealed than against England at Headingley during the semi-final match of the 1975 World Cup tournament when his 12—6—14—6 spell decimated the England batting line-up.

Although he played in only 15 Tests (54 wickets at 26.03) Gilmour was selected for Australia on close to 30 occasions. But, as he has himself once put it, he was 'vying continually with Max Walker for the honour of *not* carrying the drinks'.

Gilmour relied to a certain extent on his great strength to obtain bowling results; fellow left-handed pace-man Geoffrey Dymock used a smooth and classic approach and delivery. As Queensland's greatest wicket-taker, Dymock acted as combination stock and strike bowler and carried his immense but quiet enthusiasm forward into 21 Tests for Australia. Using a 16-stride approach, Dymock swung mainly towards the slips (to a right-handed batsman) and varied his speed to excellent effect.

Having already made his debut against New Zealand in 1973—74, Dymock was a more seasoned player than some of his non-WSC colleagues, but he managed to keep his place in the Australian team when the 'rebels' were 're-legitimised' in 1978—79. Dymock's 21 Tests produced 78 wickets at 27.12.

Australia's Test match spin bowlers during the 1970s were mostly relegated to the outfield and only brought on to bowl when the quickies needed a rest, or the wicket was abnormally unsuited to seam bowling. Old fashioned leg-spin and googly bowlers like Terence James Jenner and Kerry James O'Keefe were at times included together in the same eleven, but were seldom given an opportunity to carry the attack for Australia; theirs was essentially a supportive role. Both went to the West Indies in 1972—73 but, apart from a couple of lengthy spells at Port-of-Spain, were scarcely used. The third leg-spinner in the 1972—73 Caribbean party, John Russell Watkins, was hardly given a chance and should perhaps have never toured in the first instance. Jenner ended his career with 24 wickets in nine Tests at 31.20. O'Keefe was given more opportunities and bowled at a quicker pace that most leg-spinners to take 53 wickets at 38.07 in 24 Tests.

Before Kerry Packer and his friends caused a division in world cricket of unprecedented proportions, a few other new bowlers came and went for Australia, some of them to return another day after a stint with World Series Cricket. One of the latter was Leonard Stephen Pascoe, the son of Yugoslav migrants and a fiery right-arm fast bowler who came nearest to matching Dennis Lillee in speed and temperament.

Len Pascoe (he was born Durtanovitch) may have made more of an impact on Test cricket if he had not joined the WSC 'circus'. A straight-forward up-and-at-'em fast bowler with no frills, Pascoe was noted for his tendency to 'boil' if taunted by his opponents. Although he struggled at times with a recurring knee problem, Pascoe took 64 wickets in 14 Tests at 26.06. Unfortunately his behaviour on the field sometimes matched his combustible bowling. Lennie Pascoe was the first Australian player to be censured by his own team-mates under the new code of behaviour, and suspended for one month after sending down a beamer to Kim Hughes and then verbally abusing the Western Australian captain.

A man of more gentle mien and less volatile pace was the tall right-arm medium-pace swing bowler Michael Francis Malone. One of the players whose Test career suddenly ended when he was recruited for World Series Cricket, Mick Malone appeared in only one game for Australia but achieved bowling figures of $47-20-63-5$ and $10-4-14-1$ (plus an innings of 46 not out at number 11) in the fifth Test at the Oval in 1977.

A third eventual WSC recruit was one of those rare oddities in Australian cricket, an orthodox left-arm spinner. Raymond James Bright is nicknamed 'Candles' and his light was still burning bright after re-instatement to the Australian team in $1985-86$ when he and the world thought that his Test days were over. An accurate and canny bowler, Bright's best Test match remains his 7/87 versus Pakistan at Karachi in $1979-80$.

A string of Sheffield Shield bowlers were forced into prominence as overnight Test players when the wholesale defection of existing internationals to World Series Cricket began in earnest during $1977-78$. When veteran Bobby Simpson came out of retirement to lead Australia against India in $1977-78$, his first Test eleven contained only two recognised bowlers with previous Test experience, Jeff Thomson, who was still to join the Packer group, and another right-arm fast bowler, Alan Hurst, who had played in one Test against New Zealand four seasons previously.

The well-built Alan George Hurst was, by all reports, equally as fast as Lillee and Thomson, but the comparison ended when he was seen to spray too many of his deliveries down the leg-side. Hurst did, however, enjoy one particularly fine summer, against England in $1978-79$, when he backed up a rampant Rodney Hogg with 25 wickets at 23.08 runs apiece.

Jeff Thomson's new-ball partner in the first Test versus India in $1977-78$ was the right-arm fast-medium Wayne Maxwell Clark, who could send down a vicious bouncer and generally gained much movement in the air and off the pitch. Doubts about the legality of his action rose to haunt him and Clark was summarily dropped when Rodney Hogg struck form and favour the following year.

Fast-medium left-armer John Brian Gannon came in as support seamer to Thomson and Clark in three of the Tests against India, but failed to hold his place when the team was announced to tour West Indies in the same season, his place going to the younger Ian Wayne Callen. Big and strong, the right-arm fast Callen hurt his back in an off-field incident in the West Indies and did not again play for Australia.

Three spin bowlers, two leg-break exponents and one off-breaker received their opportunity to play for Australia during the WSC interlude. First to the mark was the then 32-year-old Anthony Longford Mann, leg-spinner and left-handed hitter whose main claim to fame became his whirlwind century as a night watchman versus India at Perth — the only such instance in Test cricket.

Mann's bowling did not match his batting and James Donald Higgs received the nod for the West Indies trip. The diminutive Higgs had already displayed his leg-breaks and high-bouncing googly on a tour of England in 1975, without playing in a Test. He now became, for a couple of seasons, an integral part of the Australian attack and took 15 wickets at 25.60 in the West Indies and 19 wickets at 24.63 in the 1978–79 series against England. A friendly and likeable character, Higgs took 66 wickets at 31.16 in 22 Tests.

The more temperamental Bruce Yardley was a man who twice changed his bowling style before he came to the notice of Australia's selection committee. At the age of 19, he shared the new ball for Western Australia with Ian Brayshaw at a brisk fast-medium. He then dropped out for five seasons, returning as a medium-paced outswing stock bowler before finally changing over to off-breaks. It was then that 'Roo' Yardley began to fulfill his potential. At 30, he came into the Australian team versus India in 1977–78.

Utilising more spin than most off-break bowlers, Yardley would drift the ball away from the right-handed batsman with a curling and deceptive flight, and then bring it back sharply off the track. He bowled himself into the team to tour the West Indies in 1977–78, but when the rift between the Australian Board of Control and the Packer organisation had been healed, Yardley experienced an on-off relationship with the selectors who rotated the spin-bowling berth between Yardley, left-arm spinner Ray Bright and leg-spinner Jim Higgs.

Bright got the nod for the short 1980 Centenary Test tour of England and was also Australia's main spinner on the full England tour in 1981, when medium-paced off-spinner Graeme Beard was chosen in support.

But Yardley bounced back with a vengeance against Pakistan and West Indies in 1981–82. With a total of 38 wickets at 22.23 in the six Tests played against the two countries that toured Australia, he became the undisputed 'Man of the Season'. In 32 Tests for Australia, Yardley tallied 119 wickets, with 7/98 versus West Indies at Sydney in 1981–82 his best figures.

A fiery right-arm fast bowler who, like Dennis Lillee, beat a back injury that threatened to halt his spectacular career, Rodney Malcolm Hogg was one of the few players recruited during the World Series seasons who was assured of his place in the Australian XI when the more experienced men were again available. Hogg will go down in history as a bowler who claimed an unprecedented 51 wickets in his first Test season – 41 wickets in six games against England and 10 more in two Tests versus Pakistan.

Hogg's golden summer came in 1978–79, but by 1981–82 he was forced to take a full season's break in an effort to diagnose and cure a nagging back injury. That he returned in 1982–83 to regain his Test place and once again join in a fast-bowling torment of the England batsmen was a testimony to Hogg's perseverance and fortitude.

A feature of Hogg's bowling is the sheer effort he puts into every ball, leaning foward in his run up to the wicket as if he cannot wait to get there. His eagerness to let go his deadly missile has occasionally seen him fall flat on his face, to the great amusement of his fellow players.

Hogg was already 27 when he first got the call to play for Australia and 31 when he made his way back into first-class cricket after injury. He struggled to re-establish a permanent place in the Australian team and missing out on a place in the 1985 Australian Ashes squad convinced him to join the 'rebel' Australian team that went to South Africa in the 1985–86 season. In his 38 Tests for Australia, Hogg has taken 123 wickets at 28.24.

Another 'comeback' bowler who has opted for Kruger gold is the likeable and persistent Terence Michael Alderman, who shrugged off a bad shoulder injury to regain his place in the Australian team against the 1984–85 West Indians, and a spot in the 1985 Ashes combination. When he elected to give it all away and go to South Africa instead, Australia lost a bowler who would have been a welcome bolster to the rather thin attack at skipper Allan Border's disposal in England.

Alderman has been plagued with injuries of one sort or another almost from the moment he first represented Western Australia at the age of 18. If his permanent smile is any indication of his philosophical attitude towards life, it is not surprising that he kept going so well and so long despite an abnormal portion of ill-luck on the field of play. Alderman's worst day came in Perth in Novermber 1982 when he was struck on the head from behind when a group of spectators invaded the field. He chased his attacker but dislocated his right shoulder when he launched into a rugby tackle in an effort to catch the miscreant.

Hungry for cricket, and determined to make up for lost time, Alderman played a season for Kent in the English County Championship in 1984. This was part of his comeback programme which included gymnasium work, weight-lifting, running and swimming, much in the style of Dennis Lillee's recovery programme of some years before.

The almost 6 ft 3 in (190 cm) Alderman has been unlucky sometimes but in England in 1981 his personal star was very much in the ascendent when he and Dennis Lillee between them claimed 81 of the 114 England wickets to fall in six Test matches. Alderman's 42 wickets in six games, at 21.26 runs each, beat the record of 41 for Australia-England clashes established by Rodney Hogg in 1978−79. Dennis Lillee ended the series with 39 wickets at 22.30.

Not a pace bowler in the true sense of the word, Alderman relies mainly on swing for his results. His approach to the wicket seems almost lackadaisical and ends up in a rather chest-on delivery. The softer English wickets suit his style of bowling and he thrived on the challenge of bowling into the wind, with Lillee hurtling them down from the other end.

Dennis Lillee's long reign as the king of contemporary Australian bowlers finally ended in 1984. His influence on his colleagues, particularly the younger players, had been immense and it was obvious that it would be unlikely that a replacement would become immediately available to step into his well-worn bowling boots.

Unfortunately, almost a complete generation of Australian bowlers has opted to join the 'rebel' South African venture and, although there are signs of a revival, it may take some while before the heady days of Lillee and Thomson may again be matched.

For a while it looked as if Geoffrey Francis Lawson, right-arm fast with an athletic approach and a high-leaping delivery stride, would be Australia's spearhead bowler for some time to come. But back trouble, which ruined his first England tour in 1981, has again reared its head and a question mark hangs over this talented bowler's future.

'Henry' Lawson took 7/81 in the first innings of the Lord's Test in 1981, before being sidelined by injury. He recovered and moved on to finer achievements in 1982−83 when, against the touring England team, Lawson thrust himself forward as Australia's number one strike bowler. He claimed 34 wickets at 20.20 in the five Tests, bowling Australia to victory at Brisbane, in the second encounter, after the strife-torn first match at Perth (when Alderman was injured) had been left drawn.

Against Clive Lloyd's rampant West Indians in 1984−85, Lawson was the one Australian whose skill of performance bore comparison with that of his West Indian speed counterparts, Marshall, Holding and Garner. At Adelaide in the third Test, he bowled Australia into a first possible winning position with a magnificent 8/112 (West Indies all out 356) only to see his efforts squandered by inept batting.

Like the West Indians, Lawson has never been afraid to pitch the ball short in an effort to unsettle a batsman and has shrugged off the occasional umpires' warning for intimidatory bowling. The effectiveness of his delivery has at times been off-set by his habit of throwing his high-stepping front leg sideways just before letting the ball go, but his hostility and dedication to his task are unquestioned. Apart from the one idiosyncrasy in his delivery stride, Lawson bowls with a smooth run-up and fluid action that is at once effective and pleasing to the eye.

At one time it was thought that the unpredictable Carl Gray Rackemann may turn out to be a force in Test matches for Australia. Arguably the most hostile of Australia's current crop of right-arm fast bowlers, the 6 ft 4 in (193 cm) blond and burly Rackemann has frequently suffered set-backs in his short career through a multitude of minor injuries. His decision to join Kim Hughes's 'rebels' in South Africa may have come as an initial reaction to his non-inclusion in the squad picked to tour England in 1985. In South Africa, Rackemann was an instant success and remains a great loss to Australian cricket. His best moments in Test cricket were against Pakistan in 1983–84, when he took 16 wickets in two matches; a Pakistani batsman was overheard to comment that it was 'dashed unsporting' that his team should be plagued by players like Rackemann when they had come to Australia to play against the likes of Lillee, Marsh and Chappell.

When Clive Lloyd and his West Indies team arrived in Australia in October 1984, they might have been excused if their reaction to the mention of Australia's latest fast-bowling 'find' was a puzzled 'Craig McWho?' But after viewing the young giant from a distance of 22 yards, some of the West Indian batsmen began to take a closer interest in Craig John McDermott. By the time it came to the fourth match of the Test rubber, the 19-year-old right-arm tearaway was hurling them down as first change to Lawson and Hogg and, in the final thriller at Sydney, was given first shine, opposite Lawson.

McDermott's easy and athletic action suggests that he may still, in time, become another Lillee. As was the case with Lillee, and a surprising number of contemporary Australian pacemen, McDermott has already developed signs of back trouble. Hopefully he will follow the 'Lillee formula' earlier than that great bowler and avoid serious complications.

McDermott's first Test was a dream: six wickets in the match, including the Windies' famed opening bat, Gordon Greenidge twice, for scores of 10 and 1. His bowling style is rather rudimentary; he relies mainly on his great pace and a little cut from the off. His bouncer is vicious and rears up at the batsman's throat and McDermott also uses a vicious yorker as a surprise weapon.

McDermott took over as spearhead from an ailing Lawson in England in 1985 to become Australia's chief wicket-taker (30 victims in six Tests). An heroic 8/141 in an England total of 9 for 482 at Old Trafford was a particularly memorable feat, as was McDermott's 6/70 at Lord's, which set Australia up for its one and only victory of the series.

The South African defection decimated Australia's fast bowling cupboard. Although Hogg and Alderman might be considered past their best and approaching the twilight of their international careers, bowlers like Rackemann; his Queensland team-mate John Norman Maguire, a hard-working medium-pacer of the Alderman type; and the zestful Rod McCurdy (chosen for one-day internationals but yet to play in a Test) will be sorely missed.

In his first Test against India at Adelaide, the unusually tall, 6 ft 8 in (203 cm) Bruce Anthony Reid bowled his left-arm fast-medium seamers like a gangling reincarnation of Bill Johnston. His 53−22−113−4 stint was simply amazing for a raw recruit playing in his second first-class season. Apart from his ability to pin the batsman down, Reid uses his vast height to bowl a quite alarming bouncer. Reid took 20 wickets for a struggling team in his first six Tests. The much shorter but strongly built and determined Simon Peter Davis has played with great verve and success in limited over internationals.

Latest seam bowling recruits into the Australian XI include droopy-moustached Mervyn Gregory Hughes and the young all-rounder Anthony Ian Christopher Dodemaide. A quick glance at Hughes prompts thoughts of a Lillee 'look-alike' but he has yet to overcome a tendency towards frequent injury. With Hughes hurt and unavailable, Dodemaide made a sensational Test debut versus New Zealand at Melbourne in 1987−88, taking six wickets in the match and playing an innings of 50.

Michael Roy Whitney, left-arm fast-medium, played a couple of Tests in England in 1981. Injury and poor form then kept him out of contention until 1986−87 (when he had a couple of limited over games) and 1987−88, when an injury to Bruce Reid saw him picked for two Tests versus New Zealand. At Melbourne, apart from some useful seam bowling, Whitney helped his side to a famous draw and a series win — and inscribed his name in cricketing legend — when he successfully played out a fiery final over bowled by the much-feared Hadlee.

When it comes to spin bowling, there are a couple of interesting contemporary Australians around, but none who look likely to be termed consistent match-winners. The form of leg-break and googly

The towering 6 ft 8 in (203 cm) left-armed Bruce Reid is one of Australia's men of the future and uses his immense height to gain disconcerting bounce off the pitch.

veteran Robert George Holland declined after he made his Test debut aged 38 versus West Indies in 1984−85. He and left-arm spinner Murray John Bennett bowled Australia to a famous win at Sydney in the final Test of the 1984−85 series but, other than one occasion at Lord's in 1985 when Holland won another Test for Australia, they have done little since. Holland has now retired while Bennett looks unlikely to regain his Test place.

Another orthodox slow left-hander, Tom Hogan, opted for the 'rebel' road to South Africa after a promising start to his Test career, which brought back into contention a spin bowler who had been left on the shelf for five seasons.

Peter Raymond Sleep, purveyor of leg-breaks and googlies in the old-fashioned style, was reawakened to help Australia for three Tests versus England in 1986−87 after having made his debut versus Pakistan in 1978−79. 'Sounda' Sleep belied his name by helping to win the fifth Test at Sydney in 1986−87 with a second innings analysis of 5/72 and kept his place for the next home series versus New Zealand in 1987−88, when he also made great progress as a batsman.

A previously rather obscure right-arm off-spinner, Gregory Richard John Matthews (whose deliveries have been described by veteran columnist Bill O'Reilly as 'donkey drops'), surprised the cricket world with his charismatic performances against New Zealand and India in 1985−86, as a brave and determined left-handed batsman and as an off-break bowler with the knack of making that essential breakthrough. His best Test bowling came in the amazing tied Test versus India at Madras in September 1986 when Matthews claimed a match analysis of 10 wickets for 249 runs.

When 30-year-old New South Wales off-spinner Peter Laurence Taylor was picked against England in the fifth and final Test of a depressing series for Australia in 1986−87, there were immediate queries of: 'Peter Who?' The stiff-backed bowler with a high, bounding delivery proved to be just what the doctor ordered when he claimed 6/78 in England's first innings (8-154 in the match) to ensure a morale-boosting victory for his struggling country. A fighter to his fingernails, Taylor also scored a dogged 42 in Australia's second innings, a decisive knock when one considers that the final margin was only 55 runs.

28

World Series

'World Series Cricket was fun'
– Richie Benaud

When Kerry Packer and his chief lieutenant Tony Greig made their initial forays for recruits to play in the newly-conceived World Series Cricket in Australia, they were not short of response from the best cricketers in the world. Most players who took part in the 'Packer circus' enjoyed the experience and subsequent seasons have seen a vast improvement in the status of the professional cricketer. Despite protests from the establishment, World Series Cricket also demonstrated how to bring back the crowds to the game and, although it might be claimed that limited overs cricket may now be a bit overdone, particularly in Australia, it is the truncated one-day game that has created a renewed interest by the public.

It remains a pity that there was so much suspicion and lack of foresight, vision and co-operation at the start of the 'pirate' exercise, otherwise the breach that stood between the cricket establishment and Kerry Packer and his players might not have been so deep and bitter. Hopefully, all is now forgiven and forgotten and the positive benefits generated by World Series Cricket will continue to be acknowledged and promoted by both sides.

When it came to playing the game of cricket pure and simple, World Series Cricket provided a wealth of enjoyable encounters for both players and spectators. With few exceptions, all the world's finest bowlers were on view and their skill and talent was severely tested by as brilliant an array of batsmen as had ever before gathered to perform together in one country in a single season.

The inaugural WSC season of 1977–78 was marked by particularly fine bowling performances from established players like Dennis Lillee, Lennie Pascoe and Max Walker (Australia), Andy Roberts, Michael Holding and Joel Garner (West Indies) and England's Derek Underwood and Pakistan's Imran Khan, who both played with some of the West Indians in a World XI. The best individual efforts came from West Indies fast bowler Andy Roberts, playing for the World XI (6/69 in Australia's second innings at the Sydney Showground); Max Walker, 7/88 in the World XI first innings of the same match; Imran Khan, 3/79 and 4/24 for World XI versus Australian XI at Gloucester Park, Perth; Joel Garner, 5/52 in Australia's second innings at VFL

The big, blond and fast South African Garth le Roux was the Star of the World Series Cricket season in 1978−79.

Park, Melbourne (playing for the World XI); and the match-winning bursts by Dennis Lillee (5/82) and Max Walker (5/62) in the final innings of the same match.

During the second WSC season in 1978−79 the most outstanding bowler to emerge was the tall South African fast bowler, Garth le Roux. le Roux also did well as a right-handed smiter of the ball, as did his South African colleague Clive Rice, a bustling all-rounder, hard-hitting right-hand bat, right-arm fast-medium to fast, who claimed the Player of the Series award for the limited overs games. le Roux was Player of the Series for the four-day 'Super Tests'. Another

South African bowler of note in the World XI was the Springbok Test all-rounder Mike Procter, who was surprisingly overshadowed by his younger countrymen.

le Roux captured 17 wickets at 15.88 in three 'Tests'. Dennis Lillee took 23 at 16.60, in four matches. Max Walker was again Lillee's main support for Australia, while Colin Croft joined up with the West Indies XI to complete the fearful Caribbean quartet of quick bowlers: Roberts, Holding, Garner and Croft. Imran Khan and left-arm spinner Derek Underwood again bowled well for the powerful World XI, whose attack was spearheaded by the South Africans.

In a rather stormy Australian XI-West Indies XI World Series Cricket rubber in the Caribbean later in 1978–79, Michael Holding (West Indies) took 24 wickets at 20.79, Dennis Lillee (Australia) 23 at 28.43 and Colin Croft (West Indies) 19 at 31.40.

The World Series Cricket interlude covered just two brief seasons, but its effects have been lasting. The one-day limited overs international is one innovation that has remained. The emphasis placed on speed bowling during the World Series years has continued right through to the present time, when spin bowlers in Test cricket elevens are few and far between (and sometimes left out altogether) and most countries carry three or four seam and pace bowlers.

29

Snow, Willis, Underwood and Botham's ups and downs

'Fast bowling always produces alibis from the other side.'
— Ray Illingworth

Trueman's final Test was the first for John Augustine Snow, up-and-coming heir apparent to the fast bowling master. Although he was to change his view later, Snow, in Trueman's eyes, did not even look like a fast bowler. Trueman had always felt that the prerequisites for a man of real pace were a broad back and an equally wide posterior, and Trueman possessed both attributes in abundance. John Snow, on the other hand, was 6 ft 1 in (185 cm), thin-shouldered but wiry, strong and narrow at the hips, with (as Trevor Bailey puts it in *From Larwood to Lillee*) 'a small backside accentuated by the trendy, tight trousers he wore'.

As Bailey's co-author Fred Trueman relates, he was immediately impressed when he first saw Snow bowl for Sussex and remarks on the young fast bowler's short, brisk run-up and his bowling arm that 'came over fast and high so that batsmen found they were frequently having their knuckles rapped'.

John Snow always bowled within himself. He would cover his short run with long, relaxed strides and swayed away from the stumps as he delivered the ball with a slightly open-chested action. His bouncer was a vicious, steepling one and, unlike most other fast bowlers, he used it almost as much against tailenders as he did against recognised batsmen. This practice made him the centre of controversy in Australia in 1970–71, and prompted a walk-off of the England team at Sydney in the sixth and final Test.

After Snow had been warned in an earlier Test for persistent short-pitched bowling, England captain Ray Illingworth, who led the walk-off at Sydney, claimed that the umpires had one rule for Australia and another for England. Illingworth pointed out that Australia's 'Froggy' Thomson frequently pitched short at the visiting batsmen (including a couple of bouncers directed at Snow himself) without being cautioned. The real problem was that Snow's bouncer was infinitely more potent that Thomson's, as was witnessed by the method used against the England fast bowler by one of Australia's leading batsmen, Doug Walters, of going to earth 'with his bat stuck up like a periscope', as Illingworth describes it in *The Ashes*.

The famous walk-off incident occurred after Snow had been warned by umpire Lou Rowan for persistently pitching short at Australian number nine batsman Terry Jenner, after the latter had been struck on the head when he ducked into a lifter. The crowd hooted and several began lobbing beer cans onto the field. When Snow took his place on the boundary at the end of his over he was greeted by some caustic remarks from sections of the crowd, replied volubly, and had his shirt grabbed by a drunk leaning over the fence. The drunk was pulled away but more cans, and eventually bottles, began raining onto the field. Illingworth decided to take his team off to ensure their physical safety. The match was resumed seven minutes later when the field had been cleared of debris.

John Snow was something of a loner who was frequently at odds with the establishment and with his various captains. He was also England's only real fast bowling hope of the late 1960s and early 1970s. In his two most effective Test series abroad, his speed and aggression were the major key to England's victory. Coming in for the second Test against West Indies at Kingston in 1967–68, Snow gave England an early advantage with a blistering 7/49 in the home team's first innings (some inept batting in its second innings saw England squander its chance of winning and the match ended in a draw). Snow went on to capture 27 wickets at 18.66 in four Tests and England won the only decided game of the series. In Australia in 1970–71, Snow shrugged off criticism of his use of the bouncer to take 31 wickets at 22.83 in six Tests. No Australian batsman was comfortable when playing him and his 7/40 in the host team's second innings of the fourth Test at Sydney was the decisive bowling spell of the rubber that gave England the Ashes.

In 49 Tests John Snow took 202 wickets at 26.66 and would have played for England more frequently were it not for his sometimes unpredictable and moody behaviour. His main support came from fast-medium seamers who did not approach his own pace and penetration. Against West Indies in England in 1966, Snow shared the new ball in four Tests with Lancashire's Kenneth Higgs, a studious right-arm fast-medium bowler of equable temperament and character, whose prime asset was unexpected pace off the pitch. Ken Higgs took 71 wickets in 15 Tests and, as a left-handed batsman, shared a last-wicket stand of 128 with John Snow (who also batted left-hand) for England versus West Indies at the Oval in 1966.

In the West Indies in 1967–68, Snow was the pick of a bunch that included Warwickshire's David Brown and Glamorgan left-arm quickie Ivor Jones, both of whom have been mentioned in an earlier chapter, and Higgs, who was not chosen for any of the Tests. South

African-born all-rounder Basil Lewis D'Oliveira (Worcestershire) was also a member of the England attack in the Caribbean in 1967−68 but was not a success there with his right-arm medium-paced 'wobblers'. 'Dolly' was a deceptively gentle-looking bowler with a classic side-on action who swung the ball both ways and was only three short of 50 Test wickets when he retired. He was also the centre of a political storm that saw the proposed 1968−69 England tour to South Africa cancelled because of objections to the inclusion of D'Oliveira, a coloured South African.

D'Oliveira was not originally chosen for the South African tour but was named as a replacement when Warwickshire all-rounder Thomas William Cartwright was declared unfit. Cartwright was an infinitely more talented right-arm medium-paced bowler than D'Oliveira, but nowhere near as fine a batsman. In county cricket Cartwright gained something of a reputation as unplayable when conditions favoured him, with an apparently inexhaustible variety of swing, seam and cut, but he was a comparative failure at Test level.

Surrey's well-built Geoffrey Graham Arnold, right-arm fast-medium and another master of swing and cut, replaced John Snow as Ken Higgs's new-ball partner after the first Test of a three-match series against Pakistan in 1967. 'Orse' Arnold went on to play in 34 Tests and capture more than 100 wickets, but was left out of the team that went to Australia in 1970−71 when he might have provided Snow with much-needed pace support. The Surrey fast bowler failed when he eventually did make it to Australia in 1974−75, the season during which England cricket was decimated by Lillee and Thomson. Arnold's best Test feat was his 6/45 and 3/46 to help England to a win over India at Delhi in 1972−73.

When England visited Pakistan in 1968−69 as a replacement tour for the aborted South African venture, Hampshire's Robert Michael Henry Cottam, a tireless right-arm fast-medium bowler who delivered the ball from a good height, took six wickets in his first Test at Lahore. Cottam also played in a couple of Tests in India in 1972−73 but was never picked at home.

Derbyshire's tall but slimly built right-armed Alan Ward was fancied as a fast bowling prospect of great promise when he took eight wickets in two Tests played in England against New Zealand in 1969. Taken to Australia in 1970−71, Ward returned home early because of injury. Two other right-arm pace bowlers supported John Snow on that tour with some good results and a third, flown out to replace the injured Ward, began a career that was to equal and in some ways even excel that of Snow.

The two Lancashire fast bowlers, Kenneth Shuttleworth and Peter Lever, each enjoyed some moments of glory in Australia in 1970−71. In the first Test at Brisbane, Shuttleworth took 5/47 in Australia's second innings, but lost his place through injury until the New

England's John Snow may not have been quite built for fast bowling in the classical sense but was nevertheless a formidable and hostile opponent.

Zealand leg of the tour, where he played his remaining Tests for England. Lever took some while to warm up but put in a 4/49 burst in the final Test at Adelaide that had the Australian batsmen reeling. On England's next trip to Australia, Lever took 6/38 and 3/65 in the final Test at Melbourne, the only England win of the series.

'Plank' Lever used the bouncer fairly liberally in Australia, but seldom bowled it again after one of his deliveries came close to killing New Zealand tailender Ewen Chatfield at Auckland in 1974–75. Chatfield deflected the ball onto his temple and collapsed. For a few seconds his heart stopped beating and only prompt heart massage and mouth-to-mouth resuscitation by England physiotherapist Bernard Thomas saved the New Zealand player's life.

England's 1970–71 replacement fast bowler, Robert George Dylan Willis, took 12 wickets at 27.41 in his first four Tests as third seamer to Snow and Lever. The right-arm and exceedingly quick Willis was destined to play for England into the 1980s, to captain his country and to join the exclusive club of bowlers who have taken 300 Test wickets.

Bob Willis, a 6 ft 5 in (195 cm) giant of a man with a thick mop of curly hair, began his career with Surrey and later moved to Warwickshire. When despatched to Australia in 1970–71, he was a raw-boned 21-year-old, keen and full of fire. He never lost his enthusiasm and sense of purpose, even when operations on both his knees threatened his budding Test career in 1975. Willis made a full recovery to become England's one and only fast bowling hope of genuine pace for a decade after John Snow departed the scene.

Bob Willis was a bowler of hostile intent who bounced the ball awkwardly from an open-chested action but relied, in the main, on good old-fashioned speed and straightness of delivery, with the occasional stinging yorker for variation. His match-winning spells in Test cricket were many and varied but none excelled his remarkable 8/43 burst against Australia at the third Test at Leeds in 1981.

England was one down in the series. A despondent Ian Botham had handed the captaincy back to Mike Brearley and gone on to bowl and bat like a superman. Botham had taken 6/95 in Australia's first knock, 401 for nine declared, and then scored 50 (out of 174) and 149 not out (in England's follow-on innings of 356). But despite Botham's miraculous efforts, Australia only needed 131 to win. England's cricketing colossus of the year then took another early wicket but, at 56 for one, was running out of steam and all seemed over for England. Willis then changed ends to bowl with the wind and, charging in like a charioteer, bowled with such sustained and inspired fury that wickets fell like ninepins. The comment in *Wisden* was: 'It is not uncommon to see him perform for England as if his very life depended on it, but this was something unique.'

Big-hearted Bob Willis ended the day with 8/43, Australia was put out for 111 and England won by 18 runs. The rest is history; the rubber was turned on its head and England ran out winners in the end, with Willis contributing 29 wickets at 22.96 in six Tests. In 90 Tests, Bob Willis took a phenomenal 325 wickets at 25.20. For England, only Ian Botham has bettered this figure while Fred Trueman is the only other English bowler to the 300 mark.

During Bob Willis's high-noon slaughter of the 1981 Australians at Leeds, local Yorkshire fast bowler Chris Old chipped in with one decisive wicket when he clean bowled Allan Border for a duck. Christopher Middleton Old was one of three England seam bowlers

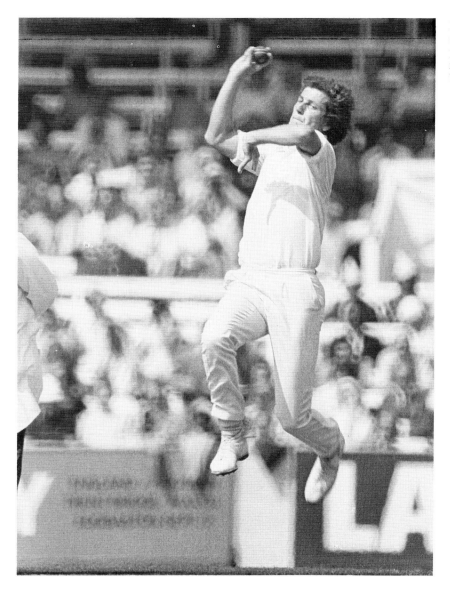

Bob Willis was a 6 ft 5 in (195 cm) English giant who performed some truly mighty deeds as a fast bowler in Test cricket.

of the late 1970s and early 1980s, two right-arm and one left, who frequently won Test matches with their combined skills. Chris Old succeeded Freddie Trueman as Yorkshire's number one strike bowler and also bowled so well in his 46 Tests for England that he took 143 wickets at 28.11. Bowling with the approved sideways action, Old moved his outswinger late, bowled the occasional devastating 'break-back' and was still something of a proposition when his pace dropped somewhat in later years. Chris Old's Test career ended effectively when he was banned from Test cricket for three years after having joined the 'rebel' English XI that toured South Africa in 1981–82.

Although never quite as fast as Old, the 6 ft 3 in (190 cm) tall

Derbyshire right-arm fast-medium seamer Michael Hendrick was a useful member of the England eleven in 30 Tests without ever really quite establishing himself. His main job was one of containment, but he was hampered for much of his career by injury. Hendrick had his best Test season in 1978—79 when, at the age of 30, he took took 19 wickets at 15.73 against a weak Austrralian team that was missing its World Series Cricket players. He also was banned from Test cricket for three years after playing in South Africa in 1981—82.

The third seamer under review was another England bowler whose Test career was interrupted when he chose to go to South Africa in 1981—82. Essex left-arm fast-medium bowler John Kenneth Lever was unlucky to have played in only 20 Tests for England. Facing strong rivalry from players like Willis, Old, Hendrick and Botham, the persevering left-armer had one outstanding series in which he was the number one choice. In India in 1976—77, Lever undermined the local batsmen with his late swing to take 26 wickets at 14.61 in five Tests, including a memorable 7/46 and 3/24 performance in the first Test at Delhi that set England off to a 3—1 series victory. Bowling with a near-perfect and very economical action, Lever was the best of an aging set of seam bowlers who did battle with the Springboks in 1981—82. In 1986 he made a surprise reappearance in the England team for one Test against India.

A fair number of seam bowlers have played for England with varying results during the 1970s and into the 1980s. Those who have had their moments of success include right-arm fast-medium Michael Walter William Selvey (Middlesex) — three wickets in 20 balls on his Test debut versus West Indies at Manchester in 1976; bespectacled, and also right-arm fast medium Paul John Walter Allott of Lancashire — 14 wickets in three Tests versus West Indies in 1984; Essex all-rounder Derek Raymond Pringle; Kent right-arm fast Graham Roy Dilley — 7/62 in two innings versus Australia at Nottingham in 1981 and a fine tour of Australia in 1986—87; right-arm fast Neil Alan Foster (Essex) — 8/107 in Pakistan's only innings at Headingley in 1987; Jamaica-born Middlesex right-arm fast Norman George Cowans — 6/77 in Australia's second innings at Melbourne in 1982—83 (England won by three runs).

Other West Indian-born fast-bowling successes for England include the pacy Gladstone Cleophas Small from Barbados who took 12 wickets at 15.00 in two Tests in Australia in 1986—87 and Leicestershire all-rounder Phillip Anthony Jason DeFreitas (born in Dominica).

Kent right-arm fast-medium Richard Mark Ellison, at 25, claimed 6/77 and 4/27 versus Australia at Edgbaston in 1985 (and a total of 17 wickets at 10.88 in just two Tests) but has since struggled to find comparable form.

Over the past 15 years or so, England's spin attack has been entrusted to the hands of very few. For most of the period, and for some time before, the Kent left-arm slow to medium Derek Leslie Underwood was England's leading spin bowler. His nickname, 'Deadly', was well earned for, on a wicket that gave him just a small amount of help, Derek Underwood could be virtually unplayable. The Australians who faced him at the Oval, where he took 7/50 to win a Test for England in 1968, will vouchsafe for it. The 24-year-old had hoped to secure the ball with which he took the seven Australian wickets in his eighth match for England, but it disappeared when the crowd invaded the pitch to congratulate him.

Other prime witnesses to Underwood's deadly skill would include six 1969 New Zealand batsmen who fell during the course of 71 balls sent down by Underwood at Lord's while only four runs were added to the total. The Pakistanis were also bundled out in very short order on a wet wicket at Lord's in 1974, when Underwood finished with 8/51, including a spell of 52 balls that gave him six wickets for two runs. And the list goes on, until a tally of Derek Underwood's Test wickets reveals a total of 297 at 25.83 in 86 games for England.

Had he not opted to play World Series Cricket in 1977–78 and 1978–79 and then to go to South Africa with the unofficial English XI in 1981–82, there is little doubt that 'Deadly' Underwood would have been way ahead in the Test wicket stakes, and well past the 350 mark reached by Lillee and Botham.

Underwood's peculiar walk back to his bowling mark, feet splayed outwards like a ballet dancer's, gives little indication of the fluid delivery to come at the end of his rather plodding eight-yard run. His length was unwavering, his direction so precise that numberless batsmen down the years have committed batting 'hari kiri' through sheer frustration at not being able to score runs off his bowling.

By the age of 25 Derek Underwood had taken his 1000th first-class wicket – only the mighty George Lohmann and Wilfred Rhodes reached this landmark at an earlier age. By the end of the 1986 English season, he had raised his total to 2420 at 20.12.

Except for the odd occasion, the presence of Derek Underwood kept the highly talented Worcestershire orthodox left-arm spinner Norman Gifford out of the England team during the 1960s and 1970s. When given a rare chance against Pakistan at Karachi in 1972–73, Gifford returned figures of 2/99 and 5/55 and was considered by some judges to be the equal of Underwood on a firm pitch.

Leg-break bowlers were considered a total luxury in first-class cricket after about 1950. Two leading batsmen, Ken Barrington and R W 'Bob' Barber, were sometimes asked to turn their wrists over, but the only leg-spin cum googly exponent chosen as such in a couple of Tests was the happy-go-lucky Robin Nicholas Stuart Hobbs of Essex, whose convivial company was much sought after on his four tours for England in the 1960s but who seldom got a bowl in a Test.

As a bit of cricket trivia, it is interesting to note that Surrey's Patrick Ian Pocock was the first player in history to make his Test debut on leap day, 29 February, versus West Indies at Bridgetown in 1967–68. W P Bradburn played his first day in a Test for New Zealand on 29 February 1964, but only because the previous day had been washed out. One other player can now claim the title 'leap year debutante', New Zealand's P E McEwan, who started his first Test on 29 February 1980.

A slow off-break bowler of high skill Pat (or 'Percy') Pocock has experienced what would have been a totally frustrating Test career for any mortal who was not blessed with his cheerful sense of humour. Aged 21, and with two Tests in the West Indies already in his bag, the tall and strong Pocock spun the ball so effectively at Old Trafford, Manchester, in 1968 that he took 6/79 in Australia's second innings. He was promptly dropped for the next game at Lord's, where the selectors preferred to play Underwood and three seam bowlers, but Pocock continued to make intermittent and widely-spaced appearances for England until 1976.

At that point Pocock really became the forgotten man of English cricket, despite the fact that he remained one of the two or three finest spinners in the land. Then came the banning of almost a generation of England cricketers following the South African defection. Still no Pocock in the Test eleven, with England generally struggling from series to series with a makeshift attack. Then came the daylight massacre of England by Clive Lloyd's West Indians in 1984, and a belated call for the 39-year-old Pocock to play in the last two Tests in an effort to stem the run tide. The veteran off-spinner responded with a 45.3–14–121–4 stint in the only West Indies innings at Manchester, did not bowl in a low-scoring final game at the Oval, but went to India the following winter with the left-armed Phil Edmonds and played in all five Tests as one of two resident spinners in the England team.

South African-born England captain Anthony William Greig bowled quickish off-turners well enough to win a couple of games for England, and to gain a reputation as a Test-class all-rounder. Tony Greig proved a popular turn on tour in India under the captaincy of Tony Lewis in 1972–73, as a brave and unrelenting batsman and as a two-in-one bowler who was given the new ball in a couple of Tests. As a Test bowler, the 6 ft 7 in (200 cm) Greig struck gold in the West Indies in 1973–74 with figures of 8/86 and 5/70 when he helped England to a famous 26-run victory at Port of Spain that levelled the series. In 58 Tests Greig scored 3599 runs and took 141 wickets at 32.20, figures that confirm his status as a highly competent international performer. He also became Kerry Packer's right-hand man in the setting up of World Series Cricket and remains totally involved in the game as a leading television cricket presenter in Australia.

Ian Botham, as aggressive with the ball as he is with the bat, has taken the most wickets in Tests.

Two other all-rounders who turned the ball successfully from the off at times were Derbyshire's Geoffrey Miller and Northampton-shire's Peter Willey. But the outstanding England off-break bowler of the period under review remains the Middlesex heir to Freddie Titmus, the laconic but eminently skilful John Ernest Emburey. Another player who lost three years in the England eleven following a trip to South Africa in 1981–82, Emburey is accepted as probably the best off-break bowler in international cricket at the moment. One of the few England players to return from the disastrous 1985–86 England tour of the West Indies with his reputation relatively untarnished, Emburey first made his mark with 16 wickets at 19.12 in four Tests in Australia in 1978–79.

Tall, and bowling with a high action similar to that of great off-spinners like Laker and Tayfield, Emburey varies his pace and trajectory with good control and also bowls a disconcerting away drifter that bites and turns in again to the right-handed batsman.

Emburey has shown a remarkable improvement in his batting in recent years and can almost claim to be a Test-class all-rounder. His long-time spin partner in both the England and Middlesex teams was the forthright orthodox slow left-hander Philippe-Henri Edmonds, a man who has frequently rubbed the establishment the wrong way with his independent ways but who was a Test-class spinner of enormous character. Edmonds surprised the 1975 Australians at Headingley when he took five wickets for 17 runs in his first 12 overs in a Test, but had to battle for his place against competition from incumbent left-hander Derek Underwood.

Another left-arm spinner, Nicholas Grant Billson Cook lost some ground despite taking 17 wickets at 16.17 in two Tests versus New Zealand in 1983. Six years younger than Edmonds, he has regained favour for the 1987−88 England winter tours following the senior player's retirement.

Also recalled at the ripe age of 38 for the 1987−88 tours was the well-proportioned off-break merchant and useful late-order batsman Edward Ernest Hemmings, who had last played in a Test in Australia in 1982−83.

One major England bowler (and possibly *the* major bowler) of the 1970s and 1980s remains to be reviewed. The tale of the mighty deeds of Ian Terence Botham have been oft repeated. So too have the many stories of his alleged misconduct. This review will concentrate solely on the marvellous cricket played by a man some people love and some people love to hate. It is perhaps one of the saddest truths about the attainment of fame in the present age that, immediately a person rises above the masses in achievement and skill, the knockers start to gather in an attempt to cut the achiever down to their own puny dimensions.

Apart from his persistent and puzzling failure to come to grips with his game when playing against West Indies, Ian Botham has risen higher than most cricketers in the history of the game. Among contemporary all-rounders he stands supreme − as a thundering striker of the ball who can turn a match in an hour, as a slip-fielder of casual brilliance, and as a right-arm fast-medium bowler who bowls with incipient hostility and has the uncanny knack of takiing a wicket with the ball that looks as if it should have been struck to the boundary fence.

Botham, it seems, reached the apogee of his Test-playing orbit during the 1981 England-Australia series and has since moved in and out of form like a satellite out of control. He keeps bouncing back from time to time in the odd Test or two to remind us all that a whole series once bore the title 'Botham's Ashes'.

The 1981 Botham saga reads like a schoolboy cricket yarn. A brief summation of that golden summer reveals that he failed utterly in the first two Tests against Australia, as batsman, as bowler and as England's captain. His form had deserted him soon after he was appointed England captain versus West Indies in the home series of 1980. It became even more depressing for Botham when he led his country in the Caribbean in 1980–81. England was outmatched at every turn and Botham averaged just 10.42 with the bat and did little as a bowler. Gone it seemed was the skill and flair that had brought him a world record all-round feat at Bombay, India in 1979–80 when he became the first (and only) player in history to score a century *and* take 10 wickets in a Test (114 in his single innings plus 6/58 and 7/48).

Botham was dismissed for a pair of ducks in his final Test as England skipper (at Lord's) and had lost his old zip as a bowler. When Mike Brearley agreed to return as England's leader for the next match at Leeds, the clouds lifted for England's ace all-rounder and his 50 and 149 not out and a bowling spell of 6/95 in Australia's first innings (plus Bob Willis's amazing 8/43 in the second) saw his side home and the series squared. England won again, by 29 runs, against the run of play in the fourth Test at Edgbaston where it was Botham's miraculous 14–9–11–5 spurt in the final innings that did the trick. In the fifth match at Manchester, the mighty Botham hit another 100 and took five wickets in the match. England was home and dry, but Botham continued to show his paces when he bowled 89 overs in the final game at the Oval to complete a 10/253 haul in the match.

So ended Botham's great year. Though his batting is nowhere near as consistently devastating as it was a couple of years ago (especially against West Indies), Botham remains a much-feared bowler who finally toppled Dennis Lillee's world record 355 Test wickets when he made a belated appearance in the final Test of the 1986 series versus New Zealand at the Oval.

Ian Botham has always been an attacking bowler who expects to take a wicket with every ball. His temperament has made him rather inconsistent and he sends down a fair number of deliveries that batsmen can safely hit away. His great strength, however, lies in his ability to send down the unplayable ball more often than most other bowlers. His late outswinger bowled on a full length frequently finds the bat's edge to create a catch behind the wicket or in the slips. He uses the width of the crease to bowl an inswinger that cramps a batsman's response. His sharp-lifting bouncer comes as a surprise from a bowler of his fast-medium pace. Above all, when he finds himself firing on all cylinders, Botham's visible confidence in his own powers tends to intimidate the less-experienced batsman as much as his actual ability with the ball.

If he had never been one of the finest attacking batsmen the game has known (and a grand all-round fielder), Ian Botham would probably have played for England as a bowler alone – a front-line attacker who can alter the pattern of a game within a few short, sharp overs. His admirers have learned to live with Botham's many ups and downs because, when he is on top, there is no player in the world to match him.

'Deadly' Derek Underwood, England's leading spin bowler of the 1960s and '70s.

30

Sri Lankan debut

*'The enthusiasm for cricket grew with the years, and Schools and
Colleges in Ceylon also began to train their youths to wield the willow . . .'*
— A W Lorenz-Andree

Organised cricket began in Ceylon in the 1830s and one of its first
famous home-born cricketers was a bowler known as the 'Wilfred
Rhodes of Ceylon'. Left-arm spinner Tommy Kelaart was reputed to
have always bowled wearing a hat. S S Perera tells us that he took
1686 wickets at 6.81 runs each in Singalese cricket. Kelaart also
opened the bowling for Colombo Colts in a strange 'international'
played against a team of Boer prisoners-of-war (including one South
African Currie Cup player, P H de Villiers) at Colombo in 1901 and
was one of the bowlers responsible for the lowest score in Ceylonese
cricket — all out for nine runs — by the ABCD Club versus Colombo
Colts in 1888 (Kelaart and C Heyn each took 5/4). Tommy Kelaart
must have been a very fine bowler indeed and was, by all accounts,
also something of a character. He certainly started a tradition of
competent and talented Ceylonese/Sri Lankan bowlers that has carried
forward down the years. A well-known bowler who followed Kelaart
was the lively leg-break and googly merchant Gamini Goonesena,
who took 674 first-class wickets for Ceylon, Cambridge University,
Nottinghamshire, New South Wales and various invitation teams
between 1947 and 1968.

It was not until February 1982 that Sri Lanka played its first Test,
versus England at the Saravanamutto Oval in Colombo. Most of Sri
Lanka's batsmen failed in that inaugural international encounter, but
its bowlers performed with unexpected skill to dismiss England for a
first innings 223. The pace of strike bowler Asantha Lakdasa Francis
de Mel (tall for a Sri Lankan and right-arm fast-medium) led the
way with 4/70. The well-flighted leg-breaks and googlies of Dandeni-
yage Somachandra de Silva and the orthodox slow left-arm spinners
of his unrelated namesake Ginigalgodage Ramba Ajit de Silva completed the damage for Sri Lanka.

At the close of the 1986—87 season Asantha de Mel, who has
modelled his action and approach on that of Dennis Lillee, was still
taking the new ball for his country as its major seam bowler, after
having played Test cricket at home and abroad and taken 59 wickets
at 36.95. The wily Somachandra de Silva, who bowled his leg-turners

Tommy Kelaart was known
as the 'Wilfred Rhodes' of
early Sri Lankan cricket.

and 'bosies' with a flat trajectory, has now retired after 12 Tests which gave him 37 wickets at 36.40. Ajit de Silva was banned for life by the Sri Lankan cricket authorities for going to South Africa with the Arosa Sri Lanka team in 1982–83. What must have been even more agonising for a sensitive and thoughtful man was the fact that the skill that had made him Sri Lanka's leading left-arm spinner for a decade so deserted Ajit de Silva in South Africa, that he looked and was treated like a third-rate club bowler.

Another spin bowler in Sri Lanka's inaugural Test side, right-arm off-breaker Lalith Wasantha Kaluperuma, also opted to tour South Africa and was banned for life. Kaluperuma did much good work for his country in unofficial 'Tests' before Sri Lanka was admitted to the official Test cricket fold. Dapper left-handed batsman Arjuna Rana-tunga also bowls right-arm off-breaks and has done well enough to merit being called an all-rounder.

For the first couple of Test series, de Mel and Somachandra de Silva virtually carried Sri Lanka's attack, but the arrival of a string of enthusiastic seamers eased their burden somewhat. One of these is the well-built and enthusiastic right-arm medium-fast Vinodhan John (whose full name is John Vindohan Bede Jeyarajasjingham but who, thankfully for the media, prefers to be called Vinodhan John). John bowls with admirable economy but has, at times, struggled with his form and fitness.

The similarly named but totally unrelated Joseph Ravindran Ratnayeke and Rumesh Joseph Ratnayake are both right-arm fast-medium bowlers who have bowled with some good effect at Test level. The former, 'Ravi' Ratnayeke, is at 6 ft 3 in (190 cm) exceptionally tall for a Sri Lankan, and uses his height well at times in order to gain lift. His most outstanding Test performance was a

Leg-break and googly exponent Somachandra de Silva was Sri Lanka's leading wicket-taker in its first dozen Tests.

623

stunning 8/83 in Pakistan's first innings at Sialkot in 1985–86. The shorter but faster Rumesh Ratnayake is very much an 'arm' bowler who can swing the ball and is not averse to using the bouncer.

When India visited Sri Lanka for its first official series in that country in 1985–86, a young unknown right-arm medium-pace bowler, Franklyn Saliya Ahangama, was a suprisingly successful Test debut opponent. As third seamer back-up to Asantha de Mel and Rumesh Ratnayake, the inexperienced Saliya Ahangama claimed 18 wickets at 19.33 in the three Tests and saw Sri Lanka take its first rubber in history. Ahangama did not keep his place for two subsequent three-match contests versus Pakistan, away and then at home, during the same season. Another young right-arm medium fast bowler, 20-year-old A K Kuruppuarachichi, could hardly get a game above third grade level when he spent part of his season in Melbourne, Australia, but took a wicket with his third ball in the second Test against Pakistan played in Sri Lanka. Unfortunately, after debut figures of 5/44 and 2/41 in a match won by Sri Lanka, Kurruppuarachichi missed the next match because of injury. His replacement, Kaushik Amalean (also right-arm), bowled very tidily in the third Test versus Pakistan to take 3/59.

Of the up-and-coming Sri Lankan bowlers, Graeme Labrooy (right-arm fast-medium), Asoka de Silva (leg-breaks and googlies), Sanjeeva Weerasinghe (leg-breaks and googlies) and Jayananda Warnaweera (right-arm off-cutters) have made their Test debuts and could be bowlers of the future.

In 1985–86 Sri Lanka gained its first Test and series win in its short history when India was defeated at the Saravanamuttu Stadium in Colombo, home of the historic inaugural Test against England in 1982. It was very much a bowlers' match in this, the second Test of the series, with seamer Rumesh Ratnayake the main hero with 4/76 and 5/49; he also took 6/65 in India's first innings in the drawn first Test. The Sri Lankans then demonstrated against Pakistan in a 1–1 drawn series later in the season that, at least on their own home turf and under familiar conditions of heat and high humidity, they would in future be no pushover in Tests. Bowling heroes of Sri Lanka's first Test win over Pakistan were Kuruppuarachichi (7/85 in the match) and J R 'Ravi' Ratnayeke (who took 2/29 and 5/37).

31

Hadlee reigns

'...there is no-one more exciting and aggressive in the game today'
— Paul Weaver

Although he has enjoyed the presence of a highly competent supporting cast, one man has dominated New Zealand's bowling stage since the mid 1970s. When Richard John Hadlee made his Test debut versus Pakistan at Wellington in 1972—73, he joined his father, Walter Hadlee, and older brother, Dayle Hadlee, as New Zealand Test match players. In 1975, the oldest of Walter Hadlee's three sons, Barry Hadlee, completed the family picture when he was picked for the New Zealand World Cup limited over international squad. Barry did not play in a Test but Richard Hadlee's wife, Karen, has played as a batswoman and medium-pace bowler on two tours of India with the New Zealand women's team. With so much cricket in the family, there is little surprise at the achievements of its most outstanding member. Richard Hadlee must be chief contender for Dennis Lillee's mantle as the best contemporary new-ball bowler in world cricket, notwithstanding the claims of a whole squad of West Indian pacemen.

At the start of the 1987-88 season, after 70 Tests, Hadlee had already taken 355 Test wickets (Lillee's total, also in 70 Tests) at 22.46. In 1985—86, he took 49 wickets during six Tests versus Australia, home and away. Against the same 'enemy' in 1987—88 he boosted his tally to equal Ian Botham's world record of 367 wickets. Hadlee had done it in 73 Tests; Botham took 92. If he continues for a couple of years in his present form, he may top 400.

As a young man, the lean and tough 6 ft (183 cm) tall Richard Hadlee was a straight forward fast bowler who came in off a 23-yard run and relied mostly on his extreme pace to beat the batsman. Like Lillee and other truly great seam bowlers before him, he has mellowed in recent years but is still as sharp as ever. He now relies more on line and length variations and movement of the ball, through the air and off the pitch.

It is hard to pinpoint his most outstanding performance in Test cricket — there have been so many. Outside Tests, Hadlee achieved in England in 1984 what everybody thought was the impossible in a drastically reduced county programme when he scored the old-fashioned double of 1000 runs and 100 wickets — the first player to do so since Fred Titmus in 1967. He is a world-class all-rounder whose belligerent left-handed batting brings added substance to New Zealand's lower order. Richard Hadlee has scored more than 2000 Test runs to add to his 334 wickets. Only Botham has bettered this. Hadlee also holds the New Zealand 'best bowling' record with his dazzling 9/52 and 6/71 performance against Australia at Brisbane in 1985–86. His maiden Test century (103) was hit off the West Indies attack at Christchurch in 1979–80.

Hadlee's main assistance over the years has come from a group of highly professional seam bowlers, none of whom possess any great pace, but all of whom are reasonably competent masters of line, length, swing and cut. The burly right-arm medium-paced Bernard Lance Cairns was, until his retirement in 1985 at the age of 36, probably New Zealand's most reliable bowler after Richard Hadlee, and a mighty smiter of the ball who was renowned for his six-hitting. A husky giant of a man, Cairns had an action that resembled a slow-motion Mike Procter and could swing the ball alarmingly in humid conditions. He took 128 wickets at 33.44 in 43 Tests and is one of only five New Zealand bowlers to top the 100 wickets mark. Lance Cairns's greatest bowling triumph came against England when he bowled his country to victory at Leeds in 1983 with an outstanding 7/74 spell. In 1979–1980, Cairns cracked the quickest century in New Zealand history – in 52 minutes off 45 balls, for Otago versus Wellington (he scored 110 out of 170).

The brave and persevering Ewen John Chatfield appears to be next in line to reach his century of Test wickets if he is picked to play in another series or two. Also right-arm and a little faster than Cairns, Ewen Chatfield made an amazing comeback to Test cricket after suffering a fractured skull from a ball bowled by Peter Lever in his debut Test versus England at Auckland in 1974–75. Chatfield recovered and got his second chance two years later and has since been a regular and consistent member of the New Zealand eleven. An industrious bowler who relies mostly on a near-perfect line and length, Chatfield had taken 88 wickets in Tests to the close of the 1986 season.

The pacier left-arm fast-medium Gary Bertram Troup found his way back into the New Zealand team for a couple of home Tests against Australia in 1985–86 after some years in the wilderness. Troup has had an on-off relationship with New Zealand's selectors since his first Test in India in 1976–77 (plus some injury problems) and has so far taken 39 wickets in 15 Tests.

Recently-retired New Zealand skipper Jeremy Vernon Coney was an all-rounder of some stature who complemented his run-getting skill with useful right-arm medium-pace seamers and cutters that gained him a reputation as a partnership breaker. Of New Zealand's current seamers, the right-arm fast-medium Martin Colin Snedden has had some days of success while the pacier, also right-arm, Daniel

Opposite: Richard Hadlee is the current 'king' of New Zealand cricket and a fast-bowling all-rounder to rank with the finest in history.

Kyle Morrison lived up to the promise of his initials 'D K' with some lively new-ball bowling during his debut series versus Australia in 1987–88.

Only five spin bowlers have played for New Zealand with any kind of regularity over the past 15 years or so. Of the two left-handers, David Robert O'Sullivan played in 11 Tests but took his 18 wickets at very high cost and soon fell away in face of competition from the steadier Hedley Howarth. When Howarth retired, the tall and slender Stephen Lewis Boock looked to be his most likely successor. Boock certainly started well with a 5/67 performance in the third Test of his debut series versus England in New Zealand in 1977–78 but, with selectorial policies opting for seam over spin, played only two first-class matches (and no Tests) on the tour of Australia in 1980–81, and actually asked if he could be sent home early. Boock has since returned to play on a more regular basis, as an occasional lone spinner in a sea of seam, and has raised his Test wicket total to 65 in 26 games. For the 1986 England tour he lost his place to all-rounder Euan John Gray whose accurate left-arm spin proved a good foil to the seam bowlers.

Of the two major New Zealand off-break bowlers of the period under review, the rather portly Peter James Petherick was already 34 when he hit the headlines in Pakistan in 1976–77 with a hat-trick in his debut Test at Lahore. Petherick's victims were the redoubtable trio of Javed Miandad (caught by Richard Hadlee off a mistimed pull for 163); Wasim Raja (a 'dolly' return catch to the bowler) and Intikhab Alam (caught at silly point by Geoff Howarth). The full list of Test hat-tricks (excluding the 'double act' by South Africa's Garth le Roux and Clive Rice versus a 'rebel' Australian team at Johannesburg in 1985–86) is:

Australia

F R Spofforth	v England at Melbourne	1878–79
H Trumble	v England at Melbourne	1901–02
H Trumble	v England at Melbourne	1903–04
T J Matthews	v South Africa at Manchester	1912
(a hat-trick in each innings)		
L F Kline	v South Africa at Cape Town	1957–58

England

W Bates	v Australia at Melbourne	1882–83
J Briggs	v Australia at Sydney	1891–92
G A Lohmann	v South Africa at Port Elizabeth	1895–86
J T Hearne	v Australia at Leeds	1899
M J C Allom	v New Zealand at Christchurch	1929–30
T W Goddard	v South Africa at Johannesburg	1938–39
P J Loader	v West Indies at Leeds	1957

New Zealand

P J Petherick	v Pakistan at Lahore	1976–77

South Africa

| G M Griffin | v England at Lord's | 1960 |

West Indies

| W W Hall | v Pakistan at Lahore | 1958—59 |
| L R Gibbs | v Australia at Adelaide | 1960—61 |

P J Petherick (New Zealand) and M J C Allom (England) are the only two players to take a hat-trick on Test debut; T J Matthews (Australia) is the only player to take two hat-tricks in the same Test — one in each innings.

New Zealand's second right-arm off-break bowler of the 1970s and 1980s has been reported to have once worked as a grave-digger. John Garry Bracewell dug his latest grave for Australia's batsmen at Auckland in 1985—86 when he took 4/74 and 6/32 to give New Zealand its first home series win against Australia and its second historic rubber against that country in the same season (New Zealand won 1—0 in New Zealand and had earlier taken the series in Australia 2—1).

An offspinner who pushes the ball through quickly, the tall John Bracewell has now taken 58 wickets at 29.86 in 20 Tests, and has sat on the 12th-man bench watching New Zealand's battery of seamers (or Stephen Boock) in operation more often than he might like to recall. He is no mean performer with the bat and at Sydney in 1985—86, Bracewell confounded Australia's bowlers by coming in at number 10 and saving his side from a disastrous start with an innings of 83 not out. Bowler Stephen Boock helped Bracewell add a New Zealand record 124 runs for the 10th wicket to further frustrate the Australians. Bracewell logged his maiden Test century versus England in 1986.

As a spin bowler, Bracewell has endured his own frustrations of seeing New Zealand so frequently taking the field with an attack consisting of four or even five seam bowlers (his younger brother, Brendan Bracewell, has on occasion been one of them) — and nary a spinner in sight. Pace and seam has formed the theme of New Zealand's out cricket for many years and, with the odd variation provided by men like Bracewell and Boock, it seems as if it will continue to do so in the forseeable future.

32

West Indian whirlwind

'...it would be naive and misleading of me to claim that I never bowl bouncers without trying to intimidate the batsman'
— Michael Holding

The story of Caribbean cricket over the past decade or so is a tale of speed in such profusion and of such frightening hostility that, until 1986–87, there were few teams in the world today capable of overcoming the West Indies XI in a single Test, let alone an entire series. The face of cricket has been altered, some say irrevocably, through the tactics devised by the urbane and determined Clive Lloyd, prompted it has been said by memories of the torment suffered by West Indian batsmen in 1975–76 against Lillee, Thomson and a couple of other Australian fast bowlers.

With the knowledge that he possessed in players like Viv Richards, Greenidge, Gomes, Haynes and himself a nucleus of batting power that would ensure a reasonable total against any attack, and under most conditions, Lloyd set out to limit as severely as possible the run-scoring ability of his opponents. The plan was two-fold — fast, short-pitched bowling that forced a batsman to frequently defend his very person instead of making a scoring stroke, and a rigid maximum 12 overs an hour by his bowlers (a total of 72 in a normal six-hour day) that would further reduce the possible run-rate so that even the best of batting sides could only hope for a maximum daily total of around 200 runs. Lloyd's battle-plan was, naturally, only made possible because he happened to always have at his command at least four bowlers who were eminently capable of maintaining high pace and extreme accuracy for sustained spells. The low daily over-rate also contributed to Lloyd's tactics by ensuring that his bowlers could be used in relatively short spells and always be fresh.

Of the current West Indies battery of Test fast bowlers, the lithe and athletic Michael Holding heads the list of wicket-takers with 249 wickets in 59 Tests. In *The Cricketer International* (August 1985), Holding comments that it is probably true that spin bowlers provide most entertainment for the public, but that there is little point in playing a spin bowler in a team if he is not as good as a faster alternative. According to Holding, 'the key question is whether that spinner is good enough to hold his place'. Holding said that, since the retirement of off-break bowler Lance Gibbs 10 years ago, there has been (until the recent rise of the youthful Roger Harper) no spin bowler of true Test class available to the West Indies' selectors. Michael Holding also admits that it would be hypocritical to claim that bouncers are not used primarily to intimidate a batsman.

A brief survey of the pace men of the past, as chronicled in this book, will confirm that almost without exception, all the great fast bowlers have used the short-pitched ball as a legitimate offensive weapon to test a batsman's nerve. The question marks that hang over the desirability of the practice as seen in today's Test cricket is, firstly, the frequency of short-pitched balls in an innings (and the resultant increase in the possibility of physical injury to batsmen) and, secondly, the tactical shortening of the daily time allowed a batting side for the accumulation of runs. The first problem is officially regulated in terms of existing laws. It remains up to individual umpires concerned as to their interpretation and implementation of them. The second query related perhaps to the spirit of the game. It is interesting to note that the 1986 England-India Test series will be played with an agreed minimum of 96 overs to be bowled each day (which at around three runs an over could result in a daily run tally approaching 300). One wonders if the West Indies team will ever agree to a similar ruling — and if other countries will have the courage to insist on such a condition.

The long line of modern West Indies pace bowlers began with Hall, Griffith and Sobers in the 1960s and early 1970s. Then, after a brief drought, a young fast bowler arrived who was to herald and then spearhead probably the most fearsome and highly skilled quick bowling group ever to be gathered together in one Test team. Peculiarly enough, all have been right-arm bowlers.

Anderson Montgomery Everton Roberts was the first Antiguan to play Test cricket for West Indies. As a well-built young man, he was a fiery bowler who ran in very quickly, put everything he had into an economical and energetic delivery action, and relied on sheer speed to send wickets cartwheeling in all directions. Roberts honed his skills until he became for five or six years the acknowledged number one fast bowler in the world. His delivery action did not quite satisfy the purists (slightly open-chested, a lower left arm than some, but a high easy-flowing right arm) but Roberts used well-hidden changes of pace, an unsettling bouncer and a good yorker to excellent effect.

Sir Garfield Sobers, for one, went on record as saying that Roberts was 'a bowler of class'. Trevor Bailey notes in *From Larwood to Lillee* that Roberts was like Lindwall, Trueman and Lillee in that his 'grooved action' gave him the ability to keep on taking wickets when he had lost some of his pace, 'compensating with increased control and guile for the slight loss of speed through the air'. Bailey considered Roberts 'a complete fast bowler'.

In 47 Tests Andy Roberts took 202 wickets at 25.61. In 1973, at 22, he travelled to England to join Hampshire. The following English

Andy Roberts, the first Antiguan to play for West Indies, helped revive fast bowling after a lapse following the retirement of Hall and Griffith.

winter he gained his first Test cap in one game against England at Bridgetown, Barbados. In 1974, Roberts took 119 wickets for his county at an incredible 13.62 apiece. By the 1974−75 season he had developed into a natural first choice new-ball bowler for West Indies and took 32 wickets in a five-Test series in India (plus a further 12 in two Tests versus Pakistan). In Australia in 1975−76, the new West Indies fast bowling hope was the one West Indian bowler to come out of the series with an enhanced reputation (his 7/54 in the second Test at Perth was superb). The rubber was dominated for the most part by Messrs Lillee and Thomson, short-pitched bowling et al.

Clive Lloyd, the West Indian captain, did a lot of thinking. Besides Andy Roberts, he had in his team a young Jamaican hopeful named Michael Holding. All he needed was another couple like him and things started coming together in England in 1976.

The tall but slimly built Michael Anthony Holding is not, at first glance, the picture of the typical West Indian fast bowler as was the case with Hall, Roberts and others. He compensates, however, with one of the most athletically rhythmical and co-ordinated bowling methods ever seen on a cricket field. Indeed, if he had chosen another sport, Holding might well have become on Olympic runner.

In his earlier days, Holding's grace of movement was always a joy to behold as he glided in to bowl with long measured strides, feet barely touching the ground. Then, leaping like a deer in his final stride, his left arm high and his right arm circling around close to his

Michael Holding must go down as one of the most athletically co-ordinated fast bowlers in history.

ear, Holding would release the ball at a terrific speed. One English player dubbed him 'Whispering Death'.

Although he has slowed down considerably, Holding remains a great bowler who, like Roberts, has so many variations of pace, length, line and swing to call upon that no batsman dare relax for a moment. One negative factor has clouded his career at times: Holding has been rather injury prone as a result of a less robust physique than some of his colleagues.

In his debut match for West Indies in Australia in 1975–76, Michael Holding was thrown in at the deep end when he was given the new ball with Roberts in the first Test at Brisbane. His final figures of 0/81 and 0/46 were scant reward for his concerted hard labour. Holding's 10 wickets in his first Test rubber cost 61.40 runs apiece, but he watched and learned – from his team-mate, Roberts, and from the wonderful opportunity to observe at first hand the methods of Lillee and Thomson. The 1976 season in England was as much Holding's year as a bowler as it was Viv Richards's as a batsman. Richards scored 829 runs in four Tests at 118.42 an innings (including two double-centuries); Holding also missed one of the five Tests through injury but bagged 28 wickets at an amazing 12.71. With strong support from a half-dozen other top-class batsmen (including skipper Lloyd) as well as fast bowlers Andy Roberts, giant newcomer Wayne Daniel and the veteran Vanburn Holder, England never had a chance. The speed bowling of Holding, Roberts and their aides was at times quite frightening. Between them, the four West Indian pacemen sent down 647.1 overs. Only 31 overs were bowled by regular spinners (with sometime bowlers like Fredericks and Gomes chipping in with a few more). Some sort of new pattern was beginning to emerge.

In the final Test of 1976, at the Oval, Michael Holding produced one of the most stunning fast bowling performances ever seen in a Test. West Indies batted for most of the first two days for 687 for eight wickets declared (Viv Richards 291). England replied with 435 (Dennis Amiss scored a memorable 203). Holding's figures of 33–9–92–8 were phenomenal, but the match looked to be heading for a certain draw. A 182-run unbroken partnership by West Indies' openers Fredericks and Greenidge in only 140 minutes raised the lead to 434 and England were left with a little over six hours to bat. On a plumb pitch that had given Andy Roberts 0/102 in England's first innings (and the home team fast bowler Bob Willis 1/121 in the match), Holding went beserk, bowling at such high speed that half England's wickets fell for 78 and the home side was eventually bundled out for 203, to give West Indies an unlikely and massive 231-run win. Holding's figures were 20.4–6–57–6, to give him 14/149 in the match.

Running into the mid-1980s Holding remains one of West Indies' most feared fast bowlers, a thinking player who has made an exceptional art of quick bowling in both Tests and limited over internationals.

Wayne Wendell Daniel arrived in England with the 1976 West Indies team as a raw giant of a youngster who could bowl very fast indeed and, with Roberts, Holding and Holder, gave England's batsmen little respite from a continuous bombardment of pace. The even-tempered Daniel took 13 wickets at 24.38 in four Tests in his first series. He still plays for Middlesex as one of the most feared right-arm fast bowlers on the English county circuit. Daniel is known as the 'Black Diamond' and has gained some sort of a reputation as a bone-cracker, albeit an unintentional one, for Wayne Daniel is by nature a kindly person, although an uncompromising opponent on the field. Competing all the time for a Test spot with a half-dozen or more other highly capable fast bowlers, Daniel has only played in 10 Tests.

When the strong Pakistan team arrived in the Caribbean in 1976–77 for a five-Test series, there was probably some relief at the news that neither Daniel nor Holding would be available because of injury. Any elation that might have been felt ended quickly when two virtual unknowns, Colin Croft (33 at 20.48) and Joel Garner (25 at 27.52), took between them 58 of the 97 Pakistani wickets to fall in a series that West Indies won 2–1. With Andy Roberts claiming 19 wickets and the three fast bowlers sending down more than 70 per cent of the overs bowled, the West Indies spin bowlers were again given little chance.

When Colin Everton Hunte Croft arrived in South Africa in 1983 to play for a 'rebel' West Indies XI, his fellow Guyana-born team companion Alvin Kallicharran was asked by a local correspondent about the man who had earned a reputation as the most fearsome fast bowler of them all. 'Crofty so bad he bounce his own mother', was Kalli's laughing reply. The little West Indian batsman then quickly corrected himself: 'No man — he *beam* his mother.' Kallicharran may have been having his little bit of fun but, for the batsmen who faced him, the 6 ft 3 in (190 cm) and hugely proportioned Croft was no joke. The big Guyanan took seven wickets in the two innings of his debut Test against Pakistan at Bridgetown and 8/29 in the third innings in which he bowled, at Port of Spain. Eventually, in only 27 Tests, Croft took 125 wickets at 23.30. He would have taken many more were it not for a persistent back complaint which prompted him to hunt a few batsmen's scalps for Kruger gold in South Africa in 1983 and 1984 before finally giving the game away.

Colin Croft was an unusual fast bowler, right-arm, with an ungainly approach and a peculiar 'high, open and ugly' action (as Trevor Bailey describes it), which saw his left foot splayed out to the off when bowling to a right-handed batsman. His line placed the ball

Colin Croft was one of the meanest of the West Indian fast bowlers; his stock ball lifted up into the batsman's ribs and throat.

well outside off-stump but it would cut into the batsman as a frightening 'rib-tickler', similar to the stock ball bowled by Australia's Jeff Thomson in his heyday. The consensus about Croft was that he literally hated the sight of batsmen and made the fact obvious. Like Wayne Daniel (and unlike Roberts and Holding), he depended more on brute strength than smoothness of style for his speed.

The giant 'Big Bird' Joel Garner from Barbados, home of fast bowling, is, at 6 ft 8 in (203 cm), one of the tallest cricketers of all time and facing his sharply lifting bowling is an extremely tall order for any but the most accomplished of batsmen. He completed the 'fearsome foursome', with Roberts, Holding and Croft who so terrorised Test batsmen for three or four seasons — they all played together for the first time during World Series Cricket and the 1979 World Cup tournament in England and split up between 1982 and 1983, when Croft's back gave way and Roberts retired. There was to be no respite for Test batting opponents with replacements like Malcolm Marshall, Winston Davis and a whole line of other young hopefuls waiting in the queue.

Joel Garner's nickname was taken from the famous television Sesame Street character of equally outrageous proportions. His performances on the cricket field are of a matching order. At the close of the 1985—86 season, he had 'Garnered' only two wickets less (247 in 56 Tests) than the leading West Indies Test wicket-taker, Michael Holding. Garner also remains, because of his enormous delivery height and equally amazing control, probably the most difficult fast bowler to score off in international cricket.

Unlike other tall bowlers of the past (Tony Greig was one), Garner does not stoop in his approach or delivery, forcing a batsman to play a normally pitched ball off his chest, instead of at waist or thigh height. Garner's steepling bouncer is an even more frightening proposition and the batsman's problems when facing Garner become further complicated by the fact that most sightscreens are not tall enough to provide a background to his abnormally high arm; the ball must be picked out from a whirl of limbs. Facing Garner in full flight is, for an average-sized batsman, an experience akin to that of a 12-year-old schoolboy squaring up to the fast bowling of a fully grown man.

Apart from the dangers created by his awesome lift off the pitch, Joel Garner has become highly feared for his blockbuster yorker. Scyld Berry once wrote: 'The only consolation of being bowled by Garner is that you haven't been hit on the boot.'

Garner took 25 wickets in his first Test series, and has scarcely looked back. His bowling in Tests in England and county games (he played for Somerset until 1986) has, for much of the time, simply scared the wits out of opposing batsmen. In 1984 he took 29 wickets at 18.62 in five Tests against England (up-and-coming Malcolm Marshall had 24 at 18.21 in four games) and his bowling was one of the prime factors in an historic 5—0 clean sweep for West Indies. In 1985—86 it became 10—0 over the last two rubbers between the two teams, with Garner taking another 27 wickets. In the Caribbean in 1983—84, he simply blew Australia's batsmen away to take 31 wickets at 16.87 in five Tests. The 'Big Bird' has bowled with equal penetration in Australia and everywhere else he has been asked to play.

Garner and Holding have now come to the end of their Test careers and it seems as if the still under 30 Malcolm Denzil Marshall, from Barbados, is set to eventually overtake the two older fast bowlers' individual Test wicket records. Marshall is now the acknowl-

At 6 ft 8 in plus (203 cm), Joel Garner is one of the tallest fast bowlers of all time and possibly the most reliable under all conditions.

edged West Indies destroyer-in-chief and, at the close of season 1986—87, had taken 240 wickets in 51 Tests at a strike rate of 4.71 wickets per Test.

Comparative figures for the major West Indies fast bowlers are (as at close of 1986—87 season — minimum 75 wickets):

	Tests	Wickets	Strike rate
M D Marshall	51	240	4.71
C E H Croft	27	125	4.63
J Garner	56	247	4.41
A M E Roberts	47	202	4.30
M A Holding	60	249	4.15
W W Hall	48	192	4.00
C C Griffith	28	94	3.36
V A Holder	40	109	2.73

(NB: G St A Sobers, who bowled fast and slow, is omitted.)

Malcolm Marshall thus leads the field and may even improve on his record before his time is up. During the early part of his Test career (Marshall made his Test debut in India in 1978—79), he was regarded, together with the older and more experienced Wayne Daniel and Sylvester Clarke, as a reserve fast bowler, ready to fill in when one of the famous four — Roberts, Holding, Garner and Croft — were unfit or unavailable. This situation changed in 1982—83 when Marshall came in for Croft versus India in the Caribbean and took 21 wickets at 23.57 in his first full series. In the West Indies in 1983—84, Marshall was again chief support bowler to Garner with 21 wickets at 22.85 in four Tests against Australia. Already a much-feared and prolific wicket-taker for Hampshire in county cricket, he became, in 1984 in England, the undisputed West Indies first-choice new-ball bowler — and the acknowledged fastest bowler around. Most of the England batsmen who escaped physical injury during 1984 were totally humiliated by Marshall (24 wickets in four Tests) whose 7/53 in England's second innings at Leeds was a unique display of courage.

Marshall broke his left thumb in two places while fielding in the gully on the first morning of the match, after bowling six overs for six runs and no wicket. He did not bowl again on the opening day but returned, heavily plastered, to bat one-handed and help Larry Gomes reach a century. Then, at first bowling flat out despite his handicap, Marshall took three quick wickets in England's second innings and added four more when he slowed down and concentrated on swinging the ball.

At 5 ft 9 in (180 cm), 'Denz' Marshall is shorter than most other West Indies fast bowlers but makes up for his lack of height by being wiry and superbly strong. Although his action is not quite side-on,

Malcolm Marshall has the
best strike-rate of all the
West Indian fast bowlers.

and he does not bowl at full stretch in his final stride in the classical
fast bowler's manner, Marshall is a thinking bowler who uses all
available variations of angle, length and movement, through the air
or off the seam. His stamina is also quite remarkable and he seems to
have overcome a back complaint.

Before Malcolm Marshall made it into the West Indies team, a
pair of new fast bowlers were hastily called up against Australia in
1977–78 when the entire World Series contingent in the West Indies
team withdrew after a dispute between skipper Clive Lloyd and the
Board of Control over team selection. Of these two, Norbert Phillip

was a raw-boned and lithe all-rounder from Dominica who bowled right-arm fast-medium and played aggressively as a right-hand batsman for West Indies in nine Tests and for Essex. A popular player, he was soon dropped when the World Series players returned in 1979–80. The second fast-bowling newcomer was Sylvester Theophilus Clarke from Barbados, who stayed around for a while as a reasonably regular choice and took 42 wickets in 11 Tests before joining the 1982–83 West Indies XI in South Africa.

Built like a heavyweight boxer, Clarke is still accepted as one of the two or three fastest bowlers in the world. He was particularly successful on two tours in South Africa (37 wickets at 16.16 in six 'international' matches) and gained a reputation there as a mean-machine who sent the Springboks scurrying for helmets and other protection; he was only mastered once or twice by veteran left-hander Graeme Pollock. The success in South Africa of three other fast bowlers from Barbados, Franklyn Stephenson, Ezra Moseley and Hartley Alleyne, none of whom have ever played in an official Test, illustrated the incredible depth of talent available to the West Indies selectors.

In recent seasons a string of young fast bowlers, all right-arm, have appeared to jostle for a place in the West Indies team. The tall and hostile Winston Walter Davis from the island of St Vincent claimed 32 wickets in his first 11 Tests, faded for a while, and was then recalled when Marshall was unavailable for the 1987 World Cup. The even taller, 6 ft 4 in (193 cm) Milton Aster Small bowls with an action reminiscent of Colin Croft, took a wicket with his first ball in first-class cricket, and played for West Indies versus Australia in 1983–84 after only four first-class games. But he did not follow through after one Test in England in 1984. All-rounder Eldine Ashworth Elderfield Baptiste, right-arm fast-medium, was given five Tests in England in 1984 but the most consistently successful of the younger West Indies fast-bowling brigade is the lanky Jamaican, 6 ft 5 in (195 cm) Courtney Andrew Walsh who first made his mark with 1/29 and 4/74 in the second Test versus England at Port of Spain in 1985–86 when fellow-Jamaican Holding was unable to play.

Another Jamaica-born demolition expert is Balfour Patrick Patterson, a young giant right-arm fast bowler whose raw strength and speed are reminiscent of the young 'Typhoon' Tyson when he 'hit' Australia back in 1954–55. By all reports, Patterson's fearsome high-bouncing 'break-back' delivery seems to follow the evading movement of a batsman like a homing missile.

And the latest West Indies 'find' certainly possesses the 'killer' instinct. Bowling in his first Test match on his ground at Kingston, Patterson first struck Phil Edmonds over the ear with a full toss, and then felled the England bowler with a short-pitched delivery the very next ball, in protest at the disallowance of an appeal for hit wicket off the first delivery.

There were cries of 'uncivilised' and 'cricket degeneration' and the London *Times* correspondent, John Woodcock, even went so far as to state after the match: 'I think I have never felt it more likely that we should see someone killed.'

In terms of speed and menace, Patterson is a worthy heir to Colin Croft. A couple of other comparative newcomers, like Trinidad's Anthony Hollis Gray and Antigua's all-rounder Winston Keithroy Mathew Benjamin have helped Walsh, Davis and Patterson to shift the fast-bowling emphasis in the West Indies away from its former almost exclusive Barbados stronghold. Gray is, at 6 ft 8 in (203 cm), the tallest of the present West Indies fast-bowling wheel of destruction and has already had some days of success in Test cricket.

Before closing this chapter about the West Indies whirlwind bowlers of the 1970s and 1980s, some mention should be made of the very few spin bowlers who have found a place in the West Indies XI during the past decade. Right-arm off-spinner Derek Ricaldo Parry from the tiny island of Nevis is one who might have thrived more in a day when spin bowling was used more freely in the Caribbean. Against Australia at Port of Spain in 1977−78, Parry marked his Test debut by bowling a wide with his first ball. In the fourth match of the series (after the World Series players left) he took 5/15 in Australia's second inningss to ensure West Indies victory. When the Packer players returned a couple of years later, Parry's opportunities became limited and there was little surprise when he chose to join the unofficial West Indies XI in South Africa.

Another right-arm off-break bowler, Ranjie Nanan of Trinidad, and Guyanan left-arm spinner Sew Shivnarine were taken to India in 1977−78 but, like Parry, were summarily dumped when the senior players returned to the fold.

The highly-talented all-rounder Roger Andrew Harper is an off-break bowler of skill who has lacked opportunities because of the West Indies emphasis on pace. A brilliant fielder and fine batsman, he has been named as a possible future West Indies captain. His stilleto-thin Guyana team-mate Clyde Godfrey Butts is also an off-spinner, whom some have compared in looks and style with the legendary Lance Gibbs and who bowled superbly for West Indies in the third Test versus Pakistan in 1986−87 for a match analysis of 60−24−95−6.

But it is patently clear that, with the various West Indies ground authorities preparing pitches to suit their fast bowlers of the day, and the seeming reluctance of West Indies umpires to act fully in accordance with existing laws limiting the use of short-pitched balls, batting in the Caribbean (and elsewhere when the Windies whirlwind is blowing) has become a rather hazardous business. Pace rules, and looks as if it will continue to do so for some time yet.

33

Best of all time

'Of course the bowler is born — who isn't?'
— E F Benson and Eustace H Miles

As no-one can claim to have witnessed all the great bowlers in cricket history, any selection of the 'best of all time' would necessarily contain some element of personal prejudice and the arbitrary judgement of the chooser, based on known statistical fact and the recorded opinions of acknowledged experts. In terms of wickets-per-match strike-rate in Test cricket, one bowler stands clearly above his fellows, and is a man whom many sound judges down the years have repeatedly named as the finest of them all.

The right-arm fast-medium Sydney Francis Barnes took 189 wickets in only 27 Tests for England between 1901 and 1914 — a strike-rate of 7.00 wickets per match. Of the bowlers who claimed 100 wickets or more in Tests, the next best is George Lohmann, also of England, who took 112 in 18 Tests, a strike-rate of 6.22. Of the post-Second World War bowlers with 100 wickets and over, Dennis Lillee of Australia, with 355 in 70 matches (strike-rate 5.07), leads the field.

Because of the limited Test programme at the time, Sydney Barnes took his 189 wickets against two countries only, Australia and South Africa. The breakdown makes interesting reading:

	Matches	Wickets	Strike-rate
v Australia in England	7	29	4.14
v Australia in Australia	13	77	5.92
v South Africa in England	3	34	11.33
v South Africa in South Africa	4	49	12.25

Barnes holds the record for number of wickets taken in a three-match series (34 v South Africa in 1912) and in a five-match series (49 in four Tests v South Africa in 1913–14 — Barnes missed the fifth Test and his chance to top 50). His closest rivals are: three-match series — R J Hadlee 33 (New Zealand v Australia 1985–86) and five-match series — J C Laker 46 (England v Australia 1956). Comparisons are indeed odious, but the bowling of Sydney Barnes (who was still actively and successfully engaged as a professional well into his 60s) appears to stand, like the batting of Sir Donald Bradman, clearly above that of his contemporaries and of those who followed him.

Sydney Francis Barnes, a pre-First World War bowler, thus gets this writer's vote as 'the best of all time', and is arbitrarily awarded the Gold Medal. This leaves the Silver and Bronze awards, but first, some honourable mention of other pre-World War One contenders: George Lohmann, Tom Richardson, Wilfred Rhodes (England); Fred Spofforth, Charles Turner, Hugh Trumble (Australia); and Aubrey Faulkner (South Africa).

Between the wars there was one bowler who participated in the major contest of the time, the Anglo-Australian Ashes series, who has been named by most of his contemporaries (some of whom are still alive) as the most skilful Test bowler of his age. Australia's William John O'Reilly, right-arm leg-break and googly bowler extraordinaire, was still active as a highly perceptive, if at times peppery, newspaper correspondent until early 1988. In 27 Tests (the same number as Barnes), 'Tiger' O'Reilly bagged 144 wickets, giving him a strike-rate of 5.33. Only one other bowler of the period who took more than 100 Test wickets betters this: Clarence Victor Grimmett, Australia's New Zealand-born right-arm leg-break and googly bowler, who took 216 wickets in 37 Tests for a strike-rate of 5.84.

And what a pair they were in Tests for Australia! 'Grimmett and O'Reilly', the sound of their linked names is itself menacing. Grimmett, the silent sleuth, the miser who hated giving away runs; O'Reilly, the ferocious predator, ready to strike the moment a batsman wavered in his concentration. No one else of their time approached the effectiveness of these two Australians, whose performances were all the more remarkable for having been achieved during a period when pitches were never plumber and there were an amazing number of high-scoring batsmen around.

O'Reilly or Grimmett? Taking into account the opinion of those who played at the time, O'Reilly would probably get the vote. So, the Silver Medal goes to William John O'Reilly (with his shadow close at his heels − 'The Scarlet Pimpernel', Clarrie Grimmett).

To remain consistent; third in line must be a post-Second World War bowler — and there are only two with, at the close of the 1986−87 season, more than 100 Test wickets and a strike-rate exceeding five wickets per match: Dennis Lillee and Richard Hadlee (both exactly 355 wickets in 70 Tests at 5.07). Ian Botham, at the same point, had 367 wickets, but in 92 matches at 3.99. Pakistan's Imran Khan had 290 in 65 matches at 4.46, while Malcolm Marshall of the West Indies (10 years younger than Hadlee and likely to outstrip them all) had 240 in 51 matches at 4.71. Of the earlier post-Second World War bowlers who reached 200 Test wickets, England's Alec Bedser took 236 in 51 Tests (strike-rate 4.63) and Freddie Trueman took 307 in 67 (strike-rate 4.58).

It remains, therefore, a toss-up between Lillee and Hadlee, but without any prejudice and partly because, in the opinions expressed by the top batsmen who have faced both bowlers, Dennis Keith Lillee is the accepted best bowler of his period, the Bronze would go to the Australian. However, to be completely fair (because of the differing conditions of play), our bowling awards system might be re-arranged into eras:

	pre-1914	1920—1939	1946 to date
Gold	Barnes	O'Reilly	Lillee
Silver	Spofforth	Grimmett	Hadlee
Bronze	Rhodes	Tate	Trueman

No Larwood? No Bedi? No Tayfield, Imran Khan or Marshall? The list of other candidates is certainly long — and open to pleasant argument.

Sydney Barnes — the best bowler of all time?

34

The great all-rounders

'...one man in his time plays many parts'
— Shakespeare (As You Like It)

Some all-rounders in cricket are immediately recognisable by their batting and bowling figures. Others are known through their ability to alter the course of a match, whether it be during a short stay at the crease for aggressive purposes or a protracted occupation to save an innings or match, plus that incisive piece of penetrative bowling that breaks a partnership and precipitates a collapse or an equally valuable containment spell when conditions favour the batsman.

To select the 'top ten of all time' in international cricket, some basic qualification criteria would have to be met. Perhaps we should first consider all players who have both scored a century in Tests and taken five wickets in an innings (not necessarily in the same match), and further reduce our number of candidates by confining the selection to players who have scored 1500 Test runs and taken 75 Test wickets. Once we have our short list, it would be prudent to add one or two players who have been universally accepted as all-rounders of unusual calibre, even though they may not fall within the categories mentioned. Then might follow a final listing of the top ten.

Looking at our candidates country by country: from England we have Trevor Bailey, Ian Botham, Tony Greig, Walter Hammond, Ray Illingworth, Wilfred Rhodes and Frank Woolley, and must add the 'Grand Old Man', W G Grace, for whom Test cricket started rather late and who cannot be left out of any list of contenders for the 'greatest all-rounder' title; from Australia we have Richie Benaud, Ray Lindwall, Keith Miller and Monty Noble — with Alan Davidson and George Giffen added from the second choice category; South Africa gives us Aubrey Faulkner and Trevor Goddard, plus Mike Procter and Eddie Barlow, who would surely have met the criteria had their careers not been cut short by politics; West Indies provides Sir Garfield Sobers plus the amazing Lord Learie Constantine; New Zealand has two players, Richard Hadlee and John Reid; representing India is Kapil Dev and Vinoo Mankad; Pakistan provides Imran Khan and Mushtaq Mohammed, with Intikhab Alam added as he falls only seven runs short.

There are 27 contenders in all. The writer's choice of the final 10 now becomes an arbitary one and has been confined to those players

Sir Garfield Sobers of the West Indies is my number one choice as cricket's best all-rounder.

who might have represented their countries as either batsman or bowler alone. The reader may care to nominate his own team. Here is mine:

1. Sir Garfield Sobers (West Indies) – scored more than 8000 Test runs and took more than 200 Test wickets *and* was a grand fielder anywhere. There can be few who will argue with the choice of Sobers as number one all-rounder in history.

2. Keith Miller (Australia) – would have been an automatic choice

for any Test team in any time period as either a batsman or a bowler and was one of the finest slip fielders in history.

3. Ian Botham (England) – despite his continued failure against West Indies (who doesn't these days?) one of the most volatile and exciting of cricketers whose 1981 performance versus Australia will go down as a classic comeback.

4. Wilfred Rhodes (England) – as a batsman at Test level, he raised himself from number 11 to Hobbs's opening partner; as a bowler he won many a Test. And how can a man be ignored who scored close on 40,000 first-class runs and still holds the world record for most first-class wickets (4187 at 16.71)?

5. W G Grace (England) – he *made* modern cricket and cannot be omitted.

6. Mike Procter (South Africa) – known as the 'White Sobers' and a dynamic all-rounder who could have walked into any Test team of his time, but was denied recognition because of his country's racial policy.

7. Lord Learie Constantine (West Indies) – the archetypal West Indian cricketer whose Constantine v Middlesex exploits at Lord's in 1928 remains as probably the finest 'one-man team' performance in history. How Constantine would have thrived in modern limited over internationals.

8. Aubrey Faulkner (South Africa) – was at one and the same time South Africa's leading batsman and leading bowler in the early 1900s.

9. Vinoo Mankad (India) – a hand in the world record opening partnership plus a Test at Lord's known as 'Mankad's Match'.

10. Monty Noble (Australia) – a 'Golden Age' all-rounder of great worth who was also one of the finest captains of all time.

Add Leslie Ames of England, the best-ever wicket-keeper/batsman, and we have an eleven to beat any other, with batting order changes depending on the run of play and a variety of bowlers for every wicket and occasion.

THE WICKET-KEEPERS
AND FIELDERS

Contents

Introduction

'A wicket-keeper and an umpire have much in common. Both must concentrate on every ball bowled...'
— Frank Chester

As each team generally only employs one of their kind, there have been fewer wicket-keepers in international cricket than batsmen and bowlers. But the importance of this central character in the great cricketing drama can never be underplayed. G D Martineau writes in his *The Valiant Stumper* that 19th century prize-fighter Jem Mace once told Surrey and England wicket-keeper Ted Pooley that he would rather be in the ring for an hour with any man in England than stand behind the stumps for five minutes, a statement that remains a lasting tribute to the oft-forgotten men of cricket who place themselves well and truly in the line of fire for every ball bowled in a long day's play. One single lapse of concentration can see the chance spilt that might represent the fine line between victory and defeat.

The bowler has respite between overs and when he is taken off. The batsman is continually crossing to the other side to relax a little and observe his partner at play. The fielder, though he must remain alert at all times, only goes into concentrated action when the ball is hit his way. The wicket-keeper has no such luck, except for a brief moment between overs when he crosses over to take his position at the other end of the wicket. He is the pivot, the hub of the wheel of cricket, concentrating all the time on the bowler, on the batsman, on the fielder making his return when the ball has been struck away. It is not surprising that so demanding an occupation has produced some of the finest characters of the game.

This section is not the history and development of the art of wicket-keeping. That task has been admirably performed by Martineau in his *The Valiant Stumper*, which erudite study remains the definitive work on the subject. Martineau's work is, in fact, a unique contribution in a field that has been sadly neglected. Apart from a number of excellent instructional and/or biographical works by famous wicket-keepers themselves (notably those by Australia's Bert Oldfield and England's Godfrey Evans and R T Stanyforth) and David Lemmon's *The Great Wicket-keepers* (a review of most, but not all, of the more prominent stumpers in history), there has been little else.

This work concentrates as much on the personality and acknowledged achievements of those wicket-keepers who have graced international cricket down the years, as on their actual techniques. The tale runs from the days of England pioneer Tom Lockyer, who was pictured behind the stumps without the protection of pads and gloves; through the early Test men from England, Australia and other countries: Lyttelton, Pilling, Lilley, Blackham, Kelly, Carter, Halliwell, Sherwell — many keeping wicket wearing the scantiest of see-through pad protection and thinly-palmed gardening-type gloves; to the master craftsmen of the 1920s, 1930s and 1940s: Duckworth, Oldfield, Cameron, Ames, Tallon, Evans, in their bulky and rather cumbersome pads, and some with slivers of steak in their huge gauntlets as extra protection; and, finally, the moderns: Knott, Taylor, Grout, Marsh, Engineer, Kirmani, Deryck Murray, Dujon, Wasim Bari, Waite, Lindsay, Wadsworth, Smith, Silva — with the latest men doing guard duty behind the stumps in ultra-lightweight, but highly protective gear made possible in an age of extruded, synthetic foams and rubbers.

With regards to fielding, there has been virtually nothing published of a definitive nature, and perhaps understandably so. It would be rather an impossible task to adequately record at a distance a department of the game which, unlike batting and bowling and, to a lesser extent, wicket-keeping, carries little in the way of meaningful statistics, and even less in the form of recorded prose. The known outstanding fielders are highlighted, with emphasis placed on those who were accepted in their time, by their peers and by watching critics, as exceptional examples of their craft, close to the wicket and on the boundary.

There is also earlier passing mention of the top fielders and wicket-keepers who played for the famous Philadelphian teams at the turn of the century. And the women are not forgotten, particularly the most adept female stumper of them all, England's Betty Snowball.

An attempt has been made to include all the outstanding wicket-keepers and fielders who have illumined cricket at international level over the years and apologies are tendered for the absence of any reader's personal favourites.

1

Early English stumpers

'Now the wicket-keeper's connection with the bowler is closest of all. It is as if the bowler were at one end of a telegraph wire and the wicket-keeper at the other.'

— K S Ranjitsinhji

In the early years of cricket the position of wicket-keeper was not necessarily occupied by a specialist. Frequently it was a resting bowler who would take over duty behind the stumps while one of his colleagues delivered the ball from the other end. Early wicket-keepers kept wickets without any of the protection offered by gloves, leg pads and abdominal guard and the position of long-stop, stationed close to the boundary directly behind the stumper, was both valued and highly necessary.

During the 18th century, certain players eventually became renowned as stumpers of great skill, and the specialist wicket-keeper was born. But it should be noted that 18th century wicket-keepers were not expected to stop every ball that passed the wicket. Their prime function was to take advantage of any catch or stumping opportunity and the important long-stop was always ready to gather any awkward ball that passed by the wicket-keeper. Nevertheless, names like William Yalden of Surrey and Tom Sueter of Hambledon, among others, became renowned as leading stumpers of the day.

The 19th century brought a revolution in bowling, when round-arm first appeared, and the art of wicket-keeping was forced to improve even further, from a 'part-time' position that relied very much upon the ability of long-stop to a highly-skilled profession that was made more complete by the introduction of pads and gloves. In the first part of the century, men like Ned Wenman (who kept without protection on uneven turf to the terrifying round-arm fast bowling of Alfred Mynn, the 'Lion of the North'), Herbert Jenner and the famous Sussex stumper Tom Box still scorned the use of pads and gloves. Wenman and Jenner played for Kent and were among the first wicket-keepers to use both right and left hands; they also pioneered the taking of bowling passing the batsman on the leg-side, but never got around to using protective gear. Tom Box, distinguishable by his broad face and ample side-whiskers, was one of the pioneer 'keepers who eventually did. He kept for Sussex and the famous All-England team led by William Clarke for 24 consecutive seasons, let through few byes and rarely missed a catch or stumping chance. Box was probably the first of the true all-round wicket-keepers but the man who has become acknowledged as the first 'modern' stumper was Surrey's Thomas Lockyer, who was, incidentally, also the first wicket-keeper to be taken on an overseas tour.

Lockyer was a member of the first-ever England touring team, which visited the United States and Canada in 1859. There can be no doubt that he was the finest wicket-keeper of his age and when he went to Australia with George Parr's team in 1863–64, Lockyer, according to a contemporary account, 'astonished everyone there'.

William Caffyn, one of Lockyer's fellow England players, describes the wicket-keeper in his *Seventy-One Not Out* as 'a big, strong, loosely-made man, nearly six feet in height, [183 cm], and with

Thomas Lockyer of Surrey, wicket-keeper for the first-ever touring side, the England team to North America in 1859.

tremendously long arms'. Lockyer's reach was apparently phenomenal and his leg-side catches and quicksilver stumpings were regarded as little short of miraculous. As Caffyn puts it, 'He was as quick as lightning and as clever as a monkey'.

Lockyer was the first of the wicket-keeping greats but was born too early to play in a Test match. However, he did play for Surrey in the famous match at the Oval in 1862 when Kent left-arm fast bowler Edgar Willsher strode off the field in protest when he was no-balled six times for delivering the ball with an over-arm action. By 1864, over-arm was officially accepted and Lockyer in his later years had to contend with the bowling of the likes of Willsher and 'Tearaway' George Tarrant on decidedly bumpy tracks. In 1866 Lockyer handed over his gloves to the up-and-coming Edward Pooley, the man who *should* have kept wicket in the first-ever Test match.

International cricket started more than a decade after Lockyer's retirement (he died aged 43 in 1869) but, ironically, because of the gambling habits of his chosen successor, Pooley, the first man to keep for England in an official Test was not even a recognised wicket-keeper.

Alfred Shaw, who bowled the first ball in Test cricket at Melbourne in March 1877, recalls in his memoirs the infamous betting incident that lost for England the services of wicket-keeper Pooley for part of the 1876–77 tour, and for the first-ever Test. Betting on the outcome of a cricket match was then still very much the vogue (with Tattersalls now evident at Lord's, the wheel seems to have turned full cycle) and, prior to a match at Christchurch, New Zealand, against an Eighteen of Canterbury, Pooley bet some locals one pound to one shilling that he could name the individual score of every member of the local team. Taking the record of Shaw and the other England bowlers into account, and the high proportion of 'ducks' made against them, Pooley reckoned himself safe by betting that each of the Canterbury players would fail to score.

After his forecast had proved pretty accurate, Pooley claimed a pound for each duck and offered to pay out one shilling for each batsman who had scored runs. The man with whom he had placed the original bet, Ralph Donkin, refused to pay stating that Pooley had tricked him. A scuffle followed and Ed Pooley was arrested and charged, together with Donkin, for 'having maliciously injured property' and for assault. Forced to stay in Christchurch to await his trial, Pooley missed the boat to Australia and his chance of playing in the inaugural Test. His place was taken by Nottinghamshire batsman John Selby.

Pooley, incidentally, set the world record for the most dismissals in a first-class match at the Oval in 1868 when he caught eight and stumped four for Surrey versus Sussex. His record was first equalled by Don Tallon (9 caught, 3 stumped) for Queensland versus New

South Wales in 1938–39 and again by Brian Taber (9 caught, 3 stumped) for New South Wales versus South Australia at Adelaide in 1968–69, a full century later.

As England's replacement wicket-keeper, John Selby took one catch in the famous Australia-England pipe-opener at the Melbourne Cricket Ground in 1877. He dismissed Tom Horan, the first Irishman to play for Australia, off the bowling of Yorkshire's Allen Hill who had earlier distinguished himself by taking the first wicket in Tests. Selby also appeared behind the stumps in the second and final Test of 1876–77 at Melbourne but Surrey batsman Henry Jupp, who took over after lunch on the first day, ended the match with two catches in his bag.

The errant Ed Pooley had meanwhile lost his chance and never kept wickets in a Test. His troubles did not end when he returned home; in 1869 he appeared in court for using 'threatening and disgusting' language to a sports reporter who had criticised his batting as lacking elegance and finish and, in 1873, Pooley was suspended by Surrey for 'insubordination and misconduct'.

During the course of his stormy career, Ed Pooley was reputed to have broken all 10 fingers and thumbs. He came into the Surrey team by chance when old Tom Lockyer had hurt his hands and was unable to take part in team practice. Pooley volunteered to take the gloves and H H Stephenson, himself a wicket-keeper of note who had toured America with Lockyer in 1859, encouraged the young player to try. Pooley was such a success that the great Tom Lockyer himself was heard to remark that he was 'born to keep wicket' and would have to be his (Lockyer's) successor in the Surrey team.

Poor Ed Pooley could not stay out of trouble and died a pauper in 1907 but was always a cheerful and humorous soul despite his many personal problems.

When England next met Australia in a single Test in 1878–79, in the absence of a regular 'keeper in the touring party, an Irishman, Leland Hone, who had never played for a first-class county, was put behind the stumps by visiting skipper Lord Harris. The next wicket-keeper picked by England (for the inaugural home Test versus Australia at Kennington Oval in 1880) was to be no stop-gap stumper but the first in a long line of outstanding English Test specialists who have set the standard for all wicket-keepers to follow.

2

Lyttelton and Pilling

'Stumping requires, above all, speed of hand and eye.'
— The Honourable T C F Prittie

England's first notable Test wicket-keeper was a member of a famous cricketing family, the Lytteltons, who produced eight top cricketers. The youngest of the brothers was destined to be the only one to play in a Test. The Right Honourable Alfred Lyttelton was a Cambridge Blue who played for Middlesex. In his book *Cricket*, W G Grace describes Lyttelton as a wicket-keeper who was a quick mover and equally adept on both sides of the wicket: 'There was no fuss or show about it, and I have rarely seen him knock the bails off unless there was a possible chance of stumping.'

England's first outstanding stumper did not tour Australia but played in four notable home Tests. He was also a commanding right-handed batsman with a preference for fast scoring and an unlikely bowler who took four wickets in the only innings in which he bowled in a first-class match.

The occasion was the third Test versus Australia at the Oval in 1884 and although the visiting team scored 551 in its only innings, the match has gone down in history as the one graced by 'Lyttelton's lobs'. According to research done by Derek Lodge (*The Journal of the Cricket Society*. Vol 11, No 1), Lyttelton was asked to bowl on the first day, and probably bowled over-arm with W W Read taking over duties behind the stumps. On the next day, Australia's innings moved inexorably onwards (Murdoch 211, McDonnell 103, Scott 102) until England's skipper Lord Harris was moved to again give the ball to his wicket-keeper. W G Grace took over the gloves this time, and soon had Billy Midwinter caught off a Lyttelton lob. Lodge records that it is possible that the regular England 'keeper actually bowled his under-armers with pads on. In any event, he ended his Test bowling debut with an analysis of 12−5−19−4, and never again bowled in a first-class match.

Other than the already mentioned instance involving W G Grace and W W Read, a number of well-known England players have substituted behind the stumps from time to time, including R H Spooner, Ken Barrington, Peter Parfitt, Tom Graveney, Brian Close and even little leg-break and googly merchant 'Tich' Freeman, who kept when his captain R T Stanyforth was injured against South

Africa at Johannesburg in 1927—28. Only three England wicket-keepers other than Lyttelton have dropped their gloves to bowl and take a wicket in a Test. Jim Parks, a more than useful leg-spinner,

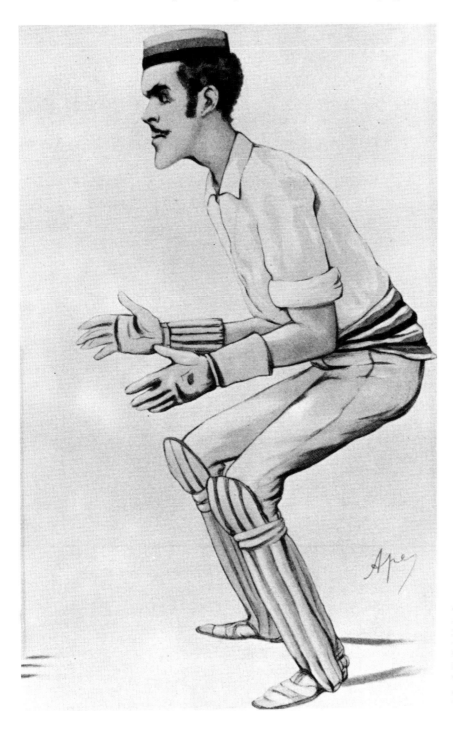

The Honourable Alfred Lyttelton of Middlesex and England. A *Vanity Fair* cartoon of the famous stumper who took eight wickets with lobs on the only occasion he ever bowled in a Test.

took 1/51 in two matches; Dick Lilley had 1/23 in the one match in which he bowled at Old Trafford in 1896; W Storer bowled in four of his six Tests to take 2/108. But none of these worthies approached the amazing analysis provided by Lyttelton at the Oval in 1884.

Tall, fair and sporting a moustache, Alfred Lyttelton was indeed an unusual character and made a perfect subject for the cartoonists of his day. He was also a keen athlete who sometimes tired of standing at the stumps all day and would prevail upon his captain to give him a spell in the outfield, where he would delight his team companions and the spectators with a dashing display of sprinting, gathering and throwing. It was hoped that Lyttelton would both captain and keep wicket when an England team sailed for Australia in 1882 but his legal work at the Bar prevented him doing so and he never ventured Down Under.

Alfred Lyttelton was a man who lived life to the full and inspired affection from all who knew him. A top Test cricketer, he was also one of the finest tennis players of his day, a soccer international and one of the few Test cricketers who have become a Member of Parliament and a Government Minister (he was Colonial Secretary for three years) and was also President of the Marylebone Cricket Club in 1898.

On his death in 1913, former Prime Minister Asquith said of the Right Honourable Alfred Lyttelton: 'He perhaps of all men of his generation came closest to the mould and ideal of manhood which every English father would like to see his son aspire to, and if possible, attain.'

Two contemporary wicket-keepers, one a trusty Lancashire professional and the other an amateur, each made his Test debut in Australia during the 1880s when Alfred Lyttelton declined to tour. The professional, Richard Pilling, became known in his lifetime as 'The Prince of Wicket-keepers'. A slightly-built and self-effacing man of around 5ft 8in (173 cm) who was for a few seasons England's undisputed best, Pilling stood very close to the stumps and scorned those wicket-keepers who did not. W G Grace claimed that the Lancashire stumper had no superior but Pilling's health was never very good and he only appeared in eight Tests, dying at the age of 36. His style was similar to that of Australia's Jack Blackham: quick, neat and unobtrusive.

In Australia in the 1881−82 season, the rather unrobust Dick Pilling survived a bout of sunstroke early in the tour to perform with high skill in four games against Australia. His earlier misfortune in the unaccustomed heat brought whispered accusations that he had succumbed because of excessive drinking, a slanderous campaign based on an ignorance that must have irked the firm teetotaller.

When the Honourable Ivo Bligh took his team to Australia in

1882−83, the place originally earmarked for Alfred Lyttelton was taken by Oxford Blue and amateur Edward Ferdinando Sutton Tylecote who had, in 1868, hit an unbeaten 404 over three afternoons in a school inter-house match at Clifton College, the first-ever score of 400 in any class of cricket to that date. A well played hundred for Kent versus the 1882 Australians apparently encouraged Bligh to include Tylecote in the England party and the new acquisition kept with great skill in the Tests, besides making a decisive 66 run out in a low-scoring match won by England at Sydney.

Like Pilling, Tylecote was an unobtrusive 'keeper who stood up to most bowling but was known to move back when combining with a genuinely fast bowler. Tylecote was one of the first wicket-keepers to entirely dispense with a long-stop (as did Australia's Blackham), relying on his own stopping ability entirely.

Yorkshire's Joseph Hunter was taken to Australia with the Shaw and Shrewsbury all-professional England team in 1884−85 and kept wicket capably, as well as sharing a 98-run last-wicket stand with little Lancashire left-hander Johnny Briggs at Melbourne in the second Test. Pilling and Tylecote replaced him for the 1886 home series against Australia and Hunter died prematurely six years later, his place in the Yorkshire XI going to his younger brother, David Hunter, who was patently unlucky never to represent England.

The massively-built Nottinghamshire stalwart Mordecai Sherwin was the next wicket-keeper to tour overseas with an England team. At something over 17 stone (108 kg) (he was 5ft 9½ins tall−176.5 cm), Sherwin was probably the largest man to keep for his country, but an unexpectedly nimble performer whom 'WG' described as capable of sprinting from the wicket to gather the ball 'as quickly as a more slenderly-built man'. Another contemporary observer, Test bowler S M J Woods, called Sherwin 'as quick as a cat' and also noted that the Notts stumper would only appeal if he was certain a batsman was out and would frequently comment 'that wasn't out' before an umpire had a chance to answer a bowler's appeal. Sherwin also delighted in displaying his agility after making a successful catch with a series of earth-shaking somersaults.

A sometime right-arm fast bowler, Sherwin was also an obdurate number 11 batsman whose unbeaten 21 in a 31-run last wicket stand with the ubiquitous Johnny Briggs at Sydney in the first Test of 1886−87 gave England the margin it needed to eventually take the match by 13 runs. The forthright Mordecai Sherwin later stood as an unsuccessful but ever-willing candidate in Nottingham Municipal elections.

Sherwin's hands were well-protected by nature and were seldom injured. For Kent's Henry Wood, who played for England against Australia at the Oval in 1888 and on two tours to South Africa, it was a different story. Although the diligent Woods sometimes suffered badly with hand injuries he preferred to stand up to fast bowlers. Poet Albert Craig was moved to pen a rhyme in his honour:

Good old Harry, bold and peerless,
Calm and cool, but brave and fearless.

A short man with a large moustache, Harry Woods kept for England in South Africa's first-ever Test at Port Elizabeth in 1888–89. On his second trip to South Africa he hit 134 not out in the only Test at Cape Town and then handed over the wicket-keeping gloves for the rest of the match to former Australian captain Billy Murdoch, who was making his debut for England.

England's next notable wicket-keeper, Scottish-born Gregor McGregor, was also the youngest of his calling ever to play for England. Capped against Australia at Lord's in 1890, the dark-haired McGregor with his striking cavalry moustache was already quite famous for his skilful combining at Cambridge with the Australian-born fast bowler S M J 'Sammy' Woods.

At 19, McGregor was considered England's best wicket-keeper after Dick Pilling. Aged 21, he proved a fine foil to England's great 'Golden Age' bowler George Lohmann and the Yorkshire left-hander Bobby Peel against Australia in England in 1890 and took five outstanding catches off fast bowler Bill Lockwood in the first two home Tests of 1893, helping his team to an edge in the series. In all, Gregor McGregor claimed 17 victims (14 caught, 3 stumped) in his eight Tests but disappointed on his only trip to Australia with Lord Sheffield's team in 1891–92 when he was replaced after two Tests by fellow Middlesex and former Oxford player Hylton Philipson.

'Punch' Philipson, an optimistic personality, was another who preferred to stand up to most bowling and he went on to share wicket-keeping duties with Cambridge amateur Leslie Hewitt Gay when A E Stoddart took his English team to Australia in 1894–95. Gay was picked ahead of Philipson for the first game versus Australia at Sydney and caught three and stumped one batsman in his only Test. Gay also kept goal for England in three soccer matches in 1893–94.

3

Blackham, Kelly and Carter

'Australia has had two heroes, each of whom the populace have familiarly called "Old Jack". One is Carbine, the equine champion, who now reigns at the stud of the Duke of Portland; the other is Jack Blackham'
— George Giffen

The first man to be called 'The Prince of Wicket-keepers' was Lancashire and England's Dick Pilling. Australia's 'Prince' of stumping was John McCarthy Blackham who emerged from the Antipodes when Test cricket was born to challenge the best of England for the royal title among stumpers of the day. George Giffen, who was himself known as the 'W G Grace of Australian cricket', named 'Jack' Blackham as the unequivocal 'Prince of Wicket-keepers', the Trumper of the stumps, who, like his rival Pilling, was one of the first of his kind to dispense with a long-stop. It was even claimed that by standing up to the stumps for even the fastest of bowling without the help of a boundary fielder behind him, Blackham upset England's country clergymen who by tradition were used as long-stops in village green cricket.

To the close of the 1985–86 season, only 24 wicket-keepers have been accorded the honour of a full Australian cap since the legendary Blackham donned his rather flimsy looking gloves for the first-ever Test match more than 100 years ago. The first man given out in that famous Australia-England encounter at the Melbourne Cricket Ground in March 1877 was a wicket-keeper, Nat Thompson, although the Australian opening batsman was not called upon to perform behind the stumps, where Jack Blackham reigned supreme. Another team-mate of Blackham and Thompson, Bransby Cooper (a cousin of W G Grace) was also a useful stumper and wicket-keepers were thus well represented on the unique occasion that gave birth to international cricket. The presence of three of the breed in the Australian team perhaps made up for the absence of an acknowledged stumper in the England XI for poor Ed Pooley was languishing in a New Zealand lock-up and batsmen Selby and Jupp had to look after the wicket-keeping chore.

Famous England wicket-keeper A F A Lilley once described Blackham as an enthusiastic performer behind the stumps whose boundless energy and agile dexterity were remarkable. Lilley also noted that when it came to a matter of fairness, Blackham's conduct was always unquestionable.

The 5ft 9½ins (176.5 cm) Blackham moved with fluid ease and his perfect movement to the ball eliminated any need for acrobatics. His greatest attribute was apparently his keen anticipation of the direction the ball would move after striking the pitch, and his ability to swiftly and smoothly position himself to take the most difficult delivery with maximum ease.

The black-bearded Australian operated behind the stumps relatively unencumbered when compared with the appearance of the stumpers who followed him into Test cricket, with their huge floppy pads and hefty-sized rubber-lined gauntlets. Things have now moved full circle in our present space age when synthetic materials have made possible adequate protection from light-weight equipment. How Blackham would have revelled in the use of the feather-light pads, gloves and other wicket-keeping aids made available through modern technology.

In his reminiscences published in 1921, notable English cricketing personality Lord Harris remarked that Jack Blackham, whom he considered the best wicket-keeper of his time, wore old-fashioned gloves manufactured from brown or yellow leather which become so hard they had to be moistened before use. Yet the mighty Blackham, according to Harris, had so fine an eye that 'at the end of his career his hands were as free from enlargements as a young lady's'.

Another contemporary account claims he hardly had a sound finger on either hand and that Blackham was once even injured when keeping to the slow bowling of Harry Trott. And in an age when dental science had not yet devised clear plastic mouthguards, most of Blackham's front teeth were at one time or another either knocked out or broken off. He was also said to have had a cavity in his chest where a fast ball had once smacked into his ribs.

The legalisation of over-arm bowling did not immediately coincide with any great improvement in the condition of pitches and, at first, a wicket-keeper was often faced with a dangerous situation. However, conditions had improved somewhat when Blackham first followed the lead given by Pilling, who refused under any circumstance to stand back, no matter the pace of the bowler.

George Giffen gives a graphic description of 'Old Jack' Blackham in his book *With Bat and Ball*: 'With eyes as keen as a hawk, and regardless of knocks, he would take the fastest bowling with marvellous dexterity, and woe betide the batsman who even so much as lifted the heel of his back foot as he played forward and missed the ball.'

A clue to Jack Blackham's personal conduct and character was given by William Cooper in a letter written in 1935 to cricket enthusiast and author Les Hill. A former Australian cricketer, Cooper maintained Blackham never appealed 'unless he thought his claim was justified' and once astounded his team-mates by dismissing a claim that he had stumped W G Grace in a match at Lord's by swiftly pointing out he had taken the ball fractionally in front of the stumps.

'WG' was an avid admirer of Blackham's skill and confirms in his *Cricket* that the Australian stumper was equally proficient taking fast or slow bowling and that he was 'marvellously quick, taking shooters and yorkers between the wicket and the pads with comparative ease'.

William Cooper saw both Blackham and Bert Oldfield in action and considered the former to be the better wicket-keeper of the two top Australians because Oldfield stood back to fast bowling and thereby missed many of the stumping chances which Blackham would have accomplished with ease.

Wearing what have been described as little more than light motoring gauntlets or gardening gloves, Blackham stood right up to 'The Demon' Fred Spofforth's bowling for much of the time, going back

John McCarthy Blackham, the Australian 'keeper who revolutionised the art of wicket-keeping, in his flimsy pads and 'gardening' gloves.

only very rarely when the Australian bowling ace was at his very quickest. The two players formed a deadly combination for many years but, strangely enough, Spofforth was at first displeased when Blackham was chosen as wicket-keeper for the Australian's inaugural Test against England. Spofforth wanted Billy Murdoch and refused to play but soon changed his opinion when he watched Blackham in action, making himself available for the second Test. Incidentally, Murdoch went on to become Australia's champion batsman of the day and occasionally acted as a substitute for Blackham when the number one wicket-keeper needed a rest. Murdoch also kept wicket for England in a Test in South Africa in 1891–92.

During his long career, Jack Blackham went to England eight times with the Australian team and played in 35 Tests at home and overseas, claiming 36 caught and 24 stumped — the interesting statistic being the high proportion of stumpings to catches. Although never a particularly reliable run-getter, Blackham enjoyed his moments as a left-handed 'slogger'. He hit his highest Test score of 74 versus England at Sydney in 1894–95 in the fateful final game in which injury forced him out of big cricket. Syd Gregory compiled the first Test double-century in this match and Blackham helped his colleague reach this landmark in a vigorous 154-run stand for the ninth wicket.

Nobody ever questioned Jack Blackham's greatness as a wicket-keeper, from the day he was first 'discovered' playing in a Second XI match by Australia's first team manager John Conway in Melbourne during the early 1870s, right up until his final Test appearance in 1894–95. After more than 20 years as Australia's stumping supremo, Blackham's exit from the first-class arena was rather tragic: he was forced to give the gloves away, aged 41, following one of his few serious injuries on the cricket field when he split a finger during the first innings of the opening Test of the 1894–95 series against A E Stoddart's England eleven. The Australian wicket-keeper was then captain of Australia, a position he had held in seven Tests. Blackham played for Victoria later in that season but was injured again in a Grade match and then retired.

When he died in 1932 at the age of 78, 'Old Jack' Blackham was something of an Australian folk hero and revered even more than the famous racehorse Carbine. As an international wicket-keeper he had set a standard of excellence that was to remain a model and goal for all future generations.

Although Blackham's imposing presence kept a number of other fine glovemen out of the Australian Test XI, two stumpers of the period did get the occasional chance to play for their country and another visited England as a reserve to the great man without playing in a Test.

Had Blackham not been around during the 1880s, there is little doubt that the South Australian stumper Arthur Harwood Jarvis would have become a permanent fixture in the Australian team. In the end, the affable 'Affie' Jarvis did manage 11 Tests, keeping wicket in nine of the games, with a dismissal haul of 8 caught and 9 stumped. He made four trips to England as Blackham's back-up and Giffen claimed that the South Australian was such a fine 'keeper to fast bowling that he had not a single unsound finger on his hands.

Jarvis was distinguishable by his habit of taking the ball and throwing it back to the bowler in one action. A couple of inches taller than the 5ft 9½in (176.5 cm) Blackham, the equally pleasant-natured Jarvis first stood erect and then stooped from the waist as the bowler came in from his mark.

Another of Australia's early stumpers was Frederick James Burton who played one game for Australia as a wicket-keeper in 1886–87, and then held his place in the team as a batsman for a further game, with Blackham taking over behind the stumps once again. Burton played for both Victoria and New South Wales but did not establish himself as either wicket-keeper or batsman and never really challenged Jarvis as Blackham's number two.

When 'Affie' Jarvis started fading as Blackham's closest rival, Alfred Ernest Johns was sent to England in 1896 as understudy wicket-keeper. Johns had hardly played for Victoria at all because of Blackham's presence and Giffen, for one, was highly critical of his choice. The 1903 *Wisden* reported that the Victorian second-string had been highly thought of in Melbourne but that his hands could not stand the strain of constant play. Johns toured England again in 1899 after Blackham retired but did not play in a Test. When it came to batting, Alfred Johns only once exceeded 50 and barely averaged 10 runs an innings in his entire first-class career.

Victoria's versatile all-rounder John Harry, batsman, bowler and more than competent stumper, was considered unlucky to miss both the 1890 and 1896 England tours. In 1890, a major selection blunder resulted in the inclusion of Tasmanian batsman Kenneth Burn on the assumption that he was also a wicket-keeper. It was only discovered when the team was already en route that Burn had never worn wicket-keeping gloves in his life!

The cool and competent James Joseph Kelly accompanied Johns as wicket-keeper on the 1896 Australian tour of England and swiftly and firmly established himself as first choice for the next decade. A Victorian by birth he moved to New South Wales where his pluck both as a wicket-keeper and as a batsman was more appreciated. Unlike his predecessor Blackham, Australia's new wicket-keeper preferred to stand back to fast bowlers like Ernie Jones and 'Tibby' Cotter. However, Kelly was a lightning-quick stumper when he came closer for the slower men. *Wisden* rated Kelly highly, without quite placing him in the same rank as Blackham, when he was chosen as one of the 'Five Cricketers of the Year' in 1903: 'It is idle to pretend that he (Kelly) could bear comparison with the greatest master of wicket-keeping the world has yet seen, but judged by any ordinary standard, he did very well.'

The rugged six-footer (183 cm) possessed great stamina and at Sydney in 1897–98, did not concede one bye in an England total of 551, becoming the first wicket-keeper to achieve such a feat when an opponent's innings exceeded 500 runs. The 12 extras consisted of 11 leg-byes and a wide.

A tough individual who wore a huge walrus moustache, Kelly was considered indestructable and weathered many hard knocks with calm stoicism. Something of an early 'ironman' among wicket-keepers, he played 36 consecutive Tests for Australia, between 1896 and 1905, collecting 43 catches and 23 stumpings along the way. Kelly was also a dogged tail-end Test batsman who always made it difficult for bowlers to take his wicket. He hit three first-class centuries and his highest score was 108 for New South Wales versus South Australia at Sydney in 1896–97. Sadly, he was forced to retire after taking a terrific blow over the heart when batting against Lancashire fast bowler Walter Brearley at Old Trafford in 1905.

Australia's reserve wicket-keeper on that 1905 tour of England was yet another of those forgotten men who has been given little or no mention in the standard works on Australian cricket. Phillip Mesmer Newland was a slightly-built stumper from South Australia, unusual for his era when the typical wicket-keeper was a rather sturdy and weather-beaten individual. A useful batsman as well as a neat and quick 'keeper, Newland did not play in a Test.

Bert Oldfield, the most notable Australian wicket-keeper after Blackham, once described his own immediate predecessor in the Australian team, Hanson Carter. According to Oldfield, Carter was 'so quick at stumping, so neat in his work and so far ahead of any other wicket-keeper I had seen up to that time'.

An undertaker by profession, the dapper 5ft 5ins (165 cm) 'Sammy' Carter was the first wicket-keeper to squat on his haunches as the bowler turned for his run-up. Earlier Australians like Blackham and Kelly had stood erect, poised like vultures over the stumps while the bowler ran in, but the highly unorthodox Carter took up his stance about four feet from the stumps to command a better view of the ball. Carter's perceptive anticipation coupled with clever footwork would then bring him into position to either catch the ball or effect a stumping.

Although he did not follow Carter's example and preferred to either stand right up to the stumps or right back for the faster bowlers, Oldfield conceded that Carter was a brilliant success despite his violation of orthodoxy. The Yorkshire-born Carter was also the last Test wicket-keeper to favour lightweight open-slatted pads to the more bulky and cumbersome equipment in general use after the First World War.

Sammy Carter was a serious competitor who carried a well-thumbed set of the Laws of Cricket in his bag and was not afraid to quote from it if an umpire or an opposing captain failed to keep to the letter. He was always in the game and his perceptive observations were sought after by his various captains. In 28 Tests, Carter caught 44 and stumped 21 batsmen. He frequently chipped in with well-made runs when the occasion demanded and his Test batting average of 22.97 was better than some of his more fancied batting colleagues. For New South Wales he hit two first-class centuries.

When the diminutive but spry Hanson Carter refused (in the company of Victor Trumper, Clem Hill, Warwick Armstrong, Albert Cotter and Vernon Ransford) to take part in the 1912 Triangular Tournament involving Australia, England and South Africa, his berth was offered to William Carkeek, his deputy on the 1909 English tour. Carkeek was another short man but possessed broad shoulders and huge hands, a product of his blacksmithing. Although a tidy player, he lacked the genius of his predecessors and, during the misconceived series that was further ruined by bad weather, the Victorian wicket-keeper struggled to maintain the high standards set by Blackham, Jarvis, Kelly and Carter. 'Barlow' Carkeek appeared in six Tests and took six catches without succeeding at a stumping and was selected for the 1914–15 tour to South Africa abandoned because of war.

Slightly-built Harold Webster went with Carkeek to England as reserve 'keeper in 1912 after playing only six matches for South Australia but was not asked to play in a Test and was never again chosen for either his country or State. After the First World War, Hanson Carter returned to play in the first two post-war series against England but breathing down his neck all the while was the next claimant to the Australian wicket-keeping 'throne', William Albert Stanley Oldfield, still regarded as the best of all Australia's glovemen.

4

Lilley, Strudwick and 'Tiger'

Wicket-keeping is an art, the skilful wicket-keeper an artist'
                                                    − 'Blazer'

At the Lord's Test in 1896, appearing for the first time was a wicket-keeper who would have few challengers for that position in the England XI during the famed 'Golden Age'. Arthur Frederick Augustus Lilley is pictured by George Beldham in his famous book *Great Bowlers and Fielders* as a relaxed and alert stumper, the centre of his body just clear of the off-stump, right foot inches behind the left, knees slightly bent, elbows resting on thighs — an eminently comfortable position as Lilley stands waiting for the bowler's delivery. In the act of stumping, Lilley is seen lifting the bails by merely straightening his body without moving his feet at all, demonstrating his absolute economy of effort. But Lilley could move if he had to, his immaculate leg-side work proved it, and he also respected the value of standing back to an express bowler, having learnt this early in his career when W G Grace pointed out that he should stand back. This was after a snorter from Tom Richardson had struck the young wicket-keeper in the chest.

Lilley gave much credit for his development as a wicket-keeper to the great Jack Blackham, whose flawless method he first observed when picked for Warwickshire versus the Australians at the age of 21. Anticipation, concentration and mobility without any histrionics became the hallmarks of 'Dick' Lilley's own glovework. Incidentally, his nickname came from his association with the Bournville company, makers of the famous Cadbury's cocoa, and with one of the principals of that firm, Richard Cadbury. As a young man Lilley worked in the cocoa warehouse at Bournville and referred frequently in conversation to 'Gaffer Dick', Richard Cadbury's own nickname among the workers. The name eventually stuck to Lilley himself and was later shortened to plain 'Dick'.

Tallish at 5ft 10in (178 cm), and a handsome man with a full, waxed moustache, Lilley looked like everybody's favourite sergeant-major and showed not a little dash of military discipline in his wicket-keeping. At Edgbaston, he developed his batsmanship under the eagle eye of England opener Arthur Shrewsbury and learnt more wicket-keeping tricks from E A Halliwell when the South Africans came to England in 1894. Halliwell had developed a good rapport with the South African fast bowler J J Kotze, who would bowl straight at the wicket-keeper as he altered his position from ball to ball, thus always placing himself in perfect line for any possible catch.

Impressed by the South African's lack of any apparent hand damage, Lilley discovered that Halliwell's secret was to place a piece of raw beef in each palm before pulling on his gloves. Halliwell was apparently the first keeper to use this rather gory protection. Lilley actually improved on it by stitching a piece of foam into the palm of each of his cotton inner gloves and wetting them before use. Unlike some other wicket-keepers of the time, Lilley preferred the freedom of not using any rubber tips in the fingers of his gloves and the very few occasions on which he injured a finger testify to his great skill.

Lilley was already 37 when he first kept wicket to the new-fangled googly bowling of B J T Bosanquet in a Test. This combination was an almost immediate success and the high point of the new bowling-'keeping partnership was reached at Sydney in the fourth match of the rubber when an England victory was for the first time based entirely on the 'bosey' bowling of Bosanquet. And Lilley, with three stumpings and one catch, helped in the snaring of four of the googly bowler's six wickets for 51 runs. When Australia came to England in 1905 and Bosanquet won another famous Test at Trent Bridge with second innings figures of 8/107, Lilley demonstrated to home spectators that he had fully mastered the intricacies of the 'wrong 'un'.

A precedent was created during the 1905 Anglo-Australian series when A O Jones became the first substitute not actually playing in the match to keep wicket in a Test (Lilley was indisposed). The normal practise was to use one of the chosen eleven. Jones took one catch as substitute 'keeper when he dismissed Australia's Warwick Armstrong off the bowling of George Hirst.

Dick Lilley eventually bagged 92 victims (70 caught, 22 stumped) in his 35 matches for England and was also a competent batsman who ended his Test career with 903 runs at an average of 20.52. Against Australia at Old Trafford in 1896, he helped prop up an ailing England innings with a determined and undefeated 65 out of 91 scored while he was at the crease. Lilley also hit a brave 55 in a partnership of 93 with Tom Hayward at Headingly in 1899 and scored 58 in a 113-run seventh-wicket stand with Hayward at Old Trafford in the next match of the same series against Australia. Then, at Sydney in 1901–02, he posted his personal best in Tests with a fine 84, adding 124 for the seventh wicket with all-rounder Len Braund in a match won by England by an innings. In the same match Lilley executed three catches and a stumping to contribute to Australia's second innings slump.

As a bowler, Lilley was used only once in a Test when England skipper W G Grace threw him the ball at Old Trafford in 1896. He sent down five tidy overs for 23 runs and bowled only one off target: his penultimate delivery was wide of the off-stump. Australian captain Harry Trott 'chased' it and was caught behind by substitute wicket-keeper J T Brown! WG took Lilley off at the end of the over with the remark that he '...must have been bowling with the wrong arm'.

Derbyshire's William Storer was the only stumper of the era who ever challenged Lilley for his place in the England team. Old William Caffyn even held Storer in higher esteem as a wicket-keeper than Lilley. Caffyn writes in his autobiography: 'To find a parallel of this great cricketer we must turn from modern players to those of ancient times — to Tom Lockyer and H H Stephenson.'

By all accounts, 'Billy' Storer must have been a very fine wicket-keeper indeed and might have played in more than six Tests if Lilley had not been so dominant. As potentially the better batsman of the two, he was included ahead of Lilley in the 1897–98 England team to Australia but faded as a run-scorer after good innings in the first two Tests. As a wicket-keeper, Storer could not be faulted and was a wonderful taker of fast bowling. England's attack in 1897–98 was built on the pace of tireless Tom Richardson and the swing bowling of George Hirst and Jack Hearne. Storer seldom let them down and his percentage of byes to runs scored was also quite remarkable — only 57 (2.12 per cent) in an aggregate of 2691. Storer was also asked to bowl his leg-breaks on a couple of occasions and bowled Charlie McLeod at Melbourne in the second Test after the Australian opener had scored a century.

The always friendly Lilley-Storer rivalry continued after the 1897–98 tour but Storer only played in one more Test, versus Australia at Nottingham in 1899.

Lilley and Storer were generally not considered for the early England teams that toured South Africa. Initially, these tours were privately organised affairs and few top Test men were considered. Of the wicket-keepers who made their way to the Cape, the first, Harry Rigden Butt of Sussex, was a sound exponent of his craft and an agile mover who always kept well behind the line of the ball. Butt seldom let through a bye and played in the historic first South Africa — England Test at Port Elizabeth in February 1896.

Gloucestershire's John Henry Board was not far behind Lilley and Storer in skill but he was limited to six Tests on two tours of South Africa, although he was taken to Australia as Storer's deputy in 1897–98. Two of Board's Tests were played in 1898–99 and he was first-choice wicket-keeper for Pelham Warner's 1905–06 side that went down to South Africa in that country's first-ever series win. Board played in four Tests in 1905–06, Leonard James Moon replacing him for the third match at Johannesburg, the only time that the Cambridge and Middlesex amateur batsman kept wicket in a Test.

Jack Board was discovered by W G Grace in 1891 at the age of 24 when he was working as a gardener's assistant. He went on to play 430 matches for Gloucestershire before the First World War put an effective end to his playing career in 1914 but emerged afterwards as a much respected coach who frequently travelled to South Africa and New Zealand. No slouch with the bat, Board topped 1000 runs in a season six times. He died aboard SS *Kenilworth Castle* en route from a coaching appointment in South Africa in 1924.

Two wicket-keepers of vastly different background and style shared duty for England in Australia in 1907–08 but neither was given any further opportunity. Derbyshire professional Joseph Humphries was noted for his ability to take quick bowling and took seven catches in his three Tests, all bar one off the faster men. Cambridge and Sussex amateur Richard Alfred Young opened the batting for England in the first Test of 1907–08 at Sydney, and kept wickets in two matches. 'Dick' Young was one of only two England Test wicket-keepers to have worn spectacles on the field (the other was Paul Gibb), played soccer for England and was a rather eccentric cricket theorist who once published a pamphlet claiming a cricket captain should be allowed to pour 100 gallons of water on any part of the pitch!

The careers of two exceptionally skilled pre-First World War England wicket-keepers, Herbert Strudwick and E J 'Tiger' Smith, are still to be highlighted, but before going on to a review of the remaining English international wicket-keepers who played before 1914, some mention should be made of the stumpers who represented the remarkable 'Golden Age' Philadelphian teams at the turn of the century and into the early 1900s.

At that time, cricket in the United States of America, and Philadelphian cricket in particular, reached a peak. At least one of the American bowlers, swing expert John Barton King, would have been an automatic selection for any World XI of the time and he and the other fine Philadelphian bowlers, like Percy Clark, combined brilliantly with a series of highly capable wicket-keepers.

The first of these Philadelphian stumpers was Frank Ralston, a neat player with a distinct military bearing, who stood up to the fast bowlers. However, Ralston suffered somewhat from tender hands and was replaced on the 1897 tour of England by J Henry Scattergood, who arrived in response to a management cable only a day before the match against Gloucestershire. In a long Gloucestershire innings, the new recruit let through only five byes and stumped England batsman C L Townsend. Later in 1897, an England side captained by Pelham Warner visited Philadelphia and after observing the American wicket-keeper at work in a match at Belmont, England's

J H Scattergood, an ace
stumper for the famous
Philadelphian teams of the
late 19th century.

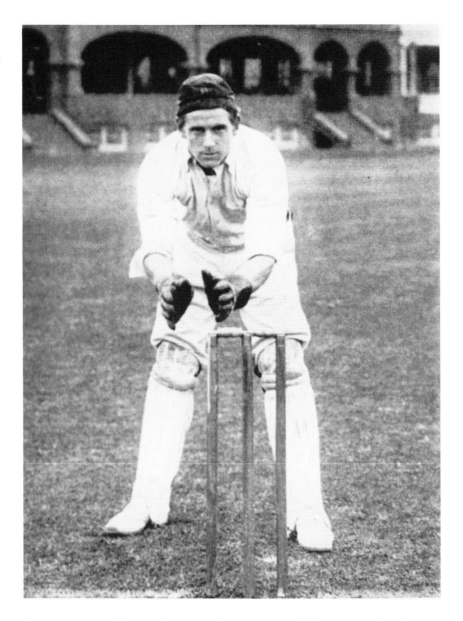

famous hitter Gilbert Jessop, who was one of Scattergood's victims,
noted: 'The wicket-keeping of Scattergood was every bit as remarkable
as was the bowling of Bart King. In the second innings he caused the
downfall of six wickets.' Jessop was himself stumped in glorious
fashion: playing forward to a swinging ball from Percy Clark, the
England batsman lifted his back foot for an instant. Scattergood took
the ball wide of the off-stump and had the bails off before the
normally quick-footed Jessop could recover.

Scattergood went to England with the Philadelphian team again in
1903, with T Carrick Jordan as an alternative stumper and when

Scattergood broke a finger against Somerset, Jordan took over. On the next tour of England in 1908, Jordan and a much younger Charles H Winter shared duties. The 18-year-old Winter immediately formed a deadly combination with Australian googly bowler H V Hordern, who was playing for the Philadelphians at the time, and developed between them what was described at the time as an 'uncanny understanding'. Hordern himself wrote later that both Jordan and Winter 'were good enough to 'keep in any company'.

Alas, Philadelphian cricket faded after the First World War and baseball took over as the national sport of America but, for a brief period, players like Ralston, Scattergood, Jordan and Winter had demonstrated at home and abroad a depth of wicket-keeping skill among the Philadelphians that was comparable to that of all but the most capable exponents of the craft produced by England and Australia before the war.

When Herbert Strudwick of Surrey and England retired from first-class cricket in 1927 at the age of 47, most of the fingers on his gnarled and oak-tough hands had been broken at some time. As Ray Robinson puts it in *From the Boundary*: '...when Strudwick faced east the tip of his right thumb pointed north.'

When Strudwick once broke the middle finger of his right hand, he said nothing to his captain. He went and had a steel plate fixed between the first and third fingers of his glove to keep the broken finger away from the ball, until the fracture knitted. In the early part of his career following his debut for Surrey in 1902, Herbert Strudwick, like Hanson Carter and others before him, kept wicket with the flimsiest of glove and pad protection. Strudwick, at the age of 80, wrote in the 1959 *Wisden*: 'Wicket-keepers used to have to put up with a good deal of knocking about then, for it was not always possible to gauge how a ball would come to you and our equipment was not what it is now.'

The canny old stumper's remark about wicket-keeping gear was in the form of an understatement for he relates also the tale of his predecessor at Surrey, Fred Stedman, who used to protect his chest with a copy of the South Western Railway timetable. Strudwick notes that on one occasion, after receiving a particularly hard blow in the chest, Stedman remarked to slip: 'I shall have to catch a later train tonight. That one knocked off the 7.30!' Ironically, Fred Stedman died in a railway accident in 1918.

Strudwick relates that it was the local vicar's daughter who told him he should be a wicket-keeper when he was playing in a choir-boys' match, and that he never doubted the authority of her prompting from the moment she first said it. Although only 5ft 5½in (166 cm) tall, he was extraordinarily nimble and frequently chased the ball to the boundary, moving as quickly in pads as most men do without. Behind the wicket he reacted like lightning, possessing the quickest feet of any of the pre-war England wicket-keepers. Being short, his customary position right on the stumps did not hamper his movement or style.

Strudwick's method was unostentatious but eminently sound. Standing square to the stumps (usually close enough to lift the bails without stretching), he balanced his weight perfectly on both feet. Strudwick's forearms rested on his pads as he crouched low when the bowler approached, and then he rose to either take the ball or watch the batsman play it. In going for a ball coming through outside the leg stump, Strudwick would move his leg to the left and slightly forward so that he almost faced mid-off when he took it, and still be within easy reach of the leg bail. He stood up to all except the really express bowlers, accepting the ball with slack arms and hands and wearing loose gloves to lessen the shock (he *never* used raw steak in his gloves).

Here was a wicket-keeper who stood up unflinchingly to a variety of bowlers, from slow to outright fast, on tracks of all kinds, for a quarter of a century, and raised a record of dismissals in first-class cricket that was only beaten for the first time almost 50 years later. Strudwick caught 1242 and stumped 254 batsmen (total 1496) in 674 first-class games. He was overhauled by J T Murray of Middlesex and England in 1975. Murray's final figures were caught: 1270, stumped: 257, total: 1527, in 635 matches. R W 'Bob' Taylor of Derbyshire and England has since beaten this figure with 1646 dismissals in 637 matches (1471 caught; 175 stumped).

Herbert Strudwick was the wicket-keeper that Bert Oldfield most admired. Oldfield was himself acknowledged as the greatest of his day and of most other days, so there could be no finer tribute. Known as 'Struddy' throughout his playing career and his many years as Surrey's scorer, he was a quiet, almost apologetic appealer, as courteous as Oldfield.

Strudwick first appeared for England in five Tests in South Africa in 1909−10. On a return visit there in 1913−14, he had 15 catches and six stumpings in a series which saw the legendary Sydney Barnes take 49 South African wickets in four matches. Strudwick went to Australia in 1903−04 but could not oust Dick Lilley. Lilley was by far the better batsman and throughout his career, Herbert Strudwick was an accredited number 11. During the 1903−04 tour, Strudwick fielded as a substitute in the second Test at Melbourne and took three fine catches. On his next excursion to Australia, he lost his Test place to 'Tiger' Smith after the first game at Sydney, having experienced some difficulty in handling the left-arm swing of Frank Foster. Smith was Foster's regular Warwickshire county 'keeper and again kept Strudwick out of the England team when his left-armed fast-bowling team-mate was picked for the Tests played during the 1912 Triangular Tournament.

After the war, Strudwick went to Australia in 1920−21 as first choice wicket-keeper and at last in 1921, at the age of 41, the old campaigner had his first game for England on English soil. Strudwick played his final Test at the Oval when England regained the Ashes in 1926. He was then already 46 years and seven months, the oldest man to be chosen as a wicket-keeper for England. Eight years later,

Herbert Strudwick of Surrey and England, the nimble, dedicated and orthodox stumper.

Frank Woolley deputised for Leslie Ames at the Oval when he was 47 years and three months.

'Struddy' Strudwick gathered 72 victims (60 caught, 12 stumped) in 28 Tests, his international career lasting longer than any other wicket-keeper. His 28 appearances for England stretched from January 1910 to August 1926. Strudwick was a man of gentle warmth and character who served his beloved Surrey faithfully for more than 50 years. During the second half of his career he was a conscientious scorer and many wondered how he gripped his pencil with those bent and swollen fingers, the legacy of his wicket-keeping craft. Herbert Strudwick died a few days past his 90th birthday, and was universally mourned as one of the few remaining links with the leisurely turn-of-the-century Golden Age of cricket.

The true character of the man was illustrated at Melbourne in February 1921 when Strudwick insisted on standing down to give his tour understudy, Yorkshireman Arthur Dolphin, an opportunity to play in what proved to be Dolphin's one and only Test. Ray Robinson recalls that Dolphin looked more like a lobster in the Australian sun and that 'his nippers were alert to seize their prey'. The broad-chested Yorkshireman had a rather ungainly stance at the wicket but was an effective performer who was unfortunate to be a contemporary of Strudwick, Smith and George Brown, who effectively kept him out of the England XI.

Neville Charsley Tufnell, a fellow Surrey player and a Cambridge Blue, stood in for an injured Strudwick during a Test against South Africa at Durban in 1909–10. Tufnell stumped the South African captain Sibley Snooke and later played his only Test match as a selected player and wicket-keeper in the final game of the series.

George Brown of Hampshire was an extraordinary tough-as-teak cricketer who replaced Strudwick for three of the five Tests against Australia in 1921. A powerful left-handed batsman, a right-arm fast-medium bowler, a marvellous and utterly fearless fielder and a Test-class wicket-keeper, Brown was a very talented all-rounder who would rather take a blow on the body than sway aside from a fast bumper (he was also known to bowl a few).

Although Brown never missed a chance as England wicket-keeper in 1921, he preferred to field in 'suicide' positions and regarded himself as a stopgap 'keeper. He batted splendidly against Australia in his first three Tests, playing successive innings of 57, 46, 31, 32 and 84 in a year when England tried 30 players in a dismally one-sided rubber that Australia won with consummate ease. Brown re-appeared as England wicket-keeper in four Tests in South Africa in 1922–23 but failed with the bat and did not again play for England.

George Benjamin Street from Sussex kept wicket in one of the 1922–23 Tests against South Africa and was one of a number of wicket-keepers whose international careers were limited to the odd game or two against the more 'unfashionable' countries whose cricket did not yet match that of the old enemy, Australia. Street was tragically killed in a motorcycle accident just over a year later.

One of the occasional England wicket-keepers was Cambridge and Kent amateur George Edward Charles Wood who had three home Tests against South Africa in 1924 after having declined a place in the team to tour Australia in 1920–21. He also kept wicket for A C MacLaren's famous scratch amateurs eleven which defeated Warwick Armstrong's all-conquering Australians at Eastbourne in 1921.

Lieutenant-Colonel Ronald Thomas Stanyforth was a great cricket enthusiast who captained England in South Africa in 1927–28 when illness caused the withdrawal of the original choice, Captain G R Jackson of Derbyshire. Stanyforth did duty behind the stumps in four Tests and was a keen student of the game who wrote an informative manual on wicket-keeping. His spell as captain was the only time he appeared as a skipper in first-class cricket.

Stanyforth's deputy in South Africa in 1927–28 was the Derbyshire stumper Harry Elliott who appeared in 194 consecutive matches for his county and in four Tests for England versus South Africa and India. Gloucestershire's Harry Smith first took up wicket-keeping as a fill-in but developed so well that he gained an England cap in a Test against West Indies at Lord's in 1928. Walter Latter Cornford of Sussex, just 5ft 3½ins (161 cm) tall and known as 'Tich', was England's wicket-keeper in the inaugural Tests versus New Zealand in 1929–30. His deputy (who did not play in a Test) was Oxford and Gloucestershire amateur Edward Turk Benson whose only tour it was in a short first-class career.

When Herbert Strudwick experienced difficulty in taking the left-arm seamers of Frank Foster in Australia in 1911–12, he was immediately replaced by Foster's own county back-up, the robust and tall Ernest James Smith who revelled in the nickname 'Tiger'. The sobriquet was given to the young colt by Warwickshire and old England wicket-keeper Dick Lilley and was based on the name of a noted boxer of the time. Ernest Smith had worked for Bournville, like Lilley before him, and lost the top joints of the third and little fingers on his right hand and the little finger of his left hand in a machine accident at the age of 14.

Ironically, 'Tiger' Smith came to the fore for Warwickshire when Frank Foster first appeared on the scene as captain and main strike bowler, and the incumbent wicket-keeper and former England number one, veteran Dick Lilley, was prevailed upon to hang up his gloves. The Foster-Smith partnership blossomed. Foster bowled a form of leg-theory and was consulted by Douglas Jardine when 'bodyline' was being conceived. Most wicket-keepers found Foster's late swing too hot to handle but Smith stood up to him with wonderful agility and skill.

Australia won the first Test of the 1911-12 series by 146 runs, despite Foster taking seven wickets. England captain Johnny Douglas had taken over the leadership from an ill Pelham Warner just before the series started and he insisted Smith replace Strudwick immediately. The move succeeded handsomely; a new dimension was added to Foster's bowling through having a wicket-keeper who was familiar with this method and understood his hand signals, and England went on to win the remaining four Tests on the trot, though not without some help from the magnificent bowling of Sydney Barnes who formed with Foster one of the most devastating attacking combinations of all time.

Tiger Smith kept remarkably well in the first three Tests he played in 1911–12 but slipped somewhat in the final match at Sydney and was criticised by Pelham Warner for letting through too many byes. However, Warner did lavish praise on Smith for his almost miraculous first-ball stumping of Australian captain Clem Hill in the first innings of the third Test at Adelaide. Smith had been standing back but moved up when Hill came to the wicket. At a prearranged signal, Foster sent the ball down the leg-side, Hill went forward, trying to glance the ball, and missed but Smith quickly had the bails off before Hill could regain the crease.

Smith went on to retain his place for the six games played by England in the 1912 Triangular Tournament but was dropped when Strudwick was preferred during the 1913–14 tour of South Africa (when Sydney Barnes decimated the South African batting line-up). Smith did play in one Test on that tour, as a batsman, but war now stopped all cricket and when play resumed in 1920 with Strudwick in fine form and fettle, Tiger Smith become a forgotten man.

His avid association with cricket certainly did not stop. Tiger Smith died in 1979, at 93 the oldest living Test cricketer. He had been a player when Warwickshire won its first County Championship title in 1911 and, as team coach, helped his county to another win in 1951. Tiger Smith's association with Warwickshire lasted a full 83 years, from the day he climbed a tree outside his beloved Edgbaston ground to watch a Warwickshire versus Kent match until the England-India Test match he attended at Edgbaston in the year of his passing. Throughout his long tenure as Warwickshire coach, the old stalwart was frequently consulted regarding matters of technique by players from all the other counties.

In his 11 Tests, E J Smith had 20 dismissals (17 caught, 3 stumped) and a total of 878 (722 caught, 156 stumped) in 496 first-class matches. He was a confident right-hand batsman who made nearly 17,000 first-class runs, including 20 centuries.

Above all else, Tiger Smith was a person who loved cricket and devoted his entire life to it. Although he accepted no nonsense from his charges, he was a kind-hearted and thorough senior adviser to many of the great players down the years, a sensitive man who had raised himself from a humble start to life and who was always willing to pass on to others the fruits of his experiences in cricket and in life.

Tiger Smith did not play for England after the First World War. Herbert Strudwick did for a while, until a successor arrived (his tale will follow later) who was as nimble behind the stumps as his predecessor, but the marked antithesis of a Strudwick when it came to physical build and manner of appealing.

5

Oldfield asks

'A more polite stumper than Oldfield was never known. It must have been a pleasure to get out to him'

— Sir Neville Cardus

In a foreword to the great Australian wicket-keeper's *Behind the Wicket*, Sir Neville Cardus sums up the work of Oldfield to perfection. He talks of '. . .a sudden swoop, a flash of the bail in the sunshine', then a quiet query to the umpire and the batsman is on his woeful way back to the pavilion. Oldfield was almost apologetic in his appealing, but sure and swift when it came to the execution of a catch, a run out or a stumping. He was the 'wicket-keepers' wicket-keeper', admired as much by his opponents as by his own colleagues.

Ray Robinson once described Bert Oldfield as 'The Gentleman in Gloves' and 'the most courtly of all wicket-keepers'. William Albert Stanley Oldfield was quite happy to be called plain Bert. Some of his team-mates preferred to use his nickname, 'Cracker', a term denoting the best, and in honour of Oldfield's numerous faultless displays in support of Australia's bowling brigade. Modest, unassuming and possessing an endearing personality, Oldfield was an undemonstrative and neat wicket-keeper who abhorred any suggestion of an exaggerated pose.

Two of Oldfield's most famous dismissals concerned Jack Hobbs, the acknowledged champion England batsman before and after the First World War until Walter Hammond took over the crown in 1928–29. Oldfield himself offers a lucid description of the two dismissal incidents involving the English batting master who was knighted for his contribution to cricket. Both events took place during the 1924–25 series 'Down Under' after Australia had overwhelmed their struggling enemy in the first three Tests.

At Melbourne in the fourth, Hobbs and his opening partner Herbert Sutcliffe began a defiant stand that took the score to 126 without loss. The England openers had already put together three partnerships of more than 100 in the series, including a marvellous 283-run stand in the second Test at Melbourne, only to see their efforts wasted by the rest of England's batsmen and a rather wayward bowling attack. Hobbs seemed to be well on his way to three figures when he missed the ball when playing forward to execute a leg-glance off medium-pacer Jack Ryder and momentarily over-balanced. All Oldfield required was that fraction of a second to take the ball and remove the bails and a bemused Hobbs was on his way to the pavilion.

England won that Melbourne Test by an innings but Australia's revenge came in the final game at Sydney when another Oldfield miracle altered the course of the game. The home side struggled to a first innings score of 295 and the England batsmen were confident they could pass this total and build a substantial lead. With just three runs on the board, Hobbs executed what to him seemed a perfectly safe leg-glance off fast bowler Jack Gregory. To the England batsman's (and everyone else's) amazement, Oldfield moved five or six yards to leg, in easy and almost unobtrusive fashion, to glove a remarkable catch just inches off the turf. Hobbs was shattered; Gregory and the rest of the Australians delighted.

Jack Hobbs later described Oldfield's movement towards square leg as being like that of a hare, or a kangaroo on the leap, and affirmed that the Australian wicket-keeper took the ball with one outstretched hand. A stunned England crumbled to 167 all out and Australia piled on the agony and won by 307 runs.

The fact that Oldfield made his great catch off Hobbs one-handed was an unusual experience. According to the outstanding England post-war stumper Godfrey Evans, Oldfield once told him that it was his practice to always place the little finger of his right hand over that of his left so that the gloves were linked together when he moved. Thus he would always be in a position to take the ball safely with two hands. Oldfield wrote in his *Behind the Wicket* that he could not go along with the method employed by wicket-keepers like England's Leslie Ames and the South Africans, Ward and Cameron, who would take good-length bowling on the leg-side by 'feeling blindly for the ball while retaining their original stance and judging the approximate height and width of the delivery'. For Oldfield, the only method was the orthodox one of covering the line of the ball with his body.

Oldfield first modelled his style on Hanson Carter, his predecessor in the Australiam team, but later changed after studying England's Herbert Strudwick at the nets. When Oldfield sought Strudwick's opinion of his wicket-keeping, the reply came: 'Keep on as you are; you're doing all right.'

Oldfield's approach to cricket in general and wicket-keeping in particular might be described as Bradman-like in its studious punctiliousness and pain-staking efficiency. Before putting on his gauntlets, he meticulously bound each of his fingers, concentrating on weak areas, and then donned two sets of wetted chamois inner gloves. Then came the placement on each finger of thimble-shaped leather tips, with rubber inserts to absorb shock, before Oldfield finally drew on leather gloves with reinforced palms.

When Herbie Collins was searching for a wicket-keeper to add to his Australian Imperial Forces team in England in 1919, he unearthed the unknown Oldfield in a dingy lodging in London and offered him the job. Oldfield at first refused but was prevailed upon to give it a go, played his first game for Collins with borrowed gear, and was so impressive that regular AIF stumper Ted Long immediately relegated himself to number two 'keeper.

At Test level, Oldfield at first competed with incumbent stumper Sammy Carter before taking over completely in 1924—25. He then proceeded over the next 12 years to break all previous Australian wicket-keeping records. He ended his career with calloused hands and gnarled fingers but an admirable record of 130 dismissals (78 caught, 52 stumped) in 54 Tests. In 245 first-class games, Oldfield had 661 dismissals (399 caught, 262 stumped).

Oldfield's handling of the fast fliers sent down by Jack Gregory and Ted McDonald was immaculate and his 'keeping to Australian googly bowlers Mailey, Grimmett and O'Reilly was marvellous to watch. If Australia's gentleman wicket-keeper ever did experience any problems in 'reading' which way a ball would turn, it was when 'keeping to left-arm googly bowler 'Chuck' Fleetwood-Smith in South Africa in 1935—36.

A notable feature of Oldfield's wicket-keeping was the small number of byes he let through. During the 1924—25 series, England topped 400 twice in the first two Tests but in each of those innings there were only four byes. At Melbourne in the fourth Test, England totalled 548 and only six of this massive total came from byes. When England next toured Australia in 1928—29, Oldfield contributed one of his most immaculate performances in the second Test at Sydney. With Walter Hammond hitting 251, the vistors totalled 636 in over two days' play. Oldfield only let through two byes during what must have been a particularly gruelling experience for the Australians. When Hammond made another double-century in the next Test at Melbourne, there was only one extra recorded in England's total of 417 — a single bye. At Melbourne in the fifth and final Test, Oldfield let through just four byes in England's score of 519. Add Oldfield's wonderful catching, stumping and backing up to his fielders, and the odd innings that helped turn a match, and there can be no cause for wonder as to why he was so highly regarded by his team-mates.

As a batsman, Oldfield averaged more than 20 runs an innings for Australia and scored six first-class centuries, three for New South Wales and three for Australian teams abroad. In his third Test, at Adelaide in 1920—21, the Australian wicket-keeper scored 50 and helped Herbie Collins in a critical ninth-wicket stand. He continued to make runs at number 10 that an opener would have been proud of. In 1924—25, Oldfield started the series against England batting at 10 with consecutive scores of 39 not out, 18, 39 not out, 39 and 47.

At Sydney in the fifth Test, he contributed 65 not out in Australia's second innings. At Melbourne in 1928–29, Oldfield was asked to open Australia's second innings against England and a responsible knock of 48 laid the foundation for his country's only win of the series.

At Adelaide during the height of the bodyline series of 1932–33, Oldfield had scored a brave 41 when he was forced to retire after being struck on the head by a Larwood thunderbolt while attempting to hook a short-pitched ball. The ball came off the pitch a fraction slower than Oldfield expected, touched his bat and smacked him in

W A 'Bert' Oldfield, Australia's 'Gentleman in Gloves'.

the temple. Larwood rushed over to the stricken Australian to tender immediate apologies but all Oldfield could say as he clutched his head and collapsed to the ground was that it was his own fault.

Larwood was bowling to a conventional off-side field at the time but the crowd were not interested and burst into a chorus of abuse aimed at the bowler, his captain, Douglas Jardine, and the rest of the England team. It was claimed that Maurice Tate, an England reserve, moved from his seat in the members' enclosure, fearful for his life! Luckily, Bert Oldfield recovered so well from a hairline fracture of the skull that he missed only one more Test and was back in the Australian team for the fifth in Sydney.

Years later Oldfield confirmed that the incident was indeed his own fault. He had off-driven Larwood to the boundary off the previous ball and had first intended to play the next one, which was pitched very much shorter and lifting, behind point. He changed his mind at the last moment and attempted to pull the ball square, but his timing was astray.

Bert Oldfield and Harold Larwood remained good friends, particularly when the former England fast bowler emigrated to Australia in 1949. The Australian wicket-keeper even once went on record to say that he thought it scandalous that Larwood had not been made an honorary member of the Sydney Cricket Ground. Oldfield himself opened a sports store in Sydney in the 1920s and used to walk the two or three miles from his shop to Sydney Cricket Ground for practice or for a match as a part of his physical fitness programme.

With Oldfield in hospital, his place behind the stumps for the fourth Test of the controversial 1932—33 series, at Brisbane, was taken by the good-natured 'Hammy' Love, formerly of Victoria, but at the time Oldfield's New South Wales deputy. The slightly-built Hampden Stanley Bray Love was noted for his fine catching and was more of a batsman than most wicket-keepers of his time. A free-scoring player, he hit seven centuries and totalled nearly 3000 first-class runs but failed in his only Test, scoring five and three. Behind the stumps he made few errors against England at Brisbane and pouched three catches, including a snick by Douglas Jardine off Bill O'Reilly.

Love also played in that famous 1926—27 match when Victoria amassed 1107 runs in a single innings against New South Wales. Oldfield's deputy stumper on the 1926 tour to England also batted in that innings — and hit the 1000th run. John Leslie Ellis was a jovial man who once shocked the establishment by keeping wicket for Victoria in brown pads. Talkative at most times, he was at his best (or worst) whenever Bradman happened to play one of his frequent big innings against Victoria. The stumper's initial remarks were generally directed at the slip fieldsmen but as a long innings pro gressed without any sign of termination, he would re-direct his comments to the batsman. When batting, Ellis was, as Ray Robinson recorded it, 'often at a loss for a stroke but never for a word'.

The ebullient 'Nana' Ellis did not play in a Test and nor did Oldfield's number two on the next tour of England, in 1930. Charles William Walker of South Australia was, like most wicket-keepers, a smiling, well-liked person but unfortunately his confidence was affected by many injuries to his fingers. For some years he vied for the number two wicket-keeping spot, after Oldfield, with Victoria's Ben Barnett, who beat him to a place in the team for the 1934 trip to England. A broken finger kept 'Chilla' Walker out of many matches when he was picked again to visit England in 1938 and Barnett took over as Oldfield's successor in the Test eleven. Walker was killed in action during a World War Two air battle, aged 33 and still to play in a Test.

Charlie Walker once broke the little finger on his right hand when 'keeping for South Australia versus New South Wales at Sydney in 1937–38 and his skipper, Don Bradman, strapped on the wicket-keeping pads. As the match was being played shortly before an England tour, opposition stumper Bert Oldfield did his utmost to dissuade the 'Don' from risking an injury by going behind the wicket. Bradman laughingly disregarded the advice and retorted that, in any event, he was going to use mainly his slow bowlers and there would be no danger. He did however follow Oldfield's advice to tape his fingers fully and wear inner gloves.

The versatile Australian captain and champion run-getter proceeded to stump O'Reilly off leg-spinner Frank Ward in the first New South Wales innings and in the second innings, Bradman took three catches in a display described by *Wisden* as 'first-rate'. According to Oldfield, Bradman's catches to dismiss fellow Test batsmen Stan McCabe and Alan Kippax were accomplished after the make-shift gloveman had made considerable ground towards square leg.

It will be a shame if Benjamin Arthur Barnett is remembered only as the man who missed Hutton when that grand batsman was on his inexorable way to a world record score of 364 at the Oval in 1938. Ben Barnett was indeed guilty of the error which allowed the England opener to proceed from 40, when he gave a stumping chance off a Fleetwood-Smith 'wrong 'un', to the 364 Hutton eventually ground out during 13 hours and 17 minutes of agony for Australia.

The 1938 Australian wicket-keeper was in fact one of the most capable of his kind and a left-handed batsman good enough to play for his country as a run-getter alone. Off the field, Barnett was something of an amateur conjurer who delighted in baffling his team-mates and on the field, his quicksilver reflexes caused many a batsman to depart for the pavilion. Barnett was particularly noted for his ability to 'read' spin bowling and his choice ahead of Don Tallon for the 1938 tour was probably prompted by the knowledge that he had handled 'Chuck' Fleetwood-Smith's puzzling 'Chinaman' with more ease than Oldfield did in South Africa in 1935–36.

The peculiar gloves worn by Barnett — webbed between thumb and forefinger — resulted in an unmarked pair of hands at the end of his career. However, there was much controversy over his 'duck's foot' creation and both the New South Wales and Queensland authorities banned use of the webbed gauntlet by their State wicket-keepers. Barnett played his first match for Victoria in 1929–30 and his final first-class outing in Australia was for that State against the MCC in 1946–47, after three and a half years as a 'guest' of the Japanese in the infamous Changi POW camp near Singapore.

Moving to England, the former Australian Test stumper led Buckinghamshire to the Minor Counties' Championship in 1952 and took a Commonwealth Team to India in 1953–54. He was still playing for Buckinghamshire in 1964, aged 56. Although he could not be compared with Oldfield, Barnett was quietly efficient. In four Test matches against England in 1938 he caught three and stumped two batsmen. As an administrator and Australia's representative at International Cricket Conferences for some 30 years, he was an urbane and tactful diplomat.

Ben Barnett was thus Australia's last Test wicket-keeper before the Second World War. His deputy in England in 1938 was Charlie Walker although many thought it should have been the 22-year-old Donald Tallon, a gloveman of such brilliance that he is still regarded by most critics as Australia's finest wicket-keeper, who was forced to wait for his moment for another eight long years, until the clouds of war had dispersed and Test cricket was resumed in 1946.

6

Duckworth demands

'His appeal was heard and famous in two hemispheres — almost simultaneously, you could have sworn.'

— Sir Neville Cardus

Sir Neville Cardus once compared the two finest post-war wicket-keepers from Australia and England: 'A more polite stumper than Oldfield was never known. It must have been a pleasure to get out to him. Once I was stumped in a club match by Duckworth and felt that I had been sandbagged.' The doyen of cricket writers goes on to confirm that Oldfield did his work stealthily and courteously but that the strident appeals of vociferous, Lancashire-born George Duckworth were the stuff that legends are made of.

Duckworth was one of the busiest and most boisterous of all Test wicket-keepers. He was also one of the most skilful. At 5ft 7in (170 cm), he was taller than either Oldfield or Strudwick, and broader in beam by far. Duckworth's pads were also the widest and bulkiest ever seen. He bustled onto the field as if there was limited time available in which to dismiss the opposition. There was no place in Duckworth's craft for the gentle niceties of style, smooth movement and clever footwork. As Ray Robinson puts it: 'He threw himself this way and that, bobbed and bounced, skidded and stumbled.' However, Duckworth was never caught falling over backwards and was as effective in his eccentricities as other more classical wicket-keepers. He would bend down on one knee to effect a stumping and hurl himself left or right like a soccer goalkeeper if there was any chance of taking a catch. His anticipation was phenomenal and there was never any safety in playing a leg-glance when he was behind the stumps.

But, above all else, George Duckworth was noted for his fierce, almost falsetto appeal when he thought a batsman was due for despatch to the pavilion. His query to the umpire was more in the manner of a demand. Duckworth was a hostile wicket-keeper and must have provided much discomfort for a sensitive batsman, breathing down his neck and willing him out.

Duckworth got his first England cap against South Africa in a rain-ruined Test at Old Trafford in 1924. The visitors' score stood at 116 for four wickets in the first innings of the game when the heavens opened and prevented any further play. The 23-year-old stumper had let through eight byes and was given no chance to voice his bugle-call of an appeal. For the next Test, Herbert Strudwick was recalled and also retained for the 1924–25 tour of Australia, taking Nottinghamshire batsman-wicket-keeper William Whysall as his deputy (Whysall did not play in a Test as a wicket-keeper). Unfortunately, Duckworth was never much of a batsman but an accredited number 11 like Strudwick and he missed out on numerous Test opportunities when England captains like Douglas Jardine preferred to play a stumper who could also help the scoreboard along.

Strudwick again held his position for the 1926 home series against Australia and R T Stanyforth and Harry Elliott were picked for the 1927–28 South African series. In 1928 the West Indies team arrived in England for its first official rubber and Elliott and Harry Smith did duty in the first two Tests. Duckworth was finally given another opportunity in the third Test at the Oval, handled the bowling of fast men Larwood and Tate and little leg-breaker 'Tich' Freeman with aplomb, and found himself as number one 'keeper for the 1928–29 Australia tour.

To protect his hands against the shock of taking fast bowling, Duckworth used thin strips of raw steak in his inner gloves, a practice that also kept his hands moist on hot days. He also wore two sets of inner gloves, binding his finger joints with tape as an additional safeguard, and a chest protector which must have helped when he went skidding along the ground after one of his famous dives to gather a snicked ball.

George Duckworth returned from his 1928–29 trip to Australia with an enhanced reputation but met with an immediate challenge from Leslie Ames of Kent, a run-scorer of such ability that he might have played for England as a batsman alone. For the next eight years, it was generally a toss-up between Duckworth and Ames. Duckworth may have had a slight edge on Ames as a wicket-keeper but there was no denying the latter's outstanding batting ability and this factor frequently weighed in his favour. George Duckworth eventually bowed out after getting only one Test in seven played in Australia and New Zealand in 1936–37. In 24 Tests he had bagged 45 catches and made 15 stumpings and with the help of not outs in about half his innings, Duckworth averaged 14.62 with the bat in Tests. In 504 first-class games he had 1095 victims (754 caught, 341 stumped), and every one of them knew with certainty when he was out. The voice behind told them so, even before the umpire had a chance to respond.

In retirement, Duckworth became a respected journalist after some time in the hotel and farming industries. He was also a popular baggage-man and scorer for several MCC sides and the genial manager of three Commonwealth teams that toured India in the 1950s.

The ebullient George Duckworth made his Lancashire debut in

England's George Duckworth on the move and exhibiting the perfect wicket-keeper's stance as Indian batsman V M Merchant plays a cut shot.

1923 and was that county's first-choice wicket-keeper for some 15 seasons. The quietly popular William Farrimond lived in Duckworth's ample shadow as reserve stumper at Old Trafford from 1924 until 1938, when Duckworth played his last county game and Farrimond finally took over at the age of 35. That he was chosen to play for England while remaining Duckworth's perpetual county deputy was a tribute to Farrimond's great skill as a wicket-keeper and that he should have stayed all the time with Lancashire was an indication of his unwavering loyalty.

Bill Farrimond had his initial chance for international honours when he was taken by the MCC to South Africa in 1930–31 as Duckworth's back-up. He ended up playing in the last two Tests when Duckworth fell ill and impressed both as a sound and confident stumper and as a determined right-hand batsman, making second top score (35) for England in a low scoring drawn Test at Durban. Farrimond's wicket-keeping was marked for its economy of movement and restraint in appeal — the exact opposite of Duckworth's aggressive and enthusiastic appealing. He played twice more for England: as reserve to Leslie Ames in the West Indies in 1934–35 and versus South Africa at Lord's when Ames was played purely as a batsman. But the loyal Bill Farrimond had only two full first-class seasons for Lancashire before the war and was too old by war's end to continue his chequered county and international career.

Strangely enough, there was a similar situation in Kent as in Lancashire. Leslie Ames played for his county from 1926 to 1951, although he did not keep wicket after the war when young Godfrey Evans arrived on the scene. From 1930 to 1947, amateur William Howard Vincent Levett filled in when Ames needed a rest or was playing for England. 'Hopper' Levett was also good enough to play for England, which he did in one Test in India in 1933—34 when he travelled as second-string 'keeper to Harry Elliott. The Kent number two wicket-keeper of the 1930s will always be remembered for the time when he was given one of his rare chances to bowl, ran up, and delivered a *bread roll*! With his Roman nose, ruddy complexion and resonant voice, Levett was a great favourite among Australian touring sides against whom he first appeared as a member of a Public School XV at Lord's in 1926.

Ames and Levett of Kent and Duckworth and Farrimond of Lancashire were for some years the undisputed top four wicket-keepers in England but there was only room for one in the England XI and two in county cricket.

Leslie Ethelbert George Ames must go down as one of the two or three finest wicket-keeper/batsmen in history, if not the very finest. He was one of the best attacking batsmen of his time, all stroke and style; a natural who hit the ball as hard as his contemporaries and was capable of making loads of runs in any company. In 47 Tests, Ames scored 2434 runs at a splendid average of 40.56 with eight centuries. In all first-class cricket, he joined the select club of those who have scored 100 centuries. In 1933, Ames hit more than 3000 first-class runs, the only wicket-keeper to ever do so. He still shares with G O Allen the world record Test partnership for the eighth wicket — 246 for England versus New Zealand at Lord's in 1931 (Ames made 137, Allen 122). Behind the stumps, Ames had 97 dismissals (74 caught, 23 stumped) in Tests and 1113 (698 caught, 415 stumped) in first-class matches to add to his claim to the title of best batsman/wicket-keeper of all time. He still holds the record of 127 dismissals in an English season, made in 1929 after claiming 121 victims the previous year. The Kent and England stumper three times performed the wicket-keeper's 'double': 1918 runs and 121 dismissals in 1928; 1795 and 127 in 1929; and a phenomenal 2482 and 100 in 1932.

Despite his extraordinary talent in two departments of the game, Leslie Ames was never quite sure of a Test place during the early part of his Test career. He was certainly good enough to play as either a batsman or as a wicket-keeper but in the 'keeping department he faced stiff competition from specialist stumper George Duckworth. Unlike the flamboyant Duckworth, Ames was one of those players who made wicket-keeping look easy. Like Strudwick and Oldfield, his skill was based on marvellous anticipation and he was able to move in two or three unobtrusive steps to quietly take a ball which would have seen Duckworth diving at full stretch.

Leslie Ames, the finest of all wicket-keeper/batsmen, plays a thundering straight drive.

Many of Leslie Ames's lightning stumpings in first-class cricket came off the bowling of 'Tich' Freeman (a man who regularly took more than 200 wickets in a county season) and the pair were a much-feared combination for Kent for many seasons. When England toured Australia in 1932–33, Douglas Jardine preferred Ames to Duckworth behind the stumps to take his bodyline bowlers, Larwood and Voce. When it came to batting, it seemed that some people found it hard to believe that a wicket-keeper could be as talented a run-maker as Ames.

During the war, Leslie Ames was a squadron leader in the Royal Air Force. After, he gave away his gloves to the up-and-coming

Evans, and played for Kent as a batsman for six seasons. Later he did grand service as a Test selector and as manager and secretary for his beloved county, Kent. Leslie Ames was a cricketers' cricketer who was probably also the greatest batsman/wicket-keeper in history.

In the last series played against Australia before war arrived, two other wicket-keepers of note each put in a brief appearance for England. The highly competent Wilfred Frederick Frank Price, who was known as 'The Rock of Gibraltar' for his stonewall batting exploits, replaced an injured Ames in the fourth Test at Headingley, took a couple of catches but failed with the bat. He was replaced by the delightfully humorous Yorkshire stumper Arthur Wood for the final famous Oval match (in which Len Hutton ground his way to 364 in England's innings). Wood was almost 40 when chosen for what proved to be his only Test but it was a memorable one: Wood scored 53 in a 106-run stand for the seventh wicket with Joe Hardstaff that 'boosted' the score to 876 (England eventually won by an innings and 579!). The fun-loving Yorkshire 'keeper feigned a tantrum when he returned to the pavilion, throwing his bat down and exclaiming: 'Joost like me. Daft. Lose me head in a crisis.'

When England made its final pre-war tour to South Africa in 1938–39, Ames went as resident wicket-keeper with another York-shireman, the then amateur Paul Gibb as his deputy. One of only three men to keep in a Test in spectacles (the others were R A Young of England and D Gamsy of South Africa), Gibb was a great success as a batsman in South Africa but wasn't called upon to don his wicket-keeping gloves. He was England's first Test stumper after the war, versus India in 1946 and kept in the first Test of the 1946–47 tour of Australia. Gibb then completed the transition from pre-war to post-war play by handing over his gauntlets to the next great England gloveman, Godfrey Evans, who was to perform in such an exciting and brilliant style as to have his name placed alongside the great wicket-keepers of the game.

7

In two minds: Cameron and other South Africans

'Wicket-keeping on matting is different altogether from keeping wicket on turf'

— A F A Lilley

Until A P F Chapman's England team toured South Africa in 1930–31, all Tests and most first-class matches in that country had been played on matting wickets. Yet in the early years South Africa produced a string of outstanding wicket-keepers who were admirably successful when taken to play on turf in England and Australia and the South African XI has nearly always possessed a wicket-keeper of class. From the beginning and unlike most other countries until more recent times, many have been above average batsmen.

South Africa has also produced more wicket-keeper/captains than any other country — four in all: Murray Bisset, E A Halliwell, P W Sherwell and H B Cameron. W L Murdoch and Jack Blackham were two Australian wicket-keepers who led their country (although the former was seldom seen in the role of a stumper) while Barry Jarman skippered Australia once when Bill Lawry was injured. England's only wicket-keeper/captain was R L Stanyforth, in South Africa in 1927–28; West Indies has had two: R K Nunes and F C M Alexander, as has Pakistan: Imtiaz Ahmed and Wasim Bari; New Zealand has had one, T C Lowry; while India and Sri Lanka have had none. Other occasional wicket-keepers like J R Reid (New Zealand), R B Kanhai (West Indies) and Hanif Mohammed (Pakistan) have captained their country when not acting behind the stumps.

South Africa's first international wicket-keeper, Frederick W Smith, was a batsman who was not an acknowledged specialist behind the stumps, and was not even aware that he was playing in what would later become known as a Test match. Smith took two catches in England's first innings of that historic inaugural encounter at St George's Park, Port Elizabeth in March 1889. In England's second innings at Port Elizabeth, W H Milton (later Sir William Milton) took over from Smith. It was something of a wicket-keeping merry-go-round in this match, for M P Bowden deputised for England's chosen 'keeper, Harry Wood, on the second day and caught Milton off the bowling of Johnny Briggs.

F W Smith kept again in the second of two Tests played in 1888−89 but, in the next England-South Africa series in 1895−96, South Africa had gained the services of its first outstanding gloveman, Ernest Austin Halliwell. Born in England, 'Barberton' Halliwell is pictured in Beldham and Fry's *Great Fielders of the World* as a sturdy man of average height with a large, drooping moustache and a style typical of orthodox wicket-keepers of his day.

Halliwell followed the family tradition: his father kept wicket for Middlesex as R Bisset and later changed his name to Bisset-Halliwell, appearing for the Gentlemen versus Players in 1879 as R B Halliwell. In 1901, Ernest Halliwell emulated his father by appearing for both Middlesex and the Gentlemen.

Halliwell the younger lived an adventurous early life. He left home at 18 for the African Gold Coast and later played much cricket in the North-west Frontier Province of India before settling at Barberton in the Transvaal. In a 'Mother Country versus Colonial Born' match at Johannesburg he once contributed 139 not out in an unbroken first-wicket stand of 289.

On South Africa's first tour of England, in 1894, no Tests were played but Ernest Halliwell was an immediate drawcard as a wicket-keeper and as a batsman of unusual ability. When the visitors played Gloucestershire, W G Grace volubly censured Halliwell for taking too long to get to the wicket when South African wickets were falling quickly. Halliwell's answer was to put together an innings of 110.

On South Africa's next trip to England, in 1901, Halliwell formed a deadly combination with his country's first great fast bowler, J J Kotze. The South African wicket-keeper had earlier first used raw steak in his gloves in deference to Kotze's thunderbolts, a practice which was later followed by England and Australian wicket-keepers.

Halliwell's captain in England in 1901 was also a wicket-keeper, Murray Bisset (later Sir Murray Bisset, sometime Chief Justice and Acting Governor-General of Rhodesia), who kept wicket and captained South Africa against England in a Test at Johannesburg in 1898−99, handing over the gloves to Halliwell for the next game at Cape Town. Bisset, who was also a fine forcing batsman, appeared in one more Test as a wicket-keeper, 11 years later versus England at Cape Town in 1909−10.

Halliwell kept in three Tests and was captain in one when South Africa faced Australia for the first time (Joe Darling's team returned home via South Africa after touring England in 1902). On the third South African tour of England in 1904, Halliwell again combined brilliantly with J J Kotze in matches against the counties but no Tests were as yet included in the South African programme. The situation was eventually rectified in 1907 when three internationals were arranged, but only after the Springbok XI had comprehensively

Opposite: E A Halliwell, South Africa's first outstanding Test wicket-keeper.

defeated Pelham Warner's 1905−06 MCC touring team in South Africa by four matches to one.

South Africa's new-found strength was based on its four outstanding googly bowlers, Faulkner, Vogler, Schwarz and White, and a new wicket-keeper who immediately impressed with his ability to handle the vagaries of the leg-break, top-spinner and 'wrong 'un'.

Percy William Sherwell captained the 1907 team and, apart from his inspired leadership and adept wicket-keeping, was also a notable batsman who favoured the late cut. He played a brilliant match-saving knock of 115 as an opener when South Africa was forced to follow on in the first Test at Lord's. The Lord's match was drawn and South Africa let England off the hook at Leeds in the next after dismissing them for 76 in the first innings. Aubrey Faulkner took 6/17 and 3/58 with his googlies. Sherwell twice stumped England opener Tom Hayward, off Faulkner in the first and off Vogler in the second innings, but England recovered to win by 53 runs in the only conclusive result in a three-match series.

Sherwell's enterprising captaincy provided as much value to his team as his wicket-keeping and batting but it was his skill in taking the four googly bowlers that caused most comment. This was a new experience for wicket-keepers and Sherwell set the standard for others to follow. Slim and sporting a full Kitchener-like moustache, he again demonstrated his stumping ability when in Australia in 1910−11, although the South African googly quartet were mastered on rock-hard tracks by the incomparable Victor Trumper and the other fleet-footed Australian batsmen. In all, Percy Sherwell claimed 36 dismissals (20 caught, 16 stumped) in his 13 Tests and averaged 23.72 with the bat.

Sherwell's deputy in Australia in 1910−11 was the neat and efficient Thomas Campbell who had played in four of five Tests against England in South Africa in 1909−10. Tommy Campbell, a typical number 11 batsman, gave way to Murray Bisset in the fifth Test at Cape Town but returned as first-choice 'keeper for the 1912 Triangular Tournament in England. In England, Campbell again lost his place, this time to the nuggety Thomas Alfred Ward who kept in five of the six Tests. Tommy Ward was a better batsman than Campbell and continued his Test career into the post-First World War period, scoring a defiant 64 against England at Johannesburg in 1922−23 when asked to open the innings on a bad wicket. Campbell had eight dismissals in his five Tests; Ward had 32 (19 caught, 13 stumped) in 23 Tests. Both Tommys met a tragic end: Tommy Campbell died in a train accident while Tommy Ward was electrocuted while working in a gold mine.

Louis Duffus once wrote that Horace Brakendridge Cameron was his country's finest aggressive batsman and 'incomparably its most skilful wicket-keeper'. The doyen of South African cricket writers penned these words before the arrival of John Waite and Denis Lindsay in the 1950s and 1960s but confirmed his opinion of Cameron in 1970, after he had seen the other two great South African wicket-keeper-batsmen in action.

Referring to 'Jock' Cameron in his *Cricketers of the Veld*, Duffus notes: 'Few, if any, cricketers have surpassed his dual ability as a batsman and wicket-keeper.' Duffus goes on to laud Cameron's strong character and infinite courage, attributes which made him one of the most-loved cricketers and captains of South Africa. The whole country went into mourning in 1935 when its beloved Jock Cameron died of enteric fever at the tender age of 30, just a few weeks after returning from South Africa's first Test series win in England.

South Africa's top cricket writer was not alone in his praise of Cameron as an all-rounder. Pelham Warner, former England captain and founder of *The Cricketer* magazine, rated the wicket-keeper/batsman as 'worthy to rank in any company'. The 1936 *Wisden* states (Cameron was one of the 'Five Cricketers of the Year' for 1935): 'Cameron, for all his fearless hitting, will be chiefly remembered for his high place among wicket-keepers not only of South Africa but in his generation. His stumping of a batsman has been likened to the "nonchalant gesture of a smoker flicking the ash from a cigarette" — an apt simile of the speed and art of his deeds.'

Cameron was a wicket-keeper who put intense concentration into his job. He was no joker like Yorkshire's Arthur Wood who quipped to Hedley Verity between overs: 'Thou hast him in two minds, Hedley — he doesn't know whether to hit thee for four or for six', after Cameron had smacked the Yorkshire and England left-arm spinner for three successive fours, followed by three successive sixes in a tour match at Sheffield. In his day, Cameron was considered second only to Oldfield as a wicket-keeper, and was similar in style. Cameron took the ball cleanly and in an unhurried manner without any hint of histrionics but was always alert for any sort of a chance. According to one report, 'some of his stumping efforts dazzled the eyesight'.

After a fine start to his Test career, at the age of 21, against the touring England side in 1927–28 (he kept impeccably and scored a couple of 50s), Cameron had just begun to show his paces in England in 1929 when he was sidelined by a fearful blow to the head from a Larwood bouncer in the second Test at Lord's. His place was taken temporarily by reserve stumper Edward Alexander van der Merwe, a grand all-round sportsman who was to play in one more Test against Australia in 1935–36, shortly after Cameron's untimely death.

Cameron came back with a vengeance later in 1929 to hit out defiantly for 83 in the fourth Test at Manchester and 62 in the fifth at the Oval, besides standing guard at the stumps in his usual reliable fashion. He took over the Springbok captairtcy from H G 'Nummy' Deane in the fourth Test against England in South Africa in 1930–31 and led his team bravely against great odds in Australia in 1931–32 when Don Bradman compiled an unforgettable 806 runs in five Test innings. Then, back in England in 1935, came triumph and tragedy.

Having handed over the leadership of the South African team to H F Wade so that he could concentrate more fully on his wicket-keeping and batting, Cameron enjoyed his finest and, sadly, final season. Apart from his plundering of Verity's normally watertight bowling at Sheffield, the South African stumper played a number of memorable innings in the Tests against England, including 90 out of 126 in only 105 minutes after four wickets had fallen cheaply in the second match at Lord's. South Africa won its first series in England by virtue of a 157-run victory in that match and Cameron signalled the end of the proceedings when he stumped England's Tommy Mitchell off Greek-born googly bowler Xenophon Balaskas.

On the boat home, Jock Cameron contracted a fever that was to prove fatal. The South African public was stunned and its cricketers were shattered and, with the exception of Dudley Nourse, failed to come to grips with the spin menace of Grimmett and O'Reilly when the Australians arrived in 1935–36, the tour starting just three weeks after Cameron's tragic passing.

Jock Cameron had 51 dismissals (39 caught, 12 stumped) in 26 Tests and scored 1239 runs at an average of 30.21. In all first-class cricket, he was one of the few South African wicket-keepers to have topped 100 dismissals, totalling 224 (155 caught, 69 stumped).

Frank 'Nipper' Nicholson was picked to replace the much lamented Cameron against Australia in 1935–36 but, try as he may, could not match his predecessor either as wicket-keeper or as a batsman and lost his place to Eddie van der Merwe for the final Test.

Two wicket-keepers appeared in South Africa's final pre-war rubber, a home series versus England in 1938–39 made famous for the 'Timeless Test' at Durban that was left drawn after 11 days so that England could catch their boat train.

Ronald Eustace Grieveson made an auspicious start in Test cricket with no fewer than seven catches and two stumpings in two Tests, plus innings of 75 and 39 in the 'timeless' epic at Durban but lost the best cricketing years of his life because of war. Walter Wareham Wade, five years younger than Grieveson, played in the first three Tests of 1938–39 and was destined to return 10 years later when England next visited South Africa in 1948–49.

John Dixon Lindsay (father of the subsequently famous Denis Lindsay), George Murray Fullerton and Douglas Ovenstone (who did not play in the Tests) shared wicket-keeping duties when South Africa toured England in 1947, but none impressed. W W 'Billy' Wade, the best batsman available among South African wicket-keepers of the time, was brought back in 1948–49 and batted with some flair against a strong England attack to score 407 runs at 50.57 in the five Tests. A rather out-of-character, cautious innings of 125 in nearly six hours in the final game at Port Elizabeth was his highest score. Wade also kept wicket fairly competently in 1948–49, but fell away the next season when Australia visited South Africa and was replaced for the last two Tests by George Fullerton, an aggressive batsman who was never a full-time wicket-keeper.

A revival in South Africa's cricket fortunes occurred during the 1950s. This grew eventually into the country's own belated Golden Age which was summarily brought to an end by political forces in the 1970s. During this era, South Africa became well-known for its outstanding batsmen-wicket-keepers.

John Henry Bickford Waite was taken to England in 1951 as a 21-year-old rookie assistant wicket-keeper. He ended the visit as South Africa's first choice stumper and a batsman of high promise who had provided veteran Eric Rowan with a reliable opening partner in four Tests. Injury kept Waite out of the final Test at the Oval where intended number one 'keeper William Russell Endean opened the batting and kept wicket. Thereafter, Waite remained first choice behind the stumps with Endean playing as a batsman in his own right and occasionally standing in as wicket-keeper (he also became one of the most remarkable of close catchers).

South Africa's veteran cricket commentator Charles Fortune (now well into his 80s but still heard on radio during important cricket matches) first came across Waite as an up-and-coming 18-year-old student — and immediately forecast a big future for the young wicket-keeper/batsman. During the 1948–49 season, when he was not yet 19, Waite played an innings of 80 against the touring M C C side that elicited high praise from the tourists. In his first Test innings at Nottingham in 1951, Waite played a mature innings of 76 (run out) that any veteran Test batsman would have been proud of. Although defence oriented, Waite used a wide range of strokes off a short back-lift and was exceptionally strong on his legs.

The young player's wicket-keeping skill was also beginning to attract as much attention as his sound batsmanship. One of the 'quiet' school of stumpers, Waite was almost self-effacing in his style, but quick and efficient when standing close and never afraid to go for a spectacular one- or two-handed diving catch when standing back. A tall man at around six foot (183 cm), Waite's flowing style was based to some extent on that of Australian's Ron Saggers whom he had observed in South Africa during 1949–50.

Waite went about his work with ice-cool concentration and an absence of flourish in 50 Tests between 1951 and 1965, the most ever played by a South African. He scored more than 2000 runs including four centuries and had 141 dismissals (124 caught, 17 stumped). His high proportion of catches to stumpings was related to the type and quality of South Africa's four-pronged attack of the day — generally

South African
wicket-keeper/batsman
John Waite has just caught
Australia's Ken Mackay off
the bowling of Kelly
Seymour at Brisbane in
1963–64. The slip fielder is
a youthful Graeme Pollock.

the two quick men, Adcock and Heine, left-arm seamer Goddard and ace off-spinner Tayfield. With these four bowlers, Waite completed one of the toughest outcricket formations in world cricket during the 1950s.

In all first-class cricket, the highly popular Johnny Waite scored nearly 10,000 runs and claimed 510 dismissals (426 caught, 84 stumped), a South African record which is something like 200 victims more than his closest rival. Many obervers claim that he was the finest wicket-keeper ever produced by his country and was certainly the most consistent wicket-keeper/batsman over an extended period of time whose only rivals are Jock Cameron and his own successor in the Springbok XI, Denis Lindsay.

It is unlikely that anyone would have taken seriously a 'Boys' Own' story in which the hero plays innings of 69 and 182 in a Test, and then gloves six catches in the opponents' first innings to equal the world record, and two more in the second for good luck. But this stunning feat was indeed achieved, for South Africa versus Australia at Wanderers, Johannesburg in 1966−67, and the home team went on to win a memorable match by 233 runs after trailing by 126 on the first innings.

The South African hero of the match was Denis Lindsay and his 182 at Johannesburg, apart from boosting South Africa's second innings score to a record 620, was only the first of three marvellous rescue 'tons' posted by the Springbok wicket-keeper in a series that saw his country beat Australia for the first time. Lindsay also created a new batting record for a wicket-keeper in a Test series with a 606-run aggregate at an average of 86.57. His energetic and acrobatic wicket-keeping brought him 24 catches in the same series to complete an incredible all-round performance. This effort put Lindsay in second place for most dismissals in a series by a South African wicket-keeper — J H B Waite's 26 (23 caught, 3 stumped) versus New Zealand in 1961−62 remains the best Springbok performance.

Lindsay's batsman/wicket-keeper record of 606 runs still stands. His six dismissals in an innings feat has since been overhauled by two players — Wasim Bari (7 catches) for Pakistan versus New Zealand at Auckland in 1978−79 and Bob Taylor (also 7 all caught) for England versus India at Bombay in 1979−80. The list of Test wicket-keepers with six or more dismissals in a match reads:

7 (all ct) Wasim Bari	Pakistan v N Zealand at Auckland	1978−79
7 (all ct) R W Taylor	England v India at Bombay	1979−80
6 (all ct) A T W Grout	Australia v S Africa at Jo'burg	1957−58
6 (5ct, 1st) S M H Kirmani	India v N Zealand at Christchurch	1975−76
6 (all ct) D T Lindsay	S Africa v Australia at Jo'burg	1966−67
6 (all ct) R W Marsh	Australia v England at Brisbane	1982−83
6 (all ct) J T Murray	England v India at Lord's	1967
6 (all ct) S A R Silva	Sri Lanka v India at Colombo	1985−86

All hands go up in appeal as Denis Lindsay gloves a catch from Australia's Tom Vievers at Johannesburg in 1966–67. The bowler in the foreground is Mike Procter.

Denis Thomson Lindsay came from a unique cricketing family. Both his father (J D Lindsay) and his grandfather (N V Lindsay) played Test cricket for South Africa. Johnny Lindsay was first-choice wicket-keeper on the 1947 tour of England while Nevil Vernon Lindsay played a Test as a batsman versus Australia at Johannesburg in 1921–22. Denis Lindsay was a tall upstanding right-handed player who favoured the pull, drive and hook. With South Africa's bowling attack of the day usually consisting of pacemen and seamers, and with only an occasional spin bowler utilised, Lindsay, as a wicket-keeper, had few opportunities to stand up to the wicket in Test cricket. Standing back, he was simply magnificent, letting very little past and ever ready to dive and take a legside snick. His record in 19 Tests of 59 victims (57 caught, 2 stumped) is unusually high — some three victims per match. In all first-class cricket, Lindsay made 333 dismissals (292 caught, 41 stumped) in 124 games. In Tests, he scored 1130 runs at 37.66 with three centuries.

When Lindsay lost form at the start of the 1969–70 season, his place was taken by Dennis Gamsy for the first two matches of a four-Test series against Australia in South Africa. Apart from being only the third international wicket-keeper to take the field wearing spectacles, the stocky Gamsy was an accomplished gloveman with great natural talent who had caught eight and stumped one on his Currie Cup debut. He was also a sound batsman, though not as competent as Lindsay. Returning to the Springbok XI for the two final Tests against Australia (which proved to be the last played by South Africa

The alert and highly mobile Ray Jennings has been kept out of official Tests by South Africa's isolation.

before its isolation from world cricket), Lindsay went out in a blaze of glory, hitting 43 and 60 and taking seven catches in the match.

Another wicket-keeper of high talent was played purely as a batsman in South Africa's farewell rubber against Australia in 1969–70. Brian Lee Irvine was a left-handed stroke-player who hit 353 runs at 50.42 in his only series and was a wicket-keeper good enough to keep in Tests. Waiting in the wings but denied any possible chance by South Africa's exclusion from Test cricket was Gavin Pfuhl of Western Province, who for some years held the Currie Cup record for most dismissals, and Natal's A J S 'Tich' Smith, a diminutive bundle of energy and a grand attacking batsman.

In more recent seasons, Transvaal's Raymond Vernon Jennings has shown remarkable form in Currie Cup cricket and in unofficial 'Tests' against a variety of rebel teams from England, Sri Lanka, West Indies and Australia. Jennings has appeared in all but one of the 14 'blockade-busting' matches played against the rebels by South Africa. In his 13 first-class matches for the South African XI, the current spring-heeled gloveman has a record of 42 dismissals (38 caught, 4 stumped) and has taken many amazingly athletic catches in one-day internationals. In an era where pace rules, the extremely mobile 'Jet' Jennings seldom stands up to the wicket: he stands back even further than most international wicket-keepers and does the job of two men, covering first slip as well. Thus the present Transvaal and South African captain Clive Rice always has an extra fielder to play with — and sometimes two as his two main slip fielders Kourie and Graeme Pollock are both ambidexterous and able to do the job of three slips.

Jennings is a fitness fanatic who puts an enormous amount of effort into hand, foot and eye co-ordination exercises. His nickname comes from the healthy advertising character 'Jet Jungle'. South Africa's current gloveman possesses almost uncanny anticipation and his unusual mobility as a wicket-keeper has seen him sprint as far as third man to take a diving catch off a skied delivery.

Ray Jennings, already in his mid-30s, will probably never have the chance of displaying his skill on a proper world stage in a genuine Test encounter for South African cricket seems as far away as ever from readmittance to the official Test arena.

8

West Indians behind the wicket

'The wickets were credited to me, but I know how much I owe to the men behind the stumps'

— Sir Learie Constantine

A fast bowler as fierce as any, and one of the two most celebrated of all pre-war Caribbean cricketers, was a great admirer of wicket-keepers. George Headley was the undisputed king of West Indies batsmanship during the 1930s. Spring-heeled Learie Constantine, the barefoot boy who became a peer of the realm, was the most renowned of the islands' bowlers and one of the most electrifying all-rounders in history. As a wily and long-headed bowler whose speed ranged from slow-medium to outright quick, Constantine was always aware of the value of a good wicket-keeper and, in his own words, said, 'a "thank you" to many fine 'keepers whose work, solid and rarely recognized at its full value, has contributed enormously to my successes'. This quotation comes from the great West Indian all-rounder's *Cricket Crackers* and applies to all bowlers, from the school-boy through to the Test match player.

Although Constantine admits that he never pulled on the gauntlets, he must have from an early age known something about wicket-keeping — his father Lebrun Samuel Constantine acted in that capacity for the first-ever West Indies XI versus A Priestley's English team in 1897. Constantine senior also shared stumper's duties with George Learmond in England in 1900 but gave his gloves away for the next trip, in 1906, when another specialist, Claude Bancroft, appeared on the scene.

There will be few who would argue with Learie Constantine about the value to a bowler of a competent 'keeper. George John, the first great West Indies fast bowler, was in full agreement although his favourite, personal club cricket stumper never had the chance to appear in international cricket.

C L R James writes in *Beyond a Boundary* that John, the 'knight-errant of fast bowling' had a 'squire' named Piggott. Known to his Stingo Cricket Club team-mates as 'Piggie', the 6ft 4ins (193 cm) Piggott was an unlikely, ambling giant of a wicket-keeper and a marvellous character whose hands were an inch behind the bails when taking the fastest stuff that John could hurl down at the quaking batsman. Piggott's unorthodox answer to a leg-side bullet from the fearsome John was to jump sideways with both feet and try to rebound the ball into the stumps, hoping to catch the batsman outside his crease.

Piggott lost his chance of higher honours when fellow-Trinidadian George Alric Dewhurst was picked to go to England as number one stumper with the 1923 West Indies team. According to C L R James, it was a case of racial prejudice, pure and simple. Dewhurst was white and a member of the prestigious Queen's Park Club; Piggott was black and 'a nobody'. As it turned out, 'Fattie' Dewhurst had a good tour and Piggott was never given a chance.

When the MCC visited the Caribbean in 1927–28, and still in the days before West Indies was granted Test status, Dewhurst was replaced by the efficient Cecil Nascimento from British Guiana. In 1928 the West Indies team sailed for its first official tour of England and, inexplicably, not a single regular specialist 'keeper was included in the party.

The West Indies skipper Karl Nunes of Jamaica stood behind the stumps as target for his fast bowlers in the three Tests. He had a dreadful time, taking only one catch in the series. Constantine and his fast bowling friends George Francis and Herman Griffith could not have been too impressed.

Robert Karl Nunes was a fine left-handed batsman who once added 271 for the second wicket with George Headley to save a Test against England at Kingston in 1929–30. A wicket-keeper of international class he was not; nor was his deputy for the 1928 tour, Claude Vibert Wight. Wight, from British Guiana, was a useful right-handed batsman and Nunes's vice-captain, although he had never captained a first-class team.

Karl Nunes was, incidentally, the first of five West Indies wicket-keepers to emerge from the Wolmer's Boys' School in Kingston, Jamaica, and was followed into the Test side in later years by Ivan Barrow, 'Gerry' Alexander, 'Jacky' Hendriks and the present incumbent, Jeffrey Dujon, all from the same school.

For England's first Test tour to the West Indies in 1929–30, the home team picked a wicket-keeper with some real credentials for the job. Trinidad's tall and energetic Errol Ashton Clarimore Hunte kept wickets in the first three Tests as well as batting number 11 in the opening match at Bridgetown. In the next, at Port-of-Spain, he opened the innings and scored 58 and 30 and made another 50 in the third Test at Georgetown. Errol Hunte went to Australia with the 1930–31 West Indies team but did not appear in a Test.

Nineteen-year-old home island wicket-keeper Ivan Barrow came in for the final Test of 1929–30 when Hunte was unable to travel to Jamaica. With a catch, a stumping and only six byes in a gargantuan England first innings of 849, Barrow immediately impressed as a player of the future and took over as first-string stumper for the Australian tour. Neat and slim, he was an unobtrusive stumper of the old school. The dapper Barrow was also an exciting right-handed batsman who preceded George Headley to the first century by a West Indian in a Test in England during the Old Trafford Test of 1933. Barrow opened the batting and made 105 before being bowled by Bob Wyatt. Headley came in first wicket down and compiled an elegant 169 not out, the pair adding 206 for the second wicket in a Test marked by an exhibition of bodyline bowling by Constantine and 'Manny' Martindale in England's innings.

Barrow had kept wickets in all five Tests played on West Indies' inaugural tour of Australia in 1930–31 but was deposed after the 1933 England tour by his number two, Cyril Marcel Christiani of British Guiana. Christiani was later to be hailed as the best pre-war West Indian wicket-keeper and kept brilliantly to the hostile West Indies all-pace attack in all four Tests versus England in the Caribbean in 1934–35 (six catches and one stumping). His brother, Robert Julian Christiani, acted as reserve wicket-keeper on a couple of post-war West Indies tours but played his 22 Tests as a batsman, only once deputising behind the stumps.

Cyril Christiani opened the batting in the final game of the 1934–35 series against England at Kingston and helped George Headley add 87 for the second wicket after Ivan Barrow, playing as a batsman, was dismissed for three runs. West Indies played no further Tests until 1939. In 1938, Cyril Christiani, at the age of 25, died of malaria and a hurried call was made by the West Indies selectors for Barrow, now resident in the United States, to return home and join the team ready to tour England in 1939. The move was not a success and Barrow's form in England was so disappointing that he was discarded after one Test and replaced by the versatile Derek Sealy. Barrow executed 22 dismissals (17 caught, 5 stumped) in his 11 Tests.

James Edward Derek Sealy was a highly-talented all-rounder — polished right-handed batsman, capable stumper and right-arm medium-paced bowler — who, according to C L R James, could drop the ball on the leg-stump and hit the off (Sealy once took 8/8 for Barbados versus Trinidad). Sealy could count four catches and a stumping as his wicket-keeping prizes in the last two Tests played by West Indies before the Second World War erupted. He scored 478 runs at an average of 28.11 in 11 Tests and is West Indies' youngest Test representative, having made his debut at the age of 17 years, 122 days.

In England in 1950, the calypso singers were all voicing their praises of those 'two little pals of mine', Ramadhin and Valentine, and the home side's leaden-footed batsmen had little respite from flight, curve and spin. And behind them, breathing down their collars, loomed a giant of a stumper who improved with every match.

The 1958 *Wisden* describes Clyde Leopold Walcott as: 'One of the pillars of West Indies cricket.' As a member of the famous batting 'W Formation' (Weekes, Worrell, Walcott), the big and burly Walcott contributed 3798 runs (average 56.68) to the West Indian Test cause between 1947 and 1960. Until halfway through the 1951–52 rubber in Australia, the 6ft 3ins (190 cm) and 15 stone plus (95 kg) Barbadian also kept wicket in 15 Test, effecting 38 dismissals (27 caught, 11 stumped) before his back gave way. Walcott recovered from a slipped disc to play in another 29 Tests as a batsman and as a sometime medium-paced bowler. His consistent scoring feats (including twice making two separate centuries in a Test in the same series) have been recorded earlier in the section on batsmen.

As wicket-keeper to the most illustrious spin-bowling combination since the 1907 South African googly quartet, the modest but commanding Walcott was always reliable. No less an authority than Godfrey Evans judges Walcott in his *Wicket-Keepers of the World*: '...he was magnificent behind the stumps. He had rapid reflexes, a huge reach and a safe pair of hands.'

Walcott gathered 16 dismissals (11 caught, 5 stumped) in four Tests versus England in the Caribbean in 1947–48. In India the following season, his record would have been better than his 11 victims (9 caught, 2 stumped) in five games had he not broken down in the third Test at Calcutta (Bob Christiani took over and stumped the last two Indian batsmen off googly bowler Wilf Ferguson). In England in 1950, particularly from the second Test at Lord's and onwards, Walcott provided the perfect back-up for the youthful spin of Ramadhin and Valentine. At Lord's, the burly West Indian 'keeper started an England slide that ended in slippery disaster when he stumped both openers — Hutton off Valentine for 35; Washbrook off Ramadhin for 36. The England innings folded like the proverbial pack of cards and the West Indians swept through to a massive 326-run victory, setting up a series win.

When doctor's orders put an effective end to Walcott's wicket-keeping days, the happy-go-lucky, extrovert son of a Trinidadian Test umpire took over. Simpson Clairmonte Guillen played four Tests for West Indies, impressed with his neat glovework and with his ever-present humour, and then emigrated to New Zealand. There the irrepressible, calypso-singing Guillen was to play three more Tests for his adopted country, all versus his old mates from the Caribbean, although it was later admitted that he had not yet qualified for residency and his inclusion in the New Zealand team was actually illegal.

New Zealand writer Dick Brittenden notes that even Roget's Thesaurus cannot provide a single word to describe the cricket of 'Sammy' Guillen: 'It was at once gay, buoyant, cheerful, animated,

Clyde Walcott behind the stumps for West Indies; Godfrey Evans batting for England.

breezy, sparkling, exhilarating and audacious, but it was not any one of these...'. During his days with the West Indies XI in Australia in 1951–52, Guillen had the 'official' post of calypso writer for the team and his melodious, lilting voice was later heard over New Zealand radio. He played a major part in New Zealand's first Test win over West Indies at Auckland in 1955–56, taking three catches in the visitors' first knock and stumping last man Alf Valentine in the second to settle the matter on the final day.

With Walcott unavailable and Guillen in New Zealand, the West Indian selectors tried a series of new men during the 1950s but none established any right of tenure in the West Indian eleven. First in the queue was Jamaica's Alfred Phillip Binns who grabbed 17 dismissals (14 caught, 3 stumped) in five Tests but failed to produce at international level his known prolific domestic batting form. Binns was Guillen's opposite number in the Test won by New Zealand at Auckland in 1955–56 and once kept through an innings of 515 for nine wickets declared by Australia at Kingston in 1954–55, letting through just three byes.

When India toured the Caribbean in 1952–53, Alf Binns was dropped after one Test to make way for the Barbados-born Ralph Archibald Legall, who was playing for Trinidad. Legall lasted four Tests (9 dismissals: 8 caught, 1 stumped) but also did little with the bat. British Guiana's Clifford Aubrey McWatt, who had travelled to India in 1948–49 as understudy to Clyde Walcott, then came in for all five Tests versus England in 1953–54. McWatt, a left-hander, batted with great aplomb to score 54 and 36 not out in the first Test at Kingston and took a couple of good catches in a 140-run West Indian win. He hit another 50 in the third game and merited mention for three good catches in the final Test at Kingston. McWatt's second Test 50, scored at his home ground of Georgetown, was marred by crowd disturbance.

Three wicket-keepers were used during West Indies' next Test rubber, versus Australia in the Caribbean in 1954—55. Binns made a pair in the first Test at Kingston and was summarily dropped, McWatt was given the next game at Port-of-Spain and Clairmonte Depeiza, an eventual but unlikely batting hero, got the nod for the remaining three matches.

In a near-faultless display, customs clerk Cyril Clairmonte Depeiza did not let through a single bye until well into his second Test. Australia scored a massive 668 in its first innings on the West Indian wicket-keeper's Barbados home ground at Bridgetown in that Test, with Depeiza bagging two catches and letting pass one solitary bye. All seemed over for the home side when West Indies slumped in its first innings to 147 for six wickets but skipper Denis Atkinson was still around and a determined Depeiza joined him at number eight to help hoist an amazing seventh-wicket world record stand of 347. Batting for almost a complete day, Depeiza hit 122 before being bowled by Richie Benaud. Atkinson made 219 and the game was saved. Depeiza's surprise effort remained his only innings of note in five Tests for West Indies and his best in all first-class cricket. The Australians, referring to his determined forward defensive stroke, named him 'The Leaning Tower Depeiza'.

Depeiza went to New Zealand in 1955—56 as Alf Binns's number two, kept wickets in one Test and bowled in another with Binns behind the stumps. Depeiza later developed into a medium-paced bowler and made a name for himself in that role in the Lancashire League.

A rather disastrous experiment took place in England in 1957 when up-and-coming young batsman Rohan Kanhai was given the gloves in three of the five Tests. It was a scene reminiscent of the 1927 wicket-keeping debacle involving West Indian skipper Karl Nunes, and Kanhai was described as little more than a stopper. Specialist 'keeper Franz Copeland Murray Alexander eventually took over and during the 1957—58 home season versus Pakistan became West Indies' second wicket-keeper/captain.

A Cambridge Blue and captain of Jamaica, 'Gerry' Alexander, became number one 'keeper for the next few years and the first West Indian wicket-keeper to play in that position for 25 consecutive Tests. He captained his team astutely in 18 Tests and gathered 90 dismissals (85 caught, 5 stumped). A strongly-built, barrel-chested individual, Alexander's style of wicket-keeping demonstrated the new vogue in a dawning age of seam bowling: standing back for just about everything except the occasional slow spinner.

Alexander held what West Indies' top cricket correspondent Tony Cozier refers to as 'some stunning catches' and formed great wicket-keeper/bowler partnerships with fast men Wes Hall and Roy Gilchrist. He also set a then West Indies record of 23 dismissals in a series against England in 1960.

Alexander enjoyed his finest rubber in Australia in 1960−61, having been relieved of the strain of captaincy by Frank Worrell after 18 straight Tests as both skipper and 'keeper. Coming in at number seven or number eight, Alexander hit at least one 50 in each of the five Tests and scored 484 runs in 10 innings in brilliantly aggressive style, including 108 in the third Test at Sydney, his only first-class hundred. He also executed three decisive catches off Wes Hall in the famous tied Test at Brisbane and 16 catches in all in the series, nine off the big Barbadian fast bowler.

A superbly talented all-round sportsman, Gerry Alexander won an England cap as a soccer player. As a wicket-keeper/batsman in particular, he was his team's first player of note since Clyde Walcott gave away his gloves a decade previously. At the height of his career, Gerry Alexander chose to retire, aged 33, and the hunt was again on for a Test-class 'keeper.

At first, the West Indies selectors did not have far to look: Alexander's deputy on two tours (to the Indian sub-continent in 1958−59 and to Australia in 1960−61) had been yet another old boy of Wolmer's School, the fourth such player after Nunes, Barrow and Alexander, and a wicket-keeper as good as any of his predecessors. Unfortunately, the Test career of John Leslie Hendriks was almost immediately interrupted by injury and although he did get to play in 20 Tests, the big Jamaican never quite lived up to his vast potential.

'Jacky' Hendriks was strongly-built in the Walcott mould and a dazzling performer behind the stumps. Some observers called him 'flawless' and he was particularly good at taking spin bowling. Poor Hendriks broke a finger in his very first Test, versus India at Port-of-Spain in 1961−62. His place for the rest of the match was taken by opening batsman 'Cammie' Smith, who must have been highly pleased with the stumping he executed off Gary Sobers in the first innings to dismiss India's top-scorer Rusi Surti.

Two specialist wicket-keepers shared duties for the remainder of the series versus India: British Guiana's Ivan Leon Mendonca came in for the second Test at Kingston, picked up four catches and a stumping and played an innings of 78. Mendonca was unavailable for the next Test at Bridgetown, Barbados, and his place was given to the home stumper, the fair-haired and strongly-built David Walter Allan. Allan also had five dismissals (4 caught, 1 stumped) in his first Test but Mendonca returned for the next match at Port-of-Spain and took his own dismissal tally to 10 in two games with another four catches and a stumping. Allan was then picked ahead of Mendonca for the fifth and final Test at Kingston and, not to be outdone, also raised his dismissal total to 10 in two matches — with four catches and a stumping! It was really a remarkable sequence of events.

With Hendriks still injured, David Allan went to England as wicket-keeper in 1963 but fell ill before the first Test and was kept out of the team for the entire series by his 19-year-old deputy, Deryck Murray of Trinidad, who made a sensational debut and about whom more will be written later. Allan played a few more Tests after that, when others were indisposed, and in his five Tests had 18 dismissals (15 caught, 3 stumped).

Deryck Murray, West Indies' longest-serving wicket-keeper, in action in a one-day match.

Jacky Hendriks made a welcome comeback when the Australians arrived in the Caribbean in 1964—65 but tragedy struck in the fourth Test at Bridgetown when he was struck on the head by a bouncer from fast bowler Graham McKenzie and ended up in hospital for urgent brain surgery. Hendriks's life was in the balance for a time and that he recovered to play in another 15 Tests was a tribute to his abundant courage and skill. Hendriks eventually boosted his dismissals to 47 (42 caught, 5 stumped) in 20 Tests, and scored more than 400 runs in good style.

An uncannily consistent performer behind the stumps, Jacky Hendriks is the only West Indian wicket-keeper to have kept through three innings of more than 500 without conceding a single bye — for West Indies versus Australia at Sydney and Melbourne in 1968—69 (Australia scored 619 and 510) and for Jamaica versus Barbados at Bridgetown in 1966—67 (Barbados 7/521 declared).

When the ill-fated Hendriks suffered a back injury in 1967—68, Deryck Murray, who had last played for West Indies in England in 1963, reappeared briefly in five home Tests versus England after a spell at Cambridge University and with Nottinghamshire. Murray experienced a rather lack-lustre series in 1967—68, his form falling well below that shown in England five years previously.

Hendriks was available for the 1969 tour of England and Murray was discarded in favour of the happy-natured Thaddeus Michael Findlay from the little island of St Vincent. With Hendriks out of form, the slim and athletic Findlay took the gloves in two Tests. Mike Findlay was a soccer goalie of note and an agile performer behind the stumps who twice toured as second-choice 'keeper and in 10 Tests totalled 21 dismissals (19 caught, 2 stumped). An average batsman only, he was dropped after two home Tests versus India in 1970—71 when Jamaican opener and wicket-keeper Desmond Michael Lewis was brought in to stiffen the West Indies batting.

Lewis experienced a wonderful first series scoring 259 runs (average 86.33) and taking eight catches in three games but was unfortunate not to be called upon again. For the next series, versus New Zealand in 1971—72, Findlay was again in favour but, in 1972—73, the intinerant Deryck Lance Murray finally settled into a groove that was to lead him to unprecedented run of 41 consecutive Tests as West Indian wicket-keeper prior to the wholesale defection of most of the West Indies eleven to the World Series Cricket cause in 1977.

When the breach was healed between the authorities and Kerry Packer in 1979, Murray returned to official international cricket to achieve a West Indies record total of 189 dismissals (181 caught, 8 stumped) in 62 Tests. In 1963, in his first series as a shy youth of 19, Murray effected 24 dismissals (22 caught, 2 stumped) in the series versus England — another West Indies record.

Deryck Murray was a thoughtful personality whose remarkable

composure on and off the field had a strong influence on his contemporaries. His wicket-keeping could best be described as workman-like and reliable. There was plenty of efficiency but nothing flashy about Murray as he mainly stood back to the West Indian battery of fast bowlers. As a batsman, he was an obdurate player who tailored his style to the needs of the day and totalled 1993 runs in Tests at an average of 22.90 without ever reaching a century. As a man, Deryck Murray's profound influence was most felt as the organiser of a Players' Association among his fellows that canvassed for better remuneration and conditions. In recent years, he was a member of Trinidad and Tobago's diplomatic representation to the United Nations.

His rather chequered early Test career saw him play in two series five years apart (in 1963 and 1967−68), and then wait another four years before finally establishing himself as unchallenged number one gloveman. Deryck Murray took with calm efficiency the bowling of a pedigree line of fast bowlers — Hall, Griffith, Roberts, Daniel, Croft, Garner — and was an integral and indispensable part of Clive Lloyd's steam-rolling West Indies teams of the 1970s. He was at times kept in the team as much for his batting as for his work behind the wicket and, just prior to his retirement in 1980 at the age of 37 Deryck Murray's wicket-keeping was beginning to be described as 'not always tidy'. His omission from the 1980−81 Port-of-Spain Test versus England initiated a boycott protest from his home crowd and those who did attend the match roundly booed his replacement in a most unsporting fashion.

Deryck Murray's immediate successor in the West Indian team was his small and neatly-built namesake David Anthony Murray, who as a lad had always insisted on keeping wicket purely because his name was the same as the then current Test 'keeper! Seven years younger than Deryck Murray, David Murray waited long for his chance, touring five times as Deryck Murray's back-up before taking over for a couple of years while the elder Murray was away playing in World Series Cricket.

When his day finally dawned, David Murray threw it all away (after touring Australia in 1981−82 as legitimate number one choice) to seek financial security in the form of two tours to South Africa with the rebel West Indies XI. In South Africa, the rather frail-looking little wicket-keeper overcame a poor start clouded by threats of losing residency rights in Australia (the land of his wife's birth) to impress as a super-efficient 'keeper and a gutsy batsman who was at his best in a crisis. In 19 official Tests for West Indies, David Murray netted 62 dismissals (57 caught, 5 stumped) and scored 601 runs at an average of 21.46. Against Australia in 1981−82, he set a new West Indian record in the second Test at Sydney of nine dismissals in the match, all caught. David Murray's departure to more financially lucrative fields cleared the way for a man who may become known as the best West Indies wicket-keeper of all time, and who is certainly the most proficient Caribbean wicket-keeper-batsman since Clyde Walcott.

West Indies' current gloveman Peter Jeffrey Leroy Dujon has continued the Wolmer's Boys' School tradition of West Indian wicket-keepers, following most ably in the footsteps of Nunes, Barrow, Alexander and Hendriks. He has also developed into one of the finest attacking batsmen Jamaica and West Indies have produced and, as an inspiring skipper of his home island, must also be on the short-list of possible future West Indian captains.

Like the pre-war Barrow and the post-war Deryck Murray, Dujon has thrived as a taker of fast bowling. Unlike Barrow and his contemporary 'keepers of the 1930s, who were conspicuous for their bulky pads and heavy gauntlets, the present West Indies wicket-keeper wears the slimmest of pads, cut off at the knees, and gloves reinforced with special light synthetic material. Times have certainly changed and there must be some support for the argument that

Jeff Dujon, West Indies' current 'keeper, flies through the air with the greatest of ease.

modern wicket-keepers are able to move much quicker than their pre-war counterparts and are more efficient, particularly when standing back to pace bowling.

Dujon made his Test debut as a batsman versus Australia at Melbourne in 1981−82 and immediately impressed with a couple of 40s. When Murray was unfit to play in the third and final Test at Adelaide, Dujon, although himself injured, took over. With four catches in Australia's first innings and seven in the match plus a blazing innings of 51, he quickly made his mark and allayed any fears of a wicket-keeping problem the West Indian selectors might have had.

A scintillating stroke-player, Jeff Dujon has scored well enough in Tests to be picked as a batsman alone. His wicket-keeping dismissal tally is highly impressive, although a rather disproportionate catches to stumpings figure (around 60 to 1) reflects the current fast-bowling times. Dujon is a superb limited overs cricketer, as a hard-striking batsman and as a highly mobile 'keeper.

His current second-string, Thelston Rodney O'Neale Payne, is also a talented limited overs performer who has toured England and Australia. A diminutive left-handed stroke-player with a string of high scores for Barbados, Payne is also a polished 'keeper who gloved five catches when finally given a Test chance against England at Port-of-Spain in 1985−86 after Dujon broke a finger.

Dujon and Payne are both rising 30 and it seems unlikely that Payne will get much of a showing other than when Dujon is unavailable. There is, however, little doubt that when Jeffrey Dujon finally hangs up his gloves, there will be a fair number of capable contenders for the post of West Indian Test wicket-keeper.

9

Like a bird of prey:
Tallon to Taber

'Tallon! The very name brings to mind an eagle swooping on its prey.'
— Ray Robinson

Argument about who was the best wicket-keeper of all time will probably continue as long as the great game is played but the name of Don Tallon will always figure high on any shortlist of contenders. Ern Toovey, former Queensland cricketer and a contemporary of Tallon, says this of the man whom many regard as Australia's top wicket-keeper and possibly the finest-ever from any land: 'It is truly amazing to think that he had to wait until he was 30 before he commenced his brilliant Test career after the war. Many of his dismissals are legend, and he did most of them without getting his trousers dirty. It may never be known why he was not taken to England in 1938.'

The young Queenslander destined for the highest achievements made his first-class debut in 1933–34 at the tender age of 17. Donald Tallon boasted just one dismissal in that first big game versus Victoria at Brisbane — the prolific Bill Ponsford, caught behind for 55. The young gloveman only played in two matches for Queensland that season and there was no thought of his being included in the 1934 Australian team to tour England (Bert Oldfield still reigned and Ben Barnett was his deputy). Two years later, when Oldfield and Barnett were busy playing for Australia in South Africa, the fledgling stumper, apart from his growing prowess behind the wicket, began to display batting talent of Test potential. In a game when Queensland struggled to avoid an innings defeat against Victoria at Brisbane, Tallon played an innings of 193 that was described as being 'in style reminiscent of Bradman'. He was still a couple of weeks away from his 20th birthday.

Tallon headed Queensland's batting table for 1935–36, and repeated the feat the following season. His wicket-keeping also continued to impress but Oldfield was still around, fit and in form and the younger player had to be content with his Sheffield Shield appearances and a match against the tourists for his State when the MCC team came to Australia in 1936–37. Oldfield, 44, was not selected in Australia's side to go to England in 1938. Ben Barnett got the nod as the wicket-keeper, and, inexplicably, Tallon was over-looked in favour of a resurrected Charlie Walker who had been Oldfield's deputy in England in 1934 but had been hampered ever since by a succession of finger injuries. As it turned out, Walker broke a finger before a single match was played and when he finally put in an appearance midway through the tour, his team-mates were prompted to ask who was the stranger in their midst.

During the final pre-war season, 1938–39, Don Tallon confirmed his credentials when he equalled a 70-year-old world record of 12 dismissals in a match set by Ed Pooley for Surrey versus Sussex at the Oval in 1868. Against New South Wales at Sydney, the 22-year-old Tallon had four caught and two stumped in the first innings and five caught and one stumped in the second. The following wicket-keepers have 11 or more dismissals in a first-class match:

12 (8ct, 4st)	E Pooley	Surrey v Sussex at the Oval	1868
12 (9ct, 3st)	D Tallon	Queensland v NSW at Sydney	1938–39
12 (9ct, 3st)	H B Taber	NSW v S Australia at Adelaide	1968–69
11 (all ct)	A Long	Surrey v Sussex at Hove	1964
11 (all ct)	R W Marsh	W Australia v Victoria at Perth	1975–76
11 (all ct)	D L Bairstow	Yorkshire v Derbyshire at Scarborough	1982

In an earlier encounter with New South Wales at Brisbane in 1938–39, Tallon caught four and stumped four in the match to give him 20 victims out of 39 New South Wales wickets that fell in the two games. Playing against Victoria at Brisbane in Queensland's final game of the season, he caught four and stumped five, most of his victims coming off the leg-break bowling of his older brother, 'Bill' Tallon. During that final pre-war Australian summer, Tallon gathered 21 catches and engineered 13 stumpings in six Sheffield Shield matches. He also scored a brilliant 115 versus South Australia. Then came war, and a long wait until 1946 when Tallon at last won an Australian Test cap.

Lean, lithe, sun-tanned and alert, Tallon certainly lived up to the image conjured up by his surname. He first practised taking spin bowling when he and his three brothers played all day long on a pitch rolled in the backyard of their home by their father. He was wicket-keeper for his school team at seven and captained a Queensland schoolboy team at 13. Known as 'Deafy' because of a slight hearing defect, Tallon was arguably the quickest of all stumpers and, in a cool undemonstrative way, one of the most agile. Modelling his approach on that of Bert Oldfield, he cut out all hint of flamboyance and concentrated completely on effect. Keith Miller once stated that Tallon was to wicket-keeping what Bradman was to batting and O'Reilly to bowling.

A master of anticipating which way a ball would move, Tallon was also uncannily adept at picking up what was going on in a batsman's mind. If he had been playing in the present age there might even have been whispers of 'mind-reading' or 'ESP'. Tallon's movement behind the stumps was all line and flowing curve. Ray Robinson recalls him as 'a master of the sway and the lean to keep eyes and hands true to the ball's course — so much so that he looks as if most of his close-up keeping could be done with a book under each

Don Tallon's spectacular catch to dismiss Len Hutton of England off the bowling of Ray Lindwall at the Oval in 1948.

armpit'. Tallon hated to be crowded by other fielders and, in England in 1953, was heard to complain at the close proximity of first slip and leg-slip in the field set by Lindsay Hassett.

Among other players, admiration for the Australian stumper's skill was universal and unqualified. Even rival wicket-keepers like Ron Saggers spoke of Tallon with awe, and both Lindsay Hassett and Ray Lindwall named him as the best that they had seen.

Tallon excelled when taking slow bowling but his hands suffered a little in the cold English weather in 1948 when he was compelled to stand back to take Australia's battery of fast bowlers. The war took away too many good years but, although Tallon's career was interrupted at a crucial point, he immediately made up for lost time in 1946—47 when he scored 92 against England at Melbourne in only 104 minutes and claimed 20 victims (16 caught, 4 stumped) in the series to create what was then a new record in Anglo-Australian Tests. In his eventual 21 Tests, Tallon had 58 dismissals (50 caught, 8 stumped).

As his old Queensland team-mate Ern Toovey puts it so succinctly: 'Tallon was never a long stop and never an actor; just a man with uncanny cricket brains, and a dry sense of humour.' Tallon's brow would furrow and he would chuckle happily whenever his humorous Queensland and Australian XI mate Colin McCool cracked a joke. The ace wicket-keeper and talented leg-break and googly bowler would have an almost permanent discussion as to 'who made who' when they were in action together. Was it Don's brilliant work that caused a dismissal from an ordinary ball or was it Colin's outstanding bowling that helped the wicket-keeper to shine?

When Lindsay Hassett made his happy trip around England with the Australian Services team in 1945, the main wicket-keeping duties revolved around the eager gloves of Stanley George Sismey, a tidy performer who had played for New South Wales before the war. Doctors had removed some shrapnel from Sismey's back after the plane he was piloting had been shot down by the Germans but the sporting 'Stan the Stoic' shrugged it all off and returned to the New South Wales side after touring England, India and Ceylon with the Services. Sismey was known to leave the field at times while playing for Australian Services in England when bits of shrapnel worked their way to the surface of his skin. Facing strong competition from Tallon and fellow New South Welshman Ron Saggers, he had to be content with a non-Test tour of New Zealand under Bill Brown in 1949—50 but gained an international cap of sorts when he appeared for Scotland in 1952.

Apart from being Tallon's deputy in England in 1948, Ronald Arthur Saggers was a remarkable look-alike when it came to physical appearance. The comparison between the two wicket-keepers ended there. Tallon was the hawk poised over the wicket, awaiting a half-chance at stumping; Saggers was more at home as a catcher of the ball, his movements as graceful as a dove.

Like Tallon, Saggers was just 22 when war interfered with his dream of playing for Australia. With his career still moving parallel to that of Tallon, his chances were eventually limited to just six Tests, five of them on tour in South Africa in 1949–50. During the five-match rubber against the Springboks, the New South Wales wicket-keeper proceeded to better Tallon's series record set against England in 1946–47 with 21 victims: 13 caught and 8 stumped. Saggers's actual Test debut had come earlier, against England at Headingley in 1948 when Tallon was injured. In his six Tests Saggers had 24 dismissals (16 caught, 8 stumped).

Two wicket-keepers can be as unalike as a fast bowler from a slow and Australia's next gloveman, Gilbert Roche Andrews Langley, was as thickset and jowly as Saggers was lean and willowy. However, when it came to speed behind the stumps, the dumpy Gil Langley of the sagging waistline was as agile and competent as his taller and slimmer predecessor in the Australian eleven.

The ruddy-faced Langley looked the picture of an old-fashioned 'Boys' Own' paper version of a soccer goalie, but his concentration and dexterity had been nurtured during his years as an Australian Rules rover. In 26 Tests for Australia, Langley claimed 98 victims (83 caught, 15 stumped) and also developed a reputation as a late-order batsman of courage. For South Australia he batted with pugnacious endeavour and hit four centuries, including a thundering 160 not out against the touring New Zealanders in 1953–54.

Langley took over as wicket-keeper for the first Test against West Indies at Brisbane in 1951–52 when an injured Saggers withdrew. The newcomer's seven dismissals in that game constituted a record for a Test wicket-keeper on debut. Langley retained his place for the series and went on to emulate Saggers's feat of 21 victims in five games. Other than when he was ill or injured, Langley kept his place in the Australian XI for five years. Against England at Lord's in 1956, with eight catches and one stumping, he created the Australian record for most dismissals in a single Test (Rodney Marsh equalled it with nine catches versus England at Brisbane in 1982–83).

The bantamweight Leonard Victor Maddocks was robust Gil Langley's ever-willing back-up. Given only an occasional chance, Maddocks effected 19 dismissals (18 caught, 1 stumped) in seven Tests. He also batted with great courage and aplomb when forced to combat England's Tyson and Statham at their fastest in 1954–55. In the third Test of the series at Melbourne, he faced Frank Tyson, destroyer of Australian confidence in the previous Test at Sydney, with wonderful fortitude to top-score with 47 out of Australia's first innings 231. Maddocks repeated his performance in the next match at Adelaide where his 69 was the only Australian score to exceed 50.

An energetic and watchful wicket-keeper, Maddocks always exhibited the perfect model for a young aspiring stumper and when he transferred to Tasmania in 1962–63, did much to lift that State's cricket.

Many thought Maddocks fortunate to get his chance against England as the injured Gil Langley's replacement in 1954–55. Queensland 'keeper Wally Grout had long been challenging for recognition and when Langley was hit in the eye during a South Australia-Queensland match at Adelaide, he immediately turned to Grout and congratulated him on his imminent Australian cap. It was not to be; Maddocks became the new Australian 'keeper and went with a recovered Langley to the West Indies later in the same season and to England and India in 1956.

Like his Queensland forerunner Don Tallon, Arthur Theodore Wallace Grout had to wait until he was 30 for his first Test chance. He and South Australia's Barry Jarman replaced Langley and Maddocks for the 1957–58 tour of South Africa and it was touch and go as to who would be chosen for the first Test at Johannesburg. Grout got the tour selectors' vote in a close contest and, with six catches in South Africa's second innings, sealed his place for the remainder of the series.

Grout twice dismissed eight batsmen in a Test and his six catches in South Africa's second innings at Johannesburg in 1957–58 remained the best such effort by an Australian until equalled by Rodney Marsh, against England at Brisbane in 1982–83. Grout is also one of only six Australian wicket-keepers to have dismissed seven or more batsmen in a single innings — eight catches versus Western Australia at Brisbane in 1959–60, a world record for all first-class cricket that was equalled by D E East for Essex versus Somerset in 1985. In 51 Tests, he removed 187 opposition batsmen (163 caught, 24 stumped). He was also a late-order batsman of skill and hit more than 5000 first-class runs, including four centuries.

For the final four years of his Test career, Wally Grout played with the secret knowledge that any match, and any moment, might be his last. After his death at the age of 41 in 1968, it was revealed by a Brisbane doctor that he had taken part in the 1964–65 tour of the West Indies only a few months after a severe heart attack. The determined and ever-cheerful Wally Grout just did not know how to give up.

His warm-hearted personality was clearly demonstrated in his actions on the field. Grout's leg-side catches were frequently the result of a spectacular dive, as if let loose by a spring from his low-crouching stance. Close to the stumps his play bore an uncanny resemblance to that of Tallon, quicksilver and effortless, be it in achieving a stumping or moving to take an impossible snick.

To have ambitions of becoming an international wicket-keeper can often lead to participation in a waiting game. There is room for only one gloveman in an eleven and, at best, two wicket-keeping spots in a touring team. The robust Barrington Noel Jarman went on five trips abroad as Wally Grout's shadow before being nominated Australia's number one. Before his elevation, he had to be content with the odd Test or two when Grout was injured or indisposed. One observer remarked that it was no wonder Jarman had weight problems.

The short but very bulky Jarman was, however, surprisingly nimble behind the sticks. He possessed all the attributes of a good wicket-keeper: anticipation, lightning reflexes and, above all, concentration. Participation in Australian Rules football kept Jarman fit and flexible, despite his heavy build. Like Grout and most of Australia's other glovemen, he was a very good-natured man who delighted in thinking up nicknames for his team-mates. Jarman's excellent humour frequently brightened a dismal day in the field and Ray Robinson once commented that, 'All knew that if everybody could a play the game like Barry Jarman it would not lack animation for a single over'.

Barry Jarman eventually played 19 Tests for his country and acted as captain on one occasion, when Bill Lawry broke a finger before the Leeds Test versus England in 1968. Jarman dismissed 54 batsmen (50 caught, 4 stumped). Many of his catches were accomplished with an acrobatic flair that belied his bulky build. A chunky, hard-hitting batsman, Jarman once hit 26 off an over from England's David Allen in a tour match and compiled five centuries in first-class cricket.

When Jarman was unavailable for the 1966−67 tour to South Africa, his place was given to the less exuberant but no less efficient Hedley Brian Taber. With five catches in the first innings of his debut outing for New South Wales versus Western Australia in 1964−65, Taber gave notice of his intentions to challenge Wally Grout and Barry Jarman for the Australian wicket-keeping position. He took his chances well against South Africa in 1966−67 and created a new record for Australia-South Africa matches with eight dismissals (7 caught, 1 stumped) in the first Test at Johannesburg. He had 20 victims (19 caught, 1 stumped) in his first series.

Brian Taber's cool and undemonstrative approach to wicket-keeping contrasted sharply with that of Grout and Jarman. Unobtrusive and neat in the Oldfield manner, and a subdued appealer, he was an especially fine catcher of the ball when standing back and a quick and decisive worker when standing up for the spinners.

With 60 dismissals (56 caught, 4 stumped) in 16 Tests, Taber's strike rate was impressive. His crowning achievement in first-class cricket came in 1968−69 for New South Wales versus South Australia at Adelaide when he equalled Don Tallon's shared world record of 12 victims in a match (originally set by E Pooley for Surrey versus

Brian Taber of Australia sits on the ground and appeals unsucessfully for a catch off South Africa's left-hander Graeme Pollock at Port Elizabeth in 1966—67. Pollock went on to score a match-winning century.

Sussex at the Oval in 1868). A chest infection and an eye injury in 1974 brought an end to the dapper little Brian Taber's playing career but, as Australia's national coach, he has put back into the game far more than it has given him.

On two visits to South Africa, in 1966—67 and 1969—70, Brian Taber enjoyed the company of a couple of second-string 'keepers who were ace players in Sheffield Shield cricket but who were never given the opportunity to display their skill in Test cricket. Gordon Charles Becker was a diligent wicket-keeper-batsman who once hit 195 for Western Australia versus India at Perth. Renowned for his catching off the numerous Western Australian seam bowlers, Becker was given few chances in South Africa and when Jarman returned, faded from the picture. Raymond Clarence Jordan (an Australian Rules football personality nicknamed 'Slug') was a tough, no-holds-barred competitor who played 79 matches for Victoria between 1959—60 and 1969—1970 as an athletic wicket-keeper and determined right-handed batsman. When Australia visited India, Sri Lanka and South Africa in 1969—70, he was only called upon for 11 matches.

Since the days of Tallon, Saggers, Langley, Jarman, Grout and Taber, only one Australian wicket-keeper has emerged who can truly be placed alongside the great glovemen of the past. The tale of the exuberant Rodney Marsh must remain the story of a current and future age of instant cricket in which more emphasis has been placed than ever before on a wicket-keeper's ability as a batsman.

10

Evans for England

'The wicket-keeper is the fulcrum of the fielding side and can transform the whole appearance of it. Godfrey realised this and revelled in it'
— Trevor Bailey

Godfrey Evans of Kent and England was possibly the most extrovert of all wicket-keepers. Not for him the quick, ghost-like movement and almost apologetic appeal of an Oldfield or Ames; Evans was all spectacular tumble and exuberant shout of triumph, more in keeping with the irrepressible extrovert George Duckworth. Evans was also one of the finest wicket-keepers who ever walked onto a cricket field.

Thomas Godfrey Evans made his first brief appearance for Kent in 1939. Six years were then wasted at war but within 12 months of its ending, England's new stumper had established a place in the Test eleven that was not to be challenged until he retired from international cricket in 1959, when he was already touching 40. The enthusiastic Godfrey Evans, who still seems to live for cricket, played his final first-class match in 1969, at the age of almost 50.

During the 30 years between his debut and final appearance, Evans claimed 219 batsmen (173 caught, 46 stumped) in 91 Tests and 1060 victims (811 caught, 249 stumped) in all first-class games. He also scored 2439 in Tests and almost 15,000 runs in all first-class games, including two sparkling Test centuries. Evans was always good value as a batsman: against India at Lord's in 1952, he came within two runs of getting his hundred before lunch. One of his most famous innings was as different from his Lord's effort as water is from a brick wall.

When England's eighth wicket fell 45 minutes from the close of the day's play in the Adelaide Test versus Australia in 1946–47, Godfrey Evans went in with instructions to stay put and give Denis Compton as much of the bowling as possible. Next morning, Evans was still 'staying put' and batted for 95 minutes before scoring his first run. Forever after, it must have delighted him to know that he held the world record for the longest period at the wicket before scoring a first run, an achievement which might have been more in keeping with the style of a 'Barnacle' Bailey or a 'Slasher' Mackay.

Evans always displayed as much stamina and concentration in his wicket-keeping as he did with his dead-bat during that Adelaide epic. But behind the stumps, he was never seen on the defensive.

Evans at work was all bustling activity and he never seemed to tire. As a young man, he was a professional boxer who never lost a bout and had brought with him into cricket the twin qualities of a boxer's footwork and fitness.

John Arlott wrote in 1952 that Godfrey Evans 'makes chances and he misses them but, faults included, he is the finest wicket-keeper in the world by a clear margin'. Like a boxer, Evans stood on the front part of his feet and Bert Oldfield, who watched him in 1946–47, remarked that the young England stumper's unorthodox style may count against an extended stay in big cricket. Luckily for Evans and England, the old Australian master's reckoning proved incorrect. Most wicket-keepers have advocated a flat-footed stance for optimum control of balance but Evans, because of his training in another discipline, proved a brilliantly successful exception to the rule.

Godfrey Evans scorned the modern practice of standing back to everything but the slow bowlers. He was, as old England 'keeper W H V Levett once put it, 'the last of the old great ones'. Evans and Bedser were a sight to see. The big England bowler pounding in to deliver his fast-medium swingers and sharp leg-cutters; the solid-looking little England wicket-keeper standing up to the stumps in the old classical style, ready for the off- or leg-side snick — and for the ghost of a chance at a stumping. Evans himself once stated that he doubted whether a wicket-keeper standing back *did* hold more catches. There is certainly very little chance of a stumping when he is located in a position that finds him rubbing shoulders with a deep first slip.

The young Godfrey Evans got his first Test chance against India at the Oval in 1946 in a match that marked his 26th birthday on the Sunday rest day. He had no luck as far as catches and stumpings were concerned but let through only one bye in India's innings of 331. England had scored 95 for three when rain washed out the third and final day. Evans had to wait until the second Test in Australia in 1946–47 for his first victim, the redoubtable Keith Miller, smartly caught off leg-spin and googly bowler Peter Smith.

England's immediately pre-war reserve stumper Paul Gibb had done duty in two of the three Tests played against India in 1946, and again in the opening Ashes Test of 1946–47. Evans took over in the next match at Sydney and never looked back. For the following dozen or so years there was no-one capable of ousting him from the England eleven.

Famous for his spectacular diving one-handed catches, Evans was a master of anticipation. One of his secrets was complete relaxation between balls and between overs. He also knew how to relax off the field and, as an inveterate party-goer, was always a cheerful companion on tour. He was in the game at every moment, urging, cajoling, demonstrating his quicksilver skills and, above all else,

Godfrey Evans provided perpetual inspiration for England's bowlers and fielders, even on the longest and hottest of days. There may never be another quite like him.

No one ever called Stuart Cathie Griffith by either of his first names; he was always known to the cricketing world as 'Billy'. After the end of his playing days, Billy Griffith was a long-serving MCC secretary but when he was still active as a first-class wicket-keeper, the strongly-built Griffith did for a while look like becoming England's number one choice. But this was before the reappearance of the ebullient Evans after the First World War.

Griffith travelled to New Zealand in 1935–36 on a non-Test tour

Godfrey Evans of Kent and England is almost airborne as he breaks the stumps.

and was picked in 1945 for all five 'Victory Tests' versus Australia. At Lord's, in the first game against Hassett's Services XI, he impressed with three catches and a stumping and, in the fifth and final celebration encounter, he pouched seven catches, six in Australia's second innings. As Evans's deputy in the West Indies in 1947−48, Griffith was pressed into service as an opening batsman for the second Test at Port-of-Spain in an injury-hit side (Evans kept wicket).

In a remarkable display of responsibility, the Sussex amateur played an innings of 140 to become the first player in history after Charles Bannerman (165 for Australia versus England in the very first Test at Melbourne in 1876−77) to record his maiden first-class century in his first Test innings. Griffith was dropped for the next Test when Len Hutton was hurriedly flown out to reinforce the MCC batting. He finally got an opportunity to go behind the stumps for England when chosen ahead of Evans for the last two games of a five-match series in South Africa in 1948−49 (Griffith had three catches in his first innings) but was never again picked for a Test.

All of Evans's deputies spent much of their time patiently waiting in the pavilion, with only the odd appearance or two when the 'ironman' was virtually on the point of being hospitalised. Surrey's Arthur John William McIntyre was one such player, and a wicket-keeper who was equally at home in taking the bowling of England's top bowler, Alec Bedser, as Evans himself. For Surrey, the McIntyre-Bedser combination was almost as famous as the Evans-Bedser partnership in Tests.

Although less exuberant and more orthodox in his method, McIntyre was as quick a stumper off the big Surrey and England bowler as was Evans. On his debut Test appearance versus West Indies at the Oval in 1950, McIntyre took three catches and let through only five byes in a massive total of 503. In Australia in 1950−51, he was picked on pre-series form as a batsman for the first Test at Brisbane. Arthur McIntyre's only other Test (this time as a wicket-keeper) came five years later versus South Africa at Leeds in 1955, where he boosted his dismissal tally to seven in two Tests (he also took one catch as a fielder in his single Test in Australia).

When Evans was injured during the 1951 rubber against South Africa, he was replaced for the last two Tests by another brilliant leg-side stumper, Yorkshire's Donald Vincent Brennan. Known as one of the characters of the game, Brennan was an amateur who only had a short career as a first-class cricketer.

Brennan went to India with the 1951−52 MCC team but was left out of the five Tests in favour of Warwickshire's Richard Thomas Spooner, a highly competent 'keeper and a sound left-handed opening batsman. Spooner played innings of 71 and 92 in the Calcutta Test and appeared again for England at Port-of-Spain in the West Indies in 1953−54 and versus South Africa at the Oval in 1955 when Evans was indisposed. In seven Tests he gathered 12 dismissals (10 caught, 2 stumped).

Northamptonshire's quietly efficient Keith Vincent Andrew might have thrived in the earlier age when good glovework was set above run-making potential in the choosing of a wicket-keeper. Despite being acknowledged as probably the best wicket-keeper in England for four or five seasons, Andrew was considered something of a 'rabbit' as a batsman and only played twice for England. He was, in effect, a man playing out of his time and reminiscent of the pre-war specialist stumpers who were frequently number 11 batsmen. Andrew had his first chance in a Test when Evans dropped out with sunstroke for the first match versus Australia at Brisbane in 1954–55. He had no dismissals but only let through 11 byes in a huge Australian total of 601 for eight wickets declared. Andrew, an avid admirer if not an emulator of Evans's jack-in-the-box style, admitted afterwards that although he did not miss any direct chances, he did, due to inexperience, miss some that he would have made at a later stage of his career.

In his only other Test, versus West Indies at Old Trafford in 1963, Andrew gloved an early catch off fast bowler Freddie Trueman. He then went through a couple of gruelling days without further success while West Indies scored 501 for six wickets declared (there were only three byes in the total). Prolific Sussex run-scorer Jim Parks, who had first kept wickets for England after only holding that position for his county for one season, then took over for the other four Tests.

James Michael Parks was perhaps one of the first England wicket-keepers who represented what E M Wellings called 'the age of stumpers turned long stops'. In an article published in *Playfair Cricket Monthly* in 1960, Wellings questioned the growing practice of keeping wicket by 'remote control, some 15 yards behind the stumps'. This new method coincided with an increase in the use of seam bowlers as opposed to spinners and the preference for a wicket-keeper who could also score runs.

The happy-natured Jim Parks was an explosive stroke-player who was twice picked to tour as a batsman alone (he suffered from double-vision at the start of the second trip to South Africa in 1956–57 and appeared in only one match). Standing back for most of the time, Parks did so well when called upon to keep for Sussex in an emergency that he was persuaded to continue.

Parks made his debut for England as a batsman in 1954; he became full-time wicket-keeper at Sussex in 1959. Brought in as a late addition to the 1959–60 MCC team in the West Indies (where he was coaching), he kept wickets in the final Test at Port-of-Spain and played innings of 43 and 101 not out. The other wicket-keepers in the party were Andrew, who was given few chances because of his poor batting, and Surrey's Roy Swetman, who played in the first four Tests.

Although he often had to vie for a place with Middlesex's John Murray, Jim Parks now became England's number one choice 'keeper for the next seven years, until he and Murray were both summarily ousted by the up-and-coming young wicket-keeping genius Alan Knott in the late 1960s.

Taking some outstanding catches while standing back to the faster men, and doing a workmanlike job when he stood up to the spinners, Jim Parks had 114 dismissals (103 caught, 11 stumped) in his 46 Tests. He added 1962 runs at 32.16, with two centuries.

Surrey's slightly-built Roy Swetman was a neat and confident player who never quite did well enough as wicket-keeper or batsman to seriously challenge Parks. He played in 11 Tests in which he totalled 26 dismissals (24 caught, 2 stumped). On the other hand, John Thomas Murray was not very far behind Parks as a batsman and was far superior behind the stumps.

John Murray was a punctilious performer who must have been extremely disappointed to be chosen for only 21 Tests. He is the only wicket-keeper other than Leslie Ames to have scored 1000 runs and dismissed 100 batsmen in a season. A purist in the pre-war sense, the Middlesex and England player was as immaculate in his glovework as he was in his dress. Murray became instantly recognisable for his ritual of touching his white-backed gloves together in front of his face before bending to wait for the bowler and looping his arms downwards in a graceful arc. Like Oldfield and a few others of earlier days, he was indeed a 'wicket-keepers' wicket-keeper'.

Graceful elegance are two epithets which describe Murray's work behind the stumps. And he was also clinically efficient and superbly agile, so much so that many contemporary players considered him the best wicket-keeper in the world. Yet the run-hungry England selectors preferred to use Parks.

John Murray's 55 victims in 21 Tests consisted of 52 catches and three stumpings — a pointer to the tactical play of the time which saw three or more seam bowlers playing together in the England team. For Middlesex, he enjoyed a fruitful partnership with off-spinner Fred Titmus. In all first-class cricket, Murray made 1527 dismissals (1270 caught, 257 stumped). Only Bob Taylor has bettered this record. As a batsman, John Murray will be remembered for his hook and flowing drive and for playing a memorable innings of 112 against the West Indian fast bowlers at the Oval in 1966.

When Murray experienced one of his few lapses in form in Australia in 1962–63, the Oxford University and Warwickshire amateur Alan Christopher Smith took over with great elan. Although he could not be categorised as being a 'keeper in the classical manner, 'A C' Smith was a sound player who also batted with verve and skill. In only six

John Murray of Middlesex and England once held the world record for the number of wicket-keeping dismissals.

Tests for England, Alan Smith took 20 catches behind the wicket and scored 69 not out in an unbroken 163-run ninth-wicket partnership with Colin Cowdrey versus New Zealand at Wellington in 1962–63 — a world record for Tests later beaten by Pakistan's Asif Iqbal and Intikhab Alam versus England at the Oval in 1967.

Two other wicket-keepers appeared for England during the Evans to Parks period, mainly on the more 'unfashionable' tours to India and Pakistan. Nottinghamshire's neat Geoffrey Millman had four Tests on the Indian subcontinent in 1961-62, and two more at home versus Pakistan in 1962. He ended with 15 dismissals (13 caught, 2 stumped), including three catches and two stumpings in his debut Test against India at Calcutta.

Yorkshire's James Graham Binks, a polished 'keeper in the classical style, had two Tests in India in 1963–64. Batting with grit and determination for 55 in the first of these matches at Bombay, Jimmy

Binks helped save an England team that, due to illness and injury, only had 10 fit players available. He also took three catches in India's first innings of the same match and five in the first innings of the next Test at Calcutta.

As mentioned, Alan Knott took over from Parks and Murray in the late 1960s and a separate analysis will be given of the years during which he surpassed all previous records for an England wicket-keeper. As the energetic and ebullient Godfrey Evans had challenged England's world-class champions of the past — Strudwick, Duckworth and Ames — for their positions of pre-eminence, so too would Knott and his faithful if less spectacular understudy, Bob Taylor, soon issue their claim for the title as best England wicket-keeper of them all.

11

Some appealing ladies

'...a Leslie Ames among women — albeit something of a pocket edition'

— G D Martineau

A description in the *Reading Mercury* of the first recorded women's cricket match, which took place near Guildford, Surrey, in 1745, includes the following words: 'The greatest cricket-match that ever was played...between eleven maids of Bramley and eleven maids of Hambleton...There was of both sexes the greatest number that ever was seen on such an occasion. The girls bowled, batted, ran and catched as well as most men could do in that game.'

It was perhaps too early an event to expect any mention of wicket-keeping but there is certainly some reference to batting, bowling and fielding and it is pleasing to note that the first known women's cricket match drew a sizeable crowd.

It is not generally known that in 1890 women's professional cricket was born. Two elevens were raised by some enterprising gentlemen to play exhibition matches (and private engagements against teams of 'Lady Amateurs') under the title 'The Original English Lady Cricketers'. One of the pioneer women professionals, Mary Willett, recalled more than 60 years later (when aged 88) that she was recruited via a press advertisement, was very good at fielding and that Mary and the other girls had been coached by county professionals George and Alec Hearne (Kent), Maurice Read (Surrey) and Fred Bowley (Worcestershire).

All members of the two teams played under assumed names and they were always accompanied by a 'matron'. Mary Willett recalled that her pseudonym was 'Miss Beckenham' and by a curious coincidence, the first known women's cricket match played before the public and which could be described as some sort of 'representative match' was staged at a place called Beckenham in 1929 between two teams dubbed 'London & District' versus 'Rest of England'.

This historic game at Beckenham also marked the debut in important women's cricket of a number of outstanding personalities. The scorecard for the match reveals that a Miss Bull scored 73 not out for Rest of England. This was Amy Bull, perhaps the first really outstanding batswoman, and it was reported of a subsequent innings played by her that with 'long, clean shots, she slogged the ball all over the ground'. Another participant in the historic match was

Marjorie Pollard, a fine all-rounder in her own right but more renowned for her pioneer work as the first broadcaster, the first reporter and the first commentator on women's matches and who is described by Netta Rheinberg in *Fair Play* as 'an institution in herself'. Then there was Con Edge, who started playing cricket with her brothers at the age of five and went up and down England bowling with an easy, natural action and 'knocking down the wickets like ninepins'.

Unfortunately, Amy Bull, Marjorie Pollard and Con Edge, amid some controversy, were not picked for England's first overseas tour by a women's team and did not appear in the first-ever women's Test, versus Australia at Brisbane in December 1934. London and District opening bowler Carol Valentine, who claimed six Rest of England wickets for 62 in 1929, did play at Brisbane. And so did her first Rest of England victim, shown on the scorecard as 'Miss Snowball', who was caught by Marjorie Pollard off the bowling of Valentine for 0.

Elizabeth Alexandra Snowball, born in Lancashire of Scottish parents, was to become one of the five or six most renowned woman cricketers since the institution of women's international cricket in 1934 and the undisputed best woman wicket-keeper in history.

Netta Rheinberg describes 'Betty' Snowball's wicket-keeping as, 'always reliable, sometimes spectacular'. Quick and impressively agile, the neat and graceful Betty Snowball kept with a sense of enjoyment of her occupation that manifested in a 'certain flourish... which often caught the eye of the spectator and made her work behind the stumps a joy to watch'. Her roaring appeal came as a surprise from a person so slight in stature and would have done George Duckworth proud.

Very fussy about her equipment, Betty preferred to keep in rubber-soled shoes, except when conditions were wet and slippery. Neither a youth's nor a man's size, her gloves and pads were made to order, the first woman player to do so. With 'never a hair out of place', Betty Snowball was also known for her immaculately creased skirts and well-groomed coiffure.

She enjoyed her first tour of Australia immensely. At Sydney, the legendary Arthur Mailey bowled a few balls to her and was delighted with her ability at picking his googly. When Betty Snowball was introduced to Bert Oldfield, she said afterwards: 'I bounced all the way back to our hotel after shaking hands with him.'

Betty Snowball admitted to being a 'cricket maniac' from an early age. She first kept wicket at school and read everything about the game that she could lay her hands on. The Lancashire League provided Betty with her first glimpse of top-class cricket and, in 1924, she had her first taste of Test cricket when taken to the Oval to watch England play South Africa. There she witnessed the great

Herbert Strudwick at work behind the stumps, and found the master on whose style she would model her own.

As a gym mistress at a Winchester girls' school, Betty was coached in her early seasons by ex-Kent pro Frank Dutnall and by that famous West Indian Test all-rounder, Learie Constantine. Her association with the latter cricketing genius fired her enthusiasm for the game for life. Constantine taught Betty to stand up to his own fast bowling. He notes in his *Cricket Crackers* that, 'She never was at all afraid of the speed and bounce, and in the end I had to advise her to use more caution. . .'. The West Indian considered Betty Snowball to be unique as a wicket-keeper and capable of taking balls that would have been treated with respect by any international 'keeper.

Besides her marvellous ability as a wicket-keeper, the small, slim and dark-haired Betty Snowball was also a prolific run-scorer. Netta Rheinberg notes that she, 'had a perfect stance and excelled in cutting and pulling'. She was a determined player whose qualities of endurance and concentration were legend. At the start of her international career, Betty made an almost immediate mark on women's international cricket during a 154-run match-winning opening partnership in the second Test of 1934-35 at Sydney. Her partner in this first-ever century stand in a women's Test was the incomparable Molly Maclagan, who scored 119 (the first Test hundred by a woman). Betty Snowball scored 71 and took a number of fine catches in this and in the first Test at Brisbane. She also executed three fine stumpings in Australia's second innings at Sydney off the tempting slow spinners of Joy Partridge.

Betty Snowball followed up with a knock of 83 not out in the third and final Test at Melbourne, an innings described in *Wisden* as her best of the tour — 'her leg-glides off the fast bowling being delightful'. Going on to New Zealand in the same season, she exceeded anything done previously in major women's cricket with an innings of 189 at Christchurch. Her 51-year-old Test batting record was finally beaten in 1986 by India's Sandyha Agarwall and bettered a year later by Australia's Denise Annetts, neither of whom is a 'keeper.

When the Australian women's team visited England for the first time in 1937, Betty Snowball continued where she had left off a couple of years previously. At the Oval, in the last game of the rubber, her finest innings in Tests ended on 99 when she was brilliantly run out by an amazing 30-yard throw from Australia's Mollie Flaherty. Mollie Flaherty was the first woman bowler to be considered as genuinely fast; she was also an amazing outfielder whose throws frequently scored a direct hit on the stumps.

Betty Snowball achieved eight dismissals (6 caught, 2 stumped) in the three-match series in England in 1937. She was still first-choice 'keeper when cricket resumed after the Second World War and

England wicket-keeper/
batswoman Betty Snowball,
the greatest woman wicket-
keeper.

sailed to Australia again with the England team in 1948–49. There
she found that wicket-keeping had not progressed very much since
before the war and her technique provided an object lesson in the art
for her opponents to emulate, as did that of her faithful deputy
stumper on two tours, Grace Morgan.

Of Betty Snowball's successors in the England XI, the blonde and
athletically-built Ruth Westbrook was a capable performer who once
shook the cricket world by becoming one of the first women to
acquire an MCC Advanced Coaching certificate (the other to do so

was former England captain Mary Duggan). During the 1960s and into the 1970s, two wicket-keepers, Shirley Hodges and Sheila Plant, vied for attention. Hodges once had five dismissals in an innings versus New Zealand at Auckland in 1968–69, including three stumpings in a row off England's ace bowler of the period, left-arm spinner Enid Bakewell. Plant came into the England side before Hodges but was unfortunate to suffer a broken finger during the 1968–69 tour of Australasia. England's current wicket-keeper is the capable June Edney, a high scorer, batting in the middle order.

In the field, English women's cricket teams have generally provided some sparkling work. Former South African opening batsman Eric Rowan, who took a great interest in South African women's cricket, was highly impressed with the out-cricket of the various English sides that visited his country, particularly the team which toured in 1960–61. One of England's most superb pre-war fields-women, Elspeth Jackson (later a president of the Women's Cricket Association), did not play in a Test. The most outstanding post-war English fielders include: Edna Barker (who was regarded as possibly the finest woman fielder of the 1960s and who had a low bullet-like throw to the wicket); June Stephenson (who will be remembered for her remarkable diving catches in the slips versus New Zealand at Auckland in 1966); and the fast-moving Jill Cruwys. Cruwys sprinted like a greyhound around the boundary edge and, according to a 1973 report in the *Sunday Telegraph*, had 'impeccable throwing from the deep which would have put many county players to shame'.

Australia's famous first Test wicket-keeper, Jack Blackham, once coached women cricketers in Victoria during the 1890s but many years were to elapse before Australia produced a woman stumper of note. In 1934, England's touring players were astonished when New South Wales 'keeper E Shevill walked onto the field wearing a wire mask, like a baseball catcher. She had apparently been hit in the face some years previously and was taking no chances. Ms Shevill kept in the first three Anglo-Australian Tests but only had a single catch to her credit after three matches. At Sydney in the second Test, coming in at number three, she batted for 45 minutes before being dismissed without scoring.

Winnie George and Alice Wegemund took over as the two Australian wicket-keepers on the inaugural 1937 tour to England. The honour of executing the first stumping by an Australian in a Test went to Winnie George when she kept wicket in the first Test at Northampton. When the gloves were handed over to Alice Wegemund for the second match at Blackpool, the replacement keeper had a marvellous match with three stumpings in England's first innings (two off Peggy Antonio, the 'Grimmett' of women's cricket) and another two stumpings (both off the spin bowling of Antonio) plus two catches in the second innings.

In more recent years, Olive Smith caught four and stumped four in the three-match rubber against England in Australia in 1968–69 and Margaret Jennings claimed six catches and two stumpings in three Tests in England in 1976. Margaret Jennings also played a solid, unhurried innings of 104 as opening batsman in the second Test at Edgbaston and averaged 40.40 for the series. The current Australian wicket-keeper, Chris Matthews, is another agile and talented performer whose two smart stumpings off left-arm spin bowler Lyn Fullston versus England at Gosford in 1984–85 did much towards assisting Australia to a 117-run victory, setting-up a home series win.

Among Australia's more notable fielders, Betty Wilson, a brilliant all-rounder who scored centuries and took wickets with equal facility, set an example for post-war Australians that produced some of the finest women's fielding teams. Described by Netta Rheinberg as 'unforgettable' in the field, Betty Wilson possessed a 'beautiful throw-in executed with easy grace'. So celebrated was she as a player that when she logged her 33rd century for Victoria in 1953, there was more than one call during a dull session of play in a men's Test match at Melbourne to 'send Betty Wilson in'. Among the many good fielders in Betty Wilson's teams were the particularly brilliant Hazel Buck and Pat Thompson and Australia's proficiency in this department of the game has continued through to current times.

Former West Indies Test wicket-keeper 'Jackie' Hendriks coached West Indian women cricketers for many years and his early inspiration showed through when the first West Indies women's team visited England in 1979 and Yvonne Geddes-Hall kept wicket so splendidly that she claimed seven dismissals (6 caught, 1 stumped) in three Tests.

Official women's cricket came rather late to India and its Women's Cricket Association was formed in 1973 but in 1969, one of the star performers for the formidable Albees women's club was wicket-keeper Tina Lalo, a cousin of the famous men's Test keeper Farokh Engineer. When the Under-25 Australian team visited India in 1975, 16-year-old Fouzieh Khalilee became the youngest-ever wicket-keeper in any international cricket.

New Zealand has produced two women's Test wicket-keepers of exceptional class. The first, Beverly Brentnall, came to notice in the mid-1960s and during a three-Test series in England in 1966 let through only one bye. She also played a grand back-to-the-wall innings of 84 not out in the second Test at Edgbaston which was the highest individual score by a New Zealander in international cricket at the time.

For some years previously, Beverly Brentnall had played in the shadow of the highly competent Joyce Clothier, but soon excelled

New Zealander Ingrid Jagersma is probably the best of today's international women wicket-keepers.

her predecessor when given her opportunity in the New Zealand women's team. In a Test at Auckland in 1968–69, Bev Brentnall caught two and stumped three in England's first innings. She added another stumping in the second innings in a match in which England 'keeper Shirley Hodges also had four stumpings and two catches to give the two wicket-keepers 12 of the 33 wickets to fall. In 1971–72, Bev Brentnall virtually dominated the series in Australia with records of four stumpings in an innings, six catches in an innings and seven dismissals in a match.

When she travelled to play for New Zealand in England in 1984, the sturdy but fast-moving Ingrid Jagersma took with her a set of gloves and pads that had taken her four years of searching to find. In the modern manner, she proceeded to twice dismiss England captain Jan Southgate with spectacular one-handed diving catches — with her left hand at Leeds in the first Test, her right at Canterbury in the final Test. Ingrid Jagersma emerged from the tour as New Zealand's player of the series and a strong challenger for the title of best wicket-keeper in contemporary women's cricket.

12

New Zealand choice

'It is a cricketing truism that wicket-keepers, like children among adults, are rarely noticed until they do something wrong'
— R T Brittenden

New Zealand's well known cricket scribe Dick Brittenden shows a great love of wicket-keepers in his writings and once remarked: 'Wicket-keeping is so pronounced a form of hard labour that the lack of a society seeking to abolish the practice is remarkable.' This expression of sympathy is based on the knowledge that the one player who must keep his wits about him for every ball bowled in an innings is the wicket-keeper. And for an occupation that is considered by some to be hard labour, it is quite surprising how many fine padded and gauntleted warriors have appeared in that role in New Zealand cricket.

The first of the Kiwi greats (and possibly the greatest) was the safe and certain Kenneth Cecil James, a smiling and friendly man who came to England as second-string wicket-keeper in 1927, and stuck around for the next four or five years as number one selection in any New Zealand XI. Brittenden writes that Ken James 'always seemed to be in position perfectly, and his sense of timing was superb'. England opening bowler Alec Bedser only saw James play in some RAF wartime matches but considered the New Zealander the best 'keeper he had ever seen. Pelham Warner wrote that James's method 'could not be improved on'.

Apart from his safe and sure catching of anything considered a chance, James was noted as a 'lightning swift' stumper and was one of the first of the top wicket-keepers of his time to habitually stand back to the fast-medium bowlers. James was also a capable forcing right-handed batsman who topped 1000 runs during 1938, one of his five seasons with Northamptonshire in the English County Championship.

In Test cricket, the cheerful James was not much of a success with the bat but held his own admirably as a classy wicket-keeper in a struggling pre-Second World War New Zealand team that was still to find its feet in international cricket. He had 16 dismissals (11 caught, 5 stumped) in his 11 Tests and 423 (311 caught, 112 stumped) in 204 first-class games.

James was actually taken to England in 1927 as reserve stumper to

New Zealand skipper Thomas Coleman Lowry, a lion-hearted utility player who could switch from attacking batsman to right-arm slow bowler and from wicket-keeper 'of the smash-and-grab type' to brilliant close-in fielder with great success.

Tom Lowry was a hardy and forthright character who, when he played as a rugby full-back, was said to have caused too many injuries by allowing his opponents to run into him instead of side-stepping out of their way. He was one of the game's most colourful characters. Referring to Lowry, R C Robertson-Glasgow writes in *Cricket Prints*: 'His comments on the run of play, had they reached the spectators, would have alone justified the Entertainment Tax...'. As a young man, Lowry went to Cambridge University but did not keep wicket there, the post being occupied by N B Sherwell, a younger brother of the famous South African. Later in his life, Lowry was president of the New Zealand Cricket Council and maintained his interest in the game until his death in 1976.

Like James, Tom Lowry was a great attraction in English county cricket when he turned out for Somerset during four seasons. He only played in seven Tests at a time when New Zealand's Test opportunities were few and far between but did not keep wicket in any of them.

Of the players available during the 1930s, the quietly efficient Eric William Thomas Tindill came closest to challenging Ken James for the wicket-keeping berth in the New Zealand team. Tindill eventually got his chance when picked for the 1937 tour of England and he played in all three Tests. A rugby All-Black (he was an accomplished half-back), Eric Tindill was noted for his rather cautious appeal, more of a high-pitched whisper than a demanding shout. He was strong on the leg-side, frequently taking the ball with a full dive, and a quick and neat stumper. Tindill was also a competent left-handed batsman who used his feet expertly and gathered runs in an unobtrusive fashion.

New Zealand's first post-war 'keeper was another man who did his job with minimum fuss and a high degree of efficiency. The rather withdrawn-looking Francis Leonard Hugh Mooney gathered 30 victims (22 caught, 8 stumped) in 14 Tests between 1949 and 1954 and played one or two Test knocks of great character and concentration. A man of easy and urbane charm, he was a cricket fanatic who loved to talk for hours about the history of the game.

Mooney was also a neat and uncomplicated wicket-keeper whose swift and sure stumping frequently surprised his opponents. He marked his Test debut against England at Leeds in 1949 with three catches and two lightning stumpings off tubby left-arm spinner Tom Burtt and batted with great courage against South Africa's demon bowler of the day, Neil Adcock, on a fast and bumpy track at Ellis Park, Johannesburg, in 1953—54. Two of New Zealand's top batsmen,

The neat and efficient Frank Mooney was New Zealand's first post-war 'keeper.

Sutcliffe and Miller, were sent to hospital for check-ups after being struck by Adcock. Mooney held the fort and made second top score of 35 before Sutcliffe returned, head swathed in bandages, to crack seven huge sixes and post a defiant 80 not out.

According to Dick Brittenden, Mooney's immediate successor as New Zealand stumper was a man who simply loved to keep wicket. Ian Alexander Colquhoun only played in two Tests but his enthusiasm was apparent all the time he was on the field in his Silver Fern cap. The size and strength of the hugely-built 'Coke' Colquhoun made him a feared rugby forward but he was surprisingly nimble behind the stumps. Colquhoun's two Tests against England in 1954—55 brought him four catches and just one run in his four excursions to the crease as number 11 batsman.

John Richard Reid, the man unchallenged as New Zealand's finest all-rounder, sometimes took the gloves in an emergency and was a competent 'keeper, as well as a brilliant world-class forcing batsman, a bowler in a variety of styles and a fielder of excellence. John Reid scored more than 3000 runs and took 85 wickets in Tests. He also claimed 43 catches, most of them in the field, and executed one stumping against England at Old Trafford in 1958, having taken over from Eric Petrie after the regular New Zealand 'keeper had been struck on the head while batting.

New Zealand included two highly capable wicket-keepers on a tour of Pakistan and India in 1955–56, T G McMahon and E C Petrie. The undemonstrative but dependable Trevor George McMahon was a regular number 11 batsman who was played for his wicket-keeping ability alone. McMahon played in four internationals in India and Pakistan, and once again in the first Test when West Indies visited New Zealand the same season. He then handed over the gloves for the remaining three Tests to former West Indies Test wicket-keeper and newly-arrived immigrant 'Sammy' Guillen. The inclusion of the talented Simpson Clairmonte Guillen in the New Zealand team was illegal as he had not yet qualified to play for New Zealand by living for four years in his adopted country. The touring West Indians raised no objections and their former team-mate revelled in his opportunity to play against his former countrymen.

The popular and jovial Eric Charlton Petrie made his debut in the second Test versus Pakistan in 1955–56, after Trevor McMahon had received his first call to the colours in the opening match of the series. Petrie was at his best in England in 1958 and, standing back for even the medium-paced bowlers, took six catches in the first Test versus England at Edgbaston and four on the following game at Lord's. In 14 Tests between 1955 and 1965, Petrie had 25 dismissals, all caught. He was also a good enough batsman to log two first-class centuries but disappointed as a run-getter in Tests, making his highest score of 55 against England at Christchurch in 1965–66 after an absence of five years from the New Zealand Test team.

Petrie's deputy on the 1958 tour of England, John Thomas Ward, was another capable wicket-keeper who had no pretensions as a batsman. Ward had been chosen for the England trip without ever having represented his province but eventually played in eight Tests and logged 17 dismissals (16 caught, 1 stumped). On occasion, he batted above his known ability as an effective night-watchman.

History repeated itself when, like Ward in 1958, Arthur Edward Dick was picked as a tour reserve 'keeper without ever having held that position in New Zealand domestic cricket. Dick's first stint behind the stumps in a first-class match came at Perth when the Kiwis played Western Australia on their voyage to South Africa in 1961–62. He thrived on the new responsibility and gained a place for the first Test against South Africa when Ward was unable to play due to a badly damaged finger.

The enthusiastic 'Artie' Dick made his international debut a memorable one by creating a new New Zealand record of seven dismissals (6 caught, 1 stumped) in a Test. This stood for 20 years, until 1982−83, when Warren Lees took eight catches in a match versus Sri Lanka at Wellington. Dick also went on to post a New Zealand series record, and equal the then existing world record, with 23 victims (21 caught, 2 stumped) in the five Tests. The unexpected wicket-keeping choice provided grand support for New Zealand skipper John Reid's battery of fast-medium bowlers that assisted materially in an historic drawn rubber. In other matches, Dick caught five and stumped three batsmen versus Griqualand West, to equal the then New Zealand record of eight dismissals in a first-class match, and claimed another seven victims in the next match against West Province.

In all, Art Dick totalled 51 dismissals (47 caught, 4 stumped) in 17 Tests for New Zealand and as an aggressive right-handed bat occasionally played an innings of great value. His highest first-class score was attained on the way home from South Africa in 1961−62 when the New Zealanders stopped over in Sydney to play New South Wales and Dick powered his way to a dashing 127 with 23 boundaries.

After Dick's retirement, the London-born Roy Ivan Harford put in a brief appearance as New Zealand wicket-keeper in a home rubber against India in 1967−68 and set a new record for his country with five dismissals (all caught) in the first innings of the third and final Test at Wellington. Adding two catches in the second India innings, Harford raised his match aggregate of dismissals to seven to equal Dick's record. Like quite a number of New Zealand wicket-keepers before him, Harford was not much of a batsman. Nor was the energetic Barry Douglas Milburn who took over from Harford when the West Indies team arrived in New Zealand in 1968−69. Milburn claimed eight victims in three matches versus West Indies and toured England in 1969 and Pakistan in 1969−70 without again playing in a Test.

A young wicket-keeper then appeared who was, in effect, the first New Zealand gloveman who might have been picked for Tests on his batting ability alone. The tragic Kenneth John Wadsworth died of cancer in 1976 after having represented his country in 33 Tests in which he scored 1010 runs at an average of 25.62 (a figure comparable with most of the New Zealand Test batsmen of his time) and accounted for 96 dismissals (92 caught, 4 stumped). He has become acknowledged as New Zealand's greatest wicket-keeper and was certainly its finest wicket-keeper/batsman.

The determined Ken Wadsworth was completely self-taught and his will to win contrasted markedly from the then rather timid approach of many of his Kiwi colleagues. According to his *Wisden* obituary, Wadsworth's outlook 'was more typical of an Australian or a Yorkshireman than a New Zealander. . . .' Always strikingly brilliant in gauntlets and pads, Wadsworth worked daily at his craft and became an eminently consistent performer who ranked with the best wicket-keepers of the past. The New Zealand stumper had not quite reached his best when he succumbed to his fatal illness at the age of 29.

In the modern manner, and because New Zealand's attack consisted of predominantly seam bowlers, Wadsworth was at his finest when standing back and his extremely high proportion of catches to stumpings reflected the out-cricket method of his age. With his long fair hair, boundless energy behind the stumps and his mainly aggressive, and sometimes dogged, batting style, the well-built New Zealand wicket-keeper was a popular and inspirational team man and a spectator favourite. His 96 Test victims represents a New Zealand record, as does his 282 victims (256 caught, 26 stumped) in all first-class cricket. Wadsworth also equalled R I Harford's five dismissals in a Test innings versus Pakistan at Auckland in 1972−73. Peculiarly enough, two of his successors in the New Zealand Test team, Warren Lees and Ian Smith, have done the same. Lees and Smith also share the honour of being the only two New Zealand wicket-keepers ever to make a century in an international match.

Warren Kenneth Lees was six years younger than his predecessor and had the unenviable task of taking over in the New Zealand XI from the recently deceased Wadsworth during an arduous and disappointing tour of Pakistan and India in 1976−77. Lees was, like Wadsworth, also a self-made wicket-keeper and he provided an immediately efficient back-up to the New Zealand bowlers and, in his debut Test series, also succeeded way beyond expectations as a batsman. A bold hooker and driver, Lees saved his side in the second match versus Pakistan at Karachi with an innings of 152, the first-ever Test hundred by a New Zealand wicket-keeper. His 185-run seventh-wicket partnership with all-rounder Richard Hadlee (86) saved the game.

In 21 Tests, Warren Lees claimed 59 dismissals (52 caught, 7 stumped) and scored 778 runs at 23.57, without ever again quite reaching the heights scaled at Karachi in 1976−77.

For a while, Lees was challenged for the wicket-keeping post by the exuberant Graham Neil Edwards. A natural comic who delighted the crowd and the players, 'Jock' Edwards was a short and bustling, stockily-proportioned player but a rather average gloveman who played some of his eight Tests as a hard-hitting batsman. Edwards scored 377 runs at 25.13 in eight Tests and had seven dismissals, all caught. In England in 1978, he experienced a rather awkward second Test at Trent Bridge and the wicket-keeping gloves were handed to left-handed opening batsman and occasional 'keeper Bruce Edgar for the final match of the series at Lord's. Edgar did quite well at his unaccustomed task, taking three good catches in England's first innings.

Lees regained his place after the 1978 England venture and went to Australia in 1980–81 as number one wicket-keeper. There he briefly lost his place for the first Test at Brisbane to a promising youngster seven years his junior. Lees was reinstated for the two remaining games against Australia but the neat, unobtrusive and highly competent Ian David Stockley Smith was not easily discouraged.

Smith performed well in the limited overs internationals played in 1980–81 and ousted Lees for the three Tests versus Australia played in New Zealand in 1981–82. The newcomer broke a finger during the Third Test at Christchurch and Lees was brought back for the 1982–83 season's matches against Sri Lanka and in the World Series Cricket competition in Australia.

Smith recovered to accompany Lees to England in 1983 for a four-Test tour and the World Cup competition and, with the two players alternating, New Zealand's wicket-keeping merry-go-round continued. The younger man then proceeded to consolidate his position when England visited New Zealand in 1983–84.

At Auckland in the third Test, Ian Smith came in at number eight and posted his maiden Test hundred during a 384-minute marathon. His 113 not out was one of three hundreds in a New Zealand innings

Kiwi Ian Smith goes down on one knee to stump Australian captain Allan Border at Melbourne in 1985–86.

of 496 for nine wicket declared and he allowed himself the luxury of hitting two sixes after he had attained three figures. In the same match, Smith equalled the record held jointly by Harford, Wadsworth and Lees when he had five dismissals in England's innings — four catches and one stumping. He has also twice achieved seven dismissals in a Test, a feat that has only been bettered by Warren Lees (eight scalps versus Sri Lanka at Wellington in 1982–83) and equalled by R I Harford and A E Dick.

Ian Smith now remains the Kiwis' number one wicket-keeper (although his present deputy, Tony Elston Blain, did play in one Test versus England in 1986 and has performed well in limited over internationals) and will very likely soon overhaul Ken Wadsworth's New Zealand record of 96 Test dismissals.

13

India's glovemen

'Like the family physician, wicket-keepers can seldom afford to be exhibitionists or to make mistakes if they are to be trusted'
— Sujit Mukherjee

India's tradition of mostly orthodox, agile and highly competent wicket-keepers started in 1932 when the diminutive Janardan Gyanoba Navle caught England captain Douglas Jardine off a medium-paced cutter from his own skipper and 'Grand Old Man' of Indian cricket C K Nayudu in the inaugural Test between the two countries at Lord's in June 1932.

The dismissal of Jardine was to be the neat and conscientious Navle's only victim of the match but he kept wicket splendidly throughout (although he did miss one definite stumping chance given by England wicket-keeper Leslie Ames) and only let through five byes in a combined England total of 534 runs. In a summing up of the 1932 India tour to England, *Wisden* recorded that the Indian team 'had a first-rate wicket-keeper, very quick in all that he did' and Sir Jack Hobbs was one observer who stated that Navle might even be placed in the same class as Duckworth and Oldfield.

J G Navle kept wicket and opened the innings but appeared in only one more Test, versus England at Bombay in the first game of the first official three-match rubber played in India in 1933–34. Ironically, the neat and tiny Navle's place was taken by the 6ft 2in (188 cm) heavyweight 'keeper Dr Dilawar Hussain. Dilawar had opened India's first innings of the second Test at Calcutta and scored 59, having returned to the wicket with his score on 11 after being struck on the head by a bouncer. He went in at number seven in India's second innings and completed a fine batting double with a score of 57. Dilawar also had one catch and a stumping in his debut match for India and a couple of catches in the third and final Test at Madras.

Dilawar Hussain was a Doctor of Philosophy whose unwearying patience was the hallmark of his rather ungainly batsmanship. While at Cambridge University in 1936, he was pressed into service as a wicket-keeper for the third Test India played against England at the Oval, scored 35 and 54 and took three fine catches off fast bowlers Amar Singh and Mohammed Nissar. In figures, the sum total of this popular player's Test career was: three Tests, 254 runs at 42.33, seven dismissals (6 caught, 1 stumped). Dilawar Hussain later became

India's first Test wicket-keeper, the tiny J G Navle, is dwarfed by first slip Mohammed Nissar. The batsman is Walter Hammond of England.

a founding member of the Board of Control of Cricket in Pakistan and served as a Pakistan Test selector.

Injuries forced India to employ a different wicket-keeper in each of the three Tests played against England in 1936. First-choice D D Hindelkar kept in the opening Test at Lord's but suffered a chipped finger bone and his place for the next game at Manchester was taken by his deputy K R Meherhomji.

What self-effacing Dattaram Dharmaji Hindelkar lacked in showmanship behind the stumps he made up for abundantly in sheer reliability and consistency. As Sujit Mukherjee says in *The Romance of Indian Cricket*: 'Much of Hindelkar's art lay in concealing art.' Although his Test appearances were limited by war and the sparse number of Indian tours, Hindelkar was India's first outstanding wicket-keeper. When the Indian team was chosen for its first post-war tour, to England in 1946, he was already a 37-year-old veteran but was picked even though he had ceased playing regular Indian domestic first-class cricket. Hindelkar was affectionately dubbed 'Handlebar' when English cricket followers had difficulty pronouncing his name.

The doughty 'Daffu' Hindelkar had rather brittle fingers and frequently suffered from broken bones; he also carried a bout of lumbago into the three Tests India played in England in 1946 and this caused a lowering of his normally high wicket-keeping standards. Hindelkar was forced to soldier on when reserve Raosaheb Babashaheb Nimbalkar fractured his thumb after only a few tour games. (R B Nimbalkar was, incidentally, a brother of the B B Nimbalkar who for 25 years held, with K V Bhandarkar, a world record second-wicket partnership of 455.)

D D Hindelkar died tragically at the age of 39. Hindelkar's 1936 deputy played in one Test in England — Khershed Rustomji Meherhomji came from an eminent Parsi cricketing family. His uncle, Rustomji Meherhomji, toured England with the 1911 All-India side and his nephew, Kersi Meherhomji, has gained some prominence in Australia as a cricket writer.

Two wicket-keepers shared Test duties when India visited Australia for the first time in 1947—48. The confident and occasionally brilliant Parsi player Jamshed Khudadaad Irani was an opening batsman in Indian domestic cricket who batted at number 11 in his two Tests. The short and stocky Probir Sen took over for the remainder of the five-match series against Australia and consolidated his place in the Indian XI for a couple of seasons. At Melbourne in the fifth Test, he took four catches and let through only four byes in Australia's innings of 575 for 8 wickets declared.

The nimble-footed and ebullient 'Khokhan' Sen possessed uncanny anticipation and ended his Test career of 14 matches with 31 victims (20 caught, 11 stumped). Sen executed five stumpings (four in the first innings) off left-arm spinner Vinoo Mankad versus England at Madras in 1951-52. He was also a useful tailend batsman and a very occasional slow bowler who once claimed a hat-trick for Bengal versus Orissa in a Ranji Trophy match.

Sen played a full five-match series against West Indies in India in 1948—49 but alternated with two rival stumpers during the next home series versus England in 1951—52. The highly capable Padmanabh Govind Joshi played in the first and fourth Tests and went on to represent India in a total of 12 Tests, gathering 27 dismissals (8 caught, 9 stumped) on the way. 'Nana' Joshi was a regular opening batsman for his state, Maharashtra (he was also captain for several years), but only once played an innings of any note in international cricket, 52 not out versus Pakistan at Bombay in 1960–61, as part of a record ninth-wicket 149 runs with fast bowler Ramakant Desai.

The second wicket-keeping debutante against England in 1951–52 was Madhav Krishnaji Mantri, uncle of renowned Indian opening batsman Sunil Gavaskar. Mantri was a sound opening batsman (although he failed in that role in Tests) and a talented 'keeper who claimed 9 dismissals (8 caught, 1 stumped) in four Tests.

Mantri went to England as Sen's deputy in 1952 but there was again much jostling among India's stumpers when Pakistan arrived for its inaugural series in India in 1952–53. Sen kept in the first and fifth Tests while Joshi was picked for the second match. Vijay Rajindernath executed four stumpings in the third match against Pakistan at Bombay, did not bat in the match, and never again appeared in a Test.

Ebrahim Suleman Maka took over for the next game at Madras, had three successes behind the wickets (2 caught, 1 stumped), also did not bat but, unlike Rajindernath, did get another chance when he travelled to the West Indies as P G Joshi's back-up in 1952–53 and played in the third Test at Port-of-Spain. Poor Maka broke a couple of bones in his hand when batting and was unable to take up his post as wicket-keeper. Top Indian batsman Vijay Laxman Manjrekar deputised so competently for Maka (two catches, a stumping and just four byes in the match) that he was again pressed into service ahead of Joshi for the final Test at Kingston. Manjrekar played notable innings of 43 and 118 in this match but apart from a stumping off little leg-spinner Subhash Gupte, he was not as successful with the gloves.

India took along a new young wicket-keeper in 23-year-old Narendra Shankar Tamhane when it toured Pakistan for the first time in 1954–55. The multi-talented Tamhane was a former slow bowler who first kept wicket as a substitute but later developed into one of India's top three or four players in that position. Neat, quick and quiet, Narendra Tamhane boasted seven dismissals (4 caught, 3 stumped) in his first international outing in an unofficial 'Test' versus the Commonwealth team at New Delhi in 1953–54.

A protégé of former Test 'keeper M K Mantri, Tamhane was unostentatious, a safe catcher and expert stumper. He enjoyed a curious early career in that he played for Combined Indian Universities before representing his own university and was picked for India in a Test before appearing for his state, Bombay. In his first series against Pakistan in 1954–55, Tamhane had 19 dismissals (12 caught, 7 stumped), combining well with ace Indian googly bowler Gupte and left-arm spinner Mankad. He also played a well-judged knock of 54 not out in the second Test at Bahawalpur (Tamhane's highest Test innings) when India was struggling for runs against Pakistan's excellent seam attack of the 1950s.

In 1955–56, Tamhane was briefly replaced for one Test versus New Zealand at Calcutta by Chandrakant Trimbak Patankar, a good all-round wicket-keeper who finished his only international game with three catches and a stumping. Tamhane returned for the remainder of the series and when Ian Johnson's Australian side visited India in 1956–57, impressed once more with nine victims in the three Tests played.

P G Joshi made something of a comeback in England in 1959 and played in three out of five Tests, with Tamhane keeping in the other two games. Tamhane then remained first choice until the arrival of B K Kunderan, the first of India's two outstanding post-war wicket-keeper-batsmen. In 21 Tests, Tamhane dismissed 51 batsmen (35 caught, 16 stumped) but barely averaged 10 runs an innings with the bat.

Budhisagar Krishnappa Kunderan was an exciting stroke-player who could bat anywhere in the order. He came within 19 runs of 1000 runs in Tests at an average of 32.70 with a determined 192 in just under seven hours versus England at Madras in 1963–64 as his best effort. 'Budhi' Kunderan's 525 runs (average 52.50) in the 1963–64 series was the best-ever effort by a wicket-keeper-batsman until overtaken by South Africa's Denis Lindsay versus Australia in 1966–67.

A sometime medium-pace bowler, Kunderan was once called upon to use the new ball in a Test against England at Edgbaston in 1967 (Farokh Engineer kept wicket) and thus became the only player to have opened both the batting and bowling in a Test and kept wicket, although not all in the same match.

However, one Indian player does hold the unique record of having batted, bowled, fielded and kept wicket all in the same Test. At Bombay in 1948–49, during the final Test of the India-West Indies series, veteran and captain Lala Amarnath (who had scored India's first Test century in his debut innings against England at Bombay in 1933–34) gave a remarkable exhibition of cricketing versatility. Regular keeper Probir Sen was injured early in the West Indies' first innings. Amarnath donned the gloves after having already bowled as first change and, not content with the role of mere makeshift 'keeper, went on to take five catches in the match.

Budhi Kunderan eventually totalled 30 dismissals (23 caught, 7 stumped) in 18 Tests. His most memorable Test wicket-keeping feat came against England at Bombay in 1961–62 when he had three catches and two stumpings in his opponents' first innings — a record for an Indian 'keeper at the time and which was bettered by S M H Kirmani (5 caught, 1 stumped) versus New Zealand at Christchurch in 1975—76. Strangely enough, Kunderan was dropped for the next Test at Kanpur in favour of a player who was to exceed his performances, both as an exciting, plundering right-handed opening batsman and as a wicket-keeper who must challenge for the crown as India's best.

Farokh Maneksha Engineer would have been worth his place in any Test side for batting alone. Dashing in his approach, he knew the value of putting bat to ball even when asked to open the innings. As a wicket-keeper, Engineer brought a new touch of flamboyance to the job that was totally unlike the workmanlike attitude of most of his Indian predecessors. An acrobatic dynamo with limitless energy, he had a touch of stylish unorthodoxy about his 'keeping that caused Lancashire skipper Jack Bond to remark: 'Farokh is so lively in the field that he makes poor returns look good and lifts everybody's game.'

Known in England as 'Rooky', Engineer played for Lancashire for nine seasons and was an expert in limited overs cricket — a version that was well-suited to his volatile and sunny temperament. He was one of cricket's characters, always ready with a thundering unorthodox stroke, a quicksilver bit of glove-work or a flashing, happy smile.

In 46 Tests, Farokh Engineer compiled 2611 runs at 31.08 with an innings of 121 versus England at Bombay in 1972—73 the best of his two centuries. He also dismissed 82 batsmen (66 caught, 16 stumped). Helped by his years at Lancashire, Engineer totalled 824 wicket-keeping dismissals (703 caught, 121 stumped), in all first-class games, far and away the most by any Indian cricketer.

When Engineer did not return to India for the 1964—65 home season, Kumar Shri Madhavsinhji Jadeja Indrajitsinhji played in all three Tests of a series versus Australia, opening the batting in his first match (scoring 4 and 0 on debut) and dropping down to number 10 for the remaining two games. The new Indian 'keeper had three catches and a stumping in his first Test and eight dismissals all told in the three games against Australia. Prince Indrajitsinhji travelled to Australia and New Zealand in 1967—68 as Engineer's understudy but did not play in a Test and his short international career ended after one more chance against New Zealand at Hyderabad in 1969—70.

With Engineer omitted because of an Indian Board of Control decision to not consider players who had been unavailable for the previous domestic season, India took two new glovemen to West Indies in 1970—71. Pochiah Krishnamurthy played in all five Tests; R A Jeejeebhoy did not get his Test cap. The tall and slender Krishnamurthy surprised everyone by standing up to even the fastest Indian bowlers. He did not appear to be quite ready for Test cricket but improved as the tour progressed, although when India visited England in 1971, Engineer was back in his rightful post and Krishnamurthy became a forgotten man.

'Rooky' Engineer was finally discarded by the Indian selectors when India went to do battle in New Zealand in 1975–76. His successor, Syed Mutjaba Hussein Kirmani, had been Engineer's understudy for a few years before playing his first Test at Auckland and he was to become India's most talented wicket-keeper in more than 50 years of Test cricket.

Syed Kirmani claims that he first kept wicket under duress when, at age seven, the older boys in his home suburb in Bangalore placed him behind the wooden plank stumps and, in the absence of more sophisticated gear, gave him a brick to stop the ball! One of Kirmani's more remarkable feats was when he did not concede a single bye during Pakistan's massive innings of 652 at Faislabad in 1982–83. Many noted batsmen will confirm that with him in action, they had what was more like a mobile brick wall behind them than a boy with a single brick.

There is just a hint of the unorthodox about his scintillating glovework and he certainly cannot be described as a total purist in terms of aesthetics. But the athletic Kirmani has had few 'keeping peers anywhere in the world, and at any time in history. Few wicket-keepers have been called upon to handle such a variety of bowling as has the Indian supremo of the 1970s and 1980s. Apart from the pace and seam of Kapil Dev and a bevy of other new-ball bowlers, Kirmani's skill behind the stumps has played a large role in the development of India's current crop of young spin bowlers: Shivara-makrishnan, Shastri, Maninder Singh and Yadav.

This comes as no surprise, for he cut his Test teeth on the unequalled flight, sharp spin and infinite variation of the incomparable Indian spin-bowling quartet of Chandrasekhar, Prasanna, Bedi and Venkataraghavan.

As a student, 'Kiri' Kirmani developed into a brilliant cricketer and was described in one report as 'a schoolboy Kanhai' during the Indian Schools' tour of England in 1967. Kirmani soon became first choice for his State side although there was criticism of the selection of Engineer, who was then fully resident in England, ahead of the developing young wicket-keeper/batsman and he then had to play second fiddle to Engineer on a couple of tours.

Apart from his world-class glove work, Kirmani has been the batsman for a crisis, a player noted for his doggedness and pugnacious-ness rather than style. He hit two Test centuries in his 2759 runs (average 27.05) scored in 88 matches for India and his innings of 102 versus England in the first Test at Bombay in 1984–85 — when he and Ravi Shastri turned the match around (India eventually won by

Syed Kirmani was a tenacious though unorthodox wicket-keeper who might go down in history as India's best.

eight wickets) in a record 235-run stand for the seventh wicket — remains one of the high achievements of his career.

Syed Kirmani was the first Indian wicket-keeper to top 100 dismissals in Tests. When he completed what was probably his final Test against Australia at Sydney in 1985—86, he had gathered 198 victims (160 caught, 38 stumped). It will take many a long year of solid grafting for any of his young successors to better these figures. Kirmani's bald dome, the reason for his nickname 'Kojak', will be greatly missed from international cricket.

The enthusiastic Bharath Reddy was for some years Kirmani's willing and capable understudy and took over from him for just one Test series, in England in 1979. A calm and undemonstrative operator, Reddy did well in four Tests to gather 11 dismissals (9 caught, 2 stumped) but his batting could not be placed in the same class as Kirmani's and he faded from consideration after the England tour.

Reddy's own deputy on the 1979 tour, Surinder Chamanlal Khanna, is still a prolific run-scorer in Indian domestic competition but has never been given a chance in a Test. A self-made cricketer, Khanna was taken to Sharjah in 1984 for a limited overs tournament where he opened the batting with verve and kept wicket capably.

Sadanand Viswanath is another competent 'keeper who was first used by India in one-day games, where he enjoyed a highly successful run behind the wicket and as a dogged late-order batsman, in the seven-nation World Championship of Cricket in Australia in 1984–85. Viswanath subsequently made his full Test debut in three matches against Sri Lanka in 1985–86 and took 11 catches in the series. He was then overlooked for the 1986 England tour, number one spot going to Kirmani's reserve on the 1985–86 tour of Australia, Kiran Shankar More.

The slightly-built but energetic Kiran More impressed in one-day games in Australia but may still have to fight off competition from Viswanath and the number two choice for the England tour, Bombay batsman/wicket-keeper, Chandrakant Sitaram Pandit. However, his new world record of five stumpings in an innings versus West Indies in the fourth Test at Madras in 1987–88 (four off new spin-bowling sensation Narendra Hirwani) places More ahead of the rest of the field.

It remains to be seen if More will remain India's regular gloveman for the next few seasons. What is certain is that, since J G Navle's dismissal of England captain Douglas Jardine back in 1932, India has seldom been short of a wicket-keeper of character and class.

14

Mr Everywhere: Rodney Marsh

'If Marsh's wicket-keeping and all its allied trappings had a marked impact on Ian Chappell's teams, and there's no way of measuring just how important it was, then so too did his batting'

— Ian Brayshaw

By the 1970s the old practice of playing one's most competent wicket-keeper, whether he could bat or not, had been all but discarded. In many instances, it seemed that the trend had actually been reversed, in that it was not an infrequent occurrence for the best batsman *who could keep wicket* to be picked for a county, state, provincial or even Test side.

When Rodney William Marsh played his first Test against England at Brisbane in 1970–71, there was something of an outcry over his selection ahead of the seasoned and apparently more capable Brian Taber. Marsh had not even kept wicket regularly for his own State and as Ian Brayshaw comments in *Warriors in Baggy Green Caps*, 'he was in such a position of siege he was battling to even convince himself he was without a shadow of a doubt the man for the job'.

This period of indecision for Rodney Marsh did not last beyond his first couple of Tests. Bill Lawry captained Australia for the first five Tests of 1970–71. Ian Chappell took over for the sixth Test and must somehow have sensed that here was a kindred spirit who, if handled correctly, would be willing to fight to the end for captain and country. A friendship was formed and, with the introduction of Dennis Lillee into the 'club', an axis was created that would transform Australian cricket over the next decade.

Thus Marsh was first selected for Australia as a batsman who could keep wicket. That this amazing bundle of energy, skill and, at times, outright impudence should shrug off his initial 'iron-gloves' image and develop into one of Australia's most outstandingly successful wicket-keepers is part of a legend. Indeed, his batting prowess peaked around 1977 and thereafter Marsh was played more for his live-wire wicket-keeping than for his run-making ability.

Accused early on in his career of being overweight and a slow mover, Marsh took the criticism to heart and worked hard and long at attaining a totally professional standard. He had to, to survive the fast bowling blitz provided during the 1970s by speedsters like Lillee, Thomson, Pascoe, Hogg and Lawson. The tough little gloveman was heard to say one day that his hands felt as if they had been belted by a hammer. He was not complaining though; Marsh was a rock-solid performer who had no time for sympathy. Yet there was no more popular cricketer in the Australian eleven — to his mates, to his opponents and to the spectators who adored his bluff humour. Marsh placed team interests above all else and once said: 'Who cares if you personally get 100 or take five wickets, but the team loses the game?'

Marsh stood back an inordinately long way to the likes of Lillee and Co. Although his method was frowned upon by the purists, it was totally effective as it gave him that extra split second to launch himself into one of his lateral movements, to right or left, in order to glove a catch. His ability to cover extra ground also allowed his captain to expand the arc of slip and leg-slip fielders without using additional men. This tactic worked particularly well when Ian Chappell had at his command such grand close catchers as himself, his brother Greg, Ashley Mallett, Ian Redpath and Doug Walters.

Any comment about the few stumpings in his career was shrugged aside by Rodney Marsh. After all, he did play in an era when most teams took the field with three or more fast bowlers, and the spinners were used mainly as fill-ins until a second new-ball could be taken. So many batsmen departed the field 'caught Marsh bowled Lillee' that it was agreeably fitting that one such dismissal gave Rod Marsh

When Australia's energetic Rodney Marsh was behind the stumps, his skipper Ian Chappell did not need a first slip. Here Marsh dives to take a catch in the first-slip position with his captain standing at second slip.

the world record for Test victims by a wicket-keeper. And in that same match at Headingly, Leeds, in 1981, Lillee became the most prolific wicket-taker in Anglo-Australian Tests.

The Lillee-Marsh partnership ultimately produced a phenomenal 95 Test dismissals. The rapport between them was uncanny and Marsh once said that he could tell from the way Lillee ran in what the angle, speed and length of the ball would be.

At Perth in 1976–77, Rodney Marsh gave an unparalleled demonstration of his all-round ability when he took 10 catches *and* scored a century in the match versus South Australia, the only instance that this feat has been accomplished since first-class cricket started during the 19th century (Sri Lanka's Amal Silva is the best in Tests so far with a century and nine dismissals versus India in 1985–86). Australia's most successful wicket-keeper also holds the world record for number of Test dismissals in a series — and also holds joint second place, with Johnny Waite of South Africa. The top international wicket-keepers in terms of dismissals per series runs as follows:

(Qualification: 20 dismissals; number of Tests in brackets)

28	(all ct) R W Marsh	Australia v England (5)	1928–83
26	(23ct, 3st) J H B Waite	S Africa v N Zealand (5)	1961–62
26	(all ct) R W Marsh	Australia v W Indies (6)	1975–76
24	(21ct, 3st) A P E Knott	England v Australia (6)	1970–71
24	(all ct) D T Lindsay	S Africa v Australia (5)	1966–67
24	(22ct, 2st) D L Murray	W Indies v England (5)	1963
23	(22ct, 1st) F C M Alexander	W Indies v England (5)	1959–60
23	(21ct, 2st) A E Dick	N Zealand v S Africa (5)	1961–62
23	(20ct, 3st) A T W Grout	Australia v W Indies (5)	1960–61
23	(22ct, 1st) A P E Knott	England v Australia (6)	1974–75
23	(21ct, 2st) R W Marsh	Australia v England (5)	1972
23	(all ct) R W Marsh	Australia v England (6)	1981
23	(16ct, 7st) J H B Waite	S Africa v N Zealand (5)	1953–54
22	(21ct, 1st) S A R Silva	Sri Lanka v India (3)	1985–86
22	(all ct) S J Rixon	Australia v India (5)	1977–78
21	(20ct, 1st) A T W Grout	Australia v England (5)	1961
21	(16ct, 5st) G R A Langley	Australia v W Indies (5)	1951–52
21	(all ct) R W Marsh	Australia v Pakistan (5)	1983–84
21	(13ct, 8st) R A Saggers	Australia v S Africa (5)	1949–50
21	(15ct, 6st) H Strudwick	England v S Africa (5)	1913–14
20	(19ct, 1st) P R Downton	England v Australia (6)	1985
20	(19ct, 1st) P J L Dujon	W Indies v Australia (5)	1983–84
20	(18ct, 2st) T G Evans	England v S Africa (5)	1956–57
20	(17ct, 3st) A T W Grout	Australia v England (5)	1958–59
20	(16ct, 4st) G R A Langley	Australia v W Indies (4)	1954–55
20	(19ct, 1st) H B Taber	Australia v S Africa (5)	1966–67
20	(16ct, 4st) D Tallon	Australia v England (5)	1946–47
20	(18ct, 2st) R W Taylor	England v Australia (6)	1978–79

It must be noted that a wicket-keeper's opportunities for dismissals are to a marked extent governed by the strength and type of bowling attack possessed by his team. Amal Silva's amazing 22 victims in only three matches represents the ultimate in wicket-keeping strike-rate per Test in a series but Marsh's five rubbers with 20 or more dismissals remains an extraordinary effort.

Marsh eventually created a new world record by sending back 355 batsmen (343 caught, 12 stumped) in his 96 Tests. He also scored 3633 Test runs, an Australian record for a wicket-keeper, including three Test centuries. No other Australian stumper has approached these figures; nor have any appeared in as many Tests as Marsh. He entered Test cricket at a time when the international programme was becoming crowded with fixtures and he took full advantage of all opportunities.

During the long reign of 'King Bacchus' Marsh, two Australian reserve stumpers who never kept wicket in Tests featured as second-string 'keepers with Australian teams. Leading batsman and out-standing fielder Ross Edwards was also a former Western Australia state 'keeper who acted as Australia's reserve in the West Indies in 1972−73. Victoria's Richard Daryl Robinson, a tall belligerent gloveman, backed Marsh up on two England tours but played his three Tests in 1977 as a batsman and close-up fielder. Tall for a 'keeper, the 6ft (183 cm) Robinson scored centuries in four con-secutive matches for Victoria in 1976−77 and was highly rated.

The man who was to take over Marsh's gloves when the Australian 'keeper defected to World Series Cricket acted as number two in England in 1981. With Marsh and most of the senior Australia players in the Packer fold, Stephen John Rixon played 10 Tests for Australia in his first season of 1977−78 — five at home versus India and then another five when veteran Bobby Simpson was recalled to lead what was virtually an Australian Third XI to the West Indies. Rixon developed a habit of scoring centuries for New South Wales after being sent in as a night-watchman, but lost his place in the Australian team because of injury during the second World Series season. With the then incumbent gloveman Wayne Phillips on the injured list, Rixon was briefly reinstated against Clive Lloyd's West Indians in 1984−85 and celebrated with seven catches in the third Test at Adelaide. Picked for the 1985 Ashes squad, he chose to cast his lot with the rebels who flew to South Africa in 1985−86. In his 13 official Tests Steve Rixon claimed the high tally of 47 victims (42 caught, 5 stumped).

Two other wicket-keepers played for Australia while Marsh was still busy with World Series Cricket. Queensland's John Alexander Maclean was picked for the first four Tests against England in 1978−79 during what turned out to be his final first-class summer. Maclean was actually nominated as Australia's vice-captain but lost his place for the remaining two Tests of the series. He took 18 catches in his four Tests and did not effect a stumping.

Western Australia's Kevin John Wright, who had been Marsh's

WA deputy, took over from Maclean and proceeded to dismiss 35 batsmen (31 caught, 4 stumped) in 10 Tests before giving way to the returning Rodney Marsh. Wright then moved to South Australia in an effort to renew his Test chances. He remained that State's wicket-keeper until just before the 1984—85 season when he was sacked after earlier being told he would be keeping wicket during the coming season. This move was initiated by the Australian selectors who wanted batsman Wayne Phillips to gain 'keeping experience at Shield level so that they could pursue their policy of playing a batsman/wicket-keeper in the Test eleven.

Wayne Phillips had gained his first taste as official Test wicket-keeper when he ousted the number-one choice, Roger Douglas Woolley, in the West Indies in 1983—84. Woolley had taken over as Tasmania's wicket-keeper in 1978—79 and had also become one of

Australia tried to make Wayne Phillips into a wicket-keeper/batsman but he was not a total success. Here he jumps for joy as the bowler hits the stumps.

the State's leading batsmen. In Rod Marsh's absence, he was sent to Sri Lanka in 1982–83 and became the first Tasmanian to play in a Test for Australia while still a Tasmanian player since L J Nash in 1931–32. Injury and the good form of Wayne Phillips kept Woolley out of all but one international in the West Indies and his brief career to date consists of two matches, five catches.

The dashing South Australian left-handed batsman Wayne Bentley Phillips scored a magnificent Test century on his debut against Pakistan at Perth in 1983–84. His good personal progress continued during a disastrous Australian excursion to the West Indies in 1983–84. Phillips's lively batting then became an important feature of the Australian eleven but he was unable, like Marsh before him, to shed his 'iron-gloves' image and develop his skills to the standard demanded of a Test gloveman.

In 27 Tests to the close of the 1985–86 season, Phillips had scored 1485 runs at 32.28 and recorded 52 catches (five as a fielder) and no stumpings. Wayne Phillips remains an example of a fine batsman whose Test prospects may have been retarded through having to assume wicket-keeping duties when he was not yet an acknowledged specialist.

When Rixon chose to go on the South African tour, Queensland's Raymond Berry Phillips, who wears photochromic 'sunglasses' in the field, was brought into the Australian party to visit England in 1985. Ray Phillips was then overlooked when the Australians went to New Zealand in late 1985–86, the position of first-choice 'keeper going to Western Australia's Timothy Joseph Zoehrer, with Wayne Phillips as reserve.

At last, Australia had picked a specialist gloveman but although he played in all three Tests, Zoehrer did not enjoy an entirely satisfactory time in New Zealand and was dogged by illness. He was, however, retained for the 1986 India tour and travelled with a new deputy (and another regular 'keeper) in Gregory Charles Dyer of New South Wales. Dyer has, at the time of writing, taken over the gloves from Zoehrer and, with some sparkling innings, has provided Australia with a useful batting bonus.

For Australia, a return to the use of the true specialist wicket-keeper was the only logical course after an experiment that worked with a thousand bonuses in the case of Rodney Marsh, failed with respect to Wayne Phillips. It should not be too surprising that the experiment did fail, for Test cricketers of the character and calibre of Rodney William Marsh are truly one in a million.

15

Pakistan and Wasim Bari

'As a wicket-keeper, Wasim Bari was almost infallible, taking his chances without fuss'

— *Wisden*, 1968

As a political, geographic and cricketing entity, Pakistan was born at the partition of India in 1947. Test cricket began for the new country just five years later. In the intervening 35 years, from Pakistan's inaugural Test versus India at the Feroz Shah Kotla ground in Delhi in 1952–53 to the present day, a fair number of highly-talented players have emerged, some rated as world-class batsmen and bowlers. Two especially long-lived wicket-keepers have been produced by the fledgling cricket nation: Imtiaz Ahmed was a batsman of great renown — the first Pakistani to notch an innings of 300 — and a safe and sound if unspectacular 'keeper; Wasim Bari was 'discovered' as an 18-year-old student by former England stumper Leslie Ames when an MCC Under-25 team visited Pakistan in 1967. Bari was taken to England as first-choice gloveman later in that year and went on to become the finest 'keeper to come from the Indian sub-continent and among the best six or seven wicket-keepers produced in all post-Second World War cricket.

The self-effacing Imtiaz Ahmed was as much a wicket-keeper made as a wicket-keeper born. As a strongly-built lad who was later to become an officer in Pakistan's Air Force, he was coached by his father, himself a wicket-keeper of some repute in Northern India cricket. However, Imtiaz preferred batting and was chosen in that role for Pakistan's inaugural Test tour to India in 1952–53, wicket-keeping duties being carried out by the 16-year-old batting genius Hanif Mohammed. Hanif could not bring to his 'keeping the same skill that marked his dedicated batsmanship and Imtiaz was prevailed upon to take over when Pakistan ventured on its first tour to England in 1954. Hanif led one more venture as Pakistan's Test 'keeper when he scored 104 and 93 and took five catches in the match versus Australia at Melbourne in 1964–65; chosen gloveman Abdul Kadir was injured when batting in the first over of the match.

Imtiaz ended up 'keeping in all four Tests and he played in 28 of the 30 scheduled first-class games. His elected deputy stumper, Shakoor Ahmed, hardly received a chance but was later the star player for a pioneering Kenya Asian XI that played a five-match

'Test' series against future England all-rounder Basil D'Oliveira's 'non-white' South Africa XI in South Africa in 1956.

Meanwhile, Imtiaz Ahmed continued in fine fettle to participate in 39 consecutive Tests for Pakistan, 36 as wicket-keeper. The enthusiastic but retiring Imtiaz experienced his first lapse in the sequence after a decade in Test cricket when he had to hand over to his deputy of the time, Ijaz Butt, for the third Test versus England at Leeds in 1962. Ijaz Butt seldom got a chance behind the stumps while Imtiaz was around but was sometimes played in Tests as an opener. In the fifth Test of 1962, at the Oval, Ijaz and Imtiaz produced a rare double when the two Test wicket-keepers opened the batting together in both innings of the match. Ijaz scored 10 and 6; Imtiaz was more successful with 49 and 98 in what proved to be his final Test. (B K Kunderan and F M Engineer did the same for India versus England at Birmingham in 1967).

As a batsman, Imtiaz Ahmed was known for his powerful hooking of fast bowling and the grandeur of his sweep shot against spin. In his 41 Tests, he scored 2079 runs (average 29.28) with his top score a remarkable 209 (Pakistan's first Test double-century) versus New Zealand at Lahore in 1955–56, after coming in at number eight. Imtiaz and his partner of the day, Waqar Hassan, added 308 runs in a record seventh-wicket stand that turned what looked to be a lost cause for the home team. As a steady 'keeper to the renowned Pakistan seam attack led by Fazal Mahmood, Imtiaz totalled 93 dismissals (77 caught, 16 stumped). He has been described as one of the pillars upon which Pakistani cricket was built.

Before the advent of Wasim Bari in 1967, two other wicket-keeper/batsmen were tried by Pakistan. Abdul Kadir was run out for 95 in his first Test versus Australia at Karachi in 1964–65 after adding 249 runs for the first wicket with a fellow Test debutante Khalid Ibadullah, the well-known Warwickshire professional. Kadir played three more Tests (only one as wicket-keeper,) without quite repeating his initial form and soon faded from the scene. Next up was the tidy Naushad Ali who had six useful outings as a wicket-keeper (three Tests each, at home and abroad) against New Zealand in 1964–65 but did not come up to scratch as an opening batsman. Pakistan's expectations had possibly been placed too high in hoping for an immediate replacement for Imtiaz Ahmed, both a competent wicket-keeper and a Test-class batsman. Kadir and Naushad emulated the 1962 feat of Imtiaz and Ijaz when they opened together in each innings versus New Zealand at Auckland in 1964–65.

When the team to tour England in 1967 was chosen, the selectors made no error, choosing the best available wicket-keeper regardless of age or batting qualifications. The teenaged Wasim Bari did not let them down, and hardly missed a Test for Pakistan for the following 16 years.

In cold figures, Wasim Bari reached a dismissal figure in his 81 Tests that will prove hard to beat — 201 caught, 27 stumped, total: 228. He was also a gritty batsman who was worth more than the number 11 tag frequently posted against his name on the scoreboard. He averaged nearly 16 runs an innings, frequently making a stand when Pakistan was in a tight corner.

In his every movement on the field, the 5ft 9ins (175 cm) Wasim Bari showed his intense enjoyment of the game. His presence in any side was worth two men and he was one of the most dedicated of stumpers. Bari's style was at once superbly balanced and wonderfully agile and his diving catches off the Pakistani fast bowlers equalled or excelled those of any other modern wicket-keeper. Bari's judgement of a chance was so superb that he only flung himself into orbit when certain a catch would not reach a fielder.

The amiable and enthusiastic Bari enjoyed himself most when handling the faster stuff (he once said that he would have loved to have kept wicket to Lillee and Thomson). The best test of a wicket-keeper's ability to cope with slow bowling is his handling of the 'wrong 'un' and here Bari passed with flying colours with his expert 'keeping to the artful leg-breaks and googlies of Abdul Qadir.

In a 1982 interview with Pakistani journalist Raiz Ahmed Mansuri, Wasim Bari claims that he did not model himself on any famous wicket-keeper. His attitude was: '. . . wicket-keeping comes naturally to a wicket-keeper. My keeping is probably more natural than anybody else's.' He goes on to suggest that if a novice wicket-keeper was looking for a player to model himself on, he should look at England's Alan Knott or Bob Taylor as his own 'keeping departed from the orthodox in a more fundamental and instinctive nature.

Wasim Bari was a giver who devoted his entire playing life to Pakistani cricket. He was even dedicated enough to take on the captaincy for an England tour in 1978 when all was not well with an inexperienced team in transition to greater things. It was not a task to thrust upon the man who remained throughout his Test career the lynch-pin of Pakistan's outcricket.

During Wasim Bari's long reign as prince of wicket-keepers, a number of challengers for the crown came and went, with some returning for a moment in the sun after the great man had departed.

Shahid Israr took a couple of catches versus New Zealand at Karachi in 1976−77, but experienced a torrid time over the chances he let slip and was never called up again. Taslim Arif was a multi-talented all-rounder who batted, bowled and kept wicket. In his third Test, against Australia on the Faisalabad featherbed in 1979−80, Taslim batted for more than seven hours to reach 210 not out. He kept wicket adequately in all three Tests against Australia and again in a couple versus West Indies the following home season, before the veteran Bari returned to his rightful post after a brief lapse.

Wasim Bari, Pakistan's
outstanding, world-class
wicket-keeper.

At various times when Bari was still number one, Ashraf Ali and
Saleem Yousuf alternated as his second string. The beefily-built
Ashraf is a big man for a wicket-keeper, although fairly agile. He is
also a useful batsman and sometimes replaced Wasim Bari for limited
overs matches. Saleem Yousuf, an athletic performer behind the
stumps, had seven dismissals (5 caught, 2 stumped) in his debut Test
versus Sri Lanka at Karachi in 1981–82 and he is also a capable
batsman. To the close of the 1985–86 season, Saleem had logged 19
dismissals (16 caught, 3 stumped) in only three Tests.

Since Wasim Bari's departure, Ashraf Ali and Saleem Yousuf
have competed with a couple of younger players for a permanent
place in the sun as Pakistan's wicket-keeper. Of these, the dapper
little Anil Dalpat impressed as a neat gloveman and plucky late-order
batsman during the World Championship of Cricket in Australia in

1984–85. Anil is the first Hindu to be chosen for a Pakistan team and to the end of the 1985–86 summer, had effected 26 dismissals (23 caught, 3 stumped) in nine Tests. Another contender for the Bari crown, Masood Iqbal, came and went very quickly when he was given just one limited overs international versus New Zealand at Multan in 1984–85 but after letting through 18 byes and failing to effect a dismissal, he faded from view.

For Pakistan's first venture to Sri Lanka in 1985–86, the selectors opted for a specialist 'keeper, Zulqarnain, who made his first-class debut in 1980–81 at the age of 16. In the three-match series against Sri Lanka, Zulqarnain stumped two and caught eight batsmen but made little progress as a run-scorer and must face continued competition from players like Salim Yousuf, Anil Dalpat and Ashraf Ali. It remains to be seen whether Pakistan will immediately produce a wicket-keeper to compare with the great Wasim Bari.

16

Only a few for Sri Lanka

'Young and old come forth to play'

— Edmund Blunden

As representatives of the newest Test-playing country, Sri Lanka's cricketers exhibit something of a boyish enthusiasm for the game that is sometimes lacking among men from the more senior cricketing lands. Since Sri Lanka's introduction to the senior league in February 1982, few of its players have had the opportunity to represent the Indian Ocean island in Test cricket, and only a handful of wicket-keepers have appeared to date.

Some observers claim that Sri Lanka's finest stumper to date has been Benedict Navaranta who represented Ceylon (as Sri Lanka was formerly known) against an assortment of touring teams during the early 1950s. His opportunities were few and far between but Ceylon's first outstanding gloveman did well enough to impress the West Indies, England and Commonwealth teams that toured the Indian sub-continent in his time and played alongside such notables as Keith Miller, Neil Harvey, Vinoo Mankad, Fazal Mahmood and Imtiaz Ahmed for a Commonwealth XI versus MCC at Colombo in 1951–52. In this match, Navaranta (his surname has also been spelled Navaratne) effected two superb stumpings off Indian left-arm spinner Mankad to help his team to an overwhelming innings and 259-runs victory.

Benedict Navaranta was a strongly-built man, a physical fitness instructor, alert and quick-moving as a wicket-keeper and always full of confidence. He was also a useful and obstinate late-order batsman and could have walked into most Test sides of his day.

Alas, Ceylon (or Sri Lanka as it became known) had to wait some years for recognition and by then Navaranta had departed this world, at the age of 63 in 1979, the year that two other well-known international wicket-keepers died, Ben Barnett of Australia and Ivan Barrow of West Indies.

To 29-year-old Hettiarachige Mahes Goonatilleke fell the singular honour of becoming Sri Lanka's first official international wicket-keeper when his country's inaugural Test was staged against England at Colombo in 1981–82. Goonatilleke immediately impressed as a polished and swift stumper who kept particularly well to the spin-based Sri Lanka attack. After playing in Sri Lanka's five Tests, he opted out to tour South Africa where he was one of only two or three players in the 'rebel' Arosa Sri Lanka team to display enough talent to be truly rated a first-class performer. Besides his neat 'keeping, Goonatilleke also displayed batting ability, scoring 27 and 56 when called upon to open against Pakistan at Faisalabad later in 1981–82. As a batsman, he averaged more than 20 in his five Tests and effected 13 dismissals (10 caught, 3 stumped) as a wicket-keeper.

Goonatilleke's punishment for playing in South Africa was a life ban from all cricket in Sri Lanka. His departure left the way open for Ronald Guy de Alwis, seven years Goonatilleke's junior, and unusually tall (6 ft — 183 cm) for a Sri Lankan. As a schoolboy, the new Sri Lankan 'keeper was noted for his heavy scoring and in 1978 compiled a match-saving 104 not out for Sri Lanka Under-19 versus Australia Under-19. He also impressed as a batsman in the 1983 World Cup in England, hitting attractive 50s against both Pakistan and England.

In a limited overs match versus Australia at Colombo in 1982–83, de Alwis claimed the Man-of-the-Match award with a record-breaking five catches to assist his side to a surprise two-wicket win over their powerful visitors. He followed up by not conceding a single bye in Australia's 514 in the Test at Kandy and, in fact, let nothing through in two Tests until 850 runs had been scored against his team.

de Alwis broke a finger just prior to Sri Lanka's first Test in England in 1984 and was forced to return home early. His place was taken by the exuberant Sampathawaduge Amal Rohita Silva, a dashing left-handed batsman and an energetic wicket-keeper who always seems to be in the game. Amal Silva had already toured Australia, New Zealand, Zimbabwe and England as reserve to de Alwis and now grabbed his chance with both gauntlets. He had failed as a batsman on his only previous Test appearance, versus New Zealand at Wellington in 1982–83, but soon made amends against England at Lord's. In a match from which Sri Lanka emerged with a much-enhanced reputation, the perky little Silva hit one of three centuries scored by Sri Lankans in the match and only let through five byes in England's innings of 370 runs.

During the World Series and World Championship matches in Australia in 1984–85, Amal Silva quickly made a name for his consistent, rapid-fire batting at the start of the Sri Lankan innings and his nifty work behind the stumps. In eight Tests to the close of the 1985–86 season, he had scored 336 runs (average 28.00) and bagged 31 'keeping victims (30 caught, 1 stumped).

Silva also set up a run of world records during the 1985-86 Sri Lanka-India series: nine catches in a Test in two successive Tests; 22 dismissals (21 caught, 1 stumped) in a three-Test series; a century and nine dismissals in a Test; and a century and 22 dismissals in a three-Test series. His work was particularly remarkable in Sri Lanka's first-ever Test win in the second match at Colombo when

Enthusiastic Amal Silva of Sri Lanka has already created a string of new Test wicket-keeping records.

Silva led off with an innings of 111, and then had three catches and a stumping in India's first innings with five more catches in the second.

When Amal Silva fell ill in 1985–86, Guy de Alwis returned to the Sri Lanka XI for two games versus Pakistan and raised his dismissal tally to 19 (18 caught, 1 stumped) in seven Tests but, for the future, it seems as if Sri Lanka's next Test wicket-keeper could be the exciting left-handed batting prospect Asanka Pradeep Gurusinghe.

A six-footer (183 cm) like de Alwis, Gurusinghe kept wicket in his debut Test versus Pakistan at Karachi in 1985–86 and gave a tidy display, including two catches off Sri Lanka strike bowler Asantha de Mel. When Pakistan visited Sri Lanka later the same season, the 20-year-old left-hander was played as a batsman (Silva and de Alwis shared 'keeping duties) and hit a resolute 116 not out in the final Test at Colombo to ensure an historic drawn series for Sri Lanka.

The bustling Don Sardha Brendon Kuruppu has already been mentioned in the batting section as having made a sensational debut with a double-century versus New Zealand in 1986—87. A livewire player like Silva, he has shown good form both behind the stumps and as a batsman in limited over internationals. Kuruppu created a particularly good impression during the 1983 World Cup after landing in England as a virtual unknown.

With four capable players (de Alwis, Silva, Kuruppu and Gurusinghe) available, all of whom can bat, Sri Lanka is certainly well-blessed with wicket-keepers for the immediate future.

17

Knott and Taylor: two of the best

'Alan Knott . . . probably the choicest wicket-keeper/batsman (as opposed to batsman/keeper) who ever pulled on a pair of gauntlets.'
— Mike Selvey

Jonathan Swift once wrote: 'Few are qualified to shine in company; but it is in most men's power to be agreeable.' Down the years there have been international wicket-keepers who could scarcely bat. There have been some stumpers who could bat quite 'usefully' in the lower order and, in recent times, there have been batsmen who have been picked because they could keep fairly competently. But of the genuine wicket-keeper *and* batsman, who might be chosen for a Test XI for his skill in either discipline, there have been very few — the emphasis here being on wicket-keeping ability first.

One would have to look hard at Australia's distinguished line of talented stumpers to find one who might have played in a Test as a batsman pure and simple. Rodney Marsh in the early part of his career would probably have qualified; so too might have Don Tallon.

Of the West Indian Test 'keepers, Barrow, Sealey, Walcott, Dujon and perhaps Deryck Murray spring to mind as Test-class batsmen but were any of these distinguished players good enough to be picked as wicket-keepers if they had been number 11 batsmen? Ivan Barrow looks to be the only one who might have made it, but his career was short, although it must be noted that he scored West Indies' first Test century.

From the Indian sub-continent have come Dilawar Hussain, Kunderan, Engineer, Imtiaz Ahmed and Amal Silva. Other than Farokh Engineer, and maybe Amal Silva, were or are any of these fine performers unshakably Test standard wicket-keepers? Of players who kept with any regularity for New Zealand, only Ken Wadsworth has some credentials for a rating.

South Africa has been most blessed and, before banishment from international cricket, produced a string of genuine wicket-keeper/batsmen: Sherwell, Cameron (the best of the lot?), Waite and Lindsay (if one includes the modern-day backstop version of the breed).

For England, Leslie Ames was the first genuine all-rounder of the classification under review, and the finest batsman of them all, from

Alan Knott, another in the long line of Kent and England wicket-keepers, makes a lightning stumping.

any country. His Kentish heir Alan Philip Eric Knott cannot be placed too far behind — as a wicket-keeper to rank with the most illustrious of the past and as a batsman who scored 4389 Test runs at an average of 32.75, and played during his 95-match international career more than one eminently decisive knock for his country.

Alan Knott also gathered a record 269 wicket-keeping victims for England (250 caught, 19 stumped). He would have had many more had he forsworn playing in World Series Cricket and, later, not searched deep into his Christian conscience and decided that the best way to help South Africans of all races would be to tour there with a 'rebel' English team in 1982. In South Africa, as in every other land in which he performed, Alan Knott gave an impeccable display of wicket-keeping of the highest order, determined and aggressive Test-class batsmanship and a demonstration of his faith in his beliefs, in himself and in his fellow man.

Off the field, Alan Knott was something of an introvert of quiet and friendly mien. In action in a match, the true steel of his character emerged in the diving, rolling catch or in the batting charge that disturbed a bowler's length and equilibrium.

Knott the wicket-keeper had his own ideas about the job. Nurtured in a school that placed pace and seam ahead of spin, he saw no visible reason to stand up to the stumps other than for the genuine slow bowler. For medium pace and up, Knott stood back. His argument was that very few stumpings were ever made by his Kent and England predecessor Godfrey Evans off the fast-medium bowling of Alec Bedser and that any snick off a seam bowler would carry sufficiently to be taken when standing back — and with more surety and comfort and less chance of converting a possible catch into unwanted byes. Knott was of the opinion that to stand up to medium-fast and fast bowlers was sheer foolhardiness and that wicket-keepers who did so risked unnecessary finger injuries while gaining scant advantage in the matter of extra dismissals.

If he had not become one of the greatest Test wicket-keepers of his time, Alan Knott could probably have become the world's best soccer goalie. Although he may have lacked the required inherent athletic quality of a top footballer, he certainly possessed application, verve and above all else, split-second reflex anticipation. His ability to change direction after having already committed himself was truly stunning and he was frequently seen diving after and catching a ball that already seemed destined to elude him. Knott was sometimes almost wraith-like in the way he moved.

A natural 'keeper, unorthodox in many ways, Knott took his weight on his toes like Evans. Former England bowler Mike Selvey, who toured India, Sri Lanka and Australia with Knott in 1976–77, once wrote in *Wisden Cricket Monthly* (November 1985): 'The little man's keeping has seen a torrent of adjectives from the realms of fantasy — elfin, impish, puckish — and they fit him perfectly, from his features to his demeanour.'

Highly respected among his colleagues for his great ability, Knott was also known for his eccentricity in style of play and manner of dress. He exercised incessantly when on the field — bending and stretching to keep fit and supple (Knott said he was not a natural athlete and needed to work at it). He covered as much of his body as possible to ward off draughts and the sun, with his shirt collar up and with sticking plaster on his cuffs in place of buttons to make for greater freedom of movement. Knott also wound tape around his pads to prevent injury if a pad should slip round. The list of eccentricities goes on: health-food fanatic; ever-present handkerchief dangling at the ready from hip pocket; touching the bails when batting; warming his hands in boiling water before taking the field.

'Knotty' was superb standing back but when he did move up to the stumps, he was equally as brilliant, particularly when 'keeping to his Kent and England mate, left-arm spinner 'Deadly' Derek Underwood. The Knott-Underwood partnership was prolific and always entertaining, as was the Ames-Freeman partnership between the wars. Knott's taking of the ball was quick and neat; his stumping like a striking cobra.

As a youngster with Kent in the 1960s, Alan Knott was a reasonably orthodox-looking batsman but as the years went by, he altered his method and became a front-on player, inelegant but supremely effective. His main attributes were unrelenting concentration and as keen an eye as any batsman has possessed. A player who genuinely seemed to enjoy facing up to the thunderbolts of Lillee and Thomson, he was, because of his fleetness of foot, just as much at home against the Indian spin quartet of Chandrasekhar, Bedi, Prasanna and Venkataraghavan, who had more leaden-footed batsman all at sea for a decade or so. His batting was sometimes quite outrageous and impudent. His 92 in 135 minutes versus Australia at the Oval in 1972 included 17 fours and was an innings in which he delighted in unmercifully hammering the swing bowling of Bob Massie. Massie had destroyed England in an earlier Test at Lord's with 16 wickets in the match but after this beating from Knott, Massie hardly took another Test wicket. Knott scored five Test hundreds — among 'keepers, only Ames has done better with eight centuries.

Alan Knott may not be classed as the most outstanding England wicket-keeper since the Second World War (there was little between him and Bob Taylor, for instance), but he was without any inkling of a doubt the best England wicket-keeper-batsman (in the true sense of the expression) since Leslie Ames.

The recently deceased Jim Laker, only bowler to ever take 10 wickets in a Test innings, claimed that Knott's understudy on many tours for England was 'the finest wicket-keeper I have ever seen'. Laker's own playing career included a sighting at close quarters of such notable stumpers as Don Tallon, Godfrey Evans and Johnny Waite. Alan Knott has himself been quoted as admitting that Robert William Taylor of Derbyshire and England, who spent so many years in the Kentish 'keeper's shadow as far as Test cricket was concerned, was the far better all-round wicket-keeper. It was really

This one got away: Knott makes a grand attempt but fails to catch Australia's Jeff Thomson off the bowling of Chris Old at Perth in 1974–75.

only Knott's far superior scoring ability that kept him in the England side and Taylor on the outside for so many years.

It was only when Knott decided to join up with Kerry Packer's World Series Cricket in 1977 that Bob Taylor was given some sort of an extended run in the England team. Before 1977–78 Taylor, five years Knott's senior, had only played in a single Test when touring as second-string to New Zealand in 1971. After two seasons in World Series Cricket in Australia, Knott returned and Taylor was again pushed to the sidelines. Then came the 1981–82 unofficial tour of South Africa by an England XI, and Knott was banned from Test cricket for a three-year period and was not again selected. Taylor was again brought into the England team and took his opportunity to raise his number of dismissals to 174 (167 caught, 7 stumped) in 57 Tests, and was still keeping wicket for England as late as 1984 when he was almost 43.

In 496 first-class matches between 1960 and his retirement at the close of the 1984 season, Bob Taylor also broke all previous records for the number of dismissals in a career. The following Test wicket-keepers have 1000 dismissals or more in all first-class cricket:

(Qualification: 1000 dismissals)		**Caught**	**Stumped**	**Total**
R W Taylor	(1960 to 1984)	1471	175	1646
J T Murray	(1952 to 1975)	1270	257	1527
H Strudwick	(1902 to 1927)	1215	253	1468
A P E Knott	(1965 to 1984)	1211	133	1344
H R Butt	(1890 to 1912)	971	291	1262
J H Board	(1891 to 1915)	852	354	1206
H Elliott	(1920 to 1947)	904	302	1206
J M Parks	(1949 to 1976)	1089	93	1182
L E G Ames	(1926 to 1951)	703	418	1121
G Duckworth	(1923 to 1947)	751	339	1090
J G Binks	(1955 to 1969)	895	176	1071
T G Evans	(1939 to 1969)	816	250	1066
R W Tolchard	(1965 to 1983)	912	125	1037
W L Cornford	(1921 to 1947)	656	344	1000

All the abovementioned were England players. Other wicket-keepers who did not play in Tests but who claimed 1000 or dismissals in first-class cricket are: F H Huish (Kent), D Hunter (Yorkshire), B Taylor (Essex), R Booth (Yorkshire and Worcestershire), H W Stephenson (Somerset), A Long (Surrey), G O Dawkes (Leicestershire and Derbyshire).

Many sound judges regarded Bob Taylor as not only the most accomplished wicket-keeper in England during the 1970s and 1980s, but as the best then available in the world. Some even rate him the best of all time and he must at least be on a short list of the greatest. For a long time there was only his county performances to judge him by but when Knott decided to stabilise his financial future by joining the Packer venture, Taylor gradually became known as the sounder if less demonstrative of England's two wicket-keeping geniuses of the day.

Bob Taylor bought his wicket-keeping gloves from the sports shop of former Australian stumper Bert Oldfield and initially modelled his method on former England 'keeper Keith Andrew. Taylor was the last of the purists and certainly no back-stopper in the contemporary vogue. A perfectionist and an unassuming but firm competitor, Taylor was in style and method reminiscent of the straight-forward, no-nonsense 'keepers of the 1920s and 1930s — like Strudwick, Oldfield and Ames.

One marked similarity Taylor had with the pre-war stumpers was that, unlike Knott and other 'moderns', he could, when the tactics of the game and the conditions warranted, be seen hovering right up at the stumps for medium-paced seam bowling in county matches for Derbyshire and in Tests. Taylor even stood up to England's rather sharp left-arm seamer John Lever in Pakistan in 1977–78. In the first Test at Lahore, he caught Javed Miandad brilliantly off a ball the batsman chopped down hard and which just touched the under

The always poised and ready Bob Taylor of Derbyshire and England claimed more victims than any other wicket-keeper in history.

edge of the bat outside the off stump. If Taylor had been standing back, it would not even have been regarded as a chance.

Taylor was always a wicket-keeper, starting his chosen career as a schoolboy aged nine. At 16 he was playing for Staffordshire in the Minor Counties league. Alan Knott had early ambitions of being a fast bowler but because of his slight build turned to spin. He only began to keep wicket after joining the Kent ground staff as a slow bowler.

Although nowhere near the same class as Knott as a run-scorer, Taylor was an effective late-order left-handed batsman who lost little in comparison with wicket-keepers from other countries. His Test match batting *pièce de résistance* was a six-hour vigil versus Australia at Adelaide in 1978–79 that brought 97 runs and ensured England's fourth victory in a series won 5–1 (he was out brilliantly caught on the leg-side by Australia's 'keeper, Kevin Wright). In his 57 Tests, Taylor scored 1156 runs at 16.28 an innings.

Throughout his long career, Taylor remained a performer whose professional pride came first and foremost. He was his own severest critic and Taylor's sense of responsibility demanded that his craft be perfectly executed in the interests of his team. A missed catch or stumping was in his view tantamount to a criminal act. Bob Taylor was the last of the traditionalists to play in Test cricket. The trend now favours the super slips fieldsman in gauntlets and pads who is also a reliable run-getter, primarily, it seems, because of the needs of the one-day limited overs game. Hopefully, the trend will be reversed and the true art of wicket-keeping will again be consistently witnessed in international cricket.

During the Knott-Taylor regime, few other English wicket-keepers could expect any chance of gaining a Test cap. One who did was the quietly efficient Leicestershire stumper Roger William Tolchard, whose nimble-footed batting saw him picked in four Tests in India in 1976–77 when he was travelling as Alan Knott's deputy. However, Tolchard was never chosen for England as a wicket-keeper.

Yorkshireman David Leslie Bairstow was an amptly proportioned, red-haired, fiery and enthusiastic 'keeper, deceivingly acrobatic for a man of his build. Taken to Australia as Bob Taylor's back-up in 1978–79, Bairstow was preferred to the senior stumper in the one-day internationals, for his robust wicket-keeping and for his belligerent batting (he is only the second Yorkshire 'keeper to score 1000 runs in a season). Bairstow eventually got a Test chance versus West Indies on his home ground, Headingley, in 1980 and played in the Centenary Test against Australia at Lord's the same season. But his performance dropped in the West Indies the following winter and the popular 'Stan' Bairstow had to be content with his four Tests for England and 13 dismissals (12 caught, 1 stumped).

Until he was replaced by his understudy after the disastrous

1985—86 England tour to the West Indies, the agile Paul Rupert Downton had enjoyed a fairly lucrative run of 26 Tests and 66 dismissals (61 caught, 5 stumped). Short in stature, Downton can occasionally be seen standing up to medium-paced bowlers and, in England, stands back only about fifteen yards to the faster stuff. As Middlesex 'keeper for some years, he gained considerable experience standing up to the county and England 'spin-twins' John Emburey and Phil Edmonds. In India in 1984—85, Downton executed the first stumping by an England 'keeper in three years when he claimed opening bat A D Gaekwad at Delhi.

Downton started his career as a teenager with Kent. With Knott still in residence, his opportunities were few and far between but he did get a round trip to Pakistan and New Zealand in 1977—78 as Taylor's second-string. Downton then waited for Taylor to retire from Test cricket and got his first Test chance during the 1980—81 series in the West Indies. He has sometimes batted with rare courage and determination, particularly against the awesome West Indies speed attack in England in 1984, without ever seriously challenging for the appellation 'wicket-keeper/batsman'.

In the home series of 1986, Bruce Nicholas French of Nottinghamshire, Downton's number two on the previous winter's tour to the Caribbean, was picked to keep wicket against New Zealand and India. It remains to be seen whether he will continue in the job in the face of competition from other young glovemen like Yorkshire's Steven John Rhodes (who in 1985—86 had a fine tour as wicket-keeper and batsman with the England B team in Sri Lanka) and Surrey's Clifton James Richards (taken to India and Sri Lanka in 1981—82 as Taylor's reserve and picked again for the 1986—87 trip to Australia).

There are others who may soon be knocking on the door but there seems to be no-one in sight destined to match Alan Knott as a genuine wicket-keeper/batsman or Bob Taylor as a specialist wicket-keeper of the old school. They remain two of the best ever to play for England and certainly two of the grandest wicket-keepers ever to appear in international cricket. Incidentally, Bob Taylor made a brief and nostalgic return to Test cricket, versus New Zealand at Lord's in 1986, as one of three substitutes after French was injured while batting. Taylor, 45, took over the gloves from batsman Bill Athey after two overs until replaced by Bobby Parks (son of Jim Parks).

18

Top of the tree?

'...comparing 'keepers from different eras is a hazardous occupation'
— Godfrey Evans

In his recently published *Wicket-Keepers of the World*, Godfrey Evans, one of England's foremost gentlemen of the gloves, expresses his trepidation at categorising wicket-keepers from different eras. He does, however, discuss some of his own personal favourites and names, among others, Alan Knott, Bob Taylor, Rodney Marsh and Don Tallon as representative of all that is best in the craft.

Naming the paramount international 'keeper of all time is indeed a hazardous task and help must be sought from some of the eminent judges of the past who were on the spot, so to speak, to note the merits and demerits of individual stumpers. And who better to consult than the players themselves and in particular the wicket-keepers who have graced international cricket down the years.

The first true international-class specialist wicket-keepers were Australia's Jack Blackham and England's Dick Pilling. Blackham, by dispensing with the hitherto customary long-stop and relying on his own skill to take the ball, revolutionised Test wicket-keeping. During a lengthy career of almost two decades he was, according to observers of his day who include W G Grace and George Giffen, the nonpareil of the 1800s. By all reports, Pilling was not very far behind Blackham in skill but only appeared in eight Tests, although he built up a formidable reputation in other first-class cricket. South Africa's Ernest Halliwell was another stumper who impressed in early matches for his country and must be mentioned in any short list of the best. Blackham, with his talent as a stumper and his remarkable longevity as a top player, must get the vote for 'greatest international stumper of the 19th century'.

The 'Golden Years' from the mid-1890s to the start of the First World War produced some outstanding 'keeping exponents. Australia had J J Kelly and Hanson Carter, England had the perennial Dick Lilley, followed by Strudwick and 'Tiger' Smith while South Africa produced Percy Sherwell, the first great stumper to master the intricacies of 'keeping to googly bowling.

Most players and writers of note seem unanimous in their praise of Australian Bert Oldfield as the most outstanding between-wars stumper. Oldfield himself rated England's Herbert Strudwick as his own model wicket-keeper from the pre-First World War period. There could be few better judges than the Australian master of the gloves so, for the Golden Years before the time of Oldfield, England's Herbert Strudwick must get the honours.

In the between-wars period, Bert Oldfield takes his rightful place, followed by such notables as George Duckworth and Leslie Ames vying for England's number one spot — with Ames perhaps getting the vote as the grandest 'keeper/batsman in history; another grand wicket-keeper/batsman is South Africa's 'Jock' Cameron; and stumpers like Ken James (New Zealand) and Ivan Barrow (West Indies).

Among those eminent playing observers of the time who rate Oldfield above all other between-wars 'keepers, we have such personalities as Sir Donald Bradman and Australia's greatest bowler of the period, Bill O'Reilly. Oldfield's opponents seemed equally impressed and there can be no quibble in any quarter if his name goes down as the best of the era — and is placed on another short list of candidates for the 'best of all time'.

Because of a dramatic increase in number of Tests played (and number of Test-playing countries), post-Second World War cricket is best divided into two eras — 1945 to 1965 and 1965 to the present day.

For the first period, the prime contenders are Godfrey Evans (England), Don Tallon (Australia), Wally Grout (Australia) and Johnny Waite (South Africa). Alan Knott was Evans's successor for Kent and England and was a great admirer of his predecessor. In his *Stumper's View*, Knott recalls watching Godfrey Evans performing at the age of 45 during an International Cavaliers tour of Jamaica and Barbados and comments that '"Godders", at 45, was still lightning fast.'

Evans, with his blacksmithy forearms and bustling ebullience must rate among the finest dozen or so 'keepers of all time but he himself bowed to Australia's Don Tallon — 'the best 'keeper I have seen'. Evans writes in *Wicket-Keepers of the World*: 'Forget Knott, Marsh or Taylor; forget Engineer, Waite or Oldfield; forget Murray, Maddocks or Langley. Magnificent wicket-keepers all of them, but Don Tallon, the unobtrusive artist from Queensland, stands supreme.' In his *Rattle of the Stumps*, published in 1954, Bert Oldfield says that when it came to picking his own successor as Australia's stumper, he regarded Tallon as 'the outstanding choice for the post' and could not understand why the young challenger was omitted from the 1938 team to England. Colin McCool of New South Wales, Queensland and Australia probably bowled more balls with Tallon as his stumper than anyone else. The Australian leg-spinner thought Evans was over-rated. For him, Tallon was the greatest, as a wicket-keeper and as a man: 'If you disliked Don Tallon there was something wrong with you.' Don Tallon must get the vote for best 'keeper for the first 20 years of the post-war era.

For the 1965 to 1986 era, the list of possibles reads: Alan Knott and Bob Taylor (England), Rodney Marsh (Australia), Farokh Engineer and Syed Kirmani (India), Wasim Bari (Pakistan), Jeff Dujon (West Indies) and Amal Silva (Sri Lanka). South Africa's livewire Ray Jennings is left out in the cold because of his country's isolation from world cricket. Engineer was certainly one of the outstanding wicket-keeper/batsmen, to rank alongside Ames, Cameron and Waite, but neither he nor Kirmani could quite match Knott, Taylor, Marsh and Wasim Bari. Jeff Dujon is another fine batsman wicket-keeper and probably the current world best on experience and ability. Alan Knott, because he *was* England's first-choice ahead of Taylor in 95 Tests, should get the nod but Taylor (and Pakistan's Wasim Bari) is a specialist of the highest quality and must rank among the top 10 'keepers in history.

Rodney Marsh can certainly not be left out of the reckoning. A poll conducted by Australia's *Cricketer* magazine in 1984 to select the best contemporary wicket-keeper called for the opinions of cricket writers and former Test players. In an exercise somewhat weighted in the number of Australians whose advice was sought, Marsh won hands down ahead of Taylor, Kirmani, Knott and Wasim Bari, in that order. Such august personalities as Bill Ponsford, Bobby Simpson, Arthur Morris, Doug Walters and Ian Johnson all voted for their own home-grown Australian hero. So too did David Frith, editor of *Wisden Cricket Monthly*, but other English writers like the highly respected John Arlott and Christopher Martin-Jenkins (editor of *Cricketer International*) placed Bob Taylor firmly in number one position. Another who chose Taylor was the noted West Indies authority Tony Cozier while John Woodock (*The Times* and sometime editor of *Wisden*) was one of only three (out of 35 panellists) to vote for Alan Knott. The writer's own view is that in terms of traditional, orthodox wicket-keeping, Taylor it must be, but in terms of the modern method that places almost total emphasis on pace, Marsh is the man. The answer might be to call it a 'dead heat' — Rodney Marsh *and* Bob Taylor.

Our short-list now reads: pre-1900 J M Blackham (Australia); 1900 to 1914 (and a little beyond) H Strudwick (England); 1920 to 1939 W A Oldfield (Australia); 1945 to 1965 D Tallon (Australia); 1966 to 1986 R W Marsh (Australia) and R W Taylor (England). Take your pick for the 'Best of All Time'.

And for the best from each Test-playing country, how about: England: Taylor; Australia: a dead-heat between Oldfield and Tallon; South Africa: Cameron; New Zealand: Wadsworth; West Indies: Dujon; India: Kirmani; Pakistan: Wasim Bari; Sri Lanka: Amal Silva. The best wicket-keeper/batsman must be Leslie Ames of England with Marsh, Engineer, Cameron, Waite and possibly Lindsay, Dujon and Walcott and Knott challenging as international wicket-keepers who were genuine Test-class batsmen.

19

Run in, pick up and throw

'The essence of good fielding is to start before the ball is hit, and to pick up and return to the top of the bails, by one continuous action'
— Rev. James Pycroft (1851)

'Patsy' Hendren, one of England's most illustrious between-wars batsmen and a grand fielder, contends in his *Big Cricket*: 'No day in the field can really be long and boring, provided the fielder takes an interest in his work.' Here speaks one of Test cricket's greatest enthusiasts, a happy-natured player who always gave 100 per cent to the task at hand. There have been many more like him down the years and to chronicle the deeds of all the fine fielders who have appeared in international cricket would take a dozen volumes and even then some important deed might still be missed.

Down the years and through the many Tests that have been played since the first at Melbourne in 1877, there have been a number of players whose skill at fielding has been so astounding as to place them far above their team-mates, and to carve for them a special niche in the annals of international cricket.

Three of the most famous fielders in history were of the canine species and members of the famous Grace cricketing household in Gloucestershire during the mid-1850s. The Grace hounds were named Noble (a retriever), Don and Ponto (two pointers). Perhaps some sixth sense prompted Dr Henry Mills Grace to call two of his dogs after *future* Australian captains. The three Grace cricket hounds were an essential part of the family's back garden practice and it was said that Ponto would, 'with classical instincts', stand at mid-off, watch the ball pitch outside off-stump, and be seen dashing towards extra-cover before the batsman played his stroke!

Perhaps the most spectacular and eye-catching fielders have been those who did patrol duty in the covers — one of the 'mid-field' positions that includes mid-off, mid-on, the various cover permutations, square-leg (if not placed right on the boundary) and short mid-wicket.

England's legendary 'Golden Age' smiter of the ball Gilbert Jessop was such a wonderful cover-point fielder that inexperienced batsmen were warned by their captains never to run when the ball was close to Jessop, unless it looked to be a certain two, and then to run only a single 'as fast as your legs will carry you'. According to S M J Woods, who played for both Australia and England, Jessop was 'the best cover-point ever seen to start with' and 'people were afraid to run if a ball went within fifteen yards of him'.

Sprinting in towards the wicket-keeper's end to take the ball, the ace England cover sometimes stunned onlookers by throwing like a flash to the bowler's end *without turning his head*. He did not throw directly at the stumps unless there was no other way of gaining a run-out, preferring instead to place the ball on the full into the wicket-keeper's or fielder's hands, just above the bails. As Jessop was also a fast bowler of some merit, as well as the most devastatingly quick scorer of all time, he was something of a one-man team. When he went in to bat after first fielding, the great Gloucestershire and England hitter had often already saved 30 or 40 runs (some say as much as 50).

Before Jessop, one of the most notable fielders was the mighty W G Grace's older brother, Dr Edward Mills Grace. Known affectionately as 'The Coroner', E M Grace was a brilliant attacking batsman and a deceiving bowler of underhand lobs. He was also an amazing

Gilbert Jessop of Gloucestershire and England, the first of the great cover-point fieldsmen.

fielder at point, sometimes standing less than eight yards from the bat even when a hitter was in and letting nothing past him, be it in the air or on the ground. E M Grace was also a swift and sure mover: the first time he fielded when A E Stoddart (captain of England at cricket and rugby) was batting, the older Grace was reputed to have taken the ball right off the bat and handed it to the wicket-keeper.

E M Grace's great prowess at point was in the long tradition established by the agile Robert Carpenter, a grand batsman and a strikingly active fielder who went with the first-ever English touring team to the United States and Canada in 1859. In America, Carpenter at point and 'Old Tom' Hayward, another leading batsman of the mid-1800s, at cover-point formed a deadly combination that dazzled the opposition. The wily Carpenter would lure an inexperienced batsman to destruction by letting the ball through for Hayward to run-out the unwary batsman.

When Test cricket began in the 18th century, England produced a series of fine mid-field experts. Lord Harris, England's captain for its first home Test at the Oval in 1880, was a swift runner and marvellous thrower. Lancashire's little jack-in-the-box Johnny Briggs, guileful slow left-hander and aggressive right-handed batsman, was another fast-moving cover-point. So too was Yorkshire left-arm spinner Bobby Peel while A N 'Monkey' Hornby, Lancashire and England opening batsman, was magnificent anywhere. W G Grace's own favourite opening partner, Arthur Shrewsbury (the Jack Hobbs of his day), was in his early years a grand performer in the deep and later an excellent point. At no time, however, could Shrewsbury be prompted to remove the cap that covered his bald pate.

Of Jesssop's contemporaries, Stanley Jackson, Yorkshire and England captain, was a keen cover-point, as was Leicestershire's Albert Knight, noted for his rather belligerent throw to the wicket-keeper. Gilbert Jessop started a tradition of brilliant cover fielding that has been carried forward in English cricket right through to the present day.

Master batsman Jack Hobbs was as fluidly effective in his run in, pick up and throw as he was in his marvellous batsmanship. Highly adept at luring batsmen to their destruction, Hobbs effected 15 run-outs during the 1911–12 MCC tour of Australia. His method was all psychology: at the start of an opponent's innings, Hobbs would field rather deep at cover-point. If a batsman played the ball gently in his direction and called for a quick single, Hobbs would respond slowly, move to the ball and eventually return it to the bowler. For a couple of overs Hobbs would let the pattern run, giving away the odd single. Then, when the batsman again played his little pat shot into the covers and started on his run, without any warning Hobbs would move like a flash, even before the ball had properly left the bat, and throw down the wicket with the bamboozled batsman well out of his crease.

Hobbs, like Jessop, did not gamble too frequently on hitting the stumps, only aiming at them when the batsman looked likely to reach his crease before the wicket-keeper or fielder could lift the bails.

Between the wars, Middlesex amateur Walter Robins took over Hobbs's cover-point crown. A quick mover to the ball, his judgement was exemplary and his back-handed pick-up, ready for the swing around and throw, was superb. The alert Robins was also noted for his great verve in the field, an attitude bordering on outright hostility that would have found favour in the present day when few mediocre fieldsmen are picked for internationals.

Had Percy Chapman not spent so much time making miraculous catches close to the wicket, the Kent and England captain of the 1920s and 1930s might have gone down in the history books as the finest cover fieldsman of them all. Chapman's long arms, long legs and seemingly inexhaustible vigour were his prime assets as a dazzling fielder who was loved by crowds and feared by England's opponents. He was Learie Constantine's favourite fielder, which says a lot when one considers Constantine himself might be handed the crown for finest fielder of all time.

The ever-increasing number of Test matches played each year since the Second World War, coupled with a growing emphasis on limited overs cricket, has resulted in a noticeable raising of all-round fielding standards at international level. Yet there remain a select few whose performances in the field have placed them ahead of their fellows. For England, the cover fielding tradition was carried on by Cyril Washbrook, Len Hutton's Lancashire-born post-war opening partner, who was as quick in his reactions and decisive in his throwing as most who came before him. Washbrook was one of the fastest runners ever to appear for England and few batsmen attempted a run when the ball was hit in his direction.

Another of Hutton's post-war partners, the Nottinghamshire batsman Reg Simpson, was also a commendable cover-point and a fast-running and reliable deep fielder. Imperious Sussex and England captain of the 1960s Ted Dexter was another highly mobile cover-point, as was one of his later successors in the 1970s, Mike Denness of Kent, a particularly athletic fielder who set a wonderful example for his team.

The two outstanding English 'moderns' in the 'glamour' positions of cover and cover-point have been Derek Randall of Nottinghamshire and the former England captain, David Gower.

Randall has become known as something of a 'clown prince' of international cricket, but there is no sign of the jester in his electric-heeled fielding. Amazingly fast and accurate, he has at all times provided inspiration for his team-mates. Randall is ever on the move and by the time the bowler delivers the ball, is running almost full-tilt, ready to swiftly change direction, cut off the ball and hurl the stumps down in one swooping motion.

David Gower is a beautifully balanced and poised natural athlete and possibly one of the greatest all-round fielders in history. Hidden behind his casual manner is a cat cruising the cover region awaiting a chance to leap on its prey. Gower possesses running speed, super-safe hands and a strong and accurate throwing arm. Former Australian captain Bobby Simpson is most impressed by Gower's 'ability to read angles'. When the need arises, Gower can field at slip, short point or silly mid-on with the same safety and skill as displayed in the covers.

Of England's other current Test players, Northamptonshire's Allan Lamb is an unusually constructive fielder in the rather un-glamorous position of third man, as attacking in his fielding attitude as he is with bat in hand. Most of the present England team are above-average fielders, not too surprising in an age of compressed cricket where runs saved in a limited overs match are as valuable as runs scored in the conventional manner.

Australia did not lack good mid-fielders in its early days in inter-national cricket. Although only a shade over five feet tall (152 cm), little Syd Gregory was in the Jessop-Hobbs class as a superlative cover point. In *Great Bowlers and Fielders*, C B Fry praises Gregory's 'electrifying pick-ups and unerring accuracy' and goes on to contend that Australia had no finer fieldsman in the late 1800s.

Syd Gregory had an unusual throwing technique: he was a below-the-shoulder thrower, whose pace of return was as much due to wrist work as to arm swing. Fry described it as 'more of a flick than a full-blooded throw'.

'Barndoor' Alec Bannerman, obdurate opening batsman in Aus-tralia's earliest Test teams, was equally famous for his fielding at mid-off. It was Alec Bannerman's catch that dismissed W G Grace in the England-Australia Test at the Oval in 1882, turning the match for his country and helping give birth to the Ashes tradition. Grace himself commended Alec Bannerman for his work at mid-off and for his ability at cover-point while Bannerman's team-mate George Giffen notes in his *With Bat and Ball*: 'At his best he was one of the most brilliant fields Australia has had . . .'.

Bannerman faded somewhat as a fielder in his later years. When the Australian team visited Philadelphia on its way home from England in 1893, a correspondent in *The American Cricketer*, referring also to the previous tour of 1878, wrote of the famed Australian mid-off: 'Bannerman has added to his weight in 15 years somewhat at the expense of his agility and power at mid-off, which was then pheno-menal and is still admirable.' Philadelphia, incidentally, beat the full

Australian Test XI by an innings and 68 runs in 1893 and possessed a fielding side of some excellence.

Bannerman's older brother Charles Bannerman was an eminently more adventurous batsman for Australia than Alec and a competent all-round fielder who could stand in any position. Other pioneer Australian Test players to impress as fielders were Billy Midwinter, who excelled in the deep and in a later period, Harry Trott at point, fast bowler Ernie Jones at mid-off and skipper Joe Darling, also at mid-off. Frank Laver, later an Australian tour manager, was a tall and strong all-rounder and another who made a name for himself at point, as did Darling's successor as Australian captain, Monty Noble. During the period before and just after the First World War, Charlie Macartney (the 'Governor-General' of Australian stroke-players) was another noted mid-off fieldsman.

Between the two world wars Australia produced a cover fieldsman to emulate little Syd Gregory and rank alongside England's Jessop and Hobbs in speed and skill. Clarence 'Nip' Pellew was as nifty a performer as his nickname suggests and together with little Tommy Andrews caused something of a sensation in the covers under Warwick Armstrong in England in 1921. Andrews later became more famous for his close to the wicket fielding but Pellew remained the superb cover-point of his day, rivalled only by Hobbs himself.

In *Warwick Armstrong's Australians*, Ronald Mason describes the young Pellew as 'a dashing sandy-haired fellow with a rather rakish fair moustache, he had the women spectatorship aswoon and the male complement on their feet with some of the cleanest and most brilliant out-fielding in the history of Test cricket'.

Commenting on the work done by Australia's two ace cover fielders of the 1920s, former New South Wales batsman Eric P Barbour writes in *The Making of a Cricketer*: 'In watching Pellew and Andrews at cover-point I was not so much struck by the difficult saves they effected, as by the large range of strokes they stopped with apparent ease.' As was the case with Gregory, Jessop and Hobbs, it was a combination of anticipation and fleetness of foot that made Pellew great. He covered more ground than any mere mortal fieldsman and like all expert fielders at cover, mid-off or third man, was able to gather and throw in one easy-flowing sideways action. Ray Robinson records in *From the Boundary* that Nip Pellew 'fielded the ball at such breakneck speed that often the heels were ripped from his boots'. A contemporary of Pellew and Andrews who also made a grand impression as a cover fieldsman was the alert Johnny Taylor, a spectacular runner and a pin-point accurate thrower.

The mighty Donald Bradman was not only the best batsman in the world throughout his playing career (and the undisputed best of all time), but a superb fielder whose anticipation made him, according to at least one notable judge, a better fielder at cover than England's

Walter Robins. Bradman was also a marvellous fielder in the deep and, close up, his unparalleled cricketing brain made him an ever-present menace in the eyes of opposition batsmen. But it was genius in the covers that put him in the same bracket as Jessop, Hobbs, Syd Gregory and the live-wire West Indian Learie Constantine.

As captain, Bradman was a master at placing his field. His tactics in England in 1948 when relying almost entirely on pace were something of an unparalleled spectacle. On unresponsive turf and when the shine was off the ball, he would close all the major scoring gaps by standing mid-on and mid-off just a few yards behind the bowler's wicket. Any ball driven straight was stopped before a run could even be contemplated. There was also a man at cover, another at mid-wicket and a square-leg (as well as third man and deep fine-leg). Lindwall could then bowl with just one slip and a gully and batsmen like Hutton, Compton and Edrich, competent as they were, could do little about it. When the new ball arrived, Bradman reverted the field to its attacking formation, packing the slips and leg-slip areas with fieldsmen in catching positions in the 'Carmody' formation — named after the West Australian captain Keith Carmody who sometimes used as many as eight men in catching positions behind the stumps.

Australia was not short of mid-field practitioners during the post-Second World War period either. In its outfielding, Bradman's team of the 1940s was one of the most organised teams ever seen and no one impressed more in England in 1948 than 19-year-old Neil Harvey. Former Australian captain Bobby Simpson for one regards Harvey as the most brilliant fielder he has seen and many other sound judges rate Harvey as a leading contender for the tag 'best of all time'.

As a left-handed shot-making batsman, Neil Harvey could be devastating; as a cover-point, his performances bore about them an aura of magic, of sleight-of-hand. Simpson writes in *Cricket — the Australian Way*: 'They said in first-class cricket that if Harvey fielded the ball and you were out of your ground... you might as well take it easy. There was no point in hustling, for it was simply a question of whether he hit the stumps or missed. If he hit them you were out, if he missed you were in, but he rarely missed by more than a foot or two.' In the outfield, Neil Harvey's anticipation was one of his greatest assets, bordering on the uncanny, and later in his career he became as expert a slip fieldsman as any produced by his country. His throwing was magnificent, rivalled among Australians in later years only by Norman O'Neill, Les Favell and Ross Edwards.

Norm O'Neill was Australia's next cover-fielding star and almost as brilliant as Harvey. The athletic and handsome O'Neill provided a grand sight as he raced in from cover to cut off the ball and return it with pin-point accuracy, either right over the bails to the waiting wicket-keeper or fielder, or to shatter the stumps. He was one of the most spectacular fieldsmen of the 1960s and like so many fine Australian fielders who threw with such stunning effect, was a baseball player of note (Neil Harvey was another). With his good looks, thunderous batsmanship and wonderful fielding, O'Neill would have become a star to rival the likes of West Indies' Viv Richards if he had played in the current era of televised cricket.

The fielding of Norm O'Neill's Australian XI successor in the covers might best be described as stylish. Paul Sheahan was an elegant if inconsistent player of strokes and a cover-point who moved to the ball with speed and panache. As a batsman, Sheahan never quite made it at Test level; as a cover fieldsman he will always be remembered.

In contrast to Sheahan, the up-and-at-'em Doug Walters scored heavily in Tests *and* fielded with controlled excellence, when patrolling the covers and when taking sizzling catches close up. Walters was a wonderful all-round fieldsman and Australian writer, broadcaster and former Sheffield Shield player Ian Brayshaw once commented that in his youth, Walters was 'so fast in the field that the only thing he could not do was keep wicket to his own bowling'. A highly manoeuvrable performer, Walters went low to the ground in his pick-up and threw fast and flat without straightening, thus saving that split-second which could mean the difference between a run out and a batsman getting safely home. Brayshaw describes Walters's returns as 'rifling in as flat as tacks' and that it was not unusual for him to hit the stumps side-on.

Walters was a member of Ian Chappell's magnificent fielding combination of the 1960s and 1970s and was not the only adept cover fieldsman in the Australian Test squad. Ross Edwards was the real star in that position and as accomplished a cover-point as most who have played Test cricket. He started life as a wicket-keeper and acted as Rod Marsh's deputy on a couple of tours but in Tests this remarkable self-made cricketer was seldom seen anywhere else but 20 or so yards on the off-side, and covering as much ground as two competent fielders.

When Ross Edwards realised that with Rod Marsh around he could never hope to attain Western Australia or Australia colours as a wicket-keeper, he resolved to make the grade as a batsman and fielder. He practised like a demon in the nets to improve his run-getting powers — and succeeded. As a fielder, he first tried the slips but there was too much competition and he did not feel quite at home there. So outfielding it was to be and the determined Edwards began a gruelling training schedule to teach himself the art of running, gathering and throwing. He even set up a pulley and weight system in his backyard to strengthen his throwing arm.

Following the example set some years before by South Africa's Colin Bland, Edwards worked out a routine of exercises that saw him hurling the ball at a single stump when on the run, spending many hours at his task to achieve accuracy from any angle. This was how a remarkable trier who was never a natural cricketer as batsman or fielder become one of his team's most reliable run-scorers, and probably its best cover fieldsman in Test cricket for a couple of years.

Since Edwards, Australia has produced a number of competent cover fieldsman without any one man quite approaching his high standard. The best of these has probably been the youngest of the three Chappell brothers. However, Trevor Chappell did not reach the same position of eminence as a Test batsman as his brothers Ian and Greg but was for some years a regular choice in limited overs international cricket, as much for his sparkling work in the covers as for his batting and bowling. Another batsman whose Test run-making ability did not quite match his excellence at cover was the rather unlucky Rick Darling who so frequently succumbed to blows to the head while batting.

The popularity of limited overs cricket — where the field spreads out after an initial attacking opening — has forced most Test players of the past decade to become athletically oriented in their fielding, and versatile in their ability to fill either close or deep-field positions. Among Australians, names like Greg Chappell, David Hookes, Kim Hughes and Allan Border spring readily to mind but the specialist outfielders will hopefully still remain, with none more gloriously visible than the man at cover or cover-point. There can be no better sight in cricket than a Harvey, Pellew or Edwards sprinting effortlessly to seize the ball and then trim the bails with a pluperfect throw.

Through the years, Test teams from New Zealand and India have produced cover fieldsmen of quality but few to rank with Jessop, Hobbs, Bradman or Pellew. For New Zealand, ace left-handed batsman Martin Donnelly was a grand cover-point who used his speed developed as a rugby player to good effect. Donnelly was also an able gully or close-catcher in the leg-trap. He toured England before and after the Second World War, as did another good cover-point Kiwi in stroke-laying batsman Mervyn Wallace.

New Zealand's immediate post-war skipper, Walter Hadlee, was an inspiration in the field and players in his team, like the wonderful all-rounder John Reid and master left-handed batsman Bert Sutcliffe, were safe fielders in any position. Of the later New Zealand players, two who shone particularly bright in the covers were Victor Pollard and Barry Sinclair, both of whom appeared in Test cricket during the 1960s.

India's first touring side to visit England in 1932 merited praise for its fielding but later Test combinations were, rather unfortunately, more notable for their slackness in the field. Naoomal Jeoomal and S M H Colah were two of the 1932 players who rated mention in

Wisden for their ground fielding while the energetic Jahangir Khan impressed with his speedy long-distance throws. Colah was quite brilliant anywhere and Naoomal was a valuable all-rounder who could bat, bowl, field and keep wicket with skill.

A few excellent cover fieldsman have appeared for India and none was better than middle-order batsman of the 1940s and 1950s, Hemchandra Adhikari. 'Hemmu' Adhikari was rated favourably against such cover-fielding giants as Harvey and Washbrook and impressed with his speed to the ball and his ability to alter direction at the last moment. Adhikari's sense of balance was remarkable and he threw down the stumps at the bowler's end far more frequently than most cover fieldsmen. He was also self-taught and developed his skill through long hours of assiduous practice. Adhikari favoured a conventional over-arm throw to the under-arm flick used by some cover exponents.

Of India's other fine cover fieldsmen, players like the little dynamo Gul Mohammed (he had the strongest of arms), all-rounders Rusi Surti and J M Ghorpade and the unrelated Ramnath and Ghulam Parker were impressive without quite reaching Adhikari's class.

In its short Test history, Pakistan has produced a series of scintillating cover fieldsmen, from Waqar Hassan and Saeed Ahmed in the 1950s and 1960s through to Wasim Raja and Javed Miandad in the 1970s and 1980s. The nimble Asif Iqbal did great things at cover and is probably Pakistan's best all-round fielder to date.

Sri Lanka has been playing Test cricket for an even shorter time than Pakistan but has produced one outstanding cover-point in the tiny Roy Dias, a bundle of energy and skill who has stood out in a team not noted for its application in one of the most important departments of the game. However, a new-look Sri Lankan team toured Australia in 1987–88 and impressed in the field, producing at least one world-class performer in Roshan Mahanama.

Two men from widely diverging backgrounds may go down in history as the most illustrious cover fieldsmen of all. The first was born in Trinidad in 1901, the black grandson of slaves, and was an all-rounder who became acknowledged as the epitome of the West Indian cricketer — big hitter, wily bowler in many styles (starting with flat-out fast) and superlative fielder in any position. The second came into this world in the year 1938 as a member of the then privileged whites of Rhodesia (now Zimbabwe), went on to play his Tests for South Africa and gained a reputation as a classy, attacking batsman and a fieldsman who has had few peers in international cricket. The two men enjoyed a mutual genius that made them drawcards for their fielding alone. Their stories are next.

20

'Electric Heels', 'Supercat' and the 'Golden Eagle'

'Fielding at cover-point or extra-cover is, like any other branch of cricket, a matter as much of brain as brawn'

— Sir Learie Constantine

Like all great cricketers, Learie Constantine, the pre-war West Indies all-rounder supreme, treated the subject of fielding as seriously as batting and bowling. He was so brilliant as a gatherer and thrower of the ball and as a taker of unbelievable catches, that he was known as 'Electric Heels'.

R C Robertson-Glasgow writes in his *Cricket Prints*: 'Constantine has always come fresh to the cricket public, re-awakening them on each rare appearance not only by the violence of genius, but by some novelty of method, some different and startling arrangement of the eight balls in the over, some unsuspected place in the field, some unbelievable device for striking an off ball to the mid-wicket boundary.' The man who began life as a plantation overseer's son and who later became a barrister and a Baron with a seat in England's House of Lords, was a cricketing law unto himself who never allowed the confines of orthodoxy to hamper his genius. As a big hitter and a fast bowler he was superb; as a spring-heeled fielder for whom the miraculous was commonplace, he was unique.

For Sir Neville Cardus, the West Indian all-rounder was one of the famous writer's favourite cricketers: 'The movements of Constantine in the field are strange, almost primitive, in their pouncing voracity and unconscious beauty, a dynamic beauty, not one of smooth curves and relaxations.' Constantine was a phenomenal catcher off his own bowling, becoming a fieldsman the instant the ball left his hand. Cardus gave him the power to be in two places at the same time and marvelled at the West Indian's swooping work at slip: 'There are no bones in his body, only great charges and flows of energy. You cannot see some of his slip-fielding, so rapid is his action.'

It was when fielding at cover-point — the position made legend by men like Jessop, Pellew and Hobbs — that Learie Constantine was seen at his most brilliant. He was so quick in movement and reaction that it was not unknown for him to hit the base of the stumps at the batsman's end with a lightning throw and then, quick-as-a-flash, dart across to short leg and retrieve the ball for a successful shy at the bowler's wicket!

For Constantine, cover-fielding became a science comprised of anticipation, athletic running to the ball and calculated footwork in pick-up to be in perfect position for a throw to either end. In his own words, it was 'a matter as much of brain' that made him the fieldsman of his age. In his *Cricket and I*, Constantine recalls that during the lunch break of the Trinidad versus MCC match at Port-of-Spain in 1926 he rather rashly bet a friend that he would soon after lunch have the two English batsmen at the wicket, Holmes and Hammond, stranded in the middle of the pitch, 'sending each other back'.

Knowing that it would not be an easy task to trick such experienced players as the MCC pair, he carefully moved his own position from cover closer to point and asked extra-cover to move around, to leave a gap between extra-cover and mid-off. Constantine then proceeded to make himself very busy at point, all the time reinforcing that this was his true position. When the bowler eventually pitched a ball on a good length on the off-stump, the wily West Indian saw that he had his chance: '...I saw the length while it was still in the air, and almost as soon as Hammond shaped to make the stroke I was off.'

Hammond had pushed the ball to extra-cover and called his partner for a leisurely single. But before he had moved 10 yards, and when he was almost abreast of Holmes, the sprinting Constantine was on the ball. Holmes saw what was happening and hastily sent Hammond back. A startled Hammond halted in his tracks, turned and scampered back towards his crease. Constantine was by now on the pitch and, keeping pace with Hammond, held back his throw, waiting for the moment when he was certain he would hit the stumps. But fate now took over and during the race down the wicket between batsman and fielder, Hammond's bat nicked Constantine's elbow and the ball flew out of his hand! Hammond was home and safe, although the disappointed Constantine still claimed his wager, pointing out to his friend that he had not said that he would actually run out either Holmes or Hammond but merely strand them in the middle of the pitch, sending each other back!

In his book, Constantine used this story as an example of what can be accomplished by a fielder who cleverly alters his position during the bowler's run-up and that the fielding position best suited for such tactics was cover-point.

Constantine was the first of a number of outstanding West Indian cover fieldsmen. Of his pre-war contemporaries, powerful opening batsman Clifford Roach was also a dazzling performer at cover-point. Immediately after the war, Frank Worrell excelled in the position but later became as accomplished in close catching positions. Worrell was also captain of West Indies in the match versus Australia at

'Electric Heels' Sir Learie Constantine of Trinidad and West Indies in his younger days.

Brisbane in December 1960, the tied Test that may well go down in history as the greatest Test of all time. It was magnificent fielding and throwing by the West Indians that saw a match moving Australia's way turned around and converted into a thrilling climax, the first tie in Test history.

Three run outs in Australia's final innings proved the decisive factor in this amazing match. The first came when little Joe Solomon threw the stumps down from mid-wicket to dismiss Alan Davidson and break what looked to be a match-winning seventh-wicket partnership between the Australian all-rounder and his skipper Richie Benaud. The remaining two run outs occurred during a dramatic, action-filled final over bowled by the big Barbadian Wes Hall.

When Hall started the last eight-ball over of the game, Australia needed six runs to win with three wickets to fall. A leg-bye was taken off the first ball; Benaud, swinging lustily at a bouncer, was caught at the wicket off the second. Ian Meckiff joined Aussie wicket-keeper Wally Grout and fended off the third ball. The fourth went through to West Indies 'keeper Gerry Alexander but the batsmen scampered a bye and a dismissal chance was missed. Grout hit the fifth ball high in the air, Hall went for the catch but the ball bounced out of his hands and another run was taken. The crowd had by now reached a fevered pitch with just three balls to go, three runs needed and two wickets to fall. Meckiff swung hard at the next ball and it flew towards the square-leg boundary. The batsmen had already run two and were going for the third and winning run when Conrad Hunte cut the ball off and threw in superbly, low and fast. Wicket-keeper Gerry Alexander made no mistake and Grout was well out of his ground when the bails were lifted.

Lindsay Kline came in to face the last two balls, with one run needed to win. The fierce Wes Hall bore down on Australia's last man like an express train. Somehow Kline hit that thunderbolt away towards leg and the batsmen bolted to take their winning run. Like a retriever after a tennis ball, Joe Solomon, 12 yards from the stumps, swooped down one-handed and with a single stump to aim at, threw almost in the same motion. The stump went over, almost simultaneously the umpire's finger went up as the West Indians appealed to a man and Meckiff was out! The scores were level, the first tie in Test history. If Solomon had paused to take aim, Meckiff would have been home and hosed. In what has become known as the typical West Indian way, Solomon had thrown by sheer instinct and hit the wicket.

Since the days of Learie Constantine, West Indians have become known for their natural ability as fielders and the quick-fire chase, pick-up and throw and miraculous catch is as much a part of their play as is their uninhibited fast bowling and stroke-playing batsmanship. Constantine will always be accorded a special niche of honour in the West Indian fielding pantheon but there is one fairly contemporary player who must come close to challenging the pre-war all-rounder for his fielding crown — a new star who annexed the position of cover-point in the West Indies XI until injury forced him into becoming one of the greatest slip fieldsmen in Test history.

The hulking, bespectacled 6ft 7in (200 cm) young Guyanese giant with exceptionally long arms was nicknamed 'Jungle Jim' when first playing for his adopted county, Lancashire, at Old Trafford in 1969. After a closer look at his remarkable fleetness of foot and lightning pick-up and throw, the big West Indian was swiftly renamed 'Supercat'.

Clive Lloyd batted with ruthless efficiency at all levels of the game for almost a quarter of a century and, in his early years in first-class cricket, fielded like two men in the covers. With his long, loping stride and unerringly straight and sure throw, he was the terror of the Test and county circuit. His Lancashire captain, Jack Bond, was once quoted as saying: 'No fieldsman prowls the covers with greater menace; no man throws with more power or accuracy!'

During the late 1970s, when advancing age and recurrent knee problems began troubling Lloyd (by now West Indies captain), he directed operations from slips — and became noted for his ability to pluck from the air snicks that would be out of reach of a normal fieldsman. Throughout his first-class and Test career, Lloyd batted and fielded wearing spectacles but never appeared to be hampered by them. In Tests, he took 89 catches to add to his 7515 runs and 19 centuries.

During Clive Lloyd's long reign as West Indies captain, two other players gained regular applause for their work in the covers. Fellow Guyanese batsman Faoud Bacchus, a highly mobile cover-point with an accurate throw, played in 19 Tests before choosing to continue his career in South Africa. Viv Richards of Antigua, the successor to Lloyd as captain, remains very much a force in Caribbean and world cricket and is one of the finest all-round fieldsmen ever to appear in international cricket.

Looking more like a world champion boxer than an ace Test cricketer, Richards is in the highest class as a cover fieldsman. He believes fielding is as important as batting and bowling and states in his *Learn Cricket with Viv Richards*: 'If you don't enjoy fielding, you may as well pack up cricket altogether.' Richards reveals that he prefers 'chasing around the boundary and then hurling the ball back...', an occupation which gives him 'an incredible sense of boyish freedom'. Just as proficient in close positions both in front and behind the wicket as he is in the outfield, Viv Richards is not only the leading West Indian cricketer of the day but can lay equal claim to the titles of 'world's greatest batsman' and 'world's best fielder'.

During the decade immediately preceding its banning from the Test arena in 1971, South Africa produced a cover fieldsman to rank with Constantine, Lloyd and Harvey and with the pre-war cover-point heroes Hobbs, Pellew and Bradman. Colin Bland was acknowledged as the finest fielder ever seen from his country and was frequently mentioned among the greatest fieldsmen to appear in international cricket.

Bland's predecessors included a number of mid-field exponents of character. The great googly bowlers Aubrey Faulkner and Ernest Vogler were two players who could be placed anywhere in the field and perform with skill and efficiency. Faulkner was particularly versatile, an especially sound slip, as were two other players who opened the batting for South Africa before the First World War, William Shalders and J W 'Billy' Zulch, while left-handed all-rounder Charles 'Buck' Llewellyn was, according to a contemporary report, 'greased lightning at mid-off'.

Between the wars, the dynamic little H G O 'Tuppy' Owen-Smith did some heroic things for his country at cover-point or in the deep during a short but busily occupied sporting career in which he played Test cricket for South Africa, captained England at rugby and gained a boxing Blue at Oxford. Heroic also was South Africa's

A sight that batsmen feared: the world's greatest post-war fielder, South Africa's 'Golden Eagle' Colin Bland completes another perfect pick up and throw.

captain in 17 Tests, H G 'Nummy' Deane, who was exceptionally brilliant at cover.

Jack Cheetham took a team of unusually agile all-round fielders to Australia in 1952–53. With the recent retirement of most of his country's top players, Cheetham knew that his side's credibility relied more than most on fielding excellence. With team-manager and former Test batsman Ken Viljoen, he embarked on a training programme that turned each of his players into a superfit athlete in the field and the crowds began turning up in their thousands just to witness the Springboks' amazing out-cricket. In the covers, no-one could out-shine pint-sized opening batsman Jacky McGlew, who made up for his lack of inches with fleetness of foot and an arm as accurate as any before seen in international cricket.

In South Africa's short-list of cover experts down the years, even McGlew must make way for the 'Golden Eagle', Rhodesian-born Colin Bland.

Bland the fielder was a self-made phenomena. Tall and splendidly-built, he combined the sprinting speed of an Olympic-class runner with the grace and timing of a ballet dancer to retrieve balls that would have passed any lesser fieldsman and hit the boundary pickets for four. His mighty and superbly accurate throw won for South Africa at least one Test series, in England in 1965.

At Lord's in the first Test of the 1965 rubber, England was heading for a comfortable lead when Ken Barrington pushed the ball firmly wide of mid-on and scampered through for what he thought was an easy single. Like a ghost, Bland materialised at mid-on from his position at mid-wicket and in one fluid movement scooped up the

Colin Bland gives a fielding exhibition before a match in England in 1965.

ball, turned and threw down the stumps at the bowler's end — with a flabbergasted Barrington still well short of his crease. Later in the same innings, when Jim Parks looked like getting on top of the South African attack, Bland performed another magical direct hit on the stumps and ran him out. From that moment on, England struggled and barely saved the game on the final day. With England's batsmen afraid to run if the ball was placed anywhere near champion fielder Bland, South Africa went on to win the series.

Wally Hammond, who saw them both in action, placed Bland firmly in the same category as Constantine. So acclaimed was the Rhodesian's fielding that Kent captain Colin Cowdrey asked him to give a fielding display before the South Africans' match against the county. Noted cricket writer Brian Chapman commented in the *Daily Mirror*: 'This man Bland is superhuman. It seems indecent that one player without bat or ball in his hand can dictate the course of a game...'. People travelled many miles just to see this lone Springbok player in the field.

Colin Bland reached his personal peak of excellence as a fielder through concentrated, gruelling practise at an hour when most of his team-mates were not yet up for breakfast. During the winter months, he continued to train each day — sprinting, picking-up and throwing at a single stump until his movements in the field were as much part of his nature as walking, eating and sleeping.

The 6ft 1in (185 cm) Bland was also a thundering stroke-player, worth his place in any Test team as a batsman (his Test average was 49.08), and a more than useful medium-paced bowler. His departure from international cricket was a tragic one — he ran into the pickets while chasing a ball at Wanderers, Johannesburg, in the first Test versus Australia in 1966–67 and seriously injured his left leg. He never again appeared in a Test but his performances in the field in South Africa, England and Australia assured him a place in cricket's memory.

Since South Africa's departure from the official world cricket scene, a number of spring-heeled fielders have appeared in the various 'rebel' Test series against teams from England, Sri Lanka, West Indies and Australia. In the covers and at mid-wicket, two of the Springboks' most effective batsmen of the day, opener Jimmy Cook and number three Peter Kirsten, have presented most threat to the opposition. Of the two, former rugby three-quarter Kirsten perhaps comes closest to Colin Bland in terms of running speed and lightning throw, although Cook, a professional soccer player, is not far behind. Both fieldsmen strive constantly to maintain the standard of excellence set by Colin Bland.

21

In the deep

'Runs lost by faulty ground fielding are just the same as runs made off the bat by the opponents...'

— Sir Donald Bradman

Deep fielders require a good pair of running legs to take them into position to cut off a boundary, a strong throwing arm to place the ball at the top of the stumps and a reliable pair of hands, allied with a safe catching technique so that any high, wide and handsome hit that does not actually land over the ropes will come to rest safely in the fielder's hands.

At the Oval in 1880, Australian George Bonnor's incredible power as a hitter set up one of the most amazing deep-field catches in Test history. W G Grace and two of his brothers, E M and G F, appeared together for England for the one and only time. George Frederick Grace was the youngest of five Grace brothers, and a thrilling out-fielder. The 6ft 6in (198 cm) and 16-stone (101 kg) Bonnor was known as the 'Colonial Hercules' and boasted a classical build. At the Oval, his exceptional hit, off the bowling of Alfred Shaw, rose so high that Fred Grace, himself a tall, fair and muscular man, was able to dash to the boundary and position himself to take the steepler when the batsmen were already into their third run! Bonnor was dismissed for two runs, Australia was forced to follow on and England went on to claim the match by five wickets. Poor Frederick Grace made a pair of ducks in his only Test. A fortnight after the Oval Test, the most charming of the Grace brothers died from congestion on the lungs following a severe cold, caught while playing in a club match.

Another of England's early outstanding fielders 'in the country' was opening batsman of the day, Albert Ward, a six-footer (183 cm) who left Yorkshire to play for Lancashire, and who was often tedious to watch at the wicket but outstanding in the deep field where his catching was ever reliable. Ward appeared during the late 1890s. Others who excelled in the deep during English cricket's turn-of-the-century 'Golden Age' included Lancashire's Reggie Spooner (the player who provided a model for 'Golden Age' batsmanship), Lancashire batsman Johnny Tyldelsey, a quick mover and equally good in the long-field or at third man, and Yorkshire's razor-keen David Denton.

Denton was an exceptionally fast and athletic runner whose gathering and throwing have seldom been bettered, and a man who believed in the virtue of constant fielding practice. E H D Sewell records in *Who Won the Toss?* that Denton 'could throw a long low ball without checking after the pick-up'. P F Warner writes in *The Book of Cricket* that the Yorkshireman was, 'one of the few cricketers about whom it could truthfully be said that he was worth his place in his team for his fielding alone'. Nottinghamshire's Joe Hardstaff senior was another dazzling fielder in the deep, less athletic than Denton but strongly built and a player who lost little in comparison.

A particularly outstanding pre-First World War all-round English fielder was Kent amateur Kenneth Hutchings, who died in the war. A scintillating stroke-playing batsman and adept slip fielder, Hutchings was fast and safe in the outfield, in the long-field or at third man, seldom missed a catch and could throw with tremendous power from the edge of the boundary. Some critics have even named him as the finest all-round fielder ever to appear in first-class cricket.

A famous catch by an early England outfielder has already been mentioned. There were also some notable ones that were dropped, of which the most notorious was perhaps that grassed by the hapless Frederick William Tate at Old Trafford in 1902. Poor 'Chub' Tate, who normally fielded at slip, ruined his only Test when he missed a straight-forward catch at deep square-leg off Australian skipper Joe Darling. Darling had scored 16 at the time, went on to make 37 and Australia won by just three runs. England skipper Archie MacLaren defended his decision to place Tate at square-leg instead of slip when he said after the match that the only alternative, K S Ranjitsinhji, was injured at the time and unable to perform in the outfield.

Fred Tate batted number 11 for England in the final innings of the match, hit one four and was then clean bowled playing an injudicious stroke with his side just four runs from victory. He was never again picked for England but the story goes that, through his tears of disappointment at the end of the match, Tate blurted out that he had 'a little lad at home who would make up for it'. His son Maurice did indeed eventually become one of England's greatest bowlers and took 155 wickets in 39 Tests.

There are indeed those days when every ball hit in the air goes to hand and is caught; and others when nothing sticks — not even the most simple little 'dolly' of a catch. Patsy Hendren tells of an incident involving England captain Johnny Douglas at the end of a long day when things did not go very well for his team in the field. Douglas turned his back when a ball was hit high in the air and the fieldsman was shaping to catch it and said to Hendren: 'Tell me the worst; I daren't look!'

Hendren, from Middlesex, was one of England's noteworthy out-fielders of the 1920s and 1930s. So too were the fierce-hitting Bryan

Valentine from Kent, fast bowler and England captain A E R Gilligan of Sussex (a remarkably brilliant mid-off) and the brave little Lancashire left-handed batsman Eddie Paynter.

Two outstanding deep-field exponents of the 1950s were Yorkshire left-handed batsman Willie Watson and all-rounder Trevor Bailey of Essex, who, as batsmen, once saved a Test versus Australia at Lord's in a famous fifth-wicket stand. Watson was an England soccer international who was a wonderful runner between the wickets and in the field; Bailey could field brilliantly in any position: slip, close-up on the leg-side or on the boundary fence.

A number of England's post-war fast bowlers gained glowing reputations as outfielders, including Lancashire's Brian Statham and Yorkshire's Freddie Trueman, who also became renowned for his catching close in at short-leg. Another Yorkshire-bred fast bowler, Chris Old, was brilliant in the deep and also a remarkable slip fielder. John Snow of Sussex was known for his fast and flat throw that was invariably placed inches above the bails and the seemingly ageless John Lever of Essex fields in the deep in a manner that is an object lesson to younger players.

For Australia, in the fledgling years of Test cricket, left-handed batting maestro Clem Hill was a highly competent long-field whose overhand throw from the deep contrasted strongly with the underhand flick used by little Syd Gregory at cover. Hill was also a fine runner and held a stunning catch in the legendary Old Trafford Test of 1902 when Fred Tate dropped Darling and Australia won by three runs. Scampering all the way from long-on to square-leg, Hill caught a skier hit by England wicket-keeper Dick Lilley off Hugh Trumble to take a catch that probably won the match.

The incomparable Victor Trumper was also an able outfielder and possessed a marvellous throw, legacy of his earlier baseball training. He used to delight fans at the fall of a wicket in Tests by hurling the ball to Clem Hill at the other end of the ground! In later seasons, Charlie Macartney's left-handed opening partner Warren Bardsley frequently drew applause for his work in the deep while another left-handed stroke-player of note, Vernon Ransford, was an exceptionally active third man or long-field and possibly the best of Australia's outfielders of the early 1900s.

Australia's immediate post-war skipper, Warwick Armstrong, was in his later years and because of his bulk not as agile a mover in the field as in his pre-war days of youth. He will however be remembered for his action against England at the Oval in 1921 when, with the game a certain draw, he retired to the deep field and started reading a newspaper. Something of a parallel incident occurred in England in 1986, although not in a Test. At Canterbury, India's Sunny Gavaskar distributed newspapers to his team's boundary fielders after Kent insisted on batting through the whole of the play available on the first two days of a rain-ruined match in which India did not even bat.

The tragic Archie Jackson, who made his Test debut at 19 in 1928–29 and died when still short of his 24th birthday, complemented his batting genius with some truly outstanding fielding in the deep that saw him running like a gazelle and throwing like the wind. Of Sir Donald Bradman's later contemporaries, opening batsman Bill Brown, who went to England on three tours, was an athletic and safe fielder in the deep while the never-say-die Stan McCabe (until foot trouble hampered him later in his career) was one of the outstanding all-round Australian fieldsmen of the between-wars period. Ray Robinson records in *From the Boundary* that Lindsay Hassett, Bradman's successor as Australian captain, 'was nearly 35 before I saw him drop a catch'. Until he became Australia's skipper, Hassett generally fielded on the leg boundary.

In the deep, in the long-on and long-off positions, at third man and square on the leg-side, Australia has, from the 1940s onwards, been well looked after by a succession of fast runners with good throwing arms. Bradman's team included such speedy and agile performers as Sam Loxton and Bill Johnston. Both were good base-ballers who threw with unerring accuracy. Another baseballer of the 1940s and early 1950s who excelled in the deep field was Ken Archer who, unfortunately, did not score enough runs to keep his place safe in the Australian team.

Running into the 1960s, men like Brian Booth and Alan Davidson were most decidedly worth their respective places as stroke-playing batsmen and bustling all-rounders, and were both unusually versatile fieldsmen whom a captain could place anywhere, from long-on to first slip. A number of good outfielders also emerged during Ian Chappell's reign of the 1970s, including fast bowlers Jeff Thomson, Eric Freeman and Gary Gilmour (a marvellous thrower and also a faultless catcher if brought close in).

In more recent times, the most electrifying Australian deep fielder has been opening batsman John Dyson whose running, diving and tumbling acts to field or to catch the impossible (and often one-handed) has brought forth visions of a soccer goalie sprinting around the boundary edge to execute save after save.

South Africa's prominent boundary pickets guardians included in the between-war days men like the swift-running Bob Catterall and the strongly-built Denys Morkel. Eric Rowan, who overcame the early handicap of a broken arm to develop a fine throw from the deep, and Ken Viljoen, another brilliant outfielder, were two who played both before and after the Second World War.

With the Springboks in England under Alan Melville in 1947, all-rounder O C 'Ossie' Dawson delighted spectators by chasing the ball to the last gasp and by hurling himself around to take impossible catches. Another grand outfielder in Melville's team was Springbok rugby fly-half Tony Harris. When Dudley Nourse brought the next South African side to England in 1951, Oxford Blue Clive van Ryneveld, an England cap as a rugby three-quarter and one of the finest of all-round athletes, impressed in any position. Nourse also had in his team two young players, Jacky McGlew and dashing stroke-maker Roy McLean, who were to become fielding heroes under Jack Cheetham in Australia in 1952—53.

McGlew's marvellous work at extra-cover has already been discussed; McLean was unsurpassed on the boundary and a fine catcher close in. Apart from McLean and McGlew, Cheetham had under his command a whole string of dazzling outfielders. As a batsman, Ken Funston at times matched McLean stroke for stroke; fielding in the deep he was almost as brilliant. The 6ft 3ins (190 cm) all-rounder Anton Murray was incredibly quick for such a giant of a man. Fast bowlers Michael Melle and Eddie Fuller were as energetic in the outfield as any of their compatriots while Russell Endean, one of the team's top 'suicide' fieldsmen, also took the outfield catch of the season in 1952—53 when he held a drive by Keith Miller in the crucial second Test, won by South Africa at Melbourne, with his back to the iron boundary fence. Jack Cheetham's remarkable team was known for its fielding ahead of its batting and bowling, and devoted three to four hours daily to fielding practice right up to the end of the tour.

Big-hitter Paul Winslow became an additional outfield star when Cheetham took his Springbok team to England in 1955. In 1960, a disastrous tour of England that saw the series lost by a big margin, the emergence of anti-apartheid demonstrations and the no-balling for throwing of young Geoff Griffin was lightened occasionally by the thrilling deep-field displays put up by Syd O'Linn and Peter Carlstein. O'Linn, a Kent professional, was also a former soccer Springbok and one of the fastest-moving of South Africa's fieldsmen in any position. Carlstein never quite made the grade as a Test batsman but was a world-class outfielder.

Pre-war West Indians who made their mark in the deep included great George Headley (the 'Black Bradman' of the 1930s), who delighted spectators with his somersault catches and fast bowler George Francis, a scintillating fielder in true West Indian style. Derek Sealy, polished batsman and agile wicket-keeper, was also a grand fielder in the country while opening batsman Jeffrey Stollmeyer was another fine outfielder who toured England in 1939 and returned to continue his Test career after the war.

Athletic fielding seems to come naturally to West Indians and there have been few picked for the Caribbean Test eleven who have not excelled in that capacity. O G 'Collie' Smith, tragically killed in a car accident in 1959, was always prominent when placed on or near the fence. Running into more recent times, the tiny Alvin Kallicharran, with his marvellously strong throw, and the all-rounders Bernard Julien, Keith Boyce and Collis King did all and more that was asked of them in any position — as have current opening batsman Desmond Haynes, fast bowler Michael Holding, and middle-order batsman Larry Gomes. Garfield Sobers, Clive Lloyd and Viv Richards are others who have proved themselves supremely versatile fieldsmen. Richards is a marvellously natural fielder with superb reflexes, covers an enormous amount of territory and has the extraordinary ability to turn and throw in one movement.

The 'Tweedledum and Tweedledee' outfielding stars of present-day West Indies' cricket are the diminutive Augustine Logie and the lanky Roger Harper. Logie is one of the fastest of cricketers on his short little legs and one of those rare players for whom people travel miles to see in the field; Harper, versus England at Lord's in 1984, actually claimed a 'Man-of-the-Match' award solely for his super-efficient groundwork and for the miraculous running catch that dismissed a rampant Ian Botham.

New Zealand's most notable outfielders among pre-war players included the alert H G 'Giff' Vivian, opening batsman John Kerr, the versatile Tom Lowry (who also acted as perennial reserve wicket-keeper), bespectacled all-rounder Denis Moloney and the energetic Gordon 'Dad' Weir. The 1949 Kiwi team in England had John Reid (brilliant anywhere in the field and in every single department of the game) and the hard-running F B 'Runty' Smith, who was something of a wizard at taking deep-field catches. During the 1950s and 1960s, men like Noel McGregor and Lawrie Miller shone in the outfield, as have left-handed opening batsmen John Wright and Bruce Edgar in more recent times. It is, indeed, an unenviable task to try and select the best fielder in the current New Zealand line-up which normally boasts 10 highly active, competent and versatile performers to back up the wicket-keeper of the day.

Of India's earlier men, googly merchant C S Nayudu made up for comparative lack of bowling success in Tests with some electrifying stuff in the deep. Good all-rounders who have frequently roamed the ropes include P R 'Polly' Umrigar and Vijay Manjrekar in the 1950s, and Abbas Ali Baig (a wonderful thrower), Hanumant Singh, Dilip Sardesai (also a fine slip) and M L Jaisimha in the 1960s and 1970s. India's one-eyed captain of the 1960s, Nawab of Pataudi junior (or Mansur Ali Khan as he later became known), was a brilliant out-fielder during his Oxford University days. India's outstanding team of the 1980s, as is the case with most other Test countries, contains a number of highly professional fielders: opening batsman Krish Srikkanth runs like greased lightning and possesses a lethal throw-in from the boundary; skipper Kapil Dev, all-rounder Ravi Shastri, leg-spinner Laxman Shivaramakrishnan, and the new young batting star

Mohammed Azharuddin are also eye-catching performers in the outfield.

Pakistan's most prominent outfielders have been Wazir Mohammed (one of the four famous Mohammed brothers who played Test cricket for their country), the highly talented all-purpose fielder Asif Iqbal and the present captain and world-class all-rounder Imran Khan.

For Sri Lanka, little Aravinda de Silva, one of his team's great batting hopes of the future, has, unlike a number of his senior and rather more portly colleagues, displayed unusual energy and skill in his outfielding endeavours.

22

Many a slip

'He leaps once more, with eager spring, To catch the brief-glimpsed, flying ball...'

— John Arlott

During the late 19th and early 20th centuries, Englishmen who were renowned for their work in the slips included dapper little Bobby Abel and his Surrey and England companion, the debonaire George Lohmann, although the former would not have dared place himself in the same class as his companion. Lohmann, the legendary master bowler who took 112 wickets in Tests at only 10.75 runs apiece, was something of a one-man band: glorious long-handled hitter, an often unplayable bowler and a fielder who held almost impossible slip catches.

Commenting on Lohmann's swift reactions, W G Grace notes it was remarkable how much ground he would cover at short slip and that, 'He rarely allows anything to pass him, and nearly everything possible in the way of a catch he brings off'.

After Lohmann's day, three unusually brilliant slip fielders, A C MacLaren (the England captain), L C Braund and A O Jones, appeared together for England at the turn of the century when another bowling giant, Sydney Barnes (many cite him as the best in history), made his first trip to Australia in 1901−02. MacLaren usually occupied the post of first slip but was not quite the equal of the remarkably quick-moving Len Braund.

At Edgbaston in 1902, Braund covered the ground from first slip to leg slip to pocket a 'safe' leg-glance played by Australia's left-hander Clem Hill off the swing bowling of George Hirst. This incredible dismissal started a slide that saw Australia bundled out for 36 runs, its lowest Test score!

The impetuous Arthur Owen Jones seldom got going as a Test opening batsman but took 15 catches in 12 Tests, most of them in exemplary style, and was an amiable, well-liked man who batted, bowled, kept wicket and fielded in Tests. He was also captain-elect of the 1907−08 MCC team to Australia but played in only two Tests because of illness. Arthur Jones, credited with the invention of a wider-placed slip position that came to be known as 'gully', was one of the greatest fielders ever in that position.

Yorkshire's 'Long' John Tunnicliffe, who took 694 catches for his county, was reputed to be the best slip fielder of the lot in the late

1800s and early 1900s but never played in a Test. The photograph of him in Beldham and Fry's *Great Bowlers and Fielders* is a model of balance and anticipation. Of the others who did represent England in an age of outstanding slip fielders, K S Ranjitsinhji and C B Fry shone for Sussex and England. Fry was also stunningly athletic in the outfield, running with antelope speed and frequently turning certain fours into twos.

R E 'Tip' Foster, whose 287 at Sydney in 1903–04 remained the highest Test score for a quarter of a century, was also a top-class slip fielder and one of seven brothers who played for Worcestershire (the county became known as 'Fostershire'). It has been claimed that when the family did their washing up, the plates and cups were rapidly thrown from brother to brother. Tip Foster's unrelated namesake, left-handed all-rounder F R Foster from Warwickshire, was also an outstanding slips fieldsman — when he was not terrifying the opposition with his fast-medium leg-theory, a forerunner to bodyline bowling.

England's two outstanding Golden Age all-rounders, Yorkshiremen George Hirst and Wilfred Rhodes, were also fine fielders — Hirst at mid-off; Rhodes yet another unusually adept performer in the slips. Both continued their careers after the First World War, as did the graceful Frank Woolley of Kent, another remarkable all-rounder who was equally capable anywhere in the field but particularly noted for his flawless work at first slip. Woolley is the only fieldsman in history to take more than 1000 catches — 1018 to be exact — in a playing career stretching from 1906 to 1938. His nearest rival is W G Grace with 877. Other Test players to have taken 800 or more catches in first-class cricket are: G A R Lock (830), W R Hammond (819) and D B Close (813) — all close fielders. Lock invariably fielded at short-leg or leg-slip, Hammond almost always at slip while Close fielded at slip or in one of the 'silly' positions in front of the batsman.

Other versatile players of the 1920s and 1930s who excelled at slip included Leicestershire's strong and cheerful George Geary, whose long reach brought him some amazing catches, and the enterprising Percy Fender (joint holder of the record for the fastest century in first-class cricket). But it was the immaculate Walter Hammond who caught the eye most frequently and whose immense natural talent was always so evident, whether batting, bowling or picking up catches at first slip.

According to some observers, Hammond was at his best when standing at short slip for slow and medium-fast bowling but lost some of his skill when the really fast stuff was in operation because he tended to stand a bit too deep. Hammond is the only fieldsman to ever have taken 10 catches in a first-class match — for Gloucestershire versus Surrey in 1928. He also scored a century in each innings!

Although there are no other instances in first-class cricket of a fielder catching 10 men in a match, the feat has been performed at other levels. One instance that took place in an international match of sorts is worth recalling. The doings of the more prominent batsmen, bowlers and wicket-keepers in the Philadelphian teams of the late 1800s and early 1900s have been touched upon in the earlier sections on batsmen and bowlers. One Philadelphia club team, the Germantown Cricket Club, defeated a strong Australian XI by four wickets at Manheim in 1913, the feature of the match being the remarkable catching of local captain and slip fielder Pete O'Neill.

O'Neill emulated Walter Hammond with 10 victims, including such notable Australian Test players as Herbie Collins, Warren Bardsley (in both innings), Arthur Mailey, E R Mayne and S H Emery. Frank Greene played for the Germantown XII and recorded afterwards that of the 15 balls hit in the air during the two Australian innings, 14 were caught by the 'Philly' fielders. The only one missed came off the second-last ball of the visitors' second innings; the batsman involved, Austin Diamond, was caught off the very next ball by Pete O'Neill — to give the ace fielder his 10th catch of the match. According to Greene, the sticky-fingered O'Neill's two best catches were those to dismiss L A Cody (O'Neill fell forward full length to take a ball that did not rise more than 18 inches from the ground) and Warren Bardsley (a catch missed by wicket-keeper Jack Stewart but taken by O'Neill moving behind him), both in the first innings.

Percy Chapman was Kent and England's debonaire captain of the 1920s and regarded by many as his country's finest slip and gully fieldsman (it has already been noted that he was also a superb cover-point). Chapman had enormous hands which let nothing through and some of his efforts in the gully area were described as superhuman.

Percy Chapman's predecessor as England captain was Nottinghamshire's uncompromising Arthur Carr, another grand close fielder who is unfortunately most remembered for the slip catch he *missed* against Australia at Headingley in 1926. Left-handed opener Warren Bardsley had been brilliantly caught in the slips, off the first ball of the match, by Herbert Sutcliffe off the bowling of Maurice Tate. On an overcast morning, Tate then found the edge of Charlie Macartney's bat with the fifth ball of the same opening over, but poor Arthur Carr grassed a very awkward chance. Macartney rode his luck, continued on his merry way to a 100 before lunch and Australia went on to compile the huge first innings of 494 runs. After the next Test, the fourth of the rubber at Manchester, Carr lost his place in the England team and the leadership to Percy Chapman.

Yet another famous slip fieldsman of the between-wars period was K S Duleepsinhji, who emulated his famous uncle, the great 'Ranji', for Sussex and England as a wristy batting artist and live-wire fieldsman whose movements at slip were described as 'panther-like'.

England has produced a fair number of first-rate slip fielders since the 1940s, some of whose performances have bordered on sheer genius when it comes to creating catches from otherwise safe-looking snicks by the batsman. Bill Edrich was a safe slip field in the 1940s and 1950s, for England and for Middlesex; Trevor Bailey (Essex) was brilliant in the same position — and anywhere else close to the wicket. The rather portly Colin Cowdrey from Kent did not fit everybody's image of the ideal slip but took 120 catches in 114 Tests, more than any other Englishman in international cricket (Hammond is next with 110 in 85 Tests).

Cowdrey moved with disarming ease at first slip and lost little in comparison with the short and stubby Phil Sharpe of Yorkshire, often been named as one of the most spectacularly efficient slip fielders of all time. His most stunning catch came when he was standing very close to medium-pacer Basil D'Oliveira at Old Trafford in 1969 and held a full-blooded slash played by West Indian left-handed opener Joey Carew as if he were picking an apple off a tree. Sharpe could frequently be seen almost casually diving to pick up two-handed a catch which any other fieldsman might not have got even a finger to.

Another fine England slip fielder of the 1960s was Lancashire fast bowler Ken Higgs and, running into the 1970s, Surrey's Graham Roope was frequently picked because of his ability at second slip even when he was not scoring as many runs as expected. Lancashire's Barry Wood was another who did not always please when it came to run-making but who seldom let his side down in the gully. Conversely, the high-scoring Surrey left-hander John Edrich kept up the family tradition started up by his cousin Bill by scoring plenty of runs for England and fielding in the gully with dedication and precision. England's current gully fielding expert is the Middlesex off-spin bowler John Emburey, who has been recently welcomed back into the fold after a three-year ban for playing in South Africa.

Slip fielders come in all shapes and sizes, as was demonstrated by South African-born Sussex and England skipper Tony Greig who used his elongated 6ft 7ins (200 cm) frame to full effect in pocketing blinders. England's contemporary slip-fielding giant is not quite as tall as Greig but broad in girth and in achievement, although unfortunately never far from controversy.

As if it were not enough that for much of his career he has been England's main batting and bowling hope, the 6ft 1in (185 cm) Ian Botham is also a 'slipfielder's slip fielder'. Since Clive Lloyd's retirement, there is just no one quite in his class in modern world cricket. More's the pity that Botham has fallen foul of authority and that a cloud hangs over his continued progress at Test level. To the close of

Ian Botham, England's current slips wizard, takes a one-hander inches from the turf. The wicket-keeper is Paul Downton. Other fielders are (left to right) John Emburey, Graham Gooch and Mike Gatting.

the 1985–86 season in the West Indies, Botham had bowled his way to within one wicket of Dennis Lillee's record 355 Test wickets; as a fielder, he had taken 96 catches — only six players in history have reached their catching 'ton'.

As in all other aspects of life, Botham prefers his own style, standing with hands on knees until the batsman plays his stroke — not an ideal model for aspiring young slip fielders who should be schooled to hold their hands out, ready for a catch. The truth is that Botham is something of a catching genius who seems to sight the ball quicker than anyone else and who moves almost with the speed of light once he has judged its flight path from the bat's edge. He is also an unusually big man for so sharp a slip fielder.

An early Australian slip-fielder of note was a cricketing character with a pair of the biggest hands in the business. Albert Trott once hit the ball over the pavilion at Lord's and performed a hat-trick twice in one innings to 'ruin' his own benefit match when playing for Middlesex. He also missed very few catches that came his way at slip or in any other position.

Australia's most famous pre-Second World War slip fieldsman was the telescopic-armed Jack Gregory, who terrified batsmen with his leaping and bounding run-up and express-paced deliveries and as a dashing left-handed batsman, also held the Test fast-scoring record for 45' years, until Viv Richards broke it at St John's, Antigua, in 1986. Gregory's brilliant catching at slip was the result of his abnormal reach and unusual anticipation and he holds the world record for most catches in a Test series — 15 versus England in 1920–21.

Another efficient pre-war slip fieldsman was the thick-set little Arthur Chipperfield and during the 1940s, Australia was particularly well-served in the slips by men like googly bowler Colin McCool, off-spinner Ian Johnson and the charismatic all-rounder Keith Miller, a man who delighted in taking 'impossible' catches in the position. During the 1950s, the tall Graeme Hole made something of a name for himself at slip, but failed as a Test batsman, while the 1960s produced a fair variety of good slips performers, including left-handed batsman Bob Cowper (the only player to score a triple-century in a Test in Australia) and Bobby Simpson, the man whom many consider to have been the best slip fieldsman of all time.

According to Simpson himself, he came to field in the slips almost by accident. During the 1953–54 Australian season he was, in his capacity as 12th man, once called on to the field by his New South Wales skipper Keith Miller and casually ordered to stand at slip. Within half an hour, the youthful Simpson had taken two fine catches (one of his victims was Neil Harvey) and was seldom again seen in any other spot on the field.

According to Simpson, 'A good slips fieldsman senses a catch just a fraction earlier than a bad one'. Simpson must have been very good indeed, if his strike rate in Tests is anything to go by; of the six fielders who have taken 100 or more catches in Test cricket, Simpson's record of catches per match is by far the best. The list reads:

	Matches	Catches	Average
R B Simpson (Australia)	62	110	1.77
G S Chappell (Australia)	87	122	1.40
I M Chappell (Australia)	75	105	1.40
W R Hammond (England)	85	110	1.29
G S Sobers (West Indies)	93	109	1.17
M C Cowdrey (England)	114	120	1.05
S M Gavaskar (India)	115	100	0.87

All the fieldsmen listed were predominantly slips fieldsmen, although Sobers, for instance, took many of his catches close up in leg-side positions. Simpson also twice took 13 catches in a five-match

Brothers in harmony: Greg
Chappell, jumping to his
left from second slip,
catches England stalwart
Colin Cowdrey at
Melbourne in 1974—75
while Ian Chappell moves
over from first slip to cover
his brother.

Test series (versus South Africa in 1957—58 and versus West Indies
in 1960—61). Only two players have exceeded this: J M Gregory, 15
catches in five Tests for Australia versus England in 1920—21 and G
S Chappell, 14 catches in six Tests for Australia versus England in
1974—75.

The contribution made to Australian cricket by the two Chappell brothers is immense. Both were batsmen of world-class status. Ian Chappell was a very good slips fieldsman; Greg Chappell was a great one. Taller and thinner than his older brother, Greg Chappell was the picture of gracefulness in all his movements, whether batting, bowling or fielding. Ian Chappell was the more down-to-earth of the two brothers and it showed in his style of play and in his manner in the field. He brought the same concentration into his performances at first slip as he did in his batsmanship. Greg Chappell, on the other hand, was more free-flowing in his style and generally stood at second slip, letting through nothing that looked the ghost of a chance. He held seven catches in that position against England at Perth in 1974–75 — a world record he shares with India's Yajurvindra Singh — and he holds the record for most catches in all Tests: 122 in 87 matches. If Ian Botham (now on 96 catches) fails to get it all together again, it may be a long time before Greg Chappell's total is beaten.

A couple of Australians have made a particularly special mark as gully fieldsmen. One was Australian skipper of the 1960s, Richie Benaud, who will be remembered for his incredible low-diving left-handed catch (he was a right-hander) to dismiss Colin Cowdrey off the bowling of Ken Mackay at Lord's in 1956. When he became Australian captain, Benaud was always a wonderful inspiration to his men in the field.

Off-break bowler Ashley Mallett was the second unusually brilliant gully fielder and an integral part of Ian Chappell's teams of the 1970s. Mallett took some unbelievable catches and was often the only spin bowler in a predominantly all-pace attack. He was particularly prominent in the gully during the 1974–75 series versus England, when fast bowlers Lillee and Thomson terrorised the opposition batsmen with their lifting deliveries, and a number of sizzling chances came Mallett's way.

Recent New Zealand teams have included a string of excellent close fielders, including former captain Geoff Howarth, big-hitting all-rounder Lance Cairns and a former captain, Jeremy Coney, who support the seam bowling of Richard Hadlee and his colleagues. Earlier New Zealand teams also produced quite a few excellent slip and gully exponents: Martin Donnelly was probably his country's best cover-point and was also a live-wire performer in the gully and, of the players who appeared before the Second World War, Albert Roberts was a very good slip. Players who have shone at slip or in the gully since 1945 include Geoff Rabone, Verdun Scott and the lanky Tony MacGibbon (in the slips) and Brian Hastings (gully) while Graham Dowling and Brian Yuille, at leg-slip, and Stephen Boock, at short-leg, have also caught the eye.

23

In the batsman's pocket

'I have always believed that half the joy of cricket is in fielding...'
— Jack Cheetham

Close-to-the-wicket fielders are generally specialists — players whose reflexes, anticipation and courage are above average and the outstanding close-catching players are those who can snap up half-chances a few yards from the bat that lesser mortals would let go by. That so many players have excelled through the years in the slips, at gully and leg-slip, or in the 'suicide' positions (silly mid-on, silly mid-off and silly short-leg), or off their own bowling, is indicative of the qualities of character and guts that go to make up the successful international cricketer.

The incomparable W G Grace was, as a young man, an athletic fielder of great note. When age and increasing girth measurements slowed him down a little, he was still reputed to be a marvellous fielder off his own crafty round-arm bowling — although there seems to be no record of the 'Old Man' having made much of an effort when someone else was turning his arm over. He was not, however, known to drop many catches that came his way. Another alert catcher to his own fast-medium bowling was all-rounder George Ulyett of Yorkshire, who played in the first-ever Test at Melbourne in 1876–77. At Lord's, Ulyett once nonchalantly caught a full-blooded drive by the giant Australian George Bonnor that left the blade of the bat like a bullet. Until Ulyett dropped the ball onto the turf to examine his hand, everyone was waiting for it to thud against the pickets behind him!

The rather rebellious 19th century Nottinghamshire all-rounder Billy Barnes, a tall and tough-as-nails character, was an early close fielder of skill and daring and England's Golden Age of cricket produced many fine close fielders to carry on the tradition.

In front of the wicket, England's most courageous fielder after the First World War was the fearless Hampshire giant George Brown, who was known to chest off bouncers when batting. He kept wicket in Tests and was an immovable, granite-hewn performer at silly mid-off or silly point, where he fielded with spectacular judgement. He was described as having 'carpet-bag hands' and was a brilliant fielder no matter where his skipper placed him. George Brown was also a belligerent left-handed batsman and sharpish right-arm fast-medium bowler — which made him one of the most versatile all-rounders ever to appear in first-class cricket.

When Douglas Jardine took his team to Australia in 1932–33 for what became known as the 'bodyline' series, his ace short-leg fieldsman, and leader of the support pack for the leg-theory bowling of Larwood and Voce, was himself a top-class fast bowler who refused to bowl in the revolutionary new style. G O B Allen from Middlesex was the next most successful bowler to Larwood in the five-match series but never resorted to bodyline tactics. As a close fielder on the leg-side, 'Gubby' Allen was superb and took seven sparkling catches, six off Larwood. The one slow bowler used regularly by Jardine in 1932–33, Yorkshire left-arm spinner Hedley Verity, was one of the most immaculate of his type to appear in Test cricket and a magnificent fielder off his own bowling and at backward point.

One of England's most prominent close fielders in the so-called 'suicide' positions (close mid-off and mid-on) was born with a name that immediately categorised him as far as his fielding was concerned. Brian Close was, indeed, the most uncaring of 'silly' fielders when it came to his own physical safety. Poised on his toes only a few yards

G O B 'Gubby' Allen, the English fast bowler who refused to bowl bodyline, was a grand short-leg fielder, seen here taking a catch in Harold Larwood's leg-trap during the controversial 1932–33 series in Australia.

from the batsman at silly mid-on, the Yorkshire and England player virtually willed the batsman to place the ball into his waiting hands. His concentration was immense; his courage was the stuff legends are made of. The story has been told and re-told of the day when a batsman swung lustily at a leg-side delivery in a blatant attempt to hit Close, who was standing in his usual 'kamikaze' spot. The ball thumped Close right between the eyes and rebounded for another fielder to retrieve. Close straightened himself casually, and then bent down again into his crouching position to await the next ball.

Close was a phenomenal fielder close up. Left-arm spinner Tony Lock was probably the greatest short-leg fieldsman seen so far and something of a genius in that position. His Surrey team-mate M J 'Micky' Stewart (himself a brilliant specialist close catcher) once admitted that both he and Lock received their early inspiration from their county captain, Stuart Surridge. Although he never played for England, Surridge was acknowledged in his time as a fearless and inspirational fielder.

Stewart notes in an article written in 1964 that when placed square to or in front of the wicket, a fielder is able to anticipate to a certain extent a batsman's stroke and the subsequent direction the ball will take. When he is standing behind square at an angle of about 45 degrees (Lock's usual spot on the legside), a fielder must calmly wait until the batsman actually plays his shot and then take the necessary action. The difference in timing may only be a split-second or so but it is enough to result in a dropped catch if a fieldsman decides to move too soon.

Tony Lock was the accepted master at judging how and when to act. He would sometimes move in a little towards the batsman while the bowler was running in but would be found 'perfectly balanced, completely still and relaxed' when the batsman went into his stroke. It was after the batsman had played the ball that Lock could be seen to move, like lightning if there was a quarter of a chance in the offing. Tony Lock was possibly the finest leg-slip fielder in history and fortunate in that he fielded regularly to the in-swing of Alec Bedser and the off-breaks of Jim Laker for both Surrey and England. Lock was also a marvel at taking catches off his own bowling, frequently hurling himself like a torpedo to grab the ball one-handed and clutch it to his chest.

Before Lock appeared for England, two other left-handers, Yorkshire spinner Johnny Wardle and Glamorgan all-rounder Allan Watkins, had impressed in Tests with their zealous close fielding. During Lock's time in the England eleven in the 1950s, trusty men like Yorkshire's Freddie Trueman gave him dynamic support at short-leg with rather brief but brilliant appearances being put in by the highly proficient Arthur Milton of Gloucestershire and Glamorgan's Peter Walker.

Tony Lock dives full length to take one of his miraculous catches at leg-slip. His Surrey and England team-mate, Micky Stewart, looks on.

England has not been wanting for short-leg fieldsmen of quality and character since Lock and Trueman played the last of their Test cricket. The tall, bespectacled Mike Smith, Warwickshire and England captain during the 1960s, was one such player. So too was tough little Middlesex left-hander Peter Parfitt, who appeared for England between 1961 and 1972. During the 1970s, the pick of the bunch was Derbyshire seam bowler Mike Hendrick, who was an exceptional performer in any position close to the batsman.

Former England captain David Gower of Leicestershire is currently a sparkling fielder in the 'suicide' positions, as well as being one of the best cover-points in international cricket. Middlesex left-arm spinner Phil Edmonds fielded so close to the batsman and so menacingly in the West Indies in 1985–86 that one of the Caribbean pace bowlers retaliated by 'beaming' him when it was his turn to bat.

The Australian tradition of fine and fearless in-fielders started as long ago as the 1880s when the full-bearded Henry Boyle stood right up to create the silly mid-on position when 'The Demon' Fred Spofforth was bowling. W G Grace, for one, considered 'Harry' Boyle 'a bit foolhardy' but acknowledged that he brought off some remarkable catches in his unique position a few yards in front of the batsman.

The vigorous and athletic Victor Richardson (grandfather of the Chappell brothers) was the premier Australian fielder between the wars. Possessed of great speed and agility, Richardson was brilliant in any position. In 1935–36 he created a world record for number of catches in a Test innings when he caught out five South African batsmen at Durban (a feat since equalled by India's Yajurvindra Singh versus England at Bangalore in 1976–77). At the time, Richardson fielded mostly in close-up positions to the bowling of googly merchants Grimmett and O'Reilly. Jack Fingleton, one of Australia's main batsmen in South Africa in 1935–36, recalls in his *Cricket Crisis* that Vic Richardson took 26 catches on the tour, 'in positions ranging from slips to cover'.

The success of Richardson's Australian team in South Africa was based mainly on the reliable opening partnerships put up by Fingleton and Bill Brown and the baffling googly bowling of Clarrie Grimmett and Bill O'Reilly. The Australian skipper took his record five catches off Grimmett and O'Reilly standing in the unusual position of very short gully, not more than two yards from the bat. Jack Fingleton recalled later: 'I have never seen a catch going in Richardson's direction without knowing that the batsman was as good as out.' Fingleton was also a grand fielder close-in, mainly at forward short-leg, and was almost as feared by the South Africans as Richardson.

South African batsman Dudley Nourse was, incidentally, rather impressed during the 1935–36 series with the cover fielding of the crafty Clarrie Grimmett who was always looking for a run-out.

Sydney Barnes was another pre-war Australian fieldsman who delighted in taunting batsmen from only a few yards away. Carrying on his career after the Second World War, he fielded so close in at point and at short-leg (seldom more than five yards from the bat) during the 1948 Australian tour of England that his tactics were criticised as being unfair. Barnes was nearly killed at Old Trafford in

Vic Richardson (centre), Australia's top all-round fielder between the wars, at practise in South Africa. The other Australian players in the picture are Ernie McCormick (left) and Morrie Sievers.

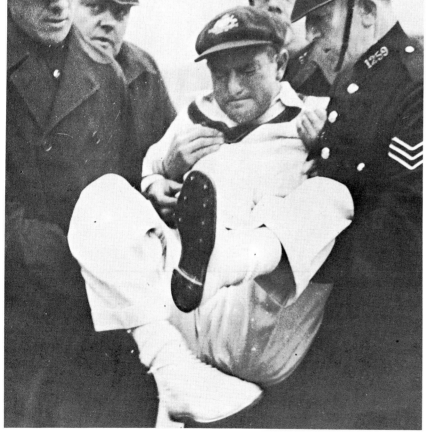

Australia's Syd Barnes is carried off the field by four policemen at Old Trafford, Manchester in 1948 after being struck in the ribs while fielding in a 'suicide' position.

the third Test when England tail-ender Dick Pollard put all of his considerable muscle into a leg-hit off a 'donkey-drop' bowled by off-spinner Ian Johnson and the Australian short-leg fielder took the ball square in the ribs and close to his heart. Barnes collapsed on the pitch like a punctured balloon and initially lost the sight of his left eye. Six policemen carried him off the field and rushed him to hospital for x-rays. Barnes wrote afterwards that the doctor had to use the full force of his machine to penetrate his ribs: 'He said he had never seen such thick ones.' Barnes missed the next Test at Leeds but was back for the final game at the Oval.

Other noteworthy post-war Australlian 'suicide' fielders have included players like left-arm unorthodox spinner George Tribe, the multi-talented and tireless all-rounder Alan Davidson and chunky opening batsman Keith Stackpole.

Jaswantsingh Wala Yajurvindra Singh must have enjoyed his debut Test for India versus England at Bangalore in 1976—77. Standing fearlessly right up at short-leg, in the batsman's hip-pocket so to speak, he displayed complete faith in the skill and pin-point accuracy of India's famous spin bowlers Bedi, Chandrasekhar and Prasanna to gather five catches in the first innings (equalling Vic Richardson's 1935—36 record against South Africa) and seven in the match (to emulate Greg Chappell's feat versus England in 1974—75). Unfortunately, Yajurvindra Singh's batting ability did not match his fielding prowess and he only appeared in three Tests for India.

India has produced a number of brilliant close-catching fieldsmen to support its spin bowlers down the years. During the 1930s, all-rounders Lala Amarsingh and Lala Amarnath were outstanding, as were Hemu Adhikari (also a brilliant cover) and Bapu Nadkarni during the 1950s and 1960s. But none achieved the fame that came to the ever-dependable Eknath Solkar, one of those small band of players who have been picked for Test matches virtually for their fielding alone. As an obdurate left-handed batsman and left-arm bowler, the only honest description of Solkar's prowess could be contained in the word 'useful'. As a short-leg fielder who habitually stood within handshake distance of the batsman, he was little short of a genius and comparable with anyone from any country who has occupied the same daring position down the years.

'Ekki' Solkar was a highly disciplined player who through sheer graft and determination lifted his craft as a batsman and a bowler beyond the limits of his own ability and who, as a fielder, demonstrated a concentration that was monumental. India's spin bowlers were always full of praise for the part he played in their own success. Leg-spinner Bhagwat Chandrasekhar was once heard to remark: 'Solkar caught those which others could catch and caught a few which others wouldn't even try.' Perhaps only England's Tony Lock has been the equal of Solkar at short-leg.

The amazing Eknath Solkar of India dives full length to take a leg-side catch offered by England's Alan Knott.

Since Solkar's retirement in the mid-1970s, India's best short-leg fielder has been opening batsman Chetan Chauhan, a man with remarkable reflexes. Record-breaking opener Sunil Gavaskar has also done well in that position and at silly mid-off and was fielding in the latter position at the Oval in 1982 when a monstrous drive by Ian Botham broke a bone in Gavaskar's left shin.

In its short history, Pakistan's most notable close fielders have been Nazar Mohammed (he hit the first Test century for Pakistan), his son Mudassar Nazar (scorer of the slowest Test hundred in history) and left-arm spin bowler Iqbal Qasim. Sri Lanka has yet to produce a noteworthy close catcher.

When Jack Cheetham set sail with his 1952–53 South African team he knew from the start that, on paper at least, they would probably be outgunned in batting and bowling by a far superior Australian team. He made it his business to turn his side into the finest-ever Springbok fielding combination. Cheetham ended up leading one of the greatest fielding combinations of them all. Its success was based on speed in the outfield and accurate throwing and superb catching, on the boundary and close to the wicket, and some of Cheetham's catching specialists can be numbered among the all-time best.

In the slips, cheery John Watkins and the bespectacled Percy Mansell provided an inspiration for South Africa's bowlers that was quite in keeping with the tradition laid down by old Dave Nourse, in the early part of the century, and carried forward by South Africa's between-the-wars slips specialist Bruce Mitchell. Dave Nourse had such enormous hands that they were referred to as his landing net;

Left: South African captain Jack Cheetham, fielding at silly mid-off, knocks a drive by Australian left-hander, Arthur Morris into the air for the bowler, Hugh Tayfield to complete the catch (see next photo).

Right: Tayfield moves about five yards and dives to his rear to take the catch.

Mitchell, the man who scored most Test runs for South Africa, was also its finest close fielder for many years. Another outstanding pre-war Springbok close fielder was Mitchell's 1935 South African captain, Herby Wade, who led his country to its first series win in England.

During the Cheetham era, off-spin expert Hugh Tayfield was a brilliant fielder in any of the 'silly' positions, and unsurpassed off his own bowling. His catch to dismiss Australia's left-handed opener Arthur Morris in the second Test of 1952–53 at Melbourne was a dazzling affair when he dived full length at a distance of seven yards beyond the bowler's wicket after Cheetham, at short mid-off, had deflected a full-blooded drive up into the air. Also at Melbourne, in the final Test (which South Africa won to square the series), Tayfield claimed another miraculous rebound catch to dismiss Richie Benaud, this time after the ball had bounced off John Watkins, fielding at silly mid-on.

When Tayfield was bowling his accurate off-breaks, Cheetham often placed four men in 'suicide' posts — two on each side of the wicket in a menacing crescent that crossed the pitch midway. Cheetham sometimes fielded there himself and the others included the team's leading run-scorer, Russell Endean; sturdy little opener Jacky McGlew; the tall 6ft 2ins (188 cm) rugby player Anton Murray;

and, in the final Test, left-handed batsman Hedley Keith. Ray Robinson dubbed the threatening formation the 'Four Just Men' and the best of the lot was Russell Endean, whose reflexes bordered on the supernatural. His eyes were so sharp that an optician once advised him to wear glasses to tone them down to the level of the normal person!

Cheetham's Springbok teams of the 1950s set a standard of fielding excellence which South Africa maintained through to its last Test against Australia in 1970. The marvellous work of Colin Bland and other outfielders of the period has already been reviewed. Players like South African captains in its final decade, Peter van der Merwe and Ali Bacher, all-rounders Trevor Goddard and H R 'Tiger' Lance, fast bowlers Peter Pollock and Mike Procter, were outstanding in any of the close positions. In the slips and at gully, opening batsmen Eddie Barlow and Barry Richards and bowlers Pat Trimborn and Graham Chevalier were all of such a high standard that it would be nigh impossible to name the best. Since isolation, the amply-proportioned left-arm spinner and all-rounder Allan Kourie has become known as 'The Flytrap' because of his slip catching and the evergreen 42-year-old batting genius Graeme Pollock has also made a habit of catching anything at slip that comes within two or three yards of him.

A remarkable shot of Transvaal and future South African captain Ali Bacher taking a one-handed catch at 'suicide' mid-on, off Australian left-hander Bob Cowper at Johannesburg in 1966–67.

For something like nearly two decades (his Test career ran from 1953 to 1974), Sir Garfield Sobers was not only the greatest all-rounder in the world but also the finest batsman, among the best half-dozen or so bowlers and the number one fielder taking part in international cricket. Almost as a necessary by-product to all this activity, the Barbados' wonder was also a successful West Indies captain.

Sobers's unique feats with bat and ball have been covered in earlier sections; as a close-to-the-wicket fieldsman, he had no equal in his time, and few from any other era in international cricket can lay challenge to being his master. Like a number of the very best leg-side close fielders, including Tony Lock and Eknath Solkar, he was left-handed. His reflexes at short-leg were those of a striking cobra. When compelled to field in any other position, there were still very few who would dare claim to be his peer. Sobers is one of the famous seven fieldsmen who have taken more than 100 Test match catches. He also scored 8032 runs and took 235 wickets in Tests. Not even Ian Botham has approached Sobers in terms of personal pre-eminence in each of the departments of the game of cricket.

In pre-war days, another great West Indies cricketing knight, Sir Learie Constantine, was the premier all-round fieldsman in the world. He was one of the classic cover-points of all time, and as agile and effective anywhere else on the field. Other prominent West Indies close fielders of the time included the Trinidad-born Grant brothers, G C ('Jackie') and R S (Rolph). Jackie Grant was brilliant at gully; Rolph Grant was a grand short-leg. Gerry Gomez, whose career

Sir Garfield Sobers of Barbados and West Indies, one of the finest close fielders of all time, picks up a slip catch off the bat of England's Brian Close at Old Trafford in 1963. The jubilant bowler is off-spinner Lance Gibbs.

straddled the war years, was also from Trinidad and another superb close catcher. So too were John Goddard (Barbados and West Indies captain), Robert Christiani (British Guiana) and Prior Jones (Trinidad), who all played with Gomez in England in 1950 when Ramadhin and Valentine were spinning their web of destruction.

Gary Sobers's cousin, David Holford, was a one-time Barbados captain and all-rounder who only occasionally showed his best form in Tests but who always excelled when fielding close in. Batsmen Conrad Hunte and Seymour Nurse (both Barbados) and Roy Fredericks (British Guiana) were other Sobers contemporaries noted for their close-to-the-stumps fielding.

Of the newer generation of West Indies fielders, Viv Richards has taken over as the outstanding contemporary fielder in any position while Gordon Greenidge, although approaching veteran stage, remains the most reliable West Indies slip fieldsman.

Now, to complete the picture, I select 10 great fielders to support my first-choice wicket-keeper Don Tallon of Australia and, in the process, endeavour to select a balanced team able to bat and bowl with the best available.

Moving around in a circle, we have: slips, Bobby Simpson (Australia) and Sir Learie Constantine (West Indies); gully, Richie Benaud (Australia); third man, Neil Harvey (Australia); cover-point, Colin Bland (South Africa); bowler, Freddie Trueman (England); mid-on, Sir Donald Bradman (Australia — captain); forward short-leg, Sir Gary Sobers (West Indies); leg-slip, Tony Lock (England); deep fine-leg, Viv Richards (West Indies); wicket-keeper, Don Tallon.

With Simpson and Constantine in the slips who needs a third? Opening bowler Trueman was equally at home in the deep or as a close catcher. Harvey, Richards and Bradman can all field close up if needed, and Bradman is only one of four superb cover fieldsmen in the team (Bradman, Bland, Harvey and Constantine). For 12th man we must have Clive Lloyd (West Indies) — the younger version to field in the covers, and the elder statesman to take his place in the slips. Here, then, is my ultimate team, in batting order: R B Simpson, I V A Richards, D G Bradman, R N Harvey, G S Sobers, K C Bland, R Benaud, L N Constantine, D Tallon, G A R Lock, F S Trueman, C H Lloyd (12th man)

The bowlers are Trueman, Constantine, Sobers, Lock and Benaud (with Simpson and Richards as change bowlers), an attack which should be able to cope with most conditions and which would certainly not be an easy one to collar. There would also be little chance of their being let down in the field, close-up, mid-field or in the deep, with each player chosen a specialist of the highest calibre and a worthy representative example of the finest fielders ever assembled to participate in an international match since the first cricket Test was played at Melbourne in 1876.

Bibliography

Altham, H S and Swanton, E W, *A History of Cricket*, George Allen & Unwin, London, 1947.

American Cricketer, The, various issues 1877 to 1929.

Arlott, John, *Days at the Cricket*, Longmans, Green, London, 1951.

Arlott, John, *Gone to the Cricket*, Longmans, Green and Co, London, 1948.

Arlott, John, *Gone to the Test Match*, Longmans, Green, London, 1949.

Arlott, John, *Indian Summer*, Longmans, Green and Co, London, 1947.

Arlott, John, *Jack Hobbs – Profile of 'The Master'*, Murray, London, 1981.

Arlott, John, *John Arlott's Book of Cricketers*, Angus & Robertson, Sydney, 1979.

Arlott, John and Brogden, Stanley, *The First Test Match*, Phoenix House, London, 1950.

Armstrong, Warwick W, *The Art of Cricket*. Methuen, London, 1922.

Ashley-Cooper, F S, *Cricket Highways and Byways*. George Allen & Unwin, London, 1927.

Association of Cricket Statisticians –
   The Cricket Statistician – various issues.
   First-class Cricket Matches – 1861–1891.
   New South Wales Cricketers – 1855–1981.
   Queensland Cricketers – 1892–1979.
   South Australian Cricketers – 1877–1984.
   Victorian Cricketers – 1850–1978.
   Western Australian Cricketers – 1892–1983.

Australasian The, 1866 to 1947, Melbourne.

Australian Cricket and *Australian Cricket Yearbook* – 1970 to 1985. Various editors/publishers, Sydney.

Australian Cricketers' Guide – 1856 to 1859. Editors H Biers and William Fairfax, Fairfax, Melbourne.

Australian Cricketers' Guide – 1879 to 1884. Editors H F Boyle and David Scott, Boyle & Scott, Melbourne.

Barbour, Eric P, *The Making of a Cricketer*, The Sydney and Melbourne Publishing Co, 1933

Bailey, Trevor and Trueman, Fred, *From Larwood to Lillee*, Queen Anne Press, London, 1983.

Barker, Ralph, *Innings of a Lifetime*, Collins, London, 1982.

Barker, Ralph, *Ten Great Bowlers*, Chatto & Windus, London, 1967.

Barker, Ralph and Rosenwater, Irving, *England v Australia, 1877/1968*. Wm Heinemann, Melbourne/London, 1969.

Barnes, Sidney, *It Isn't Cricket*, Kimber, London, 1953.

Bassano, Brian, *South Africa in International Cricket*, Chameleon, East London, 1979.

Batchelor, Denzil, *Days Without Sunset*, Eyre & Spottiswoode, London, 1949.

Batchelor, Denzil (editor), *Great Cricketers*, Eyre & Spottiswoode, London, 1970.

Bean, Ernest, *Private Diaries and Notebooks*. Melbourne Cricket Club Library.

Beldham, G W and Fry, C B, *Great Batsmen – Their Methods at a Glance*, Macmillan & Co, London, 1905.

Beldham, G W and Fry, C B, *Great Bowlers and Fielders — Their Methods at a Glance*, Macmillan & Co, London, 1906.

Benaud, Richie, *On Reflection*, Collins, Sydney, 1984.

Benaud, Richie, *Spin Me a Spinner*, Hodder & Stoughton, London, 1963.

Benaud, Richie, *Willow Patterns*, Hodder & Stoughton, London, 1969.

Bettesworth, W A, *Chats On the Cricket Field*, Merritt & Hatcher, London, 1910.

Bowen, Rowland, *Cricket — A History of its Development and Growth*, Eyre & Spottiswoode, London, 1970.

Bradman, Sir Donald, *The Art of Cricket*, Hodder & Stoughton, London, 1984.

Bradman, Don (Sir Donald), *Don Bradman's Book*, Hutchinson, London, 1930.

Bradman, Don (Sir Donald), *Farewell To Cricket*, Theodore Brun, London, 1950.

Brayshaw, Ian, *Caught Marsh, Bowled Lillee*, ABC, Sydney, 1983.

Brayshaw, Ian, *The Chappell Era*, ABC, Sydney, 1984.

Brayshaw, Ian, *Warriors In Baggy Green Caps*, Currawong Press, Sydney, 1982.

Brittenden, R T, *New Zealand Cricketers*, Timmins, Cape Town, 1961.

Brodribb, Gerald, *Next Man In — A Survey of Cricket Laws and Customs*, Pelham, London, 1985.

Brown, Lionel H, *Victor Trumper and the 1902 Australians*, Secker & Warburg, London, 1981.

Browne, Frank, *Some of it was Cricket*, Murray, Sydney, 1965.

Caffyn, William (with R P Daft), *Seventy-one Not Out*, Blackwood, London, 1899.

Campbell, R H, *Cricket Casualties*, ABC, Sydney, 1933.

Canynge Caple, S, *The All-Blacks at Cricket 1860–1958*, Littlebury, Worcester, 1958.

Cardus, Sir Neville, *Australian Summer*, Cape, London, 1937.

Cardus, Sir Neville, *Cricket All The Year*, Collins, London, 1952.

Cardus, Sir Neville, *Days In The Sun*, Grant Richards Ltd, London, 1924.

Cardus, Sir Neville, *Days In The Sun*, Rupert Hart-Davis, London, 1949.

Cardus, Sir Neville, *Good Days*, Rupert Hart-Davis, London, 1948.

Cardus, Sir Neville, *The Summer Game*, Rupert Hart-Davis, London, 1949.

Carman, Arthur H, *New Zealand International Cricket 1894–1974*, Sporting Publications, Tawa, NZ, 1974.

Cashman, Richard, *'Ave A go Yer Mug — Australian Cricket Crowds From Larrikin to Ocker*, Collins, Sydney, 1984.

Cashman, Richard, *Patrons, Players and the Crowd*, Orient Longman, New Delhi, 1980.

Chapman, A P F & others, *The Game of Cricket*, Seeley Service, London, 1930.

Chappell, Ian, *Chappeli*, Hutchinson, Melbourne, 1976.

Cheetham, Jack, *Caught by the Springboks*, Timmins, Cape Town, 1952.

Cheetham, Jack, *I Declare*, Timmins, Cape Town, 1956.

Chester, Frank, *How's That?* Hutchinson, London, 1956.

Close, Brian, *Close On Cricket*, Stanley Paul, London, 1966.

Close, Brian, *I Don't Bruise Easily*, McDonald and Jane's, London, 1978.

Constantine, L N (Sir Learie Constantine), *Cricket and I*, Philip Allan, London, 1933.

Constantine, Learie (Sir Learie Constantine), *Cricket Crackers*, Stanley Paul, London, 1950.

Constantine, Learie (Sir Learie Constantine), *Cricket in the Sun*. Stanley Paul, London, 1946.

Corrie, R T ('A Barracker'), *The Barracker at Bay*, Keating Wood, Melbourne, 1933.

Cowdrey, Colin, *MCC – The Autobiography of a Cricketer*, Hodder and Stoughton, London, 1976.

Cricket (A Weekly Record of the Game) – 1883 to 1912, 'Cricket', London.

The Cricketer and *The Cricketer International* – 1921 to 1985, Various editors/publishers, UK.

Cricketer and miscellaneous *Yearbooks* – 1973 to 1985. Various editors/publishers, Melbourne.

The Cricketer, Karachi, Pakistan.

Cricket Lifestyle, Sydney, Australia.

The Cricket Player, Auckland, New Zealand.

Cricket World, Sydney, Australia.

Crowley, Brian, *A History of Australian Batting*, Macmillan, Melbourne, 1986.

Crowley, Brian, *A History of Australian Bowling and Wicket-keeping*, Macmillan, Melbourne, 1986.

Crowley, Brian, *Calypso Cavaliers*, Ibbotson, Cape Town, 1983.

Crowley, Brian, *Calypso Whirlwind*, Ibbotson, Cape Town, 1984.

Crowley, Brian, *Cricket's Exiles – The Saga of South African Cricket*, Don Nelson, Cape Town, 1983.

Crowley, Brian, *Currie Cup Story*, Don Nelson, Cape Town, 1973.

Crowley, Brian M, *The Springbok and The Kangaroo*, Blue Crane, Johannesburg, 1967.

Crowley, Brian, *World Championship of Cricket*, Playbill, Sydney, 1984.

Darling, D K, *Test Tussles On and Off the Field*, Private, Hobart, 1970.

Davidson, Alan, *Fifteen Paces*, Hutchinson, Sydney, 1963.

Darwin, Bernard, *W G Grace*, Duckworth, London, 1978.

Dexter, E R, *From Bradman To Boycott*, Queen Anne Press, London, 1981.

D'Oliveira, Basil, *D'Oliveira – An Autobiography*, Collins, London, 1968.

D'Oliveira, Basil, *The D'Oliveira Affair*, Collins, London.

D'Oliveira, Basil, *Time To Declare*, Macmillan, Johannesburg, 1980.

Docker, Edward. *History of Indian Cricket*, Macmillan, Bombay, 1976.

Duffus, Louis, *Cricketers of the Veld*, Sampson, Low, Marston, London, 1947.

Duffus, Louis, *South African Cricket 1927–1947*, SACA, Johannesburg, 1948.

Duffus Louis, *Play Adandoned*, Timmins, Cape Town, 1969.

Dunstan, Keith, *The Paddock That Grew*, Cassell, Australia, 1974.

East, Laurence, *Australian Cricketers*, Herbert Jenkins, London, 1930.

Ellis, Clive, *The Life of Charles Burgess Fry*, Dent, London, 1984.

Emery, David, *Who's Who in International Cricket*, Queen Anne Press, London, 1984.

Evans, Godfrey, *Wicket-keepers of the World*, New English Library, London, 1984.

Eytle, Ernest, *Frank Worrell*, Hodder & Stoughton, London, 1963.

Faulkner, G A, *Cricket: Can it be Taught?*, Chapman & Hall, London, 1926.

Fingleton, J H, *Batting From Memory*, Collins, London, 1981.

Fingleton, J H, *Brightly Fades The Don*, Collins, London, 1949.

Fingleton, J H, *Cricket Crisis*, Cassell, London, 1946.

Fingleton, J H, *Fingleton On Cricket*, Collins, London, 1972.

Fingleton, J H, *The Greatest Test of all*, Collins, London, 1961.

Fortune, Charles, *Cricket Overthrown*, Timmins, Cape Town, 1960.

Frindall, Bill, *Frindall's Score Book — The Centenary Test, 1977*, Lonsdale Universal, Birmingham, 1977.

Frindall, Bill, *The Wisden Book of Test Cricket*, Macdonald & Jane's, London, 1978.

Frith, David, *The Archie Jackson Story*, The Cricketer, London, 1974.

Frith, David, *The Fast Men*, Richard Smart Publishing, Sydney, 1981.

Frith, David, *The Slow Men*, Richard Smart Publishing, Sydney, 1984.

Fry, C B, *The Book of Cricket*, Newnes, London, 1899.

Fry, C B, *Life Worth Living*, Eyre & Spottiswoode, London, 1939.

Giffen, George, *With Bat and Ball*, Ward, Lock & Co, London, 1898.

Gilligan, A E R, *Collins' Men*, Arrowsmith, London, 1926.

Goodwin, Clayton, *Caribbean Cricketers*, Harrap, London, 1980.

Goodwin, Clayton, *West Indians at The Wicket*, Macmillan, London, 1986.

Grace, W G (with W Methven Brownlee), *Cricket*, J W Arrowsmith, Bristol, 1891.

Grace, W G (with Arthur Porritt), *"W G": Cricketing Reminiscences and Personal Recollections*, J Bowden, London, 1899.

Gregory, Kenneth (with Ray Illingworth), *The Ashes*, Collins, London, 1982.

Gregory, Kenneth, *In Celebration of Cricket*, Granada, London, 1978.

Greyvenstein, Chris, *Springbok-Seges in Krieket en Rugby*, Buren, Cape Town, 1968.

Grout, Wally (with Frank O'Callaghan), *My Country's Keeper*, Pelham, London, 1965.

Grimmett, C V, *Getting Wickets*, Hodder & Stoughton, London, 1930.

Grimmett, C V, *Grimmett on Cricket*, Nelson, London, 1948.

Grimmett, C V, *Tricking the Batsman*, Hodder & Stoughton, London, 1934.

Gurdeep Singh, *Cricket in Northern India*, Cosmo, Delhi, 1966.

Hammond, Walter R, *Cricket, My World*, Stanley Paul, London, 1948.

Hammond, Walter R, *Cricketers' School*, Stanley Paul, London, 1950.

Harris, Lord, *A Few Short Runs*, Murray, London, 1921.

Hattle, Jimmy (ed), *Graeme Pollock — King of the Willow*, Acme, P Elizabeth, 1970.

Hazare, Vijay, *A Long Innings*, Rupa, Calcutta, 1981.

Headley, George (with Noel White), *George 'Atlas' Headley*, Inst. of Jamaica, 1974.

Hendren, 'Patsy', *Big Cricket*, Hodder & Stoughton, London, 1934.

Heyhoe Flint, Rachel & Rheinberg, Netta, *Fair Play — The Story of Women's Cricket*, Angus & Robertson, London, 1976.

Hill, Les R, *Australian Cricketers on Tour*, Lynton, Blackwood SA, 1974.

Hill, Les R, *The Arthur Richardson Story*, Private, Mt Gambier, 1966.

Hobbs, J B, *The Fight for The Ashes 1932–33*, George G Harrap, London, 1933.

Hordern, H V, *Googlies — Coals from a Test Cricketer's Fireplace*, Angus & Robertson, Sydney 1932.

Howat, Gerald, *Learie Constantine*, Allen & Unwin, London, 1975.

James, Alfred, *Averages & Results of Australian First-class Cricket 1850–51 to 1914–15*, Private, Wahroonga, 1985.

James, C L R, *Beyond A Boundary*, Hutchinson, London, 1963.

Jardine, D R, *Cricket*, Dent, London, 1936.

Jardine, D R, *In Quest of The Ashes*, Hutchinson, London, 1933.

Johnson, Ian, *Cricket at the Crossroads*, Cassell, London, 1957.

Journal of the Cricket Society (various issues), The Cricket Society, UK.

Joy, Nancy, *Maiden Over*, Sporting Handbooks, London, 1950.

Kidson, Hayward, *Over and Time,* Howard Timmins, Cape Town, 1983.

Knott, Alan, *Stumper's View*, Stanley Paul, London, 1972.

Labouchere, P G G, Provis, T A J & Hargreaves, Peter S, *The Story of Continental Cricket*, Hutchinson, London, 1969.

Larwood, Harold, *The Larwood Story*, Allen, London, 1965.

Laver, Frank, *An Australian Cricketer on Tour*, Chapman & Hall, London, 1905.

Laver, Frank, *The Frank Laver Collection of Press Cuttings and Photographs 1899–1930*, Melbourne Cricket Club Library.

Lawry, Bill, *Run-Digger*, Souvenir, London, 1966.

Leader, The – 1882 to 1916, Melbourne.

Lemmon, David, *The Great Wicket-keepers*, Stanley Paul, London, 1984.

Le Quesne, Laurence, *The Bodyline Controversy*, Secker & Warburg, London, 1983.

Lester, J A, *A Century of Philadelphia Cricket*, University of Pennsylvania, Philadelphia, 1951.

Lillee, Dennis, *My Life in Cricket*, Methuen, London, 1982.

Leveson-Gower, H D G, *Off and On the Field*, Stanley Paul, London, 1953.

Lilley, A A, *Twenty-four Years of Cricket*, Mills & Boon, London, 1912.

Lillywhite's Cricketers' Annual – 1872 To 1900 (Editor C W Alcock), Lillywhite, Froude, London.

Lillywhite, Fred, *The English Cricketers' Trip to Canada and The United States in 1859*, Lillywhite, London, 1860.

Lindwall, Ray, *Flying Stumps*, Hutchinson, Sydney, 1954.

Lippincott, Horace Mather, *A History of the Philadlephia Cricket Club*, Private, 1954.

Litchfield, Eric, *Cricket Grand Slam*, Howard Timmins, Cape Town, 1970.

Luckin, M W, *The History of South African Cricket*, Horter, Johannesburg, 1915.

Luckin, M W, *South African Cricket 1919 to 1927*, Luckin, Johannesburg, 1928.

Lyttelton, Hon R H (with W J Ford, C B Fry & G Giffen), *Giants of The Game*, Ward Lock, London, 1910.

Macartney, C G, *My Cricketing Days*, Wm Heinemann, London, 1930.

McCool, Colin, *Cricket is a Game*, Stanley Paul, London, 1961.

McDonald, Trevor, *Viv Richards*, Pelham, London, 1984.

Mackay, Ken (with Frank O'Callaghan), *Slasher Opens Up*, Pelham, London, 1964.

MacLaren, A C, *Cricket Old and New*, Longmans, Green, London, 1924.

McLean, Roy, *Sackcloth Without Ashes*, Timmins, Cape Town, 1958.

McLeary, G F, *Cricket With The Kangaroo*, Hollis & Carter, London, 1950.

Mailey, Arthur, *10 For 66 And All That*, Phoenix Sports Books, London, 1958.

Mankad, Vinoo, *How To Play Cricket*, Rupa, Calcutta, 1976.

Marder, John I, *The International Series*, Kaye & Ward, London, 1968.

Marsh, Rod, *Gloves, Sweat and Tears*, Penguin, Melbourne, 1984.

Martineau, G D, *Bat, Ball, Wicket and All*, Sporting Handbooks, London, 1950.

Martin-Jenkins, Christopher, *The Complete Who's Who of Test Cricket*, Orbis, London, 1980.

Martin-Jenkins, Christopher, *Wisden Book of County Cricket*, Queen Anne Press, London, 1981.

Mason, Ronald, *Ashes In The Mouth*, Hambledon, London, 1982..

Mason, Ronald, *Warwick Armstrong's Australians*, Epworth Press, London, 1971.

Meher-Homji, Kersi, *Cricket's Great Families*, Sparke, Melbourne, 1980.

Meckiff, Ian (with Ian McDonald), *Thrown Out*, Hutchinson, London, 1961.

Miller, Keith, *Cricket Crossfire*, Oldbourne, London, 1956.

Miller, Keith, *Cricket From The Grandstand*, Oldbourne, London, 1959.

Miller, Keith & Whitington, R S, *Bumper*, Latimer, London, 1953.

Modi, Rusi, *Some Indian Cricketers*, NBT, New Delhi, 1972.

Moody, Clarence P, *Australian Cricket and Cricketers*, C P Moody, Adelaide, 1894.

Morawalla, Mahiyar, *Cricket Cavalcade*, Jaico, Bombay, 1976.

Morrah, Patrick, *The Golden Age of Cricket*, Eyre & Spottiswood, London, 1967.

Moyes, A G, *Australian Batsmen*, Harrap, London, 1954.

Moyes, A G, *Australian Bowlers*, Harrap, London, 1953.

Moyes, A G, *Australian Cricket − A History*, Angus & Robertson, Sydney, 1959.

Moyes, A G, *The Changing Face of Cricket*, Angus & Robertson, Sydney, 1963.

Mukherjee, Sujit, *The Romance of Indian Cricket*, Orient, Delhi, 1968.

Mullins, Pat, & Derriman, Philip, *Bat & Pad − Writings on Australian Cricket 1804−1984*, Oxford, Melbourne, 1984

Mulvaney, D J, *Cricket Walkabout*, Melbourne University Press, 1967.

Mustaq Ali, S, *Cricket Delightful*, Rupa & Co, Bombay, 1967.

Naik, Dr Vasant, *Vijay Merchant*, Bandodkar, Bombay, 1981.

Nelson, Don (ed), *Giants of South African Cricket*, Don Nelson, Cape Town, 1971.

New South Wales Cricket Association, *Cricket Year Book* − various editions 1936 onwards.

Nicole, Christopher, *West Indian Cricket*, Phoenix, London, 1957.

Noble, M A, *The Game's The Thing*, Cassell, London, 1926.

Nourse, Dudley, *Cricket In The Blood*, Hodder & Stoughton, London, 1949.

Odendaal, Andre, *Cricket In Isolation*, Odendaal, Cape Town, 1977.

Odendaal, Andre, *God's Forgotten Cricketers*, SA Cricketer, Cape Town, 1976.

Oldfield, W A, *Behind the Wicket*, Hutchinson, London, 1938.

Oldfield, W A, *The Rattle of the Stumps*, Newnes, London, 1954.

O'Reilly, W J, *Cricket Task Force*, Werner Laurie, London, 1951.

Padwick, E W, *A Bibliography of Cricket*, The Cricket Society, London, 1977.

Page, Michael, *Bradman − The Illustrated Biography*, Macmillan, Melbourne, 1983.

Pakistan Book of Cricket, Karachi, Pakistan.

Parker, John, *Cricket Styles & Stylists*, Angus & Robertson, Sydney, 1979.

Parkinson, Michael; *Cricket Mad*, Stanley Paul, London, 1969.

Pavilion, Australian Cricket Society, Melbourne.

Peebles, Ian, *Spinner's Yarn*, Collins, London, 1977.

Peebles, Ian, *Straight From the Shoulder*, Hutchinson, London, 1968.

Playfair Cricket Monthly — 1960 to 1969, Editors Gordon Ross & Roy Webber, Playfair, London.

Pogson, Norman J, *International Wicket-keepers of Three Countries*, Lincoln, Williams, London, 1932.

Pollard, Jack (ed), *Australian Cricket — The Game and the Players*, Hodder & Stoughton/ABC, Sydney, 1982.

Pollard, Jack, *Bumpers, Boseys & Brickbats*, Murray, Sydney, 1971.

Pollock, Graeme, *Down the Wicket*, Pelham, London, 1968.

Pollock, Peter & Graeme, *Bouncers and Boundaries*, Sportsman Enterprises, Johannesburg, 1968.

Pollock, Peter, *The Thirty Tests*, Don Nelson, Cape Town, 1978.

Pullin, A W, *Alfred Shaw, Cricketer*, Cassell, London, 1902.

Puri, Dr Narottam, *Portrait of Indian Captains*, Rupa, Calcutta, 1978.

Raiji, Vasant, *L P Jai*, Tyeby, Bombay, 1976.

Rait Kerr, R S, *The Laws of Cricket — Their History and Growth*, Longmans, Green, London, 1950.

Ramchand, Partab, *Great Indian Cricketers*, Vikas, Sahibabad, 1977.

Ranjitsinhji, K S, *The Jubilee Book of Cricket*, Blackwood, London, 1897.

Ranjitsinhji, K S, *With Stoddart's Team in Australia*, James Bowden, London, 1898.

Reddick, Tom, *Never a Cross Bat*, Don Nelson, Cape Town, 1979.

Richardson, V Y, *The Vic Richardson Story*, Rigby, Adelaide, 1967.

Robertson-Glasgow, R C, *Cricket Prints*, T Werner Laurie Ltd, London, 1943.

Robertson-Glasgow, R C, *More Cricket Prints*, T Werner Laurie Ltd, London, 1948.

Robinson, Ray, *Between Wickets*, Collins, London, 1948.

Robinson, Ray, *From The Boundary*, Collins, London, 1950.

Robinson, Ray, *Green Sprigs*, Collins, Sydney, 1954.

Robinson, Ray, *On Top Down Under*, Cassell, Australia, 1975.

Rosenwater, Irving, *Sir Donald Bradman*, Batsford, London, 1978.

Shell Cricket Almanack of New Zealand, Editor Arthur Carman, various issues, Wellington.

South African Cricketer (Original), Editor John Hetherington, Cape Town.

South African Cricketer (Existing), Editor Richard Whittingdale, Cape Town.

South African Cricket Review — 1956 to 1958, Editor Norman Howell, Cape Town.

Simpson, Bobby, *Captain's Story*, Hutchinson, London, 1966.

Sportsweek's World of Cricket, Bombay, India.

Standing, Percy Cross, *Cricket of Today and Yesterday* (2 vols), Caxton, London, 1904.

Swanton, E W and Woodcock, John, *Barclay's World of Cricket*, Collins, London, 1980.

Swanton, E W, *Follow On*, Collins, London, 1977.

Swanton, E W, *Swanton in Australia*, Collins, London, 1975.

Trueman, Fred, *The Thoughts of Trueman Now*, McDonald and Jane's, London, 1978.

Vaidya, Sudhir, *Vinoo Mankad*, Thacker, Bombay, 1969.

van der Bijl, Vintcent (with John Bishop), *Cricket in the Shadows*, Shuter & Shooter, Pietermaritzburg, 1984.

Victorian Cricket Association, Annual Report, various editions.

Victorian Cricketers' Guide — 1858 to 1862, Various editors, Sands & Kenny, Melbourne.

Warner, Sir Pelham, *Cricket Between Two Wars*, Sporting Handbooks, London, 1942.

Warner, Sir Pelham, *Lord's 1787 to 1945*, Harrap, London, 1946.

Warner, Sir Pelham, *The MCC in South Africa*, Chapman & Hall, London, 1906.

Whitington, R S, *Keith Miller – The Golden Nugget*, Rigby, Adelaide, 1981.

Whitington, R S, *The Quiet Australian – The Lindsay Hassett Story*, Heinemann, Melbourne, 1969.

Whitington, R S, *Time of the Tiger*, Hutchinson, Melbourne, 1970.

Winch, Jonty, *Cricket's Rich Heritage*, Books of Zimbabwe, Bulawayo, 1983.

Wisden Cricketers' Almanack – 1864 to 1984, John Wisden & Co, J Whitaker & Sons, Sporting Handbooks, Macdonald & Jane's, Queen Anne Press, Macdonald Queen Anne Press, all London.

Wisden Cricket Monthly – 1979 to 1985, Editor David Frith. Wisden Cricket Magazines, London.

Woods, S M J, *My Reminiscences*, Chapman & Hall, London, 1925.

World Cricket Digest, Wollahra, NSW, Australia.

Wynne-Thomas, Peter, *England on Tour*, Rigby, London, 1982.

Wynne-Thomas, Peter, *The Rigby A-Z of Cricket Records*, Rigby, Sydney, 1983.

Wynne-Thomas, Peter (with Philip Bailey and Philip Thorn), *Who's Who of Cricketers*, Newnes/Association of Cricket Statisticians, London, 1984.

Comparative, era-by-era statistics of leading Test batsmen, bowlers and wicket-keepers

QUALIFICATIONS:

BATSMEN:
1. All players who scored a century in a Test.
2. All players who scored a thousand runs or more in Tests.

Information is listed in this order; abbreviations in brackets: Player; country (A — Australia; E — England; SA — South Africa; N — New Zealand; W — West Indies; I — India; P — Pakistan; SL — Sri Lanka); career starting and ending year (CAREER SPAN); matches (M); innings (I); not outs (NO); runs (RUNS); highest score (HS); average (AVGE); centuries scored (100); and half-centuries scored (50). * indicates 'not out' scores.

BOWLERS:
1. All players who took five or more wickets in an innings in a Test.
2. All players who took fifty or more wickets in Tests.

Information is listed in this order; abbreviations in brackets: Player; country (A — Australia; E — England; SA — South Africa; N — New Zealand; W — West Indies; I — India; P — Pakistan; SL — Sri Lanka); career starting and ending year (CAREER SPAN); matches (M); balls (B); maidens (MDS); runs (RUNS); wickets (W); average (AV); five wickets in an innings (5); 10 wickets in a match (10); and best bowling (BEST).

WICKET-KEEPERS:
All players who were selected to keep wickets in a Test. Players who substituted for the official wicket-keeper during a Test are not included, although some performed quite admirably. 'Keeping statistics are listed country by country.

Information is listed in this order; abbreviations in brackets: Player; career starting and ending year (CAREER SPAN); matches (MATCH); runs (RUNS); average (AV); catches (CATCH); stumpings (STUMP); total dismissals (DIS).

All statistics are correct to the end of the Australia versus Sri Lanka Test in February 1988, but exclude the first Test between New Zealand and England at Christchurch in 1988.

ALL STATISTICS © CRICKET STATS PUBLICATIONS 1988.
Correspondence to PO Box 248, Prahran 3181.

The batsmen

TABLE A: 1876-77 to 1899

PLAYER	CAREER SPAN		M	I	NO	RUNS	HS	AVGE	100	50
A E Trott(A)	1894-95		3	5	3	205	85*	102.50	0	2
H Wood(E)	1888	1891-92	4	4	1	204	134*	68.00	1	1
A J L Hill(E)	1895-96		3	4	0	251	124	62.75	1	1
C Bannerman(A)	1876-77	1878-79	3	6	2	239	165*	59.75	1	0
F S Jackson(E)	1893	1905	20	33	4	1415	144*	48.79	5	6
K S Ranjitsinhji(E)	1896	1902	15	26	4	989	175	44.95	2	6
C Hill(A)	1896	1911-12	49	89	2	3412	191	39.21	7	19
V T Trumper(A)	1899	1911-12	48	89	8	3163	214*	39.04	8	13
Albert Ward(E)	1893	1894-95	7	13	0	487	117	37.46	1	3
R Abel(E)	1888	1902	13	22	2	744	132*	37.20	2	2
F A Iredale(A)	1894-95	1899	14	23	1	807	140	36.68	2	4
J T Brown(E)	1894-95	1899	8	16	3	470	140	36.15	1	1
A E Stoddart(E)	1887-88	1897-98	16	30	2	996	173	35.57	2	3
A Shrewsbury(E)	1881-82	1894	23	40	4	1277	164	35.47	3	4
A G Steel(E)	1880	1888	13	20	3	600	148	35.29	2	0
T W Hayward(E)	1895-96	1909	35	60	2	1999	137	34.45	3	12

PLAYER	CAREER SPAN		M	I	NO	RUNS	HS	AVGE	100	50
A C MacLaren(E)	1894-95	1909	35	61	4	1931	140	33.87	5	8
W G Grace(E)	1880	1899	22	36	2	1098	170	32.29	2	5
C B Fry(E)	1895-96	1912	26	41	3	1223	144	32.18	2	7
W L Murdoch(A)	1876-77	1890	18	33	5	896	211	32.00	2	1
J T Tyldesley(E)	1898-99	1909	31	55	1	1661	138	30.75	4	9
M A Noble(A)	1897-98	1909	42	73	7	1997	133	30.25	1	16
W Rhodes(E)	1899	1929-30	58	98	21	2325	179	30.19	2	11
H Graham(A)	1893	1896	6	10	0	301	107	30.10	2	0
P S McDonnell(A)	1880	1888	19	34	1	950	147	28.78	3	2
J Darling(A)	1894-95	1905	34	60	2	1657	178	28.56	3	8
W W Read(E)	1882-83	1893	18	27	1	720	117	27.69	1	5
H J H Scott(A)	1884	1886	8	14	1	359	102	27.61	1	1
J J Lyons(A)	1886-87	1897-98	14	27	0	731	134	27.07	1	3
S E Gregory(A)	1890	1912	58	100	7	2282	201	24.53	4	8
G Ulyett(E)	1876-77	1890	25	39	0	949	149	24.33	1	7
P F Warner(E)	1898-99	1912	15	28	2	622	132*	23.92	1	3
C E McLeod(A)	1894-95	1905	17	29	5	573	112	23.87	1	4
W Barnes(E)	1880	1890	21	33	2	725	134	23.38	1	5
G Giffen(A)	1881-82	1896	31	53	0	1238	161	23.35	1	6
J H Sinclair(SA)	1895-96	1910-11	25	47	1	1069	106	23.23	3	3
A C Bannerman(A)	1878-79	1893	28	50	2	1108	94	23.08	0	8
G H S Trott(A)	1888	1897-98	24	42	0	921	143	21.92	1	4
G L Jessop(E)	1899	1912	18	26	0	569	104	21.88	1	3
W Gunn(E)	1886-87	1899	11	20	2	392	102*	21.77	1	1
T P Horan(A)	1876-77	1884-85	15	27	2	471	124	18.84	1	1
J Briggs(E)	1884-85	1899	33	50	5	815	121	18.11	1	2
G J Bonnor(A)	1880	1888	17	30	0	512	128	17.06	1	2

Combined figures of players who represented more than one country:

PLAYER	CAREER SPAN		M	I	NO	RUNS	HS	AVGE	100	50
A E Trott(A/E)	1894-95	1898-99	5	9	3	228	85*	38.00	0	2
W L Murdoch(A/E)	1876-77	1891-92	19	34	5	908	211	31.31	2	1

TABLE B: 1899 to 1913-14

PLAYER	CAREER SPAN		M	I	NO	RUNS	HS	AVGE	100	50
J B Hobbs(E)	1907-08	1930	61	102	7	5410	211	56.94	15	28
C P Mead(E)	1911-12	1928-29	17	26	2	1185	182*	49.37	4	3
F S Jackson(E)	1893	1905	20	33	4	1415	144*	48.79	5	6
J Sharp(E)	1909		3	6	2	188	105	47.00	1	1
R E Foster(E)	1903-04	1907	8	14	1	602	287	46.30	1	1
K S Ranjitsinhji(E)	1896	1902	15	26	4	989	175	44.95	2	6
R J Hartigan(A)	1907-08		2	4	0	170	116	42.50	1	0
C G Macartney(A)	1907-08	1926	35	55	4	2131	170	41.78	7	9
G A Faulkner(SA)	1905-06	1924	25	47	4	1754	204	40.79	4	8
H W Taylor(SA)	1912	1931-32	42	76	4	2936	176	40.77	7	17
W Bardsley(A)	1909	1926	41	66	5	2469	193*	40.47	6	14
G Gunn(E)	1907-08	1929-30	15	29	1	1120	122*	40.00	2	7
C Hill(A)	1896	1911-12	49	89	2	3412	191	39.21	7	19
V T Trumper(A)	1899	1911-12	48	89	8	3163	214*	39.04	8	13
W W Armstrong(A)	1901-02	1921	50	84	10	2863	159*	38.68	6	8
V S Ransford(A)	1907-08	1911-12	20	38	6	1211	143*	37.84	1	7
C Kelleway(A)	1910-11	1928-29	26	42	4	1422	147	37.42	3	6
R Abel(E)	1888	1902	13	22	2	744	132*	37.20	2	2
F A Iredale(A)	1894-95	1899	14	23	1	807	140	36.68	2	4
J T Brown(E)	1894-95	1899	8	16	3	470	140	36.15	1	1
F E Woolley(E)	1909	1934	64	98	7	3283	154	36.07	5	23
R A Duff(A)	1901-02	1905	22	40	3	1317	146	35.59	2	6

PLAYER	CAREER SPAN		M	I	NO	RUNS	HS	AVGE	100	50
T W Hayward(E)	1895-96	1909	35	60	2	1999	137	34.46	3	12
A C MacLaren(E)	1894-95	1909	35	61	4	1931	140	33.87	5	8
J W Zulch(SA)	1909-10	1921-22	16	32	2	985	150	32.83	2	4
W G Grace(E)	1880	1899	22	36	2	1098	170	32.29	2	5
C B Fry(E)	1895-96	1912	26	41	3	1223	144	32.18	2	7
R H Spooner(E)	1905	1912	10	15	0	481	119	32.06	1	4
J T Tyldesley(E)	1898-99	1909	31	55	1	1661	138	30.75	4	9
M A Noble(A)	1897-98	1909	42	73	7	1997	133	30.25	1	16
W Rhodes(E)	1899	1929-30	58	98	21	2325	179	30.19	2	11
G C White(SA)	1905-06	1912	17	31	2	872	147	30.06	2	4
A W Nourse(SA)	1902-03	1924	45	83	8	2234	111	29.78	1	15
J W H T Douglas(E)	1911-12	1924-25	23	35	2	962	119	29.15	1	6
J Darling(A)	1894-95	1905	34	60	2	1657	178	28.56	3	8
K L Hutchings(E)	1907-08	1909	7	12	0	341	126	28.41	1	1
F L Fane(E)	1905-06	1909-10	14	27	1	682	143	26.23	1	3
J W Hearne(E)	1911-12	1926	24	36	5	806	114	26.00	1	2
L C Braund(E)	1901-02	1907-08	23	41	3	987	104	25.97	3	2
S E Gregory(A)	1890	1912	58	100	7	2282	201	24.53	4	8
P F Warner(E)	1898-99	1912	15	28	2	622	132*	23.92	1	3
C E McLeod(A)	1894-95	1905	17	29	5	573	112	23.87	1	4
P W Sherwell(SA)	1905-06	1910-11	13	22	4	427	115	23.72	1	1
J H Sinclair(SA)	1895-96	1910-11	25	47	1	1069	106	23.23	3	3
S J Snooke(SA)	1905-06	1922-23	26	46	1	1008	103	22.40	1	5
G L Jessop(E)	1899	1912	18	26	0	569	104	21.88	1	3
W Gunn(E)	1886-87	1899	11	20	2	392	102*	21.77	1	1
D Denton(E)	1905	1909-10	11	22	1	424	104	20.19	1	1
J Briggs(E)	1884-85	1899	33	50	5	815	121	18.11	1	2
C M H Hathorn(SA)	1902-03	1910-11	12	20	1	325	102	17.10	1	0

TABLE C: 1920-21 to 1928

PLAYER	CAREER SPAN		M	I	NO	RUNS	HS	AVGE	100	50
H Sutcliffe(E)	1924	1935	54	84	9	4555	194	60.73	16	23
W R Hammond(E)	1927-28	1946-47	85	140	16	7249	336*	58.45	22	24
J B Hobbs(E)	1907-08	1930	61	102	7	5410	211	56.94	15	28
C A G Russell(E)	1920-21	1922-23	10	18	2	910	140	56.87	5	2
G E Tyldesley(E)	1921	1928-29	15	20	2	990	122	55.00	3	6
J Ryder(A)	1920-21	1928-29	20	32	5	1394	201*	51.62	3	9
G B Legge(E)	1927-28	1929-30	5	7	1	299	196	49.83	1	0
C P Mead(E)	1911-12	1928-29	17	26	2	1185	182*	49.37	4	3
W H Ponsford(A)	1924-25	1934	29	48	4	2122	266	48.22	7	6
D R Jardine(E)	1928	1933-34	22	33	6	1296	127	48.00	1	10
E H Hendren(E)	1920-21	1934-35	51	83	9	3525	205*	47.63	7	21
M Leyland(E)	1928	1938	41	65	5	2764	187	46.06	9	10
W M Woodfull(A)	1926	1934	35	54	4	2300	161	46.00	7	13
H L Collins(A)	1920-21	1926	19	31	1	1352	203	45.06	4	6
C G Macartney(A)	1907-08	1926	35	55	4	2131	170	41.78	7	9
G A Faulkner(SA)	1905-06	1924	25	47	4	1754	204	40.79	4	8
H W Taylor(SA)	1912	1931-32	42	76	4	2936	176	40.77	7	17
W Bardsley(A)	1909	1926	41	66	5	2469	193*	40.47	6	14
G Gunn(E)	1907-08	1929-30	15	29	1	1120	122*	40.00	2	7
C N Frank(SA)	1921-22		3	6	0	236	152	39.33	1	0
W W Armstrong(A)	1901-02	1921	50	84	10	2863	159*	38.68	6	8
A Sandham(E)	1921	1929-30	14	23	0	879	325	38.21	2	3
R H Catterall(SA)	1922-23	1930-31	24	43	2	1555	120	37.92	3	11
C Kelleway(A)	1910-11	1928-29	26	42	4	1422	147	37.42	3	6
C E Pellew(A)	1920-21	1921-22	10	14	1	484	116	37.23	2	1
J M Gregory(A)	1920-21	1928-29	24	34	3	1146	119	36.96	2	7

PLAYER	CAREER SPAN		M	I	NO	RUNS	HS	AVGE	100	50
A F Kippax(A)	1924-25	1934	22	34	1	1192	146	36.12	2	8
F E Woolley(E)	1909	1934	64	98	7	3283	154	36.07	5	23
J M Taylor(A)	1920-21	1926	20	28	0	997	108	35.60	1	8
J W H Makepeace(E)	1920-21		4	8	0	279	117	34.87	1	2
J W Zulch(SA)	1909-10	1921-22	16	32	2	985	150	32.83	2	4
R E S Wyatt(E)	1927-28	1936-37	40	64	6	1839	149	31.70	2	12
A J Richardson(A)	1924-25	1926	9	13	0	403	100	31.00	1	2
C A Roach(W)	1928	1934-35	16	32	1	952	209	30.70	2	6
H B Cameron(SA)	1927-28	1935	26	45	4	1239	90	30.21	0	10
W Rhodes(E)	1899	1929-30	58	98	21	2325	179	30.19	2	11
A W Nourse(SA)	1902-03	1924	45	83	8	2234	111	29.78	1	15
J W H T Douglas(E)	1911-12	1924-25	23	35	2	962	119	29.15	1	6
A P F Chapman(E)	1924	1930-31	26	36	4	925	121	28.90	1	5
I J Siedle(SA)	1927-28	1935-36	18	34	0	977	141	28.73	1	5
F R Martin(W)	1928	1930-31	9	18	1	486	123*	28.58	1	0
J W Hearne(E)	1911-12	1926	24	36	5	806	114	26.00	1	2
M W Tate(E)	1924	1935	39	52	5	1198	100*	25.48	1	5
V Y Richardson(A)	1924-25	1935-36	19	30	0	706	138	23.53	1	1
W A S Oldfield(A)	1920-21	1936-37	54	80	17	1427	65*	22.65	0	4
S J Snooke(SA)	1905-06	1922-23	26	46	1	1008	103	22.40	1	5
H S T L Hendry(A)	1921	1928-29	11	18	2	335	112	20.93	1	0

TABLE D: 1928-29 to 1939

PLAYER	CAREER SPAN		M	I	NO	RUNS	HS	AVGE	100	50
D G Bradman(A)	1928-29	1948	52	80	10	6996	334	99.94	29	13
C S Dempster(N)	1929-30	1932-33	10	15	4	723	136	65.72	2	5
B H Valentine(E)	1933-34	1938-39	7	9	2	454	136	64.85	2	1
S G Barnes(A)	1938	1948	13	19	2	1072	234	63.05	3	5
G A Headley(W)	1929-30	1953-54	22	40	4	2190	270*	60.83	10	5
H Sutcliffe(E)	1924	1935	54	84	9	4555	194	60.73	16	23
E Paynter(E)	1931	1939	20	31	5	1540	243	59.23	4	7
K S Duleepsinhji(E)	1929	1931	12	19	2	995	173	58.52	3	5
W R Hammond(E)	1927-28	1946-47	85	140	16	7249	336*	58.45	22	24
K H Weekes(W)	1939		2	3	0	173	137	57.66	1	0
J B Hobbs(E)	1907-08	1930	61	102	7	5410	211	56.94	15	28
L Hutton(E)	1937	1954-55	79	138	15	6971	364	56.67	19	33
G E Tyldesley(E)	1921	1928-29	15	20	2	990	122	55.00	3	6
A D Nourse(SA)	1935	1951	3	62	7	2960	231	53.81	9	14
M P Donnelly(N)	1937	1949	7	12	1	582	206	52.90	1	4
A Melville(SA)	1938-39	1948-49	11	19	2	894	189	52.58	4	3
C F Walters(E)	1933	1934	11	18	3	784	102	52.26	1	7
J Ryder(A)	1920-21	1928-29	20	32	5	1394	201*	51.62	3	9
P G van der Bijl(SA)	1938-39		5	9	0	460	125	51.11	1	2
D C S Compton(E)	1937	1956-57	78	131	15	5807	278	50.06	17	28
G B Legge(E)	1927-28	1929-30	5	7	1	299	196	49.83	1	0
C P Mead(E)	1911-12	1928-29	17	26	2	1185	182*	49.37	4	3
B Mitchell(SA)	1929	1948-49	42	80	9	3471	189*	48.88	8	21
W H Ponsford(A)	1924-25	1934	29	48	4	2122	266	48.22	7	6
S J McCabe(A)	1930	1938	39	62	5	2748	232	48.21	6	13
D R Jardine(E)	1928	1933-34	22	33	6	1296	127	48.00	1	10
V M Merchant(I)	1933-34	1951-52	10	18	0	859	154	47.72	3	3
E H Hendren(E)	1920-21	1934-35	51	83	9	3525	205*	47.63	7	21
A Jackson(A)	1928-29	1930-31	8	11	1	474	164	47.40	1	2
W A Brown(A)	1934	1948	22	35	1	1592	206*	46.82	4	9
J Hardstaff jnr(E)	1935	1948	23	38	3	1636	205*	46.74	4	10
A L Hassett(A)	1938	1953	43	69	3	3073	198*	46.56	10	11
M Leyland(E)	1928	1938	41	65	5	2764	187	46.06	9	10

PLAYER	CAREER SPAN		M	I	NO	RUNS	HS	AVGE	100	50
W M Woodfull(A)	1926	1934	35	54	4	2300	161	46.00	7	13
A H Bakewell(E)	1931	1935	6	9	0	409	107	45.44	1	3
P A Gibbs(E)	1938-39	1946-47	8	13	0	581	120	44.69	2	3
C Washbrook(E)	1937	1956	37	66	6	2569	195	42.81	6	12
E A B Rowan(SA)	1935	1951	26	50	5	1965	236	42.66	3	12
J H W Fingleton(A)	1931-32	1938	18	29	1	1189	136	42.46	5	3
J B Stollmeyer(W)	1939	1954-55	32	56	5	2159	160	42.33	4	12
H G Vivian(N)	1931	1937	7	10	0	421	100	42.10	1	5
H G Owen-Smith(SA)	1929		5	8	2	252	129	42.00	1	1
H W Taylor(SA)	1912	1931-32	42	76	4	2936	176	40.77	7	17
L E G Ames(E)	1929	1938-39	47	72	12	2434	149	40.56	8	7
W J Edrich(E)	1938	1954-55	39	63	2	2440	219	40.00	6	13
G Gunn(E)	1907-08	1929-30	15	29	1	1120	122*	40.00	2	7
A Sandham(E)	1921	1929-30	14	23	0	879	325	38.21	2	3
R H Catterall(SA)	1922-23	1930-31	24	43	2	1555	120	37.92	3	11
C Kelleway(A)	1910-11	1928-29	26	42	4	1422	147	37.42	3	6
J M Gregory(A)	1920-21	1928-29	24	34	3	1146	119	36.96	2	7
A F Kippax(A)	1924-25	1934	22	34	1	1192	146	36.12	2	8
F E Woolley(E)	1909	1934	64	98	7	3283	154	36.07	5	23
E H Bowley(E)	1929	1929-30	5	7	0	252	109	36.00	1	0
C J Barnett(E)	1933	1948	20	35	4	1098	129	35.41	2	5
J A J Christy(SA)	1929	1931-32	10	18	0	618	103	34.33	1	5
K E Rigg(A)	1930-31	1936-37	8	12	0	401	127	33.41	1	1
A G Chipperfield(A)	1934	1938	14	20	3	552	109	32.47	1	2
S Mushtaq Ali(I)	1933-34	1951-52	11	20	1	612	112	32.21	2	3
E L Dalton(SA)	1929	1938-39	15	24	2	698	117	31.72	2	3
R E S Wyatt(E)	1927-28	1936-37	40	64	6	1839	149	31.70	2	12
C A Roach(W)	1928	1934-35	16	32	1	952	209	30.70	2	6
G E Gomez(W)	1939	1953-54	29	46	5	1243	101	30.31	1	8
H B Cameron(SA)	1927-28	1935	26	45	4	1239	90	30.21	0	10
W Rhodes(E)	1899	1929-30	58	98	21	2325	179	30.19	2	11
W A Hadlee(N)	1937	1950-51	11	19	1	543	116	30.16	1	2
T S Worthington(E)	1929-30	1936-37	9	11	0	321	128	29.18	1	1
A P F Chapman(E)	1924	1930-31	26	36	4	925	121	28.90	1	5
Nawab Pataudi snr(E)	1932-33	1934	3	5	0	144	102	28.80	1	0
I J Siedle(SA)	1927-28	1935-36	18	34	0	977	141	28.73	1	5
F R Martin(W)	1928	1930-31	9	18	1	486	123*	28.58	1	0
K G Viljoen(SA)	1930-31	1948-49	27	50	2	1365	124	28.43	2	9
W W Wade(SA)	1938-39	1949-50	11	19	1	511	125	28.38	1	3
G M Carew(W)	1934-35	1948-49	4	7	1	170	107	28.33	1	0
J E Mills(N)	1929-30	1932-33	7	10	1	241	117	26.77	1	0
R W V Robins(E)	1929	1937	19	27	4	612	108	26.60	1	4
M W Tate(E)	1924	1935	39	52	5	1198	100*	25.48	1	5
M L Page(N)	1929-30	1937	14	20	0	492	104	24.60	1	2
L Amarnath(I)	1933-34	1952-53	24	40	4	878	118	24.38	1	4
G O B Allen(E)	1930	1947-48	25	33	2	750	122	24.19	1	3
V Y Richardson(A)	1924-25	1935-36	19	30	0	706	138	23.53	1	1
W A S Oldfield(A)	1920-21	1936-37	54	80	17	1427	65*	22.65	0	4
H S T L Hendry(A)	1921	1928-29	11	18	2	335	112	20.93	1	0
I Barrow(W)	1929-30	1939	11	19	2	276	105	16.23	1	0
C L Badcock(A)	1936-37	1938	7	12	1	160	118	14.54	1	0
X C Balaskas(SA)	1930-31	1938-39	9	13	1	174	122*	14.50	1	0

TABLE E: 1945-46 to 1957

PLAYER	CAREER SPAN		M	I	NO	RUNS	HS	AVGE	100	50
A G Ganteaume(W)	1947-48		1	1	0	112	112	112.00	1	0
D G Bradman(A)	1928-29	1948	52	80	10	6996	334	99.94	29	13

PLAYER	CAREER SPAN		M	I	NO	RUNS	HS	AVGE	100	50
S G Barnes(A)	1938	1948	13	19	2	1072	234	63.05	3	5
G A Headley(W)	1929-30	1953-54	22	40	4	2190	270*	60.83	10	5
R H Shodhan(I)	1952-53	1952-53	3	4	1	181	110	60.33	1	0
K F Barrington(E)	1955	1968	82	131	15	6806	256	58.76	20	35
E D Weekes(W)	1947-48	1957-58	48	81	5	4455	207	58.61	15	19
W R Hammond(E)	1927-28	1946-47	85	140	16	7249	336*	58.45	22	24
G S Sobers(W)	1953-54	1973-74	93	160	21	8032	365*	57.78	26	30
C L Walcott(W)	1947-48	1959-60	44	74	7	3798	220	56.68	15	14
L Hutton(E)	1937	1954-55	79	138	15	6971	364	56.67	19	33
A D Nourse(SA)	1935	1951	34	62	7	2960	231	53.81	9	14
M P Donnelly(N)	1937	1949	7	12	1	582	206	52.90	1	4
A Melville(SA)	1938-39	1948-49	11	19	2	894	189	52.58	4	3
D C S Compton(E)	1937	1956-57	78	131	15	5807	278	50.06	17	28
F M M Worrell(W)	1947-48	1963	41	87	9	3860	261	49.48	9	22
M L Apte(I)	1952-53	1952-53	7	13	2	542	163*	49.27	1	3
B Mitchell(SA)	1929	1948-49	42	80	9	3471	189*	48.88	8	21
R N Harvey(A)	1947-48	1962-63	79	137	10	6149	205	48.41	21	24
V M Merchant(I)	1933-34	1951-52	10	18	0	859	154	47.72	3	3
V S Hazare(I)	1946	1952-53	30	52	6	2192	164*	47.65	7	9
R B Kanhai(W)	1957	1973-74	79	137	6	6227	256	47.53	15	28
W A Brown(A)	1934	1948	22	35	1	1592	206*	46.82	4	9
P B H May(E)	1951	1961	66	106	9	4537	285*	46.77	13	22
J Hardstaff jnr(E)	1935	1948	23	38	3	1636	205*	46.74	4	10
A L Hassett(A)	1938	1953	43	69	3	3073	198*	46.56	10	11
A R Morris(A)	1946-47	1954-55	46	79	3	3533	206	46.48	12	12
J D B Robertson(E)	1947	1951-52	11	21	2	881	133	46.36	2	6
A F Rae(W)	1948-49	1952-53	15	24	2	1016	109	46.18	4	4
R S Modi(I)	1946	1952-53	10	17	1	736	112	46.00	1	6
P A Gibbs(E)	1938-39	1946-47	8	13	0	581	120	44.69	2	3
T W Graveney(E)	1951	1969	79	123	13	4882	258	44.38	11	20
M C Cowdrey(E)	1954-55	1974-75	114	188	15	7624	182	44.06	22	38
Hanif Mohammad(P)	1952-53	1969-70	55	97	8	3915	337	43.98	12	15
C Washbrook(E)	1937	1956	37	66	6	2569	195	42.81	6	12
E A B Rowan(SA)	1935	1951	26	50	5	1965	236	42.66	3	12
J B Stollmeyer(W)	1939	1954-55	32	56	5	2159	160	42.33	4	12
P R Umrigar(I)	1948-49	1961-62	59	94	8	3631	223	42.22	12	14
D J McGlew(SA)	1951	1961-62	34	64	6	2440	255*	42.06	7	10
A J Watkins(E)	1948	1952	15	24	4	810	137*	40.50	2	4
B Sutcliffe(N)	1946-47	1965	42	76	8	2727	230*	40.10	5	15
W J Edrich(E)	1938	1954-55	39	63	2	2440	219	40.00	6	13
Nazar Mohammad(P)	1952-53		5	8	1	277	124*	39.57	1	1
C C McDonald(A)	1951-52	1961	47	83	4	3107	170	39.32	5	17
V L Manjrekar(I)	1951-52	1964-65	55	92	10	3208	189*	39.12	7	15
P J P Burge(A)	1954-55	1965-66	42	68	8	2290	181	38.16	4	12
D S Sheppard(E)	1950	1962-63	22	33	2	1172	119	37.80	3	6
F G Mann(E)	1948-49	1949	7	12	2	376	136*	37.60	1	0
P E Richardson(E)	1956	1963	34	56	1	2061	126	37.47	5	9
K R Miller(A)	1945-46	1956-57	55	87	7	2958	147	36.97	7	13
S J E Loxton(A)	1947-48	1950-51	12	15	0	554	101	36.93	1	3
J K Holt jnr(W)	1953-54	1958-59	17	31	2	1066	166	36.75	2	5
C J Barnett(E)	1933	1948	20	35	4	1098	129	35.41	2	5
C L McCool(A)	1945-46	1949-50	14	17	4	459	104*	35.30	1	1
J Moroney(A)	1949-50	1951-52	7	12	1	383	118	34.81	2	1
J W Burke(A)	1950-51	1958-59	24	44	7	1280	189	34.59	3	5
T L Goddard(SA)	1955	1969-70	41	78	5	2516	112	34.46	1	18
W R Endean(SA)	1951	1957-58	28	52	4	1630	162*	33.95	3	8
K D Mackay(A)	1956	1962-63	37	52	7	1507	89	33.48	0	13
R T Simpson(E)	1948-49	1954-55	27	45	3	1401	156*	33.35	4	6
J R Reid(N)	1949	1965	58	108	5	3428	142	33.28	6	22

PLAYER	CAREER SPAN		M	I	NO	RUNS	HS	AVGE	100	50
Pankaj Roy(I)	1951-52	1960-61	43	79	4	2442	173	32.56	5	9
D G Phadkar(I)	1947-48	1958-59	31	45	7	1229	123	32.34	2	8
S Mushtaq Ali(I)	1933-34	1951-52	11	20	1	612	112	32.21	2	3
J M Parks(E)	1954	1967-68	46	68	7	1962	108*	32.16	2	9
D S Atkinson(W)	1948-49	1957-58	22	35	6	922	219	31.79	1	5
O G Smith(W)	1954-55	1958-59	26	42	0	1331	168	31.69	4	6
N J Contractor(I)	1955-56	1961-62	31	52	1	1611	108	31.58	1	11
Waqar Hassan(P)	1952-53	1959-60	21	35	1	1071	189	31.50	1	6
A J Pithey(SA)	1956-57	1964-65	17	27	1	819	154	31.50	1	4
M H Mankad(I)	1946	1958-59	44	72	5	2109	231	31.47	5	6
S C Griffith(E)	1947-48	1948-49	3	5	0	157	140	31.40	1	0
G O Rabone(N)	1949	1954-55	12	20	2	562	107	31.22	1	2
C C Depeiza(W)	1954-55	1955-56	5	8	2	187	122	31.16	1	0
H R Adhikari(I)	1947-48	1958-59	21	36	8	872	114*	31.14	1	4
J H B Waite(SA)	1951	1964-65	50	86	7	2405	134	30.44	4	16
G E Gomez(W)	1939	1953-54	29	46	5	1243	101	30.31	1	8
R A McLean(SA)	1951	1964-65	40	73	3	2120	142	30.28	5	10
W A Hadlee(N)	1937	1950-51	11	19	1	543	116	30.16	1	2
F C M Alexander(W)	1957	1960-61	25	38	6	961	108	30.03	1	7
T E Bailey(E)	1949	1958-59	61	91	14	2290	134*	29.74	1	10
Imtiaz Ahmed(P)	1952-53	1962	41	72	1	2079	209	29.28	3	11
W Place(E)	1947-48		3	6	1	144	107	28.80	1	0
K G Viljoen(SA)	1930-31	1948-49	27	50	2	1365	124	28.43	2	9
W W Wade(SA)	1938-39	1949-50	11	19	1	511	125	28.38	1	3
G M Carew(W)	1934-35	1948-49	4	7	1	170	107	28.33	1	0
A G Kripal Singh(I)	1955-56	1964-65	14	20	5	422	100*	28.13	1	2
Wazir Mohammad(P)	1952-53	1959-60	20	33	4	801	189	27.62	2	3
D J Insole(E)	1950	1957	9	17	2	408	110*	27.20	1	1
L E Favell(A)	1954-55	1960-61	19	31	3	757	101	27.03	1	5
R J Christiani(W)	1947-48	1953-54	22	37	3	896	107	26.35	1	4
W Watson(E)	1951	1958-59	23	37	3	879	116	25.85	2	3
R G Nadkarni(I)	1955-56	1967-68	41	67	12	1414	122*	25.70	1	7
Alimuddin(P)	1954	1962	25	45	2	1091	109	25.37	2	7
A K Davidson(A)	1953	1962-63	44	61	7	1328	80	24.59	0	5
G S Ramchand(I)	195	1959-60	33	53	5	1180	109	24.58	2	5
R G Archer(A)	1952-53	1956-57	19	30	1	713	128	24.58	1	2
R Benaud(A)	1951-52	1963-64	63	97	7	2201	122	24.45	3	9
L Amarnath(I)	1933-34	1952-53	24	40	4	878	118	24.38	1	4
G O B Allen(E)	1930	1947-48	25	33	2	750	122	24.19	1	3
F J Titmus(E)	1955	1974-75	53	76	11	1449	84*	22.29	0	10
P G Z Harris(N)	1955-56	1964-65	9	18	1	378	101	22.23	1	1
A R A Murray(SA)	1952-53	1953-54	10	14	1	289	109	22.23	1	1
B H Pairaudeau(W)	1952-53	1957	13	21	0	454	115	21.61	1	3
R R Lindwall(A)	1945-46	1959-60	61	84	13	1502	118	21.15	2	5
J W Guy(N)	1955-56	1961-62	12	23	2	440	102	20.95	1	3
P L Winslow(SA)	1949-50	1955	5	9	0	186	108	20.66	1	0
T G Evans(E)	1946	1959	91	133	14	2439	104	20.49	2	8
S N McGregor(N)	1954-55	1964-65	25	47	2	892	111	19.82	1	3
I W Johnson(A)	1945-46	1956-57	45	66	12	1000	77	18.51	0	6

TABLE F: 1957-58 to 1969-70

PLAYER	CAREER SPAN		M	I	NO	RUNS	HS	AVGE	100	50
B A Richards(SA)	1969-70		4	7	0	508	140	72.57	2	2
R G Pollock(SA)	1963-64	1969-70	23	41	4	2256	274	60.97	7	11
K F Barrington(E)	1955	1968	82	131	15	6806	256	58.76	20	35
E D Weekes(W)	1947-48	1957-58	48	81	5	4455	207	58.61	15	19
G S Sobers(W)	1953-54	1973-74	93	160	21	8032	365*	57.78	26	30

PLAYER	CAREER SPAN		M	I	NO	RUNS	HS	AVGE	100	50
C L Walcott(W)	1947-48	1959-60	44	74	7	3798	220	56.68	15	14
C A Davis(W)	1968-69	1972-73	15	29	5	1301	183	54.20	4	4
B L Irvine(SA)	1969-70		4	7	0	353	102	50.42	1	2
F M M Worrell(W)	1947-48	1963	41	87	9	3860	261	49.48	9	22
K C Bland(SA)	1961-62	1966-67	21	39	5	1669	144*	49.08	3	9
R N Harvey(A)	1947-48	1962-63	79	137	10	6149	205	48.41	21	24
K D Walters(A)	1965-66	1980-81	74	125	14	5357	250	48.26	15	33
E R Dexter(E)	1958	1968	62	102	8	4502	205	47.89	9	27
G Boycott(E)	1964	1981-82	108	193	23	8114	246*	47.72	22	42
S M Nurse(W)	1959-60	1968-69	29	54	1	2523	258	47.60	6	10
R B Kanhai(W)	1957	1973-74	79	137	6	6227	256	47.53	15	28
W M Lawry(A)	1961	1970-71	67	123	12	5234	210	47.15	13	27
R Subba Row(E)	1958	1961	13	22	1	984	137	46.85	3	4
R M Cowper(A)	1964	1968	27	46	2	2061	307	46.84	5	10
R B Simpson(A)	1957-58	1977-78	62	111	7	4869	311	46.81	10	27
P B H May(E)	1951	1961	66	106	9	4537	285*	46.77	13	22
C Milburn(E)	1966	1968-69	9	16	2	654	139	46.71	2	2
C H Lloyd(W)	1966-67	1984-85	110	175	14	7515	242*	46.67	19	39
D L Amiss(E)	1966	1977	50	88	10	3612	262*	46.30	11	11
P J Sharpe(E)	1963	1969	12	21	4	786	111	46.23	1	4
E J Barlow)SA)	1961-62	1969-70	30	57	2	2516	201	45.74	6	15
N C O'Neill(A)	1958-59	1964-65	42	69	8	2779	181	45.55	6	15
C C Hunte(W)	1957-58	1966-67	44	78	6	3245	260	45.06	8	13
Zaheer Abbas(P)	1969-70	1985-86	78	124	11	5062	274	44.79	12	20
G M Turner(N)	1968-69	1982-83	41	73	6	2991	259	44.64	7	14
T W Graveney(E)	1951	1969	79	123	13	4882	258	44.38	11	20
M C Cowdrey(E)	1954-55	1974-75	114	188	15	7624	182	44.06	22	38
Hanif Mohammad(P)	1952-53	1969-70	55	97	8	3915	337	43.98	12	15
G Pullar(E)	1959	1962-63	28	49	4	1974	175	43.86	4	12
J H Edrich(E)	1963	1975	77	127	9	5138	310*	43.54	12	24
I R Redpath(A)	1963-64	1975-76	66	120	11	4737	171	43.45	8	31
B F Butcher(W)	1958-59	1969	44	78	6	3104	209*	43.11	7	16
M Amarnath(I)	1969-70	1987-88	69	113	10	4378	138	42.50	11	24
R C Fredericks(W)	1968-69	1976-77	59	109	7	4334	169	42.49	8	26
I M Chappell(A)	1964-65	1979-80	75	136	10	5345	196	42.42	14	26
P R Umrigar(I)	1948-49	1961-62	59	94	8	3631	223	42.22	12	14
B C Booth(A)	1961	1965-66	29	48	6	1773	169	42.21	5	10
D J McGlew(SA)	1951	1961-62	34	64	6	2440	255*	42.06	7	10
G R Viswanath(I)	1969-70	1982-83	91	155	10	6080	222	41.93	14	35
P H Parfitt(E)	1961-62	1972	37	52	6	1882	131*	40.91	7	6
Saeed Ahmed(P)	1957-58	1972-73	41	78	4	2991	172	40.41	5	16
B Sutcliffe(N)	1946-47	1965	42	76	8	2727	230*	40.10	5	15
B L D'Oliveira(E)	1966	1972	44	70	8	2484	158	40.06	5	15
K W R Fletcher(E)	1968	1981-82	59	96	14	3272	216	39.90	7	19
M H Denness(E)	1969	1975	28	45	3	1667	188	39.69	4	7
C C McDonald(A)	1951-52	1961	47	83	4	3107	170	39.32	5	17
D N Sardesai(I)	1961-62	1972-73	30	55	4	2001	212	39.23	5	9
Mushtaq Mohammad(P)	1958-59	1978-79	57	100	7	3643	201	39.17	10	19
V L Manjrekar(I)	1951-52	1964-65	55	92	10	3208	189*	39.12	7	15
Majid J Khan(P)	1964-65	1982-83	63	106	5	3930	167	38.91	8	19
Asif Iqbal(P)	1964-65	1979-80	58	99	7	3575	175	38.85	11	12
P J P Burge(A)	1954-55	1965-66	42	68	8	2290	181	38.16	4	12
D S Sheppard(E)	1950	1962-63	22	33	2	1172	119	37.80	3	6
D T Lindsay(SA)	1963-64	1969-70	19	31	1	1130	182	37.66	3	4
P E Richardson(E)	195	1963	34	56	1	2061	126	37.47	5	9
K R Stackpole(A)	1965-66	1973-74	43	80	5	2807	207	37.42	7	14
J K Holt jnr(W)	1953-54	1958-59	17	31	2	1066	166	36.75	2	5
Sadiq Mohammad(P)	1969-70	1980-81	41	74	2	2579	166	35.81	5	10
C G Borde(I)	1958-59	1969-70	55	97	11	3061	177*	35.59	5	18

PLAYER	CAREER SPAN		M	I	NO	RUNS	HS	AVGE	100	50
R W Barber(E)	1960	1968	28	45	3	1495	185	35.59	1	9
Nawab Pataudi jnr(I)	1961-62	1974-75	46	83	3	2793	203*	34.91	6	16
J W Burke(A)	1950-51	1958-59	24	44	7	1280	189	34.59	3	5
T L Goddard(SA)	1955	1969-70	41	78	5	2516	112	34.46	1	18
M C Carew(W)	196	1971-72	19	36	3	1127	109	34.15	1	5
J S Solomon(W)	1958-59	1964-65	27	46	7	1326	100*	34.00	1	9
W R Endean(SA)	1951	1957-58	28	52	4	1630	162*	33.95	3	8
A P Sheehan(A)	1967-68	1973-74	31	53	6	1594	127	33.91	2	7
K D Mackay(A)	1956	1962-63	37	52	7	1507	89	33.48	0	13
J R Reid(N)	1949	1965	58	108	5	3428	142	33.28	6	22
A P E Knott(E)	1967	1981	95	149	15	4389	135	32.75	5	30
B K Kunderan(I)	1959-60	1967	18	34	4	981	192	32.70	2	3
Pankaj Roy(I)	1951-52	1960-61	43	79	4	2442	173	32.56	5	9
D G Phadkar(I)	1947-48	1958-59	31	45	7	1229	123	32.34	2	8
B E Congdon(N)	1964-65	1978	61	114	7	3448	176	32.22	7	19
J M Parks(E)	1954	1967-68	46	68	7	1962	108*	32.16	2	9
D S Atkinson(W)	1948-49	1957-58	22	35	6	922	219	31.79	1	5
O G Smith(W)	1954-55	1958-59	26	42	0	1331	168	31.69	4	6
M J K Smith(E)	1958	1972	50	78	6	2278	121	31.63	3	11
Khalid Ibadulla(P)	1964-65	1967	4	8	0	253	166	31.62	1	0
N J Contractor(I)	1955-56	1961-62	31	52	1	1611	108	31.58	1	11
C P S Chauhan(I)	1969-70	1980-81	40	68	2	2084	97	31.57	0	16
Waqar Hassan(P)	1952-53	1959-60	21	35	1	1071	189	31.50	1	6
A J Pithey(SA)	1956-57	1964-65	17	27	1	819	154	31.50	1	4
M H Mankad(I)	1946	1958-59	44	72	5	2109	231	31.47	5	6
M G Burgess(N)	1967-68	1980-81	50	92	6	2684	119*	31.20	5	14
Hanumant Singh(I)	1963-64	1969-70	14	24	2	686	105	31.18	1	5
G T Dowling(N)	1961-62	1971-72	39	77	3	2306	239	31.16	3	11
H R Adhikari(I)	1947-48	1958-59	21	36	8	872	114*	31.14	1	4
F M Engineer(I)	1961-62	1974-75	46	87	3	2611	121	31.08	2	16
A L Wadekar(I)	1966-67	1974	37	71	3	2113	143	31.07	1	14
M L Jaisimha(I)	1959	1970-71	39	71	4	2056	129	30.68	3	12
M L C Foster(W)	1969	1977-78	14	24	5	580	125	30.52	1	1
J Burki(P)	1960-61	1969-70	25	48	4	1341	140	30.47	3	4
J H B Waite(SA)	1951	1964-65	50	86	7	2405	134	30.44	4	16
R A McLean(SA)	1951	1964-65	40	73	3	2120	142	30.28	5	10
B F Hastings(N)	1968-69	1975-76	31	56	6	1510	117*	30.20	4	7
F C M Alexander(W)	1957	1960-61	25	38	6	961	108	30.03	1	7
T W Jarvis(N)	1964-65	1972-73	13	22	1	635	182	29.76	1	2
T E Bailey(E)	1949	1958-59	61	91	14	2290	134*	29.74	1	10
B W Sinclair(N)	1962-63	1967-68	21	40	1	1148	138	29.43	3	3
Imtiaz Ahmed(P)	1952-53	1962	41	72	1	2079	209	29.28	3	11
R F Surti(I)	1960-61	1969-70	26	48	4	1263	99	28.70	0	9
A G Kripal Singh(I)	1955-56	1964-65	14	20	5	422	100*	28.13	1	2
L E Favell(A)	1954-55	1960-61	19	31	3	757	101	27.03	1	5
J H Hampshire(E)	1969	1975	8	16	1	403	107	26.86	1	2
E D A S McMorris(W)	1957-58	1966	13	21	0	564	125	26.85	1	3
B R Knight(E)	1961-62	1969	29	38	7	812	127	26.19	2	0
W Watson(E)	1951	1958-59	23	37	3	879	116	25.85	2	3
R G Nadkarni(I)	1955-56	1967-68	41	67	12	1414	122*	25.70	1	7
S A Durani(I)	1959-60	1972-73	29	50	2	1202	104	25.64	1	7
C A Milton(E)	1958	1959	6	9	1	204	104*	25.50	1	0
E D Solkar(I)	1969-70	1976-77	27	48	6	1068	102	25.42	1	6
Alimuddin(P)	1954	1962	25	45	2	1091	109	25.37	2	7
A K Davidson(A)	1953	1962-63	44	61	7	1328	80	24.59	0	5
G S Ramchand(I)	1952	1959-60	33	53	5	1180	109	24.58	2	5
R Benaud(A)	1951-52	1963-64	63	97	7	2201	122	24.45	3	9
V Pollard(N)	1964-65	1973	32	59	7	1266	116	24.34	2	7
A A Baig(I)	1959	1966-67	10	18	0	428	112	23.77	1	2

PLAYER	CAREER SPAN		M	I	NO	RUNS	HS	AVGE	100	50
R Illingworth(E)	1958	1973	71	90	11	1836	113	23.24	2	5
Mohammad Ilyas(P)	1964-65	1968-69	10	19	0	441	126	23.21	1	1
D L Murray(W)	1963	1980	62	96	9	1993	91	22.90	0	11
D A J Holford(W)	1966	1976-77	24	39	5	768	105	22.58	1	3
F J Titmus(E)	1955	1974-75	53	76	11	1449	84*	22.29	0	10
Intikhab Alam(P)	1959-60	1976-77	47	77	10	1493	138	22.28	1	8
P G Z Harris(N)	1955-56	1964-65	9	18	1	378	101	22.23	1	1
J T Murray(E)	1961	1967	21	28	5	506	112	22.00	1	2
K J Wadsworth(N)	1969	1975-76	33	51	4	1010	80	21.48	0	5
R R Lindwall(A)	1945-46	1959-60	61	84	13	1502	118	21.15	2	5
J W Guy(N)	1955-56	1961-62	12	23	2	440	102	20.95	1	3
T G Evans(E)	1946	1959	91	133	14	2439	104	20.49	2	8
B R Taylor(N)	1964-65	1973	30	50	6	898	129	20.40	2	2
S Abid Ali(I)	1967-68	1974-75	29	53	3	1018	81	20.36	0	6
P T Barton(N)	1961-62	1962-63	7	14	0	285	109	20.35	1	1
S N McGregor(N)	1954-55	1964-65	25	47	2	892	111	19.82	1	3
Sarfraz Nawaz(P)	1968-69	1983-84	55	72	13	1045	90	17.71	0	4
Nasim-Ul-Ghani(P)	1957-58	1972-73	29	50	5	747	101	16.60	1	2
Wasim Bari(P)	1967	1983-84	81	112	26	1366	85	15.88	0	6

TABLE G: 1970-71 to 1977

PLAYER	CAREER SPAN		M	I	NO	RUNS	HS	AVGE	100	50
R E Redmond(N)	1972-73		1	2	0	163	107	81.50	1	1
G S Sobers(W)	1953-54	1973-74	93	160	21	8032	365*	57.78	26	30
C A Davis(W)	1968-69	1972-73	15	29	5	1301	183	54.20	4	4
G S Chappell(A)	1970-71	1983-84	87	151	19	7110	247*	53.86	24	31
Javed Miandad(P)	1976-77	1987-88	89	136	18	6339	280*	53.72	15	35
I V A Richards(W)	1974-75	1987-88	92	137	9	6767	291	52.86	21	30
S M Gavaskar(I)	1970-71	1986-87	125	214	16	10122	236*	51.12	34	45
K D Walters(A)	1965-66	1980-81	74	125	14	5357	250	48.26	15	33
C G Greenidge(W)	1974-75	1987-88	80	134	14	5769	223	48.07	14	30
G Boycott(E)	1964	1981-82	108	193	23	8114	246*	47.72	22	42
R B Kanhai(W)	1957	1973-74	79	137	6	6227	256	47.53	15	28
W M Lawry(A)	1961	1970-71	67	123	12	5234	210	47.15	13	27
R B Simpson(A)	1957-58	1977-78	62	111	7	4869	311	46.81	10	27
C H Lloyd(W)	1966-67	1984-85	110	175	14	7515	242*	46.67	19	39
D L Amiss(E)	1966	1977	50	88	10	3612	262*	46.30	11	11
D B Vengsarkar(I)	1975-76	1987-88	98	158	22	6256	166	46.00	17	30
L Baichan(W)	1974-75	1975-76	3	6	2	184	105*	46.00	1	0
A I Kallicharran(W)	1971-72	1980	62	103	9	4319	187	45.94	12	21
Zaheer Abbas(P)	1969-70	1985-86	78	124	11	5062	274	44.79	12	20
G M Turner(N)	1968-69	1982-83	41	73	6	2991	259	44.64	7	14
J Benaud(A)	1972-73	1972-73	3	5	0	223	142	44.60	1	0
M C Cowdrey(E)	1954-55	1974-75	114	188	15	7624	182	44.06	22	38
L G Rowe(W)	1971-72	1979-80	30	49	2	2047	302	43.55	7	7
J H Edrich(E)	1963	1975	77	127	9	5138	310*	43.54	12	24
I R Redpath(A)	1963-64	1975-76	66	120	11	4737	171	43.45	8	31
M Amarnath(I)	1969-70	1987-88	69	113	10	4378	138	42.50	11	24
R C Fredericks(W)	1968-69	1976-77	59	109	7	4334	169	42.49	8	26
D Lloyd(E)	1974	1974-75	9	15	2	552	214*	42.46	1	0
I M Chappell(A)	1964-65	1979-80	75	136	10	5345	196	42.42	14	26
D S Steele(E)	1975	1976	8	16	0	673	106	42.06	1	5
G R Viswanath(I)	1969-70	1982-83	91	155	10	6080	222	41.93	14	35
G N Yallop(A)	1975-76	1984-85	39	70	3	2756	268	41.13	8	9
P H Parfitt(E)	1961-62	1972	37	52	6	1882	131*	40.91	7	6
Mudassar Nazar(P)	1976-77	1987-88	68	103	8	3876	231	40.80	10	17
A W Greig(E)	1972	1977	58	93	4	3599	148	40.43	8	20

PLAYER	CAREER SPAN		M	I	NO	RUNS	HS	AVGE	100	50
Saeed Ahmed(P)	1957-58	1972-73	41	78	4	2991	172	40.41	5	16
R Edwards(A)	1972	1975	20	32	3	1171	170*	40.37	2	9
B L D'Oliveira(E)	1966	1972	44	70	8	2484	158	40.06	5	15
K W R Fletcher(E)	1968	1981-82	59	96	14	3272	216	39.90	7	19
M H Denness(E)	1969	1975	28	45	3	1667	188	39.69	4	7
H A Gomes(W)	1976	1986-87	61	91	11	3171	143	39.63	9	13
R B McCosker(A)	1974-75	1979-80	25	46	5	1622	127	39.56	4	9
D N Sardesai(I)	1961-62	1972-73	30	55	4	2001	212	39.23	5	9
Mushtaq Mohammad(P)	1958-59	1978-79	57	100	7	3643	201	39.17	10	19
Majid J Khan(P)	1964-65	1982-83	63	106	5	3930	167	38.91	8	19
Asif Iqbal(P)	1964-65	1979-80	58	99	7	3575	175	38.85	11	12
J V Coney(N)	1973-74	1986-87	52	85	14	2668	174*	37.57	3	16
K R Stackpole(A)	1965-66	1973-74	43	80	5	2807	207	37.42	7	14
K J Hughes(A)	1977	1984-85	70	124	6	4415	213	37.41	9	22
G A Gooch(E)	1975	1987-88	62	111	4	3971	196	37.11	7	23
Wasim Raja(P)	1972-73	1984-85	57	92	14	2821	125	36.16	4	18
B W Luckhurst(E)	1970-71	1974-75	21	41	5	1298	131	36.05	4	5
Sadiq Mohammad(P)	1969-70	1980-81	41	74	2	2579	166	35.81	5	10
Nawab of Pataudi jnr(I)	1961-62	1974-75	46	83	3	2793	203*	34.91	6	16
I T Botham(E)	1977	1987	94	150	5	5057	208	34.87	14	22
Haroon Rashid(P)	1976-77	1982-83	23	36	1	1217	153	34.77	3	5
D W Hookes(A)	1976-77	1985-86	23	41	3	1306	143*	34.36	1	8
M C Carew(W)	1963	1971-72	19	36	3	1127	109	34.15	1	5
A P Sheehan(A)	1967-68	1973-74	31	53	6	1594	127	33.91	2	7
D W Randall(E)	1976-77	1984	47	79	5	2470	174	33.37	7	12
R A Woolmer(E)	1975	1981	19	34	2	1059	149	33.09	3	2
Imran Khan(P)	1971	1987	70	101	17	2770	135*	32.97	4	11
A P E Knott(E)	1967	1981	95	149	15	4389	135	32.75	5	30
A R Lewis(E)	1972-73	1973	9	16	2	457	125	32.64	1	3
G P Howarth(N)	1974-75	1984-85	47	83	5	2531	147	32.44	6	11
B E Congdon(N)	1964-65	1978	61	114	7	3448	176	32.22	7	19
C L King(W)	1976	1980	9	16	3	418	100*	32.15	1	2
M J K Smith(E)	1958	1972	50	78	6	2278	121	31.63	3	11
C P S Chauhan(I)	1969-70	1980-81	40	68	2	2084	97	31.57	0	16
M G Burgess(N)	1967-68	1980-81	50	92	6	2684	119*	31.20	5	14
Hanumant Singh(I)	1963-64	1969-70	14	24	2	686	105	31.18	1	5
G T Dowling(N)	1961-62	1971-72	39	77	3	2306	239	31.16	3	11
I T Shillingford(W)	1976-77	1977-78	4	7	0	218	120	31.14	1	0
F M Engineer(I)	1961-62	1974-75	46	87	3	2611	121	31.08	2	16
A L Wadekar(I)	1966-67	1974	37	71	3	2113	143	31.07	1	14
B D Julien(W)	1973	1976-77	24	34	6	866	121	30.92	2	3
M L Jaisimha(I)	1959	1970-71	39	71	4	2056	129	30.68	3	12
S Amarnath(I)	1975-76	1978-79	10	18	0	550	124	30.55	1	3
M L C Foster(W)	1969	1977-78	14	24	5	580	125	30.52	1	1
B F Hastings(N)	1968-69	1975-76	31	56	6	1510	117*	30.20	4	7
A D Gaekwad(I)	1974-75	1984-85	40	70	4	1985	201	30.07	2	10
T W Jarvis(N)	1964-65	1972-73	13	22	1	635	182	29.76	1	2
A Turner(A)	1975	1976-77	14	27	1	768	136	29.53	1	3
B P Patel(I)	1974	1977-78	21	38	5	972	115*	29.45	1	5
G J Cosier(A)	1975-76	1978-79	18	32	1	897	168	28.93	2	3
R J Hadlee(N)	1972-73	1987-88	73	117	17	2728	151*	27.28	2	13
S M H Kirmani(I)	1975-76	1985-86	88	124	22	2759	102	27.04	2	12
P Willey(E)	1976	1986	26	50	6	1184	102*	26.90	2	5
J H Hampshire(E)	1969	1975	8	16	1	403	107	26.86	1	2
I C Davis(A)	1973-74	1977	15	27	1	692	105	26.61	1	4
R W Marsh(A)	1970-71	1983-84	96	150	13	3633	132	26.51	3	16
G Miller(E)	1976	1984	34	51	4	1213	98*	25.80	0	7
S A Durani(I)	1959-60	1972-73	29	50	2	1202	104	25.64	1	7
E D Solkar(I)	1969-70	1976-77	27	48	6	1068	102	25.42	1	6

PLAYER	CAREER SPAN		M	I	NO	RUNS	HS	AVGE	100	50
R S Madugalle(SL)	1981-82	1987-88	20	37	4	1006	103	30.48	1	7
C J Richards(E)	1986-87	1987	6	9	0	272	133	30.22	1	0
A D Gaekwad(I)	1974-75	1984-85	40	70	4	1985	201	30.07	2	10
B P Patel(I)	1974	1977-78	21	38	5	972	115*	29.45	1	5
S Wettimuny(SL)	1981-82	1986-87	23	43	1	1221	190	29.07	2	6
G J Cosier(A)	1975-76	1978-79	18	32	1	897	168	28.93	2	3
J Dyson(A)	1977-78	1982-83	27	52	7	1282	127*	28.48	2	5
S A R Silva(SL)	1982-83	1985-86	8	14	2	336	111	28.00	2	0
J J Crowe(N)	1982-83	1987-88	33	55	4	1401	128	27.47	3	6
R J Hadlee(N)	1972-73	1987-88	73	117	17	2728	151*	27.28	2	13
S M H Kirmani(I)	1975-76	1985-86	88	124	22	2759	102	27.04	2	12
P Willey(E)	1976	1986	26	50	6	1184	102*	26.90	2	5
P A De Silva(SL)	1984	1987-88	14	26	2	640	122	26.66	2	1
R W Marsh(A)	1970-71	1983-84	96	150	13	3633	132	26.51	3	16
Mansoor Akhtar(P)	1980-81	1987	18	27	3	636	111	26.50	1	3
Shoaib Mohammad(P)	1983-84	1987-88	14	19	1	472	101	26.22	1	2
S F A F Bacchus(W)	1977-78	1981-82	19	30	0	782	250	26.06	1	3
G Miller(E)	1976	1984	34	51	4	1213	98*	25.80	0	7
J M Parker(N)	1972-73	1980-81	36	63	2	1498	121	24.55	3	5
C J Serjeant(A)	1977	1977-78	12	23	1	522	124	23.72	1	2
C W J Athey(E)	1980	1987-88	21	37	1	851	123	23.63	1	4
A L Mann(A)	1977-78		4	8	0	189	105	23.62	1	0
W K Lees(N)	1976-77	1983	21	37	4	778	152	23.57	1	1
D M Wellham(A)	1981	1986-87	6	11	0	257	103	23.36	1	0
D L Murray(W)	1963	1980	62	96	9	1993	91	22.90	0	11
J M Brearley(E)	1976	1981	39	66	3	1442	91	22.88	0	9
S Madan Lal(I)	1974	1986	39	62	16	1042	74	22.65	0	5
J F M Morrison(N)	1973-74	1981-82	17	29	0	656	117	22.62	1	3
I D S Smith(N)	1980-81	1987-88	40	55	11	945	113*	21.47	1	2
J G Bracewell(N)	1980-81	1987-88	27	40	9	657	110	21.19	1	2
M D Marshall(W)	1978-79	1986-87	51	62	5	1063	92	18.64	0	7
Sarfraz Nawaz(P)	1968-69	1983-84	55	72	13	1045	90	17.71	0	4
R W Taylor(E)	1970-71	1983-84	57	83	12	1156	97	16.28	0	3
Wasim Bari(P)	1967	1983-84	81	112	26	1366	85	15.88	0	6

Updated record of those who played in New Zealand v England & West Indies v Pakistan series 1987-88:

PLAYER	CAREER SPAN		M	I	NO	RUNS	HS	AVGE	100	50
M J Greatbatch(N)	1987-88		2	3	1	186	107*	93.00	1	1
Javed Miandad(P)	1976-77	1987-88	92	141	18	6621	280*	53.82	17	35
I V A Richards(W)	1974-75	1987-88	94	141	9	7045	291	53.37	22	31
A H Jones(N)	1986-87	1987-88	5	9	1	423	150	52.87	1	2
C G Greenidge(W)	1974-75	1987-88	83	140	14	5904	223	46.85	14	30
B C Broad(E)	1984	1987-88	21	36	2	1508	162	44.35	6	5
M D Crowe(N)	1981-82	1987-88	42	70	6	2774	188	43.34	9	9
R B Richardson(W)	1983-84	1987-88	33	54	5	2102	185	42.89	6	8
Saleem Malik(P)	1981-82	1987-88	44	65	11	2140	119*	39.62	6	10
Mudassar Nazar(P)	1976-77	1987-88	71	109	8	3991	231	39.51	10	17
D L Haynes(W)	1977-78	1987-88	72	122	13	4298	184	39.43	9	25
M W Gatting(E)	1977-78	1987-88	65	111	14	3810	207	39.27	9	18
P J L Dujon(W)	1981-82	1987-88	50	69	8	2301	139	37.72	5	10
R T Robinson(E)	1984-85	1987-88	27	45	4	1536	175	37.46	4	6
J G Wright(N)	1977-78	1987-88	58	103	4	3343	141	33.76	7	14
C L Hooper(W)	1987-88	1987-88	6	10	1	303	100*	33.66	1	1
Imran Khan(P)	1971	1987-88	73	106	18	2860	135*	32.50	4	11
Rameez Raja(P)	1983-84	1987-88	22	36	2	1001	122	30.33	2	5
A L Logie(W)	1982-83	1987-88	23	34	2	931	130	29.09	2	5
Shoaib Mohammad(P)	1983-84	1987-88	17	25	2	661	101	28.73	1	4
R J Hadlee(N)	1972-73	1987-88	74	118	17	2770	151*	27.42	2	13

PLAYER	CAREER SPAN		M	I	NO	RUNS	HS	AVGE	100	50
J J Crowe(N)	1982-83	1987-88	35	59	4	1441	128	26.20	3	6
Ijaz Faqih(P)	1980-81	1987-88	5	8	1	183	105	26.14	1	0
C W J Athey(E)	1980	1987-88	22	39	1	892	123	23.47	1	4
J G Bracewell(N)	1980-81	1987-88	30	45	10	809	110	23.11	1	3
I D S Smith(N)	1980-81	1987-88	43	59	13	1037	113*	22.54	1	2
J E Emburey(E)	1978	1987-88	53	78	17	1363	75	22.34	0	7
M D Marshall(W)	1978-79	1987-88	53	66	6	1143	92	18.96	0	7
K R Rutherford(N)	1984-85	1987-88	14	23	3	331	107*	16.55	1	2

The bowlers

TABLE A: 1876-77 to 1896

PLAYER	CAREER SPAN		M	B	MDS	RUNS	W	AV	5	10	BEST
J J Ferris(E)	1891-92		1	272	27	91	13	7.00	2	1	7/37
C A Smith(E)	1888-89		1	154	16	61	7	8.71	1	0	5/19
F Martin(E)	1890	1891-92	2	410	30	141	14	10.07	2	1	6/50
G A Lohmann(E)	1886	1896	18	3821	364	1205	112	10.75	9	5	9/28
T P Horan(A)	1876-77	1884-85	15	373	45	143	11	13.00	1	0	6/40
W H Ashley(SA)	1888-89		1	173	18	95	7	13.57	1	0	7/95
J J Ferris(A)	1886-87	1890	8	2030	224	684	48	14.25	4	0	5/26
T Kendall(A)	1876-77		2	563	56	215	14	15.35	1	0	7/55
W Barnes(E)	1880	1890	21	2289	271	793	51	15.54	3	0	6/28
W Bates(E)	1881-82	1886-87	15	2364	282	821	50	16.42	4	1	7/28
C T B Turner(A)	1886-87	1894-95	17	5195	457	1670	101	16.53	11	2	7/43
C Heseltine(E)	1895-96		2	157	3	84	5	16.80	1	0	5/38
R Peel(E)	1884-85	1896	20	5216	444	1715	102	16.81	6	2	7/31
J Briggs(E)	1884-85	1899	33	5332	384	2094	118	17.74	9	4	8/11
A Rose-Innes(SA)	1888-89		2	128	8	89	5	17.80	1	0	5/43
F R Spofforth(A)	1876-77	1886-87	18	4185	416	1684	94	17.81	7	4	7/44
J Middleton(SA)	1895-96	1902-03	6	1064	61	442	24	18.41	2	0	5/51
F Morley(E)	1880	1882-83	4	972	124	296	16	18.50	1	0	5/56
H F Boyle(A)	1878-79	1884-85	12	1744	175	641	32	20.03	1	0	6/42
G Ulyett(E)	1876-77	1890	25	2627	299	1020	50	20.40	1	0	7/36
W H Lockwood	1893	1902	12	1910	100	884	43	20.55	5	1	7/71
W Flowers(E)	1884-85	1893	8	858	92	296	14	21.14	1	0	5/46
A E Trott(A)	1894-95		3	474	17	192	9	21.33	1	0	8/43
G E Palmer(A)	1880	1886	17	4517	452	1678	78	21.50	6	2	7/65
H Trumble(A)	1890	1903-04	32	8099	452	3072	141	21.78	9	3	8/65
E Peate(E)	1881-82	1886	9	2096	260	682	31	22.00	2	0	6/85
J T Hearne(E)	1891-92	1899	12	2976	211	1082	49	22.08	4	1	6/41
R G Barlow(E)	1881-82	1886-87	17	2456	315	767	34	22.55	3	0	7/40
S T Callaway(A)	1891-92	1894-95	3	471	33	142	6	23.66	1	0	5/37
A Shaw(E)	1876-77	1881-82	7	1099	155	285	12	23.75	1	0	5/38
W E Midwinter(A)	1876-77	1886-87	8	949	104	333	14	23.78	1	0	5/78
J J Lyons(A)	1886-87	1897-98	14	316	17	149	6	24.83	1	0	5/30
W H Cooper(A)	1881-82	1884-85	2	466	31	226	9	25.11	1	0	6/120
T Richardson(E)	1893	1897-98	14	4497	191	2220	88	25.22	11	4	8/94
T W Garrett(A)	1876-77	1887-88	19	2708	297	970	36	26.94	2	0	6/78
G Giffen(A)	1881-82	1896	31	6325	434	2791	103	27.09	7	1	7/117
J W Sharpe(E)	1890	1891-92	3	975	61	305	11	27.72	1	0	6/84
E Jones(A)	1894-95	1902-03	19	3748	160	1857	64	29.01	3	1	7/88
C B Llewellyn(SA)	1895-96	1912	15	2292	55	1421	48	29.60	4	1	6/92
G A Rowe(SA)	1895-96	1902-03	5	998	50	456	15	30.40	1	0	5/115
T Emmett(E)	1876-77	1881-82	7	728	92	284	9	31.55	1	0	7/68
J H Sinclair(SA)	1895-96	1910-11	25	3598	110	1996	63	31.68	1	0	6/26
R W McLeod(A)	1891-92	1893	6	1089	67	384	12	32.00	1	0	5/55

PLAYER	CAREER SPAN		M	B	MDS	R	W	AV	5	10	BEST
F S Jackson(E)	1893	1905	20	1587	77	799	24	33.29	1	0	5/52
C E McLeod(A)	1894-95	1905	17	3374	171	1325	33	40.15	2	0	5/65

Combined figures of players who represented more than one country:

PLAYER	CAREER SPAN		M	B	MDS	R	W	AV	5	10	BEST
J J Ferris(A/E)	1886-87	1891-92	9	2302	251	775	61	12.70	6	1	7/37
A E Trott(A/E)	1894-95	1898-99	5	948	54	390	26	15.00	2	0	8/43
W E Midwinter(A/E)	1876-77	1886	12	1725	183	605	24	25.20	1	0	5/78

TABLE B: 1897-98 to 1913-14

PLAYER	CAREER SPAN		M	B	MDS	RUNS	W	AV	5	10	BEST
A E Trott(E)	1898-99		2	474	37	198	17	11.64	1	0	5/49
S F Barnes(E)	1901-02	1913-14	27	7873	356	3106	189	16.43	24	7	9/103
J Briggs(E)	1884-85	1899	33	5332	384	2094	118	17.74	9	4	8/11
W S Lees(E)	1905-06		5	1256	69	467	26	17.96	2	0	6/78
G H Simpson-Hayward(E)	1909-10		5	898	18	420	23	18.26	2	0	6/43
J Middleton(SA)	1895-96	1902-03	6	1064	61	442	24	18.41	2	0	5/51
C Blythe(E)	1901-02	1909-10	19	4546	231	1863	100	18.63	9	4	8/59
A Warren(E)	1905		1	236	9	113	6	18.83	1	0	5/57
S J Snooke(SA)	1905-06	1922-23	26	1620	62	702	35	20.05	1	1	8/70
W H Lockwood(E)	1893	1902	12	1910	100	884	43	20.55	5	1	7/71
F R Foster(E)	1911-12	1912	11	2447	108	926	45	20.57	4	0	6/91
W Brearley(E)	1905	1912	4	705	25	359	17	21.11	1	0	5/110
W J Whitty(A)	1909	1912	14	3357	163	1373	65	21.12	3	0	6/17
J R Gunn(E)	1901-02	1905	6	999	54	387	18	21.50	1	0	5/76
H Trumble(A)	1890	1903-04	32	8099	452	3072	141	21.78	9	3	8/65
J T Hearne(E)	1891-92	1899	12	2976	211	1082	49	22.08	4	1	6/41
J V Saunders(A)	1901-02	1907-08	14	3565	116	1796	79	22.73	7	0	7/34
A E E Vogler(SA)	1905-06	1910-11	15	2764	96	1455	64	22.73	5	1	7/94
H V Hordern(A)	1910-11	1911-12	7	2148	49	1075	46	23.36	5	2	7/90
B J T Bosanquet(E)	1903-04	1905	7	970	10	604	25	24.16	2	0	8/107
C P Carter(SA)	1912	1924	10	1475	47	694	28	24.78	2	0	6/50
J J Lyons(A)	1886-87	1897-98	14	316	17	149	6	24.83	1	0	5/30
A E Relf(E)	1903-04	1913-14	13	1764	91	624	25	24.96	1	0	5/85
M A Noble(A)	1897-98	1909	42	7159	361	3025	121	25.00	9	2	7/17
T Richardson(E)	1893	1897-98	14	4497	191	2220	88	25.22	11	4	8/94
E G Arnold(E)	1903-04	1907	10	1683	64	788	31	25.41	1	0	5/37
R O Schwarz(SA)	1905-06	1912	20	2639	66	1417	55	25.76	2	0	6/47
S Haigh(E)	1898-99	1912	11	1294	61	622	24	25.91	1	0	6/11
F Laver(A)	1899	1909	15	2361	121	964	37	26.05	2	0	8/31
J D A O'Connor(A)	1907-08	1909	4	692	24	340	13	26.15	1	0	5/40
G A Faulkner(SA)	1905-06	1924	25	4227	124	2180	82	26.58	4	0	7/84
W Rhodes(E)	1899	1929-30	58	8231	365	3425	127	26.96	6	1	8/68
G R Hazlitt(A)	1907-08	1912	9	1563	74	623	23	27.08	1	0	7/25
A Fielder(E)	1903-04	1907-08	6	1491	42	711	26	27.34	1	0	6/82
C G Macartney(A)	1907-08	1926	35	3555	183	1240	45	27.55	2	1	7/59
C P Buckenham(E)	1909-10		4	1182	25	593	21	28.23	1	0	5/115
A Cotter(A)	1903-04	1911-12	21	4633	86	2549	89	28.64	7	0	7/148
W P Howell(A)	1897-98	1903-04	18	3892	245	1407	49	28.71	1	0	5/81
E Jones(A)	1894-95	1902-03	19	3748	160	1857	64	29.01	3	1	7/88
J N Crawford(E)	1905-06	1907-08	12	2203	61	1150	39	29.48	3	0	5/48
C B Llewellyn(SA)	1895-96	1912	15	2292	55	1421	48	29.60	4	1	6/92
G H Hirst(E)	1897-98	1909	24	3967	146	1770	59	30.00	3	0	5/48
J M Blanckenberg(SA)	1913-14	1924	18	3888	132	1817	60	30.28	4	0	6/76
G A Rowe(SA)	1895-96	1902-03	5	998	50	456	15	30.40	1	0	5/115
J H Sinclair(SA)	1895-96	1910-11	25	3598	110	1996	63	31.68	1	0	6/26
C Kelleway(A)	1910-11	1928-29	26	4363	146	1683	52	32.36	1	0	5/33
J W H T Douglas(E)	1911-12	1924-25	23	2812	66	1486	45	33.02	1	0	5/46

PLAYER	CAREER SPAN		M	B	MDS	R	W	AV	5	10	BEST
F S Jackson(E)	1893	1905	20	1587	77	799	24	33.29	1	0	5/52
S J Pegler(SA)	1909-10	1924	16	2989	84	1572	47	33.44	2	0	7/65
W W Armstrong(A)	1901-02	1921	50	8022	399	2923	87	33.59	3	0	6/35
F E Woolley(E)	1909	1934	64	6495	250	2815	83	33.91	4	1	7/76
L C Braund(E)	1901-02	1907-08	23	3803	144	1810	47	38.51	3	0	8/81
W M Bradley(E)	1899		2	625	49	233	6	38.83	1	0	5/67
C E McLeod(A)	1894-95	1905	17	3374	171	1325	33	40.15	2	0	5/65
D W Carr(E)	1909		1	414	3	282	7	40.28	1	0	5/146
J W Hearne(E)	1911-12	1926	24	2926	56	1462	30	48.73	1	0	5/49

TABLE C: 1920-21 to 1939

PLAYER	CAREER SPAN		M	B	MDS	R	W	AV	5	10	BEST
C S Marriott(E)	1933		1	247	8	96	11	8.72	2	1	6/59
M W Sievers(A)	1936-37		3	602	25	161	9	17.88	1	0	5/21
H Ironmonger(A)	1928-29	1932-33	14	4695	328	1330	74	17.97	4	2	7/23
G F Bissett(SA)	1927-28		4	989	28	469	25	18.76	2	0	7/29
M J C Allom(E)	1929-30	1930-31	5	817	28	265	14	18.92	1	0	5/38
A S Kennedy(E)	1922-23		5	1683	91	599	31	19.32	2	0	5/76
W H Copson(E)	1939	1947	3	762	31	297	15	19.80	1	0	5/85
S J Snooke(SA)	1905-06	1922-23	26	1620	62	702	35	20.05	1	1	8/70
H L E Promnitz(SA)	1927-28		2	528	30	161	8	20.12	1	0	5/58
J Cowie(N)	1937	1949	9	2028	65	969	45	21.53	4	1	6/40
E A Martindale(W)	1933	1939	10	1605	40	804	37	21.72	3	0	5/22
J Langridge(E)	1933	1946	8	1074	51	413	19	21.73	2	0	7/56
A E Hall(SA)	1922-23	1930-31	7	2361	107	886	40	22.15	3	1	7/63
W E Bowes(E)	1932	1946	15	3655	131	1519	68	22.33	6	0	6/33
W J O'Reilly(A)	1931-32	1945-46	27	10024	585	3254	144	22.59	11	3	7/54
C V Grimmett(A)	1924-25	1935-36	37	14513	746	5231	216	24.21	21	7	7/40
H Verity(E)	1931	1939	40	11173	604	3510	144	24.37	5	2	8/43
C P Carter(SA)	1912	1924	10	1475	47	694	28	24.78	2	0	6/50
A P Freeman(E)	1924-25	1929	12	3732	142	1707	66	25.86	5	3	7/71
M W Tate(E)	1924	1935	39	12523	581	4055	155	26.16	7	1	6/42
C I J Smith(E)	1934-35	1937	5	930	40	393	15	26.20	1	0	5/16
G A Faulkner(SA)	1905-06	1924	25	4227	124	2180	82	26.58	4	0	7/84
T W J Goddard(E)	1930	1939	8	1563	62	588	22	26.72	1	0	6/29
W Rhodes(E)	1899	1929-30	58	8231	365	3425	127	26.96	6	1	8/68
G E Gomez(W)	1939	1953-54	29	5236	289	1590	58	27.41	1	1	7/55
R W V Robins(E)	1929	1937	19	3318	77	1758	64	27.46	1	0	6/32
G A E Paine(E)	1934-35		4	1044	39	467	17	27.47	1	0	5/168
C G Macartney(A)	1907-08	1926	35	3555	183	1240	45	27.55	2	1	7/59
G G Macauley(E)	1922-23	1933	8	1701	79	662	24	27.58	1	0	5/64
W Voce(E)	1929-30	1946-47	27	6360	211	2733	98	27.88	3	2	7/40
M S Nicholls(E)	1929-30	1939	14	2565	97	1152	41	28.09	2	0	6/35
E W Clark(E)	1929	1934	8	1931	71	899	32	28.09	1	0	5/98
H C Griffith(W)	1928	1933	13	2663	89	1243	44	28.25	2	0	6/103
Mahomed Nissar(I)	1932	1936	6	1211	33	707	25	28.28	3	0	5/90
H Larwood(E)	1926	1932-33	21	4969	167	2212	78	28.35	4	1	6/32
K Farnes(E)	1934	1938-39	15	3932	103	1719	60	28.65	3	1	6/96
A R E Gilligan(E)	1922-23	1924-25	11	2404	73	1046	36	29.05	2	1	6/7
G O B Allen(E)	1930	1947-48	25	4390	116	2379	81	29.37	5	1	7/80
G Geary(E)	1924	1934	14	3810	181	1353	46	29.41	4	1	7/70
L N Constantine(W)	1928	1939	18	3583	125	1746	58	30.10	2	0	5/75
W E Hollies(E)	1934-35	1950	13	3554	176	1332	44	30.27	5	0	7/50
J M Blanckenberg(SA)	1913-14	1924	18	3888	132	1817	60	30.28	4	0	6/76
L Amar Singh(I)	1932	1936	7	2182	95	858	28	30.64	2	0	7/86
I A R Peebles(E)	1927-28	1931	13	2882	78	1391	45	30.91	3	0	6/63
F R Brown(E)	1931	1953	22	3260	117	1398	45	31.06	1	0	5/49

PLAYER	CAREER SPAN		M	B	MDS	R	W	AV	5	10	BEST
J M Gregory(A)	1920-21	1928-29	24	5582	138	2648	85	31.15	4	0	7/69
C L Vincent(SA)	1927-28	1935	25	5863	194	2631	84	31.32	3	0	6/51
D D Blackie(A)	1928-29		3	1260	51	444	14	31.71	1	0	6/94
J C White(E)	1921	1930-31	15	4801	253	1581	49	32.26	3	1	8/126
R T D Perks(E)	1938-39	1939	2	829	17	355	11	32.27	2	0	5/100
C Kelleway(A)	1910-11	1928-29	26	4363	146	1683	52	32.36	1	0	5/33
G T S Stevens(E)	1922-23	1929-30	10	1186	24	648	20	32.40	2	1	5/90
A J Bell(SA)	1929	1935	16	3342	89	1567	48	32.64	4	0	6/99
N A Quinn(SA)	1929	1931-32	12	2922	103	1145	35	32.71	1	0	6/92
L Amarnath(I)	1933-34	1952-53	24	4241	195	1481	45	32.91	2	0	5/96
J W H T Douglas(E)	1911-12	1924-25	23	2812	66	1486	45	33.02	1	0	5/46
E A McDonald(A)	1920-21	1921-22	11	2885	90	1431	43	33.27	2	0	5/32
S J Pegler(SA)	1909-10	1924	16	2989	84	1572	47	33.44	2	0	7/65
W W Armstrong(A)	1901-02	1921	50	8022	399	2923	87	33.59	3	0	6/35
A A Mailey(A)	1920-21	1926	21	6119	115	3358	99	33.91	6	2	9/121
F E Woolley(E)	1909	1934	64	6495	250	2815	83	33.91	4	1	7/76
G M Parker(SA)	1924		2	366	2	273	8	34.12	1	0	6/152
Q McMillan(SA)	1929	1931-32	13	2021	38	1243	36	34.52	2	0	5/66
C H Parkin(E)	1920-21	1924	10	2095	55	1128	32	35.25	2	0	5/38
E P Nupen(SA)	1921-22	1935-36	17	4159	133	1788	50	35.76	5	1	6/46
T W Wall(A)	1928-29	1934	18	4812	154	2010	56	35.89	3	0	5/14
X C Balaskas(SA)	1930-31	1938-39	9	1584	28	806	22	36.63	1	0	5/49
R J Crisp(SA)	1935	1935-36	9	1428	30	747	20	37.35	1	0	5/99
L O Fleetwood-Smith(A)	1935-36	1938	10	3093	78	1570	42	37.38	2	1	6/110
W R Hammond(E)	1927-28	1946-47	85	7967	300	3138	83	37.80	2	0	5/36
P M Hornibrook(A)	1928-29	1930	6	1579	63	664	17	39.05	1	0	7/92
D V P Wright(E)	1938	1950-51	34	8135	177	4224	108	39.11	6	1	7/105
N Gordon(SA)	1938-39		5	1966	28	807	20	40.35	2	0	5/103
P G H Fender(E)	1920-21	1929	13	2178	66	1185	29	40.86	2	0	5/90
O C Scott(W)	1928	1930-31	8	1405	18	925	22	42.04	1	0	5/266
J M Sims(E)	1935	1936-37	4	897	21	480	11	43.63	1	0	5/73
A B C Langton(SA)	1935	1938-39	15	4199	104	1827	40	45.67	1	0	5/58
J W Hearne(E)	1911-12	1926	24	2926	56	1462	30	48.73	1	0	5/49
B Mitchell(SA)	1929	1948-49	42	2519	26	1380	27	51.11	1	0	5/87
F A Ward(A)	1936-37	1838	4	1268	30	574	11	52.18	1	0	6/102
D C S Compton(E)	1937	1956-57	78	2710	72	1410	25	56.40	1	0	5/70

TABLE D: 1945-46 to 1956-57

PLAYER	CAREER SPAN		M	B	MDS	R	W	AV	5	10	BEST
J B Iverson(A)	1950-51		5	1108	29	320	21	15.23	1	0	6/27
J Trim(W)	1947-48	1951-52	4	794	28	291	18	16.16	1	0	5/34
R Appleyard(E)	1954	1956	9	1596	70	554	31	17.87	1	0	5/51
Zulfiqar Ahmed(P)	1952-53	1956-57	9	1285	78	366	20	18.30	2	1	6/42
H H H Johnson(W)	1947-48	1950	3	789	37	238	13	18.30	2	1	5/41
D E J Ironside(SA)	1953-54		3	982	41	275	15	18.33	1	0	5/51
F H Tyson(E)	1954	1958-59	17	3452	97	1411	76	18.56	4	1	7/27
W H Copson(E)	1939	1947	3	762	31	297	15	19.80	1	0	5/85
J H Wardle(E)	1947-48	1957	28	6594	403	2080	102	20.39	5	1	7/36
A K Davidson(A)	1953	1962-63	44	11587	431	3819	186	20.53	14	2	7/93
E R H Toshack(A)	1945-46	1948	12	3140	155	989	47	21.04	4	1	6/29
N A T Adcock(SA)	1953-54	1961-62	26	6391	218	2195	104	21.10	5	0	6/43
J C Laker(E)	1947-48	1958-59	46	12027	674	4101	193	21.24	9	3	10/53
J Cowie(N)	1937	1949	9	2028	65	969	45	21.53	4	1	6/40
F S Trueman(E)	1952	1965	67	15178	522	6625	307	21.57	17	3	8/31
J Langridge(E)	1933	1946	8	1074	51	413	19	21.73	2	0	7/56
J M Patel(I)	1954-55	1959-60	7	1725	98	637	29	21.96	2	1	9/69
E S M Kentish(W)	1947-48	1953-54	2	540	31	178	8	22.25	1	0	5/49

PLAYER	CAREER SPAN		M	B	MDS	R	W	AV	5	10	BEST
W E Bowes(E)	1932	1946	15	3655	131	1519	68	22.33	6	0	6/33
G F Cresswell(N)	1949	1950-51	3	650	30	292	13	22.46	1	0	6/168
P J Loader(E)	1954	1958-59	13	2662	115	878	39	22.51	1	0	6/36
W J O'Reilly(A)	1931-32	1945-46	27	10024	585	3254	144	22.59	11	3	7/54
K R Miller(A)	1945-46	1956-57	55	10461	337	3906	170	22.97	7	1	7/60
R R Lindwall(A)	1945-46	1959-60	61	13650	419	5251	228	23.03	12	0	7/38
W A Johnston(A)	1947-48	1954-55	40	11048	372	3826	160	23.91	7	0	6/44
Khan Mohammad(P)	1952-53	1957-58	13	3157	153	1292	54	23.92	4	0	6/21
Fazal Mahmood(P)	1952-53	1962	34	9834	563	3434	139	24.70	13	4	7/42
J B Statham(E)	1950-51	1965	70	16056	595	6261	252	24.84	9	1	7/39
A V Bedser(E)	1946	1955	51	15918	579	5876	236	24.89	15	5	7/44
P S Heine(SA)	1955	1961-62	14	3890	106	1455	58	25.08	4	0	6/58
R Pollard(E)	1946	1948	4	1102	63	378	15	25.20	1	0	5/24
R Berry(E)	1950		2	653	47	228	9	25.33	1	0	5/63
G A R Lock(E)	1952	1967-68	49	13147	819	4451	174	25.58	9	3	7/35
H J Tayfield(SA)	1949-50	1960	37	13568	602	4405	170	25.91	14	2	9/113
R Tattersall(E)	1950-51	1954	16	4228	212	1513	58	26.08	4	1	7/52
T L Goddard(SA)	1955	1969-70	41	11736	706	3226	123	26.22	5	0	6/53
C L McCool(A)	1945-46	1949-50	14	2504	44	958	36	26.61	3	0	5/41
R Benaud(A)	1951-52	1963-64	63	19108	805	6704	248	27.03	16	1	7/72
G E Gomez(W)	1939	1953-54	29	5236	289	1590	58	27.41	1	1	7/55
R G Archer(A)	1952-53	1956-57	19	3576	160	1318	48	27.45	1	0	5/53
G W A Chubb(SA)	1951		5	1425	63	577	21	27.47	2	0	6/51
W Voce(E)	1929-30	1946-47	27	6360	211	2733	98	27.88	3	2	7/40
S Ramadhin(W)	1950	1960-61	43	13939	813	4579	158	28.98	10	1	7/49
R G Nadkarni(I)	1955-56	1967-68	41	9165	665	2559	88	29.07	4	1	6/43
I W Johnson(A)	1945-46	1956-57	45	8780	330	3182	109	29.19	3	0	7/44
T E Bailey(E)	1949	1958-59	61	9712	379	3856	132	29.21	5	1	7/34
G O B Allen(E)	1930	1947-48	25	4390	116	2379	81	29.37	5	1	7/80
S P Gupte(I)	1951-52	1961-62	36	11284	608	4403	149	29.55	12	1	9/102
P E Jones(W)	1947-48	1951-52	9	1842	64	751	25	30.04	1	0	5/85
Ghulam Ahmed(I)	1948-49	1958-59	22	5650	249	2052	68	30.17	4	1	7/49
W E Hollies(E)	1934-35	1950	13	3554	176	1332	44	30.27	5	0	7/50
A L Valentine(W)	1950	1961-62	36	12953	789	4215	139	30.32	8	2	8/104
E R H Fuller(SA)	1952-53	1957-58	7	1898	61	668	22	30.36	1	0	5/66
A R McGibbon(N)	1950-51	1958	26	5659	228	2160	70	30.85	1	0	5/64
F R Brown(E)	1931	1953	22	3260	117	1398	45	31.06	1	0	5/49
J D C Goddard(W)	1947-48	1957	27	2931	148	1050	33	31.81	1	0	5/31
F J Titmus(E)	1955	1974-75	53	15118	777	4931	153	32.22	7	0	7/79
M H Mankad(I)	1946	1958-59	44	14685	777	5236	162	32.32	8	2	8/52
M G Melle(SA)	1949-50	1952-53	7	1667	20	851	26	32.73	2	0	6/71
L Amarnath(I)	1933-34	1952-53	24	4241	195	1481	45	32.91	2	0	5/96
N B F Mann(SA)	1947	1951	19	5796	260	1920	58	33.10	1	0	6/59
J R Reid(N)	1949	1965	58	7725	444	2835	85	33.35	1	0	6/60
R Howorth(E)	1947	1947-48	5	1536	61	635	19	33.42	1	0	6/124
O G Smith(W)	1954-55	1958-59	26	4431	228	1625	48	33.85	1	0	5/90
G S Sobers(W)	1953-54	1973-74	93	21599	974	7999	235	34.03	6	0	6/73
M J Hilton(E)	1950	1951-52	4	1244	65	477	14	34.07	1	0	5/61
W Ferguson(W)	1947-48	1953-54	8	2568	83	1165	34	34.26	3	1	6/92
R O Jenkins(E)	1948-49	1952	9	2118	51	1098	32	34.31	1	0	5/116
K D Mackay(A)	1956	1962-63	37	5792	267	1721	50	34.42	2	0	6/42
D S Atkinson(W)	1948-49	1957-58	22	5201	311	1647	47	35.04	3	0	7/53
T B Burtt(N)	1946-47	1952-53	10	2593	119	1170	33	35.45	3	0	6/162
D G Phadkar(I)	1947-48	1958-59	31	5994	277	2285	62	36.85	3	0	7/159
D T Ring(A)	1947-48	1953	13	3024	69	1305	35	37.28	2	0	6/72
W R Hammond(E)	1927-28	1946-47	85	7967	300	3138	83	37.80	2	0	5/36
D T Dewdney(W)	1954-55	1957-58	9	1641	65	807	21	38.42	1	0	5/21
A M B Rowan(SA)	1947	1951	15	5193	136	2084	54	38.59	4	0	5/68
Mahmood Hussain(P)	1952-53	1962	27	5910	213	2628	68	38.64	2	0	6/67

PLAYER	CAREER SPAN		M	B	MDS	R	W	AV	5	10	BEST
F M M Worrell(W)	1947-48	1963	41	7141	275	2672	69	38.72	2	0	7/70
D V P Wright(E)	1938	1950-51	34	8135	177	4224	108	39.11	6	1	7/105
G O Rabone(N)	1949	1954-55	12	1385	48	635	16	39.68	1	0	6/68
F M King(W)	1952-53	1955-56	14	2871	140	1159	29	39.96	1	0	5/74
C N McCarthy(SA)	1948-49	1951	15	3499	64	1510	36	41.94	2	0	6/43
P R Umrigar(I)	1948-49	1961-62	59	4725	257	1473	35	42.08	2	0	6/74
G S Ramchand(I)	1952	1959-60	33	4976	255	1899	41	46.31	1	0	6/49
A M Moir(N)	1950-51	1958-59	17	2644	82	1418	28	50.64	2	0	6/155
B Mitchell(SA)	1929	1948-49	42	2519	26	1380	27	51.11	1	0	5/87
L Tuckett(SA)	1947	1948-49	9	2104	47	980	19	51.57	2	0	5/68
C R Rangachari(I)	1947-48	1948-49	4	846	11	493	9	54.77	1	0	5/107
D C S Compton(E)	1937	1956-57	78	2710	72	1410	25	56.40	1	0	5/70
S G Shinde(I)	1946	1952	7	1515	59	717	12	59.75	1	0	6/91

TABLE E: 1957 to 1969-70

PLAYER	CAREER SPAN		M	B	MDS	R	W	AV	5	10	BEST
M J Procter(SA)	1966-67	1969-70	7	1514	80	616	41	15.02	1	0	6/73
L A King(W)	1961-62	1967-68	2	476	19	154	9	17.11	1	0	5/46
B F Butcher(W)	1958-59	1969	44	256	15	90	5	18.00	1	0	5/34
G B Lawrence(SA)	1961-62		5	1334	62	512	28	18.28	2	0	8/53
F H Tyson(E)	1954	1958-59	17	3452	97	1411	76	18.56	4	1	7/27
J H Wardle(E)	1947-48	1957	28	6594	403	2080	102	20.39	5	1	7/36
A K Davidson(A)	1953	1962-63	44	11587	431	3819	186	20.53	14	2	7/93
Arif Butt(P)	1964-65	1964-65	3	666	26	288	14	20.57	1	0	6/89
K Higgs(E)	1965	1968	15	4112	194	1473	71	20.74	2	0	6/91
N A T Adcock(SA)	1953-54	1961-62	26	6391	218	2195	104	21.10	5	0	6/43
J C Laker(E)	1947-48	1958-59	46	12027	674	4101	193	21.24	9	3	10/53
F S Trueman(E)	1952	1965	67	15178	522	6625	307	21.57	17	3	8/31
J M Patel(I)	1954-55	1959-60	7	1725	98	637	29	21.96	2	1	9/69
T Greenhough(E)	1959	1960	4	1129	66	357	16	22.31	1	0	5/35
P J Loader(E)	1954	1958-59	13	2662	115	878	39	22.51	1	0	6/36
L F Kline(A)	1957-58	1960-61	13	2373	113	776	34	22.82	1	0	7/75
R R Lindwall(A)	1945-46	1959-60	61	13650	419	5251	228	23.03	12	0	7/38
S F Burke(SA)	1961-62	1964-65	2	660	37	257	11	23.36	2	1	6/128
E S Atkinson(W)	1957-58	1958-59	8	1634	77	589	25	23.56	1	0	5/42
Pervez Sajjad(P)	1964-65	1972-73	19	4145	217	1410	59	23.89	3	0	7/74
Khan Mohammad(P)	1952-53	1957-58	13	3157	153	1292	54	23.92	4	0	6/21
G M Griffin(SA)	1960		2	432	14	192	8	24.00	0	0	4/87
P M Pollock(SA)	1961-62	1969-70	28	6522	268	2806	116	24.18	9	1	6/39
Fazal Mahmood(P)	1952-53	1962	34	9834	563	3434	139	24.70	13	4	7/42
J B Statham(E)	1950-51	1965	70	16056	595	6261	252	24.84	9	1	7/39
P S Heine(SA)	1955	1961-62	14	3890	106	1455	58	25.08	4	0	6/58
J N Shepherd(W)	1969	1970-71	5	1445	70	479	19	25.21	1	0	5/104
J D F Larter(E)	1962	1965	10	2172	87	941	37	25.43	2	0	5/57
G A R Lock(E)	1952	1967-68	49	13147	819	4451	174	25.58	9	3	7/35
D L Underwood(E)	1966	1981-82	86	21862	1239	7674	297	25.83	17	6	8/51
H J Tayfield(SA)	1949-50	1960	37	13568	602	4405	170	25.91	14	2	9/113
T L Goddard(SA)	1955	1969-70	41	11736	706	3226	123	26.22	5	0	6/53
W W Hall(W)	1958-59	1968-69	48	10421	312	5066	192	26.38	9	1	7/69
B R Taylor(N)	1964-65	1973	30	6334	206	2953	111	26.60	4	0	7/74
J A Snow(E)	1965	1976	49	12021	415	5387	202	26.66	8	1	7/40
R Gilchrist(W)	1957	1958-59	13	3227	124	1521	57	26.68	1	0	6/55
R Benaud(A)	1951-52	1963-64	63	19108	805	6704	248	27.03	16	1	7/72
J Taylor(W)	1957-58	1958-59	3	672	33	273	10	27.30	1	0	5/109
L J Coldwell(E)	1962	1964	7	1668	60	610	22	27.72	1	0	6/85
G G Arnold(E)	1967	1975	34	7650	284	3254	115	28.29	6	0	6/45
D J Brown(E)	1965	1969	26	5098	182	2237	79	28.31	2	0	5/42

PLAYER	CAREER SPAN		M	B	MDS	R	W	AV	5	10	BEST
Asif Iqbal(P)	1964-65	1979-80	58	3864	181	1502	53	28.33	2	0	5/48
C C Griffith(W)	1959-60	1968-69	28	5631	177	2683	94	28.54	5	0	6/36
B S Bedi(I)	1966-67	1979	70	21364	1096	7637	266	28.71	14	1	7/98
V V Kumar(I)	1960-61	1961-62	2	605	46	202	7	28.85	1	0	5/64
S Ramadhin(W)	1950	1960-61	43	13939	813	4579	158	28.98	10	1	7/49
R G Nadkarni(I)	1955-56	1967-68	41	9165	665	2559	88	29.07	4	1	6/43
K D Walters(A)	1965-66	1980-81	74	3295	79	1425	49	29.08	1	0	5/66
L R Gibbs(W)	1957-58	1975-76	79	27115	1313	8989	309	29.09	18	2	8/38
T E Bailey(E)	1949	1958-59	61	9712	379	3856	132	29.21	5	1	7/34
A N Connolly(A)	1963-64	1970-71	29	7818	289	2981	102	29.22	4	0	6/47
Mushtaq Mohammad(P)	1958-59	1978-79	57	5260	177	2309	79	29.22	3	0	5/28
R O Collinge(N)	1964-65	1978	35	7689	228	3393	116	29.25	3	0	6/63
N J N Hawke(A)	1962-63	1968	27	6974	238	2677	91	29.41	6	1	7/105
S P Gupte(I)	1951-52	1961-62	36	11284	608	4403	149	29.55	12	1	9/102
B S Chandrasekhar(I)	1963-64	1979	58	15963	584	7199	242	29.74	16	2	8/79
G D McKenzie(A)	1961	1970-71	60	17687	547	7328	246	29.78	16	3	8/71
F J Cameron(N)	1961-62	1965	19	4570	220	1849	62	29.82	3	0	5/34
A A Mallett(A)	1968	1980	38	9990	419	3940	132	29.84	6	1	8/59
Ghulam Ahmed(I)	1948-49	1958-59	22	5650	249	2052	68	30.17	4	1	7/49
A L Valentine(W)	1950	1961-62	36	12953	789	4215	139	30.32	8	2	8/104
E R H Fuller(SA)	1952-53	1957-58	7	1898	61	668	22	30.36	1	0	5/66
E A S Prasanna(I)	1961-62	1978-79	49	14353	592	5742	189	30.38	10	2	8/76
A R McGibbon(N)	1950-51	1958	26	5659	228	2160	70	30.85	1	0	5/64
D A Allen(E)	1959-60	1966	39	11297	685	3779	122	30.97	4	0	5/30
N Gifford(E)	1964	1973	15	3084	174	1026	33	31.09	1	0	5/55
R Illingworth(E)	1958	1973	71	11934	713	3807	122	31.20	3	0	6/29
J T Partridge(SA)	1963-64	1964-65	11	3684	136	1373	44	31.20	3	0	7/91
R C Motz(N)	1961-62	1969	32	7034	279	3148	100	31.48	5	0	6/63
I Meckiff(A)	1957-58	1963-64	18	3734	120	1423	45	31.62	2	0	6/38
B R Knight(E)	1961-62	1969	29	5377	204	2223	70	31.75	0	0	4/38
J D C Goddard(W)	1947-48	1957	27	2931	148	1050	33	31.81	1	0	5/31
F J Titmus(E)	1955	1974-75	53	15118	777	4931	153	32.22	7	0	7/79
M H Mankad(I)	1946	1958-59	44	14685	777	5236	162	32.32	8	2	8/52
Sarfraz Nawaz(P)	1968-69	1983-84	55	13926	485	5798	177	32.75	4	1	9/86
G A Bartlett(N)	1961-62	1967-68	10	1768	64	792	24	33.00	1	0	6/38
Mohammad Nazir(P)	1969-70	1983-84	14	3262	163	1124	34	33.05	3	0	7/99
V A Holder(W)	1969	1978-79	40	9095	367	3627	109	33.27	3	0	6/28
J R Reid(N)	1949	1965	58	7725	444	2835	85	33.35	1	0	6/60
D R Hadlee(N)	1969	1977-78	26	4883	114	2389	71	33.64	0	0	4/30
O G Smith(W)	1954-55	1958-59	26	4431	228	1625	48	33.85	1	0	5/90
G S Sobers(W)	1953-54	1973-74	93	21599	974	7999	235	34.03	6	0	6/73
E J Barlow(SA)	1961-62	1969-70	30	3021	115	1362	40	34.05	1	0	5/85
K D Mackay(A)	1956	1962-63	37	5792	267	1721	50	34.42	2	0	6/42
R M Edwards(W)	1968-69	1968-69	5	1311	25	626	18	34.77	1	0	5/84
E R Dexter(E)	1958	1968	62	5317	186	2306	66	34.93	0	0	4/10
J S E Price(E)	1963-64	1972	15	2724	90	1401	40	35.02	1	0	5/73
D S Atkinson(W)	1948-49	1957-58	22	5201	311	1647	47	35.04	3	0	7/53
H D Bromfield(SA)	1961-62	1965	9	1810	101	599	17	35.23	1	0	5/88
S A Durani(I)	1959-60	1972-73	29	6446	317	2657	75	35.42	3	1	6/73
Intikhab Alam(P)	1959-60	1976-77	47	10474	383	4494	125	35.92	5	2	7/52
D A Renneberg(A)	1966-67	1967-68	8	1598	42	830	23	36.08	2	0	5/39
S Venkataraghavan(I)	1964-65	1983-84	57	14877	696	5634	156	36.11	3	1	8/72
J W Gleeson(A)	1967-68	1972	29	8857	378	3367	93	36.20	3	0	5/61
T W Cartwright(E)	1964	1965	5	1611	97	544	15	36.26	1	0	6/94
B E Congdon(N)	1964-65	1978	61	5620	197	2154	59	36.50	1	0	5/65
D G Phadkar(I)	1947-48	1958-59	31	5994	277	2285	62	36.85	3	0	7/159
H J Howarth(N)	1969	1976-77	30	8833	393	3178	86	36.95	2	0	5/34
R S Cunis(N)	1963-64	1971-72	20	4250	140	1867	51	37.00	1	0	6/76
R B Desai(I)	1958-59	1967-68	28	5597	178	2761	74	37.31	2	0	6/56

858

PLAYER	CAREER SPAN		M	B	MDS	R	W	AV	5	10	BEST
Nasim-Ul-Ghani(P)	1957-58	1972-73	29	4406	204	1959	52	37.67	2	0	6/76
D T Dewdney(W)	1954-55	1957-58	9	1641	65	807	21	38.42	1	0	5/21
P I Philpott(A)	1964-65	1965-66	8	2262	67	1000	26	38.46	1	0	5/90
Mahmood Hussain(P)	1952-53	1962	27	5910	213	2628	68	38.64	2	0	6/67
F M M Worrell(W)	1947-48	1963	41	7141	275	2672	69	38.72	2	0	7/70
D A J Holford(W)	1966	1976-77	24	4816	164	2009	51	39.39	1	0	5/23
Munir Malik(P)	1959-60	1962	3	684	21	358	9	39.77	1	0	5/128
I J Jones(E)	1963-64	1967-68	15	3546	98	1769	44	40.20	1	0	6/118
R Surendranath(I)	1958-59	1960-61	11	2602	144	1053	26	40.50	2	0	5/75
Asif Masood(P)	1968-69	1976-77	16	3038	78	1568	38	41.26	1	0	5/111
P R Umrigar(I)	1948-49	1961-62	59	4725	257	1473	35	42.08	2	0	6/74
S Abid Ali(I)	1967-68	1974-75	29	4164	119	1980	47	42.12	1	0	6/55
R B Simpson(A)	1957-58	1977-78	62	6881	253	3001	71	42.26	2	0	5/57
A D'Souza(P)	1958-59	1962	6	1587	56	745	17	43.82	1	0	5/112
P I Pocock(E)	1967-68	1984-85	25	6650	281	2976	67	44.41	3	0	6/79
G S Ramchand(I)	1952	1959-60	33	4976	255	1899	41	46.31	1	0	6/49
C G Borde(I)	1958-59	1969-70	55	5695	236	2417	52	46.48	1	0	5/88
R F Surti(I)	1960-61	1969-70	26	3870	115	1962	42	46.71	1	0	5/74
D B Pithey(SA)	1963-64	1966-67	8	1424	67	577	12	48.08	1	0	6/58
Haseeb Ahsan(P)	1957-58	1961-62	12	2835	100	1330	27	49.25	2	0	6/202
A M Moir(N)	1950-51	1958-59	17	2644	82	1418	28	50.64	2	0	6/155

TABLE F: 1970-71 to 1977

PLAYER	CAREER SPAN		M	B	MDS	R	W	AV	5	10	BEST
M F Malone(A)	1977		1	342	24	77	6	12.83	1	0	5/63
R A L Massie(A)	1972	1972-73	6	1789	74	647	31	20.87	2	1	8/53
J Garner(W)	1976-77	1986-87	58	13169	574	5433	259	20.97	7	0	6/56
Imran Khan(P)	1971	1987	70	16358	607	6903	311	22.19	21	5	8/58
R J Hadlee(N)	1972-73	1987-88	73	19023	699	8329	373	22.32	32	8	9/52
C E H Croft(W)	1976-77	1981-82	27	6165	215	2913	125	23.30	3	0	8/29
M A Holding(W)	1975-76	1986-87	60	12680	489	5898	249	23.68	13	2	8/92
Pervez Sajjad(P)	1964-65	1972-73	19	4145	217	1410	59	23.89	3	0	7/74
D K Lillee(A)	1970-71	1983-84	70	18467	625	8493	355	23.92	23	7	7/81
R G D Willis(E)	1970-71	1984	90	17363	553	8190	325	25.20	16	0	8/43
J N Shepherd(W)	1969	1970-71	5	1445	70	479	19	25.21	1	0	5/104
W W Daniel(W)	1975-76	1983-84	10	1754	61	910	36	25.27	1	0	5/39
A M E Roberts(W)	1973-74	1983-84	47	11135	384	5174	202	25.61	11	2	7/54
D L Underwood(E)	1966	1981-82	86	21862	1239	7674	297	25.83	17	6	8/51
M Hendrick(E)	1974	1981	30	6208	248	2248	87	25.83	0	0	4/28
G J Gilmour(A)	1973-74	1976-77	15	2661	51	1406	54	26.03	3	0	6/85
L S Pascoe(A)	1977	1981-82	14	3403	112	1668	64	26.06	1	0	5/59
J K Lever(E)	1976-77	1986	21	4433	140	1951	73	26.72	3	1	7/46
G Dymock(A)	1973-74	1979-80	21	5545	177	2116	78	27.12	5	1	7/67
M H N Walker(A)	1972-73	1977	34	10094	380	3792	138	27.47	6	0	8/143
I T Botham(E)	1977	1987	94	20801	747	10392	373	27.86	27	4	8/34
A G Hurst(A)	1973-74	1979-80	12	3054	74	1200	43	27.90	2	0	5/28
J R Thomson(A)	1972-73	1985	51	10541	300	5601	200	28.00	8	0	6/46
C M Old(E)	1972-73	1981	46	8858	310	4020	143	28.11	4	0	7/50
G G Arnold(E)	1967	1975	34	7650	284	3254	115	28.29	6	0	6/45
Asif Iqbal(P)	1964-65	1979-80	58	3864	181	1502	53	28.33	2	0	5/48
B S Bedi(I)	1966-67	1979	70	21364	1096	7637	266	28.71	14	1	7/98
J M Noreiga(W)	1970-71		4	1322	47	493	17	29.00	2	0	9/95
K D Walters(A)	1965-66	1980-81	74	3295	79	1425	49	29.08	1	0	5/66
L R Gibbs(W)	1957-58	1975-76	79	27115	1313	8989	309	29.09	1	2	8/38
Iqbal Qasim(P)	1976-77	1987-88	47	12397	599	4630	159	29.11	7	2	7/49
A N Connolly(A)	1963-64	1970-71	29	7818	289	2981	102	29.22	4	0	6/47
Mushtaq Mohammad(P)	1958-59	1978-79	57	5260	177	2309	79	29.22	3	0	5/28

PLAYER	CAREER SPAN		M	B	MDS	R	W	AV	5	10	BEST
R O Collinge(N)	1964-65	1978	35	7689	228	3393	116	29.25	3	0	6/63
B S Chandrasekhar(I)	1963-64	1979	58	15963	584	7199	242	29.74	16	2	8/79
G D McKenzie(A)	1961	1970-71	60	17687	547	7328	246	29.78	16	3	8/71
A A Mallett(A)	1968	1980	38	9990	419	3940	132	29.84	6	1	8/59
K D Boyce(W)	1970-71	1975-76	21	3501	99	1801	60	30.01	2	1	6/77
E A S Prasanna(I)	1961-62	1978-79	49	14353	592	5742	189	30.38	1	2	8/76
G Miller(E)	1976	1984	34	5149	219	1859	60	30.98	1	0	5/44
N Gifford(E)	1964	1973	15	3084	174	1026	33	31.09	1	0	5/55
R Illingworth(E)	1958	1973	71	11934	713	3807	122	31.20	3	0	6/29
T J Jenner(A)	1970-71	1975-76	9	1881	62	749	24	31.20	1	0	5/90
E J Chatfield(N)	1974-75	1987-88	35	8265	375	3259	102	31.95	3	1	6/73
A W Greig(E)	1972	1977	58	9802	338	4541	141	32.20	6	2	8/86
F J Titmus(E)	1955	1974-75	53	15118	777	4931	153	32.22	7	0	7/79
Sarfraz Nawaz(P)	1968-69	1983-84	55	13926	485	5798	177	32.75	4	1	9/86
B L Cairns(N)	1973-74	1985-86	43	10628	417	4280	130	32.92	6	1	7/74
Mohammad Nazir(P)	1969-70	1983-84	14	3262	163	1124	34	33.05	3	0	7/99
V A Holder(W)	1969	1978-79	40	9095	367	3627	109	33.27	3	0	6/28
K D Ghavri(I)	1974-75	1980-81	39	7042	233	3656	109	33.54	4	0	5/33
D R Hadlee(N)	1969	1977-78	26	4883	114	2389	71	33.64	0	0	4/30
G S Sobers(W)	1953-54	1973-74	93	21599	974	7999	235	34.03	6	0	6/73
P H Edmonds(E)	1975	1987	51	12028	613	4273	125	34.18	2	0	7/66
J S E Price(E)	1963-64	1972	15	2724	90	1401	40	35.02	1	0	5/73
S A Durani(I)	1959-60	1972-73	29	6446	317	2657	75	35.42	3	1	6/73
K Shuttleworth(E)	1970-71	1971	5	1071	20	427	12	35.58	1	0	5/47
Wasim Raja(P)	1972-73	1984-85	57	4092	134	1826	51	35.80	0	0	4/50
Intikhab Alam(P)	1959-60	1976-77	47	10474	383	4494	125	35.92	5	2	7/52
Sikander Bakht(P)	1976-77	1982-83	26	4873	147	2412	67	36.00	3	1	8/69
J Birkenshaw(E)	1972-73	1973-74	5	1017	33	469	13	36.07	1	0	5/57
S Venkataraghavan(I)	1964-65	1983-84	57	14877	696	5634	156	36.11	3	1	8/72
J W Gleeson(A)	1967-68	1972	29	8857	378	3367	93	36.20	3	0	5/61
B E Congdon(N)	1964-65	1978	61	5620	197	2154	59	36.50	1	0	5/65
P Lever(E)	1970-71	1975	17	3571	92	1509	41	36.80	2	0	6/38
H J Howarth(N)	1969	1976-77	30	8833	393	3178	86	36.95	2	0	5/34
R S Cunis(N)	1963-64	1971-72	20	4250	140	1867	51	37.00	1	0	6/76
G B Troup(N)	1976-77	1985-86	15	3183	104	1454	39	37.28	1	1	6/95
B D Julien(W)	1973	1976-77	24	4542	192	1868	50	37.36	1	0	5/57
Nasim-Ul-Ghani(P)	1957-58	1972-73	29	4406	204	1959	52	37.67	2	0	6/76
K J O'Keeffe(A)	1970-71	1977	24	5384	189	2018	53	38.07	1	0	5/101
D A J Holford(W)	1966	1976-77	24	4816	164	2009	51	39.39	1	0	5/23
S Madan Lal(I)	1974	1986	39	5997	187	2846	71	40.08	4	0	5/23
G S Chappell(A)	1970-71	1983-84	87	5327	208	1913	47	40.70	1	0	5/61
R J Bright(A)	1977	1986-87	25	5541	298	2180	53	41.13	4	1	7/87
Mudassar Nazar(P)	1976-77	1987-88	68	5350	187	2321	56	41.44	1	0	6/32
Asif Masood(P)	1968-69	1976-77	16	3038	78	1568	38	41.26	1	0	5/111
S Abid Ali(I)	1967-68	1974-75	29	4164	119	1980	47	42.12	1	0	6/55
R B Simpson(A)	1957-58	1977-78	62	6881	253	3001	71	42.26	2	0	5/57
P I Pocock(E)	1967-68	1984-85	25	6650	281	2976	67	44.41	3	0	6/79
Inshan Ali(W)	1970-71	1976-77	12	3718	137	1621	34	47.67	1	0	5/59
D R O'Sullivan(N)	1972-73	1976-77	11	2744	75	1221	18	67.83	1	0	5/148

TABLE G: 1977-78 to 1987-88

PLAYER	CAREER SPAN		M	B	MDS	R	W	AV	5	10	BEST
N Hirwani(I)	1987-88		1	203	6	136	16	8.50	2	1	8/61
A K Kuruppuarachchi(SL)	1986-86	1986-87	2	272	6	152	8	19.00	1	0	5/44
F S Ahangama(SL)	1985-86		3	804	32	348	18	19.33	1	0	5/52
G C Small(E)	1986	1986-87	4	856	43	314	16	19.62	2	0	5/48
P L Taylor(A)	1986-87	1987-88	3	546	28	241	12	20.08	1	0	6/78

PLAYER	CAREER SPAN		M	B	MDS	R	W	AV	5	10	BEST
A I C Dodemaide(A)	1987-88	1987-88	3	757	37	302	15	20.13	1	0	6/58
J Garner(W)	1976-77	1986-87	58	13169	574	5433	259	20.97	7	0	6/56
M D Marshall(W)	1978-79	1986-87	51	11315	401	5194	240	21.64	14	2	7/53
C A Walsh(W)	1984-85	1987-88	17	3356	119	1548	71	21.80	3	0	5/54
V B John(SL)	1982-83	1984	6	1281	53	614	28	21.92	2	0	5/60
Imran Khan(P)	1971	1987	70	16358	607	6903	311	22.19	21	5	8/58
R J Hadlee(N)	1972-73	1987-88	73	19023	699	8329	373	22.32	32	8	9/52
C E H Croft(W)	1976-77	1981-82	27	6165	215	2913	125	23.30	3	0	8/29
Ehteshamuddin(P)	1979-80	1982	5	940	40	375	16	23.43	1	0	5/47
C G Rackemann(A)	1982-83	1984-85	5	936	31	540	23	23.47	3	1	6/86
M A Holding(W)	1975-76	1986-87	60	12680	489	5898	249	23.68	13	2	8/92
D K Lillee(A)	1970-71	1983-84	70	18467	625	8493	355	23.92	23	7	7/81
R G D Willis(E)	1970-71	1984	90	17363	553	8190	325	25.20	16	0	8/43
B P Patterson(W)	1985-86	1987-88	10	1580	37	983	39	25.20	2	0	5/24
W W Daniel(W)	1975-76	1983-84	10	1754	61	910	36	25.27	1	0	5/39
A M E Roberts(W)	1973-74	1983-84	47	11135	384	5174	202	25.61	11	2	7/54
D L Underwood(E)	1966	1981-82	86	21862	1239	7674	297	25.83	17	6	8/51
M Hendrick(E)	1974	1981	30	6208	248	2248	87	25.83	0	0	4/28
L S Pascoe(A)	1977	1981-82	14	3403	112	1668	64	26.06	1	0	5/59
J K Lever(E)	1976-77	1986	21	4433	140	1951	73	26.72	3	1	7/46
G Dymock(A)	1973-74	1979-80	21	5545	177	2116	78	27.12	5	1	7/67
Wasim Akram(P)	1984-85	1987-88	22	4289	169	1779	65	27.36	4	1	6/91
R A Harper(W)	1983-84	1987-88	20	3069	151	1103	40	27.57	1	0	6/57
I T Botham(E)	1977	1987	94	20801	747	10392	373	27.86	27	4	8/34
S T Clarke(W)	1977-78	1981-82	11	2476	81	1171	42	27.88	1	0	5/126
A G Hurst(A)	1973-74	1979-80	12	3054	74	1200	43	27.90	2	0	5/28
J R Thomson(A)	1972-73	1985	51	10541	300	5601	200	28.00	8	0	6/46
C M Old(E)	1972-73	1981	46	8858	310	4020	143	28.11	4	0	7/50
Asif Iqbal(P)	1964-65	1979-80	58	3864	181	1502	53	28.33	2	0	5/48
R M Hogg(A)	1978-79	1984-85	38	7639	230	3503	123	28.47	6	2	6/74
B S Bedi(I)	1966-67	1979	70	21364	1096	7637	266	28.71	14	1	7/98
Tauseef Ahmed(P)	1979-80	1987-88	24	5524	239	2177	75	29.02	3	0	6/45
K D Walters(A)	1965-66	1980-81	74	3295	79	1425	49	29.08	1	0	5/66
Iqbal Qasim(P)	1976-77	1987-88	47	12397	599	4630	159	29.11	7	2	7/49
Mushtaq Mohammad(P)	1958-59	1978-79	57	5260	177	2309	79	29.22	3	0	5/28
R O Collinge(N)	1964-65	1978	35	7689	228	3393	116	29.25	3	0	6/63
Kapil Dev(I)	1978-79	1987-88	92	19121	677	9452	319	29.63	19	2	9/83
B S Chandrasekhar(I)	1963-64	1979	58	15963	584	7199	242	29.74	16	2	8/79
A A Mallett(A)	1968	1980	38	9990	419	3940	132	29.84	6	1	8/59
N G B Cook(E)	1983	1987-88	12	3551	187	1407	47	29.93	4	1	6/65
R M Ellison(E)	1984	1986	11	2261	90	1048	35	29.94	3	1	6/77
E A S Prasanna(I)	1961-62	1978-79	49	14353	592	5742	189	30.38	1	2	8/76
G F Lawson(A)	1980-81	1986-87	37	8709	286	4419	145	30.47	10	2	8/112
D R Doshi(I)	1979-80	1983-84	33	9368	443	3502	114	30.71	6	0	6/102
G R Dilley(E)	1979-80	1987-88	32	6236	208	3176	103	30.83	3	0	6/154
G Miller(E)	1976	1984	34	5149	219	1859	60	30.98	1	0	5/44
Abdul Qadir(P)	1977-78	1987-88	51	13448	489	5947	191	31.13	13	4	9/56
J D Higgs(A)	1977-78	1980-81	22	4752	176	2057	66	31.16	2	0	7/143
S R Waugh(A)	1985-86	1987-88	18	1940	87	885	28	31.60	1	0	5/69
B Yardley(A)	1977-78	1982-83	33	9011	378	3986	126	31.63	6	1	7/98
S L Boock(N)	1977-78	1986-87	28	6013	296	2291	72	31.81	4	0	7/87
N A Foster(E)	1983	1987-88	22	4315	164	1977	62	31.88	4	1	8/107
E J Chatfield(N)	1974-75	1987-88	35	8265	375	3259	102	31.95	3	1	6/73
J R Ratnayeke(SL)	1981-82	1987-88	19	3342	109	1705	53	32.16	4	0	8/83
R M H Binny(I)	1979-80	1986-87	27	2870	76	1534	47	32.63	2	0	6/56
Sarfraz Nawaz(P)	1968-69	1983-84	55	13926	485	5798	177	32.75	4	1	9/86
T M Alderman(A)	1981	1984-85	22	5375	217	2597	79	32.87	5	0	6/128
B L Cairns(N)	1973-74	1985-86	43	10628	417	4280	130	32.92	6	1	7/74
Mohammad Nazir(P)	1969-70	1983-84	14	3262	163	1124	34	33.05	3	0	7/99

861

PLAYER	CAREER SPAN		M	B	MDS	R	W	AV	5	10	BEST
V A Holder(W)	1969	1978-79	40	9095	367	3627	109	33.27	3	0	6/28
K D Ghavri(I)	1974-75	1980-81	39	7042	233	3656	109	33.54	4	0	5/33
J G Bracewell(N)	1980-81	1987-88	27	5674	266	2371	69	33.57	2	1	6/32
D R Hadlee(N)	1969	1977-78	26	4883	114	2389	71	33.64	0	0	4/30
Maninder Singh(I)	1982-83	1987-88	31	8330	336	2678	79	33.89	3	2	7/27
C J McDermott(A)	1984-85	1987-88	22	4565	124	2484	73	34.02	3	0	8/141
P H Edmonds(E)	1975	1987	51	12028	613	4273	125	34.18	2	0	7/66
C Sharma(I)	1984-85	1987-88	19	2930	55	1797	52	34.55	4	1	6/58
J E Emburey(E)	1978	1987-88	50	12020	591	4261	123	34.64	6	0	7/78
Azeem Hafeez(P)	1983-84	1984-85	18	4291	173	2202	63	34.95	4	0	6/46
N S Yadav(I)	1979-80	1986-87	35	8346	337	3580	102	35.09	3	0	5/76
Wasim Raja(P)	1972-73	1984-85	57	4092	134	1826	51	35.80	0	0	4/50
Sikander Bakht(P)	1976-77	1982-83	26	4873	147	2412	67	36.00	3	1	8/69
S Venkataraghavan(I)	1964-65	1983-84	57	14877	696	5634	156	36.11	3	1	8/72
B E Congdon(N)	1964-65	1978	61	5620	197	2154	59	36.50	1	0	5/65
A L F De Mel(SL)	1981-82	1986-87	17	3518	92	2180	59	36.94	3	0	6/109
R J Ratnayake(SL)	1982-83	1986-87	14	2825	81	1523	41	37.14	2	0	6/85
G B Troup(N)	1976-77	1985-86	15	3183	104	1454	39	37.28	1	1	6/95
D S De Silva(SL)	1981-82	1984	12	3031	108	1424	38	37.47	1	0	5/59
M G Hughes(A)	1985-86	1987-88	7	1491	53	792	21	37.71	1	0	5/67
M C Snedden(N)	1980-81	1987-88	14	2313	89	1142	30	38.06	1	0	5/68
R J Shastri(I)	1980-81	1987-88	57	13044	663	4813	124	38.81	2	0	5/75
D R Pringle(E)	1982	1986	14	2411	85	1128	29	38.89	1	0	5/108
N G Cowans(E)	1982-83	1985	19	3452	113	2003	51	39.27	2	0	6/77
R G Holland(A)	1984-85	1985-86	11	2889	124	1352	34	39.76	3	2	6/54
S Madan Lal(I)	1974	1986	39	5997	187	2846	71	40.08	4	0	5/23
D R Parry(W)	1977-78	1979-80	12	1909	67	936	23	40.09	1	0	5/15
G S Chappell(A)	1970-71	1983-84	87	5327	208	1913	47	40.70	1	0	5/61
P A J DeFreitas(E)	1986-87	1987-88	7	1239	38	1239	38	40.75	1	0	4/75
Tahir Naqqash(P)	1981-82	1984-85	15	2800	109	1398	34	41.11	2	0	5/40
R J Bright(A)	1977	1986-87	25	5541	298	2180	53	41.13	4	1	7/87
Mudassar Nazar(P)	1976-77	1987-88	68	5350	187	2321	56	41.44	1	0	6/32
P J W Allott(E)	1981	1985	13	2223	70	1084	26	41.69	1	0	6/61
R B Simpson(A)	1957-58	1977-78	62	6881	253	3001	71	42.26	2	0	5/57
T J Laughlin(A)	1977-78	1978-79	3	516	16	262	6	43.66	1	0	5/101
G R J Matthews(A)	1983-84	1986-87	21	3500	140	1709	39	43.82	2	1	5/103
L Shivaramakrishnan(I)	1982-83	1985-86	9	2367	74	1145	26	44.03	3	1	6/64
P I Pocock(E)	1967-68	1984-85	25	6650	281	2976	67	44.41	3	0	6/79
T G Hogan(A)	1982-83	1983-84	7	1436	55	706	15	47.06	1	0	5/66
P R Sleep(A)	1978-79	1987-88	11	3163	95	1153	22	52.40	1	0	5/69

Updated record of those who played in New Zealand v England and West Indies v Pakistan series 1987-88:

PLAYER	CAREER SPAN		M	B	MDS	R	W	AV	5	10	BEST
M D Marshall(W)	1978-79	1987-88	53	11828	415	5478	255	21.48	15	2	7/53
Imran Khan(P)	1971	1987-88	73	17137	622	7316	334	21.91	23	6	8/58
R J Hadlee(N)	1972-73	1987-88	74	19135	702	8379	373	22.46	32	8	9/52
C A Walsh(W)	1984-85	1987-88	20	3872	133	1778	75	23.70	3	0	5/54
B P Patterson(W)	1985-86	1987-88	11	1736	39	1084	43	25.20	2	0	5/24
Wasim Akram(P)	1984-85	1987-88	25	4991	188	2098	76	27.60	4	1	6/91
G R Dilley(E)	1979-80	1987-88	35	6865	242	3386	118	28.69	5	0	6/38
E J Chatfield(N)	1974-75	1987-88	38	9016	426	3457	115	30.06	3	1	6/73
Abdul Qadir(P)	1977-78	1987-88	54	14424	510	6485	205	31.63	13	4	9/56
N A Foster(E)	1983	1987-88	22	4315	164	1977	62	31.88	4	1	8/107
S L Boock(N)	1977-78	1987-88	28	6178	305	2335	73	31.98	4	0	7/87
J G Bracewell(N)	1980-81	1987-88	30	6033	284	2464	72	34.22	2	1	6/32
J E Emburey(E)	1978	1987-88	53	12823	639	4497	126	35.69	6	0	7/78
M C Snedden(N)	1980-81	1987-88	16	2847	120	1344	36	37.33	1	0	5/68

PLAYER	CAREER SPAN		M	B	MDS	R	W	AV	5	10	BEST
D K Morrison(N)	1987-88	1987-88	6	1092	28	623	16	38.93	1	0	5/69
Mudassar Nazar(P)	1976-77	1987-88	71	5446	193	2357	58	40.63	1	0	6/32
P A J DeFreitas(E)	1986-87	1987-88	9	1786	71	827	20	41.35	1	0	5/86

The wicket-keepers

TABLE A: AUSTRALIA 1876-77 to 1987-88

PLAYER	CAREER SPAN		MATCH	RUNS	AVGE	CATCH	STUMP	DIS
B A Barnett	1938		4	195	27.85	3	2	5
J M Blackham	1876-77	1894-95	35	800	15.68	37	24	61
F J Burton	1886-87	1887-88	2	4	2.00	1	1	2
W Carkeek	1912	1912	6	16	5.33	6	0	6
H Carter	1907-08	1921-22	28	873	22.97	44	21	65
G C Dyer	1986-87	1987-88	6	172	28.66	22	2	22
A T W Grout	1957-58	1965-66	51	890	15.08	163	24	187
B N Jarman	1959-60	1968-69	19	400	14.81	50	4	54
A H Jarvis	1884-85	1894-95	11	303	16.83	9	9	18
J J Kelly	1896	1905	36	664	17.02	43	20	63
G R A Langley	1951-52	1956-57	26	374	14.96	83	15	98
H S B Love	1932-33		1	8	4.00	3	0	3
J A Maclean	1978-79		4	79	11.28	18	0	18
L V Maddocks	1954-55	1956-57	7	177	17.70	18	1	19
R W Marsh	1970-71	1983-84	96	3633	26.51	343	12	355
W L Murdoch	1876-77	1890	18	896	32.00	13	1	14
W A S Oldfield	1920-21	1936-37	54	1427	22.65	78	52	130
W B Phillips	1983-84	1985-86	27	1485	32.28	52	0	52
S J Rixon	1977-78	1984-85	13	394	18.76	42	5	47
R A Saggers	1948	1949-50	6	30	10.00	16	8	24
H B Taber	1966-67	1969-70	16	353	16.04	56	4	60
D Tallon	1945-46	1953	21	394	17.13	50	8	58
R D Woolley	1982-83	1983-84	2	21	10.50	7	0	7
K J Wright	1978-79	1979-80	10	219	16.84	31	4	35
T J Zoehrer	1985-86	1986-87	10	246	20.50	15	1	16

TABLE B: ENGLAND 1876-77 to 1987-88

PLAYER	CAREER SPAN		MATCH	RUNS	AVGE	CATCH	STUMP	DIS
L E G Ames	1929	1938	47	2434	40.56	74	23	97
K V Andrew	1954-55	1963	2	29	9.66	1	0	1
D L Bairstow	1979	1980-81	4	125	20.83	12	1	13
J G Binks	1963-64		2	91	22.75	8	0	8
J H Board	1898-99	1905-06	6	108	10.80	8	3	11
D V Brennan	1951		2	16	8.00	0	1	1
G Brown	1921	1922-23	7	299	29.90	9	3	12
H R Butt	1895-96		3	22	7.33	1	1	2
W L Cornford	1929-30		4	36	9.00	5	3	8
A Dolphin	1920-21		1	1	0.50	1	0	1
P R Downton	1980-81	1986	27	701	19.47	61	5	66
G Duckworth	1924	1936	24	234	14.62	45	15	60
H Elliott	1927-28	1933-34	4	61	15.25	8	3	11
T G Evans	1946	1959	91	2439	20.49	173	46	219
W Farrimond	1930-31	1935	4	116	16.57	5	2	7
B N French	1986	1987-88	13	285	18.30	27	1	28
L H Gay	1894-95		1	37	18.50	3	1	4
P A Gibb	1938-39	1946-47	8	581	44.69	3	1	4

PLAYER	CAREER SPAN		MATCH	RUNS	AVGE	CATCH	STUMP	DIS
S C Griffith	1947-48	1948-49	3	157	31.40	5	0	5
L Hone	1878-79		1	13	6.50	2	0	2
J Humphries	1907-08		3	44	8.80	7	0	7
J Hunter	1884-85		5	93	18.60	8	3	11
A P E Knott	1967	1981	95	4389	32.75	250	19	269
W H V Levett	1933-34		1	7	7.00	3	0	3
A F A Lilley	1896	1909	35	903	20.52	70	22	92
Hon A Lyttleton	1880	1884	4	94	15.66	2	0	2
A J McIntyre	1950	1955	3	19	3.16	8	0	8
G MacGregor	1890	1893	8	96	12.00	14	3	17
G Millman	1961-62	1962	6	60	12.00	13	2	15
L J Moon	1905-06		4	182	22.75	4	0	4
W L Murdoch	1891-92		1	12	12.00	0	1	1
J T Murray	1961	1967	21	506	22.00	52	3	55
J M Parks	1954	1967-68	46	1962	32.16	103	11	114
H Phillipson	1891-92	1894-95	5	63	9.00	8	3	11
R Pilling	1881-82	1888	8	91	7.58	10	4	14
W F F Price	1938		1	6	3.00	2	0	2
C J Richards	1986-87	1987	6	272	30.22	17	1	18
J Selby	1876-77	1881-82	6	256	23.27	1	0	1
M Sherwin	1886-87	1888	3	30	15.00	5	2	7
A C Smith	1962-63	1962-63	6	118	29.50	20	0	20
E J Smith	1911-12	1913-14	11	113	8.69	17	3	20
H Smith	1928		1	7	7.00	1	0	1
R T Spooner	1951-52	1955	7	354	27.23	10	2	12
R T Stanyworth	1927-28		4	13	2.60	7	2	9
G B Street	1922-23		1	11	11.00	0	1	1
H Strudwick	1909-10	1926	28	230	7.93	60	12	72
R Swetman	1958-59	1959-60	11	254	16.93	24	2	26
R W Taylor	1970-71	1983-84	57	1156	16.28	167	7	174
N C Tufnell	1909-10		1	14	14.00	0	1	1
E F S Tylecote	1882-83	1886	6	152	19.00	5	5	10
A Wood	1938	1939	4	80	20.00	10	1	11
G E C Wood	1924		3	7	3.50	5	1	6
H Wood	1888	1891-92	4	204	68.00	2	1	3
R A Young	1907-08		2	27	6.75	6	0	6

TABLE C: SOUTH AFRICA 1888-89 to 1969-70

PLAYER	CAREER SPAN		MATCH	RUNS	AVGE	CATCH	STUMP	DIS
M Bissett	1898-99	1909-10	3	103	25.75	2	1	3
H B Cameron	1927-28	1935	26	1239	30.21	39	12	51
T Campbell	1909-10	1912	5	90	15.00	7	1	8
W R Endean	1951	1957-58	28	1630	33.95	41	0	41
G M Fullerton	1947	1951	7	325	25.00	10	2	12
D Gamsy	1969-70		2	39	19.50	5	0	5
R E Grieveson	1938/39		2	114	57.00	7	3	10
E A Halliwell	1891-92	1902-03	8	188	12.53	9	2	11
D T Lindsay	1963-64	1969-70	19	1130	37.66	57	2	59
J D Lindsay	1947		3	21	7.00	4	1	5
F Nicholson	1935-36		4	76	10.85	3	0	3
P W Sherwell	1905-06	1910-11	13	427	23.72	20	16	36
F W Smith	1888-89	1895-96	3	45	9.00	2	0	2
E A van der Merwe	1929	1935-36	2	27	9.00	3	0	3
W W Wade	1938-39	1949-50	11	511	28.38	15	2	17
J H B Waite	1951	1964-65	50	2405	30.44	124	17	141
T A Ward	1912	1924	23	459	13.90	19	13	32

TABLE D: WEST INDIES 1928 to 1987-88

PLAYER	CAREER SPAN		MATCH	RUNS	AVGE	CATCH	STUMP	DIS
F C M Alexander	1957	1960-61	25	961	30.03	85	5	90
D W Allan	1961-62	1966	5	75	12.50	15	3	18
I Barrow	1929-30	1939	11	276	16.23	17	5	22
A P Binns	1952-53	1955-56	5	64	9.14	14	3	17
C M Christiani	1934-35		4	98	19.60	6	1	7
C C Depeiza	1954-55	1955-56	5	187	31.16	7	4	11
P J L Dujon	1981-82	1987-88	47	2117	37.14	150	4	154
T M Findlay	1969	1972-73	10	212	16.30	19	2	21
S C Guillen	1951-52	1951-52	5	104	26.00	9	2	11
J L Hendriks	1961-62	1969	20	447	18.62	42	5	47
E A C Hunte	1929-30		3	166	33.20	5	0	5
R B Kanhai	1957	1973-74	79	6227	47.53	50	0	50
R A Legall	1952-53		4	50	10.00	8	1	9
D M Lewis	1970-71		3	259	86.33	8	0	8
C A McWatt	1953-54	1954-55	6	202	28.85	9	1	10
I L Mendoça	1961-62		2	81	40.50	8	2	10
D A Murray	1977-78	1981-82	19	601	21.46	57	5	62
D L Murray	1963	1980	62	1993	22.90	181	8	189
R K Nunes	1928	1929-30	4	245	30.62	2	0	2
T R O Payne	1985-86		1	5	5.00	5	0	5
J E D Sealey	1929-30	1939	11	478	28.11	6	1	7
C L Walcott	1947-48	1959-60	44	3798	56.68	53	11	64

Updated record of those who played in New Zealand v England & West Indies v Pakistan series 1987-88:

PLAYER	CAREER SPAN		MATCH	RUNS	AVGE	CATCH	STUMP	DIS
B N French(E)	1986	1987-88	16	308	18.11	38	1	39
I D S Smith(N)	1980-81	1987-88	43	1037	22.54	120	7	127
Saleem Yousuf(P)	1981-82	1987-88	19	698	31.72	55	6	61
P J L Dujon(W)	1981-82	1987-88	50	2301	37.72	155	5	160

TABLE E: NEW ZEALAND 1929-30 to 1987-88

PLAYER	CAREER SPAN		MATCH	RUNS	AVGE	CATCH	STUMP	DIS
T E Blain	1986		1	37	37.00	0	0	0
I A Colquhon	1954-55		2	1	0.50	4	0	4
A E Dick	1961-62	1965	17	370	14.23	47	4	51
B A Edgar	1978	1986	39	1958	30.59	14	0	14
G N Edwards	1976-77	1980-81	8	377	25.13	7	0	7
S C Guillen	1955-56		3	98	16.33	4	1	5
R I Harford	1967-68		3	7	2.33	11	0	11
K C James	1929-30	1932-33	11	52	4.72	11	5	16
W K Lees	1976-77	1983	21	778	23.57	52	7	59
T G McMahon	1955-56	1955-56	5	7	2.33	7	1	8
B D Milburn	1968-69		3	8	8.00	6	2	8
F L H Mooney	1949	1953-54	14	343	17.15	22	8	30
E C Petrie	1955-56	1965-66	14	258	12.90	25	0	25
J R Reid	1949	1965	58	3428	33.28	43	1	44
I D S Smith	1980-81	1987-88	40	945	21.47	110	7	117
E W T Tindill	1937	1946-47	5	73	9.12	6	1	7
K J Wadsworth	1969	1975-76	33	1010	21.48	92	4	96
J T Ward	1963-64	1967-68	8	75	12.50	16	1	17

Index of names

All Test players are listed under their country. The South African section includes those who have appeared in unofficial internationals. Dual-country players are listed under the country for which they first played. Women international cricketers are listed separately and all other players and personalities are listed under the Miscellaneous section.

Australia

Alderman, T M 175, 342, 343, 599, 600, 602
Alexander, H H 443
Allan, F E 24, 387, 423
Andrews, T J E 89, 790
Archer, K A 182, 503, 806
Archer, R G 182, 229
Armstrong, W W 40, 48, 55, 58, 60, 63, 67, 68, 69, 86, 87, 121, 406, 407, 408, 409, 417, 431, 437, 669, 671, 679, 790, 805

Badcock, C L 119
Bannerman, A C 30, 31, 33, 182, 301, 388, 730, 789, 790
Bardsley, W 27, 60, 62, 63, 71, 86, 89, 94, 121, 178, 413, 416, 437, 805, 812,
Barnes, S G 120, 121, 178, 181, 301, 362, 363, 369, 498, 822
Barnett, B A 687, 688, 719, 770
Barrett, J E 35
Beard, G R 598
Benaud, R 47, 196, 229, 245, 246, 247, 248, 261, 271, 497, 500, 501, 502, 503, 504, 506, 508, 546, 567, 575, 585, 646, 712, 797, 817, 826, 829, 830
Bennett, M J 604
Blackham, J McC 26, 30, 304, 385, 653, 660, 661, 663-69 passim, 670, 695, 739, 782, 784
Blackie, D D 80, 444
Bonnor, G J 32, 33, 376, 803, 818
Boon, D C 338
Booth, B C 251, 252, 806
Border, A R 5, 47, 308, 313, 335-40 passim, 360, 361, 599, 793
Boyle, H F 17, 385, 386, 387, 822
Bradman, Sir D G 4, 5, 12, 37, 42, 58, 61, 75, 76, 82, 86, 90, 98, 101, 107, 111-21 passim, 122, 124, 138, 146, 149, 152, 177, 178, 181, 182, 188, 193, 203, 220, 248, 252, 256, 257, 271, 275, 278, 284, 300, 302, 313, 314, 327, 329, 331, 332, 335, 351, 354, 360, 361, 362, 363, 430, 437, 438, 452, 453, 454, 456, 457, 458, 466, 471, 475, 476, 495, 497, 498, 499, 516, 533, 547, 643, 683, 686, 687, 700, 719, 720, 783, 790, 791, 793, 799, 806, 807, 829
Bright, R J 340, 597, 598
Bromley, E H 118
Brown, W A 116-17, 118, 121, 178, 434, 498, 722, 806, 822
Bruce, W 35
Bruge, P J P 247, 248, 249
Burke, J W 182, 245, 247, 502, 534, 548
Burn, K E J 667
Burton, F I 667

Callen, I W 598
Carkeek, W 27, 412, 669
Carter, H 406, 441, 653, 663-69 passim, 675, 683, 684, 782
Chappell, G S 5, 91, 291, 299-308 passim, 310, 311, 312, 331, 335, 360, 361, 595-96, 601, 760, 793, 816, 817,

822, 824
Chappell, I M 5, 91, 252, 284, 299-308 passim, 310, 311, 363, 508, 509, 594, 760, 792, 793, 806, 817, 822
Chappell, T M 5, 91, 595, 793, 822
Chipperfield, A G 99, 119, 445, 815
Clark, W M 597, 598
Colley, D J 594
Collins, H L 27, 62, 86, 87, 88, 97, 413, 683, 684, 812
Connolly, A N 506
Cooper, B B 663
Cooper, W H 385, 387, 388, 424, 664, 665
Corling, G E 507
Cosier, G J 306
Cotter, A 406, 408, 667, 669
Cowper, R M 250, 252, 507, 815
Craig, I D 181, 182, 246, 252, 267
Crawford, W P A 503

Darling, J 26, 33, 36, 58, 59, 66, 67, 68, 118, 394, 406, 696, 790, 804, 805
Darling, W M 307, 793
Davidson, A K 246, 247, 248, 368, 502, 503, 504, 546, 646, 797, 806, 824,
Davis, I C 304
Davis, S P 602
Donnan, H 36
Dooland, B 500, 502
Duff, R A 48, 57, 58
Dymock, G 596
Dyson, J 307, 338, 806

Ebeling, H I 445
Edwards, R 303, 762, 791, 792, 793
Emery, S H 27, 412, 413, 430, 812
Evans, E 388, 405

Fairfax, A G 445
Favell, L E 248, 791
Ferris, J J 379, 387, 389, 390
Fingleton, J H 54, 68, 111, 116, 118, 119, 152, 256, 457, 550, 822
Fleetwood-Smith, L O'B 117, 434, 435, 436, 446, 684, 687, 688
Francis, B C 303
Freeman, E W 507, 806

Gannon, J B 598
Garrett, T W 17, 386, 387
Gaunt, R A 504
Gehrs, D R A 430
Giffen, G 16, 17, 19, 26, 29, 32, 33, 35, 43, 58, 60, 368, 376, 383, 388, 389, 391, 406, 646, 663, 664, 667, 782, 789
Gilbert, D R 340
Gilmour, G J 304, 596, 806
Gleeson, J W 264, 369, 506, 508
Graham, H 36
Gregory, D W 24, 57, 87, 368, 386
Gregory, E J 57
Gregory, J M 48, 57, 76, 79, 86, 87, 88, 94, 95, 97, 246, 440, 441, 442, 443, 447, 683, 684, 815, 816
Gregory, R G 119
Gregory, S E 26, 27, 36, 40, 50, 57, 58, 83, 84, 86, 396, 399, 412, 437, 448, 461, 509, 510, 591, 666, 789, 790, 791, 805
Grimmett, C V 68, 99, 102, 103, 105, 164, 256, 323, 361, 368, 369, 429, 431, 433, 434, 436, 439, 445, 493, 500, 501, 508, 510, 644, 684, 700, 739, 822
Grout, A T W 653, 724, 725, 726, 783, 797, 798

Hammond, J R 594, 595
Harry, J 667
Hartigan, R J 60, 61

Harvey, M R 181
Harvey, R N 5, 179, 181, 203, 360, 361, 498, 512, 534, 538, 770, 791, 792, 793, 794, 799, 815, 829
Hassett, A L 119, 120, 121, 176, 178, 181, 203, 216, 466, 477, 498, 518, 722, 730, 806
Hawke, N J N 506, 508
Hazlitt, G R 409
Hendry, H L 443
Hibbert, P A 306
Higgs, J D 547, 598
Hilditch, A M J 339
Hill, C 26, 33, 36, 47, 55, 58, 60, 62, 71, 138, 396, 399, 406, 417, 430, 669, 680, 805, 810
Hill, J C 503
Hoare, D E 504
Hogan, T G 604
Hogg, R M 333, 597, 598, 599, 600, 601, 602, 759
Hole, G B 181, 538, 815
Holland, R G 339, 604
Hookes, D W 306, 310, 312, 335, 793
Hopkins, A J Y 58, 67, 68, 409
Horan, T P 30, 32, 34, 35, 36, 57, 422, 424, 657
Hordern, H V 15, 28, 368, 406, 410, 417, 429, 430, 436, 439, 501, 675
Hornibrook, P M 444
Howell, W P 67, 402, 405, 444
Hughes, K J 271, 280, 307, 308, 338, 342, 532, 587, 597, 601, 793
Hughes, M G 602
Hurst, A G 597
Hurwood, A 445

Inverarity, R J 27, 302
Iredale, F A 26, 36, 57, 385
Ironmonger, H 443-44, 445
Iverson, J B 369, 500, 508

Jackson, A 92, 93, 304, 806
Jarman, B N 304, 695, 724, 725, 726
Jarvis, A H 667, 669
Jenner, T J 304, 596, 609
Johnson, I W 177, 181, 234, 495, 499, 754, 784, 815, 824
Johnston, W A 163, 445, 466, 495, 498, 499, 602, 806
Jones, D M 340
Jones, E 16, 26, 33, 46, 68, 404, 405, 545, 661, 790
Jones, S P 35

Kelleway, C 27, 30, 62, 63, 86, 121, 182, 409, 412, 416
Kelly, J J 58, 405, 653, 663-69 passim, 782
Kendall, T 386, 387, 424
Kippax, A F 92, 687
Kline, L F 256, 504, 798

Laird, B M 307, 310, 312
Langley, G R A 304, 538, 723, 724, 726, 783
Laver, F W vii, 406, 790
Lawry, W M 250, 251, 264, 268, 278, 299, 301, 302, 304, 506, 509, 695, 725, 759
Lawson, G F 323, 333, 342, 600, 601, 602, 759
Lillee, D K 113, 231, 265, 270, 275, 294, 295, 297, 298, 299, 317, 331, 332, 333, 342, 343, 353, 362, 363, 368, 431, 496, 509, 531, 568, 581, 589-604 passim, 605, 606, 607, 610, 615, 619, 621, 625, 630, 631, 632, 634, 643, 644, 645, 759, 760, 761, 767, 776, 814, 817
Lindwall, R R 57, 113, 124, 130, 154,

163, 164, 181, 185, 229, 257, 261, 363, 368, 433, 466, 495, 496, 497, 498, 499, 503, 507, 509, 522, 523, 591, 631, 646, 722, 791
Love, H S B 686
Loxton, S J E 181, 498, 806
Lyons, J J 33

Macartney, C G 5, 27, 51, 55, 58, 61, 62, 63, 86, 89, 92, 97, 121, 146, 148, 360, 361, 408, 413, 463, 790, 805, 812
McCabe, S J 99, 115, 116, 117, 118, 164, 256, 360, 361, 445, 454, 687, 806
McCool, C L 500, 722, 783, 815
McCormick, E L 443, 446, 497
McCosker, R B 303, 304, 310
McDermott, C J 601, 602
McDonald, C C 40, 247, 529, 573
McDonald, E A 40, 71, 83, 84, 86, 94, 95, 97, 102, 368, 394, 440, 441, 442, 443, 447, 448, 461, 509, 510, 524, 591, 658, 684
McDonnell, P S 31, 32, 33, 37, 376, 389
Mackay, K D 214, 245, 246, 247, 248, 502, 503, 504, 505, 727, 817
McKenzie, G D 241, 247, 271, 275, 368, 504, 505, 506, 546, 568, 715
McKibbin, T R 404, 548
MacLaren, J W 27, 67, 412
Maclean, J A 762, 763
McLeod, C E 16, 58, 405, 672
Maddocks, L V 524, 723, 724, 783
Maguire, J N 602
Mailey, A A 27, 54, 83, 86, 368, 369, 413, 429, 430, 431, 434, 436, 437, 439, 501, 684, 736, 812
Mallett, A A 508, 509, 760, 817
Malone, M F 597
Mann, A L 275, 306, 598
Marsh, G R 338
Marsh, R W 304, 312, 332, 531, 601, 653, 723, 724, 726, 759-64 passim, 774, 782, 783, 784, 792
Martin, J W 504
Massie, H H 33
Massie, R A L 594, 777
Matthews, G R J 339, 340, 604
Matthews, T J 27, 412, 430, 629
Mayne, E R 27, 412, 413, 812
Mayne, L C 506, 507
Meckiff, I 246, 256, 503, 504, 543, 546, 547, 797, 798
Midwinter, W E 379, 386, 387, 658, 790
Miller, K R 5, 112, 124, 130, 138, 154, 163, 164, 166, 176, 178, 179, 181, 185, 206, 218, 229, 232, 248, 252, 256, 257, 261, 360, 363, 368, 466, 481, 495, 496, 497, 498, 503, 509, 512, 516, 524, 538, 546, 591, 646, 647, 720, 728, 744, 770, 807, 815
Minnett, R B 417
Misson, R M 504
Moroney, J R 181
Morris, A R 120, 121, 178, 179, 181, 205, 354, 360, 466, 498, 516, 518, 534, 784, 826
Moses, H 35, 36
Murdoch, W L 29-37 passim, 133, 377, 379, 388, 412, 658, 662, 666, 695

Nagel, L E 443
Nash, L J 445, 764
Nitschke, H C 118
Noble, M A 36, 46, 47, 48, 55, 58, 59, 60, 68, 178, 368, 399, 402, 406, 416, 417, 437, 444, 477, 499, 646, 648, 790

O'Brien, L P J 118
O'Connor, J D A 409
O'Donnell, S P 338
Ogilvie, A D 306

England

Photo credits

Australian Cricket: page 173, 224, 283, 319, 320, 321, 330, 334, 574, 577, 590, 593, 613, 623, 636, 638, 640, 741; *Century of Philadelphian Cricket*: 25, 27, 411, 674; George Beldham: 13, 31, 39, 43, 45, 56, 59, 66, 384, 396, 397, 407, 418, 423, 677, 697, 786; *Cape Times/Rand Daily Mail*: 73, 165, 211, 213, 254, 262, 270, 272, 277, 279, 301, 478, 505, 582, 584, 586, 606, 704, 705, 726, 800, 801, 827; Central Press: 115, 131, 153, 156, 435, 691, 693, 721, 738, 751, 823 (bottom), 828; E. Hawkins & Co: ii, 34, 374, 381, 390, 403, 426, 665; Herald & Weekly Times Ltd: 90, 174, 177, 180, 184, 187, 192, 195, 197, 227, 230, 235, 237, 243, 253, 258, 287, 289, 293, 296, 305, 315, 326, 336, 343, 344, 346, 348, 352, 355, 358, 432, 487, 492, 497, 501, 511, 513, 517, 521, 525, 530, 535, 541, 551, 554, 567, 569, 603, 611, 617, 627, 632, 633, 647, 685, 702, 714, 717, 729, 733, 748, 760, 763, 768, 772, 775, 777, 779, 814, 816, 826 (both); *The Hindu*: 143, 147, 150, 201, 208, 219, 465, 560, 563, 565, 757, 825; *History of West Indian Cricket*: 711; *Pageant of Cricket*: 447, 620; Press Association, UK: 455; S. Ramamurthy Collection: 450; *South African Cricketer*: 331; *The Star*: 160; 823 (top); *Sydney Morning Herald*: 117; Sport & General: 77, 81, 87, 99, 103, 112, 458, 462; *Vanity Fair*: 659.